Parochial and Family History of the Deanery of Trigg Minor, in the County of Cornwall. [With illustrations.]

John Maclean

Parochial and Family History of the Deanery of Trigg Minor, in the County of Cornwall. [With illustrations.]
Maclean, John
British Library, Historical Print Editions
British Library
1872-79
3 vol. ; 4°.
10353.e.6.

The BiblioLife Network

GUIDE TO FOLD-OUTS, MAPS and OVERSIZED IMAGES

THE

PAROCHIAL AND FAMILY HISTORY

OF THE

DEANERY OF TRIGG MINOR,

CORNWALL.

THE

PAROCHIAL AND FAMILY HISTORY

OF THE

DEANERY OF TRIGG MINOR,

IN THE

COUNTY OF CORNWALL.

VOL. II.

BY SIR JOHN MACLEAN, F.S.A.,

MEMBER OF THE ROYAL ARCHÆOLOGICAL INSTITUTE OF GREAT BRITAIN AND IRELAND,
HONORARY MEMBER OF THE ROYAL INSTITUTION OF CORNWALL, ETC.

"If there be any who desire to be strangers in their own country, foreigners
in their own cities, and always children in knowledge, let them please themselves.
I write not for such humours."—*Camden.*

LONDON: NICHOLS & SONS, 25, PARLIAMENT STREET.
BODMIN: LIDDELL AND SON.

1876.

25,9

1ªºº

PREFACE TO VOLUME II.

—

The completion of the Second Volume of this work enables the Author to point out, with much pleasure, that the history of fourteen of the twenty parishes which comprised the ancient Deanery of Trigg Minor has now been issued, leaving the record of but six parishes to be embodied in a third volume. Of these six that of St. Minver is already printed, and will be issued with this paper; the history of the parishes of St. Teath and Temple, which will form Part XII, is in an advanced state, and will, it is hoped, be very soon ready for the press, whilst that of Tintagel and Trevalga has been commenced. The Author therefore feels, with gratitude, that, if it shall please God to continue to him the health and strength which has enabled him during the last ten years to pursue uninterruptedly this labour of love, he may expect, in no long time, to see the completion of his undertaking.

In a supplementary Preface to the first volume, the Author thought it right to mention that in consequence of the immense amount of original material, relating to the district whose history he had undertaken to write, which diligent search in the public Archives and elsewhere had brought to light, the work was, in some measure, exceeding in size what had been originally contemplated; but he has great satisfaction in being able to announce to the subscribers that the expense caused by printing the long family memoirs and pedigrees, which have added so much to the embellishment and value of the work, has fallen lightly upon them, for the liberality of the parties more immediately interested in these records has, in many instances, wholly, or in part, defrayed the great cost incurred by their publication. This remark is especially applicable to the memoir of the Family of Prideaux, no portion of the expense of the publication of which, through the liberal kindness of C. G. Prideaux-Brune of Prideaux Place, Esq., has fallen upon the Subscribers to the work. The same, in a less degree, might be said of several others, to whom the thanks of the Author and of the Subscribers are due.

With the last Part will be issued one or more sheets of Addenda and Corrigenda, in which will be included further materials which have been discovered since the earlier parts of the work were published; and the Author will feel obliged to his Friends and Subscribers if they will kindly direct his attention to any errors and misprints they may severally observe. That numerous errors of the nature referred to exist the Author is very conscious; for in a work of this nature, errors are, notwithstanding the utmost vigilance, almost unavoidable.

It remains now only for the Author to repeat his thanks to those gentlemen already named in the last Preface, and to others too numerous to mention in detail, though he must not fail to name his friends Jonathan Rashleigh of Menabilly, Esq., and Colonel Chester, for the assistance rendered to him in the course of his labours, and especially to the parochial Clergy, as well beyond the Deanery as within it, to whose courtesy and kindness he is under great obligations.

J. M.

PALLINGSWICK LODGE,
    January, 1876.

TABLE OF CONTENTS.

—

PARISH OF HELLAND.

PARISH OF LANOWE, *alias* ST. KEW.

PARISHES OF LANTEGLOS AND ADVENT.

TABLE OF CONTENTS.

PARISH OF ST. MABEN.

PARISH OF MICHAELSTOW.

PLATE XXX

HELLAND CHURCH.
From the South East.

PARISH OF HELLAND.

The name of this parish is popularly supposed to be derived from St. Helena the mother of Constantine, to whom, according to tradition, the Church is dedicated.[1] We do not, however, see sufficient reason for adopting this theory. In the earliest institution to the benefice upon record (1285), the Church is described as "the parish Church of Hellond," and in no instance, so far as we are aware, throughout the Episcopal Registers, is there any allusion to St. Helena in connection with this parish. Moreover, we may venture to say, that in cases in Cornwall in which the Patron Saint of the Church has given his name to the parish, the name usually appears with the word "Saint" prefixed, and that it is so used in the Episcopal Registers.[2]

In these circumstances we are inclined, in this instance, to agree with Hals, who derives the name from "Hall" *Halla.* A.-Sax. "*hal, heale, heall,*" signifying College, Temple, or Church.[3] The name also is applied to *mansion* or *manor*, and in that sense is used in Domesday, and also to the seat or habitation of the Squire or Lord of the Manor. Tonkin, following Hals, says the words "Hel," or "Hale," are the Cornish pronounciation of the English word "Hall," adding, however, that if we believe the parishioners of Helland the name is a contraction for Helen's-land, "the Church being dedicated to St. Helena."[4] Hals concludes that there was an Endowed Rectory here before the Norman Conquest. This may have been the case but unfortunately the Churches on the Cornish Manors are not named in the record.

[1] This seems to have been accepted by Dr. Oliver. Mon. Dioc. Exon, p. 439.

[2] There are several parishes which ordinarily are named without the prefix and yet derive their name from the Patron Saint, Budock, Crantock, Crowan, &c., but that prefix is not omitted in the Ecclesiastical Records.

[3] The old Cornish Vocabulary preserved in the British Museum gives "HEL, aula," *i.e.*, a hall, whether a noble mansion, or the entrance to a house.

[4] Dr. Bannister considers "that the parish takes its name from the manor, and the name of this manor in Domesday "Henland" shews that in all probability it is synonymous with the Welsh "Henllan" which is found in Cardiganshire, Denbighshire, Caermarthen, &c., and means 'old enclosure.'" "Hen" being one of the few Celtic adjectives that ordinarily precede the substantive.

B

This parish constitutes a portion of the Parliamentary Borough of Bodmin. It is bounded on the west by the parishes of Bodmin, Egloshayle, and St. Mabyn, and on the north-west by the last named parish, the river Alan forming the boundary on these sides. On the north-east it adjoins Blisland, and on the south-east Cardinham, whilst Bodmin forms the boundary on the south.

The parish contains by actual measurement 2475a. 0r. 1p., of which the Glebe comprises 28a. 2r. 9p., the portion of the river Alan within this parish, 18a. 3r. 14p.; public roads, 43a. 1r. 1p.; wastes, 9a. 0r. 33p.; and downs, 50a. 1r. 11p.[1]

With the exception of a small cloth and blanket manufactory at Clerkenwater, to be noticed presently, the parish is purely agricultural. The land is chiefly arable, though there are some rich meadows, and there is a considerable extent of woodland, both timber and coppice. A great portion of the arable land is thin and sterile, though capable of improvement.

The following abstract of the population is made from the census returns of this century:

		1801	1811	1821	1831	1841	1851	1861	1871
Population ..	.. ..	221	223	264	285	300	252	224[2]	227
Houses	Inhabited ..	33	38	44	46	52	45	49	44
	Uninhabited ..	2	3	1	..	..	4	3	3
	Building ..	..	..	..	1	..	..	1	..

		£	s.	d.
Annual Value of Real Property as Assessed in 1815	... ...	1,588	0	0
Present Gross Estimated Rental	...	2,228	0	0
Rateable Value as fixed in 1866	...	1,504	0	0
Present Rateable Valuable	...	2,041	0	0
Land Tax—Net Sum Payable, £49 15s. 5d.; Redeemed, £31 11s. 11d.		81	7	4
Assessed Taxes		*Nil.*		
Inhabited House Duty...		1	19	0
Property and Income Tax:—				
Schedule A	52	6	5	
,, B	13	8	4	
,, D	2	2	0	
		65	16	9

[1] The downs have now, to a great extent, been enclosed.

[2] Males and females exactly equal in number, 112 of each sex. The decrease in the population has arisen from emigration.

The principal Landowners are Lord Robartes, James Hayward, and Joseph Pomery, Esquires, and Mrs. Hooper.

The geological basis of this parish is of the altered Devonian series. It is, however, traversed by an elvan dyke of a somewhat peculiar character, which, emerging from the granite near Poundscawnse in Blisland, and passing in a straight course through Pennant and Trencreek in that parish, and Coldrinick and Kernick in Helland, terminates at Lymsbury. Near Kernick it resembles a coarse granitic sandstone, and at its junction with the slate both rocks are very distinct, not having any appearance of transition. It is composed of felspar, quartz, and mica, the latter being somewhat rare. There is another elvan dyke a little south of that above mentioned and running parallel to it. It extends from about a quarter of a mile north of Smith's tenement in this parish, to about the same distance north of the Church. This is more compact and porphyritic and contains hornblend, resembling the dykes on Caradon Hill, near Liskeard, situate within the granite district.

INDUSTRIAL PURSUITS.

Clerkenwater.—Towards the end of the last century a tanning business was conducted here by a person named Peake. The orchard adjoining the dwelling-house was called the "Tan-yard" until lately, and a tan-pit still exists at the east end of the house. The business had been discontinued for several years before 1794, when a lease of the premises was acquired by Mr. Richard Hawke, who established here a woollen factory; the spinning was conducted by hand. In 1800, however, the premises were all destroyed, except the "fulling-mill house," by fire, at a great loss to the proprietor. After a few years new premises were erected upon an enlarged scale, and machinery for carding and spinning was introduced, after which about 20 or 25 hands were employed for many years. In 1859 Mr. John Hawke, son of Mr. Richard Hawke, disposed of the premises to Mr. Lange of St. Kew, by whom the business is still conducted, though not on so extensive a scale. Blankets, sailors' cloth, and serge are manufactured. The wages of the women and girls employed is 8d. a day. With this exception there is no other industry practised than the cultivation of the soil. Agricultural laborers receive 12s. or 13s. a week, and sometimes cottage, garden, fuel, and potatoe ground in addition.

Villages.—Besides the Churchtown the only villages in the parish are Bodwen and Helland-Bridge, though they scarcely deserve the name, consisting of a few houses only. At the latter place is an ancient Bridge over the river Alan, consisting of four segmental arches, each of about 15 feet span, with deep cutwaters between them. The river now, on

[1] Ordnance Geological Survey of Cornwall. BOASE, Transactions of the Geological Society of Cornwall, IV. DE LA BECHE, Report on the Geology of Cornwall, Devon, and West Somerset.

B²

ordinary occasions, flows through the two arches at the south end, the third is filled with silt, and the fourth is used only for the mill leat. On the 8th July 1847, in consequence, it is believed, of the fall of a water spout on the hills between Davidstow and Lesnewith, a great flood took place, which destroyed all the bridges over the river Alan, except this bridge and Wadebridge. The water came rushing down suddenly with a great bole or head and quickly rose 15 feet. North Tamerton Bridge over the Tamar and Trekellard Bridge over the Inny were also damaged.

There was formerly an annual fair held at Helland-Bridge on the 4th October, but it has been discontinued for several years.

DISSENTERS' MEETING HOUSES.

There are two Meeting Houses in this parish pertaining to the Wesleyan Society, and to the two belong 30 registered members.

One is situate near Helland-Bridge and will accommodate 120 persons. It was built in 1813 upon a piece of ground granted on a lease of 999 years, by William Pascoe, the elder, of Lower Helland, yeoman, and was vested in Trustees for the erection of a Chapel or Meeting House in which the doctrines held by the Rev. John Wesley,[1] and none other, should be preached. This lease is dated 16th February 1813, and is enrolled in Chancery.[2]

The building, described as then lately erected, was registered by Richard Martyn, of St. Mabyn, yeoman, in the Court of the Archdeaconry of Cornwall, on 24th May 1815, as a place of religious worship by an assembly or congregation of Protestant Dissenters.[3] All the trustees under the above mentioned deed having died except one, a new Board of Trustees was formed, and the surviving trustee under the first deed, by indenture dated 1st August 1860, and inrolled,[4] made an assignment to them of the premises upon the same trusts as in the former deed.

The other Meeting House is situate by the side of the highway leading from Helland-Bridge to Cardinham, a short distance east from the Church Town. It was erected on a piece of land, part of the tenement of Lymsbury, sold for the purpose by Thomas Lawry, of Helland, yeoman, and by deed dated 11th July 1835, and inrolled,[5] was settled upon Trustees for the exclusive use of the people called "Methodists," according to the Trusts before described. Both these buildings, we learn, are now offered for sale, with the intention of erecting a new meeting house nearer the Church. This building will accommodate 90 persons.

---

[1] See Trust Deed cited pp. 402-403 and 483.
[2] Archdeaconry Records, Bodmin.
[3] Rot. Claus. 6th William IV., Part 46, No. 26.
[4] Rot. Claus. 53rd Geo. III., Part iv., No. 16.
[5] Rot. Claus. 1860, Part 129, No. 18.

Plate XXVIII.

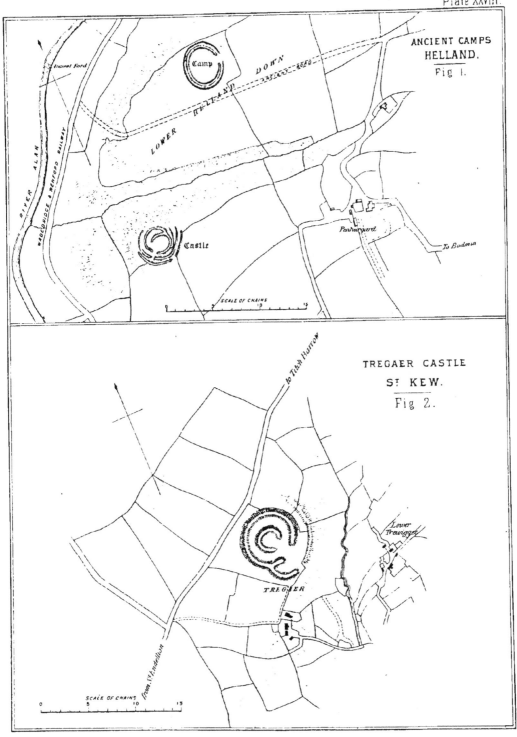

ANCIENT CAMPS
HELLAND.
Fig 1.

SCALE OF CHAINS

TREGAER CASTLE
St KEW.
Fig 2.

SCALE OF CHAINS

ANCIENT CHRISTIAN MONUMENTS.

No. 28. The only example in this parish of an ancient cross is one now set up in the Rectory grounds. It formed the threshold of the doorway to an outhouse at Boconnion, and was given to the present Rector a few years ago by the late George Pye, Esq. A portion only of the shaft remains, which scarcely measures 18 ins. in length. It is 11 in. wide, and 7 in. thick, and the head is 18 in. in diameter. The symbol is of the Greek type within a circular rim, and both sides alike.

28

PRE-HISTORIC REMAINS.

There are two ancient entrenchments, or earthworks, in this parish situate very near to each other, and evidently intended for the defence of the river Alan, of the course of which they command a view for a considerable distance, and are in sight of Pencarrow and Dunmere Camps. (See ante, pp. 113-114.) One is on the Barton of Penhargard, and the other about a quarter of a mile distant on the opposite side of a small valley springing out of the valley of the Alan.

Penhargard Castle is situate on the upper part of a wood, called Castle Wood, having a rapid slope on the north side. The fortification is of a somewhat singular character, in general form nearly circular, and about 160 feet in diameter. The circumvallation is very irregular having one curve branching out of another in an unusual manner, though on the north side the steep slope of the hill appears to have been considered a sufficient protection, defended also, as it was, on that side by the other Castle. The inner area is nearly of the form of a horse-shoe, covered on the north side by an additional rampart branching out of it. The entrance was on the south-east. On this side there is a further additional wall extending around two thirds of the whole area, but it is broached with an entrance exactly opposite to the entrance to the inner area. These entrances are, however, defended by a strong barbican. The ramparts are in some places 12 or 15 feet high.

Lower Helland Castle is of an elliptical form with diameters of about 300 and 260 feet. It consists of a single wall and external ditch, with an entrance, though not very distinct, on the upper or east side. The entrenchment is very perfect. (See Plate XXVIII.)

Ancient British Roads or Tracks.

A road or track from between the two castles, above described, may be distinctly traced in an easterly direction to the highway close to the entrance gate to Penhargard. Thence it, doubtless, proceeded, in the same direction, over the high-grounds to join the great road through the county at or near "Council Barrow" in the parish of Cardinham, just beyond the eastern boundary of Helland. As the lands, however, through which it passed have been brought under cultivation the road is not very easily traced.

Looking from Lower Helland Castle to the opposite side of the valley there would appear to be a road winding down the hill side of the wood in a direction to meet the road to which we have above referred. We conjectured that these roads or tracks would converge on the river Alan at Penhargard Ford, but we found that the ford, so called, is nearly a mile lower down the stream. On an examination of the left bank of the river, which has been disturbed by the construction of the Wadebridge and Wenford Bridge Railway, we could not discover any appearance of a ford, but on examining the right bank, in the exact place at which we expected to find the ford, we discovered the remains of one now disused, the road having been deviated and carried along the course of the river to what is now known as Penhargard Ford. The ancient dis-used ford would appear to be shewn on the Ordnance Map, and the two Castles would seem to have been well placed for its defence, the ford being situate just between them.

We may also conclude that the existing roads through the parish, from Bodmin through Clerkenwater to Helland-Bridge, and from Council Barrow to the same place, though in some parts slightly diverted, are ancient roads.

MANOR OF HELLAND, *alias* HELLAND GIFFARD, *alias* OVER-HELLAND, AND THE ADVOWSON OF THE CHURCH.

To this ancient manor the Advowson of the Rectory was formerly appurtenant. We find it recorded in Domesday under the name of Henlant,[1] at which time it was held by Seibertus under the Earl of Moreton, and in the time of King Edward the Confessor, it had been held by Ailmer. "The Earl holds one mansion which is called Henlant[2] which Ailmer held on the day on which King Edward was alive and dead, in which there is one virgate and it pays gild for one ferling. This four ploughs can plough. This Seibertus holds of the Earl, and he has thereof one acre ("agrum") in demesne and the villans hold the rest of the land and one plough. There Seibertus has two villans, and three bordars, and four acres of wood, and twenty acres of pasture. This is worth 10 shillings, and when he received it 10 shillings."

[1] Exon Domesday, vol. iv., p. 232, orig. fo. 252.
[2] In the Exchq. Domesday the name is written Henland, vol. i., p. 125.

Except that in 1283 we find the *Tithing* of Hellaund two or three times in mercy for default,[1] we do not trace any further notice of the Manor until the year 1285, when it, together with the advowson of the Church, was parcel of the possessions of the family of Giffard. In that year Ralph Giffard presented to the benefice. In 1310 Simon Giffard presented, and in 1348 Simon Giffard, probably his son, described as of Helyset, presented, and in the following year Andrew Giffard was instituted upon the presentation of John Giffard, described as son and heir of Simon. John Giffard died about the year 1375, leaving two daughters, named Ingreta and Margaret, his coheirs. He held certain lands of Reginald Bevill of Golowres, who by an indenture, dated on Wednesday next after Easter in 1376, assigned the custody of the said lands to John Colyn of Hellond, during the minority of the said heirs of John Giffard, and, in the event of their deaths, for the period of twelve years from the date of the indenture; and by the same instrument the wardship of the said heirs was committed to John Nanscavell, Parson of St. Maugan, the said John Colyn, and John Richard. Ingreta was married to Thomas Colyn son and heir of the said John, and Reginald Bevyll, by charter dated on Monday the Feast of the Conception of the Blessed Virgin Mary (9th December) granted the rent and services of the said Thomas Colyn and *Margaret* his wife and Ingreta her sister to the said John Colyn for life. Margaret,[2] the other coheir, married.........Raleigh whose arms, impaling Giffard, are still preserved in one of the windows of Helland Church (see post p. 14.)

In 1411 a fine was passed in which Robert Michel,[3] Clerk, and John Stephen, Clerk, were querists and Thomas Colyn of Helland and Ingreta his wife were deforc., whereby the said Thomas and Ingreta settled, *inter alia*, the Manors of Helland and Helset, and the advowsons of the Churches of Helland and St. Pinnock, upon the said Robert and John, to hold to the said Robert and John of the aforesaid Thomas, son of John Colyn, and Ingreta his wife, daughter of John Giffard, rendering certain rents and services to the same Thomas and Ingreta and to the heirs of the said Ingreta, and thereof made a capital fee for the said Thomas Colyn of Helland and Ingreta his wife, to hold for the whole lives of the said Thomas and Ingreta, with remainder to John son of the aforesaid Thomas son of John Colyn and Ingreta his wife, and the heirs which the said John should beget of the body of Elizabeth his wife daughter of John Nicol of Bodmyn, and in default of such issue remainder to the aforesaid Thomas Colyn and Ingreta his wife quit of the heirs of the said Robert and John Stephen, and of all other heirs of the aforesaid John son of Thomas, to be held of the Chief Lords of the fee by the rents and services thereto pertaining.[4]

John Colyn by Elizabeth his wife, daughter of John Nicol, had a son Otho, or Oto,

M

20

[1] Assize Rolls, 11th Edward I., 1 m. 8, 8d.

[2] Charter upon Inspeximus inrolled for publication. Rot. Pat. 17th Henry VII., Part II., m. 22. In this charter Margaret is incorrectly stated to be the wife of Thomas Colyn. He married her sister Ingreta as appears from other documents.

[3] Sir Robert Michell was Rector of Helland, died 1415. See post.

[4] Pedes Finium, 12th Henry IV., Hilary No. I.

who inherited the aforesaid manors, advowsons, &c., and thereof died seized on 10th September, 1463, leaving his daughter Elizabeth, aged 10 years, his nearest heir, and it appears from the inquisition taken after his death that he had conveyed all his lands to Thomas Calwodely in trust for Elizabeth daughter of the said Otho, and that at the time of the death of the said Otho, and at the time of the taking of the inquisition, the rents and profits were received by the said Thomas Calwodely to the use of the said Elizabeth.[1]

The Rectory of Helland having become vacant by the death of Sir Robert Stonard on 23rd December, 1465, by order of the Bishop an Inquisition was taken on the 16th January following as to the right of presentation, and it was found that Henry Webber, Dean of Exeter, and others, including Thomas Calwodley Senior, Sir William Ley, Chaplain of the Parish Church of Helland, and John Satchevill were the true patrons, and had the right of presentation by reason of a certain enfeoffment made to them by Otho Colyn, Esq., Lord of the Manor of Helland, to which manor the right of presentation was annexed, and that the last presentation had been made by Engredia relict of Thomas Colyn mother of John Colyn father of the aforesaid Otho.[2]

Elizabeth daughter and heir of Otho Colyn married Thomas son and heir of the above mentioned Thomas Calwodley senior, and carried the Manors of Helland, Helset, and Cassacawn into that family. Thomas her husband was alive in 1472. He died before his father but in what year we know not.[3] His widow after his death married ...... Raleigh, of the Nettlecombe family. As his widow she presented to Helland Church in 1494. She again wedded, soon after this date, Edward Ap Rice,[4] Apryse, or Preys, who in her right presented to Helland in 1499. We know not the date of her death, but by her first marriage she had a son, Humphry Calwodley, who in September 1497 embarked in the cause of the person called in history "Perkin Warbec." Though not one of those who marched to Blackheath, upon the charge of continuing assembled with others "with most traitorous and malicious purpose," he was in parliament attainted and convicted of treason, and his lands were forfeited.[5] The Colyn lands, however, not as yet being in his possession, were not affected by the attainder.

He married Johanna daughter of John Carminowe of Fentongollen and relict of John Pentyre, Jun.,[6] upon whom and her issue by him, by Charter dated 2nd January 9th Henry VII. (1493-4), he settled the Manor of Calwodlegh in co. Devon, and the

---

[1] Inq. p. m., 6th Edward IV., No. 36.

[2] Bishop Bothe's Reg., fo. 57.

[3] On 5th February 1493-4, the custody of all the lands of Thomas Calwodley, deceased, then in the hands of the King by reason of the minority of Humphry Calwodley, grandson and heir of the said Thomas, viz., the son of Thomas, son of the said Humphrey, was granted to John Ryse, Clerk, together with the wardship and marriage of the said heir. Rot. Pat., 9th Henry VII., m. 11.

[4] Rot. Pat., 21st Henry VII., Part I., m. 24.

[5] Act 19th Henry VII., Cap. 34.

[6] Of her sisters, one, Eleanor, married John Bere of Pengelly (ante p. 311); and another, Elizabeth, Nicholas Opye of Bodmyn (post Note): the wife of John Bere in the Pedigree cited is, following the records of the Heralds' College, erroneously called Elizabeth, but the brass still remaining in the Church of St. Minver (see post) in memory of Roger Opye shews that *his* mother's name was Elizabeth.

advowson of the Church thereto appurtenant.[1] By this marriage, among other children, he had a daughter, Joan, for on 16th July in that year[2] the Act of Attainder, so so far as it affected Humphry Calwodley, was reversed in favour of Joan his eldest surviving daughter, and on 14th October 1508,[3] there was a further reversal with restoration in blood and possessions to the same Joan. In this last record Humphry Calwodley is described as deceased, so that he would appear to have died between the dates of the two Acts. This Joan was born in 1496, for on the death of another Humphry Calwodley of East Stodlegh, co. Devon, on 15th November 1520, without legitimate issue, this Johanna, then the wife of Roger Arundell, was found to be his kinswoman and nearest heir.[4] Roger Arundell presented to the rectory of Helland in the following year, and died on 12th June 1536,[5] when Humphrey Arundell was found to be his son and nearest heir and to be of the full age of 23 years and more. Johanna his wife died 28th September in the following year, seized, *inter alia*, of the Manor of Over Helland with the advowson of the Church, and the Manors of Cassacawn and Helset, lands in Amaleglos, and Elwyn, her mother being then still alive, and Humphry Arundell was found to be her son and nearest heir.[6] Humphry entered into possesssion of his estates in Cornwall, and for the share which he took in the Cornish insurrection of 1549 was convicted, attainted, and executed as a rebel, and his estates became forfeited to the Crown.

The Manor of Helland with the advowson of the Church being by the forfeiture of Humphry Arundell vested in the Crown, these, and all other lands of the said Humphry in the counties of Devon and Cornwall, were, by Letters Patent dated 5th of March 1549-50,[7] granted to Sir Gawen Carew, Knight, in consideration of his good services in suppressing the rebellion. In 1553, by Letters Patent dated 13th October,[8] Sir Gawen had license to alienate the Manors of Helland and Cassacawn and the advowson of the Church of Helland to Nicholas Hele and Thomas Hele, and the manor

---

[1] Inq. p. m. of Johanna Arundell, 30th Henry VIII., No, 12. Exchequer.

[2] Rot. Pat., 22nd Henry VII., Part. 2. m. 3.

[3] Rot. Pat., 24th Henry VII., Part. 3. m. 10.

[4] Inq. p. m., 12th and 13th Henry VIII., No. 19, Exchequer.

[5] Inq. p. m. 28th Henry VIII., No. 11 Exchequer.

NOTE.—Some litigation would appear to have occurred with respect to the Manors of Helland and Helset, the exact purport of which we have not been able to unravel. In 1295 an assize of view of recognizance was taken at Launceston to enquire if William Champernoun and Walter Hay had unjustly disseized Simon the son of Ralph Giffard, of a free tenement in Helyset, when William and Walter pleaded that they held the said tenement by reason of the minority of Johanna daughter and heir of a certain Simon Giffard, who, they said, held the tenement of them by military service, and the said Johanna not being named in the writ they petitioned judgment and obtained the verdict. There was a similar assize at the same time respecting a tenement in Helland Giffard, and Simon Giffard consented to be non-suited. Assize Rolls, Cornwall and Devon, 23rd Edward I. $\frac{N}{2}$ $\}$ 5. 9

[6] Exchequer Inq. p. m. 28th and 29th Henry VIII., No. 20. Cornwall, and 29th and 30th Henry VIII., Cornwall and Devon.

[7] Rot. Pat., 4th Edward VI., Part 6.   [8] Rot. Pat., 1st Mary, p. 7. m. 29.

C

and advowson passed, as has been described (ante vol. i., p. 44) with respect to the Manor of Cassacawn, except that upon the sale of the lands of Sir John Morshead, Bart., the advowson was separated from the manor and sold to his brother, General William Morshead, by whose son, William Morshead of Lavethan, Esq., it is now possessed in "grosso."

THE RECTORY.

Under the valuation of Pope Nicholas, made between 1288 and 1291, this parish was taxed under the name of Wellonde at 40s., as it was also in 1294 under the valuation of the Bishops of Lincoln and Winchester.[1] In 15th Edward III. (1341) the Church of Hellonde was taxed for the ninth sheaf, the ninth fleece, and the ninth lamb at the same rate, and they were so sold to John Penhirgard, Jordan Waterlond, Bartholomew Fayrher, and Richard Lankearf; of 15ths there were none.[2] In the valuation of Cardinal Wolsey, 1521, the parish is rated at £9 13s. 4d. at which rate it now stands in the King's Books.[3]

The tithes were commuted into a Rent-Charge in 1840. The total quantity of land cultivated was 2186a. 3r. 39p., viz.: Arable, 1687a. 3r. 9p.; woodland, 307a. 0r. 32p.; orchard, 12a. 0r. 8p.; common, 179a. 3r. 30p. Of this the Barton of Helland, containing 507a. 1r. 32p., paid a modus of £2 per annum in lieu of all tithes.

The total value of the rent charge payable in lieu of all tithes was fixed at £212 10s. 0d., which includes the above customary payment in lieu of tithes on the Barton of Helland, and the tithe of 139a. 1r. 0p. of coppice wood amounting to £20 10s., but exclusive of the tithe of the glebe, containing 79a. 2r. 8d., the tithe of which, when not in the manurance of the Rector, was assessed at £6. The gross rent charge therefore being £218 10s.

The following terrier is not dated, but it was returned into the Bishop's Court probably in 1628, and it is still preserved in the Registry at Exeter—

Helland.

A terryer of the howses and glebe land, &c., belonging to the Rectory of Hellond, viz :—

One parlour, one hall house, one kitchen, one buttery, one larder house, one dayry, fower loft chambers, one barne, one stable, one drye house, two lynneyes, three out-

---

[1] Bishops' Reg.   [2] Inquisitiones Nonarum, p. 344.

[3] In a subsequent survey returned to the Crown by Bishop Vesey on 3rd November 1536, pursuant to a writ dated at Westminster on 20th July in that year, the value of the Rectory of Helland is stated to be £9 13s. 9d. per annum. Oliver's Ecclesiastical Antiq., Vol. ii., p. 151.

houses for piggs, one walled courtlage, three orchards, one herbour. Twoe meadowes, one called the greate meadowe, contayning fower acres; and the other called the little meadowe, contayning one acre, on the north side bounded wth the highway, on the east wth the landes of Mr. Hele of Fleete. The great Sanctuary and three parcels contaying fifteen acres or thereabouts bounded on the southside wth the highwaye, and on the east and north wth the landes of Stephen Toker, Gent^l.

GYLES HENWOOD ⎱ Wardens.
JAMES MERIFIELD ⎰

Institutions.

1285, October 3rd	- Thomas de Hendre, Chaplain,[1] was instituted to the Church of Hellond, vacant and in the presentation of Ralph Giffard, the true patron.
1310, July 20th	- John de Roscarek, Clerk,[2] was instituted to the Church of Hellaund, vacant and in the presentation of Simon de Giffard.
1348, November 10th	- Lawrence Giffard, Clerk,[3] was instituted to the Church of Helland, vacant through the death of John de Roscarrek, upon the presentation of Simon Giffard de Helyset, the true patron.
1349, June 25th	- Andrew Giffard, Clerk,[4] was instituted to the parish Church of Helland upon the presentation of John Giffard, son and heir of Simon Giffard, the true patron.
unknown	- Sir Robert Michel.
1415, January 16th	- Sir Robert Wyllet, Priest,[5] was admitted to the Rectory and Church of Helland, vacant by the death of Sir Robert Michel the last Rector, upon the presentation of Thomas Colyn of Hellond, the true patron.
unknown	- Sir Robert Stonard.[6] presented by Engredia, relict of Thomas Colyn.

---

[1] Bishop Bronscombe's Register, fo. 16.

[2] Bishop Stapelton's Register, fo. 53. On 18th September 1310, John de Roscarek, Rector of Helland, Clerk, was granted letters dismissory as regarded all minor orders. (Stapleton, fo. 56.)

[3] Bishop Grandison's Register, fo. 68.

[4] Ibid. fo. 82. In 1354 Andrew Giffard, Rector of the Church of Helland, was licensed to hear confessions in the Deanery of Trigg Minor. (Grandison, vol. i., fo. 182.)

[5] Bishop Stafford's Register, fo. 174.

[6] He was Rector in 1444 as appears from an Inquisition respecting the right of presentation to the Church of St. Tudy (Lacy, vol. ii., fo. 213) and he appears also on a Commission concerning the right of presentation to the parish Church of St. Endellion on 25th September 1462 (Nevill, fo. 86), and he resigned on 23rd December 1465 (Bothe, fo. 57).

C^2

1465, February 16th - William Ley, Chaplain,[1] was admitted to the parish Church of Helland, vacant by the resignation of Robert Stonard, the last Rector, upon the presentation of Henry Webber, Dean of Exeter, and others, the true patrons.

unknown - Sir William Radwey.

1494, February 8th - William Leigh,[2] was instituted to the parish Church of Helland, vacant by the death of William Radwey, last Rector, upon the presentation of Elizabeth Ralegh widow, the true patron.

1499, September 21st - John Hancok,[3] was instituted to the Church of Helland, vacant by the death of William Legh, upon the presentation of Edward Apryse in right of his wife Elizabeth, the true patron.

1521, February 1st - William Hockyn,[4] was instituted to the parish Church of Helland, vacant by the death of John Hancocke, last Rector, upon the presentation of Roger Arundell Esq., the true patron in right of his wife Johanna.

1555, March 20th - William Woodman, Clerk,[5] was admitted to the Church of Helland upon the presentation of Thomas Hele, gent, the true patron.

1577, June 16th - Robert Beare, Clerk,[6] was admitted to the Rectory of the parish of Helland, vacant by the death of the late Incumbent, upon the presentation of Thomas Heale gent, the true patron.

unknown - John Tucker[7] was admitted.

1602, December 14th - Roger Squire, Clerk, M.A.,[8] was admitted to the Rectory of Helland, vacant by the death of John Tucker, upon the presentation of Thomas Hele of Fleete, Esq., the true patron.

1632, April 9th - John Rous, Clerk, A.B.,[9] was admitted to the Rectory of Helland, vacant by the death of Roger Squire, Clerk, upon the presentation of Sir Thomas Hele Bart., the true patron.

1672, September 24th - Richard Hele[10] was admitted to the Rectory of Helland, vacant by the death of John Rous, A.B., the last Incumbent, upon the presentation of Samuel Hele of Fleet Damerel, Bart., the true patron.

[1] Bishop Bothe's Register, fo. 4. On 15th June 1466, William Ley, Rector of Helland, was on an Inquisition concerning the right of presentation to a Prebend in the Church of St. Endellion (Bothe, 103).

[2] Bishop King's Register, fo. 169.   [3] Bishop Redmayn's Register, fo. 11.

[4] Bishop Voysey's Register, fo. 11.   [5] Bishop Turberville's Register, fo. 9.

[6] Bishop Bradridge's Register, fo. 37. Paid Composition for First Fruits 4th February 1577-8, (Augmentation Office).   [7] Paid Composition for First Fruits 18th May, 1580 (Augmentation Office).

[8] Bishop Carey's Register, fo. 75. Paid Composition for First Fruits 19th February 1602-3 (Augmentation Office). Buried at Helland. A fragment of his gravestone remains. See post p. 15.

[9] Bishop Hall's Register, fo. 28. Matric. at Queen's College, Oxford, 1st February 1621-2, aged 18, as third son of an "Armiger" of co. Devon. No other particulars are given. He was probably son of Ambrose Rouse by Maudlyn dau. of John Osborne (Visit. Devon. Harl. Soc., p. 350). Paid Comp. for First Fruits 19th May 1632 (Augmentation Office).

[10] Bishop's Registers N.S., vol. ii., fo. 8. Son of Richard Hele of Fleete co. Devon, Gent., Matric. at Exeter College, Oxford, 23rd November 1666, aged 19. B.A., 5th July 1670.

1682, June 1st   - George Wakeham, Clerk,[1] was admitted to the Rectory of Helland, vacant by the resignation of Richard Hele, upon the presentation of the same Richard Hele of Fleet, co. Devon.

1704, August 16th   - Edward White, Clerk,[2] was admitted to the Rectory of Helland, vacant by the death of George Wakeham, last Rector, upon the presentation of Richard Hele, Esq., the true patron.

1731, March 22nd   - Ezekiel Williams, Clerk, L.L.B.,[3] was admitted to the Rectory of Helland, vacant by the death of Edward White, last Incumbent, upon the presentation of John Treise of Helland Esq., the true patron.

1778, May 30th   - Edmund Gilbert, Clerk, M.A.,[4] was admitted to the Rectory of Helland, void by the death of Ezekiel Williams, last Incumbent, upon the presentation of Sir Christopher Treise Knt., the true patron.

1817, March 26th   - Francis John Hext, Clerk, B.A.,[5] was admitted to the Rectory of Helland, void by the death of Edmund Gilbert, Clerk, the last Rector, upon the presentation of William Morshead of Lavethan, General in His Majesty's Forces, the true patron, as it is asserted.

1842, July 25th   - John Glencross, Clerk, B.A.,[6] was admitted to the Rectory of Helland, void by the death of Francis John Hext, the last Rector, upon the presentation of the Rev. William Molesworth of St. Breoke, Clerk, the true patron as it is said.

1859, June 17th   - James Hicks Glencross, Clerk, B.A.,[7] was admitted to the Rectory of Helland, void by the death of John Glencross, the last Rector, upon the presentation of Frances Susanna Molesworth widow, Sir Hugh Molesworth, Clerk and Baronet, and James Wentworth Buller, Esq., Representatives of General William Morshead, the true patron, as it is asserted.

[1] Bishop's Reg. N.S., vol. iii., fo. 25. Son of Ralph Wakeham of Southmolton co. Devon. Matric. at Exeter Coll. Oxford, 6th April 1666, aged 19. B.A. 26th October 1669.

[2] Ibid. vol. iv. fo. 110, Matric. at Pembroke College, Oxford, 16th March 1692-3, aged 19; as son of John White, "Pleb." of "Helon," co. Cornwall. B.A. as of Exeter College, 23rd March 1696. Bur. at Helland 16th November, 1731. Par. Reg.

[3] Ibid. vol. vi. fo. 111. Son of John Williams of Truro, Esq.; Matric. at Exeter College, Oxford, 1st March 1721-2, aged 17. B.A. 27th October 1725; B.C.L. 21st January 1731.

[4] Ibid. vol. ix. fo. 142. Son of Pomeroy Gilbert of St. Andrews, Plymouth, Gent. (see Ped. ante vol. i. p. 303); Matric. at Exeter College, Oxford, 14th July 1769, aged 20. B.A. 28th February 1775. He was also Vicar of Constantine.

[5] Ibid. vol. xi. fo. 90. Son of Francis John Hext of Bodmin, Gent. (see Ped. post); Matric. at Exeter Coll. Oxford, 8th April 1797, aged 17. Bur. at Helland, 3rd February 1842. Par. Reg.

[6] Ibid. vol. xii. fo. 183. Son of Josiah Glencross of Devonport. B.A. of Queen's College Cambridge 1825. Bur. at Helland 19th March 1859. Par. Reg.

[7] Son of James Glencross of Devonport, by Ann youngest daughter of General Morshead, and nephew of the preceding Rector. B.A. of Christ's College Cambridge, 1853.

THE PARISH CHURCH.

The Church, according to tradition, recognized by Dr. Oliver, is dedicated to St. Helena. It consists of a chancel, 21ft. by 14ft. 8in.; nave, 42ft. by 14ft. 8in.; south aisle, 38ft. 10in. by 14ft. 2in.; south porch, 9ft. by 8ft. 6in.; and a tower of one flight only, with a hipped roof. On the north side of the nave the Rev. F. J. Hext, during the time he was rector, erected at his own expense a sort of transept to be used as a school. (See Plate XXIX.)

The east window of the chancel is three light five fo. ogee. It is modern but of good workmanship, and was set up by Mr. Hext. There are also two modern three light square headed windows on the north side of the chancel.

The south aisle is of four bays separated from the nave by monolith pillars, supporting four-centred arches of the usual Cornish type. In the eastern bay is a priest's door. The aisle is lighted by a good three light five fo. ogee window at the east end, with tracery in the head, in one opening of which, in ancient glass, remains an escutcheon charged with the arms of Giffard of Helland: az. three fleurs de lis or.[1] There remain also in other openings of the tracery the sacred monogram, and a monogram of "Maria," both of good design. On the south side are four windows three light five fo. (See Plate XXX.) In the tracery of the second from the east is an escutcheon of arms, Gules five fusils in bend ar. with a label in chief, az. (Raleigh) impaling Giffard as above. In the third window are other remains of old glass. A portion of the figure of our Lord in Majesty. When Bodmin Church was rebuilt in 1472, one of the windows was sold to the parish of Helland, as appears from the building accounts: "Item recevyd for a wyndowe y sold to the parish of Hellond xxvj[s.]" This is probably the window so purchased. There is also a very bad modern window at the west end.

The tower is separated from the nave by a plain arch now blocked up by a singing gallery. The tower is said to have been formerly more lofty, and to have fallen down about a century ago. Building materials are found near it in digging graves. In 6th Edward VI. it contained three bells.[2] At present it has one only, which was recast by Pennington in 1805, and bears the following inscription:—" Edmund Gilbert, rector. William Neikell, Ambrose Manaton C.W. ∴ J.P. 1805." In the base of the tower we found some old

---

[1] Lysons (Mag. Brit. III., cxxxiv.) has blazoned the arms of Giffard of Helland with a pellet on each of the fleurs de lis. From an attentive examination of this glass, however, which the author has had carefully cleaned and reset, it is clear there never were any pellets. The arms do not in any respect differ from the old arms of France.

[2] The said parishners haue a Chalice. Item. iij belles yn the tower there. (Augment. Office, Church Goods 6th Edward VI. $\frac{1}{51}$)

Plate XXV.

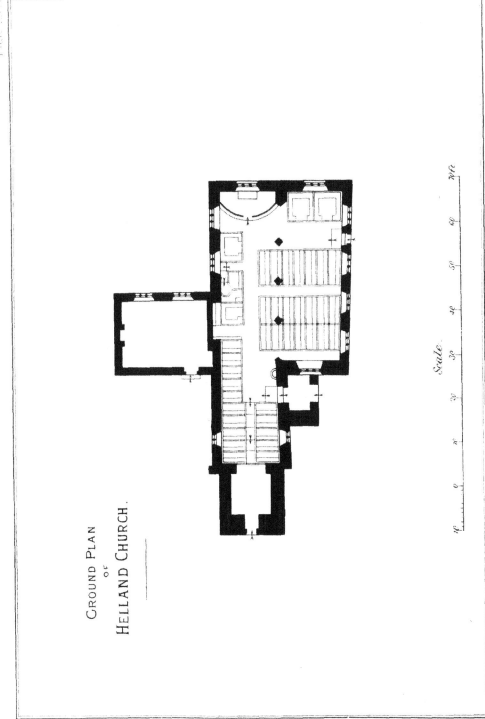

GROUND PLAN
OF
HELLAND CHURCH.

Scale.

PLATE XXXI.

HELLAND HALL
Fig 1

THE GRAVESTONE of HUMPHRY CALWODELY, in HELLAND CHURCH
Fig 2

roof timbers of oak. One wall plate, 15ft. long, being carved with quatrefoils which have been coloured alternately blue and yellow upon a red ground.

The font is in the nave near the south door, and is of granite, circular, and plain, without anything to indicate its date. It is partially set in the wall. The seating of the Church is modern, as mean and bad as can be conceived.

MONUMENTAL INSCRIPTIONS.

Against the north wall of the Chancel is a marble tablet with this inscription :—

(1). Sacred to the Memory of the Rev. FRANCIS JOHN HEXT, A.M., of Tredethy, 25 years Rector of this Parish, who died at Bath, 22nd January, 1842. Aged 62 years. Virtuous and upright, he earnestly endeavoured with true Christian Charity to do good to all around him.

On the floor of the Chancel are fragments of grave stones. On one is a portion of an inscription in old English characters :—

(2)........r Squire[1] Mr of Arts & Rector of this......(and on another portion of the same stone)......e of his age an° Dom....

(3). Lying transversely in the South aisle, just inside the Priest's entrance, is an incised slab, much worn, representing the figure of a man in a gown reaching to the ancles, with long sleeves, through slits in which the arms protrude, the hands being joined in prayer. In the dexter upper corner is a shield charged with the arms of Calwodely : or, a pair of wings conjoined in lure az. debruised by a fess gu. charged with 3 bezants ; and on the other side the same arms impaling Carminowe.

Around the margin of the stone, cut in rude letters, is the following inscription, so far as it can be deciphered :—

"Yow shall praye for the sowle of Vmfrey Calwodly son & ayre of tomas Calwodly and Eliz. daughter & ayre to Otes Colyn."

IN THE SOUTH AISLE.

(4). To the memory of ELIZABETH wife of JOHN HOOPER of Penhargard, in this Parish, who died February 6th 1839, in her 54th year.

Although a long and severe sufferer she bore her affliction with patience and exemplary Christian fortitude. As a wife few exceeded her in worth, and as a mother she was tender and affectionate.

This tablet is erected as the last testimony of affection by her bereaved and sorrowing husband and children.

[1] Roger Squire, Clerk, M.A., Rector of Helland, died 1632 (see ante p. 12)

(5). Sacred to the Memory of JAMES SANDYS, infant son of Captain G. B. KEMPTHORNE, I.N. and CHARLOTTE LOUISA his wife, who died at Aden on the 19th January 1843, aged 9 months.

His affectionate parents, in fond remembrance of his heaven-loved innocence, erect this monument to his memory in humble gratitude for the glorious assurance that of such is the Kingdom of GOD.

IN THE CHURCHYARD.

Upon the base of an obelisk:—

(6) In Memory of THOMAS LAWRY of Broads, in this Parish, who died March 24th 1861, aged 84;

And of MARY his wife, who died May 26 1856, aged 72; Also of EDMUND their son, who died May 7 1859, aged 42.

On another obelisk:—

(7) Sacred to the Memory of JOHN HOOPER of Trequites[1] in the Parish of St. Mabyn, who died May 4th 1859, aged 84.

(8). On a slab of granite:—

H . I . H.[2]
1852.

(9). In Memory of FLORENCE ELIZABETH the beloved wife of the Rev. SAMUEL ANDREWE, M.A., Rector of Halwell, Devon, and second daughter of the late JOHN HOOPER Esq. of Penhargard, died May 15th 1868, aged 68 years.

nec multis impar.

(9) ANN SLYMAN HOOPER, obt. Mar. 21 1869, ÆT 63.

(10). WILLIAM SLYMAN died at Penhargard on the 13th day of Feby 1832, aged 48 years.

PARISH REGISTERS.

The old Registers of this Parish have been lost. The earliest now in existence commences in 1722.

ALTAR PLATE.

The parishioners had a chalice in 6th Edward VI. They have now a paten and chalice of silver but modern, having been given by the Rev. F. J. Hext during the time he was Rector. The paten bears his initials and the date "1838."

---

[1] The same as is described in No. 4 as of Penhargard.

[2] This stone commemorates Henry John Hooper, only son and heir of John Hooper of Penhargard. By his wife Laura daughter of John Lyne, Esq., of Moorswater, near Liskeard, he left an only son, Henry Harding Hooper, bap. 2nd January 1852.

MANOR OF NETHER HELLAND.

This manor, together with the manor of Helland Giffard, already treated of, was probably in the Domesday Survey taxed under the name Henland. At what date Nether Helland became a separate manor we have no knowledge. It is likely the original manor became divided between coheirs.

The Fee of the manor of Nether Helland was at an early period held by the great family of Dinham. It was part of the possessions of which Joceus de Dinham died seized in the year 1300, and was then held of him by John le Seneschal. "John le Seneschal holds in Hellond a quarter part one fee and the value is 40s."[1] John le Seneschal died in 1308, and we conceive he must have held the Manor of Helland in right of his wife, for we do not find it included among his possessions in the inquisition taken after his death,[2] for among the lands held by Richard St. Margaret on his death in 1325 were certain lands in Kellinough which he held of Johanna, who was the wife of John le Seneschal, as of the Manor of Helland by rent of 2s. and suit at Court.[3]

The manor afterwards passed to the family of Merton. In Trinity term 1332[4] a fine was passed in which Richard de Merton junr., and Johanna his wife, probably the widow of John le Seneschal, were querists, and Walter de Merton and Nicholas Horlock, Chaplain, deforciants, for settling the manor on the said Richard and Johanna to hold to them and the heirs of their bodies of the Chief Lord of the fee by the services which to the said manor pertained, with remainder, in default of issue, to the right heirs of Richard. And in the statement of those who on the occasion of the king's eldest son being made a knight paid the aid of 40s. on each knight's fee, in which statement is also shewn the names of those who held the same fees when the aid was granted to King Edward I. on the marriage of his eldest daughter, "Richard de Merton is returned for the fourth part of one fee in Helland which John Seneschal[5] held before."

Soon afterwards this manor, together with other lands which had been held by John le Seneschal, had passed to Sir Richard Sergeaux, Knt., who thereof died seized on 30th September 1393,[6] when the manor of Helland devolved upon Richard Sergeaux, his son and heir, then aged nineteen years, save one third which was held in dower by Philippa his mother. Richard the son died 23rd June 1396, a minor, and his lands were inherited by his four sisters and heirs Elizabeth, Philippa, Alice, and Johanna.[7] In the partition of the lands of Richard Sergeaux the manor of Nether Helland, *inter*

---

[1] Inq. p.m., 29th Edward I., No. 56.　　[2] Inq. p.m., 2nd Edward II., No. 43.
[3] See ante vol. i., p. 273.　　[4] Pedes Finium, 6th Edward III., Trinity No. 4.
[5] Queen's Rememb. Office, Miscel. Books, Book of Aids, fo. 34.
[6] Inq. p.m., 17th Richard II., No. 53.　　[7] Inq. p.m., 1st Henry IV., No. 14.

D

alia, was allotted to his sister Philippa, who was then the widow of Robert Passele Esq., deceased, and the said Philippa in her widowhood, by charter dated at Trevellen 12th February, 8th Henry IV., granted all the said lands to William Swinborne Esq., for the term of his life to hold of the said Philippa by the rent of one red rose, by virtue of which grant the said William was seized of the said lands. Afterwards the said William took the said Philippa to wife, who died in 1420, when John Passele, her son, was found to be her nearest heir.[1] William Swinborne continued to hold, *inter alia*, the Manor of (Nether) Helland until his death, which happened on 22nd May 1422,[2] when John Passele entered into possession. Nether Helland, however, is not found among the possessions of John Passele on his death on 20th November 1468,[3] so that he must have alienated it previously. During the whole of this period it continued to be held of the Manor of Cardinham by military service.

In 1467 this manor belonged to Sir Thomas de Burgh, Knt., who petitioned against Robert Dabernoun and Johanna his wife, concerning one toft and half an acre of land Cornish, with appurtenances, in Newaton in the parish of Helland, which the said Robert and Johanna held of him as of his manor of Helland by homage and fealty, and scutage to the King of 3s., with, when it should happen, 20s., and rent of 10s. per annum, as also suit at the Court of the manor of Helland from three weeks to three weeks.[4] Very soon afterwards it was in the possession of Thomas Bodulgate, who died thereof seized, *inter alia*, on the Monday next before the feast of Easter 1471, it being held of John Dynham, Lord Dynham, as of his manor of Cardynham; and Isabella, late wife of John Roscarrock, aged 65 years, and Johanna, late wife of Edward Coryton, aged 60 years, were found to be his sisters and nearest heirs.[5]

The manor now fell to the families of Roscarrock and Coryton in moieties, John Roscarrock of Roscarrock, by his charter dated 6th January 18th Henry VIII., (1526-7), conveyed it, *inter alia*, to trustees to the use of himself for life, with remainder to Richard Roscarrock his son and heir apparent and the heirs of his body.[6] In this deed the lands are described as Nether Helland, Lancoithen, Furshaye, Helland-brigge, Bodwen, Shilwood, Newton, Killynowgh, Treverbyn, Northwood, Bery, Coldreynek, Heynond, Penkeriowe, and Rosepark. Richard Roscarrock died 26th October 1575, seized, *inter alia*, of this manor,[7] as did his son and heir, Thomas Roscarrock, on 3rd February 1586-7,[8] and Hugh Roscarrock of Pinchley on 6th December 1617, when Charles Roscarrock was found to be kinsman and nearest heir of the said Hugh, viz., the son of John Roscarrock Esq., son of Thomas Roscarrock Esq., elder brother of the said Hugh.[9] By Indenture of bargain and sale dated 25th June 1622, Charles Roscarrock conveyed all his

---

[1] Inq. p.m., 8th Henry V., No. 40.   [2] Inq. p.m., 3rd Henry VI., No. 23.

[3] Inq. p.m., 13th Edward IV., No. 43.   [4] De Banco Rolls, 7th Edward IV., Michaelmas, m. 552.

[5] Inq. p.m., 11th Edward IV., No. 17.   [6] Inq. p.m. 28th and 29th Henry VIII. (Escheator's)

[7] Inq. p.m., Wards and Liveries, 18th, 19th and 20th Elizabeth, vol. xviii. p. 33.

[8] Inq. p.m., 30th Elizabeth, Part I., No. 82.

[9] Inq. p.m., Wards and Liveries, 15th James, No. 152.

estate in the Manor of Nether Helland to Sir Richard Robartes, Bart., and by a Deed Poll dated 3rd May 1623, quit claimed all his right, title, &c., in the same premises to the said Sir Richard Robartes, his heirs and assigns for ever.

The Coryton moiety remained for a considerable period in the possession of that family. By deed,[1] dated 10th December 7th Elizabeth (1564), Peter Coryton of West Newton, Esq., son and heir of Richard Coryton deceased, granted to his mother, Ann Coryton, widow, an annuity of £32 a year payable, *inter alia*, out of his manor of Helland and other Bodulgate lands. It further appears from an abstract, in the handwriting of Sir William Coryton, of old deeds in the possession of the Coryton family in 1640, that there was a counterpart of the Conveyance, dated 3rd James, of the manor of Helland and divers lands in the parish of Helland by his grandfather, William Coryton, to Stephen Toser and his heirs for the sum of £310.

In what manner or at what date this moiety was acquired by the family of Robartes we have been unable to ascertain, but we find that soon after the accession of Charles I. they possessed the entirety, and it is now part of the possessions of Lord Robartes of Lanhydrock.

From a Rental or Extent of the Lands of Richard Roscarrock, Esq., 1569, in the possession of Francis Rodd, of Trebartha Hall, Esq.

MANERIUM DE NYTHER HELLOND.

Trigg.

Liberi Tenentes.

Hellond Brydge *wardus domini*	Thomas Luky quondam Johannes Luky olim Thomas Dygher tenet ibidem acr' terre Cornubiens' in........ Et faciet sectam communem curiæ Et reddit per annum xij⁵ solvendos ad quatuor anni terminos principales.	xij⁵
Waterlond *wardus domini*	Idem Thomas Luky quondam Thomas Dygher Et postea Johannes Luky tenet ibidem dimidiam acram terre Cornubiensem in Milicia Et faciet sectam curiæ vt supra Et reddit per annum vnum par albarum cerotecarum	j par albarum cerotecarum
Bodwen *wardus*	Idem Thomas tenet ibidem dimidiam acram terre Cornubiensem in Milicia Et faciet vt supra Et reddit per annum ij⁵	ij⁵
Kyllygnawith	Johannes Rayshleight quondam Ricardus Wynslade Et postea Johannes Wynslade Et postea Reginaldus Mohun Et postea Willelmus Mohun tenet ibidem vnam acram terre Cornubiensem in Milicia Et faciet vt supra Et reddit per annum iiij⁵	iiij⁵ Md. quod Wynslade attinctus fuit de alta proditione in anno tercio Edwardi sexti

[1] Documents at Coker Court, co. Soms.

D²

Kylmarght in Seynt Kewe	Willelmus Mohun Armiger quondam Willelmus Mohun Et postea Reginaldus Mohun tenet ibidem dimidiam acram terre Cornubiensem in Milicia Et faciet vt supra Et [reddit] per annum xiij^d	xiij^d
Newton vacat quia in convencionem	Remanet inter convencionem et est j acra terre Cornubiensis in Milicia Et solebat reddere viij^d	nil
Strykstenton in parochia de Endelyan	Ricardus Roscarrock Armiger dominus manerij quondam Johannes Trenowith Armiger postea Johannes Roscarrock Armiger solebat reddere .... sed modo dimittitur Johanni Boyth Et Thomasinæ vxori eius cum "le Towne place" de Bodanan sed non est parcella eiusdem	
le tenure et seruyce del manor	Omnia predicta terras et tenementa tenentur de ffeodo de Cardynham in feodo Mortane per seruicium quartæ partis et decimam partem vnius ffeodi militis Mortane cum parte Petri Coryngton Armigeri: Vid$^{t.}$ medietas eiusdem manerii Et releuium quando acciderit xxiij^s iiij^d	vj^d

West.

Treverbyn	Johannes Langdon Armiger quondam Thomas Trethewy Et postea Robertus Langdon tenet ibidem dimidiam acram terre Cornubiensem in Milicia Et faciet sectam communem Et reddit per annum ij^s ij^d obolum	ij^s ij^d obolum
nil quia attincti de alta proditione	heredes Bonvyle postea Marchio Dorset............Et postea Dux Suffolciæ modo in manus dominæ Reginæ tenet ibidem acram terre Cornubiensem in Milicia Et faciet sectam vt supra Et reddunt per annum	
Northwood in Treverbyn in parochia de Seynt Nyott	Bernardus Penros iure Elizabethæ vxoris sue filie et heredis Thome Enys........et heredis Thome Methros tenet ibidem vnam acram terre Cornubiensem in Milicia Et faciet duas sectas curiæ Et reddit per annum j librum piperis	j librum piperis
le tenure et serryce del tenent	Et predicta terra et tenementa tenentur de dominis de Penpoll per seruicium Militare in feodo Mortane per redditum de xiij^d per annum.	xiij^d

Summa xxj^s iij^d obolum—j par albarum cerotecarum et j libra piperis cum iiij^s pro Kyllygnowght nuper terras Johannis Wynslade[1] et nunc in manus Reginæ ratione attincturæ Johannis Wynslade[1] et solvit xvij^s iiij^d obolum

[1] Winslade was one of those who suffered with Humphry Arundell. He is mentioned by Strype (Memorials vol. ii. p. 281) as one of the "heads and captains of the rebellion." See also Journal of Royal Inst. of Cornwall, 1865, p. 36.

Trygg.

Convencionarii Tenentes.

Nyther Hellond

Henricus Beste tenet ibidem per indenturam ad terminum vite reddendo annuatim ad iiij^{or} terminos anni vsuales xxiij^s iiij^d.... dies duos cariandi unum caponem Et faciet curiæ Et erit prepositus et decennarius et heriotum quando acciderit } xxiij^s iiij^d / i caponem / ij dies cariandi

Johannes Gayche tenet ibidem per indenturam ad terminum vite Et faciet vt supra Et reddit per annum viij^s iiij^d } vi:j^s iiij^d / i caponem / i diem cariandi

Isabella Pawle vidua et Willelmus Pawle tenent ibidem Et facient vt supra Et reddunt per annum viij^s iiij^d et alia seruicia } viij^s iiij^d / i caponem / i diem cariandi

ffurshaye

Johannes Gayche tenet ibidem et reddet per annum............et heriotum &c. vt supra
....tenet ibidem et reddit per annum.....et heriotum &c vt supra } iiij^s vj^d

Isabella Pawle vidua et Willelmus Pawle tenent ibidem Et reddunt per annum vt supra et heriotum &c } iiij^s vj^d

Lancothan

Ricardus Luky tenet ibidem duo tenementa vid^t totam villam ibidem Et reddit per annum xxvij^s iiij^d diem cariandi diem autumpno caponem et heriotum &c vt supra } xxvij^s iiij^d / i caponem i diem cariandi, &c

Medietas ville de Newton

Georgius Smyth tenet ibidem medietatem ville per indenturam Et reddit per annum x^s sectam curiæ heriotum diem autumpno diem cariandi et vnum caponem } x^s / i caponem / i diem cariandi

Coldrenecke

Nicholaus Byry, Thomas Berry, et Willelmus Pawle tenent ibidem et reddunt per annum xxxiiij^s viij^d et sectam curiæ annectitur manerio per Thomam Roscarrock Armigerum dominum manerii xxvj^{to} die Novembris anno Elizabethe Regine xix[1] } xxxiiij^s viij^d

Bodwethgan

Ricardus Menhyneke tenet ibidem et reddit per annum j diem cariandi et sectam communem et reddit per annum } x^s / i diem cariandi

Robertus John tenet ibidem ...... partem et reddit per annum j diem cariandi et sectam communem et reddit iiij^s viij^d } iiij^s viij^d / i diem cariandi

Isabella Pawle vidua et Willelmus Pawle tenent ibidem........ partem et reddit per annum j diem cariandi et pro redditu iiij^s } iiij^s / i diem cariandi

Rogerus Hendy tenet ibidem .... partem Et faciet sectam communem Et ij dies cariandi Et reddit per annum viij^s } viij^s / duos dies cariandi

[1] Written in a later hand.

Shylawoode   Johannes Playe tenet ibidem et faciet communem sectam duos } vj⁕
              dies cariandi et reddit inde per annum vj⁕   ⁖ duos dies
                                                                             ⁖ cariandi

              Rogerus Hendy tenet ibidem et reddit communem sectam et vnum } ij⁕
              diem cariandi et reddit per annum ij⁕   i diem cariandi

              Ricardus Menhynek tenet ibidem et reddit communem sectam } ij⁕
              diem cariandi et melius animal quando acciderit   i diem cariandi

              Ricardus Lukye tenet ibidem et reddit communem sectam } ij⁕
              diem cariandi   i diem cariandi

Kyllygnowgh   Johannes Playe et............tenent ibidem vnam sullonem } xᵈ
              siue pecia terre vocatam " le Chapell acre " et reddunt per }
              annum xᵈ

              Summa vjˡⁱ v⁕ xᵈ quinque capones et xvj dies cariandi jamp- }
              num   }

              Suma conventionum cum Coldreneke viijˡⁱ vjᵈ

              Summa totalis receptus ixˡⁱ xxjˡⁱ obolum [1]

MANOR OF PENHARGARD.

This was an ancient manor but it is now dismembered. It was formerly a member of the Manor and Lordship of Bliston (Blisland) and was perhaps taxed under that manor in the Domesday Survey. We do not find the name of Penhargard in the record. It was long held of the Manor of Bliston in socage by a family of gentlemen who from it took their designation. The same family held also, *inter alia*, the Manor of Polhorman which for a long period accompanied the Manor of Penhargard in its frequent changes. In 1366 a fine was levied in which Robert Tresillian was querist and John Penhargard deforcient, by which the Manor of Polhorman was settled upon the said Robert to hold to him and the heirs of his body of the said John de Penhargard for ever at the rent of one red rose for all services, and in the event of the said Robert dying without heirs of his body remainder was reserved to the said John de Penhargard quit of all other heirs of the said Robert. We have failed to trace the transfer of the Manor of Penhargard to Robert Tresillian, and know not how he became possessed of it. This Robert Tresillian became Chief Justice of the King's Bench, and having incurred the

---

[1] In a later handwriting.

anger of the nobles in arms against the king, for the answer given by him and the other judges to certain questions submitted to their judgment by the king relating to the Constitution and the king's prerogative, he was attainted in Parliament and condemned to be drawn on a hurdle through the city of London and hanged at Tyburn,[1] and he suffered accordingly. By his attainder his lands fell into the hands of the king, who by Charters dated respectively on the 21st October,[2] and 23rd November 1389,[3] and 15th May 1390,[4] granted the greater part of them to John Hawley of Dartmouth, clerk, whose son John Hawley of the same place had married Emeline daughter of the said Sir Robert Tresillian (see Ped. of BURDON; BONVILLE, &c. ante vol. i., p. 394.) But the Manor of Polhorman and divers other lands, and also the Manor of Penhargard, with appurtenances and three messuages in Bodmyn, together with 108s. 8d. rent of assize in divers tenements in Penhargard and Killinowek, together with all wards, marriages, &c., had been on 27th November 1388,[5] granted to Sir Humphry Stafford Knt., and his heirs for ever, and this Charter, upon Inspeximus, was confirmed by Henry IV. on 27th November 1399.[6]

Humphry Stafford, however, in 1389 conveyed the lands which he had acquired under the above Charter to John Hawley for the sum of £300 sterling, as appears by a fine in which John Hawleigh of Dartmouth was querist, and the said Humphry deforcient.[7]

The possession by John Hawley of Penhargard was soon disputed by Walter Penhargard, who in 1392 brought an action to recover the estate. He pleaded that John Penhargard gave it to Walter his son and the heirs male of his body, in default to Ralph brother of Walter and the heirs male of his body, in default of such issue to Thomas brother of the said Ralph and the heirs male of his body, and in default of such issue to Bartholomew Penhargard brother of the said John and the heirs male of his body, and in default of such issue to Lawrence Penhargard, brother of the said Bartholomew and the heirs male of his body; and in consequence of the said Walter son of John, Ralph, Thomas, and Bartholomew having died without issue male, it ought to descend to him as son and heir of Lawrence. John Hawley, on this occasion, pleaded an informality in the writ, and Walter Penhargard consented to a non-suit,[8] but he renewed the proceedings in the following term, though the case did not come on for hearing until Michaelmas term, 1395.[9] John Hawley, in defence called Sir Humphry Stafford to warrant, who appeared and pleaded that the King by his Letters Patent had granted to the said Humphry the manor of Polhorman and other lands which had belonged

---

[1] Rot. Parl. 11th Richard II. He was hanged at Tyburn on the 19th February 1388, and was, it is believed, the first person who suffered at that place. Previous executions had taken place at Smithfield; but Nicholas Brembre, the late Lord Mayor of London, was to be hanged on the following day, and it is supposed the place of execution was changed because the Duke of Gloucester and his party hesitated to hang a late chief magistrate within the precincts of his own city. (Notes and Queries 4th Series, vol. xi., 164).

[2] Rot. Pat., 13th Richard II., Part I., m. 4.   [3] Ibid. Part II., m. 30.

[4] Ibid. Part III., m. 16.   [5] Rot. Pat. 12th Richard II., Part I. m. 6.

[6] Rot. Pat., 1st Henry IV., Part IV., m. 28.   [7] Pedes Finium, 13th Richard II., Michaelmas, No. 6.

[8] De Banco Rolls, 15th Richard II., Easter, m. 105.   [9] Ibid. 19th Richard II., Michaelmas, m. 274.

to Sir Robert Tresillian, and also the manor of Penhargard and three messuages in Bodmyn under the name of 108s. 8d. rent of assize with appurtenances in Penhargard and Kellignowek whereof the lands claimed were parcel, and that having had these tenements of the gift of the king he petitioned the aid of the king in defence. The case was postponed, and Walter Penhargard was directed by the Court meanwhile to proceed against the king. The case was deferred from term to term, but we have not found that Walter took any proceedings against his more potent adversary. John Hawley retained possession and died seized of the manors of Polhorman and Penhargard,[1] the latter being held of Richard Earl of Warwick (then Lord of the manor of Bliston) in free socage, and the net value was stated to be 100s. per annum.

Nicholas Hawley, son and heir of John above mentioned, died on 7th September 1442, s.p., seized of the Manor of Penhargard, and Elizabeth his sister, wife of John Coplestone, was found to be his nearest heir.[2] The manor thus passed into the Coplestone family. To Elizabeth succeeded her son Philip; and, in 1472, an attempt was made by Henry Penhargard, the grandson, we presume, of the before mentioned Walter, to recover the property.[3] The case was postponed at that time and we are unable to trace that it was further pursued. The estate remained in the Coplestone family until 1529, when John Coplestone, grandson of Philip, suffered a recovery, *inter alia*, in this manor to Sir Thomas Denys Knt., Philip Champernown, and others;[4] and in 1560 Christopher Coplestone, son of John, finally alienated it to Thomas Opye of Bodmyn for 260 marks of silver.[5]

Penhargard remained in the family of Opie until 1694, when Nicholas Opie, junr., and Jenophef his wife, William Hicks, Clerk, and Loveday his wife, and Michael Gyles and Johanna his wife, suffered a fine in this manor and the Manor of Parke to Thomas Hoblyn, Gent., and Edward Pearne, to hold to the said Thomas Hoblyn and his heirs for ever.[6]

Edward Hoblyn of Penhargard, son and heir of the above mentioned Thomas, left an only daughter and heir who married Samuel Peter of Percothen Esq. (see ped. of HOBLYN, ante vol. i., pp. 474-475) to whom she carried the Manor of Penhargard, by whose representatives on 15th December 1804, the capital messuage, barton, farm and demesne lands of Penhargard, and the messuage called Pimligoe, in the parish of Helland, were conveyed to Mr. John Hooper, who by his will, dated 2nd February, and proved at Bodmin on 17th May 1859, demised the whole of his estates to his wife who is now the possessor of the barton of Penhargard.

The old Manor house has been removed for many years, and is replaced by a modern farm house. C. S. Gilbert, writing of the old house *cir.* 1815, says, it " exhibits very striking evidences of its having been erected at the distance of two centuries, and the

---

[1] Inquis. p.m., 15th Henry VI., No. 25. It is remarkable that the Manors of Penhargard and Polhorman are added to the inquisition after its conclusion as if they had been overlooked.

[2] Inq. p.m., 21st Henry VI., No. 47.　　　　[3] De Banco Rolls, 12th Edward IV., Trinity m. 6.

[4] De Banco Rolls, 21st Henry VIII., m. 409.　　　[5] Pedes Finium, 2nd Elizabeth, Easter, No. 340.

[6] Pedes Finium, 5th William and Mary, Hilary. No, 8.

many carved effigies and other ornamental stone work shew it to have been a building of some note."[1]

In the parlour window, in what appears to be of 17th century glass, is set an achievement of arms: ar., upon a fess between three mullets, gules, three annulets of the field. Crest: upon an Esquire's helmet a Sagittarius; supporters two knights in sable armour. Underneath the shield is the date "1632," of which period is the armour of the knights. Notwithstanding a diligent search we have failed to identify these arms. They are unknown at the Herald's College.[2]

MANOR OF BOCONNION.

This ancient manor in Saxon times belonged to the Manor of Pendrym, near Looe, but had been taken away before the Domesday Survey,[3] when it was held by the Canons of St. Stephen's of Launceston of the Earl of Moreton, and is mentioned under the name of Bot chono am in the Exeter Domesday, and as Botconoan in the Exchequer Book.

[1] History of Cornwall, vol. ii. p. 619.

[2] There are similar coats with annulets on a fess between mullets to the names Polton, Fogg, and Maston, but none *the same*, and none of these have the same crest, which, from Lodge's Ordinary of Crests, is borne by six families only. Further, on a reference to all untitled families claiming a right to supporters, no such arms are found. They are, moreover, not the arms of any family who ever possessed Penhargard.

[3] The King holds one mansion in Paindran which Harold held on the day on which King Edward was alive and dead. In it is one hide, and it pays gild for half a hide. Six ploughs can plough this hide. Of this the King holds one virgate in demesne and one carucate, and the villans have one carucate. There the King has 13 bordars, and 3 serfs, and one league of wood in length and a half in breadth, and 200 acres of pasture, and it pays per annum 60s. by weight. From this mansion three other mansions were taken away which belonged to the aforesaid mansion on that day on which King Edward was alive and dead, whereof one was called Pennadeluuan and another Bot chono am, the third is called Bot chat uuo. In these three mansions there are two hides and a half of land; these 10 ploughs can plough. The Canons of St. Stephen's of Launceston now hold them of the Earl of Moreton, and they are worth per annum 20s., and when the Earl received them they were worth 40s. (Exon Domesday, vol. iv. p. 93. Orig. MS. fo. 101.)

E

How or when it passed from the Priory of Launceston we know not. In the 13th century it formed part of the possessions of the family of Caryhayes. Ralph son of John de Caryhayes[1] was, *inter alia*, thereof seized in his demesne as of fee, and by Matilda his wife, who after his decease became the wife of Oliver de Tregenoon, had two daughters, Margery and Johanna, who inherited his estates. Margery the eldest, in her widowhood, by her charter dated on Thursday next before the feast of St. Peter in Cathedra, 16th Edward I. (19th February 1287-8), granted to Roger Inkepenne and Emelina his wife all her Manor of Caryhayes, and all her lands in Cornwall, together with the reversion of what her mother Matilda held in dower of the gift of Ralph, grantor's father; and by their charter, dated on Wednesday next after the feast of St. Edmund the King, 18th Edward I. (15th November, 1289), John de Kallerion, who had married the abovementioned Johanna, and the said Johanna his wife, by mutual consent, granted and confirmed to the said Roger Inkepenne and Emelina all their interest in the said lands.

Roger Inkepenne, being thus seized, by his charter,[2] dated on Monday next after the feast of the Purification of the Blessed Virgin Mary, 31st Edward I. (1302), in which he describes himself as Roger the son of Richard Inkepenne, granted to Roger Inkepenne his nephew, all the lands which he had received of the gift of Margery daughter of Ralph son of John de Caryhayes, *inter alia*, all the ville and lands in Boskennan (Boconnion) with the mill there, all his lands in Canolydy (Canalizy) in Boscaer and Fentenadwen, &c. Roger the nephew married Johanna daughter and heir of John de Halton, and had issue Nicholas Inkepenne and a daughter Thomasine.

In 1317 Nicholas son of Roger Inkepenne, being within age, by Henry Tirel his guardian, recovered possession of eight messuages, one mill, four carucates of land and 20 acres of wood in Bodkonan juxta Bodmin, of which he had been unjustly disseized by Ralph Cheynduit and John Cheynduit his son.[3] By deed dated at Halton 5th February 25th Edward III. (1350-1), John de Inkepenne conveyed, *inter alia*, the manors of Boconnan and Canalesy to John Dabernon and others, who by deed dated at Halton on Monday in the feast of the translation of St. Thomas 26th Edward III. (1352), reconveyed the same lands to the said John Inkepenne and Johanna his wife and the heirs of their bodies, and in default of such issue remainder to the right heirs of the said John Inkepenne.[4]

---

[1] We conceive this John de Carhayes must have been the same as John son of Ralph, Lord of Kayryshays, first founder of the Church of the Grey Friars at Bodmin, whose obit was kept in that Church on the 3rd June. If so, his name must have been incorrectly placed in the obituary under the year 1342. If this date were read as 1242 it would in some degree clear up the difficulties to which allusion has already been made See ante, vol. i., pp. 188-189.

[2] Transcripts of this, and the two previously cited charters, are found in a Chartulary made by Chief Justice Robert Hulle in the early part of the 15th century, preserved among the Augmentation Office Records in the Public Record Office.

[3] Assize Rolls 11th Edward III. N 2 16 } 6.

[4] By an Indenture made by John Inkepenne and John de fforth and Hawisia his wife, dated at Bodmyn 20th February 30th Edward III., they granted divers lands in Boconnion with the mill there, and the services of

John Inkepenne did homage to the Prince of Wales for the Manor of Halton, which he held of the castle of Trematon on 20th August 1354,[1] and was dead in 1362; for in Easter term of that year dower was assigned to Joan his widow, *inter alia*, out of Boconnan and Canalisy; and on 28th October in the same year the wardship and marriage of the heir were granted to her in conjunction with John Ferrers and John Careswell.[1] This heir was an only daughter named Ricarda who became the wife of Sir Thomas Fichet of Spaxton, co. Somerset, and thus the manors of Boconion, Canalisy, and Halton became the property of the Fichet family, and were carried by Isabella daughter of Thomas Fichet and heir of her brother Thomas Fichet in marriage to Robert Hill, or Hull,[2] subsequently of Spaxton, and, as alleged, the ancestor of the family of the same name who several gene-rations later settled at Heligan in St. Mabyn. (See Pedigree of HILL, post.) Robert Hill, besides several manors, &c., in Cornwall, Devon, and Somerset, which he held according to the law of England in right of Isabella his wife, then deceased, died on Sunday in the feast of St. Mark the Evangelist 1423, seized of three messuages and 60 acres of land in Boconan, juxta Bodmyn, and of one corn mill there; and it was found that he held the said premises of the heirs of Thomas Peverell, by what service the jury was ignorant, and that the value of the messuage and land, in all issues, beyond reprises, was 20s. per annum; and that the value of the mill was 6s. 8d.[3] per annum. He was

divers tenants to Roger Taillor of Bodmin, to hold for the term of their lives: viz., the rents and services of Roger Taillor of Bodmyn for lands and tenements

which he held of Boconnon in Boscaer,			Richard Crenker, for lands and tenements in Bodmin.		
John Conlyng for lands and tenements in Bodmyn.			Roger Bodiniel	do.	in Penbugeldon.
Roger Martyn for	do.	do.	John de la Pole	do.	in Penbugell.
Walter Dyne	do.	do.	Richard Kyng	do.	do.
William Carhall	do.	do.	Simon Trencret	do.	do.
John Pole	do.	do.	Robert Carpenter	do.	do.
John Cotell	do.	do.	Richard Smalehall	do.	do.
Sibell de la Pole	do.	do.	William Grynnow	do.	in Boscaer.
Richard Trewy	do.	do.	Stephen le Bred	do.	at ffountynadwyll.
Walter la Bere	do.	do.	Alice de Boconnon	do.	in Boconnon.

The Courts of the Manor of Boconnion were, according to ancient custom, held in the Guildhall of Bodmin, as appears from the following record:

Boconnion   Memorandum quod curia domini de Halton de tenementis suis de Boconnion teneri debet
tenentes ibidem   ex antiquâ consuetudine in aulâ Gildhalde de Bodmyn et ibidem debent presentare tenentes &c.
et eorum servicia   In curiâ anno xj Regis Henrici IV. continetur sic. Item presentat quod Walterus Carburra qui tenuit de domino unum tenementum in Bodmyn obiit, et inde accidit domino de relevio ij^s vj^d Et distringat Ricardum Moille ad faciendum domino fidelitatem. Et de feoffamentis tenementi in Bodmyn acciderit domino de quolibet ij^s vj^d up patet in Rotulo curiæ de anno quinto Regis Henrici IV. (Chartulary before quoted.)

[1] Council Book of Edward the Black Prince. Duchy of Cornwall Office.

[2] This lady was the wife of Robert Hulle on the death of her brother, who died on the Thursday next before the feast of St. Peter ad vincula (August 1st) 1395, and was found to be aged 12 years full and complete on the vigil of the Annunciation of the Blessed Virgin Mary preceding; and it was testified that the King by letters patent, dated 29th August in the same year, had committed to John Hulle and Robert Hulle his son the custody of all the lands which Thomas Fychett had held of the heirs of Richard Poynynges, who was in the ward-ship of the King. (Inq. p.m. 19th Richard II., No. 24.)   [3] Inq. p.m. 1st Henry VI., No. 31. Remains of this ancient mill still exist in the wood about half-a-mile below Clerkenwater.

E²

succeeded by his son and heir John Hill, who died on Thursday next after the feast of St. Calixtus the Pope (14th October) 1434, leaving his son John Hill aged 10 years his nearest heir; and dower to Cecilia his widow was assigned, *inter alia*, out of this estate.[1] This lady subsequently married Sir Thomas Keryell, Knt. John Hill, son of John, died on Sunday next after the feast St. Denis (9th October) 1455 seized, *inter alia*, of two thirds of three messuages, &c., in Boconion, which he held of Sir Robert Hungerford, Knt., leaving Genoveva his daughter, aged eight weeks, his nearest heir.[2] This young lady, when she arrived at a mature age, espoused William Saye, for upon the death of Cecilia Keryell, on 19th April 1472, the said Genovefa the granddaughter of John Hill of Spaxton who had been the husband of the said Cecilia, was found to be her nearest heir and was then the wife of William Saye, and of the age of 16 years and more.[3] Sir William Saye died 4th December 1529, 21st Henry VIII. (his wife Genovefa having predeceased him s.p,) seized, as tenant according to the law of England, *inter alia*, of the aforesaid three messuages in Boconion, &c., and Thomas Hussey, Esq., William Clapton, Esq., and Elena the wife of George Babington, Esq., as representatives of Johanna daughter and coheir of John Cheyne of Pynne (Pinho, co. Devon), son and heir of Elizabeth sister of John Hille of Spaxton, father of the aforesaid Genovefa, and John Waldgrave, Esq., son and heir of Isabella the other daughter and coheir of the said John Cheyne, were found to be her nearest heirs.[4] (See pedigree post.)

The Hill estates were subsequently partitioned between the four coheirs, when Boconion and Canalizy fell to the share of William Clopton, who, in 1562, alienated the same to John Rowse, Esq., under the description of the Manors of Bucconion, *alias* Bucconyon, and Kanalesye.[5] These lands immediately passed to the family of Bligh, or Blight, of Bodmin, for in 1569 Boconion was held by Thomas Blyght of Richard Roscarrock Lord of Bodannan, who held it of the Manor of Blyston.[6] It continued in the family of Bligh for several generations. On the death of Nicholas Glyn of Glyn in 1580, it was found that he held Penbugell of John Blighe of Bodmyn, Gent. (son of the above mentioned Thomas) as of his Manor of Boconion.[7] And it appears from the custumal and rental of the Manor of Bliston, which was drawn up after 1660, that it was held by one of the same family;[8] and in January 1674-5 Richard Blight, Gent., and Gilbert Blight, Gent., suffered a fine in the Manor of Canalesye, together with Boconnion, to Tobias Scholler, Merchant.[9]

When Hals wrote (before 1736), he mentions that it was the residence of his good friend Dr. Robert Heart, who, he says, was " descended from the Hearts of Trencreek in Menhyniet, and giveth for his arms: *gu. on a chef ar. three human hearts ppr.*'[10] Dr.

---

[1] Inq. p.m. 13th Henry VI., No. 36.   [2] Inq. p.m. 32th Henry VI., No. 17.

[3] Inq. p.m. 12th Edward IV., No. 51.   [4] Inq. p.m. 22nd Henry VIII., No. 46.

[5] Pedes Finium, 4th and 5th Elizabeth, Michaelmas, No. 5,

[6] See ante vol. i., p. 520. The succession as given in the rental referred to is generally accurate, though not quite exact in details.   [7] Inq. p.m., 23rd Elizabeth, Part II., No. 14, see post.

[8] See ante, vol. i., p. 93.   [9] Pedes Finium, 26th and 27th Charles II., Hilary.

[10] Hal's History of Cornwall, p. 160.

Hart in 168— married at Lanhydrock Mary daughter of Hender Molesworth of Pencarrow,[1] and was probably then or soon afterwards settled at Boconnion. We do not know the date of his death, but he would not seem to have left issue by Mary Molesworth, and appears to have married a second time a lady named Elizabeth, who after his death married a person called Holden, for in 1722 Elizabeth Holden of Helland died, and by her will, dated 11th April 1719, directed that her body should be buried in the Church of Helland " as neare the seate there belonging to the Barton of Bocconion as may be." She gave legacies to her daughters Mary Harte and Elizabeth Harte, and, reciting a certain agreement between her son, John Harte, and herself concerning her real estate, appointed her daughters joint executors.[2]

The estate would appear to have continued in the family of Harte until 1745, when a fine was levied, in which Thomas Kniveton, Gent., and William Grigg, were plaintiffs, and John Stergotterick, Robert Hart, Gent., and Mary his wife, John Hart, Barker, Robert Hart, Barker, Martha Hart, spinster, and Richard Pellamounter, Gent., and Elizabeth his wife, were deforciants, in which, *inter alia*, the Manors of Boconion and Canalissy were acknowledged to be the right of the said Thomas and William.[3]

Boconnion afterwards passed to the family of Angove. William Angove of St. Columb Major, Esq., by his will, dated 25th February 1774, devised the Manor, or reputed Manor, of Boconnion, with the capital messuage, farm, and demesne lands to William Angove of Falmouth, cabinetmaker, subject to an annuity payable to testator's nephew, John Angove of Liskeard, and it was eventually, by indentures dated 4th and 5th June 1819, conveyed to John Harry, then residing at Brussels, Doctor of Physic. Dr. Harry subsequently returned to England, and having rebuilt the house made it his residence for a short time. By deed, however, dated 2nd July 1834, he conveyed the said manor and lands to George Woolcock, Esq., who made it his residence, and by planting and other judicious alterations greatly improved the property. By Royal License dated 23rd May 1846, Mr. Woolcock was authorised to assume the name of Pye in lieu of that Woolcock, and to bear the arms of Pye;[4] and dying in 1867 devised the Manor and lands of Boconnion to Elizabeth Pye his widow, for life, with remainder, after her death, to George Pye their son, who, by deed dated 20th December 1870,[5] conveyed the Barton of Boconnion, together with Clerkenwater and Whitley, to Joseph Pomery, Esq., the present possessor.

[1] See ante, Pedigree of Molesworth, vol. i., p. 468.

[2] Proved in Archd. Court of Cornw., 18th June 1722; original will delivered to Mary Harte the same day.

[3] Pedes Finium 19th George II., Michaelmas.

[4] The following Arms were accordingly granted and exemplified: ar. on a fesse per pale az. and gu., a talbot's head couped between two escallops of the field, a bordure wavy of the third. Crest: Upon a mount vert, a talbot's head couped ar. charged with a saltier wavy, gu. Motto, " Pietatis Causa."

[5] Deeds at Boconnion.

The Rentall of the Manor of Boconion.

	HIGH RENTS.	£ s. d.		
	The Lord Mohun for Boskyer	0 0 6	Mr. John Phillips pay	
	The heirs of .... now Hobbs ..	0 0 6	Suit and service ..	6
.... Cornish pay it ..	John Best for a house in Pool Street ..	0 3 0	Suit and service ..	6
yᵉ Lord pay it ..	The Lord Mohun for	0 1 6		
.... Jewell pay it, now Robt. Crap	James Parker, now Bouster, for a house in Boor Street	0 1 0	The suit and service ..	6
yᵉ Lord pays it ..	The Lord Mohun for a house in Boor Street ..	0 1 0	Mr. John Phillips Steward pay it }	6
	The Lord Robarts for a house in Honey Street..	0 1 9		
now John Winsouth, 2 years due	The heirs of Boskernon and Crosman, now where Christopher Hocking lives in a tenemt. in Boor Street	0 1 0	} Suit and service ..	6
Mr. Bultail pays, & pᵈ by Nichs. Pearce yᵉ 15ᵗʰ Nov.	George Spry, Gent., now Keakwich, Gent., for a close in Pools Street	0 1 0	}	
Mr. Bultail pays & pᵈ by Nichs. Pearce yᵉ 15ᵗʰ Nov.	The same Spry, now Keakwich, for a garden in Lostwithiel Street..	0 1 1		
Mr. Edward Hoblyng pays itt	......Wyot, Gent., now Hoblyn, Gent , for a stitch in Bornard's Lane	0 1 2	The suit and service ..	6
Mr. Stone pays itt ..	Opye Gent, now Stone, for a house in Pool Street	0 0 11¼	The suit and service ..	6
yᵉ Esq. Glyn does pay itt by yᵉ haᵈ of .... Gant	The heirs of Glyn, Esq., for Penbugell and the Culverhouse Parks	0 3 4	The suit and service ..	6
Peter Seymons pays it.. Mich. Ugler pay it ..	The heirs of Pearce, now Peter Seymons, for a tenement in the Fore Street	0 1 2	The suit and service ..	6
Mich. Giles pay it ..	Michael Giles for Oak Park at Boorhill ..	0 1 0	The suit and service ..	6
John Blight pay it ..	The heirs of Nichollas, now John Blight, for a Closs in Fearwash	0 1 1	The suit and service ..	6
Mr. Bultail pay it by Nichs. Pearce ye 15ᵗʰ Nov.	The heirs of Sepreey, now Keakwich, for Pitt Park	0 0 10	The suit and service ..	6
Widow Gray pay it Peter Cock and Thos. Bullock pay it	The widow Hender, now yᵉ widow Grey, for a house in Boor Street	0 1 0	The suit and service ..	6
		1 2 10¼		
	CONVENTIONARY RENTS.			
	Mr. Nichs. Opye, Junr., for pt. of Boconion at Rack	30 0 0		
	Frans. Webber, Gent., for a third pt. of Boconion	1 6 8		
	George Bond for a tenement in Widley ..	0 10 0	{ A capon 1· { One harvest day	
	Richard Bunster for his Pound ..	0 6 0	A capon and day	
	Sum ..	32 2 8		

1699   Received then by the hand of Justinian Webber 13 years' High Rent due from my Lord Mohun to the Manor of Boconion.

MANOR OF NEWTON.

Lysons mentions a manor of Newton in this parish which, he says, " belonged formerly to the Priory of Bodmin and afterwards to the Glynns," &c.[1] This, however, is an error. The manor of Newton which was held by the Priory of Bodmin was the manor of Newton St. Petrock, co. Devon.[2] In 1447 we find Newaton in Helland parcel of the manor of Nether Helland,[3] and it appears as a free tenement of that manor in the rental of 1569, though then under convention.[4] It was probably a portion of the Toker lands in Helland which passed to the Glynn family, and was afterwards sold to Mr. Treise, who converted his scattered lands in this neighbourhood into a reputed manor under the name of the Manor of Newton.

MANOR OF BODWEN.

Lysons also alleges that Bodwen in this parish was a manor held under the Prior of Bodmin by the Archdekne family, from whom it passed in marriage to the Courteneys.[5] It is true that Thomas son of Odo Lercedekne died in 5th Edward III. seized, *inter alia*, of a manor of Bodduuan, which he held of the Prior of Bodmin as of his manor of Rialton by the service of 16d. at the feast of St. Michael, and one ewe sheep with 6 hoggastres at the feast of Invention of Holy Cross, in socage, with suit at court, &c.,[6] and that this manor passed eventually to the Courtenays and Carews. We venture, however, to differ from Mr. Lysons' statement, and believe that Bodwen in Helland was never a manor and was never held of the Prior of Bodmin. In the Rental of the manor of Nether Helland of 1569, we find Bodwen as a free tenement of that manor held by Thomas Luky, then a minor, at the rent of 2s. per annum (ante p. 19), and he also held by the same tenure Helland Bridge and Waterland, and in January 1605-6 Stephen Toker, Gent., levied a fine in these tenements of John Wolffe, Gent., and Rebecca his wife, Magdalen Wolffe, widow, Richard Taverner, Gent., and John Hicks,[7] and these tenements afterwards passed, like some of the other Toker lands, through the Treises to Sir John Morshead and the late Mr. Wallis. There are several tenements, some of which are now held by the Hon[ble]. Mrs. Davies Gilbert of Trelissick, and others by James Hayward of Loudwater House, co. Herts, Esq.

There is a Bodwenn in Luxulian, which was probably the site of the manor of Boduuan held by the Archdekne family of the manor of Rialton.

---

[1] Mag. Brit. vol. iii. 131. [2] See ante vol. i., p. 139.
[3] See ante p. 18. [4] See ante p. 21.
[5] Mag. Brit. vol. iii. p. 131. [6] Inq. p.m. 5th Edward III., Part I., No. 33.
[7] Pedes Finium 3rd James, Hilary.

BRODE *alias* BRODES *alias* BROADS.

The Barton of Brodes or Broads, in this parish, without doubt, derived its name from its ancient possessors. The name of Brode, or Broad, is too general in Cornwall to admit of easy identification, but we find Henry Brode was one of the assessors of the subsidy in Helland in the time of Edward III.[1]

We have no trace of this Barton until the 15th century, when it belonged to the family of Tredenek,[2] in which it remained a considerable time. Christopher Tredenek was returned as holding lands in Helland of the value of 30s. per annum in 1522, but was not then resident.[3] In January 1606-7 Walter Tredenek, Gent., and Grace his wife, and James Tredenek, Clerk (probably their son), suffered a fine in Brodes in Helland to Hugh Roscarrock, Esq.,[4] who died at Pinchely Park in Cardinham in 1616; when his lands passed to his great nephew Charles Roscarrock, who in January 1621-2 suffered a fine in Brode, *alias* Brodes, in Helland to Stephen Toker, Gent.[5] This Stephen Toker, whose father settled in Helland at a somewhat earlier date, acquired considerable lands in the parish. In 1660-70 his grandson, of the same name, held Lymsworthy of the Manor of Bliston (ante vol. i., p. 93) which he had acquired, and which he had annexed to Brodes, with which it has passed ever since. Upon his death in 1682 his daughter and heiress carried Brodes and Lymsworthy in marriage to Hubert Glynn, whose son Robert Glynn in 1711 settled Brodes and Lymsworthy upon his marriage with Lucy Clobery. Upon the death of their only son Robert Glynn Clobery, M.D., without issue in 1800, by his will dated 7th April 1798,[6] he bequeathed these lands to the Rev. John Henry Jacob of Salisbury, eldest son of John Jacob, M.D., of that city, who sold Brodes and Lymsworthy to Mr. James Hawken. From Mr. Hawken the lands passed to Mr. Thomas Lawry, by whom, within a few years past, they have been conveyed to Lord Robartes the present possessor.

---

[1] Subsidy Rolls, temp. Edward III. — In the mayor's accounts of the Borough of Bodmin for 1508, the Receivers General take credit for 7d. which they had paid for the carriage of a tree that had been given by Sir John Brode, apparently for the repair of the Church. Ante, vol. i., p. 158.

[2] In 1484 John Carowe of Wade (Wadebridge), Smith, brought an action against Robert Tredenek of Tredenek, juxta Nansent, (in St. Breoke), Gent., *Ralph Tredenek, late of Brodys, juxta Helland, Gent.*, and John Tredenek of Trenyowe, juxta Tredard, husbandman, for having falsely accused him of having, on 3rd April 1475, at Hounslow Heath, co. Middlesex, hidden in ambush with intent to kill John Tamson, and of having beaten and wounded the said John so that his life was despaired of, and of having taken his purse containing 20s. John Carowe was arraigned at Westminster upon this accusation, and proved that he was at Wade at the time mentioned, and so was acquitted, and he now sought to recover damages. De Banco Rolls, 2nd Richard III., Michaelmas, m. 6.   [3] See Appendix.

[4] Pedes Finium, 4th James, Hilary, No. 5.   [5] Pedes Finium, 19th James Hilary.

[6] Will proved 5th March 1800. Prerog. Court of Canterbury.

KERNICK.

Kernick in this parish was formerly a place of some importance. Early in the 14th century it belonged to the family of St. Margaret,[1] and in 1336 was the residence of William St. Margaret.[2] Later we find the name " de Kernek " mentioned as the designation of a family.

In the reign of Queen Elizabeth Kernick had become divided into three or more tenements. In 1595 Stephen Plee, *alias* Playe, suffered a fine in Lower Kernick and Kayse, in Helland, to Stephen Toker, Gent.[3] In 1599 the same Stephen Toker levied a fine of Richard Mynors, Gent., and Thomas Nottell, in " Kernicke le higher,"[4] and in 1631 he acquired another tenement in Kernicke of Tristram Keen and Johanna his wife.[5]

Stephen Toker having thus acquired this messuage, it, together with the other Toker lands in Helland, was carried in marriage to Hubert Glynn, and afterwards became the residence of his son-in-law John Silly (see Ped. of GLYNN, post). Subsequently it became the property of Sir John Morshead, Bart., by whom it was sold to the late Mr. Wallis of Bodmin, and it is now, by purchase, the property of Mr. Hayward. There is upon it a small modern farm-house only.

Lancothan, alias Lecudgen, alias Lacudan. This is a pleasantly situated farm, containing about ·108 acres, on the western side of the parish. It is deserving of notice in consequence of a tradition that the Lord of the Manor having on one occasion driven a stag from Devonshire and killed it on this farm, gave the farm to his huntsman for his life as a testimony of the Lord's enjoyment of the day's sport, and also as a reward for the skill and perseverance of the huntsman. We imagine that the generous Nimrod was one of the Corytons of Newton Ferrers.

---

[1] Assize Rolls 10th Edward II. $\frac{N}{2} \left. \begin{array}{c} \\ 16 \end{array} \right\}$ 5 m. 9.

[2] Assize Rolls 9th Edward III. $\frac{N}{2} \left. \begin{array}{c} \\ 20 \end{array} \right\}$ 6. See also ante vol. i., pp. 272, 273.

[3] Pedes Finium 37th Elizabeth, Trinity, No. 5.   [4] Pedes Finium 41st Elizabeth, Trinity, No. 16.

[5] Pedes Finium 7th Charles, Easter, No. 19.

F

FAMILY HISTORY.

THE FAMILIES OF GIFFARD, COLYN, CALWODELY AND ARUNDELL, OF HELLAND.

GIFFARD.

There were two branches of the family of Giffard settled in Cornwall at a very early date. In one branch the Manor of Lanowmure, or St. Kew, was for several centuries vested. Of that branch we shall treat hereafter. The family now under our notice held the Manors of Helland and Helset, together with other possessions in the county. The earliest knowledge of this family is obtained by us from certain proceedings in Banco in January 1324[1] concerning the wardship of a certain Reginald, son and heir of Nicholas Peytenyn, which was claimed by Johanna widow of Ralph Giffard, upon the ground that the said Reginald held by military service certain lands, part of the Manor of Helset, which Johanna had in dower. On the other side it was contended that the lands had been held by an ancester of Reginald *in socage* of the grant of one Ralph, son of William Giffard,[2] ancestor of Ralph late husband of the said Johanna; but Johanna replied that Johanna the mother of Reginald during her minority had been in the wardship of John Giffard father of the last mentioned Ralph.

These proceedings give us four descents of the Giffard family ending with Ralph Giffard, but the succession would not seem to have been direct, for in 1295 there were at the Assizes at Launceston two cases of view of recognizance to enquire if William Champernon and Walter Hay had unjustly disseized Simon son of Ralph Giffard of a free tenement in Hellisete, and of another in Helland Giffard juxta Bodmin. They pleaded that they held the tenements in view by reason of the minority of a certain Johanna daughter and heir of a certain Simon Giffard, who had held the said tenement of them by military service, and had died in homage; moreover, they pleaded that the

---

[1] Assize Rolls, 18th Edward II. $\frac{N}{2}\Big\}9$

[2] It is probable that this William was the son of Ralph who in 3rd John (1202) was surety for Richard Burrel. (Coram Rege Rolls.)

said Johanna was not mentioned in the writ, and so they were discharged. From this it would appear that, irrespective of Simon the son of Johanna, there was a Simon son of Ralph in the succession to the estates.[1] This Simon was probably the eldest son of Ralph, and the brother of John the father of Ralph the husband of Johanna, the plaintiff in the case first mentioned.

In the following year Laurence de Tremur and Mabilla his wife took out a writ of novel disseizin in Titesburghdon (Titchbarrow Down) against Johanna daughter of Ralph Giffard, but they did not appear to prosecute.[2] We conclude that this Johanna was the daughter and heir of Ralph Giffard, the husband of the before-mentioned Johanna, probably by an earlier marriage, and that she died young and unmarried; for in 1302 we find a case before the Justices Itinerant in which the aforesaid Laurence de Tremur and Mabilla his wife were sued by Johanna who was the wife of Ralph Giffard of the third part one messuage, one mill, and one acre of land in Resgre, and one acre of land in Penyniton, as dower. Laurence and Mabilla pleaded that a certain Ralph Giffard had given the tenements afore-said to the said Mabilla to hold to her and her heirs for ever, and called Simon Giffard, brother and heir of the aforesaid Ralph, to warrant. Simon appeared by summons, and alleged that the aforesaid Johanna sometime before had petitioned before the Justices in Banco upon another writ against the said Laurence and Mabilla concerning her dower of the said premises, and that they had, at that time, called to warrant a certain Johanna daughter and heir of the aforesaid Ralph Giffard, and that the said Johanna, the plaintiff, had of her recovered her dower. Johanna admitted that she had sought to recover her dower in the manner stated, but that she had never been seized of it; and it was decided that she should recover the value of her dower from Simon the brother and heir of Ralph, and that Laurence and Mabilla should hold the premises in peace.[3] These proceedings would seem to confirm the above conjecture that Johanna the daughter and heir of Ralph Giffard died a minor and unmarried, and that his brother Simon succeeded to the estates; and this is further confirmed by other proceedings in the same term, wherein Simon Giffard sued the aforesaid Johanna for waste and destruction of houses and woods which she held in dower of the inheritance of the said Simon in Helliset and Hellan Giffard. It was pleaded that she had pulled down in Hellan a certain hall of the value of 10 marks, and a certain grange of the same value, and that she had cut down 40 great oaks worth 40d. each, and 200 small oaks of the value of 6d. each; the whole damage being laid at £100. The jury, however, found for the defendant.[4] This Simon presented to the Church of

[1] Assize Rolls, Cornwall, 23rd Edward I. $\frac{N}{2}$ 5. m. 13

[2] Assize Rolls, Cornwall, 24th Edward I. $\frac{N}{2}$ 8. m., 14d.

[3] Assize Rolls, Cornwall, 30th Edward I. $\frac{M}{2}$ 1 m. 22.   At the same Assize Simon Giffard of Hellisete took out a writ against William Prempa of Hehenant, sen., and others, that they should do suit for the mill at Hellisete, but did not prosecute.   [4] Ibid. m. 13.

F 2

Helland in 1310, and in 1348 Simon Giffard,[1] described as of Helset, presented to the same Church a certain Lawrence Giffard, probably his brother. This Simon married Olivia, or Olive, fifth daughter and coheir of John Shylston Lord of Penvrane,[2] by which he acquired a share in the manor of Penvrane and the advowson of the Church of St. Pinnock thereto appurtenant. He died about 1348, and was succeeded by his son and heir John Giffard, upon whose presentation in 1349 Andrew Giffard, probably his brother, was instituted to the Rectory of Helland. John Giffard died cir. 1375 leaving two daughters, his coheirs, viz., Ingreta, who married Thomas son and heir of John Colyn, and Margaret who became the wife of.........Raleigh, of the Nettlecombe family.

ARMS OF GIFFARD OF HELLAND—Az. three fleurs-de-lis or, two and one. (See ante p. 14.)

COLYN.

The family of Colyn was also of considerable antiquity in the county, and held a prominent position at an early date. John Colyn was Sheriff of Cornwall in 1388, and again in 1392.[3] This was, without doubt, the same John Colyn to whom, with Rose his wife, Bishop Brentingham granted a license, in 1379, to have Divine service celebrated in their presence in the Chapel of the Blessed Mary of Boscarne and in that of St. Catherine of Elwynse,[4] yet we find John Colyn, the father of Thomas, described as of Helland in 1376,[5] and he was again so described, as one of the Collectors of Subsidies, in 3rd Richard II. (1379-80).[6] In 1380 John Colyn of Helland was plaintiff in a suit for debt against Geoffry Commet, Vicar of Treneglos.[7] We find by a charter dated on Monday next before the Feast of St. Gregory the Pope (22nd March) 6th Richard II. (1382-3) that Richard Trenance granted to John Colyn of Bokerne all his messuages &c. in Peneton for a term of twelve years, and by a deed dated at Alwans on Saturday next before the Feast of SS. Simon and Jude (Oct. 28th) 11th of the same king's reign[8] (1387) John Colyn of Alwans appointed Thomas his son as his attorney to receive seizin of the whole ville of Peneton; and land in Elwans[9] was parcel of the possessions of which Otho Colyn died seized in 1463 and of which Johanna Arundell died seized in 1537.

---

[1] Simon Giffard was assessed to the subsidy in Helland, temp. Edward III., at 12d., being the highest assessment in the parish. Sub. Roll. $\frac{87}{37}$

[2] Of the other daughters—Margaret married Bastard; Katherine, Resethercombe; Alice, Ferrers, and afterwards Coryton; and Lucy, Boterdon (De Banco Rolls 1st Edward IV., Hilary, m. 393.) This was the origin of the partition of the manor of Penvrane and the advowson of the Church of St. Pinnock, the latter being still held jointly by the surviving representatives of the above coheirs. This John Shylston was a descendant of John Silveston (of which name it is a corruption) Lord of Penvrane in the early part of the 13th century, from which place they were sometimes called " de Penvrane." (See article by the Author in Journal of the Royal Institution of Cornwall 1873.)

[3] See ante, vol. i., p. 392.

[4] Ante, vol. i., p. 263.

[5] See ante, p. 7.

[6] Subsidy Rolls.

[7] Court Roll, Stannary of Blackmore.

[8] Deeds at Place, Fowey.

[9] Elwynse or Elwans was probably Elvans in St. Eval.

Thomas, son of John Colyn married, as above-mentioned, Ingreta daughter and co-heir of John Giffard of Helland, and, in her right, presented to the Church of Helland in 1415, the next presentation to which Church, date unknown, was made by Ingreta herself, as appears from an inquisition taken in 1465[1] to inquire into the right of presentation to a vacancy which then occurred. He was probably the rebuilder of the hall or manor house of Helland, the old hall, as we have seen above, having been destroyed by Johanna Giffard. A part of the new erection still remains[2] (Plate XXXI., fig. 1.) This house became his residence and that of his successors in the manor.[3] He had a son John[4] who espoused Elizabeth daughter of John Nicoll, or Nicholl, of Bodmin, and left a son Otho, and a daughter Elizabeth, who in 1444 became the wife of Thomas Treffry of Fowey.

Her ARMS: *Ar. a Chev. sa. between three Cornish choughs*, continue in the windows of Place House, in old glass, as do those of Giffard, to which she was entitled: *Az. three fleur-de-lis or.*, whch have been supposed to be the arms of France. In 1457 John Colsyll, Knt., John Nanfan, John Nycolle of Bodmyn, John Tremeket, and John Bere at Tregaren (feoffees of John Colyn) granted to Thomas Treffry, son and heir of Thomas Treffry of Fowey and Elizabeth his wife, the Manor of Penvrane, except their part of the advowson of the Church of St. Pinnock, which they had of the gift of John Colyn, to hold to the said Thomas and Elizabeth and the heirs of their bodies;[5] and we find another Charter dated the same day by which Otho Colyn granted the same manor to the said Thomas and Elizabeth sister of the said Otho;[6] and we have also a third Charter, by which Elizabeth relict of John Colyn, in her widowhood, granted to the aforesaid Thomas Treffry and Elizabeth his wife the interest which she had, in dower, in the said Manor of Penvrane. A portion of this Manor of Penvrane, and a third turn in the right of presentation to the Church of St. Pinnock, are now held by Dr. Treffry of Fowey as derived from Elizabeth Colyn.

---

[1] Bishop Bothe's Reg. fo. 57.

[2] The hall is 34 ft. by 21 ft. There was a door on each side, that on the south is now walled up. On that side are the remains of two ancient windows: viz, a two-light transomed window, the upper part of which has been removed, and a square headed window of two lights. In the wall is a stone inscribed "John Cock, Anno Domini 1706." The building has been occupied as a farm-house within the present century but is now an out-house. In the particulars of sale at the auction for the lands of Sir John Morshead, Bart., in 1808, it was described as a farm house called "The Hall."

[3] Thomas Colyn of Helland was witness to a Charter of Nicholas Helygan, dated at Treblethick (in St. Mabyn) on Monday next after the Feast of St. Thomas the Martyr 9th Richard II. (1385). Thomas Colyn was one of the collectors of subsidies in 16th and 21st Richard II., in 2nd and 6th Henry IV., and in 2nd Henry V.

[4] John Colyn of Helland, on 12th October 1437, was plaintiff in an action of debt against John Lymbery in the Stannary Court of Blackmoor, and on 14th November had a day given for trial. Court Rolls of the Stannary of Blackmoor 16th Henry VI. (Record Office.)

[5] Charters dated at Bodmyn on Friday next before the Feast of St. George the Martyr 25th Henry VI. (At Place, Fowey.)

[6] Dated at Bodmin the last day of May 25th Henry VI. (In the author's collection.)

CALWODELY.

Otho Colyn died 10th September 1463,[1] leaving Elizabeth his daughter, then of the age of ten years, his sole heir. She was married first to Thomas Calwodely, son and heir of Thomas Calwodely of Calwodely co. Devon, who after his marriage settled at Helland, and dying in his father's lifetime left one son named Humphry, born cir. 1472.[2] She married secondly ....Raleigh, and whilst his widow she presented to the Church of Helland in 1494. She espoused, thirdly, Edward Apryse, who in her right presented to Helland in 1499.

Humphry Calwodely, of whose misfortune and attainder we have already written (ante p. 8), married Johanna, or Jane, daughter of John Carmynowe of Fentongollen and relict of John Pentyre, jun. We do not know the date of his death, but a gravestone to his memory still remains in Helland Church (see ante p. 15, No. 3, and Plate XXXI., fig. 2.) He left a daughter and heir named Johanna, born in 1501. His widow survived to 1537.

Thomas Colwodely, who married the heir of Otho Colyn, had several brothers of whom the next in order of birth to himself was Oliver. Of this gentleman and his descendants it may be well to add a brief notice. He married Alice daughter and heir of William Monke of Padstow, by Johanna daughter and heir of Joceus Dayowe, with whom he acquired considerable estates. He settled at Padstow, and is frequently named in the Court Rolls of the Manor of Padstow down to the year 1498. Certain lands which he held in Exeter were forfeited to the Crown on account of a murder which he committed at Padstow, and for which he adjured the realm; and these lands, in 1505, were granted to Robert Holland, Esq.[3] Oliver Calwodely had two sons John and Robert. John married Catherine daughter of Robert Tredinnick of Tredinnick, and had a son John who died in his father's lifetime, s.p. Notwithstanding the above mentioned forfeiture John Calwodely in 1542 was assessed to the subsidy in Padstow upon lands of the value of £40 a-year, whilst Robert was assessed upon lands of the value of 40s. only.

Robert Calwodely married Honour daughter of ...... Lawgher, who died on 9th April 1522. A monument to her memory remains at Padstow where she was buried. John Calwodely, the issue of this marriage, succeeded to his uncle's estates, and his name occurs continually in the Padstow Manor Rolls from 1558 to 1573. In 1571 he occurs as Lord of the Manor of Trelother, and in the same year he was assessed to the subsidy upon lands of the value of £20 per annum. He married Ann daughter of Laurie; and

---

[1] Inq. p.m. 6th Edward IV., No. 36.

[2] On the death of Thomas Calwodeleigh of Calwodeleigh on 6th June 1492, Humphry Calwodeleigh was found to be his kinsman and nearest heir, viz., the son of Thomas son of the said Thomas, and to be aged 20 years and more. (Inq. p.m. 8th Henry VII., Excheq. No. 5.)

[3] Rot. Pat. 21st Henry VII., p. 1. m. 24.

inasmuch as she is mentioned as a widow in 1606 he must have been then dead. We find another John Calwodely holding the Padstow lands from 1606 to 1610, who was probably his son, though he is not shewn in the pedigree recorded in the Heralds' Visitation of 1620. The last of the name was Sir Nicholas Calwodely who is mentioned in the Manor Rolls in 1616, and was dead in 1623, when his heirs are mentioned in the same record. He was knighted in parts beyond the seas, as is shewn in the registered pedigree. He appears to have died s.p., and his heirs were the representatives of his sisters Catherine and Honour. The latter would seem to have inherited the Padstow property for in the Court Rolls of the years 1647 and 1652 we find the entry, "Heirs of Calwodely now Mr. Webber."

ARUNDELL.

Roger Arundell, who married the sole heir of Humphrey Calwodely, was the third son of Sir Thomas Arundell of Lanherne, Knight of the Bath,[1] by Catherine daughter of Sir John Dynham Knt., and sister and co-heir of John Lord Dynham of Cardynham. He died 12th June 1536, when Humphrey Arundell was found to be his son and heir and to be of the age of 23 years and more,[2] and Johanna his widow died 28th September in the following year seized, *inter alia*, of the Manor of Over Helland, together with the advowson of the Church of Helland, and the Manors of Cassacawn and Hellsett, and of lands in Amaleglos and Elwyns; the Manor of Over Helland and the advowson of the Church being held of the Marquis of Dorset as of his Manor of Tywardreth, the tenements in Amaleglos of George Earl of Huntingdon, and Elwyns of the Prior of Bodmyn as of his Manor of Ryalton; when the said Humphry Arundell was found to be her heir and to be of the age of 24 years and more.[3] Of Humphry Arundell's connection with the Cornish insurrection of 1549, and of his subsequent attainder and execution and the forfeiture of his estates we have already written. (Ante p. 9.)

[1] In 1524 Roger Arundell was assessed to the subsidy in Helland upon lands of the value of £40 a-year Sub. Rolls, 16th Henry VIII. $\frac{87}{131}$

[2] Inq. p. m. 27th and 28th Henry VIII. Exchequer No. 11.

[3] Inq. p.m. 30th Henry VIII. In 1545 Humphry Arundell, like his father in 1524, was assessed to the subsidy upon lands to the value of £40 a-year, being the largest payment in the Hundred of Trigg except that of Richard Roscarrock of Roscarrock, who was assessed upon lands of the value of £50 a-year. Sub. Roll 37th Henry VIII. $\frac{87}{179}$ The following were the assessments for the parish of Helland:—

Humphry Arundell Esq., in lands xl^li paid iiij^li			Thomas Kett	in goods v^li paid	iij^s iiij^d
John Lukye	,,	xx^s ,, ij^s	John Menhenyck	,, v^li ,	iij^s iiij^d
William Lukye	in goods v^li ,,	iij^s iiij^d	Robert Edey	,, v^li ,	iij^s iiij^d
John Edey	,, v^li ,,	iij^s iiij^d	John Hendy	,, v^li ,,	iij^s iiij^d
John Courtys	,, v^li ,,	iij^s iiij^d	Total for the parish		v^li v^s iiij^d

PEDIGREE OF GIFFARD, PENVRANE,

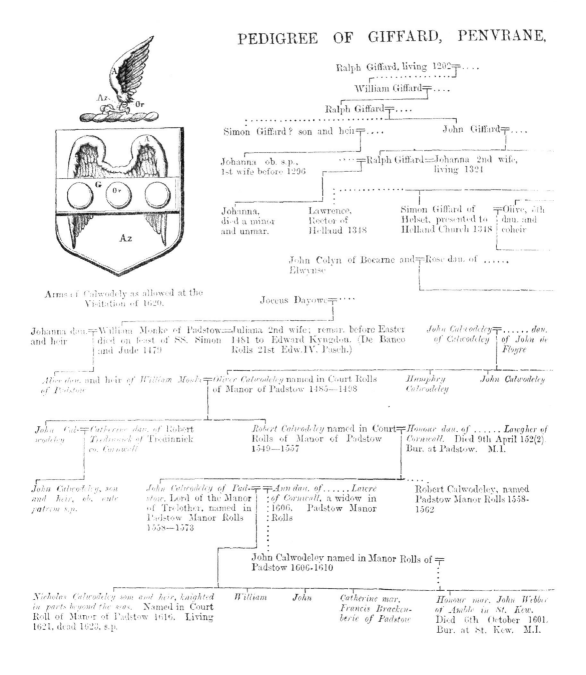

Arms of Calwodely as allowed at the
Visitation of 1620.

Ralph Giffard, living 120?⊤....

William Giffard⊤....

Ralph Giffard⊤....

Simon Giffard? son and heir⊤....   John Giffard⊤....

Johanna ob. s.p., ...⊤Ralph Giffard⹀Johanna 2nd wife,
1st wife before 1296   living 1321

Johanna,   Lawrence,   Simon Giffard of   ⹀Olive, 5th
died a minor   Rector of   Helset, presented to   dau. and
and unmar.   Helland 1348   Helland Church 1348   coheir

John Colyn of Becarne and⹀Rose dau. of ......
Elwynse

Joceus Dayowe⊤....

Johanna dau.⹀William Monke of Padstow⹀Juliana 2nd wife; remar. before Easter   John Calwodeley⹀...... dau.
and heir   died on feast of SS. Simon 1481 to Edward Kyngdon. (De Banco   of Calwodeley │ of John de
               and Jude 1479   Rolls 21st Edw.IV. Pasch.)   Floyre

Alice dau. and heir of William Monke⹀Oliver Calwodeley named in Court Rolls   Humphry   John Calwodeley
of Padstow   of Manor of Padstow 1485—1498   Calwodeley

John Cal-⹀Catherine dau. of Robert   Robert Calwodeley named in Court⹀Honour dau. of ...... Laugher of
wodeley   Tredinnick of Tredinnick   Rolls of Manor of Padstow   Cornwall. Died 9th April 152(2).
          co. Cornwall   1549—1557   Bur. at Padstow. M.I.

John Calwodeley, son   John Calwodeley of Pad-⹀⹀Ann dau. of ...... Lawre   Robert Calwodeley, named
and heir, ob. cute   stow. Lord of the Manor of Cornwall, a widow in   Padstow Manor Rolls 1558-
patron s.p.   of Trelother, named in   1606,   Padstow Manor   1562
                       Padstow Manor Rolls   Rolls
                       1558—1573

                       John Calwodeley named in Manor Rolls of⹀
                       Padstow 1606-1610

Nicholas Calwodeley son and heir, knighted   William   John   Catherine mar.   Honour mar. John Webber
in parts beyond the seas. Named in Court   Francis Bracken-   of Amble in St. Kew.
Roll of Manor of Padstow 1616. Living   berie of Padstow   Died 6th October 1601.
1621, dead 1623. s.p.   Bur. at St. Kew. M.I.

COLYN, CALWODELY, AND ARUNDELL.

John de Silveston Lord of Penvrane⊤....

Serlo de Penvrane⊤....

John de Penvrane living 1285 and 1298 ⊤

Adam de Penvrane living 1315, aged cir. 21 years ⊤

Simon Giffard, heir of his⊤ brother Ralph 1302, presented to Helland 1310

John Shylston Lord of⊤.... Penvrane

Lucy, 4th dau. and coh. mar... ..de Boterdon

Alice 3rd dau. and coh. mar. 1st Nichs. Ferrers, 2nd ...... Coryton

Katherine 2nd dau., mar. .... Resethercombe

Margaret 1st dau. and coh. mar. .. ....Bastard

Serlo de Penfrane living 1432, ob. s.p.

John Giffard of Helland son and heir, presented to Helland⊤.... 1349, died cir. 1375

Nicholas

Andrew Giffard Rector of Helland 1349

Thomas Colyn of Helland⊤Ingreta dau. living 1394-5. (De Banco │ and coh. Rolls)

Margaret dau. and = ... Raleigh of the coh. Nettlecombe family

John Colyn of Helland⊤Elizabeth dau. of John living 1437 │ Nicoll of Bodmin

From Helland Church.

Thomas Calwodeley son and heir.⊤Elizabeth dau. of Thomas Hache of Died 6th June 1492 Inq. p.m. │ Wollege co. Devon. Bur. in Church of 8th Henry VIII. No. 5 │ Friars Preachers at Exeter before 1479

Oto or Otes Colyn of Helland. Died⊤.. 10th September 1463. Inq. p.m. 6th Edward IV., No. 36.

Thomas Calwodeley son and heir,⊤Elizabeth dau. and heir =.... Raleigh, 2nd husband⊤Edward ap Rice or ob. v.p. Bur. in Church of Friars │ of Otes Colyn, aged ten │ Apryse, 3rd husband Preachers at Exeter, near his mother, │ years on her father's Will dated 1st March 1497 │ death, 1463

Humphry Calwodeley aged⊤Johanna dau. of John Carmynowe of Fentongollen, 20 years on the death of │ and relict of John Pentyre, jun. ; mar. settl. dated Jan. his grandfather 1492. At- │ 1493-4, living 24th February 1537-8, on the death of her tainted 1497 │ daughter.

Roger Arundell. Died 12th June 1536⊤Johanna dau. and heir restored in blood and possessions 1508. Died Inq. p.m. 28th Henry VIII. Excheq. No. 11 │ 28th September 1537. Inq. p.m. 30th Henry VIII. Excheq. No. 12

Humphry Arundell of Helland,⊤Elizabeth aged 23 years on his father's death 1536. Attainted and executed 1549

I certify that the portions of this Pedigree printed in *Italics*, and the Arms, except the above small Escutcheon, agree with the Records of this Office.

Herald's College, 8th April, 1873.

GEORGE HARRISON, *Windsor Herald.*

G

PEDIGREE ILLUSTRATIVE OF THE DESCENT

Compiled from Ancient

Hugh Fichet=....

Hugh Fichet=....

Robert Fichet, temp. Henry II., (Liber Niger, 1, 97)=....

Hugh Fichet, (Coram Rege Roll, 4th John)=Albreda

Geoffry Fichet=....

Hugh Fichet=.... Lord of Spaxton 1245, living 1261

Sir Nicholas Dauney, Knt., died 1332. (Inq., p.m. 6th Edward III., Part 2, No. 79)=Sir Walter Treverbyn, Knt.=Margery, dau. of Ralph Bloyowe, living a widow of Treverbyn 1307; died 9th June 1346 and bur. in Church of Grey Friars, Bodmin. See Vol. I., p. 189.=Sir John de Halton, Knt.=....

Sir William Fichet

Robert Fichet=Sarah, dau. Lord of Spaxton of ...... Estune

Sir John Dauney, Knt., aged 30 years on his father's death. Died Aug. 1346, Inq. p.m., 20th Edward III., No. 33=Sibella, dau. and heir, bur. in Church of Grey Friars, Bodmin, 1360, see ante Vol. I., p. 189.

......=.... Chalons

John Fichet, Lord=Isabella of Spaxton, living 1331

Edward Courteney, son=Emelina, dau. and heir, aged 18 years on her father's death; of Hugh 2nd Earl of died on Friday next after the Feast of St. Peter in Cath. Devon, died v.p. 1370-1, Inq. p.m., 45th Edward III., Part I., No. 15

Nicholas=Johanna, heir=John=.... Daune of Walter Chalons Langdon

Isabella, dau. of .... Chalons=Thomas Fichet of of Chalonsleigh, co. Devon, Spaxton, living 1350 mar. there

Edward Courteney, 3rd Earl of Devon. Aged 15 on his mother's death; died 5th December 1419

Robert Chalons=Martin Langdon,=Dionisia, dau. of John=Sir John Hulle *alias*=Matilda, living 1392 1st husband, ob. Durburgh; dead in 1392 Hill, Knt. s.p.

Ralph Chalons

Johanna, mar. Sir John Malet, son and heir of Sir Baldwin Malet; Mar. Settl. 5th Rich. II.

JOHN HILLE *alias* HULLE of Spaxton; aged 10 years on his father's death;=Margaret, dau. of Sir William Rodney, Knt., by died on Sunday next after the Feast of St. Denis 1455. Inq. p.m., 34th Margaret, dau. of Lord Hungerford Henry VI., No. 17

SIR WILLIAM SAYE, KNT., of Broxbourn, co. Herts; died 4th December=GENOVEVA, dau. and heir, aged 8 weeks on her father's 1529; Inq. p.m.; 22nd Henry VIII., No. 46; Bur. at Broxbourn, M.I. death. Died before her husband, s.p.

Thomas Saye of Liston Hall, co. Essex=Johanna, dau. and coheir

William Saye, died 1st August, 23rd Henry VII. Inq. p.m. 1st Henry VIII.

Robert Hussey of Sleaford, co. Lincoln; died 28th May 1538, Inq. p.m., 2nd Edward VI., No. 107=Anne, eldest dau. and coh. of her brother, aged 20 years, 1st Henry VIII.

William Clopton=Elizabeth, 2nd dau. and of Benston co. coh. of her brother, aged Suffolk 18 years 1st Henry VIII.

Thomas Hussey, son and heir, aged 21 years 1529; died 31st May 1559, s.p., Inq. 1st Elizabeth

WILLIAM CLOPTON, son and heir, aged 21 years 1529

)F THE MANOR OF BOCONNION.

)eeds, Inquisitions, &c.

The names in CAPITALS *shew those who held the Manors of Boconnion and Canalisey.*

Nicholas de Hauton *alias* Halton of Halton in St. Dominic,⹂Rosamund, dau. and heir of Henry St. George, Lord of
co. Cornw.   Dydysham, living 1257.

Sir Ralph de Halton, Knt., living 1253⹂....   Richard de Inkepenne⹂....

......de Inkepenne⹂....   ROGER DE INKEPENNE⹂Emelina

ROGER INKEPENNE of Inkepenne,⹂Johanna, dau. and heir, Inq. p.m. 5th⹂Robert Bendyn, living 1318
co. Berks, died in 1317   Edward IV., No. 50, Part 2

Henry Sampson⹂Thomasine   SIR NICHOLAS INKEPENNE, KNT., a minor in⹂Philippa, a dau. and heir of Sir
of Plymonth   1317; aged 22 years on the death of his   John Cobham, Knt.
                                  mother; dead 1350

ohnSamp-⹂......dau. JOHN DE INKEPENNE, did⹂JOHANNA, had dower Roger Thomas Nicholas William ..⹂Amicia
on of Ply-   of ...... homage for the Manor of out of Boconion and
nouth   Gorges   Halton 1353; dead 1362   Canalisey 1362

IR THOMAS FICHET, KNT., Lord of Spaxton;⹂RICARDA, dau. and heir; died⹂William Hywish, James   Richard⹂Margaret
ied on Monday next after the Feast of Nat. Monday next before the Feast of 1st husband   Sampson   Trenage
t. John Bap. 1386; Inq. p.m., 15th Richard St. Laurence, 1390, Inq. p.m., 15th
I., Part II., No. 21.   Richard II., Part I., No. 21.

ohanna, dau. and heir⹂ROBERT HILLE *alias* HULLE of Spaxton;⹂ISABELLA, heir of her brother; born   Thomas Fichet of Spaxton;
f Sir Otho Bodrigan;   Judge of the Common Pleas; died on at Halton, and bap. at St. Dominic, died on Thursday next after
ee Ped. of BODRIGAN   Sunday in the Feast of St. Mark, 1424, 24th March 1383; Prob. Etat., 20th the Feast of St. Peter ad vin.
nte, vol. i., p. 555   Inq. p.m., 1st Henry VI., No. 31   Richard II., No. 145   1395, a minor and s.p.

OHN HILLE *alias* HULLE of Spaxton, aged 21 years on⹂CECILIA, dau. and coh. of Sir John Stourton of Prest⹂Sir Thomas Keryell,
is father's death.; died on Thursday next after the feast Pucknett, Knt.; died 18th April 1472. Inq. p.m., Knt., 2nd husb.
f St. Calixtus 1434; Inq. p.m., 13th Henry VI., No. 36   12th Edward IV., No. 51

Sir John Say, Knt., of Saysbury,⹂Elizabeth, dau. of Laurence Cheyney of   John Cheyne of Pinho,⹂Elizabeth
co. Herts, died 1478   Fen Ditton, co. Camb., died 1473   co. Devon

John Cheyne, *alias* Cheyney of Pinho⹂Alice, dau. of......Stowell of Cotherstone

dward Waldgrave, of the Friers in Sudbury, co. Norfolk, 2nd son of Thomas Waldgrave of Buers in Suffolk⹂Isabella, dau. and coheir.

John Ellis, living⹂Elizabeth, 3rd dau. and coheir   John Walgrave son and heir, aged 30 years
in 1529   of her brother, dead in 1529   1529, ancestor of Earl Waldegrave

George Babyngton⹂Elena dau. and heir apparent, aged 11 years
· and 25 weeks 1529

G²

DE PENHARGARD.

The family of Penhargard was of considerable antiquity in this parish, and for a long period held the Manor of Penhargard from which they derived their name. They held also the Manor of Polhorman and other extensive possessions in different parts of the county.

The first of the name which has fallen under our notice was Bartholomew de Penhargarth who, before 1282, had married Thomasine one of the two daughters of Serlone Hay and co-heirs of their grandfather Walter Haye, Lord of Pencarrow and Amal-Eglos. Johanna the other co-heir married Sir Richard Stapledon Knt., and died s.p.[1] Bartholomew by this marriage had a son Maurice who had issue John de Penhargard, Bartholomew, and Lawrence. Bartholomew in 1351 was associated with John in an attempt to recover the Manors of Pencarrow and Amal-Eglos from Maurice de Berkeley and Johanna his wife.[2] In the same year John de Penhargard and Walter his son, Bartholomew de Penhargard and Lawrence de Penhargard, brothers of John, were found upon an assize of view of recognizance to have unjustly disseized Nicholas Helfaknyght of extensive lands in Alternon, St. Cleather, Duloe, St. Keyne, St. Pinnock, and other places.[3] In 29th Edward III. (1355) we find John Giffard of Helland and John de Penhargard appointed by Reginald Helygan of Helygan trustees under a deed of settlement of his lands.[4] In 1361 John de Penhargard presented to the Rectory of Lesnewth as the guardian of Richard son and heir of Henry Denys, to whom the patronage for that turn belonged.[5] And in 39th Edward III. (1365) we find John Penhargard witness to a deed by which Walter de Carburra of Cabilia granted to John Kylmynau of Brothek all his messuages &c. in Cabilia, Treutheret, &c.[6]

In January 1365-6 a fine was levied in which John Penhyrgard was querist and Thomas Butteburgh and Margery his wife were deforciants concerning lands in Kellignough,[7] and in the same month John de Penhirgard was deforciant in a fine levied by Robert Tresillian of the Manor of Polhorman[8] (see ante p. 22). Walter son of John in 1368 was elected one of the knights for the shire, the other being Robert Tresillian. This Walter had a daughter Rose who died within age and non compos mentis.[9] In 1372

---

[1] Assize Rolls, 2nd Edward I. $\frac{N}{2}$ 7. m. 12.
    4

[2] Assize Rolls, 25th Edward III. $\frac{N}{2}$ 6. m. 54.   See also ante vol. i. pp. 442-443.
    23

[3] Assize Rolls, 26th Edward III. $\frac{N}{2}$ 2. m. 84.   [4] Deed at St. Benet's Priory.
    24

[5] Bishop Grandison's Reg., fo. 130 b.   [6] Ante vol. i. p. 275

[7] Pedes Finium 40th Edward III. Hilary No. 1.   [8] Pedes Finium 40th Edward III. Hilary No. 9.

[9] Assize Rolls, 1st Henry IV. $\frac{N}{2}$ 2. m. 45, and 13th Henry IV. $\frac{N}{2}$ 4. m.
    36   38

John Penhargard bought of John Spencer and Alice his wife daughter and heir of Thomas Lametton the Manor of Lametton with the advowson of the Church of St. Kayne thereto pertaining, to which Church he presented one John Morsell in the time of Edward III.[1]

Ralph and Thomas, brothers of Walter, died before 1392 without issue male, as did also their uncle Bartholomew. The latter left an only daughter named Katherine, who became the wife of William Coplestone, and who, together with her husband, in January 1400-1, were sued, in a plea of debt, by John Resprenna executor of the will of Isabella relict of Stephen son of John de Trewynt of Bodmin, of which Stephen's will she had been executrix.[2] Laurence had a son called Walter who in virtue of a settlement made by his uncle John in the year 1392, endeavoured to recover from John Hawley the Manor of Penhargard[3] (see ante, p. 23); and a similar attempt was made by Henry Penhargard in 1472. This Henry we suppose to have been a grandson of the last mentioned Walter. In 1475 we find him taking proceedings against William and Richard Mayowe of Lemmanysworthy for trespass upon his closes and houses in Bodmin,[4] and in 1480 he suffered a recovery to John Penlyn of two messuages, &c., in Kylwyth, Polcan, and Bodmyn.[5]

We find other names which we are unable to connect with the foregoing, or to place in the pedigree, though doubtless, the persons who bore them belonged to the same family. In 1314, Walter de Penhargard was one of the Monks at Bodmin, as appears by certain proceedings before the Justices Itinerant at Launceston,[6] and in the same year Geoffry de Penhargard, John le Seneschal, Roger le Seneschal and others were accused of having unjustly disseized John de Treiagu of his free tenement in Dynas Caerarthyn juxta Penepons.[7] This was probably the same Geoffry who, in 1310 and again in 1311, had been Burgess in parliament for Liskeard.

In 1316-7 Laurence de Penharghard was one of the defendants in a plea of novel disseizin in Trehudreth, &c.[8] In 1416 Catherine Penhargard held some land, probably Penbugel, under Nicholas Beket and Johanna his wife.[9]

ARMS OF PENHARGARD: A saltier engrailed has been assigned as the arms of this family but, as far as we can ascertain, without sufficient authority.

---

[1] De Banco Rolls, 20th Richard II. Hil. m. 107. The Bishop's Registers give no information with respect to John Morsell, but shew that on the 30th April 1349 Philip de Cleue was admitted to the Church of St. Kayne upon the presentation of John de Penhirgart. (Bishop Grandison's Register, vol. iii. fo. 78.)

[2] De Banco Rolls, 2nd Henry IV., Trinity m. 202.

[3] De Banco Rolls, 15th Richard II. Easter, m. 105.

[4] De Banco Rolls, 15th Edward IV., Trinity, m. 223.

[5] De Banco Rolls, 20th Edward IV. Michaelmas, m. 340.

[6] Assize Rolls, 8th Edward II., 2 N } 6
   16

[7] Assize Rolls, 8th Edward II., 2 N } 1.
   10

[8] Ante p. 272, in which we regret to find that the proceedings are stated to have taken place in 10th Edward I., instead of 10th Edward II.

[9] Assize Rolls, 2nd Henry V.

PEDIGREE OF PENHARGARD.

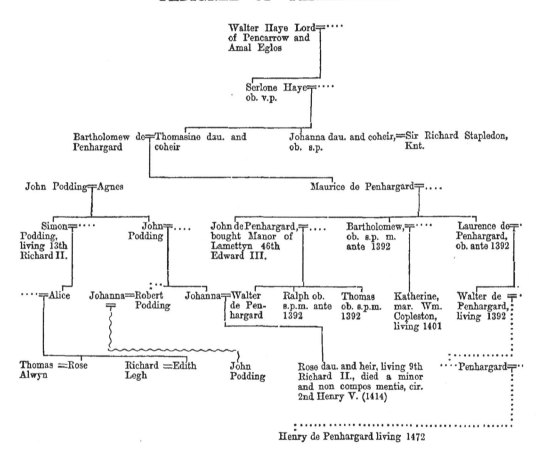

OPYE, *alias* OPY, *alias* OPIE.

The family of Opie is one widely spread and of considerable antiquity in the county of Cornwall, but of no great eminence, though about the end of the fifteenth century holding a position which justified John Carmynowe of Fentengollen in giving to Nicholas Opie of Bodmin one of his several daughters in marriage. The issue of this marriage was a son, Roger Opye, who was buried at St. Minver in 1517, where a brass to his memory still remains (see post.) We have no evidence as to other issue, but it is probable that Nicholas Opie, who was mayor of Bodmin in 1522, was another son. He appears in the return of that date[1] as possessing goods in Bodmin of the value of £40 a year, being the highest valuation in the town; and the same return shews that he possessed land in several parishes. John Opie was one of the Commissioners of Subsidies for the Hundred of Trigg in 1524, whilst at the same time Thomas Opy, Senior, and Thomas Opie, Junior, were assessed upon goods, and Martin Opy upon a stipend of 20s. a year in the Borough of Bodmin: probably the latter was town clerk. Robert Opy at the same time was assessed upon goods of the value of £10 a year, at that time a somewhat high rate, in the Parish of Bodmin.[2]

The Nicholas Opie who heads the pedigree recorded at the Visitation of 1620 was probably the same mentioned above as the son of the first named Nicholas by Elizabeth Carmynowe. He would seem to have died between 1522 and 1524, for his name does not occur in the Subsidy Roll of the latter date whilst that of his son Robert does. He would appear also to have had a son named Nicholas, who in 1565 married Honour, daughter of Thomas Bligh of Bodmin (see Ped. of BLIGH, ante vol. i., p. 289), by whom he had several children, from none of whom, however, can we trace issue. He was one of the Burgesses of Bodmin named in the Charter of 1562-3 (ibid., p. 212). In 1565 he acquired the Manor of Lancarfe, which in 1581, after his death, belonged to his brother Thomas Opie (ibid. p. 261), who also was one of the Burgesses named in the abovementioned charter.

The last mentioned Thomas was assessed to the Subsidy in Bodmin in 1546, upon an income of £20 a year in goods.[3] He purchased Penhargard in 1560, was Mayor of Bodmin in 1564, and received a grant of arms from Robert Cooke Clarencieux in 1573 In June 1588, he was granted by the Queen a lease of the tithe of wool in Bodmin, St. Minver, Padstow, and St. Cubert, for the term of twenty-one years (ibid. p. 342, not ninety-nine years as there printed). By his wife Alice, daughter of William Waye of Lostwithiel, he had a large family of whom it will be sufficient here to notice William, who succeeded him at Penhargard, and Nicholas who settled at Plymouth and is shewn at the Herald's Visitation of 1620 to have had three sons, Nicholas, Thomas, and Edward.

[1] See Appendix.

[2] Subsidy Roll, 16th Henry VIII. $\frac{87}{131}$

[3] Subsidy Roll, 37th Henry VIII. $\frac{87}{179}$

William Opie of Penhargard died in 1656, leaving a great number of sons and daughters, none of whom however seem to have been very prolific. Thomas, his eldest son, succeeded him at Penhargard and Parke. We know not the date of his death, but he was alive in 1658, when he suffered a recovery in Parke (see ante, vol. i., p. 418). He left two daughters, his co-heirs, the elder of whom, Mary, married her kinsman Nicholas Opie of Pawton, of whom presently, and the younger, Loveday, William Hicks of Cardinham, Clerk.

Nicholas Opie, the eldest son of Nicholas Opie of Plymouth, mentioned above, died in 1662. He had acquired the Barton, and some interest in the Manor, of Pawton in St. Breoke, and the Barton of Coldridge or Coleridge in the parish of Eggbuckland co. Devon, and by his will[1] he devised Pawton to his eldest son Nicholas Opie, and Coldridge to his son Richard. John became Rector of St. Breoke, and William was a merchant in Bristol.

Nicholas Opie of Pawton, as is before stated, married Mary, coheir of Thomas Opie of Penhargard, and joined in the sale of all the estates of his wife's family. He had a son Nicholas, who by Jenessphef or Jenophef, his wife, had an only son Hugh Opie, who died unmarried in 1737, when his sister, Elizabeth Treweeke, became sole representative of this branch.[2]

Returning again to the issue of Nicholas Opie of Plymouth: William Opie of Bristol, Merchant, died in 1695,[3] leaving an only son, named Nicholas, then a minor, who appears to have died s.p. William Opie mentions his brother John, late Rector of St. Breoke, and his brother Richard, lately living in Hampshire, then deceased, and Richard's son Nicholas. It was, we presume, this Richard who married Barbara, daughter of Malachi Dudeney of Upton Grays co. Hants, and heir of her brother Thomas Dudeney. He died in 1673,[4] leaving three sons, and a daughter named Barbara, who became the wife of John Came of London.

Nicholas, the eldest son of Richard Opie, was an attorney and scrivener in London, in considerable practice. He possessed Coldridge and Thornbury in Eggbuckland, and freehold property in Exeter, and died in 1704, intestate, leaving by Apphia his wife, daughter of Edward Anthony, three daughters, of whom two, Apphia and Anne died in infancy, and Barbara became the sole heir of her father, and was living unmarried in 1728.[5] Thomas the second son was a linendraper in London, and died in 1700 s.p. John, the third son, was a merchant in London. He was twice married. By his first wife, Margaret, daughter of Daniel Oley of London, he left no issue.[6] His second wife was Elizabeth Dorre of Barton upon Heath, co. Warwick, whom he married at St. Benets, Paul's Wharf, London, 19th January 1713, but we know not if by her he left issue.

---

[1] Will dated 23rd May, proved 20th December 1662. P.C.C. (Laud 156.)   [2] See ante, vol. i., p. 451.

[3] Will dated 17th, Cod. 22nd April, and proved P.C.C. 11th June 1695. (Irby 100.)

[4] Buried at Eggbuckland 28th November 1673, P.R.

[5] Chancery Proceedings Opie v. Opie, 4th June 1728.

[6] Chancery Proceedings Opie v. Oley, 9th May 1713.

The descent of Coldridge perplexes us very much. A certain Richard Opie, described in his will as " Richard Opie the elder of Plymouth, merchant,"[1] died seized of it in 1714, but we have failed to identify him. He was probably the same Richard Opie of Plymouth, Merchant, who, in conjunction with Elizabeth his wife, and Richard Opie his son and heir apparent, on 9th December 1700, demised to Richard Hancock[2] certain premises in St. Mabyn Church Town. He bequeathed to his daughter, Jane Opie, a tenement called Ford, in Eggbuckland, and the upper part of " The Hall " of Coldridge with certain chambers &c., to be divided, and he gave her also certain furniture, plate and jewels which had belonged to his three wives, including a silver tankard with the arms of Opie thereon. To his son Richard Opie he gave the other portion of " The Hall " of Coleridge and other lands in Eggbuckland. He mentions his brother-in-law Sir John Elwell, Bart.,[3] and his brother and sister Gill, and directing that his body shall be buried in the Church of Eggbuckland he gave to the Minister one guinea for preaching a sermon at his funeral.

Of John Opie, Rector of St. Breoke, it remains to say a few words. He married a lady named Mary, a kinswoman of John Paige of Plymouth, gent., a person of considerable estate, some of which she received under his will.[4] John Opie left two surviving sons, both named in Mr. Paige's will as devisees of a share of his freehold premises in Plymouth, of whom Nicholas died unmarried in 1716, and John became a citizen and haberdasher of London, and was living in 1726. Mary, widow of the Rector, " being ancient and weak," died in Plymouth in 1726, giving certain houses in Plymouth to her son John Opie, described as of the city of London, *Grocer*,[5] and mentions her kinswoman Mrs. Hannah Opie wife of her kinsman Mr. Richard Opie.

In consequence of the wide dispersion of the members of this family and the loss of the early parochial Registers of Helland we have experienced greater difficulty in tracing the descents of both branches than in the case of any other pedigree. Though we have collected a great deal of information from Parish Registers, Wills and Deeds, and Proceedings in Chancery, it is insufficient to enable us to identify all the individuals and, at present, to complete the pedigree of the Plymouth and Coleridge branch.

[1] Will dated 18th September 1713. Proved P.C.C. 30th September 1714 (Aston 179.)

[2] HANCOCK'S SEAL OF ARMS: Gu. a dexter hand. On a chief ar. three cocks; a deed in the possession of R. Hambly Andrew of Tredinnick, Esq.

[3] Sir John Elwill of the city of Exeter, knighted 28th April 1696. Created a Baronet 15th August 1709. Died 25th April 1717. ARMS: Erm. on a chev. eng. between three double-headed eagles displayed gu., each charged with a ducal coronet or, as many annulets of the last. The title became extinct in his grandson in 1778.

[4] Chancery Proceedings, Mitford, 306-44.

[5] Will dated 22nd May 1722. Proved by John Opie 1st February, 1726-7. P.C.C. (Larrant 48).

H

PEDIGREE

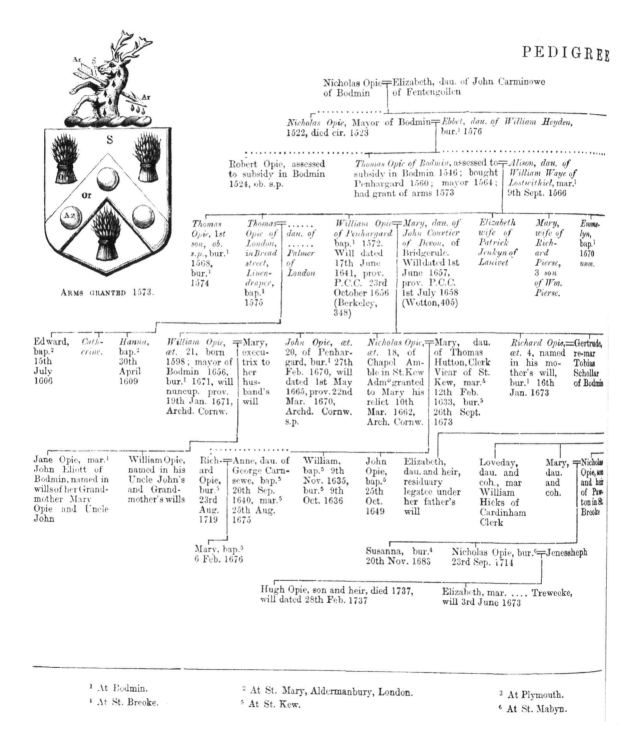

ARMS GRANTED 1573.

Nicholas Opie═Elizabeth, dau. of John Carminowe
of Bodmin   │ of Fentengollen

Nicholas Opie, Mayor of Bodmin═Ebbet, dau. of William Heyden,
1522, died cir. 1523   │ bur.³ 1576

Robert Opie, assessed   Thomas Opie of Bodmin, assessed to═Alison, dau. of
to subsidy in Bodmin   subsidy in Bodmin 1546; bought   │ William Waye of
1524, ob. s.p.   Penhargard 1560; mayor 1564;   │ Lostwithiel, mar.¹
                             had grant of arms 1573   9th Sept. 1566

| Thomas Opie, 1st son, ob. s.p., bur.¹ 1568, bur.¹ 1574 | Thomas═ ..... Opie of London, in Bread street, Liuendraper, bap.¹ 1575 | ..... dau. of ..... Palmer of London | William Opie═Mary, dau. of of Penhargard │ John Courtier bap.¹ 1572. │ of Devon, of Will dated │ Bridgerule. 17th June │ Will dated 1st 1641, prov. │ June 1657, P.C.C. 23rd │ prov. P.C.C. October 1656 │ 1st July 1658 (Berkeley, │ (Wotton, 405) 348) | Elizabeth wife of Patrick Jenkyn of Lanivet | Mary, wife of Richard Pierse, 3 son of Wm. Pierse. | Emmelyn, bap.¹ 1670 unm. |

| Edward, bap.² 15th July 1606 | Catherine. | Hanna, bap.² 30th April 1609 | William Opie, ═Mary, æt. 21, born │ executrix to 1598; mayor of │ her hus- Bodmin 1656, │ band's bur.¹ 1671, will │ will nuncup. prov. │ 19th Jan. 1671, │ Archd. Cornw. │ | John Opie, æt. 20, of Penhargard, bur.¹ 27th Feb. 1670, will dated 1st May 1665, prov. 22nd Mar. 1670, Archd. Cornw. s.p. | Nicholas Opie,═Mary, dau. æt. 18, of │ of Thomas Chapel Am- │ Hutton, Clerk ble in St.Kew │ Vicar of St. Admº granted │ Kew, mar.⁵ to Mary his │ 12th Feb. relict 10th │ 1633, bur.⁵ Mar. 1662, │ 26th Sept. Arch. Cornw. │ 1673 | Richard Opie,═Gertrude, æt. 4, named │ re-mar in his mo- │ Tobias ther's will, │ Schollar bur.¹ 16th │ of Bodmin Jan. 1673 │ |

| Jane Opie, mar.¹ John Eliott of Bodmin, named in wills of her Grand- mother Mary Opie and Uncle John | William Opie, named in his Uncle John's and Grand- mother's wills | Rich-═Anne, dau. of ard │ George Carn- Opie, │ sewe, bap.⁵ bur.⁵ │ 20th Sep. 23rd │ 1640, mar.⁵ Aug. │ 25th Aug. 1719 │ 1675 | William, bap.⁵ 9th Nov. 1635, bur.⁵ 9th Oct. 1636 | John Opie, bap.⁵ 25th Oct. 1649 | Elizabeth, dau. and heir, residuary legatee under her father's will | Loveday, dau. and coh., mar William Hicks of Cardinham Clerk | Mary,═Nicholas dau. │ Opie, son and │ and heir coh. │ of Paw- │ ton in St │ Breoke |

Mary, bap.⁵   Susanna, bur.⁴   Nicholas Opie, bur.⁶═Jenessheph
6 Feb. 1676   20th Nov. 1685   23rd Sep. 1714   │

Hugh Opie, son and heir, died 1737,   Elizabeth, mar. .... Treweeke,
will dated 28th Feb. 1737   will 3rd June 1673

F OPIE.

Roger Opie, died 13th January 1517,
bur. at St. Minver, M.I.

Nicholas Opie of Bodmin,=Honour dau. of Thomas Bligh of Bodmin
bought Lancarfe, 1565, | (see PED. OF BLIGH, ante Vol. I., p. 189)
bur. 1581 | mar.[1] 15th Jan. 1565

vard, =Amy	Nicholas Opie=Jane,	Radigan,	Joane,	Otho,	Tho-	Alice,	Nicho-	Par-	Mar-	Dor-
n bap. Small,	*of Plymouth,*2 *dau. of*	bap.[1]	bap.[1]	bap.[1]	mas,	bap.[1]	las,	sons,	garet,	othy,
7 mar.[1]	bap.[1] 1574, *John*	1566	1567,	1569,	bap.[1]	1572,	bap.[1]	bap.[1]	bur.[1]	bur.
1601,	bur.[3] 22nd *Woode*		bur.[1]	bur.[1]	150	bur.[1]	1573,	1574	1573	1577
bur.[1]	April 1640; *of*		1577	1577		1576	bur.[1]			
1624	Adm° granted *Har-*						1573			
	to son Thomas *restow*									
	11th June *co.*									
	1640 P.C.C. *Devon*									

ry, mar. Steph. Toker	Edward Opie, æt.=....	Thomas Opie,=Love-	Nicholas Opie=Susan,	Thomas =Sarah	Edward	Mar-
zabeth, mar. Wil-	10, of Bodmin,	*æt. 22, son and* day	of Plymouth, bur.[4]	Opie,		garet,
iam Webbe	named in his	*heir, of Pen-*	will dated 24th	bap.[3] 16		bur.[3]
e, mar. .... Watts	mother's will,	*hargard and*	23rd May July	Mar.		12th
lip, mar. Symonds	bur.[1] 15th Feb.	*Parke, living*	and prov. 20th 1677	1605		Dec.
ice, died an infant	1674, will prov.	*in 1658*	Dec. 1662,			1610
malyn, mar. Jobb.	6th May 1674,		P.C.C. (Laud,			
	Archd. Cornw.		156)			

Richard	John Opie, named=Mary, died	Wil-	Edward,	Stephen,	Susanna,	Anne,	Jane,	Grace,
Opie of	in his father's will, 1726, will	liam,	bap.[3]	named	bap.[6] 3rd	mar.	bap.	named in
Cole-	Rector of St. dated 22nd	bap.[3]	24th	in his	Oct. 1638	Steph.	14th	her fath-
ridge,	Breoke, died 1690, May 1722,	10th	Dec. 1650	father's	bur. 9th	Tre-	July	er's will,
co.	Adm° to Mary prov. P.C.	Nov.		will	June	ville	1639	mar. Jno.
Devon	his relict 20th C. 1st Feb.	1650			1640			Batters-
	July 1690 1726-7 (Lar-							by
	rant 48)							

Nicholas, bap.[4] 31st May   John Opie, citizen and haberdasher   John, bur.[4] April
1687, died 1716   of London, living 1720   1684

I hereby certify that the portion of this Pedigree which is printed in *Italics,*
and the Arms, agree with the Records of this Office,

Herald's College,   GEORGE HARRISON,
27th May 1873.   *Windsor Herald.*

[1] At Bodmin.   [2] At St. Mary, Aldermanbury, London.   [3] At Plymouth
[4] At St. Breoke.   [5] At St. Kew.   [6] At St. Mabyn.

H[2]

OPIE OF PARKE IN EGLOSHAYLE.

We have stated that Thomas Opie of Penhargard and Parke was alive in 1658, and that in that year he suffered a recovery in Parke to Thomas Marrett, that he died leaving two daughters and coheirs, and that they and their representatives in 1688 sold the Barton of Parke to Edward Hoblyn.[1] This Thomas Opie was probably resident at Penhargard, for we find another Thomas Opie in possession of Parke dying in the same year. In his will he describes himself as "Thomas Opie of Parke, Gent.," and therein he mentions a daughter and five sons, describing the sons in the order of their birth. He had a terminable estate only in Parke, for he gave two parts in three of it, " for such term as I now have therein," as security for the payment of certain legacies to his younger children. His wife's name was Sarah, which was also the name of the wife of Thomas Opie, son of Nicholas Opie of Plymouth, by Jane Woode (see ped. ante p. 51). The names of their children also, to some extent, agree, though they do not occur in the same order of birth, and consequently the identity is not established.

This Thomas Opie of Parke was the owner of the tithe of Hay of the parish of Bodmin, which John Opie, his son and heir, in 1668 conveyed to the Mayor and Burgesses of Bodmin.[2] John Opie married Elizabeth, daughter of William Parker of St. Mabyn, under whose will she was residuary legatee, and died in 1702, leaving two sons, John and Richard. John settled in London, and married Rachel, relict of ...... Maintree. He died in 1757, and in his will[3] described himself as "John Opie of Egloshayle, Esq., now of the City of London, Merchant," and, after giving small legacies to his "son-in-law, John Maintree,"[4] and his daughter-in-law, Rachel Maintree, he bequeathed the whole residue of his estate to his wife Rachel Opie, and appointed her sole executrix. Rachel Opie settled in Egloshayle, where she died in 1763, and by her will[5] devised to her daughter, Rachel Maintree, the whole of her lands in Egloshayle, St. Stephen's, and the Borough of Saltash, and elsewhere in Cornwall and Devon and constituted her executrix.

Of Richard Opie we have no trace subsequent to his father's death.

---

[1] See ante, vol. i., p. 448.   [2] See ante, vol. i., p. 146.
[3] Will dated 14th November 1757, proved P.C.C. 14th February 1758 (Hutton 49).
[4] John Maintree of Saltash, Gent., was one of the sureties for the administration of the effects of Elizabeth, mother of the said John Opie. Adm° Exeter, 4th September 1747.
[5] Will dated 8th June, proved 27th July 1763, P.C.C. (Cæsar 351.)

OPIE OF EGLOSHAYLE.

Thomas Opie of Parke, bur.[7]=Sarah, bur.[7] 28th
8th June 1659, will dated | Aug. 1655
30th May and prov. P.C.C.
8th Oct. 1658 (Wotton, 405)

| Sarah, named in her father's will | Nicholas Opie, 2nd son, named in his father's will | Thomas Opie, 3rd son, named in his father's will, bur.[7] 28th Jan. 1689 | Richard Opie, 4th son, named in his father's will, bur.[7] 29th April 1713 | Edward, 5th son, bap.[7] 8th June 1654, named in his father's will | John Opie, son and heir, executor to his father's will bur.[7] 25th June 1702, will dated 30th May, prov. 20th July 1702 | =Elizabeth, dau. of William Parker, of St. Mabyn, born 1st bap. there 15th April 1657, mar.[7] 1st July 1682, bur.[7] 16th April 1741, aged 85, Adm° granted to John Opie her son 4th Sept. 1747, Exeter |

| Margaret, born 10th, bap.[7] 20th June 1683, named in her father's will | William, bap. March 1684, bur. 23rd April 1688 | Sarah, bur.[7] 21st Dec. 1691 | Elizabeth, bur.[7] 13th Jan. 1692 | John Opie, son and heir, died in London, will dated 14th Nov. 1747, proved P.C.C. 4th Feb. 1758 | =Rachel, relict of .. Maintree, bur.[7] 11th July 1763, will dated 8th June, prov. 27th July 1763 | Richard Opie, 2nd son, bap. April 1693, proved his father's will |

[7] At Egloshayle.

TOKER *alias* TOOKER *alias* TUCKER.

The name Toker, or Tucker, is widely spread throughout the West of England and is very common in Cornwall. In 1329 we find Walter le Toker of Bodmin mentioned as having made default on a jury.[1] In 1395 John Wilkoc of Benbolgh recovered from John Peryn of Retoun and Margery his wife, and Meliora the sister of the same Margery, and Reginald Toker, a free tenement in Retoun juxta Kellygren.[2] In 1398 William Smith sued Robert Martyn and Johanna his wife and Stephen Toker, executors of the will of John Toker, to recover chattels of the said John of the value of 100s.[3] In 1419 John Toker had married Elena daughter and heir of Ranulph Tregone, and had a son John,[4] and in the same year an assize of view of recognizance was granted to enquire if Richard Toker and Johanna his wife, Richard Doyguan and Thomas Toker had unjustly disseized John Atte Style of his free tenement in Liskeard,[5] and in 1425 to enquire if John Hankyn had disseized Reginald Toker and Johanna his wife of a free tenement.[6]

In the middle of the 16th century, when the Parish Registers commenced, we find the name existing in many of the parishes of which we have a record, *e.g.*, Bodmin, Egloshayle, &c.

We have made these remarks to shew the antiquity of the name and its prevalence. The family of which we now propose to treat was probably distinct from any of the above, although the occurrence of the Christian names of John and Stephen, which are leading names in the early pedigree, is perhaps worthy of notice.

John Toker, or Tucker, of South Tavistock, was the father of Stephen Tucker of Lamerton, to whom, on account of some disease in his head, King Henry VIII in 1519 granted his license to wear his bonnet as well in the King's presence as elsewhere. He was twice married. By his second wife.........daughter and co-heir of.........Borlase, he had a son John Toker who settled in Helland, in which parish we find him assessed to the subsidy *on goods* of the value of £6 per annum in 1559.[7] In 1571 he was assessed *upon lands* of £3 per annum.[8] In 1594 we find Stephen Tooker his son assessed at the same rate,[9] and in 1600 Stephen Toker was assessed upon lands of £4 per annum.[10] This Stephen had a younger brother John Toker, who was Rector of Cardinham, but we have no means of identifying him with the John Tucker who was Rector of Helland and died in 1602 (ante p. 12.)

---

[1] Assize Rolls, Cornwall, 3rd Edward III. $\frac{N.2}{18}$ 4. m 10. d.   [2] Assize Rolls, Cornwall, 19th Richard II.

[3] De Banco Rolls, 21st Richard II., Easter m. 221.   [4] Assize Rolls, Cornwall, 7th Henry IV.

[5] Ibid., m. 91.   [6] Ibid., 3rd Henry VI., $\frac{N.2}{41}$ 2. m. 102. d.   [7] Subsidy Rolls, 1st Elizabeth $\frac{87}{218}$

[8] Subsidy Rolls, 13th Elizabeth $\frac{88}{228}$ [9] Ibid. 36th Elizabeth $\frac{28}{253}$ [10] Ibid. 42nd Elizabeth $\frac{88}{265}$

Stephen Toker registered his pedigree at the Herald's Visitation of Cornwall in 1620, when the arms allowed to him differed but little from those which had been granted in March 1538 by Thomas Hawley, Clarencieux, to Robert Tooker, Alderman of Exeter. We have failed, however, to trace the connection of the two families. In 1625, Stephen Toker's assessment in Helland was upon lands of the value of £6 per annum.[1] He died in 1637, and in 1641 his son and heir, Christopher Toker, who was forty years of age in 1620, was assessed at the same rate at which his father had been assessed in 1625. And Alice Toker, who was probably Alice the second daughter of Stephen, was assessed upon goods of the value of £3 per annum.

Christopher Toker by his wife, Honour, daughter of Maurice Hill of Helligan (see pedigree of HILL post) had four sons: Stephen who succeeded him at Brodes; John, who settled at Tregaddock in St. Mabyn, which his father had purchased of Nicholas Martyn 1622;[2] Joseph who married Margaret, daughter and coheir of Thomas Marrett of Blisland, and settled in that parish, and whose issue in the male line became extinct in the next generation; and Christopher who died s.p. in 1644.

Stephen Toker of Brodes died in 1682, leaving an only daughter, who became the wife of Hubert Glynn (see pedigree of GLYNN post) and carried the Toker lands in Helland into that family.

John Toker of Tregaddock had several children most of whom remained in St. Mabyn, but his son Stephen Toker sold Tregaddock in 1706,[3] and his children removed to St. Tudy, where their descendants continued to the end of the 18th century, and probably still remain in reduced circumstances.

ARMS OF TOKER.—Az. eight barrulets wary arg. over all on a chev. embattled counter embattled or, between three sea-horses naiant of the second, five guttée de poix.

CREST.—A lion's gamb erased gu., charged with three humets in pale, fesswise, or, and grasping a mace headed az. hafted of the second.[4]

---

[1] Stephen Toker acquired considerable lands in Helland from time to time. In 1594 and 1599 he bought two tenements in Kernick and other lands, in 1605 Bodwen and other lands. In 1621 Brodes, and in 1631 another messuage in Kernick, which accounts for the gradual increase in the rate of his assessment.

[2] Pedes Finium 5th Anne Michaelmas.

[3] Pedes Finium, 20th James, Michs. No. 12.

[4] The arms originally granted to Robert Tooker of Exeter are blazoned as under (Her. Col. R. 21, fo, 177[B] and F. 12, fo. 85[B]) :—"Azure & argent wave, a cheverone batteld count[r] batteld gold, dropy sabull, betweene iij shevaulx marin nawgeante, and so ar they callyd for ther nature & force as it is exprest by Aristotle, "au liure des natures," uppon his helm a torce argent & azure, on a lion's arme gulz iij humetts gold, holding in his jawe a mase of weyer heedyd argent haftyd vert—his mantel gulz dubled silver."

PEDIGREE OF

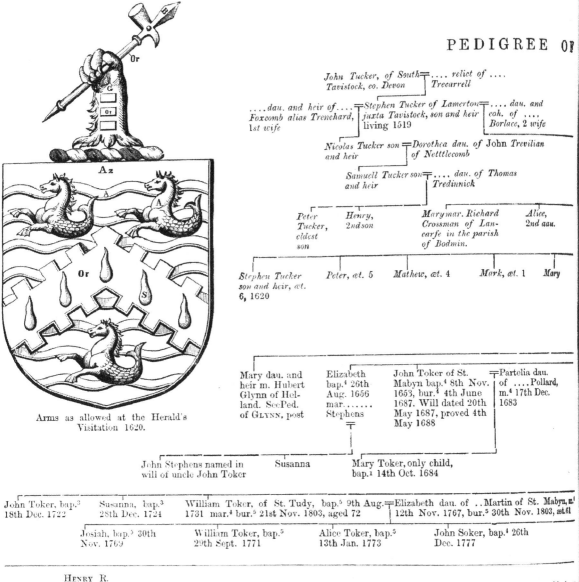

Arms as allowed at the Herald's Visitation 1620.

John Tucker, of South Tavistock, co. Devon = ... relict of .... Trecarrell

....dau. and heir of.... Foxcomb alias Trenchard, 1st wife = Stephen Tucker of Lamerton juxta Tavistock, son and heir living 1519 = ... dau. and coh. of .... Borlace, 2 wife

Nicolas Tucker son and heir = Dorothea dau. of John Trevilian of Netttlecomb

Samuell Tucker son and heir = ... dau. of Thomas Tredinnick

Peter Tucker, eldest son | Henry, 2nd son | Mary mar. Richard Crossman of Lancarfe in the parish of Bodmin. | Alice, 2nd aau.

Stephen Tucker son and heir, æt. 6, 1620 | Peter, æt. 5 | Mathew, æt. 4 | Mark, æt. 1 | Mary

Mary dau. and heir m. Hubert Glynn of Helland. See Ped. of GLYNN, post | Elizabeth bap.[4] 26th Aug. 1656 mar...... Stephens | John Toker of St. Mabyn bap.[4] 8th Nov. 1653, bur.[4] 4th June 1687. Will dated 20th May 1687, proved 4th May 1688 = Partelia dau. of ....Pollard, m.[4] 17th Dec. 1683

John Stephens named in will of uncle John Toker | Susanna | Mary Toker, only child, bap.[1] 14th Oct. 1684

John Toker, bap.[3] 18th Dec. 1722 | Susanna, bap.[3] 28th Dec. 1724 | William Toker, of St. Tudy, bap.[5] 9th Aug. 1731 mar.[4] bur.[9] 21st Nov. 1803, aged 72 = Elizabeth dau. of ..Martin of St. Mabyn, m.[4] 12th Nov. 1767, bur.[5] 30th Nov. 1803, æt.61

Josiah, bap.[5] 30th Nov. 1769 | William Toker, bap.[5] 29th Sept. 1771 | Alice Toker, bap.[5] 13th Jan. 1773 | John Soker, bap.[4] 26th Dec. 1777

HENRY R.
Henry, by the Grace of God King of England and of Fraunce and Lord of Ireland, to all manner of our subiects as well of ye spirituall preheminence and dignitye as of the temperall authoritye. These our letters hearing or seeing, Greeting. Forasmuch as we are credibly informed that our trusty subiect Stephen Tucker of Lamartyn in our county of Deuon, gentleman, for certayne diseases and infirmities which he hath and dailye susteyneth in his head, he cannot conueniently without his great danger be discouered of the same. We lett you witt that of our grace espetiall in tender consideration thereof haue by these presents licenced the sayd Stephen Tucker to vse and weare his Bonnet vpon his sayd head as well in our presence as

[1] At St. Kew.   [2] At St. Breward.   [3] At Blisland.

[4] At St. Mabyn.   [5] At St. Tudy.   [6] At Bodmin.

OKER, *alias* TUCKER.

I certify that the portions of this descent which are printed in *Italics* are faithfully extracted from the Record in the College of Arms. (1 C 2 403.)

STEPHEN TUCKER,
Rouge Croix.

John Tucker of Hellond, co. Cornwall, 2 son. Will proved=*Blanche dau. of .... Bonde*
15th Nov. 1589. P.C.C. (Leicester 84) | *of Exeter*

atherine mar. | *Stephen Tucker of Hellond juxta Bodmin in the co. of*=*Jane dau. of John* | *John Tucker Rector*=*Ann dau. of Hugh*
icholas Morecombe | *Cornwall, son and heir.* Will dated 1st August | *Conock of Liskerd* | *of Cardinnam co.* | *Pollard of North*
Bodmin | 1626, proved 5th May 1637, P.C.C. (Goare 60.) | *co. Cornwall* | *Cornwall, 2nd son* | *Moulton co. Devon*

ter Tucker,=*Catherine dau.* | *Christopher*=*Honour dau. of* | *Stephen Tucker of Hel-*=*Margery* | *Zacharia,*=*Ann dau. of*
d son, Par- | *of Maurice* | *Tucker son and* | *Maurice Hill* | *land, 3rd son, Admin°* | *dau. of* | *Tucker* | *Edmund Dow-*
n of Car- | *Hill of Helli-* | *heir, æt. 40, 1620* | *of Helligan in* | *to Margery his relict* | *Peter Marke* | *eldest* | *rish of the co.*
nham 1626 | *gan, Esq.* | *Dead 1644* | *co. Cornwall* | *18th Jan. 1640* | *of Liskerd* | *son* | *Cornwall*

ristopher | *Stephen Tucker*=*Mary d.* | *John Tucher,*=*Elizabeth* | *Jane,* | *Joseph*=*Margaret dau.* | *John* | *Sus-*
Helland, | *son and heir, æt.* | *of Wm.* | *2nd son, æt. 7,* | *dau. of......* | *æt. 2* | *Toker,* | *and coh. of* | *son* | *anna*
ll dated | *9, 1620, of* | *Opie of* | *1620, of* | *Phillipps, m.⁵* | | *bur.³* | *Thomas Marrett* | *and* |
th Nov., | *Helland Admin°* | *Penhar-* | *Tregaddock* | *21st Sept.* | | *June* | *of Blisland.* | *heir* |
oved 26th | *to Hubert* | *gard,* | *in St. Mabyn,* | *1652, bur.⁴* | | *1694* | *Vide Ped. of* | *aged* |
ov. 1644, | *Glynn of* | *mar.⁶ 27* | *bur.⁴ 15th* | *3rd Sept.* | | *(?)* | MARRETT, vol. i. | *2 yrs.* |
rchd. | *Helland, 8th* | *Nov.* | *Mar. 1697-8* | *1717* | | | p. 86 | |
ornw. s.p. | *Jan. 1682* | *1649* | | | | | | |

ephen=*Susanna dau. of* | *Daniel* | *Ann,* | Bridget, bap.³ | *Hon-* | *Jane,* | Christoph-=*Susanna dau. of* | *Joseph*
oker of | *Wllm. Mathew,* | *Toker,* | *bap.⁴* | 27th Oct., 1648, | *our,* | *bap.³ 24* | er Toker, | RichardMathew | *Toker,*
. | *Vicar of Eglos-* | *bap.⁴* | *1660* | mar. Edward | *bap.³* | *Feb.1652* | bap.³ 30th | (see Ped. of | *bap.³*
abyn, | *haile, bap. ˣ* | 19th | | Kempe of Blisland | *9th* | *mar.* | April 1665 | MATHEW, ante | 2nd
p.⁴ 6th | *16th April 1658,* | Sept. | | (see Ped. KEMPE, | *Dec.* | *William* | bur.³ 6th | vol. i. p. 570), | *Jan.*
arch | *mar, 27th April* | 1658 | | vol. i. p. 78). Will | *1650* | *Coleman* | June 1662, | Admin° 4th | 1659,
54 | *1684, bur.⁴ 6th* | | | prov. 28th Feb. | | | s.p. | June 1686 to | bur.³
| *February 1710* | | | 1714 | | | | her husband |

ne, bap.⁴ 18th | John Toker, of St. Tudy, bap.=⁴Alice dau. of .... | William Toker, | Stephen Toker,=Joane dau. of......
pt. 1688, bur.¹ | 1st February 1692-3, bur.⁴ 27th | Cole, mar. 24th | bap.⁴ 24th Oct. | bap.⁴ 20th Sept. Best, mar.ˣ 21st
th Oct. 1697 | Dec. 1775. M.I. | 1721 | 1697 | 1699 Sept. 1731

Josiah, bap. 25th Oct. 1743, of St. Tudy, | Stephen Toker, bap.⁵ 29th | Jane, bap.⁵ 27th
bur.₄ 4th Mar. 1767, M.I. | April 1735 | May 1741

Jenifer, bap.⁵ 19th | Elizabeth, bap.⁵ 12th | Ann, bap.⁵ 16th
March 1775 | Dec. 1776. | July 1780

wheare at his libertye. Wherfore we will and commaund you and euery of you to permit and suffer him soe to doe, thout any your challenges, lettes or interruptions to the contrarye, as yee and euery of you tender our pleasure. ven vnder our signet at our manor of Woodstock the 2 day of July in the 10 year of our Raigne.

A true copy from the Record (1. c. 2. fo. 404) in the Col. of Arms, London.

STEPHEN TUCKER, *Rouge Croix.*

¹ At St. Kew.   ² At St. Breward.   ³ At Blisland.
⁴ At St. Mabyn.   ⁵ At St. Tudy.   ⁶ At Bodmin.

I

GLYN *alias* GLYNN.

The family of Glyn, or Glynn, is of great antiquity in Cornwall, though we do not find the name in the list of Sheriffs, nor as Knights of the Shire, nor among those holding any public office, except as below stated, until the 17th century; nor does any member of the family seem to have held any lands in capite, hence we have great difficulty in tracing the early descents.

Richard de Glin was amerced in four marks, for a breach of the forest laws in 10th Richard I.[1] (1198-9), a large fine at that time. In 1284 we find John de Glynn and Ralph de Glyn mentioned in the Assize Rolls,[2] and in 1324-5 Peter de Glyn is named as the husband of Alice daughter of Henry de Kellygren.[3] In 1327 Thomas de Glyn was assessed to the subsidy in the parish of Cardynham at 12d.[4]

The Fee of the Manor of Glyn was long held by the family of Montacute. Sir John de Monte Acuto died thereof seized 13th Richard II. (1390), as did John de Monte Acuto in 10th Henry IV. (1409), and, under these Chief Lords, the *Manor* of Glyn, during this period, was held by the family of Carmynowe. John Carminowe held it in 1317.[5] John Carmynowe, Esq.,—son and heir of John Carmynowe, Esq., who was the son of William Carmynowe, Esq., the son of Ralph Carmynowe, who died seized of the Manor in 10th Richard II. (1409),—died thereof seized on 6th May 1418, when his uncle Thomas Carmynowe was found to be his heir.[6] On the death of Thomas Carmynowe on Wednesday next before Christmas 1442,[7] the Manor of Glynne, *inter alia*, passed to Hugh Courtenay of Haccombe, son and heir of Hugh Courtenay of the same place by Margaret one of the daughters and co-heirs of the said Thomas Carmynowe, and, though Edward Courteney suffered a recovery therein to Halnathan Maleverer in 1479,[8] it was parcel of the possessions forfeited by Henry Marquis of Exeter in 1539. It has been stated[9] that the Manor of Glyn was carried into the family of Carmynowe by the marriage of Sir John Carminowe, Knt., who died in 1331, with Joane, daughter and heir of Sir John Glyn, Knt., and we find such an alliance upon record.[10] Osbert Hameley, who died in the same year, married a daughter of Ralph Glyn, which Ralph was one of the jurors on the Inquisition *post mortem* of Edmund Earl of Cornwall in 1300.[11] This lady died in 1349. In 1302 Osbertus Hamelyn is returned as indebted to the King in 100 marks for wreck of the sea which he had received of the sureties of Geoffry de Glyn, John Hamelyn, John de Bilon and others.[12] Geoffry de Glyn is

[1] Rot. Pip. for the year.

[2] Assize Rolls, 12th Edward I. $\frac{m}{1}$ $\genfrac{}{}{0pt}{}{}{20}$ 3. m. 8.

[3] Assize Rolls, 18th Edward I. $\frac{N}{2}$ $\genfrac{}{}{0pt}{}{}{17}$ 9. m. 11.

[4] Subsidy Roll, 1st Edward III. $\frac{87}{7}$

[5] Rot. Cart., 2nd Edward II.

[6] Inq. p. m. 8th Henry V. No. 99.

[7] Inq. p.m. 21st Henry VI. No. 46.

[8] De Banco Rolls, 17th Edward IV. Trinity.

[9] Lysons' Mag. Brit. III. 57.

[10] Brit. Mus., Cotton Coll. Cl. xj.

[11] Inq. p. m. 28th Edward I. No. 44.

[12] Rot. Pip., 30th Edward I. Ibid. 32nd Edward I.

also mentioned in the same way in 1304. Eleanor, another daughter, married James de Trenages. John Giffard, son and heir of Sir Michael Giffard of Lanowmure, Knt., who died in 1340, married Jane daughter of Sir Peter Glyn, Knt., who, in 1324-5, is mentioned as the husband of Alice daughter of Henry Kellygren.[1] In 1351 William Glyn of Bodmin and Johanna his wife recovered seizin of a tenement in Bodmin against John Philip of Tredethy, William de Tredethy, John son of Roger Smith of Bodmin, and Roger Helygan of Bodmin and Dionisia his wife.[2] In 1358 Richard Glyn was defendant in a suit of novel disseizin.[3] In 1361 Richard Glyn of Bodmin and Johanna his wife sued Thomas, son and heir of Thomas Grounder of Bodmin, in a plea that he should warrant one messuage in Bodmin which William de Penquite and Johanna his wife claimed as dower of the said Johanna.[4] In 1383 Stephen Glyn is spoken of as late Mayor of Bodmin.[5] In 1384 a precept was issued to the Sheriff to arrest Richard Glyn of Helleston, together with many others, for offences against the Stannary laws,[6] and in 1387 Henry de Glyn and Johanna his wife recovered of Simon Mareys and others five messuages in Kethelsham, Wadefast, Bordonne, Borcot, and Rous in Cornwall,[7] whilst in 1394[8] we find the same Henry Glyn and Johanna his wife plaintiffs in an action of debt, as was Launcelot Glyn in the following year.[9] These notices, however, are too scanty to enable us to compile a pedigree.

GLYN OF GLYN.

By a deed dated at Bodmin on Thursday next after the Feast of St. James the Apostle, 44th Edward III. (1370) Stephen Grygge of Glyn appointed Stephen Glyn and Judkyn Lange his attornies to deliver seizin to Henry Glyn[10] and Johanna his wife of all his estate and right, &c., in the ville of Lawharne, which Olivia wife of Walter Westcote and mother of the said Henry Glyn then held in dower. And by a deed dated at Polwater on Monday next before the Feast of SS. Philip and James, 6th Henry IV. (1405) Thomas, son and heir of Henry Glyn, granted to William Westcote, of the parish of Bradok, all his messuages &c., in the ville of Polwater, to hold for the term of his life, at the annual rent of 12d, with remainder after the death of the said William to Walter Westcote, at the same rent. The Olivia here mentioned was probably the wife

---

[1] Assize Rolls, 18th Edward II. 2$\left.\begin{array}{c}N\\17\end{array}\right\}$9 m. 11.

[2] Assize Rolls, 25th Edward III. 2$\left.\begin{array}{c}N\\23\end{array}\right\}$6. m. 53.

[3] Assize Rolls, 32nd Edward III. m. 96.

[4] De Banco Rolls, 35th Edward III. m. 65.

[5] De Banco Rolls 7th Richard II. Hilary.

[6] Coram Rege Rolls, 7th Richard II. Easter. Crown Pleas.

[7] Assize Rolls, Cornwall, 12th Richard II. 2$\left.\begin{array}{c}N\\32\end{array}\right\}$1 m. 170.

[8] De Banco Rolls, 18th Richard II. Michaelmas m. 225. d.

[9] Ibid., 19th Richard II. Hilary, m. 392. d.

[10] In January 1397, Henry Glyn and Johanna his wife were plaintiffs in an action of debt against Alice Sturte and John Hunt and Alice his wife. (De Banco Rolls, 20th Richard II. Hil. m. 347.)

I²

of Thomas Glyn, who was assessed to the subsidy in Cardynham in 1327, as above stated. These deeds[1] enable us to deduce three descents ending with Thomas Glyn, who was probably father or grandfather of Thomas Glyn who heads the visitation pedigree of 1620.

How, or when, the Manor of Glynn was re-acquired by the family of its ancient possessors we have not been able to ascertain, but it appears from a deed dated at Polwater, 1st October 3rd Henry VII.[2] (1487), by which Thomas Glyn of Glyn granted and confirmed to Thomas Glyn of Lanhydrock, and Richard Denys, all his messuages &c. in Polwater and Southcarne, that Glyn was then held by the family. The possession of Polwater would seem to support the conjecture above stated that this Thomas was a descendant of Thomas Glyn (son of Henry) who held the same place in 1405. Thomas Glyn, son of the above Thomas Glyn of Glyn, had three sons of whom Nicholas would appear to have been the elder. In a deed dated 3rd December 17th Henry VIII. (1521), to which John Glyn of Lanhydrock was one of the witnesses; he is described as Nicholas Glyn of Glyn,[3] as he is also in another deed dated 27th July 20th Henry VIII. (1528), which John Glyn of Lanhydrock also attests: and also in a further deed dated 24th April 1st and 2nd Philip and Mary (1555).[4] This was doubtless the same Nicholas who is mentioned (ante. vol. i., p. 138) as being 51 years of age in 1538. Glyn would appear to have been held on lease from the Courteneys, for in 1542 Nicholas Glyn was assessed to the subsidy in Cardynham upon goods[5] of the value of £30 per annum. This Nicholas died s.p. and was probably succeeded by his brother Thomas. Thomas had two sons: Nicholas carried on the succession at Glynn and in 1558 was assessed to the subsidy in Cardynham upon lands of the value of £7 per annum,[6] as he was in 1570 upon lands in the same parish of £10 per annum.[7] In 1594 the value of the lands had increased to £12,[8] when the name of Nicholas Glyn again appears in the Roll. There is, however, an error in the name, for Nicholas Glyn died on 11th October 1580, seized inter alia of the moiety of the Manor of Treyere in Lanreath, also of the Manor of Maneleye Fleming in St. Vepe,[9] also of one messuage and forty acres of land in Cardynham called Glyn, also of one messuage in Brodoke called Polwater, also of one

[1] Deeds in the possession of William Anthony Glynn of Fairy Hill, Isle of Wight, Esq., the present representative of the Glynn family, to whose obliging courtesy we are indebted for a sight of them.

[2] Glynn Deeds.

[3] The lands of Nicholas Glyn in Cardinham in the Return, cir. 1522, are valued at 13s. 4d. per annum, and his goods as of the value of £14; and he was returned as "full harnessed." He had also lands of the value of 10s. per annum, at the same time, in St. Neot. (Augm. Office, Miscel. Books, vol. lxxvii.)   [4] Glynn Deeds.

[5] Subsidy Roll, 33rd Henry VIII. $\frac{87}{150}$ John Glyn at the same time was assessed upon goods in St. Neot of the value of £20 per annum. A leasehold or chattel estate would be described as "goods."

[6] Subsidy Rolls, 1st Elizabeth $\frac{87}{218}$ [7] Subsidy Rolls, 13th Elizabeth $\frac{88}{225}$

[8] Subsidy Rolls, 36th Elizabeth $\frac{88}{253}$

[9] The Manor of Manelye Fleming was quit-claimed by John Briand of Lansallowes, Gent., to Nicholas Glyn of Glyn, by deed dated 15th June 1st Edward VI. (Glynn Deeds.)

messuage called Penbugell &c., which latter he had settled upon his son Nicholas, and the jury say that he held Glyn of Bryan Cave and Bridget his wife as of their Manor of Glyn &c., and that William his son is his nearest heir and is aged 46 years and more.[1] Upon his son Nicholas and his heirs male he settled, as just stated, Penbugell and other lands, with remainder, in default of such issue, to his own right heirs. This Nicholas resided at St. Merrin where he died in 1602, s.p.

John, second son of the last above mentioned Thomas Glyn, founded the family of Glyn of Westcote, in Boyton, whose descendants[2] remained seated there at the time of the Heralds' Visitation of 1620, when there were three sons living: John, aged 12 years, Robert, aged 11 years, and George, aged 8 years. John married Prudence, daughter of ...... Risdon of Aston, Co. Devon, and died before 1649, s.p. George, settled at North Tamerton, and died there in 1679, s.p., and by his will, of which he made his brother Robert executor, directed that his body should be buried at Boyton. Robert, it is believed, also died s.p.

William, son of Nicholas Glyn, above mentioned, died on 6th October 1613. The inquisition taken after his death shews that he had increased his possessions in Cardynham. He was found to have been seized, in addition to the manors aforesaid, of one capital messuage and 200 acres of lands, &c., in Glyn, also of a messuage 140 acres of lands, &c., in Kingswood Hill and other places in the same parish, and that Glyn was held of Bridget Skipwith as of her Manor of Glyn, and further, that Nicholas Glyn was his son and nearest heir, and was aged 50 years and more.[3]

This Nicholas was Sheriff of Cornwall in 1620, in which year he registered his pedigree at the Heralds' Visitation. He had two sons, William and Walter—William carried on the succession at Glyn. His great grandson, of the same name, by Rose, the daughter of John Prideaux of Prideaux Place, and coheir of her brother Edmund Prideaux, had several children. His eldest son, Nicholas Glyn, married Elizabeth, daughter of Francis and sister and sole heir of John Nichols of Trewane and Davidstow. He was Sheriff of Cornwall in 1743, and died the following year leaving an infant son. John Glyn, the second son of William Glyn, by Rose Prideaux, went to the bar where he greatly distinguished himself, and was one of the most eminent constitutional lawyers of his age. In 1768, he was a candidate for the representation in Parliament of the County of Middlesex. The poll commenced at Brentford on the 8th December, and the business was carried on with tranquillity until the afternoon, when it being supposed that Sergeant Glynn had polled 'a greater number of votes than his opponent, Sir W. B. Procter, a tumult arose. The mob stormed the hustings and attempted to seize some of the poll books. Many persons were much injured, and the polling was entirely stopped for the

[1] Inq. p. m. 23rd Elizabeth. Part 2, No. 14.

[2] In 1558, John Glyn was assessed upon goods in the parish of Boyton at £9 a year, as he was again in 1594, but in 1600, the property had become divided as John Glyn the son or grandson of the first John was assessed upon goods of the value of £3 a year only, and he was assessed at the same rate in 1627.

[3] Inq. p. m., 12th James, Part I. No. 402.

day. The next day Sergeant Glynn issued a very spirited address to the freeholders, denouncing the riot and proclaiming himself a friend to the "cause of the people." He was returned by a majority of 264, and took a prominent part in the case of Mr. Wilkes. In 1772, he was elected Recorder of London in succession to Baron Eyre. The old salary of the appointment was £180 a year, which the Common Council usually made up to £400. The services of Mr. Eyre occasioned an additional £200, but those of Mr. Glynn were considered so valuable, that the stipend was increased to a £1000 a year. Mr. Glynn was also Recorder of Exeter.

The young heir of Nicholas Glynn was supposed to be of weak intellect, and Serjeant Glynn took out a commission in lunacy against him, and got himself appointed receiver of the estates. This so angered Mrs. Glynn, the mother, that at her death, her son having pre-deceased her, s.p., she bequeathed all her own manors and lands to Thomas Glynn of Helston, a distant relative, and John Bennet gent., who had been steward of the Glynn estates.

Sergent Glynn had three sons, Edmund John Glynn of Glynn, Anthony William, clerk, some time Rector of Lesnewith, and Henry Richard Glynn, who entered the Navy and rose to the rank of Admiral. Edmund John Glynn entered upon many speculative enterprises, which proved unfortunate, and all his estates were sold.[1] He died in 1840 leaving three daughters, coheirs, of whom Elizabeth Ann married William Henry Petre, then in the Enniskillen Dragoons, and eldest son of the Hon. George William Petre, second son of Robert Edmund ninth Baron Petre. Frances Mary married Charles Prideaux-Brune of Prideaux Place, and Gertrude Rose died unmarried.

Anthony William Glynn is now represented by his grandson William Anthony Glynn of Fairy Hill, Isle of Wight, Esq., who is also the representative, in the male line, of the family of Glyn of Glyn.

GLYN OF LANHYDROCK.

A short pedigree of this family is upon record in the Herald's Visitation of 1531,[2] commencing with Thomas Glyn of Lanhydrock who is shewn to have married Joan daughter and sole heir of William Clyker of Clyker, by whom he had three sons John, Thomas, and John. Of Thomas we are unable to give any account. John the younger was probably the founder of the family of Glyn of Morval, of which we shall presently treat. John the elder was perhaps the same John who we find, from about 1460, in large practice as an Attorney at Bodmin. He married Isabell daughter and heir of Ralph Arundell of Penbugell, Esq., and by deed dated at Penbugell, 11th October 23rd Henry

---

[1] Glynn is now the chief seat of Lord Vivian, Lord Lieutenant of the County.
[2] Herald's Coll. E. 15, fo. 32.

VII. (1507),[1] William Vaghan quitclaimed to him and his wife all his right and claim of right, to all his messuages, lands, and toll of tin in Penbugell and Rosmelyn, and he warranted the same against the Prior of Bodmin and all men for ever. This deed, *inter alia*, is tested by John Arundell of Lanharne, Knt., John Glyn of Morvall, Esq., and others. This John was perhaps the same who was Mayor of Bodmin in 1497.[2] He had two sons, John and Thomas. John was probably the same John Glyn who was Mayor of Bodmin in 1510, and 1520,[2] and who is mentioned as coroner in 1519.[3] He was also Collector of the Subsidy in the 6th, 7th, 13th, and 14th Henry VIII.[3] He was living in 1538, on the 17th October in which year, by deed dated at Penbugell wherein he is described as John Glynn of Lanhederock, gentylman, he mortgaged Penbugell to Thomas Mayowe, *alias* Helyer, of Lostwithiel and William his son for 40 marks. In 1543 he was assessed to the subsidy in Lanhydrock upon lands of the value of £5 per annum,[4] and was alive in January, 1547-8, when he suffered a fine in the Manor of Lancarfe, but he died before 1550, for, by deed dated at Bodmin on 9th December in that year, Bartholomew Glynn, gent., describing himself as son and heir of John Glynn of Lanhidrock, deceased, quit-claimed to Nicholas Glynn of Glynn all his title and interest in Penbugell with which Nicholas Glyn had been enfeoffed by grantee's father.[5] Of this Bartholomew we have no further notice. He was probably dead s.p. before the Herald's Visitation of 1573.

Thomas Glyn, second son of John Glyn and Isabella Arundell, married Jane, daughter and heir of James Nichol of St. Ives, who, from the arms which he was allowed to impale for her at the visitation of 1573,[6] when the pedigree was extended, would seem to have been of the same family as Nichols of Penrose—see pedigree.

The issue of this marriage was a daughter, Margery, who married Richard Tregose, and a son John, who married Jane, daughter and heir of Michael Nanskevell, of Nanskevell in St. Maugan, in whose right he held certain lands of the Manor of Padstow, and we find his name in the Court Rolls of that manor in almost every year from 1553 to 1574. In 1668, 1671, and 1684, the name of Thomas Glyn, Esq., appears in the same Rolls, and in 1687, John Glynn, junr. is appointed "Scrutator and Sigillator" of the manor, and he served in the homage until 1693.[7]

---

[1] The lands of John Arundell of Penbugyll, in the parish of Bodmyn, in the valuation cir. 1522, were returned as of the value of 40s. per annum. Augment. Office Miscl. Book, vol. lxxvij.

[2] Ante vol. i. p. 236.　　　　　[3] Ante vol. i. p. 220.

[3] Subsidy Rolls for those years. In 1524 John Glynn was assessed to the Subsidy in Bodmin upon a higher income than any other person except William Vivian. The latter was assessed upon *goods* at 40 marks per annum, the former at £20. The next highest income was £10 (Sub. Roll 16th Henry VIII. $\frac{87}{---}$). John Glynn of $\frac{131}{}$ Lanhydrock and John Glynn of Bodmin both held lands in Liskeard; the former valued at 40s. and the latter at 10s. per annum, as appears from the return of cir. 1522 before cited.

[4] Sub. Roll for this year.

[5] Pedes Finium, 2nd Edward VI., Hilary. See also ante vol. i. p. 261.

[6] Heralds' Coll. G. 2, p. 72, and E. 15, p. 32.

[7] Court Rolls, Manor of Padstow.

GLYN OF MORVAL.

The first of the name who settled in Morval was, we conceive, John Glyn, the second son of that name of Thomas Glyn of Lanhydrock, by Jane, daughter and heir of William Clyker. In 1462, he recovered from John Rumsey and Agnes his wife, who had been the wife of William Botreaux, Esq., one acre of land, Cornish, in Clis juxta Morval, which seems to have become his chief place of residence. He also, at the same time, recovered from Johanna, daughter and heir of the said William Botreaux, one acre of land, Cornish, in the same place, of which they had unjustly disseized him.[1] About the same time this John Glyn acquired lands, and the services of divers tenants, of whom Thomas Glyn was one, in the parishes of St. Neot and Warleggan.[2] In 1465, William Glyn,[3] by John Glyn, his attorney, sued John Dodding, concerning one messuage in Bodnek, whereof the said John Dodding had disseized him,[4] and in 1469, John Glyn recovered from Margaret Lady Hungerford, widow, daughter and heir of William Botreaux, the Manor of Treffry.[5]

This John Glyn of Morval was Under-Steward of the Duchy of Cornwall, having superseded in that office Thomas Clemens of Liskeard, by whom and his associates he was, after much previous persecution and illtreatment, brutally murdered at Over Wringworthy in the parish of Morval on the 29th August 1472, the chief particulars of which have been given by Davies Gilbert[6] from the petition to Parliament from Johanna widow of John Glyn, printed in the Rolls of Parliament.[7] Upon the inquisition taken after his death he was found to have died seized of West Trenaynowe, held of John Hallewyll, Richard Clyker, and William Clyker, as of their Manor of Trenode, and also of Clys and other lands; and it was found that John Glyn, Junr. was son and nearest heir of the said John Glyn, and that he was then aged 23 years and more.[8] By his charter dated 26th......4th Henry VIII. he enfeoffed Edmund

---

[1] De Banco Rolls, 1st Edward IV. Hil. m. 110. d.

[2] De Banco Rolls, 4th Edward IV. Michaelmas, m. 455.

[3] We have not been able to indentify this William Glyn so as to fix his place in the pedigree. He is mentioned again in July, 1469-70, in connection with the illtreatment of John Glyn of Morval.

[4] De Banco Rolls, 5th Edward IV. Easter, m. 51. d.

[5] De Banco Rolls, 9th Edward IV. Michaelmas, m. 138.   [6] History of Cornwall, vol. iii. pp. 246—248.

[7] Rot. Parl. printed by Record Commissioners, vol. vi. p. 36.

[8] Imq. p. m, 13th Edward IV. No. 57.   Immediately after his father's death proceedings were taken against John Glyn of Morval by Alice who was the wife of William Benaluna, for the recovery of the third part of three messuages in Penquite juxta Hole in the parish of Liskeard, which she claimed as dower of the gift of William some time her husband. (De Banco Rolls 12th Edward IV., Hilary, m. 444.) In January, 1473-4 proceedings were taken by John Mark of Liskeard against John Glyn late of London, junr., gent., Executor of the will of John Glyn late of Morval, to recover a debt of 10 marks (De Banco Rolls 13th Edward IV., Hil., m. 312 d.); and three years later John Glyn of Morval, son and heir of John Glyn late of Morval, gent, deceased, was sued for a debt by Thomas Trevarthian. (De Banco Rolls 16th Edward IV. Hil. m. 584.)

Kendall and Elizabeth his wife, and William Godolphin and Margaret his wife, which Elizabeth and Margaret were two of the daughters and heirs of the said John Glyn, in the Manor of Treffrie to hold to them and the heirs of their bodies. He also, by a charter dated 11th October 3rd Henry VIII. (1511), enfeoffed Richard Code and Thomasia his wife, another daughter and heir of the said John Glyn, in three closes of land in Clyse, and divers other lands, to hold to the said Richard and Thomasia and the heirs of their bodies.

By another charter of the same date he granted certain lands therein described to William Fulford, John Glyn of Lanhydrock, and other trustees, to hold to the use of the said John Glyn for life, with remainder to Richard Code and Thomasia his wife and the heirs male of their bodies, and in default of such issue to the use of the said John Glyn and his heirs for ever. And the jury found that the said John Glyn died 3rd May 4th Henry VIII. (1512), and that Thomasia wife of Richard Code, aged 30 years, Elizabeth wife of Gilbert Beket aged 28 years, and Margaret wife of William Godolphin aged 25 years, were his nearest heirs.[1]

GLYNN OF HELSTON.

We now return to William Glynn, younger son of William Glynn of Glynn by Ann Crewes. That gentleman married Mary, the daughter of —— Roscrow of Roscrow, and settled at Wendron, where he died and was buried in 1613. He left a son of his own name, who settled at Helston, and whose son Thomas married Mary,[2] daughter and heir of Otho Polkinhorn of Polkinhorn in Gwinear, by whom he acquired the Manor and Barton of Polkinhorn. The family remained at Helston until 1794, when Thomas Glynn, the last of the line, died unmarried, and his sister, wife of Richard Gerveys Grylls of Helston, became his sole heir. (See Pedigree of GRYLLS, post.)

GLYNN OF BROADS IN HELLAND.

This family derived its descent from Walter, second son of Nicholas Glynn, which Walter was aged 10 years in 1620. He married and settled in St. Neot, where several of his children were born. Hubert, his son, married Mary only daughter of Stephen Toker of Broads in Helland, where Hubert Glynn[3] eventually established himself, and

---

[1] Inq. p.m. 5th Henry VIII., No. 117. We find John Glyn of Morval in the Commission of the Peace for the county from 1493 to 1509. He doubtless held the office until his death.

[2] This Thomas Glynn, described as of the Scilly Islands, by deed dated 31st October 1640, conveyed certain lands in the parish of Feock to one Thomas Hendra, which lands, it is recited, formerly belonged to Nicholas Glynn, Esq., deceased, and had been conveyed by him to William Glynn, Gent., deceased, father of the said Thomas.

[3] Dennis Glynn of Glynn, by his will dated 13th August 1704, bequeathed a legacy of 30 Guineas to his *cousin* Hubert Glynn, and also a legacy of 20 Guineas to his *cousin* Jane Glynn, which Jane was the daughter of Nicholas brother of Hubert.

K

where he died in 1705. The issue of this marriage, together with daughters, was one son, Robert Glynn of Broads, who by Mary daughter and co-heir of John Clobery of Bradstone left a son Robert Glynn.

This eminent man was educated at Eton on the foundation, and was admitted a scholar of King's College, Cambridge, in 1733. Became B.A. 1741, and proceeded M.A. 1745, M.D. 1758, and 1763 was elected Fellow of the Royal College of Physicians. He practised physic first at Richmond, and afterwards he removed to Cambridge, where he continued until his death. He is described as a "disinterested, virtuous, and consummate scholar," and his life is said to have been "one uniform course of integrity and benevolence."[1] It was his practice to invite the young men of the University to drink tea in the afternoons in his rooms, by which he exercised a most beneficial influence over many of them. Testimony to this is borne by Mr. Chaffin, the author of "Anecdotes of Cranborne Chase." In his Life he makes mention of the advantage he gained from an introduction to Mr. Burford, a Fellow of the same College, and to the good and learned Dr. Glynn. "These good friends," he says, "were very indulgent to me, and I was invited to their rooms two or three times in the week to afternoon tea drinkings, when they examined me respecting my college lectures, and gave me, in the most pleasing manner, such instructions as were of the greatest benefit to me through all my exercises in the schools."[2] Dr. Glynn's tea parties were frequented by young men of the highest rank and character, many of whom afterwards attained the first places in Church and State. Among these was Mr. Pitt, who, when he became Chancellor of the University, expressed himself gratified at the repeated invitations which he had received from Dr. Glynn, and offered him the Professorial chair, which Dr. Glynn declined in consequence of his advanced age.

Many anecdotes are preserved of Dr. Glynn's eccentricity, coupled with his kindness of heart. It has been said that his love for his native county led him never to accept a fee from a Cornishman. Davies Gilbert records a story of a tame bird which, having been given to the Doctor by a poor woman who had nothing else to bestow for his kindness and attendance on her family in sickness, the Doctor accepted the present, and afterwards, upon the plea that he could not keep the bird in his College rooms, gave the woman half-a-crown a week to keep it for him. Among his other peculiarities Dr. Glynn considered that the belief that the tendency to gout was hereditary was a popular error. On one occasion he was consulted by a young gentleman in his nineteenth year, in his first attack of gout. He observed: "My young friend, you call this gout; pooh! pooh! you have not earned the costly privilege. You must drink your double hogshead first." "But my father, sir——it's in my blood by right of inheritance." His reply was strong: "You talk nonsense! You may as well tell me that you have a broken leg in your veins by right of inheritance." Nevertheless the writer adds "that notwithstanding reasonable temperance he was a martyr to the disease at forty, and doubted not he should die crippled."

[1] Pursuits of Literature.   [2] Gentleman's Magazine, lxxxviii. i. 11.

Dr. Glynn greatly interested himself in the Chatterton controversy, and is said to have been some time confined from a violent cold caught in visiting the depository of the Rowleian MSS. He is understood to have assisted Mr. Matthias in his learned and comprehensive essay upon the subject, as also the erudite and profound Jacob Bryant."[1]   In compliance with the testamentary injunction of his maternal uncle, Mr. Clobery of Bradstone, Dr. Glynn, assumed the name of Clobery in addition to and after that of Glynn,[2] but he still continued to be usually designated by his more familiar paternal name.

Dr. Glynn died from gradual decay on the 8th February 1800.   During his illness resignation and kindness to others were the marked traits of his character, and he expired without a struggle or a groan.   Agreeably to his wish he was interred in the vault of King's College Chapel in a private manner, at night, when the members of the College only attended.   He was so greatly beloved and esteemed in Cambridge as to be styled the "*Deliciæ*" of that famous University, and the general feeling was so strong that one who had set so bright an example should be treated with some special mark of respect, that the Vice-Chancellor, Dr. Mansel, communicated to the gentlemen of the University his intention to accompany Dr. Glynn's friends, in mourning, from Trinity College to St. Mary's Church on the Sunday following the funeral, and accordingly a procession of the Heads of Houses, the Noblemen, and a numerous body of the Masters of Arts, were present.   A sermon was preached on the occasion by Mr. Michell, a Fellow of King's College.

Though Dr. Glynn's practice for a long series of years was very extensive, and his establishment, confined within the walls of the College, very small, the value of his effects after his death, including the bequest from his uncle, was comparatively of little amount.   In what manner he applied the principal part of his professional emoluments was best known to those who were supported or assisted by his beneficence.

By his will, dated 7th April 1798, and proved 5th March 1800, he bequeathed £9000 to his College, and £5000 to the Rev. Thomas Kerrich, his executor.   His lands in Helland he left to the Rev. John Henry Jacob, sometime a Fellow of King's College, son of John Jacob of Salisbury, M.D., who had been a particular friend of the deceased.

Dr. Glyn left but little literary evidence of his great learning and ability.   His principal work was a poetical essay on the Day of Judgment, for which he obtained the Seatonian prize in 1756.   This was first printed in the University press and afterwards in various forms.   A portrait of him by Dr. Kerrich was engraved by Facius in 1783, but it is now very rare.

---

[1] The Author has in his library a treatise in "Vindication of the Appendix of the Poems called Rowleys" by Thomas Tyrwhitt.   It was a presentation copy to Dr. Glynn, and bears his autograph, "R. Glynn, C." on the cover, and some notes by the Doctor in short hand on the margins of some of the leaves.

[2] We cannot find any Royal License or Act of Parliament authorising the change.

K²

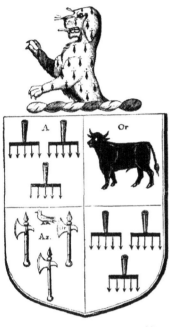

Arms as allowed at the Herald's
Visitation 1620.

PEDIGREE OF

(Thomas?) Glyn,⊤Olivia, living⊤Walter
assessed to the subsidy, 1327. Died 1370 | 1380　　Westcote

Henry Glyn, living⊤Johanna, living
1370　　　　　　 | 1370

Thomas Glyn, son and heir,
living 1405　　⊤

Thomas Glyn of Glyn,⊤....
born cir. 1427

Thomas Glyn of Glyn,⊤Rose, dau. of ......
born cir. 1457　　　 | Trecaren

Nicholas, ob. s.p., born 1487,　　Thomas Glyn⊤Alice, dau. and　　Henry, a
aged 51 years in 1538, (see　　of Glyn　| heir of Richard　Priest
ante vol. i., p. 138)　　　　　　　| Dennys

John Glynn,⊤Thomasine, dau. of Nicholas
2nd son　| Carlyon of Carlyon in Key,
　　　　　 | Cornw.

John Glynn⊤Mary, dau. of Robert　　Nicholas Glyn, 2nd son, mar. Joane
of Boyton | Trewdick of Stednans　dau. of John Bonithon of St. Mer-
　　　　　　| in Cornw.　　　　　　rin, will dated 10th March 1602,
　　　　　　　　　　　　　　　s.p.

Leonard,　　Philip, wife to ....　John Glyn of⊤Ann, dau. to　William,
bap.[1] 11th　Pierse of Tamerton　Boyton, ano.　| Rob. Menwynick　3rd son,
Dec. 1578　in Cornw., bap.[1]　1620, bap.[1] 10　| of Menwynick　bap.[1] 4th
　　　　　　10th Sep. 1582　　Feb. 1577　　| in Cornwall　Aug 1581

Robert 2nd, bap.[1]　John Glyn, second son, æt.,　George 3rd, bap.[1] 23rd Sept. 1612, of North Tamerton. Will dated
20th Jan 1610.　12, Anno 1620, bap.[1] 5th　13th Nov. 1679, pro. 28th April 1680. His bro. Rob. Executor.
　　　　　　　Aug. 1609.　　　　　To be bur. at Boyton. s.p.

Nicholas, son and heir, Sheriff of⊤Gertrude, dau. and coh. of　John Glynn, 2nd son, bap.[3] 1605,⊤....
Cornw. 1675, bap.[3] 1633, bur.[2] 26th | Anthony Dennis of Orleigh,　admo. granted at Exon 20th May |
Mar. 1697, M.I.　　　　　| bur.[1] 29th Sept. 1675.　1689, bur.[1]　　　　|
　　　　　　　　　　a　　　　　　　　　　　　　　　　　　b

[1] At Boyton.　　　　　[2] At Cardinham.　　　　　[3] At Bodmyn.
[4] At St. George's, Bloomsbury, London.　　　　[5] At Bideford.

LYN OF GLYN.—Table I.

I certify that the portion of this pedigree which is printed in *Italics* and
the Arms agree with the records of this Office.

Herald's College,   GEORGE HARRISON,
29th May, 1873.   *Windsor Herald.*

Nicholas Glyn, mar. Constance, dau. and heir of John ═ *Elizabeth, dau. of John* │ *Thomasine,* │ *Joane, wife*
Bryan, who died s.p. Died 11th Oct. 1580, Inq. │ *Talkerne of Goodacott,* │ *wife to William* │ *to Richard*
p.m. 23rd Elizabeth, p. 2, No. 14 │ *2nd wife* │ *Langesford* │ *Doune*

William Glyn, eldest son, aged 46 years on his father's death ═ *Ann, dau. of* │ *Mary, wife of John* │ *Margery, wife*
in 1580, died 6th Oct. 1613, Inq. p.m. 12th James, Part I., │ *Anthony Crewes* │ *Harrie alias Trehrok* │ *of John*
No. 102, bur.[2] M.I. │ of Liskeard │ (Trebarrock ?) │ *Treuedon*

George, appointed executor to │ *Nicholas Glyn of Glyn an°* 1620, ═ *Jane, dau. of* │ *William,* (?) │ *Jane.* │ *Phillip,* mar.
Uncle Nicholas' will 1602, living │ aged 50 years on his father's │ *Walter Ken-* │ settled at │ │ John Incleden
in 1615. Witness to his brother's │ death. Sheriff of Cornw. 1620 │ *dall of Pelyn,* │ Wendron, │ │ of Bratton, co.
will. Mar. Denet, dau. of John │ Died 20th Dec. 1615. Will prov. │ bur.[2] 8th │ see Table │ │ Devon. (Visit.
Bligh of Bodmin 1595, (ante vol. i. │ 13th Jan. 1626 in Archd. Court │ *April* 1634. │ III. │ │ Devon 1620.)
p. 280.) Bur.[3] 20th Nov. 1628. s.p. │ of Cornw.

Walter 2nd, æt. │ *William Glyn, son and heir, æt.* 21 1620, ═ *Alice, dau. of* Arthur Harris of │ *Loueday, wife to*
10, of St. Neot. │ bur.[2] 5th Aug. 1664, M.I., will dated 29th │ Haine co. Devon. Adm° to Nicholas │ *Thomas Hearle*
See Table IV. │ Jan. 1656, prov. 12th Jan. 1665, Exon. │ Glyn, son of decd., 11th Aug. 1677. │ *of Trenouthe.*

William, 3rd son, will dated 19th June 1671, died │ Cordelia, bap.[3] │ Philip, │ Ann Hearle, named in her
1672, prob. granted in Archd. Court of Cornw. │ 1634. │ 4th son. │ grandfather's will.
28th Aug. 1672.

---

[1] At Boyton.	[2] At Cardinham.	[3] At Bodmyn.
[4] At St. George's Bloomsbury, London.		[5] At Bideford.

William, bur.[2] 16th
May 1668, M.I.

Nicholas, bur.[2] 13th
Aug. 1670, M.I.

Gertrude, bur.[2] 8th
June 1669. M.I.

William,
bap.[2] 22nd
Aug. 1716,
bur.[2] 13th
Feb. 1717.

Nicholas Glynn of
Glynn, son and heir,
born 5th and bap.[2]
22nd Jan. 1713;
Sheriff of Cornw.
1743. Died 22nd
June 1744.

Elizabeth, sister and heir
of John Nichols of
Trewane. Mar. settl.
dated 5th and 6th Sept.
1734, will dated 10th
April, proved 24th May
1771, P.C.C.

John Glynn, 2 son, bap.[2] 3rd Aug.
1722, matric. at Exeter Coll., Oxf.
17th May 1738, Serg.-at-Law,
Recorder of London and Exeter,
M.P. for Middlesex, died 16th
Sept. 1779, intestate, bur.[2] 23rd
Sept. 1779.

Susanna Margaret, 3rd
dau. of Sir John Oglander
Bart., born 1st Sept. 1744,
mar. settl. 9th July and
mar. 21st July 1763, died
at Bath 20th May 1816.

William Glynn, of
Glynn, born 29th
Sept. bap[2]. 11th
Nov. 1735, died
intestate and un-
mar., bur.[2] 28th
Dec. 1762.

Edmund John
Glynn of Glynn,
son and heir, born
22nd, bap. 28th
June 1764. Sheriff
of Cornw. 1799,
Died 27th July
1840.

Elizabeth Anne, eldest
dau. of Edward Meaux
Worsley of Gatcombe,
Isle of Wight, mar. 9th
Nov. 1790, mar. settl.
5th and 6th Nov. 1790,
died June 1797.

Anthony William Glynn, born
1st and bap.[4] 3rd Oct. 1766,
matric. at Bal. Coll., Oxford,
15th Dec. 1784, Ordained Priest
19th Dec. 1790, Inst. to Rectory
of Lesnewth 2nd Feb. 1791,
Civilian Fellow of New Coll.,
Oxford.

Sukey Margaret,
eldest dau. of Sir
William Oglander,
Bart., sometime
M.P. for Bodmin,
mar. Jan. 1800, died
5th April, 1840.

Elizabeth Anne,
born 2nd Sept. 1791,
mar. 1st July 1818
Henry Petre of
Dunkenhalgh, co.
Lanc. Died 13th
Sept 1828.

Susan Jane,
born 29th
July 1793,
died in
infancy.

Francis Mary,
born 23rd May
1795, mar. Charles
Prideaux-Brune
of Prideaux Place,
co. Cornw. 29th
Feb. 1820. Died
22nd July 1863.

Gertrude
Rose, born
6th June
1797, died
unmar.
6th Sept.
1853.

William Anthony Glynn of
Fairy Hill, Isle of Wight,
born 22nd May 1807, matric.
at Wadham Coll. Oxf. 25th
June 1824, aged 17, B.A. as
of Magdalen, Hall, 17th Oct.
1833, M.A. as of Merton
Coll. 26th May 1847, D.C.L.
1851, died 19th May 1865.

Anne, dau. of ....
Goodall, born Sept.
1808, mar. 29th May
1828, died 21st Oct.
1864, bur. St.
Helens, Isle of
Wight.

William Anthony
Glynn of Fairy
Hill, Isle of
Wight, son and
heir, born 5th
Nov. 1842.

Margaret Anderson,
only dau. of Robert
Wigram Crawford,
M.P. for London,
mar. 5th Sept. 1865.

John Henry Oglander,
born 7th Mar. 1847,
Barrister-at-Law,
matric. Trinity Hall,
Camb. Oct. 1864, B.A.
1868.

Anne Matilda, born
6th July 1829, mar.
22nd July 1852
Francis Price of
Longlands, co.
Glamorgan, Esq.

Elizabeth.

Susan.

Margaret
Gertrude
Frances,
died
unm.

---

a   *b*

ridget, dau. of Edw. Hoblyn of Bodmin, 2nd=Dennis Glynn of Glynn,=Elizabeth, dau. of Samuel Foot   William Glynn, bap.[2]
ife, bap.[3] 22nd June 1666, bur.[2] 10th Nov.   will dated 13th Aug. 1704, | of Wemworthy, near Tiverton,   4th Aug. 1668, bur.[2]
595. (See ped. of HOBLYN, vol. i., p. 475.)   bur.[2] 14th April 1705. | 1st wife, bur.[2] 31st Jan. 1629.   17th Feb. 1719.

William Glynn of Glynn. Will dated 20th=Rose, dau. of John Prideaux of Prideaux Place, bap. at Padstow 25th
Nov. 1727, bur.[2] 22nd Nov. same year. | June 1683, mar. there 15th Sept. 1709, bur.[2] 3rd Mar. 1736.

Edmund Glynn, 3rd son, bap.[2]	Ann,[2] bap. 4th	Gertrude,	Elizabeth, bap.	Bridget, bap.[2] 25th
20th April 1725, died unmar.	Sept. 1711, died	bap.[2] 8th	2nd July 1715.	April 1720, bur.[2]
Will dated 17th Nov. 1736, his	unmar. 16th	Feb. 1714.		7th Jan. 1736.
brother John residuary legatee,	Mar. 1736.			
bur.[2] 29th Nov. 1746.				

Maria, dau. of=Henry Richard Glynn, born=Maria dau. of William Batt of   Susan Margaret, born
Spicker, 2nd | 17th Sept. 1768, bap.[4] 26th | Moditonham, relict of William   14th Nov. 1770, died
wife, died s.p. | Feb. 1769, Admiral R.N., died | Turguard, Capt. R.N., 1st wife.   unmar. 16th July
         | 20th July 1856. | 1855 ; aged 87.

=Mary, daughter of Rob. Incle-
don, Capt. R.N., mar. 14th June
1825, died 16th April 1853, s.p.

Henry	=Anne, dau. of	Jane, dau.=	=John	=Harriet	Edmund	=Laura	Susan	Elizabeth Jane,
Richard,	Colonel Kear-	of Adam	Edmund,	Wells, 2nd	Anthony,	Georgina,	Margaret,	born 6th May
born at	ney. Mar. at	Reid, mar.	born 26th	dau. of	born 6th and	dau. of John	born 6th	1807, mar. 26th
Bath 10th	Ryde Is. of W.	1829, died	Sept. 1809,	Henry	bap. at Ply-	Templer,	Jan. 1806,	Mar. 1836
June 1805,	11th June	2nd Jan.	Major,	Narcissus	mouth 26th	Clerk Vicar	unmar.,	Francis Richd.
died July	1836, died	1842 at	E.I.C.S.,	Hatherley,	Sept. 1812, ?	of Cullomp-	bapt. at	Bagbie Clerk,
1849, s.p.,	26th July	Bangalore,	died 9th	Colonel	Comr. R.N.	ton, co. Dev.	Poole, co.	Vicar of Dise-
bur.[5]	1872, at Chel-	E.I.	March	Madras	28th Nov.	mar. 17th	Dorset.	worth, co.
	tenham, and		1864, bur.	Native	1848, Capt.	Nov. 1845,		Leic., died 17th
	bur. there.		at Abbots-	Infantry,	1866.	at Genoa.		Sept. 1845, she
			ham, co.	mar. 9th				died 29th Oct.
			Devon.	May 1848.				1846, bur.[4]

Jane Williamson,	Maria Elizabeth,	John Glynn,	Henry Oglander	Sophy Louisa, born 1st	Harriet
born 20th Jan.	born 7th April	born 1st Oct.,	Seymour, born	March 1844, mar. 8th Aug.	Catherine,
1837, mar. 10th	1941, unmar.	bap.[5] 5 Nov.	5th March, bap.[5]	1866 Walter Collyns Baker,	born and
May 1866 Wm.		1849, died	14th April 1852.	Clerk, Vicar of Shipton	died 14th
Harris of Inche-		20th Jan.		Bellinger, co. Hants.	April 1853.
wen, co. Perth, Esq.		1859.			

[1] At Boyton.   [2] At Cardinham.   [3] At Bodmyn.
[4] At St. George's, Bloomsbury, London.   [5] At Bideford.

PEDIGREE OF GLYN
OF LANHYDROCK AND MORVAL.
TABLE II.

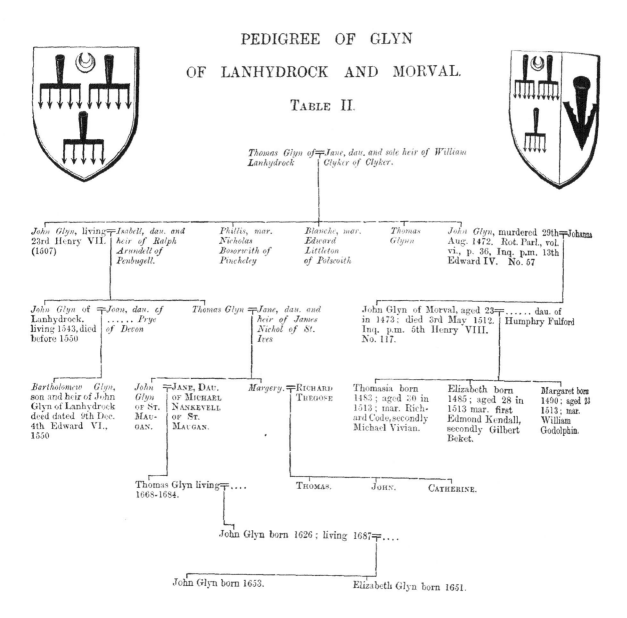

Thomas Glyn of=*Jane, dau. and sole heir of William*
Lanhydrock | *Clyker of Clyker.*

John Glyn, living=*Isabell, dau. and*   *Phillis, mar.*   *Blanche, mar.*   *Thomas*   *John Glyn, murdered 29th*=*Johanna*
23rd Henry VII. | *heir of Ralph*   *Nicholas*   *Edward*   *Glyn*   Aug. 1472. Rot. Parl., vol.
(1507) | *Arundell of*   *Bosorwith of*   *Littleton*   vi., p. 36, Inq. p.m. 13th
| *Penbugell.*   *Pincheley*   *of Polscoith*   Edward IV. No. 57

John Glyn of=*Joon, dau. of*   *Thomas Glyn*=*Jane, dau. and*   John Glyn of Morval, aged 23=*......* dau. of
Lanhydrock. | *..... Prye* | *heir of James*   in 1473; died 3rd May 1512. | Humphry Fulford
living 1543, died | *of Devon* | *Nichol of St.*   Inq. p.m. 5th Henry VIII.
before 1550 | *Ives*   No. 117.

Bartholomew Glyn,   *John*=JANE, DAU.   *Margery.*=RICHARD   Thomasia born   Elizabeth born   Margaret born
son and heir of John | *Glyn* OF MICHAEL | THEGOSE   1483; aged 30 in   1485; aged 28 in   1490; aged 23
Glyn of Lanhydrock | OF ST. NANKEVELL   1513; mar. Rich-   1513 mar. first   1513; mar.
deed dated 9th Dec. | MAU- OF ST.   ard Code, secondly   Edmond Kendall,   William
4th Edward VI., | GAN. MAUGAN.   Michael Vivian.   secondly Gilbert   Godolphin.
1550   Beket.

Thomas Glyn living=....   THOMAS.   JOHN.   CATHERINE.
1668-1684.

John Glyn born 1626; living 1687=....

John Glyn born 1653.   Elizabeth Glyn born 1651.

MEMORANDUM.

    The portion printed in *Italics* and the Arms are from the Herald's Visitation of 1531.

    The addition in CAPITALS was made at the Visitation of 1573 (G. 2. p. 72 and E. 15. p. 32).

    The additions in "Roman type" have been made from Inquisitions and other evidence.

PEDIGREE OF GLYNN OF HELSTON.—TABLE III.

John Polkinghorne of Polkinghorne═*Elizabeth, heir of Thomas Oliver of*
in Cornwall | *Bodmyn in Cornwall*

Thomas Polkinghorne, of Polkinghorne, son and heir. On 25th═*Katherine, dau. of Richard Pellamouner*
Sept. 1571 enfeoffed John Polkinghorne his son and heir of | *of Cornwall*
lands in Polkinghorne

William
Flynn of
Vendron,
ur. there 3
Feb. 1613
═Mary, dau.
of ......
Roscrow of
Roscrow

*Thomas,
2nd, æt.
40, 1620*

*Richard,
3rd, æt.
38, 1620*

*John Polkinghorne of
Polkinghorne, son and
heir, died 30th Oct.
1638, Inq. p.m., 21st
Aug. 1639*
═*Alice, dau.
of Otes
Edye of
Bodmyn*

*James,
4th, æt.
33, 1620*

*Margery,
wife of
Warin
Pryor of
Guendron*

*Grace,
æt. 34,
1620*

Donett,
ur. at
Constan-
ine,
8th May
612

Thomas
Glynn of
Helston
═Mar-
garet,
dau.
of ..
Ken-
yon

*Thomas,
2nd, æt. 18.
Bur.at Sith-
ney, 28th
March 1629*

*John,
3rd,
æt. 16.*

*Oates Polkinghorne,
eldest son, æt. 20, 1620.
Aged 30 years and more
at the time of his
father's death, Inq.
p.m. Died 1665*
═*Alice*

*William
4th, æt.
15.*

*Roger,
5th,
æt. 14.*

*Ralph,
6th, æt.
12.*

*Katherine,
æt. 13
Margery,
æt. 4.*

William Glynn of
Bodillyvean

Thomas Glynn of Helston,═Mary, dau. and heir
living 1662

Thomas Glynn,═Elizabeth
ur. at the | Snow, dau.
nner Temple | of ......
725. | Croke

William

Otho Glynn═Elizabeth, dau.
of Helston, | of ...... Pen-
bur.[1] 8th | darves of Gwin-
April 1723 | ear, bur.[1] 3rd
| July 1730

John Glynn,
Vicar of Crow-
an, bur.[1] 28th
Aug. 1731

Susanna,
mar.
William
Hearle

Mary,
mar.
......
Penhal-
low

Lucy,
mar.
Thos.
Vivian

Elizabeth Glynn, mar.[1]
3rd June 1735 to John
Henwood. Bur.[1] 12th
Feb. 1749.

Thomas Glynn of Polkinhorne,═Cordelia, dau. of Thomas Trewren
afterwards of Helston, bur.[1] | of Trewardrevah bap.[1] 28th June
9th Sept. 1777, aged 79, will | 1710, mar.[1] 26th April 1731.
dated 27th May 1771.

Richard Gerveys═Cordelia, only
Grylls of Helston. | dau. Heir of
| her brother.

Thomas Glynn, bap.[1]
2nd July 1737, died
unmar.

Elizabeth,
bap.[1] 2nd
May 1741,
died young

Jane, bap.[1] 24th
Dec. 1744, bur.[1]
20th Mar. 1746.

Thomas, bur.[1]
2nd Aug. 1740.

I certify that the portion of this Pedigree printed in *Italics* agrees
with the record in this Office.

Heralds' College,
30th May 1873.

GEORGE HARRISON,
Windsor Herald.

[1] At Helston.

L

PEDIGREE OF GLYNN OF HELLAND.—TABLE IV.

Walter Glynn, of=Agnes, bur.[1] 11th Dec. 1672,
St. Neot, bur. | will dated 2nd Sept. 1672, prov.
30th Oct. 1662. | 26th June 1673.

| Jane, bur. 3rd Aug. 1642 | Walter, bur. 30th Oct. 1644 | William bap.[1] 8th June 1645 | Hubert Glynn, bap.[1] 9th=Mary, dau. and April 1648, of Brodes in | heir of Stephen the parish of Helland. | Toker of Brodes Named in the will of Den- | bur. 16th Nov. nis Glynn of Glynn 1704. | 1702, (see ped. Will dated 13th May, prov. | of TOKER ante. 28th May 1705. | p. 56) | Tho- mas, bap.[1] 12th Aug. 1650 | Mark, bap.[1] 2nd Aug. 1653 | Love- day, bap.[1] 7th July 1657 | Nicholas, of=Thomas- St. Neot, | ine, bur.[1] named in his | 28thMay mother's will. | 1704 Bur.16th May | 1716 |

| Robert Glynn, of Brodes, bur.[2] 26th April 1761 | =Lucy, dau. of John Clobery, of Brad- stone | Mary Glynn, bap.[2] mar. John Silly of Kernick in Helland. Admo. to her husband's effects 26th Mar. 1784, (see Ped. of SILLY, post.) | Loveday Glynn, mar. William Pennington, Clerk,(see Ped.of PEN- NINGTON, ante. vol. i., p. 202), mar.[3] 4th Mar. 1706. | Alice Glynn, named in her father's will. | Jane Glynn, bap.[1] 6th Nov. 1677. Named in the will of Dennis Glynn ofGlynn in 1704. | Loveday, bap.[1] 11th May 1680 |

| Robert Glynn, afterwards Robert Glynn Clobery, having taken the name of Clobery in addition to that of Glynn. Born at Brodes 5th Aug., bap.[2] 16th Sept. 1719, M.D. Cambridge. Will dated 7th April 1790, prov. 5th Mar. 1808, s.p. | Mary, bap.[2] 18th Aug. 1713, bur.[2] 27th Jan. 1718. | Margaret, bap.[2] 31st January 1716-7 | Hubert, bap.[2] 16th Dec. 1722, bur.[2] 6th Feb. 1838. | Elizabeth, bur.[2] 11th Feb. 1738. | William, bap.[1] 15th Mar. 1725. |

[1] At St. Neot.   [2] At Helland.   [3] At Cardinham.

APPENDIX.

A return for the Hundred of Trigg, shewing the names of all spiritual men in each parish and the annual value of their possessions, together with the value of their goods and chattels; also the names of all landowners, and the annual value of their lands and tenements; also the names of all the inhabitants of each parish, the value of their goods &c., and the number of arms in their possession; also the names of all *aliens* and the value of their goods, &c., taken under the King's Commission.

Parochia de }
Helland }

Valencia Spiritualium possessionum ibidem per Annum.

Willelmus Hockyn, Rector ibidem, valet in proficuis } x^li
et emolumentis ejusdem ecclesie per annum }

Summa   -   -   £10

Valencia terrarum et tenementorum ibidem per Annum.

Rogerus Arundell Armiger[1] valet ibidem per annum				-	v marcas
Johannes Rescarek[2]	-	-	-	-	xl^s
Thomas Luky -	-	-	-	-	xviij^s
Ricardus Corynton[2] -	-	-	-	-	iiij^s
Alicia Marke vidua	-	-	-	-	xxxvj^s viij^d
Willelmus Wyndslad[3]	-	-	-	-	x^s
Willelmus Saye miles[4]	-	-	-	-	xxx^s
Johannes Coplestone[5]	-	-	-	-	xxvj^s viij^d
Johannes Yeogge[6] -	-	-	-	-	vj^s viij^d
Christopherus Tredenek[7]	-	-	-	x^s	x^s
Thomas Cok · -	-	-	-	-	vj^s viij^d
Ricardus Russell -	-	-	-	-	vj^s viij^d

Summa   -   -   £13 15 2

---

[1] Held the Manor of Helland.
[2] Held the Manor of Nether Helland in moieties.
[3] Probably the father of the Wynslades who were attainted. He appears to have been non-resident.
[4] Held the Manor of Boconion.
[5] Held the Manor of Penhargard.
[6] There is now a tenement in Helland called Yogg's Parks.
[7] Held Brodes but appears to have been non-resident.

Valencia bonorum et catallorum dicta parochia et de eorum armis.

Idem Willelmus Hockyn Rector ecclesie, predicte valet in bonis iiij^{li}
Robertus Cok Capellanus ibidem in stipendio vij marcas in bonis x marcas

Rogerus Arundell Armiger in bonis	-		l^{li}
Thomas Nuton	-	-	-	iiij^{li} arma pro uno homine
Johannes Melyonek	-	-	-	c^{s}
Johannes Best	-	-	-	c^{s}
Johannes Hendy	-	-	-	iiij^{li}
Thomas Penhale	-	-	-	liij^{s} iiij^{d}
Robertus Bawdyn	-	-	-	xl^{s}
Johannes Vdy	-	-	-	xl^{s}
Johannes Smith in bonis nil quia pauper tenens Ricardi Coryngton			
Johannes Pawle	-	-	-	x marcas arma pro vno homine
Nicholaus Hockyn	-	-	-	xl^{s}
Johannes Chaptor	-	-	-	c^{s}
Stephanus Walke	-	-	-	xl^{s}
Johannes Tredwen	-	-	-	xx^{li} arma pro vno homine
Ricardus Balke	-	-	-	xl^{s}
Johannes Walke	-	-	-	xl^{s}
Gilbertus Curtes	-	-	-	iiij^{li}
Johannes Skele	-	-	-	xl^{s}
Thomas Vdy	-	-	-	xl^{s}
Johannes Curtes	-	-	-	c^{s}

Summa

Numerus armorum
Numerus hominum habilium
Numerus alieneginorum nullus

This return is not dated, nor can we find upon record the commission under which the survey was made. It is evident, however, from internal evidence that it was made between 1521 and 1523. It was designed to ascertain the quantity of arms, the number of able-bodied men, and the number of *aliens* in each Hundred. The returns from several of the Hundreds in Cornwall are wanting. That for the Hundred of West is very full and interesting. It details every bow and arrow, every salett and splint in the Hundred. The survey was probably made in connection with the musters taken upon the breaking out of the war with France in 1522. It is of considerable interest as it shews the name and condition of every inhabitant head of a family within each parish.

PARISH OF LANOWE,

ALIAS ST. KEW.

This Parish was anciently called Lanho, sometimes written Lanhohou, and more recently Lanowe. In the Exchequer *Domesday* it appears as Lanehoc; and in the Exeter Book it is written Lannoho. It derives its name of St. Kew from the dedication of the Church. In form it is an irregular parallelogram lying transversely to the meridian north-east and south-west, and is bounded on the north-west by St. Minver, Endellion, and St. Teath; on the north-east by St. Teath; on the south-east by St. Tudy and St. Mabyn; and on the north-west by Egloshayle and St. Minver.

The following particular perambulation of the boundaries of the parish in 1613 is preserved in the Register Office of the Bishop of Exeter, to which it was officially returned at the time. It will be of interest and may be useful.

Cornwall.—The Bounde and lymittes of the parishe of St. Kew veiwed and seen by the Mynister, Churchwardens, and other the pishioners the forteenth day of June in Anno Dni 1613.

Imprimis. begyninge on the west side of the pishe aforesaide at Trevarthen Yeate, wch boundeth wth Endelyan pish, and from thence passeth streight west dividinge Endellyon from St. Kew till it cometh against Rowke Myll meadow to a conduite at thentrance whereof joyneth Two little Brookes, wch bounde St. Kew, Endellyon and St. Mynver, from the said conduit St. Kew joyneth wth St. Mynver and boundeth wth the said water downewarde till it cometh to Smeethe's hedge corner, and then it is divided from St. Mynver aforesaid by the said hedge, wch leadeth upp streight west from the said water to Poldowes, and soe poynteth still westwarde till it cometh to Dynhames gutt, and from thence, turninge south-ward by Trewornan, it passeth to a little plot of marrishe grounde, wch plot boundeth St. Kewe in the east, St. Mynver on the west, and Eglosaile on the south; from the said plot St. Kew joyneth with Egloshaile and boundeth south-east wth Chapple Amble grounde till it cometh to the River, and then the River divideth the said pishes soe far vpp as Downeinge marshe saving one little plott of marrishe grounde lying on the north side of the River, wch ptayneth to Egloshail pish; ffrom Downeinge marrishe it crosseth the River and so

M

boundeth vp southwarde betwixt Penpont and Tregorden to Wrangshefordes Yeate, and from thence, passinge still southwarde by a hedge that leadeth to Kelly Berrye and so keeping still southwarde by the same hedge till it cometh to a River at the foote of the Rock Parck, wch divideth the pishes aforesaide from St. Mabyn; ffrom the said Rocke pcke St. Kew joyneth wth St. Mabyn vpp Eastwarde by the said River till it cometh to an other brooke on the south side of the said River that falleth into the same Right against Tretawne woode, saving one plott of lande lying on the south side of the River Right against Tre-theaven woode wch ptayneth to St. Kewe; And from thence it boundeth wth St. Tudy pish vp Eastwarde by the same River till it cometh to Pollrode bridge, saving on little plot of land that lyeth on the south side of the River against brighter woode, belonging to St. Kew. ffrom Pollrode bridge, leaving the River, it boundeth by a hedge northeast that leadeth direct to the leate of Pengennow myll, and then keepinge due east by the saide leate to foxhole hedge corner, wch place boundeth St. Kew, St. Tudy, and St. Teath. ffrom thence St. Kew joyneth with St. Teath and boundeth vp northwarde by the said hedge till it cometh to the hedd of foxhole woode, wch joyneth wth Treburgate landes, and soe keeping still northwarde betwixt Pengennowe and Treburgate so to a Yeate that joyneth wth Tre-weythan, and then boundeth northwarde by Treweythan hedge to the highway Right against ffentengoge lande, and then passeth by ffentengoge hedge to Trekey water, and from thence it is divided by the said water to a hedge corner of Trekey landes called the Meane pcke, and then turneth northeast by the said hedge to a way at the hed of Trewigget landes that leadeth to hendra Cross from Trekeer (*sic*) beforesaid, and from thence streight west to hendra Crosse, and thence boundeth by a lane southwest to the skuttle parcke corner wch place boundeth wth St. Kew, St. Teath and Endellyon. ffrom Shuttle pcke corner St. Kew joyneth wth Endellyon, and boundeth streight west by a hedge that leadeth to Bodanan ground fast by St. Trillick yeate, and then turneth southwarde by Pendoggett landes to the higheway, and then passeth west by the said higheway to Trentenny yeate and from thence southwarde by a hedge that leadeth to Trewathen yeate wher we first begann.

The total area of the parish is stated to be 7514 acres 2 roods and 31 perches, and the following table will shew the population and number of dwelling houses at the several periods of the census.

		1801	1811	1821	1831	1841	1851	1861	1871
Population	.. ..	1095	1113	1218	1316	1429	1337	1182	1178
	Inhabited ..	206	215	234	257	281	268	255	251
Houses	Uninhabited ..	8	1	11	7	28	19	25	18
	Building ..	..	4	3	6	2	..	1	1

Besides the " Church Town " the villages in this Parish are: Highway, Amble or Amel, Tregoyde or Treguite, and Trelill.

The chief Landowners are Lord Robartes, The Hon^blo G. M. Fortescue, the representatives of the late Sir William Molesworth, Bart., S. M. Grylls Esq., and Mr. Grose.

	£	s.	d.
The annual value of real property as assessed in 1815	8598	0	0
The Gross Estimated Rental in 1872	9606	0	0
The Rateable Value	8823	0	0
Land Tax—net sum, £356 18s. 10d.; redeemed, £245 2s. 10¾d. =	601	18	8¾
Assessed Taxes (not known)			
Inhabited House Duty	4	14	6

Property and Income Tax—

		£	s.	d.
Schedule	A	141	17	5
„	B	24	5	0
„	C	nil		
„	D		16	8
„	E	nil		
		166	19	1

GEOLOGY.

The general geological character of St. Kew resembles that of the surrounding parishes, and consists of slates of the Devonian period intersected by courses of greenstone running in parallel lines east and west, and by at least two ranges of a felspathic and horblendic character. Probably, according to De la Beche, the entire mass is underlaid by a conglomerate composed of fragments of slate cemented by argillo-calcareous matter. An elvan course traverses the parish. It is formed of a felspathic base containing disseminated quartz and imperfect crystals of felspar, the whole being of a granitic appearance, and it may be traced from near Treburget in St. Teath, and passing east of Trehill, and a little north of St. Kew Church town, extends thence in nearly a straight line to Penwarne, in St. Minver.

INDUSTRIAL PURSUITS AND WAGES.

A few years ago a mine was worked on the north side of the parish, but it is now abandoned. At present no other industry is exercised than the cultivation of the soil. The latter somewhat varies in character, and is well suited to the several kinds of grain, and the harvest is usually early. Until the present year (1873) laborers received about nine or ten shillings a week, now they get twelve or thirteen shillings, and occasionally a cottage in addition or a shilling a week more if they have cattle to attend to beyond the ordinary period of daily labour.

M²

PRE-HISTORIC REMAINS.

Tregaer.—On the high table land on the north side of this parish is a fine earth-work, or encampment, which has not, we believe, heretofore been described. It is situate close to the great road leading from Warbstow and Titchbarrow on the north-east of the county to St. Minver, which has been already noticed (ante vol. i., p. 484) and it commands a view of the important work at Warbstow as well as of Michaelstow Beacon, Castle Canyke, &c., &c. The main work at Tregaer is circular in form and consists of two embankments, a short distance apart from each other, strengthened by deep external ditches. The approach is from the lower, or south-eastern side, and the entrance is protected by a bastion or external wall, which, springing out of the outer of the two embankments above-mentioned, encircles the whole of the work on the southern and eastern sides until it debouches upon the great road above-mentioned, which passes on the north side of the work. The entrance is opposite to those leading to the inner circle. This external wall is in some places very high, and was originally defended by a ditch which has now been filled up; and on the north-eastern side the wall itself has been removed under the processes of cultivation, but the site is easily traceable across the field numbered 591 on the parish map; and probably the remains of the ditch yet exist for a short distance along the south side of the road. The outer gate is approached by a ditch or covered way from the valley below, which covered way still remains crossing a field numbered 600 on the parish map. This important work, which is numbered 592 and 593 on the map, has given its name to the farm on which it is situate. (See Plate XXVIII., Fig. 2.)

Close to the same road, and about 1½ miles further west, in a field on the farm of Trevinnick, may be found the remains of a quadrangular encampment measuring about 100 yards on each side. It has now become nearly levelled down by agricultural operations, but the sites of the walls are very clearly defined on the northern and eastern sides. There is a tradition that it formed a military position in the time of the civil war of the 17th century, and pieces of swords, &c., in a very advanced state of decay, have been found in great quantities in ploughing the field. It has never been ploughed very deep, and it is thought by the farmer that by deeper ploughing further discoveries would be made. We do not learn that any coins, or pieces of pottery, have been noticed, nevertheless we are disposed to give to this work a far higher antiquity than has been ascribed to it. Its position, close to the great road leading from the north-east of the county to the Roman settlement which undoubtedly existed in St. Minver, of which we shall hereafter treat, seems to point it out as a Roman work. It is not unlikely that it may have been occupied by one or other of the contending parties in the civil war; and tradition says a great battle was fought in the neighbourhood, and human remains have not unfrequently been found, though we are not aware that any engagement in this neighbourhood has been mentioned in the history of the period. This circumstance is not, however, inconsistent with the higher antiquity we claim for this work.

ANCIENT ROADS AND TRACKS.

Several ancient roads, or tracks, intersect the parish of St. Kew. Of these, perhaps, the most important, after the great road from the north-east of the county described ante Vol. i., p. 484, is the road from the ancient ford at Wade leading to the north, alluded to ante Vol. i., p. 405. This road entered the parish about two furlongs from "Three Hole Cross," and passing through Highway and Trelill and near to the great earth work at Tregaer, to which there was an entrance on the south, it formed a junction with the north-east road, mentioned above, within the parish of St. Teath.

In addition to the road from Dinham's Bridge through "Kelly Rounds" to "Three Hole Cross," mentioned ante Vol. i., p. 405, two other roads proceeded from the former place. One led over the hill, in nearly a direct line, to Penpons, alias Penpont, and thence to St. Minver; and the other crossed the road first above-mentioned, and passing near Hendra it crossed the river at Cakeval and united with the great north-east road at St. Endellion.

A fourth road entered the parish from St. Tudy at Kellygren, and crossing the road first above described at Whitehall, it passed through Tregoyd and St. Kew Church town, and proceeded over, or near, the elvan dyke which extends through the parish, before mentioned, (ante p. 79) to Rooke Mill where it entered the parish of St. Minver.

A fifth road entered the parish from St. Teath at Great Treveran, and crossing the road first above described joined the great north-east road at Pendogget.

ANCIENT CHRISTIAN MONUMENT.

No. 29. The only example of an ancient cross which we have discovered in this parish is used as a portion of a bridge over a gutter in the road leading from the turnpike-road to Polrode Mill. It is a fine example, but one side of the head has been cut away. The head measures 2ft. 3in. in diameter, and the shaft is 3ft. 2in. in length, 1ft. 6in. in breadth, and 9 inches in thickness. The symbol is of the Greek type within a marginal ring and has a boss in the centre. The angles of the shaft are rounded, and there is an incised line forming a border on each face. Both sides are alike.

No. 29.

MEETING HOUSES OF DISSENTERS.

Bible Christians.—The earliest Meeting House in this parish is one erected at Dinham's Bridge, at the south-east angle of the parish, two miles from the parish Church. A piece of ground, being portion of a tenement called "Rock Parks," with a building partially erected thereon, was granted by John Martyn Bligh of St. Mabyn, Gent., by deed dated 25th Aug. 1815,[1] for a term of 999 years at the rent of 1s. per annum, and was vested in George Northey and Digory Northey, maltsters, and others, as trustees, for the purpose of erecting thereon a chapel, or place of worship, to be used by Wesleyan Methodists upon the special trust, that they should finish the said building, and thenceforth, from time to time permit such persons as might be appointed by the yearly conference of the people called Methodists, specified in a deed dated 28th Feby. 1784, to preach and expound God's Holy Word, and perform other ministerial acts of religious Worship in the said Chapel.[2] Power was granted to appoint one of themselves as treasurer to receive seat rents, to appoint new trustees in succession to such as might die or cease to be members of the body, to raise money for building or repairing—to sell the said premises and discharge incumbrances and debts, the surplus to be expended in the purchase of another building to be used under the same limitations, or to be applied to such other charitable uses as the society of Wesleyan Methodists might think proper. We do not know when this building ceased to be used by the Wesleyan Methodists, or in what manner the trust terminated; but it appears that in 1862 the building belonged to Mrs. Mary Perry, now of Liskeard, who in that year granted its use to the Bible Christians upon the payment of a high rent of 2s. 6d. per annum, and it is still occupied by that denomination. The building will seat about 100 persons. Soon after it was opened by the Bible Christians they had more than twenty members attached to it, but the members are now reduced to nine.

United Methodist Free Church.—This community has the following five Meeting Houses within the parish, affording, in the aggregate, accommodation for 590 persons, and attached to these Chapels are 104 registered members.

Trelill.—In the year 1817 a Meeting House was erected in the village of Trelill, on the east side of the parish, on a piece of ground 31 feet by 26 feet, parcel of a field called Trewane Park, granted in fee by a deed dated 24th June 1817[3] by Richard Grose of St. Kew, Gent., to Thomas Pope Rosevear of Botreaux Castle, merchant, and others, upon the same trusts as in the last recited deed. Accommodation is afforded here for 150 persons, and there are 25 registered members.

---

[1] Rot. Claus. 56th George III., Part xix., No. 2.   [2] See special limitations, Vol. i., p. 402.
[3] Rot. Claus. 57th Geo. III. Part xiii., No. 3.

Pendogget.—Another building was erected at Pendoggett on the northern side of the parish in 1830, upon a piece of ground 30 feet by 20 feet, sold in fee by James Philp of Tremere in St. Tudy, Gent., by deed dated 29th May 1830,[1] to William Grose, Gent., and others, upon the usual trusts for "the people called Methodists" as stated above. There is seat accommodation here for 80 persons, and the number of registered members is eight.

Amble.—A Meeting House was erected at Chapel Amble in 1840 upon a piece of land called "Jane Hewit's Garden," containing 5 perches, granted by deed dated 16th January 1840 for the term of 1000 years, at the rent of one pepper corn, by Thomas Grose of St. Kew, yeoman, to William Grose and others, to hold upon trust for such persons as were then, or should thereafter become, shareholders in the said premises, for the purposes of public and social worship and Sunday schools, and also for other sacred purposes and services as the said persons, or the majority of them, should appoint, and including a power of sale.[2] This building is now appropriated to the United Methodist Free Church connection. The building affords accommodation for 130 persons, and there are 30 registered members.

Treguite.—There is another Meeting House of the same body at Treguite *alias* Tregwide, built upon a piece of ground given by Lord Robartes. This will seat 80 persons, and to it are attached 16 registered members.

St. Kew Highway.—A fifth was erected in 1840 near St. Kew Highway which affords sittings for 150 persons, and there are attached to it 25 registered members.

The two last mentioned have not been settled under legal Trusts, but we are informed that the whole are about to be transferred to new Trusts in accordance with the objects of the "United Free Church Connexion."

MANOR OF LANNOHO, *alias* LANOWE.

The Manor of Lanowe was anciently of considerable extent and importance and was a part of the royal demesne, being so held at the time of the *Domesday Survey*, even at which date two manors had been taken away from it. It is recorded in the *Exeter Domesday*:[3] "The King holds one manor which is called Lannoho which was held by Harold on the day on which King Edward was alive and dead. In the same are five

---

[1] Rot. Claus. 1st William IV. Part ix., No. 5.　　　　[2] Rot. Claus. 1840, Part xxvii., No. 4.

[3] In the Exchequer Book, as printed by the Record Commissioners, the name is given as Lanehoc: "The King holds Lanehoc. There he has five hides, for two hides it is gilded. The land is twenty-two ploughs but of this is demesne one hide, and there are two ploughs, and eight bond servants, and seventy villains, and twenty-six bordars with twenty ploughs. There is one acre of meadow, forty acres of pasture, wood one league long and three quarters of a league broad. It pays six pounds by weight and for burning. From this manor is taken away two manors Podestoc and Sanguinas. There is one hide and half of land and twelve ploughs. Jouuinus holds it of the Earl of Moreton. Formerly it was worth 60s. now the value is 40s."

hides and it pays gild for two hides. This twenty-two ploughs can plough. Thereof the King holds one hide in demesne and two ploughs, and the villans hold four hides and twenty ploughs. There the King has sixty villans, one miner, and twenty-six bordars, and eight bond servants, and nine animals, and 120 sheep, and one league of scrubwood in length and three quarters in breadth, and one acre of meadow, and forty acres of pasture, and it renders per annum six pounds by weight and [wood] for burning.

"From this manor two manors have been taken away which belonged to it on the day on which King Edward was alive and dead, one called Podestok (Poundestock) and the other called Sanguinas (St. Gennys). In this manor is one hide and half of land. Twelve ploughs can plough the whole land of these two manors. These Jouuinus now holds of the Earl of Moreton and the value per annum is 40s., and when the Earl received it the value was three pounds."

The Manor of Lanowe itself very soon after this became subdivided. The two carucates of land held by the King in demesne, together with the Advowson of the Church were granted by King Henry I., to the Bishop of Exeter, and the remainder of the manor was granted by King Richard I., to Simon de Pincerna. The former became designated Lanhosaint or Holy Lanho, from its appropriation to religious purposes, and the latter Lanhomur, or Great Lanho. We propose, in the first instance, to treat of:

THE MANOR OF LANHOSAINT AND THE ADVOWSON OF THE CHURCH OF ST. KEW.

The King Henry I. having granted a portion of the manor as above stated to the Church of Exeter, William Warelwast, who was consecrated on 11th August, 1107, and died 1137, granted the same lands and the Advowson of the Church in free alms to the Canons regular of Plympton. Henry II. confirmed this grant, which was also subsequently confirmed by Bishops Robert Chichester (1138-1155), Robert Warelwast (1155-1160), Bartholomew (1161-1184), and John (1161-1191) with all the lands, tithes, liberties, and appurtenances thereof, as appears from Charters printed by Dr. Oliver.[1]

From this date the Manor and Advowson would seem to have been enjoyed in peace by the Prior and Convent of Plympton, the offices of the Church being performed by the Canons detached from that house, but in the year 1283 Bishop Bronescombe admitted a certain Raymond de Lanhoho, Priest, probably one of the Canons of Plympton who had acquired his name from continuous residence in this parish, as Vicar, and with the assent and consent of the Prior and Convent assigned to him and his successors, Vicars of this parish, as their stipend, the whole altarage of the said Church, together with the lands and possessions which Roger Sors and Richard Fitz-Ralph sometime held of the demesne

[1] Mon. Dioc. Exon., p. 135 Charter No. III., and p. 138 Charter No. XIV.

of the sanctuary of that Church, the tithe of the sheaf of the whole parish excepted, never-theless reserving the power to increase or decrease the same.[1] In 1302, however, upon the visit to the county of the Justices Itinerant, the Jury presented that King Edgar gave the Church of Lannoseynt, which was of the value of £40 per annum, and two carucates of land and 100s. rent, to support two Canons to celebrate divine service and to give alms to the poor and afford hospitality to travellers, for the benefit of the souls of the King and his suc-cessors; and that during 15 years they had not performed these duties. A precept was issued to the Sheriff that he should cause the Prior to appear. Afterwards the Prior came and said that a certain William, Bishop of Exeter, granted in perpetual alms, with the assent and consent of the Chapter of Exeter, the said Church to the Prior and his Canons serving God in the Church of Plympton, so that when the Clerks of the same Church (Lanhoho) die, their prebends should go to the use of the Canons of Plympton, and he proffered the Charter in Court to witness the same, as also the Charter of Confirmation of King Henry (II.), the grandfather of the King; and he said that he and his predecessors had held the said Church quietly and quit of the services and alms as aforesaid, and he petitioned judgment. The Jury found that the Prior and his predecessors had held the aforesaid Church and land of the Lord the King and his ancestors time out of mind, and continued the chantries and alms until the time the aforesaid was subtracted by the pre-decessors of the said Prior; and it was concluded that the aforesaid chantries, &c., should be continued, and a precept was granted to distrain the said Prior to compel him to do so.[2]

It would appear that the Prior refused to comply with this injunction, and that the benefice was seized into the King's hands, for in the same year the Prior petitioned the King and Council, setting forth that he and his predecessors had had two carucates of land and 100 shillings rent in Laneuhouseynt, otherwise called Landoho, and the Church of the same place in pure and perpetual alms of the gift of William Warwast sometime Bishop of Exeter, and under the confirmation of King Henry, great grand-father of the then King, without doing any kind of service until the iter of Sir John de Berwyk and his associates in Cornwall in Michaelmas term, 30th Edward I., before whom it was presented that the said lands, rents, and services were given to the said Prior and Canons in the same place serving God for the sustenance of two Canons to celebrate divine service there, and to give alms and shelter pilgrims and other wayfarers by a certain King called Edgar, but that the same people confessed there was little likelihood in the allegation, because that forty years after the death of the said King Edgar there was neither Prior, nor Canon, nor Convent at Plympton, that could have received the property, for that Bishop William, to whom King Henry son to William the Conqueror rendered and returned to our Lady and to St. Peter

---

[1] Bishop Bronescombe's Register, folio 122. (See Appendix No. I., A.) The altarage included not only the obventions and offerings made at the altar, but also the tithes of wool, lambs, colts, calves, &c., known as small tithes.

[2] Assize Rolls, Cornwall, 30 Edward I. $\left.\begin{array}{c} M \\ 1 \\ 26 \end{array}\right\}$ 1 m. 6s.

of the Church of Exeter the said lands, rent, and Church, founded the Priory of Plympton, and gave to it the said lands, &c., and Church of Landoho, which gift was confirmed by King Henry, great grandfather of the then King. And the Prior prayed the King for the sake of his soul and the souls of his ancestors, that he, the Prior, and his Convent might hold his the said lands, &c., &c., for their sustenance, and to maintain their hospitality at Plympton, according to the said Charters and according to the custom which had existed from the foundation of the Church until the iter aforesaid, for since that iter they had not received anything for their sustenance nor to maintain hospitality there.[1] A writ was ordered to Sir John de Berwick to produce the record and process of his last iter in Cornwall before the Treasurer and Barons of the Exchequer, that when the same had been examined right might be done. The result was that on the 26th March 35th Edward I. (1307), the King granted a Charter to the Prior and Canons exempting them from personal service at Landoho, provided they had there one fit and proper secular priest as Vicar, and one Chaplain, to celebrate divine offices, and to give alms to the poor and afford hospitality to travellers in behalf of the Prior and Convent for ever.[2]

Disputes, however, arose respecting the maintenance of the Chaplain between the Prior and Convent and the Vicar; the former contending that the Chaplain's stipend should be paid from the revenues of the vicarage, and that latter urging that such revenues were inadequate for the support of the Vicar and one Chaplain, and for paying the dues to the Bishop and Archdeacon and the other burdens incident to the vicarage. The parties appeared before the Bishop at Chudleigh on 17th January 1354, and a compromise was agreed to, viz., that the Vicar (Henry Tresodorn) and his successors should be found and paid at the expense of the Prior and Convent for ever, and that the Vicar and his successors should be bound to repair the chancel of the said Church from time to time as need required, and to bear all other burdens; and for the support of the said vicar the tithes of certain lands should be assigned in augmentation of the vicarage, viz., the great tithes of the lands of Benbolgh, Trewarthenyer, Cropping Hill, Tretheven, Dale, Nyweton, Redsmyth, and Pelengarou, beside the manse, sanctuary and altarage which the said Vicar and his predecessors had received according to ancient custom.[3]

Notwithstanding the Royal Charter above cited, matters were not allowed as yet to

---

[1] This petition, which is in Norman French, has been printed by Dr. Oliver from the Rolls of Parliament, Vol. i. p. 461, (Monasticon Exon. p. 140, No XIX.) but he does not seem to have been cognisant of the previous proceedings.   [2] Rot. Pat. 31st Edward I., m. 20.

Note.—In 1283, John Aston, then escheator, on Saturday next after the feast of S. Ambrose (6th Decr.) took an inquisition at Bodmyn ex-officio upon the oaths of Stephen Glyn, Henry Cavel, Roger Treury, John Bere, and others, who found that the Prior of Plympton held of the King in Capite, two carucates of land in Lannoseynt, and that Robert, sometime Prior of Plympton, had granted the same to John Treury, Richard and Roger his sons, William Caly and Petronilla Parsons, without license of the King: viz., on Monday next after the feast of the Nativity of S. Mary the Virgin, 35th Edward III., for their whole lives, and the jury say that the said John and Richard are dead, and that Roger, William, and Petronilla, are still alive; and they say further that the true value of the land is £4 4s. 4d. per annum, and that the Escheator had taken it into the hands of the King. (Escheats. 6th Richard II., No. 185.)   [3] Bishop Grandisson's Reg. p. 180.

rest in peace.[1] In 1391 John Hauley the King's Escheator, in virtue of his office, held an inquisition at Bodmin, and the jury found that King Edgar had granted to the Prior of Plympton and his successors the Manor of Lanouseynt and the advowson of the Church of Lanowe with the tithes and all profits for ever to maintain two Canons at Lanoweseynt there to celebrate for the souls of the king and his ancestors, and to distribute alms twice every week, on Wednesday and Friday, to forty poor persons, for the souls of the King and his ancestors for ever, and one of the Chaplains to celebrate in the Chapel in the cemetery of the said Church, and the said Chapel to be kept in repair at the charge of the Prior and Convent: and that inasmuch as sixty years had elapsed since the said services were performed, the said Manor ought to become forfeited to the King. And they said that the value of the said Manor was 100s. per annum, and that the value of the Rectory was £50 per annum (sic). They also presented that the Prior and Convent had bought one messuage and one acre of land, Cornish, after the statute of religion, in Talcogow, juxta Lanowseynt, and one messuage and one ferling of land in Treaynek, of William ffoote of Hale without the license of the King.

We are enabled to lay before our readers a Court Roll of the manor of about this period. It is for the eighth year of King Henry IV. (1406-7) and shews the value of the manor at that date. It will be seen that the gross amount of the rents received for the year was £10 10s. 9¾d., which, with £2 14s. 9d. arrears for the previous year, and 17s. 9d. perquisites of the courts, made the aggregate income £14 2s. 4d. Of this was paid to the Lord at several times £10 9s. 5d., which gives a balance of £3 13s. 11d., of which sum was allowed of the arrears to Richard Yache, late prepositus, 4s., and of the same arrears of Richard Gaggar paid to the steward 7s. 0½d., of John Pleyer 38s. 4d., and forgiven by the Lord to the same John 5s, whereof the sum allowed was 54s. 5d. and the decrease 19s. 6d., whereupon the Prepositus accounted for 12s.

We have before us another Court Roll of the manor for one year from Michaelmas, 2nd Henry VIII., the aggregate of which year was £11 4s. 4¾d., and the perquisites of the Courts, 7s., so that, without reckoning the difference in the value of money, irrespective of fines, the revenue from the manor remained much the same.[2]

Court Roll of the Manor of Lannowseynt, 8th Henry IV., 1406-7.

Lannow	..	.. Compotus Ricardi Porthquyn Prepositi ibidem a festo Sancti Michaelis Archangeli anno regni regis Henrici iiij^ti vij^mo usque idem festum eiusdem Sancti Michaelis anno regni regis Henrici supradicti viij°.
Arreragia ..	..	Idem reddit compotum de liiij^s ix^d quadrante de arreragiis vltimi compoti anni precedentis.

Summa liiij^s ix^d quadrans.

[1] Escheats. 14th Richard II., No. 97. see Appendix No. I. F.
[2] These Manor Rolls are in the possession of C. G. Prideaux-Brune of Prideaux Place, Esq.

N²

Redditus .. ..   Et de x^{li} v^s x^d obolo quadrante de redditibus ibidem tam liberis quam convencionalibus per annum vt patet per extentum   Et de xij^d de incremento redditus de Colverparke dummodo Johannes Trethyvan ocupat ibidem. Et de ij^s de incremento redditus terre dominicæ dimissæ Johanni Trethyvan et Rogero Belle.   Et de v^d de incremento redditus pro tenemento quod modo Ricardus Gagau tenet quondam Ricardus Cok pretenuit sub redditu v^s vij^d per annum.   Et modo conceditur eidem Ricardo pro vj^s per annum et sic incrementum redditus patet vt supra.   Et de xij^d de incremento redditus tenuræ quondam Calway in Hale et vbi solebat reddere per annum xij^s modo conceditur Ricardo Ynch sub redditu xiiij^s et sic incrementum redditus patet vt supra.   Et de vj^d de incremento redditus tenementi Roberti Bertlot quod solebat reddere per annum viij^s modo conceditur Willelmo Mule pro viij^s vj^d et sic incrementum redditus patet vt supra.

Summa x^{li} x^s ix^d obolus quadrans.

Perquisitus Curiæ ..   Et de xvij^s ix^d de perquisitis iiij^{or} curiarum ibidem hoc anno tentarum cum finibus et releuiis in eiisdem.

Summa xvij^s ix^d.

Summa totalis receptionis cum arreragiis xiiij^{li} iij^s iiij^d.

Allocancia ..   De quibus in allocanciis tenuræ nuper Petronullæ Wadyne concessis Roberto Daundell per Cartam Domini et vbi solebat reddere per annum xxj^s iiij^d modo dimittitur eidem Roberto pro xx^s et sic decrementum redditus xvj^d. Et in pergameno pro Rotulo Curiæ hoc anno empto i^d.

Summa xvij^d.

Penciones .. .. ~~Et soluitur Nicholao Bokelly seneschallo ibidem pro pencione sua per annum xiij^s iiij^d.~~

~~Summa xiij^s iiij^d.~~

Liberacio denariorum   Et liberata Nicholao Selman seneschallo de redditu ibidem termino natalis domini per manus Nicholai Bokelly..   xl^s

Et eidem seneschallo per manus Nicholai Bokelly   vj^{li} xiij^s iiij^d

Et eidem pro decimis solutis Priori Launceston   xv^s viiij^d

Et eidem super hunc auditum .. .. .. xix^s

Summa x^{li} viij^s

Summa totalis receptus et liberationis x^{li} ix^s v^d. Et decrementi lxxiij^s xj^d· de quibus allocatur eidem de arreragiis Ricardi Ynche nuper prepositi ibidem iiij^s obolus quadrans condonati per dominum Et ei de arreragiis Ricardi Gaggu solutis seneschallo vij^s obolus Et eidem de arreragiis Johannis Pleyer solutis seneschallo xxxviij^s iiij^d. Et eidem de arreragiis eiusdem Johannis v^s condonati per dominum. Quarum summa allocationum liiij^s v^d. Et decrementa xix^s vj^d. Vnde super predictum Ricardum nunc compotantem xij^s.

---

[1] It is curious to know the cost of the vellum upon which this record is written. The size is 16½ inches by 9 inches.

Respectuata   .. Inde respectuantur eidem de releviis Johannis Lanhergy filij et heredis Johannis Lanhergy pro dimidio acre terre in Tregelest quousque peruenerit ad plenam etatem qui nunc est etatis xvj annorum vj^s iij^d Et eidem de amerciamentis heredum de Brygcher et Nicholai Gyfford hoc anno xv^d.

xxiij^s vij^d obolus.

From this time the Prior and Convent would seem to have held peaceable possession until the dissolution of the religious houses. The Priory of Plympton was surrendered by Prior John Howe on 1st March 1538-9, and all its possessions fell into the hands of the King.[1]

The Ecclesiastical revenues of this parish, according to the valuation of Pope Nicholas, 1280-1291, were as under:

Ecclesia de Lannow - - - - - viij^{li} xiij^s iiij$^{d.}$	xvij^s iiij^d
Vicarius ejusdem - - - - - ij^{li}	

According to the valuation made under the King's commission in 1522, we have:

Prior de Plympton Rector Ecclesie ibidem valet per annum -	xij^{li}
Mr Johannes Mane,[2] Vicarius ibidem, valet in proficuis -	x^{li}

In the Valor Ecclesiasticus, 36th Henry VIII we find:

Priory of the Apostles Peter and Paul at Plympton.[3]

Manerium de Lanowe Seynt

Redditus assisie et conventionalium tenencium ibidem per annum -	xj^{li}	xv^d q.
De perquisitibus curiæ et aliis proficuis manerij per annum communibus annis - - - - - - - - }	vij^s	xj^d q.
Rectoria de Lannow *alias* Seynt Kewe[4] - - -		
Decima garbarum ibidem valet per annum xx^{li} sic dimissa per indenturam Nicholao Pridyaux pro termino annorum - }	xx^{li}	

Rectorie, Vicariæ, Prebendæ in Decanatu de Trigg Minor.[5]

Seynt Kuee

Proficua prouenientia de Rectori ibidem non respond' hic, eo quod appropriata est Prioratui de Plympton et respondetur inde in valore suo }	nil
Vicaria ibidem valet per annum tam in decimis majoribus quam minoribus cum agistamento glebe ultra viij^s ix^d solutis procuratione }	xix^{li} xj^s
Decima inde - -	xxxix^s j^d q.

[1] Mon. Dioc. Exon, p. 132.

[2] See Appendix II. Mr. John Mane, Vicar, was also returned for goods of the value of £40, and Richard Penny, Chaplain, for stipend seven marks, and goods 60s.

[3] Valor Ecclesiasticus, Vol. ii., p. 376.   [4] Ibid., p. 377.   [5] Ibid., p. 401.

The Manor and the Rectory, after the dissolution of the Monastery, became separated. We will first endeavour to trace the descent of the former. It did not long remain in the hands of the king, for we find that by Charter, dated 29th March 1546, the Lordship and Manor of Lanoweseynt, otherwise called Seynt Kewe, was, *inter alia*, granted to John Woollacombe, Clerk, and Roger Prideaux, Gent.,[1] to hold to them and their heirs and assigns for ever, to hold, in capite, by the 40th part of one knight's fee, and the annual rent of 23s. 2d.[2]. Roger Prideaux had two sons: Nicholas his heir, the ancestor of Mr. Prideaux-Brune of Padstow, and Edmund, who was created a Baronet in 1622, and was the ancestor of Sir Edmund Prideaux of Netherton, Bart. Nicholas inherited the family estates, including the Manor of Lanowe. He was thrice married. By his first wife he had a son, Humphrey, and by his second wife, Chester, daughter and co-heir of William Vyell of Trevorder, a son, John. Humphrey inherited Solden; but in 1611 Sir Nicholas Prideaux, who in 1606 had received the honour of knighthood, obtained a Royal Licence to alienate the Manors of Lanowe and the Manor of Padstow, together with the advowson of the Church of Padstow and the free fishery in the water of Eyle, to John Arundell of Trerise, Esq., and Richard Crossman, Gent., to hold to the use of the said Sir Nicholas, for life, with remainder to John Prideaux Esq., his son, and the heirs of his body, and in default of such issue to the right heirs of the said Sir Nicholas.[3] The said John Prideaux having no issue sold the Manor of Lanoweseynt to Nicholas Prideaux his nephew, eldest son of his half brother Humphrey, whilst the Manor of Padstow, &c. was settled upon Edmund, younger brother of the said Humphrey, whose direct descendant Charles Prideaux-Brune Esq. at present enjoys it.

Nicholas Prideaux had three sons, Nicholas, Roger and Humphrey. He was slain at Modbury,[4] fighting on behalf of the king in 1642, and by his will[5] he bequeathed the two great Bartons of St. Kew, and the mill there, to his son Humphrey for the term of 99 years. To his daughter Elizabeth Prideaux he gave the sole inheritance of his manor of St. Kew, *alias* Lannowsant, as security for the payment of £1400, as her portion, with remainder, in case of her death, to the said Humphrey. Humphrey died in 1692 leaving Ann Prideaux his sole daughter and heir, who was then the wife of John Prideaux, third son of Sir Peter Prideaux, of Netherton, Bart., grandson of the first Baronet, by which marriage the two lines of Prideaux became re-united. Humphrey Prideaux, by his will dated 5th March 1692,[6] gave all his lands in Devon and Cornwall to his said son-in-law John Prideaux and the daughter of testator. And we find that in 1706 John Prideaux was seized of the following manor and lands in Cornwall.

---

[1] Roger Prideaux was of Solden near Holsworthy, which he inherited from his uncle, Nicholas Prideaux.
[2] Rot. Pat. 37th Henry VIII. Part vij. m. 2.   [3] Rot. Pat. 9th James, Part xlij, m. 21.
[4] So stated in family records, but we have been unable to verify it. He was perhaps killed in some skirmish not noticed in general history.
[5] Proved at Exeter 31st January 1643.   [6] Proved at Exeter.

The quantity of each Tenement in the Mannor of St. Kue in Cornwall.

				A. R. P.		A. R. P.
THE	S. Kue ..	The South Barton in hand ..	..	191 .2 37	Both Bartons ..	277 3 06
MANOR	Church Town..	The North Barton in hand ..	..	086 0 9		
OF	Hall ..	William Archer, his tenement	..	018 3 3	The whole Village	042 1 03
ST. KUE	.. ..	James Clement, *alias* Webber's Tenement		023 1 2		
IN	Treago ..	James Pauley, his tenement ..	..	041 3 6		
ST. KUE	Trevenick ..	The Burrough tenement ..	..	028 3 00	Mr. George Spreye and his mother tenants for both tenements.	057 2 23
PARISH.	.. ..	Benet's tenement there ..	..	028 3 23		
		The Mannor of St. Kue	..	0419 1 38		
ST. TEATH	Treronsall ..	The Manor of Lanovzant ..	..	000 1 35	Being the whole of the Manor	
		Robert Physick the tenant ..	..			
ST. EVAL	Treburtheck ..	George Spreye, Esq., ye tenant	..	088 3 ·10		

			A. R. P.		
The Mannor of St. Kue in Cornwall	..	..	0419 1 38	Cornish Measure, at 18 feet to the yard.	
The Mannor of Lannozant	..	..	0000 1 35		
The Barton of Treburtheck in St. Evall ..	..	0088 3 10		
Cornish Lands	..	..	0508 3 03		

Teste—Geo. Withiell of Holsworthy-Philomath, Anno 1706.[1]

This terrier discloses the fact that as early as 1706 the manor was in a state of confusion. Some lands would appear to have been sold off. The two Bartons, Hall, &c., are designated "the Manor of St. Kue," and the ancient Manor of Lanoweseynt is reduced to a few perches of land in the parish of St. Teath, stated to be "the whole of the manor." John Prideaux died soon afterwards. By his will dated on 10th July 1703,[2] and with the intent that his lands "should remain in the name and blood of Prideaux," he devised the whole of his lands, *inter alia*, the Manor of St. Kew, to his nephew Peter Prideaux of the Inner Temple, Esq., and the heirs males of his body, in default of such issue remainder to testator's brother Peter Prideaux of All Souls College, Oxford, with several remainders over. Peter Prideaux by deed dated 7th June in the following year conveyed all his lands, *inter alia*, the Manor and Lordship of St. Kew, *alias* Lezant, unto Edward Tregenna of the Middle Temple, Gent, to the intent that

[1] Original in the possession of Sir Edmund Prideaux of Netherton, Bart.
[2] Proved P.C.C. 19th June 1707, Poly 149.

one or more recoveries might be obtained settling the said lands upon the said Peter Prideaux, his heirs and assigns for ever in fee-simple. Peter Prideaux being thus in possession, by his will dated 23rd November 1710,[1] devised the whole of his lands to his uncle the abovementioned Peter Prideaux of Oxford, and his issue male, and in default of such issue he desires that his uncle will convey the lands to the uses mentioned in the will of testator's uncle John Prideaux. The last mentioned Peter enjoyed the estates a still shorter time than his predecessor. By his will, dated 15th July 1712,[2] he devised all his lands in Devon and Cornwall to his brother Sir Edmund Prideaux, Bart., and his brother-in-law Mr. Charles Harward, in trust to sell or grant leases of such portions as they thought proper, for the purpose of paying the debts of his brother John Prideaux, deceased, and of his nephew Peter Prideaux deceased, and upon the further trust that they should stand seized of the remainder to the use of testator's nephew John Prideaux and his heirs for ever, and in default of such issue to the uses prescribed in the wills of testator's brother John Prideaux and his nephew Peter Prideaux.

This John Prideaux of Soldon, the nephew, afterwards the 6th Baronet, sold the Manor of Holsworthy and the Advowson of the Church to Thomas Pitt Earl of Londonderry in 1620, and probably Lanowe was sold about the same time to Sir John Molesworth. It was in the possession of the Molesworth family in the year 1753, as appears from a deed dated 19th September in that year, wherein it is described as the Manor of St Kew, *alias* Lanowzant *alias* Lazant, situate in the parish of St. Kew, and in the following year it formed a portion of the lands settled on the marriage of Sir John Molesworth.[3] It still remains in the family but Manor Courts have long ceased to be held.

THE RECTORY.

In anticipation of the spoliation of his house, Prior Howe had been for some time previously engaged in obtaining fines for long leases of its property, and in charging it with pensions for those who had previously rendered service to the Priory. Among others, on the feast of St. Michael, 30th Henry VIII. (1538) a lease was granted, under the Conventual seal, of the Rectory of Lannowe to Humphrey Fortescue for the term of 25 years at the rent of £20 per annum, and Humphrey accounted for this rent in 2nd and 3rd Edward VI.[4] On 30th August 1563, a lease for 21 years, at the same rent, was granted by Letters Patent to John Tailor and Elizabeth his wife,[5] to com-

---

[1] Proved P.C.C., 1st February 1711-12. Barnes 35.   [2] Proved P.C.C., 8th September, 1712. Barnes. 174.

[3] Deeds in the possession of the Trustees of the Molesworth Estates.

[4] Ministers' Accounts of the possessions of Monasteries and other lands in the possession of the Crown. Cornwall, 2nd and 3rd Edward VI., No. 10.

[5] The Queen gave instructions that a lease of this Rectory should be made to John Cryller and Elizabeth his wife, Her Majesty's laundress, but it was not carried out, and on 17th February 1562, an order was given to make a lease to Roger Prideaux and Edmund and Nicholas Prideaux, his sons, for the term of their lives, and this also failed of execution. (Augm. Office, Particulars for Leases, Roll 5, No. 25.)

mence from the expiration of the lease above cited, reserving all great trees and also the advowson of the Vicarage;[1] and, previously to the expiration of this lease, a further lease was granted by Letters Patent dated 30th July 1579,[2] to Hugh Miller, one of the Queen's footmen, for the term of 21 years, to commence from the time that the aforesaid demise should cease, at the annual rent of £21, with the same reservations as before, but granting to the said Hugh Miller the Chancel of the Church and sufficient housebote, hedgebote, firebote, ploughbote, and cartbote.

By Patent dated 11th May 1608[3] a grant of the Rectory with all its members, rights and appurtenances, and all oblations, obventions, &c., together with the advowson of the parish Church or Vicarage of St. Kew, *alias* Lanowe, to the said Rectory pertaining, was made to Francis Philips and Richard Moore of London, gentlemen, their heirs and assigns for ever, to be holden of the Manor of East Greenwich, by fealty in free and common socage and not in capite nor by military service, at the rent of £20 per annum. This rent formed parcel of the dower assigned to Anne, Queen of James I.,[4] and afterwards to Queen Henrietta Maria;[5] but upon the overthrow of the Monarchy it was seized, and by Indenture dated 29th July 1651 was conveyed, *inter alia*, for a valuable consideration, by Thomas Coke and others, nominated by an Act of Parliament "for selling the fee farm rents belonging to the Commonwealth of England," to a certain Robert Merring of Stonehouse in co. Devon, Merchant, and his heirs for ever.[6] On the Restoration, however, of course, this alienation was annulled and the rent again vested in the crown. In 23rd[7] Charles II., this, and divers other fee farm rents, were vested in Francis Lord Hawley and others as Trustees for sale, and this rent, *inter alia*, by Indenture dated 23rd March, 23rd Charles II. (1670-1) was granted to John Grenville, Earl of Bath, and his heirs for ever.[8]

In no long while after the abovementioned grant of the Rectory and the Advowson of the Vicarage both came into the possession of Nicholas Sprey of Bodmin, Gent., who assigned the next presentation to William Inch of St. Kew, Gent.[9] Nicholas Sprey also in his life-time settled some of his estates, for in his will proved 6th November 1624, he mentions that he had already conveyed sufficient estate of inheritance to Nicholas Sprey, son of testator's eldest son Christopher (who died in his father's life-time) by Joane, daughter of Richard Courtenay of Tremeer in Lanivet.[10] The lands so settled embraced

---

[1] Rot. Pat. 5th Elizabeth, Part ij., m. 41.   [2] Rot. Pat. 21st Elizabeth, Part iv., m. 19.

[3] Rot. Pat. 6th James, Part xxx., No. 8.   [4] Rot. Pat. 11th James, Part xiij., No. 4.

[5] Rot. Pat. 2nd Charles, Part iv., No. 3.

[6] Fee Farm Rents. Counterparts of Deeds of Sale. Augment. Office, Bund. M. 1, No. 17.

[7] In the previous year the fee farm rent of £20 a year, paid by Nicholas Sprey out of the Rectory of Lanow was granted, *inter alia*, as part of her dower, to Queen Katherine. (Rot. Pat. 12nd Charles, Part vi.)

[8] Rot. Claus., 23rd Charles II. Part ii., m. 3.

[9] It should be here noted that on the 30th March 1630-1, a caveat was lodged in the Bishop's Court against the institution of any person to the Vicarage of St. Kew without first calling James Parker of Warlegh, Esq., the true (as is asserted) and indubitable patron of the said Vicarage, to shew cause against it by his proctor, Christopher Babb. (Act Book B, Bishops' Registry, Exeter.)

[10] See account of the Sprey family, Vol. I., p. 293, and Ped. p. 294.

O

the estates of Nicholas Sprey in St. Kew, and included the Rectory and Advowson of the Church, or at least a moiety of the former. He presented to the Vicarage on 23rd May 1640 upon the death of Robert Belmaine who held the benefice for a few months only.[1] Philip Sprey, upon his marriage in 1641, settled at Trevinnick, in this parish, and adhering to the King in the great rebellion of the seventeenth century his estates were sequestrated, and not being comprised in any exception or qualification of the propositions sent to Hampton Court, on 22nd May 1649 he paid a composition of £188.[2]

Not long after this the Rectory of Lanow came into the possession of John Tregagle of Trevorder, Esq., who acquired considerable possessions in the County. He became, in conjunction with Sir Peter Kelligrew, Receiver General of the Duchy of Cornwall, and died in 1680 largely indebted to the crown and several other persons. The office of Receiver General was transferred to his son, John Tregagle, who became still more involved. The Rectory of Lanow was mortgaged to Robert Corker of Falmouth, Esq., and eventually after the death of John Tregagle, the son, a private Act of Parliament was obtained for the sale of the whole of his estates for the purpose of paying his debts and making some provision for his family.[3] By the Trustees under this Act the impropriate Rectory of Lanow was conveyed to the above-mentioned Robert Corker, who also became possessed of the office of Receiver General of the Duchy of Cornwall, but would seem not to have prospered in it more than his predecessors. By indentures of lease and release, dated 28th and 29th July 1729, Robert Corker conveyed to John Hedges, Treasurer and Receiver General of the Duke of Cornwall, all his estate, including this Rectory, for the purpose of sale to pay, in the first instance, a sum of £11,000 due to the Prince on account of this office.

Robert Corker died about 1st March 1730, s.p., without having paid the sum due, and by his will dated 27th September 1728, his estates were devised to certain persons therein named. By deed dated 11th December 1735, the whole estate was conveyed to Hugh Gregor, of the Middle Temple, Gent., his heirs and assigns for ever,[4] by the Prince of Wales, John Hedges, Esq., described as above, Jane Parker of Falmouth, widow, only surviving sister and heir at law of Robert Corker, Mary Corker, theretofore called Mary Rowcliffe, relict of the said Robert Corker, William Pennicott of St. Dunstan's in the West, London, Surgeon, Chambre Corker and Degory Pearce, executors &c., of the will of the said Robert Corker, for the sum of £13,175; and from a further deed, dated 2nd June 1736, it appears that the said Hugh Gregor had made the said purchase on behalf of Edmond Prideaux of Padstow, Esq., and Sir John Molesworth of Pencarrow, Bart.; and it further appears that, *inter alia*, the Barton of Trevorder in St. Breoke was bought on behalf of Edmond Prideaux, and the Barton of Bokelly the messuage of Lanseage, &c., together with the Impropriate Rectory of Lanow, *alias*

---

[1] See post, p. 99.   [2] Royalist Comp. Papers, 2nd series, Vol. xxxviij., fo. 505.

[3] Act, entitled "An Act for the sale of the estate of John Tregagle, Esq., deceased, in the Counties of Devon and Cornwall, for payment of his debts, and making provision for his children." 13th Anne, September, No. 17.   [4] Deed at Prideaux Place, Padstow.

St. Kew, and the tithes of corn and grain thereto belonging, valued at £150 a year, subject to a fee farm rent of £20 a year, on behalf of Sir John Molesworth. With the paper is a rough schedule of the lands forming the estate, and against the "Advowson of the Vicarage of St. Kew" is a memorandum stating that it was "not sold, the title not being cleared up to the satisfaction of Sir John Molesworth." The Rectory of St. Kew thus came into the possession of the Molesworth family, in which it still continues, and the Advowson of the Vicarage became severed therefrom.

The total quantity of all the lands chargeable with tithes is 6087a. 0r. 24p., viz.:

				A.	R.	P.
Arable	..	..	..	5666	0	39
Meadow and Pasture	..	..	..	116	3	30
Woodland	..	..	..	192	0	16
Orchards and Gardens	..	..	..	44	3	10
Common Land	..	..	...	21	0	9
Waste and Brake	..	..	..	46	0	0
				6087	0	24

The tithes of corn and grain arising from the undermentioned lands have been merged in the said lands.

	A.	R.	P.		A.	R.	P.
Carclase	67	3	36	Bokelly	176	3	28
Carkavils	50	0	15	Barn	76	0	29
South Barton	165	1	31	Lanseague	9	3	31
Little Barton	14	2	4	Rooke	154	0	12
North Barton	93	3	33	Pengenna	181	3	2
Great and Little Hall	56	3	13	Trewigget	165	2	21
Tregillis Parks	19	3	39	Pengenna Mills	6	3	8
Little Trevinnick	29	2	34	Jobs	60	2	19
Tregillis	18	3	17				
Bound's Close	5	2	8		1405	3	30
Trecugoe	51	0	20				

The trustees of the late Sir William Molesworth, Bart., are entitled as Impropriators to the tithes of all the unmerged corn and grain, except those hereunder mentioned, and the Vicar of the parish is entitled to all the unmerged small tithes and the tithes of hay, and also to the tithes of corn and grain arising from the following lands, viz., Pollingarrow, Penbole, Trethevy, Dinham's Bridge, Bove Hills, Dinham's Bridge Tenement, Trethevan, Parish Lands called Smeeth's, Newton, and part of Tretane containing by estimation 405 acres. The small tithe and the tithe of hay of the glebe lands, containing by estimation 26a. 0r. 22p., have been merged in the said lands.

O²

	£	s.	d.

The value of the tithes awarded to the Impropriator, including the tithes of corn and grain, amounting to £3 10s., when not in the occupation of the Vicar is　　…　　　…　　　…　　　…　　.741 10 0

And the value of the tithes awarded to the Vicar, including the tithes of 172a. 2r. 0p. cultivated as coppices fixed at £20 3s. 9d., is　　520 3 9

　　　　　　　　　　Total value …　　　…　　　…　　£1261 13 9

The following terrier shewing the boundaries of the Glebe lands is preserved in the Bishop's Registry Office at Exeter:

"*St. Kew Parish Gleeb Lande.*" { The gleeb lande of the saide parishe vewed and taken by the Mynister, Churchwardens, and other the parishioners the sixteenth day of June in Anno Domini 1613.

"The gleebe lande, contayninge by estymation twenty-eight akers or thereabouts, is bounded by a way leading out southwarde from the viccarage house, and is bounded on the west side from a yeate belonging to the viccarage wth the grounde of Nicholas till yo^u come to the corner of a garden of the viccarage belowe the well, and from thence it boundeth wth the same lande till it come to a River that runneth westward, and then it boundeth eastwarde by the Church way till it comes to Skesine garden, and from thence till it come to the grounde of one Smythe called Skesine, and then it boundeth by an other lake that leadeth by the grounde of Tregoyde till it come to a peece of land called "Creekes," and from thence it leadeth till it come to an other peece of land called "seven akers," and from thence it leadeth till it come to the yeate belonging to the Vicarage wher first we began. There is an other close belonging to the said Viccarage by himself wch is bounded from a yeate that lyeth westwarde wth the grounde of Simon Rundell till it comes to the grounde of Richard Carnsew, Esq., and from thence it is bounded with the said grounde northwarde till it come to the highway on the east side, and then it boundes wth the said highway till it comes to an other way on the south side that leadeth westwarde till it comes to the said yeat where we first began."

The Vicarage House is a very convenient residence, having been rebuilt during the incumbency of the Rev. J. S. Scobell. Near the gate is a fine spring of water called the "Holy Well," mentioned in the above terrier.

THE ADVOWSON OF THE VICARAGE.

We have seen that until the dissolution of the Priory of Plympton both the Rectory and the Advowson of the Vicarage were appurtenant to the Manor of Lanowsaint, and that upon the grant of the Manor in 1546 to John Wollacombe and Roger Prideaux the two latter were reserved. In 1608 the Rectory, with the Advowson of the Vicarage annexed, was granted to Francis Philips and Richard More, and the 'latter continued appurtenant to the Rectory until after the death of John Tregagle in 1680, but in the Act of Parliament for selling his lands no particular mention is made of the Advowson of the Vicarage, nevertheless, Robert Corker presented in 1724. This omission was, perhaps, the cause of the difficulty as to the title to the Vicarage to which Sir John Molesworth took exception in 1735, and the advowson reverted to John Tregagle, by whom it is probable the next presentation was sold to Richard Hollings of Lincoln's Inn, who presented in 1737.

By lease and release dated respectively 6th and 7th March, 1748, the Advowson was conveyed by Francis Tregagle, brother and heir at law of John Tregagle, described as then late of Melchet Park, co. Wilts,[1] to John Bennet of St. Neot, co. Cornwall, Gent. in fee, who, by deed of grant dated the 18th of the same month, conveyed the Advowson in fee to the Honorable Thomas Pitt, sometime Governor of Fort St. George in the East Indies, and the fortunate possessor of the " Pitt Diamond," whose steward he at that time was for the Mohun Estates in Cornwall which Mr. Pitt had recently purchased. Mr. Pitt left issue three sons and two daughters, of whom the eldest, Robert Pitt, was of Boconnoc. He left two sons: Thomas Pitt of Boconnoc, and secondly, William, who became the great Earl of Chatham. Thomas Pitt had a son Thomas, who, in 1784, was created Baron Camelford, and his only son and heir at law, the second Lord Camelford, by his will dated 24th May 1799, devised all his real estates to his mother, Anne, Lady Camelford, for life, with remainder to his sister Anne the wife of William Wyndham Lord Grenville. As Lady Camelford predeceased her son the estates devolved upon Lady Grenville, and by deed dated 1st June 1822, Lord and Lady Grenville conveyed the Advowson of the Vicarage of St. Kew, to the Revd. Nicholas Every, Vicar of St. Veep, co. Cornwall, and he, on his death in 1836, devised all his real estates to his wife, Mrs. Elizabeth Hickes Every,[2] the present patron of the benefice.[3]

LIST OF INSTITUTIONS.

1283, Feast of St. Luke	Reymond de Lanhoho,[4] was admitted as Vicar to the Church of Lanhoho, and had a stipend assigned to him out of the benefice. (See Appendix No. 1. A.)
1349, April 4th	- Sir Nicholas de Penhal,[5] was instituted to the Vicarage of Lannohou, upon the presentation of the Prior and Convent of Plympton.

[1] See account of TREGAGLE family post.   [2] See Note * Vol. i., p. 171.

[3] In consequence of some family arrangement the next presentation to the Vicarage, vested in the Rev. John Glencross, Rector of Helland, who had married Mr. Every's sister, and Mr. Glencross conveyed the same to John Scobell, Esq., who presented in 1837. (Vide List of Institutions, p. 100.)

[4] Bishop Bronescombe's Register, fo. 122.   [5] Bishop Grandisson's Register, Vol. iii., fo. 76.

1349, May 23rd	-	Henry Tresedron,[1] was instituted to the Vicarage of Lannow, upon the presentation of the Prior and Convent of Plympton.
1361, April 3rd	-	Sir Walter Polyt, Priest,[2] was instituted to the Vicarage of Lannov, upon the presentation of the Prior and Convent of Plympton.
unknown	-	John Rescarek, Vicar of Landohou, on 29th March 1383, had licence from the Bishop to celebrate divine offices in the Chapel of St. Aldhem at Ammal.
unknown	-	Nicholas Tresulgan was Vicar on 20th September 1388,[3] when he, and John Cresse, Chaplain, were licenced to hear the confessions of debtors and outlaws. (Bishop Brantyngham's Register.)
·unknown	-	Richard Castell.
1443, April 25th	-	Richard Portelond, B.LL.,[4] was instituted to the Church of St. Kew (de Sancta Kewa) vacant by the death of Richard Castell, last Vicar, upon the presentation of the Prior and Convent of Plympton.
1466, April 20th	-	Robert Rike, Chaplain,[5] was instituted to the Vicarage of St. Kew (de Sancta Kewa) vacant by the death of Richard Portlond, last Vicar, upon the presentation of the Prior and Convent of Plympton.
1500, October 21st	-	John Manz[6] was instituted to the Vicarage of St. Kew, vacant by the resignation of Robert Ryke, upon the presentation of the Prior and Convent of Plympton.
1523, May 11th	-	Roger Sherman, Chaplain,[7] was instituted to the Church of St. Kew of Lannowsente upon the death of John Mane, the last Vicar, upon the presentation of the Prior and Convent of Plympton.
1525, November 12th	-	Anthony Fortescue, Clerk, M.A.,[8] was instituted to the Vicarage of St. Kew, vacant by the death of Roger Sherman, last Vicar, upon the presentation of the Prior and Convent of Plympton.

[1] Bishop Grandisson's Register, Vol. iii., fo. 80.   [2] Ibid., fo. 141.

[3] In 1412 the Church of St. Kew (Lannow) was under interdict, from what cause we know not, but the interdict was removed on 11th June in that year, John Burgh being Chaplain. The Vicarage would seem to have been vacant.

[4] Bishop Lacy's Register, Vol. ii., fo. 204. In 1445, Richard Portlond, B.L., Vicar of St. Kew, was placed upon a Commission concerning the right of patronage of the Church of Michaelstow. (Bishop Lacy's Register, Vol. ii., fo. 217.).

[5] Bishop Booth's Register, fo. 5. 1489, Robert Rike, Vicar of St. Kew, was on an Inquisition concerning the patronage of Lesnewth, and again in 1498 concerning the patronage of Tintagel.

[6] Bishop Redmaine's Register, fo. 18. He was also Vicar of St. Teath, and Rector of St. Tudy. See also Appendix II.   [7] Bishop Voysey's Register, fo. 16.   [8] Ibid., fo. 26.

1536, September, 20th - Nicholas Nycholls, Priest,[1] was instituted to the Church of St. Kew, vacant by the resignation of Anthony Fortescue, upon the presentation of the Prior and Convent of Plympton.

1554, September 6th - John Langman, Clerk, was instituted to the Vicarage of St. Kew, vacant by the deprivation of Nicholas Nicolls, Clerk, Priest, last Vicar, upon the presentation of Mary Queen of England.

1576, June 4th - John Goldsmith, Clerk,[2] was instituted to the Vicarage of St. Kew, vacant by the death of the last Incumbent, upon the presentation of the Queen.

1601, October 21st - Richard Wall, Clerk, M.A.,[3] was admitted to the Vicarage of St. Kew, vacant by the deprivation of John Goldesmith, last Incumbent, upon the presentation of the Queen.

1606, January 10th - Thomas Hutton, Clerk, S.T.B.,[4] was instituted to Vicarage of' St. Kew, vacant by the death of the last Incumbent, upon the presentation of the King.

1639, December 23rd - Robert Belmaine, M.A.,[5] was admitted to the Vicarage of Lanow, *alias* St. Kew, vacant by the death of Thomas Hutton, Clerk, last Incumbent, upon the presentation of William Inch, Gent., of St. Kew, for this turn the true patron by the assignment of Nicholas Sprey of Bodmin, Gent.

1640, May 23rd, - John Orchard, Clerk, M.A.,[6] was admitted to the Vicarage of St. Kew, *alias* Lanow, vacant by the death of Robert Belmayne, Clerk, last Incumbent, upon the presentation of Philip Sprey of Bodmin, Gent., the true patron.

1675, April 22nd - Thomas Jane, Clerk,[7] was admitted to the Vicarage of St. Kew vacant by the death of John Orchard, Clerk, last Incumbent, upon the presentation of William Treuill of Buttshead, Esq., the true patron.

[1] Bishop Voysey's Reg., fo. 85.   [2] Bishop Bradridge's Register, fo. 26.   [3] Bishop Carey's Register, fo. 73.

[4] Ibid. fo. 84. Matriculated at St. John's College, Oxford, 2nd July 1585, aged 19, "Pleb. fil," London, Fellow of St. John's College, Oxford, Prebendary of Exeter, and Rector of Northlew, buried at St. Kew, 27th December, 1639. (See M. I., No. 5.)   Will dated 2nd April, 1639, and proved at Exeter 10th January 1639-40. Mr. Hutton took an active part in the controversy with the Puritans on the accession of King James I., and between 1605, and 1608 published several volumes of Essays and Sermons, more especially relating to the subject of "Subscription." (See Bibliotheca Cornubiensis, sub. HUTTON.)   His descendants returned to Devon. (See post TRETHEVY.)

[5] Bishop Hall's Register, Vol. ii., fo. 21. Second son of Robert Bellmayne of Dallamore, co. Devon. Matriculated at Exeter College, Oxford, 20th July 1621, age. 17.   His grandfather was Richard Bellmayne of Bellmayne Banck, co. Westmorland. (*Vide* Ped. Visitation of Devon, Harl. Soc. Pub. Vol vi., p. 23.)   Buried at St. Kew, 6th February 1639-40, M.I., No. 5.

[6] Ibid., fo. 25. Matriculated at Gloucester Hall, 5th February 1629-30, aged 17, son of John Orchard of Mary Week, Cornwall, "Pleb.,'   In the Parish Registers of Week St. Mary, we find "John son of John Orchard, lawier, was baptized 6th September, 1612." In the Church of Poughill is a monument in memory of Mr. Charles Orchard, Vicar of that Parish, who was buried 2nd January 1756, aged 63, and of John his son and Patience his wife.   He was probably of the same family.   The monument is surmounted by a shield of arms: ar. a chev. Erm. between three pears gu.

[7] Bishop's Register, N.S., Vol. ii., fo. 32. Buried at St. Kew 23rd September 1693, P.R.

1693, March 17th - John Nation, Clerk, M.A.,[1] was admitted to the Vicarage of St. Kew, vacant by the death of Thomas Jane, upon the presentation of John Mill of Okehampton, co. Devon, Gent., *hac vice*, with the assent of John Tregagle, patron of the same.

1724, May 27th - Edward Stephens, Clerk, B.A.,[2] was admitted to the Vicarage of Lanow, vacant by the death of John Nation, upon the presentation of Robert Corker, of Falmouth, Esq., the true patron.

1737, May 19th - James Read, Clerk, M.A.,[3] was admitted to the Vicarage of St. Kew, void by the death of Edward Stephens, Clerk, last Incumbent, upon the presentation of Richard Hollings, of Lincoln's Inn, Middlesex, Esq., the true patron.

1760, December 23rd - Henry Bennett, Clerk, B.LL.,[4] was admitted to the Vicarage of Lanow, *alias* St. Kew, void by the death of James Read, upon the presentation of Thomas Pitt, of Boconnoc, Esq., the true patron, as is said.

1777, October 15th - Joseph Pomery, Clerk, M.A.,[5] was admitted to the Vicarage of St. Kew, vacant by the death of Henry Bennet, upon the presentation of Thomas Pitt of Boconnoc, Esq., the true patron, as is said.

1837, March 7th - John Samuel Scobell, Clerk, B.A.,[6] was admitted to the Vicarage of St. Kew, *alias* Lanow, vacant by the death of Joseph Pomery, upon the presentation of John Scobell of Halwell House, in the parish of Whitchurch, co. Devon, Esq., for this turn the true patron, as is said.

1849, July 5th - John Glencross, Clerk, B.A.,[7] was admitted to the Vicarage of St. Kew, vacant by the death of John Samuel Scobell, Clerk, upon the presentation of Elizabeth Hickes Every, of Cambridge, the true patron.

[1] Bishops' Registers N.S. Vol. iii., fo. 137. Matric. at Balliol College, Oxford, 3rd May 1672, aged 16, son of Francis Nation of Parkham, co. Devon, (his brother Francis, matric. the same day) B.A. 29th January 1675; M.A. 17th December 1678; Buried at St. Kew 29th January 1723-4. Will dated 24th May 1720, and proved at Exeter 27th June 1724. (See Ped. post.)

[2] Ibid. Vol. vj., fo. 17. Matric at Exeter College, Oxford, 11th March 1715-6, Son of Edward Stephens Gent., of Falmouth, Cornwall, B.A., 11th October 1719.

[3] Ibid. vij., fo. 10. Matric. at St. Mary Hall, Oxford, 29th October 1724, aged 18; son of Thomas Read "Pleb." of Farmborough, co. Somerset; B.A. 27th November 1728; M.A. 29th April 1731; bur. at St. Kew, 12th September 1760, M.I., Nos. 5 and 17.

[4] Ibid. Vol. viij., fo. 99. Matric. at Balliol College, Oxford, 14th January 1744-5, aged 18, son of Henry Bennett, Gent. of St. Neott, Cornwall; B.A. 11th October 1748.

[5] Ibid. Vol. ix., fo. 136, Matric. at Exeter College, Oxford, 26th March 1768, aged 18; son of John Pomery, Gent., of Liskeard, Cornwall; B.A. 7th December 1771; M.A. 2nd July 1774. He was buried at St. Kew, just outside the Priest's door, in a granite coffin which had been prepared and laid in the ground during his lifetime.

[6] Ibid., Vol. xij., fo. 122; of Peterhouse, Cambridge; B.A. 1830; died 26th February 1849; bur. at St. Kew, M.I., No. 33. [7] Ibid., Vol. xiii., fo. 61. Rector of Helland also. See ante p. 13.

St Kew Church.

GROUND PLAN

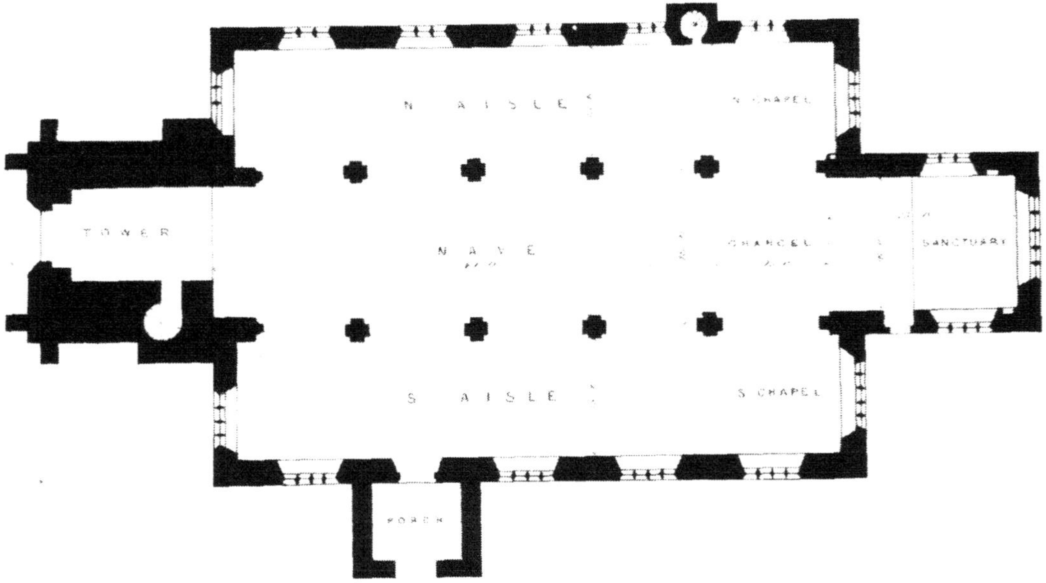

Plate XXII

SANCTUARY

N CHAPEL

CHANCEL

S CHAPEL

N AISLE

NAVE

S AISLE

PORCH

TOWER

1852, February 10th   -   Nicholas Thomas Every, Clerk, B.A.,[1] was admitted to the Vicarage of St. Kew, vacant by the resignation of John Glencross, Clerk, upon the presentation of Elizabeth Hickes Every, of St. Kew aforesaid, the true patron.-

THE PARISH CHURCH.

The Parish Church, which is dedicated to St. Kewa, is favourably situate in a valley, and is surrounded by some good trees, having a plantation of timber on the rising ground on the north side. It consists of a sanctuary, disengaged, 23ft. by 16ft.; Chancel, 15ft. by 16ft.; north and south Chapels, the former being 13ft. 6in. wide and 16ft. long, and the latter of the same width and 15ft. 6in. long; Nave, 61ft. long and 18ft. 9in. wide; with north and south aisles of the same width as the Chapels above-mentioned; south porch, 9ft. 9in. by 8ft. 9in.; and western tower, 15ft. by 10ft. These are all internal measurements. (See Plate XXXII.) The gables are surmounted by crosses.

The sanctuary is lighted by three windows. The east window has 5lt, ogee, without foliation and with plain tracery, north window 3lt. 5fo. with tracery, and south window four-light in two divisions 5fo. with tracery in the head. There is a Priest's door and a small 5fo. piscina in the south wall. The sanctuary is raised one step above the Chancel, at the communion rails is a second, and a third within, whilst the altar stands upon a footpace.

The north Chapel has two windows. That on the east is 4lt. 5fo. in two compartments, with tracery in the head. In this window remains a considerable quantity of good ancient glass. According to tradition this is the window sold to the parish of St. Kew on the rebuilding of Bodmin Church, which sale is recorded among the receipts in the building accounts of that Church, in these words: "for a wyndowe of Seynt Kewa xxij[s] vij[d]." In the upper opening are the royal arms, France and England quarterly. In the opening on the left hand side a shield charged on the dexter side with ar. a bear sa; but the impalement is lost. On the right hand side ar. a chev. between three birds, black, with white breast (magpies? Kingdon) impaling az. a bend or, in chief a label with 3 points gu. (Carminowe). In the body of the window are represented incidents in the life of Our Lord.

The south Chapel is lighted by two windows. That on the east is very handsome. It is of 5lt. 5fo. under a flat four-centered arch, and contains considerable remains of old painted glass. The south window is of 4lt. 5fo. In this is an escutcheon of the arms of Arundell: sa. six martlets ar. 3, 2, and 1, differenced with a crescent. There is a small piscina in the south wall of the Chapel.

---

[1] Bishops' Registers, N.S. fo. 82. Son of Nicholas Every, Vicar of St. Veep. Of Clare Hall, Cambridge; B.A. 1850.

P

The Chancel and Chapels are raised one step above the nave and aisles, and there are remains of the Chancel screen and parcloses. The rood loft staircase continues in the north wall, and has recently been opened out by the Vicar, as have also been the openings in the spandrels of the arches. The Chancel is blocked up on one side by a large square pew, erected by the Nichols family of Trewane. On it are carved several escutcheons of arms pertaining to that family: *e.g.* sa. three pheons ar. (Nichols) impaling: or. a lion ramp. gu., within a bordure eng. sa., differenced with a mullet (Pomeroy). Nichols, impaling or, a cross eng. sa. (Mohun). Nichols, impaling az., a bend eng. ar. Cotised or., and differenced with a crescent (Fortescue of Fallapit).

The nave is of four bays separated from the aisles by monolith granite pillars supporting four centered arches of the usual Cornish type, and both nave and aisles have good wagon roofs. The aisles are lighted by a window in each bay, of the same character as those in the chapels, though smaller, and by larger windows in the west ends 3lt. without cusping. (See Plate XXXIII).

The font, which is of the Third Pointed period, is octagonal, each face being sculptured with a quatrefoil.

There is a wooden tablet set up at the west end of the Church with the following record painted thereon:

"This is to record that within a small Tin Box deposited in the Parish Chest are contained the Deeds, Writings, &c., relating to the Estate called the Church land, bequeathed and appropriated by the family of Trewarne in aid of the repairs of St. Kew Parish Church for ever."[1]

"There is also deposited a Copy of the Clause in Mrs. Nation's Will, by which she has given and devised to the Vicar and overseers of the Parish of St. Kew, One Hundred Pounds to be placed out at interest, which Interest is by them to be distributed annually to those poor Housekeepers who receive no regular pay from the parish. The Hundred Pounds is vested in three per cent. Consols from whence the Vicar and Overseers receive yearly Three Pounds through the East Cornwall Bank. Jos. Pomery, Vicar."

The tower, the arch of which rests upon plain abaci and is open to the Church, is a lofty structure of three stages. It is embattled and decorated with croketted pinnacles, and is buttressed on the square. The stair turret is at the south east corner, and is raised above the battlements. In the ringing, or basement, floor over the entrance door on the west, is a large 3lt. window with tracery in the head without foliation, and in the next stage on the west side are two square headed 2lt. 3fo. windows under equilateral arches. The bell chamber has a large 3lt. window on each face, the head being filled with tracery, except on the south side, on which side the window is square headed. In 1552 there were four bells in the tower; in 1818 they were recast into six by Rudhall of Gloucester, the third and sixth have been again recast; see the following inscriptions. The fourth is now cracked.

---

[1] Through the courtesy of the Vicar and Churchwardens we were allowed to inspect the parish chest. We found therein the little tin box secured by a padlock, and in it the deeds relating to the Church Estate. The grant however was not by the "Family of Trewarne," but by John Dagg. See post *Charities.* The name of Trewarne does not occur in the deeds.

	Diameter at the mouth.	
1st Bell	2ft. 5¼in.	Iohn Rudhall Fecт., 1818.
2nd ,,	2ft. 6¾in.	I. Rudhall Fecт., 1818 Keep Attentively your time.
3rd ,,	3ft. 8¾in.	Mears and Stainbank, Founders, London. Every Sabbath mind to chime.
4th ,,	2ft. 9½in.	Rev. Joseph Pomrey, Vicar. John Rudhall, Fecт. 1818. 'Ring Changes oft in Proper Season.'
5th ,,	3ft. 1½in.	I. Rudhall Fecт. ⁙ Abм. Hambly and Richᴰ. Worden, Churchwardens, 1818. 'Never drink to hurt your reason.'
6th ,,	3ft. 4¾in.	C. and G. Mears, Founders, London, 1845.

Over the south door are the Royal Arms, with the initials "C. R. 1661," and underneath "God save the King."

CHURCH PLATE.

In the return of plate and bells appertayning to every pish Church wᵗʰin the sayd hundred (Trigg) made by William Carnsew and Henry Cheverton in 6th Edward VI.[1] (1552) we find for :

The pish off St. Kue.   The sayd pishners hath a Chalice of Sylver through gilted.

It. a chalice of sylver pcell gilte

It. iiij belles in the tower there

The present condition of the bells we have stated above.

The Church Plate now consists of the following articles :

1. Chalice and cover, silver gilt and much embossed. The cover adapted for a paten, made probably 1578.

2. An elegant cup, of a secular pattern, enriched with two scrolls supporting the stem and the upper rim by four bearded human figures in relief. On the rim is the following inscription :

"*Ex Dono Mariæ Nicholls Ecclesiæ de St. Kew in comitatu Cornubiæ obijt 19th Januarij 1723.*" The cup would appear to be of much earlier date.

3. A flagon silver gilt, with the inscription :

"*To the Holy Communion Service in Church of St. Kew this humbly devoted by Elizᵗʰ daughter of Jnᵒ Nicholls, Esq. by Elizᵗʰ his wife daughter of Sʳ Joseph Tredinham and Dame Elizᵗʰ his wife daughter of Sʳ Edward Seymour, 1729.*" Hall mark of the same year.

4. A paten silver gilt with the same inscription as the last except the date which is 1732. Hall mark of the same year.

5. An alms dish silver gilt, with this inscription :

"*The gift of Mrs. Mary Webber, Spinster to the Church of St. Kew. Who died 19th Octʳ 1763, aged 81.*"[2] Hall mark of the same year.

---

[1] Augmentation Office, Church Goods $\frac{1}{51}$.

[2] By her will dated 30th June 1762, proved 28th January 1764, she gave "£10 to be laid out in the purchase of a piece of plate for the Communion of St. Kew."

P²

MONUMENTS AND GRAVE STONES.

IN THE CHANCEL.

1. In a Vault beneath are deposited with those of her three Infants the Remains of MRS. MELLONEY POMERY, Eldest Daughter of GEORGE SCOBELL, ESQ' PENZANCE, and wife of JOSEPH POMERY, A.M., Vicar of this Parish. After a long series of Bodily afflictions, on y⁰ 30ᵗʰ August 1799, in the 47ᵗʰ year of her Age, her spirit returned to the GOD whom she adored. As the last grateful Tribute of affection to the Memory of a faithful Wife and tender Mother this Monument is erected by an afflicted Husband.

> How lov'd how valu'd once avails Theo not
> To whom related, or by whom begot
> From human passions now for ever free
> In love divine, Oh! mays't thou perfect be.

2. Beneath are deposited the mortal Remains of Grace youngest daughter of the REVᵈ JOSEPH POMERY and MELLONEY his wife, who departed this life June 5 1816. She was exemplary in the faithful discharge of all Her Relative and Social Duties: A Dutiful and tender Child, an affectionate Sister, a sincere sympathizing Friend, Benevolent to the Poor, Obliging to All, Cheerful in Health, patient and resigned in Sickness. Under the influence of a lively Christian Faith and Divine Love, she lived in daily Communion with Her Creator and died rejoicing in the animating and certain Hope of a Resurrection to Eternal Life through the Death and Merits of her Redeemer.

3. Sacred to the Memory of the REVᵈ JAMES READ, A.M., many years Vicar of this Parish, who was buried 12ᵗʰ September, 1760, aged 55.

And of his wife JANE who was buried 25ᵗʰ May 1752, aged 46, with two of their infant Children.

Also their son JAMES READ, M.D., of Tremeare in St. Tudy, who departed this life 12ᵗʰ November 1800, aged 52.

And his wife Loveday, eldest daughter of Trehane Symons, Esqʳᵉ of Trevine in St. Minver, who departed this life 25ᵗʰ March 1821, aged 71, with several of their infant children.

Also in Memory of the sons of James and Loveday Read, the Revᵈ TREHANE SYMONS READ, A.B., who departed this life 21ˢᵗ May 1809, aged 27. And of Lieut. JOHN READ, of the Royal Marines, who fell gallantly fighting in his Country's Service at the reduction of Cayenne, 8th January 1809, aged 20, and was buried in the Ocean.

4. Underneath lieth the body of George one of the twin Sons of the Rev. Joseph Pomery and Melloney his Wife, who was buried the 28ᵗʰ day of March 1782, aged 8 months.

> Let no rude hand disturb his dear remains.

Here lieth also Joseph his brother, who died December 16ᵗʰ 1783, aged 11 weeks.

5.
Hic vna suauiter obdormiunt
Thomas Hutton Filiolus Dulcis Puellus
Willielmus Opye[1] Nepotulus Infantulus Tenerrimus
Nec Non
Thomas Hutton Pater Londinensis S.S.
Theol. Bacc. Coll. D. Joan. Bap. Oxon. Socius Eccliæ
Cathed. Exon. Præbend. Rect. Parochiæ N. Lew in Agro
Devon. Hujus Vicariæ Incumbens, Vir optima Fide et
Moribus XL Annos Eccles. nulli opere Evangelico
Secundus Eccliæ et Musæi Captivus, sacris Lectione
Precibus assiduus septuagenarius illæso visu: Memoria
Acumine Literar: Sanctæ, Græc. Lat. Gal. Ital. Callen
tiss[us] Ad Facetias Rhetoricen et Poeticen Præsenti Impetu
Theologus omni Literaturâ Instructiss[us] Apparatiss[us] Demum
PRÆDICATOR NUNQUAM SATIS PRÆDICANDUS ET DENIQ:
Robert Bellmain M[r.] Art. Ætatis Flore Placidissimi Ingenij Soeri vix prius successor in Ecclia
quam tumulo cum uxore
Philippâ[2] Thomæ Primogenita Fœminâ Eleganti Forma raris
Moribus et Multum Desideratâ.
AVE VIATOR ET CAVE
Ætatis omnis sexûs et Aliquor Hic jacent
obiit Thomas Hutton P. Prid. D. Thomæ

 Æt

D N I

10[bris]

 74

40

20

Huttonianis Manibus sacrum vides
Gnatus neposq. prodromi Medius pater
Filia Generq. vt asseclæ juxta Hic cvbant
Templo et Sepulchro proximum nacti locum
In Patrem Opt
E Lacrymis utinam solidarer petra salilli
vt Lapis Imponar Te super alme pater
Nil super Ingenij est subtus iacet Inq. sepulchro
Conditur omne tuo. nos tibi saxa sumus
Jam Vacua Ecclesia est Tumulusq. hæc saxea moles
Si non in Tumulo Hoc Ecclesia ipsa jacet
aliud
Londini cum sole Oreris mediâ Oxoniæ stas
Luce. Diem et Noctem Das Pater occiduis
W[mus.] Hutton Fil.
Posuit
Composuit

ARMS: 1. Guttee a cross flory. 2. On a fess 3 bucks' heads cabossed, differenced with a
crescent, impaling: a chev. betw. 3 covered cups. 3. Upon a Chev. between 3 garbs 3 hurtes (Opie).

[1] Mary daughter of Thomas Hutton married Nicholas Opie of Chapel Amble in St. Kew, and their son
William was buried there 9th October 1636, aged 11 months. See Pedigree of OPIE, ante p. 50.
[2] 1636, Robertus Belmayne, Clericus, et Philippa Hutton Nupt. 20 Oct.—1639, Philippa uxor M[ri] Roberti
Belmayne, hujus Ecclesiæ Vicar, sepult 6 Februarij.—1640, Robertus Belmayne, hujus Ecclesia Vicarius, sepult, 20
Aprilis.—P. R. St. Kew.

6. Around the margin of a well-cut slab:

Here lyeth yᵉ Bodie of John Cavell Esquier who departed this Life one the Tenth ⌊day⌋ of Januarie Anno Domini 1602. (Within the margin, Charitas crvde litatem Constringit.)

ARMS: 1. In the first compartment, quarterly 1st and 4th erm; a calf passant (Cavel). 2nd and 3rd an Old English 𝕿 crowned (for Treharrick). In the second compartment, Cavell impaling 3 roundels differenced with a mullet (Courtenay?) and on each side is a small escutcheon, that on the dexter Cavell impaling a two-headed eagle displayed between 3 fleurs de lis (Godolphin). On the sinister, Cavell impaling a lion ramp within a bordure eng (Pomeroy).

IN THE SOUTH CHAPEL.

7. Is a slate slab with a fragment of a large incised foliated cross together with the following inscription, and a shield bearing tho Carnsewe arms........Wiłłm Carnsuysuwe armig' qui...........die Aprił anno dni Milimo quingentessimo........

8. There is also another slab the inscription on which is almost illegible, all that can be deciphered is........Wiłłm..............January anno domini 1634.

9. Here lyeth John the son of John Hickes of Trewiggett of this Parish, born November yᵉ 20ᵗʰ, Baptized Decembʳ yᵉ 7ᵗʰ 1714, Dyed October yᵉ 7ᵗʰ, Buried yᵉ 9ᵗʰ 1715.

> Blest Innocents remou'd so soon
> We too officiously bemoan
> Tho Hoary headed one day may
> Enuy this—This Babe its short stay.

IN THE SOUTH AISLE.

10. Set in the sill of the second window from the east is a stone bearing the following inscription and arms:

Sacred to the Memory of Thomas Treffry, Esq., of Rooke anᵈ Place in Fowey, anᵈ Elizabeth his Wife, Daughter of John Kelligreᵂ, Esqʳ, he Dyed the 31ˢᵗ of Janʳʸ 1563. John Treffry his son married Jane daughter of Reginald Mohun, Esqʳ, had one Daughter, his Second Wife Emblyn Daughter of John Tresithnye, Esq., Nine Sons And Seven Daughters, he Dyed 28 January 1590. Mathew Treffry and Elizabeth his wife, Daughter of Somester he Dyed in the reigne of King James the First.

Thomas Treffry and Jane his Wife, Daughter of John Vivian of Trewan, Esq., he Married 1641.

Edward Treffry Married Susanna, Daughter of John Davie of Devon, had Five Sons and Five Daughters, he Dyed tho 18 July 1727.

Nicholas Treffry, youngest son of Edward and Susanna, he Dyed Decʳ 25th 1767, aged 60.

John Treffry, Esqʳ, Son of Nicholas and Mary his Wife, he Dyed April 1ˢᵗ 1770, aged 24.

ARMS: 1. Quarterly, 1st and 4th: sa. a chev. between three hawthorn trees in full bloom (Trefry) 2nd and 3rd az. 3 fleurs de lis or. (Giffard of Helland).

2. Treffry impaling three mascles (Kelligrew). 3. Treffry impaling a cross eng. (Mohun) 4. Treffry quartering: ar. a chev. sa. betw. 3 roses gu. (Tresythney). 5. Treffry impaling: 3 eagles' heads erased, upon a chief 3 martlets (Vivian). 6. Treffry quartering: ar a chev. sa. betw. 3 mullets pierced gu. (Davie).

11. Underneath this pew lyeth the body of Mary Treffry, Widow, of this Par⁴ʰ, who was buried the 22 day of July 1775, aged 63, and by her Will hath Expressly ordered that the ground under this pew shall never be open⁴ or broke up.

IN THE NAVE, ON THE FLOOR.

12. Here lies yᵉ Body of James the son of Constantine and Prudence Moyle of Trethevan of this Parish, who was buried yᵉ 25 day of May An° Dni 1744, Ætatis suæ 25.

Here also lies yᵉ Body of yᵉ above Constantine Moyle, Bury'd yᵉ 11ᵗʰ Day of April 1746, aged 76.

The above Prudence Moyle was Bury'd here yᵉ 7ᵗʰ of Jan. 1750, aged 73.

13. Here lyeth yᵉ Body of John the son of John and Mary Lang of Trevinnec in this parish who was buried yᵉ 23ʳᵈ of April 1742.

> My friends forbeare to grieve for me so sore
> I'm gone from hence you ne'er will see me more
> My life was short (you'l say) gone like a blast
> But now my trouble's o're my pains are past.

IN THE NORTH AISLE.

14. Neare this place Lye the Bodys of Margery the Wife of John Wills of this prish, who was buryed the 11ᵗʰ Day of Decbr. 1725, And Letticia Froade, her Grand-daughter, who was buryed the 24ᵗʰ Day of March 1720.

> Vertuous they lived whilst with us here
> And now yᵉ are gone to live with Christ their Saviour dear.
> All is vanity but Vertue.

16. In the sill of one of the windows is a slab bearing, in low relief, the recumbent figure of a woman, and below it three figures, two male and one female, kneeling. Around the margin is the following inscription deeply and clearly cut:

Here lyeth yᵉ body of Honor yᵉ wife of John Webber of Ambel, daughter to John Calwodley Esquire of Padsto, who died yᵉ vjᵗʰ of October 1601, and had issve Honor, Richard & Mathew.

IN THE CHURCHYARD.

16. Sacred to the Memory of John Treffry of this Parish, who was buried Feb^y· the 18th 1808, aged 40 years; also of Ann his wife, who was buried July the 6th 1809, aged 34 years; together with their four children:

John, was buried the 5 Nov^r· 1795, aged 9 weeks.

John Wilce Treffry, was buried the 26 of Oct. 1798, aged one year and 24 weeks.

Mary, was buried the 24th June, 1804, aged 24 weeks.

John, was buried the 15 March 1808, aged 27 weeks.

17. Around the margin of a slab on an altar tomb is the following inscription:

Here lyeth the body of John the sonne of John Bellamy of Drewstenton in the County of Devon, Gent, and Lucy the Daughter of John Nicholls of Trewane, Esq., who departed this Life on Tuesday the Seventh day of July 1702, aged 21.

In the middle, surmounted by the words "Remember Eternity," is an Escutcheon of Arms. On a bend three Crescents (Bellamy) impaling Nichols, and the following lines:

> Weep reader weep and let thy mournful eyes
> With tears embalm this young man's obsequies
> On his blest shrine, who had the ecchoing prays
> Of those that knew him. Studious were his ways.
> His Heart so rarely good, Piety did rest
> Within the Closet of his serious Brest.
> No oath, nor curse, was from his mouth ere known,
> Drunkeness and Pride by him was never shewn.
> Take Pattern all young men, Extoll his Prays,
> Bellamy deserved a double wreath of Bayes.
> All is Vanity but Virtue.

18. Underneath this Stone lies the Body of the Revd James Read, A.M., Vicar of this Par^sh who was buried the 12 day of Sept. Anno Domini 1760, Ætatis suæ 55. Also,

Here lies the Body of Jane wife of the aforesaid James Read, who was buried ye 25th Day of May 1752, Ætatis suæ 46; also,

Here lie the Bodies of Thomas and Judith Ann, Son and Daughter of the aforesaid James and Judith Read; Thomas was buried May 5th 1752, aged seven months. Judith Ann was buried May 16th 1752, aged 9 years.

19. Beneath this Stone lies the Body of James Read, M.D., of Tremeare, in the Parish of St. Tudy, who departed this life Novr the 12th 1800, aged 52.

Also under the Tomb of his father, the Rev. James Read, lies the Body of Loveday, wife of the abovementioned James Read, M.D., and eldest daughter of Trehane Symons, Esqr of Trevine in St. Minver, who departed this life March 25th 1821, aged 71.

19. On an altar tomb:

Here lyeth the Body of John Carne of this Parish, Gent., who departed this Life the 4ᵗʰ day of March Anᵒ Dom. 1709, Ætatis suæ 53.

> When I consider'd new Jerusalem
> Wherein's reserv'd my Crown, my diadem,
> Oh then I long'd the same for to enjoy
> And leave this world which doth my peace anoy!
> I come dear Lord, the floods here rise,
> These troubled seas, some nought but mire!
> Farewel false world Heaven's my desire.

Arms: A pelican in her piety. The shield is surmounted by an Esquire's helmet and wreath but there is no Crest.

20. In memory of Edward Grigge [Gent.] of Skisdon, who departed this life the 27ᵗʰ of [April] 1789, aged 78. Also of Mary his wife, who departed this life the 15ᵗʰ day of May 1757, aged 56.

21. Sacred to the memory of Rev. Joseph Bennett, ʟʟ.ʙ., late of Skisdon in this County who died the 17ᵗʰ of May 1789, aged 49.

22. Underneath this stone are deposited the Remains of the Rev. Trehane Symons Read, ᴀ.ʙ., who departed this life the 21 day of May 1809, aged 27 years: son of the late James Read, ᴍ.ᴅ., of Tremeare, in the parish of St. Tudy, and grandson of the Rev. James Read late Vicar of this Parish.

23. Against the south wall of the Church, outside, is a broken slate tablet with the following inscription around the margin:—

Here lyeth the Body of [Barb]ara the wife of [Wil]liam Brown of.................... of her age. May she rest in peace. Within the border:

Also, Here lyeth the Body of the said William Brown of this Pᵇʰ who Departed this Life yᵉ 9ᵗʰ day of May 1738, in the 72ⁿᵈ year of his age.

Also here lyeth the Body of Ann, yᵉ Daughter of the said William Browne and Barbara his wife, was buried yᵉ 27ᵗʰ ....

24. In memory of Nicholas, Father of John Phillips of the North Barton, Saint Kew, in this Parish, Gent., Was buried the 30ᵗʰ day of Janʸ anno domini 1779, in the 71 year of his age.

Also In Memory of Susanna, wife of the said John Phillipps, who departed this Life the 13ᵗʰ Day of Oct., anno dom. 1781, in the 51 year of his age.

Also, In Memory of Jane the 2ⁿᵈ Daughter of the said John and Susanna Phillipps, Was buried the 30ᵗʰ Day of March anno dom. 1781, in the 20 year of her age.

Also, In Memory of Gertrude her sister who died the 19 day of July 1785. In the 17 year of her age.

Q

25. Here Lyeth the Body of Phillippa the Daughter of Richard Hickes of this P.ʰ who was buried the 4ᵗʰ day of January 1724, in the 43ᵈ year of her age.

26. Here lyeth the Body of John Hickes of Trewigget, in this Parish, who was Buried on the 23 of April 1754, in the seventy-second year of his age.

Likewise here Lyeth the Body of Elizabeth the daughter of John Hickes, who was buried on the 16 of december 1753, in the thirty-seventh year of her age.

27. Near this Place lies the Body of Constantine Moyle of Trethevan in this Parish, Esqʳ·, who was buried the 6 Day of Febʳ· 1781, in the 80ᵗʰ year of his age.

Also, underneath this Tomb lies the Remains of Constantine Moyle of Trethevan in this Parish, Esqʳ, nephew of the above Constantine, who departed this Life 29 day of December 1800, aged 50.

Also, near this Place lie the Remains of Richard Moyle Esqʳ, Brother of the above named Constantine Moyle, who died the .... day of March 1802, aged .... years.

Also, near this Tomb on the north side lie the remains of Ann Hambly, the Widow of the last above named Constantine Moyle and Edmund Hambly Esqʳ· late of the parish of Menheniott in the County of Cornwall, who died the 22 day of July 1820, aged 73 years.

28. This stone is erected to the Memory of James Curgenven, late of Tretane in this Parish, who departed this life on the 15ᵗʰ day of Oct. 1846, aged 47 years.

29. To the Memory of Samuel Warne of Tregildren of this Parish, Gent., who departed this Life the 7ᵗʰ day of April in the year of our Lord 1779, in the 78ᵗʰ year of his age.

Also to the Memory of Samuel Burton of this Parish, who departed this Life yᵉ 3 day of Oct. 1802, aged 47 years.

Also in Memory of Samuel, the Son of the said Samuel Burton, who departed this Life April yᵉ 30 1805, aged 23 years.

30. In Memory of William Norris, Esqʳ, of Newton in this parish, youngest son of the late Rev. John Norris and Ann his wife, of Dulverton in the County of Somerset, who, after a lingering illness, departed this life the 12ᵗʰ day of August 1827, aged 34 years.

31. John Arscot Tickell, died Sept. 10 1856, aged 70.

Harriet Tickell, died July 17 1869, aged 79.

32. Sacred to the memory of the Rev. J. Scobell, Vicar of this Parish, who died suddenly the 26 day of February in the year of our Lord 1849, aged 43 years.

33. In Memory of Abraham Hambly, J.P., who died at Treharrock Oct. 13, 1827, aged 49 years.

Eliz. Hambly, wife of the above, who died Janʸ 11, 1831, aged 56 years.

Emma Hambly, 3 daughter, who died July 27, 1829, aged 20 years.

34. Here lies the Body of William, yᵉ son Richard and Jane Webber of this Par. who was buried yᵉ 17ᵗʰ day of Feb. 1762, in yᵉ 22 year of his age. Also in Memory of Rich. Webber of this Par., who departed this life yᵉ 19 day of May 1791, aged 93, the father of the above William.

35. Sacred to the Memory of Thomas Webber of this Parish, who departed this life the 1st of Feb. 1804, in the 74th year of his age. Also to the Memory of Ann, the wife of the above said Thomas Webber, who departed this life the 27 May 1780, in the 37 year of her age.

36. Sacred to the Memory of Elizabeth Webber, the wife of William Webber of Chapel Amble in this Parish, who departed this life the 16 Day of Oct. 1828, aged 65 years.

Also to the Memory of John Webber, son of the above said William and Elizth Webber, who departed this life the 12 Day of Sept. 1828, aged 25 years. Also to the Memory of the above William Webber, who died on the 31st Day of Decr. 1849, aged 87 years.

37. Sacred to the Memory of Richard Webber of Chapel Amble in this Parish, who departed this life on the 12 Day of Feb. 1832, in the 68 year of his age.

38. Sacred to the Memory of John Webber of Lands in this Parish, who departed this life on the 22 Day of April 1830, aged 63 years.

Also to the Memory of Nicholas Webber of Lower Amble in this Parish, brother of the above, who departed this life on the 22 day of August 1821, aged 49 years.

39. In Memory of Elizabeth the Wife of Samuel Webber of this Parish, who died the 14 Day of February 1832, aged 44 years; Also of Ann daughter of the above, who died 22 Day of Oct. 1840, aged 14 years; Also of John son of the above, who died 1 Day of June 1843, aged 12 years; Also to the Memory of the above Samuel Webber, who died on the 1 Day of Decr. 1846, aged 53 years.

PARISH REGISTERS.

The old registers consist of two volumes. The first commences in the year 1564, and the entries are transcribed in the same hand, in accordance with Act 1st James I, and Canon 70, from earlier records down to the year 1598. The pages in the early part are divided into four columns, and the entries of baptisms, marriages, and burials, are made indiscriminately as they occur. Arabic numerals are used throughout. The writing is in fair condition and the volume has recently been carefully rebound upon the old oak boards. The second volume extends from the year 1680 to 1794 and the entries are made in Latin until 1695, after which date English is used.

The earliest names are: Lynam,* Wade, Blake, Alee, Webber,* Inch,* Heyward, Trewboddie, Frode,* Harper, Britton,* Mathew,* Lymscott, Carnsewe, and Sobye, of which those marked with an asterisk are still found in the parish.

Q²

CHAPELS, CHANTRIES, ORATORIES, &c.

There was anciently a Chapel in the Cemetery, or Churchyard, in which the King's Priest celebrated for the benefit of the soul of the King and of his ancestors. It is mentioned in the Inquisition taken in 1391, from which Inquisition it appears that the Prior of Plympton was bound to keep it in repair. It it probable that when the Church was rebuilt, and doubtless greatly enlarged, this Chapel was absorbed into the edifice, and the Chapel on the north or south of the Chancel appropriated to the use of the King's Priest.

It appears from the certificate of the commissioners appointed to enquire into the value of the possessions of Chantries, Colleges, &c., dated 13th February 2nd Edward VI., "that a certyn tythe goyinge owte of certeyn townships on yᵉ north syde of yᵉ sayd paryshe were gyven by yᵉ prior of yᵉ late Monastary of Plemton, as yt shall appere by a composc'on thereof remaynyng in the said late Monastary to yᵉ Vicar of yᵉ sayd paryshe of Kue to fynde a prest to syng in yᵉ sayd Church, and to praye for the sowles of yᵉ Kyngs of the realme; whych prest is comenly called yᵉ Kyng's prest."[1] This confirms the opinion expressed above that the King's Chantry had been removed to within the Church. The endowment remained in abeyance for several years, but on 17th February 1562, directions were given for the preparation of a lease of the same to Roger Prideaux and Edmund and Nicholus Prideaux his sons, for the term of their lives successively, at the rent of 44s. per annum, which was stated to be the annual value of the endowment, but inasmuch as the same had not been paid for thirteen years, and Roger Prideaux "must try the title for the Queen's Majestie, and answer the rent, &c."[2] no fine was required.

The certificate above quoted shews also that there was "an obyte in yᵉ parysh Churche. Thomas Pore, executor to Thomas Reynolds, ys bound to paye yerely iijˢ iiijᵈ for keepyng of an obytt, of yᵉ profytts of the lands, goods and catalls of yᵉ sayd Reynolds, during v yeres to come."[3]

This endowment is charged upon an estate called Upton, *alias* Tupton, *alias* Tipton in this parish. We are unable to trace its proprietorship back to Thomas Reynolds. In the early part of the seventeenth century, or perhaps still earlier, it was parcel of the possessions of Francis Harper, and descended to his nephew and heir William Harper, whose son, of the same name, by deed dated 10th March 19th James (1621-2) sold the premises to Thomas Carne of St. Austell, Gent. It remained in the Carne family for more than a century, and by deed dated 10th April 1732, Richard Carne of Calstock, Yeoman, conveyed it to Stephen Hickes of Blisland, which Stephen Hicks, by deed dated 5th May 1st George III. (1761)[4] sold it to Christopher Lean of Blisland, Yeoman, whose descendant, of the same name, is now the possessor.

---

[1] Augmentation Office, Cert. 9, No. 40.   [2] Augmentation Office Particulars for Leases, Roll 5. No. 25.
[3] Augmentation Office, Cert. 9, No. 40.   [4] Deeds in possession of the proprietor.

Notwithstanding that on 13th February 1547-8, the Royal Commissioners certified that the stipend in question was payable for five years then to come only, it has been regularly paid down to the present time. The late proprietor made an application to the Commissioners of Woods and Forests and Land Revenues, objecting to the title of the crown to the continuance of this payment, and submitting that the land should be discharged, and was informed that, "without discussing the terms of the certificate, the subsequent payment for 300 years is a sufficient evidence that the rent did not cease at the end of five years mentioned in the Certificate, and that it is payable in perpetuity!"

Besides the Chapels in the Parish Church, there were two other Chapels situate in the parish. One was at Ammel, or, as it is now called, Amble, and the tenement on which the Chapel stood is from it designated, "Ammal Eglos" or "Chapel Amble." This Chapel was dedicated to St. Aldhelm. Our first notice of it is on 29th March 1383, when we find that the Bishop granted a license to Mr. John Roscarrek, Vicar of Landohou, to celebrate divine offices in the Chapel of St. Aldelam of Ammell, situate within that parish. And on 23rd May 1405, Bishop Stafford licenced Nicholas Helygan and Emmot his wife, and Roger and Nicholas their sons, also Richard Chousyng, Edmund Smith, and Isote his wife, Nicholas Soby and Johanna his wife, Richard Waltey and Juliana his wife, Walter Burat and Margaret his wife, William Gebus and his wife, to have divine service celebrated in their presence by a fit priest in the Chapel of St. Aldelm of Ammel in the parish of Lannow, provided no prejudice, or inconvenience, arose to the mother Church. Ammel is two miles distant from the Parish Church, and these parties, we presume, were the chief inhabitants of the hamlet at the time.[1]

The exact site of this Chapel is not known, though it was doubtless in or near a field called "Chapel Meadow." Contiguous to this field human remains have frequently been found. Not long since in digging the foundations for a house a skeleton was disinterred; the skull was quite perfect with all the teeth firmly set.

Several pieces of window tracery of Early Third-Pointed work in Catacluse stone, shewing the excellence which characterised this style on its first introduction towards the end of the fourteenth century, are built up in the walls of cottages and outbuildings near the supposed site of the Chapel.

Chapel of St. Wenne. We do not know the site of this Chapel. On 11th October 1379, John Huda and Dionisia his wife had licence for the celebration of Divine Service in their presence in the Chapel of St. Wenne in the Parish of Lanowe for one year.[2] This was afterwards renewed, and in 1425 a similar license was granted to Robert Estcote of St. Kew for the Chapel of St. Wenne and in other Chapels and Oratories within his Manor of Pengywe (?).

[1] Bishop Stafford's Reg. fo. 75.   [2] Bishop Brantingham's Reg. fo. 76.

On 26th August 1387, Henry Cavell and his wife had licence for a Chapel or Oratory within their Mansion of Trehanget (? Treharrek) in the Parish of Lannowe,[1] and on 5th September 1400, Nicholas Bokelly and Alice his wife had a like licence for his Oratory in his Mansion of Bokelly.[2]

CHARITIES.

By his charter dated at St. Kew 16th March 37th Elizabeth (1594), John Dagg of Trewyget, Gent., for divers good causes and considerations him thereunto moving, granted to Richard Carnsewe, Esq., William Cavell, Gent., John Nicholl, Gent., John Lynam of Treverian, William Can, Nicholas Inch, and Richard Dagg, all those messuages, &c., in Smythe's Land, *alias* Smythes, juxta Rosenvallen, in the Parish of St. Kew, to hold to the said Richard Carnsewe and the others and to their heirs and assigns for ever to their sole use and profit, and he appointed John Webber of Amell and John Mathy his lawful attornies to deliver seizin. There is an indorsement stating that possession was taken of the land on 26th September 38th Elizabeth (1596.)

By indentures dated 20th November 39th Elizabeth (1596), the above mentioned grantees, upon the surrender of an old lease by John Lobb of Hender, granted the said premises to the said John Lobb and Haniball his son under the description of all those messuages, &c., called Smythes, otherwise Reddy Smythe, and stated to be abutting on the east part with the middest of the highway, on the south with the hedges of the land called Hender, being now the inheritance of one Crewes, and once the land of Glyn of Lanhedrock, on the west with Rosenvallen, and on the north with the lands of Newton, being the west side of the aforesaid highway.

These records do not shew the purpose of the grant, but this is disclosed by a deed dated 25th February 18th Charles (1642-3), reciting a grant of the same premises by William Cavell of Trehaverock, Esq., possibly the last survivor of the above-mentioned grantees, to Thomas Treffry, John Lynam, William Inche, John Blake, George Carnsewe, Richard Archer, and Richard Webber, these grantees declare that the said premises were granted and conveyed to them, in trust only, for and to the use of the reparations of the Parish Church of St. Kew.

These lands appear in the parish map as two enclosures, numbered respectively 1703 and 1704, and called "Great Smeators" and "Little Smeators," containing together 14a. 3r. 28p., and the premises are now let at £20 a year, the rent being applied as above directed.

Mr. Degory Dagge of St. Kew, Yeoman, by his will dated 8th October 1622,[3] gave to the parish of St. Kew £20, to be paid to the gentlemen, eight men, and the Vicar, to be invested, and the use thereof to be divided amongst the poor of the said

---

[1] Bishop Brantingham's Reg.   [2] Bishop Stafford's Reg.
[3] Proved, 21st October 1626. Helc. 134.

parish hereafter for ever. He made also a similar bequest to the parish of St. Minver, and gave "to the poor people of the Alms House or Chapell of Bodmin called St. Anthonye's Chapell, 40ˢ."

By his will dated 15th June 11th Charles (1635),[1] William Inch of St. Kew, the elder, bequeathed towards the reparation of the Church of St. Kew £10, to be invested for that purpose; and also to the poor of the parish £20, to be invested, and the interest disposed of at the discretion of the Vicar for the time being. He also gave 40ˢ to each of the following parishes towards the reparation of the Churches, viz., Endellion, St. Tudy, Michaelstow, and Minster.

Mrs. Diana Nation, widow, by her will, dated 12th January 1775,[2] bequeathed the sum of £100 to the Vicar and Overseers of the Poor of the Parish of St. Kew, to be laid out as described ante p. 102.

Schools.—There is a National School adjoining the churchyard gate on the west of the Church, which will accommodate eighty children. It is conducted on the mixed principle, and is now (1873) nearly full. It is reported that further accommodation is required for ninety-three children. These are at the outlying hamlets of Amble and Trelill, each of which places is distant two miles from the Parish Church.

MANOR OF LANNOWMURE.[3]

This manor, as we have already stated (ante p. 84), was taxed in *Domesday* together with Lanowseynt under the name of Lannoho. Two carucates of lands held by the king

---

[1] Proved P.C.C., 17th November, 1637 (152 Goare.)

[2] Proved in Archd. Court of Cornw. 18th August, 1784.

[3] Lannowmure, like most other important ancient manors, was a tithing of itself, *e.g.*, "Stephen Grazelen slew Mark Sweta at Lannomur, and forthwith put himself in the Church of Sancte Tethe de Lannomur. Therefore his goods were confiscated for a fugitive, and the sheriff answered for 20s. 1d. And the same Stephen afterwards rendered himself to peace and was presently taken and set at liberty by Robert de Stokkeye then Sheriff. Therefore he to answer for him. Afterwards it is witnessed that the said Stephen abided in the County. Therefore he should be taken. Afterwards came the aforesaid Robert Stokkey and said that he was not Sheriff of this county when the same Stephen rendered himself in prison but Theobald de Nevill. Afterwards the same Stephen came, as appears in the gaol delivery." (Assize Rolls, 30th Edward I., Crown Pleas, Hund. Trigg, m. 57) From this it would appear that the Church of St. Teath was at this time within the Manor of Lannomur. "The jury presented that John Scott ̣of Trelulla and Alice the wife of Thomas Collan were indicted before the Sheriff at his court of stealing crowbars and wool and of committing other robberies, and were presently taken and delivered to the custody of the tithing of Lannomur, which same John and Alice from the custody of the same tithing escaped. Therefore to judgment of escape of the said John and Alice upon the tithing of Lannomur and upon the Hundred of Trigg; and the said John and Alice presently after had escaped and were fugitives. Therefore the chatels of the said John to be taken, and the Sheriff answered for 14s. And it was in the tithing of Lannomur. Therefore in mercy, and the aforesaid Alice had no chattels, therefore in mercy." Idem, m. 57d.

in demesne, and the advowson of the Church having been given by King Henry I. to the Bishop of Exeter, the residue remained vested in the Crown[1] until 7th Richard I. (1196), when Richard Reuel, then Sheriff, accounted for the sum of £10 2s. 6d. which he had received for three quarters of a year from Simon Pincerna (the butler) for lands given him by the king in Lanho.[2] We conclude that the lands were granted in this year. During the remainder of the reign of Richard, Simon paid the rent of £13 10s. per annum; but on the accession of King John, the rent appears to have been reduced. In the 2nd of that King[3] (1201) 105s. only were paid, and the rent of £10 10s. per annum was afterwards paid during the reign of King John, and scutage for half a knight's fee when it happened.

Simon was dead in 1213, for we have a record that in that year Simon, son of Simon le Butiller, offered the king one palfrey for his relief of half a knight's fee which Simon his father held of the king in Lanhowe.[4] This appears to have been refused, for in the following year the sheriff accounted for 30 marks or 6 palfreys given by Simon Pincerne for lands in Lanho of the inheritance of Simon his father; and in the same year Simon de Pincerne paid 12s. 6d. scutage for half a fee.[5] In 7th Henry III. (1223) Simon de Pincerna paid £10 10s. rent in Lanho, and 3s. 4½d. scutage for half a fee, and in the following year 8s. 4d.; whilst in 10th Henry III. he gave half a mark to have an inquisition against Margaret de Newburgh. In 19th Henry III., the collectors of the aid granted to the king upon the marriage of Isabella his sister to the Emperor Frederick accounted for 8s. 4d. for half of a small fee of Simon Pincerna in Lanho.[6] In 29th Edward I. Simon Pincerna paid rent at £10 10s. per annum in Lanho, and in the following year the sheriff accounted for 8d. of wreck of the sea, which he had received in the tithing of Lanhoumur. The annual rent of £10 10s. continued to be paid in the name of Simon Pincerna down to 1314,[7] after which we find no further trace of it.

Notwithstanding, however, that the rent in question continued to be paid to the date above stated, in the name of Simon Pincerne, as early as the year 1283 Lanhomur was vested in Ralph Reynward, who suffered a fine in two messuages and two carucates of land in Lanomur and Lanyvet, and the Advowson of the Church of Lanyuet to Hugh de Munckton and Katherine his wife, whereby it was settled that the premises should be held to the use of the said Hugh and Katherine and the heirs of their bodies, and in default of such issue remainder to Nicholas Munckton, uncle of Hugh and Margery his wife and the heirs of their bodies, and for this fine the said Ralph gave the said Hugh one sparrow hawk fully fledged.[8]

In 1299 a fine passed in the same lands in Lanhoumur, in which Robert Gyffard and Katherine his wife were querists, and Martin Gyffard deforciant, whereby they were

---

[1] The men of Lanho paid 48s. 2d. as Tallage of Gift in 1st Richard I., Rot. Pip.

[2] Rot. Pip., 7th Richard I.   [3] Rot. Pip., 2nd John.

[4] Abbrevatio placitorum, p. 91.   [5] Rot. Pip., 16th John.

[6] Testa de Nevill, p. 201.   [7] Rot. Pip. 7th Edward II.

[8] Pedes Finium, 11th Edward I., Easter No. 2.

settled upon the said Robert and Katherine for their lives, with remainder to Nicholas son of the same Robert and his heirs,[1] and in 1300 the land was vested in Robert Giffard who, upon the death of Edmund Earl of Cornwall, was returned as holding one fee of the Earl, of the value of £10, in Lanhoghau;[2] and two years later, at the assizes at Launceston, Robert Giffard and Katherine his wife petitioned against Roger Gentilcors of one messuage in Lannohmur of the right of the said Katherine, in which he alleged the said Roger had no entrance except through the intrusion into it after the death of Peter Gentilcors to whom Roger Pentec the father of the said Katherine, whose heir she is, demised it for the life of the said Peter, and that after the death of the said Peter it ought to revert to the said Robert.[3] At the same assize Robert Giffard and Katherine his wife petitioned against Gilbert de Condre concerning one messuage and one carucate of land in Treuentheuyn juxta Lanhomur as of the right of Katherine, and into which, he said, the said Gilbert had no ingress except by Isolda, who was the wife of Thomas Prideaux to whom Roger Prideaux demised it, who thereof unjustly disseized Laurence Pentec, brother of the aforesaid Katherine, whose heir she is. And Gilbert appeared and said that he held the tenement by the law of England for his life of the inheritance of a certain Roger, son and heir of the aforesaid Isolda de Pridias. Roger appeared upon summons and said that the aforesaid Roger de Pridias did not disseize the aforesaid Laurence de Pentec the brother of Katherine. The jury gave their verdict for Robert and Katherine who recovered seizin, and Gilbert and Roger remained in mercy for a false claim.[4] At the same assize the jury of the County in their presentments stated that Robert Giffard and Katherine his wife held the Manor of Lannomure of the gift of the King in capite, and that the value was £10 per annum.[5] In the next year Robert Giffard was associated with Thomas de la Hyde, then Sheriff, to make inquisition as to the number of Knights' fees in the County, and in full assembly of the County at Lostwithiel, on Monday next after the feast of the Nativity of the Blessed Mary 31st Edward I., and upon the oaths of Robert le Brune, Benedict Reynward, Henry Cavel, Richard Roscaret, John Billun, John le Seneschal, Baldwin Roscaret, and others, it was found, *inter alia*, that Robert Gyffard held in Lannowmur half a fee.[6]

In 5th Edward II. Laurence de Tremur recovered seizin against Katherine, who was the wife of Robert Giffard, and Nicholas Giffard of the third part of one messuage, one

---

[1] Pedes Finium, 27th Edward I., Michaelmas No. 1.

[2] Inq. p. m. Edmund, Earl of Cornw., 28th Edward I., No. 44.

[3] Assize Rolls, Cornwall, 30th Edward I., $\frac{M}{1}$ $\frac{}{21}$ 1 m. 17

[4] Assize Rolls, Cornwall, 30th Edward I., $\frac{M}{1}$ $\frac{}{21}$ 1 m. 6 d.   [5] Ibid. m. 58d.

[6] Original Inquisitions taken upon fees in co. Cornwall, 31st Edward I., Sub. Rolls $\frac{87}{4}$

R

mill, two carucates of land, six acres of meadow, twenty acres of wood, and £10 rent in Lanhomur.[1]

On the aid of 40s. for each knight's fee granted in 1346 on the king's eldest son being made a knight, the return of which shews the names of those who held the same fees when the aid was granted to King Edward I. on the marriage of his eldest daughter, the Lord Duke was returned for half a fee in Lanoumur by reason of the minority of the heir of John Giffard, which Robert Giffard sometime held, and paid 20s.[2]

John Giffard was dead in 33rd Edward III.[3] (1359), and Roger his son had entered into possession, for on 2nd July in that year it was ordered that proof of age should be obtained of Roger Giffard, son of John Giffard of Lannovmur, and on 26th November in the same year, he was summoned to attend the Prince's council concerning his age. It is presumed he did not appear, for on 13th February following it was directed that the lands should be resumed because livery had been given before he became of full age. On 2nd May 1361, however, it was commanded that livery of seizin should be given notwithstanding that he was still a minor.[4] He appears, however, not to have lived long to enjoy it, for on 23rd May in the following year, a writ was ordered for taking an inquisition, *inter alia*, on the deaths of John Giffard and Roger Giffard.[5] This inqusition is not in existence, but in 1392, Roger had been succeeded by Henry Giffard, probably his brother, who sued John Osbert of Trelull and others for trespass and breaking down his trees and underwood in Lannomur.[6] Henry Giffard, by deed dated on Tuesday next after the feast of Holy Trinity 5th Henry IV. (1404) granted, *inter alia*, the Manor of Lannovmur to John Boscawenros[7] from which date we have no trace of the family of Giffard being connected with the Manor.

Soon after this the manor would seem to have passed, in some way which we have not discovered, to the family of Lanhergy, but what estate that family held in it is not very clear. On the inquisition taken after the death of John Lanhergy, who died on Monday next after the feast of All Saints 8th Henry IV.[8] (1406), the jury found that he was seized of two parts of a rent of £6 0s. 6d., growing out of the Manor of Lannowmeur, which he held in capite of the Duke of Cornwall by the third part of one Knight's fee, and that John Lanhergy was his son and nearest heir, and was of the age of 21 years and more. In 16th Henry VI. (1438) Thomas

---

[1] Rot. Orig. m. 23 (Vide Abbrev. Rot. Orig. p. 192.)

[2] Queen's Rem. Office, Misc. Books—"Book of Aids," fo. 34.   [3] Nevertheless, upon the inquisition taken in 1378, after the death of Edward Prince of Wales, among the fees in Cornwall is returned half of one knight's fee in Lannowmur which John Giffard holds, value £12 per annum. (Inq. p.m. 2nd Richard II., No. 57.) It is not unusual, as we have before observed, to retain on the king's books the name of a tenant long after his decease.

[4] Council Book, Edward the Black Prince, pp. 412, 435, 470, 476 (Duchy of Cornwall Office).

[5] Ibid. p. 495.   [6] De Banco Rolls, 15th Richard II., Hil. m. 67.

[7] Assize Rolls, 8th Henry Henry IV. 2 $\frac{N}{37}$ } 4 m. 90. See post, FAMILY OF GIFFARD.

[8] Inq. p.m., 2nd Henry V., No. 5.

Lanhergy, supposed to be the son of the last named John, as Lord of Lannomur received the relief of Nicholas Colapyn due to the Lord of the Manor upon the death of John Colapyn the tenant of Tretawne.[1] This Thomas Lanhergy was Burgess in Parliament for the Borough of Bodmin in the 15th, 27th, and 28th Henry VI.[2] It is presumed that he must have obtained some change in the tenure by which he held this manor, for upon the usual inquisition taken at Launceston on 2nd November 1465, after his death, the jury found that on the day of his death he held no lands in Cornwall of the King in demesne or in service, that he died on the last day of April preceding, and that Johanna, wife of Edmund Beket, was his sister and nearest heir and was aged forty years and more.[3]

After the death of Thomas Lanhergy the manor appears to have descended to the Bevilles, as the heirs of Edmund Beket. In the return of 1522 (Appendix ii.) Peter Bevill, who married Phillippa Bere, great grand-daughter of Edmund Beket,[4] held lands in St. Kew of the value of £9 a year. He also appears to have been resident in the parish, and to have possessed goods of the value of 100 marks, and arms for one man.

By deed, dated 12th March in 40th of Elizabeth, Philip Bevill of Brenne, Esq., and John Bevill, of Poltreworgie, Gent., conveyed, *inter alia*, the manor of Lanowmuer to Barnard Greynville of Stowe, Esq., for the term of twenty-one years, with remainder to the Queen and her heirs and successors, subject, however, to the proviso that if the said Philip and John should tender to the said Barnard the sum of £20 in the church-porch of Kilkington, the bargain should cease.[5] It coming, however, to the knowledge of King James I. that the object of this conveyance was to disable Sir William Bevill, Knt., and the heirs of his body of the power which they then had to convey the premises to any party they should think meet, and detesting all indirect covenant practices, especially such as tend to overthrowing of common assurance of lands, he granted to Sir Francis Manners, Knight of the Bath, and Philip Beville of Brenne, all the reversion which was then vested in the crown by reason of the aforesaid conveyance.[6]

Bernard Grenville, in 1592, married Elizabeth daughter and heir of Philip Beville, and was the father of the illustrious Sir Beville Grenville[7] who in right of his mother eventually inherited this manor, and by deed dated 24th December 3rd Charles I.[8] (1627), sold the same to William Noy, Esq., afterwards (1631) attorney-general to King Charles I. Dying in 1634 it descended to his son Edward Noy, who, in 1636, was killed in a

---

[1] See post sub TRETAWNE. [2] Ante Vol. i., p. 242.

[3] Inquisition p.m. 5th Edward IV. No. 50.

[4] See Pedigree, ante Vol. I., p. 311, in which, however, following the Pedigree recorded into the Heralds' College, Johanna Lanhergy is stated to have been the *daughter* and heir of Thomas Lanhergy, whereas the Inquisition proves that she was his *sister*, so that he died s. p.

[5] Deed inrolled in Common Pleas Recovery Roll, 46th Elizabeth, Easter, m. 6.

[6] Rot. Pat. 3rd James, Part 10, m. 4.

[7] "Barnard Grenvile, Esq., et Elizabetha Beville nupt. 10th July 1592." "Bevill, filius Barnardij Grenfille, armiger, bapt. 1st March 1595." Withiel Par. Reg.

[8] Inrolled at the Assizes at Launceston and fine thereon paid.

R²

duel by a Captain Byron,[1] and the lands passed to his brother Humphry Noy of Carnanton, though incumbered by heavy legacies under his brother's will.[2] For the payment of these legacies Humphry Noy mortgaged the manor of Lanowe, and, *inter alia*, a messuage in Tregeare, then or late in the occupation of .... Loveys, widow, and Sir Samuel Rolle, Knt., for the sum of £1500, and having been included in the Commission of Array by the king, his estates were sequestrated. On the 6th February 1646, he was allowed to compound for them by the payment of a tenth of the value under the Articles of Truro, the mortgage being allowed.[3]

After the restoration Sir John Grenville, Knight, subsequently created Earl of Bath, son of Sir Beville Grenville, claimed, *inter alia*, this Manor from Humphry Noye, and served his tenants with writs of ejectment compelling them to pay double their accustomed rents, as the condition of holding their leases. The case was tried at the assizes at Launceston, and the Earl of Bath obtained the verdict. Humphry Noy appealed to the Court of Chancery, complaining of the wrong which he had sustained in the loss both his purchase money and estate, and a decree was issued for a new trial at Common Law. When the cause came on for hearing Noy proved that Sir Bevill Grenville was tenant in tail of the lands in question, and that he levied a fine and executed a deed declaring the same to be to the use of William Noy and his heirs and assigns for ever, and thereupon obtained the verdict. The Earl of Bath, however, filed a cross bill against Noy, praying a writ of injunction to stay further proceedings, and retained possession of the estate. Noy being weary of the controversy sold his interest to Mr. Christopher Davies of Burnewall in St. Burian, and the suit was eventually compromised, leaving the manor in possession of the Earl of Bath. The details are fully related by Hals.[4]

This manor was subsequently sold to John Lord Mohun whose great grandson Charles 5th Lord Mohun of Okehampton dying 1712,[5] s.p., his title became extinct, and he devised all his real estate to Elizabeth Lady Mohun his widow. She subsequently married the Honorable Charles Mordaunt, who, on 30th July 1720, joined with her in the sale of the Cornish estates to Thomas Pitt of Old Sarum, co. Wilts, Esq., *including the Manors of Lanowe and Ammal*, from whom, as described ante p. 97, they descended to Anne Lady Grenville, who dying without issue in 1865, bequeathed Boconnoc and all her Cornish lands to her husband's nephew, the Honorable George Mathew Fortescue, second son of Hugh first Earl Fortescue by Hester daughter of the Right Honorable George Grenville.[6]

---

[1] Davies Gilbert's History of Cornwall, iii. 156.

[2] Will dated 16th March 1635, proved 7th April, 1636.

[3] Royalist Comp. Papers, 2nd series, vol. xxxvi., ff. 253—280.

[4] Davies Gilbert's History of Cornwall, ii., pp. 332—335.

[5] He was slain in a duel with the Duke of Hamilton which proved fatal to both antagonists.

[6] Deed at Boconnoc.

Rental of the Manor of Lanow, 1748. From the Muniments at Boconnoc.

Tenants.	Tenements.	Total of Rents.		
		£	s.	d.
CHIEF RENTS.				
Archer, William, Esq.	Polgarrow	0	0	1
Bawden, Hugh	Treburgett	0	11	0
Cheney, Edmund, Esq.	Bodwine	0	1	2
Dingle, Mr., his heirs	Lower Suffenton	0	4	0
Ditto	Hills	0	0	2
Glynn, Madam	Trewane	1	4	5½
Glynn, Madam, the same	Watt's Tenement in Treburgett	0	3	0
Keigwyn, Esq., his heirs	Tatawn	0	6	8
Lang, Mr. John, his heirs	Tregellist	0	0	2½
Ditto	Fentengoge	0	0	1
Ditto	Hockin's Tregellist	0	0	2½
Lyne, Mr. John	Suffenton	0	5	8
Molesworth, Sir John	Bokelly	0	5	0
Peter, Mr. John, his heirs	Treharrick	0	0	2
COVENANT RENTS.				
Brown, William	Penquite	2	1	0
Ditto	Hockin's Penquite	1	0	4
Burton	Trewethan and Jagoe's Close	0	19	0
Dancaster, John	Penventinew	2	2	10
Ditto	Little Treverra	0	10	0
Doble, Mr. Stephen	Barton of Lanow	3	8	4
Hamley, John, Esq.	Poltreworgey	2	0	0
James, Philip	Barton of Clifton	2	0	0
Lang, John, his heirs	Trecugoe	2	1	4
Moyle, Mr. Constantine	Tregildras	2	0	0
Philip, Mr. Thomas	Lanow Mill, 3 little closes, a moor and a house	0	13	4
Ditto	Hockin's Lanow	1	10	0
Ditto	Butten's Lanow	1	0	0
Ditto	Tinney's Lanow	0	15	0
Warn, Mr. Samuel	Tregildras	2	2	10
In hand. N.B. Mr. Lewis	Fox in Bodmyn	..	..	..
		£27	5	10½

The manor is now dismembered, and courts have ceased to be held for many years.

THE MANOR OF AMAL, *alias* AMMAL, *alias* AMBLE.

The Manor of Amal was one of the 248 Manors in Cornwall granted by the Conqueror to the Earl of Moreton. At the time of the Domesday Survey it was held of the Earl by one Turstin.[1] "The Earl holds one manor which is called Amal, which was held by Grim on the day on which King Edward was alive and dead. There he has half a hide and it renders gild for two ferlings. This three ploughs can plough. This is held by Turstin of the Earl, and he has thereof one ferling and one carucate in demesne, and the villans have the rest of the land. There Turstin has four bordars, and five bond servants, and twenty acres of pasture, and the value is six shillings, and when the Earl received it 10 shillings."[2]

Turstin held also the Manor of Pencarrow and the fee of these two manors became vested in the family of Dynham, of which fee Joceus de Dynham died siezed in 29th Edward I. (1301). At this time it seems to have been divided, Richard de Stapledon holding of Joceus in Pencarrow and Ammel half a fee of the value of 100s., and John the son of William holding in Ammel of Richard the ninth part of a fee worth 60s.[3] This manor was derived by Sir Richard Stapledon from Walter Hay (see ante, Vol. i., p. 442) and it became designated Amal-eglos from the Chapel founded thereon, whilst the other part was called Amal Richard.

Sir John Dauney, Knight, died in the feast of St. Lawrence (10th August) 1346, seized, *inter alia*, of six acres of land and a half, Cornish, in Ammalmur which he held to him and the heirs male of his body, in default of such issue remainder to Richard son of Alice who was the wife of John Daumarle and the heirs male of his body, in default of such issue remainder to Thomas son of Isabell de Kilgath and the heirs male of his body, and in default to William Dauney and the heirs male of his body, in default remainder to John brother of Nicholas Dauney and the heirs male of his body, and in default of such issue remainder to the right heirs of the said John Dauney; and the jury say he held Amalmur of Margaret de Donedale as of her Manor of Cardynan by the third part of one Knight's fee, and that the value per annum, in all its issues, was £12 15s. The jury say further that he held lands in Ammalgres, &c., of John de Arundell, in pure socage as of his Manor of Trembleith.[4]

---

[1] The same (Turstin) holds Amal. Grim held it in the time of King Edward, and it is gilded for two ferlings, now there is half a hide of land and three ploughs. There is one plough, and four bordars, and five bond servants, and twenty acres of pasture. Formerly it was worth 10s. now 6s. Excheq. Domesday. Vol. i. p. 22b.

[2] Exon Domesday Vol. iv., p. 219. Orig. m. 239.

[3] Inq., p.m. 29th Edward I., No. 56, and extent of the possessions of Joceus de Dynham which he held of the King in capite on the day on which he died.

[4] Inquisition, p.m. 20th Edward III., No. 33st (1st Nos.).

In the following year at the Assizes at Launceston, an Assize of view of recognizance was granted to enquire of Sibella who was the wife of John Dauney, Chr., Richard son of Alice Daumarle, Edward de Courtenay and Emma his wife, John Bereware, Parson of Cornwood, Adam Bryan, Parson of Lamana, Hugh de Arwoythel, and John Daberon had unjustly disseized Reginald de Mohoun of his free tenements, *inter alia*, in Ammalmur, Ammalgres, Ammaleglos, Arwoythel juxta Restronget, and Trecradek juxta Seynt Ethe. Sibella and the others appeared by their attorney and said the assize ought not to proceed because the lands had been seized into the King's hands by John Daberon the Eschaetor, who, being in Court, was examined and said that the lands had been so seized under the King's writ upon the death of John Dauney, Chr., and an inquisition taken thereupon, and that from this cause the lands remained in the King's hand. The jury found that John Bereward had unjustly disseized the aforesaid Reginald to his damage to the extent of £372 13s. 4d., and that the others were not culpable. Reginald thereupon recovered his seizin and damages, and John Bereward was in mercy, whilst Reginald Mohun was in mercy for a false claim against the others.[1]

The manor continued to be held by the family of Mohun for a considerable time. Sir William Mohun, Knt., died thereof seized on 6th April 1588, as held of John Arundell and others as of their Manor of Cardinham, leaving Reginald Mohun his son, aged 23 years, his heir.[2] On the inquisition taken 12th June 1588, after the death of Thomas Roscarrock, it was found that he held Trethavake of Reginald Mohun as of his Manor of Ambell Richard.[3] Reginald Mohun here mentioned was created a baronet in 1612, and in 1628 his son John Mohun was raised to the dignity of a peer as Baron Mohun of Okehampton. Warwick Lord Mohun his son, the third baron, having adhered to the king in the rebellion of the 17th century was in 1650 admitted to compound for his estates at two years' value (the fine amounting to £2090), *inter alia*, the Manor of Amell which was returned as worth £22 per annum before the year 1640,[4] and to be improvable after lives to £275 per annum. From Lord Mohun this manor has descended to the Honble. G. M. Fortescue as before described with respect to the Manor of Lanowmure, ante p. 120.

---

[1] Assize Rolls, Cornwall, 21st Edward III., $\frac{N}{2}$ } 3 m. 3.
  22 }

[2] Inq. p.m. 30th Elizabeth, Part 2, No. 43.

[3] Inq. p.m. 30th Elizabeth, Part i., No. 82.

[4] Royalist Composition Papers, 2nd series, Vol. xxx., fo. 439—465.

Rental of the Manor of Ammell, 1748. From the Muniments at Boconnoc.

Tenants.	Tenements.	Total of Rents.		
		£	s.	d.
CHIEF RENTS.				
Bennett, Thomas, his heirs.	Carnmarrow-	0	14	0
Cock, Mr. Joseph	Carnmarrow-	0	11	0
Darrell, Esq., his heirs	Trewornan -	0	18	0
Hambly, Esq., his heirs	Trefrecke -	0	1	0
Hodge, Thomas	Trefrean -	0	5	0
Radnor, Lord, his heirs	Middle Amel	0	1	4
Rawling, his heirs	Rosewin -	0	3	6
COVENANT RENTS.				
Basset, Madam	A Messuage and Tenement in Trevanger -	1	1	0
Bullock, Mr. Richard, his executors	Trund's Tenement in Lower Amel -	2	2	0
Cann, James	Smith's Tenement in Porteath	1	8	8
Collins, William	Hender's Tenement in ditto	0	14	4
Ditto	Plain Street, alias Gunvena	0	9	6
Harry, Mr. John	John Webber's, Tenement in Lower Amel -	2	2	0
Ditto	Thomas Webber's, Tenement in Lower Amel	2	2	0
Higgs, Jonathan	A Moiety of Trevego Fields in Porteath -	0	14	4
Hodge, Thomas	Trevesoc, Dallie's Tenement -	1	8	8
Ditto	Rounsevall's Tenement in Trevesoc -	1	8	8
Kent, Philip	Bradford's Tenement in Trevesoe -	1	8	8
		£17	16	8
Moyle, Mr. Constantine	Nicholl's Tenement in Trethevan -	0	14	0
Proffitt, Joseph	Downing's Tenement in Chapple Amel -	1	1	6
Rebouse, John	Long's Tenement in Porteath -	1	8	8
Triplett, Elizabeth	Jeffery's Tenement in Lower Amel	2	3	0
Webber, Ezekiel, Esq.	Amel Greys, alias King's Tenement in Middle Amel	2	3	0
	Total of the Manor of Ammell -	£25	6	10

MANOR OF PENPONS, *alias* PENPOWNTE, *alias* PENPONTE.

One knight's fee in the manors of Boconnoc, Glyn and Penpont, as pertaining to the manor of Lantyan, was held by the family of Monthermer. In 1283 Penpon is mentioned as a separate tithing in the hundred of Tryggeshyse.[1] Ralph de Monthermer, who married Joane Plantagenet, daughter of king Edward I., and in her right and during her life was summoned to Parliament as Earl of Gloucester and Hertford,

[1] Ass. Roll 11th Edward I., m. 8.

granted the manor of Lantyan and the fees thereto pertaining to his son, Edward Monte Hermer, and the heirs of his body. Edward died s. p., and the said manor remained to Thomas Monte Hermer son of the said Ralph and brother of Edward, and the heirs of his body. Thomas died s. p., seized of one knight's fee in Boconnoc, Glyn and Penpont, leaving a sole daughter and heir who became the wife of Sir John de Montacute,[1] second son of William, first earl of Salisbury, which John was summoned to Parliament as "John de Montacute, Chr." He died 4th March 1390, seized, *inter alia*, of the said fee, the value of which was stated to be 66s. 8d. per annum; and also of one fee in Deliaboll, Hamet and Tracorn, value 100s. per annum; and John de Montacute his son, aged 34 years and more, was found to be his nearest heir.[2] After the death of John de Montacute, the father, the above fees remained to Margaret his relict as of her inheritance. She died 24th March 1394-5, thereof seized, and the above-mentioned John de Montacute, the son, was found to be her nearest heir and to be of the age of forty years and more.[3] This John de Montacute succeeded his uncle William as Earl of Sarum, and was attainted and beheaded in 1400; nevertheless the aforesaid fees descended to his son and heir Thomas de Montacute, who was aged twenty-one years and more in 1408,[4] in tail. He was restored to the Earldom as early as 1409, in which year he was summoned to Parliament as "Thomæ Comiti Sarum." He died in 1428 s.p.m., leaving Alice his sole daughter and heir who married Richard Nevill, third son of Ralph Earl of Westmoreland, upon whose attainder, in 1460, his estates were forfeited to the crown.

The *Manors* of Boconnoc, Glyn, and Penpont were held of the Manor of Lantyan by the family of Carminowe. On the death of Ralph Carmynou, Chr., on the 9th October 1386, it was found that he was seized in fee and demesne, *inter alia*, of the Manors of Bodconnok, Glyn, Penpont and Tregesteyntyn which he held of John Montagev, Chr., by military service, and the value per annum was £40, and that William Carmynov, brother of the said Ralph, was his nearest heir and was aged thirty-one years and more. Thomas Carmynow, second son of William and heir of his nephew John Carminow, son of John who died 6th May 8th Henry V., s.p., died in 1423, leaving two daughters, coheirs, Margaret, the elder, being the wife of Hugh Courteney of Boconnoc, son and heir of Sir Hugh Courteney late of Haccombe, Knt., aged twenty years and more, and Johanna wife of Thomas, son of Sir Nicholas Carew, Knt., aged fifteen years and more. Upon the inquisition taken after his death it was found that he had by several Charters settled his estates upon his two daughters and their respective husbands, and the heirs of their bodies, and that he was entitled to the reversion, *inter alia*, of the Manor of Penpont, which Johanna wife of Thomas Bodulgat, late wife of John Carminow, son and heir of John Carmynow, Esq., brother of the said Thomas, and then living, held in dower of the heirs of the said Thomas, and which to the said Thomas descended by the death of the aforesaid John, son of

---

[1] Inq. p.m. 14th Edw. III., No. 35.
[3] Inq. p.m., 18th Richard II., No. 31.

[2] Inq. p.m. 13th Rich. II., No. 34.
[4] Inq. p.m., 10th Henry IV., No. 54.

S

John as uncle and heir of the said John, and it was found that the said manor was held of the Earl of Sarum, as of his Manor of Lantyan.[1] Johanna wife of Thomas Bodulgat died 17th March 1453-4, and it was found upon the usual inquisition that she held in dower, *inter alia*, the Manor of Penpont of Sir Hugh Courteney, Knt., and Margaret his wife, and Thomas Carew, Esq. and Johanna his wife, as of the right of the said Margaret and Johanna, daughters and heirs of the aforesaid Thomas Carminow.[2] In the partition of the estates the Manor of Penpont, *inter alia*, fell to the share of Sir Hugh Courteney, whose son Sir Edward Courteney, Knt., was created Earl of Devon in 1485. His son, Sir William, married the Princess Katherine of York, seventh daughter of King Edward IV., and had a son Sir Henry Courteney, eleventh Earl of Devon, who, in 1525, was created Marquis of Exeter, and being attainted and beheaded on 9th January 1538-9, his estates, *inter alia*, the Manor of Penpont, became forfeited to the Crown. Queen Mary, however, in the first year of her reign, restored the Earldom of Devon to his son Sir Edward Courteney and *his heirs male;*[3] and for the better support of his dignity, by Letters Patent dated 28th September 1554,[4] granted divers lands and manors, *inter alia*, the Manors of Tynten, Penpont, Glyn and Brodoke, to hold, unlike the limitation of the Patent for the Earldom the dignity of which the lands were designed to support, to him and the *heirs male of his body.* He died at Padua, of the ague, on the 18th December 1556, unmarried, when his lands reverted to the Crown, and a Commission was issued to Sir Thomas Dennys, Knt., Sir John St. Leger, Knt., and others, to seize the same. We find them accordingly brought upon the Minister's accounts for the years 1557-8 in the following form as regards the Manor of Penpont.[5]

Terræ et Tenementa nuper Edwardi Comitis Devoniæ modo ad manus dominorum Regis et Regine devenientia per Mortem eiusdem Comitis nuper defuncti pro eo quod domina Regina nunc Maria per literas suas patentes datas (28 September 1553) anno regni sui primo dedit et concessit easdem Terras et tenementa eiidem Comiti ac heredibus de corpore suo legitime procreatis remanentia inde ob defectum hujusmodi exitus eidem domine Regine heredibus et successoribus suis prout in dictis literis patentibus inter alia continetur. Qui quidem Comes obiit apud Padway (Padua) in partibus Transmarinis xviii die Decembris Annis predictis dominorum Regis et Regine tertio et quarto sine aliquo hujusmodi herede de corpore suo legitime procreato eaque de causa in manum dominorum Regis et Regine nunc capta et seseita virtute cujusdam commissionis quibusdem Thome Dennys Militi Johanni St. Leger Militi et aliis Commissionariis dominorum Regis et Regine in hac parte assignatis.

---

[1] Inq. p.m. 21st Henry VI., No. 46.   [2] Inq. p.m. 33rd Henry VI. No. 10.

[3] The succession to the Earldom was not as usual limited to the grantee and the heirs male of his body but to hold to him, "*et heredibus suis masculis in perpetuum.*" Nevertheless the earldom remained unclaimed until 1831, when it was recovered by Sir William Courtenay, Bart., third Viscount Courtenay, upon whose death unmarried in 1835, the title descended to his second cousin, the father of the present Earl.

[4] Rot. Pat. 1st Mary, Part x. m. 28.

[5] Minister's Accounts, Devon and Cornwall, 4th and 5th Philip and Mary. No. 6.

PENPOUNT -   -   Compotus Henrici Spiller Ballivi ibidem per tempus predictum.

Arreragia   -   -   Nulla. Quia est primus compotus ad usus dominorum Regis et Regine post mortem Edwardi nuper Comitis Devoniæ.

Summa Nulla.

Redditus Assisarum libe-   Sed responditur de xxiiˢ xᵈ de redditu assisarum liberorum Tenencium
rorum Tenencium   -   Domini ibidem per annum soluendo ad duos anni terminos principales.

Summa xxiiˢ xᵈ

Redditus Assisarum   Et de xxiiiⁱⁱ jᵈ de redditu Assisarum Tenencium Domini ibidem
Custumariorum Tenen-   per annum soluendo ad quatuor anni terminos equaliter.
cium soluendus

Summa xxiijⁱⁱ jᵈ

Incremento Reditus   -   Et de xxᵈ de Incremento redditus in Penpount doune ultra xiiijˢ iiijᵈ de antiquo redditu dimissos Tenentibus domini ibidem. Et de xxᵈ de Incremento Redditus vnius parcelle vocatæ Wengelly downe dimissos eisdem Tenentibus vltra xvˢ de antiquo redditu.

Summa iijˢ iiijᵈ·

Perquissita Curiæ   -   De aliquo proficuo prouenenti siue crescenti de perquissitis curiæ ibidem hoc anno tentæ non respondit. Eo quod nulla extracta siue rotuli curiæ Auditoris certificantur.

Summa nulla.

Summa omnium predictorum xxiiijⁱⁱ vjˢ iijᵈ quibus allocatur ei xiijˢ iiijᵈ pro feodo dicti ballivi causa officij sui exercendi et occupandi hoc anno. Et eidem ijˢ pro decremento redditus unius tenementi in Crocklargus superius onerati in titulo redditus assisarum ad xxixˢ xᵈ per annum et modo dimittitur Johanni Spernell pro xxviiˢ ixᵈ per annum. Et sic in decrementis hujusmodi hoc anno. Et eidem xiiijˢ pro decremento redditus vnius Molendini bladii domini ibidem superius in titulo redditus assisarum onerati. Eo quod dictum Molendinum stetit vacuum et inoccupatum per totum tempus hujus compoti. Et sic in decremento vt super. Et eidem ijˢ pro stipendio clerici auditoris scribenti hunc compotum hoc anno vt in precedenti. Et debet xxijⁱⁱ xiiijˢ xjᵈ· quos liberauit Johanni Ailworth armigero Receptori ibidem. Ex Recognitione dicti super hunc compotum coram auditore.

The estates of the Earl of Devon being thus in the possession of the Crown, Queen Elizabeth, by her Letters Patent dated 3rd July 1564,[1] granted the Manor and Lordship of Penponte, *alias* Penpownte, with all its members and appurtenances, together with all works and mines of tin, lead, iron, coal, and all other minerals whatsoever, and all liberties and franchises, to Philip Cole, Esq., and Johanna his wife. The franchises are very fully described, *inter alia*, farms, fee farm and annuities,

[1] Rot. Origin. 6th Elizabeth, Part I. m. 114.

S²

knight's fees, wards, marriages, escheats, reliefs, waifs, goods and chattels of felons. and fugitives and felos de se and outlaws, wreck of sea, pannage, free warren, liberties, native men and women, also villans with all their children, (nativos nativas ac villanos cum eorum sequelis), also tolls of markets and other tolls and customs, with courts leet, view of frank-pledge, and assize of bread and beer, with all that to Courts Leet and view of Frank-pledge pertain, &c.

This Philip Cole was son and heir of William Cole, by Elizabeth the daughter of Sir Philip Champernoun of Modbury, Knt., and Catherine, daughter of Sir Edmund Carew, Knt., last Baron Carew of Mohuns Ottery. He married Joane, daughter of Thomas Williams of Stowford, Esq., and died in 1595 leaving a son, Richard, aged 28 years, who married Radigon, daughter of Nicholas Boscawen of Bliston, co. Cornwall, Esq., He died s.p. in 1614, and by his will, dated 7th January 1612, devised all his lordships and manors in the counties of Devon and Cornwall unto Capt. John Cole of London, Gent., and the heirs male of his body, in default of such issue to Gregory Cole of the Middle Temple, London, Esq., and the heirs of his body, with other remainders over. Captain John Cole died soon afterwards without issue male, and the estates devolved upon the said Gregory Cole who was in possession of them in 1630. From Gregory Cole the lands descended to his grandson, Henry Cole, who settled, *inter alia*, the Manor of Penpont on his marriage in 1687. Edward Cole, son and heir of the said Henry, dying in 1756 s.p., demised all his lands to his brother Potter Cole, Clerk, and his heirs, with remainder to his sisters and their heirs on the condition that each person upon entering into possession shall take the name and arms of Cole and use none other. Potter Cole died in 1802, when the estates devolved upon William Loggin, Clerk, son and heir of Johanna, one of the sisters of the aforesaid Edward Cole, and wife of William Loggin of Bewley, co. Warwick. William Loggin, the son, upon inheriting the estates, in compliance with the will of his uncle Edward Cole, obtained an Act of Parliament[1] to enable him to bear the name and arms of Cole. He left a son of the same name, by whom the Manor of Penpont was sold in parcels. In 1809 the barton, which is a very valuable estate, was sold by Mr. Loggin to Mr. Richard Grose, who died in 1831, whose son, Mr. William Grose, is the present owner. The remains of the manor pound still exist.

---

[1] 42nd George III.

Terrier of the Manor of Penpont, Compiled from a Deed dated 21st November 1791.

Tenement.	Parish.	Tenants.	Area.		
			A.	R.	P.
Benbole -	St. Kew	Samuel West - - -	96	0	32
Tregline and Breusne	St. Minver	Richard Blake - - -	167	0	30
Carwan - -	,,	John Legoo - - -	61	0	35
Messmear -	,,	Joseph Collings - - -	52	0	30
Carey's Messmear	,.	Joseph Collings - - -	78	2	7
Treble's Messmear	,,	Robert Martin - - -	61	3	35
Guy's Trebetherik	,,	Anthony Guy - - -	42	3	12
Tregare's Trebetherik	,,	Joan Mably, Widow - -	41	0	8
Donathan -	,,	Jane Gibbs and Joan Gibbs on lease for the life of the survivor of them	163	2	4
Coles Sandy Commons	,,	.. ..	99	3	14
Parcel of Land from the Cliff to Low Water Mark	,,	.. ..	171	0	30

The *Barton* of Penpont does not seem to be included. This was divided into Great Penpont and Little Penpont, but the whole now forms one compact estate, the property of Mr. William Grose.

TREGOIDE *alias* TREGWIDE.

We do not find this Manor mentioned in *Domesday* and probably the land was taxed under Lanho. Our earliest notice of the name is in 47th Henry III. (1263), at which date John de Tregoyd held of Luke de Cadano one acre of land in Tregoyd rendering for the same 30s. 1½d. rent per annum, and making suit at the Court of the said Luke from three weeks to three weeks at Nanwythan.[1] In 24th Edward III. (1350) John Treury, Junr., and Johanna his wife levied a fine on Richard de Kelsent of five messuages, one dovecote, &c., &c., and 40s. rent, and one pair of gloves, with appurtenances in Tregoydvean, Tregoydmur, Reskesan, Crickly, Oppatone and Rosonuallan, whereby the lands were settled on the said John Treury and Johanna his wife and the heirs of their bodies, and in default of such issue remainder to the right heirs of the said John.[2] In 1475 Elizabeth who was the wife of Thomas Treffry, Esq., petitioned against John Treffry of the third part, *inter alia*, of the Manors of Tregwyed and Treffry, which she claimed as of dower.[3] It continued to be held by the Treffry family until 1648, when, by deed dated 24th November in that year,[4] under the description of the Manor of Tregoid, or Tregwite, it was sold by John Treffry of Fowey, Esq. and Bridget his wife, to the Honorable John Robartes son and heir apparent of the Right Honorable John Lord Robartes, Baron of Truro. In the fine passed on the occasion the lands are described as in Tregoid *alias* Tregwyte, Tregoid *alias* Tregwyte magna, Tregoid *alias* Tregwite parva, Rosenvallens, Lampill, Carwithers, *alias* Carwithered, Trewithick, Trelightes *alias* Trelightres, Trevederock, St. Kew, Brewar, *alias* Simon Ward, Endellion and St. Minver; also an annual rent of 8s. issuing out of one messuage and forty acres of land in Trenwith in Michaelstow. From that date to the present time the manor has been held by the family of Robartes and it is now the property of Lord Robartes of Lanhydrock, though in 1703 a fine was levied in which John Symkyn, merchant, was querist and Mesech Matthew, Gentlemen, deforciant of two messuages in Tregwide, *alias* Tregwite, *alias* Tregoyde, *alias* Tregwyde, *alias* Tregwhite, in St. Kew.

The following Rent Roll of the manor will shew of what tenements it was composed in 1656 :

[1] Pedes Finium, 47th Henry VI., Michaelmas, No. 13.

[2] Pedes Finium, 24th Edward III., Michaelmas, No. 3.

[3] One of the messuages on which she claimed dower was, as alleged by John Treffry, in Blysland, and was, on the day of the issue of the writ, held of the King by Richard Duke of Gloucester as of his Manor of Blisland, which same manor was, and from time immemorial had been, ancient demesne of the Kings of England, and that all the messuages and lands held of that manor had, from time immemorial, been impleaded in the court of the manor, held within the manor, by a small writ of the Lord the King of right closed (*per paruum breve Domini Regis de Recto Clausum*). De Banco Rolls, 15th Edward IV., Easter 126.

[4] Deed at Lanhydrock.

Mannor of Tregoide ⎱ *A rent Roll of the ffree and Convenc'onary Tenm^{ts} of the Mannor*
alias Tregwite ⎰ *aforesaid for the yeare ended at Mich'as 1656.*

		HIGHRENTS.	£	s.	d.	
Tregoide Magna	-	The heires of Atta Park, yearly	..	..	..	
there	-	The heires of Nicholls of Trewane	00	00	00	ob'
there	-	The heires of ffrancis Hocken	00	00	02	ob'
there	-	The heires of Randall	..	..	..	
ffarthing Downe	-	The heires of Warren	00	00	00	ob'
Vpton Hill	-	The heires of Pentire now Roscarrocke	00	00	00	ob'
there	-	John Carne	00	00	00	ob'
Rossenvallen, *alias* Rossenwallen		William Inch, Gent.	00	01	06	
there	-	Richard Lynam, Clerk	00	01	06	
there	-	William Hutton, Clerk	00	01	00	
Rosemenant	-	The heires of Barronett Carew	00	01	06	
Saventon	-	The heires of John Dagge	00	12	00	
		CONVENC'ONARY RENTS.				
Tregoid Parva		Humphrey Arthur payeth yearly	04	00	00	Cap' 1ˢ Day 6ᵈ out 7ˢ
Tregoid Magna in St. Kew		Humphrey Bath now Henry Bath	00	11	04	Cap' 1ˢ Day 6ᵈ hen 6ᵈ out 1ˢ 6ᵈ
Lampill in Breward		John Mathew late Broad	01	06	08	Cap' 1ˢ Day 6ᵈ hen 6ᵈ
there	-	John Warren	00	13	04	Cap' 1ᵈ Day 4ᵈ hen 6ᵈ }out
there	-	Thomas ffox, Clerk	00	13	04	Cap' 1ˢ Day 4ᵈ hen 6ᵈ } 4ˢ 6ᵈ
Carwithers, *alias* Carwithered in Breward		John Vivian, Esq.				
Trewithicke in Endellion		John Hambly	00	10	00	Cap' 8ᵈ Day 4ᵈ hen 4ᵈ out 2ˢ
Trelightres	-	Robert Goade	00	10	00	Cap' 10ᵈ Day 4ᵈ out 1ˢ 3ᵈ
Trevedrock in Minver		Purchased as in hand, the ould rent of it was yearly 1ˡⁱ 2ˢ Cap' & harvest day				
Rossenvallen in St. Kew		Tom Hutton, Clerk	00	05	04	
Trenowth in Michaelstow		The heires of Broad for a dry rent there	00	08	00	
			11	01	04	8 Cap's 6 hens 7 daies

Theise are to will and require you Thomas ffox, Clerk, Reeue of the Mannor aforesaid, to Collecte and Gather the seuerall sums above written with the Extracts annexed, and for default of payment to distraine for the same. And that you make retowrne hereof and passe in your full accompte for your yeare ended at Mich'as 1656 to mee at Lanhidrock on Monday the 17th Nov. next.

Giuen vnder my hand this 29th 7ᵇᵉʳ 1656.

J. ROBARTS.

To Thomas ffox, Clerk
     Reeue of the
       Mannor aforesᵈ

MANOR OF TRELULLA, *alias* TRELULL, *alias* TRELILL.

The earliest mention which we have found of this place is in 32nd Edward I. (1304), when Warinus de Trelulla recovered seizin against Roger Morsell and Anastasia his wife of a piece of land, six perches in length and six perches in breadth, with appurtenances in Trelulla, juxta Trewena (Trewane).[1] A few years later John le Keu of Trelulla recovered seizin against John Morsel of Trelulla, Junior, probably the son of Roger, of certain profits arising out of ten acres of wood, inclosed in Trelulla juxta Trewana, and of all his corn and of sufficient timber (maeremium) for rests for his ploughs and sixty men's burden of firewood every year.[2]

In 1317, Nicholas Giffard, in consideration of the sum of 40 marks, suffered a fine to Lawrence de Tremur in five messuages, 21s. 10d. rent, and a rent of five sheep, with appurtenances in Trelulla, Pelengarou, Tregellest, Lanseuegy, Vppeton deythyn, Hendra, and Trewyget,[3] which having been done without a license, the lands being held in capite, Laurence de Tremure was obliged to make fine to the King in five marks for his pardon and to have a license.[4] Laurence died in 1326[5] seized of these lands which he held of the King in capite as in socage by fealty and service, and 12s. 6d. of relief after the death of each tenant, for all services. He also held of Stephen de Podiford one messuage and one acre of land Cornish in Tremure (in Lanivet) by fealty and service, rendering to the said Stephen a rent of 1lb of cummin annually, and John de Tremure, son of the said Laurence, was found to be his nearest heir and to be of the age of 26 years and more; and in the same year John Tremure, upon payment of 12s. 6d. relief and making fealty, had seizin in the above lands.[6]

In 1391 John Tremure sued Robert Duck, Robert Jekelney, Robert Dag and others for trespass in breaking down the trees of the said John in Tremure and Trelulla.[7]

John Tremure, or Tremere, died without issue male, leaving two daughters co-heirs, the elder of whom married John Bray, son and heir of Thomas Bray of St. Cleer in this County, whose son, through that marriage, inherited Tremere and Trelulla. His great grandson, Reginald Bray, designated in the Pedigree[8] as of Tremere, was seized of Trelulla and all the abovementioned lands, now described as the Manor of Trelull,

---

[1] Rot. Originalia, 32nd Edward I., m. 14.　　　[2] Ibid. 8th Edward II., m. 34, and 9th Edward II., m. 24.

[3] Pedes Finium, 11th Edward II., No. 5.　　　[4] Rot. Fin. 11th Edward II.

[5] Inq. p.m. 1st Edward III., Part I., No. 63. The warrant to the escheator for taking the lands of Laurence de Tremure into the King's hands was tested at Kenilworth 6th January, (Rot. Fin. 20th Edward II. m 1.) "John le Ku de Treluila" was one of the jury on this inquisition, as he had been, as "John le Cu de Trelulla," on the inquisition taken after the death of Alan Bloyou on 23rd May, 9th Edward II.

[6] Rot. Origin. 1st Edward III. m. 17, and Rot. Fin. same year. Warrant tested at York 25th June, m. 11.

[7] De Banco Rolls, 14th Richard II., Easter, m. 184.　　　[8] Heralds' College, 2, c. 1, 441b.

and being so seized in 1545, suffered a recovery to Nicholas Bowyer of Bodmin, Merchant, probably for the purpose of settlement.[1]

From the family of Bray the Manor would seem to have passed to that of Nicoll of Penvose. Nevertheless the family of Nicoll would seem to have possessed lands in Trelulla previously to the last abovementioned date. In 1533 John Shewys and others levied a fine of Henry Nycoll of the Manors of Penvose and Carkele, and thirty messuages, *inter alia*, Trelulla.[2] On 27th December 1597, Humphry Nicoll of Penvose, Esq. died seized, *inter alia*, of the Manor of Trelulla which he was found to have held of George Breye (son of the abovementioned Reginald. He was aged seventy-one years in 1699), but by what service the jury declared themselves ignorant. They found his son Humphrey Nicoll to be his nearest heir, and to have been aged twenty years, twenty-one weeks, and five days at the date of his father's decease,[3] which said Humphrey Nicoll was living in 1620. His son Anthony suffered a fine in this manor in 1652, to John Nicoll, Gent.,[4] probably his brother. In 1676, William Beale petitioned against Humphrey Nycoll (son of the last named Anthony) in the Manors of St. Tudy and Trelill,[5] and in 1705 Peter Kekewich petitioned against Rebecca Nicolls, widow (relict of the last named Humphrey), *inter alia*, of the same manor and a moiety of the Manor of Lannozook, when Anthony Nicolls was called to warrant,[6] and the lands in Trelill still continue in the Kekewich family though not as a manor.

MANOR OF TREGAER *alias* TREGEARE.

There is a reputed Manor of Tregeare in this parish possessed by the Honorable G. M. Fortescue of Boconnoc, of which we annex a rental dated in 1748. The name of Tregear is found in many places in the county, and is not easily identified, but we have not been able to discover any evidence to establish Tregaer in St. Kew as an ancient manor possessing any special rights or franchises. Tregaer, or " Tregayr Castre," as it was called in ancient times, belonged to the family of Chenduit, as parcel of the Manor of Bodanan.[7] It does not, however, appear in the Rent Roll of that Manor in 1569.[8] In 1642 it was held by Humphrey Noye, Esq., who, by deed dated 25th April in that year,[9] in addition to the Manors of Lanowe and Trevelwith, conveyed " all that messuage and all those lands and tenements in Tregeare now or late in the occupation of — Loveys, widow, Sir Samuel Hele, Knt., &c., &c." to Daniel Harvey of London, Esq., Elizabeth Harvey and Michael Harvey of London, Merchant, by way

---

[1] Recovery Roll, 37th Henry VIII., Michs. 413.
[2] Pedes Finium 25th Henry VIII., Trinity.
[3] Inq. p.m. 43rd Elizabeth, No. 133.
[4] Pedes Finium 1652, Michaelmas.
[5] Recovery Rolls, 27th and 28th Charles II., Hil. 130.
[6] Ibid. 4th Anne, Trinity, 146.
[7] Pedes Finium, 3rd Henry VI., Easter.
[8] Ante, Vol i, pp. 519, et seq.
[9] Rot. Claus. 18th Charles I., No. 33.

T

of mortgage, and a fine was levied between the parties in the same year.[1] We presume these lands passed from Mr. Noye to the Earl of Bath, together with the Manor of Lanow, and were designated a manor while in the possession of Mr. Pitt, from whom they descended to Mr. Fortescue as before described.[2] No courts are now held.

Rent Roll of the Manor of Tregeare, 1748. From the Muniment Room, Boconnoc.

Tenants.	Tenements.	Total Rents.		
		£	s.	d.
CHIEF RENTS.				
Cann, Samuel	Tregavern	0	1	3
Parsons, John	Ditto	0	1	3
COVENANT RENTS.				
Bear, Walter	Hocking's House	0	4	0
Brown, Abraham	Pichen's Park and Long Park	0	12	0
Burton, William	Part of Inche's House and Garden	0	1	0
Brown, John	A Meadow	0	4	0
Burton, Willm. or John Dancaster	A Watering	0	3	0
Dancaster, John	Marrow's Tenement	0	10	10
Ditto	Dagg's Meadow	0	2	0
Ditto	Marrow's Tenement, Old Walls	0	2	0
Ditto	Part of Inche's House	0	2	0
Hickes, Mr. John	Barton of Tregeare	2	14	10
Ditto	Higher Tenement in Trewigett	0	15	0
Ditto	Home Tenement, or Lynham's Tenement in ditto	1	1	6
Ditto	Grey's Tenement in ditto	0	10	6
Lang, Elizabeth	Inche's House and Garden	0	1	6
Roose, Richard	Little Hendra Ruddon	0	4	0
Ditto	Great Hendra Ruddon	0	8	0
Ditto	Chollacott	0	8	0
Thomas, Nicholas	A House, Garden, and Meadow	0	4	0
Burton, William	Marrow's Meadow	..	..	..
	Total	£8	10	8

[1] Pedes Finium, 18th Charles, Easter.

[2] Ante, p. 97.

MANOR OF TREHAVEROCK, *alias* TREHARROCK.

These lands gave name to a family of gentlemen who, at a very early date, are supposed to have founded one of the prebends in the Church of St. Endellion. The prebend was in existence as early as the thirteenth century; but we do not find it specifically described as the Trehaverock Prebend until the beginning of the seventeenth. The earliest patrons whom we can trace were of the family of Modret.[1]

Lysons states Treharrick to be a manor, and says that it once belonged to a family of that name, whose heiress brought it to the Cavalls in the reign of Henry VII.[2] In the latter statement he is correct, except as regards the date. The marriage between Robert Cavell and Sibell daughter and heir of John Treharrock took place about the end of the fourteenth century, for Nicholas Cavell, the issue of this marriage, presented to the Trehaverock prebend in 1428, and was dead in 1464.[3] We cannot, however, trace that Trehaverock ever possessed any manorial rights or privileges.

In 1425, Trehaverock was parcel of the Manor of Bodannan, and it appears as a free tenement in the Rent Roll, or Terrier, of the same manor in 1568,[4] as it does also in 1588.[5] In 1642, it would seem to have become annexed to the Manor of Lannomuer, and was parcel of the tenements included in that manor, which Humphrey Noye conveyed to Daniel Harvey and others.[6]

As to the estate itself, it was doubtless held by a family who from it took its designation. In 1st Edward III. (1328) John de Treauerok was assessed in St. Kew on a subsidy of a 20th at 9d.[7] From this family, like the prebend in Endellion Church, it passed to Nicholas Cavell in the latter part of the fourteenth century.[8] In 1615, William Cavell and Jane his wife suffered a fine, *inter alia*, in Trehaverock, *alias* Treaverock, and in the Prebend of Trehavarock, in St. Endellion to Andrew Pomeroy, Esq., Richard Carter, Esq., Pascoe Vivian, Esq., and John Dagg, Gent.[9] It thus became a part of the possessions of the family of Vivian of Trewan upon the marriage of John Vivian of Trewan with Mary the eldest daughter and coheir of the said William Cavell, and so continued until the end of the century, when an Act of Parliament was obtained to enable John Vivian, Esq., and Thomas Vivian his son to sell a part of their estate.[10] On 27th June 1699, articles of agreement were entered into between Thomas Vivian of Trewan, Esq., of the

---

[1] See ante Vol. i., p. 503.   [2] Mag. Brit. Vol. III. p. 162.

[3] Ante Vol. i., p. 505.   [4] Ante vol. i., p. 516.

[5] Inq. p.m., of Thomas Roscarrock, 30th Elizabeth, Part i., No. 82.   [6] Ante p. 133.

[7] Subsidy Roll, 1st Edward III. $\frac{87}{7}$. — On the payment of the aid of 10s. for each Knight's fee, 20th Edward III. (1346) John Trehaverek held half a fee in Treonek which Mathew and Agnes Treonek sometime held.

[8] Ante Vol. i., p. 584.   [9] Pedes Finium, 13th James I., Michaelmas.

[10] Act 5th William and Mary.

T²

one part, and John Peter of Treator of the other part, for the purchase of this estate, which was accomplished by a deed of bargain and sale dated 21st September in the same year.[1] In 1727, John Peter of Treharrock, Gent.,[2] conveyed it to John Hamley, Gent. After various transactions of mortgage, it was eventually sold by Indentures of Lease and Release, dated respectively 17th and 18th November 1786, by Edward Hamley to Francis Brown of Endellion, Gent., from whom, in 1802, it passed to Abraham Hambly of Endellion, Esq., who was no relation of the beforementioned Hamleys.[3] Mr. Hambly greatly improved the property by planting, &c., and built thereon a new and commodious house, which he made his residence. The family continued to reside there until 1872, when the property was sold to the Rev. Francis Basset.

BOKELLY.

Bokelly is very favourably situate upon rising ground on the east side of the parish, and possesses a south aspect. The site is well adapted for a gentleman's seat. Leland says of it: " From Trelill to.........wher Master Carniovies (Carnsiouie?) *alias* Carnsey hath a praty house, fair ground, and praty wood about it."[4] The house is now removed and a modern farm house built upon the site. Little of its former beauty remains except what nature has given to the situation. There is a remarkably fine old barn, and the stables, also, are old, with granite mullioned windows.

Bokelly is now parcel of the Manor of Lanowmure, and was held of that Manor by William Carnsuyowe on his death 1528 ; nevertheless it would appear from a fine levied in 1432,[5] in which Walter Pollard, John Mulys, and others were querists, and John Wyndeslade and Elizabeth his wife, and Stephen Trenewyth and Isabella his wife, deforc., concerning the Manor of Treglasta, that at that date Bokelly and Tregellest pertained to that Manor ; though the fine is not very clear upon the subject. In 1748 it was held of the Manor of Lannowmure by Sir John Molesworth at the chief rent of 5s. per annum.[6] Courts of the Manor have now ceased to be held, and the rent in question has been allowed to drop.

The nature of the tenure under which Bokelly was held renders it difficult to trace its early history, but we find that as far back as the reign of King Edward III., it had given its name to a family of gentlemen who long continued to possess the estate. We find Roger de Bokelly mentioned in the Roll of the Assize at Launceston in 1347.[7] In 1429 Richard Nicholas and Thomas Smith, citizens and painters of London,

[1] Inrolled.
[2] Recovery Roll, No. 146.
[3] Deeds at Treharrock.
[4] Leland's Itinerary.
[5] Pedes Finium, 10th Henry VI., No. 5.
[6] Rent Roll, ante p. 121.
[7] Assize Roll, Cornwall, 21st Edward III., m. 8.

sued Nicholas Bokelly for a debt of £40, and ten years later Nicholas Bokelly sued John Watta of Amal Eglos in a similar plea.[1] In 1461 John Bokelly, described as late of Bokelly, Gent., was attached to reply to Sir John Marny, Knt, on a plea that he had broken the banks of the mill pond of the said Sir John Marny, at Overdeny;[2] and in the following year John Bokelly, described as late of Bokelly in the parish of St. Kewy, Gent., was summoned and replied to William Munck in a plea of debt of £40.[3]

In 1464 we find that William Carnsuyowe, described as of Bokelly, Gent., and Henry Cavell, described as late of Bokelly, Gent., were attached and replied to William Mohun in a plea of trespass upon the lands of the said William in Delyowemure.[4] The case was postponed from term to term for a year when a verdict was given for the defendants.[5]

From this date Bokelly would seem to have been in the possession of the family of Carnsewe.[6] William Carnsewe by his Charter dated at Bokelly on Monday next after the feast of the Conception of the Blessed Virgin Mary, 15th Henry VIII. (1523) settled his estates, *inter alia*, Bokelly and other lands in St. Kew,[7] and the estate continued in the same family until the year 1653, when George Carnsewe and Ann his wife suffered a fine in four messuages, two corn mills, one fulling mill, &c., in Bokelly and Lanseage to Jane Carew, widow;[8] and, in 1656, the same George and Ann, together with Richard Carnsewe, Gent., suffered a fine in two messuages, &c., in Bokelly, to the same Jane then described as Jane Tregagle,[9] widow, and three years later Nicholas Courteney, Gent., and Jane his wife, suffered a fine in the same premises to John Mill, Esq.[10] By Indenture dated 22nd May, 14th Charles II.[11] (1662), George Carnsewe of Bokelly, Gent., and Ann his wife, and Richard Carnsewe, son and heir apparent of the said George, conveyed all that *Manor* (sic) of Bokelly, and all those messuages called Lanseage, &c., and Langeage Mills, and all royalties, &c., together with the Estrays of the Hundred of Trigg[12] to Sir Peter Kelligrew of Arwenack, Knt. In the following Trinity term a fine[13] was levied in which Sir Peter Kelligrew, Knt., was querist, and George Carnsewe, Gent., and Ann his wife, Richard Carnesew, Gent., and John Mill, Esq., and Ithemar his wife, and Nicholas Courteney, Esq., and Jane his wife, were deforc. relating to the same premises. This was probably a transaction of mortgage, as it appears that the estate was purchased by John Mill, in trust for

---

[1] De Banco Rolls, 18th Richard II., Michaelmas, m. 557.

[2] De Banco Rolls, 2nd Edward IV., Michaelmas, m. 373.

[3] Ibid. 3rd Edward, IV., Easter.   [4] Ibid. 4th Edward IV., Michaelmas m. 302.

[5] Ibid., 5th Edward IV., Michaelmas, m. 53.

[6] Norden mentions "Bockellie the howse of Mr. Carnsew frutefully sett." (Speculi Britanniæ Pars, p. 82.)

[7] Inq. p.m., 15th Henry VIII. No. 64.   [8] Pedes Finium, 1653 Trinity.

[9] Pedes Finium, 1656, Easter.   [10] Pedes Finium, 1659, Trinity.

[11] Deed in the possession of the Rev. T. Carnsew of Flexbury near Stratton.

[12] The wayfs and strays of the hundred of Trigg anciently pertained to the Manor of Bodanan. (See account of that Manor, ante Vol. i., pp. 515—523.)   [13] Pedes Finium, 14th Charles II., Trinity.

John Tregagle of Trevorder, son of the abovementioned Jane Tregagle, afterwards Courteney. Bokelly subsequently passed to Sir John Molesworth, under the deed of 2nd June 1736, together with the Advowson of the Vicarage of St. Kew. (See ante p. 97.)

TREWANE.

This estate is parcel of the Manor of Lanowmure, of which, from ancient times, it was a free tenement. Our earliest notice of it is in 1314, in which year, at the assizes at Launceston, an assize of view of recognizance was held to enquire if Thomas, the son of Richard, Bomite of Trewana and Walter de la Hill had unjustly disseized John, the son of Richard, Bomite of his free tenements in Trewana and Treveryon juxta Trelulla. It appears from the pleadings that Richard Bomite had died seized of the premises, and that after his death the said Thomas had entered as son and heir. John alleged that the said Thomas was not born in wedlock and obtained a verdict, and Thomas was left in mercy.[1]

Trewane afterwards, at an early date, became the property and residence of a family called Nicoll, or Nicholls. In the Return 1521-3 (Appendix II.) Henry Nicol[2] is shewn as having possessions in St. Kew of the value of 40s. per annum, and John Nicol as possessing goods of the value of £20, and arms for one man, and in 1524, the same John Nycoll was assessed to the subsidy in St. Kew, at the same rate per annum. Trewane continued in the same family for many descents.[3] John Nichols[4] was possessed of it at the beginning of the 18th century, and, passing over the issue of his eldest son, John Nicholls of Davidstow, then deceased, he settled, *inter alia*, Trewane in succession upon his grandsons James and Erisey, sons of James Nicholls of St. Neot, his second son, and their heirs for ever. Both soon afterwards died s.p., and the estates devolved upon Elizabeth the only child of John Nicholls of Davidstow, grandson of the John Nicholls first abovementioned, as heir at law. This young lady married

---

[1] Assize Rolls, 7th Edward II. $\frac{N}{2}$ $\Big\}$ 6 m. 2 d.
$\frac{}{15}$

[2] This Henry was Henry Nicoll of Penvose, who held lands in Trelulla. See ante p. 133.

[3] Norden, under St. Kew, mentions "the howse of John Nycolls." (Speculi Britanniæ Pars, p. 73.)

[4] He died in 1709, and in his will dated 9th October 1707, we find the following bequest: "I do leave to the great parlour of Trewane house, which I use, all the pictures and family pieces that use to hang there, to be used with that room, and not alienated or otherwise disposed of, and in like manner I leave to the hall the great brass candlestick that use to remain there." He also directed that his "great emerald ring or jewell shall remain in Trewane house to be used and worn only by such such woman or women, as my grandsons James Nicholls and Erisey Nicholls shall intermarry with." C. S. Gilbert states that when he wrote the hall was ornamented with some curious carved work, and that there were in the house several good portraits of the Mohuns and Nichollses, together with fragments of ancient tapestry, and that near the house were remains of good gardens and fish ponds. (History of Cornwall, Vol. II., p. 611.)

Nicholas Glynn of Glynn, Esq., by whom she had a son who predeceased her,[1] and dying s.p., by her will, dated 10th April, and proved 24th May 1771,[2] devised, *inter alia*, her barton of Trewane to Thomas Glynn then of Helston, Esq., whose daughter carried it in marriage to Richard Gerveys Grylls of Helston, Esq., from whom it has descended to his great grandson, Shadwell Morley Grylls of Lewarne in St. Neot, Esq., now (1873) Sheriff of the County.

At Trewane is a fine and handsome old mansion house with large mullioned and transomed windows. There is said to have been another story which has been taken off. It is now converted into a farm house. In the principal bed-chamber is a representation, in plaster in high relief, of the offering of Isaac with the following legend on a scroll:

> Old Abraham hold thine hand, it doth suffice,
> God loveth obedience better than sacrifice.

Over the fire place in the adjoining room there is an escutcheon of arms, viz., Nicholls, thrice repeated, impaling: 1st?.................. 2nd. Three bendlets. 3rd. A cross humettée. In another room, now converted into a passage, is a second escutcheon: Nicholls impaling Mohun. And there is an old hatchment: Nicholls impaling a bend lozengy gules.[3]

There is a tradition that Charles II. was sheltered here, and made the family a present of two silver warming pans.

RETON, *alias* TRETON, *alias* TRETAWNE.

Tretawn is parcel of the Manor of Lanowmur, and at an early date was held by the family of Tretheven. John son of William de Tretheven by his charter granted all his lands and tenements in Vale an Kua wyll to Walter Golapyn, which charter was, upon inspeximus, ratified and confirmed by John de Tretheven son of Walter de Tretheven by charter dated on Monday next after the feast of St. John ante porta Latina 10th Edward II. These lands thereafter would seem to have been held by the family of Golapyn for a considerable time. In 16th Henry VI. Thomas Lanhergy, Lord of Lannomur, acknowledged to have received of Nicholas Colapyn, son and heir of John Colapyn, also called Power, by the hands of John Bere of Tregaren and others, the sum of vjs. and iijd. for relief upon the death of the said John Colapyn, for the whole ville of Tretoun which he held of the Manor of Lanomur in socage.[4]

Tretawne, in the 16th century, was part of the possessions of Francis Carnsew, Esq.,

---

[1] See Pedigree of Glynn, ante p. 70, in which, however, Elizabeth is erroneously described as *sister* and heir of John Nichols of Trewane.

[2] In Prerogative Court of Canterbury.   [3] Additional M.S., 9419, p. 228.

[4] Deeds in the possession of J. Brendon Curgenven, Esq.

from whom, in the reign of Queen Elizabeth, it passed to the family of Kestell. By deed dated 20th September 3rd James (1605), Thomas Kestell of Trevegan in the parish of Egloshayle, Esq., and Theophilus Kestell, Gentleman, alienated it to John Molesworth of Pencarrow, Esq., it being described as, "all that capital messuage, barton, and demesne lands called or known by the name of Reton, *alias* Treton, *alias* Tretoune." And, by deed dated 6th October 1612, the said John Molesworth acquired of Francis Carnsewe of Philly, Gent., all that wood called Trethevan, *alias* Trethevy Wood in the parish of St. Kew.

By deed dated 1st May 1633, John Molesworth granted the said lands to his four daughters, Martha, Phillippa, Honour, and Grace, by his marriage with Phillippa, daughter of Henry Rolle of Hampton,[1] provided they married with his consent. By various deeds of divers dates, the said several shares became vested in John Godolphin of Doctors' Commons, Doctor of Laws, who by deed, dated 30th May 1659, under the description of "all that capital messuage, &c., called Reton, *alias* Treton, *alias* Tretawne, and all those lands called Cuell an Dale" and "Penhendra in St. Kew," conveyed the whole to William Keigwin of Mousehole in co. Cornwall, Gent. It continued to be held by this family for nearly a century. James Keigwin of Mousehole, Gent., by his will dated 1st February 1734, devised all his estates to trustees for the sale of such portions as might be necessary beyond the amount of his personal estate to pay his debts; the remainder to George Keigwin, his eldest brother and heir, and, dying unmarried, the whole of his lands, *inter alia*, Reton, *alias* Treton, *alias* Tretawne, Cuell an Dale, Penhendra, and Tupton in St. Kew were, under a decree in the Court of Chancery, pronounced 30th March 1745, directed to be sold, and, by Indentures dated respectively 1st and 2nd May 1752, were conveyed to George Veale of Penzance, Gent., who, in the same year, sold Tretawne and the other lands in this parish to Mr. John Curgenven of Lelant, who settled at Tretawne. By his grandson John Brendon Curgenven, Gent., in 1867 the whole, except a small cottage, called Tretawne Cottage, at Highway, was sold to Reuben Magor of Lamellen, Gent., a descendant of the above-mentioned William Keigwin and of John Curgenven (see Pedigree post), whose brother is the present possessor.

There is an interesting old house at Tretawn of the Jacobean period, built probably by the Molesworths. There is a granite stone built into the wall near the fire place in the back kitchen, about twelve inches square, which has carved in on its surface:

PHIL^A· MOLESWORTH

1620

---

[1] See Ped. ante vol. i., p. 468.

BETHBOLE, *alias* BENBOLGH, *alias* BENBOLL, *alias* PENPOLL.

This estate would seem to have been a free tenement held of the Manor of Penpont. Our earliest knowledge of it is derived from a Roll of Assize for the County in 1337, from which we find that, at that date, it had given its name to a family who possessed it. At the visit of the justices intinerant to Bodmin an assize of view of recognizance was granted to enquire if Johanna, who was the wife of John Carmynou, Knt., and Walter son of the said Johanna, and John de Dyngelli had unjustly disseized Nicholas son of John de Bethbole of his free tenement in Bethbole juxta Trethevan; but Nicholas took nothing by his writ and was in mercy for a false claim.[1] Before the close of the century, however, Benbolgh was held by one Roger Coton. He had two sisters, the youngest of whom, called Petronilla, married John Bandyn, and had a son of the same name, who upon the death of his uncle without heirs entered into possession. In 1399, however, an assize of view of recognizance was granted to Richard Hendre and Margery his wife to enquire if John, the son of John, Bandyn, and Alice who was the wife of John Bandyn, had unjustly disseized them of the said premises, and they claimed the same as the right of the said Margery as kinswoman and heir of the aforesaid Roger, viz., as daughter of Meliora, sister of the said Roger. In defence it was alleged that the said Margery was born before the espousals of the said Meliora and John Atte Wode, late her husband, were celebrated. The jury found that Margery was born within marriage, and Richard Hendre and Margery recovered seizin.[2]

We are obliged now to leap over a long period. In the reign of Queen Elizabeth Benbole was held in moieties, one moiety being in the possession of the Beville family, and the other in that of persons called Lapp. In 1593 John Beville, Gent., suffered a fine in three messuages in St. Kew, viz., Trewarthey Croppe, Penboll, and St. Kew, to Nicholas Dagge, for which the said Nicholas gave him £40.[3] The other moiety was sold to Nicholas Dagge by Philip Lapp, Gent. Thus he held the entirety which he granted to his son Degory Dagge. Degory Dagge died in 1622 s.p., and on 26th April in the following year, John Archer, with the consent of Nicholas Dagge, attorned and became tenant to Richard Dagge for such lands as Degory Dagge his brother had died seized of in Benboll *alias* Penboll, which the said John Archer held under a lease made to him jointly with his brothers Edward and William by the aforesaid Philip Lapp.[4] We do not

---

[1] Assize Roll, Cornwall, 10th to 14th Edward III., $\frac{N}{2} \frac{}{20}$ 4 m. 111.

[2] Ibid. 22nd Richard II., $\frac{N}{2} \frac{}{32}$ 1 m. 207.

[3] Pedes Finium, 35th and 36th Elizabeth, Michaelmas.

[4] Memorandum in possession of Edward Archer of Trelaske, Esq.

U

quite understand the tenure by which the Dagges held Benboll, but we find that before the end of the century a moiety was held as freehold by the family of Archer, and the other moiety was vested in Harry Cole as Lord of the Manor of Penpont. Upon the marriage of John Archer of Trelewack, in 1708, he settled, *inter alia*, Benboll, *alias* Penboll, in the parish of St. Kew.[1] By indentures of lease and release, dated respectively 12th and 13th April 1737,[2] William Archer of Trelewack, Gent., disentailed all his estates, *inter alia*, Penboll *alias* Benboll, Pollagarrow and other lands in St. Kew, and settled the same upon himself and his heirs and assigns for ever, and a fine was levied accordingly.[3] Certain complications and family disputes occurred which were eventually settled by an award on arbitration, made in 1789, in accordance with which, by indentures of lease and release dated respectively 1st and 2nd January 1790,[4] Edward Archer of Trelaske, heir at law and devisee under the will of Swete Nicholas Archer, conveyed to Addis Archer, only son and heir of Addis Archer then late of Plymouth, deceased, *inter alia*, all that undivided moiety of Benboll; and Addis Archer, described as of Leighan, co. Devon, being so seized, by indentures of lease and release dated 4th and 5th January 1803, conveyed the same to the Rev. William Cole of Long Marston in co. Gloucester, to whom had descended, as Lord of the Manor of Penpont, the other moiety. Mr. Cole died in 1805, and the property devolved upon his son William Loggin, who, in the following year, by deed dated 5th September, conveyed the entirety to Samuel West, whose grandson, Mr. James West of Benboll and of Camelford, is the present possessor.[5]

TRETHEVY, *alias* TREWARTHEVY.

We have already stated under Benboll (ante p. 141), that John Beville, in 1593, suffered a fine to Nicholas Dagge in, *inter alia*, Trewarthey Croppe (*alias* Trethevy.) This messuage descended to Richard Dagge of Trevinnick, son and heir of the said Nicholas, who, by charter dated 20th May 2nd Charles (1626), in consideration of the sum of 5s., and for divers other valuable, important and good considerations him thereunto moving, granted, remised, and quitclaimed to Thomas Hutton, Clerk, Bachelor of Divinity and Vicar of St. Kew, all that messuage called Trethevie, *alias* Trethevie Crapp, *alias* Trewarthevie Crapp, to hold to the said Thomas, his heirs and assigns for ever.[6] Thomas Hutton died in 1639 (see ante p. 99, note 3) leaving three sons and four daughters, and by his will, dated 2nd April in the same year, after granting certain legacies, demised all his lands, &c., to his son William Hutton, Bachelor of Laws, and Rector of Northlew, co. Devon. By indentures of lease and release, dated respectively 7th and 8th October 1696, Thomas Hutton of Newton Bushell, Gent., believed to be the son of the aforesaid William,

---

[1] Deed at Trelaske.   [2] Ibid.
[3] Pedes Finium 11th George II., Trinity.   [4] Deed at Trelaske.
[5] Deed in possession of Mr. West.   [6] Deed in the possession of Mr. West.

granted to William Hutton his son and heir apparent the said message of Trethevy Crapp, and by indentures of lease and release, dated respectively 2nd and 3rd October 1704, the said William Hutton, then described as of the parish of Lustleigh, co. Devon, Clerk, conveyed the same to Digory Froad of St. Mabyn, yeoman. Digory Froad being thus seized in fee, by his will dated 7th November 1709, devised to his daughter and heir at law, Elizabeth Froad, all his goods, lands, &c. The said Elizabeth Froad married Hender Mounsteven of Lancarfe, Gent.[1] From Hender Mounsteven the premises descended to his grandson, John Mounsteven, who, by indentures of lease and release dated respectively 10th and 11th May 1786, conveyed the same to his son and heir Hender Mounsteven, who, by deed dated 6th January in the following year, sold the same to Samuel West, whose grandson, Mr. James West of Benboll, is the present possessor.

SKISDON LODGE.

This pleasantly situated house is comparatively of recent creation as a gentleman's residence. It is parcel of the Manor of Tregoide, and we first find it mentioned as a tenement of that manor, under the form of Reskesen, as early as 24th Edward III. (1350).[2] It appears from the terrier of glebe lands,[3] that in 1613 it belonged to one Smyth. In 1707 it was part of the possessions of John Nicholls of Trewane, and was devised by his will to trustees for the use of his grandson, James Nicholls the younger of St. Neot.[4] It was afterwards the property, under lease, of the Rev. John Nation, Vicar of St. Kew, who resided here. In his will, dated 27th June 1724,[5] he says "to my said daughter (Elizabeth) my messuage called Skizzen, near St. Kew Church Town, in which I now dwell." It was afterwards the property of Edward Grigg who married Mary, another daughter of the aforesaid John Nation, and resided here, whose daughter Jane married the Rev. Joseph Bennett, sometime curate in charge of the parish; and when the Rev. Joseph Pomery, the Vicar, came into residence, Mr. Bennett removed from the Vicarage into the house at Skisdon with his father-in-law. Mr. Bennett added a wing to the cottage, built the garden walls, increased the land by purchase, and otherwise improved the property.[6] Mr. Grigg died 27th April 1789,[7] and Mr. Bennett very soon afterwards, having devised Skisdon, *inter alia*, to trustees for his son John Bennett then a minor. It was soon afterwards sold to Major William Clode of the Hon. E. I. Company's Service, son of William Clode of Camelford, Attorney at Law, and Sarah Phillis his wife, daughter of John Holder. Major Clode added other lands to Skisdon

---

[1] Pedigree of Mounsteven, ante Vol. i., p. 300, where the lady is erroneously called Judith (which was her mother's name) instead of Elizabeth. [2] See ante p 130.

[3] See ante p. 96. [4] Will proved in Archd. Court of Cornwall, 11th May 1710

[5] Proved at Exeter, 20th June 1724, see Pedigree of NATION, post.

[6] Additional MSS. 9418, fo. 230. [7] See Monumental Inscriptions, No. 20 and 21, ante p. 109

U²

by exchange with Molesworth, and dying in 1807 s.p., Skisdon, and his other property, passed to Sarah Phillis his sister, wife of Henry Braddon Esq., who made Skisdon his residence, and it is now the property and residence of his grandson, William Clode Braddon, Esq., who has recently made further additions to the house.

POLTREWORGIE.

Poltreworgie in this parish is parcel of the Manor of Lannowmur, and probably formed the barton of that manor. Whilst the manor was in the possession of the family of Bevill Poltreworgie was occasionally the residence of a member of the family, but would not appear to have been so continuously. In the return (Appendix II.) Peter Bevyll appears as being possessed of lands of the value of £9 per annum, and of goods of the value of 100 marks and arms for one man, and he was assessed to the subsidy in St. Kew, 1525,[1] at 100 marks *upon goods*, and John Bevill was assessed at £3 per annum upon lands in 1593,[2] and upon £5 per annum in 1600.[3] John Bevill, on his death 1609,[4] held, *inter alia*, a lease of Poltreworgie granted by his brother Philip Bevill on 4th June 4th James (1606) for a term of ninety-nine years determinable upon the deaths of John Grenville and William Prideaux second son of Humphry Prideaux of Crediton. By his will dated 10th May 1609,[5] he bequeathed the reversion of Poltreworgie, after the death of Johan his wife, to John Hodges, described as "a little boy who lives in my house," to hold to him and the heirs of his body, and in default remainder to the abovementioned William Prideaux.[6] Norden mentions "Poltreworgie the howse of Mr. John Beuill," and in 1642,[7] it is spoken of as having been late in the occupation of Joane Bevill widow. It passed from the family of Bevill to that of Grenville with the Manor of Lannowmur, and is now the property of the Honorable G. M. Fortescue of Boconnoc.

TREWIGGET.

There having been more than one messuage in Trewigget, it is difficult, at all times, with certainty, to identify them. As early as 1280 one of those messuages

---

[1] Subsidy Roll, 16th Henry VIII. $\frac{87}{131}$

[2] Subsidy Rolls, 36th Elizabeth $\frac{88}{273}$　　　　[3] Subsidy Roll, 42nd Elizabeth $\frac{88}{273}$

[4] "Mater Johannes Bevill Armiger sepult. 3 Julij 1609." P.R. By his will he directed that he should be buried in the Parish Church where he should happen to die.

[5] Proved 8th September 1609. Arrhd. Court of Cornwall.

[6] Speculi Brit. Pars. p. 75.　　　　[7] Pedes Finium, 18th Charles, Easter.

belonged to the family of Smith, whose heiress, in the early part of the 14th century, carried it by marriage into the family of Dagge, which family continued seated here at the time of the Herald's Visitation of 1620.[1] In 1627 John Dagge and Dorothy his wife suffered a fine in Trewigget to John Webber and John Lynam.[2] This would seem to be Lower Trewigget, and in this, under the description of the *Manor* of Trewigget neather *alias* Trewigget Roy, John Hicks in 1708 suffered a fine to Thomas Morrice senior, and Thomas Morrice junior.[3]

There was, however, another Trewigget. John Geffrey of Trewigget was one of the jurors on the Inquisition *post mortem* of Ralph Carminow held at Bodmin in 1386,[4] and he was also one of the jurors on the Inquisition taken at Bodmin in 1391, concerning the right of the Priory of Plympton to the Manor of Lanowseynt, adverted to ante p. 87.[5] This was, we presume, Higher Trewigget, which pertained to the Manor of Trelulla in 1308,[6] and is mentioned as pertaining to that Manor in 1545.[7] It was afterwards the inheritacce of John Blake and one Richard Averye. Catherine the only sister and heir of John Blake married George Sprey of St. Kew,[8] but we find that in Hilary term 1668-9,[9] Thomas Blake and Dorothy his wife suffered a fine in one messuage in Higher Trewigget to John Arscott, Esq. It afterwards passed to the family of Phillipps of St. Kew. By deed dated 31st October 1703,[10] Nicholas Phillips of St. Kew, Gent., settled it upon his second son Nicholas Phillips who by his will dated 20th April 1773 directed that it should be sold. It is now the property of the Honorable G. M. Fortescue.

TREGILDREN.

This place, in the 16th century, was parcel of the possessions of the family of Mathew, and was given by William Mathew of Pennytinny to his younger son Nicholas Mathew who died here in 1608. William Matthew, son of Nicholas, compounded for it in 1652. Being a conventionary tenement of the Manor of Lannowmure, it was probably held only on a lease for lives. In 1748 it was held by Mr. Constantine Moyle, at a rent of £14 14s., who was buried at St. Kew on 16th February 1781. He was the son of Mr. Constantine and Prudence Moyle of Trethevan, in this parish, who are commemorated by the gravestone in the floor of the nave of St. Kew Church, ante p. 107, No. 12. Mr. Constantine Moyle by a will dated 3rd August 1780,[11] charged Tregildren with an annuity

---

[1] See Account of Dagge Family, ante Vol. i., pp. 295-97.
[2] Pedes Finium, 3rd Charles, Michaelmas. .
[3] Pedes Finium, 7th Anne, Michaelmas.
[4] Inquisition p.m., 10th Richard II., No. 11.
[5] See also Appendix No. I. F.
[6] Pedes Finium, 2nd Edward II., No. 5.
[7] Recoveries, 37th Henry VIII., Michaelmas m. 413.
[8] Deed in possession of S. M. Grylls, Esq.
[9] Pedes Finium, 21st and 22nd Charles II., Hilary.
[10] Deed in Arthur's Collection.
[11] Proved in Court of Archd. of Cornwall, 10th February, 1781.

of £5 to his sister, Alice Moyle. Nevertheless Tregildren would appear to have been the residence of Samuel Warne, Gent., who was one of two surviving trustees of the Church Charity in 1772 (Constantine Moyle of Trethevan, Esq., being the other) when new trustees were appointed.[1] He died 7th April 1779. (See M. I. No. 29, ante p. 110.)

PENVENTINEW *alias* PENNYTINNY.

Penventinew, or Pennytinny as it is, and has long been, usually called, is parcel of the Manor of Lannowmure, and in the middle of the 18th century was held in convention by one John Doncaster at the rent of £1 16s. 10d. per annum (see p. 121). It was the original seat in this parish of the gentle family of Matthew. It is probable that John Mathew was resident here in 1540, when he was Bailiff for the King of the Manor of Lanho, and it continued to be the seat of the elder branch of the Mathew family until the great grandson of the above John, William Mathew of Pennytinny, having obtained the Barton of Tresunger, in St. Endellion, by the bequest of his uncle of the half-blood removed thither (ante, Vol. i., pp. 565, 569, 570.)

TRETHEVEN.

In 1302, Roger Giffard and Katherine his wife recovered from Gilbert de Condre one messuage and one carucate of land in Treuentheuyn juxta Lanhomur (see ante p. 117).

A family, the members of which we have found repeatedly mentioned in the records, derived its name from this place. We have noticed that John, son of Walter de Tretheven by a charter dated at Tretheuen in 1317, which charter was witnessed by Adam de Tretheuen, confirmed the grant of his ancestors of Vale an Kua Wyll (ante p. 139), and in 1387 Ralph de Tretheuen recovered from Robert Cavell a messuage in Tregellest, and from Elizabeth who was the wife of Robert Huchen two messuages in Tregellest.[2] In 1472 John Bokelly, upon leaving Bokelly, appears to have settled at Trethevyn.[3]

In the early part of the seventeenth century Trethevan was parcel of the possessions of Francis Carnsew, who granted it to Valentine Rolle of Tretawne, who, by deed dated dated 11th April 1640, conveyed it to his sister Phillippa Molesworth and her heirs for ever, and in the same month the said Phillippa settled the same to her own use for life, with remainder to her daughter Mary, the wife of Richard Porter of Launcels, Esq., who, upon his composition, under the articles of Truro, returned two tenements in Trevethan *alias* Tretheven in St. Kew, as of the value of £9 per annum.[1]

[1] Deed in Parish Chest.   [2] De Banco Rolls, 11th Richard II., Easter, m. 159.
[3] De Banco Rolls, 12th Edward IV., m. 33.

In the latter end of the seventeeth century, Tretheven was parcel of the possessions in St. Kew of the family of Keigwin; and upon the marriage, in 1697, of Prudence, daughter of John Keigwin with Constantine Moyle she had this estate as her marriage portion. By Lease and Release dated respectively 22nd and 23rd March 1736, Constantine Moyle the elder of Tretheven, Gent., and James Nichols, described as "formerly of St. Kew, and now of North Petherwyn, co. Devon, Gent.," only surviving trustees of the Church lands in St. Kew, appointed other trustees, among whom was named Constantine Moyle, the younger, of Tretheven; and by a further deed, dated 2nd November 1772, and reciting the last recited deed, Constantine Moyle, of Tretheven, and Samuel Warne, being then the only surviving trustees of the said Church Estate, appointed others, among whom we find named Constantine Moyle, the younger, of Tretheven. The last mentioned Constantine Moyle was the nephew of the former, who by his will, dated 3rd August 1780, devised to him his messuage called Tretheven, to hold to him and the heirs male of his body, and in default of such issue remainder to testator's nephew Constantine Bradford. The last mentioned Constantine Moyle died in 1800, leaving by his wife, Ann daughter of John Curgenven of Tretawne, an only child, Ann, who became the wife of John Furnis of Lamellen in St. Tudy, Gent., by whom she had an only daughter, Elizabeth Ann Moyle, who married John Penberthy Magor of Redruth, Gent., and is still (1874) living at Lamellen, which estate she inherits from her father. After the death of her first husband, Mr. Furnis, who died in 1804, Ann Moyle re-married Richard Hoskin of Carvineck in the parish of Cubert, and is still (1874) living at Elenglaze in that parish, a widow, aged 92 years, and under her marriage settlement with Mr. Furnis holds Tretheven in dower with reversion to her daughter, Mrs. Magor, and her heirs. The Magor family hold another estate in Tretheven, purchased of the Trustees of the late Lady Grenville.

TREVINNICK.

Trevinnick, on the accession of Queen Elizabeth, was the residence of Nicholas Dagge, and his son Richard Dagge was resident there in 1604. By him, or his brother, it was probably sold to Nicholas Sprey of Bodmin in the early part of the seventeenth century, whose grandson, Philip Sprey, was seized of it in 1649, and it formed a portion of the possessions for which, in that year, he compounded with the parliament for the share which he had taken in support of the King. It was then, with other tenements in St. Kew, returned as having been worth £10 a year before the troubles.[2] Philip Sprey,

---

[1] Royalist Composition Papers, Second Series, Vol. liii., fo. 871.

[2] Royalist Comp. Papers, Second Series, Vol. xxxviii., fo. 505.

by his will, dated 8th November 1657, bequeathed to his wife Wilmot, "my mansion house wherein I now dwell, called Trevinnick, during her widowhood, as an increase of joincture," with reversion to his eldest son Nicholas Sprey.[1] Wilmot Sprey died in 1699, when, it is presumed, Trevinnick devolved upon her grandson, son and heir of the above Nicholas, who dying intestate in 1729, we have no further trace of Trevinnick in this family. Perhaps before this date it had become the property of the family of Lang. In 1706 John Lang married Mary daughter of Samuel Mathew of St. Kew, younger brother of Richard, to whose effects he administered in 1668, and son of Andrew Mathew by Philippa Dagge (see Pedigree of Mathew, ante Vol. i., p. 570, see also ante p. 107). Upon the death of John Lang, in 1748, Trevinnick passed to his heirs Ezias Lang and Jane Buckingham, who disposed of it by will. It is now the property of the Molesworth family.

RUGOG *alias* ROWGOG, *alias* ROUKE, *alias* ROOKE.

In the year 1333, John the son of Mauger the son of Lawrence, for the sum of 100 marks of silver, alienated to Ranulph de Albo Monasterio (Blanchminster) one messuage, one mill, one carucate of land, and six acres of meadow with appurtenances in Rugog,[2] and Ranulph died seized of the same lands on 23rd June 1348, leaving John, son of Godwyn Albo Monasterio, son of the said Ranulph, aged ten years and more, his nearest heir. It was then held of the Prior of Launceston, in socage, and the value of it per annum, in all its issues, near the true value, was 100s.[3]

We have not discovered any further trace of this estate until the fifteenth century, when Rugog was part of the possessions of the family of Kelligrew, and was acquired by Thomas Treffry of Fowey by marriage with Elizabeth daughter of John Kelligrew of Penryn, eldest son of John Kelligrew of Arwinneck. By the marriage contract dated 29th September 21st Henry VII. (1505) the parents undertook to settle a competent estate upon their respective children, and John Kelligrew conveyed to Thomas Treffry and Elizabeth, daughter of the said John, all those messuages and lands called Rowcok, with the mill, &c., to hold to the said Thomas and the heirs of his body begotten of the said Elizabeth, and this grant was confirmed by John Kellygrew of Ardwennek, Esq., son and heir of John Kelligrew of Penryn, by charter dated 1st March 3rd Edward VI.[4] (1548-9). Thomas Treffry died in 1563. By deed dated September 31st Elizabeth (1589),[4] John Treffry of Fowey, Esq., conveyed to his younger sons, John Treffry the younger, Mathew Treffry, and Tresithney Treffry for their future maintenance, all that messuage and lands called Rouck, *alias* Rewgog, and the mill thereto pertaining, to hold for the term of their lives, at the rent of £4 per annum. John and Tresithney probably died soon after-

---

[1] Proved January 1658. (83 Wotton) P.C.C.   [2] Pedes Finium, 7th Edward III., Michaelmas 3.
[3] Inq. p. m. 22nd Edward III., No. 36. 1st Nos.   [4] Deeds at Place, Fowey.

wards for Mathew Treffry would seem to have been possessed of it solely, and to have taken up his residence there upon his marriage. His eldest son was baptized at St. Kew in 1624.[1] Upon the surrender of this lease his nephew, John Treffry of Fowey, eldest son of his eldest brother, by deed dated 14th January 1616, granted to him, the said Mathew, the messuage, lands, &c., known by the name of Rowke, *alias* Rewgog, with the grist mill and the toll of the tenants of his Manor of Tregoyd, for the term of the lives of him, the said Mathew, Elizabeth his wife and Thomas their son. Mathew Treffry died in 1626, and was succeeded by his son Thomas, to whom his cousin, John Treffry of Fowey, by deed dated 10th November 1638, sold Roouk, in fee, and Thomas Treffry settled the property by deed dated 28th April 1641, upon his marriage with Jane, daughter of John Vivian of Trewan, Esq. The said John afterwards dying s.p., demised all the lands which descended to him from his grandfather to the said Thomas, who, thereupon, seated himself at Place. He left a son, John Treffry of Place, who sold Rooke to Edward Treffry of Mevagizzy, whose connexion with the family, if any, cannot be traced. Edward Treffry, by deed dated 11th July 1711, charged Rooke with an annuity of £5, payable to the said John Treffry for life. Edward Treffry died in 1727, and John Treffry, by deed dated 2nd May 1728, though never executed, proposed to relieve John Treffry of St. Kew, Gent., upon whom the barton and lands of Rooke had descended by the death of his father and elder brother without issue, of the said annuity, and by a further deed, dated 30th January 1728, also unexecuted, proposed further to relieve the said John Treffry and Edward Treffry from all debts owing to him the said John Treffry, by their father deceased and their deceased elder brother.[2] And further the said John Treffry of Fowey, who died s.p. in 1731, by his will confirmed the sale of Rooke to the aforesaid Edward Treffry. He left several children who had an interest in the estate, for on 11th July 1768, a conveyance was executed by John, Walter, and Constance Treffry,[3] sons and daughter of the aforesaid Edward, to John Treffry, Junior, son of Nicholas Treffry, another son of the aforesaid Edward then recently deceased. John Treffry, Junior, died two years afterwards unmarried. By his representatives Rooke was sold to the Molesworth family by whom it is now possessed.

NEWTON.

Newton, in St. Kew, in the last century belonged to the family of Carew, and was sold by Dame Dorothy Carew and others to James Read, M.D., of Tremeare in St. Tudy, who died thereof seized in 1801. By his will dated 25th October 1800[4] he devised it, *inter alia*, to his wife Loveday Read in trust for his younger children, Susanna Read, Hannah Read, Barbara Read and John Read. By Indentures dated 3rd and 4th April

---

[1] Thomas filius Mathei Treffrye de Rooke bap. 21st Octobris 1604.—P.R.
[2] Deeds at Place. [3] Mr. George Browne's Diary. [4] Proved 27th March 1801.

V

1809, the said Loveday Read sold Newton to Trehane Symons Read, eldest son of the abovementioned Dr. Read. He dying s.p. in the same year, by his will dated 23rd April 1809 [1] devised Newton to his sister Hannah Read. In 1820 Hannah Read married William Norris, son of George Pool Norris, Clerk, and by the marriage settlement, dated 27th May 1820, Newton was settled upon her to her own separate use. William Norris died 12th August 1827, at Newton, and Hannah his wife died s.p. and intestate, leaving her surviving sisters, Susanna, then wife of James Philp, and Barbara, then wife of William Hext, her heirs at law (her brother John having died unmarried) who on 30th May 1828 were granted letters of administration of her effects, and entered upon the possession of the said premises. By Indentures dated 12th and 13th September 1832, the said Susanna Philp and Barbara Hext, with the approbation of their respective husbands, conveyed the said premises to John Arscott Tickell, Gent., who made Newton his residence, and died there on 10th September 1856. By his will dated 12th March 1852,[2] he devised Newton to William Hext of Tredethy, Esq., and to his brother Trehane Symons Tickell of Wade-bridge, Surgeon, in trust for sale when they should deem it desirable, who by deed dated 24th June 1857, sold the same to Mr. Nathaniel Lang, by whose representatives, on 10th January 1872, it was conveyed to the Rev. John Every, late a Chaplain in the Royal Navy, and brother to the Vicar of St. Kew.[3] Mr. Every has lately married Ada Ruth, second daughter of Sir Henry Onslow, Bart. of Hengar, and having rebuilt the house, makes Newton his residence.

PENGENNA.

Is said to have been a seat of the Beale family, and subsequently became the property of Morice, from whom it descended to the Molesworths.

---

[1] Proved 14th October 1809.   [2] Proved 7th October, 1856.
[3] Deeds in the possession of the Rev. John Every.

FAMILY HISTORY.

GIFFARD OF LANOWMURE.

This family is of high antiquity, but has left on our records scarcely sufficient evidence to enable us to trace with certainty its history. In all probability it is of the same stock as the family of Giffard of Helland, of which we have already treated (ante pp. 34 and 40), though we have not succeeded in tracing the connection. In 1299, Robert Giffard and Katherine his wife, through the intervention of Martyn Gyffard, probably the brother of Robert, settled one messuage and two carucates of land in Lannohoumur upon themselves for their lives, with remainder to Nicholas their son and his heirs for ever.[1] This Robert married Katherine the daughter of Roger Pentec,[2] and sister and heir of Laurence Pentec,[3] and he held, together with the Manor of Lannowmure, the Manor of Lanivet, and the advowson of the Church of that manor, which would appear to have been of the inheritance of Katherine, for in the year 1285, Robert and Katherine suffered a fine in Laniueth and Kylelan to Bartholomew Giffard, who settled the same upon the said Robert and Katherine and the heirs of Robert of the body of the said Katherine begotten, and in default of such issue remainder to the *nearest heirs of Katherine.*[4] And in 1299 Robert and Katherine suffered a fine in one

---

[1] Pedes Finium, 27th Edward I., Michaelmas.

[2] Probably the same who was Prepositus of Bodmin temp. Henry III. (see ante, Vol. i., p. 235.)

[3] This lady was probably the relict of Hugh de Muncton (see ante Vol. i., p. 494 n*, and Vol. ii., p. 116.) In 1302 an assize of view of recognizance was granted to enquire if Robert Giffard and Katherine his wife, and Nicholas son of the said Robert had unjustly disseized William, son of Nicholas de Reton (Retin in St. Enoder ?) of a messuage in Bodmin. The jury found that the said messuage had been sometime in the seizin of Nicholas Muncton, father of the said William, and that he had thereof died seized, and that after his death William had entered as son and heir and thereof had been seized for three weeks and more until the said Robert and the others disseized him; and the jury found that the said Robert, after that he had disseized the said William, assigned a third part of the said messuage to Margery who was the wife of the said Nicholas de Muncton to hold as dower, and that she still held it. William recovered the other two-thirds and 60s. damages. (Assize Rolls, 30th Edward I., M 1 21 } 1. m. 5.)

[4] Pedes Finium, 13th Edward I., Trinity No. 1.

V[2]

messuage and one carucate of land in Lannevet, and the Advowson of the Church of the same ville to Nicholas Gyffard and Isabella his wife and the heirs of the said Nicholas.[1] Robert died before 1312,[2] for a vacancy then falling in the Church of Lanivet, a presentation thereto was made by "Waltero Giffard, Sacre Theologiæ Doctore," and others,[3] who were doubtless trustees under some deed of settlement, or will, of Robert. Bartholomew Martyn and Walter were probably brothers of Robert. A vacancy again occurring in 1330, Nicholas Giffard presented Mr. John Giffard, probably his brother.[4] We are inclined to conclude that this Nicholas, whose wife we have seen above was called Isabella, was identical with Sir *Michael* Giffard (erroneously so called in an old pedigree Harl. MSS. 4031) who married Isabella daughter of Sir Richard Hywys, Knt. by Maude daughter of Sir Alan Bloyou, Knt., and is said to have died in 1334. An assize of view of recognizance was granted at the assizes at Bodmin in 1337, to enquire if Isabella Giffard, Stephen de la Monck, and others had unjustly disseized Mr. John Giffard, Parson of the Church of Lanneuet, of his free tenement in "Le Park," juxta Lanneuet, and upon a technicality they were discharged.[5] Sir Michael, otherwise Nicholas, Giffard left a son, John Giffard, who was one of the assessors and venditors of the ninth fleece, &c., in St. Kew in 1341[6] He married Jane, daughter of Peter de Glyn (see ante p. 59) which John presented to the Church of Lanivet in 1349, and was clearly the heir of Nicholas.[7] He died before 1359, and was succeeded by his son Roger who died soon afterwards, and was succeeded by Henry Giffard, probably his brother (see ante, p. 118), who presented Alfred Giffard, perhaps another brother, to the Rectory of Lanivet in 1384. Soon after the accession of King Henry IV., Henry Giffard being about to proceed on a voyage for the defence of the seas, enfeoffed Richard Giffard, bastard, in the Manor of Lanneuet, &c., under the conditions that if the said Henry did not go on the voyage, or if he returned safely to England, he should re-enter upon the lands as in his former state. He did return and became seized of his estates, and being so seized, by his charter dated at Lostwithiel on Tuesday next after the feast of Holy Trinity 5th Henry IV. (1404), he granted the Manors of Lannomur and Lanneuet with the Church of Lanneuet to John Boscawenros, described as "fratri meo," to hold to him his heirs and assigns. Henry Giffard, however, seems soon to have re-entered upon the Manor of Lanivet, for at Launceston, in March 1406-7, an assize of view of recognizance was granted to enquire if Henry Giffard, Richard Giffard, bastard, and Henry Giffard Junior, who was then aged seven-and-half years only, had unjustly disseized the aforesaid John

•

---

[1] Pedes Finium, 27th Edward I., Michaelmas, No. 2.

[2] We find Robert Giffard among the dealers in tin in 1305-6. Stannary Roll, 34th Edward I. Journal of the Royal Institution of Cornwall 1870, p. 242.   [3] Bishop Stapeldon's Register, fo. 70.

[4] Bishop Grandisson's Register, Vol. iii., fo. 16.   [5] Assize Roll, 10th to 14th Edward III., 2 $\genfrac{}{}{0pt}{}{N}{20}$ } 4 m. 110.

[6] Nonarum Inquisitiones. p. 345.

[7] Bishop Grandisson's Register, Vol. iii., fo. 79.   [8] Bishop Brentingham's Register, Vol. ii., fo. 85.

Boscawenros of his Manor of Lanneuet, and John recovered.[1] In the following year Isolda wife of Henry Giffard and the said Henry together were complainants against Stephen Talpyn and Rose his wife, in an assize of new disseizin, and not appearing to prosecute were ordered to be arrested.[2] We have no evidence whether or no the abovementioned Henry Giffard, Junior, was the son of Henry and Isolda. If he were both his father and himself would appear to have died s.p. before 1423, in which year, upon the death of Alfred Giffard, Rector of Lanivet, Benedict, described as " cousin and heir of Robert Giffard and Katherine his wife," presented.[3] This reference to his title as derived from so remote an ancestor would seem to imply that he was not very nearly related to Henry, or, at least, that he did not derive his title through him; nevertheless we find that he was resident in St. Kew long before the death of Henry. In 1384 the Prior of Plympton sued Benedict Giffard for a debt of £8. The Prior alleged that Benedict had, at Lannoweseynt, on Monday next after the feast of Easter 1st Richard II. (1378) bought up all the tithe of the corn growing in Hendre and Trenentony for the sum of 46s., to be paid at the feast of All Saints following, and, further, that at the feast of Trinity the 4th of the said King (1381) the said Benedict had bought of the same Prior the tithe sheaf of all the corn growing in Hendre, Treamelys and Trenentony for the sum of 114s., to be paid at the feast of All Saints following; and that the same had not been paid. Benedict denied the debt and put himself upon the country.[4] He may probably have been an uncle of Henry and a younger son of Nicholas Giffard by Isabella Hywys. In 1398 we find him sued as Benedict Giffard, Senior, together with Thomas Bempet, by Richard Groundy of Bodmin in a plea of debt;[5] and the Manor of Lanowemur ceased to belong to the family. We find the name, however, connected with St. Kew in 1425, when an assize of view of recognizance was granted to inquire if John Jop of Tregellest and Isolda his wife, Benedict Gyffard, Junior, and Thomas Harry of Tregellest had unjustly disseized Geoffry Gregor of Bosiny, of his free tenement in Tregellest juxta Lannoumur. John Jop pleaded that the assize ought not to be had against him, because, he said, a certain Entoa, daughter of John Ive, was lately seized of the tenement and died seized without heirs, and that the tenement had devolved upon the said Isolda as cousin and heir of Entoa: viz., as daughter of John, son of Petronilla, son of John, son of Margery, sister of Richard, father of the said Entoa; by which the said John and Isolda into the said tenement entered in right of the said Isolda.[6]

---

[1] Assize Rolls, 8th Henry IV, $\frac{N}{2}\}$ 4 m. 90.   [2] Assize Rolls, 8th Henry IV. $\frac{N}{2}\}$ 4 m. 107d.
                   37   37

[3] Bishop Lacy's Register, Vol. ii., fo. 57. It may be here observed that there was no subsequent presentation made by the Giffard family. The next was in 1430, by Remfry Arundell.

[4] De Banco Rolls, 8th Richard II., Easter, m. 354d.

[5] De Banco Rolls, 22nd Richard II., Michaelmas, m. 294.

[6] Assize Rolls, 3rd Henry VI. $\frac{N}{2}\}$ 1 m. 68d.
                             42

GIFFARD OF LANOWEMURE.

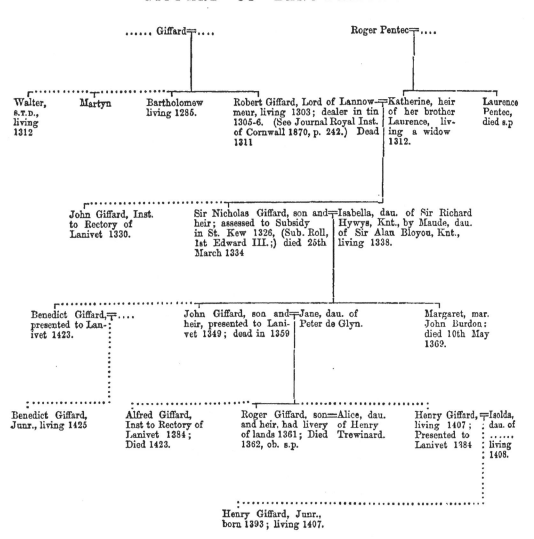

...... Giffard=....   Roger Pentec=....

Walter, s.t.d., living 1312.   Martyn   Bartholomew living 1285.   Robert Giffard, Lord of Lannow-=Katherine, heir meur, living 1303; dealer in tin 1305-6. (See Journal Royal Inst. of Cornwall 1870, p. 242.) Dead 1311   of her brother Laurence, living a widow 1312.   Laurence Pentec, died s.p

John Giffard, Inst. to Rectory of Lanivet 1330.   Sir Nicholas Giffard, son and=Isabella, dau. of Sir Richard heir; assessed to Subsidy in St. Kew 1326, (Sub. Roll, 1st Edward III.;) died 25th March 1334   Hywys, Knt., by Maude, dau. of Sir Alan Bloyou, Knt., living 1338.

Benedict Giffard,=.... presented to Lanivet 1423.   John Giffard, son and=Jane, dau. of heir, presented to Lanivet 1349; dead in 1359   Peter de Glyn.   Margaret, mar. John Burdon: died 10th May 1362.

Benedict Giffard, Junr., living 1425   Alfred Giffard, Inst to Rectory of Lanivet 1384; Died 1423.   Roger Giffard, son=Alice, dau. and heir, had livery of Henry of lands 1361; Died Trewinard. 1362, ob. s.p.   Henry Giffard,=Isolda, living 1407; dau. of Presented to ...... Lanivet 1384 living 1408.

Henry Giffard, Junr., born 1393; living 1407.

DE TREHAVEROCK, *alias* TREAVEREK.

The ancient family of Trehaverock, which derived its name from Trehaverock (now Treharrick) in St. Kew, and gave it to one of the prebends in the Church of St. Endellion, requires some notice at our hands.

The earliest bearer of the name of whom we have any knowledge is Matthew Treauerek, who was one of the dealers in tin in 1305.[1] In the following year he was surety for William Roscarrekmuir,[2] and in 1310 he gave half a mark to have a writ of assize.[3] By his charter he granted all his lands in Trehonek, Trevarthian, and Botconek to John de Tynten for the life of the said John, at the rent of twelve marks per annum, to be paid to the said Matthew and Johanna his wife during their lives, remainder to Johanna, sister and heir of the said Matthew, and wife of John le Run.[4] John Treauerok was assessed to the subsidy in St. Kew in 1327, (vide Appendix III.) He was one of the assessors and venditors of the ninth fleece &c., in St. Kew, 15th Edward III. (1341).[5]

In 1350, Philip de Treauerek was concerned with Henry Cavel in a case of disseizin of lands in St. Teath;[6] and in the following year John de Treauerek, Henry Cavell, and Hugh de Trewyntyn were defendants in a similar suit against Robert de Treaverek, Senior, concerning lands in Trewygtrey, &c., in which Robert recovered.[7] In 1346, this John Trehauerek held one fee in Treonek, which Matthew and Agnes Treonek sometime held.[8] He was witness to a charter dated at Bodmin, 27th Edward III. (1353), and to another dated at the same place the following year,[9] and to a third dated at Treweythek in 1361.[10] He was probably the same John whose daughters married Bray of Treworlas, Cavel, and Tregose.[11]

DE TRELULLA.

Thomas de Trelulla, Clerk, was witness to a charter dated 1269.[12] Roger de Trelulla held lands in Trelulla towards the end of the thirteenth century, of which he was unjustly disseized by Roger Morsell and Anastasia his wife, and in 1302 Warine de

---

[1] Journal of Royal Inst. of Cornwall, 1870, pp. 253, 364.   [2] Assize Roll, Cornwall, 35th Edward I.

[3] Rot. Pip., 3rd Edward II.   [4] Assize Rolls, Cornwall, 14th Edward II. $\frac{N}{2}_{17}$ m. 12. d.

[5] Nonarum Inquisitiones, p. 345.

[6] Ibid, 24th Edward III., $\frac{N}{2}_{23}$ 6. m. 51. d.   [7] Ibid. 25th Edward III., $\frac{N}{2}_{23}$ 6. m. 54.

[8] Aid, 20th Edward III.   [9] Tregothnan Deeds.

[10] See ante, Vol. i., pp. 232, n. 7 and 543 n**   [11] See ante, Vol. i., pp. 503, 504, and n*

[12] Oliver's Monasticon, p. 18.

Trelulla, his son and heir, recovered seizin.[1] Warine, by his wife Dionisia, left two sons, Peter[2] and John, against whom, in 1317, Richard Totybussh and John his brother recovered a free tenement in Trekyou juxta Polrodda.[3] In 1321, John son of Warine de Trelulla, who had taken out a writ of assize of new disseizin against Beatrice relict of Adam Webber, of a tenement in Robsupton, juxta Pollingargorou, did not prosecute and was in mercy with his pledges, of whom one was his brother Peter de Trelulla.[4] And four years afterwards, we find that an assize of new disseizin, in which Dionisia relict of Warine de Trelulla was defendant against John Cheynduit and others concerning a tenement in Dormaen, juxta Trelulla, was postponed for default of jury.[5] In 1334, Peter de Trelulla was sued by Johanna relict of Henry de 'Kellygren, and John son of Henry Kellygren, and others in a plea of assize of new disseizin, which was postponed.[6] Eight years later we find John brother of Peter de Trelulla appointing the said Peter his attorney in a suit against John de Kellygren and others;[7] and in 1344, Peter de Trelulla, himself, sued Johanna relict of Henry de Kellygren and others concerning a tenement in Trekyogh and failed to recover upon a technicality.[8]

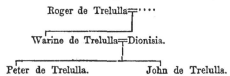

Roger de Trelulla=....

Warine de Trelulla=Dionisia.

Peter de Trelulla.   John de Trelulla.

DE BOKELLY.

We have already stated (ante p. 136) that Bokelly at an early date had given its name to its possessors, many of whom we have mentioned in our account of the estate, which would seem to have passed out of the family of Bokelly about the end of the reign of King Henry VI. The latest occurrence of the name, of which we have any knowledge, is in 1473, in which year John Bokelly, in an action brought against him for trespass, is described as of Trethevan in the parish of St. Cua.[9]

[1] Assize Roll, Cornwall, 30th Edward I. $\frac{M}{1}$ $\frac{21}{}$ 1. m. 7.

[2] In January 1315-16, Nicholas Doden of Treukyhogh suffered a fine in one messuage and one carucate of land in Treukyhogh to Peter de Trelulla, Clerk, for which the said Peter gave him 100s.

[3] Ibid. 11th Edward II. $\frac{N}{2}$ $\frac{16}{}$ 9. m. 21.

[4] Ibid. 14th Edward II., $\frac{N}{2}$ $\frac{17}{}$ 2. m. 22.

[5] Ibid. 18th Edward II. $\frac{N}{2}$ $\frac{17}{}$ 9. m. 12.

[6] Ibid. 8th Edward III., $\frac{N}{2}$ $\frac{19}{}$ 7. Essoins.

[7] Ibid. 16th Edward III., $\frac{N}{2}$ $\frac{21}{}$ 6. m. 26.

[8] Ibid. 17th Edward III., $\frac{N}{2}$ $\frac{21}{}$ 6. m. 15.

[9] De Banco Rolls, 12th Edward IV. Hilary m. 33. (see ante p. 146.)

CAVELL.

The family of Cavel was originally seated in the parish of St. Teath. Upon the marriage of Eleanor, eldest daughter of King Edward I.,[1] Henry Cavel paid the aid for his one fee in Deliomur. In 1283 Henry Cauvel was fined one mark for a trespass on the plea of Richard le Fleming and Oliver de Arundel,[2] and in the same year he and Lucas de Penhal were accused of an indignity offered to the person of the Prior of Bodmin, but it being shewn that they had acted under the authority of the Sheriff they were acquitted.[3] In the following year Henry Cavel was in mercy for selling ten tuns of wine contrary to the assize.[4] In 1286 William, Vicar of St. Teath,[5] on an assize of view of recognizance recovered from Henry Cavel a free tenement in Sayntcs doune, of which the said Henry had unjustly disseized him.[6] Two years later (1288) Henry Cauvel, who had taken out a writ of novel disseizin against Hugh Peverel and Daniel Wof of common of pasture in Hamadethy (Hamatethy), which he claimed as pertaining to his free tenement in Leuedon, did not appear to prosecute and was in mercy.[7] In 1302 a contention, which had been for some time before the courts of law, was decided, wherein Johanna who was the wife of Henry le Stiner recovered her dower out of certain land in Setfenton juxta Trekyogh against Agnes who was the wife of John Cauvel, and which, Agnes stated, had been sometime held by a certain Henry Trehonek her grandfather whose heir she was.[8] In 1329 Henry Cavel was, with others, a defaulter on a jury, and it was ordered that he should be distrained.[9] Henry Cavel died about this time, and was succeeded by his son and heir Roger, who heads the pedigree recorded in the Heralds' College,[10] and is described as " of Trerake."

In 1329 an assize of novel disseizin, which had been granted to Thomas de Trehonek against Roger Cavel and John Weryng, concerning a tenement in Deliomure, was placed in respect for default of jury.[11] In 1340 an assize of view of recognizance was granted to enquire if Nicholas Cavel and Johanna his wife had unjustly disseized William son of Sampson de Yulmouthe of his free tenement in Yulmouth.[12] In 1342 Johanna, daughter of

---

[1] She was affianced to Alphonso, King of Arragon, who dying before marriage, she espoused John Earl of Bar in 1294.

[2] Assize Rolls, Cornwall, 11th Edward I., m. 7. Note—Henry Cavel and Michael Trehauerock were on the jury in December 34th Edward I. (1305) for taking an extent of the lands of Alan Bloyou on his death. Inq. p.m., 34th Edward I., No. 44.

[3] Ibid. m. 8d. See also Vol. i., p. 126.   [4] Assize Rolls, Cornwall, 12th Edward I., $\frac{M}{20}$ } 1 } 4

[5] Sir William de Methe, collated on the day of St. Agnes the Virgin (21st January) 1279. See post St. Teath.

[6] Assize Roll, 14th Edw. I., Hilary $\frac{N}{6}$ } 2 } 4 m. 8.   [7] Ibid., 16th Edw. I. $\frac{N}{6}$ } 2 } 6 m. 8, See also ante Vol, p. i., 355.

[8] Assize Rolls, 30th Edw. I. $\frac{M}{21}$ } 1 } 1 m. 20.   [9] Ibid. 3rd Edw. III. $\frac{N}{18}$ } 2 } 4 m. 19d.   [10] 2 c. 1, p. 386b.

[11] Assize Rolls, Cornw. 3rd Edw. III., $\frac{N}{18}$ } 2 } 4. m. 19d.   [12] Assize Roll, 14th—21st Edw. III., $\frac{N}{21}$ } 2 } 3. m. 21, 23d.

W

Henry Cavel of Haylond, who took out a writ of assize of novel disseizin against John de Tynten and others of a tenement in Haylond, juxta Delioboll, was amerced for default.[1] In 1346, Stephen Cavel who took out letters of assize of new dissezin against John Podding of Treneglos and others of a tenement in Westregre, juxta Oterham, did not prosecute;[2] and in the following year Hamon Peter and Agnes his wife, upon an assize of novel disseizin, recovered a free tenement in Trewynan, juxta Treurosel, against Stephen Cavel and Alice his wife and Stephen de Regre, with damages 40s.; and Stephen Cavel and Alice his wife afterwards made fine with the King of 2s., for the said disseizin.[3] In 1346, when an aid was levied for making the king's eldest son a knight, Roger Cavel was rated for one small fee in Deliomur which Henry his father had held on the marriage of the eldest daughter of King Edward I.[4] In 1350 an assize of view of recognizance was granted to enquire if Henry Cavel, Philip de Treaurek, John Houtham and Stephen Houtham had unjustly disseized Margaret wife of John Westcarne of her free tenements, in Brademor, Wylletus, Haylond, magna Hendre, and Nywehall, juxta Deliouboll, in Delioumur, and John Westcarne and Margaret recovered seizin of all the tenements except Brademor;[5] and in the following year Robert Treauerek, senr., recovered seizin of his free tenements in Trewygtrey and Treuarthyon, juxta Treuentenyn, against John de Treauerek, Henry Cavel of Trewythyon, William Cheyndut, Ralph Cheyndut and Henry Dynan.[6] In 1362 there was a plea of novel disseizin in which Henry Cavel was plaintiff and John Langeston defendant, which was put in respect for default of jury.[7]

It is very probable that the above-mentioned Nicholas, Stephen, and Henry Cavel, as well as Johanna, were younger children of Henry first mentioned, but we have not sufficient evidence to place them upon the pedigree. Robert Cavel, great grandson of the said Henry, is shewn in the Visitation pedigree to have married Sibella, one of the daughters and coheirs of John de Treharrock, *alias* Trehaverock It is clear that Elizabeth, daughter of John de Trehaverock married William Bray of Treworlas, who in her right exercised the patronage of the advowson of the Trehaverock prebend in the Church of St. Endellion in 1392.[8] He died before 1400 when the said Elizabeth, as his relict, presented. The right of the advowson, after the death of Elizabeth, descended to Nicholas Cavel and Peter Tregose, but whether derived immediately from marriage with the coheirs of Trehaverock, or indirectly through coheirs of Bray, is not very clear. Nicholas Cavel presented in 1428, and the next turn, in 1461, devolved upon Peter Tregose. We conclude that the Tregose line became extinct, for the entire patronage devolved upon Nicholas Cavel, son of the above named Robert, and the heir of Trehaverock. Robert must have held the Knight's fee in

---

[1] Assize Roll, Cornwall, 14th—21st Edward III., $\frac{N}{2}$, 21. 3. m. 15*d*.   [2] Ibid. m. 8*d*.

[3] Assize Rolls, 21st Edw. III., $\frac{N}{2}$, 22. 3. m. 5.   [4] Queen's Remb. Off. Misc. Bks. Bk. of Aids, fo. 34, and ante p.135, n.7

[5] Assize Rolls, Cornwall, 24th Edward III., $\frac{N}{2}$, 23. 6. m. 51*d*.   [6] Ibid. m. 53*d*.

[7] Ibid. 36th Edward III., $\frac{N}{2}$, 26. 6. m. 24.   [8] Ante, Vol. i., pp. 503, 505.

Delioumur in 3rd Henry IV. when the aid was levied for the marriage of Blanche, the King's eldest daughter, though the land still stood in the King's books in the name of Henry Cavel.[1]

John Cavel, whom we suppose to have been the brother of this Robert, was one of the manucaptors for Henry Bandyn, one of the Burgesses in Parliament returned for the Borough of Bodmin in 12th Richard II.[2] (1411.)   Nicholas Cavel, son of Robert, presented to the Prebend in 1428 a certain John Cavel, a lay scholar, aged seven years, whom we suppose to be his son.   Nicholas Cavel married Alice, daughter and coheir of John Trecarren, or Trecarne, and relict of William Carnsew of Bokelly.   She would seem to have held Bokelly in dower, and Nicholas Cavel, after his marriage, resided there with her until his death, before 1464.   He is several times mentioned in the de Banco Rolls as "of Bokelly," or as "late of Bokelly."[3]   He must have been twice married, for his daughter Isabella married William Carnsew of Bokelly son of Alice, and William could not have married his half sister.   By Alice he left, with other children, a son and heir Henry Cavel, who, in 1465, is described as "late of Bokelly," in an action brought against William Carnsuyowe late of Bokelly, gent., and himself, by William Mohun, for forcible entry upon the lands of the said William Mohun at Delyowemure.   The case was heard in Michaelmas term the same year, and a verdict given for William Carnsuyowe and Henry Cavel, and William Mohun was left in mercy; and in the same term, William Mohun sued him as "Henry Cavel son and heir of Nicholas Cavel late of Bokelly, gent.,"[4] in a plea of debt of £40 which the said William Mohun alleged was secured to him by a bond given by the said Nicholas Cavel, the father, dated 28th May 20th Henry VI. (1442). Henry denied that the writing was made by his father, and pleaded that as son and heir of the said Nicholas he was not indebted, because, he said, that he had nothing by the decease of his father of inheritance in fee simple.   William Mohun, on the other hand, contended that he ought not to be precluded from his action, because, he said, that on the day of the issue of the writ: viz., 10th September 1465, the said Henry held sufficient lands in fee simple, descended to him from his father: viz., at Trehanek, Trehavereck, Genegan, Newehall, Lanegan, Lanlawren and others, and petitioned an inquiry.   The case was postponed and a jury given.[5]   In the same term William de Mohun, *alias* Sir William de Mohun, summoned Alice who was the wife of Nicholas Cavel late of Bokelly, widow, William Carnsuyowe of Bokelly, gent., and Isabella his wife, executors of the will of Nicholas Cavell, on a plea that they owed him £20, and he alleged that Nicholas, the testator, had given him a bond, dated at Bodenek on 28th May 20th Henry VI. (1442), for the payment of the said sum on the feast of St. Michael following, and that it had not been paid, and he produced the bond in evidence; and the said Alice, William Carnsuyowe and Isabella defended themselves, and said the action ought not to be held against them, because, they said, the same William Carnsuyowe and Isabella his wife were not executors of the will of the said Nicholas Cavel, and had no goods and chattels belonging to him at the time of his death, or since, as executors or administrators, and petitioned judgment; and the aforesaid Alice said

---

[1] Subsidy Rolls, 3 Henry IV.   [2] Ante, Vol. i., p. 242.   [3] De Banco Rolls, 4th to 6th Edward IV.
[4] De Banco Rolls, 5th Edward IV., Michaelmas, m. 461.   [5] Ibid. 6th Edward IV., Easter, 342.

W²

that before the issue of the writ full administration of the goods and chattels of the
said Nicholas had been made, and that nothing remained in her hands.   William de
Mohun rejoined that he ought not to be precluded from his action by these allegations,
because, he said, as to the plea of William Carnsuyowe and Isabella, that after the death
of the said Nicholas the testator, they had administered to divers goods of the said
Nicholas at the time of his death as executors of his will: viz., at Trehavereck and
other places; and as to the plea of Alice, he said that on the day of the issue of the
writ: viz., 12th September 5th Edward IV. *(1465)* the aforesaid Alice had divers goods
which belonged to the said Nicholas in her hands as administratrix, and sufficient to
satisfy the debt: viz., at Bokelly and other places, and he petitioned judgment; a day
was given in Trinity term to hear the case.[1]   It was again postponed, and we have not
further pursued it.   In 1482 Ralph Cavell, late of Lostwithiel, yeoman, was summoned
to reply to John Hopkyn of Bossewe, on a plea that he owed him £5 5s 8d., on a bond
dated at Bossewe, 14th January 1472-3.[2]   Henry Cavel died 2nd November 1485, and
upon the inquisition, *post mortem*, taken at Treaverek on the 27th February following,
it was found that he died seized of 200 acres of arable land in Gomecrau, which he held,
in demesne as of fee of the Castle of Launceston and Duchy of Cornwall by the third
part of one Knyght's fee of the fee of Moreton, and that he held no other hands of the
king in demesne or in service on the day on which he died, and that Nicholas Cavel was
son and nearest heir of the said Henry, and on the day of taking the inquisition was
aged ten years and twenty-four weeks.[3]

Nicholas Cavel, on 1st May 1497, presented his brother William to the Prebend
of Trehaverock in the Church of St. Endellion, the said William being then a lay
scholar of the age of seven years, and he was duly instituted by the Bishop of Exeter,[4]
but the record of the institution is not found on the Bishop's Register.   He was
ordained Priest 20th January 1518-19.   Nicholas Cavel was assessed to the Subsidy
upon lands of the value of twenty marks in 1524.[5]   William Cavel, Prebendary of
Endellion, having died on 20th February 1552-3, and the Prebend being thus vacant,
Nicholas Cavel presented his son William, then a lay scholar and unmarried, and he
was accordingly admitted by the Bishop, but his institution, like that of his uncle, is
not found recorded in the Bishop's Register.   William Cavel, by Elizabeth daughter of
John Godolphin, Esq., had two sons, of whom John the eldest succeeded him at Treharrock, and Andrew, the second son, settled at Creed and died in 1608 without issue,
and William Cavel of Treharrock, his nephew, administered to his effects.   The last
named William Cavel died in 1647 leaving two daughters and co-heirs, of whom Mary,
the eldest, married John Vivian of Trewan, and Johanna, the youngest, became the
wife of John Hore of Trenouth, and both had issue in 1620.   Treharrock descended
to the issue of the former, and was sold by Thomas Vivian in 1699.

Ralph Cavell was Mayor of Lostwithiel on 11th November 1476, on which day he

[1] De Banco Roll, 6th Edw. IV., Easter, m. 393.   [2] Ibid. 22nd Edward IV., Michaelmas, m. 112.
[3] Inq. p. m., 1st Henry VII., No. 28.   [4] Exchequer Lord Treasurer's Memd⁹. 13th Elizabeth.
[5] Subsidy Roll, 16th Henry VIII.

was witness to a deed[1] whereby John Netherton, late of Bodmyn, mercer, and Florence his wife, granted certain messuages in Launceston and in Temple juxta Blisland, to William Oliver and Johanna his wife.[2] And we find that William Cavell, Esq., probably the son, or grandson, of the above-mentioned Ralph, was in 1558 assessed to the subsidy upon lands in St. Winnow of the value of £16,[3] and in 1571 William Cavel, probably the same William, was assessed in St. Veep at £12 a year, in each case being the highest assessment in the parish.[4] In the same year John Cavell was assessed upon land in the Borough of Liskeard.

A Stephen Cavell, Cler., in 1616, made the inventory and valuation for the Will of William Lynam of St. Kew, and in 1621 was witness to a deed between Charles Roscarrock of Roscarrock, Esq., and William Paul of Helland, relative to certain messuages in St. Mabyn Church Town.[5]

In 1592 a fine was levied in which Nicholas Sprey, Gent., was quer. and Dorothy Cavell, widow, Francis Courtenay, Esq., and Elizabeth his wife, Richard Courtenay, Gent., and Oliver Carminowe[6] and Mary his wife were deforciants, by which one messuage in Temple, called Donnaton, and a messuage in Bodmin were conveyed to the said Nicholas Sprey.[7]

In 1555 Humphry Cavell, Robert Bekket, Nicholas Carmynowe, Esq., and John Courteney, Gent., levied a fine of Sir William Godolphin, Knt., and Lady Blanche his wife, of the Manors of Lelant, Trevethowe, and Penventan.[8]

Samuel Cavell of Southpetherton Co. Somerset, Esq., by his will dated 19th March 1698 (Prov. 22nd April 1699, Pett. 55) charged his estates in Devon, Somerset, Wilts and *Cornwall*, with an annuity of £138 to his wife Elizabeth during her life, in addition to lands and tenements in Co. Somerset of the value of £362 per annum, which he had already settled upon her, the whole making up an income of £500 he had agreed to settle upon her in his marriage articles, by way of joincture. He was probably descended from this family.

We have no evidence to enable us to place these persons on the pedigree, though of the same family as the Cavels of Treharrock, as were also, we imagine, the Cavells of St. Tudy, whose name we find in the Registers of that parish at their commencement in 1559 They gradually became reduced until we find the burial of Elizabeth Cavell, in 1764, described as a " pauper."

---

[1] Deed in the possession of Mr. Roger Bate of Cardinham.

[2] William Olyver described as of Lonk, and Johanna his wife and Henry his brother, by their Charter, dated 6th December 18th Henry VI. (1439) granted all their messuages in Temple and Carwen to Trustees, to secure the payment sum of 40d· annually to the Warden of the Stock of the Gild of the Blessed Mary of Blyston. Deed in the possession of Mr. Roger Bate.

[3] Sub. Roll, 1st Elizabeth — $\frac{87}{218}$ [4] Sub. Rolls, 13th Elizabeth — $\frac{88}{225}$ [5] Deed in the Author's collection.

[6] Oliver Carminow of St. Michael Penkevil, died December 1597, leaving by Mary his wife, daughter of Peter Coryton, three daughters co-heirs.

[7] Pedes Finium, 34th Elizabeth, Trinity.   [8] Pedes Finium, 1st Philip and Mary, Easter, No. 13.

PEDIGREE OF CAVELL

Arms of the Family of Cavell as allowed at the Visitation 1620.

Henry Cavell, held one fee in Delioumur time of Edward I.; ⊤ Alice, (Ped Fin. 15th
assessed to subsidy in St. Teath 1st Edward III. (1326). | Edward III., Trinity.)

Roger Cavell of Trerake in ⊤ Anne dau. of John Bodulgate   Johanna, dau. of Henry Cavell
co. Cornw., held one fee in | of co. Cornw., Esq.   1342, (Ass. Roll. Cornw.
Delioumur in 1346.   14-21 Edward III.)

Stephen Cavell of Trerake, ⊤ Johanna, dau. and coh. of Robert
son and heir | Boniface, Esq.

Robert Cavell of Trerake, son and heir, ⊤ Sibella, dau. and coh. of John
Coll. of Subsidies 1407, (Tax Accts. | Trehaverock, Esq.
9th Henry IV.)

..... ⊤ Nicholas Carell of Trehaverock ⊤ Alice, dau. and heir
son and heir, of Bokelly; | of John Trecarren, Esq.,
Dead 1464. | widow of William Carnsewe.

Isabell, mar. William Carnsewe of Bokelly, see Ped. of
CARNSEW, post.

Henry   Richard   William, born 1490; Inst. to Preb. of Trehaverock   John
1st May 1497, then aged 7 years, ordained Priest
20th Jan. 1518-9; Died 20th Feb. 1552-3.

John,   William Carell of Trehaverock, son and heir; ⊤ Elizabeth, 3rd dau. of
2nd son   Assessed to Subs. 1542, admitted to the Preb. | John Godolphin, Esq.
of Trehaverock 21st April 1555.

John Vivian of ⊤ Alice, dau. and heir of   Dorothy, mar.   Philippa,   Anne,
St. Columbe | Tresaster of St.   Thomas Woode.   2 dau.   ob. s.p.
Major. | Wenn in Cornw.

Thomas Vivian of ⊤ Anne, dau. and coh. of   Nicholas, eldest son, ob. s.p.; Adm⁰ in   Katherine, bap.[1]   Mary
St. Columb Major. | Peter Lower of Truro.   Court. of Archd. of Cornw. 9th May   9th Jan. 1570.
1594 (Act lost).

Frances, dau. of Francis Buller ⊤ John Vivian of St. Columb, co. Cornw. Bap.[2] 26th Feb. 1582; bur.[2] ⊤ Mary 1, dau. and coh.;
of Pelint, Cornw., 1st wife. | Will dated 18th Jan. 1641, Prov. 18th Nov. 1647. | mar.[1] 18th April 1615.

Ann, æt. 9   Anne, dau. of Sir ⊤ John Vivian, son and heir, æt. ⊤ Mary, dau. of   Thomas   Mathew, bap.[2] 1625, ⊤ Julian, dau.
1620; bap.[1]   John Trelawny of | 5 years 1620; bap.[2] 9th June | Sir John Glan-   2, bap.[2]   of Advent; will | of Anthony
30th Oct.   Trelawe; died | 1616; sheriff of Cornw. 1668; | ville of ......   10th   dated 14th Sept. | Tanner; mar.
1613.   17th Mar. 1638, | Presented to the Preb. of | co. Devon; mar.   Aug.   1664, prov. 8th | at St. Ewe
s.p. s. | Trehaverock 1675; bur.[2] 12 | at Tavistock,   1617.   April 1665, Archd. | June 1655.
May 1691. | 18th Oct. 1642.   Court of Cornw.

John, bap.[2]   Frances, sister to ⊤ Thomas Vivian of ⊤ Sarah, dau. of ..   Anne, dau. of ⊤ John Vivian ⊤ Mary, dau.
25th Nov.   William Blaithwaite | Truan, son and heir; | Dodson of Haye;   Mathew Halse | of Truan, 2nd | of Joseph
1638; bur.[2]   of Detham, co. | bap.[2] 13th Nov. 1645; | mar.[2] 8th June   of Efford, co. | son; bap.[2] | Sawle of
17th Mar.   Glouc.; bur.[2] 16th | sold Treharrock 1699 | 1710, 2nd wife.   Devon; bur.[2] | Oct. 1647. | Penrice.
1638-9.   Mar. 1707. | bur.[2] 8th June 1716,   19th May 1682. | Barrister at
    s.p.   Law.

John Vivian of Truan,   Thomas Vivian, bap.[2] 12th Sept. 1689;   Mary, only dau.
son and heir.   bur.[2] 1723; unmarried.

[1] At St. Kew.   [2] At St. Columb Major.

AND VIVIAN.

I hereby certify that the portions of this Pedigree which are printed in *Italics* and the Arms agree with the Pedigree and Arms of the families of Cavell and Vivian recorded in this Office. 2. C. 1. fo. 386*b* and fo. 338.

Heralds' College,
6th February 1874.

STEPHEN TUCKER,
Rouge Croix.

Henry Cavell of Trehaverock, son and heir, Died 2nd Nov. 1485, (Inq. p.m. 1st Henry VII. No. 28). ═ *Jane, dau. of John Trevillian of Nettlecombe in co. Som., Esq.*

John Cavell, Inst. to the Prebend of Treharrock upon the presentation of Nicholas Cavell, 18th Dec. 1428; Died 14th Dec. 1460.

Thomas

Nicholas Cavell of Trehaverock, son and heir, aged 10 years and 24 weeks in 27th Feb. 1485-6; Assessed to Subs. 16th Henry VIII. ═ *Thomasine, sole dau. and heir of William Knight of Fowey*

Robert *Alice*

Mary 5, mar. John Roscarrock

Dorothy 3, mar. John Dagge.

Milicent 4, mar. John Wolf
Jane 1, mar. Edw. Winter

Philippa 6

Elizabeth 2, mar. Gregory Bunn

Andrew Cavell, 2 son, of Creed; Died 1608; Adm° granted to nephew Wm. Cavel of Treharrock 31st May 1608, Archd. Court of Cornw.

John Cavell of Trehaverock, son and heir; Died 10th Jan. 1602, M.I. ═ *Philippa, dau. of Lawrence Courteney of Ethy in St. Winnow.*

William Cavell, 2 son, heir to his bro. of Treharrock, living 1620; Bap.[1] 25th Nov. 1569; bur.[1] 19th Dec. 1647; Presented to the Prebend of Trehaverock in 1605 and 1618; Adm° to relict Jane Cavell. ═ *Jane, dau. of William Pomeroy Esq. of co. Devon;* Bur.[1] 26th June 1652; Adm° to estate of her husband, further Adm° of his estate and her own to dau. Mary Vivian, Widow, 14th Sep. 1652.

Elizabeth 2. *Frances 3.* *Isabell 4.* *Dorothie 5, dau.* *Thomasine 6, dau.;* mar.[1] 14th Jan. 1595 Roger Kellie.

Johanna 2, dau. and coh. ═ *John Hore of Trenouth in Cornw.;* mar.[1] 10th Aug. 1618.

Francis, bur.[1] 20th Nov. 1607.

William 3, bap.[2] 1 Nov. 1618; bur. 14th June 1641.

Richard 4 bap. 19th May 1619; living 1653.

Francis, bap.[2] 1st. Feb. 1622.

Edward, bap.[2] 1627; living 1653.

Peter, bap.[2] 12th Sept. 1630; living 1653.

Jonathan Charles Elizabeth Bernard, died in childhood.

Jane, mar. John Treffry of Fowey See Ped. of TREFFRY post.

Mary

John Hore, son and heir, æt. 1 year 1620.

Daughter unchristened 9th Oct. 1620.

Francis Vivian of Coswarth, in right of his wife, 3rd son, bap.[2] 6th Oct. 1649. ═ Anne, only dau. and heir of Henry Maynard of Coswarth, Contract before mar. 20th April 1681.

William, bap.[2] 16th Oct. 1659; bur.[2] 26th June 1663.

Richard, bap.[2] 16th Oct. 1659.

Dorothy 1, named in will of grandfather Anthony Tanner 1688.

Julian 2

Mary 3, named in will of grandfather Anthony Tanner 1688.

Matthew Vivian.

Sir Richard Vyvyan of Trelowarren, Bart. ═ Mary only dau. and heir.

---

[1] At St. Kew. [2] At St. Columb Major.

NICHOLLS OF TREWANE.

We find the family of Nicholls settled at Trewane in the early part of the reign of King Henry VIII. In the return of 1522 (Appendix II.) the name of John Nicol appears as possessing goods of the value of £20, and arms for one man; and three years later[1] he was assessed to the subsidy in St. Kew upon the same amount. In 1543 his name again appears upon the Subsidy Roll as John Nycoll, senior, assessed upon goods at £8, and John Nycoll, junior, is assessed upon £19.[2] The latter died in 1593, leaving five sons, of whom the eldest, John Nicholls, recorded his descent from his grandfather at the Herald's Visitation of 1620. He married Elizabeth, daughter of Edmund Fortescue of Vallapit, and died and was buried the same day, viz., 15th August 1633.[3] Upon the Inquisition taken after his death at Bodmin on 29th October 9th Charles (1633)[4] it was found that he died seized, *inter alia*, of the Manor of Truthen and of certain premises in Lanteglos by Camelford; of a capital messuage, or barton, called Bodulgatt in Lanteglos, also the Manor of Bodulgatt with appurtenances in Delyehennon, Treverlidge, Medrose, Nowallopp, Pinkwalls, Torr, and Trecarlock, in Lanteglos, Advent, and St. Breward; and also of one messuage called Trewane in St. Kew. And the jury say that he held the Manors of Truthen and Bodulgatt of the king as of his Manor of Helston in Trigg, in socage; that he held land in Treburtheke of William Noye as of his Manor of Lannomeere; that he held land in Pendethye and llanseague of Humphry Nicholls as of his Manor of Trelill; that he held land in Tregellest of John Prideaux as of his Manor of St. Kew; that he held a tenement in Treguide of John Treffry as of his Manor of Treguide; and that he held a tenement called Lewynes, *alias* Leweanes, in St. Kew, of Sir Henry Spiller, Knight, as of his Manor of Colquite; and the jury further say that Elizabeth, wife of the said John Nicholls is still living at Trewane, and that John Nicholls his son, aged twenty years five months and eight days, is his nearest heir.

Trewane continued in the name of John Nicholls until 1700, when the then possessor (his eldest son John Nichols, and John Nicholls, son of the said John, having died during his lifetime), by his will devised all his estates to his grandsons James Nicholls, the younger, and Erisey Nicholls, sons of his second son James, in tail male, to the disinherison of his infant granddaughter Elizabeth Nicholls the heir of line. The said James and Erisey, however, died soon afterwards, s.p., and the estates devolved upon the aforesaid Elizabeth as heir at law. She married Nicholas Glynn of Glynn, Esq.,[5] and dying without surviving issue her line became extinct.

---

[1] Subsidy Rolls, 16th Henry VIII. $\frac{87}{131}$

[2] Ibid. 35th Henry VIII., $\frac{87}{154}$

[3] According to the Inquisition and Parish Register.

[4] Inquisition, p. m., 9th Charles, Wards and Liveries, Bund. 53, No. 249.

[5] See Pedigree of Glynn, ante p. 70.

Confirmed to John Nicholls
of Trewane by Wm. Camden
Clarenceux. 2. C. 1. 394.

I certify that the portion of this Pedigree which is printed in *Italics*
and the Arms agree with the Records of this Office. (2. C. 1. 394.)

Heralds' College,   STEPHEN TUCKER,
10th February, 1874.   *Rouge Croix.*

PEDIGREE OF NICHOLLS OF TREWANE.

John Nicholls of Trewane in the parish
of St. Kue, in co. Cornw. Assessed to
Subsidy in St. Kue in 1525 and 1545

John Nicholls of Trewane, son and heir = *Katherine, dau. of John Trobridge of Tro-* | Thomasine,
Assessed to Subsidy 1543. Bur.¹ in the | *bridge, co. Devon.* Bur.¹ 5th July 1607. | mar. Geo.
Church 17th Feb. 1593; Will dat. 17th | Will dated 4th June 1607, prov. 17th | Carnsewe,
Jany. 1593, Prov. 10th May 1594, P.C.C. | Oct. 1708, Archd. Court of Cornw. | see Ped. of
| | CARNSEWE.

Thomas 4	*Nicholas 5,*	John Nicholls of Trewane, *living* = *Elizabeth, dau. of Edmund*	Roger = *Sibell,*	Constance, = *Robert*
named	named	1620, *son and heir.* Executor to	*Fortescue of Fallapitt, co.*	Nicholls, dau. of	dau. of Hugh	Nicholls,
in his	in his	his mother's will. Died and was	*Devon.* Mar. settl. 30th Sep.	2nd son, John	Pomeroy of	3rd son.
mother's	mother's	bur.¹ 15th Aug. 1633; will dat.	43rd Elizab.; executrix to	named Killi-	Tregony.	Named
will.	will;	10th Aug., and prov. 2nd Oct.	her husband's will. Bur.¹	in his owe of	Married at	in his
	bur.¹ 10th	1633, Exon. Inq. p.m.	28th Nov. 1634; will dated	mother's Laun-	St. Minver	mother's
	Sept.	9th Charles I., Wards and	15th Nov. and prov. 11th	will. celles.	13th Nov.	will.
	1622.	Liveries, Bundle 53, No. 249.	Dec. 1634.		1604.

Nicho-	Doro-	*John Nicholls, son* = Brid-	Valen-	Francis Nicholls, 2nd	Sibella 1,	Grace 2	Mary 3	Eliza-	Sibella	Roger
las,	thy,	*and heir, æt. 7*	get,	tine,	*son;* named in his	bur.¹		bap.¹	beth,	bur.¹	Nich-
bap.¹	Kath-	1620, bap.¹ 7th	dau. of	named	fath's will. Barrister	20th		29th	bap.¹	11th	olls,
1st	erine,	Mar. 1612; nam.	......	in	at Law of the Middle	Nov.		June	11th	Aug.	bap.¹
Sept.	bap.¹	in his father's	remar.	fathr's	Temple, and of Tre-	1661,		1620;	Jany.	1604.	26th
1622;	9th	will; aged 20	Sir	will.	hane in Davidstow;	unmar		named	1616.		Feb.
bur.¹	July	years on his fa-	James		bur. at Davidstow	named		in			1605.
10th	1626,	ther's death;	Smith.		18th June 1674, aged	in		fathr's			
Sep.	named	bur. ¹11th Mar.			56. M.I. Adm° grant-	fathr's		will.			
1622.	in	1646-7. will dat.			ed at Exon 26th	will					
	fathr's	6th Mar. 1646-7,			June 1674 to nephew						
	will.	prov. 1st July			John Nicholls of						
		1647, (Fines160)			Trewane.						

John Nicholls, bap.¹ 1st April 1638; bur.¹ 13th = Lucy, dau. of ...... Bur.¹ 7th	Reginald, bap.¹ 5th	Ferdinando,
Jan. 1709; will dated 9th Oct. 1707, prov. 11th	Aug. 1669. Adm° granted at	May 1639; bur.¹	bap.¹ 13th
May 1709 Archd. Court of Cornw.	Exon 1669 to husband.	11th May 1640.	April 1645.

John Nicholls, = Mary, dau. of	James Nicholls, = Dionisie, dau. of Richard Erisie of	Bridget,	Lucy, bap.¹ 4th	Eliza-
bap.¹ 3rd	John Pearse	bap.¹ 31st May	Trevenna; born 26th April and bap.²	bap.¹ 5th	Dec. 1662; mar.	beth,
Mar. 1658. Of	of Davidstow,	1660. Of Chelsea	17th May 1659; mar.² 27th Nov.	Jany.	John Belamy of	mar.
Davidstow.	mar. settl 10th	College and of	1681; bur.² 6th Dec. 1700;	1664.	Drewstenton co.	......
	Sept. 1675	St. Neot.	settl. after mar. 20th Oct. 1688.		Devon.	Belamy.

Henry, namd.	John Nic- = Elizabeth, eld. dau. and	Mary,	James = Lætitia,	Bridgett,	Erisey	Mary, bap.²
in his brothr's	holls of	coh. of Sir Joseph	mar.	Nicholls, dau. of	born 12th	Nicholls,	25th Nov.
will, and in	Davidstow;	Tredenham of Trego-	Yeo,	born 9th Stephen	and bap.²	born 2nd	1696; died
that of his	will dated	nan; mar. settl.	nam'd in	and bap.² Northleigh	22 April	and bap.²	unmar.;
sister-in-law	17th July	20th June 1701; mar.	her	22nd mar. settl.	1688;	19th	will dated
Elizabeth	1707, prov.	at St. Veep 24th July	mother's	March 30th Sept.	bur.¹	Aug.	10th Jany.
Nicholls, dat.	10th Nov.	same year. Will dated	will 1720	1684. Of 1710.	24th	1693.	1723-4.
1714, ob. s.p.	1707, P.C.C.	27th Dec. 1714, Codl.		Trewane	Dec. 1700.	ob. s.p.	
		5th May 1720.		ob. s.p.			

Elizabeth Nicholls, dau. and heir; mar. Nicholas Glynn of
Glynn; named in her mother's will.

---

¹ At St. Kew.   ² At St. Neot.

X

ARMS OF Nicholls as confirmed to John Nicholls of Trewane by William Camden Clarencieux : sa. three pheons ar.

The same arms, with a crescent or in fess point as a mark of Cadency, and impaling : gu. upon a fess between three mascles or, three escalops, the whole within a bordure engrailed of the second charged with torteauxes, are, or were, surmounting a tablet in the north transept of the Abbey Church of Bath, commemorating Mary the wife of Sir Augustine Nicols of Foxton co. Northampton, one of the Justices of the Common Pleas, which Mary died in 1614.[1] Sir Augustine was the second son of Thomas Nicholls of Pichley in the same county. He died s.p., and was succeeded by his nephew, Francis Nicholls of Hardwick and Foxton. It should, however, be observed that the arms allowed at the Herald's Visitation of Northamptonshire in 1618 to this family were the reverse of those of Nicholls of Trewane : viz., ar. three pheons sa.[2]

WEBBER OF MIDDLE AMBLE.

The name of Webber was so common in the parish of St. Kew that we have found it impossible to trace the family in all its ramifications. The names of John Webber and Richard Webber appear in the Return of 1522 (Appendix II.), and the latter was assessed to the subsidy upon goods, three years later, of the value of ten marks.[1] In 1545 Richard Webber and Nicholas Webber were assessed upon goods of the value of £5 each.[2] In 1549 Nicholas Webber was assessed upon £10.[3] In 1559 Nicholas Webber was assessed upon £7 and William Webber upon £6.[4] This William was the same who as " William Webber of Amell," heads the pedigree recorded at the Herald's Visitation of 1620.

In the Parish Registers the name of Webber is one of the first which occurs, and the entries are so numerous that an attempt was made to distinguish the different parties by their respective places of residence. In 1565 we find the marriage of John Webber of Penpont and Margery Trewbodie, and then occur the baptisms of numerous issue of this marriage. We can, by means of the Registers, trace the Penpont Branch for five or six descents, though not with that exactness which is necessary for the compilation of a pedigree.

In 1570 occurs the burial of John Webber, but his place of residence is not given.

In 1571 we find the marriage of John Webber and Johanna Trewbodie, and the recorded pedigree enables us to identify this John as the son of William Webber of Amell, mentioned above, and the children of this marriage, in the record of their baptisms are described as those of " John Webber of Amble."

[1] History from Marble compiled in the reign of Charles II. by Thomas Dingley, Gent. Part I., p. 30.
[2] Harl. MS. 1553 fo. 175.

[1] Sub. Roll, 16th Henry VIII. $\frac{87}{131}$

[2] Ibid. 37th Henry VIII. $\frac{87}{179}$

[3] Ibid. 3rd Edward VI. VI. $\frac{87}{198}$

[4] Ibid. 1st Elizabeth $\frac{87}{218}$

These two families would seem to stand alone (and they certainly were then and continued to be the most opulent and important, and, only, are described as gentlemen) until 1590, when we find John Webber of St. Kew mentioned, and in the next year John Webber of Trethevie and Richard Webber of Amble, which Richard is not named in the pedigree of Webber of Middle Amble. In 1594 we have William Webber of Trelill named, and two years later John Webber of Trelill, and in 1599 Nicholas Webber of *Lower* Amble. The occurrence of all these different branches, and several others, with the same Christian names prevailing throughout the whole, has baffled us in our attempt to disentangle the web.

John Webber of Amble, mentioned above as having married Johanna Trewbodie, had a son of his own name, who by his first wife Honour, the daughter of John Calwodeley of Padstow, had two sons Richard and Mathew, both of whom matriculated at Exeter College, Oxford. Of the former we have no further certain knowledge. He probably died young, for his younger brother inherited his mother's property at Padstow, where he settled and where his younger children were baptized between 1652 and 1659.

John Webber, by his second marriage with Susanna daughter of Digory Polwhele, had a son Digory who succeeded his father at Middle Amble, and left a son, Jonathan, mentioned by Hals[1] as of Middle Amble, who had two sons Ezekiel and John. The latter matriculated at New Inn Hall, Oxford, in 1711, from which time we lose sight of him. He must have died s.p., before his brother, who died intestate in 1760 possessed of considerable estates,[2] and administration was granted to Mary Webber, spinster, his sister and next of kin. She died in 1764, and by her will devised the chief part of her lands to her great nephew John Treffry; residue to her niece, Mary Treffry wife of Nicholas Treffry, and mother of the said John. John Treffry died in 1770, s.p., and the said Mary Treffry having in her will named her brother, John Phillipps, residuary legatee, further adminstration of the effects of the said Ezekiel Webber, left unadminstered to by the said Mary Webber and by the executors of the will of the said Mary Webber, and by Mary Treffry, was granted on 3rd June 1797, to said John Phillipps, his mother Gertrude Phillipps having died without having taken upon herself letters of administration.[3]

Arms of Webber of Middle Amble: gu. upon a chevron engrailed or, between three plates, three annulets az. These arms are not recorded on the pedigree in the Heralds' College, but they are "tricked" on the Visitation pedigree in Harl. MS. 1079, fo. 138, and were allowed to John Webber of Amble, under the certificate of Sir John Borough, Knight, Garter Principal King of Arms, dated 8th March 1638. Original in the possession of Major-General Hamley.

[1] Hals's MSS. History of Cornwall, now the property of the author. See also Davies Gilbert's History of Cornwall, Vol. ii., p. 366.

[2] He possessed lands in the parishes of St. Kew, St. Minver, St. Merrin, Egloshayle, Endellion, Tintagel, Camelford, St. Teath, Padstow, and Temple, a rental of which is now before us dated in 1771.

[3] Act Books, P. C. C.

x²

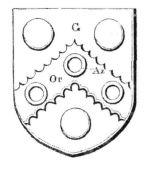

PEDIGREE OF

WEBBER OF MIDDLE AMBLE.

William Webber of Amell in the parish of St. ⊤ *.... dau. of William Mathew of St.*
Kew, co. Cornwall. Bur. 13th Sept. 1595. | *Kew, relict of Harper of St. Kue.*

John Webber of Amell, son and ⊤ *Johanna dau. of ...... Trewbody of Trengate in the parish of St. Cleer*
heir. Bur.[1] 3rd Oct. 1606. | *Mar.[1] 20th June 1571; bur.[1] 4th Sept. 1614.*

| Margaret mar. Alexander Hauley of Trebbethick in St. Mabyn. | *George 2, Webber bap. 22nd Sept. 1588.* | *Susanna dau. of Digory Polwhele of Trewargan in Cornw. 2nd wife. Bur.[1] 8th March 1661* | ⊤*John Webber of Amell living 1620. Bap.[1] 2nd May 1578; bur.[1] 10th April 1648.* | *Honour dau. of John Callowalley of Padstow in Cornw. Esq. 1st wife. Bur.[1] 6th Oct. 1601, M.I. No.9.* | Elizabeth, bap.[1] 10 Jan. 1579 | Matilda, bap.[1] 13th Oct. 1583. | Johanna bap.[1] 1st May 1586 |

| Katherine bap. 24th Dec. bur. 27th Dec. 1609. | *Katherine æt 9 Bap.[1] 3rd Nov. 1611; mar.[1] William Rawle of St. Juliot, 4th March 1632.* | *Joane at 6. Bap.[1] 23rd June 1615.* | *Susanna, æt. 3 Bap.[1] 20th April 1618.* | *Digory Webber,* ⊤*.... 3rd son, æt. 4 yrs. Of Middle Amble; Matric. at Wadham Coll. Oxford, 19th Jan. 1637-8, æt. 18; bur.[1] Jan. 1699.* | *Richard Webber, eldest sonn æt. 20 ano 1620, bap.[1] 22nd Jany. 1599; matric. at Exeter Col. Oxf. 3rd May 1621.* | *Matthew 2nd, æt. 19. Bap.[1] 25th Sept. 1601; Matric. at Exeter Col. Oxf.10th Oct. 1623, aged 19 (sic); bur.[1] 14th June 1683.* ⊤Johanna | Honour bap. 22nd Jan. 1599. ob. s. p. |

| Willm Rawle, bap.[1] 20th June 1635. | Katherine bap.[1] 15th July 1656; mar.[1] 14 Sept. 1680, William Grey of St. Minver. | Elizabeth, bap. 30th July 1657; bur. 29th Mar. 1659. | Jonathan ⊤.... of Middle Amble, bap.[1] 4th June 1659; bur.[1] 12th Sept. 1731. | Susanna, bap.[1] 8th May 1665 | John, bap. 25th June 1667 | Matthew, born 25th, bap.[2] 28th Aug. 1652. | Elizabeth born 26th April; bap.[1] 9th May 1655 adm[d.] 8th Oct. 1683 to her mother, Jane Webber. | Mary, born 14th Dec., bap.[2] 5th Jany. 1659. | John Webber, bap.[1] 14th Mar. 1610; bur.[1] 6th June 1642. | John Webber, bap.[1] 2nd May 1643. | Charity bap.[1] 29th Jan. 1652. | Honour bap.[1] 29th June 1645; bur.[2] 10th Nov. 1664, unmar. |

| Mary, bap. 14th Oct 1682; died unmar. By a cod. to this will dated 30th June 1762, gave £10 to be laid out in the purchase of a piece of plate for the communion of St. Kew; proved 28th Jany. 1764. (Simpson 34.) | Gertrude, bap.[1] 17th June 1684, mar. Humphry Phillips of Trewigget in St. Kew; mar.[1] 20th February 1706. ⊤ | Ezekiel Webber, bap.[1] 18th March 1685; died 1760 unmar. Adm[c.] to his sister Mary Webber, spinster, 11th November 1760. Further adm[o.] to Exr. of her will, Sept. 1764, and further adm[n.] to John Phillips, 3rd June 1797. | Anne, bap. 18th Sept. 1688. | Susanna, bap. 24th April 1690. | John Webber, bap.[1] 17th Aug. 1693; Matric. at New Inn Hall, Oxf. 8th May 1711, aged 17. |

Nicholas Treffry of Rooke, died 25th ⊤ Mary Phillips bur.[1] 22nd
and bur.[1] 28th Dec. 1767. | July 1775.

John Treffry of Rooke, bap.[1] 9th July 1745;
died 1st and bur.[1] 4th April 1770, æt. 24, s.p.
See ped. of TREFFRY post.

I certify that the portion of this Pedigree which is printed in
Italics, agrees with the Records of this Office.   2. C. 1. fo. 442*b*.

Heralds' College.

10th February, 1874.

STEPHEN TUCKER,

Rouge Croix.

---

[1] At St. Kew.   [2] At Padstow.

CARNSUYOWE *alias* CARNSEWE.

This ancient family derived its name from Carnsewe in the parish of Mabe, which it long possessed. At our first knowledge of them, however, they were seated at Trembrise (Trehembris usually called Trembrase) in St. Kevern. Watkyn Carnsew of Tenbryse (see Pedigree Table I,) married Honour the daughter of ....Tregose. Their great grandson married Alice, daughter and heir of John Trecarne of Trecarne, in Advent, and thereby acquired that estate which remained in the family many descents. In the Carnsew pedigree he is called *Richard*, but Alice after his death, married Nicholas Cavel of Trerake, (Treharrock) and in the pedigree of Cavel she is described as the "widow of *William* Carnsewe," and this is confirmed by several entries in the records. How, about this time, Bokelly passed to the family of Carnsew we know not, but Alice would seem to have possessed it either of inheritance, or dower, and here her husband, William Carnsew, resided with her until his death in 1464, when it devolved upon William Carnsew, son of the above William, who, in the same year is described as "William Carnsewe of Bokelly." He was Sheriff of Cornwall in 1478, and in the following year a precept was issued to his successor to distrain him on account of some debt to the Crown arising out of his office.[1] He married Isabella, daughter of his step-father, of course by an earlier marriage, and had two sons and two daughters.

William, son and heir of the last mentioned William, was in the commission of the peace during the reign of Henry VII, and in the 8th year of that King he had license to alienate his land without the payment of a fine, being about to accompany the King in his voyage to France.[2] In the following year he was in the commission of Oyer and Terminer, and in 1511 he served the office of Sheriff. In the Return (Appendix II,) he is stated to have lands and tenements in St. Kew of the value of £3 6s. 8d. per annum, and goods of the value £40. Upon the inquisition taken after his death it was found that by his charter, dated at Bokelly on Monday next after the feast of the Conception of the Blessed Virgin Mary (December 8th,) 15th Henry VIII (1523), he had settled his manors of Trehembris and Newlyn, and all his lands, including Bokelly, Lanseage, Upton, Trecarne, Trewint, &c., upon trustees to the use of himself for life, and after his death to the use of William his son, begotten of the body of Elizabeth the daughter of Richard Tregose, and the heirs of his body, in default of such issue remainder to Johanna, late the wife of John Beauchympe and Milicent Gaveregan his daughters, which he begat of Juliana daughter of Lawrence Sherston, and the heirs of their bodies; in default of such issue remainder to John Carnsuyowe brother of grantee and the heirs of his body; in default, remainder to Alice Polgreen and Johanna Nanskevell his sisters and the heirs of their bodies; and in default of such issue, as regarded Bokelly and Lanseage, &c. with the mills, &c. remainder to James Luke and his heirs and assigns for ever; which lands,

---

[1] De Banco Rolls, 19th, Edward IV., Hil. m. 185.　　[2] Rot. Pat. 8th, Henry VII., m. 8

&c. he held of Peter Bevyll and Philippa his wife and others. And it was found that the said William Carnsuyowe died 20th June 20th Henry VIII. (1528) and that William Carnsuyowe was his son and heir and was aged 31 years and more.[1] Accordingly, in consequence of the conveyance, William Carnsew, the elder, was not assessed to the subsidy in 1525, but William Carnsuyou, junior, was assessed upon lands of the value of £4 per annum.[2]

William Carnsew, last mentioned, married Johanna daughter and co-heir of Edmund Stradling of St. Dominick, or St. Dometts, co. Glamorgan, by Katherine one of the daughters and co-heirs of John Trenowith,[3] by whom he had several children. He was assessed to the subsidy in St. Kew in 1543[4] upon £20 a year in lands, as he was again in 1545 and 1550.[5] A Privy Seal was directed to him in 1570, but on the 15th April in that year it was reported to the Council that it could not be delivered because he was dead.[6] He was buried on the 11th of that month.[7] He left four sons of whom William, the eldest, succeeded him at Bokelly; John, the second, settled at Trecarne in Advent; of Thomas we are unable to give any information; and George, the fourth, was of Brighter in St. Kew. William and George were assessed to the subsidy in St. Kew in the year of their father's death, the former in £7 in lands, and the latter on £3 in goods. William Carnsew left three sons and two daughters of whom Matthew, the second, died unmarried in 1613.

William, the third son of the above-mentioned William, married Ann daughter of John Arundell of Trerise, and resided at St. Anthonye (in Meneage?) There are several letters from him among the State Papers, addressed to his brother Richard, and to his brother-in-law John Arundell. It appears from one of the former, dated 17th March 1615, that his wife was rebuilding Carnsew house, and he expresses a desire to obtain from his brother a lease of a certain close.[8] He died s.p. in 1627, his wife having pre-deceased him, and administration of his effects was granted to his brother Sir Richard Carnsew.

Richard Carnsew succeeded his father at Bokelly. In 1613, he was Treasurer for the Eastern Division of the county. In 1619, he married Grace, daughter and heir of Arthur Fowell of Fowellscombe, co. Devon, and relict of Richard Barrett of Tregarden in St. Mabyn, and soon afterwards attained to the degree of knighthood. In 1621, as Sir Richard Carnsew, he was one of the Commissioners for collecting the Fine for the Prince.[9] He was sometime resident in London, for, on 2nd July 1623, there was a writ of Proclamation of Outlawry against him (under the description of Sir Richard Carnsew, formerly of London now of Buckelly co. Cornwall), unless he appeared and answered to a claim

---

[1] Inq. p. m. 21st Henry VIII., No. 64.   [2] Sub. Roll. 16th Henry VIII. $\frac{87}{131}$ [3] See Ante Vol. i., p. 546.

[4] Sub. Roll. 35th Henry VIII. $\frac{87}{154}$ [5] Ibid. 37th Henry VIII. $\frac{87}{179}$ and 3rd Edward VI. $\frac{87}{198}$

[6] State Papers, Dom. Corr. Vol. lxvii. 63 .   [7] Parish Registers.

[8] "If you do sett Park Angue I will geve you for my wife's life therein as much as any reasonable man will. She hath her life on nothing by my procurement, and that lieth fittest for Carnsew, wher the little demains can hardly keep a house, if she have but that close she will be willing to bestow a good deal on building Carnsew house; thus leaving you to God,   Your loving brother,   WILLIAM CARNSOW.

To the wor' my loving brother Richard Carnsow, Esq., these." (State Papers, Dom. Corr., Vol. lxxx., 53.)

[9] State Papers, Dom. Corr., Vol. cxxiii., 87.

for £40. He died in 1629 s.p., when administration of his personal estate, with the assent of Dame Grace his widow, was granted to Margaret Hill of Advent, widow, cousin and next of kin, who was the only child and heir of John Carnsew, his eldest uncle; and his lands passed to the issue of his uncle George. In 1662, Bokelly was sold by George Carnsew, grandson of the said George, and Anne his wife, and Richard their son and heir. See ante p. 137.

ARMS of Carnsew:—Sa. a goat passant ar. attired or.

THOMAS, *alias* CARNSEW.

There is another family bearing the name of Carnsew, and, we believe, the only persons in whom the name now resteth. Tonkin says: "One of the Carnsews of Bokelly, in the reign of Queen Elizabeth, granted a lease of the barton of Carnsew to William Thomas, which William Thomas from thenceforth took the name of Carnsew; and I have in my possession a grant of arms from Sir Richard St. George, Clarenceux King-at-Arms, to Henry Carnsew of Trewoon, jun. dated the 2nd December 1633, recognising this assumption of a new name from his place of residence."[1] This assumption had, however, been previously recognised by the Heralds in the record of the pedigree of this family at the Visitation of Cornwall in 1620, see pedigree Table II annexed. We have no knowledge of the lease referred to by Tonkin but it had evidently expired before 1615, when we find William Carnsew rebuilding the house at Carnsew (ante p. 170), and in the Visitation pedigree of 1620 Henry Thomas, *alias* Carnsew, is described as of "Treune" (Trewoon) in St. Budock. His son married Gertrude daughter of John St. Aubyn of Clowance Esq., and had a large family. John his eldest son died in 1675, s.p., and by his will, dated 13 April 1670, devised his manors of Trewoon and Trevenna and other considerable lands to Trustees (of whom John St. Aubyn of Clowance, created a Baronet in the following year, was one) for the uses of his brothers Henry, Francis, Thomas, William, and Nicholas, in successive tail male, and in default of such issue to the right heirs of testator. The above mentioned Thomas, fourth son of Henry Thomas, *alias* Carnsew, by Gertrude St. Aubyn, who succeeded to the estates and sold Trewoon to —— Trewinard, is now represented by the Rev. Thomas Stone Carnsew of Flexbury in the Parish of Poughill, and Vicar of that parish.

ARMS.—There does not appear to be any record in the Heralds' College of the "Grant" referred to by Tonkin, from which fact we are inclined to think that Sir Richard St. George's licence, or recognition, related to the assumption of the name only. Hals says: these Carnsews give for their Arms, ar. a chev. between three talbot sa. but that is a coat of Talbot and Cowderon; while the same charges, with colours reversed, were borne by the family of Lanhergy, before mentioned (ante p. 119); facts which confirm our discredit of the statement of Hals.

[1] Davies Gilbert's History of Cornwall. Vol. ii., p. 61.

Arms as allowed at the Herald's Visitation 1620.
2. C. 1. 399*d*.

1. CARNESEW.
2. TRECARNE.
3. STRADLING.
4. TRENOUTH.
5. NANFANT.
6. TREJAGUE.
7. CHENDUIT.
8. CARNESEW.

PEDIGREE OF

Watkyn Carnesew of ═ *Honor, dau. of* ...... *Tregose of*
Tenbryse. │ *co. Cornw.*

John Carnesew of Tenbrise, ═ ......
son and heir.

John Carnesew, son ═ *Jane, dau. and heir of*
and heir. │ *John Nulinge.*

(William) Richard Carnesew, son and ═ *Alice, dau. and heir of John Trecarne*
heir; died 1464. │ *of Trecarne.*

William Carnesew, son and heir ═ *Isabella, 2nd dau. of Nicholas.*
Sheriff of Cornwall 1478 │ *Carell of Trehaverock.*

Jane or Joane, ═ *William Carnesew, sonne and heir.* ═ *Eliza, 2nd dau.*
dau. and coh. of │ Sheriff of Cornw. 1511. Died │ *of Rich. Tregose,*
Laurence Shers- │ 20th June 1528, Inq. p.m., 21st │ *2nd wife.*
ton, 1st wife. │ Henry VIII., No. 64.

Jane, 1st wife to John Beauchamp of │ *Millicent wife to John*
Beere, and 2ndly to Rich. Langdon. │ *Gaueregan of Gaveregan*
│ *in Corn and hath yssue*
│ *Jane and Millicent*

John and Thomas Beauchamp.

George Carnesew ═ *Thomasine, dau.* │ *John Carnesew* ═ *Ann, dau. of*
of Brighter; │ *of John Nicoll, of* │ *of Trekare,* │ *Gilbert Ashhurst*
of St. Kue, in │ *St. Kue in co.* │ *(Trecarne in* │ *of Lancash.;*
Cornw. 4th sonne │ *Cornw.; bur.* │ *Advent,) 2nd* │ *bur. St. Kew*
bur. 1604. │ *25th Oct. 1603.* │ *sonne.* │ *1579.*

George bap. 19th Oct. 1565.	William, bap.[1] 17th Feby. 1567.	Ann, wife of Hugh Prust of Hart-land, in Devon.	Honour wife to John Joliff. Mar.[1] 5th Nov. 1582	Francis Carnesew of Phil-ley in co. Cornw. 1620. Bap.[1] 10th Nov. 1572.	Mary, dau. of John Webber of St. Kue. Mar.[1] 26 Jan. 1601 bur. 29th Jan. 1647.	Marga-rett, wife to John Lukie of Helland in Cornw. Mar.[1] 4th June 1599.

Mathew Carnesew, ═ *Mary dau. of .. Webber;*   *Philippa*, bap.[1] 9th June   *Mary 2.*
2nd son. │ *mar.*[3] *1625.*   1606.

Margery bap.[3] 19th Feb. 1635; mar.[1] William Shoule 1681.	Ann, bap.[1] 27th Aug. 1637.	Mary, bap.[1] 8th Feb. 1646; bur.[1] 13th May 1647.	Phil-ippa, bap.[1] 1st Feb. 1648.	John Carn-sew, bap.[1] May 1651.	Frances bap.[1] 24th March 1638; bur.[1] 1st Dec. 1643.	Mary, bap.[1] 30th Jan. 1640.	Martha bap. 26th Dec. 1642.	Mary, bap.[4] 7th Nov. 1613.	Johan-na, bur. 9th	Mathew Carnsew, bap.[1] 2nd Oct. 1644 of St. Tudy; bur.[5] 26th Apr. 1712.	Mary, dau. of ...... Leverton of St. Tudy; mar.[3] 31st July 1673; bur.[5] 18th May 1679.

Phillippa, bap.[5]   *Eve*, bap.[5] 1686;   Mathew Carnsew, bap.[5] 1674;
1st April 1687.   bur.[5] 1687.   bur.[5] 24th May 1684.

[1] At St. Kew.   [2] At St. Mabyn.   [3] At Michaelstow.   [4] At St. Teath.   [5] At St. Tudy.

CARNESEW.—Table I.

I hereby certify that the portions of this Pedigree which are printed in *Italics*, and the Arms agree with the Records of this Office. 2. C. 1. 399*b*.

Heralds' College,
12th February, 1874.

STEPHEN TUCKER,
Rouge Croix.

Ihon 2, living 1524.
Jane 1, Mar. ...... Nanskevel.
Alice 2, Mar .... Polgreen.

Edmond Stradling=*Katherine dau. and heir of John Trenouth.*

William Carnesew of St. Kue in Cornw.=*Jane, dau. and heir* (coh.) *of Edw. Stradling of St. Donetts in Wales; sonne and heir; aged 31 years on his father's death; buried at St. Kew 11th April 1570.* | *bur. at St. Kew 1566. Found to be one of the coheirs of John Trenowith, Inq. p. m., 15th Henry VIII., No. 77. See ante, Vol. i., p. 546.*

William Carnesew of Bokelly, co. Cornwall, sonne and heir; bur. 26th Febry. 1588.=*Honor, dau. of John Fitz, of Tavistock, in co. Devon.*

Thomas, 3.

Margery wife of Robert Flamock, re-mar. John Whitston of Whitston. He made a will and constituted Wm. Carnsew, his father, and Margery his wife Exrs. She was living a widow 19th June, 2nd Edward VI.
Margaret.
Mary mar. Wm. Langford, 2ndly, Rich. Wills.

| Grace, bap.[1] 31 Oct. 1582; mar.[1] Richd. Carne of St. Kew, 20th June 1603. | Joane, bur.[1] 25th March 15̃5. | *Margaret,* mar Morris Hill of Heligan (see Ped. of HILL, post), adm° to the effects of Sir Richard Carnsew as cous. &nearest of kin, 30th Nov. 1629; then a widow. | *Mat-hew, 2nd son* Bur.[1] 30th Sept. 1613. | *Sir Rich. Carnsew,* *Knt. sonne and heir;* bur.[1] 13th May 1629; adm° grant. 30th Nov. 1629, with the consent of Lady Grace his relict, to Margaret Hill of St.Advent, widow, cousin and nearest of kin, P.C.C. | =Grace, dau. and heir of Arthur Fowell of Fow-lescombe, and relict of Richard Barrett of Tre-garden; mar. lic.dat.11th and mar.[2] 24th Sept. 1619; died 7th and bur.[2] 8th July1656 æt.73. | *William* of St. Anthony died s.p. adm° to his bro. Sir Rich. Carnsew, 5th July 1627. | =Ann, dau. of John Arun-dell of Trerise. | *Frances,* died unmar. will dated 11th May 1605; prov. 4th Feb. 1605-6. Archd. Court of Cornw. | *Grace.* |

George Carnsew, eldest sonne of Advent; bap.[1] 2nd March 1602; will dated=Ann dau. of Humph. May, mar[2] 1st Dec. 1690; prov. 9th Sept. 1691. Exon | 25th Nov. 1631.

Francis, 3rd sonne.

| Mary, bap.[1] 16th Sept. 1632; bur.[1] 17th June 1650. | Richard, bap.[1] 17th October 1635, son and heir; named in father's will, 1690. | Ann, bap.[1] 24th June, 1638; bur.[1] 10th Sept. 1640. | George Carnsew, bap.[1] 18th July 1642, of St. Tudy in 1671. | =Mary. | Grace, bap.[1] 3rd Sept. 1643. | Frances, bap.[1] 28th Aug. 1645; execu-trix to father's will 1691, then unmar. | Thomasine, bap.[1] 31st Jan. 1646. |

John, bap.[5] 1679; bur.[5] 26th May 1746.

Mary, bap.[5] 1676

Mary, bap.[5] 1669.

---

[1] At St. Kew. [2] At St. Mabyn. [3] At Michaelstow. [4] At St. Teath. [5] At St. Tudy

Y

PEDIGREE OF

William Thomas, alias Carnsew, of Carnsew,⸗Matilda, dau. and heir of ...... Drew
in co. Cornwall. | of Trigney.

Henry Thomas, alias Carnsew, of Carnsew,⸗Juliana, dau. of ...... Tubb of St. Niott,
son and heir | in co. Cornwall.

Henry Thomas, alias Carnsew, of Treune, in co. Cornwall; died 8th March 1605; bur.[1]⸗Charity, dau. of James Tripcunnye.
M.I.; will proved at Exon 1605; names all his children and Margaret his sister
and her children

Henry Thomas, alias Carnsew, son and heir, aged 23, 1620, of⸗Gertrude eld. dau. of John St. Aubyn of Clowance;
Trewoone; will dated 17th March 1642, proved at Exeter | aged 15 in 1620, bur.[2] 14th Dec. 1667
1648, but now lost

| John Carnsew, bap.[1] 13th June 1630, of Trewoone; bur.[2] 24th Nov. 1674; will dated 13th April 1670, proved 12th June 1675, P.C.C. (Dycer 145) s.p. | Henry Carnsew, named in brother John's will 1670 | Johan, mar. ...... Taylder named in Sister Gertrude's will. | Francis named in bro. John's will⸗Martha. of Christ Church, Barbadoes; will dated 13th July 1671, proved 1st April 1673 (Pye 41) s.p. |

| Gertrude, bap.[2] 3rd Feb. 1667; bur.[2] 29th Nov. 1685. | Catherine, bap.[2] 25th Feb. 1672. | Thomas Carnsew, bap.[1] 20th Oct. 1663; bur.[3] August 1717. Supervisor of Excise⸗Margery, dau. of ...... Hooper. |

| Anna, bap.[3] 1712. | John Carnsew, bap.[3] June 1715, of Lostwithiel⸗Elizabeth, dau. of ...... Couch, mar.[4] 13th Feb. 1737. |

| Mary, bap.[4] 9th August 1743. | John Carnsew, bap.[4] 1st May, 1746; bur.[4] 17th March 1751. | William, bap.[4] 10th Nov. 1751; bur.[4] 7th Aug. 1768. |

Thomas Carnsew bap.[4] 7th Feb. 1779; died 15th March; bur.[7]⸗Ann, dau. of John Morgan. Esq.; mar. St.
20th March 1860; will proved 14th April 1860, at Bodmin | Lawrence Jewry, London 1812.

| Ann, born 26th Sept. 1813; bur.[7] 5th April 1873. | Gertrude, born 1815; mar.[7] R. B. Cowie, Clerk, now (1874) Dean of Manchester. | Margaret, born 14th April 1816. | Elizabeth, born 7th Dec. 1817; mar.[7] Henry Vyvyan, Clerk, Vicar of Seaton, Devon. | James, born April 1819; bur. 1847, at Adelaide, New South Wales. |

| Frances, bap.[7] 27th Nov. 1861. | Walter Henry, bap.[7] 29th Nov. 1862 | Emma Marian, bap.[7] 20th Feb. 1864. |

---

[1] At St. Budock.   [2] At Mabe.   [3] At St. Mary Magdalene, Taunton.

[4] At Lostwithiel.   [5] At Bodmin.   [6] At Stratton.   [7] At Poughill.

CARNSEW.—TABLE II.

I hereby certify that the portions of this Pedigree which are printed in *Italics* agree with the Records of this Office. 2. C. 1. 391.

Heralds' College,
12th February, 1874.

STEPHEN TUCKER,
Rouge Croix.

Thomas Thomas, alias=*Sibella dau. of Edward*
Carnsew, 2nd son   *Kestell of Kestell.*

Margaret, mar.
and had issue.

James, 2nd son, living 1670, named in will of nephew, John ;   *Grace, mar. John Chenowith*   *Elinor.*
will dated 19th May 1673 ; proved Exon; bur.² 19th July 1673.   *Juliana.*
                                                                                                            Johanna.

| Thomas Carn-=sew, bap.¹; named in bro. John's will; died at Falmo. adm°toFlorence his relict, 24th Feb. 1695. | Florence dau. of ...... Paskoe; mar. 2Cth Oct. 1663, under licence dated 4th July, same year. | William, named in bro. John's will. Of St. Clement Danes, Middlesex, adm° 8th July 1671, to Brother John. | Nicholas named in bro. John's will | Grace, named in her Sister Gertrude's will, 1692, then unmar. | Kath-erine | Gertrude, diedunmar. will dated 1st July 1692, prov. 8th July 1694. Exon. | Charity. | Anne, bur.² 7th Sept. 1671 adm° 20th June 1672 to bro. John Carnsew of Trewoone. |

Henry, bap.² 27th June 1670.   William, bap.¹ 6th Jan. 1679. bur.³ 26th June 1695.

Elizabeth, bap.⁵ 1700 ; bur.⁵ 1701.   Grace, bap.⁵ 1702.

| James Carnsew, bap.⁴ 2nd Feb. 1748 ; died 30th Jan.=Elizabeth, dau. of Nichs. 1823, aged 76 years ; bur.⁶ M.I. ; will proved 10th May Norway of Lostwithiel; 1823 ; Archd. Court of Cornwall | bap.⁴ 1755 ; mar.⁴ | Joseph, bap.⁴ 24th June 1751 | Philip, bap.⁴ 29th Sept. 1758. |

Betsey, bap.⁶ 2nd Feb. 1781. bur.⁶ 21st March 1859, unmar.   Anna, bap.⁶ 12th Sept. 1782. bur.⁶ Nov. 13th 1784.

| Thomas Stone Carnsew, Clerk, bap.=Frances Hallett, dau. of Sir J. at Stoke Newington, Middlesex E. Honywood of Evington, co. 1825 ; matric. St. John's Coll. Kent, Bart., mar. at St. Camb. 1851 ; Inst. to Vicarage of Michael's, Chester Square, Poughill, Jan. 1857, of Flexbury in London, 22nd Jan. 1861 that Parish. | William, born 1824 ; midship-man in the Navy ; bur. at Calcutta 1849 | Henry, born April 26th 1826 | Emma, bap.⁷ 27th Oct. 1830 ; bur.⁷ 4th April 1848, unmar. |

Mary Gertrude, bap.⁷ 29th July 1865.   Florence Hilden, bap⁷ 5th July 1868.   John Honywood, bap.⁷ 12th Jan. 1873.

---

¹ At St. Budock.   ² At Mabe.   ³ At St. Mary Magdalene, Taunton.

⁴ At Lostwithiel.   ⁵ At Bodmin.   ⁶ At Stratton.   ⁷ At Poughill

Y²

TREGAGLE.

The family of Tregagle, which sometime held the advowson of the Rectory of St. Kew and the Barton of Bokelly, in the beginning of the seventeenth Century was residing at Bosvallack in St. Allen. John Tregagle is said[1] to have married a daughter of...... Polwhele and to have had a son of the same name who was bred to the law and became Steward to the family of Robartes, Earls of Radnor. He purchased of Edmund Prideaux the estate of Trevorder in St. Breoke, long before parcel of the possessions of the family of Billing, and which was carried by Elizabeth daughter and co-heir of Richard Billing of Trevorder in marriage to George Vyell, and by the co-heir of Vyell to Nicholas Prideaux. Tradition states that this John Tregagle was a very arbitrary, unscrupulous and unjust man. He certainly was very unpopular, and his name has been handed down to us with infamy. According to the superstitious belief of the peasantry he, for his evil deeds, has been doomed to the never ending task of emptying Dosmary Pool by means of a limpet shell with a hole in its bottom. His son, John Tregagle, became Receiver General of the Duchy of Cornwall, in which office he was succeeded by his son of the same name, but they seem not to have prospered, and their lands were sold. John Tregagle, the younger, married the daughter of Sir Paul Whichcote, Bart., by whom he had three sons, John, Francis, and Nathaniel, and a daughter Jane.[2] Their aunt, Susan Coleman of Melchet Park, co. Wilts (supposed to have been a sister of their mother,) by her will dated in 1719, settled the Melchet Park Estate upon her nephews John Tregagle, Francis Tregagle, and Nathaniel Tregagle, and their heirs, in succession in tail male, and in default of such issue remainder to their sister Jane Tregagle the wife of Thomas Whichcote of Harpwell. The latter had a daughter Jane who, surviving her mother, her uncles, and their male issue, inherited the estates, and having married Christopher son of Sir Francis Whichcote, Baronet, whom he afterwards succeeded to the title, was empowered by an Act of Parliament, passed before 1775, to sell the Manor of Melchet.[3]

Arms. Lysons attributes to this family the arms: ar. three bucks trippant or; which is false heraldry. The same arms, however, are found on a Tregagle monument in the Church of White-parish, co. Wilts, in which parish Melchet Park is situate, impaling: ar. a saltier sa. on a chief gu. three woolpacks of the first. The arms assumed by John Tregagle of St. Allen were, however, disclaimed at Bodmin at the Heralds' Visitation of 1620,[4] and he pronounced ignoble; and no subsequent grant of arms can be traced in the College of Arms.

[1] C. S. Gilbert's Hist. of Corn. Vol. II., p. 279.

[2] C. S. Gilbert says a daughter married .... Brewer of St. Breoke. Hist. of Corn., Vol. II., p. 280.

[3] Hoare's Wilts. Hund. of Alderbury, Vol. V., p. 78.   [4] 2. C. I., fo. 308*b*.

PEDIGREE OF TREGAGLE.

John Tregagle of Bosvallack══...... dau. of ......
in St. Allen.   Polwhele.

John Tregagle of Trevorder══Jane, dau. of Sir══Nicholas Courteney, mar.[3]
in St. Breoke, Steward of │ Thomas   Grenville,   28th April 1656.
Lord Robartes; bur.[3] 3rd │ Knt.
Oct. 1655.

Richard Tregagle.   Grenville.   John Tregagle of Trevorder══Elizabeth, dau. of Sir   Jane, mar.
and of the Inner Temple, │ William Hooker, mar.   Bryan Rogers
London ;   Receiver-General │ licence 27th April 1667, of Helston;
of the Duchy of Cornwall. │ to marry at St. Botolph, mar.[3] 24th
Burg. in Parliament for the │ Bishopsgate or St. Cath. May 1704.
Borough of Bosinny 1679; │ Cree, London, then aged
bur.[3] 7th Feb. 1679-80, M.I. │ 19 ; bur.[3] 19th May
Will dated 15th July 1678; │ 1679, M.I.
proved 17th March 1679-80.
(Bath 42.)

John, bur.[3]   Elizabeth, mar. at   John Tregagle of Trevorder,══Jane dau. of Sir Paul   Richard
3rd April   St. Minver, 30th Oct.   Receiver General of the │ Whichcote of Quy Hall   named
1672, s.p.   1701, to William   Duchy of Cornwall; Burg. │ co. Camb. Bart., sett[l]   in his
Reed, Clerk, Rector   in Parl. for Bor. of Bosinny │ after mar. 21st April   father's
of St. Breoke.   1698-1700.   Adm° granted │ 1699,[3] died 19th March will.
to Francis Tregagle, 3rd Dec- │ 1708, aged 27, and bur.[3]
ember, 1753, P. C. C.   │ M.I.

John Tregagle   Francis, bap.[3]   Nathaniel,   Thomas Whichcote══Jane, heir   ....
of Trevorder and   24th May   3rd son. of   of Harpwell co. │ of her   mar.......
of Melchet Park   1704; heir   Melchet   Linc.   │ brothers.   Brewer of
Wilts; bap. at St.   at law of his   Park. a   St. Breoke.
Anne's, Soho Lon- brother John. merchant
don, 16th Jany.   Sold Advow.   in South
1699-70.   of St. Kew   Carolina.
1748.

Christopher, son of Sir══Jane Whichcote
Francis Whichcote Bart. dau. and heir of
her mother and
uncles.

[3] At St. Breoke.

DAGGE OF TREWIGGET AND TREVINNICK.

We have already given some account of this ancient family (Vol. I., pp. 295—297) with such portion of the pedigree as was recorded at the Herald's Visitation of 1620, and a continuation of the descents from Abel, third son of John, Dagge of Trewigget by Margery the daughter of William Webber. We now return to John Dagge, eldest son of the same John, who had a son and heir Richard, aged eight years, in 1620—who was assessed to the subsidy in St. Kew in 1641.[1] Richard married, but died in 1642 s.p., his wife Johanna having pre-deceased him in 1635. And his brothers are not traced to have left issue.

Nicholas Dagge, second son of John Dagge of Trewigget, grandfather of John Dagge first above-mentioned and Dorothy his wife daughter of William Cavell, was settled at Trevinnick, in the beginning of the reign of Queen Elizabeth. He is described as of Trevinnick in the Parish Register in the record of the burial of his son John in 1565. He was assessed to the Subsidy in St. Kew in 1571,[2] again in 1594, at the rate of £16 a year,[3] being the highest assessment in the parish except two, and again in 1597, when he was assessed in £18 a year which was then the highest rate; the assessment of John Webber of Amble, only, being equal to it.[4] Nicholas Dagge had a large family of whom Richard, the eldest, succeeded him at Trevinnick. To his son Degory he gave a moiety of Benboll, who dying without issue it devolved upon his elder brother Richard who was living in 1623,[5] but appears to have died without surviving issue. Degory Dagge devised to his brothers George and Nicholas the impropriate Rectory of St. Austle for the term which he had therein. It would appear from the Will of Richard Dagge of Endellion that his father, George Dagge, was dead in 1625. This Will is of some interest. He bequeathed to his mother Elizabeth Dagge, *inter alia*, "a cup made with a nutt and bound with silver," and his "best gould Cuppe." To his brother Nicholas he gave his estate for term of years in the Sheaf Tithe of St. Austle, and also his inlaid sword and the hangers on it. To his brother Hazael certain apparel and one trunk of books in his chamber in London and his silver sword with the hangers. To his sister Mary Dagge certain apparel, plate and jewels, and "a great old trunk in his chamber in London and all that is in it." To his sister Chestyn Dagge apparel, plate and jewels, and the goods which he had in a trunk at Sir Gerard Sammes's. To the parish of Endellion "as a means to keep the poor on work for ever 40s." He would appear to have been in some way connected with Sir Gerard Sammes to whom he gave £20 and certain diamond rings; and to Lady Sammes the elder he gave £10.[6] To Mr. Reginald Billinge of St. Mabin, Gent, he gave certain rich furniture from his chamber in London and £10 to buy him a piece of plate.

[1] Sub. Roll, 17th Charles $\frac{88}{334}$ [2] Sub. Roll, 13th Elizabeth $\frac{88}{228}$

[3] Ibid, 36th Elizabeth $\frac{88}{253}$ [4] Ibid, 39th Elizabeth $\frac{88}{261}$ [5] See Ante, p. 141.

[6] Sir Gerard Sammes, Knight, died 1630, adm°. to his mother Dame Isabel Sammes during minority of Richard Sammes son of deceased, the relict Dame Ursula renouncing. P. C. C.

PEDIGREE OF DAGGE.

IN CONTINUATION OF PEDIGREE Vol. I., pp. 295-297.

Nicholas Dagge of Trevinnick in St. Kew, assessed to sub. in St. Kew, 1591, 1594, and 1597. = Elizabeth dau. of ....

George Dagge of St. Columb, named in his brother Degory's Will. Dead in 1625. = Elizabeth, named in her son Richard's will, to whom she admo.

John bur.[4] 22nd Aug. 1565.

Degory, bap.[4] 3rd Nov. 1569; bur.[4] 5th Nov. 1622, s.p. Will dated 8th Oct. 1622; Prov. 11th Feb. 1622-3 (Swann11).

Nicholas Dagge, bap.[4] 27th Dec. 1575 assessed to Sub. in St. Kew, 1625, 1637; bur.[4] 15th Mar. 1643 = Mary, dau. of ...... Crom, mar.[4] 15th Oct. 1611; bur.[4] 14th Feb. 1674.

Chesten, bap.[4] 17th Aug. 1578; mar.[4] 5th Feby. 1595; Thomas Raw of Endellion.

John Dagge bap.[4] 17th Dec. 1581, of Penpont. = ...

Elizabeth, bap.[4] 8 June 1984; mar.[4] 3 Feb. 1601, of Humphry Maye. = ...

Richard Dagge, eldest son of Trevinnick, living 1623. = ...

Margaret mar. 20th Mar. 1583, Walter Jeffrey.

Richard Dagge, of Endellion named in his uncle Degory's will, dated 17th Aug. 1625; prov. 21st Oct. 1626. (Hele 134)

Nicholas Dagge named in Bro. Richard's will.

Hazael Dagge named in his Bro. Richard's will. = Alice, dau. of Christ. Moyle of St. Minver, bap.[5] 1603; mar.[5] 23rd Jan. 1633

Mary, named in Bro. Richard's will.

Hanna, named in Bro. Richard's will.

Chestyn, named in Bro. Richard's will.

Elizabeth, named in Bro. Richard's will.

Catherine bap.[5] 3rd Mar. 1634

John, bap.[5] 9th Feb. 1635

Jane bap.[4] 19th Dec. 1613.

Johanna bap.[4] 17th, and bur.[4] 18th Aug. 1617.

William Dagge bap.[4] 8th Dec. 1612; will dated 5th July 1654; proved 3rd April 1666. = Joane dau. of

Nicholas, bap.[4] 25th Feb. 1620; bur.[4] 15th Aug. 1639.

Anne bap.[4] 9th Aug. 1629.

Jane, bap. 10th July 1640.

Richard bap.[4] 6th Nov. 1608 and bur. following day.

Thomas bur.[4] 14th Mar. 1604.

Elizabeth bap.[4] 6th Jan. 1594.

Nicholas Dagge bap.[4] 10th Dec. 1647. Exr to his father's will; bur.[4] 31st May 1667.

Mary bap.[4] 16th April 1650; bur.[4] 14th 1676.

Thomas Dagge, named in his father's will, bur.[4] June 1666.

Richard, bap.[4] 25th Dec. 1647; died before his father, in whose will he is not named.

[4] At St. Kew.

[5] At St. Minver.

LE ARCHER, *alias* ARCHER.

The family of Le Archer held in ancient times the lordship of the Manor of Lizard, and we find the name in connection with that district at a very early date. The family seat was probably at a place still called "Archer's Hale," or "Archer's Hall," in the parish of Landewednack. In 1283 Flora, the relict of Peter Le Archer, petitioned against Godfrey de Penros and Mary his wife, concerning the third part of one acre of land in Boffrantam; and against Dionisia, the daughter of Richard de Penros, concerning the third part of two parts of one carucate of land with appurtenances, (except the third part of two parts of five acres of land in the same ville); and against Nicholaa, daughter of Richard de Penros, of the third part of two parts of one carucate of land and a half (except as above.) Godfrey and Mary appeared and said that they held the said tenements in right of dower of the said Mary of the inheritance of the said Dionisia, Nicholaa, and a certain Johanna their sister, who were within age;[1] and Flora was non-suited. At the same assize the said Flora, who had taken out a writ of ingress concerning certain tenements in Rosesyon, was in mercy for failing to prosecute.[2] And at the same time Henry Le Archer, who was probably the son and heir of the aforesaid Peter, was presented for not taking up his Knighthood, he holding one entire Knight's fee and being of full age.[3]

In 1290, William Le Archer was defendant in a suit with others brought against them by Joan daughter of Fenicia de Bosworwetwoeles and Lucy her sister, for the recovery of a certain free tenement in Treures, juxta Pendu, of which the said Joan and Lucy recovered seizin.[4]

In 1302 a certain John Le Archer was charged with striking a man on the head with a stick in the Ville of Lyzard, and killing him on the spot. "Johannes Le Archer percussit Johannem de Sancto Rumone quadam baculo in capite in Villa de Lyzard ita quod statim obiit." He was taken and delivered to the Tithing of Lyzard to be kept in custody, but he escaped and the Sheriff seized his lands and goods. He afterwards surrendered himself, and pleaded that he was a clerk and could not answer for the offence before the civil tribunal, and John de Middelwode, the official of the Bishop, came and demanded him as a clerk. The facts, however, were inquired into by a jury who found the said John guilty of felony, and he was delivered up to the Bishop as a convict. His lands and goods were accordingly forfeited, the former being in the Hundred of Penwith

---

[1] Assize Roll, Cornw. 12th Edward I. 1 $\frac{M}{20}$ 4. m. 9d.

[2] Ibid, m. 10.

[3] Ibid, m. 11.

[4] Ibid, 16th to 18th Edward I., 2 $\frac{N}{7}$ 2, m. 15.

and worth per annum 25s. 9d.[1]   In the same year (1302) we find Dionis, the daughter of Henry le Archer, who had taken out a Writ of novel disseizin against Amadeus son of John Archer, Emeranda who was the wife of Henry le Archer, and John the son of Henry le Archer of Lulyn, concerning the tenement called Porthenes juxta Brewyn, in mercy for not appearing to prosecute.[2]

In 17th Edward II, (1323-4) Henry de Mingois and Johanna his wife recovered against John Archer, junior, and others, two messuages, one acre of land Cornish, and one acre of meadow in Hensiwen and Treneglos, juxta Luddre;[3] and in 1327 we find John Le Archer amerced in 6d. for default on a jury.[4]

In 1331 John Le Archer, senior, recovered against Richard de Bello Prato (Beauchamp) Parson of the Church of St. Just, and William Mabernal, a certain tenement in Bosseghan Kynysieks;[5] and in 1337 the same John Le Archer, junior, took proceedings against Peter de Kemyel and Henry de Kemyel for having diverted a watercourse in Kynyseik belonging to the said John, and thereof it was enquired whether the said John had mills in Bosseghan, and whether the mill called Kynysiek was damaged by the diversion of the water.   The jury found for the plaintiff and he recovered damages.[6]

We do not find any further trace of the family until the year 1387,[7] a period of fifty years, when John Archer was lord of Lesard, but whether he was John Archer, junr. who was living in 1323, or John Archer who made a certain deed in 1400, to which we shall presently refer, or whether there was another John Archer between them, we cannot with certainty shew.   There can, however, be no doubt, from the identity of the lands named in the below mentioned records, that the succession continued unbroken.   We have John Archer of Liszeard again mentioned in 1394.[8]

John Archer of Lyzard, on 10th September 1st Henry IV. (1400) confirmed to John Archer, under the description of "John Archer my eldest son," for the period of his life, all the grantor's messuages, &c., in the ville of Karallek, with his mill of Bosseghan, with the multure of all his tenants in Dovran, and Bosseghan, and Kanserow, with the reversion of the tenements which Henry Magor held for the life of the grantor in the ville of Arghansawth, with remainder over, successively, to grantor's son Roger; to his son John by his wife Isolda; to his son John by his wife Hyngryn Pegersek, and lastly to Thomas Curteys. On the 20th of the same month he

---

[1] Assize Roll, Cornw. 30th Edward I., $\frac{N}{1}$ m. 49.   [2] Ibid.
$\quad$ 21

[3] Ibid. 17th Edward II.   [4] Ibid. 1st Edward III.

[5] Ibid. 4th Edward III., $\frac{N}{2}$ 2, m. 13.   [6] Assize Roll, Cornw., 10th to 14th Edw. III., $\frac{N}{2}$ 4. m. 111
$\quad$ 19   20

[7] Thomas, son of Thomas Marsely of Treureythyowe sued Thomas Treworgy and others that they should acquit him of services due to John Archer of Leshard, for a free tenement which the said Thomas Treworgy and the others held in Leshard and Gurfoys.   (De Banco Rolls, 18th Richard II., Trinity.)

[8] John Archer of Liszeard versus Richard Rosmodres, John Caru of Treuronek and Johanna, who was the wife of Thomas Trenewith, on a plea why they had taken and appropriated the goods of the said John Archer at Segblan.   (De Banco Rolls, 18th Richard II., Michaelmas, m. 236.)

Z

confirmed to his son Roger all his messuages, &c., in the villes of Lysard, Seglanmoer, Botreagh, and Touran; except a messuage and land in Touran which John Sare held for the life of grantor in Porthmure, Carallek, Luddre, and numerous specified tenements in divers specified villes, to hold to the said Roger and the heirs of his body, and, in default of such issue, remainder in succession, in tail mail, to grantor's eldest son John Archer; to his son John begotten of the body of Isolda Roger; to his son Randulph; to his son John begotten of the body of Hyngryn Pengersek; and to Thomas Corteys with remainder over to grantor's right heirs. By a separate instrument, of the same date, he appointed John Pascov of Lulyn, his attorney, to give to his son Roger seizin of the said lands, &c. Roger Archer being thus in possession, by deed dated 1st November 8th Henry IV. (1407), confirmed to John son of King Henry (John Duke of Bedford) Thomas Sentaustell, Parson of the Church of St. Rumon, and several others, all his messuages, &c., in the villes of Lesard, Seglanmoor, Botregh, Touran and Boscassell, &c., for the life of the said Thomas Sentaustell.

Roger Archer died before 1422, s.p., for in that year a claim was set up by Hervey Tregoys for the recovery of the estates upon the ground of the illegitimacy of the abovementioned John Archer, who, in virtue of his remainder under the above recited deed, had, upon the death of Roger, entered upon the Lesard estates. An assize of view of recognizance was granted to enquire if John Archer of Lysard, bastard, senr., and John Archer, junior, had unjustly disseized the said Hervey of the said lands. John Archer protested that he was legitimate and cited the above recited deed of the 20th September 1400, which he proffered in Court, in which John Archer of Lysard, kinsman of the said Hervey Tregoys: viz., brother of Johanna, mother of Peter, father of the said Hervey, whose heir he is, had granted the said lands as before described, and bound his heirs to warrant the same; and petitioned judgment upon the warrantry. Hervey Tregoys denied all knowledge of the charter, and alleged that John Archer, his ancestor, died seized of the said lands in his demesne as of fee. It is unnecessary to follow the pleadings, which extend to considerable length in detail, suffice it to say that the case was ordered to go to a jury on Monday in the feast of St. Lawrence next following, before the justices at Launceston, on which day the said Hervey and the said John Archer, junior, appeared in person, but John Archer, senior, did not appear, being, in obedience to the Lord the King in company Richard Haryngton, Esq., in France, under letters patent of protection, dated 27th of April 10th of the King, extending for three quarters of a year then next following.[1]

In the year following these proceedings the case came again before the Justices Itinerant at Launceston, when John Archer, senior, and John Archer, junior, appeared in person, and said that the aforesaid Hervey Tregoys, for his manifest contumacy in a certain case in which he had violently beaten John Archer, Clerk, had been excommunicated with the greater excommunication, and the case was postponed.[2]

---

[1] Assize Rolls, Cornwall, 10th Henry V. 2 $\left\{\begin{array}{c} \text{N} \\ 40 \end{array}\right\}$ 1. m. 31.   [2] Ibid. 1st and 2nd Henry VI. m. 30.

Soon after the above proceedings the case between the parties was referred to arbitration, and on 6th December 1st Henry VI., John Archer of Lysard entered into a bond of 400 marks to abide by the decision, and eventually, by deed dated 21st September 3rd Henry VI. (1424), Hervey Tregoys, under the description of Hervey Devryon *alias* Tregoys, confirmed to John Archer of Lesard, senior, all the lands in dispute, to hold to him and the heirs of his body, in default remainder to John Archer of Dovran, junior, and the heirs of his body, in default remainder to Ralph, brother of the said John, junior, and the heirs of his body, and in default of such issue, remainder to the heirs of Tristram Courteys.

The fact of there being so many Johns, sons of the same father, renders it extremely difficult to identify them with any degree of certainty, but we are inclined to believe that the John Archer, senior, of Lysard, who was alleged to have been illegitimate, is the same mentioned in an ancient pedigree [1] as having married Alice the daughter of John Beauchamp, which is in some measure confirmed by John Beauchamp of Benerton being one of the arbitrators appointed on his behalf in the dispute concerning the lands. In this case his mother, according to the pedigree, would have been Alice the daughter of John Penrose.

John Archer, junior, married Elizabeth, daughter of Richard de Tresebell, who, by deed dated 25th June 10th Henry VI. (1432), confirmed to "John Archer, son of John Archer of Lysard, and Elizabeth my daughter," all his messuages in the ville of Henforth, to hold to them and the heirs of their bodies during the life of the grantor. Richard Tresebell was dead in 1445, for by deed dated 24th July 23rd Henry VI. (1445) John Archer of Lesard, junior, granted a moiety of his fulling mill of Tresebell to John Dywy, Tookkyer; and by a deed, dated 27th July in the same year, between John Archer of Lysard, junior, of the one part, and Thomas Masseley of the other part, the lands which were David Halep's and Richard Tresebell's were divided, whereby the messuages in the ville of Trevyhan, juxta Trevythian, half the messuages in the villes of Chygurthy and Trevasek, with the reversion of half the messuages which Matilda, relict of James Halep, held in dower, also a tenement in the ville of Tresebell, and a moiety of the fulling mill of Tresebell, and the whole ville of Hensforth and certain other lands, were assigned to John Archer, and the remainder to the said Thomas Masseley and Pentecost, his wife, who was the other daughter and co-heir of Richard Tresebell.

John Archer, senior, died in 1446, for we find, under the date of 12th September in that year, a receipt, given by William Clerk and the Lady Philippa his wife, late the wife of Sir William Bodrygan deceased, for ten marks paid by John Archer of Lesard for a relief on the death of his father John Archer, for two Knights' fees in Lisard, Bosogan, St. Rumon, Luddre, Boschim, &c., which the said John held of them as of their manor of Restronget. One of these fees was, in 1424, held of John Archer of Lesard by William Bryt, and we have an acknowledgment, dated 3rd August 29th Henry VI.

---

[1] Harl. MSS., 4031.

Z²

(1451), that Richard Uydeslade had done homage to John Archer for one Knight's fee, which of the said John he held in right of his wife, Mary, the cousin and co-heir of William Bryt late of Bochym, in Lesard. The other fee was held of John Archer by the aforesaid Thomas Masseley, for on 11th October 3rd Edward IV. (1463), John Archer acknowledged to have received the homage of the said Thomas for one Knight's fee which the said Thomas held of him in Lysard worvus, of St. Rewan, by Knight's service.

By deed dated 8th December 4th Edward IV. (1464), John Archer of Lisard conveyed to George Duke of Clarence, John Archer of Hastyng, Richard Archer, Chaplain, and others in trust for the life of the said George, all his lands in Arkansawyth, Karallok, Lisard, Seglanmoer, &c., remainder to grantor's two daughters Joan and Agnes and the heirs of their bodies, in default, remainder to Robert Drakys and the heirs of his body, in default, remainder to John Courteys and the heirs of his body, in default of such issue remainder to King Edward IV. and the heirs male of his body, rendering to the said John Archer and his heirs the rent of £10 per annum.

It is probable that the reason for giving the King an interest in these lands was to obtain his assistance in the dispute as to the title, which, from a bond given by John Devryon for £200 to John Archer and Thomas Archer to abide by the arbitration of certain persons named concerning the title to lands in Lessard, Seglanmoer, &c., &c., it is evident had again been revived; and on 4th March 12th Edward IV. (1471-2), a similar Bond was given by John Devryon in the same matter, as he also again did under the date of 2nd August 13th Edward IV. (1473).[1] By deed dated 12th February 12th Edward IV. (1472-3), Pentecost widow of Thomas Masseley confirmed to John Archer of Lesard all her messuages in the ville of Lesard for the term of her life.

John Archer was dead before 1483 for in that year (1st Richard III.) Elizabeth his widow conveyed all her lands in Tresebell and other places named to John Levelis, to hold to him and the heirs of his body, and in default of such issue remainder to Joan wife of James Levelis and the heirs of his body, in default, remainder to grantor's right heirs; and by another deed,[2] dated 12th December in the same year, she granted all her messuages in Spernan, Trevasek, Melynanter, and the homage of John Reskymmer for what he held

---

[1] John Archer also gave a Bond to John Deueryon and William Deueryon dated 19th December 11th Edward IV., which became the subject of litigation. In 1475 John and William Deueryon sued John Archer of Seghlanmor, Gent, for the recovery of £40 upon his Bond of the above mentioned date. John Archer defended himself and said, that the money upon the Bond in question was not due because the bond had been given upon a conference between them upon the condition that if the said John Archer should abide by the arbitration ordinance and judgement of Thomas Lucombe and other persons named as arbitrators, upon all actions and controversies between them, to be given before the feast of the Purification of the Blessed Virgin Mary then next following, then the said Bond should be of none effect; and the said John said, that as the Bond produced did not contain that condition it was not his and put himself upon the country, and the said John Deueryon and William Deueryon likewise. (De Ban. Rolls, 15th Edward IV., Trinity. m. 125.)

[2] The deeds here cited are in the muniment room at Tregothnan. The Archer and Levelis lands were acquired by Richard Vosper of Liskeard in marriage with Prudence, sole heir of Arthur Levelis. He left a son, Arthur, who died in 1679, leaving two infant daughters his co-heirs, one of whom, Elizabeth, married Joseph Marke of Woodhill, and the other Prudence, became the wife of George Dennis of Liskeard, from whom the estates passed to the Boscawen family.

in the ville of Trelanvyan, &c., to John Lavelys and Florence daughter of Thomas Erysey and the heirs of their bodies.

By the above marriage of Joan, heir of John Archer, the extensive Lizard possessions passed to Levelis, the male lineage of the elder branch having become extinct. Younger branches however, whom we are unable lineally to connect and place in the pedigree, had located themselves in the county. In the reign of Richard II. John Archer of Truro frequently appears on the Assize and De Banco Rolls. He was dead in 1425, in which year an action was pending in which Henry Stykyer and others were plaintiffs, and Johanna, who was the wife of "John Archer of Truro," and others defendants in a case of novel disseizin.[1] In 1452 we find a John Archer Burgess in Parliament for Helston.

In 1382, John Archer was one of the jurors on an Inquisition held at Camelford after the death of John Walesbrewe.[2] He was most likely the progenitor of the Archers of St. Kew.

Absence of Records obliges us now to leap over a considerable period. In the Return of 1522 (Appendix II.) we find the name of John Archer as residing in St. Kew, and both his name and that of William Archer are found in the Subsidy Roll for that parish in 1525,[3] the latter appearing at the head of the roll, though the amount at which he was assessed is illegible. This was probably the same William Archer who was Lord of the Manor of Helston Tony,[4] and who, by his charter dated at Perynvoos 10th May 36th Henry VIII. (1544), granted to John Thomas all his messuages and tenements in Perynvoos, parcel of the abovementioned manor, for the term of twenty-one years, at the rent of 8s. per annum, the said John Thomas to make suit at the court of the said William within the manor aforesaid.[5]

The parish registers of St. Kew open with three branches of the name: viz., Richard Archer of Benbole, Nicholas Archer of Trecogoe, and John Archer of Hale, who were probably grandsons of the abovementioned William, and, perhaps, the sons of John Archer, who was assessed to the Subsidy in St. Kew upon lands of the value of £20 in 1558,[6] who might have been the same who was assessed in 1525. It may be here noticed as corroborative of the descent of the Archers of St. Kew from the Archers of Lizard, that the seal of Arms appended to the wills of John Archer, Rector of Carhayes, dated 1675, and of Edward Archer, Vicar of Manaccan, dated 1682, are the same as the arms quartered by Levelis for Archer of the Lizard on a monument erected in the Church of St. Buryan in 1671; and which arms were allowed to Levelis at the Heralds' Visitation of 1620.

The issue of Nicholas Archer of Trecogoe would seem to have become extinct in his

---

[1] Assize Rolls, Cornw., 2 $\{$ $\frac{N}{41}\}$ 2. m. 98.   [2] Inq. p.m., 6th Rich. II.   [3] Subsidy Rolls, 16th Henry .VIII. $\frac{87}{131}$

[4] He must have held this Manor under *Lease*, for it reverted to the crown by the death of Sir Richard Nanfan, s.p.m., before the 12th Henry VIII., and was not again granted in fee until 6th Elizabeth, though meanwhile several leases had been granted (see ante Vol. i., p. 32, and post sub. LANTEGLOS.)

[5] Deed in the possession of Edward Archer of Trelaske, Esq.   [6] Subsidy Roll, 1st Elizabeth $\frac{87}{218}$

son John Archer.   The descendants of John Archer of Hale we can trace for three generations.   John Archer of Hale, grandson of the last mentioned John, died in 1615.[1]   He
had two sons undisposed of but we are unable to trace them further.

Richard Archer of Benbole had three sons, John, Edward, and William.   Edward
would seem to have died s. p.   John succeeded his father at Benbole.   He married a
lady named Patience who was a legatee of plate, &c., under the will of Thomas Mallett
of Lanivet in 1593,[2] and was buried at St. Ewe in 1595.   He left a son Richard Archer
who died s. p., and devised his estate in Benbole and Trelewack in St. Ewe to his kinsman
Nicholas Archer, which Nicholas was the son of John Archer, Rector of St. Michael Carhayes,
son of William Archer the third son of Richard Archer of Benbole first above mentioned.
Nicholas Archer died s. p. in 1700 and his lands, *inter alia*, Trelewack and Benboll,
devolved upon his nephew John Archer, eldest son of his brother Edward Archer, Vicar of
Manaccan.

John Archer of Trelewack married Sarah daughter of John Addis of Whitford, co.
Cornwall, who brought in a great descent (see pedigree) and no inconsiderable estate.   By
her he had a large family.   William Archer, the eldest son died s. p. and by his Will,
dated 16th May 1749, devised his estates to his widow Ann Archer for life, remainder to
his brothers Swete Nicholas Archer and Addis Archer and their heirs for ever.   Addis
Archer died in 1780, and by his will devised his estates to his brother Swete Nicholas,
for life, with remainder to his nephews Edward Archer and Samuel Archer, as tenants in
common.   Swete Nicholas inherited also, in 1741, from his uncle Samuel Addis, Trelaske,
and dying in 1788, devised all his lands to his nephew, the aforesaid Edward Archer,
his heir at law, who succeeded him at Trelaske, and a few years afterwards an arrangement was come to between him and his cousin, son and heir of the aforesaid Addis
Archer, for the partition of the lands which they held in common, and the termination
of their joint tenancy.   Edward Archer died in 1802, and was succeeded by his brother
Samuel, Lieut.-Colonel 3rd Foot Guards, whose son Edward succeeded him in 1822, was
Sheriff in 1832, and dying in 1834, was succeeded by his eldest son Edward, the present
possessor, a Justice of the Peace and Deputy-Lieutenant for the County of Cornwall, and
Lieut.-Colonel of the Duke of Cornwall's Volunteers.

ARMS of Archer as allowed to Levelis at the Herald's Visitation of 1620, were:—sa.
a chev. engrailed between three pheons argent; and the same arms have since that date
been used by the family of Archer of Trelewack and Trelaske, with the charges or
instead of argent, probably as a difference to distinguish them from the elder branch of
the family.

CREST: a quiver fesswise, head to the sinister, stringed and full of arrows.

[1] It is not quite clear whether the person whose burial here recorded as "John Archer, Senior", was John
Archer of Hale or John Archer of Trecogoe.

[2] John Archer, Rector of St. Michael Carhayes, by his will dated 1st September 1675, gives to his eldest
son Nicholas Archer his Silver Cup with cover given him by Mrs. Mary Mallett, deceased, to remain in the keeping
of the eldest of his family for a memorial of her.   (Prov. 5th June 1676.)

PEDIGREE OF LE ARCHER, *alias* ARCHER OF LIZARD.—TABLE I.

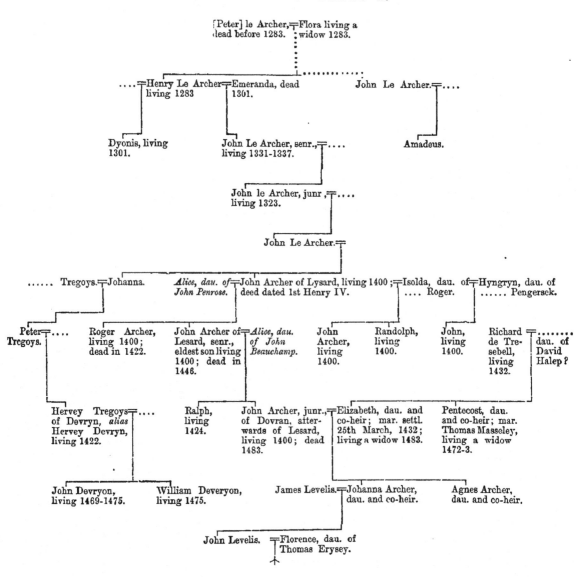

[Peter] le Archer, dead before 1283. ⊤ Flora living a widow 1283.

....⊤Henry Le Archer living 1283 ⊤ Emeranda, dead 1301.

John Le Archer.⊤....

Dyonis, living 1301.

John Le Archer, senr.,⊤.... living 1331-1337.

Amadeus.

John le Archer, junr , ⊤.... living 1323.

John Le Archer.⊤

...... Tregoys.⊤Johanna.

Alice, dau. of John Penrose. ⊤ John Archer of Lysard, living 1400 ; deed dated 1st Henry IV. ⊤ Isolda, dau. of .... Roger. ⊤ Hyngryn, dau. of ...... Pengersek.

Peter⊤.... Tregoys.

Roger Archer, living 1400; dead in 1422.

John Archer of Lesard, senr., eldest son living 1400; dead in 1446. ⊤ *Alice, dau. of John Beauchamp.*

John Archer, living 1400.

Randolph, living 1400.

John, living 1400.

Richard de Tresebell, living 1432. ⊤........ dau. of David Halep ?

Hervey Tregoys of Devryn, *alias* Hervey Devryn, living 1422. ⊤....

Ralph, living 1424.

John Archer, junr., of Dovran, afterwards of Lesard, living 1400; dead 1483. ⊤ Elizabeth, dau. and co-heir; mar. settl. 25th March, 1432; living a widow 1483.

Pentecost, dau. and co-heir; mar. Thomas Masseley, living a widow 1472-3.

John Devryon, living 1469-1475.

William Deveryon, living 1475.

James Levelis.⊤Johanna Archer, dau. and co-heir.

Agnes Archer, dau. and co-heir.

John Levelis. ⊤ Florence, dau. of Thomas Erysey.

PEDIGREE OF ARCHER OF ST. KEW, TRELEWACK, AND TRELASKE.—TABLE II.

ROYAL DESCENT OF ARCHER.

BASILIUS, or GEORGE⊤....
King of Russia.

HENRY I. King of France,⊤Agnes.
ob. 1060

MALCOLM III.⊤Margaret, sole heiress
King of Scot- | of the Crown of Eng-
land, ob. 1093. | land (Saint Margaret).

Hugh Magnus, 2nd son, Count⊤Adelheld, dau. and heir
of Vermandois, Valois, Cha- | of Herbert, Count of
mont, and Amiens. | Vermandois, ob. 1101.

DAVID I. King⊤Maud, dau. of Waltheof Earl of
of Scotland, ob. | Northumberland by Judith, niece
1153. | of William the Conqueror.

William Warren Earl⊤Elizabeth.
of Surrey.

Henry, Prince of Scotland, 1182.⊤Adama, 2nd dau.

WILLIAM, the Lion King of
Scotland, ob. 1214.

David, Earl of Huntingdon,⊤Maud, dau. of Hugh
3rd son, died 1219 | Earl of Chester.

Henry Hastings Earl of Huntingdon, died 1250.⊤Ada.

Humphry de Bohun, died 1182, v.p.⊤Margaret.

Henry de Bohun Earl of Hereford,⊤Maude, dau. of Geoffry Fitz Piers Earl of Essex,
created 1199; died 1220. | and heir of her brother.

Humphry de Bohun Earl of Hereford and Essex,⊤Maude, dau. of Earl of Ewe.
Lord High Constable; died 1273; Inq. p.m. 1st.
Edw. I. No. 1.

FERDINAND III. King of Castile,⊤Beatrix, dau. of the
died 1252. | Emperor Philip II.

Humphry de Bohun,⊤Eleanor, dau. and coh. of William de
aged 34 yrs. on his fa- | Braose, Lord of Brecknock.
ther's death, ob v.p.

EDWARD I. King of England,⊤Eleanor of Castile, 1st wife;
died 1307. | mar. 1254, died 1290.

Humphry de Bohun Earl of Hereford⊤Maud, dau. of William
and Essex, Lord High Constable. Died, | de Fienles.
1297. Inq. p.m. 27th Edw. I. No. 142.

Elizabeth, Relict of John Earl of⊤Humphry de Bohun Earl of Hereford and Essex; aged
Holland and Zealand; died 5th | 22 years on his father's death; gave Powderham to his
May 1316, aged 32. | daughter as a marriage portion; killed at Borough
Bridge 1322.

Hugh de Courtenay, 2nd Earl⊤Margaret de Bohun, mar. 11th Aug. 1325, died 16th Dec. 1391, bur. in
of Devon, K.G.; died 2nd May | Cathedral at Exon. By her will, dat. 28th Jan. 1390, she settled
1377; Inq. p.m. 51st. Edw. | Powderham upon her fourth son Sir Philip Courtenay.
III. No. 6.

a

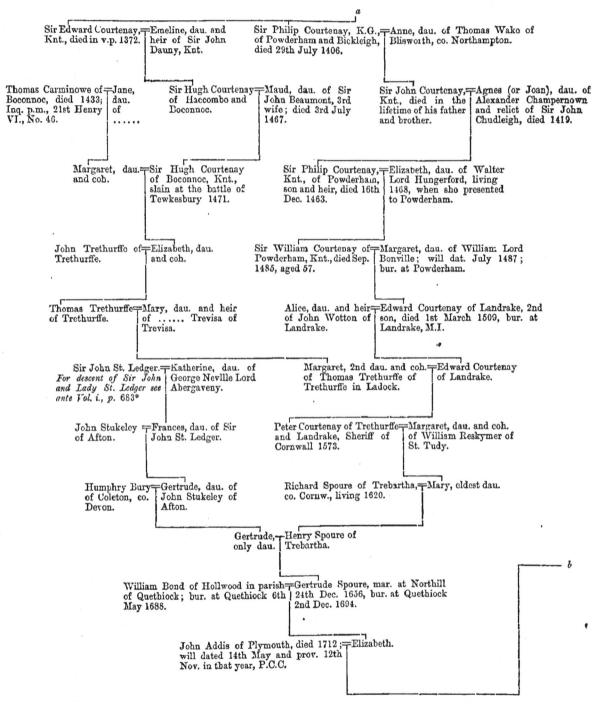

a

Sir Edward Courtenay,=Emeline, dau. and
Knt., died in v.p. 1372. | heir of Sir John
| Dauny, Knt.

Sir Philip Courtenay, K.G.,=Anne, dau. of Thomas Wake of
of Powderham and Bickleigh, | Blisworth, co. Northampton.
died 29th July 1406.

Thomas Carminowe of=Jane,
Boconnoc, died 1433; | dau.
Inq. p.m., 21st Henry | of
VI., No. 46. | ......

Sir Hugh Courtenay=Maud, dau. of Sir
of Haccombe and | John Beaumont, 3rd
Boconnoc. | wife; died 3rd July
| 1467.

Sir John Courtenay,=Agnes (or Joan), dau. of
Knt., died in the | Alexander Champernown
lifetime of his father | and relict of Sir John
and brother. | Chudleigh, died 1419.

Margaret, dau.=Sir Hugh Courtenay
and coh. | of Boconnoc, Knt.,
| slain at the battle of
| Tewkesbury 1471.

Sir Philip Courtenay,=Elizabeth, dau. of Walter
Knt., of Powderham, | Lord Hungerford, living
son and heir, died 16th | 1468, when she presented
Dec. 1463. | to Powderham.

John Trethurffe of=Elizabeth, dau.
Trethurffe. | and coh.

Sir William Courtenay of=Margaret, dau. of William Lord
Powderham, Knt., died Sep. | Bonville; will dat. July 1487;
1485, aged 57. | bur. at Powderham.

Thomas Trethurffe=Mary, dau. and heir
of Trethurffe. | of ...... Trevisa of
| Trevisa.

Alice, dau. and heir=Edward Courtenay of Landrake, 2nd
of John Wotton of | son, died 1st March 1509, bur. at
Landrake. | Landrake, M.I.

Sir John St. Ledger.=Katherine, dau. of
For descent of Sir John | George Neville Lord
and Lady St. Ledger see | Abergaveny.
ante Vol. i., p. 683*

Margaret, 2nd dau. and coh.=Edward Courtenay
of Thomas Trethurffe of | of Landrake.
Trethurffe in Ladock.

John Stukeley=Frances, dau. of Sir
of Afton. | John St. Ledger.

Peter Courtenay of Trethurffe=Margaret, dau. and coh.
and Landrake, Sheriff of | of William Reskymer of
Cornwall 1573. | St. Tudy.

Humphry Bury=Gertrude, dau. of
of Coleton, co. | John Stukeley of
Devon. | Afton.

Richard Spoure of Trebartha,=Mary, eldest dau.
co. Cornw., living 1620.

Gertrude,=Henry Spoure of
only dau. | Trebartha.

b

William Bond of Hollwood in parish=Gertrude Spoure, mar. at Northill
of Quethiock; bur. at Quethiock 6th | 24th Dec. 1656, bur. at Quethiock
May 1688. | 2nd Dec. 1694.

John Addis of Plymouth, died 1712;=Elizabeth.
will dated 14th May and prov. 12th
Nov. in that year, P.C.C.

William Archer, Lord of — ....
Helston Tony, living in
St. Kew 1522, and liv-
ing in 1544.

John Archer, assessed to the — ....
subsidy in St. Kew 1558.

Richard Archer of Benbole in the parish of St. Kew, assessed — ....
to the subsidy in St. Kew upon lands 1594 (Sub. Roll., 36th
Eliz. $\frac{88}{253}$). Bur. 25th March 1597.

John Archer of Benboll. Attorned to Richard — Patience,   Edward, bur.[3]   William — ....
Dagge as tenant for land in Benboll 26th April   dau. of   14th Aug.   Archer
1625, names his brothers Edward and William   ....   1636.   of
and his son Richard ; assessed to subsidy in St. bur.[3] 9th   Blaseley,
Kew 1600 (Sub. Roll, 42nd Elizab. $\frac{88}{265}$ and again Feb. 1595.   co.
                                                                                             Cornw.
upon lands in 1622 (Sub. Roll, 20th Jas. $\frac{88}{289}$).

Susanna,   Dorothy, dau. of Humphry — Richard Archer of Benbole, bap.[1] 16th May 1593. Assessed to — ....
bap.[1]   Nicol of Penvose, bap. at   the sub. in St. Kew 1641 (Sub. Roll, 17th Charles $\frac{89}{388}$.) Bur.[1]
29th   St. Tudy Feb. 1613, mar.   22nd Nov. 1664 ; will dat. 9th April 1660, prov. 8th April
Sep.   there 24th May 1656, 2. wife. 1665, Archd. Court of Cornw. s.p.v.
1588.

John Archer,   Nicholas Archer of Trelewack and — Thomasine, eldest sister and   Edward Archer, matric. at — Judith, dau. of
bap.[1] 29th   Benboll ; devisee of those and   coh. of William Inch of   Exeter Coll. Oxf. 13th July   John Swete,
June 1623,   other lands under the will of his Lanow in St. Kew ; mar.[1]   1660. Inst. to Vicarage of   Clerk, Vicar of
bur.[1] 25th   kinsman Richard Archer of Ben-   8th Dec. 1665, bur.[3] 26th   Manacean 1st June 1666 ;   St. Kevern.
Sept. 1636.   boll and Trelewack, prov. 8th Apr. June 1704.   bur.[1] 9th April 1683 ; will
               1665 ; bur.[3] 12th Mar.1700-1 ; will   dat. 27th Feb. 1682. Adm[o]
               dat. 1st Feb. 1700-1, s.p.   widow Judith 16th June 1683.

b

                Sarah, dau. and coh. of John Addis — John Archer of Trelewack, bur.[1] 30th
                of Whiteford, co. Cornw. ; mar.[3] 8th   Dec. 1726, will dat. 15th Dec. 1726,
                June 1708, bur.[3] 31st Oct. 1731 ; will prov. May 1727. Adm[o] to his son
                dat. 13th July 1731, prov. 3rd Jan.   William on attaining his majority 6th
                1731-2, Archd. Court of Cornw.   June 1735.

                                         c

---

[1] At St. Kew.   [2] At St. Michael Carhayes.   [3] At St. Ewe.

[4] At Egloshayle.   [5] At Lewanick.   [6] At Egg Buckland.

[7] At South Petherwin.   [8] At Plympton St. Maurice.   [9] At Bishopsteignton.

OF ARCHER

TRELASKE.—Table II.—Continued.

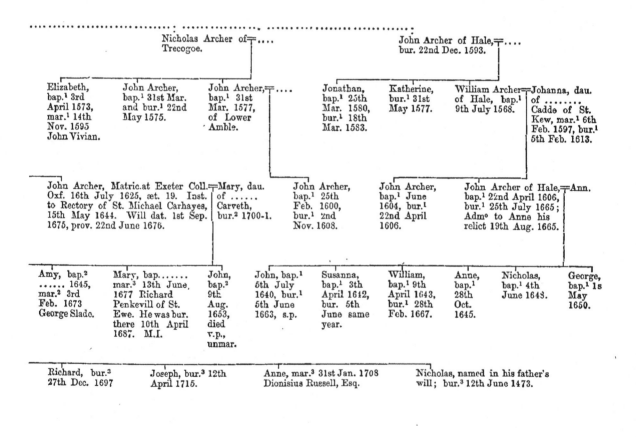

[1] At St. Kew.   [2] At St. Michael Carhayes.   [3] At St. Ewe.
[4] At Egloshayle.   [5] At Lewanick.   [6] At Egg Buckland.
[7] At South Petherwin.   [8] At Plympton St. Maurice.   [9] At Bishopsteignton.
    2 A[2]

c

| Elizabeth Anna, born 10th, bap.[3] 29th May 1710, died 25th April 1736. | Judith, born 10th March, bap.[3] 14th April 1713, died 12th March 1732. | William Archer, born and bap[3] 10th April 1714, died 16th and bur.[3] 19th May 1749, s.p.; will dat. 16th May, prov. 18th May 1749, P.C.C. | =Anne, 2nd dau. of Philip Lyne; mar. at Liskeard 23rd Dec. 1742, remar.[3] Richard Haydon, Clerk, 27th Dec. 1753, died 1783. | John Archer, bap[3]. 10th April 1714, died 6th Mar. 1733. | Swete Nicholas Archer, born 18th Oct. bap.[3] 8th Nov. 1715, of Tre-lewack and Trelaske; devisee under the will of his bro. William. Sheriff of Cornwall 1758; died 5th Nov. and bur.[3] 15th Nov. 1788, s.p. Will dat. 28th May 1783, devised all his estates to his neph. Edward Archer. s.p. | =Anne, dau. of Francis Basset of Tehidy, Esq., mar. at Illogan 31st Dec. 1747. | Edward Archer, bap.[3] 27th Feb. 1716, bur. at St. Andrews Plymo. 30th Aug. 1746. | =Jane. dau. of Wm. Lockett of Charlton Marshall, Dorset, mar. at St. James, Piccadilly, London. 29th Aug. 1741, remar. .... Morshead, died 2nd Nov. 1775. |

Edward Archer of Trelaske, born 15th May,=Theophila, dau. of ...... Freno of and bap. St. Andrew's, Plymouth 15th June Plymstock, Devon; mar. settl. 16th 1742; Sheriff of Cornw. 1794, died 11th and Oct. 1784, and mar. at Plymstock 23rd bur.[5] 19th Nov. 1802. same month.

Nicholas Addis, born 4th and bur. 14th Oct. 1743.

| Elizabeth Anne, born 25th June, bap.[6] 26th July 1788, mar. at Plympton St. Maurice 1st July 1819 R. B. Hunt, Major R.A.; died 29th Aug. and bur. at Modbury 2nd Sep. 1854. | Jane, born 9th Feb., bap. at Plympton St. Mary 15th Mar. 1790; died 12th June and bur.[5] 20th June 1818. | Edward Archer of Trelaske, born 25th April 1792, bap. at Plympton St. Mary 1st Jan. 1792; Educ. at Winch.: Gent. Com. of C.C.C. Oxf. 12th Mar. 1811, Sheriff of Cornw. 1832, Lieut.-Colonel North Cornwall Hussars. | =Charlotte Catherine, only child of Charles Harward of Hayne House, Dev. (only son of Charles Harward, D.D., Dean of Exeter) Capt. 3rd Foot Guards, Gent. in Waiting to Queen Charlotte, by Charlotte Augusta, 3rd dau. of Sir William Chambers, Surveyor Genl. of H.M. Works; died 16th May, bur.[5] 28th May 1834. |

| Charlotte Dorothea, born 15th June, bap. 2nd August 1815 at Dawlish; Mar.[5] 15th Jany. 1846 Francis John Hext Kendall, Clerk, Rector of Talland; died 18th April and bur. at Lostwithiel 22nd April 1871. | Edward Archer of Trelaske, born 8th Nov. 1816, bap.[8] 15th January 1817; Educ. at Win-chester, & Oriel Coll. Oxford; Matric. 30th October 1834; Lieut.-Colonel Duke of Corn-wall's Volun-teers. | =Sarah Lydia, eld. dau. of Walter Rad-cliffe, Clerk, of Warleigh Hall, Devon; mar. at Tam-erton Foliot, co. Devon, 24th July 1838. | Jane, born 2nd Jany., bap.[9] 6th Mar. 1818; mar. at Launceston William Henry Anderson Mors-head, C.B., Vice-Adml. of H.M. Navy, of Widey Court, Devon; died 22nd and bur.[6] 28th Feb. 1851. | Charles Harward Archer, born 6th Aug. 1819, bap.[9] 2nd Feb. 1820; Inst to Vicarage of Lewanick 24th Nov. 1844. | =Jane, 2nd dau. of William Rash-leigh of Menabilly mar. at Tyward-reth 21st October 1845. | Samuel Harward Archer, born 9th Jany, bap.[9] 25th April 1821; Inst. to Rectory of Throw-leigh 22nd Nov. 1852. | =Charlotte Hester, 2nd dau. of Walter Radcliffe, Clerk, of Warleigh Hall, Dev.; mar. at Tamerton Foliot 3rd Oct. 1850. |

| Emma Augusta, born 18th Oct. 1841, bap.[5] 3rd April 1842, died 27th Feb., bur.[5] 4th Mar. 1843. | Alice, born 29th Oct., bap.[5] 20th Dec. 1843, died 14th and bur.[5] 20th Nov. 1855. | Edward Radcliffe, born 11th Mar., bap.[5] 18th April 1845, died 28th Mar., bur. at Tamerton Foliot 1st April 1848. | Charles Gordon Archer, son and heir, born 1st and bap.[5] 24th Nov. 1846; Educ. at Eton; in Comm. of Peace for co. Cornw. |

---

[1] At St. Kew.   [2] At St. Michael Carhayes.   [3] At St. Ewe.

[4] At Egloshayle.   [5] At Lewanick.   [6] At Egg Buckland.

[7] At South Petherwin.   [8] At Plympton St. Maurice.   [9] At Bishopsteignton.

c

Samuel Archer, born 23rd Jan. bap.[3] 15th Feb. 1717, died 28th Aug. 1730.	Addis, born 9th May, bap.[3] 16th May 1719, of Plymouth; died 13th Dec. 1780; will dated 3rd May 1753. = Rebecca, 2nd dau. of William Lockett of Charlton Marshall, co. Dorset; mar. settl. dat. 24th Mar. 1742.	Sarah, born 12th May, bap.[3] 22nd June 1721, died and bur.[3] 29th Dec. 1722.	Nicholas Archer of Plymouth, born 16th, bap.[3] 26th Mar. 1723, died 11th June 1743; will prov. 20th Aug. 1743.	Margaret, born Jan. 11th, bap.[3] 4th Feb. 1724, mar. at Truro 9th June 1673, Edward Stillingfleet, Clerk, P.C. of West Bromwich, co. Staff. died 14th Oct. and bur. 18th Oct. 1776 at West Teignmo., co. Devon.

Samuel Archer of Trelaske, born 22nd Feb. and bap. at St. Andrew's, Plymo. 1st April 1745; Lieut. Col. 3rd Regt. Foot Guards, Major Commandant of Launceston Volunteers, Lieut. Col. South Devon Volunteers; died 6th June and bur.[5] 14th June 1822. = Dorothy Ayre, eld. dau. of John Yonge, Clerk, of Puslinch, Devon, mar.[6] 15th June 1787.	Addis Archer, of ......, born 1752, bap...... , died 1822 and bur. at St. Budeaux, co. Devon, 3rd June 1822, aged 70.	Maria Elizabeth, mar. Richard Julian, Major 44th Regt., died 1831.

Anne, born 9th Mar. bap.[7] 3rd June 1794; mar. at Plympton St. Maurice 25th Feb. 1823 Richard Davie, M.D.; died 11th Sep. and bur. at Plympton St. Maurice 16th Sep. 1864.	Samuel Archer, born 18th Nov. and bap.[7] 16th Dec. 1795; Inst. to Vicarage of Lewanick 24th Sep. 1822, died 9th Jany and bur.[5] 18th Jany. 1831.

Ann Augusta, born 17th Feb., 1822; mar. at Brompton 3rd Sep. 1850 Dominic Sarsfield Greene, C.B., R.A.	Elizabeth, born 7th April, bap.[9] 26th July 1823, mar.[5] 24th May 1849 Major Edward Bond, H.M. 53rd Regt.	Fulbert Archer of Canterbury, New Zealand, born 14th April, bap.[9] 20th July 1825. = Mary, dau. of William Cave, mar. at Westbury on Trym 24th Sep. 1856; died 27th Oct. 1871.	Catherine, born 18th Sept. 1826, bap. at Bisopsteignton 26th Jan. 1827, mar. at Heavitree 27th Sep. 1860 Henry Tolcher of Harewood, co. Devon.	Marianne, born 14th Jan., bap.[5] 1st April 1829, mar. at Heavitree 28th Dec. 1854 Mansfield Turner, H.M. 20th Regt.	William, born 23rd Aug., bap.[5] 5th Nov. 1830, bur.[5] 31st March 1832.	Henry Swete, born 18th Jan., bap.[5] 18th Nov. 1834. = Fanny, dau. of John Prestwood Bellew, mar. at Stockleigh 6th Sep. 1860.

Emily Augusta, born 27th Nov., bap.[5] 25th Dec. 1848, mar.[5] 9th Jany. 1873 George Badely Marke of Woodhill, co. Cornw.	Addis Edward, born 18th Aug., bap.[5] 12th Sep. 1851; Educ. at Eton.	Sarah Constance, born 9th April, bap.[5] 17th May 1853.	Dora Kate, born 27th Aug., bap.[5] 26th Sep. 1855.

[1] At St. Kew.
[4] At Egloshayle.
[7] At South Petherwin.
[2] At St. Michael Carhayes.
[5] At Lewanick.
[8] At Plympton St. Maurice.
[3] At St. Ewe.
[6] At Egg Buckland.
[9] At Bishopsteignton.

FAMILY OF DE PRIDIAS *alias* PRIDEAUX.

The name and family of Prideaux is of great antiquity in Cornwall. Soon after the Norman Conquest we find the family seated at Prideaux Castle in the parish of Luxullion, and some have attributed to it a British origin.[1] The first of the name of whom we have any record is Paganus, or Pagan, Predieux who in the pedigree registered in the Heralds' College is described as "Pagan Prideaux, Lord of Prideaux in the Conquest time." From him the third in descent was Nicholas Predieux, Lord of Predeaux,[2] who, in addition to a son Richard, is stated in an old family pedigree, to have had a son called Hickedon or Herdon[3] twin brother of the said Richard[4] from whom, according to family pedigrees, Prideaux of Orchardon descended; but this is manifestly incorrect, for it appears from record evidence that Geoffry de Pridyas married the heiress of Orcharton, for in 1220 a fine was levied in which Alina who was the wife of John Orcherton was petitioner and Geoffry de Pridyas and Isabella his wife, by Reginald[5] de Pridyas as attorney for the said Isabella, of the third part of two parts of one Knight's fee, &c., in Orcherton, and the third part of two parts of one Knight's fee in demesne, and the third part of two parts of the services of two Knights, &c., in Brethok (Brodoke), in Cornwall, which Alina claimed as of dower of the gift of the said John sometime her husband, and she remised and quitclaimed her whole right in the same to the said Geoffry and Isabella and the heirs of the said Isabella for ever.[6]

The Heralds' Visitation of 1620 (Harl. MSS. 1080, fo. 412*b*.) commences the pedigree of Prideaux of Orcharton with Sir Richard Prideaux (described as of Orcharton) said to be the father of Sir Geoffry Prideaux of Orcharton. We think that Sir Richard is erroneously described as "of Orcharton" for there was no Richard of that place until 1408, and we believe the former to be identical with Richard Prideaux, who is shown in the authorised Visitation Pedigree (Heralds' Coll.) to have died in 1250. The dates will agree very well.

---

[1] Polwhele Hist. of Cornw., Vol. ii., 61. Whitaker.

[2] This Nicholas is stated to have died in 1169, but we find in 1182 the Sheriff of Cornwall accounted for half a mark paid to Nicholas de Pridias, who had come to London to cross the sea in the King's service. In 1189 he was amerced half a mark for making a false claim, and again in 1195 he was amerced 2s. for the same cause. (Pipe Rolls of these years).

[3] May not "Hickedon" have been a corruption of "Orcherdon" and Herdon of "Hickedon.

[4] It should be noted that in 1218, Sir Thomas de Pridias, Knt., was placed in remainder in default of issue of John Bevill and Agnes his wife, *inter alia*, in the manor of Wolfyston co. Cornwall. (Ped. Fin. Div. Cos. 3rd Hen. III.) Somewhat later we find Thomas de Pridias several times mentioned, and on one occasion with Sibella his wife. This last Thomas is not described as a Knight, and therefore must have been a different person. We are unable to place either of them in the pedigree.

[5] This Reginald was probably the brother of Geoffry, and the father of Sir Thomas who held Truromarche.

[6] Pedes Finium 8th Henry III., Easter. Cornw. No. 1.—The Pipe Roll of 8th Henry III. shows that Geoffry de Pridyas gave the King one mark to have a licence of concord with Ailena who was the wife of John de Orcherton.

The pedigree of the elder branch of this ancient house, as recorded in the Heralds' College, gives only the direct line and is very defective in dates. There are no fewer than six descents from Richard Pridieux mentioned above as dying in 1250, and Richard Predieux who died in 3rd Edward III. (1329), a period of less than seventy years, and of the names mentioned we have very scant information. By a Charter, without date, but which must be very early, Osbert, Prior of Tywardreth, we believe the first of that name, who ruled the Priory about the middle of the twelfth century, with the favour and council of the Lord Robert Fitz William, granted to Baldwin de Pidias (Pridias) one Knight's fee in the manor of Pidias, to hold to him and his heirs, except an acre of land in Carnubelbanathel for which the monks of Tywardreth rendered annually to the said Baldwin 20d. for all customs, &c., as written in the Charter of convention between Ordagar the Canon, and Richard de Pidias father of the said Baldwin.[1] This we conceive must refer to Richard de Prideaux who is said to have died in 1122, and Baldwin his son who died 1165. In an exchange of lands in 1234, between Andrew de Cardinan and Emma relict of Robert de Cardinan[2] the said Andrew granted to the said Emma, *inter alia*, the whole services of Richard de Pridias and his heirs of the fee of one Knight and a half with appurtenances in Pridias.[3] This Richard was probably the same who is mentioned above as having died in 1250. We find him again as witness to a Charter, by which Odo son of Walter de Treverbyn granted certain lands to the Priory of Tywardreth and which, though undated, we can, from internal evidence, fix between 1230 and 1240. He is shewn to have left a son Baldwin who carried on the succession at Prideaux, and we believe Geoffry who married the heiress of Orcharton as stated above, and Reginald who was attorney for Isabella in the fine cited, were also his sons.

Of Baldwin we have no notice, but Reginald was probably the father of Thomas to whom John de Ripariis (Rivers) granted, under the designation of Thomas son of Reginald de Prydyas, Knt., one messuage and one garden in Trurue Marche, with the advowson of the Church of the Blessed Mary of Trurue appertaining to the same garden and house, and one place of land called the Castle, together with the moiety of the free Borough of Trurue Marche with fairs, markets, tolls, stallages, riverage, sac and soc, toll and them, infangenethef, utfangenethef, with all the liberties to the said borough pertaining, &c., &c., and the services of Thomas Davy for the moiety of the mill which he holds of him in Trureu, to hold to the said Thomas de Pridyas his heirs and assigns of him the said John de Ripariis and his heirs and assigns for ever of the King in capite by the accustomed services. This Charter is not dated, but it was just preceding 1302, for in that year an inquisition ad quod damnum was taken to enquire if any prejudice would arise to the King, or to any one else, if Thomas de Pridias were allowed to hold the manor of Truro Marche together with the advowson of the Church, &c., &c., which had been granted to him by John de Ripariis who held the same of the King in capite, and the jury

---

[1] Deed at Wardour Castle, Oliver's Mon. p. 41.

[2] Robert de Cardinan was alive 1224, Rot. Fin. 8th Henry III.

[3] Pedes Finium, 18th Henry III., Trinity No. 4. p. 41.

found that no damage would occur.[1]　Thomas de Pridias was appointed attorney for Isolda wife of Thomas de Tracey in certain proceedings respecting the dower of Ela relict of Andrew de Cardinan in 1256.[2]

We believe this Sir Thomas to be identical with the Sir Thomas shewn in the Visitation pedigree as the son of Baldwin, the latter name being written in error for Reginald; for at the searching iter of John de Berewic and his associates in 30th Edward I., (1302) Thomas de Pridias was summoned and answered to the King upon a Writ Quo Waranto by what right he claimed to possess the franchises enumerated above in the Borough of Truro, and likewise why he claimed to hold the Bailiwick of the Hundred of Poudreshire.[3]　As regarded the latter he said, that he held the Bailiwick of the King in capite rendering per annum to the King, as of his manor of Tybesta, 40s. per annum; and that he and all his ancestors had held that bailiwick from a time beyond the memory of man without any interruption, and his claim upon inquisition was accordingly admitted by the court and jury.　This would point back to a possession by his ancestors at a very remote period, and would show that he was the direct lineal representative of those ancestors.　Thomas de Pridias, in 1294, was summoned from the County of Cornwall to perform military service against the Welsh, and, in the same year, he was appointed one of the Assessors and Collectors of the subsidy for the County, as he was again in 1309. In 1297, as Sir Thomas Pridias, he was returned from Cornwall as holding lands or rents of the value of £20 a year or upwards, and as such was summoned under the general writ to perform military service, with horses and arms, beyond the seas.[4]　In the following year he was returned as Knight for the shire of Cornwall at the Parliament held at York, and in 1301 he was summoned from Cornwall to perform military service in person against the Scots.　He died in 1311 seized, *inter alia,* of a moiety of the Borough of Truro, and of the Manor of Nywenen (Newnham) and Geoffry his son was found to be his nearest heir and to be of the age of 23 years and more, who, in the same year, made fealty for the moiety of the Borough of Tryuru which Thomas de Pridias his father held of the King at the rent of 4d. per annum.[5]

---

[1] Escheats, 30th Edward I., No. 117.　In this document the land pertaining to the Castle is described as 40 perches in length and 40 perches in breadth.

[2] Rot. Coram Rege. 40th Henry III., A. 3, No. 20, m. 13d.

[3] It appears from the proceedings that whilst Thomas de Pridias held one moiety of the Manor and Borough, &c., under the grant of John de Ripariis cited in the text, the remainder was held by Matilda the relict of Richard Hewissh, who held one third in dower, and Richard their son, who claimed as the assigns of one Robert son of Walter de Wodeham; and Thomas de Tregaminion and Elena his wife and John de Hellaund whose ancestors, they said, had held the franchises in question from time immemorial.　The Burgesses of Truro however appeared and claimed the aforesaid franchises under a Charter of Reginald Earl of Cornwall (De Dunstanville illegitimate son of King Henry I.) and Charters of confirmation of King Henry II. and of the then King (Edward I.) which they produced in court and which witnessed the same.　Upon a Certificate to this effect the said liberties were confirmed to the Burgesses by Letters Patent dated at Westminster 16th Nov. 42nd Edward III., and which, upon inspeximus, was ratified and confirmed by Letters Patent dated at Westminster 9th Nov. 1st Richard II. (Rot. Pat. 1st Richard II. Part II. m. 27.)

[4] Brit. Mus. Cott. M.S., Claud. C. II., fo. 64.　　　　[5] Rot. Orig. 4th Edward II., m. 11.

Geoffry de Pridias, described as son of Thomas, was party to a deed concerning Tregoth-nan in 1306.[1] In another deed, dated 2nd Edward III (1328), it is recited that Geoffry de Pridias had enfeoffed Ralph Cowling and Robert Person of Truro in one messuage and all his land in Clunikeck, together with his fulling mill, &c. We do not know the date of his death but he was alive in 1330 when John son of John Ripariis petitioned against Geoffry de Pridias concerning two parts of the moiety of Truru March, and against Rose relict of Thomas de Pridias concerning the third part of the same manor which she held in dower of the gift of the said Thomas, sometime her husband, and of the inheritance of the said Geoffry, which the said John alleged John de Ripariis his great-great-grandfather had given to plantiff's grandfather, and that the right had descended to him (the plaintiff). Geoffry pleaded that the said John Ripariis (plaintiff's grandfather) had alienated the manor long before the statutes concerning gifts. The case was ordered to go before a jury and Geoffry obtained a verdict.[2] He died in 1347, for in that year Thomas de Prydeaux, believed to be the son of Geoffry, granted to Alice who was the wife of Thomas Pedycrue, Knt., and William Brett of Bossom, two parts of the manor of Newnham and the mills of Clynych (Calenick?) and the reversion of the third part of the said manor which Rose de Prideaux held in dower, together with the profits of the market town of Truru and the advowson of the Church of St. Mary, and at the same time the said parties re-granted the said premises to the said Thomas Prideaux and Margaret his wife and the heirs of their bodies. Thomas de Pridias attained the degree of a Knight, and died in the year last aboved named. His will was proved at Winchester on 28th August 1347,[3] and administration granted to his executors Richard Pedegrew and William Trevayn. It appears from an old pedigree in the British Museum that his wife was Margaret daughter of Thomas Pedicru, and that he left a son named Thomas whose wife was called Grace. They are all commemorated in an ancient Bede Roll of some monastery, not identified, in the possession of the author.

Thomas Pridias, the younger, would appear to have died s.p. before 1367, when the estates devolved upon Robert his uncle, for in that year an Assize of view of recognizance was held at the Assizes at Launceston, on Saturday next after the feast of St. Peter ad Vincula,[4] to enquire if Robert de Pridias and Margery his wife, Otto Bodrigan and Johanna his wife, Nicholas Wonford, Thomas Collan, and John Restourek of Nansulwaster unjustly disseized Reginald de Pridias and Thomas Geveyley of their free tenement in Truro March, the Manor of Nywenham, &c. The Jury found that the said Robert was seized in his demesne of fee and right of the aforesaid manor, &c., and granted the same to the aforesaid Reginald and Thomas Geveyley, on the condition that they should find the said Robert and Margery his wife in food and clothing, during their lives, and pay for the said Robert all the debts which at that time he owed, and that after the payment of the debts they should re-enfeoffe in the said manor the said Robert and Margery and the

---

[1] Tregothnan Muniments, No. 1366.

[3] Bishop Eddington's Reg. fol. 10b.

[2] De Banco Rolls, 4th Edward III., Michs. m. 396d.

[4] Assize Roll, Cornw. 41st Edward III. 2 $\left.\begin{matrix}N\\27\end{matrix}\right\}$ 7. m. 72d.

2 B

heirs of their bodies for ever, and in default of such issue, reversion to the said Reginald. The Jury further found that Reginald and Thomas Geveyley were seized of the said manor and paid on behalf of the said Robert a certain Richard Peticru, executor of the will of Margaret who was the wife of John Manerown, £20, part of a debt of £300, which the said Robert had bound himself to pay to the said John Manerown and Margaret his wife, on this condition, that provided the said Margaret held peacably for her whole life certain tenements which belonged to a certain Thomas de Pridias, sometime her husband, which was of the inheritance of the said Robert, the bond should be of no effect; and they say that the said Margaret held the said premises during her whole life, and that the said Reginald and Thomas paid for the said Robert divers debts, and that they held the said manor for a quarter of a year when the said Robert and Margery removed them, and that the profits for that time were 100s. and that the damages were £40.

Two years afterwards Robert Prideaux, described as son of Geoffry, released to Otho Bodrigan and his heirs all his right to the manor of Newnham, the mills of Clunyck, and the profits of the market town of Truru March with the advowson of the Church, and the place called the Castle. It was, perhaps, this Robert who was one of the manucaptors for the Burgesses of Bodmin in 1327, though we have no means of identifying him with certainty, nor are we able, notwithstanding the mass of evidence which we have collected, to trace any thing further respecting either him or Reginald de Pridias, nor have we been much more successful as regards the Visitation pedigree. In 1324 a Roger Prideaux was returned as holding lands worth £40 a year.[1] He may have been the Roger who is stated to have married Alice Podysford though we have no means of identifying him, and the succession would seem to be incorrect. Nor have we been more fortunate with respect to the succession of the Richards. Neither of their names once appears in the Public Records. This may, in some measure, perhaps, be accounted for from the fact of their holding the Manor of Predeaux of the Priory of Tywardreth, and their not holding any other lands of the King in capite, consequently their Inquisitions post mortem do not appear among the Chancery or Exchecquer Records. The pedigree, however, has been admitted by the Heralds, and in the absence of other evidence must be received.

PRIDEAUX OF ORCHARTON. TABLE I.

We now return to the Orcharton branch, with which we are more immediately concerned. Reverting to Geoffry Pridyas, we find that by a fine levied in 1247, in which Roger Pridyas was querist and Geoffry de Pridyas and Isabella his wife were defendants, the said Geoffry and Isabell settled on the said Roger and his heirs for ever two carucates of land with appurtenances in Orcherton, in Devon, one carucate of land in Brothek (Brodoke), and the service of one Knight's fee in Rodewall, in Cornwall, at the rent of one pair of white

---

[1] Brit. Mus. Cotton, MSS., Claud. C., 2. fo. 45.

gloves, or one penny, during the lives of the said Geoffry and Isabella, with remainder in fee.[1] There seems to have been a dispute between the aforesaid Geoffry and Isabella and Henry Bonathelek concerning the service due from the said Henry for half-an-acre of land with appurtenances, which, of them, he held in Bonathelek; and it was agreed that the said Henry should render yearly the reaping of one man for one day, and the ploughing of one man for one day; that he should find for them one man to hoe their land; and perform for them the service of the nineteenth part of one Knight's fee; that he should find for them one horseman at their summons within the county of Cornwall at his cost, and without the said county one horseman with a lance in the army at the cost of the said Geoffry and Isabella; and for this agreement they remitted all arrears of these services and gave the said Henry five marks of silver.[2]

We find Geoffry de Pridias mentioned in 1255, and he was, probably, identical with Geoffry the son of Sir Richard before mentioned (p. 194). We do not know the date of his death, but he was succeeded by his son Roger, whom we find as Sheriff of Devon for three parts of the year 1271, when Ralph de Teygnemue and John de Wilton, Clerk, acted as his deputies; in the year 1272, when he acted for the King of Almaine, the same persons being his deputies; and in the year 1273, when he himself acted for the King of Almaine.[3]

In 1281, for the rent of £60 a year during his life, he settled one messuage and two carucates of land in Orcherton, and one messuage and one carucate of land in Brothek on Peter his son and the heirs of his body, in default remainder to Reginald, brother of the said Peter, with the same limitation, in default remainder to Margery, daughter to John Chartrey[4] and the heirs of her body, paying to the said Roger £30 per annum, in default of such issue to revert to the said Roger quit of all other heirs of the said Margery, in default of heirs of the body of Reginald remainder to Richard Reskymer and Alice his wife, Benedict Rereward[5] and Lucy his wife, and to the heirs of the bodies of the said Alice and Lucy begotten by the said Richard and Benedict, under limitations similar to those in the case of Margery, and in default of such issue to Roger and his heirs, quit of all other heirs of either Alice or Lucy.[6]

He was alive in 1290[7] but we know not when he died. He was succeeded by his son Peter whose wife was Elizabeth daughter of Sir Hugh Treverbyn.[8] He died in 1316 leaving Sir Roger de Pridias, Knt., his son and heir aged 22 years and more,[9] who did homage for his lands 6th October in the same year, and it was directed that seizin should be given to him upon his payment of his reasonable relief,[10] but payment was not made until 1322, when we find that Roger de Prideaux, son and heir of Peter de Prideaux,

---

[1] Pedes Finium, Div. Cos., 31st Henry III., Easter No. 4.   [2] Pedes Finium, 28th Henry III., Easter.

[3] Pipe Rolls.

[4] It is presumed that Margery Chartrey was affianced to Reginald, and that she died before marriage, when Reginald became a priest.

[5] Benedict Rereward was probably identical with Benedict Reynward whom we find dealing largely in tin in Cornwall in 1305-6. (Stannary Roll; Journal of Royal Inst. of Cornw. 1870, p. 244.)

[6] Pedes Finium, 10th Edward I., Easter.   [7] Pipe Roll, 19th Edward I.

[8] Pole's Devon, p. 302.   [9] Inq. p. m. 9th Edward II., No. 15.   [10] Rot. Fin. 10th Edward II.

2 B[2]

paid five marks for his relief for the hamlet of Orcharton, in the County of Devon, which he held of the King[1] in capite by the service of one Knight's fee of the fee of morteyne.[2] His wife was named Claricia by whom had a son of his own name who married Elizabeth daughter and heir of John de Clifford and Claricia his wife, and cousin and heir of Odo Treverbyn. By a fine levied in 1332, in which John de Clyfford, Knt., and Claricia his wife were querists and Roger Prydeaux, Knt., was deforc., whereby reversion of the Manor of Combeintynhyde and the advowson of the Church there, after the death of the said John and Claricia, were settled upon Roger Prideaux, son of the said Roger, and Elizabeth his wife, the daughter of the said John Clyfford and the heirs of their bodies, and in default of such issue remainder to the right heirs of Roger the son of the said Roger.[3] By Charter dated 26th September 18th Edward II. (1324) the King, upon inspeximus of a Charter by which Richard Earl of Poitou and Cornwall granted to Odo Treverbyn the Borough of Porbuan, confirmed to Roger Prideaux and Elizabeth his wife, cousin and one of the heirs of the aforesaid Odo, and to John Dauney and Sibella his wife, the cousin and other heir of the said Odo, and to the heirs of the said Elizabeth and Sibella, all the franchises and liberties pertaining to the said Borough.[4] Roger had a brother Ralph upon whom his father appears to have settled the moiety of the Manor of North Alyngton which had descended from the Cardinan family,[5] and Ralph, in 1330, conveyed the same to his brother Roger for his life, with remainder to John son of the said Roger and the heirs of his body, in default, remainder to Roger, brother of the said John and the heirs of his body, in default, remainder to Ida, sister of the said John and Roger, and the heirs of her body, in default, remainder to the right heirs of Roger Prideaux.[6]

Sir Roger Prideaux presented to Alyngton in 1341, and to Brothek (Brodoke), upon the death of Reginald Prideaux, in 1343.[7] We have no evidence of the exact date of his death, but in 1357 it was directed by the Council of the Prince of Wales upon a petition of Joan Prideaux that it should be enquired into, and that the Council should be informed what estate she had in certain lands in Orcharton and la Wode settled by her husband on her and their child, but seized into the Prince's hands by reason of the non-age of the child.[8] On the 18th July in the same year the wardship and marriage of Peter Prideaux, son and heir of Roger Prideaux, son and heir of Monsieur Roger Prideaux, together with the advowson of the Church of Come in Thinhide, were granted to Walter de Wodeland during the minority of the said Peter;[9] and in the following year a further return was

---

[1] Pedes Finium, 14th Edward III., Easter, Div. Cos.   [2] Rot. Fin. 16th Edward II.

[3] Ped. Finium, Devon, 6th Edward III., Easter.

[4] Rot. Pat. 18th Edward II., Part 1. m. 22. Translation printed in Bond's Hist. of Looe, p. 56.

[5] This manor was held in dower in 1234, by Emma who was the wife of Robert de Cardinan. (Ped. Finium, 18th Henry III., Trinity.)   [6] Ped. Fin., 4th Edward III., Devon.

[7] Bishop Grandisson's Reg. fo. 49.   [8] Council Book of the "Black Prince," fo. 320. (Duchy of Cornwall Office.)

[9] Ibid. fo. 325. On 5th May 1361 Mr. Walter Bacheler, Clerk, was admitted to the Church of Combe in Tynhide upon the presentation of William Smale of Dartmouth, he having acquired the right of presentation from Sir Walter de Wodeland, Knt. who acquired it of the King in whose hands it was by reason of the minority of Peter de Prideaux of the same Church the true patron, son and heir of Roger Prideaux deceased. Bishop Grandisson's Reg. Vol. iii. fo. 50.

made to the Council from which it appears that an annual rent of 100s. out of lands in Orcharton, la Wode, &c. had been granted by Monsieur Roger Prideaux to Roger Prideaux his son and Johan his wife for the term of their lives.[1] On 4th December 1361 it was directed that the age of Peter Prideaux should be certified to the Council,[2] and at this time he probably attained his majority. He died, however, before 1363, for on 6th June in that year the wardship of the body of John Prideaux and the lands of the said heir in the King's hands by reason of the minority of the said heir, together with his marriage, were granted to John de Montague; nevertheless in 1361 Sir John Dynham, Knt., presented to the Church of Alyngton by reason of the custody of the lands of John Prideaux, a minor, son and heir of Roger Prideaux deceased.[3] In 1368 John Prideaux made a grant of lands to Walter Dabernon,[4] and in 1384 John Prideaux, Knt. charged his lands in Combe in Thynhyde, being the lands of Clifford, with an annual rent of £20.[5] This Sir John was Knight for the Shire of Devon in 1383 and 1386, and he presented to the Church of Combe in Tinhead in 1391.[6]

There is a tradition that this Sir John Prideaux slew his relation Sir William Bigbury at a place called "The Five Crosses," near Modbury, and being one of the party of the "White Rose" against Henry IV. in order to secure his pardon was obliged to part with several considerable manors, e.g., Cullom John and Comb in Tynhead.[7] No one of the name of Prideaux ever again presented to the Church of the last named manor. He died in 1403, and in his will, dated 5th June in that year, he directs that his body should be buried in the aisle (ala) of the Church of St. Peter at Modbury,[8] and gives to the same Church 100s. under the condition that if the parishioners of the said parish Church shall buy within two years a set of Vestments they shall be paid, but if not then the gift shall go for the picture lately bought for the High Altar of Modbury; gives to his daughter Thomasia all his pearls; residue to Elizabeth his wife, whom, with his said daughter Thomasia, John Copleston, John Raleigh of Fardel and others he makes executors,[9] who proved his will on 7th August following.[10] He left a son Richard, whom he does not name in his will, but who succeeded him at Orcharton, and presented to the Church of Brodoke on 21st July 1403, and to Alyngton in 1407.[11] He died on Wednesday next after the Feast of the Blessed Virgin Mary 1408, seized of the manor of Orcharton which he held of Sir John Cornwall, Chr., and Elizabeth his wife as of their Castle of Trematon, and of no other lands in Devon, leaving John his son his nearest heir, aged 17 years.[12]

[1] Council Book of the "Black Prince", fo. 336.   [2] Ibid. fo. 484.

[3] Bishop Grandisson's Reg., Vol. iii., fo. 135.

[4] Deed dated Monday next after the Feast of St. Matthew. (Heralds' College, C. 1, fo. 55. Prideaux MSS. 2nd Edward III.)

[5] Deed dated 9th May, 8th Richard II.   [6] Bishop Brentingham's Reg. Vol. ii. fo. 138.

[7] With reference to this tradition Leland says: "There dwellith one Prideaux in Modburi, a Gentilman of an auncient stoke and fair landes ontil by chaunce that one of his parentes killed a man; whereby one of the Courtencis Erle of Devonshire had Colum John, and other landes of Prideaux." (Itinerary, Vol. iii., p. 25.)

[8] "Prideaux Isle in Modbury Church" is mentioned by Leland. Ibid.   [9] Exeter. Bishop Stafford's Register.

[10] His monument remains in the Church of Modbury, and has lately been restored.

[11] Bishop Stafford's Register.   [12] Inq. p.m. 9th Henry IV., No. 2.

John Prideaux presented to the Church of Brodoke in 1413. In 1429, John Prideaux of Orcharton and Elizabeth his wife settled the manors of Orcharton and North Alyngton, and the advowson of the Church of Alyngton, and the manor of Brodoke, and the advowson of the Church of the said manor, to hold the said manors of Orcharton and North Alyngton to their own use for life with remainder to Martyn, brother of the said John, and the heirs of his body, in default, remainder to William Prideaux and the heirs of his body, in default, remainder to the right heirs of the said John Prideaux; and as regards the manor of Brodoke to the use of the said William Prideaux and the heirs of his body, he paying to the said John Prideaux and Elizabeth his wife, during their lives, the annual rent of 100s., in default of issue to revert to the right heirs of the said John Prideaux.[1] In 1432, however, John Prideaux of Orcharton, Esq., and Elizabeth his wife suffered a fine in the manor of Brodoke and the Church of the said manor to Thomas Carminowe, Esq., to hold to the said Thomas and his heirs of the said John and Elizabeth at the annual rent of one rose, in default of issue remainder to Nicholas Carminowe and his heirs, in default to Walter Carminowe and his heirs, in default to revert to the said John and Elizabeth and the heirs of John Prideaux of Orcharton.[2] He attested a deed in 1437. In virtue of the last of the above recited fines the manor and advowson of Brodoke passed to Thomas Carminowe of Boconnoc, and from him descended to Sir Hugh Courtenay, who married Margaret one of the two daughters and co-heirs of the said Thomas Carminowe, which Sir Hugh Courtenay presented to the benefice in 1464. The manors of Orcharton and North Alyngton rested with John Prideaux who presented to East Alyngton in 1443. A vacancy again occurring in 1453, an inquisition was held to enquire into the right of presentation, and it was found that under the above recited fine of 1429, Elizabeth relict of John Prideaux was the true patron, and she presented accordingly.

From this date, for one or two descents, we are dependant upon Pole's Devon and the pedigree recorded at the Heralds' Visitation of 1620.[3] John Prideaux,[4] last mentioned, is stated to have had a grandson of the same name. He died a little before 1522, leaving Thomas[5] his son and heir who died on 10th May in that year, and upon the inquisition taken thereupon, in which he is described as Thomas Prideaux of Orcharton, son and heir of John Prideaux recently deceased, it was found that he had died seized in fee of the manor of Orcharton, and that he had settled the same upon certain trustees to the use of himself and Margaret his wife, daughter of John Copleston of Yalhampton, and the survivor of them, with remainder to the right heirs of the said Thomas; and it was found that John Prideaux was his son and nearest heir.

---

[1] Pedes Finium, Div. Cos., 8th Henry VI., Easter.   [2] Pedes Finium, 11th Henry VI., Michs. 1.

[3] Harl. MSS. Nos. 1080, fo 123.

[4] William Prideaux, described as of Thurleston, contested the legitimacy of this John Prideaux and the case was tried in the court of the Bishop, and it was found on the 11th October 1428, that Richard Prideaux was canonically and legally married in the parish Church of Milton to Johanna Lercedekne, and that John Prideaux was their lawful son and heir, (Bp. Lacey's Reg., Vol. iii., fo. 77, see also Oliver's Mon. p. 298.) William Prideaux might have been the person named in the text, and possibly the uncle of John Prideaux, but his relationship is nowhere stated.

[5] This Thomas is erroneously called John in the registered pedigree.

By inquisition taken at Exeter on 12th September 1567, after the death of the said John Prideaux, the jury found that he died on the 25th May preceding, seized of the manors of Orcharton and East Allington, and that Thomas Prideaux was his son and nearest heir, and was aged thirty years and more.[1] This Thomas, by deed dated 25th January 1567-8, granted a rent charge of £5 per annum, payable out of a tenement called Washwells, parcel of the manor of Orcharton, towards the repair of the Parish Church of Modbury. He left a son Robert Prideaux, who by deed dated 1st September 1590,[2] confirmed his father's grant. Being the last survivor of his family in the male line he sold the manor of Orcharton, which the family had possessed for fourteen descents, to Sir John Hele, Serjeant at Law.[3]

PRIDEAUX OF ADESTON AND THEUBOROUGH, Table II.

John Prideaux, second son of Sir Roger by Elizabeth daughter of John Clifford, married Joane daughter and coheir of Gilbert de Adeston, with whom he acquired the manor of Adeston and there seated himself. After his death his relict re-married John Mules. On her death she left her son Giles Prideaux her heir.[4] John Prideaux died before 1358, for in that year we find Simon de Longbrook guardian of his son Giles. Giles was Burgess in Parliament for the Borough of Dartmouth in 1368, and in 1404 had licence to proceed to Acquitaine. He married the daughter and heir of Gunstone (Pole p. 308, says of John de Goneton) of Shilston and left a son Sir John Prideaux of Adeston.[5] We find him serving on a jury in 1413. On 18th June 1415 he had a licence to go abroad in company with the King,[6] and in 1423 he had licence to be abroad whilst in company with Sir John Robessart, Knt., Captain of the castle of Saint Sauvieur le Viscont.[7] He was thrice married. By his first wife Isabella, sister and heir of John Bromford, with a daughter, he had a son John Prideaux, who, upon the death of his uncle, the said John Bromford, was found to be his nearest heir and to be of the age of 15 years and more.[8] Dying s.p. his half brother, William Prideaux, son of his father by his third wife Ann daughter of John Shapton of Shapton, co. Devon, became his father's heir. William is described as of Langford and Adeston. Like his father, Sir John Prideaux, he was thrice married. By his third wife Alice, daughter and heir of Stephen Gifford of Theuborough, in the parish of Sutcombe, co. Devon, he had, with a daughter, two sons Fulke and John. In 1462 William Prideaux and Alice his wife suffered a fine in which they settled upon certain trustees the manors of Yewe and Myddelmyswode, in Devon, to hold to the use of themselves during their lives, with

[1] Exchequer, Esch. 8th and 9th Elizabeth, No. 10.
[2] Deeds in the parish chest of Modbury.
[3] Deed dated 47th Edward III. (1373), Prideaux MSS.
[6] French Roll, 3rd Henry V., m. 18
[8] Inq. p. m., 9th Henry VI., No. 40. See also Rot. Claus., 8th Henry VI., m. 14.

[4] Pole's Devon. p. 311.
[5] De Banco Roll, 1st Henry V.
[7] French Roll, 1st Henry VI., m. 6

remainder to Fulke their son and the heirs of his body, in default, remainder to John brother of the said Fulke and the heirs of his body, in default, remainder to the heirs of the body of the said William and Alice, with other remainders over.[1]

Fulke Prideaux seated himself at Theuborough, and had nine sons, of whom it will be sufficient to mention here Nicholas, his second son, who became a famous lawyer and amassed considerable wealth. In 1549 he purchased Soldon, near Holsworthy, and other estates in Devon. He also, in 29th Henry VIII. (1537), was granted a lease for seventy-seven years of the Rectories of Bodmin, St. Minver, Padstow, and St. Cuthbert in Cornwall, which was confirmed under the great seal in July 1544. This lease would seem, however, to have been surrendered, for we find that in 1578 the said rectories were granted to Roger Prideaux and Philippa his wife and Edward their son and the survivor of them, with remainder after their decease to Humphry Prideaux, nephew of Edmond.[2] Nicholas settled Soldon upon his nephew Humphry. Humphry Prideaux, son and heir of Fulke, died at Theuborough in 1550 leaving three sons: Richard who carried on the succession at Theuborough, William who settled himself at Trevose in St. Merryn, co. Cornwall, and Roger who was the progenitor of the family of Prideaux of Soldon (See Table III.)

Richard Prideaux of Theuborough, by his second wife Katherine, daughter of Sir John Arundel of Trerise, had several sons, of whom Richard was his successor, and George, of whom hereafter. Richard Prideaux of Theuborough was twice married: by his first wife, Grace, daughter of Nicholas Carminowe of Resprin, he left a son Jonathan, and other children; and by his second wife, Zenobia, daughter and coheir of James Nansperian, he had, with other children, a son William who inherited Gurlyn and settled there, and had a son John who married Honour daughter of James Praed of Trevetho, and had issue two daughters Joane and Honour, the eldest not above two years old at the time of her father's death. He died 15th February 1649, a little over twenty-one years of age. In September 1650 his estates were sequestrated on a charge of delinquency, when it was stated that he died seized of the manor of Gurland and divers other lands and rents in the country of Cornwall.[3] Of his daughters, Joane became the wife of Francis Gregor of Trewarthenick, co. Cornwall; and Honour married Arscot Bickford of Dunsland, co. Devon, who, after her death, took to his third wife Bridget, daughter of Edmund Prideaux of Padstow.

Jonathan, son of Richard Prideaux of Theuborough by Winifred daughter and coheir of Tristram Gorges of Budeaux Head, co. Devon, was the father of Sir Richard Prideaux, who marrying Mary daughter and one of the co-heirs of Richard Barret of Trecarne (now called Tregarden) in St. Mabyn, settled himself there. He was Sheriff of Cornwall in 1644, and was a man of great ability and prudence. He took part with the King in the civil war against the Parliament, nevertheless he had a letter of protection from Fairfax on 16th March 1645.[3] He was at Truro at the time of the capitulation, under the articles of which,

---

[1] Pedes Fin., 2nd Edward IV., Easter, Devon.

[2] See ante Vol. i., p. 143, where in lines 25 and 27, *Nicholas* is erroneously printed for *Roger*.

[3] Royalist Comp. Papers, 1st Series, Vol. lii., p. 673-691. Vol. xc., fo. 1.

confessing his delinquency, in 1649 he petitioned to be allowed to compound for his estates, which was granted, and a full discharge given to him, with the exception of all advowsons of Churches, or Chapels, to the patronage of which he was entitled.[1] Upon the Restoration in August 1660 he was appointed a Vice Warden of the Stannaries of Devon and Cornwall and Surveyor General of the Duchy of Cornwall,[2] and immediately set himself to make a new and exact survey of the Duchy whereby His Majesty's revenue was increased to nearly £3000 a year, and in 1666 a special warrant was granted for the reimbursement of £300 spent by him on this service. In the following year he died suddenly whilst hawking, and was succeeded by his eldest son of the same name, who dying soon afterwards the property devolved upon his brother Jonathan Prideaux. The latter married Ann, daughter of Sir Francis Clarke of London, by whom, as well as seven daughters, he had one son, Richard Prideaux, a Counsellor-at-law, who pre-deceased his father, unmarried, when this branch became extinct in the male line. The two elder daughters died unmarried. Frances, the third became the wife of Charles Davie of Bideford, to whom she carried the Theuborough estate.[3]

PRIDEAUX OF SUTCOMBE.

George Prideaux, fifth son of Richard Prideaux of Theuborough by his second wife Katherine Arundel, settled at Sutcombe, but we regret that we are unable to give much account of him or his descendants. He died in 1657 leaving a son, Richard Prideaux, and several daughters. Richard Prideaux, through the means of Alderman Barnes of Newcastle upon Tyne, settled in that town. He was one of a sect called "The Congregational Judgment", to which the Alderman also belonged. It is said that he conformed and became Vicar of Newcastle, but the statement is very questionable, and he does not describe himself as a "Clerk" in his will. He died in 1663, and bequeathed to his son Richard Prideaux £100 and all his estate in Devonshire, and names his other sons George, John, and Peter, and several daughters, appointing Sir William Morrice and Sir Richard Prideaux to decide any disputes which might arise. Richard was a merchant at Newcastle, and dying unmarried, he bequeathed all his land in Devonshire to his brother John Prideaux, described as Vicar of Long Houghton, co. Northumberland.[4]

[1] Royalist Comp. Papers, 1st Series, Vol. lii., fo. 671 and 676.
[2] Magna Brit. Vol. iii., p. vii.   [3] State Papers, Dom. Corr., Vol. xi., Grants.
[4] N.B.—This account is derived from the Memoirs of Ambrose Barnes, late Merchant and sometime Alderman of Newcastle-upon-Tyne, published by the Surtees Society, p. 129. There is a note to page 253 referring to the wills cited, and to the will of Alderman Barnes himself in these words; "This will (that of Barnes) and other testaments of the family, and the will of Richard Prideaux were abridged and indexed by Sir Cuthbert Sharp, who was employed by Bishop Barrington to index the Durham wills. But Raine tells me that they are not now to be found. The index bears opposite to their mention a + the favorite mark of the knight." Richard Barnes is described as Pastor of All-Hallows in Newcastle, p. 375.

2 c

PRIDEAUX OF TREVOSE AND ST. ISSEY.

William Prideaux of Trevose, in the parish of St. Merryn, married Johanna daughter of John Munday of Rialton, brother of the last Prior of Bodmin, through whose influence he was granted by the convent a lease, dated 20th October 29th Henry VIII. (1537), to him and Johanna the daughter of John Munday, whom he, "God permitting, intends to marry", and the survivor of them, of the manor of Padstow, together with the advowson of the Vicarage of the Church,[1] which lease was afterwards confirmed in the Court of Aug-mentation.   The term unexpired in this lease, by deed dated 24th February 1544-5 (36th Henry VIII.), he assigned to Nicholas Prideaux his uncle, who had, meanwhile, been granted the manor in fee.   He afterwards settled at St. Cadoc in Padstow, where he died on 27th June 1564, and upon the inquisition taken after his death on 17th January 1564-5, it was found: that he died seized in his demesne as of fee of all the tithe fish and fishery of the parish of Paddestowe, and of a tenement called Trebartheke in St. Eval ; that by his will he gave to his wife Johanna two-thirds of these possessions to pay his debts and portion his daughters; that his wife died at St. Cadoc the day following the death of her husband; and that Richard Prideaux and Roger Prideaux (his brothers) and William Munday (his brother-in-law) administered to his effects; and further that John Prideaux was his eldest son and was of the age of eighteen years seven months and sixteen days.[2]   William Prideaux is several times mentioned as a tenant in the Court Rolls of the manor of Padstow between 1553 and 1563.   At a Court held on 20th October 1564 the jury present his death; and in 1566 John Prideaux is presented as a conventionary tenant.   By an Indenture dated 15th August 25th Elizabeth (1583) Degory Polwhele of Polwhele granted to John Prideaux of Padstow Esq., John his son, and Anne his wife, and the survivor of them certain houses, &c. in Padstow, and by a deed dated 24th May 1st James (1603), by which Degory Polwhele of Treworgan conveyed to Nicholas Prideaux of Padstow Esq., *inter alia*, the reversion of these houses, it appears that John Prideaux and John his son were still living, but that Anne, the wife of John Prideaux, was deceased.[3] John Prideaux *senior*, Gent, is mentioned in a Court Roll of the 18th October 1606, and the name of John Prideaux frequently occurs in the rolls down to 1623.   In 1604 John Prideaux married at Padstow,.........the name of his wife not being given, and he died in March 1633-4.   Johanna Prideaux, perhaps his widow, is mentioned as being seventy years of age in 1657, and she died in 1665.   They had two children, if not more, Richard baptized at Padstow in 1615 and Elizabeth baptized and buried at St. Merryn in 1617. We have no further trace of his issue.

We find a Richard Prideaux, Gent, settled in the contiguous parish of St. Issey, who

---

[1] See Ante, Vol. i., p. 137. n.

[2] Inq., p. m. 7th Elizabeth, No. 113.

[3] Deeds at Prideaux Place.

was, probably, a younger son of John Prideaux the son of William and Johanna Munday. He died in 1625, and in his will names two sons and two daughters. His eldest son, William, continued to reside at St. Issey, and had several children and grandchildren baptized there.

PRIDEAUX OF SOLDON AND PRIDEAUX PLACE.—TABLE III.

We now arrive at the most important part of the genealogy of this ancient family, inasmuch as the branches of which we shall now treat still continue and flourish. They are also of the greater interest to us as they were intimately connected with the district of which we write. Roger Prideaux, third son of Humphry Prideaux of Theuborough by Jane his wife, daughter of Richard Fowell of Fowellscombe, settled at Soldon, in the parish of Holsworthy, which he inherited from his uncle Nicholas. He married Philippa daughter of Roger Yorke, Sergeant at Law, and had two sons and two daughters. His eldest son, Sir Nicholas Prideaux, carried on the succession at Soldon, and was the ancestor of the Prideauxes of Prideaux Place, Padstow; and his second son, Edmund, was the founder of the family at Netherton, from which sprung that of Ford Abbey.

Sir Nicholas Prideaux was thrice married. By his first wife, Thomasine daughter and co-heir of John Henscot of Henscot, in the parish of Bradford, co. Devon, he had one son, Humphry. He married, secondly, Cheston, third daughter and co-heir of William Viell of Trevorder in St. Breoke (which estate the Viells inherited from George Viell who married Elizabeth daughter and co-heir of Richard Billing of Trevorder)[1] by whom he had a son, John Prideaux, upon whom his father settled all his Cornish lands, and who served the office of Sheriff of Cornwall in 1631. Sir Nicholas Prideaux, by his third wife, had no issue.

Humphry, eldest son of Sir Nicholas Prideaux, married, in 1600, Honour daughter of Edmond Fortescue of Fallowpit, when his father surrendered to him the estate of Soldon, having previously, in 1588-1592, built the fine mansion at Padstow, since called Prideaux Place, where he seated himself. He was seized with the small pox and died in the prime of life, leaving his youthful family to the care of their grandfather, Sir Nicholas. His eldest son, Nicholas Prideaux, carried on the succession at Soldon, and his representation eventually vested in Anne daughter and heir of his second son Humphry, who married her cousin John Prideaux, third son of Sir Peter Prideaux, of Netherton, Bart.

Edmund Prideaux, third son of Humphry and Honour Fortescue, settled at Prideaux Place, which had devolved upon him under the deed of settlement upon the death of his uncle John Prideaux in 1649, as above-mentioned. He had a large family, all of which may be seen in the annexed pedigree (Table No. III). John, his eldest son, left issue three

---

[1] See Ante, Vol. i., pp. 387, 389.

sons, all of whom died s.p., and Edmund, the second son, had issue one daughter. Humphry, the third, carried on the succession and was one of the most remarkable men of his family in modern times.

Humphry Prideaux was born at Padstow in 1648, and received his elementary education at Liskeard and Bodmin, and was from the latter place removed to Westminster, under the famous Dr. Busby, where he soon became King's scholar. From thence he was elected to Christ Church, Oxford, and was admitted a Student in that College on 11th December 1668 at the age of 18. He took his degree as B.A. in 1672. About this time Lord Henry Howard, then Earl of Norwich, afterwards Duke of Norfolk, having given to the University of Oxford the Arundell Marbles collected by his grandfather, Thomas Earl of Arundell, it was thought desirable to have the inscriptions on them published with explanations, and Mr. Prideaux, though at that time very young and only a Bachelor of Arts, was selected for the work, which he published in folio two years afterwards, viz.: in 1676, under the title "Marmora Oxoniensia", being then just of one year's standing as Master of Arts. This work gained for him a great reputation. Being ordered, upon the first publication of the book, to present a copy to Lord Chancellor Finch, it procured him an introduction to his Lordship, who, in 1679, presented him to the Rectory of St. Clements in Oxford, and continued his patron to the end of his life. In 1681 he was appointed to a Prebend in the Cathedral at Norwich, and in the following year proceeded B.D., and was instituted to the Rectory of Bladen cum Capella de Woodstock, which he held with his Studentship of Christ Church in virtue of his being Librarian of his College. On 16th February 1685-6 he married, and immediately afterwards proceeded D.D. and thereupon exchanged the benefice of Bladen for the Rectory of Saham Tony in Norfolk, and settled upon his Prebend at Norwich. In 1688 he was collated by Dr. Lloyd, Bishop of Norwich, to the Archdeaconry of Suffolk, and in 1702 he was appointed to the Deanery of Norwich. He was an earnest and able man, and in every office which he filled he not only strove zealously to perform his own duties but endeavoured to remove all abuses which he found existing. He was the author of several works of learning and ability, among them the "Original Divine Right of Tithes", and "Instructions to Churchwardens," but that by which he is chiefly known is his "Connection of the History of the Old and New Testaments", the two latter of which still continue to be esteemed as standard works. In his later years Dr. Prideaux was afflicted with a distressing and painful disease, and towards the end of his life he could no longer use his books. He died at Norwich 1st November 1724, and was buried in the cathedral.[1]

Dean Prideaux left an only surviving son, Edmund, who on the death of his cousin Edmund Prideaux of Prideaux Place in 1728, s.p., succeeded to his estates, and dying in

---

[1] From this family of Theuborough and Soldon John Prideaux, Bishop of Worcester, would also appear to have derived his descent, though we have failed to trace the connection, for in 1621, he dedicated his two Sermons entitled " Christ's Council for ending Law Cases", to "The Worshipful my very worthy *Kinsman* Edmund Prideaux Esq., Counsellour at Law, and Mrs. Mary Prideaux his vertous and religious wife." This Edmund was created a Baronet of Netherton the next year.

1745, was succeeded by his son Humphry Prideaux of Prideaux Place, who married Jenny second daughter of Nevill Morton Pleydell of Shitterton, co. Dorset, by Betty daughter of Charles Brune of Plumber, in the same county. By this marriage Humphry Prideaux had a large family. His eldest son Charles Prideaux, on the death of his uncle Charles Morton Pleydell-Brune, succeeded to the Brune estates, and, in conformity with the testamentary injunction of his maternal great uncle, Charles Brune, assumed the name and arms of Brune in addition to that of Prideaux. For continuance of this branch see account of the family of BRUNE post.

PRIDEAUX OF NETHERTON, BARONET.—TABLE IV.

The founder of the family of Prideaux of Netherton was Edmund, second son of Roger Prideaux of Soldon (see Table III). Edmund Prideaux was born in 1554 and was educated for the profession of the law. In 1598 he was appointed Autumnal Reader of the Inner Temple, in 1608 Treasurer of the same, and five years later Double Reader. He acquired in his profession not only distinction but wealth, and purchased the manor of Netherton in the parish of Farway, co. Devon, where he built a handsome mansion and settled himself, which place has continued the chief residence of his family to the present time. Netherton had been parcel of the possessions of the Priory of Canon's Leigh, co. Devon, to which house it was granted in the 12th century by Walter de Claville. Nevertheless the family of Prideaux would seem to have held it in the 14th century, for we have a note of a petition by John de Prideaux, dated 10th November 29th Edward III., to the Duke of Cornwall to have the manor of Netherton restored to him.[1] Edmund Prideaux was created a Baronet under the title of Sir Edmund Prideaux of Netherton on 17th July 1622. He was twice married. By his second wife, Katherine daughter of Piers Edgcombe of Mount Edgcombe, he had two sons, Peter who succeeded him in his title and estates, and Edmund who became the founder of the family of Prideaux of Ford Abbey. (See Table V.)

Sir Edmund Prideaux, the third in descent from Sir Peter, and the fifth Baronet, was twice married but died without surviving issue male, and the title and estates devolved upon his half brother Sir John Prideaux, who having succeeded to Soldon under his uncle John Prideaux's will sold the same. By Anne, eldest daughter of John Vaughan Viscount Lisburne, by Lady Mallet Wilmot, daughter of John Wilmot Earl of Rochester, he had two sons who attained to man's estate, both of whom were slain in battle. Saunderson, the eldest son, was killed, on the 9th April 1741, in the attack on Fort Lazare at Carthagena, in South America, whilst yet in the flower of his youth, being only just over 21 years of age. John, the second son, became a distinguished officer the friend and companion in arms of Wolfe and Amherst. He attained the rank of Captain in the 3rd Regiment of Guards

---

[1] Council Book of Edward the "Black Prince", p. 236. Duchy of Cornwall Office.

in 1748. On 28th October 1759, he was appointed Colonel of the 55th Regiment. This Regiment formed a portion of the Army in North America under Major General Amherst. Colonel Prideaux served in the campaign with the rank of Brigadier, and was appointed to command a body of troops, re-inforced with a considerable number of friendly Indians under the command of Sir William Johnston, appointed to invest the French fort erected at the falls of Niagara. He conducted his expedition with great success, and invested the fortress about the middle of July, and carrying on his approaches with untiring vigour until the 20th, when, visiting the trenches, he was unfortunately killed by the bursting of a cohorn. By his wife Elizabeth, sister of Sir Edmund Bayntun Rolt, of Spye Park, Wilts, Bart., he had several children, the eldest of whom, Sir John Wilmot Prideaux, Bart., succeeded his grandfather in 1766, whose second son, Sir Edmund Saunderson Prideaux, the ninth Baronet, a Major in the Army and Honorary Colonel of the Exeter and South Devon Rifle Volunteers, is at present the highly respected and greatly esteemed representative of this branch of the family.

PRIDEAUX OF FORD ABBEY, Co. DORSET.—Table V.

Ford Abbey is in the Parish of Thorncombe now in the County of Dorset. Thorncombe was formerly in Devon but transferred to Dorset by Act of Parliament in 1842. Ford Abbey was purchased of Sir Henry Rosewell in 1649 by Edmund Prideaux second son of Sir Edmund Prideaux the first Baronet. This gentleman was educated in the University of Cambridge where he proceeded M.A. He was admitted a Student at the Inner Temple on 12th May 1616, and was called to the Bar on 23rd November 1623. Having been returned as Burgess in Parliament for Lyme Regis he took part against the King. On 10th Nov. 1643 he was appointed one of the Commissioners of the Great Seal, and on 1st Oct. 1646 he was granted by the Parliament the privileges of a King's Council, the combined offices being worth between £6000 and £7000 a year, and he was allowed to retain his seat in the House of Commons notwithstanding his holding the former office. On his relinquishing the Great Seal the House of Commons ordered, as a mark of honour and as an acknowledgement of the value of his services, that he should practice within the Bar and have precedence next after the Solicitor General. He then continued his private practice until 1648, on 25th November in which year he took the oath as Solicitor General. He appears, however, to have been less rancorous against his Sovereign than his coadjutors for he took no part in the King's trial, nor in the subsequent trials of the Duke of Hamilton and others; nevertheless, a few weeks afterwards, he accepted the office of Attorney General from the dominant party, which he retained during the remainder of his life. In 1644, by a resolution of the House of Commons, Edmund Prideaux, a Member of the House, was constituted

Master of the Post Messengers and Carriers, and in 1649 he established a weekly conveyance to every part of the kingdom, in lieu of the former practice under which letters were sent by special messengers whose duty it was to supply relays of horses at a certain mileage. In 1658 Cromwell made him one of his Baronets. He acquired great wealth. It is said that his emoluments in connection with the Post Office were not less than £15,000 a year. Edmund Prideaux was twice married. By his first wife Joane, daughter and sole heir of Henry Collins[1] of Ottery St. Mary, he had a daughter Mary. By his second wife Margaret, daughter and co-heir of William Ivery[2] of Cotthay co. Somerset, he had a son, Edmund, and three daughters.

Edmund Prideaux succeeded his father at Ford Abbey. He was a highly educated gentleman having had for his tutor John Tillotson, afterwards, upon the deprivation of Archbishop Sancroft, made Archbishop of Canterbury. He does not appear to have taken any part in politics after the restoration. Our first notice of him is as the entertainer of the unfortunate Duke of Monmouth, upon whose journey of pleasure to the west, at the latter end of 1680, he paid a visit to Mr. Prideaux at Ford Abbey and was magnificently received.[3] In 1681 he was returned to Parliament as one of the Burgesses for Taunton. But his connection with the Duke of Monmouth after the Rye House affair rendered him suspected, and his house was searched for arms under the general warrant for searching the houses of dangerous and disaffected persons. In the memorable year 1685, when the Duke of Monmouth landed at Lyme Regis, it is said Mr. Prideaux remained quietly at his own house, which was visited by a party at night for horses and arms, and that one person drank the health of Monmouth. On this becoming known in London a warrant was issued to arrest Mr. Prideaux, which was carried into effect on the 19th June, and he was eventually committed a close prisoner to the Tower on a charge of high treason. Nothing was ever proved against him, nevertheless he could not obtain his release until he had paid a sum of £15,000 to the infamous Judge Jefferies. His pardon was signed on 20th March 1685-6.[4] On the accession of William III. Mr. Prideaux petitioned Parliament for leave to bring in a Bill to charge the estates of Judge Jefferies with the restitution of the £15,000 he had paid, but the Act did not pass. Edmund Prideaux had several children by his wife Amy, daughter and co-heir of John Fraunceis of Combe Florey, co. Somerset, all of whom pre-deceased him except his daughter Margaret, who had married her cousin Francis Gwyn of Llansannor co. Glamorgan, and who, in her right, inherited Ford Abbey, and by whose descendants it has recently been sold.[5]

---

[1] Arms: ar. a chev. betw. three mulletts pierced gu.

[2] Arms: ar. three chevronels gu. same as *Every.* Monuments in Ford Abbey Chapel.

[3] Roberts's Life of Monmouth, Vol. ii., p. 254.   [4] Rot. Pat., 2nd James II., Part 8, No. 3.

[5] Francis Gwyn's mother was Eleanor daughter of Sir Francis Popham, whose other daughter, Catherine, became the wife of John Fraunceis, whose daughter Amy was the mother of Margaret.

PRIDEAUX OF NUTWELL AND ASHBURTON.—TABLE VI.

According to the Visitation of 1620 the ancestor of this family, Thomas Prideaux of Ashburton, was Thomas the fourth son of Humphry Prideaux of Theuborough by his second wife Edith, the daughter of William Hatch of Aller. It is, however, impossible to reconcile this statement with known facts. Joane Prideaux, the first wife of the said Humphry, did not die until 31st October 1623, as shewn by the inquisition taken upon her death,[1] therefore this Thomas, by a second marriage, could not have been born earlier then 1524, and, consequently, could not have been the father of John Prideaux, Sergeant at law, who died on 29th September 1558, leaving his son and heir Thomas Prideaux aged nine years three months and eight days (born 21st June 1549).[2]

We find, however, that a certain Thomas Prideaux, described as of Aysshton, died 22nd January 1547 seized of lands and tenements called Scrobbyscomb, magna and parva, in Kingston, the Manor of Credywygger held of the Bishop of Exeter, and a messuage in Aysshton, which latter was stated to have been granted by a certain Thomas Predyaux, senior, by his charter, dated 20th September 12th Henry VIII. (1521), to a certain Johanna Predyaux, relict of John Predyaux, brother of the said Thomas Predyaux, senior, to hold to the said Johanna and the heirs of her body; and it is stated that it descended to the said Thomas, the subject of the inquisition, as son and heir of the said Johanna, and that it was held of William Jackson and Ricarda his wife, the said Ricarda being kinswoman and heir of the said Thomas Predyaux, senior : viz. the daughter and heir of John Predyaux son and heir of the aforesaid Thomas, senior, and the jury further find that John Predyaux, then living at Ayssheton, was son and heir of the said Thomas mentioned in the writ, and that he was aged twenty eight years and more. This John could not have been any other than the Serjeant, for upon the death of the latter, on 29th September 1558, it was found upon inquisiton[3] that in addition to the manors of Nutwell, Woodberie, and Lympston, which he is known to have purchased, he was seized of the manor of Creditwiger held of the Bishop of Exeter of the manor of Crediton, and lands called Stebbiscombe magna and parva held of the manor of Kingston in free soccage : and that Thomas Prideaux was son and heir of the said John, and was aged nine years three months and eight days.

We find also a will of a certain Richard Pridyaux, described as of Tavistock,[4] dated 21st October 1529,[5] in which he makes a bequest of 3s. 4d. to the Church of St. Andrew at Asheberton, thus shewing his interest in that place, and making bequests to Margaret, Dorothy and Alice Webb, the children of William Webb, and to his first [*sic*] sister Alice

---

[1] Inq. p. m., 16th Henry VIII., No. 144.   [2] Inq. p. m., 1st Elizabeth, Part III. No. 31.

[3] Inq. p. m. 1st Elizabeth, Part II. No. 31.

[4] Richard Prideaux was assessed to the Subsidy at Tavistock in 1523, upon goods of the value of £304.

Sub. Roll. 14th Henry VIII. $\frac{97}{186}$ [5] Proved 12th February 1529, P.C.C., (15th Jankin).

the wife of Adam Williams, to his brother-in-law Adam Williams,[1] and £100 sterling to each of his daughters Grace and Phillip, he declares that in the event of his two daughters dying before marriage, it is his will that £40 of the said £200 shall be "bestowed in fynding of some honest priest to sing for me and Agnes my wife and all my children, and for the soules of Joane (Jane) my late wife and William Webbe her late husband, &c. and for the soules of Thomas Predyaux and Elizabeth his wife, my father and mother and all their children, and for all good dooers and well wyllers." It further appears from the inquisition taken after his death that he died 13th October 1529, seized of lands in Tavistock and elsewhere, and that his daughters, Grace aged five years, and Phillip aged one year, were his nearest heirs.[2] It thus is manifest that the name of the father of Thomas Prideaux, father of the Serjeant, was John and not Humphry as stated in the Visitation Pedigree, and, perhaps, Thomas Prideaux the father of Richard was a younger son of this ancient house whose name is not shewn in the old pedigrees.

Thomas Prideaux of Ashburton had two sons, John Prideaux, Serjeant at Law, already mentioned, and Robert Prideaux who seems to have succeeded his father at Ashburton.

John Prideaux, as we have already stated,[3] purchased Nutwell and settled there. He received a grant of Arms on 16th May 1558 materially differing from the ancient arms of Prideaux, and died on the 29th September in the same year, and was succeeded by his son Thomas, who, in 1594, obtained an alteration in the Arms previously granted, bringing them nearer to the Prideaux Arms. He died in 1605 and was succeeded by his son Thomas who received the honour of Knighthood in 1603, whose son Amias Prideaux sold Nutwell in 1647, and dying in 1676, s. p. this branch of the family became extinct.

Robert Prideaux of Ashburton, the second son of Thomas, died in 1578, and in his will names his sons Thomas, George, Robert, and Harry, and Elizabeth his daughter. A John shewn in the Visitation pedigree of 1620 as eldest son is not named in the will, and Harry does not appear in the pedigree. Thomas, described in the pedigree as second son and of Totnes, carried on the succession, and by deed dated 14th December 7th James (1610) charged certain lands in Ashburton with a rent charge of £2 12s. per annum for the benefit of thirteen poor persons of the parish of Ashburton.[4] John Prideaux his eldest son was aged twenty one years in 1620, and Thomas his second son settled at Ugborough and died in 1639 leaving issue which we give to the third descent.

ARMS. Ar. upon a chevron sa. between three Eagles' feet, couped, gu. a Book, or, purfled vert, between two Bowyers' knots ar. Granted by William Hervey, Clarenceaux, 16th May 1558.

[1] Adam Williams by Alice daughter of Thomas Prideaux of Ashburton, was the father of Thomas Williams, Speaker in the House of Commons 1562. (Pole's Devon, p. 320.) Elizabeth Prideaux, widow, was assessed in 1523, upon goods in Ashburton of the value of £180. (Sub. Roll 14th Henry VIII, $\frac{97}{186}$. And the Williams pedigree. (Harl. 1080. 241.) describes Alice wife of Adam Williams, as daughter of Thomas Prideaux of Ashburton.

[2] Inq., p.m. 21st Henry VIII., No. 11 Chanc.

[3] On 29th October 1553, George Ford obtained a Royal License to alienate a fourth part of the Manor of Nutwell to John Prydeaux of Upton Pyne, Gent.   [4] Charities of Devon, (1826) Vol. II., 145.

In 1594 the Arms were altered by Lea, to: Ar. a chev. sa. charged with two bars gemelles wavy of the first, a label of three points gu. with this note: " The arms and creast of Thomas Predyaux of Nutwell, in the County of Devonshire, Esquire, first given by William Harvye, *alias* Clarentzaulxe, with a book between two Bowyers knottes on the cheveron, now altered thus by Robert Lea *alias* Clarenceulx 1594. The creast is as it was at the first." (Heralds' Coll. Miscl. Grants I., 19*b*.)

LE BRUN *alias* LE BRUYN, *alias* BRUNE.

This ancient and distinguished family was at an early date settled in Essex. The first of any prominence which we are able to trace is Sir William Le Brun who was Chamberlain to King Edward I., and probably was in the service of that Prince before his succession to the throne, for we find that in the fifth year of his reign (1277) he granted to Sir William Le Brun and Isolda his wife, which Isolda was one of the Maids of Honor to Queen Eleanor, certain manors in the counties of Dorset and Southampton of which Fordingbridge, Rughenore, and East Perle still remain in the family. He also granted them extensive rights of free warren. This Isolda is said to have been the daughter and co-heir of Philip de Rupellis, *alias* de la Rokele, but this is clearly a mistake, as we shall presently shew. In the year 1300 William le Brune was returned from the county of Southampton as holding lands in capite, or otherwise, of £40 yearly value, or upwards, and as such was summoned under the general writ to perform Military service in person against the Scots, and in the same manner he was returned from the counties of Somerset and Dorset.[1] Sir William le Brun died in the year 1300, and upon the usual inquisition taken thereupon Maurice le Brun his son was found to be his nearest heir, and to be of the age of twenty one years and more.[2] Isolda survived her husband and died in 1307, and by the inquisition taken after her death it was found that she held, *inter alia*, the manor of Rouenore by serjeantry: viz. by the service of finding one man for the defence of Porchester Castle for forty days in time of war, for which service she paid 40s. to provide a substitute, and it was found that Maurice le Brune was her son and heir and of the age of thirty years and more.[3]

Maurice le Brune was a man of great eminence. In 1308 he was summoned, together with his consort, from the county of Essex to attend the coronation in the train of the King and Queen.[4] In 1313 he was summoned to Parliament as one of the Barons of the Realm,[5] as he was again in the same year and in 1315,[6] and continued to be during the remainder of his life, though his descendants were never afterwards summoned.

In the civil commotions which distracted the country during the greater part of the reign of Edward II. Sir Maurice le Brun seems to have been tolerably stedfast in his

---

[1] Rot. Parl. Writs, Vol. i. pp. 337, 338.   [2] Inq., p. m. 29th Edward I., No. 44.
[3] Inq., p. m., 1st Edward II., No. 64.   [4] Rot. Claus. 1st Edward II., m. 10*d*.
[5] Rot. Claus. 6th Edward II., m. 16*d*.   [6] Ibid, 9th Edward II., m. 22*d*.

loyalty to the King. In 1321 when the Earls of Lancaster and Hereford arose in arms on account of the Spensers we find Maurice le Brune among those who were requested to co-operate in appeasing the disturbances, and also to refrain from attending illegal confederacies or assemblies,[1] and on the 12th November in the same year he was ordered to abstain from attending the meeting of the " Good Peers " convened by the Earl of Lancaster to be held at Doncaster,[2] and on 6th February following he was enjoined to raise as many men at arms and foot soldiers as he could, and to hold himself in readiness to march with them to the King when summoned to do so,[3] and on the 14th of the same month he was summoned to appear with his forces at Coventry on the 28th for the purpose of marching against the rebels.[4] On 13th November 1324 he became one of the manucaptors for the good behaviour of John de Wroxhale on his discharge from imprisonment as an adherent of the Earl of Lancaster.[5] In the following year he was appointed one of the Conservators of the Peace for the county of Southampton,[6] and in the next year he was addressed in that capacity and commanded to disperse seditious assemblies and to apprehend offenders.[7]

It was this Sir Maurice, and not his father, who formed an alliance with the family of de la Rokele. He married Matilda daughter and heir of Sir Philip de la Rokele, with whom he acquired the Manor of Beckinham in Kent, Okendon in Essex, and other lands.

The family of de la Rokele was one of great eminence in Essex. Philip de la Rokele, the father of Matilda, was the son of Sir Richard de la Rokele, Justiciary of Ireland, who died in 1276,[8] being grandson of Sir Richard de la Rokele, who died at South Okingdon in 1222. This last, Morant says, " was son of Geoffry de la Rokele *alias* William de Ou to which the registry of the Priory of Hatfield Peveril is voucher, and this William, uncle to the Earl of Angus, is said to have lived in the reign of King Stephen." He seems to be the person meant in the Red Book when it is said " Hugh de Ou held one Knight's fee, and William de Rochelle three parts of a Knight's fee, under Geoffry de Mandeville of the new feoffment in the reign of Henry II ".[9] Sir Philip de la Rokele died 18th October 1295, when Matilda his daughter was found to be his heir and to be of the age of nine-and-a-half years.[10] A special inquisition was taken concerning her age five years afterwards, when the jury found that she was then the wife of Maurice le Brun and was aged fourteen years on 9th October 1300, but added that they had no other evidence than the voice of the country because the said Matilda was born in Ireland.[11] Sir Maurice le Brun died 17th March 1354-5, and was succeeded by his son Sir William le Brun who died in 1362, leaving a son Sir Ingelram le Brune whose son, Sir Maurice le Brun, was Sheriff of Herts and Essex in the 2nd and 14th years

---

[1] Rot. Claus. 14th Edward II., m. 7*d.*, Writ tested at Bristol 21st April.

[2] Ibid, 15th Edward II., m. 23*d.*
[3] Ibid, 15th Edward II., m. 19*d.*

[4] Ibid, m. 17*d.* in ced.
[5] Rot. Fin., 18th Edward II.

[6] Rot. Pat., 19th Edward II., Part I., m. 29.
[7] Ibid, 19th Edward II., Part II., m. 19*d.*

[8] Inq. p.m., 5th Edward I., No. 6.
[9] History and Antiquities of Essex, Vol. ii, p. 477, *n.*

[10] Inq. p.m., 23rd Edward I., No. 39.
[11] Inq. Prob. Etat., 28th Edward I., No. 157.

2 D²

of King Henry VI.   By his wife Elizabeth, daughter and co-heir of Sir Henry Radford of Irby, co. Lincoln, he had two sons, Henry and Thomas.

Henry Bruyn married Elizabeth, daughter and co-heir of Robert Darcy of Maldon, and was Sheriff of South Hants in 1447.   There is extant a receipt given by him for certain dues payable to the King by the men of Southampton, dated 5th May in that year, and sealed with his official seal, a seal of a class of which specimens are very uncommon considering the number which must at one time have existed.   Henry Bruyn's

seal is a very fine example and elegantly designed.   It is of a circular form and has the device of a castle, usual in these seals, and in front of it a shield, couched, charged with the arms of Bruyn and Rokele quarterly.   His initials **h. b.** are given just above the shield on each side of the gateway.   Henry Bruyn was knighted soon after this date, and was again Sheriff of this county in 1458.   He died in 1461 v.p., leaving two daughters and co-heirs: Alice wife of John Berners, and Elizabeth wife of Thomas Tyrell.[1]   The latter afterwards married Sir William Brandon Knt., and was the mother of Charles Brandon Duke of Suffolk; and thirdly she married William Malory.

Thomas Bruyn, upon his father's death in 1467, was found to be his son and nearest heir.[2] On 30th January 1481-2, as son and heir male of Maurice Bruyn Knt., deceased, and heir male of Henry Bruyn Knt., deceased, son of the said Maurice, he had license to enter upon all the lands, &c., separately held of the King in capite by the said Maurice and Henry.[3] He left two sons, William and John.[4]   William, married Katherine daughter and heir of William Rengebourn, grandson of Agnes, daughter and co-heir of Sir William Sturmy of Wolfall, co. Wilts.   Matilda, the other co-heir, married Roger Seymour ancestor of Jane Seymour, Queen of Henry VIII., and of the present Duke of Somerset.   Upon the death of their son, Sir John Seymour Knt., in 1464, he was found to have died seized, *inter alia*, of a moiety of the manor of Wolfall, the other moiety being held by Robert Rengebourn son of William, son of the abovementioned Agnes, who dying s.p. in 1485 his brother William was found to be his heir.   Upon the death of William Rengebourn in 1512, his grandson, Thomas Bruyn, was found to be his nearest heir.   He died in 1539 s.p., seized *inter alia* of a moiety of the Sturmy lands,[5] and his uncle John Bruyn was found to be his heir.[6]

Henry Brune, grandson of John, by his wife Elizabeth, daughter and co-heir of Nicholas Martin of Athelhampton, co. Dorset, had three sons, Sir John Brune, his eldest son and heir died s.p.: Nicholas, the third, died unmarried; Charles, the second, married Mary daughter of Robert Coker of Mapowder in the same county, and had two sons John and Charles.   John, on the death of his uncle, Sir John Brune, was found to be his heir.

---

[1] Inq. p.m., 1st Edward IV., No. 27.   [2] Inq. p.m., 8th Henry IV., No. 24.

[3] Rot. Pat., 21st Edward IV., Part I.   [4] Inq. p.m., 14th Henry VII., No. 48.

[5] Inq. p.m., 4th Henry VIII., No. 79.   [6] Record Office, Primus Lib. ced. 86.

He married Mary daughter of Edward Hooper of Boveridge, in the same county, and, having previously settled the ancient family inheritance upon his brother Charles and his heirs, died leaving an only daughter and heir who married Sir Ralph Bankes of Corfe Castle. Charles, second son of Charles Brune, purchased the manor of Plumber, co. Dorset, and settled there. Dying in 1703 he left issue one only surviving son who succeeded to the estates. He married Betty daughter and heir of Lorenzo Jeffery of West Bagborough, co. Somerset, by whom he had four sons, the three younger of whom died unmarried, and three daughters, the elder of whom, Betty, became the wife of Nevill Morton Pleydell of Shitterton, co. Dorset.

Charles Brune, the eldest son of the aforesaid Charles, succeeded his father in the estates. He married Elizabeth daughter and co-heir of William Boulting of Wells, but having no issue devised his estates to his nephew Charles Morton Pleydell, and his heirs male, on condition that he and his issue should assume the surname of Brune in addition to that of Pleydell, with remainder to his great nephew Charles Prideaux, eldest son of Humphry Prideaux of Prideaux Place by his second wife Jenny Pleydell, eldest niece of testator, and to his issue.

Charles Morton Pleydell-Brune died s.p. in 1785, and Charles son of the aforesaid Humphry Prideaux succeeded to the Brune estates, and, in conformity with the testamentary injunction of his maternal great uncle Charles Brune, by Royal License, dated 11th July 1799, assumed the name and arms of Brune in addition to those of Prideaux. He died in 1833, leaving, by his wife Frances, daughter of Thomas Patten, of Bank Hall, co. Lancaster, an only son Charles Prideaux-Brune of Prideaux Place, co. Cornwall, and of Plumber, co. Dorset, who is the present representative of the ancient families of Brune and Prideaux. His son and heir, by Frances daughter and co-heir of Edmund John Glynn of Glynn, co. Cornwall, Charles Glynn Prideaux-Brune of Prideaux Place, by his wife the Honorable Ellen Jane, second daughter of Robert Shapland, first Baron Carew, has numerous issue, who it is hoped will carry on the succession for many future generations.

THE ARMS used by Mr. Prideaux-Brune are: Quarterly, 1. Az. a cross moline or. BRUNE. 2. Ar. a chev. sa., in chief a label of three points gu. PRIDEAUX. 3. Party per pale ar. and gules three castles counterchanged. Old arms of PRIDEAUX. 4. Lozengy erm. and gules. ROKELE.

CRESTS—BRUNE: A goat passant, per pale indented, ar. and sa. armed and unguled or. Pendant from a collar or, a shield charged with the arms of Brune.

PRIDEAUX: A man's head in profile couped at the shoulders ppr., hair and beard or, on the head a chapeau gu. turned up ar.

MOTTOES—BRUNE: "*Toujours prèt*", which is found on the monument of Sir John Brune, Knt., who died 1559, Rowner Church, co. Dorset, in this form "*Tours jours pres.*",

PRIDEAUX OF PRIDEAUX PLACE, "*Prudentium arma Providentia est.*"

PRIDEAUX OF NETHERTON, "*Deus providebit.*"

Arms as allowed at the Heralds' Visitation, 1620.

1. PRIDEAUX.	6. HUDDY.
2. OLD ARMS OF PRIDEAUX.	7. GOULSTON.
3. GIFFORD OF THEUBOROUGH.	8. HUGWORTHY.
4. ESSE.	9. CARMINOW.
5. SPENCER.	10. as 1.

On the Escutcheon of pretence GORGES.

PEDIGREE OF PRIDEAUX

ORCHARTON, co.

Pagan Prideaux Lord of Prideaux ⊤ ....
in the Conquest time.

Philip, 2.   *Richard Prideaux, Lord of Prideaux,* ⊤ ....
died 1122, temp. Henry I.

Baldwin Prideaux, Lord of Prideaux, died 1165. ⊤ ....
Had a grant in fee of the Manor of Prideaux
from Prior of Tywardreth.

Nicholas Prideaux, Lord of Prideaux, died 1169? ⊤ ....
Amerced in half a mark 1189, and again
amerced 1195.

Richard Prideaux, Lord of ⊤ ....
Prideaux, son and heir.

Richard Prideaux, Lord of Prideaux, ⊤ ....
died 1250. Witness to a charter
dated between 1230 and 1240.

.... ⊤ ....

Baldwin Prideaux, Lord of ⊤ ....   Reginald. ⊤ ....
Prideaux, son and heir.

Sir Thomas Prideaux, Knt., ⊤ *Jane, dau. of*
Lord of Prideaux, son and   *Philip Brodrygan.*
heir.

Robert Prideaux, Lord of ⊤ ....   *Godfrey.*   Geoffry Pridias, son and heir ⊤ ....   Reginald,   Alice, wife of Sir
Prideaux, granted to the   aged 23 years on his father's   rector of   Richard Reskymer.
Monastery of Tywardreth   death; did fealty for Borough   Brodoke   (Ped. Finium, 10th
certain lands in Frank   of Truro 1311; living 1330,   died 1343.   Edward I., Easter.)
Almoigne.   dead before 1347.

Geoffry ⊤ ....   Thomas Pridias granted profits of ⊤ Margaret, dau. of   Robert Pridias, son of ⊤ Margery.   Reginald,
Prideaux,   Truro Market 1347. Presented   Thomas Pedicrue,   Geoffry, granted Manor   Rector of
Lord of   Reginald Prideaux to St. Mary's   remar. John Man-   to Newnham 1369, manu-   St. Mary's
Prideaux.   Truro 1333. Will prov. at Win-   croun.   cap. for Burgesses of   Truro,
   chester 28th August 1347.   Bodmin 1327.   1333.

OF PRIDEAUX, co. CORNWALL, AND OF DEVON.—TABLE I.

I hereby certify that the following Pedigree of Prideaux, Lords of Prideaux, agrees with the Record in this Office. 2. C. I. 344.

Heralds' College,
9th March, 1874.

STEPHEN TUCKER,
Rouge Croix.

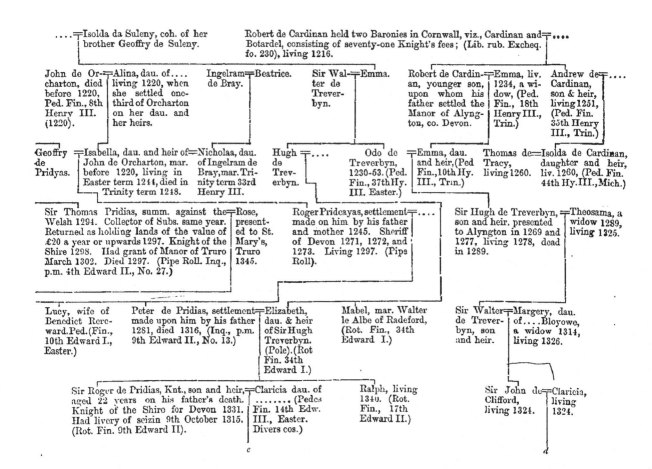

c   d

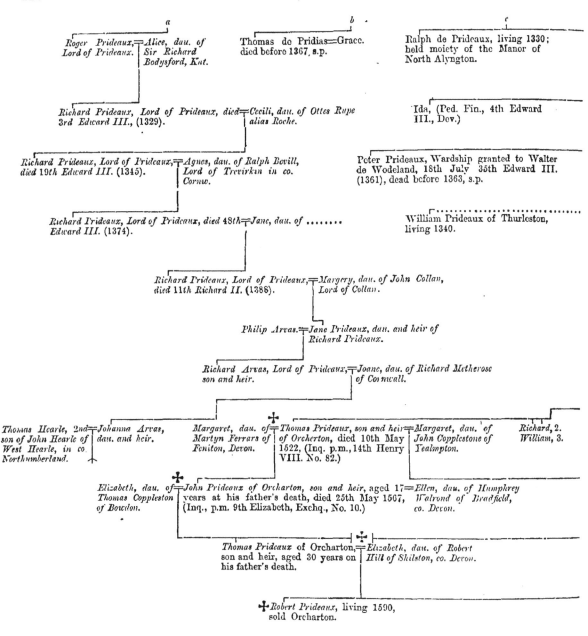

The descents marked thus ✠ are not upon Record in the College of Arms, but they appear upon the Heralds' Visitation, preserved in the Harleian MS., No. 1080, fo. 423.

_c_   _d_

Sir Roger de Prideaux, Knt., son and heir. ═ Elizabeth, dau. and heir of John   Sibella,
John de Clifford settled upon him the Manor   de Clifford and Claricia his wife,   mar.
of Combe in Tynhyde, &c. 1332. Sheriff of   cousin and heir of Odo de Tre-   John
Devon 1340. (Rot. Fin.)   verbyn, mar. before 1324.   Dauney.

Sir Roger Prideaux, son and heir; died ═ Joane, dau. of Sir   John Prideaux had grant from his uncle in 1330, of a moiety
before 1357, leaving his son a minor.   William Bigbury.   of the Manor of North Alyngton. (See TABLE II.)

Sir John Prideaux, Knt., a minor in 1363, Wardship granted to John ═ Elizabeth.   Edith. ═ Sir Thomas Scrobbahull.
Montague. Knight for the Shire of Devon 1383 and 1387; Will dated
5th June and prov. 7th August 1403, (Exon. Bp. Stafford's Reg.)

Sir Richard Prideaux, of Orcharton, Knt., ═ Jane, dau. of .... Lercedekne, mar. in South   Thomasia, named in
died 28th March 1408. (Inq., p.m. 9th   Milton Church, Devon. (Oliver, 298. Lacy's Reg.   her father's will.
Henry IV., No. 2.)   Vol. iii.,fo. 77.)

John Prideaux of Orcharton, son and heir, aged seventeen ═ Elizabeth, presented to   Martin Prideaux. (Pedes
years on his father's death. Presented to North Alyngton   North Alyngton 1453.   Fin., 8th Henry VI.,
1443. Dead before 1453.   Easter.)

John Prideaux of Orcharton, (Pole). ═ ....

✠

.... _dau. of Sir Thomas_ ═ _John Prideaux of Orcharton._ Suffered a ═ _Joan, dau. of John Fortescue of Wymstone, co._
Wortley, co. York, 1st wife.   recovery in 1497, to John Fortescue of   _Devon, relict of Thomas Cotterell of Washbourne,_
            Wymston, (De Banco Rolls, 12th Henry   _who after the death of her 2nd husband married_
            VII., Easter, m. 100d.) Died recently,   _Richard Troblefeld of Oure, Dorset._
            before 1522.

John ═ _Agnes, dau. of William_   _Joan, wife of Thomas_   _Elizabeth, or Isabell, wife_
Prideaux.   _Honychurch of Daystock._   _Paxwell, co. Dorset._   _of William Cosby, of_
                     Dartmouth.

Elizabeth, mar.   _Elizabeth, the younger, mar._   _Alice, mar. Christopher_
Robert Stretchley.   _John Steepe._   _Pytts._

Philip 2nd.   _Agnes 1st._

Philip 2nd.   _Elizabeth._

The descents marked thus ✠ are not upon record in the College of Arms, but they appear upon the Heralds' Visitation
reserved in the Harleian MSS. No. 1080, fo. 423.

2 E

PEDIGREE OF PRIDEAUX

John Prideaux, 2nd son of Roger Prideaux of Orcharton, by Elizabeth, dau. of Sir John Clifford, Knt., dead before 1358. — Joan, *dau. and coh. of Gilbert Adexton*, mar. 2ndly. John Mules. Died leaving a son, Giles Prideaux, her heir. Deed dated 47th Edward III. (1373.) (Prideaux MSS.)

Nicholas Bromford of Horilake, grandson and heir of Robert de Horykke, died on Friday in the feast of St. Luke the Evang. 1401., (Inq., p.m., 4th Henry V., No. 45.) — ....

John Bromford of Horilake, Devon, aged 30 years on his father's death, died 17th November 1429. John Prideaux, son of Isabella, sister of the said John Bromford, his nearest heir. (Inq. p.m, 8th Henry VI., No. 20.)

John Prideaux, aged 15 years on the death of his uncle, John Bromford. Died 27th February 1431-2, (Inq., p.m. 9th Henry VI., No. 40.) s.p.

Joan, sister and heir of John Prideaux, aged 23 years on her brother's death, *mar. Robert Stretchley of Stretchley*, before 1431.

John Prideaux, in remainder for certain lands.

Edith, *dau. of William Hatch of Aller, co. Devon.* — *Humphry Prideaux of Theuborough*, aged 44 years on his father's death, died 8th of May 1550, (Inq. p.m. 4th Edward VI., Part I, No. 52.) Will dated 4th July 1549, prov. 10th January 1550-1. (15 Code). — Joane, *dau. of Richard Fowell of Fowellscomb*, and relict of Philip Courtenay of Longtor, Devon, died 31st October 1523, (Inq. p.m. 16th Henry VIII., No. 144,) 1st wife.

Nicholas, died 1560, s.p., purchased Soldon 1549, (Rot. Pat.,3rd Edward VI., Part 5.,) and Padstow. **(a) (b)**

Thomas, living in 1574, was married and had a daughter. See his letter, S. P. Dom. Corr., Vol. lixviiii., 17.

Elizabeth, *wife of Robert Drake of Wiscombe.*

Joane, *dau. of Thomas Gilbert*, 1st *wife died s.p.* — *Richard Prideaux of Theuborough*, aged 50 years on his father's death. Died 11th December 1603, (Inq. p.m. 4th James, Part 1, No. 170.) **(a) (b).** — *Katherine, dau. of Sir John Arundel of Trevise, Knt., and Mary, dau. and heir of John Bevill of Gwarnick, heir of her Nephew John Bevill of Gwarnick.*

Arms as allowed at the Visitation, 1620.

1. PRIDEAUX.
2. OLD COAT OF PRIDEAUX.
3. GIFFORD.
4. ESSE.
5. SPENCER.
6. HUGWORTHY.

N.B.—Those marked thus **(a)** are named in the will of Richard Prideaux of Tormerton; and those marked thus **(b)** in that of Humphry Prideaux of Theuborough; and those marked thus **(c)** in that of Richard Prideaux 1614.

OF ADESTON AND THEUBOROUGH.—TABLE II.

John Gifford.=*Ingrett, dau. and coh. of Alan Esse of Theuborough, co. Devon, Knt.*

Giles Prideaux, son and heir, of Adeston, Burgess in Parl. for Dartmouth 1368 ; had license to proceed to Aquitaine 1404. =*........ dau. and coh. of .... Gunstone of Shilston.*

John Gifford.=*Alice, dau. and heir of John Hugworthye.*

Isabella, *sister and heir of* John *Bromford, 1st wife,* died before 1429. =*Sir John Prideaux of Adeston,* Knt., returned by the Sheriff to take the oaths 1433. =*Maude, dau.* and heir of *Robert French of Sharpham,* Devon, 2nd wife. =Anne, *dau. of John Shapton, 3rd wife.*

Stephen Gifford.=*Joan, dau. of John Spencer of Tedborne, co. Devon.*

Jane, mar. 1st William Drew, 2ndly. Baldwin Acland of Acland, co. Devon.

Elizabeth, mar. Wm. *Somaster.*

Julian, wife of Adam Somaster, (Camden).

Rose, *dau. of Hugh Michelstow,* 1st wife, died, s.p. =*William Prideaux of Adeston* and of Langford. Escheator for Cornw. 1461. =Ethelred, *dau. of John Fortescue of Buckland Filleigh, 2nd wife, died s.p.*

=*Alice, dau. and heir of Stephen,* Gifford of Theuborough 3rd wife, mar. 2ndly. William Wollacombe. Died 24th February 1511-12, (Inq. p.m. 3rd Henry VIII., No. 8.)

Katherine, dau. of Sir Humphry Poyntz, Knt., of Langley, co. Devon. =*Fulke Prideaux, son and heir, of Adeston and Theuborough,* aged forty years on his mother's death. Died 15th January 1520-1, (Inq , p.m. 22nd Henry VIII., No. 12.) =*Jane, dau. and heir of Sir Richard Edgcumbe, Kt., 1st wife, died s.p.*

Jane, mar. William Wyke of North Wyke.

=Thomas Wyke. **(a)**

Robert, rector of Esseraff, (now called Roseash) and Newton St. Petrock. **(a)**.

Richard of Tormerton, co. Glouc., died 1541, s.p., will dated 7th January 1540, proved 12th May 1541, (28 Alenger) **(b)**.

Five other sons all of whom died s.p.

Margaret, mar. 1st *John Williams of Treworgy ;* 2ndly. *Leonard Tremayne.* **(a)**

Alice, mar. Thomas ...... co. Cornw. **(a)**.

Elizabeth, married Robert Yeo of Sheabeer. **(a)**.

Joane, mar. 1st *Thomas Hussey of Shipwick, co. Dorset,* and 2ndly. *Charles Vaughan of the* same place.

Catherine, wife of Robert Trowbridge.

Margery, wife of Robert Gibbs of Horington, co. Warwick.

Mary, wife of Henry Tremayne of Bodrugan.

Roger Prideaux of Soldon, TABLE III.

William Prideaux of Trevose, 2nd son of Humphry Prideaux of Theuborough, (Vide TABLE II.) of Trevose in St. Merryn, co. Cornw., died 27th June 1564, (Inq. p.m., 7th Elizabeth, No 113.) =Johanna, dau. of John Munday of Rialton, mar. 1537, died 28th June 1564.

b

N.B.—Those marked thus **(a)** are named in the will of Richard Prideaux of Tormerton ; and those marked thus **(b)** in that of Humphry Prideaux of Theuborough ; and those marked thus **(c)** in that of Richard Prideaux 1614.

a

Grace, dau. and heir of Nicholas Carminow of Resprin, co. Cornw. ══ Richard Prideaux, son and heir, of Theuborough, aged 57 years on his father's death, will dated 17th July 1614, prov. 19th February 1618-9, (17 Parker). ══ Zenobia, dau. and coh. of James Nansperian of Gurlyn, in St. Earth, (Harl, MS. 1079, fo. 213.)

Humphry Prideaux of Westwood in Crediton, Counc. at law, will dated 7th January 1603-4, prov. 3rd February same year (16 Harte). ══ Johanna, dau. of John Bevill of Kelligarth, in parish of Talland, Cornw. Will dated 14th November 1612, prov. 9th January 1612-3, (2 Capel.)

John, ob. s.p.

Jonathan Prideaux of Theuborough, son and heir, living 1620, Exor. to his father's will. M.P. Bosinny, 1625. Will dated 27th June and prov. 31st October 1637. ══ Winnifred, dau. and coh. of Tristram Gorges of Budeaux head, mar. lic. dated 7th Sept. 1597, (Exon.)

Charles.

Francis.

Hugh (c) married Honour, dau. of Alex. Rolle of Stevenston, co. Devon.

Benjamin.

Elizabeth, mar. Edw. Chapman of Resprin, (c).

Philippa, married Hichens Wadham, (c).

Prudence, mar. Peter Spry of Newran, in Maugan, (c).

Jane, mar. Thomas Cauderowe (c).

Susan, unmar. 1614, (c).

Frances, married William Dennis of .... (c).

William Prideaux of Gurlyn. ══ Johanna, dau. of John Roscarrock, mar. at St. Martins in the Fields, London, 13th Dec. 1624, (see History of Trigg, Vol. i., p. 563).

Wilmot. Will prov. Exon, 1634, unmar. (c).

Helena, unmar. 1614. (c).

Anne, (d).

Zenobia, wife of Richard Bowdon. (d).

Grace, (d).

Margaret, (d).

Sir Richard Prideaux, executor to his father's will. Matric at Baliol Coll., Oxf. 13th Dec. 1622, aged 16; M.P. Bodmin 1639, died 1667, will dated 16th May 1660, prov. 22nd Sept. 1668, (Exon.) ══ Mary, dau. and coh. of Richard Barrett of Trecarne, (Tregarden) in St. Mabyn, Mar.[3] 31st Dec. 1634.

John Prideaux, died 15th Feb. 1649, aged 21 years. ══ Honour, dau. of James Praed of Trevetho.

Catherine.

Richard Prideaux, son and heir, bap.[3] 20th August 1641, Matric. at Christ Church, Oxford, 31st July 1658, died 1670, will dated 22nd March 1669, prov. 10th May 1670, s.p.

Charles, bur.[3] 14th May 1644.

Jonathan Prideaux, exr. to brother Richard's will. M.P. Callington 1689, bur.[5] 7th April 1710, aged 64, M. I. ══ Anne, dau. of Sir Francis Clarke of London.

Mary, bap.[3] 31st January 1635, bur.[4] 14th July 1715, unmar. (e).

Richard Prideaux, Counc. at Law. Matric at Baliol Coll. Oxford, 19th March 1686-7, aged 17, bur.[5] 18th October 1702, died unmar.

Frances, born and bap.[5] 22nd January 1670, bur.[5] 29th January 1672.

Thomasine, born 14th April, bap.[5] 4th May 1671.

N.B.—Those marked thus (a) are named in the will of Richard Prideaux of Tormerton; and those marked thus (b) in that of Humphry Prideaux of Theuborough; and those marked thus (c) in that of Richard Prideaux 1614; those marked thus (d) in that of Jonathan Prideaux of Sutcombe, dated 1637; those marked (e) in that of Sir Richard Prideaux, dated 1660; those marked (f) named in the will of Humphry Prideaux of Westwood, 1603, and those marked thus (g) in that of Johanna, wife of the said Humphry; those marked thus (h) in the will of George Prideaux of Sutcombe, dated 1649; and those marked (i) in that of Richard Prideaux of Newcastle.

---

[1] At Padstow.   [2] At St. Issey.   [3] At St. Mabyn.   [4] At Holsworthy.   [5] At Sutcombe.

a   *b*

| Robert, Rector of Newton Saint Petrock. | George Prideaux of Sutcombe, will dated 1st May 1649, prov. 2nd April 1651, (71 Grey). | =Jane, married Jasper Stowell, bap. 1560 at Buckland Monachorum. | Charity, mar. Nicholas Turberville of Crediton. | John Prideaux, born 1547, had lease from Oliver Polwhele, in 1583, of premises in Padstow for the lives of himself, Anne his wife, and John his son. Living 1606. | =Anne, dau. of, ... dead in 1603. | .... daughters. |

| Beville Prideaux, executor to his mother's will. (f) (g). | =Elizabeth, dau. of ...... | William Prideaux, named in the will of John Bevill of Poltreworgy, his uncle, dated 10th May, prov. 8th Sept. 1609, (Archd. Court of Cornw) (f) (g). | =Thomasine, dau. of ...... Chapell, mar. lic. 20th August 1614. | Jane, married Thomas Holcombe of Crediton (f). | Charity, wife of John Lynam of St. Kew, see LYNAM Pedigree post. (f). Mary, (f). | Richard Prideaux, Matric. Exeter College, Oxf., 2nd Dec. 1631, aged 18, Fell. of same Coll. 1635-43. Of Newcastle upon Tyne. Will dated 17th May 1661, prov. 1663 (Durham). (h). | =.... | Honour, (h). Frances, (h). Jane, mar. ...... Knill, (h). | ...... mar. .... Jeffries, (h). mar. Emanuel Phayer, (h). mar. .... Townsend, (h). | John Prideaux, born before 1583, bur.[1] 15th May 1633. | =.. |

| Humphry Prideaux. | Bridget, wife of Sir John Skelton, Governor of Plymouth, who died 24th December 1673. Bur. at St. Andrews' Plymouth, M.I. | Frances. | Richard Prideaux of Newcastle, Merch., will dated 27th February 1677, gave his lands in Devon to his brother John. (i). | John Prideaux, matric. St. Edmund's Hall, Oxford, 17th May 1667, aged 16. Vicar of Long Howton, Northumb. (i). | George, (i). Peter, (i). Rebecca, (i). Sarah, (i). Hannah, (i). Mary, (i). Anne, (i). | Elizabeth, bap. at St. Merryn 10th Sep. 1617, bur. there the same month. | Richard, bap.[1] 5th Nov. 1615. |

| Anne, bap.[3] 5th April 1637, died in infancy. | Anne, bap.[3] 6th May 1638, died in infancy. | Elizabeth, (e). | Winifred, mar. Edward Butler of Exeter, died 27th July 1673, Monmt. in St. Martin's Church, Exon, (e). | Joane Prideaux, wife of Francis Gregor of Trewarthenick. | Honour Prideaux, wife of Arscot Bickford of Dunsland, co. Devon, who after her death mar. Bridget, dau. of Edmund Prideaux of Padstow. |

Frances, mar. Charles Davie of Bideford; she died 15th January 1764, s.p.; he died 11th July 1742 bur.[5] M.I.

Mary, mar.[5] Degory Slade, rector of Holsworthy, 25th February 1702-3; he died 22nd October 1712, bur.[4]

I hereby certify that those portions of the above Pedigree which are printed in *Italics*, agree with the Records of the Heralds' Cottage, London.

STEPHEN TUCKER,
Rouge Croix.

N.B.—Those marked thus (a) are named in the will of Richard Prideaux of Tormerton; and those marked thus (b) in that of Humphry Prideaux of Theuborough; and those marked thus (c) in that of Richard Prideaux 1614; those marked thus (d) in that of Jonathan Prideaux of Sutcombe, dated 1637; those marked (e) in that of Sir Richard Prideaux, dated 1660; those marked (f) named in the will of Humphry Prideaux of Westwood, 1603; and those marked thus (g) in that of Johanna, wife of the said Humphry; those marked thus (h) in the will of George Prideaux of Sutcombe, dated 1649; and those marked (i) in that of Richard Prideaux of Newcastle.

[1] At Padstow.   [2] At St. Issey.   [3] At St. Mabyn.   [4] At Holsworthy.   [5] At Sutcombe.

PEDIGREE OF PRIDEAUX OF SOLDON

PRIDEAUX PLACE, co.

Roger Prideaux of Soldon, Eschæ. for Devon and Cornwall,=*Phillippa, dau. of Richard* [Roger] *Yorke*, 1550, Sheriff of Devon 1577, died 18th January 1581-2, will *Serjeant at Law*, bur. at Holsworthy 15th dated 13th May 1579, cod. 2nd January 1581, prov. P.C.C. November 1597, will dated 3rd of March 19th February 1581-2, (7 Tyrwhit,) Inq. p.m., 24th Eliza- 1589, prov. 25th January 1597-8, P.C.C. beth, Part II., No. 37. (2 Lewys).

Thomasine, dau. and=*Sir Nicholas Prideaux of Soldon, co. Devon,*=*Cheston, 2nd dau. and coh. of William Viell of St. Breoke, heir of John Henscot* | *Knt., son and heir*, aged 32 on his father's | *Cornw.* 2nd wife, mar. at St. Breoke 24th September *of Henscot in Brad-* | death, Knighted 22nd Nov. 1606, M.P. | 1576, bur.[4] 5th September 1610. *ford, co. Devon*, died | Camelford 1570, Sheriff of Cornw. 3rd | = *Mary, dau. of John Castell of Ashbury, co. Devon*, 3rd 16th August 1575, | James (1605), died at West Putford, Devon, | wife, mar. license dated 26th September 1611, relict of Dr. bur.[1] M.I. | 25th Jany. 1627-28, will dated 1st Jany. | Evan Morice, died 2nd October 1647, bur. at West Put- 1624, prov. P.C.C 1628, (46 Barrington) | ford, will dated 28th September 1640, prov. 10th Feby. Inq. p.m. 5th Charles I., Part I., No. 64. | 1647-8. P.CC (24 Essex).

Humphry Prideaux, son and heir, of Soldon, born cir. 1573, matric. at=*Honour, dau. of Edmund Fortescue* of Fallopit, Devon, mar.[2] Broadgate Hall, Oxford, 21st November 1589, aged 16, died v.p. 31st | 30th March 1600, rem. Sir Shilston Calmady, mar. license March 1617, will dated 14th July 1615, prov. 7th July 1617, P.C.C. | dated 14th September 1618, she died 17th December 1663, (74 Weldon), Inq. p.m. 15th James, Part II., No. 188. | bur. in Bridestow Church, Devon, M.I.

Nicholas Prideaux, son and heir, of=*Ann, dau. of William* | *John Prid-* | *Edmund Prideaux* of Pad-=Bridgett, dau. of John Soldon, aged 14 years 7 months and | Coryton of Newton | *eaux*, bap.[2] | stow, born 15th Sept. | Moyle of Bake, mar. at St. 17 days on his father's death, bap.[2] | Ferrers, Cornw. mar. | 9th Sept. | 1606, bap.[2] same month, | Germans 24th March 1638, ..August 1620, died 21st February | cir. 1621, admd. to | 1605, died | M.P. for Saltash 1658-9, | bur.[4] 9th October 1690, will 1642-3, will dated 10th Feby. 1642-3, | Nicholas Prideaux | in Holland, | Sheriff of Cornwall, 1664. | dated 1st April 1690, prov. prov. 31st Jany. 1643-4, Exon., Inq. | of Holsworthy, Esq., | s.p. | Died 15th October 1683, | 3rd February 1699-1700, p.m., 19th Charles, Part I., No. 4. | 21st February 1648. | | bur.[4] M.I. | P.C.C., (28 Noel).

Nicholas Prid-=Margaret. dau. | Roger, | Humphry =dau. of | Eliza- | John =Anne, | Edmund =Anna, eaux, son and | of ...... Lane | ob. s.p. | Prideaux, | .... | beth, | Prideaux | dau. of | Prideaux of | dau. of heir, aged 19 | and relict of.... | | born 1636, | Hobbes? | wife of | of Prid- | Roger | London, a | ...... years 4 months | Hunt, will dated | | died 15th | | George | eaux | Mallock | Smyrna | Hopkins. and 2 days at | 9th Mar. 1697-8, | | Mar. 1692, | | Luttrell | Place. | of Cock- | Merchant, | Will dat. his fath's. death. | admº with will | | æt. 56, bur.[1] | | of Dun- | Matric. | ington, | born 1644, | 7th Dec. Will nuncupat. | annex. granted | | 18th Mar. | | ster | at Exeter | Devon, | died 2nd | 1723, dated 4th Feb., | to Jane Gibbs | | 1692-3, will | | Castle, | Col. Oxf. | mar. | Oct 1706, | prov. admº to Marga- | during minority | | dated 5th | | co. | 12thJuly | settlt. | will dated | 19th ret his relict | of John Gibbs, | | Mar.1692-3 | | Somer- | 1661, æt. | 7th Dec. | 20th June | January 27th February | 18th October | | proved at | | set. | 18, bur.[4] | 1669, | 1699, prov. | 1724 1653, s.p., (28 | 1698. Exon. | | Exon. | | | 2nd Dec. | æt. | 11th Oct. | P.C.C., Alchin). | Will proved 7th | | | | | 1704. | bur.[4] 4th | 1706 P.C.C. | (17 Rom- | August 1704. | | | | | | August | (218 Ec- | ney.) | | | | | | | 1688. | cles.) |

a   *b*   *c*

[1] At Sutcombe.   [2] At East Allington.   [3] At Bradworthy.
[4] At Padstow.   [5] At St. George's, Hanover Square.   [6] At St. Breoke.

IN co. DEVON AND OF PRIDEAUX OF CORNWALL.—TABLE III.

I hereby Certify that those portions of the following Pedigree which are printed in *Italics*, agree with the Records of the Heralds' College, London.

Heralds' College,　　　　　　　　STEPHEN TUCKER,

Rouge Croix.

ARMS OF PRIDEAUX-BRUNE.

1. BRUNE.　　　2. & 3. PRIDEAUX.

4. De la ROKELE.

Edmund Prideaux of Netherton, see TABLE IV.	Elizabeth, wife of Sir John Periam of Exeter.	Wilmot, mar. at Kilkhampton 8th January 1584, Anthony Mapowder. Proved her mother's will.

John Prideaux of Breoke, 2nd son. Bap.[6] 1583, Sheriff of Cornwall 1631, died 1649, adm° to his nephew Edmund Prideaux 13th December 1649, P.C.C., s.p.	*Anne, dau. of Robert Moyle of Bake, Cornw.* bur. at St. Breoke, 28th March 1639.

Humphry Prideaux of Hankford, bap.[2] 21st Aug. 1611, died 9th April 1664 and bur.[1] M.I. Will dated 14th October 1663, prov. 7th May 1664, Exon.	*Elizabeth, dau. of Henry Waldron of Bradfield, Devon, relict of Edmund Specott of Anderton,* 1st wife, died 14th and bur. at Launcells, March 1645, M.I.	Frances, dau. of Ralph Berrie of Eastleigh, Devon, died 23rd July 1671, bur. St. Merryn, M.I.	*Tomasine,* bap.[2] 23rd October 1603, wife of John Fortescue of Buckland Filleigh.	*Elizabeth,* wife of Sir William Morice, Sec. of State to King Charles II

Humphry Prideaux, born at Padstow 3rd May 1648, D.D., Dean of Norwich, died there 1st Nov. 1724 and bur. in the Cathedral.	Bridget, dau. and sole heir of Anthony Bokenham of Helmingham, Suffolk, mar. 16th February 1685-6, died at Norwich November 1700.	Walter, born 12th, bap.[1] 24th Nov. 1654, died in infancy.	Nicholas, born at Simpson, co. Devon, 3rd July 1657, Matric. at Christ Ch. Oxf., 29th Mar. 1672, æt. 15, Student of Corp. Christi Coll., died 17th June 1675, æt. 18, and was there buried M.I.	Roger died in infancy.	Admonition, bap. at St. Germans 25th August 1639, mar.[4] 23rd May 1667, William Pendarves of Pendarves who died 22nd Dec. 1683,s p. Mar. 2ndly, Edm. Pollexfen of Kitley, Dev.	Anne, mar.[4] Richard Coffin of Portledge, 2nd May 1673, died 19th Aug. 1705, Monu- ment in Alwington Church, Devon.	Honour, born cir. 1649, mar. 1699, ... Bardew of London and died s.p. 1700. Bridget, mar.[4] 8th July 1683, Arscott Bickford of Dunsford, co. Devon.	A dau. mar. John Hawkey of Fowey, Cornw.	Penelope, mar. Rev. William Edbrooke of Sidmouth co. Devon

b

---

[1] At Sutcombe.	[2] At East Allington.	[3] At Bradworthy.
[4] At Padstow.	[5] At St. George's Hanover Square.	[6] At St. Breoke.

a   *b*

Humphry Prideaux bap.[3] 14th January 1664-5, died in infancy.	Ann Prideaux, bap.[3] 10th Feb. 1663-4, mar. her cous. John Prideaux, third son of Sir Peter Prideaux, 3rd Bart., of Netherton.	Edmund Prideaux bap.[4] 19th Jan. 1672 Sheriff of Cornw. 1699, bur.[4] 27 Dec. 1728, will dat. 19th Oct. 1728 prov. 1729, s.p., (Exon). ═ Susanna, dau. of John Pate, and coh. of her bro. Robert Pate of Cowick, Devon. Mar. St. Thomas, Exon, 25th July 1695.	Roger Prideaux, bap.[4] 13th December 1674, died in infancy.	John Prideaux bap.[4] 17th March 1677, Capt. in the Army, bur.[4] 29th June 1728, unmar., will dated 26th June 1728, prov. 12th Nov. 1728, (Exon) Referred to in adm° granted in Aug. 1737, (Exon.)	Admonition, bap.[4] 15th Oct. 1671, mar. at Charles' Church, Plymouth, 29th July 1697, John Elford of Longstone, Devon. Bur. at Sheepstor, Devon 16th October 1717, adm° 28th February 1728-9 to her husband

Mary, eld. dau. and coh. of Sir George Chudleigh of Haldon, Devon, Bart., mar. 11th Feby. 1747-8, mar. settlt. 6th Feby. 1748, 1st wife ═ **Humphry Prideaux**, born 1719, Sheriff of Cornw 1750, died at Bath 24th April 1793, bur.[4] 6th May 1793, aged 74, will dated 15th November 1792, prov. 10th May 1793, P.C.C. ═ Jenny, 2nd dau. of Nevill Morton Pleydell of Shitterton, Dorset, mar. settlt. 12th July, 1759, died at Bath 14th August 1819, aged 84, bur at Walcot Church, M.I. Will dated 24th June 1811, prov. 17th September 1819, P.C.C.

George Prideaux of Haldon, born there 10th April 1750, died unmar. bur.[4] 9th September 1784, aged 34, will dated 3rd November 1781	Charles Prideaux, born 15th and bap. at St. James', Bath, 25th June 1760, of Clare Hall, Cambridge, Clerk in Holy Orders. By Royal License dat. 11th July 1799, assumed the surname of Brune in addition to that of Prideaux, died at Bath 28th April and bur.[4] 11th May 1833, will dated 18th September 1821, prov. 13th June 1833, P.C.C.	═ Francis, 4th dau. of Thomas Patten of Bank Hall, co. Lancaster. Mar. at Warrington in that co., 1st August 1784, died at Cheltenham 23rd March and bur.[4] 14th April 1831	Humphry Prideaux born 4th, bap. 12th January 1762, Lieut. R.N., died 1st and bur.[4] 8th December 1809, aged 47, will dated 24th June 1807, s.p. ═ Elizabeth dau. of Sir John St. Aubyn, Bart, and coh. of her brother Sir John St. Aubyn. Died 21st June and bur.[4] 4th July 1804, aged 47.	Edmund Prideaux of Hexworthy, born 5th and bap.[4] 6th October 1766, Barrister at Law, died 20th October 1819, will dated 8th September 1819 prov. 2nd May 1820, P.C.C. ═ Hebe Elizabeth, dau. of Sir John St. Aubyn Bart., mar. at St. Martins in the Fields, Lond. 9th Novmbr. 1797, died January 1844.

Charles Prideaux-Brune, born 7th December 1798 and bap. at Walcot, Bath, 27th May 1799, Sheriff of Cornw. 1834. Living 1874. ═ Frances Mary, 2nd dau. and coh. of Edmund John Glynn of Glynn, Cornw. mar.[4] 28th Feb. 1820, died in London 22nd July 1868 and bur. at Kensall Green.	Dorothea Prideaux Prideaux-Brune, born 12th December 1790 and bap. at Queen's Square Chapel, Walcot, Bath, 14th March 1791, mar.[4] 7th December 1815, Joseph Sawle Sawle, afterwards Sir Joseph Sawle Graves-Sawle, Bart., died 23rd October 1853, bur. at St. Austell. M.I. He died 13th January 1865.	Frances Prideaux Brune, born 5th August and bap. at Clifton 11th September 1794, mar. at Walcot Church, Bath, 10th May 1823, Charles Du Cane, Commander Royal Navy, of Braxted Park, Essex. Died in London, 2nd July 1871, and bur. at Braxted. He died at Bath 17th November 1850.	Anna Maria Prideaux-Brune, born at Bath, 13th December 1795, bap.[4] 18th October 1796, died at Cheltenham 9th and bur.[4] 25th February 1831, Adm° 6th December 1833, P.C.C.

Charles Glynn Prideaux-Brune, born in London, 2nd April and bap.[4] 11th October 1821, a J.P. and D.L. for Cornw. Living 1874. ═ Hon. Ellen Jane, 2nd daughter of Robert Shapland 1st Baron Carew, mar.[5] 21st July 1846	Ernest Augustus, born 17th June and bap.[5] 16th July 1839, Lieut. 29th Regiment, died in London 22nd January 1868, and bur. at Kensall Green, will dated 4th August 1865. ═ Frances Josling, 2nd dau. of George Sayle Prior, Clerk, Rector of St. Breoke, Cornw., mar. there 21st Sept. 1864.	

Charles Robert Prideaux-Brune, born at Bodmin 10th October 1848, bap.[4] Lieut. Rifle Brigade.	Edward Shapland, born 14th June 1853, bap.[4] Comm of Christ Church, Oxford.	Francis Ernest, born 5th February 1863, bap.[4]	Ellen Frances, born 24th July 1851, bap.[4]	Gertrude Rose, born 29th Oct. 1855, bap.[4]

---

[1] At Sutcombe.   [2] At East Allington.   [3] At Bradworthy.

[4] At Padstow.   [5] At St. George's, Hanover Square.   [6] At St. Breoke.

_b_   _c_   _d_

Bridget bur.[4] 23rd April 1696

Anne, bap[4] 2nd August 1680, both died in infancy.

Rose, bap.[4] 25th June 1683, mar.[4] 15th Sept, 1709, William Glynn, of Glynn, Cornw. bur. at Cardinham 19th March 1736.

Ann, bur. in Julius Cæsar's Vault in St. Helen's Church 1702. Bond given to the Parish. (Malcolm's, Lond. Redevivum, Vol. iii, p. 553.) Nam. in her father's will.

Thomas, named in grandmother's will, died young, v.p.

And several other children who died young v.p.

Edmund Prideaux, bap. at Saham Tony, Matric. at Claro Hall, Camb. 22nd February 1693, bur.[4] 23rd June 1745, will dat. 4th January 1743, last codl. 12th June 1745, adm° with will annexed granted Charles his son 22nd November 1745, P.C.C., (307 Seymer). = Hannah, dau, of Sir Benjamin Wrench, Knt., of the City of Norwich, mar., settl. dated 17th April 1717.

Charles, died s.p. 17th September, bur.[4] 24th September 1783, æt. 63, unmar.

Edmund, died at Truro, 11th November, 1737, s.p.

Benjamin, of the Inner Temple, died 22nd July 1795, s.p.

Rebecca, mar. 4th December 1749, Sir Horatio Pettus of Rackheath, co. Suffolk, Bart. Died 17th November 1780, aged 50, s.p., bur. at Rackheath.

Nevill Richard Prideaux, bap.[4] 30th November 1769, died at Bath 17th and bur. Bathwick, Somst. 23rd Sept. 1808, adm° 5th October 1808

William Brune Prideaux, bap.[4] 6th August 1773, died 7th and bur.[4] 13th December 1802, will dated 20th December 1801 = Frances, dau. of General Ogle of Cawsey Park, co. Northumberland, relict of Capt. Courtenay, R.N., Mar.[5] 1800, died 11th March 1849

Thomas Prideaux, bap.[4] 29th January 1778, died at Totnes 16th Dec. 1859 and bur. there = Jenny Phillips mar. at St. Breoke Cornw. 25th April 1809, died at Totnes 2nd June 1865

Nicholas Prideaux, bap.[4] 11th August 1771, bur.[4] 4th May 1772.

Jane Prideaux, bap.[4] 28th March, bur.[4] 11th October 1763.

Mary Prideaux bap.[4] 16th Nov. 1764, mar. Thomas Ball of Seaford co. Waterford, 1st August 1795, mar. settl. dated 5th July 1795.

Mary Jenny Prideaux-Brune, born 27th March and bap.[4] 22nd July 1808, died in London 10th and bur.[4] 16th May 1872, will dated 17th September 1868, prov. 5th June 1872, P.C.C.

Caroline Prideaux-Brune, born 19th April and bap.[4] 11th August 1808, mar.[4] 14th August 1838, Capt. afterwards Rear Admiral The Hon. George John Cavendish 3rd son of 2nd Baron Waterpark. He died 23rd October 1865. Living 1874.

Elizabeth Jenny, dau. and coh. born 8th March 1799, bap. Lawhitton, Cornw., mar. at Aveley, Essex, 7th November 1820, George 3rd son of Sir Thomas Barrett Lennard of Belhus, Essex,

Hebe Dorothy, dau. and coh. born 20th April 1800, mar. 25th April 1821, at Aveley, Essex. Henry Barrett Leonard, Clerk, 4th son of Sir Thomas Barrett Lennard of Belhus, Essex, Bart.

Jenny Pleydell Prideaux, died 15th December 1801, aged 1 year and 6 months.

Caroline Frances, bap.[6] 8th April 1810, mar. June 1826, Capt. Frederick T. Michell afterwards Adml Sir Frederick Michell, K.C.B. She died 14th November 1856.

Frances Mary, born 11th August 1824 and bap. at St. Mary le Bone, mar[5] Hon. George Augustus Browne 3rd son of 2nd Baron Kilmaine, a Major in the Army, 28th October 1853.

Caroline Dorothea, born 23rd October 1827, mar.[5] 9th December 1858, Capt. afterwards Rear Adml. Sir William George Legge Hoste, Bart., by whom, who died 10th September 1868, she has issue; mar. 2ndly at Hawstead, Suffolk, 8th November 1871, Edward Greene of Ixworth Abbey, Suffolk, M.P.

Beatrice Anne, born at Cheltenham 4th June 1831, mar.[5] 15th July, 1856, The Rev. Sir Hugh Henry Molesworth of Pencarrow, Bart., Rector of St. Petrock Minor, Cornw. He died 6th January 1862, bur. there, s p.

Mary Katherine, born 2nd October 1857, bap.[4]

Beatrice May, born 2nd May 1860, bap.[4]

Isolda Blanche, born 2nd Feby. 1865, bap.[4]

Mildred Maria, born 1st Nov. 1866, bap.[4]

George Ernest, born 5th Feby. 1867, bap.[6]

Frances Mary, born 7th July 1865, bap.[6]

---

[1] At Sutcombe.

[2] At East Allington.

[3] At Bradworthy.

[4] At Padstow.

[5] At St. George's, Hanover Square.

[6] At St. Breoke.

2 G

PEDIGREE OF PRIDEAUX OF

Bridget, dau. of John Chichester of Raleigh, 1st wife.	=I. *Edmund Prideaux of Netherton,* 2nd son of Roger Prideaux of Soldon. Barrister at Law, created a Baronet 17th July 1622, died 28th February 1628, (Inq. p.m., 5th Charles, Part III., No. 32,) bur.[1] 12th March 1628-9. *Jure Consult. Duplex Reader to Inner Temple.*	=Katherine, dau. of Piers Edgcombe of Mount Edgcombe, 2nd wife.	=Mary, dau. of Richard Reynell, of East Ogwell, and relict of Arthur Fowell of Fowellscombe, Devon. mar. at Ugborough 22nd July 1606, 3rd wife.

Timothy, named in his grand-mother's will, 1589.	*Tabitha* mar, *Thomas Ayl-worth of Ben-allack, Cornw.*-named in grandmother's will 1589.	*Sara, mar. John Fortescue of Fallowpit,* named in grandmoth's. will 1589	*Admonition,* mar.[1] *John Moyle of Bake,* 8th September 1612, mar. lic. dated 1st Sept. Died 29th November 1675 and bur. at St. Germans, M.I.	II. *Sir Peter Prideaux,* Bart., son and heir, aged 30 years on his father's death, M.P. for Honiton, 1661, Sheriff of Devon 1662, died at Netherton and Bur.[1] 3rd February 1681-2.	=Susan, dau. of Sir *Anthony Powlet of Hinton St. George, Somerset,* and sister of John, Lord Poulet of Hinton St. George. Bur.[1] 10th October 1673.

John Prideaux, 2nd son, bap.[1] 23rd March 1619, Matric. Exeter Coll. æt. 17. April 1635, died v.p.	Thomas, Matric. Exeter Coll. Oxford 17th April 1635, æt. 14, died s.p. and v.p.	*Edmond Prideaux, son and heir,* æt. 2, 1620, bap.[1] 6th July 1618, Matric. Exeter Coll. Oxford 17th April 1635, æt. 17, died s.p. and bur.[1] 9th October 1643, adm° to his father 26th February 1655. P.C.C.	*Mary,* bap.[1] 9th July 1617 died unmar. adm° granted to her father 25th Feby. 1655-6, P.C.C.	III. *Sir Peter Prideaux,* Bart., bap.[1] 13th July 1626, M.P. for Liskeard 1661, died 22nd and bur.[1] 24th November 1705, aged 79, M.I. Will dated 11th Sept. and proved 9th Dec. 1705, P.C.C. (251 Gee.)	=Lady Elizabeth, eldest dau. of Sir Bevill Gren-ville of Stowe, and sister of John, Earl of Bath. Granted precedency as an Earl's dau. 27th August 1675. (I. 25, 161), mar. at Kilkhampton 17th Nov. 1645, bur.[1] 28th May 1692, M.I.

IV. Sir Edmund Prideaux, Bart., Matric. Oriel Coll. Oxford, 10th April 1663, æt. 16, M.P. for Tregony, 1714, died 6th February and bur. at Great Stanmore, Middle-sex, 1st March 1719-20. Will dat. 24th Jany. 1716, prov. 4th June 1720, P.C.C. (141 Shalter.)	=Susanna, eld dau. of James Winstan-ley of Braunston, co. Leicester, relict of .... Austin of Derhams, co. Mid-dlesex, mar. lic. dated 23rd Feb-ruary, 1672-3, 1st wife, bur. at Great Stanmore, Mid-dlesex, 29th Oct. 1687, adm° to her husband 8th Feby. 1687-8, P.C.C.	= Elizabeth, dau. and coh. of George Saunderson of South Thor-esby, co. Linc. son of Nicho-las Viscount Castleton, 2nd wife, bur. at Great Stan-more 14th May 1702, adm° to her husband 22nd May 1702, P.C.C.	=Mary, dau. of Spencer Vincent, Alderman of London, relict of Sir John Rogers of Wiscombe, co. Devon, 1st Bart., mar. at St. Andrews', Plymo. 5th Sept. 1710; remar. Col. John Arundell of Kensington, 31st Jany. 1722-3, died 17th March follow. Will prov. 21st March, 1723, P.C.C. (67 Bolton.)	Peter Prideaux, bap.[1] 2nd Dec. 1651, Matric. at ExeterColl. Oxf. 7th May 1668, æt. 16, Fell. of All Souls Died unmar and, bur.[1] 21st July 1712. Will dated 15th July, prov. 8th September 1712, P.C.C. (174 Barnes.)	John Prideaux, born 22nd July bap.[1] 2nd Aug. 1655, Mat. at Ex. Coll. Oxf. 12th July 1672, æt. 16. M.P. New-port, Corn., 1700 Died 16th and bur. 25th June 1706. Will dat. 10th July 1703, Prov. 29th June 1707, P.C.C. (149 Poley), s.p.	=Anne, dau. and sole heir of Humph. Prideaux of Soldon 1st wife. Died 8th and bur. 11th March 1702-3.	=Katherine, dau. of John Kelland of Painsford, Devon, and relict of John Coffin of Port-ledge, Dev. remar. Peter Prideaux of Soldon, see next page.

a   *b*

---

[1] At Farway, Devon.   [2] At Sutcombe.

NETHERTON, BARONETS.—TABLE IV.

1. & 2. PRIDEAUX.   3. GIFFORD.   4. ESSE.

Escutcheon of Pretence.
———
1. & 4. BODLE.   2. & 3. SCOTT.

Edmund Prideaux of Ford Abbey. See TABLE V.

Mary Prideaux, bap.[1] 15th October 1598, bur. St. Dunstan's in the West, London, 16th June 1612, *d. s. p.*

Margaret, bap. at Farway 27th September 1631, mar.[1] 14th May 1661 Thomas Drewe of Grange, Devon, died 21st May 1695, bur. Broadhembury M.I.

| Roger Prideaux born[1] 26th March 1657, Matric. at Exeter Coll. Oxford, 12th July 1672, æt. 14, bur.[1] 15th February 1684-5. | Susan, eld. dau. bap.[1] 22nd April 1649, bur.[1] 21st Decembr. 1710. Will dated 23rd November 1710, prov. 6th February 1710-1 at Exeter. | Elizabeth, bap.[1] 27th September 1650, living 1710. | Grace, bap.[1] 7th June 1653. Died unmar. and bur.[1] 28th Dec. 1677. | Mary, born[1] 30th July 1658, mar.[1] 16th April 1705, Sir William Drake of Ashe, Knt. and Bart. Her will dated 30th April 1729, prov. 3rd June 1730, P.C.C. (155 Auber.) | Katherine, mar.[1] 14th February 1698, Charles Harward of Hayne, Clerk, Rector of Tallaton. | Anne, bap.[1] 2nd August 1664, mar.[1] 21st July, Roger Cheeke of Madford, co. Devon. |

———

[1] At Farway, Devon.   [2] At Sutcombe.

a

| Mary, dau. of Samuel Reynardson of Hillingdon, Beds., ob. 1710. 1st wife. | =V. Sir Edmund Prideaux, Bart., born 3rd November and bap. St. Giles in the Fields, Middlesex, 21st November 1675, Matric. Exeter Coll. Oxford, 19th May 1694, aged 18. Died s.p.m., 26th February 1728-9, and bur. in Westm. Abbey, M.I. Will dated 3rd April 1722 prov. 3rd May 1729, P.C.C., and again 10th Oct.1743, (144 Abbot.) | =Anne, dau. of Philip Hawkins of Pennans, Cornw., mar. lic. 6th May 1714. Died 10th May 1741, aged 55. Will dated 20th Feby. 1738, prov. 14th June 1741, by Ann Basset, widow, dau. and only child of deceased. (26 Trenley.) | | Katherine, relict of his uncle John Prideaux, died 10th and bur.[1] 15th April 1709. | =Peter Prideaux, of Soldon, died 3rd & bur.[2] 11th December 1711, M.I. Will dated 23rd November 1710, prov. 1st February 1711-12, (35 Barnes.) | =Dorothea, eld. dau. of Clement Petitt of Dentyleon, Isle of Thanet, s.p. Will dated 28th November 1711, living 1712. |

| Mary, dau. and coh. mar. James Winstanley of Braunston, co. Leicester. Died 1758. | Peter, died in infancy, M.I. | Anne, dau. and coh. mar. John Pendarves Basset of Tehidy Cornwall, who died 25th September 1739, leaving her pregnant with a son and heir John Prideaux Basset, who died unmar. 28th May 1756. | Susanna, mar. Charles Evelyn, 2nd son of Sir John Evelyn of Wotton, Bart. | Saunderson bap.[3] 5th November 1719, killed in the attack on Fort St. Lazare, Carthagena, South America, 9th April 1741, unmar. Adm° to his father, 23rd November 1742. | John Prideaux Brigadier General and Col. of 55th Regt. of Foot, killed at Niagara, 19th July 1759. Will dated 2nd April 1748; Prov. 19th May 1760. P.C.C.(Lynch 70.) | =Elizabeth, dau. of Edward Rolt, of Sacombe Park Herts, and Sister of Sir Edmund Bayntun Rolt of Spye Park Wilts, Bart., living 1760. |

| VII. Sir John Wilmot Prideaux, Bart., Born 13th Feb. and bap.[4] 6th March 1747-8. Died 4th, bur.[1] 10th March 1826. M.I. | =Anne Phœbe, dau. of William Priddle, of Farway, mar.[1] 28th January 1791, 1st wife. Died 2nd September 1793, aged 23. M.I.[1] | =Sarah, dau. of ...... Smith, of Farway, and widow of .... Ellis, mar.[1] 19th May 1804. Died at Sidbury, 22nd September, and bur. there 27th September 1851, aged 79. |

VIII. Sir John Wilmot Prideaux, Bart., born 29th September 1791. Capt. H.I.C. Service. Died at Calcutta, 13th May 1833, aged 42 years. M.I.[1]

| Edmund Gardiner, Born 1st September 1832, bap. at Awliscombe 22nd March 1833. Died 1st September and bur.[1] 6th September 1833. | John Rolle Prideaux, Born 13th January, bap.[1] 25th December 1835. Lieut. 23rd Foot. Died at Ceylon 14th May 1855. M.I.[1] |

---

[1] At Farway, Devon.   [2] At Sutcombe.   [3] At Holsworthy.   [4] At St. George's, Hanover Sq.

b

Susanna, mar. lic. 1st. and mar.[1] 4th October 1706, Phineas Cheeke of Lion's Inn, Middlesex. He living 1716, She 1722.

VI. Sir John Prideaux,=Anne, eldest dau. of John Bart., born 17th, and bap. 24th June 1695, at St. James' Westminster, succeeded his half-bro. as 6th Bart. Bur.[1] 29th August 1766. Will dated 13th March 1763; Proved 24th December 1766.

=Anne, eldest dau. of John Vaughan Visct. Lisburne by Lady Mallet Wilmot, dau. of John Wilmot Earl of Rochester, mar. at St. Anne's Blackfriars' 4th February 1718-9. Will dated 11th February 1767; Proved 4th November 1770. (404 Jenner.)

Edmund Prideaux, bap.[1] 5th January 1729-30, bur.[1] 6th April 1730.

Edward Prideaux, bap.[1] 31st March and bur.[1] 8th April 1731.

Elizabeth, bap.[1] 26th April 1732, mar.[1] 19th Nov. 1766, Edward Chichester of Northover, Somst, mar. settl. 14th same month.

Anne, bap.[1] 26th April 1734, mar.[1] 23rd March 1770, died at Bath and there buried.

=William Windsor Fitz Thomas, Rector of Arrow and Beaudesert, co. Warwick.

Edward Baynton,=...... a minor, 1767. dau. of Commander R.N. ...... Bur. at Fowey Gilbert. 8th June 1797.

Edmund Prideaux, 18th Regt. of Foot, a minor 1767. Died in West Indies unmar.

Elizabeth Constantia, died unmar.

Maria, died unmar.

William =Maria, dau. of ...... Edward Holland, M.D., of Fitz Hinckley, co. Leic. Thomas, Clerk of Awliscombe.

IX. Sir Edmund Saunder-=Frances Mary Anne, 3rd=Caroline, 3rd dau. of=Francis, youngest dau.=Louisa, dau. and coh. of son Prideaux, Bart. born 21st January, and bap.[1] 8th April 1793. Major in the Army, and Hon. Colonel of 1st Battalion Exeter and South Devon Rifle Volunteers.

=Frances Mary Anne, 3rd dau. of William Edward Fitz Thomas, Clerk, of Awliscombe, born 15th January 1814, mar. at Awliscombe, 19th Jany. 1832. Died 1st and bur.[1] 9th June 1836, aged 22. M.I.

=Caroline, 3rd dau. of James Barnard of Combe Flory, Clerk, mar. at Sidmouth 29th April 1841. Died 3rd and bur.[1] 10th August 1841, aged 45. M.I.

=Francis, youngest dau. of Edward Irton, of Irton Hall, Cumberland. Mar. at Walton, Bath, 6th October 1842. Died 17th Nov. 1852. M.I.[1]

=Louisa, dau. and coh. of Robert Bodle, of Woolston Hall, Essex, and relict of George Watlington, of Caldecot House, Aldernham, Herts, mar. at St. James,' Westminster, 7th August 1855.

Frances Mary Anne, born 24th February, bap. at Sidmouth 3rd July 1834. Died 28th January, bur.[1] 3rd February 1844.

I hereby certify that those portions of the above Pedigree which are printed in *Italics*, agree with the Records of this Office

Heralds' College.
London, 14th March, 1874.

STEPHEN TUCKER,
Rouge Croix.

[1] At Farway, Devon.   [2] At Sutcombe.   [3] At Holsworthy.   At St. George's, Hanover Sq

2 H

PEDIGREE OF PRIDEAUX OF ASHBURTON,

Richard Predyaux, died 1515-6,⚭Elizabeth.
bur. at Ashburton. | died 1528-9.

John Predyaux,⚭Johanna.　　Thomas Predyaux,⚭....　　Adam Williams⚭Alice.
Churchwarden　　　　　　　Senr. Churchwarden　　　of Stowford, co.
of Ashburton　　　　　　　of Ashburton 1511-12.　　Devon.
1502-4.

Thomas Prideaux of Ashburton co. Devon, Church-⚭....　　Thomas Williams, Speaker
warden there 1528-30. Died 22nd Janv. 1547-8,　　of the House of Commons,
(Inq. p.m. 1st Edward VI., part 1, No. 29.)　　　　1562.

John Prideaux, Sergeant at Law, aged 28 years on his father's death,⚭*Mary, dau.*
bought Nutwell and settled there. Knt. for the Shire of Devon, 1st | *of Sir Hugh*
Mary. Died 29th September 1558, Adm⁵. 12th May 157², 28th January | *Stuckley, Knt.*
1607-8, 21st April 1608 and 30th October 1633. (Inq. p.m., 1st
Elizabeth, Part III., No. 31.)

| Anne mar. Elias Crymes of Buckland, Monachorum Harl. MS. 1080, fo. 289. | *Catherine mar. Richard Duke of Otterton, Dev. Harl. MS. 1080, fo. 141.* | *James, died s.p.* | *Jane, mar.* James Courtenay of Cheriton Fitz Pain. Bur.² 28th February 1596. | Thomas Prideaux, son and heir, of Nutwell, æt. 9 years 3 months and 8 days at his father's death. Died 21st, and bur.² 25th April 1605. (Inq. p.m., 3rd James, No. 27.) | *Margaret, dau. of Richard Cooper of Winscombe co. Somerset.* | *John Prideaux, of Nutwell, s.p.* | Barbara, dau. of ...... Woodcock of Totnes, mar. lic. 4th October 1596, mar. at St. Thomas, Exeter. |

| *Margaret, mar. John Allet of Iwood, Somerset. Harl. MS., 1559, fo. 342 and 1141, fo. 116.* | *Morice, ob. s.p.* | *Christopher,* matric. at Exeter College, Oxford, 24th Oct 1595, æt. 20. Bur.² 22nd May 1639. | *Mary, mar.* John Spratt, B.D., Canon of Exeter. | *Sir Thomas Prideaux, Knt. of Nutwell,* son and heir, æt. 30 years at his father's death. Bur.² 3rd March 1640, adm⁵ to son Amos, 13th Dec. 1641 and 4th June 1650. | *Joan, dau. and coh. of John Cole of Buckland Tout Saints, Devon,* mar. license 9th February 1595-6. | Florence, bur.² 23rd October 1589. | *Francis, bur.² 21st May 1652.* *John, slain at Ostend. s.p.* *William. s.p.* | *Margery, o. s.p.* |

| *Margaret,* born 1603, bur.² 23rd December 1648. | *Eleanor,* bur.² 24th Sept. 1607. | *Anne,* born 1605, mar. Edward Rowe, Rector of Lympston 1640, died 1671. | *Thomas,* æt. 24 1621, bur.² 6th May 1637, unmar. | *Arthur,* born 1606, died s.p. | *John,* bur.² 25th Janv. 1619. s.p. | *Joane,* born 1613, bur.² 24th June 1636. | *Edward,* bur.² 4th October 1618. s.p. | *James,* born 1615, bur.² 3rd April 1641. s.p. |

Thomas, bap.¹ 14th October
1665, bur.¹ **3rd December**
same year.

Thomas Prideaux, born 27th
December 1666, and bap.¹
15th January following.

NOTE.—Since the Memoir of this branch of the family on pp. 212—213 was printed, we have derived further information respecting it from a little work courteously lent to us by the Rev. J. H. Butcher, Curate of Ashburton. This work consists of extracts from the accounts of the Churchwardens of Ashburton, extending from 1479 to 1580. Richard Prideaux is mentioned in 1486, and in 1515-6 3s. 8d. is credited on his death "for a cross at his house and in the Church." Elizabeth Prideaux, widow, on her death in 1528-9 "gave £5 13s. 4d. for the part purchase of a best cope." Richard and Elizabeth were probably the parents of John and Thomas, and, possibly, the brother of Thomas father of Richard Prideaux of Tavistock. There are many entries relating to the family.

¹ At Ugborough.　　　　　　　　　　　　² At Woodbury.

NUTWELL, AND UGBOROUGH.—TABLE VI.

Thomas Prydeaux = Elizabeth.
of Ashburton.

Joane, dau...... = *Richard Prideaux of Tavistock*, died 13th Oct. Will = *Agneta, dau. of*
Relict of William   dated 12th Oct. 1529, prov. 12th Feby. 1529-30. P.C.C. | *John Arscott, of*
Webb, s.p.   (15 Jankin.) (Inq. p.m. 21st Henry VIII., No. 11.) | *Holdesworthy.*

John Predyaux = ...   Grace, born   Philippa,
son and heir.   1524.   born 1528.

Robert Prideaux of Ashburton. = *Ann, dau. of John*   Ricarda, dau. and heir,
Attorney at Law 1666-8. | *Ridgway of Torr,*   mar. William Jackson,
Will dated 2nd March 1573, | *co. Devon.*   both living 1547.
proved 5th February 1578-9,
P.C.C. (5 Bacon.)

Thomas Prideaux = *Agnes, dau. of Walter*   *John*, not   Harry, named   *George.*   *Robert.*   Elizabeth,
of Totnes, living | *Kellan of Totnes,* Bur.[1]   named in   in father's   mar. Richard
1620. | 17th November 1647.   father's   will, bur.[1]   Dolbeare of
             | Will dated 29th October   will.   6th May,   Ashburton.
             | 1647, proved 24th Jany.   1635.
             | 1647-8. Exon.

Thomas Prideaux of Ug- = Ann, dau.   John Prid- = Jane,   *Agnes,*   Elizabeth,   Dennis,   Mary,   *Sarah.*   Anne,
borough, Matric. at | of ......   eaux, born   dau. of   *mar. John*   mar.   mar.   mar.[1]   named
Exeter College, Oxford, | Glas.   1599, æt.   ......   *Braken*   JohnFoxe-   John   Peter   in
2nd December 1614. | mar.[1]   21, 1620,   (Brook-   worthy,   Horsham,   Osborne,   mother's
Bur.[1] 18th December | 14thAug.   named in   ing).   named   Clerk,   Clerk   will,
1638. Will dated 2nd | 1642, bur.   mother's   named   in   named   30th   bur.[1]
October. Codl. 17th De- | 28th   will. Bur.[1]   in   mother's   in   July   11th
cember 1638, proved 5th | January   19th Sept.   mother's   will.   mother's   1633.   July
February 1638-9. P.C.C. | 1668.   1680.   will.   will.   1669,
                                                                               unmar.

Dennis Prideaux, Fellow of Exeter = Mary, dau. of   *Amias Prideaux,* admr = Sarah,   Thomas Prid- = Mary.   Elizabeth, bap.[1]
College, Exeter 1618-30. Proctor | John Tuckfield   his father's effects, | dau. of   eaux, bap.[1]   21st January
of Oxford 1626. Inst. to Rect. of | of Little Ful-   Died 1667, admr to | ......   8th Sept.   1633, bur.[1] 28th
Lympstone, 23rd August 1630. Preb. | ford, mar. lic.,   his Nephew, ex. | Ford.   1638, bur.[1]   March 1651.
of Exeter, 10th Mar., 1633-4. Inst. | 9th May 1638,   sorore and nearest | 29th January
to Rect. of Bishops Morchard, 6th | died 17th June   kinsman Edmund | 1694-5, of   Agnes, bap.[1]
March 1638-9. Bur.[2] 12th Nov. | 1663, bur. at   Rowe. Sold Nutwell | Ugborough.   27th September
1640. s.p. Will dated 1640. | Crediton. M.I.   1647.   1634.

Nicholas, bap.[1] 12th   Roger, bap.[1] 5th   Nann, bap.[1] 5th January 1663,
October 1668.   July 1670.   mar.[1] 2nd February 1693-4,
                                            Richard Savory.

I hereby certify that the portions of this Pedigree which are printed
in *Italics*, agree with the Records of this Office.

Heralds' College,   STEPHEN TUCKER,
     London, 14th March, 1874.   *Rouge Croix.*

---

[1] At Ugborough.   [2] At Woodbury.

PEDIGREE OF PRIDEAUX OF FORD ABBEY.

TABLE V.

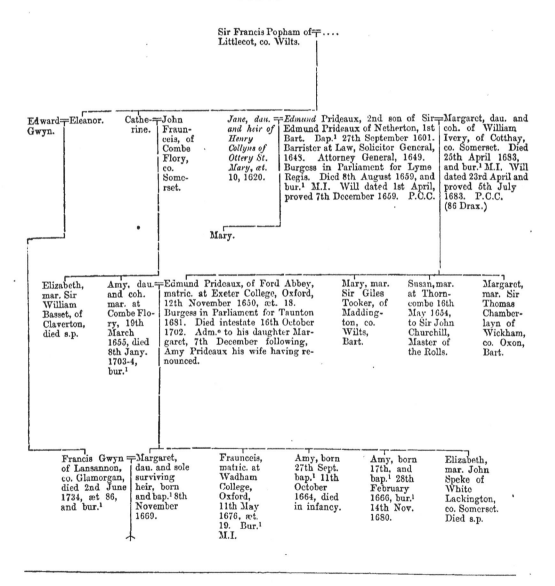

Sir Francis Popham of⊤.... Littlecot, co. Wilts.

Edward⊤Eleanor. Gwyn.

Cathe-⊤John rine. Fraun-ceis, of Combe Flory, co. Somer-rset.

Jane, dau. ⊤Edmund Prideaux, 2nd son of Sir⊤Margaret, dau. and and heir of | Edmund Prideaux of Netherton, 1st | coh. of William Henry | Bart. Bap.[1] 27th September 1601. | Ivery, of Cotthay, Collyns of | Barrister at Law, Solicitor General, | co. Somerset. Died Ottery St. | 1648. Attorney General, 1649. | 25th April 1683, Mary, æt. | Burgess in Parliament for Lyme | and bur.[1] M.I. Will 10, 1620. | Regis. Died 8th August 1659, and | dated 23rd April and | bur.[1] M.I. Will dated 1st April, | proved 5th July | proved 7th December 1659. P.C.C. | 1683. P.C.C. | (86 Drax.)

Mary.

Elizabeth, mar. Sir William Basset, of Claverton, died s.p.

Amy, dau.⊤Edmund Prideaux, of Ford Abbey, and coh. | matric. at Exeter College, Oxford, mar. at | 12th November 1650, æt. 18. Combe Flo-| Burgess in Parliament for Taunton ry, 19th | 1681. Died intestate 16th October March | 1702. Adm.º to his daughter Mar-1655, died | garet, 7th December following, 8th Jany. | Amy Prideaux his wife having re-1703-4, | nounced. bur.[1]

Mary, mar. Sir Giles Tooker, of Madding-ton, co. Wilts, Bart.

Susan, mar. at Thorn-combe 16th May 1654, to Sir John Churchill, Master of the Rolls.

Margaret, mar. Sir Thomas Chamber-layn of Wickham, co. Oxon, Bart.

Francis Gwyn ⊤Margaret, of Lansannon, | dau. and sole co. Glamorgan, | surviving died 2nd June | heir, born 1734, æt 86, | and bap.[1] 8th and bur.[1] | November | 1669.

Fraunceis, matric. at Wadham College, Oxford, 11th May 1676, æt. 19. Bur.[1] M.I.

Amy, born 27th Sept. bap.[1] 11th October 1664, died in infancy.

Amy, born 17th, and bap.[1] 28th February 1666, bur.[1] 14th Nov. 1680.

Elizabeth, mar. John Speke of White Lackington, co. Somerset. Died s.p.

[1] Chapel of Ford Abbey.

ARMS OF PRIDEAUX-BRUNE.

1. BRUNE. 2. & 3. PRIDEAUX.

4. DE LA ROKELE.

PEDIGREE OF BRUNE.

TABLE VII.

Sir William le Brun, Chamberlain to King Edward I., received from the King, by Charter dated 6th February 6th of his reign, a grant of several Manors in Hants and Dorset to him and Isolda his wife and the heirs of their bodies. Died 1300. Warrant to take his lands into the King's hands dated 4th March 29th Edward I., (Rot. Orig.) Inq. p.m., 15th April 29th Edward I., No. 44. ═ *Isolda*, Maid of Honour to Queen Eleanor, died 1307. (Inq. p.m., 27th September 1st Edward II., No. 64.)

Richard de la ═ Maud Rokele, Justiciary of Ireland, died 7th December 1276. (Inq. p.m., 5th Edward I., No. 6.)

Sir Philip de la Rokele, aged 30 ═ .... years on his father's death. Died 18th October 1295. (Inq. p.m., 23rd Edward I., No. 39.)

Sir Maurice le Brun, aged 21 years on his ═ *Matilda*, dau. and heir, aged 9½ father's death. Summoned to Parliament as a Baron of the Realm 7th Edward II. 8th Edward II., 9th Edward II., and 11th Edward II. &c. *Lord Chamberlain to Edward III.* Died 17th March 1354-5. (Inq. p.m., 29th Edward III., No 38.) years on her father's death. By Inq. 28th Edward I., found to have been of the age of 14 years on 9th October 1300.

Sir William le Brun, son and heir, aged ═ *Alice, dau. and heir of* 40 years on his father's death. Had *Richard Lacer, Alder-* seizin of his lands 17th April 1355. *man of London, remar.* (Rot. Fin. 29th Edward III.) Died *Sir Robert Marney. Liv-* 24th February 1361-2. (Inq. p.m., 36th *ing 45th Edward III.* Edward III., Part 1., No. 31.)

Sir Edmund ═ Elizabeth, sister de la Pole and heir of Sir died 1418. Edmund de Handlo of Borstal.

William Sturmy ═ Johanna, ob. of Wolfall, Knt., 20th Febry. ob. 23rd March 1428-9. (Inq. 1426-7. (Inq. p.m. p.m. 7th 5th Henry VI. Henry VI., No. 22). No. 44.)

Rich-ard 2nd son 1371 (Rot. Claus. 45th Edw. III. m.36d | Johanna, mar. 1st, William Wayte, (Inq. ad quod dam. 32nd Edw. III., Part 2, No. 53.) 2ndly, Thomas de Overton, son and heir of Sir William de Overton, Knt., who was Sheriff of Hants 1355, and died 13th Oct. 1361, his son and heir being aged 19 years. Thomas de Overton had grant from Sir William Brun of the Manor of Fordingbridge, (Inq. ad quod dam., Esc. 44th Edward III., No. 31, Part 2.) He had a son Michael, who died 19th Oct. 1389, s.p., and a daughter Elizabeth, wife of Robert Tawke, who was found to be her brother's nearest heir and aged 23 years. (Herald and Geneal. Vol. i., p. 214).

Sir Ingelram le Brun, ═ *Elizabeth* Knt.,† son and heir, aged *dau of* 8 years on his father's death. *Sir* By Inq. dated 1st Sept. *Edmund* 1375, found to have been *de la Pole,* of the age of 21 years on *coh. of* 6th Dec. 1374, having *her moth.* been born at Titchfield, *died 14th* and bap. in the Chapel of *Decr.* Chark in the parish of *1404.* Titchfield, on feast of St. *(Inq.* Nicholas 1353, died 12th *p.m. 8th* August 1400. (Inq. p.m., *Henry* 1st Henry IV., Part 1, *IV., No.* No. 39.) Bur. at South *18.)* Okenden, Essex.

William, ═ Agnes, ═ John Renge-bourne dau. Hol-1st hus. and combe. ob. 8th coh. 2nd Sept. æt. 40 hus. 1422. in ob. (Inq. 1426, 14th p.m., 1st rem. Oct. Henry before 1455. VI., No. 1427. (Inq. 39). p.m., 34th Henry VI. No. 2).

Matilda, ═ Roger dau. and Sey-coh. mour.

a *b* *c*

---

† The name of Ingelram le Brun leads to the inference that this family was of the lineage of the le Bruns, Counts of Poictou, Lusignan, de Couci, and la Marche, who had a footing in this country at an early date. Ingelram le Brun had summons to Parliament from 23rd Edward I. to 15th Edward II. He had a son Ingelram le Brun, Lord of Couci, who married Katherine, daughter of the Duke of Austria, and had a son, also named Ingelram, Lord of Ghisnes and Couci, who married the Princess Isabella, and was created by her father, Edward III., Earl of Bedford and K.G., ob. 1397. s.p.m.

2 J

a   *b*   *c*

Sir *Maurice Bruyn*, aged 14 ═ Elizabeth, dau. and coh. of Sir | Eliza- | William Rengebourn ═ Elizabeth, | John Seymour, ═ Isabella,
years on his father's death. | *Henry Radford* of Irby, co. Lincoln, | beth. | son and heir, aged 15 | remar. John | Knt., son and | dau. of
Born at South Wokyndon | coln, Knt. Died 26th May, 1471. | | in 1422, ob. 10th | Blake. Ob. | heir æt. 26 in | Mark
14th Sept. 1385. Prob. Etat., | (Inq. p.m., 11th Edward IV., | | March 1449. (Inq. | 30th Sept. | 1426, ob. 1464. | William
8th Henry IV., No. 83. Died | No, 27.) Will dated 4th Feb. | | p.m., 28th Henry | 1459. (Inq. | (Inq. p.m., 4th | of
8th Nov. 1467. (Inq. p m., | 1470-1, proved 17th June 1471 | | VI., No. 18). | p.m., 38th | Edward IV., | Bristol,
8th Edward IV., No. 24). | P.C.C., (Wattis 2.) | | | Henry VI., | No. 32). | Mercht.
                                                                    | | No. 27).

Sir *Henry Bruyn*, ═ Elizabeth, dau. | Kath- | Jane, | Mercy ═ *Thomas Bruyn*, 2nd son and | William ═ Mar- | Robert ═ Eliz.
son and heir. | and coh. of | erine, | mar. | (Ped. | heir, Esch. for South Hants | Rengebourn | garet. | Rengebourne
Sheriff of Hants, | *Robert Darcy* | mar. | John | Fin. | and Wilts, 35th Henry VI., | died 23rd | | son and heir,
25th & 26th & 37th | of Maldon. | Rich. | Digges | 18th | aged 27 years on his father's | Oct. 1512. | | aged 13 in
& 38th Henry VI. | (Harl. MS., | Dry- | of | Edw. | death. Had lic. to enter | (Inq. | | 1449, ob. 6th
Died v.p. 30th Nov. | Davy's Suff. | land. | Digges | IV., | upon his fath's. and broth's. | p.m., 4th | | Oct. 1485,
1461. (Inq. p.m., | Coll. Ped. | Namd. | Court, | Mich.) | lands. (Pat. Rot., 21st Edw. | Henry | | s.p. (Inq.
1st Edward IV., | Vol. i., | in | co. | | IV., Part 1.) Died 27th | VIII., | | p m., 1st
No. 27.) | letter D.) | moth's. | Kent. | | April 1497. (Inq. p.m., 15th | No. 67). | | Hen. VII.,
                     | will. | | | Henry VII., No. 48.) | | | No. 87.)

Elizabeth, dau. and coh. aged 17 years | Alice, dau. and coh., aged | John Bruyn ═ Anne, dau. | William Bruyn, ═ Katherine,
on her father's death. *Wife of Thomas Tyrell*, Esq. of the Herons and Okenden, | 18 on her father's death. | uncle and heir | of Nicholas | son and heir, | dau. and
den, Essex, by whom she had a | Mar. 1st John Berners, | of Thomas | Tichborne | aged 25 years | heir of
son and heir, Hugh. Mar. 2ndly Sir Wm. | Esq., by whom she had a | Bruyn. Died | of | on his father's | William
Brandon, Knt., by whom she was mother | son and heir, John. Mar. | 24th Sept | Tichborne, | death. Died | Rengebourn.
of Charles Brandon, Duke of Suffolk; | 2ndly Robert Harleston. | 1544. (Inq | Hants. | 19th September | ob. v.p.
and 3rdly, William Malory. Died 26th | 3rdly Sir John Heveningham, | p.m., 36th | | 1512. (Inq.
March 1474. (Inq. p.m., 9th Henry | died 15th February | Henry VIII., | | p.m., 4th Henry
VII., No. 12.) | 1472. (Inq. p.m., 13th | No. 128.) | | VIII., No. 79.)
                     | Edward IV., No. 59.)

Elizabeth, | Sir John Brune, Knt., son and heir, ═ Jane, dau. of ...... | Thomas Bruyn, son and heir,
wife of | aged 25 years on his father's death. | Bampfield, Exec. to | aged 14 years on his father's
Henry | Died 10th November 1559. (Inq. | husband's will. Remar. | death. Found kinsman and heir
Bickley. | p.m., 2nd Elizabeth, No. 9, Exq.) | Charles Wingfield. | of William Rengebourn. (Inq.
          | Will dated 27th August 1559. Proved | | p.m., 4th Henry VII., No. 67).
          | P.C.C., 16th May 1560. (Mellershe 30.) | | Died 7th May 1539. Rec. Office,
                                                    | | Primus., Lib. Ced. 86.

Nicholas *Martin of Athelhampton*, died 24th March ═ Margaret, dau. and heir of John, and sister of
1595-6. (Inq. p.m., 39th Elizabeth, Part 1, No. 76. | Nicholas Wadham of Merifield, Somerset.

Elizabeth, dau. and coh., of full age on ═ Henry Brune, son and heir, aged 8 years and 6 | Stephen Brune, | Jane, wife of
death of her father. Mar. 2ndly at | months on his father's death. Had livery of | named in | ...... Rugge.
Piddleton 1595, Sir Thomas Hamon of | seizin 1573. ob. 13th March 1593-4. (Inq. p.m., | father's will. | named in
Parley. | 36th Elizabeth, Part 1, No. 112). Bur. at | | father's will.
          | Piddleton.

Sir *John Brune*, born 5th ═ Bridget, dau. of | Charles Brune, ═ Mary, dau. of | Nicholas, | Elizabeth, | Grace, | Anne,
Aug. 1577, Kntd 1619, | Sir Edward | died 17th Oct. | Robert Coker of | 3rd son. | wife of John | wife of | wife of
Sheriff of Dorset 13th James | Seymour, Bart., | 1637, aged 50, | Mapowder, mar. | | Scrope, of | Sir | Edward
Died 1st March 1639, bur. | settlement after | bur. at Piddle- | there 1620. Died | | Castlecumbe | Edward | Dukcombe
at Piddleton, M.I. s.p. (Inq. | marriage 20th | ton, Dorset. | 2nd April 1636, | | Wilts. | Lawrence | of Corfe
p.m., 15th Charles, No. 235. | November 1599. | M.I. Will dated | bur. at Mapowder. | | Mary, wife | of Creeck | Castle,
W. & L.) Adm.n to his | | 10th Oct. 1637. | M.I. | | of John Hall | Grange, | Dorset.
relict 12th March 1639-40 | | Prov. 29th Jan. | | | of Bradford | Dorset.
                            | | 1637-8. (Lee 7). | | | Wilts, mar.
                            | | P.C.C. | | | 1591.

b

b

John Brune, heir of his Uncle, Sir John Brune, bap. at Mapowder 1622, aged 16 years and 10 months at his Uncle's death. Died 24th March 1645, Will dated 16th January 1645, proved 10th June 1646. Bur. at Piddleton, Dorset. M.I. **=** Mary, daughter of Edward Hooper of Boveridge, Dorset.

.... **=** Charles Brune of Plumber. Married Margaret, daughter of John Dennis of Pucklechurch, Gloucester. Sheriff of Dorset, 35th Charles II., 2nd James II. Died 21st October 1703, Will dated 6th November 1699, Cod. 6th June 1702, proved at Blandford Forum, 20th Nov 1703. **=** Jane, daughter of Henry Collier, marriage settlement 16th December 1674. Will dated 15th January 1707-8, proved 13th July 1708, P.C.C., Buried at Fifehead Nevill, Dorset, 1707, aged 58.

Mary, only daughter and heir, married Sir Ralph Bankes of Corfe Castle.

John Brune, ob., s.p.

Mary, wife of William Lewys of Stoke Gayland, Dorset.

Charles Brune of Plumber, only surviving son. Bap.[1] May 1677. Sheriff of Dorset, 7th Anne. Died 31st May 1726, aged 49, buried at Fifehead Nevill. M.I. Will dated 11th November 1724, Cod. 28th May 1726, proved 14th January 1727. **=** Betty, daughter and heir of Lorenzo Jeffery, of West Bagborough, Somerset. Marriage Settlement 13th and 14th May 1703. Died 1732, aged 47. Buried at Fifehead Nevill. M.I.

Jane, bap.[1] 25th Aug. 1680, bur.[1] 6th July 1753.

Betty, bap.[1] 17th June 1682, wife of Wm. Weston of Cullen, Dorset.

Charles Brune, son and heir, bap.[1] 30th Sept. 1707. Sheriff of Dorset 1731. Died 23rd November 1769, s.p. Buried at Fifehead Nevill, Will dated 15th June 1768, proved 16th[1] January 1770. **=** Elizabeth, daughter and coh. of William Boulting of Wells, Marriage Art. 12th September 1750. Settlement 30th May 1752. Died 16th September 1758, aged 58, buried at Fifehead Nevill, M.I.

John, died 21st Sept. 1757, aged 48, buried at Fifehead, Nevill. Will dated 29th January 1754, proved 1st July 1758. s.p.

Harry, bap.[1] 31st Aug. 1716, died 12th March 1748, aged 23, adm° to his bro. John 2nd June 1740.

James, bap.[1] 10th June 1720. ob. s.p.

Betty Brune. bap.[1] 18th May 1704. **=** Nevill Morton Pleydell.

Jenny, married Robert Browne of Frampton, Dorset. Died 1st July 1760, aged 49, buried at Fifehead Nevill, M.I.

Mary. bap.[1] 31st Dec. 1714.

Charles Morton, afterwards Charles Morton Pleydell Brune, having, in conformity with the testamentary injunction of his Maternal Uncle Charles Brune, assumed the name of Brune in addition to that of Pleydell. Died 18th September 1785. s.p.

John Gape **=** Betty.

Humphry Prideaux, of Prideaux Place. **=** Jenny.

Cornelia.

Charles Prideaux, who, on the death of his Uncle, Charles Morton Pleydell Brune, succeeded to the Brune Estates, and in conformity with the testamentary injunction of his Maternal Great Uncle Charles Brune, assumed the name and arms of Brune, in addition to those of Prideaux.

I hereby certify that those portions of the above Pedigree which are printed in *Italics* agree with the Records of this Office.

Heralds' College,
16th April 1874.

STEPHEN TUCKER,
Rouge Croix.

[1] At Lydlinch, Dorset.

ROYAL DESCENT OF PRIDEAUX,

TABLE VIII.

Rhys ap Tudor Maur, Prince of South Wales, eleventh in direct =....
descent from Cadwalader the last King of Britain, sl. 1090.

Griffith ap Rhys, Pr. of S. Wales, ob. 1136. = Gwenlhian, dau. of Griffith ap Conan, Pr. of N. Wales.

Rhys ap Griffith, Lo. = Gwhelian, dau. of Madoc ap
ap Rhys, ob. 1197.   Meredith, Pr. of Powis.

Gerald Fitz Walter de Windsor, = Nesta, had Cærau and other
Constable of Pembroke.   lands as marriage portion.

William Fitz Gerald, = ...
lived at Pembroke.

Maurice Fitz Gerald, from whom the
Earls of Kildare and Desmond.

EDWARD I., King = Eleanor, of Castile
of England, ob.   and Leon, ob. 1290.
1307.

Griffith ap = Maud, dau. of Wm.
Rhys, ob.   de Broase, Lord of
1202.   Brecnock.

Odo = Margaret, dau.
Carrio.   of Richard son
of Tancred.

Humphry de Bohun, = Elizabeth Planta-
Earl of Hereford and   genet, widow of
Essex, killed at   John, Earl of
Borough Bridge 1322.   Holland, ob. 1316.
(See Descent ante, p.
188.)

Gilbert Talbot. = Gwenhlian,
   sole heir.

William, Lo. de Carrio, = ...
to whom K. JOHN restored
the Lordship of Mulles-
ford in Berks.

Ric. Talbot, only = Sarah, dau. of Will. Beau-
son, 1296.   champ, Earl of Warwick.

Hugh Courteney, = Margaret
Earl of Devon,   de Bohun,
K.G., ob. 1377.   ob. 1391.

Richd. Talbot = Joane, dau. and heir
of Richard's   of Hugh de Mortimer
Castle.   of Richard's Castle.

Nicholas, = Katherine, dau.
infr. æt. 15th   and coh. of Myles
Henry III.   Lord Courcy.

Sir = Ann, dau.
Philip   of Thomas
Court-   Wake of
eney,   Blisworth,
ob.   Northton.
1406.

Sir = Emeline,
Edw.   dau. and
Court-   heir of
eney,   Sir John
ob.   Dauney.
1372.

Eliza- = Sir An-
beth   drew
Court-   Lutterell
eney,   ob. cir.
ob.   1374.
1395.

John Talbot, = Joane, dau. of
ob. 1356.   Roger Ld. Grey
   of Ruthyn.

Nicholas de = Avicia,
Carrio,   sister
Lord of   and heir
Mullesford   to John
ob. 1286.   son of
   Hugh
   Peverell.

John Talbot. = Catherine.

Sir John = Agnes
Courte-   or Joan,
ney,   dau. of
o.v.p.   Alex.
   Cham-
   pernon.

Sir Hugh = Philippa,
Courteney   dau. and
of Hac-   heir of
combe and   Sir
Boconnoc,   Warren
ob. 1425.   L'Erche-
   dekne.

Sir Hugh = Catherine,
Lutterell,   dau. of
ob.1427-8.   Sir John
   Beau-
   mont of
   Shirwill,
   Devon,
   ob. 1436.

Sir Waren = Eliz. Talbot,
L'Erche-   coheir, ob.
dekne of   3rd August
Cornwall.   1407, Inq.
   p.m. 9th
   Henry IV.,
   No. 39.

William = ...
de
Carrio.

Nicholas = Amicia,
de Carrio   dau. and
Lord of   heir to
Mulles-   Ric. Tuit
ford,   the
ob. 1312.   younger
   Knt.

Sir Philip = Elizabeth,
Courteney,   dau. of Wal-
ob. 1463.   ter, Lord
   Hungerford,
   living 1468.

Sir John = Margaret,
Lutterell   dau. of
ob. 1431.   John, Lord
   Audley, ob.
   1439.

Joan = John Baron Carew,
Talbot.   ob. 1324.
2nd wife.

John Baron Carew, = Margaret, dau. of John
ob. 1362.   Lord Mohun.

SirPhilip = Elizabeth,
Cour-   dau. and
teney,   heir of
living   Robert
1488.   Hengston.

Elizabeth = James Lut-
Courteney,   terell, slain
mar. lic.   at St.
dated 13th   Albans,
Jan 1450-1,   1461.
ob. 1493.

Leonard de Carew, = Alice, dau. and heir of Edmund Fitz Alan de Arundel,
ob. 1395.   Knt., younger bro. of Richard, 13th Earl of Arundel.

Thomas de Carew, = Elizabeth, dau. of Sir William
ob. 1430.   Bonville of Shute.

Joan Courteney, heir = Sir Nicholas, Baron
of her mother.   Carew, ob. 1460.

Sir Thomas, Baron = Joan, dau. and heir of Thomas
Carew, ob. 1461.   Carminow, born 1423.

a   *b*   *c*

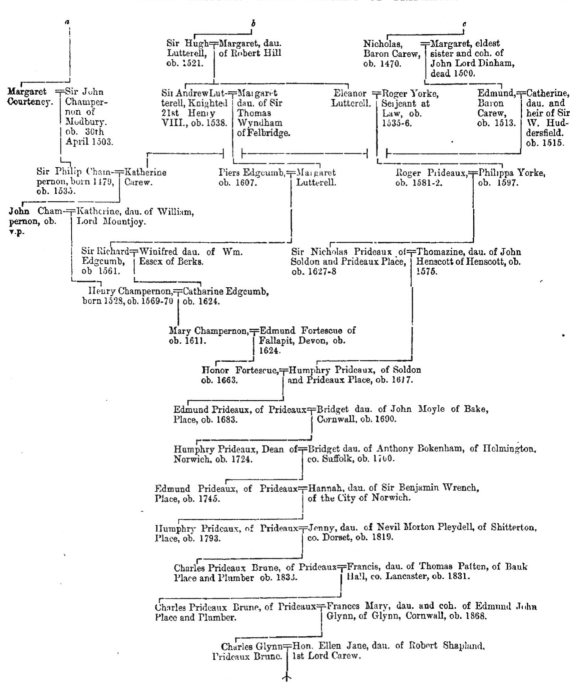

TREFFRY.

The name of Treffry is undoubtedly of very great antiquity in the county of Cornwall, and is said, in the family records, to have been derived from the Manor of Treffry in the parish of Linkinhorn, which records also state that the family existed anterior to the conquest by Duke William of Normandy. The Pedigree in the Heralds' College, recorded at the Heralds' Visitation of Cornwall in 1620, commences with Roger Treffry de Treffry, without date. From this Roger the seventh in descent was Sir John Treffry, Knt.. son of Thomas Treffry and Alice daughter and co-heir of ...... Searle of Penyerance, co. Cornwall. We have failed to discover any evidence on record to support these descents, and, in fact, do not find the name of Treffry to occur at all until late in the fourteenth century. Some of the matches were, however, supported by old paintings of Arms in the pannelling of a room at Place, to which we shall presently refer. And this record is, to some extent, suported by the account given by Symonds, who visited " Trefray house on Munday 1st September 1644,"[1] and describes the " coates and writing" as being then " old :" to this we shall refer hereafter.

With reference to the above-mentioned Sir John Treffry a tradition exists that he was at the battle of Cresey with the Black Prince, and was there so fortunate as to capture the Royal Banner of France, and that, in recognition of his valour, the king made him a Knight Banneret on the field. " In memory of which service by speciall commandment from the king, who sent his warrant to the Heralds that the said John Treffry, Banneret, and his heirs should quarter the Armes of France with their own atchievement, with supporters to the said armes, willing and requiring them to publish the same authentically under their hands and seals for continuance of the memory thereof to posterity ensuing, which was performed accordingly."[2] In support of this statement it is averred that the Arms : az, three fleurs-de-lys or, which occurred in ancient painted glass formerly in the Hall windows and were emblazoned in the above-mentioned old room " in Place house upon wainscot pannels, which room, being in a state of decay, was, about 1750, repannelled, but, previously to the removal of the old pannels, the arms and all the inscriptions from the pannels which contained a record of the arms and 'of all the marriages, and the issue from them, were carefully copied into a regular pedigree book which is still at Place, and that the said arms are quartered with Treffry on a tombstone in Fowey Church."[2] We do not doubt that this record was made, from tradition, in perfect good faith, though we apprehend the alleged facts will not bear investigation. The battle of Cresey was fought on the 26th August 1346, whilst Roger Treffry, the great grandson, according to the pedigree claimed, of John who is said to have been at that battle, died in 1391, leaving his son and heir a minor ; but supposing Roger to have died at the early age of 25, his great grandfather in 1346, if alive, must have been a very aged man. Secondly : It is

---

[1] Symond's Diary, pp. 68, 69. Camden Society.   [2] Treffry MSS., Place, Fowey.

bore as sovereign of that kingdom, to any subject whatever. Thirdly: the arms of France, at that date, were semée of fleurs-de-lys, and not three fleurs-de-lys only, the latter not having been adopted until the time of Henry IV. or Henry V. Fourthly: it is not likely the Heralds would have been required at that early period to take special notice of heraldic insignia, as their first chapter was held at Rouen in 1420, seventy-one years after the battle of Crescy. Fifthly: Supporters were unknown in the reign of Edward III.

The Arms referred to: Az. three fleur-de-lys or, unquestionably existed of ancient date at Place in various forms, but their presence there is more easily accounted for than by supposing them to be the Royal arms of France. Elizabeth Colyn, who married Thomas son and heir of Thomas Treffry of Fowey in 1444,[1] was the daughter of John Colyn of Helland, the son and heir of Ingreta, the elder of the co-heirs of John Giffard of the same place by Elizabeth daughter of John Nicoll of Bodmin. The Arms of Giffard were: Az. three fleur-de-lys or, as still remaining in one of the windows of Helland Church.[2] These arms Elizabeth Colyn was, of course, entitled to quarter, and their earliest occurrence at Place is found to be on the same shield with the arms of Colyn: ar. a chev. sa. betw.

three Cornish choughs ppr. This shield was in one of the windows of the hall, but being much broken was taken down about fifty years ago. A drawing of it is preserved, and it affords a very singular instance of marshalling. It is paly of four, Treffry, Giffard, Colyn, and Nicoll. According to modern practice it should have been Treffry, impaling, *quarterly* instead of *paly*, Colyn, Giffard, and Nicoll—provided Elizabeth Nicoll were an heiress, of which we have no direct evidence, though there is some reason to believe such was the case. Symonds does not mention this shield in the windows of the hall, but he blazons four old shields, in two of which the disputed coat is found in connection with the arms of Colyn, and in one with those of Nicoll also (see post). In objection to the questioned arms being the arms of Giffard it has been urged, that in the arms of that family the fleurs-de-lys are charged with annulets, or pellets; a careful examination however of the Giffard arms in Helland Church shews that there was no such surcharge, nevertheless it is remarkable that Symonds, in blazoning one of the old shields in the hall windows at Place when he visited it, describes one as impaling, az. three fleurs-de-lys or, *the bend sa charged with three roundels.* From this we conclude that the surcharge was not an essential part of the blazon, but was sometimes used as a difference; moreover, it may be further noticed that in the great achievement of Treffry the questioned coat occurs in the eighth quarter instead of being in the first, or at least second, as it would have been had it been a royal augmentation, and that the fleurs-de-lys are charged with pellets.

We should mention that there is here a great discrepancy between the pedigree now

---

[1] See ante p. 37, where Elizabeth Colyn is noticed, but her name was accidently omitted in the pedigree, page 41.   [2] Ante p. 14 and Note.

2 K²

in the possession of the family and that upon record in the College of Arms. The Heralds identify the John Treffry of whom we have been writing with Sir John Treffry who died s.p. in 16th Henry VII. (1500), whose brother Thomas carried on the succession, omitting no fewer than five descents. There is no record in the Heralds' College, or elsewhere, of which we have any knowledge, of a *Sir* John Treffry in the time of Edward III.   There was a John Treffry, however, living at that period, for on 7th February 1356-7, ten years after the battle of Crescy, a payment of three marks was directed to be made to John Trevery, (doubtless the same name in a different form), for remaining with the Prince's Council in Cornwall during the time of their session.[1] This gentleman, however, was not a Knight. In the annexed pedigree I have given a parallel genealogy of this family, which is supported by the documentary evidences appended.   Except in the matches it does not widely differ from the authorised pedigree in the Heralds' College—indeed by rolling two of the Thomases, in the latter, into one, the two lines would be in perfect accord.

The Heralds' Visitation of 1531 shews two descents of Treffry. "John Trevry of Trevry, co. Cornwall, married Jane, second daughter and part inheritor to Richard Petyt of Trengwaynton, in the said county, and had issue John,—John married Elizabeth, second daughter of Nicholas Colan of St. Colan in the said County." The first John is shewn, in the Place pedigree, as the son and heir of the supposed Sir John Treffry, and if this be granted these two descents are confirmed, though we have no evidence as to date unless we accept the first John and Jane as identical with the John Treury and *Johanna* his wife, who levied a fine in Tregoyd vean, &c., in 24th Edward III. (1350), and identical also with the John who heads my alternative pedigree, which is not improbable.

Roger Treffry, son and heir of John the younger, married in 3rd Richard II. Maude, daughter of Richard[2] Juyll of Bodmin, merchant. In Trinity term 8th of the same king (1385) a precept was directed to the Sheriff to take him and keep him safely in prison until he should satisfy the claim of John Hellygan to £32 which the said Roger on the 15th January 6th of the same king (1381-2) before John Kendall, then Mayor of Lostwithiel, and Nicholas Pego, Clerk, acknowledged himself to be indebted. The Sheriff produced a certain extent taken before him upon the oaths of a jury of twelve men, who say that the said Roger Treffry had lands, messuages, and tenements in Tregoyd Minor worth 20s.; and lands in the ville of Grywys worth 6s. 8d.; and one messuage and lands in Tregoyd Major of the value of 7s.; land in the ville of Reskesik worth 2s.; one messuage and land in ville Fentengotes worth 10s., in ville of Tregenewen. one messuage and land worth 5s.; in ville Syntfenten one messuage and land worth 7s.; in ville Treuylyder one messuage and one acre of land Cornish worth 13s. 4d.; In ville Carwetherett one messuage and land worth 15s.; in ville Trebighan one messuage and land worth 10s.; In Lanhiderok one messuage and land worth 10s.; In ville Trefleytts one messuage and land worth 6s. 8d.; in ville Treglasta land worth 2s.; In ville Trewythek one messuage and land worth 10s.;

---

[1] Council Book of "the Black Prince," fo. 282. Duchy of Cornwall Office.

[2] This Richard Juyll was the founder of the elegant Chapel of St. Thomas the Martyr in the Churchyard at Bodmin. See ante, Vol. i., p. 184 and Plates VII. and VIII.

in ville Bodmyn one messuage and land worth 30s.; and they say he had no more lands. He was dead in 1391, for we find a suit was instituted by Thomas Peverell against William Calaway, Thomas Bere, and John Nichol and Emma his wife, and Roger Calaway, for having at Bodmyn,[2] forcibly abducted Thomas, son and heir of Roger Treffri, being within age, whose marriage belonged to the said Thomas Peverell because the said Roger held two messuages in Carwederet by homage and fealty and scutage of 40s. to the king, when it happened, and by the service of 6s. each year, and that he died in homage, and that the said Thomas had been in peaceable seizin of the said heir from Monday next before the feast of St. Peter ad Vincula 15th Richard II., until Wednesday in the same feast, when he was forcibly abducted. In the following year a suit was instituted by William Treffry, probably the brother of Roger, against the aforesaid William Calaway, John Bere, and John Nicholl and Emma his wife, executors of the will of the said Roger, in a plea of debt.[3] This Thomas, son and heir of Roger Treffry, is the same who, with Avisia his wife, is commemorated as Thomas Treffry, senior, by a brass in the Church of Fowey, unfortunately without date and destitute of the two shields of arms, which originally adorned it and served · to identify the persons to whose memory it was erected. The above Amicia is said to have been the daughter of Philip Michelstow by Margery the eldest daughter and one of the co-heirs of Robert Boniface by which marriage the Treffrys acquired a considerable portion of the Boniface estates. Thomas Treffry, senior, left a son and heir of the same name, who, in 1444, contracted marriage with Elizabeth daughter of John Colyn of Helland. In conjunction with the Burgesses of Fowey, he erected the blockhouse at the entrance to the harbour, and he built the house at Place which, during his absence, as related by Leland, his wife Elizabeth gallantly defended against the French.[4] In 1464, Thomas Treffry of Fowey made fine with the king to be allowed not to take up his knighthood, in which year, also, he received a general pardon,[5] and he was dead at Easter 1475. Elizabeth his wife survived him, and instituted a suit against John Treffry for the recovery of her dower of a third part of the manors of Tregwyed and Treffry.[6] He left three sons, the above-mentioned John, William and Thomas, and was buried at Fowey, together with his wife Elizabeth, where they were commemorated by a brass in the Church.

In 1476 John Treffry, executor of the will of Thomas Treffry of Fowey, had taken out a writ against William Dabernon of Treundyn, ffrankelyn, executor of the will of Robert Dabernon of the same place, and Henry Ley of St. Bruard, Clerk, in a plea of debt, but did not prosecute and was in mercy with his pledges.[7] In January 1478-9 we find him as John Treffry of ffowey, Gent., attached to reply William Mohun concerning the passage of the ferry of Bodenek.[8] In 1482, being the last year of King Edward IV.,

[1] De Banco Rolls 8th Richard II., Trinity, m. 329.

[2] De Banco Rolls, 15th Richard II., Easter, m. 202, and 17th Richard II., Mich., m. 319 d.

[3] Ibid. 17th Richard II., Michs. m. 295.

[4] The Frenchmen in diverse tymes assailed this town and last most notably about Henry VI. tyme, when the wife of Thomas Treury the 2nd with her men repelled the French out of her house in her husbandes absence. Leland's Itin., Vol. v., fo. 17. Hearne's Edit. [5] Rot. Fin., 4th Edward IV.

[6] De Banco Rolls, 15th Edward IV., Easter, m. 126. [7] Ibid. 16th Edward IV., Trinity, m. 325.

[8] Ibid., 18th Edward IV., Hilary, m. 456.

he was appointed Sheriff of Cornwall, and filled that office from Michaelmas in that year until the following Michaelmas in 1st Richard III.[1] The Treffrys would appear to have been of the Lancastrian party. The red rose, and other badges of that party, frequently occur in the ancient glass, and elsewhere, at Place House and in Fowey Church. John Treffry zealously supported the pretensions of the Earl of Richmond, and, accompanied probably by his brother William Treffry, hastened to meet the Earl and was present at Milford Haven to receive him on his landing on 7th August 1485, on which occasion he was dubbed a Knight.[2] Soon after Henry was established on the throne, viz., on 4th March 1485-6, he granted to Sir John Treffry, in tail male, the manor or lordship of Rode Langham, alias Redelagham, in Somerset and Wilts, and also the manor or lordship of Launden, co. Bucks, which were in the hands of the crown by reason of the attainder of John Lord Zouche, who had supported King Richard III.[3] In the same year we find him in the commission of the peace for the county of Cornwall. In 5th Henry VII. (1490) he was again appointed Sheriff, as he was also, for the third time, in 1499,[4] but he died on the 18th September in the following year before he had quite completed his third term of office.[5]

Upon the death of Sir John Treffry, the estates devolved upon his brother William. He also partook of the gratitude of the new king. Within a month after the entry of the latter into London; viz: by Privy Seal dated 21st September 1485, and by letters patent dated 16th October, he granted to William Treffry for life the offices of Surveyor of Customs and Subsidies within the city of London,[6] and on the following day, " in consideration of the services he had done at his great cost and expenses," he was granted for life the office of Controller of the Coinage of Tin in the counties of Cornwall and Devon, and the custody of the gaol at Lostwithiel.[7] His name does not appear in the pedigree recorded in the Heralds' College, but upon the death of his brother he succeeded to the

---

[1] Pipe Roll.

[2] Cotton MSS. Claudius C. III., fo. 3.

[3] Inrolled 19th January, Rot. Pat., 3rd Henry VII.

[4] Pipe Rolls.

[5] In his will, dated 24th June 1500, he directs his body to be buried within the gild near the Altar of St. Mary the Virgin in the Church of St. Finbara (? Finbar of Crimlen commemorated 5th July) of Fowey, and he gives to the building of the said Gild of St. Mary £20 sterling. He gives, *inter alia*, 22 marks to the Prior and Convent of Tywardreth to settle his name in the mortclege with their founders, and to say, after his decease four times placebo and dirige, and four masses at four times in the year for his soul and all the souls that he is bound to pray for, and after to be prayed for daily and yearly as their founders are there prayed for; and he stipulates that the Prior and Convent shall be bound to him and his heirs by the Convent seal for the performance of the same in £20. Among other similar legacies he gives £10 to the Friars of Bodmin for the same purpose. According to the above direction, we find his name in the Bede Roll of the Priory of Tywardreth under the month of September—" 7, obitus Johannis Treffry militis bone memorie, qui obiit viij id. et vij die Septemb' M.D. cujus anime propicietur Deus. Amen." (Oliver's Mon. Exon. p. 37.) The original Roll is now (1874) the property of Mr. Kerslake of Bristol. It is somewhat uncertain if Sir John Treffry left a daughter. In his will he bequeaths a piece of plate, &c., " to my son-in-law John Tregodek and to Ann his wife." This scarcely appears to be a bequest to an only child, and it is probable that John Tregodek was his step-son. This will was proved P.C.C. 19th February 1500 (Moone 20).

[6] Rot. Pat., 1st Henry VII., Part 2, m. 21.

[7] Rot. Pat., 1st Henry VII., Part 1, m. 3.

Shrievalty of Cornwall, and served the office during the following year.[1] He died[2] in 1504, and it appears that besides the above offices, he held some place in the Royal Household.[3] In addition to his possessions in Cornwall, he had lands in Coventry and Berkeley, in all of which he was succeeded by his younger brother Thomas Treffry, who by Janet his wife, daughter of William Dawe, had a son of his own name who was appointed Captain of the Castle of St. Mawes, and he held that office at the time of Leland's visit to Cornwall, who records that he had made certain inscriptions at the request of Master Trewry at the Castelle of St. Mawes.[4]

By his marriage with Elizabeth, daughter of John Kelligrew of Penryn, he acquired the estate of Rooke to him and his heirs, and she brought the family also a royal descent from King Edward I. and Margaret of France. John his son was twice married. By his second wife Emeline, daughter and co-heir of John Tresithney, he had nine sons and seven daughters. His eldest son William Treffry had a son John, who in 1648 sold the Manor of Tregoyde (see ante p. 130). Dying s.p. in 1658, his estates devolved upon Thomas Treffry of Rooke whose wife was Jane daughter of John Vivian of Trewan. His son John Treffry sold Rooke to Edward Treffry of Mevagissy. John Treffry married Katherine daughter of Henry Stephens of Fowey, and dying in 1731 s.p., devised his estates to William Toller eldest son of John Toller of Fowey, merchant, by Jane, sister of the said John Treffry, on condition that he and his issue succeeding to the property should assume and use the name and arms of Treffry only. William Toller, by Act of Parliament 8th George II., complied with this injunction, and dying in 1735 left a

---

[1] Pipe Roll.

[2] Michael Vyvyan, one of the Gentlemen Ushers of the Privy Chamber, appointed Controller of the Coinage of Tin, vice William Treffry dec. (Rot. Pat., 20th Henry VII.)

[3] The will of William Treffry, dated 1504, is a document of considerable interest, and shows that he was very rich in plate and jewels. He directs that his "body shall be buryed in the Amlatorye on the south side of Our Lady Chapel in the Church of Saynt Barre at Fowy, if it please God that I dye there, and assone as the Amlatorye ys made I will that myn Executors cause to make a tombe with three ymages, oon for my broder, another for me, and another for my wife, after their discrecions, and lyke vnto a tombe which lyeth on M. Brown, in the Croched freers in london, with the pitie of Saynt Gregory, and such sculptures as myn Executors can devise after the apparell of the same." He afterwards directs that "the tombe shall be made of the yle of Purbec Stone and sent to ffowy." We do not know if the design for this Ambulatory, or Cloister, was ever carried out, but the rude stone described by Symonds (post) was not the tomb which the testator directed to be made. He names his younger brother Thomas, and his nephews Thomas, Henry, and William, sons of Thomas, all then minors; his eldest sister, Gennet, wife of William Trevanion, and his nephew John Trevanion, whom he makes one of his executors, and he bequeaths certain money that his "biclding at ffowy may go forth according as it is begonne," adding "my nevewe John Trevanion can shew you the playnness thereof." He makes numerous bequests of plate and jewels, and gives several legacies for religious and charitable objects, inter alia, "at Tregwyte to such poore tennants as I have in that quarter iij li." Addressing his "felowe Hugh Denys, and Mr. Weston of the king's chamber, he says: "I beseche you commende me vnto my soueraine lord the king that he be good and gracious vnto my nevewes, and shew his grace that I never had non of his money vntruely in all my life." Dr. Oliver (Mon. Exon, p. 439), states that the Church of Fowey on 3rd July 1336, then described as "de nova constructa," was dedicated to St. Nicholas, but that "S. Fimbarr was patron of the old Church," nevertheless, this will and that of Sir John Treffry (ante) shew that at the beginning of the sixteenth century the ancient dedication still obtained.

[4] Itin., Vol. iii., p. 46, (Hearne's Edit.)

son Thomas Treffry, who left a son William Esco Treffry and two daughters.   Jane the eldest daughter was twice married.   By her first husband, Nicholas Austin, she had no issue.   By her second husband Thomas Dormer, she had two daughters.   Susanna Ann the second daughter married Joseph Austin, brother of her sister's first husband, and, William Esco Treffry, her brother, dying s.p., settled his estates upon her and her issue.   She had a son Joseph Thomas Austin, who, in 1836, by royal license assumed the name and arms of Treffry, and dying, unmarried, in 1850, devised his estates to his kinsman, Edward John Wilcocks, Clerk, D.C.L., the grandson of his aunt the aforesaid Jane Dormer, who, in compliance with the above-mentioned testamentary injunction, has, by royal license dated May 1850, assumed the name and arms of Treffry.

Notes on the Church of Fowey, made in 1644 by Richard Symonds.   "Diary of the Marches of the Royal Army during the Great Civil War, kept by Richard Symonds," pp. 69, 72.—Camden Society, 1859.

"In the south yle of the Chancel, the picture of a man and woman in brass, and this inscription, two shields gone (temp. Edward II. at least)":[1]

"Orate pro animabus Thome Trefry senioris armigeri et
Avisie uxoris ejus et omnium benefactorum suorum."

"Another with the pictures of a man and woman, two shields, top gone:

"Orate pro animabus Thome Trefry Armigeri filij Thome Trefry
et Elizabeth uxoris ejus et omnium filiorum (Temp. Edwardi 2di.)"[1]

"A flat stone there, the picture of a man in armes scratched in the stone; the inscription is round about imperfect.........: dyed 1590, 28th January.   Trefry, Esquire.

"TREFRY impaling a cross engrailed.

Quarterly 1 and 4 Trefry; 2 and 3, a chevron between three roses.   [TRESITHNEY.]"[2]

"Another hugh large stone, three pictures of men in armes scratcht upon the stone, these two shields, and the inscription circumscribed.

"TREFRY—Quarterly, 1 and 4 TREFRY; 2 and 3, three fleur-de-lys.

"Here lyeth the bodyes of Sir John Trefry, Knight, William Trefry, and Thomas Treffry, Esquires, bretheren; they dyed in the moneth of September, the said Sir John in the 16th yeare, the said William in the 20th yeare of the reighne of King Henry ye 7, and the said Thomas Trefry the first-yeare of the reighne of King Henry ye 8."

[1] Mr. Symonds's conjecture as these dates is probably incorrect.

[2] The stone would seem to have been recut without the incised figure, for we find in the family book a description of the slab; surrounding the margin, "Here lyeth the body of John Treffry, Esquire, who dyed the 28th of January, 1590, he had issue by Jane the Daughter of Reginald Mohun, Esquire," (and within, below the two shields of arms described above, filling the space formerly occupied by the figure) "one Daughter, and by Emblym, his second wife, the daughter of John Tresithnye Esq., nine sons and seven Daughters, for whose Godly end the Lord be Praised."   This inscription would appear to have been cut towards the end of the last century.

"Another flat stone there:

"Quarterly 1 and 4, TREFRY; 2 and 3, three lozenges, a crescent for a difference.

"Quarterly 1 and 4, TREFRY; 2 and 3, quarterly, 1 and 4, four lozenges; 2 and 3, a lion rampant.

"Quarterly 1 and 4, TREFRY; 2 and 3, on a chevron between three roundles as many (? annulets or roundles.)[1]

"Here under lyeth buried the body of Thomas Treffry, Esq., and of Elizabeth his wife, daughter of John Killigrew. Esq., the which Thomas dyed the yere 1563, the 24 of Jan., for whose godly departing the Lord be praysed. Amen."

"A course (*sic. orig.*) monument against the east of the said yle:

"TREFFRY; a mullet for a difference.

"Quarterly, 1 and 4, TREFRY; 2 and 3, MAYOW.

"Here lyeth the body of Thomas Trefry, Esq., Councellor at Law, who tooke to his wife Katherine one of the daughters and heires of Thomas Hellyer, Esq., who died the 1 of March 1635."

"Dum Deo placuerit."

"In an Escocheon on the wall over this monument aforesaid:

"TREFRY, impaling, gules, three human arms conjoined at the shoulder in the fesse point, the fists closed, argent." [TREMAYNE.]

"This is also in a paper (*sic. orig.*) on the wall:

"A shield of nine coats, viz.: 1, TREFRY; 2, argent, an eagle displayed sable, within a bordure (KILLIGREW); 3, argent, a fret raguly sable; 4, MICHELSTOWE; 5, a chevron between three eagles' heads erased; 6, gules, three fleur-de-lys or; 7, vert, on a bend three [? doves volant[2]]; 8, gules, 3 mascles or [? argent]; 9, TRESITHNEY; impaling, quarterly, 1 TREMAYNE; 2, or, a chevron azure between three escalops; 3, argent, a saltier azure between four cross crosslets fitchy; 4, argent, on a chevron between three "hogs" sable, three roses of the field.

"WILLIAM TREFRY and URSULA his wife.

"There hang two pennons, mantle, helme, and crest, old:

"On a wreath, an eagle's head erased sable, holding in the beak an oak branch slipped vert." [Crest of TREFRY.]

---

[1] Ar. on a chevron sa. between three torteauxes, as many bezants. BOLIGH (Heralds' College, C. 1. 471.) Killigrew married Boligh.

[2] Should be "daws," for Dawe of Plymouth.

2 L

EVIDENCES IN SUPPORT OF THE PEDIGREE OF TREFFRY OF FOWEY.

No. 1.

Ceste endenture fait perentre Richard Juyl, Merchaunt de Bodmyn dun part et Roger Treury fitz et heir Johan Treury dautre part, tesmoigne qe le dit Richard Juyl doyt trouer le dit Roger et Maude sa femme a son table de mesne honestement del jour del confeccion de cestes tanqe le iour de Seynt George prochain ensuaunt et eux vestier encountre le feste de Nowell, Roger a sa seute de mesne et Maude al saute sa miere. Et quant le dit Roger se propose daler a soun mesoun de mesne le dit Roger (*sic* for Richard) eux apparila de vesture et de lit pour soun Chambre honestement come appertient a son degre. Et a ces couenauntȝ bien et loialment destre tenuȝ et performez les parties avaunt dit obligent euz lour heires et lour executours: en tesmonaunce de quel chose les partiez avauntditȝ entrechaungeablement ount mys lour seals. Tesmoigne John Lange, mere de Bodmyn, John Symon, Roger Martyn, John ffol, John Jowy, John Richard et altres. Done a Bodmyn le Vendirdy prochein deuant le feste del Nativite Seynt John le Baptiste lan du regne le Roy Richard le second apres le conqueste Dengleterre Tierce (1397.)

No. 2.

Sciant, &c., quod ego Oto Colyn Armiger dedi, &c. Thome Treffry filio et heredi Thome Treffry de Fowy et Elizabetæ uxori sue sorori mee totum manerium meum de Penvrayn cum omnibus suis pertinentiis, &c., habendum, &c., perfato Thome filio et heredi predicti Thome et Elizabetæ uxori sue sorori mee et heredibus de corporibus eorum legitime ex-euntibus de me et heredibus meis, &c. In cuius, &c. Hiis testibus Otone Nycoll, Thoma Bere, Roberto Dyer, Johanne Smale, Johanne ffenell Capellano et aliis. Datum apud Bodmyniam die Veneris proximo ante festum Sancti Georgii Martyris, anno Regni Henrici sexti post conquestum Anglie vicesimo quinto (22 April 1447).

No. 3.

Omnibus, &c., Elizabeta relicta Johannis Colyn salutem, &c. Noveritis me prefatam Elizabetam in pura viduitate mea et libera protestate remississe, &c., Thome Treffry filio et heredi Thome Treffry de ffowy et Elizabete uxori sue filie mee et heredibus inter eos legitime procreatis totum ius meum, &c., ratione dotis mee Manerii de Penffrayn cum suis pertinentiis, &c. In cuius, &c. Hiis testibus Thoma Bera, Roberto Dyer, Johanne Smale et aliis. Datum Bodmyniam penultimo die Maij anno regni Regis Henrici sexti post conquestum Anglie vicesimo quinto (30 May 1447).

No. 4.

Omnibus, &c. Johannes Kyllygrew de Ardwennek Armiger filius et heres Johannis Killygrew nuper de Penryn Armigeri defuncti salutem. Cum in quibusdam Indenturis ante hac inter quendam Thomam Treffry Seniorem Armigerum defunctum ex parte vna et predictum Johannem Kyllygrewe patrem meum ex altera parte, conuentum fuit de et super quoddam maritagium inter quendam Thomam Treffrye juniorem Armigerum tunc filium et heredem apparentem dicti Thome Treffrye senioris et quandam Elizabetham vnam filiarum dicti Johannis Kellygrew patris mei habendum et celebrandum prout in dictis Indenturis gerentibus...........vicesimo nono die Septembris anno R. Domini Regis Henrici septimi post conquestum Anglie vicesimo primo magis plene liquet et apparet. Sciatis me prefatum Johannem Kellygrew in.................dictis indentur' et specificat' ex parte dicti patris mei et heredum suorum superimplend' dedisse, &c., prefato Thome Treffry filio omnia illa mesuagia, &c., &c., in Rowcok in Comitatu Cornubiæ habenda et tenenda omnia predicta mesuagia terras tenementa et molendina, &c., prefato Thome Treffry filio et heredibus de corporibus eiusdem Thome et dictæ Elizabethæ quondam vxoris eiusdem Thome sed modo defunctæ legitime procreatis imperpetuum, &c., Datum 1° Marcii Anno R. D. Edwardi VI. 3°.

TREFFRY OF MEVAGISSEY AND OF ROOKE.

We are unable to connect this family with that of Treffry of Fowey, from whom Edward Treffry of Mevagissey purchased Rooke about 1711, though they claim descent. The parish registers of Mevagissey do not shew that the Treffrys were of long standing in that parish, for, with the exception of the burial of a Collambe Trefry in 1603, the name is not traced to occur until the baptism of the eldest son of the above-mentioned Edward Treffry in 1700. Edward Treffry had several other children baptized there between that date and 1707, soon after which he removed to Rooke. He is said to have had a younger brother, named Thomas, who married Jane only daughter of......... Roskelly, and to have had issue Richard, Thomas, Henry, and Anne. Anne died young; Richard married the daughter of William Thomas of Trenkreek in Veryan, and left issue. Thomas died a bachelor, but Henry married.[1] Of this branch we have no further information. For the issue of Edward Treffry we refer to the pedigree, page 256.

---

[1] MS. at Place, Fowey, compiled by John Treffry of Rooke who died 1787, and which is in many respects inaccurate.

2 L²

1. TREFFRY.
2. FLAMANK.
3. KILLIGREW.
4. POLGRENE.
5. BONIFACE.
6. MICHAELSTOW.
7. SEARLE.
8. GIFFARD.
9. DAWE.
10. KILLIGREW.
11. TRESITHNEY.
12. TREMAYNE.

PEDIGREE OF TREFFRY

EDWARD I., King, of England.=Margaret, dau. of PHILIP IV., King of France.

Edmund of Woodstock, 6th son, Earl of Kent, beh. 1329.=Margaret, dau. of John Lord Wake.

Thomas Holland, Earl of Kent, died 1360.=Joan Plantagenet, "The Fair Maid of Kent," heir of her brothers.

Sir Oliver Carminow, bur. at Grey Friars, Bodmin, 1345.=Elizabeth Holland, bur. at Grey Friars, Bodmin, 1332.

Sir John Petit, Lord of Trenerth, died 1362. (Inq. 6th Richard II., No. 267.)=Johanna, dau. of Sir Oliver Carminow.

Sir Michael Petit, aged 30 years on his father's death.=Amicia, dau. of Sir John Bloyou, by Margaret, dau. and heir of John Tynten. (Inq. p.m., of her grandson, John Petit).

John Petit of Ardevora.=Margaret, dau. and heir of Ralph Resoryk.

John Petit of Ardevora, died 10th June 1455. (Inq. p.m., 33rd Henry VI., No. 27.)=Margaret, dau. of Ralph Trenowith of Trenowith.

John Kelligrew of Penryn.=Jane, dau. and coh. Relict of Thomas Trevanion.

Elizabeth, dau. of John Kelligrew of Penryn, mar. settl. 29th September, 21st Henry VII. Deed No. 4 ante. Dead 3rd Edward VI., Bur.[1] M.I.=Thomas Treffry, son and heir of Thomas Treffry, named in will of uncle William. Capt. of St. Mawe's Castle, 3rd Edward VI., Knt. of the Shire for Cornw. 1555. Died 31st January 1563, bur.[1] M.I.

Jane, dau. of Reginald Mohun, 1st wife.=John Treffry of Treffry, son and heir, Died 27th January 1590-1 (Inq. p.m., 33rd Elizabeth, Part 1, No. 59.) Bur.[1]=Emblen, dau. and coh. of John Tresithney, 2nd wife. Bur.[1] 30th June 1604.

| Loro, mar. .... Trenewith of Trene-with. | William Treffry of Treffry, son and heir, bap.[1] 18th Feby. 1559, aged 30 years on his father's death. Mar. settl. 12th Janv. 1558-9; Burg. in Parl. for Fowey 1584 and 1596.=Ursula, dau. and coh. of William Tremayne of Upcott, co. Devon, mar.[1] 3rd April 1589. | Tresith-ney. bap.[1] 23rd July 1571. | Deborra, bap.[1] 30th April 1570, mar.[1] 1609 Henry Peters. | Matthew Treffry of Foy, 2nd son, bap.[1] 20th Feb. 1566. Of Rooke in St. Kew, bur.[2] 3rd Nov. 1626.=Elizabeth, dau. of John Sumaster of Peinsford, bur.[2] 19th September 1656. | Sara, bap.[1] 25th June 1568. |

a

b

[1] At Fowey.   [2] At St. Kew.

OF FOWEY AND ROOKE.

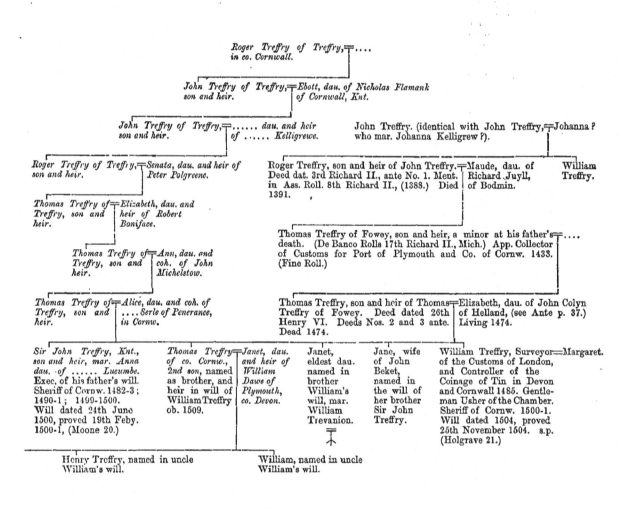

Roger Treffry of Treffry, ⫪ ....
in co. Cornwall.

John Treffry of Treffry, ⫪ Ebott, dau. of Nicholas Flamank
son and heir. | of Cornwall, Knt.

John Treffry of Treffry, ⫪ ...... dau. and heir | John Treffry. (identical with John Treffry, ⫪ Johanna ?
son and heir. | of ...... Kelligrewe. | who mar. Johanna Kelligrew ?). | William Treffry.

Roger Treffry of Treffry, ⫪ Senata, dau. and heir of | Roger Treffry, son and heir of John Treffry. ⫪ Maude, dau. of
son and heir. | Peter Polgreene. | Deed dat. 3rd Richard II., ante No. 1. Ment. | Richard Juyll,
in Ass. Roll. 8th Richard II., (1388.) Died | of Bodmin.
1391.

Thomas Treffry of ⫪ Elizabeth, dau. and | Thomas Treffry of Fowey, son and heir, a minor at his father's ⫪ ....
Treffry, son and | heir of Robert | death. (De Banco Rolls 17th Richard II., Mich.) App. Collector
heir. | Boniface. | of Customs for Port of Plymouth and Co. of Cornw. 1433.
(Fine Roll.)

Thomas Treffry of ⫪ Ann, dau. and | Thomas Treffry, son and heir of Thomas ⫪ Elizabeth, dau. of John Colyn
Treffry, son and | coh. of John | Treffry of Fowey. Deed dated 26th | of Helland, (see Ante p. 37.)
heir. | Michelstow. | Henry VI. Deeds Nos. 2 and 3 ante. | Living 1474.
Dead 1474.

Thomas Treffry of ⫪ Alice, dau. and coh. of
Treffry, son and | .... Serle of Penerance,
heir. | in Cornw.

Sir John Treffry, Knt., | Thomas Treffry ⫪ Janet, dau. | Janet, | Jane, wife | William Treffry, Surveyor ⫪ Margaret.
son and heir, mar. Anna | of co. Cornw., | and heir of | eldest dau. | of John | of the Customs of London,
dau. of ...... Lucumbe. | 2nd son, named | William | named in | Beket, | and Controller of the
Exec. of his father's will. | as brother, and | Dawe of | brother | named in | Coinage of Tin in Devon
Sheriff of Cornw. 1482-3 ; | heir in will of | Plymouth, | William's | the will of | and Cornwall 1485. Gentle-
1490-1 ; 1499-1500. | William Treffry | co. Devon. | will, mar. | her brother | man Usher of the Chamber.
Will dated 24th June | ob. 1509. | | William | Sir John | Sheriff of Cornw. 1500-1.
1500, proved 19th Feby. | | | Trevanion. | Treffry. | Will dated 1504, proved
1500-1, (Moone 20.) | | | | | 25th November 1504. s.p.
(Holgrave 21.)

Henry Treffry, named in uncle | William, named in uncle
William's will. | William's will.

| Martha, bap.[1] 14th March 1572; mar. Thomas Dickwood alias Peters June 1594, mother of the notorious Hugh Peters; bap.[1] 29th June 1598. | Henry, bap, 2nd Feby. 1575. Abel, bap.[1] 15th Octr. 1577. | Rebecca, bap.[1] 29th March 1579. | Mary, bap.[1] 1st April 1581. | Henry, bap.[1] 20th June 1583. | Benjamin, bap. 26th June 1585. | Thomas Treffry of. Lostwithiel ⫪ Katherine, Councellor at Law; Mayor of Lostwithiel 1604, 1625, 1631; died 1st March 1635, will dated 6th February 1631. (Inq. p.m. 12th Charles, bundle 58, No. 226, Wards and Liveries). Bur.[1] M.I. | dau. and coh. of Thomas Hellyer alias Mayow of Lostwithiel. |

c

[1] At Fowey.   [2] At St. Kow.

a

John Treffry of Treffry, son and heir, bap.[1] 26th January 1594; Matric. at Exeter Coll. Oxf. 14th June 1611, æt. 16. Bur. 24th Sept. 1658,s.p.Burg. in Parl. for Fowey 1620. == Bridget, dau. of Sir Philip Champernon of Modbury, Knt. Mar.[2] 17th October 1619, bur. 15th April 1650.

Mary, bap.[1] July 1593.

Emeline, 2nd, bap., 20th August 1596, bur.[1] 23rd October 1644; Adm° to only sister Ursula, wife of Thomas Trefusis 8th December 1656.

Bridget, 3rd.

Jane, bap. 5th March 1591, mar.[1] John Trefusis 29th May 1611.

Ursula, bap.[1] 23rd January 1603; mar. Thomas Trefusis.

William, bap.[1] 20th March 1605.

John Tollar of Fowey, son of William Tollar of the same place; bur.[1] 21st October 1652. == Jane Treffry, bap.[2] 28th May 1646, bur.[1] March 1701.

Mary, bap.[2] 3rd April 1644, bur.[2] 22nd November 1676.

Bridget, bap.[2] 4th March 1647, bur.[2] 30th April 1650.

Thomas Treffry, died s.p.

...... dau. of ...... Fortescue of Spiddleston, co, Devon. 1st wife. == William Tollar of Fowey, bap.[1] 27th Dec. 1676; assumed the name and arms of Treffry by Act of Parl. 8th George II. Bur.[1] 5th March 1735. Will dated 15th February 1735. == Rebecca, dau. and coh. of John Weymouth relict of Daniel Hyde, Clerk, Vicar of Barnstaple, who died 1709; also relict of ...... Mason, 2nd wife.

John, bap.[1] 6th Sept. 1714, bur. July 1715.

Henry, bap.[1] 1717, bur.[1] May 1719.

Thomas Treffry of Place, bap.[1] 1724. Sheriff of Cornwall 1766. Bur.[1] 12th December 1776. == Susanna, dau. of Thomas Pipon, Mercht. and Alderman of Fowey.

William Esco Treffry, bur. 19th November 1779.

Nicholas Austin, Lieut. R.N., youngest son of Jacob Austen, s.p. == Jane Treffry, eld. dau. and coh., bap.[1] 11th August 1747, bur.[1] 3rd December 1786. == Thomas Dormer, mar.[1] 15th March 1782, bur.[1] 22nd May 1800.

...... Mills of Warkleigh. == Susan Treffry Dormer, dau. and coh.

Edward Wilcocks of Exeter, born 3rd January 1785, mar. at Warkleigh, co. Devon. Bur. at Jersey. == Jane Treffry Dormer, dau. and coh., born 24th August 1785, mar. 22nd September 1806, bur.[1] 11th March 1864, aged 78. M.I.

Jane Treffry, born 21st July 1807, mar. 10th February 1835, James Jones.

Selina Dormer, born 31st December 1810, died 10th January 1811.

Ellen Dormer, born 25th February 1812, died 9th September 1830, unmar.

Henry Dormer, born 24th July 1815, mar. ...... dau. of .... Pengelly, and relict of ...... Oxenbury.

Thomas Austin Treffry, born 21st September 1819, mar. 1st July 1847 Elizabeth Mary, dau. of ...... Joyce.

Edward, born 21st Sept. 1838, died 21st September 1844, bur.[3]

Ann Ellen, born[3] 16th April 1840, mar.[1] 24th July 1866 Handfield Noel Purcell, Clerk, now (1874) Vicar of Fowey.

Charles Edward, born[3] 1st May 1842. == Baroness Udney Von Bretton, dau. of Baron Joseph Von Bretton. Mar. at St. George's, Hanover Square, 30th August 1866.

George Steel, born[4] 12th Feby. 1844.

Reginald Heber, Clerk, born[4] 30th March 1846.

Blakeley von Bretton, born at Padstow, 11th August 1867.

Edward Treffry, born at Newquay, 1st March 1869.

Florence, born at Newquay, 5th March 1871.

---

[1] At Fowey.   [2] At St. Kew.   [o] At St. Mary's, Scilly Islands.   [4] At Berkhamstead, Herts.

b   *c*

Thomas Treffry, eld. son, æt. 13 1620; of Rooke and of Fowey. Bur.[1] 21st October 1604,	*Jane, dau, of John Vivian of Trewan; mar, settl. 28th April 1641; bur.[2] 2nd December 1654, see Ped. of CAVELL and VIVIAN ante p. 163.*	*Elizabeth,* bap.[2] 18th March 1606.	*Jane,* bap.[2] 14th March 1607.	*John Treffry* bap.[2] 1st June 1608.	*Mary, dau.* of ...... Bowdon, mar.[1] 20th June 1634, bur.[1] 12th July 1672.	*Emlyn, mar. Nicholas Kendall of Pelyn; aged 30 years on her fath's. death.* *Blanche, aged 22 years on her father's death; mar. Thomas Wood of Orchardon, Devon.*

(Thomas Treffry = Jane; John Treffry = Mary)

John Treffry of Fowey, bap. 28th March 1650; Matric. at Exeter Coll. Oxf. 10th July 1668 æt. 17. Burg. in Parl. for Fowey 1679 and 1685. Sold Rooke to Edward Treffry cir. 1711; bur.[1] 2nd April 1731. s.p.	Katherine, dau. of Henry Stephens of Fowey; bur.[1] March 1724.	Martha, bap. 3rd July 1652, mar.[1] John Hamley of Trefreake 26th November 1673, s.p. (See Ped. ante Vol. i., p. 577.)	Elizabeth, mar. ... . Spry; will dated 15th Dec. 1743, s.p.

(John Treffry = Katherine)

John Tollar.   Mary.

Elizabeth, bap.[1] 14th October 1715, bur.[1] July 1715.	Jane, bap.[1] 26th February 1716.	Margaret, bap.[1] 5th July 1719.	Rebecca, bap.[1] 5th June 1720.	William, bap.[1] 7th October 1720, bur.[1] November 1721.

Elizabeth, bap. 23rd October 1739, bur.[1] August 1753.	Rebecca, bur.[1] May 1747.	Susanna Ann, 2nd dau. and coh. bap.[1] 6th October 1748, mar.[1] 17th April 1780, bur.[1] 15th December 1850.	Joseph Austin, son and heir of Jacob Austin of Plymouth.

(Susanna Ann = Joseph Austin)

Susanna, born at Plymouth 7th Jany. 1784, bur.[1] 14th June 1800.	Sarah Shaw, born 20th February 1788; died young.	Joseph Thomas Austin, bap. at Plymouth 1st May 1782. By Royal License dated 23rd February 1836 assumed the name and arms of TREFFRY. Sheriff of Cornwall same year. Bur.[1] 29th January 1850. Will proved 5th April 1850.

Edward John Wilcocks, Clerk, D.C.L., of Place, Fowey, bap. at St. Sidwell's, Exeter, 8th May 1809. By Royal Licence dat. 16th May 1850, assumed the name and arms of TREFFRY in conformity with the testamentary injunction of his cousin Joseph Thomas Treffry.	Ann, dau. of Charles Steel, Inspecting Commander of H.M. Coast Guard. Born 19th October 1815 at Harwich, Essex; mar. at St. Mary's, Scilly Isles, 30th August 1835.	Charles Treffry Dormer, born 12th June 1821, mar. 1st May 1849 Jane, dau. of ...... Boultbee.

(Edward John Wilcocks = Ann)

Harry, born[4] 8th March 1848.	Zoe, born[4] 11th Dec. 1849.	Joseph Thomas, born[1] 29th December 1851.	Edward Lambert, born[1] 29th April 1854.	Spencer Thornton, born[1] 14th December 1856.	Maria Stuart, born[1] 4th December 1860.	John de Cressy, born[4] 3rd April 1859.

I hereby certify that the portions of this Pedigree printed in *Italics*, and the Arms agree with the Records of this Office.

Heralds' College,   STEPHEN TUCKER,
23rd March, 1874.   *Rouge Croix.*

---

[1] At Fowey.   [2] At St. Kew.   [3] At St. Mary's, Scilly Islands.   [4] At Berkhamstead, Herts.

PEDIGREE OF TREFFRY OF ROOKE.

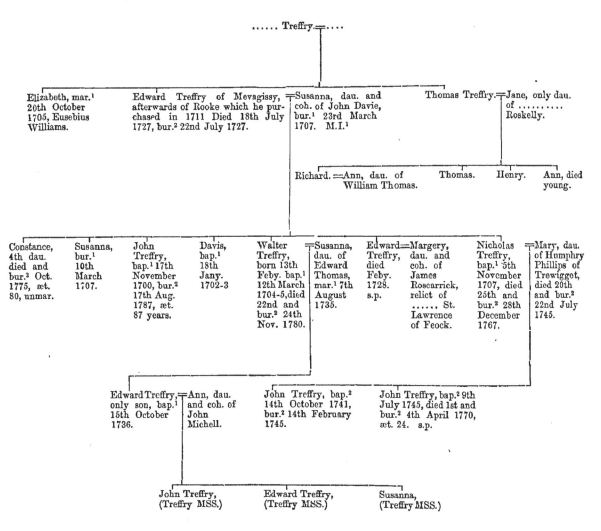

...... Treffry.=....

Elizabeth, mar.[1] 20th October 1705, Eusebius Williams.

Edward Treffry of Mevagissy, afterwards of Rooke which he purchased in 1711 Died 18th July 1727, bur.[2] 22nd July 1727.=Susanna, dau. and coh. of John Davie, bur.[1] 23rd March 1707. M.I.[1]

Thomas Treffry.=Jane, only dau. of .... Roskelly.

Richard.=Ann, dau. of William Thomas. Thomas. Henry. Ann, died young.

Constance, 4th dau. died and bur.[2] Oct. 1775, æt. 80, unmar.

Susanna, bur.[1] 10th March 1707.

John Treffry, bap.[1] 17th November 1700, bur.[2] 17th Aug. 1787, æt. 87 years.

Davis, bap.[1] 18th Jany. 1702-3

Walter Treffry, born 13th Feby. bap.[1] 12th March 1704-5, died 22nd and bur.[2] 24th Nov. 1780.=Susanna, dau. of Edward Thomas, mar.[1] 7th August 1735.

Edward Treffry, died Feby. 1728. s.p.=Margery, dau. and coh. of James Roscarrick, relict of ...... St. Lawrence of Feock.

Nicholas Treffry, bap.[1] 5th November 1707, died 25th and bur.[2] 28th December 1767.=Mary, dau. of Humphry Phillips of Trewiggot, died 20th and bur.[2] 22nd July 1745.

Edward Treffry, only son, bap.[1] 15th October 1736.=Ann, dau. and coh. of John Michell.

John Treffry, bap.[2] 14th October 1741, bur.[2] 14th February 1745.

John Treffry, bap.[2] 9th July 1745, died 1st and bur.[2] 4th April 1770, æt. 24. s.p.

John Treffry, (Treffry MSS.)

Edward Treffry, (Treffry MSS.)

Susanna, (Treffry MSS.)

[1] At Mevagissy.　　　　[2] At St. Kew.

INCH.

The family of Inch was settled in this parish at an early period. Richard Ynch held Hale of the Prior and Convent of Plympton, as of their Manor of Lanowseynt, in 8th Henry IV. (1406).[1] In the beginning of the sixteenth century the Inches were people of some substance and consideration in the parish. In the Return (Appx. II.) William Inch appears as possessing goods of the value of £20 and arms for one man, and Robert Inch is returned for £7. In 1525, William Inch was assessed to the subsidy upon goods of the value of £20,[2] as he was also again in 1546,[3] and members of the family continued to be assessed upon goods at the highest rates in the parish down to the end of the reign of Queen Elizabeth. In the reign of James I., William Inch farmed the Manor of Lanow of the Crown at the rent of £20 per annum,[4] and in 1622 this William Inch is for the first time assessed *upon lands;*[5] and the same name appears upon the Rolls until 1641.

William Inch of St. Kew by his will, dated in 1635, gave £10 to be invested and the proceeds to be applied towards the repair of the Church of St. Kew; and he also gave £20 to be invested for the benefit of the poor of the parish. He further made similar bequests to several other parishes. Dying in 1637, s.p., he bequeathed the residue of his property to his nephew William Inch, son of his brother Robert. This William presented to the Vicarage of St. Kew in 1639 (ante p. 111,) and he was one of the Trustees of the parish lands in 1642-3 (p. 114).

Some members of this family settled at Camelford. In 1753, William Inch married Arminel one of the daughters and coheirs of Robert Hodge of that town. This lady and her sister Ann Hodge in 1804, as cousins and coheirs of Mary the relict of Nicholas Connock of Treworgey, in St. Cleer, inherited her estates which had been settled upon her by her husband, who died 1757 s.p. She was the daughter of Ambrose Hodge of Stoke Damerel, brother of the aforesaid Robert. Upon the death of Ann Hodge, the survivor of the sisters, the property passed by bequest to her niece Ann Inch,[6] who dying in 1826 unmarried, it devolved, under a settlement, upon the present possessor, William Marshall of Treworgey Esq., son and heir of the Rev. Lewis Marshall, Vicar of Davidstow and Rector of Warleggan, by Arminel sister of the said Mrs. Ann Inch.

John Inch, son of another William Inch and Susanna his wife, was Mayor of Camelford in 1805, and died one of the Aldermen of the borough in 1821, aged 77.

[1] Ante p. 88.

[2] Subs. Roll. 16th Henry VIII. — $\frac{87}{131}$

[3] Ibid 37th Henry VIII. — $\frac{87}{179}$

[4] Ministers' Accounts, Cornw.

[5] Subs. Roll, 20th James — $\frac{88}{289}$

[6] C. S. Gilbert says this lady was the lineal descendant of William Inch of Lanow in St. Kew, and that the arms of Inch are: Ar. 3 torteaux in bend between two cotises sa. (History of Cornwall, Vol. ii, p. 948 note †). We know of no authority however for these Arms.

2 M

LYNHAM *alias* LYNAM.

The name of Lynam has existed in the parish of St. Kew, and in the neighbouring parishes, from an early date. Our first notice of it is in 1341, when Henry Cavel and Alice his wife suffered a fine to Margery, daughter of John Lynham, concerning one messuage and one carucate of land in Northbertiscote, whereby the said land was settled upon the said Henry and Alice during the life of Alice at the rent of one rose, and after her death to revert to the said Margery and her heirs quit of the heirs of the said Alice.[1]

John Lynam was one of the jurors upon the Inquisition post-mortem of Otho Colyn, held at Lostwithiel on 20th August 1466.[2]

The family would seem to have been very numerous in the early part of the fifteenth century, and to have held a substantial position. On reference to Appendix II., it will be seen that five persons of the name were returned for the parish of St. Kew, three of them possessing arms for one man each; and one is returned as poor and not assessable. In 1525, Richard Lynam was assessed to the subsidy upon goods in St. Kew of the value of 40s., and Henry Lynam upon 10s. in St. Teath.[3] These were small assessments, and it is difficult to account for the disappearance of the names found in the Return of two or three years earlier. It is the more remarkable, inasmuch as in 1543 Robert Lynam is assessed upon goods of the value of £17, almost the highest rate in the parish, and George Lynam upon £4.[4] Two years afterwards, Robert Lynam was assessed at the same rate as before, and John Lynam upon £16.[5]

The above-mentioned Robert is the person who heads the pedigree recorded at the Heralds' Visitation of 1620,[6] and was, perhaps, the son of Henry Lynam, whose name, as well as his own, appears in Appendix II. His son, John Lynam, described in the Parish Register as " of Penpont," was buried in 1574, leaving, together with three daughters, a son, Richard Lynam, who registered his pedigree in 1620. He had two sons, John and Richard; the latter became Vicar of Quethiock, where he died in 1657, leaving by his wife Elizabeth, daughter of Henry Chiverton of Trehunsey in that parish,[7] many children, most of whom were, however, dead s.p. before 1676. By his will he bequeathed to his first born son, Richard Lynam, his estate in Rosenvallen in St. Kew, and the choice of his books to the value of £5.[8] Richard, however, died s.p. before 1668.

---

[1] Pedes Finium, 15th Edward III., Trinity, No. 3.

[2] Inq. p.m., 6th Edward IV., No. 36.

[3] Sub. Roll, 16th Henry VIII. — $\frac{87}{131}$

[4] Ibid, 35th Henry VIII. — $\frac{87}{154}$

[5] Ibid, 37th Henry VIII. — $\frac{87}{179}$

[6] Heralds' Coll., 2. C. 1., fo. 412. *b.*

[7] Henry Chiverton, grandfather of this Henry, acquired Trehunsey by marriage with Alice, daughter and heir of ...... Kingdon of that place. ARMS OF CHIVERTON: Ar. on a mound vert a castle triple-towered sa. KINGDON: ar. a chev. sa. betw. 3 magpies ppr.

[8] He appointed his brother-in-law Richard Chiverton, Alderman of London, overseer of his will. Richard

John, the eldest son of Richard Lynam of Penpont, married Charity, eldest daughter of Humphry Prideaux of Crediton, (see Prideaux Ped., ante p. 225) and Richard his eldest son was nine years of age in 1620. He had two other sons then living, Matthew and John, and another, named Philip, born afterwards. Richard, last mentioned, was twice married. After his second marriage he resided at Cant in St. Minver,[1] in which parish all his children by that marriage were baptized, nevertheless, he was brought to St. Kew for burial. His relict, Joane, after his death returned to Penpont, where she died in 1680.[2] In 1653 a fine was levied in which Richard Lynam was querist, and Robert Myll deforc., concerning the fourth part of two messuages in Porthylly greys and Porthylly eglos, in the parish of St. Minver.[3]

Richard Lynam, by his first marriage, had an only son, John Lynam, who married Helen, daughter of Thomas Pyne of Dunsbeare, co. Devon, and by his marriage settlement, dated 29th July 1677, settled Cant, Porthylly and Treverrow in St. Minver, and a moiety of Trewethan in St. Kew. He had five daughters born to him, of whom, Diana married Charles Nation of St. Kew; of the others we are unable to give any further information. He had also a son who succeeded him at Cant, and died in 1765, apparently s.p., his widow surviving him thirty years. There was also a Jacob Lynam resident in St. Minver in the middle of the eighteenth century, he may have been a brother of the last mentioned John, though we have failed to identify him.[4]

Matthew Lynam, next brother of the last abovementioned Richard, after the baptisms of his three elder children, settled in Egloshayle. In 1677, as Matthew Lynam of Egloshayle, Gent., he was trustee under the marriage settlement of his nephew, John Lynam of Cant. Besides daughters he had two sons, Matthew and Thomas; the latter was a sailor on board H.M.S. "Antelope," and died in 1692, s.p. Matthew lived to 1735, but we have no trace that he had issue.

Philip, younger son of John Lynam and Charity Prideaux, it is believed settled in

---

Chiverton belonged to the Skinner's company, to which company by his will dated 15th December 1677, (Prov. P.C.C. 25th November 1679. King, 146), he gave "£100 to be bestowed in plate and kept in remembrance of him." He was Sheriff of London and Middlesex in 1650-1, and Lord Mayor in 1657-8. On the 29th October 1657, a pageant was performed in his honour at the cost of the Company, entitled "*Londinum Triumpham.*" He was knighted by King Charles II., on 12th October 1663. It is believed he was the first Cornishman who was ever Lord Mayor of London. Sir Richard Chiverton left two daughters and coheirs, Elizabeth who married John Coryton, Esq., who afterwards succeeded his father in the Baronetcy, and Anne who married Francis Charleton, Esq.

[1] By deed dated 14th August 8th James, (1610), William Matthew of Endellion, gent., granted to Richard Lynam of Penpont, gent. a lease of a close of land in Cant, in St. Minver, for a term of 99 years, if John Lynam, Richard Lynam, and Katherine Lynam, sons and daughter of the said Richard Lynam, or either of them, so long should live.

[2] "Domina Joane Lynam de Penpont, sepulta 28° die Junii 1680." (St. Kew, Par. Reg.)

[3] Pedes Finium 1653, Michs.

[4] We find the following entries in the St. Minver Register:

1749, Jacob Lynam and Mary Kent were married 31st December.
1750, John, son of Jacob Lynam and Mary his wife, bap. 14th October.
1751, John, son of Jacob Lynam, buried 14th December.
1752, William, son of Jacob Lynam and Mary his wife, bap. 22nd March.
1754, John, son of Jacob Lynam and Mary his wife, bap. 20th May.

2 M²

London, and died before 1688. It appears from the will of his widow, dated in that year, that he had three sons and a daughter, of whom William, the eldest son, was supposed by his mother, when she made her will, to be dead.

There were other branches of the same family, descended probably from younger sons, settled in St. Kew and the adjoining parishes, which we have no sufficient evidence to connect with the Visitation pedigree. A Richard Lynam is described in the Parish Register, under the year 1564, when he had a daughter baptized, as "Richard Lynam de Treverin," also in other places called Treverian. He was, perhaps, a younger son of Robert, who heads the Visitation pedigree. From this Richard we trace the following descents:

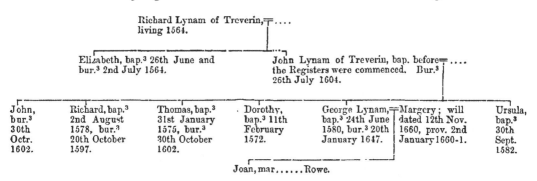

We also find a Richard Lynam of Trewitherd, in Endellion, which is not far distant from Treverin, who was probably grandson of the abovementioned Richard, as in his will he mentions his cousin, George Lynam, whom we can identify with George Lynam of Treverin. We can trace four descents of this line ending in an only daughter who married .... Henwood. The loss of the early Registers of the parish of Endellion increases our difficulty in respect to this branch.

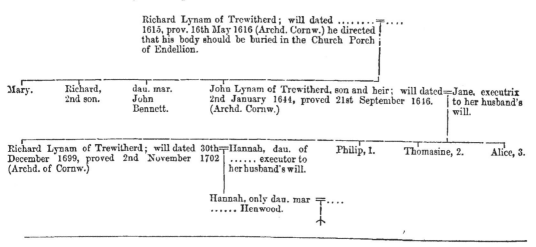

---

³ At St. Kew.

There was also a William Lynam of Tregavern in Endellion, who died in 1625. He was probably a brother of the first Richard of Trewitherd. We can, by Wills and Parish Registers, trace his descendants for five generations.

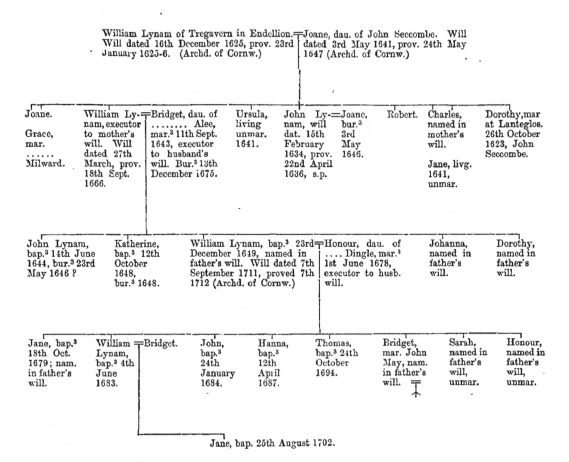

Jane, bap. 25th August 1702.

There are numerous entries in the Parish Registers of St. Kew, extending down to a recent date, which we have been unable to appropriate.

A branch of the family was also settled in St. Teath, in the middle of the sixteenth century.

[3] At St. Kew.

PEDIGREE OF

Henry Lynam, living⊤‥‥
1520, see Appendix II.

Robert Lynam of St. Kew in co. Cornw.⊤‥‥
Assessed to Subs. in St. Kew, 33rd
and 37th Henry VIII.

John Lynam of St. Kew, son and heir,⊤Johanna, dau. of ‥‥‥
assessed to Subs. in St. Kew 3rd Edward │ Blewett of Eggleshayle,
VI., of Penpont, bur.[1] 28th April 1547. │ bur.[1] 4th March 1602.

Martha, wife of   Elizabeth, wife of
John Newton of   John Hamm of
Eggleshayle.   Dewstone.

Frances, bap.[1] 4th July 1595.	Ursula, bap.[1] 9th April, bur.[1] 12th August 1587.	John Lynam, son and heir, æt. 30 years 1620, bap.[1] July 1589.⊤Charity, dau. of Humphry Prideaux of Kirton, bur.[1] 17th October 1663.

Anne, dau. of ‥‥‥ bur.[1] 1st March 1648, 1st wife.⊤Richard Lynam, son and heir, æt. 9, 1620, bur.[1] 27th January 1673.	Johanna, dau. of ‥‥‥ bur.[1] 28th June 1680, will dated 9th June 1680, prov. 27th June 1681.	John, 3rd, bap.[1] 27th March 1618.	Matthew Lynam, 2nd, bap.[1] 29th Decem. 1615, bur.[1] Novem. 1690.⊤‥‥	Johanna.	Martha, bur.[1] 11th Dec. 1651. Ursula, bap.[1]18th April 1625.	Katherine, bap.[1] 20th Jan. 1627. Thomasine, bap.[1] 14th Oct. 1620.	Philip, bap. 24th Nov. 1629, of St. Paul's, Covent Garden, London, died before 1688.	Sarah. Will dated 18th December 1688, prov. 2nd Jany. 1688-9 (Ent. 12).

Mary, bap.[1] 27th August 1642, mar.[2] Richard Fillis of St. Minver, 12th July 1664.	John Lynam, bap.[1] 28th February 1643, of Cant, in St. Minver; bur.[2] 22nd December 1698. Adm⁰ to Peter Day of St. Columb, Helen, relict of dec., having renounced, 28th April 1699.⊤Helen, dau. of Thomas Pyne of Dunsbeare, co. Devon, mar. settl. 29th July 1677. Will prov. 17th April 1737 (Archd. Cornw.)	Agnes, bap.[1] 9th June 1645, mar.[2] Edward Cornish, Clerk, 30th May 1677.	George, bap.[2] 17th May 1655, bur.[2] 19th May 1656.	Thomas, bap.[2] 2nd April 1657.	William, bap.[2] 29th August 1659; named in mother's will.	Joane, bap.[2] 12th January 1660; execut⁰ to mother's will, and adm⁰ to bro. Hugh.

Joane, bap.[2] 5th April 1681.	Frances, bap.[2] 29th November 1683.	Mary, bap.[2] 11th May 1686.	Hellyn, bap.[2] 16th September 1692, mar.[1] 27th June 1719 Richard Elvans.

[1] At St. Kew.   [2] At St. Minver.   [3] At Egloshayle.   [4] At St. Tudy.   [5] At Quethiock.

LYNAM.

I hereby certify that the portions of this Pedigree printed in *Italics* agree with the Records of this Office. The Arms of Lynam (as on page 262) are entered in a MS. entitled "Devon and Cornwall Arms," fo. 48.

Heralds' College,   STEPHEN TUCKER,

23rd March, 1874.   *Rouge Croix.*

Agnes, wife of John Beer of Eggleshayle, see ante vol. i., p. 311.

Richard Lynam of St. Kue, living 1620, of Penpont, bur.[1] 29th January 1630. = *Thomasine, dau. of ...... Fursland of Bickington, bur.[1] 24th August 1636.*

Richard, 2nd son, bap.[1] 18th Feb. 1592. Coll. Rect. Quethiock. 4th February 1627. Bur.[5] 7th October 1657, will dated 8th April, prov. 30th November 1657 (Ruthen 488). = Elizabeth, dau. of Henry Chiverton, mar.[5] 20th November 1628, bur.[5] 12th June 1674, will dated 23rd November 1668, prov. 9th October 1676 (Archd. Cornw.)

Dorothy, bap.[1] 30th May 1585, wife of John Dagge of Trewiggett, see Pedigree of Dagge ante vol. i., p. 296.

Catherine 2nd dau., named in deed dated 8th James.

Elizabeth, bap.[5] 4th Oct. 1629, bur.[5] 30th May 1637.

Tamson, bap.[5] 13th Feby. 1630-1.

Richard Lynam, eldest son, bap.[5] 20th February 1630-1, dead before 23rd Nov. 1668, s.p.

Elizabeth, bap.[5] 2nd January 1633, bur.[5] 30th May 1639.

Joseph, bap.[5] 21st January 1637, living 1668.

George, bap.[5] April 1640; was a legatee in the will of his uncle Sir Richard Chiverton dated in 1677.

John, bap.[5] 26th April 1642, died in childhood.

Charles, bap.[5] 11th June 1643.

Edward, bap.[5] 5th January 1645.

Henry, bap.[5] 13th June 1648, bur.[5] 22nd June 1676; will dated 19th June prov. 9th Octr. 1676 (Archd. Cornw.) s.p.

Isabell, bap.[5] 31st Jan. 1635, mar.[5] 9th Decr. 1658, Samuel, son of Hugh Hawkyn; widow 1668, living 1676.

Tabitha, bap.[5] 31st Jany. 1635-6 living unmar 1676.

Hugh, bap.[2] 20th January 1692, named in mother's will, adm° to sister Joane 4th July 1681.

Richard, named in his mother's will.

Elizabeth, mar.[2] Alex, Hill 31st January 1678, named in mother's will.

Charles, bap.[1] 14th Decr. 1665, bur.[1] 29th Novem. 1676.

Charity, bap.[1] 29th January 1652.

Ann, bap.[1] 26th Nov. 1655.

Mary, bap.[1] 7th Nov. 1658.

Matthew, bap.[3] 25th February 1660, bur.[3] 14th June 1735.

Thomas, bap.[3] 10th May 1644; will dated 1690, prov. 12th Dec. 1692, (Fane 226. s.p.)

William, supposed to be dead in 1688.

Philip.

Matthew.

Charity.

Diana, bap.[2] March 1695, mar.[2] Charles Nation of St. Kew, see Ped. of Nation post, p. 266.

John Lynam, named in his mother's will. Bur.[2] 12th February 1765, s.p.? = *Christiana, dau. of William Prophet of St. Minver, bap.[2] 3rd June 1718, mar.[2] 12th May 1741, bur.[2] in the South Church, 5th June 1795.*

---

[1] At St. Kew.   [2] At St. Minver.   [3] At Egloshayle.   [4] At St. Tudy.   [5] At Quethiock.

PEDIGREES OF KEIGWIN, MOYLE, CURGENVEN, AND

Jenkyn Keigwin of Moushole in Cornw. Gent.=Thomasine, dau. of ......
Slain in an attack by the Spaniards and bur.[2] | bur.[2] 1st October 1616.
24th July 1595, M.I.[2]

Richard Keigwin of Moushole, Merchant; died 21st and=Elizabeth, dau. of ...... bur.[2]
bur.[2] 23rd April 1636, æt. 74. Will dated 18th Sept. | 27th November 1637.
1632, prov. 1st December. 1636, (Pile.)

John Keigwin of Moushole, mar. 1615, living 1632.=Dorothy, dau. of ...... Borlase.

WILLIAM KEIGWIN of Mousehole, born 1625=Prudence, dau. of James Praed
bought Tretawne in St. Kew, 1659. | of Trevethow, Cornw.

JOHN KEIGWIN of Moushole, died at Huish, co. Devon 1693. Will=Margaret, dau. of John Gifford of Brightley, born 1st February
dated 19th June 1693, Adm° 12th March following to Relict. | 1648, bap. at Chittlehampton, mar. there 29th Mar. 1686.

John Keigwin, Clerk, born 18th Aug.=Isabella, dau. of John | JAMES KEIGWIN of Moushole,=Julian, eldest dau. of George
1689; Ordained 21st February 1713; | Keigwin, by his wife | bap.[2] 10th January 1673, died at | Musgrave of Nettlecombe, co.
Vicar of Landrake 1732. Died 3rd | Mary Penrose, bap.[2] | Bath 12th July 1710, æt. 37; will | Somerset; Bar. at Law, exe.
March 1761, bur. at Landrake; will | 5th March 1680, bur.[2] | dated 21st June 1710, prov. 30th | to her husband's will; bur.[2]
dat. 4th May 1759. | 4th November 1720. | September following at Exon. | 18th April 1718.

| John, bap.[2] 9th April 1706, died young. | James Keigwin of Moushole, bap.[2] 29th Oct. 1697, died s.p. Will dated 1st February 1734, prov. 6th July 1741 (Archd. Cornw.)=Florence Penrose of Penrose, bur.[2] | George Keigwin of Moushole and afterwards of Crowan, 2nd surviving son, bap.[2] 8th April 1707, Exr. to his brother's will. Died at Crowan 1781 and bur.[2]=Anne, dau. of Thomas Hoblyn of Tresadern; died at Moushole, bur.[2] 24th July 1759. | John Keigwin, youngest son, bap.[2] 12th November 1708; Exr. to his brother's will 1734, living 1735; mar. Elizabeth Townsend. | Mary, bap.[3] 23rd July 1717, mar.[3] John Lobb 22nd September 1747. Prudence, bap.[3] 19th October 1714, mar. ...... Eades. | Sarah, bap.[3] 18th May 1712, mar.[3] Charles Nicholl 11th May 1749. Alice, bap.[3] 28th December 1709. Elizabeth, bap.[3] 4th Nov. 1707. |

| Sarah, mar. William Thomas; named in wills of brother and sister. | Susanna, bap.[4] 1731. | Richard, bap.[4] 1734; named in wills of his brother and uncle, bur.[3] March 1802, M.I. s.p. | Frances, named in the wills of her brother and uncle Constantine, bur. 1801, will dated 23rd November 1800, prov. 18th December 1801 (Archd. Cornw.) | Prudence, bap.[4] 1736. | Elizabeth, bap.[4] 1739. |

John Furnis of Lamellen in St. Tudy,=Anne, only child and heir, bap.[3] | John Curgenven of Tregoide,
bap.[7] 7th August 1772, mar. settl. 19th | 5th November 1782. She remar. | bap.[3] 28th December 1785.
and mar. 20th December 1803. Died | Richard Hoskins of Carenis in | Bur.[3] 24th May 1850, aged 65.
29th May 1804, æt. 31, bur.[7] M.I. | Cubert. Living 1874.

John Penberthy Magor of Redruth and afterwards=Elizabeth Ann Moyle, only child and heir, bap. 22nd
of Lamellen, bap. 22nd November 1804. Died 5th | November 1804, mar. settl. dated 8th and mar. 13th
July 1862, æt. 62. M.I.[7] | December 1825, at Cubert, living 1874.

John Furnis Magor, bap.[6] 20th | REUBEN FREDERICK MAGOR of Lamellen,
October 1830. Died at Madeira, | bap.[6] 20th October 1831, purchased Tre-
28th October 1854, æt. 26. M.I.[7] | tawne. Bur.[7] 27th Feb. 1872.

---

[2] At St. Paul.   [3] At St. Kew.   [4] At Bodmin.

[5] At St. Minver.   [6] At Redruth.   [7] At St. Tudy.

MAGOR, SHEWING THE DESCENT OF TRETAWNE.

N.B.—The Names of those who have held Tretawne are printed in CAPITALS.

Thomas Moyle of St. Minver,=Mary, dau. of ...... bur.[5]
bur.[5] 24th December 1616.   10th May 1621.

Thomas Moyle of St. Minver, bap.[5] 30th=Jane, dau. of Thomas Kent; bap.[5] February 1600, mar.[5]
May 1590; bur.[5] 5th March 1657.   9th February 1624, bur.[5] 12th December 1637.

Constantine Moyle of Tretheven, bap.[5] 24th April=..
1631, bur.[3] 14th November 1705.

Prudence, dau. of John Keigwin and sister=Constantine Moyle of Tretheven, son
of James Keigwin of Mousehole; bap.[2] and heir; bur.[3] 11th April 1746, æt.
21st September 1677, mar.[3] 26th September 76. Will dated 17th January 1745-6,
1697, settl. after mar. 23rd June 1699, bur.[3] prov. 26th April following (Archd.
7th January 1750, æt. 73. M.I., No. 2. Cornw.) M.I. No. 12.

John Curgenven=Anne, dau. of
of Uny Lelant.   ...... Richards
of Lelant.

Margaret, bap.[3] 9th March 1702, mar.[3] William Browne 25th December 1733, named in brother's will.

James, bap.[3] 8th September 1719, bur.[3] 25th May 1744, æt. 25, M.I. No. 12.

John Moyle of Bodmin, bap.[3] 28th Sept. 1705.=Susanna, dau. of ...... Bullock, mar. at Lanivet 2nd May 1731.

Constantine Moyle of Tretheven, eldest son, bap.[3] 18th March 1700, bur.[3] 16th Feby. 1781, æt. 79; Will dated 23rd August 1780, prov. 10th February 1781 (Archd. Cornw.) M.I. No. 27. Died 1780, s.p.

JOHN CURGENVEN=Anne, dau. of
of Tretawne   ...... born
which he purchas- 1713, bur.[3]
ed in 1752; will 14th January
dated 12th Feby. 1786, æt. 73;
1773, prov. 29th will dated
October 1779. 20th April
(Archd. Court of 1785.
Cornw.)

Constantine Moyle of Tretheven, bap.[4] 28th January 1747, died 29th December 1800, æt. 50; will dated 19th November 1800, prov. 9th February 1801 (Archd. Cornw.) M.I.[3] No. 27.=Anne, dau. of John Curgenven of Tretawne, mar.[3] 26th June 1781, remar. Edmund Hambly of Menhenniot, died 12nd July 1820, æt. 73, bur.[3] M.I. No. 27.

Thomas of Tretawne, eldest son, bur. 29th December 1804, aged 60, s.p.

JOHN CURGENVEN=Ann, dau.
of Tretawne, born of John
1752, bur.[3] 11th James of
January 1828, Towednack
aged 76; will bap. 23rd
dated 26th April February
1827, prov. 17th 1766, mar.
January 1828 1782.
(Archd. Court of
Cornw.)

Catherine, mar. Abr. Coger.

Elizabeth, mar.[3] James Wilton of St. Kew 16th September 1788; will dated 31st August 1825, prov. 14th October 1826 (Archd. Cornw.)

JAMES CURGENVEN of Tretawne.=Peggy, dau. of John Brendon of
Died 15th and bur.[3] 19th October Chillaton, co. Devon, born 27th
1840, aged 47. M.I. No. 28. May 1800, and bap. at Milton
Intestate.   Abbot, living 1874.

Peter.

JOHN BRENDON CURGENVEN of Tretawne=Josephine, daughter of Joseph Sadler of London,
and London, born 28th March, bap.[3] 6th bap. at St. Pancras, London, mar. at Christ
April 1831.   Church Paddington, 26th September 1860.

EDWARD AURIOL MAGOR,=Mary Caroline, second daughter of John
of Lamellen, bap.[6] 3rd Gilbert Chilcott of Gwendroc, near Truro,
October 1849.   mar. 1st May 1873.

[2] At St. Paul.	[3] At St. Kew.	[4] At Bodmin.
[5] At St. Minver.	[6] At Redruth.	[7] At St. Tudy.

2 N

PEDIGREE OF NATION.

Francis Nashion of West⹂....
Buckland, co. Somerset.

Francis Nashion *alias* Nation, born at Bishop's Lydiard, co. Somerset, matric. at Balliol College⹂Joane, daughter of Oxford, 1zth May 1637, æt. 18. Held a Military command in the Army, and obtained the ...... executrix to Rectory of Inwardleigh, co. Devon in 1652, which he held about two years. He then filled the her husband's will. Vicarage of Lewannick in Cornw. until 1660, when he returned to Inwardleigh. In 1666 he became Rector of Parkham, co. Devon, where he died and was bur.[2] 19th May 1702. Will dated 25th May 1669, prov. 12th June 1702. Exeter.

| Eliza-beth, mar. ...... Cummer, named in fath.'s will. | Charles Nation, a Lieut. Bur.[2] 2nd Dec. 1695, named as dec. in fath's. will. ⹂Pru-dence, dau. of .... | Sibella, daughter of ...... Inch, mar.[5] 5th October 1717, bur.[6] 19th March 1748. ⹂John Nation, Mat. at Ball. College, Oxf.3rd May 1672, æt. 16 ; B.A. 29th Jany. 1675, M.A. 17th Decr. 1678, Inst. to Vicarage of St. Kew 1693; bur.[5] 19th May 1723 ; will dated 27th May 1720. prov. 50th June 1724, Exon. ⹂Eliza-beth, bur.[5] 1st Sept. 1711. | Susan, mar. Richard Nicholls, Vicar of Brad-worthy, Inst. to Rectory of Inward-leigh 20th Sept. 1702. He was bur.[4] | Francis Nation, Clerk, Mat. at Ball. Coll. Oxf. 3rd May 1672, æt. 16 ; Rector of Inwardleigh, bur.[3] 23rd Mar. 1701-2, Admᵒ to Ann Nation Relict 21st Mar. 1702. ⹂Ann, dau. of ...... remar.[3] Jeremiah Hussey, Vicar of Oke-hampton, 29th April 1707. | Lewis Nation named in fath's. will. ⹂Mary, dau. of ...... | Jane, mar.[2] Philip Potter named in fath's. will. |

| Charles, bap.[2] 30th Nov. 1692, named in grand-father's will. | John, bap.[3] Feby. 1694, bur.[2] 2nd March 1695. | Mary, bap.[5] 21st Octr. 1717, bur.[5] 23rd April 1720. | Mary, bap.[5] 28th Aug. 1721, mar.[5] Edw. Grigg 14 May 1743, died 15th May 1757. He died 27th April 1789, aged 78 M.I. No. 20. | Eliza-beth, died in in-fancy. | Anthony, bap.[3] 13th April 1699. | Elizabeth, bap.[3] 23rd February 1700. | Hugh, bap.[2] 3rd June 1699. John, bap.[2] 14th Feby. 1685. | Francis, bap.[2] 10th May 1688. Charles, bap.[2] 15th July 1690. |

| Francis Nation, Matric. at Ball. College, Oxford, 12th March 1707-8 æt. 18 ; Vicar of St.Cle-ther, Cornw. Named in his fath's will ; bur.[6] 1st July 1752, will dated 15th June and prov. 18th July 1752. Exeter. ⹂Mary, dau. of ...... extrix. with dau. to husb.'s will. | Charles Na-tion, bap.[5] 4th October 1700; nam. in father's will ; bur.[5] 20th April 1741, Admᵒ to relict Diana 14th December 1741. ⹂Diana, dau. of John Lynam of St. Minver, bap.[7] March 1695, mar.[7] 27th Feby. 1739, bur.[5] 16th July 1784; will dat. 12th Jany. 1775, prov. 18th August 1784. | Richard, bap.[5] 23rd Mar. 1702, bur.[5] 30th July 1751; will prov. 20th Oct. 1752 by Sentence, died unmar. | Samuel, named in his father's will. ⹂Elizabeth, dau. of ...... Gilbert of Padstow, mar. at Padstow 19th Feb. 1722. | John of St. Kew, mercer ; will dat. 5th Sep. 1717, prov. 27th Oct. 1718, Exeter. | Eliza-beth, bur.[5] 24th Sept. 1700. | Elizabeth, bap.[5] 28th May 1706, mar.[8] 4th April 1728 William Prideaux of Lanteg-los by Camelford. ⹁ |

| Francis Nation, named in father's will. | John Nation, bap.[9] 1724, died before 1752, not named in father's will. | Elizabeth, bap.[9] 1721, executor to father's will, then unmar. |

---

[2] At Parkham.   [3] At Inwardleigh.   [4] At Bradworthy.   [5] At St. Kew.

[6] At Advent.   [7] At St. Minver.   [8] At Lanteglos.   [9] At St. Teath.

BRADDON OF SKISDON.

The family of Braddon was settled in Devon at an early date. In 1478 Alice, relict of John Braddon and executrix of his will, summoned Alice Prideaux of Orley in that county, relict and executrix of the will of William Prideaux, in a plea of debt.[1] Stephen Braddon was returned as one of the Burgesses for the Borough of Bossiny in the Parliament which met on 23rd January 1558-9.[2] This Parliament was dissolved in the following May, and Stephen Braddon was returned again for the same Borough to the Parliament which met on 16th January 1562-3.[3] A Robert Braddon was married at Kilkhampton to Agnes Beare in 1569. Stephen is said to have been settled at Treworgey in St. Gennys,[4] in the middle of the sixteenth century; the name of Braddon, however, does not occur in the Subsidy Rolls for that parish down to the time of Charles I. A William Braddon was married at Launcells to Margaret Bayly in 1618; a Richard Braddon was buried at Egloshayle in 1605, and a John Braddon was resident in that parish early in the seventeenth century; he had three children baptized between 1613 and 1620. The name appears to have been much scattered in the counties of Devon and Cornwall in the sixteenth and seventeenth centuries.

William Braddon of Treworgey joined in the great rebellion, and was a Captain in the Parliamentary army. He was returned to Cromwell's Parliament of 1656 as one of eight persons for the county of Cornwall; and again he was returned for Camelford in 1658-9.[5] His name appears two or three times in the Royalist Composition Papers as Captain William Braddon, and as holding leases of the sequestrated estates of the Royalists.[6] In October 1660, it was certified that "during the whole time of the late war, and ever since, he had been a violent enemy to his sacred Majesty and all his party, and was in arms and did act in the time of the Committee of safety." It was also certified that he held the Barton of Bradridge, worth per annum clear £90, and the messuage and tenement called Treworgey, and the tenement adjoining thereto, worth per annum clear £70.[7] He rebuilt the mansion house at Treworgey as shewn by his initials thereon and the date 1694, in which year he died and was buried at St. Gennys, where a monument to his memory, with a quaint inscription, still exists. Ann his wife, predeceased him in 1678, and is also commemorated by a monument in the Church of St Gennys. William Braddon left two sons, Henry and Lawrence. Lawrence was a Barrister of Inner Temple. The Earl of Essex having been committed to the Tower on a

[1] De Banco Roll, 18th Edward IV., Trinity, m. 116.   [2] Browne Willis, Not. Parl., Vol. iii., Part 2, p. 62.
[3] Ibid fo. 72.   [4] C. S. Gilbert's Hist. of Cornw., Vol. II., p. 37.
[5] Browne Willis, Not. Parl., Vol. iii. part 2, fo. 28'.
[6] Royalist Comp. Papers, First Series, Vol. lxxxiv. fo. 499, and lxviii, fos. 211, 229.
[7] State Papers, Dom. Corr., Vol. xix., No. 107.

charge of High Treason, on 13th July 1683 committed suicide by cutting his throat, as found by an Inquisition taken the following day; and it was charged against Lawrence Braddon and Hugh Speke that,[1] not being ignorant of the premisses, with the intention of bringing the Government into disgrace, they had falsely conspired to make the subjects of the king believe that the said Inquisition had been unduly taken, and that the Earl was killed by those in whose custody he was placed, and having been found guilty on this charge he was sentenced to pay a fine of £2,000, and to give sureties for his good behaviour during his life.   He afterwards wrote two or three pamphlets in vindication of the Earl of Essex, and some other small works.[2]

Henry Braddon, the eldest son of William Braddon, died in 1711, and was buried at St. Gennys, where he also is commemorated by a monument in the Church.   His great-grandson, Henry Braddon, Gent., described as of Lifton, in 1782 married Sarah Phillis daughter of William Clode of Camelford, and sister and heir of her brother Major William Clode of Skisdon, which place, through this alliance, the Braddons inherited and have since made their principal residence.

Henry Braddon had a large family.   His eldest son, William Braddon, held a high judicial office in the Civil Service of India.   Having retired from the Service and settled in Cornwall he was brutally attacked in his bed by burglars and soon afterwards died of the injuries he received, and is now represented by his eldest son William Clode Braddon of Skisdon Esq., whose son, Captain William Clode Braddon, late 75th Foot, is Adjutant of the Brecknockshire Rifle Volunteers, and grandson, Edward Henry Clode Braddon, son of the last mentioned, is a Lieutenant in the 55th Regiment.

---

[1] Cobbett's State Trials, Vol. ix. 1127-1128.   [2] Bibliotheca Cornubiensis, Vol. i., p. 40.

APPENDIX I.

A.

Universis, &c., Petrus, &c., Salutem in Domino sempiternam. Ad universitatis vestræ noticiam tenore presentium volumus pervenire quod nos ad præsentationem religiosorum virorum Prioris et Conventus Plymptoniæ ecclesiæ de Lanhoho in Cornubia verorum patronorum, Reymundum de Lanhoho præsbyterum ad taxandam vicariam ejusdem ecclesiæ admittentes intuitu caritatis ipsum vicarium canonice instituimus in eadem assignantes eidem Reymundo et successoribus ejus qui pro tempore fuerint de expressa voluntate et assensu dictorum Religiosorum nomine dictæ vicariæ totum altilagium ejusdem ecclesiæ cum suis pertinentiis vna cum terris et possessionibus quas Rogerus Sors et Ricardus filius Radulphi aliquando tenuerunt de dominico sanctuariæ ecclesiæ supradictæ, decima garbarum totius parochiæ duntaxat excepta. Ita tamen quod dictus Reymundus et successores sui qui pro tempore fuerint, omnia onera debita et consueta omnino sustineant et angnoscant reservata nichilominus nobis potestate ordinandi et disponendi de dicta vicaria augendo vel minuendo prout nobis videbitur expedire. In cujus rei testimonium præsentibus literis sigillum nostrum duximus apponendum. Datum apud Ylsteworth die sancti Lucæ Evangelistæ, anno domini M C C. octogesimo tercio, et Consecrationis nostræ tercio.

Bishop Bronescombe's Register, fo. 122.

B.

Juratores presentant quod Rex Edgarus dedit Ecclesiam de Lannoseynt que valet per annum xl libras et duas carucatas terre centum solidos redditus Canonicis de Plympton pro sustentatione duorum Canonicorum ad diuina ibidem celebranda et elemosinam pauperibus erogandam et pro peregrinis et aliis hospitandis pro anima Regis et successorum suorum Que quidem celebracio et elemosina iam quindecim annis elapsis subtractæ sunt Ideo preceptum est Vicecomiti quod venire faciat priorem predicte domus, &c. Postea venit predictus prior et dicit quod quidam Willelmus Episcopus Exoniensis concessit et dedit perpetualiter in elemosinam assensu et consensu Capituli Exoniensis G. Priori et omnibus Canonicis Deo seruientibus in Ecclesia de Plumpton ecclesiam predictam et quicquid ad eam pertinet in omnibus rebus ita ut decedentibus eiusdem ecclesie clericis prebende eorum in vsus Canonicorum de Plumpton cedant, &c., et profert cartam ipsius Episcopi que hoc testatur. Profert eciam confirmationem domini Henrici Regis proaui domini Regis nunc que testatur quod idem Dominus Rex concessit et confirmauit ecclesiæ et canonicis regularibus de Plomptona ecclesiam de Landoho cum omnibus appendiciis suis ita ut decedentibus eiusdem ecclesie clericis prebende eorum in vsus Canonicorum Regularium de Plomptona cedant Et dicit quod ipse et omnes predecessores sui a confectione predicte carte tenuerunt predictam ecclesiam cum terra predicta quietam de predicta celebratione et elemosina pauperum eroganda aut peregrinis hospitandis et petit Judicium, &c. Et Johannes de Mutford

2 O

qui sequitur &c., dicit quod Dominus Rex Edwardus pater &c., et Dominus Rex nunc fuerunt seisiti de cantaria duorum canonicorum et elemosina supradicta pro animabus progenitorum suorum facienda usque iam xv. annis elapsis quando predictus prior illa subtraxit Et hoc petit quod inquiratur et prior similiter.   Et juratores dicunt super sacramentum suum quod predictus prior et omnes predecessores sui tenuerunt predictas ecclesiam et terram de Domino Rege et antecessoribus suis a tempore quo non existat memoria et semper continuauerunt predictam cantariam et elemosinam in forma predicta vsque ad tempus predictum quando subtracte fuerunt per predecessores dicti prioris.   Ideo consideratum quod predicta cantaria de cetero fiat Et preceptum est Vicecomiti quod distringat eundem Priorem ad cantariam illam de cetero faciendam Et Prior in misericordia quia contra placitauit.—

Assize Rolls, Cornwall, 30th Edward I. $\left.\begin{array}{c} M \\ 1 \\ 21 \end{array}\right\}$ 1 m. 58.

C.

Petitio Prioris de Plympton in Parliamento de terris et ecclesia de Landoho Anno regis Edwardi Primo 30mo.

A nostre seignur le Roi et a sun consail mustre le Priour de Plympton, que come luy et ses precedessours eyent ew deus carrueyes de terre, cent Soudeyes de Rente en Laneuhouseynt, que par autre noun est apele Landoho en Cornwaille, et le Eglise de meisme le lyeu, en pure et perpetuele amoune, du doun William Warwast, jadis Evesque de Excestre, et par confermement le Roi Henri, Besael nostre seignur le Roi que hore est, saunz nule maniere de servise fesaunt; des ques a l'heyre Sire John de Berewyk et ses Compaignouns, en Cornewaille, a la feste S. Michel, l'an du Regne nostre Seigneur le Roi que hore est trentisme : devant lesqueux presente fuist, per gentz meins conyssauntz, qe les ditz Terres, Rente et Eglise, esteyent donetz al dit Priour et as Chanoignes, en meisme le lyeu Dieu seruantz, pur la sustenaunce de deus Chanoignes a devyn servyse ylesques celebrer, et a almongne a Povres doner, et pur Pelryns et autre ylesques herberger, par un Roi Edgar; et per meismes ceux de meisme le servise conuyct, qe ne semble mie acordaunt a verite, par le resoun que quaraunte aunz apres la mort le dit Edgar Roi, n'y avoit il Priour, ne Chanoyngne, ne Covent, a Plympton, par quei la chose poet estre a eux par le dit Roi Edgar done. Kar le dit Evesque Williame, a qui le Roi Henri, fuiz William le Conquerour, rendi et retourna a nostre Dame et a Seint Piere de l'Eglise Excestre les ditz Terre, Rente et Eglise, founda la dite Priorie de Plympton, et les diz Terre, Rente, et Eglise de Landoho lur dona, par confermement le Roi Henri, besail nostre Seignur le Roi que hore est, sicum est avaundit. Prie le dit Priour a l'avaundit nostre Seignur le Roi, pur s'alme et les almes ses auncestres, qu'il e sun Covent, puissent les ditz Terre, Rente, et Eglise tenir a la sustenance de eux, et a meyntenir lur Hospitalite, a Plympton, solem la forme des Chartres avaunditz, et solom ceo que eux les unt tenuz de la fundacion de lur eglise des ques a l'heyre avaundit ; kar puis cele heyre rien ne unt resceu pur lur Sustenaunce, ne pur la hospitalite ylesques memtenir.

Responsio.   Habeant breve in Cancellaria, Domino Johanni de Berewik, ad faciendum venire recordum et processum ultimi itineris Cornubiæ coram Thesaurario et Baronibus de Scaccario et examinatis processu et chartis, fiat eis secundum quod fuerit faciendum.

Petition to King and Council, No. 6826.

D.

Rex omnibus ad quos, &c., Salutem. Sciatis quod cum nuper in Curia nostra coram dilectis et fidelibus nostris Johanne de Berewyk et sociis suis Justiciariis nostris ultimo itinerantibus in comitatu Cornubiæ presentatum fuisset quod quidam bone memorie Edgarus quondam Rex Angliæ predecessor noster dedit Canonicis de Plympton duas carucatas terre centum solidatas redditus cum pertinentiis in Landoho et Eccles'am eiusdem ville pro sustentatione duorum canonicorum ad divina ibidem celebranda et elemosinam pauperibus erogandam et pro peregrinus et aliis hospitandis pro anima dicti Regis et successorum suorum et quod huiusmodi celebracio et elemosinarum erogacio a tempore donationis predicte ibidem facte fuerunt vsque ad principium quindecim annorum dictum iter Justiciariorum nostrorum predictorum precedentium quo celebracio et elemosinarum erogacio predicte subtracte fuerunt ac Prior dicti Prioratus de Plympton in dicta Curia nostra coram prefatis Justiciariis nostris super subtractione huiusmodi allocutus asseruit quod quidem Willelmus quondam Exoniensis Episcopus de assensu capituli sui Exoniensis dedit ecclesiam predictam cuidam G. tunc Priori de Plympton et canonicis eiusdem loci et quod dictus Prior et predecessores sui per donum dicti Episcopi et confirmationem celebris memorie domini Henrici quondam Regis Angliæ proavi nostri predictos terram redditum et ecclesiam tenuerunt absque celebratione diuinorum elemosinarum erogatione seu peregrinorum hospitatione inde faciendis. Cumque per inquisitionem in dicta curia nostra coram prefatis Justiciariis nostris de premissis captam in qua dictus Prior se posuit compertum fuisset quod quidam ...... Predecessor predicti Prioris habuit predictos terram redditum et ecclesiam de dono predicti Regis Edgari pro Cantaria elemosinis et hospitalitate sustentandis in forma supradicta et quod eedem cantaria elemosine et hospitalitas a tempore donationis predicte per predecessores predicti Prioris sustentate fuerunt quousque subtracte extiterant vt est dictum per quod dicta curia nostra considerauit quod predicte cantaria elemosine et hospitalitas sustentarentur et quod Prior predictus ad hæc distringetur sicut per recordum et processum coram prefatis Justiciariis nostris inde habita que coram nobis venire fecimus est compertum. Nos licet Prior et Canonici predicti ad sustentationem dictorum duorum canonicorum elemosinarum erogationem et hospitalitationem iuxta considerationem curie nostre predicte teneantur accendentes nichilomnius cultum diuinum adeo honeste et congrue per presbiteros seculares quam per religiosos extra conuentum in loco priuato commorantes posse exerceri et sustentari ad requisionem dictorum Prioris et Canonicorum volumus et concedimus pro nobis et heredibus nostris quantum in nobis est quod predicti Prior et Canonici et eorum successores decetero habeant ad dictam ecclesiam de Landoho vnum vicarium et vnum capellanum seculares divina ibidem celebraturos et elemosinarum erogationem et hospitalitatem nomine dictorum Prioris et Canonicorum pro terra redditu et ecclesia predictis facturos imperpetuum. Uolentes quod iidem Prior et Canonici vel successores sui ad aliquos canonicos seu alios vltra dictos Vicarium et Capellanum in dicta ecclesia de Landoho ad predicta pietatis opera excercenda sunt predictum est inueniendos decetero teneantur aut per nos vel heredes nostros Justiciarios Escaetores Vicecomites aut alios Balliuos seu ministros nostros quoscunque ad hoc aliqualitur compellantur. In cuius, &c. Teste apud Karlin xxvj° die Marcij, per petitionem de consilio.[1] [1307.]

[1] Rot. Pat. 25th Edward I., m. 20.

2 o[2]

E.

Universis &c., Johannes &c., universitati vestre innotescimus per presentes quod cum inter religiosos viros Priorem et conventum Plympton ordinis Sancti Augustini nostrorum patronatus et diocesis ecclesiam parochialem et curatam de Lannou dicte nostre diocesis in vsus proprios obtinentes ex parte vna et dominum Henricum Tresodorn dicte ecclesie perpetuum Vicarium ex parte alia super inuentione et sustentatione vnius Capellani in eadem ecclesia pro domino nostro Rege Angliæ progenitoribus ac successoribus suis Angliæ Regibus perpetuo celebrantur qui eodem dicto vicario in diuinis officiis assidue et animarum cure exercicio quociens opus esset assisteret, suborta fuisset materia questionis, prefatis Religiosis viris asserentibus inuencionem seu sustentationem dicti Capellani ad dictum Vicarium et onus vicarie sue huius pertinere debere ipsumque ad subeundum illud onus cogendum fore rationabiliter et artandum dictoque vicario contrarium asserente pro eo quod porcio vicarie sue predicte quam in manso et sanctuario que ipse et predecessores sui ibidem Vicarii habet et habebant necnon in altilagio totius parochie de Lannou excepto eo quod de dominico dictorum Religiosorum per eosdem ex culto vel alias occupato prouenit annuatim solummodo consistere pretendebat insufficientem fore notorie ad ipsius Vicarii et unius Capellani sustentationem iuraque Episcopalia et Archidiaconalia persoluenda ac cetera onera sibi incumbencia supportanda. Ac nos super premissorum veritate voluissemus in figura iudicii seruato iuris ordine informari ut sic omni ambiguitate sublata fecissemus vtrique parti iusticie complementum partes supradicte Prior videlicet et Conuentus per dominos Nicholaum Wellesforde et Ricardum ffairwode dicti Monasterii Canonicos et eorumdem Prioris et Conuentus procuratores per suas certi tenoris literas sigillo eorum communi sigillatas ad infrascripta sufficienter constitutos dictus vero vicarius personaliter in aula manerii nostri de Chuddelegh xviiº die mensis Januarii anno domini millesimo CCCᵐᵒ quinquagesimo quarto coram nobis pro tribunali sedentibus comparentes et ut dixerunt anfractus licium exercentes super dissentione et discordia supradicta per viam transactionis et pactionis initarum inter eos per modum qui sequitur concordarunt videlicet quod dictus vicarius et successores sui ibidem futuri vicarii perpetui capellani de quo superius fit mentio ad celebrandum et deseruiendum vt predictur in Ecclesia memoratai inueniet et inuenient imperpetuum suis sumptibus et expensis. Item dicti vicarii onus constructionis reparationis et confectionis cancelli ecclesie supradictæ et inventionis librorum per loci Rectorem ibidem de iure ut de consuetudine inueniendorum quod ad dictos Religiosos spectare hactenus consueuit necnon onera ordinaria et extraordinaria quecunque supradicte ecclesie et eius nomine Rectori loci incumbencia de cetero insolidum supportabunt et ipsorum quilibet suis temporibus supportabit.   In subsidium vero inuentionis et sustentationis dicti capellani ac supportationem ceterorum onerum predictorum memoratus vicarius ac successores sui antedicti decimas maiores quarundam terrarum infra limites predicte parochie de Lannou situatarum, vidz: decimas maiores terrarum de Bethbolgh Trewarthenyer Croppyng Hille Tretheuen Dale Nyweton Redsmyth et Peulengarou vltra mansum sanctuarium et altilagium que ut prefertur idem vicarius qui nunc est et precessores ac predecessores sui illius loci vicarii percipere consueuerant ab antiquo recipient imperpetuum et habebunt. Et ut premissa omnia coram nobis iudicialiter confessata et in scriptis eciam recitata perpetuis futuris temporibus inuiolabilem optinerent roboris firmitatem partes supradicte a nobis cum instancia petiuerunt vt eisdem nostrum consensum prebere nostramque auctoritatem pontificalem apponere dignaremur.   Nos itaque Johannes Exoniensis Episcopus antedictus cupientes inter partes supradictas sicuti inter quoscunque subditos nostros pacis et quietis vincula confouere ac licium quarumcunque subtrahere strepitus et fomenta compositionem transactionem supradictas vt reales fiant perpetuis temporibus duraturum ad petitionem dictarum partium vt præmittitur nobis porrectam authoritate nostra pontificali approbamus auctorizamus ac tenore presentium confirmamus. Tenor vero literarum de quibus superius fit mencio sequitur in hec verba.

Pateat vniuersis per presentes quod nos Prior et Conuentus monasterii Apostolorum Petri et Pauli Plymptoniæ ordinis sancti Augustini Exoniensis diocesis ecclesiam parochialem de Lannou dicte diocesis in vsus proprios obtinentes dilectos nobis in Christo dominos Nicholaum Wellesforde et Ricardum ffayrwode concanonicos nostros ordinamus et constituimus nostros veros et legitimos procuratores et nuncios speciales coniunctim et diuisim et vtrumque eorum in solidum. Ita quod non sit melior condicio occupantes sed quod vnus eorum inceperit alius prosequi valeat et finire. Dantes et concedentes eisdem et eorum vtrique potestatem in solidum et mandatum speciale ad tractandum nomine nostro et monasterii nostri supradicti cum Henrico Tresodorn supradicte ecclesie de Lannou perpetuo Vicario super inuentione cuiusdam capellani ibidem perpetuo celebraturi necnon super constructione refectione ac reparatione cancelli dicte ecclesie et aliis oneribus tam ordinariis quam extraordinariis eidem ecclesie incumbentibus per eum et successores suos prefate ecclesie futuros vicarios perpetuo supportandis ac eciam pro supportatione onerum huius et inuentione dicti capellani assignando et concedendo decimas quarumdam terrarum infra fines parochie de Lannou existencium in augmentationem portionis vicarie sue videlicet: decimas maiores terrarum de Bethbolgh Tywarthenyer Cropping Hille Tretheuen Dale Nyweton Redsmyth et Pelengarou sibi et successoribus suis ibidem vicariis imperpetuum ac omnia alia et singula facienda speciale ratum et gratum perpetuis temporibus habituri quicquid iidem procuratores nostri aut eorum alter fecerit seu gesserit in premissis seu alio premissorum sub ypotheca omnium bonorum nostrorum non intendentes per presentem procurationem nostram quecunque per nos prius facta aliqualiter reuocare. In quorum omnium testimonium sigillum nostrum communi presentibus est appensum. Datum Plymptoniis in domo nostra capitulari sextodecimo die mensis Januarii anno domini Millesimo CCC^{mo} quinquagesimo quarto. In quorum omnium et singulorum testimonium atque fidem has litteras nostras sigilli nostri appensione fecimus communiri. Data in dicto manerio nostro xviij^o die dicti mensis Januarii sub anno domini supradicto consecrationis vero nostre vicesimo octauo.

Bishop Grandisson's Register, Vol. i., p. 180.

F.

Extract from an Inquisition so far as it relates to the Church of St. Kew.

Inquisicio capta apud Bodmyn die Jouis proxima ante festum Sancti Georgii anno regni Regis Ricardi secundi quarto decimo coram Johanne Hauley Escaetore domini Regis in comitatu Cornubiæ ex officio suo per sacramentum Henrici Giffard, Johannis Burgh, junr., Johannis Geffry, Trewyget, Ricardi Andrew, Benedict Giffard, Johannis John, Johannis Trethuuen, Johannis Bera, Treburthek, Willelmi Hichon, Thome Nanfan, Johannis Trewen et Henrici Tregeriok, qui dicunt per sacramentum suum quod Edgarus quondam Rex Anglie dedit et concessit Priori et Conuentui de Plympton et successoribus suis manerium de Lanouseynt et aduocacionem ecclesie de Lanowe cum decimis et omnibus proficiis imperpetuum ad sustentamdum duos canonicos ibidem apud Lanowe Seynt ad celebrandum ibidem pro animabus eiusdem Regis et successorum suorum et ad distribuendum ibidem qualibet septimana bis videlicet diebus mercurii et veneris elemosina xl. pauperibus pro animabus predicti Regis et antecessorum suorum imperpetuum duratura quorum vnus Canonicus deberet celebrare in capella in cimiterio predicte ecclesie existenti et dictam capellam sustentare debent predicti Prior et Conuentus Sumptibus suis propriis Qui Prior et Conventus Canonicos et Elemosinam et reparacionem eiusdem capelle per sexaginta annos elapsos subtraxerunt per quod dictum maneriem forisfacere debent domino Regi. Et predictum manerium valet per annum Cˢ· Et aduocatio ecclesie predicte valet per annum lˡⁱ· Item dicunt quod predictus prior et conuentus de Plympton adquisiuerunt sibi et successoribus suis post statutum religiosorum vnum mesuagium et unam acram terre cornubiæ in Talcogow iuxta Lanowseynt et unum mesuagium et j ferliegum terre in Treaynek de Willelmo ffoot atte hale sine licencia domini Regis et valet per annum xiijˢ iiijᵈ

Escheats, 14th Richard II., No. 97.

APPENDIX II.

RETURN OF THE POSSESSIONS OF THE INHABITANTS OF ST. KEW, 1521-1523.

Augmentation Office, Miscellaneous Books.

Parish of } The yerely valor of the spirituall men is possessions wᵗ yn the seid parysche
Seynt Kue. } accordyng to the kinges commission.

Prior de Plympton Rector Ecclesie ibidem valet per annum	.. ..	xi ɫi
M. Johannes Mane Vicarias[1] ibidem valet in proficius	.. ..	x ɫi

Summa

Valencia terrarum et tenementarum ibidem per annum.

Willelmus Carnsuyowe habet terras et tenementa ibibem per annum -	iijɫi vj s viij d	Thomas Trote -	-	v s
		Johannes Smyth de Bodmyn -		v s
Nicholaus Cavyll -	c s	Thomas Gilbert -	-	x s
Willelmus Byle -	xvj s	Arturas Kemys -		x s
Prior de Plympton predicta -	vj ɫi	Johannes Calwodleigh	-	xx s
Petrus Bevyll -	ix ɫi	Thomas Treffry -	-	xl s
Ricardus Code -	vj ɫi	Johannes Pentyre	iij ɫi vj s viij d	
Henricus Nicol -	xl s	Johannes Worthevale	-	xij s
Rogerus Arundell Armiger -	x s	Johannes Skuys	-	viij s
		Johannes Rouell	-	viij s

[1] Also Vicar of St. Teath and Rector of St. Tudy.

Willelmus Hopkyn	-	xxx s
Edwardus Chechester	-	xiij s
heredes Wullecombe	-	xxx s
Johannes Vyall -	-	vj s
Jacobus Kestell	-	xxxiij s iiij d
Henricus Marney Miles	-	xl s
heredes Johannes Mone	-	c s
Johannes Luke	-	xvj s
Dominus ffitzwaryn	-	viij s
Dominus Henricus Courtenay	vj li xiij s iiij d	
Willelmus Cullow	-	viij s
heredes Edwardi Arundell		
Milites	-	vj li xiij s iiij d

Johannes Rescarek	-	c s
heredes Johannes Cok	-	vi s viij d
Cary de Cokyngton	-	xxvj s viij d
Johannes Helyer	-	xxx s
Margareta Stowell vidua	-	xl s
Domina de Hastynges	-	xvj s
Johannes Carmynow	-	xiij s iiij d
Johannes Glyn	-	viij s
Ricardus Nuton	-	vj s viij d
Johannes Donesyll	-	xiij s iiij d
Johanna Specot Vidua	-	xiij s iiij d
Johannes Kestell	-	xiij s iij d
Johannes Tallan	-	x s

Valencia bonorum et Catallorum dicta parochia et de eorum armis.

Idem M. Johannes Mane Vicarius ibidem valet in bonis xl li

Ricardus Penny Capellanus ibidem in stipendio vij marcas in bonis lx s

Willelmus Carnsuyowe	-	xl s
Nicholaus Cavell	-	- xx li
	arma pro vno homine	
Petrus Bevyll	-	- c marc
	arma pro uno homine	
Johannes Nicol	-	- xx li
	arma pro vno homine	
Johannes Mathew	-	- xx li
	arma pro vno homine	
Johannes Pethek	-	- xl s
Willelmus Inche	-	- xx li
	arma pro vno homine	
Ricardus Parkyn	-	- xl s
Willelmus Emot	-	x marcas
Matheus Hutchyn	-	x marcas
	arma pro vno homine	
Willelmus Hutchyn	-	- xx li
	arma pro vno homine	
Willelmus Hogge	-	- xl s
Willelmus Hobbe	-	- lx s
Johannes Clerk	-	- xl s
Johannes Triplat	-	- viij li
Willelmus Ayer	-	- vij li
Johannes Hawkyn	-	- iiij li
Johannes Jenkyn	-	- xl s
Willelmus Polgrene	-	- viij li
Johannes ffycke	-	- xl s

Johannes Lynam, Junioris		x marcas
	arma pro vno homine	
Johannes Lynam, Senioris	-	c s
	arma pro vno homine	
Johannes Marlond	-	- iiij li
Robertus Inche	-	- vij li
Nicholaus Morlond	-	c s
Johannes Dagge	-	- xl s
Ricardus Kendall	-	- xl s
Henricus Lynam	-	- x li
	arma pro vno homine	
Thomas ffyke, Senioris	-	- x li
Thomas ffyke, Junioris	-	- vj li
Nicholas Hayward	-	- xl s
Willelmus Brym	-	- xl s
Johannes Archer	-	- xl s
Robertus Hogge	-	- xl s
Ricardus Mathy	-	- lx s
Willelmus Betty	-	- xl s
Thomas Paket	-	- xl s
Johannes Walys	-	- c s
	arma pro vno homine	
Johannes Smyth	-	- c s
Davidus Danger	-	v marcas
Thomas Ronold	-	- c s
	arma pro vno homine	
Stephanus Martyn	-	- xl s

Ricardus Strowte, Junioris	-	xl s
Ricardus Strowte, Senioris	-	xl s
Ricardus Kestell	-	- viij li
arma pro vno homine		
Johannes Hawkyn	-	- xl s
Johannes Parson	-	x marcas
arma pro vno homine		
Philipus Tregyon	-	- xl s
Johannes Crome	-	- iiij li
Johannes Taverner	-	xx marcas
Ricardus Mathu	-	- xl s
Johannes Sutton	-	x marcas
arma pro vno homine		
Willelmus Burnard	-	- iiij li
Willelmus Hutchyn	-	- xv li
arma pro vno homine		
Ricardus Hutchyn	-	- viij li
Thomas Adam	-	- xl s
Robertus Ronall	-	x marcas
Johannes Moyle	-	- x li
Johannes Harper	-	- xx li

Johannes Webber	-	- c s
Robertus Lynam	-	- iiij li
Ricardus Webber	-	x marcas
Willelmus ffrode	-	- x li
Robertus Martyn	-	- xl s
Johannes Calwaye, Junioris	-	xl s
Johannes ffyke	-	- xl s
Thomas Hutchyn	-	xx marcas
arma pro vno homine		
Willelmus Mathy	-	- x li
Johannes Harry	-	- iiij li
Johannes Blake, Senioris	-	xl s
Johannes Blake, Junioris	-	xl s
Willelmus Philipp	-	- xl s
Johannes ffycke	-	- iiij li
Willelmus Hogge nil quia pauper tenens Prioris de Plympton		
Johannes Emot nil quia pauper tenens Alexandri Cary		
Robertus Lynam nil quia pauper tenens Domini Devon		

APPENDIX III.

Subsidy Roll, 1st Edward III., granting a twentieth to the King.   Augmentation Office, Miscl. Books, Vol. 431, p. 42.

Parochia de Lannou.

Johanne de Carmynou	-	ij s
Reginaldo de Moun	-	- ij s
Nicholao Giffard	-	- ij s
Nicholao Tregellest	-	- xij d
Roberto Tregeller	-	- ix d
Hugone Trewythian	-	- ix d
Johanne Penguynna	-	- ix d
Johanne Lony	-	- ......
Johanne Coc	-	- vj d
Radulpho Prigou	-	- xij d
Johanne Trevethan	-	- vj d
Thoma Taloogan	-	- ix d
Johanne Tregoyth	-	- ix d

Ricardo Nikelyn	-	- vj d
Ricardo Soby	-	- vj d
Thoma Gerny	-	- ix d
Johanne Treauerok	-	- x d
Willielmo Criket	-	- vj d
Johanne Simon	-	- xij d
Reginaldo Coykyn	-	- vj d
Johanne Pyl	-	- ix d
Ricardo Heket	-	- vj d
Henrico Trewenek	-	- ix d
Johanne Marsel	-	- xij d
Taxatoribus { Willielmo Trethynau		xij d
{ Ricardo de Hendre	-	xij d

LANTEGLOS JUXTA CAMELFORD, AND ST. ADWEN *ALIAS* ADVENT.

These two parishes, being consolidated into one benefice, we propose to treat of together, though distinguishing each as far as practicable. Both are situate in the Hundred of Lesnewith; Lanteglos is bounded on the north by the parish of Minster, on the east by Davidstow, Advent and St. Breward, on the south by Michaelstow, and on the west by St. Teath. The following perambulation, signed by the Minister and Churchwardens and principal inhabitants of the parish, is preserved in the Bishop's Registry at Exeter.

LANTEGLOS JUXTA CAMELFORD.—A note of the Lymites and Boundes of the p'ish of Lanteglose juxta Camelford, vewed by the Inhabitants thereof, together wth the Minister thereof, Anno d'ni 1613.

Imprimis. From Helesbery yeate the Bounds runn north-west along by the hedg between Helstone ground and Helsebury downe till you come to a lake wch riseth in John Harvies doune, wch lake, or Brooke, is the very Bound between Michaelstowe and Lanteglosse till it come to a Bridge neere Knight's Mill; and from the sayed Bridge the bound runneth all alonge by the river northeast until it come vnto newall Bridg, beinge the verye bound between Lanteglosse and St. Teath; and from newall Bridg the bound run all along upward by the river until it come vnto a Tenem^t in St. Teath called Trevihen, and from thence the bounds run along by the east hedg of the sayed Tenem^t vnto Chapples hedg, and by Chapples hedg the Bounds run along vnto Castlegoe hedg, and by that hedg the bounds run north vnto a place called "roses," being the bound between Lanteglosse, St. Teath, and Minster; and from "roses" to brewers gate, and from Brewer's gate the bounds run westward vntil they come vnto Hornawinke wheare the bounde between Lanteglosse and St. Teath end: and from Hornawinke the bounds run by a small riuer between Lanteglose and Tintagel, wch runneth northward vnto Cockell's Coome, and from thence the boundes run alonge eastward, between Tintagel and Lanteglose, vnto the field Bridg att Bruers; from the Bridge it runneth southward vntil it come vnto Brewer's gate aforesayed: ffrom the river betweene Lanteglosse and Minster aforesayed vnto Trewilla Parke, and from the River as the hedg runneth betweene Trefredoe doune, Trevilla parke, and Collen eastward, the Bounds runn

2 P

alonge by the hedg vnto the head of Collen Lane, and joining with one hedg of Copsen heath, Bounding betweene Lanteglosse and Minster; and from thenc the bounds runn alonge by the hedg of Trewassoe downe, in Davidstow, vnto Hendra Walles southeast, being the Bound between Lanteglosse and Davidstow, and soe from Hendra Walles hedg the bounds runn alonge by the hedg westward vnto little Collen, which one John Hunny holdeth; and from thence the bounds runn between Trenarth and Trevarlidg by the southeast hedg vnto a tenemᵗ called Couldcada, and from thence the bounds runn alonge by the highway, westward, vnto the Bridg in the sayed highway, and from the bridg the bounds runn all along by the river vnto Trevarlidg hedg, which is the bound betweene Lanteglosse and Advent; and from the hedg, southward, the bounds runn vnto Lancarne water, and from thenc the bounds runn alonge by the river, westwarde, vnto Worthaker hedg, and so alonge the hedg, northward, vnto the highway, and soe the Bound runneth all alonge the high way vntil it come vnto hoary Stone, and from hoary Stone alonge by the south hedg vnto Helsbery gate aforesayed. There is alsoe belonginge vnto the parish of Lanteglosse some part of Helsbery parke, as it is reported, but how much wee know not. But these are the Trew bounds of all the rest of oʳ p'ish to oʳ knollegde.

Signed,

    Samuell More, per me Nathanaelem More substitut' ibidem.

Henry Allye, Walt' Hay, } Churchwardens.		Hugh Hockine.
John Wallys, Will. Edwards, } Sidesmen.		Hugh Wilkye.
Jonn Joyce, Nicholas Coleman, } Constables.		William Pearse.

Henry Allye, ⎫
Walt' Hay, ⎬ *Churchwardens.*

John Wallys, ⎫
Will. Edwards, ⎬ *Sidesmen.*

Jonn Joyce,   ⎫
Nicholas Coleman, ⎬ *Constables.*

Hugh Hockine.
Hugh Wilkye.
William Pearse.
Hugh Dann....
John White.
Adryan Bastard.
John Cocke.
   wᵗʰ the rest of the pⁱˢʰᵉ.

    The total area of the parish of Lanteglos is, according to the Tithe Survey, 395. acres and 6 perches. The whole of the parish is, geologically, within the altered Devonian district though an elvan dyke extends from Greenlake, near Camelford, in a southwestern direction to Tregreenwell near the border of St. Teath, where it abuts upon a greenstone vein running almost perpendicular to it, which intersects this parish and extends into St. Teath. The elvan dyke runs parallel to, and close upon, the turnpike road leading from Camelford to Wadebridge, chiefly on the south side. Near Greenlake this dyke is a porphyry with a grey-white quartzo-felspathic base containing crystals of quartz and specks of mica; but at Tregreenwell it becomes a granite having a base of light-coloured felspar, quartz and mica containing disseminated crystals of light-coloured felspar.[1] The northern part of the parish possesses rocks of the calcareous series, among which are slates of an excellent quality for roofing, which have been worked to some extent at Bodwithick.

    The land generally is fertile, though better adapted to pasture than corn. The chief Landowners are His Royal Highness the Prince of Wales in respect to the Manor of Helston, S. M. Grylls of Lewarne, Esq., and Miss Pearse of Launceston.

---

[1] De la Beche. Report on the Geology of Cornwall, Devon and West Somerset, p. 181.

INDUSTRIAL PURSUITS.

A considerable wool trade was formerly carried on in Camelford, but it has now ceased and some of the premises are used as a small tannery. Many of the labouring men who reside in this town are employed in the slate quarries at Delabole. For many years a slate quarry was worked at Bodwithick, in this parish, but its operations have now ceased.

At Trethian, in Advent, a mine was opened a few years ago, called "The Great North Caradon," but it has now stopped working, as have also certain China-clay Works at Stannon, though others at Poldu are in operation. With these exceptions the only Industry is agriculture, in which the wages of labourers is about 12s. a week, with, occasionally, a house, rent free, in addition, and food during harvest.

The Parish of Advent, which derives its name from the dedication of the Church, has been, from ancient times connected with Lanteglos either as a Chapelry or consolidated Parish. We find it separately assessed to the Subsidy as early as 1st Edward III (1327,) as "Parochia de Adwyn."[1] It is bounded on the west by Lanteglos, from which it is separated on this side by the river Camel; on the north and northeast by the same parish and by Davidstow; on the east by the last mentioned parish; and on the south east and south west by St. Bruard. The river Alan takes its rise from numerous springs in Crowdy Marsh, which is partly in Davidstow and partly in Advent. It forms two streams, one of which flows north and the other south of a hill on Advent Moor. The latter forms the boundary between Advent and St. Breward from near its source to Trecarn, where it receives the waters of the Camel. The two streams abovementioned unite at Alan Ford and flow through a picturesque valley, on the opposite sides of which are two singular formations of granite rocks, which, from a distance, cause the valley to have the appearance of a deep rocky chasm, which is called the "Devil's Jump." Tradition says, that when his Satanic Majesty visited Cornwall he was chased out of the county by St. Michael, who had his residence on the top of Roughtor, and was glad to effect his escape by leaping over the chasm.

The area of this parish is somewhat larger than that of Lanteglos, extending to 4059 acres 1 rood, but nearly one half is rough moor.

The whole of this parish, except a small area on the western side forms a portion of the extensive granite district of Brown Willy, the remainder is of the altered Devonian series, composed of felspar and hornblend rocks. The Elvan dyke, described under Lanteglos, intersects the north west corner of Advent. It has been pointed out that the various slates, &c., which surround the granite bosses, existed previously to the intrusion of the granite, as shown by the displacement of these rocks by the latter, and by the injection

[1] Sub. Roll $\frac{87}{7}$

2 P²

of granite veins into the cracks caused by the upheaving and disruption of the earlier rocks. The junction of the granite with the slate, in this parish, is concealed by marsh and bog, adjoining which is an extensive range of moor resting on an irregular bed of quartzose gravel derived from the granite hills, and evidently of diluvial origin. In some districts this is extensively worked for China-Clay.[1]

The eastern, or granitic, portion of this parish is sterile and uncultivated, affording only coarse pasture for cattle and sheep during the summer months; the other portion consists of fine meadow land of deep soil. It is remarkable for its verdant appearance. The land never burns up in the driest summer, but always preserves a particularly green and fresh appearance. The soil is better suited for pasture than corn. The principal landowners are S. M. Grylls, Alexander Marshall and W. Teague, Esquires, and Mrs. Abbott.

The following table will shew population and number of houses in the two parishes, respectively, at the several periods of the Census within the present Century.

Parishes.	Description.		1801	1811	1821	1831	1841	1851	1861	1871
LANTEGLOS	Population		912[2]	1100	1256	1359	1541	1740	1620[3]	1718
	Houses	Inhabited	188	216	229	249	320	352	328	328
		Uninhabited	8	15	9	10	24	21	12	12
		Building	nil.	3	1	nil.	6	2	1	1
ADVENT	Population		170	219	229	244	291	252	208	246
	Houses	Inhabited	37	42	55	50	63	56	45	45
		Uninhabited	4	6	2	8	5	3	10	10
		Building	nil.	nil.	1	1	1	1	nil.	nil.

The following table will shew the Annual Value of real property in 1815 and the present assessment :

Parishes.	Annual Value of Property as assessed in 1815.	Present rateable Value	County Assessment.	Land Tax. Amount Assessed.			Land Tax. Amount Redeemed.			Assessed Taxes.	Inhabited House Duty.			Property and Income Tax. Schedule. A			B			D			E		
	£	£	£	£	s.	d.	£	s.	d.		£	s.	d.	£	s.	d.	£	s.	d.	£	s.	d.	£	s.	d
Lanteglos	4141	7090	5600	163	11	8	48	15	9½	Nil.	23	15	3	80	6	4	20	7	10	27	9	8	1	19	0
Advent ..	1396	1873	1768	61	17	0	19	0	9¼	Nil.	..		..	..		..	..		..	..		..	..		..

[1] De la Beche, Geological Survey ; and Dr. Boase. Davies Gilbert's History of Cornwall.

[2] It would appear from the number of housling people in 37th Henry VIII. (1545) that the population then was about 300, see post, p. 323.

[3] This decrease is attributed, mainly, to migration.

PLATE XXXIV.

30

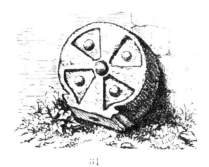

31

32

ANCIENT CHRISTIAN MONUMENTS.

We find in these parishes the following ancient crosses, the most remarkable and interesting of which is:

No. 30. This, for several years, was used as a prop, or buttress, to support the tottering wall of an out-building in the farm yard of Castlegoff, but it has recently been purchased by the Rev. J. J. Wilkinson, and set up in the Rectory grounds. Its original site is stated to have been near the earthworks at Castlegoff, and it is said that its base, with the socket therein, remained in situ within living memory, though now lost. At one end is formed a tenon to fix it in the socket of the base, and from the shoulders of this tenon it tapers to the top, which was squared, though now broken; there is, however, nothing to shew that it was ever surmounted by a cross. From the shoulders to the top it measures 7 ft. 2 ins.

Prefaced by a cross, there is an inscription in Saxon characters, consisting of two lines on the face of the stone and another line on one of the sides. It reads: + ÆLSELTH & GENERETH WROHTE THYSNE SYBSTEL FOR ÆLWYNEYS SAUL & FOR HEYSEL, that is—Ælselth and Genereth wrought this family pillar for Ælwyne's soul and for themselves. It is uncertain whether the first letter of the second line should be read as "W" and "R" conjoined, or as "W" only. There is a depression under the loop of the "W" which was probably an incision. The "W" is certain, and the word can be no other than *wrought*. At an earlier period than that to which this inscription is assigned the third person plural, imperfect tense, of the verb to wyrcan would have been written "worhton," but wrohte is also plural and only a later form than "worhton."

The only other word which requires special remark is the last in the second line. Fortunately the letters forming this word are particularly distinct, but being a compound word it could not easily be found in a Saxon dictionary. Those who are familiar with German know how hopeless it is to look for such words in German dictionaries. We must search for its component parts and seek its actual application when in composition. The word before us is formed of two roots: "sib" and "stel." The first is used, with various terminations, to signify family, kindred, relationship. The second means pillar or column. "Stele" is from the Greek word $\sigma\tau\acute{\eta}\lambda\eta$ == a "pillar." In Ainsworth's dictionary we find *stela* "a square or flatsided pillar, set up for a memorial, with an inscription; any monument set up in the high way; a tombstone."—Pliny vi, 28. The first definition is an exact description of the monument before us.[1]

The inscription is doubtless of the eleventh century. The omission of the letter "f"

---

[1] The Author is indebted to his friends Hans Claude Hamilton, Esq., F.S.A., of the Public Record Office, and the Rev. W. Iago of Bodmin, for valuable assistance in the elucidation of this monument, and to the latter for making the drawing on wood for the engraver.

in some of the names and words, and the form "wrohte" for "worhton," shew that it is late in the century, while "þysne" shews that it is not very late. (Plate XXXIV, fig. 30).

No. 31. This is the head of a fine cross. The symbol is of the Greek type within a circular rim, in the centre is a boss, and the same ornament is found upon the sunk panels between the limbs of the cross. The head measures 2 ft. in diameter, and it is 6 ins. thick. Both sides are alike. This cross crowns a little rocky island in a fish-pond in the grounds of Lanteglos Rectory. (See Plate XXXIV, fig. 31.)

No. 32. This cross is situate at the junction of three roads near Trewalder. It formerly stood in the hedge at the corner of the field called "Great Bovetown," marked 1235 in the parish map. When the hedge at the corner of this field was taken down a few years ago for the purpose of widening the road, the cross was, together with its base, placed upon the hedge on the opposite side of the road, where it still remains. The base of this cross is about 4 feet square, and the cross is fixed in a socket therein. The shaft is 11 inches high, and the head is an irregular circle without a rim. The symbol is of the Greek type, the lower arm widening out to the breadth of the shaft, and it has a hole sunk in the centre. (See Plate XXXIV, fig. 32.)

No. 33. Within the Rectory grounds is also a large cross the shaft of which measures from the ground to the head 4 ft., the head is 1 ft. 6 in. in diameter, and the stone is eight inches thick. The symbol is of the Greek type irregularly and rudely cut. It would appear to have been used as a gate post as it has a hole sunk in one of its sides. (See Plate XXXV, fig. 33.)

No. 34. This monolith cross is of a somewhat unusual type. It is very rude in character, and is remarkable for the size of the head and the projections below it. The symbol, which is of the Greek type, is within a circular rim. Both sides are alike, the symbol leaning to the left. It is probable that its original site was at the cross roads at a place called "Valley Truckle," about half-a-mile west of Camelford. It was found set in the ground, with its head downwards, at a smith's shop, immediately contiguous to the supposed site. It had been in the position described for several years, and had been used for the purpose of bending the tires of wheels, for which purpose a part of the shaft had been rounded off and pierced through for fixing a strong iron staple. From this position it has recently been rescued by the Rev. J. J. Wilkinson, and set up in the Rectory grounds at Lanteglos. The head measures 2 ft. 4 ins., and the projection below 2 ft. 8 ins. in breadth, the shaft below the arms is 1 ft. 8 ins. and at the bottom 1 ft. 6 ins. in breadth, and the total length, including the head, is 7 ft. 6 ins. At the head it is 6 ins. thick, and at the bottom of the shaft 8 ins. (See Plate XXXV, fig. 34.)

No. 35. At Trevia is another cross which now forms the post of a gate. It is much mutilated, the sides having been cut away and the top broken off. The shaft is now four feet above the ground. The portion of the head which remains measures 1 ft. 4 in. in addition. On one side is an incision which somewhat resembles the bowl of a chalice, but we have not been able to detect anything like a stem or foot. (See Plate XXXV, fig. 35).

No. 36. In the open field on the west side of the Parish Church of Advent is a tall elegant monolith cross remaining in situ. The shaft is 6 ft. 9 ins. in length out of the

PLATE XXXV.

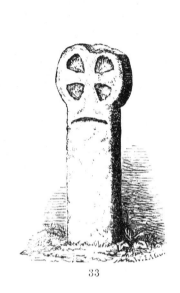

33

36

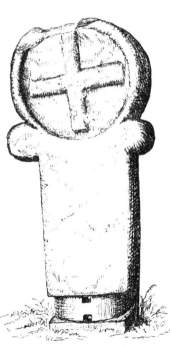

34

35

ground, and 1 ft. 3ins. wide at the bottom, tapering to 1ft. at the neck, and it is 8 ins. thick. The symbol is of the Greek character, somewhat irregular, within a circular rim. The ancient road, which has been deviated, passed close by it, and was intersected here by the Church path. (See Plate XXXV, fig. 36.)

ANCIENT ROADS AND TRACKWAYS.

In our account of the parish of Minster (ante vol. i. pp. 586, 587), we alluded to the ancient roads passing through that parish, and mentioned the great road leading from Stratton and the north, through the site of the town of Camelford, to Michaelstow Beacon. The ancient road from Warbstow Beacon, passing close to Davidstow Church, fell into this road about half-a-mile before it entered the parish of Lanteglos. About half-a-mile on the south of Camelford it received a trackway, which, diverting from the road from Warbstow Beacon, just mentioned, at Hallworthy, pursued a more southerly course through Davidstow and over Middle Moor in Advent. At this junction the main road divided, one branch leading to St. Teath and thence through St. Kew and Egloshayle to Wade (see ante vol. i. pp. 405, 484), and the other continuing its course to Michaelstow Beacon, as before described. About half-a-mile before entering the parish of Michaelstow, another trackway fell into this road. It, also, branched off from the great Warbstow road at Hallworthy, taking a more southerly circuit by Trevillian gate and Lanlary rock, a mile north of Roughtor. Near the rock it divides, one branch leading through St. Breward by " Arthur's Hall," which we have described (ante vol. i., p. 353), and the other through Advent. About half-a-mile after entering that parish a road branched off to Camelford, and the other continuing its course by Watergate and through Tresinny near Advent Church, crossed the Camel at Kentistock mill and formed the junction above-mentioned; and crossing the great road pursued its course to St. Teath. There was also a still more southerly track which branched out of the one we have last mentioned about midway between Watergate and Tresinny, which passed through Trewint and Trecarne, and fell into the Michaelstow road just before it entered the parish of Michaelstow.

Another ancient road, now forming, through the greater part of its length, the turn-pike road leading from Boscastle to Camelford, though it does not, itself, pass through the former place, crosses the road described (ante, p. 586), and passing by Lanteglos Church and Trewalder leads to St. Teath.

Previously to the construction of the railways, the road which we have mentioned as passing from Hallworthy by Davidstow Church to Camelford, formed a portion of the turnpike road leading from Exeter to Falmouth through Launceston and Wadebridge. After passing out of the parish of Lanteglos at Knight's mill into St. Teath, it entered upon a new road constructed down the valley of the Kestell, which united again with the ancient road at St. Kew highway and proceeded thence to Wadebridge.

PRE-HISTORIC REMAINS.

Castlegoff. On the top of a hill about a quarter of a mile on the west of Lanteglos Church, about 2 miles north by west from Michaelstow Beacon and 3½ miles north east from Tregaer (in St. Kew) is an entrenchment called Castlegoff. It consists of a single rampart and ditch about 200 ft. in diameter. On the west side is an outwork or barbican, the length of which is about 300 ft. and the breadth about 120 ft. After branching out on each side of the principal work a short distance the rampart is nearly concentric with that of the inner circle. The principal entrance appears to have been through this out-work, though there is an opening, resembling an entrance, on the opposite side.

About 350 yds. north of this entrenchment, on the slope of the hill, on a tenement called Newberry, in the parish of St. Teath, is another circular work doubtless pertaining to the former. It consists of a rampart and ditch about 500 ft. in diameter. The greater part of the rampart is entire and forms the fence of a circular meadow, numbered 1218 on the Tithe map of St. Teath. On the north side it is intersected by an occupation road and a cottage is built within the area. (See Plate XXXVI, fig. 1.)

There is another circular entrenchment on the north side of the parish, on a tenement called Bury Ground belonging to Helstone. It is situate on the high ground 400 or 500 yards west of the turnpike road leading from Camelford to Bodmin, about a mile north east of Michaelstow Beacon, from which, of course, it can be distinctly seen as also from Castle-goff. It is in a field numbered on the parish map 897, and called Higher Bury Ground, and for about two-thirds of its circuit forms the fence of a field, within this enclosure, omitted in the map. The entrenchment consists of a single Vallum with external ditch, the whole of which has been filled up in agricultural operations except about 150 yds on the north side which is clearly distinguishable. This entrenchment, like that last mentioned, has not, heretofore, been noticed. (See Plate XXXVI, fig. 2.)

MEETING HOUSES OF DISSENTERS.[1]

Wesleyan Methodists.—By an Indenture dated 1st November 1784 Gertrude, Duchess of Bedford, and other devisees in trust of the real estate of John Duke of Bedford then

---

[1] On 8th March 1819, William Mason, of Ashwater, registered in the Archdeacon's Court a Building situate in the village of Camelford, in the parish of Lanteglos, then in the occupation of William Rowe, as a Meeting House for Protestant Dissenters, and on 12th July in the same year, the same person registered a Building situate in the village of Trezenny, in the parish of Advent, for the same purpose. We do not know by what denomination these buildings were used.

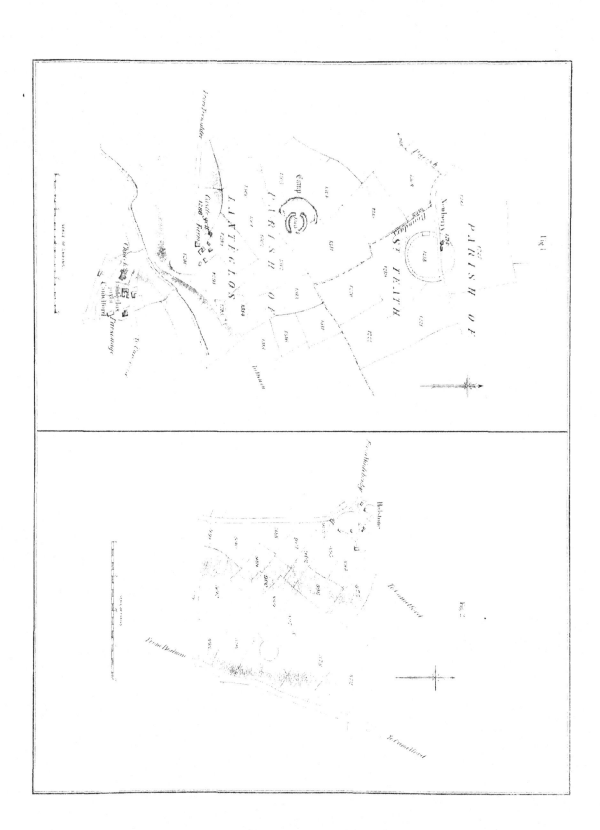

lately deceased, granted, for a term of 99 years determinable upon the deaths of three lives, to Richard Mabyn of the Borough of Camelford, currier, and John Rosevear of the same Borough, shop-keeper, a plot of ground called "Tom's Hay," behind the Back Street in the said Borough, cotaining in length about 60 feet and in breadth about 30 feet;[1] and upon this plot a building was soon afterwards erected, which, on the 25th May 1787, was registered as a Meeting House for Protestant Dissenters in the court of the Archdeacon of Cornwall.[2]   By deed dated 30th June 1797 Richard Mabyn and John Rosevear conveyed these premises to John Cock of Port Isaac, Esq. and others, in Trust for the uses limited in the foundation deed, dated 28th February 1784 and enrolled, of the people called Methodists.[3]   Afterwards, by Indenture dated 24th December 1812, a lease was obtained for the term of 99 years of a piece of ground, contiguous to the above, to be used as a burial ground; and by deed dated 16th March 1833 the Duke of Cleveland, who had now acquired the property in Camelford, in consideration of the sum of £283, conveyed the above-mentioned premises, together with a dwelling-house, malt-house, and stable, all contiguous, to James Rosevear, draper, and others, to hold in fee in trust for the uses above described.[4]

This building is licensed for the celebration of marriages.   It contains sittings for 400 persons, and there are now attached to it 51 registered members.

The Wesleyan Methodists have also a Meeting House at Helston, which was built about the year 1830, and by deed dated 24th June 1867 was conveyed upon the trusts of the Wesleyan model deed dated 3rd July 1832.   It affords accommodation for 140 persons and there are eight registered members attached to it.

United Methodist Free Church.—Messrs. Thomas Pope Rosevear, Richard Harris Burt and others, erected a proprietary building at Camelford in 1837. This is probably the same building which, on 19th December 1840, was registered in the Court of the Archdeacon by Walter Treleaven of Lanlivery, under the description of a Chapel in the Borough of Camelford, on the east side of Fore street and on the Launceston side of the Market house, as for the use of the Wesleyan Methodist Association.   In 1871 it was conveyed to the uses contained in United Methodist Free Churches model deed. It affords accommodation for 300 persons, and there are attached to it 60 registered members.

Trewalder.—The same body possesses an old Meeting House at Trewalder in which John Wesley is said to have preached.   There are here 130 sittings and 37 registered members.

Tresinney.—They have another at Tresinney in the parish of Advent, not long since erected.   This will accommodate 80 persons, and there are 13 registered members belonging to it.

---

[1] Rot. Claus. 37th George III., Part 6, No. 7. [2] Archdeaconry Records.
[3] Rot. Claus. 37th George III., Part 6, No. 7. [4] Rot. Claus. 4th William IV., Part 6, No. 7.

2 Q

Bible Christians.—The Bible Christians, under their original designation of "Brianites," would appear to have been particularly active, from their first organization in 1819, in the parishes of Lanteglos and Advent. On 30th December 1820, William Baily, described as of Jacobstow, Minister, registered in the Court of the Archdeacon of Cornwall a house, in the occupation of Honora Perse, at Trewean (Trewen) in the parish of Lanteglos by Camelford, as a place for meetings of Brianites; and also another house at Helstone, in the same parish, in the occupation of William Danning. On 10th March 1821 he registered a house at Trevye, in the occupation of William Waken, for the same purpose, and on the 19th April following a house at Witwalls, in Advent, in the occupation of William Allford. On 12th March 1821 Simon Orchard of Advent registered a house in his own occupation at Treclego, in that parish, for a like purpose, and on 9th May 1828 William Runnalls, described as "of Minster, Minister," registered for the same purpose a house at Helstone, in the occupation of George Hockin.[1]

The Bible Christians have now two Meeting Houses in these parishes.

On 23rd June 1841 Thomas Libby of St. Teath registered in the above-mentioned court a building at Victoria Row in Camelford as a place of meeting for Protestant Dissenters,[1] and, by deed dated 24th December in the same year, William Fillis Pearce of Camelford, Gent., conveyed to the said Thomas Libby and others, for the sum of £16, a piece of ground, 81½ ft. in length and 50 in breadth, being part of a field called Turnpike Meadow, situate on the road leading from Camelford to Launceston, with the house, chapel, and building lately erected thereon, to hold to the said Thomas Libby, and the others, in trust, to permit all such persons as should be appointed by the Annual Conference of the people called Bible Christians to preach therein, and no other without the consent of the pastor or superintendent of the circuit, provided that such persons preach no other doctrines than those contained in the Rev. John Wesley's notes and sermons.[2] From this it appears that there was no difference in the religious opinions of the Bible Christians and the Wesleyan Methodists. This meeting house contains sittings for 200 persons, and there are thirty registered members.

The other meeting house of this Connexion is at Helston, built, it is presumed, in succession to the meetings in private houses above-mentioned. This will accommodate 100 persons, and there are nine registered members.

MANOR OF HELSTON IN TRIGG.

This manor, called Helston in Trigg to distinguish it from other manors of the same name, appears in Domesday under the name of Henlistona. In the time of Edward the Confessor it was held by Algar, and was given by William to the Earl of Moreton. "The Earl

---

[1] Records of the Archdeaconry Court of Cornwall.   [2] Rot. Claus. 1841. Part 22, No. 5.

has one manor which is called Henlistona, which Algar held on the day on which King Edward was alive and dead. In it are two hides, and it rendered gild for one hide [these two hides fifteen ploughs can plough] whereof the Earl has one hide and four ploughs in demesne, and the villans have one hide and eight ploughs. There the Earl has twenty villans and fifteen bordars, and eighteen serfs, and eighteen unbroken mares, and ten animals, and 150 sheep, and five hogs, and twelve she goats, and ten acres of brushwood, and pasture three leagues in length and two in breadth. This renders £16, less twenty pence, and when received it [rendered] as much."[1]

This was one of the 248 manors granted by the Conqueror to his half brother Robert Earl of Moreton, whom he created Earl of Cornwall. From him it descended to his son William, who having taken offence against King Henry I. for refusing to him the Earldom of Kent, which had been bequeathed to him by his uncle Odo, in 1105 he took part with his maternal uncle, Robert de Belesme, against the king, and consequently forfeited all his lands.[2] This manor subsequently passed with the Earldom of Cornwall to Reginald de Dunstanville, illegitimate son of K. Henry I., afterwards to Henry Fitzcount,[3] illegitimate son of Reginald; and, eventually, by charter dated 10 August 1231,[4] to Richard Earl of Poictou and Cornwall, as already stated under *Bliston*.[5] Richard Earl of Cornwall died in December 1271, and was succeeded by his son Edmund.

In December 1275 the Bishop of Exeter committed the Church of Lanteglos to the charge of Sir Ralph de Hengham for the Earl of Cornwall until the Kalends of April following, and upon the presentation of the said Earl, on the 6th May next afterwards, the said Ralph was admitted to the Rectory of the said parish, which was then appurtenant to the Manor, as it still continues to be. Earl Edmund died in 1300, and from the usual inquisition taken thereupon we find the following particulars of the Manor. In the list of the Jurors on this inquisition appear the following names: Henry de Bodrigan, Ralph Bloyou, John Reskemmur, Ralph de Glyn, Walter Tremur, John Trelouny, Richard Rescarekmur, Stephen de Trewint, Michael Bráy, Robert le Brun, &c., who say: as concerning "the Manor of Helleston in Tregasbire with the Borough of Camelford and Hamlet of Penmayn[6] that there is a certain pasture which is called Knottlesford, which is worth by the year 20s, and a certain other pasture which is called Gosehull, (Goosehill) worth by the year 8s., and the turbary in the same pastures is worth by the year 20s.; and there is there a certain park with deer, and the herbage in the same is worth for the deer 40s.

"And there are there in the hamlet of Penmayn 39 free tenants who render by the year 115s. 6d. at the feast of St. Michael, and for the aid of the same 2s. 11d. at the same term. And Stephen de Trewaynt holds by deed three water mills at fee farm, and

---

[1] Exon Domesday, Add. p. 216, origin. fo. 237. See also Exch. Domesday, vol i., p. 121 *b*.

[2] Ordericus Vitalis, vol. iii. 358.

[3] In 1189 the manor was in the hands of the King and the men of the manor owed 31s. 2d. of Tallage (Rot. Pip. 1st Richard I.)   [4] Rot. Cart. 15th Henry III. p. 4.   [5] Ante vol. i., p. 29.

[6] Penmayn was not originally parcel of this Manor, but having escheated to the Crown, was included in the grant to Earl Reginald and was by him annexed to this Manor. Rot. Hund. vol. ii, p. 56.

2 Q²

he renders therefore by the year £6 13s. 4d. at the feasts of Easter and St. Michael;' and there are there 33 conventionary tenants who hold 10 acres and 1 ferling of land Cornish, and 9 landyok,¹ and they render by the year £9 14s. 5d. at the four principal terms; and there are there and in the hamlet aforesaid seventy-eight villans who hold 38½ acres and the third part of one ferling of land Cornish, and twenty-five landyok, and two plots of meadow, and render by the year £22 5s. 4d. at the four principal terms, and for aid at the feast of St. Michael 56s.; and there is at Penmayn a certain ferry which is worth by the year 10s., and two tenants there for multure of mill and one plot of land at the feast of St. Michael render 3s. 6d., and the chevage of natives there are worth 3s. 8d. The pleas and perquisites of courts there are worth by the year 66s. 8d. Also there are in the borough of Camelford sixty-two burgesses who hold sixty-two burgages and render by the year £4 4s. 4½d. The fairs there once a year are worth 5s. The pleas and perquisites there are worth by the year 13s. 4d. *Sum.* £61 2s. 3d."

The jury also found that the said Earl died seized " of the advowson of the Church of St. Michael of Hellesbiry of the value of 10 marks, and of the Church of ' Nanteglos' of the value of 40 marks per annum." ²

As Earl Edmund died s.p. the Earldom of Cornwall became extinct, and the lands which had been granted by King Henry III. to support its dignity reverted to the crown and continued in the hands of the King during the remainder of the reign of King Edward I. Edward II. however, on his accession, created his favorite, Peter de Gaveston, who had married the widow of Earl Edmund (Margaret daughter of Richard de Clare Earl of Hereford and Gloucester, who had been divorced from her husband) Earl of Cornwall, and granted to him the whole of the honours, manors, lands, advowsons, &c., &c., of which Earl Edmund had died seized.³ And two years afterwards the King confirmed the same to the said Peter and Margaret his wife.

Hence Peter de Gaveston presented to the Church of Lanteglos in 1307 one Thomas de London.⁴ Into the question of the unpopularity of Gaveston and his tragical fate at Scarborough, on 19th May 1312, we need not here enter. Suffice it to say that after his death this manor, *inter alia*, again fell into the hands of the King, and two years afterwards we find the Sheriff accounting for the profits of the same. We need not here enter into the details, but may remark that the gross receipts, including the issues of the Manor of Helleston together with the borough of Camelford, and the hamlet of Penmain amounted to £33 15s. 10¾d.; and that the expenditure, including the reparation, and in part new making, of the palings around the park of Lanteglos, and the wages of the parker there for 137 days at 1½d. per day, amounted to 37s. 5½d., so that the net revenue was £31 18s. 5¼d.⁵

¹ "Yokelands"—small farms.   ² Inq. p.m. 28th Edward I., No. 44.   ³ Rot. Cart., 1st Edward II.
⁴ It may be noted that Thomas de London would seem to have been much attached to his patron. When Gaveston fell into trouble we find the Rector of Lanteglos asking for, and obtaining, license of non-residence, and on 16th November 1315 he obtained a license to remain at the house of his lady the Countess of Cornwall until the end of Michaelmas term, and soon afterwards he finally resigned the benefice. (See post, List of Institutions.)
⁵ Rot. Pip. 9th Edward II.

In 1328 King Edward III. created his brother John of Eltham Earl of Cornwall, and by Charter, dated 10th October 1331, in addition to two annuities, one of £20 and another of 2000 marks, payable out of the issues and profits of the County of Cornwall, granted to him certain castles, manors, lands, &c., in Cornwall, *inter alia*, the Manor of Helleston in Trigg with the park and other its appurtenances, to hold to the said Earl and the heirs of his body, in default of such issue to revert to the King and his heirs.[1]

It would, perhaps, be convenient here to advert to the tenures under which the lands of this manor were from ancient times held. It has from beyond legal memory been called one of the Assessional Manors of the Earls and Dukes of Cornwall. There were seventeen of these manors, but in 1798 four or five of them were sold under Act 38th George III, for the redemption of the land tax. These manors have been designated assessional from the tenements within them, which were not held in free tenure, being let from time to time at certain assessed rents in convention. The process was this: a commission was issued either by the King, or the Earl, as the case might be, to certain persons of eminent station to let the lands. The first commission extant is that of Earl John, dated 20th November 6th Edward III. in which, after reciting that he had the power, without doing wrong to any one, to retake all the lands into his own hands and make thereof his profits, he empowers the Commissioners to let the lands in convention for term of life or lives, or for years, as shall seem to the said Commissioners for the good of the tenants who then held the same, or, in their default, to others who would give more, as should be most for the profit of the Lord. Accordingly the Commissioners assessed all the lands in the several manors for seven years from the feast of St. Michael following (excepting the lands which the natives held in villanage) and not beyond, because it seemed not to the advantage of the lord to let them for a longer term. The Assession Roll, under this commission, which is dated 29th March 7th Edward III, is still extant in the Duchy of Cornwall Office, but it is clear from it that it established no new principle.

The names and lands of the *free tenants* are not shewn on this Roll. At that date it was not considered necessary, for the free tenants were not concerned with the assession. There were three other classes of tenants, viz., free conventionaries, native conventionaries, and natives of stock.

The *Free Conventionaries* took their tenements for the term of seven years at an assessed rent, to be paid quarterly, and were bound to serve the offices of prepositus, tythingman, and bedel when elected, and when the Lord, or any one in his name, wished to hunt they were to chase and find litter When the ancient parks were broken into arable land they were bound to plough there each year according to the quantity of their tenure: viz., they who held half an acre of land Cornish half an acre of land English, and were paid for the ploughing one penny, and they were to reap there in Autumn with one man for one day and received for diet one penny. The tenant had no power to devise his tenement without the license of the Lord, and when he died the lord was entitled to his best animal as a heriot, but to no other of his chattels; and the tenant made fealty.

[1] Rot. Cart, 5th Edward III.

The *Native Conventionaries*, whose condition was that described as *villans regardant*,[1] held their tenements by precisely the same tenure, except that when the tenant died the lord had all his chattels, and his youngest born son, then living, made fine at the will of the lord, and had the tenement for the remainder of the term, in native convention.

The *Natives of Stock*, equivalent to *villans in gross*, held their lands in villanage and paid rent at the four usual terms, and performed all the same services as the native conventionary tenants. Indeed, in some respects, they appear to have been in a more favourable situation, for the son succeeding to the tenements was not to be amoved there-from during his life.

In the caption of seizin upon the creation of Edward the Black Prince Duke of Cornwall 1337, all these tenures are fully set out, together with the names of the tenements and of the tenants, as well of the free tenants as the conventionary. Of the former there were in number twenty-eight, who paid a certain rent and were obliged to do suit at the Lord's court three weeks by three weeks. The rents then paid were:

	£	s.	d.
Rents of 23 Free Tenants	11	19	10
„ of 38 Free Conventionaries	8	19	9
„ of 68 Native Conventionaries	24	19	7
„ of 8 Natives of Stock	3	1	7

Other casual payments, *e.g.* Recognition, Pasture, Turbary, Customary aids, Chevage of Natives, &c., amounted to £7 11s. 3d.; and there were some other small payments. From Penmayn was received 111s. 9½d., and the Borough of Camelford rendered in the whole 105s. 3½d.[2]

From this date there would not appear to have been any legal alteration of the relations of the Lord and tenants, though in process of time, from the leniency of the Commissioners, or Stewards, or from other causes the tenants came to believe that they held an estate of inheritance in their conventionary tenements renewable from seven years to seven years by the payment of a fixed fine, at a fixed rent. We shall not enter here into any discussion of this subject. It will be sufficient to refer the reader to a most interesting paper upon the customs of the assessional manors, drawn up very early in the seventeenth century, which we discovered in the Muniment Room at Coker Court, co.

---

[1] Ante Intro., p. 17.

[2] In 32nd Edward III. at a court of the Manor of Helleston in Trigg the homage of the manor presented that the tenants' of the said' manor ought to have common of all sorts over all the wastes of Rowetorre, which is parcel of the manor of Hamaethy; upon this presentment John Dabernoun, then Steward of the manor of Helston, commanded the said tenants to use the rights so claimed, and they put, from day to day, 500 beasts upon the said wastes. Hugh Peverel, Lord of the manor of Hamatethy, complained to the Prince, alleging that he and his ancestors had, immemorably, been seized of the manor of Hamatethy, which they held by military service, and that no man had any commons on any part of the said manor. The Petition was ordered to be referred to the Steward to certify. (Council Book of the Black Prince). We have no information as to the result, but the claim of the tenants would seem to have been disallowed.

Somerset, printed in Appendix I. It may, however, be observed that in the Parliamentary Survey, hereafter to be mentioned, the claims of the tenants seem to have been recognised.

The Assession Rolls shew, however, a gradual softening and decay of the spirit of serfdom. In the earlier Rolls the several classes of conventionary tenants were kept quite distinct. Very soon the natives of stock disappear entirely, and the free conventionaries and the native are thrown promiscuously into the same class, and their condition is not always stated. Serfdom, however, continued to exist as late as 1575, when a commission was issued under the great seal to Lord Burleigh, then Lord High Treasurer, and Sir William Mildmaye, Knight, Chancellor and under Treasurer of the Exchequer, reciting that divers and sundry of the Queen's poor faithful subjects, being born bond in bludde and regardant to divers of her manors, &c., had made humble suite be manumised, enfranchised, and made free with their children and sequells, by which they, their children and sequells, might become more apt and fit members of the commonwealth; and considering the same acceptable to Almighty God, who in the beginning made all mankynd free, and for the tender love and zeal which Her Majesty bore to her said subjects, authority is given to the said Commissioners to accept, admytt and receive to be manumitted, and made free, such, and so many, of the Queen's bondmen and bondwomen in bloude, with all and every of their children and sequells, their goods, tenements and hereditaments, as are now pertaining, or regardant, to any of the Queen's manors, &c., in Cornwall, Devon, Somerset, and Gloucester, as to the discretion of the Commissioners should seem meet, compounding with them for such reasonable fines, or sums of money, for their manumission and enfranchisement, and for the possessions, and enjoying of all and singular their manors, lands, tenements, hereditaments, goods and chattels as the Commissioners and they could agree for the same.[1] Accordingly, under this commission, an arrangement was come to with divers bondsmen of this manor, and by deeds dated 10th November 19th Elizabeth, (1577) Henry Hicks of Fentenwannen, and Robert Werring and others of Trevie, in Lanteglos, natives regardant of the manor of Helston, were granted their manumission, and by similar deed, dated 12th February 1577-8, in the same regnal year, Nicholas Werring and others of Trevie were also emancipated.

After the death of Queen Elizabeth and the accession of James the Dukedom of Cornwall devolved upon Prince Henry, the eldest born son of the latter, and after his death, in 1612, his brother Charles, afterwards King Charles I., though not in accordance with the terms of the charter creating the Duchy, which limited the succession to Prince Edward and "to the first begotten sons of him Kings of England and Dukes of the said place," was made Duke of Cornwall. Upon the birth of his eldest son Prince Charles in 1630, he, in virtue of his birthright, became Duke of Cornwall, and inherited the honours, castles, manors, and lands thereto belonging, *inter alia*, this manor with its appurtenances. Upon the murder of Charles I. and the overthrow of the kingdom all the estates of the King, Queen, and the Prince of Wales were seized by the Parliament, and an act was

---

[1] Draft in Burleigh's handwriting, Lands. M.S. 105, No. 42.

passed vesting them in Trustees for sale. This led to a survey being made in 1650, called the "Parliamentary Survey," which gives a particular account, *inter alia*, of this manor. It states that there was no manor, or mansion house, and that the demesnes, consisting of the two parks, had been let on lease to Sir Richard Buller (see post); that the total amount of the rents was £83 3s. 9¾d., and the fourth part of a farthing; that the improved rents of the lands in lease, beyond the then rent, was £126 8s. 8d., and that the timber, underwood, &c., on the lands on lease was then worth, to be sold, £256 12s. 6d.

The boundaries of the manor are thus stated :

The said manor is bounded on the south and south-east with the manor of Hamatethy, being the lands of John Billing, Esq., Anthony Nicholl, Esq., Humphry Lower Esq., ...
Elcot Gent., Thomas Lower Esq., and [Christ'] Walker Gent.; on the east with the lands of John Trevillian Esq.; and thence with the lands of........; on the north with the lands of Richard Hockin Gent.; from thence by the lands of John Lampen Esq.; from thence by the barton of Worthyvale, being the land of Christopher Worthyvale Esq.; thence with the lands of Hender Molesworth Esq.; thence with the lands of William Glynn and Christopher Worthyvale, Esqs.; thence with the lands of Anthony Nicoll Esq.; from thence on the north-west with the Manor of Tintagell, parcell of the ancient Duchy; from thence by the Manor of Trebarrow being the lands of...........Harrington Esq.; from thence with the lands of William Scawen Esq.; on the west with the lands of William Scawen Esq.; on the west with the lands of the heirs of John Nicoll Esq.; from thence with the lands of John Davis Esq., and Thomas Lower Esq.; thence with the lands of John Chappel; thence with the lands of the heirs of John Nicholls Esq., thence with the Manor of Newhill, being the lands of John Lord Roberts; thence with the lands of John Nicoll Esq.; thence with the lands of Taverner Langford; thence with the lands of Warwick Lord Mohun; thence with the lands of Tavernor Langford Gent; thence with the lands of Carminow Esq.; on the south side the Manor of Polrode, being the lands of Warwick Lord Mohun; thence with the Barton of Hengar, being the lands of John Billing Esq., thence with the lands of the heirs of John Davis Esq., until the aforesaid bounds come to the Manor of Hamatethy whence they did begin.

Accordingly on 2nd July 1650 a contract was entered into for the sale in fee simple of the Manors of Helston in Trigg and Tintagel, except the parks of Helsbury and Lanteglos, to one Thomas Hearne, on behalf of Robert Bennett of Lawhitton, co. Cornwall Esq., at fifteen years' purchase at the then annual rents, which, for the purpose of the sale, so far as relates to this manor, was estimated at the exact sum £72 10s. 5¾d. and seven parts of a farthing; and by an Indenture, dating 7th August following, between William Steele Esq., Recorder of London, and other of the Trustees for the sale of the lands, &c., lately belonging to Charles Stewart Duke of Cornwall, now vested in the Commonwealth, of the one part, and the aforesaid Robert Bennett of the other part, the said Manors of Helston and Tintagel, except as before excepted, were conveyed to the said Robert Bennett in fee simple to hold to him the said Robert and his heirs and assigns for ever.

Of course, upon the restoration of the monarchy 1660, all the irregular grants made during the the usurpation were resumed by the crown, and, *inter alia*, the Manor of Helston in Trigg, which, from that date, remained vested in the crown, or the successive Dukes of Cornwall, under the ancient tenures, until the year 1844, when an Act of Parliament was passed to enable the confirmation and enfranchisement of the estates of the conventionary tenants of the ancient assessional manors of the Duchy of Cornwall, whereupon three Commissioners were appointed who, on 28th July 1846, awarded a certain sum to be paid by the tenants in lieu of all arrears of rent, &c., and of all heriots and services, amounting in the whole to £307 17s. 6¾d.; and they further agreed with the tenants for the payment of an annual sum, thenceforward, for each tenement in lieu of all rents, heriots and services; and as the tenants claimed, and had been accustomed to enjoy, certain rights of common of pasture and turbary on the wastes of the said manor, portions of Advent Moor were awarded to each tenement in proportion to its extent.

THE PARKS.

There was an adjunct to this important manor which we must not omit to notice, for it is, perhaps, a feature of greater local interest than any other. We allude to the extensive royal parks with which the manor was honoured and adorned. Of these there were two, the most ancient of which, perhaps by several centuries, was the Park of Lanteglos. This, in 1337, is spoken of as one ancient park containing 102 acres, English, of profitable land, worth 4d. per acre, per annum, ten acres of meadow, worth, per annum, 18d. per acre, and eleven acres of wood whereof the pasture and underwood were worth, per annum, 3s. The great antiquity of this park is shewn from the fact that the conventionary tenants of the manor were, by ancient custom, extending back beyond legal memory, which reached to the accession of King Richard I. (1189), under the obligation of ploughing it when any portion was broken for cultivation. The other park, that of Hellesbury, was in 1337 called the "New Park" and was said to contain in its circuit four groves wherein were 180 wild animals, but it was added that it would sustain 200 wild animals, and if the animals were not there the agistment was worth, per annum, 50s. One Richard Golalmynge was at this time Parker for the term of his life under a charter from the King, and received for his wages 2d. a day and 13s. 4d. annually for his robe. This was the condition of the parks on the creation of the Duchy of Cornwall in the person of the "Black Prince," and they do not appear to have altered their character for a considerable period. On 29th October 1351 the office of Parker of the parks of Lanteglos and Kerribullock was granted to John Logardyne, at the request of Bartholomew Burghersshe the father, and Bartholomew Burghersshe the son;[1] and in 1354 William de

---

[1] Council Book of the Black Prince, fol. 175. (Duchy of Cornwall Office).

2 R

Tottebusshe was appointed Parker of the parks of Lanteglos and Hellesbury, and received for himself and his boy 3d. per day wages.[1]   On the 7th September 1355 there was a warrant to him to deliver the custody of these parks to Walter Smale and Walter Vencor.[2] On 7th May 1361, the custody of these parks was granted to John the son of Robert Dabernoun ;[3] and on 9th June 1363, Nicholas Hunt was appointed Keeper.[4] The parks at this date would seem to have been well stocked, for in the following year an order was given for furnishing divers deer from the Duke's parks in Cornwall, and whilst the other parks, in general, supplied two only, four " deyms " (fallow deer) were taken from Lanteglos and Helsbury and six from Restormel.[5]

Again we find that in 1397 John Colyn of Helland was attached to reply to Sir Richard Abberbery, Knight, who, at the time, we presume, was Parker, for having, together with Robert Hervy, Simon Warde and others, entered the parks of the same Richard at Lanteglos and Hellesbury, on Monday next after the feast of St. John Baptist, by force with swords, bows and arrows, &c., and without his licence hunted and taken game, viz., twenty bucks and forty does, and carried them away, to the value of £20.[6]

In 1456 the office of Parker of the parks of Hellesbury and Lantegules was granted by King Henry VI, to John Arundell, together with the herbage, pannage, and dead wood, for the term of his life,[7] but, whether by the death of the said John or in consequence of forfeiture upon the overthrow of King Henry we cannot say, it was again in the hands of the crown in 1462, for at the Court of Assession in that year the agistment of the pannage of these two parks was taken by William Menwynnek and Nicholas Loure, for the term of seven years, at the rent of 40s. per annum, but they were bound to leave sufficient pasture for the wild animals.[8]

By Letters Patent dated 1st March 4th Edward IV. (1464-5) the office of Keeper of the Parks of the King at Hellesbury and Lanteglos was granted to John Penfoune, Esq., to have and occupy the said office by himself or his sufficient deputy or deputies, for the term of his life, and to receive the profits and emoluments to such office due and accustomed. Salary iiij[li] xj[s] iij[d] [9] On the overthrow of the house of York, this grant was annulled, and on 24th of September 1485, the custody of the parks was granted for life to Henry Lee one of the King's Guard. [10]

On 6th July 1509, the office of Keeper of the Parks of Lanteglose and Heylesbury was granted to Sir John Arundell, Knt.: [11] and in 1539 he took at the assession court the agistment of the pannage.[12]

On a survey of the park of Hellesbury, made on the 2nd April 1549 by the King's surveyor, it is said " that there ys growing forty-six acres set thinlie wth oke, no timber short and shrubbed, of 100 or 200 yer grow[t], wherof the topp and lopp of 10 acres,

---

[1] Council Book of the Black Prince, fol. 175. (Duchy of Cornwall Office).

[2] Ibid., fo. 232.   [3] Ibid., fo. 476.   [4] Ibid., fo. 522.

[5] Ibid., fo. 528.   [6] De Banco Rolls, 20th Richard II., Hil. m. 406.

[7] Rot. Claus., 24th Henry VI, Part i, m. 37.   [8] Assession Roll, 2nd Edward IV.

[9] Inrolled in the Exchequer, 5th Edward IV., Easter.   [10] Rot. Pat. 1st Henry. VII, Part i, m. 8.

[11] Rot. Pat., 31st Hen. VIII., Part i. m. 7.   [12] Assess. Roll, 31st Henry VIII.

of one yeres grow[t], & 36 acres residue, one w[t] an other, valued at 40s. the acre.   The outwood, set with underwood of oke and hazil,[1] contains six acres, whereof 3 acres of 12 & 14 years grow[t], & 3 acres residue of one, twoo 3 & 4 years grow[t], worth, at 20 yer grow[t], 26s. 8d. thacre."[1]   It was about this time that the Parks were disparked and the timber was, probably, cut, for in 1617 a jury of tenants, in reply to certain interrogatories, state upon oath, at a court held at Lostwithiel in August, that there were then growing in Lanteglos Park four acres of wood, and in Hellesbury Park four acres of wood and timber, or there-abouts, and that some were more than thirty years' growth, and some less.   At this time both parks were in the tenure of Sir William Killigrew.   On 20th October 1625, Roger Palmer, Esq., accounted for half a year's rent due to the King's Majesty at Michaelmas preceding, amounting to £5 6s. 8d.[2]

On 5th May 1627 King Charles I. granted a lease of the Parks of Lanteglos and Hellesbury to Sir Richard Buller for the term of ninety-nine years, if John Buller, Anthony Buller, and William Buller, sons of the said Sir Richard Buller, so long should live, at the rent of £10 13s. 4d. per annum, all great trees, woods, underwoods, mines, wards, marriages, &c., &c., being excepted, and the lessee being bound to plant yearly twelve trees of oak, ash or elm, and he was allowed to have all sorts of " botes " to be expended on the premises.   On the taking of the Parliamentary Survey in 1650 this lease continued in existence, Anthony Buller, aged twenty-five years, and William Buller, aged twenty-four years, being still alive.

The Park of Lanteglos, described as then lately disparked, was said to contain 126 acres then divided into several enclosures of meadow, pasture and arable ground ; and Hellesbury Park to contain 306 acres of land similarly divided.   The timber trees, pollards, sapplins, &c., in the Park of Lanteglos were valued at £13 2s. 6d., and those in the Park of Hellesbury at £82 10s., whilst the value of the underwoods in the same park, in which were valued divers sapplins and timber trees, were estimated as worth, in ready money, £180.   At the same time it was stated that Sir Richard Buller had recently cut six acres of coppice wood which he sold for £5 an acre.   The surveyor further stated that these parks were worth at an improved value, besides the then rent, as above stated, £126 8s. 8d. per annum.

Upon this survey, on 21st August 1650, a contract was entered into by the Trustees for the sale of the Estates of the King, Queen, and Prince of Wales, for the sale of these parks to John Holwell of Plymouth, Gent., in fee simple, at twenty years' purchase, based upon the above-mentioned survey, and, accordingly, by Indenture dated 28th October following, in consideration of the sum of £1247 11s. 2d., the said premises were conveyed to him, his heirs, and assigns, for ever.   This sale, like that of the manor, became void at the restoration.

In the last century the parks of Helsbury and Lanteglos were held under lease from the Duchy by the family of Denithorne.   Isaac Denithorne of the city of Hereford, Clerk,

---

1 Augm. Office, Miscell. Books vol. 431, p. 42.
2 Miscl. Books, vol. 73, Augm. Office. Duchy of Cornwall.

2 R[2]

by deed dated 9th September 1766, granted to Joseph Pope of Michaelstow, yeoman, all those fields or closes of land called Deer Parks, in the parish of Lanteglos, and all those other fields of closes of land called Helsbury, in the parishes of Advent and Michaelstow, with the dwelling house, gardens, &c., in the village of Helston, to hold to the said Joseph Pope, from the expiration of a former grant which had eight years to run, made by the said Isaac Denithorne to the said Joseph Pope, for the further term of ninety-nine years, if the said Isaac Denithorne aged fifty-six years, James Denithorne aged twenty-three years, and Nicholas Denithorne aged twenty-two years, sons of the said Isaac Denithorne, so long should live, at the yearly rent of £60; and by deed dated 3rd October 1778, the said Joseph Pope assigned the said lease to Giles Jory of St. Tudy, yeoman, for the remainder of the said term.[1]

In August 1871, Helsbury Park, described as containing 287a. 1r. 32p., whereof about fifty-two acres consisted of thriving oak timber and coppice and fir plantations, together with the minerals and the exclusive right of fishing in the river Camel, within the limits of the estate, was advertised to be sold by auction, under the provisions of Act 26th and 27th Vic., cap. 49. It was not sold at the auction, but, by deed dated 10th May 1872, the property was conveyed to Mr. John Gatley of St. Erme. On his death, in February of the following year, the estate passed in equal shares to his nephews, Mr. Charles Ralph Gatley and Mr. John Gatley of Her Majesty's Customs. The latter has purchased his brother's moiety, and is now the sole proprietor of this interesting and historical estate.

FREE WARREN.

At the Assession Court held on 12th August 1617, the Commissioners granted to Richard Billing and Nicholas Cock, Esquires, a licence of hunting, hawking, and fishing throughout the manor at the rent of 3s. 4d. per annum, and fine of 12d., until the next assession; and at the following assession the sole and entire privilege was granted, at [the like rent, to the same persons and Christopher Worthevale until the following assession. At an assession on 1st October 1658, similar rights of Free Warren were granted, at the same rent, &c., to William Lower and Hugh Carew, Gentlemen, reserving, however, to the Lord of the Manor, at this time Mr. Bennett, (see ante p. 292) and his heirs, and his, and their, retinue, free liberty of fishing, fowling, and hawking within the said manor. After the Restoration it continued to be let, to different persons, without the above reservation, in the same manner, until the assession of 21st September 1742, when the same rights were granted, as they had been before, to Edward Elliot and others; and at the same time William Flamank Esq., took a weir upon the river Camel, near Boskearne, by grant from the Commissioners, to hold to the next assession at the pleasure of the Duke, at the rent of 12d.; and at the following assession, on 25th September 1750, Edward

---

[1] Deed in the Author's collection

Elliot took the same rights, and also, saving the right of Mr. Flamank, he took the weir upon the Camel, above mentioned, at the said rent of 12d, and had also a licence for several waters within the lordship of Helston, beginning in a certain place called Lastwen and extending to a certain bridge called ffelliford bridge, containing in circuit three miles, together with the fishing of the same water called Lancrowe bridge, which had been recovered and charged at the assession in 9th Elizabeth and granted by the Commissioners to John Cock and Humphry Hendy, Gentlemen, to hold from year to year during pleasure. At the Assession of 27th September 1756, the rights of Free Warren and fishing were granted, as before, but no mention is made of the weir at Boscarne, nor is there any reservation of the rights of Mr. Flamank. The right of Free Warren continued to be let to various persons, and has now for several years been held by the Rev. J. J. Wilkinson

THE RECTORY AND ADVOWSON OF LANTEGLOS.

The advowson of the Church of Lanteglos has been appurtenant to the manor from the beginning, at least it has been so annexed from beyond the period of legal memory. The Earl of Cornwall presented in 1276, and in 1299, upon the death of Earl Edmund, under the name of "Nanteglos," it was returned as of the value of forty marks per annum.[1] In the taxation of Pope Nicholas 1288-1291, it is valued at £13 per annum, under the name of its dedication, viz., "Ecclesia Sancte Julitte." In 1340 the ninth of the sheaf, wool, and lambs, of "Ecclesia Sancte Julutte de Lanteglos, cum Capella Sancte Athewenne," was taxed at £12 and so sold to Warine Bodulgat, Roger Abbot, Walter Renaud, and Stephen Trethyan; and of the fifteenths, it was said, there were none.[2]

In the Valor Ecclesiasticus (1535) the two parishes of Lanteglos and Advent are taxed at £34 2s. 11d.; Bishop Vesey's valuation, returned to the crown in pursuance of a writ dated 20th July in the following year, makes it one penny less.[3]

Both Lanteglos and Advent possess extensive and valuable glebes, of which the following old Terriers remain in the Bishop's Registry at Exeter.

LANTEGLOSSE.—Lanteglosse wth the Chapple appendant of St. Tawne, *alias* Adven—Incumbent Thomas Moore, presented by Mr. Tristram Arscott who had it of Mr. Arthur Arscott, &c. The glibe and parcells of lande.

A Range of grownde called the Middle Sentrie .... acres, to this grounde lieth bordering rownde about wth y[e] Queen's lande, the Duke's lande in tyme, and one Mr. Roscarrokes. Another parcell of grounde .... acres whereof som parte of it bordereth on the Deere parke which was the Duke's. Also another Rough parcel of grounde .... acres 14, w[ch] bordereth, as the rest, rownde aboute the Duke's lande and Heirs of Roscarrocke, in this grounde was

---

[1] Inq. p.m., 28th Edwards I., No. 44.

[2] Lay Subsidies, Cornw., 15th Edward III, $\frac{87}{16}$ m. 3 d., being the original record of the Inquisiones Nonarum, but the name was rendered as "Julitte" in the printed Volume, p. 346.

[3] Bishop Vesey's Reg., vol. ii, fols. 86-100.

sometime a mylle, I suppose the auncient mill of the Lo. shipp, and for wch is paied yet still sixe pence per annum.[1] Another parcell of grounde ... acres 34, and where is a little grove of wood, bordering on the right hand on the Duke's land and the other side on the heires of Dilkes and Roscarrock.

Also some waste growndes about the Church of Lanteglosse wth a small meadowe nier the Deere Parke, acres 2. Also about the Chapple of St. Advene Land, acres 30, bordering, as the rest, on the Dukes, heires of Mr. Dilkes one way, and the other way next vnto the moores.

In all there is som 160 [acres.] The Patrons still be the same Tristram Arscott Esqr. for this nexte donation onely, and ever after Arthure Arscott Esq., and his heirs, as was layed doun in the last ending of the letigeous title by the Lords of the Council and others.

THO. MOORE,[2]

(Not dated but earlier than the accession of James I.)

A Terrier of the houses, Gardens and Gleebe lands belonging to the Parsonage of Lanteglos and Aduent, within the county of Cornwall, in the Diocese of Exeter, made by us James Beaufort, Rector, John Batten, Godfrey White, Churchwardens.

Imprimis.—One parlour floored with Boards, one Hall, one Kitchin, a Brewhouse, a Seller, seauen Chambers, one Barne, one Stable, two gardens, and one orchard contayning about one acre of land, one close of land called the Broome Close, being seauen acres, the great downe, being twenty acres, the higher Whitely, twenty acres, the Middle Close and the Brocks, twenty acres, the North Parks being 26 acres, the Butt Park, the Upper quillett and two quilletts adjoining to the Churchyard there three acres, wch said Gleebe lands are bounded on the North wth Lanteglos Parke (being the King's Land) one the southeast and east with the grounds of Christopher Hocken, and Edward Seccombe, and John Wallis, on the north with the lands of John Nicholls, Esq., called Treuy downes, and alsoe wth the grounds of Edw. Seccombe, on the west with the grounds of Abraham Basterd, Richard Cocke, John Bennett, and Elizabeth Wilcocke; Two Closes of Land called Worthacres, one grove, and one moore, parte of the Gleebe Lands of Advent, being twenty-ffower acres, bounded on the East with the ground of Charles Rickard and Julian Vivian, Wid., on the north with the lands of John Wallis, on the west with the King's Highway, and on the south with the ground of John Batten. And three other closes of land called Aduent Sanctuary, being eleauen acres, bounded on the west side with the King's high way and partly with the grounds of George Basterd, on the east with the grounds of Charles Rickard and Ambrose Cowle, and on the north side with the grounds of Julian Vivian Widow.

March 20th 1679.

James Beaufort, *Rector*.

John Pearse,   } *Churchwardens,*
Godfrey White, }   *Lanteglos.*

John Batten of Advent.

[1] This mill was situate in a close of still rough land which has been recently sub-divided, but contains altogether, according to the tithe survey, including a marsh at the bottom, 19a. 3r. 37p., statute measure. It adjoins Jetwells, parcel of the Manor of Bodulgate, which in 1613 was parcel of the possessions of the family of Roscarrock. Traces of the mill and mill leat are still visible, especially the "mill run." The original close is numbered on the parish map as 1369 and 1370. The mill was not the ancient manor mill as suggested in the text. The rent of 6d. per annum is still paid.

[2] Thomas Moore died 2nd March 1612, and was buried 28th June 1613. P.R.

Another Terrier was made in 1727. After giving a description of the then condition of the Parsonage House, and the Glebe Lands, &c. It states:

Item 4. That no one payes less for offering then two pence, or for marriages, churchings, and burials than one shilling, but what more as the persons please. No mortuaries paid.

Item 6. A font of Stone with a good cover thereunto, a decent Communion table Railed in, with a Carpett of Green Cloath and a Cloath of white Linnen to spread thereon, a communion Cup, or Chalice, of Silver with a silver cover, weighing eleven ounces, a peuter flagon, and one peuter Bason. A Bible of the last edition, two Books of Common Prayer, a Book of Homilies, a Table of Marriages, a large Surplice, a Register Book of parchment, a Church-wardens Book, a strong Chest with three locks and keys, four bells with all materials and in good order and a Velvet Chushin.

Signed   Daniel Lombard, *Rector.*

Nath. Hender,	John Seccombe,
Wm. Carew,	William Coleman, junr.
William Sloggett,	
Will Prideaux and others.	

} *Churchwardens.*

The Glebe hath right to Commons on the Homer and Midelle Moors, commonly called the King's Moor, belonging to the Manor of Helston in Trigg, parcel of the Antient Dutchey of Cornwall, for such and so many cattle in the summer as the Glebe will maintain in the winter; and six pence per annum is payable out of the said Glebe lands to the said Manor of Helston in Trigg. There are two ash trees in the home state worth five shillings, and thirty-six ash and succomore trees in the Churchyard worth twenty-eight shillings.

These terriers shew us, with much clearness, what was the condition of the benefice in the seventeenth century, and we will now proceed to review its present state.

The estimated area of the parish of Lanteglos, subject to tithes, except the glebe, is 3160a. 2r. 12p., viz.:

					A.	R.	P.
Arable	...	...	...	...	1674	1	8
Meadow	...	...	...	...	400	2	20
Pasture	...	...	...	...	1065	3	16
Woodland	...	...	...	...	19	3	8

The tithes arising from the glebe lands, containing by estimation 133a. 0r. 3p., have been merged in the freehold.

The lands undermentioned are exempt from the payment or tithes, except tithes of corn and grain, by several, prescriptive or customary, payments in lieu.

			A.	R.	P.	MODUS.
Great Tregarth	...	...	36	3	24	5s. 8d.
Little Tregarth...	...	...	29	1	24	5 4
Penpethy	...	...	66	0	0	5 0
Trethern	...	...	6	0	0	4
Trevie Parks	...	...	48	0	0	1 0
Piskey	...	...	9	2	16	10

	A.	R.	P.	MODUS.	
Trevarledge Hill and Bridge Park ...	12	0	0	1s	3d
Little Trethern	15	2	16		4
Trethern	54	3	24	1 10	0
Bodulgate	157	0	32	7	6
Polmere	14	1	24	3	4
Penhale	50	1	24	1	0
Part of Bowithick late Northey's Bowithick	40	3	8	2	6
Bowithick	25	0	32	2	0
Parish Lands	38	1	24		6
Penpethy	42	0	0	5	4
Jetwells	14	1	24	4	0
Part of Trenuth	73	0	32	5	4
Trevarledge	61	0	32	3	4
Penpethy	76	3	8	4	8
Town Mills and Curtlage			2	3	4
	866	1	26	£4 12	7

The tithes of corn and grain arising out of certain lands called Part of Trewalder and Part of Castle Goff is now the property of Mr. Richard Parson of St. Austell; and the Vicar of St. Teath, in right of his benefice, is entitled to the tithe of hay arising on the same lands.

In 1841, the tithes were commuted in the undermentioned proportions:

To the Rector	£353	0	0
To George William Lyon, Esq. (now Mr. Parson) ...	5	13	6
To the Vicar of St. Teath	2	12	0
Total	£361	5	0

The titheable land of the Parish of St. Adwen, or Advent, consists of the following quantities, viz.:

	A.	R.	P.
Arable	1080	2	16
Meadow	97	2	0
Pasture	622	3	8
Woodland	21	2	16
Common	2400	0	0[1]
	4222	2	0

[1] Returns have lately been published by the Tithe Commissioners, carefully compiled from maps, agreements, awards, apportionments, &c. in their custody, and shewing the extent and situation of the waste lands in Cornwall, subject to the rights of common, and the common field lands of which the tithes have been commuted. After deducting any lands which have been enclosed since the commutation of tithe, the returns shew the waste land now remaining in every parish, and distinguishes the commons apparently capable of cultivation, from the apparently mountainous, or other lands unsuitable for cultivation, and the common field land, &c. So far as the Deanery of Trigg Minor is concerned, the following is the result:—

The Glebe lands contain, by estimation, fifty-four acres statute measure, and the tithe arising therefrom has been merged in the freehold. The undermentioned lands are covered from the render of all tithes (except the tithes of corn and grain) in kind by the several prescriptive, or customary, payments here stated, viz.,

	A.	R.	P.	£	s.	d.
Trevarlege	258	0	0	1	10	0
Furr house Tenement	25	0	32		2	8
Kenningstock Mill and Courtledge ...			12		3	4

The Rector is entitled to all the tithes, which, in 1841, were commuted at £137 per annum.

The Glebe of Lanteglos, exclusive of what the Rector keeps in his own tenure, is let for £178 per annum, and the remainder is estimated to be worth £22 per annum, and that of Advent at £80 per annum.

The Parsonage house having become dilapidated, and the Rectors for a considerable period non-resident altogether, or residing in Camelford, the late Rector, Mr. Roger Bird, in 1847 erected a large and commodious Parsonage House from designs of that famous architect Mr. E. W. Pugin. It is beautifully situate, the grounds being adorned with fine old timber and flourishing young trees and shrubs.

ANCIENT SAXON FONT PRESERVED IN THE RECTORY GROUNDS.

Parish.			Total Quantity.	Improvable.	Un-Improvable.	Common Field Land.
Advent	..	..	1704	777	927	—
Blisland	..	..	1715	615	1100	—
Bodmin	..	..	363	363	—	—
St. Breward	..	..	2801	1160	1641	—
Forrabury	..	..	63	17	—	46
St. Kew	..	..	43	43	—	—
Temple	..	..	211	161	50	—
Tintagel	..	..	24	24	—	—

2 S

INSTITUTIONS.

1275, Tuesday next after the feast of St. Lucy -	Sir Ralph de Hengelham.[1] The Bishop committed the custody of the Church of Lanteglos to the keeping of Sir Ralph (who the same day was appointed Chancellor of Exeter) for the Earl of Cornwall, until the kalends of April following.
1276, Feast of St. John ante porta Latina	Ralph de Engleham,[2] was instituted to the Church of Lanteglos upon the presentation of the Earl of Cornwall.
1307-8, March 15th	Thomas de London, Clerk,[3] was instituted to the Church of Lanteglos, vacant, upon the presentation of Peter de Gaveston Earl of Cornwall.
1317, July 10th -	Thomas Sweyneseye, Clerk,[4] was instituted to the Church of Lanteglos, on the presentation of the King, vacant by the resignation of Thomas de London.
1356, July 17th -	Sir John de Gyppeswych[5] (Ipswich) was admitted to the Parish Church of Lanteglos, vacant, upon the presentation of Edward Prince of Wales and Duke of Cornwall.
1358, June 15th -	Robert de Waltham[6] was admitted to the Church of Lanteglos, upon the presentation of the Duke of Cornwall.
1360-1, February 18th	William de Berton[7] was instituted to the Church of Lanteglos, upon the presentation of the Duke of Cornwall.
1372, June 19th -	John de Tiverton.[8] Commission to Simon de Withiel, Archdeacon, for the induction of John de Tiverton to the Church of Lanteglos, upon the presentation of the Prince.
1376, August 30th -	William de Aylesham,[9] Clerk, was admitted to the Church of Lanteglos, vacant by the death of John de Tiverton, last Rector, upon the presentation of the King.
1376, November 17th	Richard Bolham,[10] Rector of Wyke St. Mary, was admitted to the Rectory of Lanteglos upon exchange with William Aylesham. He resigned on 26th November 1382.

[1] Bishop Bronescombe's Reg., fol. 67.

[2] Ibib. 72. This is the same person as the above. He appears in the list of the Chancellors of Exeter as Ralph de Hengham. (Fasti Exonienses. Oliver.)

[3] Bishop Stapeldon's Reg., fos. 31 and 37. 1310, October 27th, Thomas de London, Priest, Rector of Lanteglos, had licence of non-residence. 1315, November 16th, Thomas, Rector of Lanteglos, obtained licence to remain at the house of his lady, the Countess of Cornwall, to the end of Michaelmas term, in obedience to his patroness.

[4] Ibid., p. 120.   [5] Bishop Grandison's Register, fo. 109. He was probably the same person who, upon the presentation of the Prince of Wales, was admitted to the Rectory of Blisland in 1347, and ceased to be Rector of that Parish in 1354, (see ante vol. i, p. 51.)

[6] Ibid., fo. 116.   [7] Ibid., fol. 124.   [8] Bishop Brentingham's Reg., fol. 19.

[9] Ibid., fo. 42. Writ of presentation tested at Plesei, 24th August 50th Edward III. Ibid., vol. ii., Part 2, fol. 17.   [10] Ibid., fol. 44. He was Vicar of Gwennap on 12th August 1392.

1383, March 27th - Robert Bolham,[1] Priest, was admitted to the parish Church of Lanteglos, vacant by the resignation of Richard Bolham, last Rector,
upon the presentation of Richard King of England.

1384 - - Thomas Clyfforde,[2] whose institution is not traced, exchanged with
1401-2, February 28th Richard Aldryngton,[3] Rector of the Church of Stoke in Tynhide.

1416, July 27th - William Trebel,[4] Rector of Maugan in Pyder, was admitted to the
Church of Lanteglos upon exchange with Richard de Aldryngton
alias Colomb.

[1] Bishop Brentingham's Reg. fo. 79, Presentation dated 13th January 1382-3. Rot. Pat. 6th Richard II. p. 2, m. 24.

[2] He was collated to a Canonry in the Cathedral of Exeter; by his will, dated 18th December 1418, and proved before Bishop Stafford at Clist in 28th February following, he desires to be buried in the Cathedral, and gave to the Church of St. Andrew at Stokeinteinhede a suit of vestments of red velvet.

This institution led to some litigation—Johanna, Princess of Wales, brought an action of Quare Impedit against Robert Bolham in respect to this Benefice. Reciting that Edward, late Prince of Wales, sometime her husband, being seized of the advowson of this Church presented a certain John Teuerton, who, upon that presentation, was admitted, that afterwards the said Prince died, after whose death the said advowson, *inter alia*, was seized into the King's hands, and afterwards the Church becoming vacant by the death of the aforesaid John Teuerton the King presented a certain William Ayleshame, who was admitted, and afterwards the Church became vacant by the resignation of the said William, and the King presented a certain John (*sic*) Boleham, who upon such presentation was admitted, afterwards the King died and the said advowson came into the hands of the then King, and, together with other advowsons, &c., was assigned to the said Princess as Dower, and afterwards the said Church became vacant by the resignation of the aforesaid Richard and is now vacant.

Robert Bolham appeared by his attorney and denied all knowledge of the presentation alleged to have been made by the Prince of Wales, and said that the Church became vacant by the resignation of the aforesaid Richard Boleham on 26th November 1382, and that the King presented the said Robert on 13th January following, and that he had been duly admitted by the Bishop of Exeter and that he had not impeded the said Princess.

The Princess rejoined that before the vacancy the advowson had been assigned to her as dower, and that the said Robert, knowing the title of the said Princess, had craftily persuaded the King and his Council that the King was the true patron and procured the presentation, the King being ignorant of the right of the Princess. And afterwards, and before the institution of the said Robert, he approached the Princess at Walyngford on 10th March 1382-3, and said the Church was vacant, and that she had the presentation which he begged. The Princess knowing, however, his fraud, refused and presented a certain Thomas Clifford, but the said Robert procured his presentation by the King and obtained institution; whereupon the Princess asked the King to revoke the grant of the presentation, which was done by letters patent dated 3rd July 1384. The jury found for the Princess, and a writ was issued to the Bishop of Exeter not to object to the removal of the said Robert, and to admit the afore-said fit person presented by the Princess of Wales (De Banco Rolls, 7th Richard II, Hilary, m. 317). A volume of Bishop Brentingham Registers, covering the time of the admission of Thomas Clifford, is lost, so that the actual date of his institution is not known.

[3] Bishop Stafford's Register, p. 56.

[4] Ibid, fo. 178. On 24th September 1431, William Trebell, Rector of the Parish Church of Lanteglos, had license to preach throughout the Diocese (Lacy, vol. iii., fo. 96) and on 9th January 1447, he had licence to celebrate the divine offices in the oratories and all honest places within his Rectory. It appears from an inqui-sition taken on the 18th August 1448, that, whereas upon a previous inquisition in that behalf taken, it was found that Master William Trebell, Rector of the Parish Church of Lanteglys, was so broken in health and weak in mind as to become incompos mentis, it was now found that of late times, by divine mercy, he had obtained so much benefit that he was so restored to his pristine sanity of mind that he is able to govern both himself and his concerns, and the cure committed to him, without a coadjutor, but that, on account of his bodily weakness, he was not able to discharge the duties of his cure. Bishop Lacy's Register, vol. iii., fo. 301.

2 s²

1448, August 18th   -   John Wylet,[1] Chaplain of the Church of Trevalga, was admitted to the Church of Lanteglos juxta Camelford in exchange with William Trebel, B.L., Rector.

1452 December 26th   Henry Huchyn, B.L.,[2] was instituted to the Church of Lanteglos, vacant by the death of John Wylet, upon the presentation of Henry King of England, the said Henry Huchyn having resigned the Church of Stamford Courtney.

1454 February 26th   -   Robert Kyrkham,[3] Keeper of the Hanaper in Chancery, was instituted in the Parish Church of Lanteglos, vacant by the death of Henry Huchyn, the last Rector, upon the presentation of the King.

1466 June 15th   -   John Moreton,[4] Rector of Lanteglos, was included in a Commission, concerning one of the Prebends of Endelion.

1488 March 6th   -   Thomas Mades, S.T.B.,[5] was instituted to the Church of Lanteglos, vacant by the death of John Moreton, upon the presentation of Henry King of England.

1489 October 7th   -   Thomas Moreton, B.C.L.,[6] upon the resignation of Thomas Maddeys.

1511 August 18th   ·   Edward Higgyns, Clerk,[7] was instituted to the Church of Lanteglos, vacant by the death of Thomas Morton, last Rector, upon the presentation of King Henry VIII.

1538 July 3rd   -   George Woilsset, Doctor of Laws,[8] was instituted to the Church of Lanteglos, vacant by the death of Edward Hygons, last Rector, upon the presentation of the King Henry VIII.

1548-9 February 8th   George Woolset[9] was admitted to the Rectory of Lanteglos, vacant, upon the presentation of King Edward VI.

1554 September 7th   John Kyrkebye, Clerk,[10] was admitted to the Rectory of Lanteglos by Camelford and Adven, vacant by the death of George Wolsleytt, Doctor of Laws, last Rector, upon the presentation of Edmund Walter, Esq., for this turn only the true patron by reason of a grant from John Arscott, of the Middle Temple, London, Esq., the original true patron.

1563 March 23rd   -   William Roll, B.A.,[11] was instituted upon the presentation of Brownn, Esq.

---

[1] Bishop Lacy's Reg., fo. 238. It should be here noted that, on 14th February 1449, the name of Sir Robert Symon, of Adwen, is included in a List of Priests of the Deanery of Trigg Minor, who subscribed 6s. 8d. each, to the King for the defence of the Church and Kingdome. (Bp. Lacy's Reg. vol. iii., ff. 352-337.) He was probably Chaplain or Curate.

[2] Ibid, fo. 272. Presentation dated 7th October 1452. Rot. Pat. 31st Henry VI., Part 1, m. 15. 1455, February 27th. Sequestration of the goods and fruits of Mr. Henry Huchyn, late Rector of Lanteglos, deceased.

[3] Ibid, fo. 287. Presentation dated 18th February 1454-5, Rot. Pat. 33rd Henry VI., part 1, m. 11.

[4] Bishop Booth, fo. 103. John Watta, of the Parish of Lanteglos juxta Camelford, Holywaterclerk, is mentioned in 1467, De Banco Roll, 7 Edward IV, Easter 172 d.   [5] Ibid, fo. 119.

[6] Presentation dated 6th October 1489, Rot. Pat. 5 Henry VII, m. 31.

[7] Bishop Oldham Reg., fo. 44. Presentation dated August 1511. Rot. Pat. 3rd Henry VIII, part 1, m. 11.

[8] Bishop Veysey's Reg., fo. 93.   [9] Ibid 128.   [10] Bishop Coverdale's Reg., fo. 26.

[11] Bishop Turberville's Reg., fo. 84.

not traced . . Thomas More,[1] D.D.

1612 June 2nd - Daniel Price[2] was admitted to the Parish Church of Lanteglos, vacant by the death of Thomas More, D.D., last Incumbent, upon the presentation of the Prince of Wales.

1621 Novr. 11th - William Forde, Clerk S.T.B.,[3] was admitted to the Parish Church of Lanteglos juxta Camelford, with the Chapel of Adven annexed, vacant by the death of Daniel Price, S.T.P. last Incumbent, upon the presentation of Edmund Arscott of Tetcott, co. Devon, the true patron.

1632 Aug. 16th - George Gillingham, Clerk, M.A.,[4] was admitted to the Rectory of Lanteglos cum Adven, vacant by the death of the last Incumbent, upon the presentation of the Duke of Cornwall.

1633 April 15th - Godfrey Price, Clerk, M.A.,[5] was admitted to the Rectory of Lanteglos and Adven, vacant by the resignation of George Gillingham, Clerk, last Incumbent, upon the presentation of the King.

1635 Oct. 28th - William Todd, Clerk, M.A.,[6] was admitted to the Rectory of Lanteglos and Advent, vacant by the death of Godfrey Price, last Incumbent, upon the presentation of the King.

John Wills[6] (intruded?)

James Lake.[6]

[1] The Chapel of Adven was under sequestration, which was relaxed on 25th May 1568. (Bishops' Act Book.) It was probably at this time that Dr. More was admitted. Thomas More, Doctor Theologiæ, Mortuis est 21° Marcii, et sepult. 28° Junii 1612. (Par. Reg.)

[2] Bishop Cary's Reg., fo. 98. One of this name, son of a Shropshire minister, matric. at St. Mary Hall, Oxford, 14th October 1597, aged 16 years.

[3] Bishop Hall's Reg., fo. 26. 1625, Nicholas Trefrye, Clerk, buried yᵉ 25th day of ffebruary. (Par. Reg.) Probably he was Curate. The benefice of the Church of Lanteglos and Advent was under sequestration, which was relaxed 30th March 1629-30. Bishop's Act Book, A 2.

[4] Ibid fo. 29. One of this name signed the Subscription Book at Oxford 16th April 1613, but is not in the Matriculation Register. Presentation dated 8th February 1631. Rot. Pat. 7th Charles, Part 20, No. 161.

[5] Ibid fo. 32. One of this name matriculated from Hart Hall, Oxford, 13 December 1622, aged 20, "Gen. fil." Presentation dated 29th March 1633. Rot. Pat. 9th Charles, Part 18, No. 14.

License to serve the Cure of Lanteglos was granted to John Trethewy, Clerk, 26th March 1634, and at the same time a similar license for the Chapel of Advent, annexed, was granted to Hugh White. (Bishop's Act Book, A 2.)

[6] Ibid., fo. 41. Presentation dated 21st February 1634. Rot. Pat. 10th Charles, Part 36, No. 34. Walker (Sufferings of the Clergy, Part 2, p. 375) states, with some uncertainty, that this Rector was sequestrated by the Puritans, and it appears from Calamy's "Nonconformists' Memorial," vol. i., p. 354, that Mr. Jonathan Wills, described as a Fellow of Exeter College, Oxford, son of Mr. John Wills, Rector of Morval, was Rector of this parish, and was ejected under the Act of Uniformity of 1662. We find, however, the following entry in the Parish Register, under the year 1654:—"John Wills, Clerk, Rector of this parish, dyed the 20th day of ffebruary 1654, and was buried the 23rd day of the same month." (See also Mon. Inscrip., No. 25, post, p. 313.) But neither Jonathan nor John Wills were of the University of Oxford. Whether or not John Wills were an intruder is not certain. The next Rector of whom we have any trace is James Lake, and of his presentation and institution we have no knowledge. We find, however, the following entry in the Parish Register under the year 1664: "Charles the son of James Lake, Clerk, was buried the 20th of March." As Rector he was present at the Visitation at Bodmin in 1671. He was subsequently collated to a Canonry in Exeter Cathedral, and, resigning this benefice, died in Exeter on 30th September 1678, and was buried next day near the Lady Chapel. The Cathedral Register shews that he married Mary Gibbyns on the 27th January 1641.

1677 Decr. 24th - James Beaford, Clerk, M.A.,[1] was instituted to the Rectory of Lanteglos and Advent, vacant by the resignation of James Lake, last Rector, upon the presentation of Charles II. King of England.

1690 Decr. 2nd - Henry Whitaker, Clerk,[2] was admitted to the Rectory of Lanteglos juxta Camelford, "legitime vacantem," upon the presentation of William and Mary King and Queen of England.

1717 Feby. 24th - Daniel Lombard, Clerk, S.T.P.,[3] was admitted to the Rectories of Lanteglos and Advent, vacant by the death of Henry Whitaker, upon the presentation of George Prince of Wales.

1747 April 22nd - William Phillipps, Clerk,[4] was admitted to the Rectories of Lanteglos and Advent, vacant by the death of Daniel Lombard, Clerk, upon the presentation of H.R.H. Frederick Prince of Wales.

1794 Aug. 14th - Coryndon Luxmore, Clerk, M.A.,[5] was admitted to the Rectories of Lanteglos and Advent, vacant by the death of William Phillipps, Clerk, upon the presentation of George Augustus Frederick Prince of Wales.

[1] Bishop's Reg. N.S. vol. ii., fo. 84. Matric. at Exeter Coll., Oxford, 10th July 1668, aged 15, son of Rev. John Beauford of St. Columb, mar. Jane dau. of John Vivian of Truan. Presentation dated 14th December 1677. Rot. Pat. 29th Charles II, Part 11, No. 6.

To the honour of this Rector, and the Rev. Thomas Polwhele, Rector of Newlyn, they stood alone of all the Cornish clergy firm in refusing to violate their oath of allegiance to King James II. For such conscientious fidlity both were deprived. (Hal's M.S. History of Cornwall.) Mr. Beauford was buried in the Church of his native parish, where a monument to his memory still remains with the following inscription:

H. S. E. Reverendus ille vir literatus Jacobus Beauford, A.M., ecclesiæ de Lanteglos quondam Rector sapientâ vitæ integritate et consummatâ eruditione tam merito quam publice celebratus. Quippe utriusq. peritus pharmaceutices et corpori et animæ medelam feliciter adhibuit. In matrimonio duxit Janiam, Johannis Vivian arm. filiam: atq. ea defuncta Annam Josephi Sawle de Penrice, arm. Obiit gemiter generali xix Martii, A.D. MDCCXX; ætatis suæ lxix.

[2] Ibid., vol. iii., fo. 103 and 107. We cannot trace him either at Oxford or Cambridge. 1717, Henry Whitaker, late Rector of this Parish, was buried the ninth of October (Par. Reg.)

[3] Ibid., vol. v, fo. 114. This Rector was the son of a French Protestant Minister, who took refuge in this country after the revocation of the Edict of Nantes in October 1685. In a list of many persons being aliens born, in whose favour a warrant was issued on 16th December 1687 for making them free denizens of this kingdom by Letters Patent under the great seal, without fees or charges, occur the names of "John Lombard, Clerk, Francis his wife, Daniel and Phillip their children." (Lists of Foreign Protestants and Aliens resident in England, 1618-1688 p. 51. Camden Soc. Pub. 1862.) Dr. Lombard received his elementary education at Merchant Taylor's School in London. Matriculated from St. John's College, Oxford, 7th July 1694, aged sixteen, son of Rev. John Lombard, born at Anjou in France, B.A. 17th May 1698, M.A. 16th March 1701-2, B.D. 26th April 1708, and D.D. 23rd April 1714. Of his learning and simplicity much has been written. (See Davies Gilbert's History of Cornwall, vol. ii, p. 407.) He is said never to have assimilated himself to the manners nor the society of this country, and spent much time abroad. He died, however, at Camelford, and was buried at Lanteglos, 2nd January 1746, leaving a valuable library and his portrait to his successors. Dr. Lombard published several small treatises and sermons, and his correspondence with Mr. Gregor of Trewarthenick remains in M.S. During the greater portion of his incumbency, viz., from 1722-1740, the curacy of the parish was held by the Rev. John Farnham (Bibl. Cornub.) see also ante, vol. i, p. 577.

[4] Ibid., vol. vij., fo. 119. 1794 Rev. William Phillipps (buried) April 27th (Par. Reg.)

[5] Ibid., vol x., fo. 95. Of St. John's Coll. Camb. B.A. 1782, M.A. 1785. He was also Rector of Bridestow and Sourton, co. Devon.

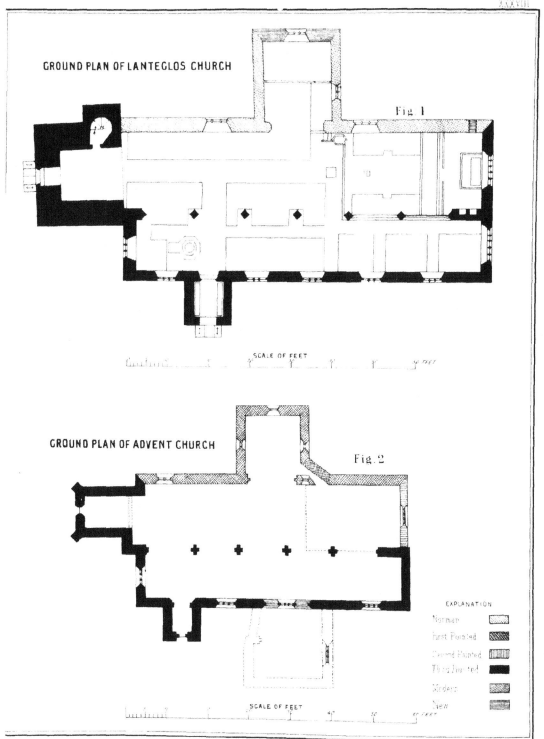

GROUND PLAN OF LANTEGLOS CHURCH

Fig. 1

SCALE OF FEET

GROUND PLAN OF ADVENT CHURCH

Fig. 2

EXPLANATION

Norman
First Pointed
Second Pointed
Third Pointed
Modern
New

SCALE OF FEET

1845, October 31st - Roger Bird, Clerk, B.D.,[1] was admitted to the Rectories of Lanteglos and Advent, void by the death of Coryndon Luxmore, Clerk, last Incumbent, upon the presentation of Albert Edward Prince of Wales.

1852, November 17th John James Wilkinson, Clerk, M.A.,[2] was admitted to the Rectories of Lanteglos and Advent, vacant by the cession of Roger Bird, Clerk, upon the presentation of the Prince of Wales.

PARISH CHURCHES.

The Parish Church of Lanteglos is situate in a deep picturesque valley, about one and-a-half miles west of the town of Camelford, and is surrounded by some fine old timber, chiefly ash and sycamore, probably some of the trees mentioned in the foregoing terrier of 1727 (ante p. 299). It is dedicated to St. Julitta. We have not, however, observed the patron saint of this Church anywhere mentioned in the Bishop's Registers. It has been usually thought that it commemorates St. Julitta, a noble lady who suffered martyrdom in the Diocletian persecution at Cæsarea in Cappadocia, on 30th July 303. The Celtic form of Julitta is "Ilid," and there was a daughter of Brechan named Ilud, whose designation in Latin would also be *Julitta*. As a group of Brechan's numerous children settled on the north coast of Cornwall, and founded several of the Churches in this Deanery, it becomes a question whether St. Julitta of Lanteglos may not be identical with her.

The Church consists of Chancel (not constructional) 35 ft. × 19 ft. 6 in., Nave 54 ft. × 19 ft. 6in., North Transept 21 ft. 9 in. × 16 ft. 9 in., South Aisle 85 ft. × 13 ft. 6 in., Western Tower 15 ft. 6 in. × 11 ft. 9 in., and South Porch 8 ft. 3 in. × 7 ft. 3 in. It has recently been restored under the care of Mr. J. P. St. Aubyn, to whose courtesy we are indebted for the accompanying plan (Plate xxxviii, fig. 1).

The Church was originally a cruciform Norman structure, but of that the only remains are the north walls of the chancel and nave, and the east and west walls of the transept. On the recent restoration it was found necessary to rebuild the north wall of the latter. Some additions would appear to have been made in the Second-Pointed period, as a doorway in that style was inserted in the tower on its erection in the Third-Pointed period. The south wall of the aisle and porch is of very good granite ashlar of the later Third-Pointed character.

The Chancel consists of two bays, divided from the aisle by the usual Third-Pointed

---

[1] Bishop's Reg. N.S., vol. xii., fo. 32. Matric. from Queen's Coll., Oxford, 6th December 1816, aged 16. Son of Robert Bird of Andover, Gent. B.A. 22nd May 1820; M.A. 29th June 1823; B.D. 3rd February 1837.

[2] Ibid., vol. xiii., fo. 87. Born 1818. Queen's Coll., Oxford, B.A. 1842; M.A. 1845. A Justice of the Peace for the County of Cornwall. Eldest son of the Rev. George Wilkinson, Rector of Whicham, co. Cumberland, and a Justice of the Peace for that County.

columns, supporting fourcentred arches. It is lighted by an east window of five lights with tracery in the head of a flamboyant type, and on the north side by a window of three lights of a- late and poor character, having plain circular heads. There are in this window some small fragments of ancient painted glass set in lozenges, and among them is a modern escutcheon of arms: quarterly first and fourth sa. a goat's head erased, ar. attired or; second and third, ar. five ermine spots. In the north wall are two sedilia of a very plain character. A priest's door formerly opened into the sanctuary on the north side, which was walled up in 1853. The chancel and sanctuary are properly arranged. The altar is new and of oak. It is erected in memory of Archer Gilbert Harvey, a child of Mr. Charles Harvey, whose family was long resident at Tregoodwell in this parish, who died on 15th December 1872. The nave is of four bays, separated from the aisle in the same manner as the chancel. It has a poor three-light window inserted in the north wall.

The aisle is lighted by a fine five-light traceried window at the east end; five three-light cinquefoil windows in the north wall; and by a new window of the same type at the west end. In the tracery of some of the windows on the south side remain some ancient glass, chiefly figures. The roofs throughout the Church are of the cradle type. Upon the wall plates in the aisle, at the feet of the principals, are some small escutcheons charged with chevrons and crosses in various forms, but it is very doubtful if they are armorial.

The nave and aisle are now seated with plain benches of red pine. The old benching had been long removed before the restoration, and no part of it remained, except one bench end, which was of late date and inferior workmanship. On it was carved an escutcheon of Arms: Worthevale impaling Billing, rudely cut, commemorating the marriage, in 1616, of Christopher Worthevale of Worthevale, Esq., and Philadelphia, daughter of Richard Billing of Hengar, Esq. The font is on the west side of the south door. It is made of Pentewan stone, octagonal, of Third-Pointed work, the panels and shaft carved, the former resembling the tracery of the Chancel window. The ancient font, which is of Saxon character, having interlaced knots sculptured on it, is preserved in the Rectory grounds (see fig. p. 301) The north transept is separated from the nave by a large circular arch resting upon pilasters, with square abaci hollowed below and on the face. In the east wall has been inserted a small square-headed two-light window of debased work, and in the north wall is a new window of three lights resembling those in the north aisle.

The tower is lofty, of three flights, embattled and pinnacled. It measures 70 ft. from the ground to the top of the battlements. The stair turret, which is lighted by five round-headed loop holes, is at the north east corner, and rises some 2 ft. above the battlements. The tower does not stand parallel with the nave, into which it opens by a lofty pointed arch having square abaci, but leans southward. The external door, as we have before stated, is of Second-Pointed work. The ends of the label mouldings are carved with heads, the one on the left side being that of a female, and the one on the right a man's head. Above it is a new window of three lights of the same pattern as the one which it replaced.

In 3rd Edward VI the tower contained three bells, but they have been recast and their number increased to six. According to tradition the casting took place in a field, near Helston, which is still called " the Bell Field," now converted into a garden. The owner has seen the ashes where the bells were recast.

The Bells now bear the following inscriptions:

1. I. P ⦂ C. P ⦂ 1783.

2. I. P ⦂ C. P ⦂ 1783.

3. I. P ⦂ C. P ⦂ 1783.

4. EDWARD SECCOMBE & NICHOLAS POPE P. W. ⦂ I 🔔 P ⦂ C 🔔 P ⸭ 1783.

5. CHARLES PHILLIPS AND WILLIAM JEFFERY C. W. ⦂ I 🔔 P ⦂ C 🔔 P ⸭ 1783.

6. WILLIAM PHILLIPS, RECTOR ⸭ JOHN MARSHALL, GENT. I 🔔 P ⸭ C 🔔 P ⸭ 1783.

THE PORCH.

Both the external and internal doorways are of good Third-pointed work. Above the latter is a cinquefoil niche, now empty, and on the right hand side was a Benatura, now walled up. The porch has a cradle roof like the Church, and at the bottom of the principals are escutcheons, one of them being charged with four fusils in fess (the arms of Dinham) and another with a taw cross.

MONUMENTAL INSCRIPTIONS.

ON THE WALLS IN THE CHURCH.

On a plain marble tablet:

1. CHRISTIAN CARPENTER born in 1730, died Oct' 24th 1802, aged 72.

2. Mary relict of Ralph Cresswell, died 22nd April 1825, aged 62.

3. To the memory of CATHERINE CARPENTER whose remains lie in a vault near this spot. This memorial is erected by her deeply afflicted Husband CHARLES CARPENTER of the Borough of Camelford and of Moditonham in this County Esquire, Obiit x Jan' MDCCCX, Ætatis XLIV.

ARMS: Party per pale gu. and sa. an eagle displayed of the last.

CREST: An armed arm, embowed, holding a staff.

MOTTO: Spernit pericula vertus.

2 T

4. On a marble tablet surmounted by the arms of Carpenter:

In the vault beneath are deposited the remains of Charles Carpenter Esqr an old and faithful Officer of the Duchy of Cornwall, and a magistrate of that county. He died on the 1st day of March 1831, aged 74 years.

ARMS: Party per pale or and gu. an eagle displayed of the last; impaling : sa. a cross flory betw. 12 billets. CREST as above, but without the staff. MOTTO the same.

5. Sacred to the memory of the Reverend William Phillips, Clerk, M.A., who died on the 20th day of April 1794, being Easter Sunday, in the 71st year of his age, and 47th anniversary of his institution as Rector of this Parish, a period which will ever be held dear by its inhabitants.

Reader stop! and contemplate with awe this simple marble consecrated to the ashes of a worthy individual, to whose remains it is erected by his nephew, John Phillips Carpenter, as a small but grateful tribute to a generous benefactor.

"Of no distemper, of no blast he died;
But, like Autumn fruit mellowed long, he fell,
And even wondered, that he dropped no sooner;
Fate seemed to wind him up for three score years,
But freshly ran he on to ten years more,
Till like a clock worn out with eating time,
The wheels of weary life stood still."   (Lee.)

6. Near this place lie also deposited the remains of John Phillips Esquire, and Elizabeth his wife. And John Phillips, Elizabeth Phillips, and Charles Phillips their children.

ARMS: Or, a lion ramp. collared and chained.

CREST : A lion passant, tail extended.

NORTH WALL.

7. On a white marble tablet surmounted by an urn draped.

Sacred to the memory of Lydia Rosevear Bastian, the wife of James Bastian, Merchant of Truro, died Aug. 6th 1826, aged 25 years.

See from the earth the fading lily rise,
It springs, it grows, it flourishes, and dies,
So this fair flower scarce blossomed for a day,
Short was the bloom, and speedy the decay.

SOUTH WALL.

8. Sacred to the memory of John Lawrence Esqr of the Borough of Camelford, who died Novr 22nd 1824, aged 63.

Also to the memory of GRACE relict of JOHN LAWRENCE Esqre, who died October 4th 1828, aged 76 years.

9. This tablet is erected in remembrance of Rebecca Pearce of Helstone, in this Parish. She died (alas that she is dead) October xxvii. mdccccxxxix. æt lxxvi beloved by all who knew her.

Also of her husband John Pearce, who died April xxi. mdccccxli. æt lxxxvi.

10. On a tablet of white marble surmounted by a female figure weeping over an urn, in relief.

Sacred to the memory of WILLIAM INCH, of the Borough of Camelford and Armenall his wife. The former died Febry 19th 1798; aged 78. The latter April 25th 1814, aged 89.

This tribute of respect is erected by their affectionate daughter Ann Inch.

Also to the memory of Ann Hodge, late of Treworgey in this County, who departed this life May 23rd 1615, in the 87th year of her age.

They are not lost, but taken from the evil to come.

11. On a tablet of white marble under the above.

Sacred to the memory of

ANN INCH, spinster, late of Treworgey, near Liskeard, in this County, Daughter of WILLIAM and ARMENELL INCH, who departed this life 27th January 1826, aged 65.

Also of ARMENELL, wife of the Revd. LEWIS MARSHALL, Vicar of Davidstow in this County, and sister to the said Ann Inch, who departed this life 2nd July 1831, aged 67.

Also in memory of ROBERT, the second son of Tristram and Ann Hodge, of this Parish, who was born 14th Decr 1698, died 20th Decr 1733, aged 35.

Also of Arminell his wife who was buried 17th Octr 1749, aged 60 years.

12. In memory of William Fillis Pearce, Esquire, one of the Magistrates of this County, who, having passed the greater part of a life of much usefulness in this Parish, died at Tremeddan in the Borough of Liskeard the 17th day of February 1862, in the 63rd year of his age, Deservedly beloved and esteemed by all who knew him.

The memory of the just is blessed. Prov. 10, 7.

13. In memory of Robert Bake, gent. of Delabole Quarry in the Parish of Saint Teath, who died 10th day of October 1810, aged 84 years.

As Principal Proprietor of the said Quarry for upwards of sixty years, He justly bore the Character of An honest Man.

IN THE CHURCH YARD.

14. Here lyeth ye mortal r[emains of] Diggory Wallis, of Fento[roon] who was buried December........,1560.

And also of John Wallis, his descendant, a man of Singular Humanity & Integrity, & who lived beloved & died lamented by all that knew him. He was buried ye 29th of Oct. 1726. Ætat 70.

[1] The Wallis who was buried in 1560 was named Thomas. His son Digory died in 1591, as is shewn by the Register of Burials. The descendant who erected the monument subsequent to 1726 appears not to have known the name of his ancestor.

15. A flat stone circumscribed as follows:

William [Edward] was buried the [19 July in the year of our Lord] God 1589 E.R. 31. [Joan Edward] was buried [the 9th day of September 16¹] 35. C. R. xi. 11: c:

16. A flat stone circumscribed:

Thomas Budge was buried the xx day of January in the yeare of oure Lord God 1635 C.R. xi.

17. [John?] Hocken *alias* Tregarth, Gentleman.

> Vita fugax hominis miseris. repleta
> Fœlis cui requiem mors cito sancta.

18. Two fragments of grave stone bearing a female figure in low relief between the initials M.W., and the following imperfect inscription:

Here lyeth the Bod[y of Mary the dau]ghter of Christopher Wort[hyvale who was buried 10th August 1639.]²

> Beavty ¡vertve, youth and gentry
> All at Grave post make their entry,
> And the custome we must pay
> Dissolving us to dust and clay,
> But the comfort of us all
> Rests in our Lord High Admiral
> Jesus, who in his good time
> Will refine our dust and slyme,
> And assume us to his joyes
> Past fear, past care, past all alloyes.

19. Also on a circumscribed stone:

✠ Here lieth buried the bodie of Christopher Hocken Gentleman [who was buried 4th Nov. in the year] of our Lord God 1620.

⚕ R. A : XVIII : E I : S LIII.

20. Also on a circumscribed stone:

✠ Here Lieth The Body of Renald Robey who was Buried the 22 day of May in The year of our Lord God 1639. C. R. 14.

21. Also on a circumscribed stone:

Margaret the wife of Hugh Hocken . . . ay in the year of our Lord God 1643.

22. On an altar tomb, a granite slab, with letters in relief:

MARGERY EDWARD WAS BVRIED THE VII DAY OF MAY ANO DOMINI 1622.
JOHN EDWARD WAS BVRIED THE XXV DAY OF APRIL IN THE YEAR OF OUR LORD GOD 1642.

23. Against the side of this tomb is the following inscription on a slate:

¹ The defects are supplied from the Registers.
² Mary yᵉ daughter of Christopher Worthevale was buried yᵉ 10th August 1639.—P. R.

EDWARD : SECCOMBE : WAS : BURIED : UNDER : THIS : TOMB : THE XXIIIITH OF NOVEMBER IN THE YERE OF OUR LORD GOD 1694.

IN : THIS : MOST : PVRE : AND : BLESSED : SHADE :
SUCH : BY : THIS : SECREAT : A : SO MADE.

24. On a circumscribed slab :

Gunnet the wife of John Bennet

She was buried on the 4th of September in yᵉ year of our Lord 1652.

The Poor, the World, the Heavens, and the Grave

Her Alms, her Praise, her Soul, and Body have.

25. On a circumscribed slab :

Here lyes the Body of John Wills late Reverend Minister [of this Parish who was buried the 23 day of Febʸ 1654 P. R.]

Within the margin the following lines :

Come Reader reckon wʰ lyes here
And for a counter dropp a tear
Wᵗʰ God a powerful Israell
Wʰ men a playn Nathaniell
A comforter yet thunderer
A Planter and a Waterer
And in yᵉ Churches darkest night
Her burning and her shining light
No man more lowe none more aboue
When mounted by yᵉ heavenly Dove.

He Jesus bosom lith a John
Claymed by Impropriation
And thence yᵉ fountain head so nigh
Preach'd spirits of Divinity
These speake him turn'd up all in on
A grace possessed Legion
Too high for us, these qualify
For th' Church Triumphants Ministry
Thither hee's called wee cant refuse
Hees gone but to receive his dues.

26. On a stone circumscribed in double lines, formerly on an altar tomb in the Churchyard :

HERE LYETH THE BODY OF AMBROSE WADE WHO DIED THE X OF MARCH IN THE YERE OF OUR LORD GOD ANNO 1669.

HERE LYETH THE BODY OF MARGARET THE WIFE OF AMBROSE WADE ʷHO DIED THE 8 Dʸ OF NOVEMBER IN THE YERE OF OUR LORD GOD ANNO 1680.

Within the margin :

BY FAITH SO FERM
BY HOPE SO BOLD
BY LOVE SO TRUE
WEE CHRIST BE - HOLD.

27. On an altar tomb circumscribed :

Here lyeth the body of Christopher HODGE who was buried the xxiiii Day of October in the yere of our Lord God Anno Do. 1680.

Within the margin :

Romanes the viiith and the 19th. For the earnest expectation of the Creature waiteth for the manifestation of the sons of God.   Being his funerall text.   C. H.

28. Also on an altar tomb:

Here lyeth the body of Mary the Wife of Edward hodge of the Towne of Cammellford who was buried the 9 day of October 1684.

And allsoe here lyeth William the son of Edward hodge and of Mary his wife who was buried the 2 day of October in the year of our Lord 1699.

29. On an altar tomb circumscribed:

Here lyeth the body of Catherine Gayer. She was bvried the 17 day of November in the year of our Lord God 1688.

Against the head:

Nere this place lyeth the body of Beniamen Gayer Gent which was bvried the 31 day of March Anno Domi 1697.

Against the foot:

Contiguous this tomb are deposited the remains of Thomas Gayer who departed this life the 17th day of January 1805 in the 25th year of his age.

Beneath this tomb are deposited the remains of Anna Maria Gayer, who departed this life the 10th day Feb' 1824 in the 13 year of her age.

30. Here lyeth Mary the wife of Richard Taprill which was buried yᵉ 27th day of M . . 1696.

> Originall from dust wee came
> To dust we must Return again
> The common fate of all mankind,
> Teach us our mortallity to mind
> To look for a better state than this
> Of immortality and endless bliss.

31. Here lyeth the body of Ann Honey she was . . . . . yere of our Lord 1691.
Here lyeth the body of William Honey . . . . . .
Thomas Honey was buried - . . . . . the 20th day of March.

32. On an altar tomb on the south side of the Church circumscribed:

Here lyeth the body of Joan the wife of William Greenway and her Daughter, of this Parish who were buried the 16th of April in the year of our Lord 1711.

In the centre:

> Stay passers by and here behold
> how wee do ly inclosed in mould
> And hungry worms wee daily wast
> and so they shall by you at last
> But though our Body's here do ly
> our souls do dwell with God on high.

33. Here lyeth the body of Katherine the wife of John Phillipps Gent, who was buried october the 13th 1711

> In life she feared God
> In death she show'd the same
> In life & death she did him praise
> And blest his holy name.

Also here lyeth Sarah and Elizabeth his daughters. The one was buried y⁰ 5th day of October, y⁰ other y⁰ 10th 1711.

> In remembrance of my wife and children dear
> this Tombe I have erected on them here.

34. Beneath this stone lye interred y⁰ mortall remains of Mary daughter of Samuel & Mary Jackson who departed this life (of the small pox) y⁰ 28th day of July in y⁰ year of our Lord 1721 aged 27.

And also Samuel her Brother, who died of y⁰ same distemper, y⁰ 13th day of August 1721, in y⁰ 17th year of his age.

> He was blest with large endowments o' y⁰ mind
> She wanted no grace of woman kind,
> ....what they are, what they were, express best
> ....is and tombs turn like ourselves to dust,
> Our glass is run, yours runs whilse looking on,
> So do your work or else you are undone.

35. Here lyeth the Body of Catherine the wife of Joseph Wilkey, who was buried the 23rd day [of September 1714.]

Here lyeth the Body of Joseph Wilkey of this Parish and Town of Camelford, was buried the 26th day of May in the year of Our Lord 1715.

Here Lyeth the Body of Mary Wilkey their Daughter, who was Buried the 22nd day of July Anno Domini 1716.

> The Mother and the Father hee,
> Likewise the Daughter maketh three,
> Under this Tomb they all do lye,
> As you may read that do pass by ;
> Even as they be so must you all—
> Therefore repent and on God call,
> While in this world good time you have
> For it's too late when in the grave.

36. Here lyeth the body of Elizabeth the wife of John Ford of Camelford, who was buried the 25th day of July in the year of our Lord 1721.

> Life leads to death, so nature saith,
> Death is the way to life, so faith.
> Thus let us think of both say I,
> He that desireth to live must die.

37. Here lyeth the Body of James Willcocks, son of Robert Willcocks, Officer of Excise, who was buryed January y⁰ 10th 1731, aged eight months.

> Cropt in my bud by fate, cut clear away
> From human ills to peace and endless day.
> Praise be to Thee that freed me from these cares,
> This anxious world with all its gilded snares,
> Which oft proves fatall unto riper years.

38. In memory of Edward Seccombe of this Parish who was buried here Dec. ye 16th 1732, ætat suæ 47.

39. Here lye ye bodies of Mary and James ye wife and Son of James Tronhayl of this Parish. Mary his wife was buried ye 19th of March 1735, etat suæ 63.

James their son was buried ye 24th of Septber 1716, in ye first year of his age.

40. Here lyeth ye body of Gonnet Peathick who was buried ye 16th of July 1741, aged 89.

41. Sarah the wife of Walter Mallet was buried the 12th day of April 1744, aged 79.

Thomas the son of John Mallet was buried the 15th day of May 1746, aged two years.

Walter Mallet was buried the 12th day of November 1747, in the 73rd year of his age.

Here also lieth the body of John, the son of John Mallet of the Borough of Camelford, who departed this life the 9th day of September 1769, aged 43.

42. Here lyeth the body of Mary Prestridge who was buried the 30th of July anno dom. 1746, aged 23.

Edward Prestridge was buried here the 12th day of July, anno domini 1752, aged 66.

Edward the son of Edward and Jane Prestridge, was buried the 22nd day of March 1753, aged 27 years.

43. Here lies the bodies of Arminel and Arminel, Robert and Ambrose the sons and daughters of William and Arminal Inch, of this Parish.

Arminel was baptized the 15th and buried the 17th day of November, anno dom. 1755.

And Arminel was baptized the 4th day of June 1758, and was buried the 20th day of August, 1759.

Robert was baptized the 23rd day of June 1761, and was buried the 27th day of May 1763.

Ambrose was baptized the 29th day of August 1762, and was buried the 27th of May 1763.

44. In memory of Nathaniel Hender of the Borough of Camelford in the county of Cornwall, gentleman. He was born the 15th day of September 1674, and dy'd the 14th day of June 1755. He married Esther the daughter of William Edwards, the 20th day of November, in the year of 1708. She dy'd the 27th day of January 1745.

45. Underneath this stone are deposited the Remains of Eliz. Pearce, daughter of Par^s and Mary Pearce, who died 6th of June 1798, aged 6 weeks

Also the body of Edward Pearce who died 16th August 1802, aged 3 months.

Also Lies here inter' Mary the Wife of Parmenas Pearce, who died August 27th, 1803, aged 32 years.

Also the said Parmenas Pearce, who died the 8th day of Dec. 1807, aged 47 years.

46. Here lies the body of Will: the son of William and Eliz: Grigory of this P^h who was buried the 4th day of April 1758 in the 16th year of his age.

Also the body of Eliz: the wife of William Grigory was buried the 20th day of August in the year of our Lord 1760, aged 57.

47. On an altar tomb:

Here lieth the body of Thomas the son of Hugh Broad and of Ann his Wife, who was Buried the 22nd day of October, in the year of our Lord 1758, aged 20.

Also the body of Hugh Broad, of this Parish, who was buried Septr. the 12th 1796, aged 87.

And Ann, the wife of Hugh Broad, who was buried Decr. the 11th 1784, aged 80.

48. Here lieth the Body of Margaret Pearce, Daughter of Edward and Honor Pearce, of this Parish, who was buried the 2nd day of October, in the year of our Lord 1759, aged 3 years and 3 months.

Here lie the remains of Honor Pearce, wife of Edward Pearce, who died September 22nd 1787, aged 65.

Edward Pearce, Gent., died the 17th of Oct^t 1810, aged 85 years.

49. Here lies the body of Sarah the wife of William Stonard. She was buried on Good Friday, the 4th day of April, in the year of our Lord 1760, aged 63.

50. Here lyeth the Body of William the son of Henry and Catherine Smith of this Parish, who, on Sunday the 6th of Nov. 1762, was accidentally and casually snached from hence to the other world in the bloom of his youth, having scarce reached his 18th year.

51. In memory of John Barnes Esq., of the Borough of Camelford. He departed this life the 31st day of January anno domini 1764, aged 35.

52. Upon an altar tomb:

Here lieth the Body of Sarah Phillis Clode, wife of William Clode, Gent., Alderman of the Borough of Camelford, who departed this life March the 27th 1788, in the 75th year of her age.

An affectionate wife and tender mother.

Here also lieth the Body of William Clode, sen^r., Gent., Alderman of the Borough of Camelford, who departed this life Nov. the 2nd 1788, in the 77th year of his age.

An affectionate husband and tender father.

53. Upon an altar tomb:

In memory of Ann the wife of Robert Bake of Camelford, who departed this life the 31st Day of Dec. 1767, in the 51st year of her age.

Also in memory of Samuel Bake, son of Robert and Ann Bake, aforesaid, who departed this life the 21st day of Jan. anno dom. 1784, in the 27th year of his age.

54. Upon an altar tomb:

Sacred to the Memory of Richard Gayer, Late of Trethin in the Parish of Advent, who departed this life on the 10th day of April 1858, aged 71 years.

Also in memory of Jenifer the beloved wife of Richard Gayer, aforesaid. She departed this life on the 28th day of March 1865, aged 71 years.

2 U

55. Upon an altar tomb:

Sacred to the memory of James Hurdon, youngest son of the late John Hurdon Esq., of Egloskerry, who Departed this life on the 28th of April 1859, aged 60 years.

56. This stone is erected in memory of Mr. John Clode, who departed this life the 11th day of January 1765, in the 27th year of his age.

57. Here lyes the body of William the son of William and Susanna Inch of this Pᵃ who departed this life the 11th day of June anno dom. 1766, in the 20th year of his age.

And also the mortal remains of John Inch one of the Aldermen of the Borough of Camelford, son of the above William and Susanna Inch, who died the 26th day of April 1821, aged 77.

THE CHURCH OF ST. ATHEWENNA, *alias* ADVEN, *alias* ADVENT.[1]

This Church is annexed to that of Lanteglos of which it was anciently a Chapel. It is, according to the Inquisitiones Nonarum, dedicated to Sancta Athewenna, but, on account of its dependent position, we do not find it named in the ancient Episcopal Registers. Among the names of the clergy, however, assessed to a Subsidy temp. Henry VI, we find that of Dominus Rogerus Capellanus Sancti Audoeni, a name equivalent to Owen, as is also Adwen or Athwen. From the close connexion which has always existed between this Church and that of Lanteglos we should naturally anticipate a relationship between the founders, and such, it is likely, was the case. Leland says that Advent was founded by one of Brechan's family.[2] Brechan had a son called Adwen,[3] and a daughter Arianwen, which latter might, probably, be latinised into Athwenna. They would, of course, be brother and sister to St. Julitta, or Julutta, of Lanteglos, and to the founders of many of the Churches on the north coast of Cornwall. We confess our inability, in the conflicting evidence, to determine the sex of the founder of this Church, and the Charter by which Walter Bodulgate, in 1435, founded a chantry at Camelford (Appendix II.) does not help us, for although the name of the saint is therein mentioned, the doubt which, perhaps, even then, existed, was eluded by the use of the English word " Seint," which expresses either sex.

The Church consists of Chancel and sanctuary, 18 ft. 6 in. by 14 ft., nave, 44 ft. 3 in. by 14 ft., north transept, 12 ft. 6 in. by 11 ft., south aisle, 61 ft. 6 in. by 10 ft. 6 in., western tower and north porch.

[1] In certain deeds in the Author's collection the parish is described in 1559 as St. Tawthan; in 1572 as St. Adwen; in 1601 as St. Tathene, *alias* Adventte, and St. Tathen, *alias* Advent; and in 1621 as St. Adven, *alias* Awthin.

[2] Coll. III, 183. This view is adopted by the Rev. John Adams, Vicar of Stockcross, co. Berks, the learned Cornish hagiologist.

[3] St. Adwen, son of Brechan, had several Churches in Wales dedicated to him. Another St. Audoen, *alias* Owen, was consecrated Bishop of Rouen in 648, and died 683. He was commemorated on 24th August. (Acta Sanctorum.)

VIEW OF ADVENT CHURCH.

The chancel occupies more than one bay. It is lighted by an eastern window of three-lights Second-pointed date. There is a small piscina in the south wall. A large hagioscope opens into the chancel from the north transept of a somewhat peculiar character; from it spring the stairs to the roodloft, and the same opening is now used for access to the pulpit. There is no ancient window on the north side of the nave, but a modern one has been opened near the west end, over the north door, which door has been walled up. The south aisle is divided from the chancel and nave, eastward of which it projects in a somewhat unusual manner, by four columns of the ordinary Cornish tyye. The roof is of a good cradle pattern, the principals being richly painted and gilt, though it is now in very bad condition. The aisle is lighted by a three-light window at the east end, of a flamboyant and good character, and by a modern insertion at the west end. In the south wall are two windows three-light, cinquefoil, ogee, with openings in the head. They are of good workmanship, in catacluse stone. There was formerly a large chapel on the south side of a somewhat peculiar construction but a few years ago, when laden with a heavy fall of snow, the roof fell in. The window on the east side was of the same character as those just above mentioned, and when it was resolved not to restore the chapel, the window was placed in the archway, when walled up. The details of this chapel are not now known.

The north transept is of the First-pointed period, and has a single lancet window in each wall, those on the north and west being slightly foliated. At the north end an ancient stone bench extends across the transept. The font is of Norman work, the bowl is round, and is supported by a thick octagonal shaft standing upon a square base. (See fig. annexed.)

The tower is of three flights, embattled and ornamented with eight pinnacles, three on each side. The ground has been raised several feet on the west side, so as not to admit of ingress by the west door, which has, accordingly, been walled up. It has an equilateral pointed arch with poor shallow mouldings. Over it is a plain square-headed window of three-lights. In the bell chamber flight is a two-light cinquefoil window on each face of the tower. There is no stair turret, and access to the upper part of the tower is of an unusual character. From the nave a flight of steps leads up to the first chamber, and into this passage a door formerly opened from the outside, which has been walled up. The tower opens into the Church by a lofty arch.

There are four bells, the fourth of which, bears the following inscription:

J. TAYLOR, FOUNDER, OXFORD: 1831: J. BROWNIN C: W:

The others are not inscribed, but all were recast at the same time.

The internal door of the porch, which, like the greater part of the Church, is late Third-pointed, is of very good workmanship in catacluse stone. It has a square hood moulding. The mouldings of the door are continuous, the deep cavetto being filled with

2 U²

quatrefoils, marrigolds, and other ornaments. In the spandrils are quatrefoils. The whole is well cut and as sharp now as when first executed.

Since the foregoing notes were made the edifice became in such bad condition as to render considerable repairs immediately necessary. The whole of the north walls of the nave and chancel and the walls of the north transept were found to be so decayed as to lead to their being entirely rebuilt. The ancient windows were re-inserted in the transept, but the special features mentioned in connection with that part of the Church have been lost. The remainder of the Church has been renovated, and a new roof constructed for the nave, whilst that of the south aisle has been thoroughly repaired and reset. The Church has been benched throughout with red pine.

This Church is not mentioned by the Commissioners on Church ornaments of 3rd Edward VI.

MONUMENTAL INSCRIPTIONS.

IN THE CHURCH.

1. Here lieth the Body of Elizabeth, the w..............Bennet who was Buried the xv Day of September in the...........Lord God 1643. C. R. 19.

2. Here lyeth the Boddy of.............. ....Bvried the six and twentieth day of May Anno Domini 1667.

3. On a flat granite slab, in the north transept, in raised capitals some conjoined:

WILLIAM MICHEL WAS BVRIED. IN 1650
AGNIS HIS WIFE: WAS BVRIED 85 THEIR SEED
ELYZABETH. ANNE. MARGERY. GRACE.

4. Sacred to the Memory of Edmund Dinham of Newton in the Parish of St. Kew, who died August 13. 1831, Aged 66; also of Anne, wife of the above, Died July 19th 1860, aged 83.

5. John Batten, the elder, of this Parish, Gent, was Buried the 22 day of February Anno Dom. 1710.

This tomb contains a Father and a son
whose deaths were sudden and they quickly gon,
Say not I'm young my Parent yet I have
Since Parents follow oft the child to grave,
wrapt vp in ....les of night they silent lye
till summon'd by the last trump's dreadful cry
Before the grand tribunal to appear
And render an account of all done here,
Oh happy they who all accounts can clear.

IN THE CHURCH YARD.

6. In raised letters on a granite slab.

HVGH HONEY | WAS BVRIED T | HE V DAY OF IANVA | RY 1704. +

7. A broken slab removed from the Church is thus circumscribed in capital letters:
HERE LIETH THE BODY OF ANTHONY WADE DECEASED WHICH WAS BURIED THE TWENTIE FIFTH
DAY OF MAY ANNO DOMINI (1667 ?)

PARISH REGISTERS.

The old Registers of the Parish of Lanteglos consist of four volumes; the first volume
was commenced on the accession of Queen Elizabeth, though there are entries of four
marriages which were solemnized sometime before the registers were begun, the dates of the
years of which are not recorded. From the beginning until 1725, when the first volume ends,
the dates of the several weddings, christenings and funerals are entered in parallel columns,
and seem to have been usually made with regularity, except in the period of the interregnum,
during which few entries occur. In the autumn of the year 1591 great pestilence appears
to have prevailed, whole families were carried off by this scourge, as shown by the following
entries:

—— filius —— Netherton sepultus 14° Augusti.
Duo liberi Glanfield ex pest' sep. 12ⁿ Septembris.
Henricus Greene et uxor ex peste sepult' 16° Sept.
Nicholaus Hender et familias ex pest' sepult' eodem tempore.
Christopher Collman vx' et tres liberi sep'. 16° Octobris.

The first volume was begun under the 70th Canon of 1603, when the old registers, or
records, were copied into this book. It is in fair condition though in some places the writing
has become faint. The present Rector has made a fair copy for ordinary reference. The
second volume commences in 1726, and contains entries from that date until 1791, which
are made in parallel columns as in volume i. This volume requires rebinding. The third
volume commences in 1791 and contains entries of baptisms and burials until 1812, and of
marriages until 1799, when, for marriages, was opened vol. iv., in which entries are made
until the new Act came into operation in 1812. The earlier names which occur in the first
volume are Cock, Collman, Hendy, Tregoddick, Wallis, Lanxon, Tucker, Sloggett, Harper,
Baylye, Roobye, Peverell, Worthevale, &c.

The old registers for the Parish of Advent have been lost. The earliest now in existence
contains baptisms from 1709 to 1812; burials, 1781 to 1812; and marriages, 1731 to 1798.
The marriages from 1801 to 1812 are recorded in a second book.

ALTAR PLATE.

In 3rd Edward IV., according to the return of the Commissioners, the Church of Lanteglos possessed one chalice of silver. It now has a silver chalice with a cover, bearing the date "1576," the same referred to in the terrier of 1727, and a broken silver gilt bason for alms, upon which are engraved the arms of Phillips and the following inscription " The gift of Charles Phillips, Esq., M.P. for Camelford."

CHAPELS AND CHANTRIES.

In 1311 the Burgesses of Camelford, having erected a Chapel[1] in that Borough, petitioned Bishop Stapeldon to licence it for divine worship, which he accordingly did on the 4th January afterwards, as appears from the following record :

Dominus concessit Burgensibus Ville de Camelford, ut in Oratorio seu Capella, quam in eadem Villa in honorem beati Thome martyris construi fecerunt de novo, per capellanum ydoneum suis sumptibus in omnibus sustinendum, juxta formam Constitutionis Synodalis super hoc edite (Exon, April 1287) Divina facerent celebrari, ut ipsi et ceteri duntaxat habitantes in eadem villa, hujusmodi ibidem audire possint, duntamen in libris, ornamentis et aliis, in hoc necessaria invenerint; voluntas quoque dicte ecclesie de Nanseglos ad id accesserit et consensus, ita quod nullum prejudicium ipsi Matrici ecclesie generetur.[2]

On 10th June 1381 Richard Bolham, Rector of Lanteglos, had licence to celebrate by a proper priest in the Chapel of St. Thomas the martyr at Camelford.[3]

By his charter dated at Trecorm̃ 20th January 1434-5 (13th Henry VI.), Walter Bodulgate founded a chantry in this Chapel, and conveyed to John Jaybren and Stephen Trenewith, all his messuages, &c., in Mochil-Trewint, Tresterleck, Torre and Algarsmylle in the parish of " Seint Athwanne," and Souther Treworder in the Parish of Egloshaile, to hold for the life of the said Walter, with remainder to Thomas Bodulgate and the heirs of his body, on condition that the said Thomas and the heirs of his body within one year next following the death of the said Walter should, from the profits of the said lands, provide a fit chaplain to celebrate mass daily within this Chapel, according to the use of Sarum, or some other mass at his discretion, for the soul of the said Walter, and for the souls of his parents, ancestors, and benefactors, and also for the souls of all those whose names should be inserted in a tablet, or schedule, over the high altar in the said Chapel, with this proviso, nevertheless, that on every Wednesday throughout the year, the priest should say the mass *De Requiem et placebo* and *Dirige cum commendatione animarum,* and the prayer *Absolve quæsumus Domine* for the souls aforesaid, together with the

---

[1] This Chapel stood near the river on the site of the present Cow Market, where, until lately, there was a cottage called " Chapel House."

[2] Bishop Stapledon's Register, fo. 68.   [3] Bishop Brantyngham's Register.

psalm *De profundis;* daily, unless he could shew reasonable cause for omitting the same. For this the said Thomas Bodulgate was to pay the said priest seven marks annually; and if it should be found before the Rector of Lanteglos for the time being, that the Chaplain had failed to fulfil the said services without reasonable cause, sixpence sterling should be deducted from his salary for each default, and paid towards the fabric of the said Chapel: and in default of the said Thomas and his heirs to sustain the said services the lands to remain to Thomas Roscarrock and Isabella his wife, and their heirs under like condition, and, in default, remainder to Edward Coryton and Johanna his wife in the same manner, and, in default, remainder to the right heirs of the said Walter Bodulgate; and if, through the default of any one, any of the said services should de omitted, the person culpable should answer to the said Walter for the default at the bar of the Almighty God and his angels, and his soul should go away into the place where there is wailing and gnashing of teeth, &c. This deed is sealed with the seal of the said Walter, and because his seal is not so well known, it is sealed also with the seal of John, Prior of St. Germans.[1]

This Chapel, though erected by the inhabitants of Camelford as a place of public worship, and licensed by the Bishop for that purpose, was seized by the king under the act for suppressing the chantries, colleges, &c., and in the certificate of the Commissioners appointed 14th February 37th Henry VIII, to survey and value the possessions of such chantries, &c., its state is given in the following words.

"The stipendary in the Parish Church of Lanteglos, in Camelford, housling people 200. This towne is one mile from the Church. Roberte Babington, incumbent, for his salary yearly £4 13s. 4d. Scoles and preachers none. Pore people having any relief out of the premises none." And the Commissioners propose that Robert Babington should continue to receive his stipend as a pension.[2]

A further commission was appointed on 14th February 2nd Edward VI. when it was stated by the Commissioners that "The stipendary called Camelford Stipendary, in the Parish of Lanteglos, was founded by the ancestors of Bodulgate, who had certain lands entailed upon them and their heirs for ever upon condition that they should find a Priest to minister Divine Service to the inhabitants within the Town of Camelford, in a Chapel there, distant from the Parish Church of Lanteglos, aforesaid, one mile and more, paying unto such Priest, in perpetuity, for his salary yearly £4 13s. 4d., going out of the lands and tenements lying in Mocheltrewynt (Great Trewint), Tresterleke, Torr, Aldersmyll, Southertre and Wourdranghe, with their appurtenances." It appears further that this endowment had been seized by the King under the Act for disolving colleges, chantries, &c. And the Commissioners certify that the pension and yearly stipend, Robert Babington, now Incumbent there, hath for the maintenance of his living, "No charge going out of the same other than the x[h] payable to the Kings maiestie w[ch] is not here reprysed." And they certified that the ornaments, jewels, plate, &c., appertaining to the said stipendary was of the value of 35s.[3]

[1] Deed in the possession of John Jope Rogers of Penrose, Esq. (See Appendix II.)
[2] Augmentation Office, 37th Henry VIII., Certificate No. 15.
[3] Augmentation Office, 2nd Edward VI., Certificate No. 9, 78.

In 1592 the endowment of this chapel, under the description of all that late Chantry founded within the Parish Church of Camelford, (fundatam infra ecclesiam parochialem de Camelford) was granted, *inter alia*, to William Tipper and Robert Dawe of London, Gentlemen, and to their heirs and assigns for ever,[1] at a mere nominal rent.[2]

There was also an obit founded in the Parish Church of Lanteglos which fell into the King's hands in the same manner as the Camelford Stipendary. It was of the value of 22s. 1¼d. per annum, payable out of lands and tenements in Camelford, Calabegyn, and Trewynen. This was granted, *inter alia*, in 3rd Edward VI., to Sir Thomas Pomeroy, Knt. and Hugh Pomeroy.[3]

CHARITIES.

Sir James Smith's Charity.—By indenture, dated 24th May 1679, James Smyth, described as of Chelsea, Knt.,[4] as well for and in consideration of the goodwill and respect which he had for the Borough of Camelford, and for the better erecting of a School House and maintenance of a School there, and for discharging such other necessaries as might, or should, happen in the said borough, as also in consideration of the sum of £50, to him paid by the Mayor and Burgesses, and for divers others good and valuable considerations him thereunto moving, conveyed to John Nicholls and Ambrose Manaton, and their heirs and assigns, and the survivor of them and his heirs and assigns for ever, the moiety of one messuage or tenement called Great Tregarth,[5] in the Parish of Lanteglos by Camelford, to the intent that they should stand seised of the said premises to the use of the mayor and burgesses of the said borough for the time being, their successors and their assigns for ever, and that the said mayor and burgesses, and their successors, should for ever take and receive the rents, &c., of the said premises for the purposes aforesaid.

In consequence of the mayor and burgesses of Camelford having appropriated the whole, or the greater part, of the income derived from this property to their own uses instead of applying it to the support of a school, an information was filed against them in the Court of Chancery in 1813. The suit was compromised and withdrawn, and

---

[1] It is remarkable that a fee farm rent of precisely the same amount reserved out of certain lands and tenements in Camelford, by indenture dated 22nd September 23rd Charles II. (1671), were conveyed, *inter alia*, by Francis Lord Hawley and others, Commissioners for the sale of Fee Farm Rents of the Crown, to Hugh Boscawen of Tregothnan, Esq. (Rot. Claus. 23rd Charles II, Part 7, m. 8.)

[2] Rot. Pat., 34th Elizabeth, Part 4, m. 21.

[3] Particulars for grants, Edward VI.

[4] Sir James Smith was also of Trehanick in St. Teath. He married Bridget, relict of John Nicholls of Trewane, (vide ped. ante p. 165.) He had been just previously returned as one of the Burgesses in Parliament for Camelford. See post.

[5] This property, by deed dated 1st January 1671, was conveyed to Sir James Smith by Hugh Carew of Trevye, Gent., and Dorothy his wife. (Deed among the records of the Corporation of Camelford.)

consequently no decree was made, but a schoolroom was erected, on some land belonging to the Corporation, by the then patron of the borough. The trust property consists of about twenty-eight acres, and is now let at the annual rent of £35 per annum, the proceeds being given towards the salary of the master of a National School, built in 1853, of which the Rector and Churchwardens, and the members of the corporate body, are joint managers. Since the year 1829 the accounts have been kept by the Town Clerk, and are in good order.

EYRE CHARITY.

The origin of this charity we have not succeeded in tracing. It is believed to have been a bequest of a pious lady of the name of Eyre of Davidstow. It originally consisted of one messuage and thirty acres of land in the village of Trelill in St. Kew, the annual proceeds whereof were directed to be applied to the reparation of the Church of Lanteglos, and to the relief of the poor of the said parish. The feoffees, however, by deed dated 29th September 1708, exchanged these lands with John Nicholls of Trewane, in St. Kew, Esq., for certain tenements in Trevia, in this parish, containing about forty-eight acres, to be holden of the chief lords of the Manor of Bodulgate, at the rent of 1s. 5d. per annum. This is now let in parcels to different tenants at an aggregate rental of £103 per annum. For several years the rents were carried to the credit of the parish in the accounts of the Overseers of the Poor, in aid of the poors' rates, out of which the expenses of Churchwardens were defrayed, no Church rate having been made. The profits are now applied in accordance with the intention of the founder, one moiety being appropriated towards the reparation of the Church, and the other distributed at Christmas by the Churchwardens and Overseers among poor housekeepers of the parish. The estate is vested in eight trustees.

ALMS HOUSE, TREVIA WALLS.

At Trevia Walls is an Alms House erected in 1709, the money for building which was partly contributed by the Honble. Hugh Boscawen and John Nicholls, Esq., as testified by two tablets of slate affixed to the front of the house. Surmounted by escutcheons of arms: Boscawen, impaling three horses' heads crowned; and Nicholls, impaling Mohun; are the following inscriptions:

"Anno 1709
The Honourable Hugh Boscawen gave towards the building of this house Ten Pounds."

"Anno 1709
John Nicholls of Trewane, Esq., gave towards the building of this house Ten Pounds.
James Nicholls his grandson, Esq., gave Three Guineas."

2 v

Near to this alms house in 1791 the parish built a workhouse in accordance with Act 22nd George III. The cost of this building was about £500, which was borrowed on the security of the rates; having ceased to be used as a workhouse it became the resort of the idle and dissolute, and, in 1859, was taken down.

PHILLIPS' CHARITIES.

CHARLES PHILLIP'S CHARITY.

Charles Phillips, Gentleman, one of the Aldermen of the Borough of Camelford, by his will, dated 6th October 1804, devised to Charles Carpenter of the same borough the sum of £170, and directed that he should lay out the same for the benefit of the poor of the parish of Lanteglos by Camelford, or to such of them as shall not have regular pay or relief from the said parish. Charles Carpenter having received the said sum, in order to give full effect to the purpose of the testator, by deed dated 13th April 1808,[1] charged his estate, called Moditonham, in the parish of Botusfleming, with the sum of £8 10s. per annum, being the value of the said capital sum at the rate of £5 per cent. per annum, and gave power to the Recorder of Camelford to receive the said rent-charge at Christmas in each year, and if not duly paid, to distrain for the same, and distribute it annually to the poor not in receipt of parochial relief.

WILLIAM PHILLIP'S CHARITY.

William Phillips, sometime Rector of this parish, by his will dated in 1790, charged his estate of Trefrew, in the parish of Lanteglos, with the sum of £5 per annum to be distributed among the poor in bread. The estate passed to Mr. Phillip's nephew, Charles Carpenter, by whose son John Phillips Carpenter of Mount Tavy, in co. Devon, Esq., it has recently been sold to Miss Pearse of Launceston, chargeable with the said rent-charge, which is duly paid, and the amount is expended in bread, which is distributed by the Rector every Sunday during the winter months after divine service.

NATIONAL SCHOOL.

The National School at Camelford was built in 1853, and is the only school in the parishes of Lanteglos and Advent. It is conducted upon the mixed principle, and will contain 220 children. There are now about 200 under instruction. In April 1854, the school building was licensed for divine service, and for the convenience of the inhabitants of Camelford, extra services are held there on Sunday evenings.

[1] Deed in the Corporation Chest.

THE BOROUGH OF CAMELFORD.

This town is situate in the parish of Lanteglos, and undoubtedly derives its name from a ford of the river Camel, whose source is in the parish of Davidstow, about four miles north of this town. It has been called by other names as " Gafulford," " Cablan," and " Cambala " as already noticed (ante vol. i, pp. 583, 584, and notes), but these names seem to be corruptions of the proper name, derived from the river on which it is situate, which river empties itself into the river Alan near the southern extremity of this parish. We have also treated, at the place above cited, of the tradition concerning the great battle between Arthur and Modred, fought near Camelford.

There is nothing remarkable in the early history of this place. In the year 1259, Richard Earl of Cornwall and King of the Romans by his charter made it a free Borough, and granted to the burgesses a weekly market on Friday, and a fair on the eve, day, and morrow of St. Swithen, which liberties, upon inspeximus of the charter, were confirmed by the Earl's brother, King Henry III, on 12th June 1260, as appears from his charter following :

Henricus dei gratia Rex Anglie Dominus Hiberniæ et Dux Aquitaniæ Archiepiscopis Episcopis Abbatibus Prioribus Comitibus Baronius Justiciariis Vicecomitibus Prepositis Ministris et omnibus Balliuis et fidelibus suis salutem. Sciatis nos ad instanciam domini Regis Illustris Alemaniæ fratris nostri de gratia nostra speciali concessisse et hac carta nostra confirmasse pro nobis et heredibus nostris quod villa sua de Camelford in Cornubia quam idem Rex per cartam suam nuper fecit liberum Burgum cum mercato singulis septimanis per diem Veneris et cum feria singulis annis per tres dies duratura videlicet in vigilia et in die et in' crastino Translationis Sancti Swythuny remaneat liberum Burgum cum predictis mercato et feria et omnibus libertatibus et liberis consuetudinibus ad huiusmodi Burgum mercatum et feriam pertinentibus imperpetuum. Hiis testibus Ricardo de Clare comite Gloucestriæ et Herefordiæ. Rogero le Bygod comite Norfolkiæ et marescallio Angliæ. Hugone le Bygod Justiciario Angliæ, Philippo Basset, Johanne Maunsell Thesaurario Eboracensis, Waltero de Merton, Gilberto de Preston, Imberto Pugeys et aliis. Datum per manum nostram apud Westmonasterio duodecimo die Junii anno regni nostri quadragesimo quarto.[1]

This charter was again confirmed by King Richard II on 20th April 1398, by King Henry IV on 5th February 1400-1,[2] by King Henry VI on 20th May 1449,[3] and by King Edward IV on 23rd May 1475.[4]

Upon the Inquisition taken on 13th November 1300, after the death of Edmund Earl of Cornwall, it was found that, *inter alia*, he died seized of the Borough of Camelford, and that in the said borough there were sixty-two burgesses who held sixty-two burgages, and paid annually to the Lord of the Manor of Helston £4 4s. 4½d.

[1] This Charter is not inrolled.
[2] Rot. Pat., 2nd Henry IV, Part 2, m. 38.
[3] Rot. Pat. 27th Henry VI, Part 2. m. 11.
[4] Rot. Pat., 15th Edward IV, Part 1, m. 4.

2 v²

That the fair produced to the Lord five shillings, and that the pleas and perquisites of the courts were worth by the year 13s. 4d. It was also found that he had died seized of the Church of Nanteglos, and that the value per annum was forty marks.[1]

The town, however, must have been very poor, or have fallen greatly into decay soon afterwards, for when in 1327 a subsidy of a twentieth was levied upon all who possessed moveable goods of the value of ten shillings, or upwards, eleven persons only were found to be assessable in the borough, and the aggregate amount paid by them was no more than ten shillings.[2]

It appears from the caption of seizin of Edward the Black Prince, 1338, that the Burgesses made fealty with the Duke, and gave him for his recognition 40d., and that they claimed to hold the borough of the Duke by the payment of a rent of £4 5s. 4d. and to be free burgesses of the said Duke. And being questioned by what warrant? they said that they and their ancestors and predecessors, Burgesses of the borough from a time beyond the memory of man, had been free Burgesses, holding the borough in the form aforesaid of the Lord the King and his progenitors, and of all others who had the lordship. At that time the toll there was of the value of 8s. per annum, and the pleas and perquisites of the borough were worth 10s. per annum.

On the accession of Henry IV. as King, his eldest son was created Prince of Wales, and was invested with the Dukedom of Cornwall, and a writ for the delivery of seizin to him of, *inter alia*, the Manor of Helston in Trigshire, with the Park of Helsbury and other appurtenances, was issued in 1399,[3] and on 6th April 1401 this Prince, by the stile and titles of Henry eldest son of the King of England, Prince of Wales, Duke of Lancaster, Cornwall, &c., granted to John Cornwaille and Elizabeth his wife, Countess of Huntingdon,[4] *inter alia*, the Borough of Camelford, to hold to the aforesaid John and Elizabeth for the whole life of the said Elizabeth, without any payment whatever to the Prince or his heirs. They obtained livery of seizin of the said lands, but in the same year again surrendered them into the Prince's hands, probably because under the charter creating the Duchy no power exists, or can exist, for the alienation of any portion of the possessions.

In 1467 Thomas Donnecombe, Prepositus of the Borough of Camelford, accounted to the Exchequer for the rent of £4 5s. 4½d.[5]

In the 6th year of King Edward VI, the borough was first allowed the questionable privilege of sending two burgesses to Parliament. The franchise was never defined, but

---

[1] Inq. p.m., 28th Edward I, No. 44.   [2] Subsidy Roll, 1st Edward III, see also Appendix III.

[3] Rot. Claus, 1st Henry IV., Part I., m. 27.

[4] This Lady was the sister of the King, and therefore aunt of the Prince, being the second daughter of John of Gaunt and Blanche his first wife, coheir of Henry Plantagenet, great grandson of Henry III., created Duke of Lancaster. She married first, John Holland, created Earl of Huntingdon, and afterwards Duke of Exeter, by his half-brother, Richard II., but was deposed from the latter title by his brother-in-law Henry IV., and afterwards beheaded by him. She married secondly, this Sir John Cornwall, a man famous in his age, and created K.G. by Henry IV.

[5] Minister's accounts, Duchy of Cornwall, 6 and 7, Edward IV., $\frac{95}{9}$

became vested in freemen, being inhabitants and paying scot and lot. A contest took place in 1660. By indenture dated 25th April in that year, Peter Kelligrew and Samuel Trelawny were returned, but the election was declared void upon the ground that the poll had not been duly taken. The other candidates were Thomas Vivian and Henry Nicoll. Another election took place, and by three several indentures, dated 30th June in the same year, William Cotton of Botreaux Castle, Thomas Vivian, and Henry Nicoll were returned. The return of Mr. Vivian seems to have been undisputed, and upon petition, on 3rd August, a Committee of the House reported that the freemen and inhabitants paying scot and lot had the right of election, and that comparing the number of votes given to Henry Nicoll, who was returned by one indenture, and to William Cotton, who was returned by another indenture, the Committee found that Mr. Nicoll had a greater number of votes of freemen, but that as divers of them did not pay scot and lot, and therefore had no right to vote, they decided that Mr. Cotton was duly elected. This was confirmed by the House by 103 to 98, and Mr. Cotton declared duly elected.[1] The charter of 1699 made no change as to the right of voting for the Members of Parliament, nevertheless the resident Capital Burgesses for some time claimed and exercised the exclusive privilege. A Court was held annually within a month after Easter, at which a jury of freemen was impannelled and sworn before the Mayor and Recorder, or his Deputy, who presented fit persons to be freemen. Their number was indefinite, and varied from fifteen to thirty. By their venality Camelford obtained an unenviable notoriety.

The question of the right voting again arose upon a petition in 1796, when a Committee of the House decided that the right of election was in the freemen who were inhabitants paying scot and lot, and that the capital burgesses had no right to vote for members for the borough, unless they were also free burgesses, inhabitants, and paying scot and lot.[2]

The present charter was granted by King Charles II. on 24th July 1669, on the application of the then mayor and burgesses.[3] By it the body corporate consists of nine aldermen, or capital burgesses, of whom one is to be annually elected mayor, a recorder, deputy recorder, a common clerk, and a common serjeant at mace. The mayor is to be elected on the Monday next after the feast of St. Michael the Archangel, the recorder and common clerk to be chosen by the mayor and burgesses, the common serjeant by the mayor for the time being, and the burgesses, whenever a vacancy occurs, by a majority of the mayor and burgesses. The mayor and recorder, or deputy recorder, are empowered to hold a court of record once in three weeks, to try all manner of pleas, actions, suits and plaints, provided that the sum in such pleas, &c., does not exceed fifty pounds. In addition to the ancient fair on the 14th, 15th, and 16th July, two new fairs are granted by this charter, to be held yearly; one on the 14th, 15th, and 16th May, and the other on the 25th, 26th, and 27th of August; the tolls and profits of such fairs to be received by the mayor and burgesses, and the mayor and burgesses are empowered to hold lands, &c., to the value

[1] Journals, vol. viii., p. 110.
[2] Journals, vol. lii., p. 109. See also Brady's History of Boroughs, pp. 1751, 1639 and 2115.
[3] Rot. Pat., 21st Charles II., Part I., No. 4.

of £50 per annum. In addition to the sergeant-at-mace formerly, according to ancient custom, the mayor appointed, annually, constables, bread-weighers, triers of weights and measures, ale taster, scavenger, pig-ringer, and pound-keeper; but as many of these offices had, in process of time, become superseded, and others had fallen into desuetude, they have, of late years, ceased to be filled.

It appears from the return made by Charles Dinham, then mayor, to the circular of the Home Office, dated 24th November 1831, that at that date there were 110 houses within the borough, and that the amount of assessed taxes paid by the borough for the year ending April 1831 was £110 17s. 7d. Accordingly, as the number of inhabitants was under 2000, the town was placed in Schedule A of the Reform Act of 1832, and wholly disfranchised as regarded Parliamentary representation.

In 1764, shambles and a yarn market were erected adjoining the Town Hall at a cost of £140, which was raised by the mayor and burgesses on mortgage of "The Clease" or Fair Park, and Town Tregarth, for which latter they were trustees for the purposes mentioned (ante, p. 324); and the Town Hall having become dilapidated, in 1806 the Duke of Bedford, then patron of the Borough, erected, at his own cost, the present hall over the Market House. The hall is a commodious room surmounted by a cupola, containing a clock and a bell. In this room the Judge of the County Court and the County Magistrates for the Hundred of Lesnewith hold their sessions.

In 1833, the Duke of Cleveland gave by deed to the mayor and burgesses for ever a tenement called Carvabins, containing 9a. 1r 30p. on condition that the markets should thenceforward be free from tolls. This land, with "The Clease," or Fair Park, which contains something less than three roods, and the tolls of the fairs are the whole of the property possessed by the Corporation, except Tregarth, for which the mayor and burgesses are trustees for the purposes before stated.

BOUNDS OF THE BOROUGH.

"The bounds and limits of the Vill or Borough of Camelford, in the county of Cornwall, were perambulated and viewed on the sixteenth day of April 1805, by Parmenas Pearce, Gentleman, Mayor, Charles Carpenter, Esq., William Dinham, Gentleman, John Lawrence, Gentleman, John Inch, Gentleman, Thomas Jago, Gent., Charles Dinham, Edward Penhallow, John Harvey, John Gist, and Richard Gayer.

The said Perambulators and viewers began from the white thorne in the Warren, growing opposite the back kitchen window of the late Rev. William Phillipps's Dwelling house, to the Warren stile, and out strait across the King's Highway and turn'd into Jonathan Harvey's Tan-yard, and up in a strait line to the old Linhay door the north side of the pound-house there, and thence out over the wall into the King's Highway,[1] and up the

---

[1] The highway being the boundary of the borough on that side.

highway so far as Samuel Cock's dwelling house, and thence into the little lane (opposite the said Samuel Cock's house) leading to Tregoodwell, and along by the hedge of Daw's ground (but NB not inside the said hedge) and across the other lane leading to Tregoodwell, by the white thorne on the hedge of the Duke of Bedford's Beef Parks,[1] and along by the *inside* of that hedge, in a strait line, to the corner of the cross hedge, and over that corner of the said cross hedge by the *inside* of the hedge of the late William Gregory's above-town,[2] and turn the corner of that hedge down to the little lane leading from the above town to Tregoodwell, until you come to the slate or ragstone on the top of the hedge, and then over that hedge by the side of that stone down *inside* of the hedge of Mr. Bant's west grounds, and down to the water or Rivulet, and by the side of the said water to the moorstone at the bottom of the Duke of Bedford's Beef Parks, and down by the inside of the water till you come to the Burrow of stones, and then over the hedge into William Phillipps's Coloden, and then over the hedge of Coloden into the Duke of Bedford's out-ground,[3] and over the hedge of said out-ground into[4] Mr. Thomas Pearce's Out-ground, down to the (four beech trees) two waters, and then over the hedge by the said trees into Fenteroone ground, and across the said two waters at the corner into Tucking Mill ground, and down by the side of the river to Tucking Mill pool, otherwise Rockwell's Pool (and here the borough ends as to the going down by the side of the river). And from thence along by the hedge up into the corner of Tucking Mill Moor, and over the said corner of the said into Hodge's or Puddacombe's wood, and by the side of the Leat down to the hedge, and thence up by the side of that hedge to the spring or well, to Fenteroone second stile, and over the hedge by the side of the said stile, into the late Mrs. Hamline's ground, and up by the side of the hedge into the King's Highway, called Cawse End, and across the said Highway into John Pearce's field, called Lobb's ground, heretofore belonging to Jonathan Rundle, which used formerly to be called Cawse End Field, and thence up by the inside of the hedge to the corner, and over the hedge at the said corner by the stile on the inside, into Davey's field, formerly called Old Lloyd's field, and along by the inside of said Davey's field hedge next to the Highway,[5] through and over all the other fields and cross hedges thereof, and across the lane by Chapman's Turnpike until you come to Town Tregartha, and then over the hedge into, and down by the side of the hedges of Harvey's and Hodge's ground, 'till you come to the Badger Rock near the river, and then down along by the side of the river 'till you come to the Flood gate opposite the Fore Kitchen Window of the said Rev. William Phillipps' said dwelling house, and through the said Fore Kitchen Window into the said Kitchen, and out through the said Back Kitchen Window to the White Thorne before mentioned, from whence the said Perambulators sat off."

[1] Known by the name of Wade's Beef Parks.   [2] Known by the name of Bant's Above Town.
[3] Query if the south part of the said field over the river is in the borough.
[4] Query as above.
[5] The lane or highway doth not belong to the borough.

LIST OF MAYORS.[1]

1552, Christopher Cock	1613, Christopher Cock	1665, Richard White
1553, (25th September) Do.	1614, Christopher Cock	1668, Ambrose Wade
1555, (1st October) Do.	1621, Christopher Cock	1678, Rodolphus Pike
1562, 13th December) Do.	1623, Christopher Cock	1680, Richard White
1572, (April) John Cock	1625, Christopher Cock	1684, Ambrose Wade
1588, (1st November) John Cock	1630, Christopher Cock	1687, Ralph Pike
1597, John Cock	1631, Christopher Cock	1689, William Prideaux
1604, John Cock	1632, Christopher Cock	1695, William Prideaux
1605, Christopher Cock	1635, Christopher Cock	1699, Samuel Jackson
1607, Christopher Cock, Esq.	1646, Christopher Worthevale	1700, Edward Cloake
1608, Christopher Cock	of Worthevale, Esq.	1701, Edward Hodge
1610, Christopher Cock	1659, Christopher Worthevale	1702, Ralph Pike.
1611, Christopher Cock	1660, Christopher Worthevale	1704, Godfrey White.

The above names are derived from the Indentures returning Burgesses to Parliament.

ELECTED.

1707, October 6th, Edward Hodge, Gent.[2]
1708, October 4th, Geffrey White, Gent.
1709, October 3rd, Edward Cloake, Gent.
1710, October 2nd, Edward Cloake, Gent.[3]
1711, October 1st, Samuel Jackson, Gent.[4]
1712, October 6th, John Phillips, Gent.
1713, October 4th, John Phillips, Gent.
1714, October 4th, Ralph Pike, Gent.[5]
1715, October 3rd, William Carew, Gent.
1716, October 2nd, James Prideaux, Gent.
1717, September 30th, William Rowe, Gent.
1718, October 6th, John Phillips, Gent.
1719, December 3rd, Ralph Pike, Gent.
1721, ... Samuel Jackson.
1726, ... Ralph Pike.

ELECTED.

1729, Ralph Pike, Mayor, buried 3rd December, 1729, P.R.
1731, William Rowe.
1732, October 2nd, Jonathan Pomery, Gent.
1733, October 1st, John Phillips, Gent.
1734, October 30th, Charles Hamline, Gent.
1735, October 6th, John Rowe, Gent.
1736, October 4th, Nathaniel Hender, Gent.
1737, October 3rd, William Carew, Gent.[6]
1737, March 14th, Jonathan Pomery, Gent., vice Carew deceased.[7]
1738, September 26th, John Phillips, vice Jon. Pomeroy, deceased.[8]
1738, October 2nd, Charles Hamline, Gent.
1739, October 1st, John Rowe, Gent.

[1] The days on which the mayors were elected prior to the Charter of Charles II, is not known.
[2] Buried 22nd February 1713.   [3] Buried 17th December 1713.   [4] Buried 22nd July 1736.
[5] 1699, August 18th, mar. lic. between Ralph Pike of Camelford, and Mary Jefery of Launceston, spinster.
[6] Buried 7th March, 1737.
[7] Buried 29th August 1738.

ELECTED.

1740, October 6th, John Phillips, Gent.
1741, October 5th, no election, J.P. continued.
1742, October 4th,   do.   do.
1743, October 3rd, Charles Hamline.
1744, October 1st, William Phillips, Gent.
1745, September 30th, Nathaniel Hender.
1746, October 6th, John Rowe, Gent.
1747, October 5th, Joseph Pomeroy, deceased.[1]
1748, May 26th, Charles Phillips.
1748, October 3rd, William Rowe.
1749, October 2nd, John Phillips.
1750, October 1st, Jonathan Phillips.
1751, September 30th, John Phillips.
1752, October 2nd, William Phillips, Senr.
1753, October 1st, Charles Phillips.
1754, September 3rd, no election (a tie)
1755, October 6th, Rev. William Phillips.
1756, October 4th, Jonathan Phillips.
1757, October 3rd, William Clode.
1758, October 2nd, John Phillips.
1759, October 2nd, William Clode.
1760, October 6th, Jonathan Phillips.
1761, October 5th, John Phillips.
1762, October 4th, William Clode.
1763, October 3rd, Jonathan Phillips.
1764, October 1st, John Phillips.
1765, September 30th, William Clode.
1766, October 6th, Charles Dinham.
1767, October 5th, Rev. William Phillips.
1768, October 3rd, William Clode.
1769, October 2nd, Charles Phillips.
1770, October 1st, John Phillips.
1771, September 30th, Charles Dinham.
1772, October 5th, William Clode.
1773, October 4th, Charles Phillips.
1774,   Rev. William Phillips.
1775, October 2nd, Charles Dinham.
1776, September 30th, Charles Phillips.
1777, October 6th, William Clode.
1778, October 5th, Charles Phillips.
1779, October 4th, Charles Dinham.
1780, October 2nd, William Clode.

ELECTED.

1781, October 1st, Thomas Phillips.
1782, September 30th, William Clode.
1783, October 6th, Charles Phillips.
1784, October 4th, Charles Dinham.
1785, October 3rd, Charles Phillips.
1786, October 2nd, William Clode.
1787, October 1st, Charles Dinham.
1788, October 6th, William Clode, Junr.
1789, October 5th, William Dinham.
1790, October 4th, Henry Braddon.
1791, October 3rd, William Dinham.
1792, October 1st, John Phillips Carpenter.
1793, September 30th, William Clode.
1794, October 6th, William Dinham.
1795, October 5th, Thomas Winsloe, Junr.
1796, October 3rd, William Dinham.
1797, October 2nd, William Phillips.
1798, October 1st, Henry Braddon.
1799, October 1st, William Clode.
1800, October 6th, William Dinham.
1801, October 5th, William Phillips.
1802, October 5th, William Clode.
1803, October 3rd, John Lawrence.
1804, October 1st, Parmenas Pearce.
1805, September 30th, John Inch.
1806, October 6th, William Clode.[2]
1807, May 9th, Henry Braddon, vice Clode,
          deceased.
1807, October 5th, John Lawrence.
1808, October 3rd, Mathew Pope the younger.
1809, October 2nd, Richard Mabyn.
1810, October 1st, Charles Dinham.
1811, September 30th, no election, C.D. continued.
1812, October 5th, William Dinham.
1813, October 4th, John Carpenter.
1814, October 3rd, Mathew Pope, Jun.
1815, October 2nd, George Wharton.
1816, September 30th, Charles Dinham.
1817, October 6th, Mathew Pope, Junr.
1818, October 5th, John Dent.
1819, October 4th, James Rosevear.
1820, October 2nd, Charles Dinham.

[1] Buried 24th May 1748.   [2] William Clode, Esq., late of Skisdon, buried 7th February 1807.

2 X

ELECTED.

1821, October 1st, Mathew Pope, Junr.
1822, September 30th, James Rosevear.
1823, October 6th, William Fillis Pearce.
1824, October 4th, Charles Dinham.
1825, October 3rd, John Dent.
1826, October 2nd, Edward West.
1827, October 1st, Mathew Pope.
1828, October 6th, William Henry King
1829, October 5th, James Robson.
1830, October 4th, Richard Watts.
1831, October 3rd, Charles Dinham.
1832, October 1st, James Rosevear.
1833, September 30th, Edward West.
1834, October 6th, John Clode Braddon.
1835, October 5th, William Henry King.
1836, October 3rd, Mathew Pope.
1837, October 2nd, James Robson.
1838, October 1st, Richard Watts.
1839, September 30th, James Rosevear.
1840, October 5th, John Clode Braddon.
1841, October 4th, William Henry King.
1842, October 3rd, Edward West.
1843, October 2nd, Warwick Guy Pearse
1844, September 30th, William Braddon.
1845, October 6th, Mathew Pope.
1846, October 5th, James Robson.
1847, October 4th, John Clode Braddon.

ELECTED.

1848, October 2nd, William Henry King.
1849, October 1st, Edward West.
1850, September 30th, Warwick Guy Pearse.
1851, October 6th, Rev. Roger Bird.
1852, October 4th, William Dinham King.
1853, October 3rd, Charles Augustus West.
1854, October 2nd, Rev. John James Wilkinson.
1855, October 1st, William Henry King.
1856, October 6th, Edward West.
1857, October 5th, Warwick Guy Pearse.
1858, October 4th, William Dinham King.
1859, October 3rd, Francis Barton Rowe.
1860, October 1st, Rev. John James Wilkinson.
1861, September 30th, Edward James Hurdon.
1862, October 6th, William Henry King.
1863, October 5th, Thomas Pope Rosevear.
1864, October 3rd, Edward West.
1865, October 2nd, William Dinham King.
1866, October 1st, Rev. John James Wilkinson.
1867, September 30th, Edward James Hurdon.
1868, October 5th, William Henry King.
1869, October 4th, Nicholas Male, Junr.
1870, October 3rd, Thomas Pope Rosevear.
1871, October 2nd, William Hender Sowdon.
1872, September 30th, William Dinham King.
1873, October 6th, Rev. John James Wilkinson.
1874, October 5th, Nicholas Male.

	Recorders.	*Deputy Recorders.*	*Town or Common Clerks.*
1669,	Francis Lutterell.		Anthony Cosen, continued.
1711,	Henry Manaton.		1712, October 6th, William Phillips appointed.
		1715, Daniel Budger.	
1716, May 11th	Francis Manaton, Elected.	1716, August 21st, John Phillips, sworn.	
1735, May 6th,	Thomas Pitt, Esq.	1736, October 7th, Joseph Pomery, Gent.	1745, May 2nd, Charles Phillips; resigned 3rd October 1761.
1761, October 6th	Charles Phillips.		
1775,	Jonathan Phillips.		
1794			1794, June 19th, Thomas Jago.

Recorders.	Deputy Recorders.	Town or Common Clerks.
	1797, September 26th, Charles Phillips appointed deputy to Sir Jonathan Phillips, who resigned 16th January 1798	
1803, January 13th, Charles Carpenter appointed vice Sir Jonathan Phillips deceased.		
1803, October 25th, Robert Adair.	Charles Carpenter,	
	1812, April 7th, Charles Rashleigh.	1812, April 7th, John Lawrence. vice Thomas Jago resigned.
1813, January 13th, John Phillips Carpenter vice Adair resigned.	Charles Rashleigh.	
1813, July 22nd, John Carpenter, vice John Phillips Carpenter, deceased		
1818, Mark Milbank, vice J. Carpenter, resigned.		
	1819, May 4th, John Darke.	1824, William Fillis Pearce, vice John Lawrence, deceased.
		1850, November 18th, Richard Harris Burt, vice W. F. Pearce resigned.

BURGESSES ELECTED TO SERVE IN PARLIAMENT.

(Compiled from Crown Office Records.)[1]

Date of Indenture of Return.	Place and date of Meeting of Parliament.	Names of Burgesses.		
	WESTMINSTER.			
1552-3, Feb. ..	1st March 1552-3	Robert ..cke [2] ..	.. ..	Nicholas Seyntjohn.
1553, 20th Sept.	5th Oct. 1553	Francis Roscarrock	..	Ambrose Gilbert.
Missing ..	2nd April 1554	*Thomas Arundell* ..	..	*George Stafford.*
1554, 22nd Oct.	12th Nov. 1554	Francis Roscarrock, Gent. ..	..	Clement Trefford, Gent.
1555, 1st Oct...	21st Oct. 1555	William Cavyll, Gent. ..	..	George Tadlowe, Gent.
Missing ..	20th Jan. 1558	John Carnsuyowe ..	..	John Smith.[3]

[1] The names printed in *italics* are not found in the Crown Office Returns, and are taken from Browne Willis and other sources.

[2] The first two letters of this name are illegible, but "Chyke," as printed by Browne Willis, is certainly inaccurate. The name is probably "Cocke."

[3] 1558, February 24th, John Smith, returned burgess for Camelford, upon a declaration made by Mr. Marshe that he had come to the house being outlawed, and also had deceived divers merchants of the city of London, taking wares of them to the sum of £300, minding to defraud them of the same under the colour of the privilege of this house. Question raised whether he should have the privilege of the house: Ayes 112, Noes 107. Ordered that he still continue a member of this house. (Journals, vol. i, p. 55.)

2 X²

Date of Indenture of Return.	Place and Date of Meeting of Parl. WESTMINSTER.			Names of Burgesses.
Missing ..	23rd Jan. 1559	William Partridge..	.. ..	Drew Drewry, Esq.
1562, 13th Dec.	11th Jan. 1563	William Partridge ..	.. ..	Drew Drewry, Esq.
Missing ..	2nd April 1571	*Edward Williams, Gent.*	..	*Nicholas Prideaux, Gent.*
1572, 27th April	8th May 1572	George Graynefylde, Junr., Gent.	..	John Gifford, Esq.
Missing ..	23rd Nov. 1584	*Richard Trefusis, Esq.*	..	*Emanuel Chamond, Gent.*
Missing ..	15th Oct. 1586	*Geoffry Gale, Esq.* ..	..	*Richard Trefusis, Gent.*
1588, 1st Nov.	12th Nov. 1588	Arthur Gorge, Esq.	..	Richard Trefusis, Gent.
Missing ..	19th Feb. 1593	*Humphry Michell, Esq.*	..	*Richard Leeche, Esq,*
1597, 4th Oct.	24th Oct. 1597	William Carnesew, Esq.	..	Jerome Horsey, Esq.
1601, 1st Oct.	27th Oct. 1601	Anthony Turpin, Gent.	..	William Carnsew, Gent.
Missing ..	19th March 1604	John Good, Esq. ..	..	Anthony Turpin, Gent.
.. ..	5th April 1614	No Return ..	.. ..	
Missing ..	30th Jan. 1621	*Henry Carey, Knight*	..	*Edward Carre of London, Esq.*
Missing ..	12th Feb. 1624	Edward Carr, Esq.	..	Francis Cottington, Bart.[1]
	17th May, 1625	*Henry Hungate, Knight*	..	J. Cottcele, Esq.
1625-6, 12th Jan.	6th Feb. 1625-6	Edward Lindsey, Esq.	..	Thomas Monck of Woode, Knight.[2]
Missing ..	17th Mar. 1628	Evan Edwards, Esq.	..	Francis Crossing
Missing ..	13th April 1640	Edward Reade, Esq.	..	Pierce Edgcumbe, Esq.[3]
Missing ..	3rd Nov. 1640	William Glanvill, Esq.	..	*Pierce Edgcumbe, Esq.*
1647, 12th April		William Sey, Esq., in the place of William Glanville, Esq., adjudged by the House of Commons to be no longer a member		
Legislative Assembly called a Parliament	4th July 1653	No Return ..	.. ..	
Missing ..	27th Jan. 1659	*J. Maynard, Serjeant at Law.*	..	*William Braddon, Esq.*
		Thomas Vivian, Esq.	..	Peter Kylligrew, Esq.
	25th April 1660	Henry Nicoll, Esq.	..	Samuel Trelawny, Esq.[4]
1660, June 30th		Thomas Vivian, Esq.	..	William Cotton, Esq.[5]
	8th May 1661	Thomas Coventry, D.C.L.[6]	..	Charles Roscarrock.

[1] Created a Baronet 16th February 1623, Lord Cottington of Hanworth, co. Middlesex 1631. Was sometime Chancellor and under Treasurer of the Exchequer. Ambassador to Spain, and Lord Treasurer during the civil wars. Died at Valladolid in Spain 1653, s p.

[2] 1625 March 24th. Upon Mr. John Drake's information in the House that Sir Thomas Moncke, a burgess elected for Camelford, was in execution before, and at the time of, his election. Ordered a new writ to issue for a new choice in his room. (Journals, vol. i, p. 840.) We have no record that his place was filled, and it would appear from the returns in the Crown Office, that one burgess only sat for Camelford in this Parliament.

[3] The name of Pierce Edgcumbe does not appear in the Crown Office Returns, but is given by Browne Willis. He was sent for on 12th November 1642, as a delinquent, and again on 5th January following, and desired to lend £1000 ; and a person was appointed to receive the sum assessed upon him. (Journals, vol. ii, p. 23.) In the same month both he and his colleague were disabled from sitting in the House for deserting the Parliament service and adhering to the King's cause. (Journal vol. iv, p. 285.)

[4] This election was declared void the poll not having been duly taken.   [5] See ante p. 652.

[6] Bernard Grenville Esq., who was returned by another indenture of the same date, petitioned against the return of Thomas Coventry and Charles Roscarrock Esqrs. As the Mayor, Christopher Worthyvale, said that he would take his own time in bringing the books &c , he was committed to the custody of the Serjeant-at-Arms for contempt, but was released upon his conformity and on the payment of the fees. The petition of Mr. Grenville was dismissed.

Date of Indenture of Return.	Place and date of Meeting of Parl.	Names of Burgesses.	
1665, Oct. 27th		William Godolphin, Esq., vice Charles Roscarrock, Esq., deceased.	
1678-9, 20th Feb.	6th Mar. 1679	James Smith of Trehannick, Knight...	William Harbord, of Grafton Park, co. Northants, Esq.
1679, 8 Sept.	17th Oct. 1679	Robert Russell, Esq.	James Smith of Trehannick, Knt.
	OXFORD.		
	21st Mar. 1680	*Robert Russell, Esq.*	*James Smith, Knt.*
	WESTMINSTER.		
1685, April 28th	19th May 1685	Humphry Langford of Hill, Esq.	Nicholas Courteney, of the Inner Temple, Esq.
1685, Sept. 11th		Charles Scarborow, Knt., M.D., vice Humphry Langford, deceased.	
1688, 17th Jan.	22nd Jan. 1688	Ambrose Manaton, Esq.	Henry Manaton, Esq.
1695 Nov. 11th	22nd Nov. 1695	Ambrose Manaton of Kilworthy, co. Devon.	*Robert Molesworth.*
1696, April 1st		Hon. Sidney Wortley, *alias* Montague, vice Ambrose Manaton, elected also for Tavistock.	
1700, Jan. 13th	6th Feb. 1700	Henry Manaton of Harwood, Esq.	Dennys Glynn of Glynn, Esq.
1701, Dec. 1st	30th Dec. 1701	Henry Manaton of Harwood, Esq.	Denis Glynn of Glynn, Esq.
1702, July 27th	21st Aug. 1702	Henry Manaton of Harwood, Esq.	Denys Glynn of Glynn, Esq.
1703, Jan. 17th		William Pole, Esq., in place of Henry Manaton elected for Tavistock.	
1705, May 21st	14th June 1705	Henry Pinnell, Esq.	William Pole of Shute, co. Devon, Esq.
1708, 17th May	8th July 1708	Richard Munden, Esq.	*John Manley, Esq.*[1]
1710, 19th Oct.	25th Nov. 1710	Hon. Bernard Grenville, Esq.	Jaspar Radcliffe, Esq.[2]
1711, 26th Mar.	28th Nov. 1710	Paul Orchard, vice Jaspar Radcliffe, deceased.	
1711-12 20th Feb.	25th Nov. 1710	Sir Bouchier Wray, Bart., in place of Barnard Grenville.[3]	
1713, 7th Dec.	12th Nov. 1714	Sir Bouchier Wray, Bart.	James Nicols, Esq.
1714-5,17th Jan.	17th Mar. 1714-5	James Montague, Esq.	Richard Coffin, Esq.
1722, 13th April	10th May 1722	Hon. Henry Earl of Drogheda.	William Sloaper, Esq.
1727, 23rd Aug.	28th Nov. 1727	Thomas Hales, Esq., son of Sir Thomas Hales, Bart.	Colonel Thomas Pitt.
1734, 2nd May	13th June 1734	Hon. Sir Thomas Littleton, Bart.	The Hon. James Cholmondley, Esq.
1741, 12th May	25th June 1741	William Earl Inchiquin of the Kingdom of Ireland.	Charles Montague, Esq.
1747, 1st July	13th Aug. 1747	Hon. Ridgeway Pitt of Soldon, co. Devon, Esq., Earl of Londonderry in Kingdom of Ireland.	Samuel Martin of the Inner Temple, Esq.
1754, 17th April	31st May 1754	Samuel Martin of the Inner Temple, Esq.	John Lade of Hendley, co. Dorset, Esq.
1759, 25th May		Bartholomew Burton, Esq., in place of Sir John Lade, Bart., deceased.	

[1] A petition was presented by Henry Manaton, Esq., against the return of John Manley, Esq., alleging various acts of bribery and corruption, but Mr. Manley's election was confirmed. (Journals, vol. xvi, pp. 274, 275.)

[2] Upon the death of Jasper Radcliffe an election took place, and Henry Manaton, Esq., then recorder, was returned by Mr. White claiming to be Mayor. Paul Orchard was returned by Edward Cloake, also claiming to be Mayor. The validity of the election of the Burgess turned upon the fact as to whether Mr. White or Mr. Cloake had been duly elected Mayor. The House determined in favour of Mr. Cloake, and as under the poll taken by that gentleman Mr. Orchard had a majority of votes he was declared duly elected. (Journals, vol. xvi, pp. 643, 644.)

[3] Appointed Lieut.-Governor of Hull.

Date of Indenture of Return.	Place and date of Meeting of Parl.	Names of Burgesses.	
1761, 30th Mar.	19th May 1761	Samuel Martin of Westminster, Esq...	Bartholomew Burton of the City of London, Esq.
1768, 19th Mar.	10th May 1768	Charles Phillips of Camelford, Esq.	William Wilson of Keythorpe, co. Leicester, Esq.
1774, 16th Oct.	31st Oct. 1774	John Amyand of London, Esq. ..	Francis Herne, of Harrow, co. Middlesex, Esq.
1776, 4th Nov.		Sir Ralph Payne of Charles Street, Westminster.	
1777, 13th June		Sir Ralph Payne of Charles Street, St. James, one of the Clerks of the Household.	
1780, 11th Sept.		John Pardoe, Junr. of Layton, co. Essex, Esq.	James Macpherson, Manchester Buildings Westminster, Esq.[1]
1784, 6th April	18th May 1784	James Macpherson	Jonathan Phillips of the Borough of Newport.
1784, 5th July		Sir Samuel Hannay of Putney Heath, Bart., in the place of Jonathan Phillips Esq., who had accepted the Stewardship of the Chiltern Hundreds.	
1790, 21st June	10th Aug. 1790	James Macpherson of Putney Heath, Esq.	Sir Samuel Hannay of Putney Heath Bart.
1791, 8th Jan.		William Smith of Clapham, co. Surrey, Esq., vice Sir Samuel Hannay, deceased.	
1796, 19th Mar.[2]		Lord William Cavendish Bentinck, vice James Macpherson, Esq., deceased.	
1796, 30th May[3]		William Joseph Dennison, Esq. ..	John Angerstein, Esq.
1802, 7th July	31st Aug. 1802	Robert Adair of 24, Great Marlborough Street, Esq.	John Fonblanque of Lincoln's Inn, Esq.
1806, 1st Nov.	15th Dec. 1806	Robert Adair of Hertford St., Mayfair, Esq.	James Viscount Maitland
1807, 11th May	22nd June 1807	Robert Adair of Hertford St., Mayfair	Lord Henry Petty of Downing Street.
1810, 2nd Feb.		Henry Brougham, Junr.,[4] of Brougham Hall, co. Westmorland, vice Henry Petty now Marquis of Lansdown.	
1812, 10th Oct.	24th Nov. 1812	William Leader of Putney Hill, Surrey, Esq.	Samuel Scott of Sunbridge Park, Kent,
1818, 17th June[5]	4th Aug. 1818	Mark Milbank of Thorpe Hall, North Riding of co. York.	John Bushby Maitland of Eccles, co. Dumfries.
1819, 17th April[6]		John Stewart of Albany, Westminster.	Lewis Allsopp of Lincoln's Inn Fields.
1820, 9th March	1st April 1820	Mark Milbank of Thorpe Hall, Esq.	Francis Charles Seymour Conway commonly called Earl of Yarmouth.
1822, 26th June		Sheldon Cradock of Harforth in North Riding of York, vice the Earl of Yarmouth. succeeded to the Peerage as Marquis of Hertford.	
1826, 12th June	26th July 1826	Mark Milbank of Thorpe Hall, Esq.	Sheldon Cradock of Harforth, Esq.
1830, 30th July	14th Sept. 1830	The same.	The same.
1831, April 29th[7]		The same.	The same.

[1] Translator of Poems attributed by him to Ossian, and author of several Historical Works and Political Pamphlets.   [2] Writ ordered 7th March. (Journals, vol. li, p. 484.)

[3] A petition against this election was presented by the unsuccessful candidates, Lord Preston and Robert Adair, but without success. (Journals, vol. lii, p. 109.)

[4] This was the first step in political life of the famous Lord Chancellor.

[5] These members were said to have given the Patron £800 for their seats, of which each freeman received £100 besides other privileges.   [6] Indenture missing.

[7] The Candidates at this election were Mark Milbank and John Bushby Maitland Esq., in the Darlington interest, and John Stewart and Thomas Hanmer, supported by the Earl of Yarmouth. The two former were returned by a

POLSTON-BRIDGE, *alias* POLSTONEL-BRIDGE.

It appears from the caption of seizin of Edward the Black Prince, that in 1337, John the son and heir of Henry de Kellygren held two acres of land Cornish,[1] in petty serjeantry, viz., by the service of meeting the Duke on his coming into Cornwall at Poulstonelbridge, and there receiving a certain grey cape (capam gris) and carrying it after the Duke through all Cornwall, at the expense of the Duke, for forty days.[2] And on 13th September 1354, we find an order given for the purchase of a grey riding coat at an expense of 2s. 2d. to be carried by John Keligryn, on the Prince's entering Cornwall.[3]

The names of the free tenants appear for the first time on the Assession Rolls of 9th Edward IV. (1468) wherein we find that the land was then held, by the same service, by ——— heir of John Michaelstow, kinsman and heir of John son of Henry de Kelligren, and we may notice that the name is still written Polstonelbrigge. In

majority of three : Milbank and Maitland 13, Hanover and Stewart 10. There was much bribery, in consequence of which several votes were struck off the poll, leaving the numbers even, when the election was declared void. A new writ having been issued six candidates entered the field, namely, Messrs. Milbank and Maitland in the Darlington interest, Mr. Polhill and Colonel Hanmer in the Yarmouth interest, and Messrs. Stewart and Allsopp in the interest of a Mr. Hallett, a druggist of St. Mary Axe, London, who brought down £6000 to be divided among 15 voters provided they returned his candidates. As the four last named gentlemen were all of the same politics they adopted the somewhat novel expedient of selecting two by lot, the tickets being drawn out of a tea pot. At the close of the poll the numbers were for Stewart and Allsopp 14, Milbank and Maitland 12. A petition was immediately presented, the election was declared void, and Mr. Stewart incapacitated for sitting in that parliament for the Borough of Camelford. Upon the issue of a new writ the Earl of Yarmouth and Mr. Milbank were returned without opposition.

[1] In our Introduction to this work (p. 5), we briefly remarked upon land measures, observing that a *hide* of land was an indeterminate quantity. Being designed for the support of one family it must necessarily have varied in extent in different localities according to the greater or less fertility of the soil, and we suggested that the modern customary Cornish acre of 5760 yards must have very closely approximated to a Saxon acre. The Cornish acre, however, there alluded to, was not the same as is mentioned in the text. The latter was unquestionably much larger, but the number of English or statute acres contained therein is not easily determined. Mr. (now Sir Edward) Smirke, in an Essay on the subject read at a Meeting of the Royal Institution of Cornwall, on 23rd May 1862 (pub. twenty-fourth Annual Report, p. 29) of which Society he was then the President, has very carefully considered this subject, and after an exhaustive search satisfied himself that the extent of a Cornish acre cannot be represented by any corresponding modern measure of surface, or area, which can be relied upon as of universal application. He came to the conclusion that an "acre of land Cornish" was equivalent to a carucate of land, or plough land, that is, such quantity of arable land as could be ploughed by a single plough and its team in a year, referring to Testa de Nevill, p. 204, as supporting that view. In these circumstances a Cornish acre, like a *hide* of land, must have varied in area according to the fertility of the soil; but Mr. Smirke came to the conclusion that in ordinary circumstances a Cornish acre would contain in area about sixty-four English or statute acres, and that the number would be governed by the quality of the soil, *e.g.*, in rough, mountainous, or moor land, the area would be much greater than in well cultivated districts.

[2] Caption of Seizin, Record Office. It is remarkable that the Manor of Cabillia was held by a similar service, viz., of rendering a grey cape as often as the *King* should cross Poulston Bridge into Cornwall (see ante, vol. i, p. 273 and note).

[3] Council Black Prince, fo. 184. The original is among the records of the Receipts of the Exchequer, Record Office.

1553, the tenant was Richard Copleston, described as heir of John Michaelstow. In 1602, John Wood was tenant, which John Wood was the heir of Richard Wood by Isabella his wife, the heir of Richard Copleston. The tenement disappears from the Assession Rolls from this date until 1742, when it is again entered, but without the name of a tenant, with the following memorandum appended :—" This land *is said* to lye near Polston-bridge and called St. Leonard's, and near the Cockpit. 9th Elizabeth held by Richard Copleston, Esq.; 15th Charles I by Christopher Wood, Esq." In 1756 Thomas Dark was the tenant by purchase from Gwyn Spry, a legatee to William Spry, from whom it passed to John Roe, Esq., who held it by the same tenure in 1777. In 1798, John Cudlip, M.D., was the tenant, and the tenement is described as " late Anthony Roe's." In 1819, it was in the tenure of the heirs of John Cudlip, M.D., as it was in 1826. Of the heirs of Cudlip it was purchased by Mr. Cowlard, Solicitor, of Launceston, who is the present proprietor.

It will be observed that in the above quoted memorandum the identity of the land is qualified by " is said." It was clearly a mistake, and we have yet to discover where the land held by the abovementioned interesting tenure was situate. The land purchased of the heirs of Cudlip is undoubtedly the land referred to in the later Assession Rolls, but it was never parcel of the Manor of Helston, but belonged formerly to the Lazar Hospital of St. Leonard, at Launceston, and is held of the Mayor and Burgesses of that borough. We are indebted to the courtesy of Mr. Christopher Cowlard of Launceston, for this information.

BODULGATE IN TRIGG.

In 1337, William Chenduit held two acres of land Cornish in Bodulgate of the Manor of Helston in Trigg, at the rent of 6s. per annum, fealty, and suit at Court; whilst a further half acre, in the same ville, was held by Richard Tynden at the rent of 18d, and similar services. William Chenduit died leaving a son Thomas, and two daughters, Johanna, who married Stephen Trejago, and Alice who became the wife of Thomas Roscarrock. The legitimate issue of Thomas Cheynduit became extinct in his grandson, John Cheynduit. John had two illegitimate children, Richard Cheynduit and Johanna, wife of John Pengelly, upon whom, by a fine levied in 1425, he settled, *inter alia*, Bodulgate, which appears then to have been annexed to the Manor of Bodannan, with various remainders over. John Cheynduit died two years afterwards, and it was found upon the Inquisition taken after his death, that William Cheynduit being seized of this manor settled the same upon himself and his wife Elizabeth for life and the heirs of their bodies, and that he had issue Thomas, Johanna, and Alice, and that the said Thomas had the manor, and that it descended to the said John, who died without issue, and that the manor descended to certain Ralph Trenowyth and Thomas Roscarrock as kinsmen and heirs of the said John, viz., the said Ralph as son of Johanna daughter of the aforesaid Johanna, one of the sisters of the aforesaid Thomas son of William, and the aforesaid Thomas Roscarrock as son of Alice, the other sister of Thomas son of William.[1] Accordingly we find in the Assession Roll of 1461, that the abovementioned two acres of land in Bodulgate were held by John Trenewith, described as kinsman and heir of William Cheynduit. He was the grandson of Ralph Trenewith abovementioned. In the same roll, the other tenement in Bodulgate is stated to be held by Thomas Bodulgate, kinsman and heir of Warine Bodulgate, and kinsman and heir of Richard Tynden.

John Trenowith died in 1496, s.p.m., when the Bodulgate lands reverted to the Roscarrock family as the male representatives of William Cheynduit, and in the Assession Roll of 1539, it is stated that the said two acres were held by John Roscarrock as kinsman and heir of William Cheynduit, and that the other tenement in Bodulgate, abovementioned, together with two acres of land Cornish in Penkerowe, which in 1337 were held by Warine Bodulgate, at a rent of 4s. per annum, were held by Richard Roscarrock, son and heir of John Roscarrock, as kinsman and heir of Warine Bodulgate.

The statement that any portion of the lands was held in 1539 by *John* Roscarrock was a clerical error, for the said John died on 26th October 1537, and upon his inquisition, *post mortem*, the jury found that before his death he was seized of certain lands in Bodulgate in his demesne as of fee, and being so seized by his Charter, dated 6th January 18th Henry VIII, had conveyed the same to William Lower, Esq., and Richard Penros, guardians of Isabella Trevenor, one of the sisters and heirs of William Trevenor, to the use of Richard Roscarrock, son and heir apparent of the said John Roscarrock and the said Isabella, and the heirs of their bodies, in virtue of which grant the said Richard and Isabella entered upon the said lands, and were thereof seized in fee tail; and the jury say that the said *Manor* of Bodulgate together with the Manor of Delaboll were held of the Prince as of his Manor of Helston in Trigg by fealty and rent of 21s. 3d., and suit at Court, in pure socage, and that the value was £26 13s. 4d.[2] This is the first occasion on which these lands had been designated a *Manor*,[3] but it seems improbable that they possessed any ancient manorial franchises. The condition of the manor and the lands forming it during the tenure of Richard Roscarrock will be shewn by the following terrier, dated in 1569.[4]

---

[1] Inq. p.m., 5th Henry VI, No. 57. See also Pedigree of CHEYNDUIT, ante vol. i., p. 546.

[2] Escheator's Inq., 28th and 29th Henry VIII.

[3] We are told that no new manors have been created since the passing of the Statute *Quia Emptores* in 13th Edward I.

[4] Roscarrock Rent Roll, in the possession of Francis Rodd of Trebartha Hall, Esq.

2 Y

HUNDRED DE TRYGGE.

Manerium de Bodulgate.

Liberi Tenentes.

Penkerowe	Willelmus Carnsuyowe Armiger et Nicholaus Glynne Armiger tenent ibidem vnam acram terræ Cornubiensem in soccagio Et facient Et reddunt per annum.	iiij^d Domino Duci Cornubiæ Manerio suo de Helston in Trygge iiij^s
TheRoseParke	Johannes Langdon Armiger tenet ibidem dimidiam acram terræ Cornubiensem in soccagio sine secta. Et reddit per annum.	vi^d
Downe	Willelmus Grylles de Tavistoke tenet ibidem vnum ffarlingum terre Cornubiensem in soccagio et faciet sectam ad duas curias legales. Et reddit per annum.	iij^s xj^d
Camelforde	Willelmus Carnsuyowe et Nicholaus Glynne Armigeri tenent ibidem Et reddunt per annum.	xx^d

Summa x^s j$^d\cdot$

Convencionarii Tenentes.

The Mayne Parke	Johannes Nycholls de Bodwene tenet ibidem Et reddit per annum.	xij^d
Delyowcarle-bon	**Johannes Webber.** Alicia Roche vidua tenet ibidem ....tenementum per indenturam reddendo per annum xxxiiij^s vj^s Et heriotum quando &c. Et faciet sectam curiæ Et erit prepositus et decennarius quando &c. Et soluendo redditum ad quatuor anni terminos magis vsuales viz ad festum Natalis Domini Annunciacionis Beate Marie Virginis, Natalis Sancti Johannis Baptiste et Michaelis archangeli equis porcionibus et ij capones diem autumpno et alia seruicia sicut &c.	xxxiij^s vj^d ij capones et vnum diem autumpno vel xij^d pro defectus
Delyowcarle bullion *alias* Dely	**Johan Joce.** Johanna Slogett vidua tenet per indenturam ad terminum vitæ suæ Et reddit per annum xxvj^s x^d Et faciet vt supra et j diem autumpno vel xij^d pro defectu eiusdem j caponem et inhabitabit super premissa Et habebit jampnum et brueria super dominiam de Delyobell Et stirpes jampnum ad focalia.	xxvj^s x^d j caponem j diem Autumpno vel xij^d pro defectu

Camelforth ~~Polysgton~~ Georgius Tome
~~Robertus~~∧Capellaneous ∧ tenet ibidem j tenementum cum pertinentiis et reddit per annum xxj⁵ j caponem j diem autumpno Et
sectam vt supra. } xxj⁵
j caponem j diem autumpno

tenentur domino
Duce Cornubiæ
per redditum
iiij⁵ vj⁴ oboli vt
de Burgo de
Camelford.
Johannes Cokke tenet ibidem j ortum cum tofto cum pertinentiis et reddit per annum vj⁴ } vj⁴

Georgius Tome tenet ibidem j toftum et ortum et reddit per
annum viij⁴ } viij⁴

Idem Georgius tenet ibidem j toftum et ortum cum pertinentiis et faciet sectam vt supra Et reddit per annum. } xx⁴

Trevarlyche Antonius
~~Ricardus~~ Roskarrocke Armiger dominus manerij tenet ibidem
medietatem eiusdem ville et solebat reddere. } xxiiij⁵

pro altero redditu
domino Duce
viij⁵
Elizabeth hoidge vidua tenet ibidem medietatem eiusdem ville
cum pertinentiis Et faciet sectam vt supra Et reddit per annum
xxiiij⁵ j caponem j diem autumpno et alia seruicia &c. } xxiiij⁵
j caponem j diem autumpno.

The Downe Dominus tenet ibidem medietatem et solebat reddere. iiij⁵ vj⁴

Nicholaus Mighell.
Elizabeth hodge vidua tenet alteram medietatem Et faciet
vt supra Et alia seruicia Et reddit per annum iiij⁵ vj⁴ } iiij⁵ vj⁴

Newhall Thomas Cowlyng tenet ibidem per indenturam Et faciet vt
supra Et reddit per annum xvj⁵ j caponem et j diem autumpno. } xvj⁵
j caponem j diem autumpno.

Attorre Stephanus Trereby tenet ibidem vt supra Et faciet vt supra
Et reddit per annum........j caponem j diem autumpno. } iiij⁵ vj⁴
j caponem j diem autumpno

The Myllonde Idem Stephanus tenet ibidem Et reddit per annum. iiij⁵ vj⁴

Pokewalles Hugo Colman tenet ibidem medietatem eiusdem et faciet vt
supra Et reddit per annum v⁵ j caponem j diem autumpno. } v⁵
j caponem j diem autumpno.

Thomas Black tenet ibidem alteram medietatem Et faciet vt
supra Et reddit per annum v⁵ j caponem j diem autumpno. } v⁵
j caponem j diem autumpno.

Katerina Dawe vidua.

Trevya downe Willelmus Wylles iure uxoris
Johannes Joce ∧ tenet ibidem tenuram predictam cum pertinentiis Et faciet sectam vt supra Et reddit per annum vj⁵ viij⁴
j caponem et j diem autumpno. } vj⁵ viij⁴
j caponem j diem autumpno.

2 Y²

Nicholaus Dagg.

Trevya   Ricardus Roskarrocke Armiger dominus Manerij predicti } xl*
tenet ibidem medietatem eiusdem ville Et solebat reddere per { solebat reddere.
annum xl*

Seynt Gylt   Johannes Joce tenet ibidem alteram medietatem ville predicte Et } xl*
Parkes   faciet sectam &c. j caponem Et j diem autumpno Et reddit per annum. { j caponem j diem
                                                                                    autumpno.

                Johannes Nycholl de Seynt Kewe.
Dominicum de   *Ricardus Roskarrocke* Armiger dominus Manerij predicti tenet ibi- } lxxviij* iiij^d
Bodulgate   dem omnia pastura in orientale parte mansionis reddit lxxviij* iiij^d

tenetur de   Johannes Rycarde tenet ibidem omnia pastura iu occidentale   lxj* viij^d
Domino Duce   parte mansionis Et faciet sectam &c. j caponem j diem autumpno   (lxvj* viij^d)
Cornubiæ per   Et reddit per annum lxj* viij^d   j caponem j diem
redditum de vij*   autumpno.
vj^d et sec tam
communem xiij^d

                Johanna Slogett vidua tenet ibidem quandam peciam terre } ....
                Et reddit per annum.

Tresterloke   Henricus Cowlyng tenet ibidem tenementum predictum Et } xj*
tenetur de do- faciet sectam &c. j caponem j diem autumpnalem Et reddit per { j caponem j diem
~~dominus de Hama-~~ annum xj*   autumpno.
~~thethyperredditum~~
hereui Willelmi
Kayle per reddi-
tum xxij^d oboli
quadrantis

Fenterwonwith   Degorius Walys tenet ibidem tenuram predictam et molen- } xlvj* iiij^d
tenetur de   dinum ffullonicum reddendo per annum xlvj* iiij^d Et faciet sectam { j caponem j diem
eisdem heredibus vt supra j caponem et vnum diem autumpno.   autumpno.
scilicet Et per
vij^d de receptis
pro beda molen-
dini fullonici. Et
ij sectas curiarum
vel vj^d

Tresolet   Robertus Garrowe et Johannes Hokkyn tenent ibidem j } xiiij*
tenetur de do- tenementum cum pertinentiis Et facient sectam &c. ij capones { ij capones ij dictas
minis de Hama- et duos dies autumpnales Et reddunt per annum.   autumpuales.
tethe per redditum
xij^d Et xiij^d pro
fine sectam curiæ
cum feodo clerici

Trewynte   Elizabeth Hokkyn vidua tenet ibidem tenementum cum per- } xx*
tenetur de do- tinentiis Et faciet sectam &c. j caponem j diem autumpno Et { j caponem j diem
minis predictis reddit per annum xx*   autumpno.
per redditum v^d

Camelforde   Robertus Babyngton Capellanus et Robertus Penwaren tenent } vj*
                ibidem j domum ibidem hic inscriptum vj^to Novembris anno {
                Elizabethe Regime xix°

ffngacio de Tre- In manibus domini Et reddit per annum aliquando plus } xl* olim
wynte Moure   aliquando minus.
tenetur de
Georgio Tubbe
de Maneris de
Trenaye per
redditum ij* iiij^d

South Tre-
worde
tenetur de Man-
erio de Burnayre
per redditum vj⁸
et sectam com-
munem

Hugo Roskarrocke tenet ibidem tres acras terre Cornubienses ⎫ lxxiij⁸ iiij⁴
in convencione Et reddit per annum. ⎭

Delyoboll

Vmfridus Roskarrock et Nicholaus Roskarrock dominus ⎫ xx^li
tenet totam terram ibidem in manibus propriis et solebat reddere. ⎭

Lytell Bodulgate
alias le lytell
pere extra sepes
de Bodulgate

Johannes Slogett reddit per annum Et pro heriotum iij⁸ iiij ⎫ xij⁴
quando &c. de Fine x⁸ ⎭

Summa convencionarii tenentes vltra Trewent more lij^li x⁸ xvij
capones et xvj dies antumpno vel xij⁴ pro quolibet defectu.

Resolucio
Redditum

Inde in reddituum resolucione domino Duci Cornubiæ pro altero redditu
totius Manerij de Bodulgate. Viz., Manerio suo de Helston in Trygge. Cum
iiij⁸ pro Penkarowe. Et cum viij⁸ pro altero redditu de Trevarlyche Et cum
vij⁸ vj⁴ pro altero redditu de Bodulgate Et cum xiij⁴ pro ffine sectæ j⁴ pro
feodo Clerici pro intracione eiusdem Et cum iiij⁸ vj⁴ obolo solutis Burgo de
Camelforde pro diuersis Burgagiis ibidem Et ei xxij⁴ obolo quad^r solutis heredibus Willelmi Kayle pro altero redditu de Tresterloke Et ei v⁸ solutis eisdem
heredibus pro altero redditu ·de ffenterwonwith Et ei vj⁴ eisdem heredibus
pro gurgite molendini fullonici ibidem Et ei vj⁴ solutis eisdem heredibus
pro ffine sectæ curiæ ad duas curias legales Et ei xij⁴ solutis dominis de
Hamatethe pro altero redditu de Tresolette Et ei v⁴ eisdem Dominis pro altero
redditu de Trewynte Et ei xiij⁴ solutis eisdem pro ffine sectæ curiæ cum j⁴ pro
feodo clerici pro intracione eiusdem Et ei vj⁸ solutis domino Episcopo Exon-
iensi manerio suo de Burneyre pro altero redditu de South Treworder.

It would seem clear from this Rent Roll, that Bodulgate was not an ancient manor,
though it is so described as early as 13th Edward IV, but a reputed manor formed in the
way described in section v, clause 5, of Appendix I.

Richard Roscarrock died in 1575, seized, *inter alia*, of the *Manors* of Bodulgate and
Delioboll, and Thomas Roscarrock was found to be his son and heir,[1] whose son John
Roscarrock, by indenture dated 20th February 33rd Elizabeth (1590-1), granted to John
Nicholls of St. Kew, Gent., all that the Manor of Bodulgate, situate in the Parishes
of Lanteglos and St. Adveny, that is to say Lytill Bodulgate, St. Jellettwell Park, Trevie
Higher Closes, Trevie Lore Closes, Trevie Down, Torre, Powkenalls, Trescarleck, Newhall,
and one tenement in Camelford, and also all the suits and services which the heirs of
Trecarne, to wit, Richard Carnsewe and William Glynn, Esquires; and the heirs of
Langdon owe for certain lands in Camelford, Penkeyrow, and Rose Park, which they held

[1] Inq. p.m., Wards and Liveries, 18th, 19th, and 20th Elizabeth, vol. xviij, p. 33.

of the said John Roscarrock, as of his Manor of Bodulgate.[1] And in Trinity Term following, the said John Roscarrock and Katherine his wife suffered a fine to the said John Nicholls, and quit-claimed the said manor, &c. to him and his heirs for ever.[2] John Nicholls died thereof seized in 1633,[3] from whom it descended to Elizabeth Nicholls, sole heir of her family. She married Nicholas Glynn of Glynn, Esq., and dying without surviving issue, by her will, dated 10th April 1771,[4] devised these lands, *inter alia*, to Thomas Glynn, of Helston, John Bennett, her steward, and others, in trust for sale, for the payment of the costs in a suit between Testator and Serjeant Glynn, and certain debts and legacies, with the proviso that any lands remaining unsold after the payment of the above claims should go to the use of the said trustees. Bodulgate remained vested in these trustees and their heirs as late as 1826, but eventually passed to the sole possession of the heir of Thomas Glynn, from which family it passed by the marriage of Cordelia, sister and heir of Thomas Glynn, with Richard Gerveys Grylls, of Helston, Esq., to the latter family, and is now inherited by Shadwell Morley Grylls, of Lewarne, Esq., its representative.

JETWELLS.

Jetwells contains about eighteen acres of rich meadow land. It derives its name from a Holy Well which formerly existed on the premises, and which has been ruthlessly torn down and the place desecrated within the last twenty years. The abundant spring is still known by the name of "The Holy Well." The two stones which formed the ancient equilateral arch still lie on the spot, as also do other stones which formed the building. In early times the tenement was called "St. Giltwell Parks," which is a corruption, or abbreviation of "St. Julitta's Well Parks." In 1569 it is mentioned, under the name of "St. Giltwillpark," as parcel of the Manor of Bodulgate, to which reputed manor it had been annexed (see ante p. 344). Upon the demise of Mrs. Glynn, of Trewane, above referred to, Jetwell Parks, as the tenement was then called, vested in Joseph Bennett, of Skisdon, Clerk, under whose will, dated 31st August 1788, it passed to his son John Bennett, who, in conjunction with certain trustees, by indenture dated 28th and 29th April, 1796, conveyed the same to Thomas Davey, yeoman. By indenture dated 6th and 7th July 1815, Mr. Davey sold the premises to Charles Carpenter, Esq., who built thereon a large and comfortable residence in the cottage style. Mr. Carpenter, during his life, from the natural affection which he bore towards his nephew Frederick Cresswell, Gent., by indenture dated 25th and 26th September 1829, conveyed to him all the said tenement with the dwelling house, lodge, stables, &c., which gift he afterwards confirmed by his will. By indenture dated 12th and 13th January 1838, the said Frederick Cresswell conveyed the premises in fee simple to Frederick Pym,

---

[1] Deed in the possession of S. M. Grylls of Lewarne, Esq.
[2] Pedes Finium, 33rd Elizabeth, Trinity.
[3] Inq. p.m., 9th Charles I, Bundle 53, No. 249.
[4] Prov. P.C.C., 24th May 1771.

Clerk, and Charles Cobley Whiteford, Gent., the latter of whom, by deed dated 15th April 1858, sold it to Samuel Graham Bake, Esq., who, by deed dated 16th June 1873 demised it to Frederick Cecil Holder, Esq., who had for some years previously held a lease of the premises, and resided there, and is now the possessor in fee.

TREVTHNOUTH, *alias* TREYVTHOUT, *alias* TREYTHEN.

The manner of writing the name of this place has varied exceedingly, nevertheless there cannot be any doubt as to its identity. We find it first mentioned in 1337. John de Treuthnouth held of the Manor of Helston in Trigg, one acre of land Cornish in Treyuthent, and another acre of land Cornish in Tregartha which adjoins it. In 1469 Richard Buketon, in right of Nicholaa, daughter and heir of William Sewyington, kinsman and heir of John de Treyuthouth, held one acre of land Cornish in Tregartha, and another acre of land Cornish in Treyuthouth, *alias* Trenewith, juxta Trewarlich. The lands, however, would not seem to have been held in entirety for John Trecarne, in right of Thomasie, daughter of Edward Tregarthen, and Thomas Edward, kinsman and heir of John Treyouthent, held seven acres of land (English?) in Trenowith,: viz., the said John Trecarne two parts, and the said Thomas Edward four parts. In 1491 Richard Buketon still held the lands as above described, in right of Nicholaa his wife, and in 1539 the lands in Tregarthin and Trenouth, held by Thomas Edward, had passed to William Carnsew and Nicholas Glynn, as kinsmen and heirs of John Trecarne. The entirety, however, not long afterwards, would appear to have passed to the family of Langdon, probably by marriage with the heiress of Buketon. John Langdon, of Buketon, Co. Cornwall, by his charter dated 10th March 1574, granted to John Connock, of the Borough of Liskeard, Gent., all his *Manor*[1] of Trewthand, with all its rights, members, and appurtenances, with all messuages &c. in Lanteglos and St. Teath, Trewthand, *alias* Trewythand, Rosepark, Netherose, and Trevyly, which had formerly been the lands of inheritance of his father John Langdon of Buketon, Esq. By his Charter dated 22nd January 1579, John Connock the younger of the Borough of Liskeard, Gent., granted all his Manor of Trewthand to John Nicholls of St. Kew, Gent., which was further confirmed by a subsequent Indenture dated 8th January 1580-1, in which the manor and lands pertaining thereto are described as " All that Manor of Trewthand, and the barton or demesne lands called Treythen, *alias* Trevythen, within the parish of Lanteglos juxta Camelford, with all their appurtenances in the towns, villages, fields, and hamlets of Trewthand, *alias* Treythen, *alias* Trevythen, Roseparks, *alias* Resparek, Brewers, *alias* Brewys, Metherose, *alias* Mederose, being in the several parishes of Lanteglos, Dewstow, *alias* Davydstow, and St. Teath, heretofore known

---

[1] This is the first instance in which these lands had been described as a manor. They could not have been any more than a conventional manor, as before described. Ante.

as the inheritance of Richard Langdon,[1] Esq., and lately purchased by the said John Connock, one tenement called Trevyly Park, in the Parish of St. Teath being excepted. John Nicholls of St. Kew, Gent., son of the abovementioned John, upon his marriage with Elizabeth daughter of Edmund Fortescue of Fallapit, by deed dated 30th September 1601, settled his Manors of Treuthen and Bodulgate in the parish of Lanteglos, to provide a joincture for his wife. John Nicholls died 15th August 1633, and it was found by inquisition taken after his death,[2] that he had died seized, *inter alia*, of the Manor of Truthen, which he held of the Manor of Helston in Trigg in socage; and that John Nichols his son was his nearest heir.

From John Nichols the lands have descended to the present possessor, Shadwell Morley Grylls of Lewarne Esq., in the manner described under Bodulgate, ante p. 346.

TREWENT, *alias* TREWYNT, *alias* TREWINT.

This is one of the many places in the county so designated, more than one of which, perhaps, gave its name to its possessors. Of Trewint in Blisland, we have already treated,[3] and it is often difficult, and sometimes impossible, from the notices in the Public Records, to identify the several places. With respect to Trewint in Advent, however, the description of Michell or Muchell Trewent, sometimes applied to it, enables us, on those occasions, to identify it, as we can, also, occasionally, do from the lands associated with it.

On the levy of the Aid granted in 18th Edward I. (1290) on the marriage of the King's eldest daughter, we find, under the Hundred of Lesnewyth, that William Wytham and John de Carminow were assessed for one knights fee in Trewynt and Westdisart; and in the 20th Edward III. (1346) when the King's eldest son was knighted, John Wytham and Ralph de Carminow paid the aid for the same fee.[4] In 6th Henry VI, Inquisitions were taken for the purpose of levying another aid, and at an Inquisition taken at Camelford on Monday next after the feast of St. Barnabas the Apostle 1346, it was found that Thomas Carminow held the quarter part of one knight's fee in Trewynt, and Westsydar, which John Wytham and Ralph Carminow had formerly held. This fee, therefore, seems to have become subdivided, and inasmuch as persons holding less than the quarter part of one fee were not required to contribute to this aid, and, moreover, as many of the fees in this Hundred are very indefinitely described, we are unable to identify, at this date, the other three parts of the fee in Trewynt and Westdysart. Under these chief Lords of the fee, Trewynt was undoubtedly held by a family which from it derived its name.

---

[1] Richard Langdon of Keverell, son of John Langdon of Bicton, co. Cornwall, by Elizabeth daughter of Sir William Godolphin. He married Agatha daughter of Robert Hill of Helligan, Esq. (Visitation of Cornwall, Harl. Society's Pub., p. 119.)

[2] Inq. p.m., 9th Charles I, Wards and Liveries, Bundle 53, No. 249.   [3] Ante, vol. i, p. 47.

[4] Book of Aids, Exchequer, Queen's Rememb. Office.

At the place above cited we have referred to several fines undoubtedly connected with this place. It seems certain that Stephen de Trewint, who was returned in 1297, from the County of Cornwall, as possessing lands or rents of the value of £20 a year or upwards,[1] held it, as did several of his descendants, but when it passed out of the name we have no knowledge. John de Trewynt suffered a fine in La Wales, and other lands in the neighbourhood, in 1361.[2]

In 1421, however, a fine was levied, in which Ralph de Botreaux, Knt., William Halle and John Darell, Clerk, were querists and Thomas Reed and Margery his wife and Stephen Melowarn, deforciants, concerning the manors of Trewynnek and Trewent, including fifty messuages, seventeen carucates of land, 600 acres of pasture, 2000 acres of moor, &c., in Torre, lytel Trewynt, Resterlek, Treclegou, Camelford, and Trewyntmore and ffowymore, whereby, in consideration of the sum of 200 marks of silver, the said lands were settled upon the said Ralph, William, and John, and the heirs of the said Ralph for ever.[3]

In 1435, these lands had become parcel of the possessions of the family of Bodulgate, and in that year Walter de Bodulgate charged his lands in Mochel Trewint, Tresterleck, and Algarismylle in the parish of St. Athwanne, with a stipend for a chantry chaplain in the Chapel of St. Thomas the Martyr at Camelford. (See ante p. 322.)

Before the middle of the seventeenth century Trewint was possessed by the Hocken family, and at that period was held by William Hocken, Gent., with other tenements, of the Manor of Hamatethy at the annual rent of 2s. 1½d.[4] By Indentures dated 28th and 29th October 1691, William Hocken, probably grandson of the abovenamed William, for the sum of £360 conveyed to Christopher Sloggatt of Lanteglos by Camelford, yeoman, all those messuages, &c., called Trewint, *alias* Trewints, *alias* Trewint the higher, and Trewint the lower, and Michael (Muchel) Trewint, then in the occupation of the said William Hocken and William Hocken of Michaelstow, to hold to the said Christopher and his heirs for ever; and the said William Hocken and Mary his wife, suffered a fine to the said Christopher Sloggatt accordingly. By his will, dated 26th December 1699, Christopher Sloggatt devised all his lands in Trewint to Mary his wife, who, by her will, dated 8th December 1721, devised the said lands to Francis Sloggatt her eldest son. The probates of these wills have not been found, and in their absence the said Francis, as heir at law of his father and mother, would inherit the estates. Francis Sloggatt died s.p., and by his will, dated 28th September 1756,[5] devised Trewint to his nephew Thomas Sloggatt and his heirs for ever. Thomas Sloggatt died intestate, leaving an only son, called William, who died a minor, and the estates devolved upon his uncle Christopher Sloggatt, described as of East Stonehouse, tidewaiter, who, upon the death of his nephew, took possession. By his will dated 8th June 1775, he devised the said messuage to trustees to the following uses: viz., to his wife Jane Sloggatt for life, remainder to his

---

[1] Parl. Writs, vol. i, p. 285. [2] Pedes Finium, 35th Edward III, Michaelmas, No. 1.
[3] Pedes Finium, 9th Henry V, Trinity 5. [4] See Ante, vol. i, p. 365.
[5] Prov. Archd., Cornwall, 3rd December, 1762.

2 Y

two daughters Ann Tallant, widow, and Elizabeth Sloggatt, for the term of seventy years, if Phillippa wife of Oliver Gregory should so long live, and after the determination of that estate to the said trustees for sale, for the payment of debts, &c., residue to his two said daughters. Ann Tallant died intestate, leaving an only child, John Tallant, who by his will, dated 29th January 1813,[1] devised all his estate in these lands to his wife Rebecca Tallant. In 1817, the lands were vested in the said Rebecca Tallant and Elizabeth Ivey (the beforenamed Elizabeth Slogget, who had married, and was then the widow of, Henry Ivey of East Stonehouse, shipwright) who, in conjunction with the trustees of the will of Christopher Sloggatt, by indentures dated 23rd and 24th December 1817, in consideration of the sum of £1400, conveyed the estate in fee to William Hocken of Michaelstow, yeoman,[2] said to have been a descendant of the first mentioned William Hocken, who, a few years afterwards, sold it to Richard Marshall, M.D., of Totnes, by whose son Alexander Marshall of the Priory, Totnes, Esq., it is now possessed.

Some portions of the old house remain, having four-light square-headed windows. It was probably built by William Hocken in the early part of the seventeenth century. That gentleman married, in 1634, Jane daughter of Edward Lower of Tremere in St. Tudy.

PEDIGREE SHEWING THE LATER DESCENT OF TREWINT.

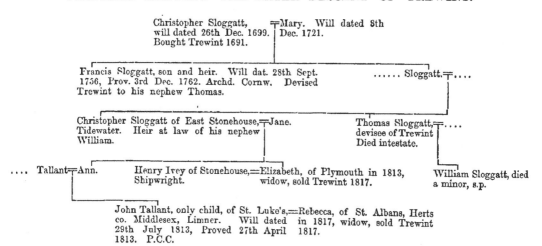

[1] Prov. P.C.C., 27th July 1813.   [2] Abstract of Title in possession of Alexander Marshall, Esq.

FENENWETHENWYTH *alias* FENTONWONWITH *alias* FENTENATHWILL *alias* FENTENWOON.

In 1302, one acre of land in Fentenwenweht was held by Stephen de Trewint,[1] and in 1337, William son of Geoffry de Bodbran, held three acres of land Cornish, in Fenenwethenwyth, Restarlek, and Hendrewalle, at the annual rent of 5s. 10d., suit at Court, &c. In 1469, these lands had become divided in property between Sir Walter Moyle, in right of his wife, William Rosmodres, in right of his wife, and John Devyok, described as coheirs of William son of Geoffry de Bradbran.[2] These gentlemen married, respectively, Margaret, Alice, and Elizabeth, daughters and coheirs of John Lucombe, by Isabella daughter and heir of Henry Ilcombe, who, probably, married the heir of Bodbran: and the same persons were possessed thereof in 1491.[3] The lands afterwards passed to Oliver Carminow.[4] In 1596, Oliver Carminow and Mary his wife, and William Salter and Ann his wife, suffered a fine to Nicholas Sprey of Bodmin, *inter alia*, in lands in Resterlack, Hendrawalls and Venternoon, in Adven and Lanteglos,[5] who, in 1602, under Reskerlek, held three acres of land Cornish in Fentenathwell, Reskerlek, and Hendrewell, which Oliver Carmynow had taken at the previous assession.[6] The family of Sprey possessed these lands for several descents. Nicholas Sprie, great grandson of the abovenamed Nicholas, died seized in 1673, when they passed to his brother George, who is returned as possessing them in 1683.[7] It is shewn, under Reskerleke, in 1756, that Edward Elliot, Esq., holds three acres of land Cornish in Fentonathwill, Reskerleck and Hendrewell, paying a rent of 6s. 3d. To which is added the following note: "It is alleged that this tenement is held as follows: viz., John Wallis, Gent., by purchase from .... Spry, Clerk,[8] Lord of the Messualty, of one acre of land Cornish in ffentenwonwith, under the rent of 3s.; Elizabeth Glynn, widow, holds one acre of land Cornish in Roskerlick, rent 23½d.; Edward Elliot, Esq., holds one acre of land Cornish in Hendrewell, under the rent of 15½d." At the following assession in 1763, John Wallis is returned as holding one acre in Fentonathwill, and he continues to be so returned until 1791, when Ann Wallis, widow, appears as tenant after the death of her late husband, John Wallis.

In 1806, Fentonathwill had passed to Lovell Todd, and in 1819, it was in the

---

[1] Pedes Finium, 20th Edward I, Trinity, No. 2.

[2] Assession Roll, 9th Edward IV., Duchy Office. For further account of Geoffry de Bodbran, or Brodbran, see ante vol. i, p. 41, and 41 *n*.

[3] Assession Roll, 7th Henry VII, Record Office.

[4] Oliver Carminow was son and heir of John Carminow of Fentengollen. He married Mary daughter of Peter Coryton, in 1597, and dying left two daughters, Ann who married William Salter of Dorsetshire, and Margaret who was wife of Philip Cole of Devon.

[5] Pedes Finium, 38th and 39th Elizabeth, Michaelmas.

[6] Assession Roll, 44th Elizabeth, Duchy Office.   [7] Assession Roll, Duchy Office.

[8] Philip Sprey, Vicar of St. Issey, died 1729.—See Pedigree of Sprey, ante, vol. i, p. 294.

2 Y²

possession of the Earl of Darlington, by purchase of the devisees in trust under the will of John Phillips Carpenter, and in 1823, it was sold by the Duke of Cleveland, sometime Earl of Darlington, to Richard Marshall and William Sloggatt, and it now forms a portion of the estate in this parish of Mr. Alexander Marshall beforementioned.

The old house has been recently taken down, and a large and convenient farm house erected on the site.

TRECLEGOU.

Treclegou at an early date was held by a family whose heiress, Isolda, carried it in marriage, together with other lands in the neighbourhood, to Gilbert de Goudray, who, apparently, resided at Lostwithiel. In 1292, a fine was levied in which Gilbert de Coudray and Isolda his wife were petitioners, and Stephen son of Stephen de Trewint, whom Margaret, relict of Stephen de Trewint, called to warrant, and who warranted one acre of land in Fentenwenweht, whereby Gilbert and Isolda quitclaimed for themselves and the heirs of the said Isolda, the said premises to the said Stephen and his heirs for ever, and for this fine and quitclaim the said Stephen gave the said Gilbert and Isolda one sparrow hawk.[1]

By his Charter, dated at Lostwithiel on Tuesday in the feast of St. John ante portam latinam 21st Edward I. (6th May 1293) Gilbert de Coudray, with the consent of Isolda his wife, conveyed to Stephen de Trewynt one acre of land in Fyntenenet, one acre of land in Treklegou, and one fuller's mill and six acres of land in Treklegou, together with the weir head and free water course to the said mill pertaining, with all houses, &c., to hold to the said Stephen and his heirs, of the said Gilbert and Isolda and their heirs and assigns for ever, at the annual rent of 6d., and by their hands to pay to the chief Lord of Helleston for one acre of land in Fentenwynenet 2s. due to the said manor; and to the Lord of Resterlek by their hands annually 2s. 11½d. due to him; and for one half acre of land and one fuller's mill with appurtenances in Treklegou to the chief Lord of Helleston 10d. annually, due to the said manor for all services saving to the said Gilbert and Isolda and their heirs suit at court twice a year at Brutem de Treuenien. Witnesses: William de Trewynt, John de Trelowni, Thomas de Tredyen, John de Grenehant, Stephen de Bodulgate and others.[2]

In the following Trinity Term, the said Gilbert and Isolda suffered a fine in the same premises to Stephen the son of Stephen. In the same term the said Gilbert de Goudray and Isolda his wife, levied several fines conveying divers lands, including several tenements in Treklegou juxta Camelford, to divers persons, viz., to Nicholas Bony one acre of land with appurtenances in Treklegou; to Robert de Trefreu one messuage and one acre of land

[1] Pedes Finium, 20th Edward I, Trinity.
[2] Copy of Deed in Roscarrock Rent Roll, in the possession of Francis Rodd of Trebartha, Esq.

in the same place; to Thomas Haymes, one messuage and the moiety of one acre of land in the same place; and to Richard Parmenter one messuage and one acre of land in the same place; also to Thomas Humphry of Kellynoran one messuage and one acre of land in Goenweylok; the whole to be held, in the usual manner, of the chief Lord of the fee.[1]

It appears from the caption of seizin of the Black Prince, that in 1337, Henry de Welyngton held three acres of land Cornish in Utlegou, and that he also rendered for a mill weir in Treclegou 6d. per annum. In 1469, Thomas Southwode, in right of Alice his wife, daughter of Isabell daughter of Henry Richard, cousin and heir of Henry Welyngton, held three acres of land Cornish, in Utlegeu, *alias* Treclegowe, at the rent of 5s. per annum, suit at court, &c.,[2] and in 1553, the premises had passed to Christopher Cock, who is described as the heir of Thomas Southwode. At the next assession, in 1567, John Cock had succeeded. In 1621, Richard Billing of Hengar, and Abigail Stonying, widow, levied a fine of Richard Marke and Francis his wife, of the third part of the *Manor* of Treclegou, for which they gave the said Richard Marke and Frances £100,[3] and in 1624, it had become sub-divided in the following manner: John Billing, Gent, after the death of Richard Billing, Esq., his father,[4] by purchase from Ralph Cosens and Patience his wife, held one third part, Emanuel Davies, in right of Abigail his wife, relict of William Sonning, held another third part. John Billing by purchase from Richard Marke and Frances his wife, held one sixth part, and the said Richard Marke and Francis his wife held the other sixth part.

In 1650 the entirety had become vested in the heirs of John Davis,[5] and in 1683 was held by Dame Ann Smith, widow, after the death of Sir James Smith her husband. In 1717 it had become the property of John Phillips, Gent., and continued in the same name until 1750, when it was held by Charles Phillips after the death of his father John Phillips. On the death of Charles Phillips, in 1774, s.p., it passed, with the rest of his lands, to his brother William Phillips, Clerk, Rector of Lanteglos and St. Cleather, upon whose demise, unmarried, in 1794 it passed, by bequest, to his nephew John Phillips Carpenter, son of his sister Christian, who held it at the assession in 1805. From him it descended to John Carpenter Garnier, Esq., by whom, in 1868, it was sold to Mr. William Hocken of Tregenna in Michaelstow.

---

[1] Pedes Finium, 21st Edward I, Trinity.   [2] Assession Roll, 9th Edward IV.

[3] Pedes Finium, 19th James, Trinity 22.

[4] Richard Billing, died 22nd July 1624 (see Ped. vol. i, p. 389), seized, *inter alia*, of a moiety of the Manor of Treclegoe, with his rights, members, and appurtenances, and common of pasture for all manner of beasts, unto the said manor belonging, in and upon Goosehill, Curdown, and Cotehill, in the parishes of Lanteglos, Advent, and Davidstow, which he held of the Lord Duke of Cornwall, as of his Manor of Helston in Trigg, in free socage, and by suit to the Court of the said Manor from three weeks to three weeks. (State Papers, Dom. Corr., vol. clxxv, No. 12.)   [5] Parl. Survey.

TALCARNE, *alias* TRECARNE, *alias* TRECAREN.

In 1337, William Cole held one acre of land Cornish in Trecarne of the Duke of Cornwall, parcel of the Manor of Helleston, in free tenure, at the annual rent of 2s. 6d. and aid 6d., and made suit at Court.[1] In 1469, it was held by John Trecarne in right of Thomasia, daughter of Edward Tregarthen, kinsman and heir of William Cole, at the same rent, &c. John Trecarne left two daughters, co-heirs, of whom, Alice, married William Carnsew, and Rose became the wife of Thomas Glynn of Glynn, and in 1539 Talcarn was held in moieties by William Carnsew, Gent., great grandson of the abovementioned William, and Nicholas Glynn, grandson of the aforesaid Thomas.[2] It continued to be held in moieties by these families until near the end of the sixteenth century, but at the assession preceding 1602, the entirety had become vested in Richard Carnsew, Gent., afterwards Sir Richard Carnsew, Knight, of Bokelly, who died in 1629, s.p. Administration of his personal estate was granted to his cousin, Margaret Hill, relict of Morice Hill of Heligan, described as of Advent, only child of his uncle, John Carnsew, who had been resident at Trecarne. By her charter, dated 14th August, 1635, the said Margaret Hill described as of Trecarne, widow, in conjunction with Humphry Hill of Helligan, the elder, son and heir apparent of the said Margaret Hill, Richard Hill, Gent, youngest son of the said Margaret and Humphry Hill, the younger, son and heir apparent of the said Humphry Hill, the elder, in consideration of the sum of £500, conveyed the said capital messuage barton, demesne lands, &c., to Richard Turney of Bodmyn, merchant;[3] nevertheless Richard Carnsew, in the lifetime of his father George Carnsew, who died at Advent in 1691, held it in 1688.[4] It was part of the possessions of which William Beale of Trewinnell, in St. Teath, died seized in 1713, who by his will, dated 1st May 1712,[5] devised this estate and other lands in Advent to his son John and his issue in tail male, from whom, in 1756, it had passed to Charles Phillips, and descending with the other Phillips' estates eventually vested in John Carpenter Garnier, Esq., who, by deed dated 14th January 1868, conveyed the same to Mr. Nicholas Parnell, the present possessor.

A portion of the old house with its mullioned windows still remains, though considerably modernised. There are also fragments of earlier window tracery.

TRETHYAN, *alias* TRETHYN, *alias* TREWETHAND, *alias* TREWEYTHEN.

In 1337, William de Treythian held of the Duke of Cornwall three acres of land Cornish in Treithian, Langaston, and Wyndesore, at the annual rent of 9s., and 6d. of

---

[1] Caption of seizin.   [2] See Pedigrees of Glynn and Carnsew, *ante*, pp. 68 and 172.
[3] Deed in possession of John Coode of St. Austell, Esq.   [4] Assession Rolls.
[5] Prov. Archd. Cornwall, 22nd March 1713.

aid; and he also held one acre of land at Mighelstow (in the parish of Advent) at the annual rent of 3s., and aid of 6d., and made suit at court, &c. In 1440, Robert Bruyn,[1] suffered a fine in five messuages, one mill, three carucates of land,[2] and 4d. rent in Trethyan, Camelford, Wyndsore, and Penfrane to Thomas Dannant and Nicholes Stephyn whereby the lands were settled to hold to the said Robert and the heirs of his body, and in default of such heirs remainder to Nicholas Aysshton and Margaret his wife and the heirs of their bodies, in default, remainder, after the deaths of the said Nicholas and Margaret, to the right heirs of the said Robert Bruyn. In 1469 John Brewen, as kinsman and heir of William de Trethyan, held the lands in Trethyan, Langeston and Wyndsore; but the land at Michaelstow was then described as held by Philip Copleston, as kinsman and heir of William Trethyan. In 1526 the lands in Trethian, Langeston, and Wyndssor, formerly held by William Trethyan were held by Edward Aston, as kinsman and heir of John Broune, and they were held by the same person in 1539. Ralph Aston, Gent., in 1567, held by this manor one acre of land at Michaelstow, which the heirs of Edward Aston, kinsman and heir of John Broune, had taken at the previous assession; and in 1602, the same lands had passed by purchase from Thomas Dilke to Robert Rooles (Rolle). In 1624, one acre of land Cornish at Michaelstow, as of Trethian, was held by Robert Rolles, and in 1650, three acres in Trethian was vested in the same name.[3] It afterwards passed to Samuel Rolle, who held it in 1717, but in 1731, it had passed to Robert Trefusis of Trefusis, who in 1735, by recovery, cut off the entail, from whom in 1742, it had passed to his son, Robert Cotton Trefusis, who in October 1766, sold it to Robert Lovel of Roscrow, and Ann Gwatkin, of the city of Bristol, widow. By the death of Robert Lovell it became vested in the said Ann Gwatkin, his only daughter and heir, by whom it was held in 1770. It remained in the Gwatkin family until 1814, when it was sold by Robert Lovell Gwatkin and Theophila his wife, and others, to Allen Searell of Staverton, co. Devon, who in the following year sold it to Richard Marshall of Totnes, co Devon, Doctor of Physic, and John Toms of the same place, who, in 1834, sold it to Thomas Graham of Penquite, co. Cornwall. Thomas Graham, by his will executed in 1835, devised it to his great nephew Thomas Graham Graham, who, in 1870, sold it to the late Mr. William Ward Abbott,[4] whose widow now holds it.

According to Tonkin, who wrote in the year 1715, a lease of this estate was granted by Sir Henry Rolle to Mathew Vivian, third son of John Vivian of Truan, by Mary daughter and co-heir of William Cavell of Bokelly. He married Julian daughter of Anthony Tanner in 1655,[5] and, thereupon, either enlarged or rebuilt the house, as is witnessed by the house itself. In front of a wing of the building, which yet remains, is a four-light square-headed window, with the letters "M and V," being the initials of

---

[1] It appears from certain proceedings in 1477 that, in the time of Henry IV, litigation had occurred between Stephen Bodulgate and Johanna his wife *versus* Robert the son of Margaret Trethyan, *alias* Robert Bruyn, and Thomas Trethyan, concerning seven messuages &c., in Lamelyn, and that Robert Bruyn and Thomas Trethyan had been imprisoned. (Lord Treas. Rem. Excheq. 25th Henry VI. Easter m. 15.)

[2] It should be noticed that the lands heretofore described as *three acres of land Cornish*, are here called *three carucates of land*, thus confirming the hypothesis in Note 1, p. 339 ante.

[3] Parliamentary Survey.   [4] Abstract of Title.   [5] See Pedigree, ante vol. ii, p. 162

Mathew Vivian, on the drop ends of the hood-mouldings; and over the mantel piece, which is modern, is a granite slab, bearing the letters and date as in the margin, in relief, being the initials of Mathew Vivian and Julian his wife. Mathew Vivian died before 19th September 1664, and by his will, dated 14th September 1664,[1] after making certain bequests to his three daughters and Mathew Vivian his son,

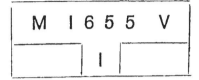

he left the residue of his property to Julian his wife, and made her sole executrix, directing that his son's life should be taken up upon Trethyan, Winser, and Longstone unto himself only, in reversion of herself and testator's brother Francis Vivian; and in the terrier of 1679, the glebe of Advent is stated to be bounded on the east by the ground of Julian Vivian,[2] widow (ante p. 298). Mathew Vivian, the younger, died s.p., and Julian the second daughter of Mathew Vivian having married William Beale of Trewinnell, in St. Teath, carried to him the lease of Trethyn. William Beale died in 1713, and by his will, dated 1st May 1712,[3] devised to his eldest son, William Beale, his estate in these lands for the term of seventy years, and the same for his child or children for the term testator had therein. We do not know when this lease terminated, or if William Beale assigned it to his brother Mathew, but it appears from the Parish Registers that Mathew Beale, Esq., was buried at Advent on 15th August 1727.

TRESINNEY.

Tresinney was formerly the residence of the Dinham family. The house has been rebuilt, but over an old doorway is a stone with the following letters in raised characters, being the initials of William Dinham and Mary his wife:

It was sold by Mr. William Dinham in 1770 to Mr. Thomas Pethick, and it is now held by Mrs. Mary Gillard, widow, relict of Mr. George Gillard, deceased, and daughter of Mr. Thomas Pethick the son of the purchaser.

[1] Will proved 8th April, 1665, Archd. Cornw.

[2] Mathew Vivian, the younger, was a burgess of Camelford in 1679, and as such signed the Indenture by which Bernard Grenville, Esq., was returned as burgess in Parliament for the borough. We know not when he died.

[3] Proved 22nd March, 1713-4. Archd. Cornwall.

FAMILY HISTORY.

DE TREWYNT, *alias* TREWINT, *alias* TREWENT.

The difficulties to which we have alluded in identifying the several places called Trewynt are obviously still greater in repect of persons, and we cannot hope to escape error in our attempt. Trewynt, in Advent, certainly gave its name to a family of considerable distinction in early times. Of this family was Stephen de Trewin (Trewint) who with Johanna his wife, in 1256, quitclaimed to Nicholas Tregyer and others certain lands in Tregyer, Treniegar dha, and Trenewid, in exchange for one acre of land in Pelaworgan, and that acre which Roger Perou held, to hold to the said Stephen and Johanna and the heirs of the said Johanna for ever.[1] In 1292, a fine was levied in which Gilbert de Coudray and Isolda his wife were petitioners, and Stephen son of Stephen de Trewint, whom Margaret, who was the wife of Stephen de Trewint, called to warrant and who warranted one messuage and one acre of land in Fentenwenweht, and Gilbert and Isolda acknowledged the said tenement as the right of Stephen, and as those quitclaimed to him by the said Gilbert and Isolda and the heirs of Isolda, and for this fine Stephen gave one sparrowhawk.[2] Stephen, the younger, mentioned in this fine, was probably the grandson of Stephen, who was party to the one previously cited, and identical with Stephen de Trewint,[3] who, in 1297, was returned by the Sheriff of Cornwall as possessing lands or rents of the value of £20 a year or more, and as such was summoned from Cornwall with horses and arms to accompany the king across the sea. His wife's name was Johanna, with whom he acquired Wyndsore juxta Trewent (in Advent) and which he held jointly with her in 1302.[4] He had a brother named Richard who, in this year, under the description of Richard the son of Stephen de Trewynt, took out letters of assize of novel

---

[1] Pedes Finium, 40th Henry III, Michaelmas, No 9.   [2] Pedes Finium, 20th Edward I, Trinity, No. 2.

[3] In 1300, Stephen de Trewynt was one of the jurors on the Inquisition p.m. of Edmund Earl of Cornwall, at which date he held three water mills of the Manor of Helston in Trigge, see ante.

[4] Ass. Roll, 30th Edward I, $\frac{M}{1} \bigg\} 1$, m. 7.
21

2 z

disseizin against Stephen the son of Stephen de Trewynt, senior, concerning a tenement in Camelford, but failing to prosecute was in mercy with his pledges.[1]   It was, probably, this Richard de Trewynt who, in 1323, as one of the pledges of Richard de St. Margaret, was amerced on account of the failure of the said Richard de St. Margaret to prosecute a writ of novel disseizin, which he had taken out against Johanna, who was the wife of Alan Bloyou, concerning a tenement in Trewassa juxta the Church of St. David.[2]

In 1327, Stephen de Trewynt was assessed to the Subsidy in Lanteglos, at the highest rate in the parish. He, or one of the same name, was also assessed in Advent.[3]

At the Assizes at Launceston in 1335, before I. Inge and I. de Trevaignon, Justices, an assize of novel disseizin was taken to enquire if William de Trelouny,[4] Johanna de Whalysbreu, Isabella who was the wife of Stephen de Trewynt, and others, had unjustly disseized Robert de Trewynnok,[5] and William Crowen of their free tenements in Camelford, Lyteltreuya, Treuilyas, Bodmin, Pelaworgan, Lytel-Trewynt, Niwehalle, Fentenweynneth, Polbartha, Colaelake, Dynmur, Treclegou, Lostwithiel, Algerismylle, and Trewynt juxta Camelford, and thence it was complained that they had disseized them of thirty messuages, four mills, &c.

Isabella, by her guardian, appeared, but the others did not appear, but one John Aldestowe answered for them as their attorney, and said that they had no interest in the said lands, and did not claim to have any, and had not done any injury or disseizin, and put themselves upon the assize, and the aforesaid Robert and William Crowen likewise. And Isabella, as tenant, said that the lands in question were in the seizin of a certain Stephen de Trewynt, Knight, kinsman of the the said Robert and William Crowen whose heirs they are, who thereof had enfeoffed the said William de Trelouny and Johanna de Whalysbrou, to hold to them and the heirs and assigns of the said Johanna for ever; that afterwards, before the Justices at York, a fine was levied between the said Stephen and Isabella, plaintiffs, and the aforesaid William de Trelouny and Johanna, as deforciants, whereby the said William and Johanna surrendered the said premises to the said Stephen and Isabella, to hold to the said Stephen and Isabella and the heirs of their bodies, remainder to the right heirs of the said Stephen.[6] Which said charter and fine were produced in court, by which charter, dated at Trewynt on Wednesday next after the feast of St. John Baptist 7th Edward III. (1333) the said Stephen de Trewynt, Knight, granted to William de Trelouny and Johanna, who was the wife of William de Walesbrew, and the heirs and assigns of

[1] Assize Rolls, 30th Edward I, $\genfrac{}{}{0pt}{}{\text{M}}{1\,26}$ } 1, m. 32 d.   [2] Ibid., 16th Edward II, $\genfrac{}{}{0pt}{}{\text{N}}{2\,17}$ } 6, m. 10.

[3] Subsidy Roll, Appendix III.

[4] William de Trelouny was the son of John Trelawny by his wife Joan de Boterell. He married Joane daughter of Stephen Trewynnick, and had with her lands in feetail in Trelawny, Overagonan, and the mill called de la Morgans.

[5] Robert de Trewynnick was one of the witnesses to a charter, by which Henry Osmer conveyed certain lands to John Trelawny, father of the abovementioned William Trelawny. (Archives at Trelawne.) Robert de Trewynnick was also a witness to a charter of 11th Edward III, of Mabilla, relict of Lawrence de Tremure, relative to lands in Peneton and Tettesburgh-down.

[6] Pedes Finium, 7th Edward III, Michaelmas, No. 4.

the said Johanna, all his messuages, lands, &c., in Trewynt, Liteltreuya, Camelford, Algeris-
mille, Liteltrewynt, Newehalle, Treclogou, Fentonwonet, Polwartha, Cheldelake, Treuilias,
Bodmin, Dynmoer, and Lostwithiel, together with the reversion of all lands in Peleworgan
coming by the death of Johanna,[1] who was the wife of Richard de Stapeldon, Knight,
and all rents and services of Adam de Treclegou of one messuage and one half an acre
of land Cornish in Treclegou, and the rents and services of Thomas de Trefreu, except
his mills in Camelford and Kenstock. Robert de Trewynnok and William Crowen could
not deny that the aforesaid charter was made by their kinsman, whose heirs they were,
or that the said lands were the estate of the said Isabella.[2]

These documents shew the extinction of the elder branch in the main line, and the
transfer of the estates to other names. Junior members, however, still continued to own
property in Camelford and its neighbourhood, and it is probable that the Trewynts, who
held a good position in Bodmin, were of the same stock. In 1310, Nicholas de Trewent
was one of the manucaptors for Walter Flegard, one of the Burgesses in Parliament for
Bodmin.[3]

In 1314, there was a remarkable case tried at Launceston, which turned upon the
spelling of the name. An Assize of view of recognizance was held to enquire if John
the son of Robert Martyn, Roger Godbegynnyngs, and several others had disseized Stephen
de Trewent of Bodmin, merchant, of his free tenement in Bodmin. John, son of Robert,
appeared for himself and the others, and refused to answer to the writ because, he said,
that the said Stephen was called Stephen de Trewynt and not Stephen de Trewent. The
jury found it as pleaded, and the defendants were discharged *sine die*, and Stephen was
amerced for a false claim[4]

In 1342, Michael Trewynt was manucaptor for John Treworgie, one of the burgesses
in Parliament for Bodmin.[5]

In 1388, a precept was issued to the Sheriff of Cornwall to arrest Stephen Treiagou
and Ralph his father, and to keep them in prison at the suit of John Reprenna, executor
of the will of Isabella, who was the wife of Stephen the son of John Trewynt of Bodmin,
late executor of the will of the said Stephen son of John, for a debt of £40,[6] and in
1401, John Reprenna, as executor as above, sued William Copleston and Katherine his wife,
daughter and heir of Bartholomew Penhirgard, for a debt of 100s.[7]

[1] This Johanna was daughter and co-heir of Serlone Haye. Her sister Thomasine married Bartholomew
de Penhargard, and left issue. (See Pedigree, ante, p. 46.) It is not known in what way Stephen de Trewynt
inherited from her.

[2] Assize Rolls, 9th Edward III. $\frac{N}{2}$ $\left.\begin{array}{c} \\ \\ 20 \end{array}\right\}$ 6

[3] See ante, vol. i, p. 240.

[4] Assize Rolls, 7th Edward II, 2 $\frac{N}{\left.\begin{array}{c} \\ 15 \end{array}\right\}}$ 6, m. 2.

[5] See ante, vol. 1, p. 241.

[6] De Banco Rolls, 12th Richard II, Michaelmas, m. 596.

[7] Ibid. 2nd Henry IV, Trinity, m. 202.

2 z[2]

In 1384-5, Richard de Trewynt was a defendant in an assize of view of recognizance concerning a tenement in Camelford;[1] and in 1390-1, we find Stephen Trewynt and Isolda his wife mentioned,[2] who were, probably, the same Stephen Trewynt and Isolda his wife, that in the fourteenth century held the Lordship of West Newton, subject to the payment to Martin de Ferrers of an annual rent of £20; and to whom the said Martin de Ferrers, by charter dated at Byrferrers in the Vigil of the Purification of the Blessed Virgin Mary, 46th Edward III. (1371-2) relinquished the said rent, after the expiration of two years from that date, on the condition that the said Stephen and Isolda did not make alienation of any part of the said manor without the license of the said Martin, and suffered a fine recognising an annual rent of 100s. in the said manor, and allowed the said Martin, or any one in his name, free ingress and egress to remove all trees in their forest of West Newton, which might be blown down by the wind. This deed would seem to be a counterpart. It is sealed with two seals, one of which is charged with the arms of Trewynt, circumscribed by the legend: S. RICHARD' TRAIWYNT, and the other with an eagle displayed.[3]

DE BODULGET *alias* DE BODULGATE.

The earliest persons of this name, of whom we have any knowledge, are Richard Bodulgate and Margery his wife, of whom, in 1302, Baldwin de Roscarrockbighan recovered a messuage in Trewythreges near the village of Endellion, of which Johanna, who was the wife of Richard Rannon, great grandmother of the said Baldwin, had died seized.[4] It is probable that this Richard was of Bodulgate in Lanteglos, and that his heiress carried that estate to Richard Tynden, who held it in 1337, but would appear to have died s.p.[5] At this date, however, Warine de Bodulgate held Penkayerou, Trewalrygge, and other lands of the Manor of Helston in Trigg, which Warine was probably the younger

[1] Assize Roll, 8th Richard II, $\frac{N}{2} \Big\} 3$, m. 35.   [2] Assize Roll, 14th Richard 11, $\frac{N}{2} \Big\} 1$, m. 175 d.

[3] This Charter was printed by the late Mr. John Gough Nichols, F.S.A. in the Top. and Genealogist, vol. iii, p. 35, and was purchased at the sale by Messrs. Sotheby and Wilkinson, 12th December 1874, of his library and collections by the Author.

[4] Assize Rolls, 36th Edward I, $\frac{M}{1} \Big\} 1$, m. 17 d. See also vol. i, p. 556.

[5] Caption of Seizin, Edward Black Prince.

brother, or nephew, of Richard. He was assessed to the Subsidy in Lanteglos in 1327.[1] Pencarowe was held by this family for a long period, though we do not possess sufficient information at present to compile, with certainity, a continuous pedigree. It seems, however, desirable to place upon record the following notes which may assist other genealogical enquirers towards that object.

In 1387, a trial on a plea of waste brought by John Bere of Tregaren (in St. Maben) against John Bodulgate and Johanna his wife was put in respect for default of jury;[2] and in the following year Walter Bodulgate sued Stephen Oppton in a matter of trespass at Cabilia, &c.[3] John Bodulgate died cir. 1392, leaving a son and heir, Stephen, who in that year sued William Carpenter and others in a plea of trespass at Fentennans,[4] and at the same assize Johanna, relict of the said John, sued the said Stephen of the third part of three messuages in 'Bodulgate, &c., which she claimed of dower against him.[5] This action continued for some years, and was not concluded in January 1395-6,[6] though a year afterwards we find the same Johanna prosecuting Walter Chubba atte Forde, and others, for trespassing upon her closes at Bodulgate;[7] and at the same assize John Bodulgate sued Simon Trote in a plea of debt.[8]

We find John Bodulgate mentioned in 1398,[9] and in the following January, John Bera of Tregarn took proceedings against Stephen Bodulgate for the recovery of a certain pix containing charters and other muniments. He did not appear, and was ordered to be attached and produced in Court in Easter term.[10] In the same year, William Tregarra took proceedings against Stephen Bodulgate, Thomas Tettebush, probably son of William Tottebush appointed parker of Lanteglos and Hellesbury Parks in 1354,[11] and others in a plea of trespass.[12] In 1404 an action of novel disseizin was commenced against Stephen Bodulgate and Johanna his wife and others.[13] In the same year, 1399, both Stephen and Walter Bodulgate were jurors on the Inquisition p.m. of Sir Richard Sergeaux,[14] as Stephen was on that of Phillippa Swynburne, and Thomas Marny, 1408. In 1410, Stephen Bodulgate and Johanna his wife suffered a fine to Richard Resprenna and Walter Bodulgate, of fifteen messuages, &c., in Trevia, Fentenwonwyth, Newehall, Trefullet, Tresterlak, &c., whereby the said tenements were settled upon the said Stephen and Johanna, to hold to them and the heirs of their bodies, in default remainder to the right heirs of the said Johanna.[15] Stephen Bodulgate and Walter Bodulgate were jurors on the Inquisition p.m. of John Lanhergy, held at Launceston in 1415.[16] By deed dated 20th June in this year,

[1] Subsidy Roll, 1st Edward III.

[2] De Banco Roll, 10th Richard II, Trinity, m. 236.

[3] Ibid. 11th Richard II, Hilary, m. 369.

[4] Ibid. 15th Richard II, Easter, m. 444.

[5] Ibid. 444 d.

[6] De Banco Roll, 19th Richard II, Hilary, m. 257.

[7] Ibid. 20th Richard II, Hilary, m. 249.

[8] Ibid. m. 436.

[9] Ibid. 22nd Richard II, Michaelmas, m. 294 d. John Bodulgate was one of the jurors of the Inquisition held at Bodmin, 1387, Inq. p. m. 10th Richard II, No. 11.

[10] Ibid. Hilary m. 172 d.

[11] See ante p. 294.

[12] De Banco Roll, 23rd Richard II, Trinity, m. 155.

[14] Inq. p.m., 1st Henry IV, No. 4.

[13] Assize Roll, Cornwall, 5th Henry IV.

[15] Pedes Finium, 11th Henry IV, Hilary.

[16] Inq. p.m., 2nd Henry V, No. 5.

Walter Bodulgate was appointed one of the trustees of the estates of Sir William Marny of Colquite, and he was still living in 1460.[1] Stephen and Walter were clearly brothers.

Stephen Bodulgate died after 1448, leaving a son and heir, Thomas Bodulgate, who in 1470, as kinsman and heir of Warine Bodulgate, held two-and-a-half acres of land Cornish in Penkeyrowe, and as kinsman and heir of Richard Tynden half an acre in Bodulgate, and also two acres in Treualrygge.[2] He was one of the farmers of the king of the Manor and Castle of Restormel and other manors and boroughs. In 1456, he was exonerated of 100s. 4d., a portion of £33 6s. 8d., which he owed the king;[3] and two years later he was again exonerated, together with John Trevillian, of divers sums in similar circumstances.[4] It was, probably, these and other debts which brought him into difficulties, for we find that in 1461, under the description of Thomas Bodulgate, late of London, Esq., *alias* the said Thomas Bodulgate, late of the County of Cornwall, Esq., he was summoned to reply to Guleatto Centurion, merchant of Jauua, in a plea of debt of £60;[5] and in 1468, we find a writ was issued to the Sheriff of Cornwall,[6] to take Thomas Bodulgate, late of Trencruke in the aforesaid county, Esq., made an outlaw in London, on Monday next after the feast of St. Swithin the Bishop, 5th of the King, at the suit of Edward Luke, late citizen and brewer of London, and Robert Spayn, Scryvener, executors of the will of William Luke, late citizen and brewer of London, and Richard Phippes and Alice his wife, who was the wife of William Luke, co-executor with the said Edward and Robert, in a plea of debt.[7]

Thomas Bodulgate died on Monday next before Easter 11th Edward IV. (1471) seized of the manors, *inter alia*, of Trencruk, Yeolland, and Nether Helland, and Isabella late wife of Thomas Roscarrock and Johanna late wife of Edward Coriton, were found to be his sisters and nearest heirs.[8]

Nevertheless in the Assession Rolls of 1492 and 1498, the name of Thomas Bodulgate as kinsman and heir of Warine Bodulgate appears as holding 2½ acres of land Cornish in Penkeyrowe at the rent of 4s. per annum, as it had appeared in the Assession Roll of 1470.

In letters patent dated 18th March 13th Edward IV. (1472-3) it is recited that (the abovementioned) Stephen Bodulgate, Esq., was seized in his demesne as of fee of the manors, *inter alia*, Trencreek, Helland, Bodulgate, Delioboll, Treuarlicke, &c., and being so seized enfeoffed certain trustees to hold to the use of the said Stephen and his heirs for the fulfilment of his last will—that the said Stephen had issue, Thomas Bodulgate, Esq., and died, afterwards the said Thomas died, and that certain of the trustees continued seized of the premises, for that the will of the said Stephen was not yet fulfilled; but that certain of the king's officers, under colour of certain offences supposed to have been committed, claimed on the king's behalf a certain interest in all the said manors and

---

[1] See ante, vol. i, p. 442-443.   [2] Assession Roll, 9th Edward IV.

[3] Lord Treas. Rememb. of the Excheq., 34th Henry VI, m. 111, Trinity.

[4] Ibid. 36th Henry VI, Michaelmas, m 16.   [5] De Banco Roll, 1st Edward IV, Hilary, m. 301 d.

[6] Ibid, 7th Edward IV, Michaelmas, m. 317 d.   [7] Ibid. m. 512.

[8] Inq. p.m. 11th Edward IV, No. 17.

lands, as well as the annulment of the will of the said Stephen as to the disinheriting of the heirs of the said Thomas who had never transgressed against the king; therefore the king, wishing to do justice to everyone, pardons all the said offences and remits to the trustees, and also to Joan Coryington and Isabella Roscarrock, sisters and heirs of the aforesaid Thomas, son and heir of the aforesaid Stephen, and their heirs, all his right and title to the aforesaid lands and manors, and grants that the said Thomas shall not be impeached in Parliament or elsewhere in respect of anything heretofore done by him.[1]

Walter Bodulgate appears to have resided at Trecarren in Advent, (?) at which place, on 20th January 1435, he dated his charter for the endowment of a chantry priest in the chapel of St. Thomas at Camelford. He would appear to have had no issue, and devised his estates, subject to the above endowment, to his nephew Thomas Bodulgate, with remainder to Thomas Roscarrock and Isabella his wife, and Edward Coryton and Johanna his wife.

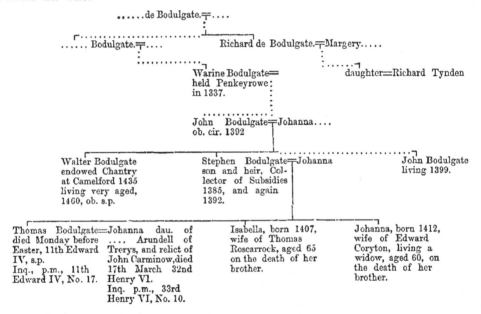

[1] The original of this document, with the great seal attached, was found by the author in the muniment room at Coker Court, Co. Somerset, the seat of William Hawker Helyar, Esq., derived from the family of Coryton of Newton Ferrers from which Mr. Helyar is descended. An indorsement on the instrument in a modern hand makes the date the 13th Edward *First* which is clearly a mistake. The handwriting is not of that period, and the Royal Seal has the arms of France quartered with those of England, and the rose and star, the badge of the House of York, clearly shewing that the seal is that of Edward IV. The seal is of white wax and in tolerably good preservation.

PHILLIPS.

In the early part of the last century Mr. John Phillips of Treveanes in St. Teath settled in Camelford, and, availing himself of the political advantages of the town, obtained much influence in the Borough, and acquired a considerable fortune. He had six sons and a daughter. The two eldest sons died young. The third, Charles, married one of the co-heiresses of Long of Penheal, and, dying s.p., transmitted her ample fortune to his brother. Charles Phillips was appointed Recorder of Camelford in 1761, and in 1769 was returned as one of the burgesses in Parliament. He was also Lieut.-Colonel of the Cornwall Militia. The fourth son, William, entered Holy Orders and became rector of the parishes of Lanteglos and St. Cleather, and died at Camelford, unmarried, in 1794. Jonathan, the fifth son, in early life was a surgeon in the Navy. He married Grace, daughter and co-heir of Cotton Amy of Botreaux Castle by Anna Maria, daughter and coheir of Samuel Gilbert of Tackbear. (See Ped. of COTTON, ante vol i., p. 652.) In 1775 he was appointed Recorder of Camelford in succession to his brother, and in 1784 was returned one of the burgesses in Parliament. Three months afterwards, however, he accepted the stewardship of the Chiltern Hundreds. Having, as Recorder, taken up from the Borough an address of congratulation on the king's escape from the attack upon his life by Margaret Nicholson in 1786 he received the honour of knighthood. Sir Jonathan Phillips died in 1798, and was buried at Minster, where he, his wife, and five children, who all pre-deceased him, are commemorated by a tablet in the chancel. (See ante vol. i., p. 608, No. 3.) Christian, the only daughter of Mr. John Phillips, married Mr. John Carpenter of Mount Tavy, near Tavistock. To her Sir Jonathan Phillips bequeathed the moiety of his estates for life with remainder to Thomas Winsloe (See ante vol. i., p. 621) and to her son, John Phillips Carpenter, the Rev. William Phillips, by his will dated 18th August 1793, devised all his property in Camelford and the neighbourhood.

CAREW OF LANTEGLOS.

George Carew, the fourth son of Richard Carew of Antony, Esq., the celebrated author of the "Survey of Cornwall," having married Jane daughter and heir of John Hocken, *alias* Tregarth, of Trevya, settled there, and his descendants continued in some repute for several generations.

The Hockens, it is presumed, were originally of Tregarth, as they were sometimes called by that name, either as an *alias* or otherwise, and Great Tregarth descended to Hugh Carew, who in 1671, demised it to Sir James Smith (see ante, p. 324 n. 5). John Hokyn, however, held a messuage in Trevia, of the Manor of Helston, as early as 1427. In 1539, Robert Hockyn held the same messuage. In 1553, Hugh Hockyn, son and heir of Robert Hockyn, held it, in which year he was one of the jurors. In 1574, it was held by Margaret Hockyn, *alias* Tregarth, on the death of Hugh Hockyn her husband; and it continued in the family until it passed to George Carew as above stated.

George Carew, Gent., was returned as one of the freeholders of the Manor for Tregarth and other lands in 1650. He died in 1661, and at the next assession, in 1668, Hugh Carew appears on the Assession Roll, after the death of George his father. Hugh left two sons · George who succeeded him, and William Carew, Gentleman, who was mayor of Camelford in 1715, as he was again in 1737, the year of his death. The issue of this William settled in St. Teath, where they remained for several descents. Thomas Carew of St. Teath was married there in 1832, and had issue, and afterwards emigrated to America.

The property held by the family in Lanteglos and Advent gradually diminished until upon the death of George Carew of Trevye, great grandson of the last mentioned George, in 1826, but little remained, which was sold by his only surviving son, Samuel Carew, who, like his cousin of St. Teath, emigrated to America. We know not whether in the new world they have carried on, in the male line, the representation of a family which for many centuries has been so illustrious in the old.

ARMS: Or, three lions passant, in pale, sa. armed and langued gu.

3 A

PEDIGREE OF CAREW

Alexander Carew, 4th son of Sir Nicholas Carew, Baron Carew,=Joane dau.
by Joane dau. and heir of Sir Hugh Courtenay of Haccombe. | of ....
Founder of the family of Carew of Antony, died 20th Sept. 1492. | Hatch.

John Carew of Antony, son and heir,=Thomasine dau. of
Sheriff of Cornwall 1488. | .... Holland.

Sir Wymond Carew of Antony, Knt., died 22nd=Martha, sister of Sir
Aug. 1549. Inq. p.m., 3rd Edward VI., No. 98. | Anthony Denny.

Thomas Carew of Antony, aged 22 on his=Elizabeth dau. of Sir
father's death. Died 12th Feb. 1563-4. | Richard Edgcombe,
Inq. p.m., 6th Elizabeth, No. 14. | Knt. Living 1564.

Richard Carew of Antony. Aged 8 years and 213 days,=Julia dau. of Sir John
on his father's death. Historian of Cornwall, born 1555. | Arundell of Trerice, Knt.
Sheriff of Cornwall 1583. Died 6th Nov. 1620. Inq. | and coh. of her mother,
p.m., Wards and Liveries, bund. 27, No. 53. | Catherine Cosworth.

| Gertrude, mar. Richard Silly of St. Minver. Mar. Lic. 1st Dec. 1636. | Sir Richard Carew, created a Baronet 1641. | Martha mar. Francis Rouse of Brixham, Mar. Lic. 27th Dec. 1638. | Elizabeth, mar. William Pearse of Holwell, in Davidstow. | Ann, mar. Lic. 16th, mar. 18th Nov. 1616, Francis Godolphin. | John Carew of Penwarne, 2nd son.=Alice dau. of .....Hillman of Drewsteignton. Mar. Lic. 22nd Nov. 1616. | Hobbie Carew of Liskeard, 3rd son, died there. Will dated 8th Feb. 1640. Prov. 22nd January 1644. Archd. Cornw.=.... |

| Richard Carew. Bur.[2] 16th April 1640, aged 17 years, M.I. | Candace. Mary. Grace. | Ann mar.[3] 14th July 1663, Richard Hoblyn of St. Columb. | Bridget, mar. settl. dated 1st April 1647. Mar.[2] 8th Aug. 1659, Edward Hoblyn son of Edward Hoblyn of Nanswyddon. | | Thomas. Titus. | John. Christopher. | Ann. Grace. |
| | | | | | All named in father's will. |

| Grace dau. of .... Gust. mar.[4] 1684. Bur. 27th Oct. 1742. | George Carew, bap.[1] 2nd Sept. 1661. Bur.[1] 5th July 1710.=Mary dau. of William Hender of Lanteglos, bap.[1] 1665. Mar.[1] 22nd April 1685. Bur.[1] 21st Aug. 1736. | Elizabeth, bap.[1] 17th Sept. 1662, mar.[1] 3rd April 1706, Edward Cloake, Mayor of Camelford 1709, 1710. He bur.[1] 17th Dec. 1713. She bur.[1] 27th Aug. 1729. | Jane, bap.[1] 4th Oct. 1664. | John Carew, bap.[1] 9th Jan. 1666. | Frances, bap.[1] 9th April 1669, bur.[1] 26th Oct. 1687. |

| Mary, mar.[4] Wm. Inch, 1735. | Peter bap.[4] 3rd May 1685, bur.[4] 30th Oct. 1687. | John Carew of Lanteglos, bap.[1] 17th Jan. 1689. Bur.[1] 4th Nov. 1777.=Thomasine, d. of John Hawkins of Quethiock, bap. 19th July, 1689, mar.[1] lic. dated 21st & mar.[1] 26th Jan. 1720. Bur.[1] 3rd Feb. 1762. | Samuel, bap.[1] 18th Sept. 1690, bur.[1] 23rd March 1693. | Elizabeth, bap.[1] 4th July 1693, mar.[1] 21st May 1719, John Ward. | Samuel, born 19th, bap.[1] 28th May 1696. Bur.[1] 26th April 1763. | Mary, born 6th, bap.[1] 22nd Feb. 1698, bur.[1] 1st Jan. 1712. | George, b. 20th, bap.[1] 28th April 1702, bur. 4th Nov. 1722. |

| John Carew, bap.[1] 17th June 1722.=Deborah, dau. of ...... Bur. 6th June 1790. | George, bap.[1] 27th April 1724, bur.[1] 27th Oct. 1724. William, bap.[1] 2nd Oct. 1725. | Elizabeth, bap.[1] 7th May 1725, mar. her cous. George Carew. Mary bap.[1] 28th Oct. 1727, mar.[1] 19th June 1761, Thomas Wakeham. Thomasine bap.[1] 28th Oct. 1730, bur.[1] 3rd Feb. 1762. | Jane, bap.[1] 10th Jan. 1735, mar.[1] William Dannon of Tyntagel, 9th Mar. 1763. | Thomas Carew of Lanteglos, bap.[1] 8th Oct. 1738, bur.[1] 28th July 1766.=Elizabeth, dau. ...... remar. 27th Jan. 1776, Wilm. Davey | Ann, bap.[1] 1744. | William, bap. 8th Feb. 1746, bur. 13th Aug. 1766, s.p. |

| Mary bap.[6] 17th Dec. 1750. | Elizabeth, bap.[6] 1st Feb. 1753. | George Carew of Treyvo, bap.[1] 11th Feb. 1752. Bur.[1] 8th August 1826.=Frances, dau. of ...... Parken. Bur.[1] 11th Oct. 1809. | John Tingcombe.=Elizabeth, bap.[1] 24th May 1767, mar.[1] 5th Feb. 1796. | Honour, bap.[1] 18th Jan. 1794. | William bap.[4] 3rd July 1796, bur.[1] 15th July 1798. |

| John Carew, bap.[1] 12th Mar. 1780, bur.[1] 8th Jan. 1799. | Deborah bap.[1] 29th Aug. 1781, bur.[1] 6th June 1790. | Elizabeth bap.[1] 27th April 1783, died at St. Germans. | Sarah bap.[1] 27th Mar. 1785, mar.[1] Roger Northey 1817. Bur.[1] 27th Jan. 1847. | Mary bap.[1] 1st April 1787. Mar.[1] William Hawken 1814. Bur. 6th Nov. 1864, aged 77. | Thomasine bap.[1] 1st March 1789. Mar. N. Horswell 1819. |

* On 7th May 1729, a Caveat was lodged in the Bishop's Court against the issue of a licence to marry between William Carew, described as.

[1] At Lanteglos.   [2] At Mevagissey.   [3] At St. Columb Major.   [4] At St. Teath.   [5] At Tyntagel.   [6] At St. Kew.

F LANTEGLOS AND ST. TEATH.

John Hockyn held⹀.... in Trevia 1427.

Robert Hocken held⹀.... in Trevia 1539.

Hugh Hocken, son and heir of Robert Hocken,⹀Margaret Hocken, *alias* Tregarth, held in Trevia on the death of her husband, Hugh Hocken, 1574. Bur.[1] 21st Dec. 1575.
held in Trevia 1553, bur.[1] 1563.

Christopher Hocken, *alias* Tregarth, held lands in Trevia⹀Elizabeth dau. of .... Harvy, mar.[1] 22nd July on the death of his mother, Margaret Hocken, 1602. | 1573. Bur.[1] 29th June 1622.
Bur.[1] 4th Nov. 1620.

Humphry Tregarth, bap.[1] 25th March 1575, bur.[1] Oct. 1600.	Ann Tregarth, bap.[1] 15th Oct. 1578, bur.[1] 26th Sept. 1600.	John Tregarth, *alias* Hocken. Bur.[1] 31st Dec. 1612.⹀Frances dau. of .... Crossman. Mar.[1] 25th Jan. 1600.	Hugh, bap.[1] 24th Nov. 1592.⹀Margaret, bur.[1] 7th July 1643.

Sibella dau. of.... Carkick of Meva-gissey. Mar. Lic. 25th Jan. 1639-40. Bur.[1] 15th May 1648.⹀George Carew of Trevia in Lanteglos, 4th son. Bur.[2] 2nd Sept. 1661. M.I. 2nd wife.⹀Jane dau. and coh., bap.[1] 11th Oct. 1607, mar[1] 11th Feb. 1624. Bur.[1] 22nd Dec. 1630. 1st wife.	Ann, bap. 16th Jan. 1605.	Frances, bap. 16th Jan. 1610.	Christopher, bap.[1] 18th March 1601, bur.[1] 2nd May 1602.	Humphry, bap.[1] 3rd July 1603, bur.[1] 30th June 1605.	Elizabeth, bap.[1] 23rd Jan. 1630, bur.[1] 12th Oct. 1632.

Dorothy dau. of .... Bur.[1] 22nd March 1710. 2nd wife.⹀Hugh Carew of Lanteglos. Bur.[1] 19th March 1693.⹀Florence dau. of ...... Bur.[4] 11th Nov.1656.M.I. 1st wife	Gartered, Mar.[1] 22nd April 1651, Walter Tingcombe.	Ann Carew, bap.[1] 30th Aug. 1629.

Gartered bap.[1] 8th June 1675, mar.[5] 4th March 1700, Richard Creese.	William Carew, bap.[1] 25th April 1671. Mayor of Camelford 1715, 1737. Bur.[1] 7th March 1737-8.⹀Susanna d. of Oliver Horndon of Calling-ton. Mar. lic. dated 12thDec.1693.Mar.[7] 11th Jan. 1694., Bur.[1]24th March 1712. ⹀Gracedau.of..Hodge, m. at Lesnewith 1st Dec. 1719. Bur.[1] 27th Oct. 1742.	Hugh, died in infancy. Bur.[1] 7th Sept. 1679.	Elizabeth, bap.[4] 28th Dec. 1655, bur.[4] 11th Mar. 1655.	John, bap.[4] 11th Nov. 1656, bur.[4] 1st Feb. 1656-7.

William Carew * of Trevia, bap.[1] 8th May 1707. Bur.⹀Elizabeth, dau. of .... Sloggett mar.[1] 14th April 1734. Bur.[1] 2nd March 1782.	Hugh Carew, born and bap.[1] 29th Oct. 1697.	Mary, dau. of ...... Buried 3th April 1760.⹀William Carew, born 3rd Dec., bap.[1] 5th Jan. 1695, of St. Teath. Bur.[4] Admo. to Mary his relict, 20th June, 1732.

Elizabeth, bur.[4] 21st Nov. 1735.	William Carew.⹀Elizabeth, dau. of Thomas Bonney, bap.[4] 25th Feb. 1736, mar.[4] 30th May 1768.

George Carew bap.[1] 11th August 1743, bur.[1] 4th Sept. 1801.⹀Elizabeth, dau. of John Carew, mar.[1] 8th July 1764. Bur.[1] 6th Feb. 1817, aged 73.	John Carew bap.[1] 3rd Aug. 1750, bur.[1] 5th Aug. 1792, s.p.⹀Bridget, dau. of ...... Hender, mar.[1] 10th Sept. 1770, bur.[1] 31st May 1774.	Jenefer, bap.[4] 19th Feb. 1771.	Thos. Carew of St. Teath, bap.[4] 26th Sept. 1769, bur.[4] 23rd March 1837, aged 68.⹀Mary, dau. of William May, bap.[4] 31st Oct. 1773, mar.[4] 12th July, 1794. Bur.[4] 20th Dec. 1818, aged 44.	Elizabeth, bap.[4] 25th Feb. 1774, mar.[4] John Kernick, 25th Dec. 1793.	Mary, bap. 13th Nov. 1775, bur.[1] 4th Oct. 1795.	Honor bap.[4] 11th June 1778, bur.[4] 7th Oct. 1786.

...ry, bap.[4] ...h Dec. ...7, bur.[3] 1Oct.1805.	Elizabeth, bap.[4] 2nd Feb. 1800.	Catherine, bap.[4] 3rd Oct. 1802.	Jane, bap.[4] 25th Dec. 1804, bur.[4] 2nd Oct. 1805.	Thomas Carew,bap[4] 16th March 1806.⹀Mary Stanbury dau. of John Inch of St.Teath, bap.[4] 9th Dec. 1812, mar.[4] 28th July, 1832.	Mary. Jenefer. Bap.[1] 8th April 1809.	Anne, bap.[4] 29 Nov. 1812.

Samuel Carew of Trevia, bap.[1] 22nd March 1792.	Deborah bap.[1] 22nd March 1792, mar. H. Hocken 1814. Bur.[1] 7th Aug 1859.	Mary Jane, bap.[4] 17th Feb. 1833.	Ann bap.[4] 1st April 1835, mar. .... Camps.	Elizabeth bur.[4] 1st December 1851. Æt 14.

St. Stephens by Saltash, and Ann Bluett of Lanteglos by Camelford, before William Dinham of Tresinny, in Advent, had been first called..

[1] At Lanteglos. [2] At Mevagissey. [3] At St. Columb Major. [4] At St. Teath. [5] At Tyntagel. [6] At St. Kew. [7] At Callington.

COCK OF CAMELFORD.

The family of Cock is of considerable antiquity in this neighbourhood. John Cock was one of the jurors at the court of assession of the Manor of Helston in Trigg 5th Henry VI. John Cock was assessed to the subsidy in Advent in 1st Edward III., and in 33rd Henry VIII. Christopher Cock was assessed upon goods in Lanteglos at the highest rate. This was doubtless the same Christopher who, as son and heir of John Cock, at the assession court of 1539 took the mill at Camelford, which his father had taken at the previous assession. The Cock family would appear to have been the leading inhabitants of the Borough for a considerable period. The above mentioned Christopher Cock was Mayor of Camelford in 1552, being the earliest date of which we can find any record, and he and his son and grandson would appear to have held that office, continuously, for nearly a century. He died in 1566, and in 1572, there being no record between, we find John Cock, his son, was mayor, who died as mayor in 1604, and was succeeded in the mayoralty by his son Christopher Cock, who, apparently, continued to hold that office without interruption until after 1635. He lived until 1651, and died at the advanced age of 80 years.

John Cock, son of the first Christopher, would seem to have registered his pedigree at the Heralds' Visitation of 1573, embracing, however, only three descents, and it was not extended at the subsequent Visitation of 1620. At the assession court of the Manor of Helston in 1553, Christopher Cock, heir of Thomas Southwode, kinsman and heir of Henry Welyngton, took three acres of land, Cornish, in Treclegou, which Christopher Cock, heir of Thomas Southwode, kinsman and heir of Henry Welyngton, had taken at the previous assession; and John Cock again took it at the assession in 1567, at which assession, as John Cock, gent., he was one of the jurors. In 1578 John Cock, acquired the advowson of the rectory of Bliston, and, as John Cock of Camelford, gent., presented to that benefice in 1581, while in 1606, Christopher Cock, his son and heir, sold the advowson to William Parker, afterwards Archdeacon of Cornwall.[1] John Cock, Esq., and Christopher Cock, gent., were both jurors at the assession court in 1602. This Christopher had several children baptized at Lanteglos between 1597 and 1619. To Nicholas, his eldest son, he surrendered the mill at Camelford, and at the assesion of 1624, as Nicholas Cock, Esq., he took the said mill, as, in conjunction with John Billing and Christopher Worthevale, gentlemen, he took also the right of Free Warren of the Manor of Helston.[2] We have no further notice of him. His father, as Christopher Cock Esq., was buried on 28th January 1651, from which date we are unable to distinguish the members of this family from others of the same name, who are numerous in the parish.

---

[1] Ante, vol. i. pp. 49, 50, 52.   [2] Assession Rolls of the Manor of Helston of various dates.

PEDIGREE OF COCK OF CAMELFORD.

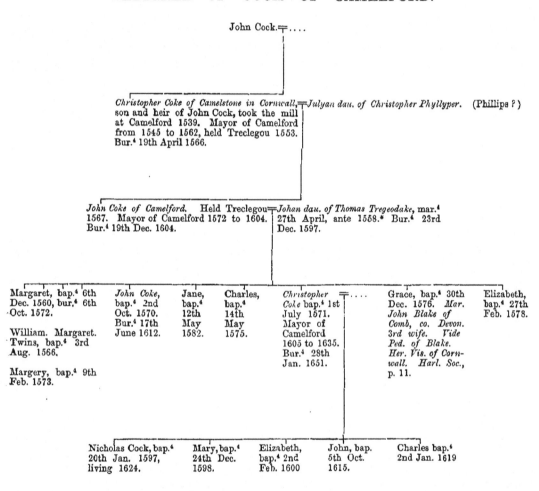

I hereby certify that the portions of the above Pedigree which are printed in *Italics*, agree with the Books of this Office. G. b. vi.

Herald's College,
    December 1874.

STEPHEN TUCKER,
Rouge Croix.

---

⁴ At Lanteglos.   * See ante, p. 321.

WALLIS OF FENTENWOON.

In this parish in the 16th century resided the family of Wallis. It would appear from a gravestone in the churchyard (ante p. 311, No. 14) that Degory Wallis of Fento[nwoon] was buried in December 1560. This stone, however, was evidently set up by a descendant after the death of John Wallis who died in 1726, and is inaccurate many particulars. The register shows that the Wallis who was buried in December 1560 was named Thomas. He was the father of Degory, who died in 1591. We do not find the name of Wallis in the subsidy rolls for Lanteglos until 32nd Henry VIII (1540) when Thomas Walys was assessed upon goods, who was doubtless the same Thomas who died in 1560. In 1591 Degory Wallis and John Hockying, *alias* Tregarth, levied a fine of John Roscarrock and Katherine his wife of two messuages, one mill, four gardens, 50 acres of land, 20 acres of meadow, 40 acres of pasture, and 30 acres of furze and heath in Tresalett, Trewynt, Fentonwonwith, *alias* Fentonwonwill, Milland, Lanteglos, Advent, and St. Bruer, whereby the said premises were quit-claimed to the said Degory to hold to him and his heirs for ever.[1]

At the assession in 1602 Christopher Wallys, son of John Wallys, took in convention a portion of a tenement in Trevia, in right of Johanna his wife, on the surrender of John Durnand, on the surrender of Christopher Wallys, on the surrender of John Wallys. This John, the father of Christopher, was probably the son of Thomas and brother of Degory above mentioned. We do not find the name of Wallis again in connection with Fentonwonwill until 1683, at the assession in which year John Wallis, great-grandson of the above mentioned Degory, acquired the fourth part of a tenement in Fentenwansen.[2] He married Mary, eldest daughter of Ferdinando Wallis of Trewall in St. Germans, (of whom presently), by whom he had a son of his own name, who in 1742, under the description of John Wallis, gent., held the fifth part of a tenement in Fentenwansen. In 1756 it was alleged that John Wallis, gent, by purchase from [Phillip] Spry (Sprey) clerk, lord of the messualty, held one acre of land Cornish in Fentonwonwith. By Sarah, daughter of John Barrett, of St. Tudy, this John Wallis had three sons and a daughter. John, his eldest son, continued to hold the above mentioned land in Fentenwonwith until his death in 1780. He married Ann, daughter and co-heir of John Rowe of Cullinwith in Landrake, by whom he had an only child named Ann, who married Captain John Thomas Duckworth, R.N., afterwards Admiral Sir John Thomas Duckworth, G.C.B., created a baronet in 1813. Ann Wallis, relict of the last mentioned John, after the death of her husband, continued to hold the above mentioned premises until her death in January 1806.

Samuel Wallis, the third son of John Wallis and Sarah Barrett, was the famous circumnavigator. The biographers of this celebrated officer have avowed themselves totally

---

[1] Pedes Finium, 23rd Elizabeth, Trinity.   [2] Assession Roll.

ignorant of his parentage, but it is certain that he was born in this parish, and baptized at the parish Church on 25th April 1728. He probably entered the Navy in early life under the patronage of Admiral Boscawen, who was frequently a resident at Worthevale in the immediate neighbourhood of his father's house. In 1755 we find him a lieutenant of the Gibraltar (20), from which he was promoted to be a lieutenant of the Torbay (74), Admiral Boscawen's flag ship. On 8th April 1757, he was commissioned as captain of the Portmahon (20), and was ordered to North America under Admiral Holburne, who commanded the expedition against Louisburg. In 1760 he was ordered to Canada in command of the Prince of Orange, a reduced third rate, on his return from whence he is said to have been employed on the Home Station, in command of a third rate, until the conclusion of the war.

On 19th June 1766, he was commissioned to the Dolphin (24) as successor to Commodore Byron, and sent out on a voyage to the Pacific, as his predecessor had been before him, to extend the discoveries of that officer. Captain Wallis informs us that he hoisted the pendant the day he received his commission, on the 26th day of the same month sailed down the river, and on 16th August entered into Plymouth Sound. On the 19th he received his sailing orders with directions to take the Swallow sloop, and Prince Frederic storeship, under his command, and having completed his equipment, sailed on the 22nd at four o'clock in the morning, thus showing a promptness and decision of character which augured well for the success of the voyage.

The Swallow sloop (14) was commanded by Captain Carteret, but she was soon found to be a bad sailor, and having retarded her consorts, they did not arrive at Maderia until the 7th September. Sailing again on the 12th they visited Cape Virgin Mary on the coast of Patagonia, where they had friendly intercourse with the natives. On 23rd January the ships anchored under Cape Gallant in the Straits of Magellan, and after a variety of occurrences, they cleared the Straits on 12th April, after a passage of nearly four months, and on the night of the same day the Swallow parted company, and the two ships never afterwards met until their return to England. After parting company with his consort Wallis discovered Easter Island on 3rd June 1767, and on the 19th of the same month Tahite, or Otaheite, being the first who had visited that Island after the Spanish navigator Quiros, in 1605, assuming that Quiros's Sagillari is Tahite, which is doubtful. Very interesting particulars of Captain Wallis's visit to this place, and of his communications with the Queen and natives of the Island, at first hostile and afterwards very friendly, will be found in Hawkesworth's voyages. Captain Wallis shewed great courage, tact, and prudence, in which he was ably seconded by his officers, especially his second lieutenant, Tobias Furneaux,[1] the first lieutenant being ill the greater part of the time. The Dolphin arrived in the Downs on 13th May 1768. Wallis has the character of being a painstaking, sensible, and veracious man. He was the first to bring down the fabulous stature of the Patagonians to its real altitude. It was Captain Wallis who recommended Taheite as the station for observing the transit of Venus over the sun's disc in 1769.

---

[1] Lieut. Tobias Furneaux was great uncle of the Rev. Tobias Furneaux, Vicar of St. Germans lately deceased.

We have no trace that Captain Wallis was again employed until 1771, when, upon the equipment of a naval force in consequence of an apprehended rupture with Spain respecting the Falkland Islands, he was commissioned to the Torbay. He retired from active service in the following year, and never again commanded a ship, except for a short time in 1780, at the end of which year he was appointed an extra Commissioner of the Navy, an office which he held until the peace, when it was discontinued. In 1787 it was again revived and Captain Wallis was appointed to fill it, which he did until his death in 1795. Captain Wallis married Betty, one of the daughters and co-heirs of John Hearle of Penryn, Esq., by whom he had a daughter named after her mother, who, on 22nd October 1796, married Samuel Stephens, Esq., barrister-at-law and left issue. For some time after his marriage Captain Wallis resided at Trelissick, but in 1791, upon the death of his cousin Mydhope Wallis, clerk, he succeeded, under the will of Ann Wallis of Trethill, in Sheviock, to that property.—Charnock's Biographia Navalis; Hawkesworth's Voyages; Annual Register; Gent.'s Magazine; and Penny Cyclopædia.

ARMS: John Wallis, in executing a deed, dated 26th December 1738, by which he granted a lease of premises in Camelford, used an armorial seal: gu., a fess and canton erm. impaling: a chev. engrailed between three bears passant (Barrett of Tregarren); and the same arms were used by his son John Wallis, who impaled therewith three stags' heads, cabossed (for Rowe). The arms: gu., a fess and canton erm., were granted in the year 1590, by Robert Cooke, Clarencieux, to Lewis Wallis, *alias* Darte of Mevagissey, *and his issue*, from whom it is evident, from the subjoined pedigree, the Wallises of Fentenwoon could not be descended.

WALLIS OF TREWALL IN ST. GERMANS AND TRETHILL IN SHEVIOCK.

A family of Wallis was resident in St. Germans in the early part of the 17th century. John and Ferdinando Wallis, probably brothers, were respectively having children baptized 1614—1620. Ferdinando, son of John Wallis, baptized in 1620, appears from his will, dated 14th November 1687, to have held lands in Trewall and other places in St. Germans, and at Nether Blarich and other places in Sheviock. He left two sons and two daughters. To his eldest son Ferdinando he devised his estates in St. Germans, and to Henry those in Sheviock. Rhoda, the youngest daughter, died unmarried, and Mary the elder became the wife of John Wallis of Fentenwoon.

Francis Wallis, eldest son of Ferdinando Wallis the younger, above mentioned, married the daughter and co-heir of Roger Mydhope of Trenant in Duloe,[1] with whom

---

[1] Hals states that he is informed that these Mydhopes are descended from the Mydhopes of Essex. He says that the father of — Mydhope, then of Trenant, married Porter, and that his grandfather and his great grandfather had both been rectors of St. Martins-by-Looe. Arms: Erm. A lion ramp. Az. Crowned or. (Davies Gilbert's Hist. Cornwall, vol. i· p. 320.) Roger Mydhope, Gent., about forty years old, was baptized at Duloe on 9th January 1710, and was buried there 23rd March in the same year. Par. Reg.

he acquired Penhale in the parish of St. Martins-by-Looe. He had a son named Mydhope Wallis who matriculated at Balliol College, Oxford, in 1735, aged 16 years, and was instituted to the rectory of Endellion and the Prebend of Trehaverock in the same Church in 1753,[1] holding also the curacy of Sheviock in 1769 and 1776. The Prebend he resigned in 1754, and the Rectory in 1774, and afterwards, in 1776, became Rector of St. John's, Antony. Henry Wallis the second son of Ferdinando Wallis, the elder, added to his possessions in Sheviock by the purchase, *inter alia*, of Trethill in that parish where he erected a convenient mansion. He left two sons and a daughter named Ann. Of his sons John, the younger, died a minor in 1714, and Ferdinando, the elder, served the office of Sheriff of Cornwall in 1736, and died unmarried two years later, when the estates devolved upon his sister Ann Wallis. By her will, dated 29th May 1756, she demised the Barton of Trethill and other lands to her cousin Mydhope Wallis, clerk, for life with remainder to his first and other sons in tail male. In default of such issue remainder to John Wallis of Fentenwoon for life, with remainder to his issue in tail male; in default of such issue remainder to Samuel Wallis for life remainder to his sons in tail male; and in default of all such issue remainder to the right heirs of the said testatrix. The said Ann Wallis died soon afterwards and Mydhope Wallis, clerk, entered into possession. John Wallis, who resided chiefly at Stoke Damerel, died s.p.m. at Trethill in the lifetime of Mydhope, whilst on a visit to him there, and was buried at Sheviock, where a monument to his memory still remains. On the death of Mydhope Wallis, who is said to have been an excellent Classical and Hebrew scholar, in 1790, without issue male, but leaving two daughters Ann and Elizabeth, the estates devolved upon Captain Samuel Wallis, then one of the Commissioners of the Navy. He also died s.p.m. in 1795, when, under the settlement in the will of Ann Wallis, above cited, the estates devolved upon the aforesaid Ann and Elizabeth, the daughters of Mydhope Wallis, as heirs-at-law of the said Ann. Ann, the elder, married the Rev. Bryan Roberts, LL.D., rector of Drewsteignton, co. Devon, by whom he left issue, now residing at Trethill, and Elizabeth became the wife of the Rev. John Bennett, vicar of Mawgan, who soon afterwards succeeded to his uncle Mr. Gully of Tresillian House, Newlyn. These ladies are still alive, and enjoy Trethill and the other lands in equal moieties.

---

[1] See ante Vol. i, pp. 493, 493, n. 507.

PEDIGREES OF THE FAMILIES OF WALLIS

Thomas Wallis of Lanteglos.=Phillippa dau. of ......
Bur.[2] 26th Dec. 1560, M.I.   Bur.[2] 15th Sept. 1560.

Phillis.   John Wallis.=Margery, dau. of .... Hodge. Mar.[2] 27th Nov.
                         1572.   Bur.[2] 8th July 1605.

| Thomasine, bap.[2] 1st Feb. 1575. | Christopher Wallis of Trevia, bap.[2] 28th Aug. 1574. =Johanna. | William Wallis, bap.[2] 28th Jan. 1559. Bur.[2] 18th April 1624. Admo. to Jone his relict. Archd. Cornw. =Jone dau. of ..... Hoper. Mar.[2] 25th June 1593. | Johanna, bap.[2] 19th Nov. 1561. Mar.[2] George Robye 5th Aug. 1585. | Margaret, bap.[2] 26th March 1563. Bur.[2] 7th Jan. 1591. |

Christopher, bap.[2] 16th Dec. 1601. Ann, bap.[2] 15th June 1600.

Hugh, bap.[2] 12st March 1604, bur.[2] 24th May 1613. Jessey, bap.[2] 19th April 1607.

Henry, bap.[2] 13th Sept. 1610. Hugh, bap. 21st April 1620, bur.[2] 28th Oct. 1620.

Silvester, bap.[2] 4th May 1599.

Agnes, bap.[2] 3rd Jan. 1601.

Hugh, bap.[2] 7th May 1606.

Johanna, bap.[2] 27th Oct. 1601.

John Wallis, bap.[2] 15th Feb. 1601. Bur[2] 14th May 1653.

Ann, bap.[2] July 1625. Mar.[2] Edward Secumbe 29th June 1648.

John Wallis, bap.[2] 1st July 1627, bur.[2] 13th May 1648.

Mary, bap.[2] 6th Nov. 1661, bur.[2] 26th Sept. 1683. Admo to Bro. John, 4th Oct., 1683.

Milicent dau. of =John Wallis of Fenton-=Mary dau. of Fer-
.... Roupe. Mar.[2] wonwith, bap.[2] 4th Sept. dinando Wallis,
12th Aug. 1697,   1656 Died 26th and bap.[5] 19th Aug.
2nd Wife. Bur.   bur.[2] 29th Oct. 1726. 1656. Bur.[2] 21st
3rd Jan. 1623.   Æt 70. M.I. No. 14.   Dec. 1693.

| Samuel Wallis, bap.[2] 14th Oct. 1679, bur[2] 11th March 1680. | Ann, re-lict of ... Gyles of St. Austell. Mar. lic. 20th Oct. 1733, 2nd wife =John Wallis of Fenton-wonwith, bap.[2] 20th March 1680. Bur.[2] 15th Dec. 1768. | Sarah, dau. of John Barrett of St. Tudy. bap.[6] 27th Sept. 1689 Mar.lic. 9th March1719 and m.[6] 21 April 1720. Bur.[2] 1 Oct. 1731. | Samuel, bap.[2] 21st Oct. 1682 Bur.[2] 1st May 1683. Mary, bap.[2] 11th March 1683. | Francis Wallis of London, bap.[2] 30th Sept. 1688. Rhoda, bap.[2] 11th Jan. 1690, bur.[2] 10th Nov. 1718, unmar. | Elizabeth bap.[2] 11th July 1693, bur.[2] 9th Aug. 1693. | Ferdinando, son and heir, b. 1694. Sheriff of Cornwall 1736, ob. s.p. 14th July 1738, aged 44. Bur.[3] M.I., unmar. | John. Died 30th Oct. 1714, aged 19. Bur.[3] M.I. ob. s.p. |

Mary, bap.[2] 24th Aug. 1723, mar...Dyke, Lieut. R.N., and had one child, Mary, mar. William Prater, and left one son, William, who died unmar.

John Wallis of Fen-=Ann dau of Thomas
tonwonwith, bap.[2] Rowe of Cullinwith,
30th Nov. 1721, died and of Stoke
at Trethill, June Damerel. Mar. lic.
1780, buried at She- 13th Dec. 1748. Died
viock, aged 59, M.I. 20th Jany. 1806,
                      buried at Sheviock
                      1806, aged 70, M.I.

Francis Wallis, bap.[2] 30th Nov. 1725.

Samuel Wallis, bap.[2]=Betty,
23rd April 1728. dau. and
The circumnavigator coh. of
Com[r]. of the Navy. John
Died at Devonshire Hearle
St., London, about of
1795.   Penryn.

Ferdinando, bap.[2] 21st Sept. 1730.

John Thomas=Ann Wallis only child and heir, bap.
Duckworth, 30th June 1751. Died at Stoke,
Capt. R.N., 20th Aug. 1797, buried at Sheviock,
1797.   aged 46, M.I.

Samuel Stephens=Betty Hearle,
Barrister at Law, only child
of Tregenna and heir.
Castle, Cornw.

---

[2] At Lanteglos.   [3] At Sheviock.   [4] At St. Martin's juxta Looe.   [5] At St. Germans.   [6] At St. Tudy.

OF FENTENWOON AND TRETHILL.

Digory Wallis of Fentonwonwith.=Margery, dau. of John Hocken, *alias*
Bur.[2] 1591.　Tregarth. Mar.[2] 9th Oct. 1558.

| Phillippa, bap.[2] 15th Oct. 1566, bur.[2] 25th Sept. 1623. Will dated 19th Sept. and Prov. 3rd Nov. 1623. Archd. of Cornw. | Humphry, bap.[2] 28th March 1570. | Elizabeth, bap.[2] 28th March 1570. | Robert, bap.[2] 26th Aug. 1573. | John Wallis of Fentonwonwith, bap.[2] 3rd July 1564. Will dated 10th, Prov. 14th May 1631, Arch. Cornw. =Ann dau. of ....Pawle Mar. April 1592. | John Wallis of St. Germans.[4] =.... |

| Mary, dau. of (Henry ?) Allin, mar.[2] 24th Nov. 1616, I.W. Bur.[2] 16th May 1653. =Samuel Wallis of Fentonwonwith, bap.[2] 18th March 1603. =Florence dau. of .... Bennett of St. Neot. Bur.[2] 3rd March 1675. Will dated 23rd Feb., 1675. Prov. 28th May 1676. | Ferdinando Wallis of Trewall in St. Germans, bap.[5] 2nd April 1620. Bur.[5] 15th Aug. 1692. Will dated 14th Nov. 1687, Prov. Exon. =Frances, dau. of .... Jory of Lanjore in St. Germans. Mar.[5] 26th Nov. 1646, bur.[5] 18th June 1665. |

| Rhoda, bap.[5] 16th Nov. 1663, bur.[2] 26th Feb. 1715, unmar. | Henry Wallis, 2nd son, bap.[5] 4th Oct. 1654. Purchased Trethill in Sheviock, died 12th Oct. 1701, aged 49. Bur.[3] M.I. =Elizabeth, dau. of John Hodge, of St. Germans, mar. setl. 26th Oct. 1692. Died 7th Nov. 1743, aged 85. M.I. | Ferdinando, son and heir, bap.[5] 10th Oct. 1647, bur.[5] 31st Dec. 1703. =Eleanor, dau. of .... Easton of Bickleigh, co. Devon. Bur.[5] 2nd Aug. 1700. | Francis, bap.[5] 20th Nov. 1652, bur.[5] 14th Oct. 1653. |

| Ann Wallis, heir of her brothers, settled Trethill upon her cousin Mydhope. Will dated 29th May 1756. Bur.[3] 17th Feb. 1760, unmar. | Frances, bap.[4] 1676, mar.[4] 26th June 1705, William Davy. | Francis Wallis of Penheale, bap.[4] Dec. 1684, died 27th and bur.[3] Dec. 1765, aged 81. =Jane dau. of Roger Mydhope of Trenant and Penheale, born 1688, mar. at Duloe 17th Nov. 1712. Died 28th March, and bur.[3] 3rd April 1761, aged 73. | Eleanor, bap.[5] 24th May 1675. Mar.[4] Nov. 1712, Richard Durnford. Mary, bap.[4] Dec. 1682. | John Wallis, bap.[4] 17th Oct. 1678, eldest son named in his grandfather's will and app[d]. exr. Died Nov. 1701, aged 21. | Samuel, bap.[4] Jan. 1686. Henry, bap.[4] mar. 1689. Jonah, bap.[4] 1st Sept. 1691. |

| Mydhope Wallis, Clerk, bap.[4] 7th Oct. 1718, matric. at Balliol College, Oxford, 20t May 1735, aged 16. Inst. to Rectory and Prebend of Endellion, 7th April 1753, resigned 1774, became Rector of St. John's by Antony 1773, died at Trethill Dec. 27th 1790, buried at Sheviock, Jan. 4th, 1791.' Will proved 28th April, 1791. P.C.C. =Elizabeth, dau. of .... .. Palmer of ...... died cir. 1780. | Jane, bap.[4] 23rd Nov. 1721. | Henry, bap.[4] 26th Nov. 1726. | John, bap.[4] 23rd Nov. 1714, bur.[4] 9th Jan. 1714-5. | Jane, bap.[4] 5th March 1715. |

| Ferdinando Wallis, bap.[5] 1761, bur.[3] 6th May, 1762. | Ann born June 1768, mar. Rev. Bryan Roberts, LL.D. 1788, mar. settl. 30th Aug. 1791., died May 1836, buried at Sheviocke, M.I. ☥ | Elizabeth, born Feb. 1770, died at Drewsteignton, mar. 1791, at Stoke, Revd. John Bennet, Bur. at Newlyn, 1805. ☥ |

---

[2] At Lanteglos.　[3] At Sheviock.　[4] At St. Martin's juxta Looe.　[5] At St. Germans.

3 B[2]

PEDIGREE

John Dinham of═Joan dau. of ...... Hamlye,
St. Kew.   : mar.[4] St. Kew 1580.
   ....
    John Dinham of St. ═ ....
    Kew.

Philip Dinham, B.A., matric. at Exeter Coll., Oxford, 1st April 1642,═Jane.   Executrix to husband's
aged 18. Inst. to Rectory of Blisland 21st Dec. 1660 and to Preb.   will.   Bur.[4] 10th July 1717.
of Endellion 4th April 1678. Bur.[4] 30th Jan. 1708-9. Will dated
12th Dec. 1704, Prov. 25th Aug. 1709, Exon.

| John Dinham, born 1st, bap.[4] 10th Dec. 1663, named as "Clerk" in father's will. Matric. at Exeter Coll. Oxford, 8th March 1680-1. Æt. 17. Vicar of Rogate, Sussex, living 1732, ob. s.p. | Mary, born 16th, bap.[4] 24th Oct. 1665. | Ursula. Mar.[7] NicholasPhillips 1791, named in father's will. | Jane, bap.[4] 29th Aug. 1666. Mar. .... Thomas, named in father's will. | Richard Dinham, bap.[4] 21st June 1681. Matric. 7th April 1698, at Exeter Coll. Oxford. Æt 17. B.A. 14th Oct. 1701. Named as "Clerk" in father's will. |

| John Dinham, bap.[5] 16th March 1709. Mat. at Queen's College, Oxford, 20th March 1727-8. Æt. 18. | William, bap.[5] 12th Aug. 1712. | Elizabeth, bap.[5] 17th May 1715. Mar.[6] 2nd Sept. 1745, Edmund Prideaux of Hatton Garden, London. | Charles Dinham, bap.[5] 29th Oct.═Sarah, dau. of 1717. Of Camelford. Mayor there │ ...... Stacey. 1766, 1771, 1775, 1779, 1784, │ Mar.[6] 6th May 1787. Bur.[5] 21st Aug. 1795. │ 1751. |

| Mary, bap. 15th Sept. 1751. Mar. 6th June 1735, Thomas Symons of Tintagel. | William Dinham, bap.[6]═Sarah, dau. of James Pulmon of Liskeard, bap. there 30th Jan. 1754. Mayor │ of Camelford 1789, │ 13th April, 1763. Mar.[6] 1791, 1794, 1796, 1800. │ 8th Dec. 1794. bur.[6] 15th Bua.[6] 21st Aug. 1820. │ June 1815, Æt. 52. | Anne, bap.[6] 12th May 1756, bur.[5] 22nd Dec. 1759. | Elizabeth, bap.[6] 3rd May 1759. | Anne, bap.[6] 16th Jan. 1763, bur.[6] 15th April 1848, Æt. 86. |

| Jane, bap.[6] 28 Feb. 1797, mar. William Henry King of Camelford. Bur.[6] 9th July 1867. Æt 70. ┬ ┴ | Caroline, bap.[6] 8th Aug. 1799,[6] mar.[6] Samuel James Evans of St. Breoke, 25th April 1825. | William Phillips, bap.[6] 19th Nov. 1795, bur.[6] 7th Nov. 1798. | Charles, bap.[6] 28th Oct. 1801, bur.[6] 23rd May 1815. Æt 14. | Ann, bap.[6] 21st Oct. 1804. Mar.[6] 5th Nov. 1832. William Shilson of Launceston. ┬ ┴ | William Dinham,═...... bap. 12th July   relict of 1803. Emigrated   ...... to Australia, and   Harvey, died there s.p. |

| Eliza, born 5th Jan. 1790. Bap.[8] Mar. John Pearce of Camelford, living 1874. | Charles, born 1st Mar. 1794, bap.[9] Master of Bancroft's School, Mile End, London. Died there cir. 1853. William, born 6th Dec. 1791, bap.[8] Died Dec. 1873, at Manchester. | Edmund, born 10th June 1796, bap.[5] liv. 1874. | ═Margaretta═Elizabeth Mary, dau. of   dau. of ...... John   Chambers, mar. Pearce of   21st Sept. 1874, Camelford,   at Keppel Street July 1st   Baptist Chapel. 1821. Died 27th July 1872. | John, born 11th Aug. 1798, bap.[9] mar. twice. Died cir. 1853. ┬ ┴ | Sarah, born 9th July 1800, bap.[9] died 9th March 1809. Bur. at Hockley, co. Essex. |

---

³ At St. Kew.   ⁴ At Blisland.   ⁵ At Advent.   ⁶ At Lanteglos.   ⁷ At Bodmin.

⁸ At St. Andrew's, Holborn, London.   ⁹ At St. Giles in the Fields, London.

OF DINHAM.

Philip Dinham, born 17th, bap.[4] 30th Nov. 1671.	Ann, bap.[4] 29th Sept. 1674.	Elizabeth, bap.[4] 21st Aug. 1676, bur.[4] 25th June 1677.	William Dinham, bap.[4] 29th Jan. 1677, named in father's will. Of Tresinney in Advent. Bur.[5] 7th Jan. 1742.	=Mary dau. of .... Bur.[5] 27th April 1750.

Anne, bap.[5] 3rd Nov. 1719, bur.[5] 8th Nov. 1755.	Jane, mar.[5] 7th Feb. 1733, Mr. Hugh Prideaux.	Mary, mar. John Rowe of Lanteglos, mar. lic. 1st July and mar.[5] 30th Sept. 1731.	Philip Dinham held a thirty-eighth part in Tresinney in 1742.

Jane, bap.[6] 31st March 1768, bur.[5] 26th July 1808, unmar.	Charles, bap.[6] 14th Sept. 1770, bur.[5] 14th May 1772.	Charles Dinham, bap.[6] 30th May 1775 Mayor of Camelford 1810, 1816, 1820, 1824, 1831, bur. 25th Jan. 1839. Æt 63.	=Elizabeth, dau. of .... Taylor, mar. 17th May 1802, bur.[6] 14 May 1846.	Rebecca dau. of John Jones of Eagle St., Holborn, Mar. 23rd April 1789, at St. George the Martyr, Queen Square.	=Edmund Dinham, bap.[6] 2nd July 1765. Of Newton in St. Kew. Bur.[5] 18th Aug. 1831, M.I.	=Ann, dau. of George Green of Brentford. Mar. 17th Feb. 1814, at St. George's, Bloomsbury. Bur.[5] 25th July 1860. M.I.

Sarah, bap. 16th Nov. 1804, mar. 2nd June 1826, John Lukey of London.	Mary, bap. 13th July 1806, mar. ...... Windsor of	Barbara, bap.[6] 3rd April 1808, bur.[6] 5th April 1808.	Charles =.... dau. of Dinham, ... Taylor bap.[6] 9th of Lancast. April 1809.	James, bap. 24th Nov. 1811, bur.[6] 19th Jan. 1813, aged 15 months.	John Hocken Codrington Wharton, bap.[6] 27th Dec. 1814.

Joseph, born 26th April 1802, mar. Anna, dau. of .... Pritchard of Gray's Inn Lane. Died cir. 1872.	Jane, born 2nd Mar. 1804, bap.[9] Mar. F. E. Trush, Surgeon. living at Hobart Town, 1874, a widow. Henry, b. 10th June 1806, bap.[9] Died 2nd May 1810. Bur.[9]	George, born 22nd Aug. 1808, bap.[9] living at Hobart Town 1874.	=Elizabeth, dau. of .... Linney of Pimlico, London.	Anna Sophia, born 10th Dec. 1814, bap.[9] living unmar. 1874.	Sarah Lucy, born 9th Aug. 1816, bap.[9] living unmar. 1874.	Mary Rebecca, born 25th April 1818, bap.[9] mar. Robert Anderson. Died 1872.

---

[3] At St Kew.   [4] At Blisland.   [5] At Advent.   [6] At Lanteglos.   [7] At Bodmin.

[8] At St. Andrew's, Holborn, London.   [9] At St. Giles in the Fields, London.

PRIDEAUX.

In our memoir of the family of Prideaux (ante p. 206), we have given some account of William Prideaux of Trevose, second son of Humphry Prideaux of Theuborough, and of his descendants by Johanna daughter of John Munday of Rialton, brother of the last Prior of Bodmin. Since that account was published we have discovered evidence, as well by the will of William Prideaux himself, dated 25th June 1564,[1] as by certain proceedings in Chancery, to shew that we were correct in our conjecture that Richard Prideaux of St. Issey was the second son of the aforesaid William. These discoveries, and the result of further researches, enable us to present to our readers a more full pedigree than appears ante pp. 223 and 225.

Richard Prideaux died in 1625, leaving, besides daughters, two sons, William Prideaux of St. Issey and John. Of the latter we are unable to give any further account, unless he was the same John Prideaux of Bodmin, Gent., who died in 1686 intestate, and administration to whose effects, on 30th August in that year, was granted to Elizabeth Prideaux, spinster, his daughter, his relict, Sussanna, having renounced.

William Prideaux left several children, of whom John married and had issue, baptized at St. Issey; and William, baptized at St. Issey on 19th October 1628, who was probably identical with William Prideaux, whom we find about 1670, settled in Camelford, and who was one of the burgesses who signed the indentures returning the burgesses to Parliament in the year 1679, and was mayor of that borough in 1698. He died in 1705, leaving several children. James Prideaux son of William was mayor in 1716. He had also many children. William, his eldest son, married in 1728, Elizabeth daughter of John Nation, Vicar of St. Kew, and had grandchildren baptized at Lanteglos after 1760. James Prideaux, described as of Camelford, Gent., whom we suppose to have been another son of the abovenamed James, died in 1765, when administration of his effects was granted to his son Edmund Prideaux of Hatton Garden, London, watchmaker, which Edmund, in 1745, had taken to wife Elizabeth daughter of William Dinham of Tresinney in Advent, by whom he appears to have had a daughter named Elizabeth who was buried at St. Andrew's Holborn, in 1753. Edmund Prideaux survived until 1796. Edmund Prideaux of the Inner Temple, and afterwards of Hexworthy, on the fly leaf of a family Bible, under the date of 30th September in that year, records the death of his ever dear friend and kinsman, Richard Coffin, Esq., formerly Bennett, and on the following day we find the entry "dyed his worthy ffriend and namesake Edmund Prideaux of Hatton Garden." Adding: "It was the pleasure of Almighty God to take two such dear ffriends within 14 hours of each other. His will be done." Elizabeth, widow of Edmund Prideaux, was buried in Advent Church, 30th August 1797.

---

[1] Proved at Exeter, Old Book of Copies of Wills, proved in the Court of Bishop's Peculiars.

PEDIGREE OF PRIDEAUX OF TREVOSE AND ST. ISSEY.

TABLE I.

William Prideaux, will dated 25th June 1564,=Johanna, dau. of John
to be buried in the Church of St. Petroc of │ Munday of Rialton.
Padstow, see ante p. 223.

John Prideaux,=Anne.	Richard Prideaux, bur.[2] 3rd=Jane, dau. of	Catherine, named	Another
son and heir, │ Dead in	Aug. 1625. Will prov. │ execx. to her husband,	in her father's	daugh-
born 1547, │ 1603.	29th Aug. 1625, Exon. │ bur.[2] 30th Aug. 1639.	will as married.	ter.
living 1615.			

John Prideaux,*=Abigail,	Grace,?	William =Eleanor,	John =Alice dau.	Mary, nam.	Elizabeth,
born before │ dau. of	mar.[4]	Prideaux │ dau. of	Prid- │ of Swim-	in father's	named in
1583, bur.[4] │	John	of St. Issey, │	eaux, │ mor, Bur.[2]	will.	fathers
15th May │ bur.[2] 20th	Threner,	named in │ Langdon	named │ 18th June		will. Bur.[2]
1633. │ Dec.	25th	father's │ mar.[3] 1st	in │ 1659,Adm°	Richard,	4th Dec.
│ 1653.	Nov.	will. Admo. │ May	fath's. │ to husband	bap.[4] 20th	1641.
		1611.	to Relict │ 1619.	will. │ 1659.	April	
			15th Feby. │	│ P.C.C.	1606.	
			1641.			

Elizabeth, bap.	Richard,	Richard Prid-	Joan =John Prid-=Eliza-	William, bap. 19th	Edith,
at St. Merryn	bap.[4] 5th	eaux, bap.[2] July	Gros, │ eaux, bap.[2] │ beth.	Oct. 1628. Probably	bap.[2]
10th Sept. 1617.	Nov.	1620.	mar. │ 25th July │ Bur.[2]	WILLIAM PRIDEAUX	19th
Bur. there the	1615.		1660. │ 1624. │ 22nd	OF CAMELFORD.	Nov.
same month.		Elizabeth, bap.[2]	│ │ Sept.	(See following	1630.
		March 1622.	│ │ 1653.	Pedigree.)	

Mary, bap.[2] 17th	John Prideaux, bap.[2] 12th June
Oct. 1648.	1651. ? Mr. John Prideaux, bur.
	at Lanteglos, 20th Jan. 1722.

---

[2] At St. Issey.   [3] At St. Mabyn.   [4] At Padstow.

* John Prideaux, Junior, Gent., and Abigail his wife (the said John Prideaux being son and heir apparent of John Prideaux, Senior, Esq.,) had licence to alienate the Manors of Trewosal and Treburthick to Humphry Prideaux his heirs and assigns, April 1st 1615. Rot. Pat., 13th James, Part 33, No. 39.

PEDIGREE OF PRIDEAUX OF CAMELFORD.

TABLE II.

Elizabeth, dau. of=William Prideaux of Camelford, Mayor of Camelford, 1689, 1695. Signed Parl. Indres.=Loveday.
...... bur.[5] 7th 1679, 1700. Will dated 10th April 1705. Prov. 22nd Jan. 1705. Archd. Cornw. Bur.[5] 5th
Mar. 1729. May 1705. [? Of St. Mabyn in 1662, as Agent or Steward of Sir William Godolphin]
(Chanc. Proceed. "Whitington," B. and A. Trinity 1662. Prideaux v. Bennett).

William Prideaux Bur.[5] 24th Sept. 1685.	James Prideaux of Camelford=Susanna, dau. of	Grace, named in father's will. mar.[5] 7th Aug.1703, Humphry Westlake.	Loveday named in father's will.	Margaret named in father's will.	Johanna, bap[5] 12th Feb.1667 named in father's will. mar.[5] 20th May 1690. NicholasDennithorne.	Francis, bap[5] 27th April 1671, bur.[5] 1st April 1677.

James Prideaux of Camelford Signed Parl. Indres. 1700, 1702, 1703, 1705, 1708, 1714. Mayor 1716. Bur.[5] 2nd July 1725. Admo. granted to Susanna his relict 22nd Oct. 1725. Executor to his father.=Susanna, dau. of .... .. Angow, mar. 8th May 1698. Admo. to Edmund Prideaux her son and one of the next of kin, 13th Jan. 1762, P.C.C.

William Prideaux of Camelford, bap.[5] 25th June 1699. Bur.[5] 3rd July 1765.=Elizabeth, dau. of John Nation, Vicar of St. Kew. Mar. lic. 24th June 1727. Mar.[5] 4th April 1728. Bur.[5] 30th March 1771. (See Ped. of NATION ante vol. ii, p. 266.)	Elizabeth, bap.[4] 23rd March 1706 bur.[5] 13th April 1728. John Elliott.	Edmond, bap[5] 4th Dec. 1709, bur.[5] 16th June 1711. Mary. bap.[5] 25th Aug. 1711, bur.[5] 13th April 1788, unmar.	Edmond Prideaux, bap.[5] 2nd April 1713. Admo. to his mother 13th Jan. 1762. John, bap.[5] 1st Dec. 1700.	George, bap.[5] 20th Oct. 1714, bur.[5] 3rd April 1715. Susanna, bap.[5] 19th Sept. 1708, bur.[5] 23rd Dec. 1712.	Hugh, bap.[5] 12th Nov. 1705, mar.[4] 7th Feb. 1733, Jane dau. of William Dinham of Tresinney. Vide Ped. of DINHAM.	Richard, bap.[5] 8th May 1704, bur.[5] 25th April 1725.	James Prideaux of Camelford. Admo. granted 1765, to Edmond his son.

William, bap.[5] 18th Oct. 1729, bur.[5] 10th July 1730.	William, bap.[5] 11th July 1731.	James Prideaux, bap.[5] 19th Aug. 1733.	John Prideaux of Camelford, bap[5] 28th Oct. 1735. Signed Parl. Indres. 1790,1791,1796. Bur.[5] 10th Jan. 1802.=Susanna, dau. of James Mallett, of Lanteglos, bap.[5] 29th May 1733, mar.[5] 11th May 1761, Bur.[5] 6th Aug. 1807.	Johanna, bap.[5] 6th Sept. 1740.	Edmond Prideaux of Hatton Garden, Watchmaker. Admo. to his father. Died 1st Oct. 1796.=Elizabeth, dau. of William Dinham of Tresinney. Mar. lic. 20th Aug. 1745. Mar.[5] 2nd Sept. 1745. Bur. in Advent Church 30th Aug. 1797. Vide Ped. of DINHAM.

James Prideaux, bap.[5] 29th May 1762.	Ann, bap.[5] 5th Oct. 1763. Mar.[5] 23rd June, 1793, Richard Besanko.	Johanna, bap.[5] 1st Jan. 1766, mar.[5] 28th May 1793, Nicholas Burt of St. Stephen's by Launceston.	Elizabeth, Bur. at St. Andrew's, Holborn, 12th Nov. 1753.

[5] At Lanteglos.

APPENDIX I.

THE ASSESSIONINGE LANDS IN CORNWALL.[1]

Ducatus Cornubiæ
$\left\{\begin{array}{l}\end{array}\right.$
Breiffe colleccions concerninge those Manners of the Dutchie of Cornewall wch are comonly called assessionable, or Antient Dutchie.

SECTION I.

The said Manners are in Number xvij , viz., Rillaton, Stokeclimsland, Calstocke, Trematon, Liskeard, Restormell, Penknight, Penlyn, Tewington, Tibesta, Talskedie, Moreske, Helston in Kerrier, Tywarnhayle, Helston in Trigg, Penmayne, and Tyntagle; wthin which there have benne in former tymes three castles, j forrest, fiue parkes, and a Court of Escheqr for the Receivinge of the Revennewes and Triall of Sundry Causes wthin the sd Dutchie. And are called Antient Dutchie because they belonged vnto the Earldome of Cornewall before it was made a Dutchie.

v. 12th Elizabeth, Rott. Assess. et 40th, 44th Elizabeth vis. Asses.

Att this present All the Tennantes wthin the said severall Manners doe clayme a Customarie estate of Inheritance in such lands as are in theire severall Tenures from vij yeres to vij yeres, to them and their heires for ever ; and to pay such Rent & Fyne for the same as by this present is noted vpon theire heads in the Ascession Rolls, and noe fine where noe menccion is made of any in the said Rolls; and to pay one Heriott at the death of every Tennt though the same Tennt enioy six or more Tenementes which are Herietable, and there fine to be six yeres a payinge. They likewise affirme that they can comitt noe such Forfeiture whereby the duke may seize there lands, neither the said Duke make other Grant thereof then for vij yeres to vij yeres accordinge to the said Custome.

But by the Antient Records of the said Dutchie, and also diverse Records of Latter Tyme, the state of the said Manners appeareth to be in Manner followinge :

The said mannrs did consist of free Tenntes free Convencionarie Tenntes Bound Convencionarie Tenntes, Bond men in Bloud, or Villens, Tenntes for terme of life, and Lands remayninge in the Duke's handes vnlett, or, as the Terme is, vnassessed.

---

[1] From the Muniment Room, Coker Court, Somerset.

3 c

SECTION I.   The ffree Tenn^{tes} are such as enioy the land wch they hold of theise Mann^{rs} to them and theire heires by the Rents & Services particulerlie expressed.

v. 40 & 44 Rott. Assess., &c.   The free Convencionarie Tenn^{tes} (so called to distinguish them from the bond convencionarie) are such as hold theire estates by Covenant and agreem^t made wth the Duke's Commissioners, who were therefore called Assessers or Assessioners, because they did assesse and tax what Rent and ffine everie Tenn^t should pay. The most common kind of estate which they so tooke was for vij yeres, at thend whereof the said commission was new granted by the Duke, and it was at the Commissioners Choyce to decrease or increase the fine & Rent, and at the Tenn^{tes} pleasure to take and leave the Land. The Services whereby they held them, and wch are at this day mencioned in theire Takings, were Suite at Courte, performance of Offices w^{th}in the Mann^r, Carryinge of the Lord's letters, drivinge of distresses when they should be therevnto required by the bayliffe of the hundred in which they dwelt, repayringe of theire tenem^{tes}, and paym^t of an Heriott for everie tenem^t which they hold.

v. 7th Edw. III. 20th Hen. VIII, 45th Edw. III, 7th Hen. IV, Rott. Assess. in Manner deStokeclimsland, Talskedy, &c. 7th Edward III.   The bond Convencionarie Tenn^{tes} were such Bondmen, or Villeins, as tooke estates of the Commissioners at the Tyme of the assession, as the former Tenn^{tes} did for vij yeres or more. There services were such as those of the Tenn^{tes} bond in Bloud next followinge, only differinge in this that they hold theire estates at the Lord's will, and theise by Convencion and agreem^t.

3rd Edward III. &c.   The Tenn^{tes} bond in bloud are, as the Record calls them, Natiui de Stipite, were such as were villeines by descent, and so were there whole Race or sequela (as the record calls it). Theise had only an estate at the wille of the Duke in theire Tenem^{ts}, and did not pay any certaine some for theire Rent or fine by Convenccion or agreem^t, as the former; but sometymes more and sometymes lesse accordinge to theire abilitie, for both theire goods and bodies were the lord's. Theire Services were (besides those of the free Convencionarie Tenn^{tes} formerly mencioned) that they should not professe any sort, or set theire sonnes to schoole, nott marry theire daughters without the lords leaue first obtayned. That they should doe worke dayes vpon the Lord's Demeasne lands. That the Lord at theire death should haue all theire goods and theire youngest sonne should haue the Tenem^t & pay a fine for the same at the Lord's pleasure.

20h Hen. VIII. 27h Hen. VIII. 17h Hen. VIII.

3rd Edward III. 45th Edward III.   The Tenn^{tes} for life were such as either by Deed from the Duke or his Councell, or by takinge at the Assessiens, tooke an Estate for life.

7th Henry IV. Rott. Assess.   The Landes which remayned in the Lord's hands were such as no man would take at the former Rents, or ffines, and therefore, after the assession ended, they were either letten by the Steward, or bayliffe, to the duke's best profitt; or else the Reiue of the Manner remayned chardgable wth the yerelie valewe of them.

But nowe both the ffree Convencionarie Tenures and the bond (which seem to remayne accordinge to the old Tenure, though the Tenn^tes be enfranchised,) and all those Lands wch were granted for Terme of life, or of a greater or lesse number of yeres then vij, together wth all such as remayned in the Lord's hands at any Tyme, beinge Refused by the Tenn^tes themselues, or came by Escheate, fforfeiture, or Attainder, or were inclosed & taken in out of the Lord's Wastes, either by the appointm^t of the Comissioners or incrochm^t of the Tenn^tes, and Lord's Demeasne Lands w^thin the said Manner, except the parkes, are all claymed and enioyed by the Tenn^tes as theire Inheritance in a like Nature and by the same Custome.

The Custome of Settinge theise Lands from seuen yeres to vij yeres seemeth to haue had the first beginninge in the vijth yere of King Ed. 3, in the Tyme of John Eltham, brother to the same King Edward, and the Earle of Cornwall, which was aboute foure yeres before the ereccion of the said Earldome into a Dutchie, whose Comission to that purpose, because it proues most parte of that which is said before, I haue inserted the same verbatim as it is in the record.

Johan fils a noble Roy d'Angleterre Counte de Cornewall a toux Viccountes, Conestables, &c., Salut. come plusors de nos Tennantes de nostre seigneure de Cornewall, &c. Whereas sundry of our Tenn^tes of our Lordship of Cornewall haue longe tyme held in diverse Manners a greate quantitie of our Demeasne Lands in those partes be convencionarie estates, payinge for the same lands certain yerely Rents, and theire Termes do wholie expire at Michaelmas next followinge, as it is, and ought to be matter knowne in the Countrie; and albeit we might, w^thout doinge wronge to any manne, resume the said Lands into our hands, and make our best proffitt thereof, wch thinge perchaunce would turne to the disquiet and damage of our said Tenn^tes, We will, not-w^thstandinge soe theire case, that they by newe covenants hold the same Lands in a convencionarie estate, yet so that they yeild vnto vs the true valewe of them as shalbe agreed betweene them and our Ministers whome we send thither for that Cause. Thus we give ye^m all to vnderstand that we have by theise our letters attourned and put in our steed our deere and loved Batchelor Sr Richard Champernoun, and our deere Serv^tes John of Herland, Auditor of our Accompts, Richard of Bachampton, our Steward of Cornewall, and Thomas of Hockele, givinge full power to them fowre joyntlie, or to three of them, whereof the said John alwayes to be one, to assesse our Lands aforesaid, and to lease them in convencionarie estates by Indentures or Enroll-ments for Terme of life, liues, or yeres accordinge as they shall thinke meete vnto our Tenn^tes, who nowe hold our said Lands, or in theire defaults to others who will give vs more, and as it shalbe best for our profitt Ratefyinge and Confirminge whatsoever the said Sr Richard, John, Richard, & Thomas, &c., shall doe in our name in the matters aforesaid.

Pretextu quarum literarum dicti domini Ricardus, Johannes, Ricardus, et Thomas asserunt omnes terras infrascriptas per septennium proximo post

SECTION II.   dictum festum S. Michaelis tantum preter terras quas natiui tenent in villenagio vt de
Stipite, et non ultra, quia videbatur dictis assessoribus commodum domini fuisse
illa vice alterius illas dimisisse ex pluribus causis eisdem tunc apparentibus: et ex
aliquibus ipsarum causarum et aliis concesserunt quod quilibet eorum qui de dictis
terris sic recepit solvat de fine suo ea occasione faciendo terciam partem ad festum
paschæ, &c. Et super hoc omnes infrascripti ceperunt terras subscriptas per mensuram
aeræ Angliæ per eosdem mensuratas sed quilibet eorum suam particulam ex
precepto et monitione dictorum assessorum, &c. Ita quod si plus inueniatur in
tenementis que sic receperint de terris predictis ultra messuagium et dictam
mensuram acrarum illum superplusagium ad opus domini per Seneschallum
suum approprietur exceptis tenementis tentis in villenagio, &c. Et inceperunt
primo apud Helston in Kerrier in forma subscripta, viz.:

SECTION III.   Helston in Kerr xxxiiij Feb. An° 7° Ed. 3.
liberi conuen-   Ricardus de Glynn cepit unum messuagium xxxiij acrarum terræ vnde
tionarii.   viij acras prati in j parcela terræ quam Willelmus de Tresprisoun tenet in
fine lxiij viij   Tresprisoun. Tenendum in conuencionarie a festo Sancti Michaelis proximo futuro
post confeccionem presencium vsque ad finem vij annorum proximo sequentium
Reddendo inde per annum xx ad quat terminos vsuales equaliter, vnde de nouo
Incrementum iiij incremento iiij faciet sectam, &c. Et omnia alia seruicia secundum consue-
tudines conuencionales, &c. Et dabit domino de fine, &c., faciet fidelitatem,
&c., plegium, &c.

7 H. 4.   The same tenem in the seventh yere H. 4, was lett for xx
rent & xxxiij iiij fine, whereof vj viij was an increase of the
said fine more then was at the former assession.

5 E. 4.   The same tenem in the fifth yere of Ed. 4, remayned in y
Lord's hands, the rent beinge but xvj, and noe fine because no
man would take it.

27 H. 8.   The same Tenem in the 24th yere of H. 8 was let for xvij
rent and iiij acknowledgment, given by tennt to take it so:

40 Eliz.   The same Tenem in the xl[th] yere of the late Queenes Ma[tie]
which was the last assession, was let for xx rent and 26 8[d]
fine, and by that rent and fine it is nowe claymed as inheritance.

The like difference is to be found in all the Tenemt[s] within the said
xvij manners, yf the new and old takinge be compared together of the par-
ticulers, but it may be more easilie be guessed by comparcinge the Totall somes
of the said Manner, and thereby it may likewise appere how much is lost vnto
the King's Mat[ie] by the said Custome, so pretended, for that land which was
worth xij[d] in 7 Edw. 3, is now worth ten shillings, & yet the fines are
scarcelie the 4th parte of what they were then: for example the said manner
of Helston in Kerrier.

SECTION III.   7 E. 3.   In the vijth yere of Ed. 3, the rents of the said Manner were in all lxiij^{li} xv^s iij^d ob. qr., besides the rents of such Tenem^{ts} as remayned vnletten. The fines did in all amount vnto iiij^{xx} iiij^{li} vj^s viij^d

20 H. 8.   In the xxth yere of Hen. 8, the rents of the said Manner wth those things that remayned in the King's hands for want of takers, wch was above v^c acres, amounted but vnto xliij^{li} vj^s v^d, the fines none, and the old acknowledgm^t, which came instead of the fines, were but xvj^s ij^d.

19 Eliz.   In the xixth yere of Queene Elizab the rents of the said Manner were 45^{li} xij^s iij^d, the fines xxiiij^s ix^d, the old acknowledgm^t xvj^s ij^d

40 Eliz.   In the xlth yere of the said Queene the rents of the said Manners were 47^{li} xviij^s vj^d, the fines xxxiij^{li} vj^s x^d, and the old acknowledgm^t xvj^s ij^d.

SECTION IV.   Out of theise and other the like records there may be gathered these proffes ag^t the pretended Custome.

Clause 1.   That the lands and Tenem^{ts} wthin the said Manner are no Inheritance as the Tenn^{tes} nowe Clayme them : but may be sett to the Lord's best proffitt, and to whome he will.

7 E. 3.   The Commission of John Eltham before recited.

45 E. 3.   A Tenem^t granted vnto the Tenn^{tes} brother because the Tenn^t himselfe came not to the Assessions.

30 E. 3.   William de Levenhill tooke a Tenem^t by Deed of the prince for life which at the former Assession was taken for seven yeres by another.

vj H. 8.   Robert Walsh, the second sonne, tooke the Tenem^t in the life of his elder brother, because he came not.

7 H. 4.   The Commission granted vnto William Stourtonne and others by Hen. 5, then prince, gives them power to lease all his lands in the Countie of Cornewall to any Convenable & Sufficient persons for terme of life or yeres.

20 H. 8.   Walter Bohay, a straunger, tooke a Tenem^t wch Wm Cornish tooke in the former Sessions; the like in many more presidents in like nature.

9 Eliz.   A Tenem^t granted to the Deputie of the bayliffe Itinerant for his good service.

Clause 2.   That the Tenn^{tes} of these Seventeene Manners Cannot prescribe in an Estate from vij yeres to vij yeres, but that it is at the Duke's pleasure to grant any Estate to them for liues or yeres.

7 E. 3.   The Commission of John Eltham before recited.

3 D

SECTION IV.   45 E. 3.   Thomas Barton tooke a Tenem^t for Terme of life by Deed from the prince. Climsland, this is now Customarie Inheritance.

          5 E. 4.   The Tenm^{tes} of the Manner of Restormell & Penlyn parte leased for xxi yeres and parte for vij yeres.

          45 E. 3.   The Commission directed to the Assessioners gaue them power to lease the princes land in Cornewall & Devon for Terme of life or yeres, and to put the fines of such Tenem^{tes} as they should lease for life, and which were formerlie letten for seven yeres, amonge other Rents yerelie payable to them, no Tenn^t might alien his Tenem^t wthout license, And that yf the Reiue were behind for the space of a moneth after the Terme assigned, and no Sufficient distresse, it might be lawfull for the prince and his heires to enter.

          45 E. 3.   The Rentes of iiij^{or} Tenn^{tes} for life were xij^s vj^d and theire fines xx^{li}

          30 E. 3.   xxx^{li} made of Tenem^{tes} letten for Terme of life.

                        iij^{or} mess: & 90 acres taken for life of the princes Councell were enioyed as Customary Inheritance, beinge parte of the Demeasnes of the Manner of Calstock.

          45 E. 3.   The Tenem^t of a Tenn^t for life granted vnto another for vij yeres, wth a Clause of Redemption yf the Tenn^t for life would come & pay his fine wthin a half a yere.

          1 H. 4.   There are fewe Assessions before his tyme wherein some Estates for life are not granted.

          38 E. 3.   A Tenem^t leased for life in 36 Ed. 3, by the rent of xxij^s after the death of that Tenn^t for life was let vntill the next Assession for 28^s Rent, & the Increm^t of v^s ix^d sett downe.

Clause 3.   That thestates so graunted doe determyne at thend of seven yeres and are noe Estates of Inheritance.

          7 E. 3.   The grants made by the Commissioners at that tyme.

          9 Eliz.   A condicion that the Tenn^t should leave his Customary Tenem^t sufficientlie repayred at thend of his terme.

          18 H. 8.   The same condicion in grant of 2 mils.

          45 E. 3.   The Tenn^t would not pay a heriott because yf he died wthin vij yeres for which he tooke it the lord should have his Tenem^t againe.

Clause 4.   That the Rents and fines were not Certaine but might be either increased or abated at the pleasure of the Duke or his Comissioners, as they sawe Cause.

          17 H. 8.   The Mill of Tywarnehaile was let at the Assessions, Redditus viij^s iiij^d et ante non fuit nisi iij^s et Tempore Ed. 3. 26^s 8^d

SECTION IV.

Tibesta.

John Tregian tooke iiij^{xx} acres for ix^s wch was before x^s Rent which all the Tenn^{tes} tooke in the fformer Assession.

7 H. 4.

The Increase of the ffines in Rillaton, one of the smallest Manners, was iiij^{li} xvij^s vj^d

19 Eliz.
Rott. 14.

A Tenem^t let for vij yeres by the Rent of xx^s, which was demeasne land and leased for life by the Rent of xxvij^s

26 Eliz.

The Mill of Tyntagle let for cvj^s viij^d which, in the xixth yere Eliz. remayned in her Maties hand, & 27° H. 8, there was only xxiij^s Rent paid for it.

44 Eliz.

A ffine newlie Imposed one the Tenn^t at the Assession, whereas none was paid before

viz. : assess. fol. 16, before.

45 E. 3.

The ffine was decreased vj^s viij^d because some straunger for mallice had made an Increase at the last assession.

7 E. 3.
45 E. 3.
30 E. 3.
7 H. 4, &c.

All the Antient Records doe set downe increase of Rents and ffines and decrease of them at everie Assession, And yf the Rent were abated they shewe a reason for it, as the povertie of the Tenn^t, or such like.

Molendiuum de Wallen, Mollendinum de Porthmelyn, Landa de Wallyn quæ continet clx acras vastum et pasturam in bosco quam Willelmus de Pafford nuper tenuit sicut continet' in extento vnde reddere solebat per annum iiij^{li} xiij^s iiij^d per parcell, nondum dimittit' quia tenentur ad totum nec ad parcell eiusdem pro tanto Redditum adhuc invenire potuerunt eo quod dicta terra et predictum Molendinum fuit totum crematum Molendinum multum debilitatum vt dicit' &c. Ideo dimittat' per seneschallum meliori modo, &c., sin autem prepositus de exitibus oneret' &c.

Clause 5.

That it is the Duke's pleasure and in the discretion of his Comissioner to let the said Landes vnto the Tenn^{tes} vnder what Condiciones & Limitacions they please.

10 Eliz.

All the Estates of the Manner of Helston in Kerr^r granted vpon Condicion of repayringe, and also on the Condicion yf the Lord Treasurer and Chauncell^r of thexcheq^r should like of it.

20 H. 8.

A Tenem^t letten vpon Condicion the Tenn^t should repaire, dwell, and keepe hosspitallitie vpon it, vpon paine of fforfeitur of the said Tenem^t, and for more. And that yf he died wthout heire of hes bodie lawfullie begotten it should remayne to William Wrey vnder the same Condicion.

9 Eliz.
Tywarn-
hayle.

A Condicion that yf the Tenn^t should refuse to pay for a quarry the Queene might enter into all other the Tenem^{ts} wch the same Tenn^t held wthin that Manner.

9 Eliz.

A Condicion to Re-edyfie, and another Condicion that the Tenn^t should cut downe noe Trees sub Pena fforisfacturœ.

SECTION IV.   9 Eliz.   A Condicion That the Tenn* should build a newe house.

             3 E. 3.   A Covenant that the Tenn* should repaire his Mill.

            19 Eliz.   A provisoe that the Tenn* should not alien his Customary Tenem* to any other then to his owne heire.

            7 H. 4.   The Tenn* bound to build a newe house vpon paine of
Tibesta.   fforfeiture of the Tenem* & 40ˢ more.

   Clause 6.   That for breach of the said Condicions, or vpon Attaind', the Tenn* doth forfeite his Customarie estate & the duke may lawfullie enter.

           19 Eliz.   A Tenem* forfeited because the Tenn* did not dwell vpon his Customary holdinge, & did set the same to a straung' by Indenture, & the same letten at the Assessions to one Bawdon by a newe Rent and a new ffine.

           19 Fliz.   Two Tenem*ᵗᵉˢ & xxvj acres of land let by Custome wᶜʰ came
Rott. 9, 6.   by Attaind' of a Customarie Tenn* in 4 Mar.

           19 Eliz.   Two Tenem*ᵗᵉˢ not taken at the Assession but stayed by Sir
Rott. 3.   Walter Mildmaye's letter, because the Tenn*, one hellier, had forfeited them.

           20 H. 8.   The Customary Terme forfeited & let to another.
Restormell.

           Ibm.   A Tenem* forfeited for lettinge it to diverse ⎱ Nanslo
Helston in   persons.   ⎰ Grigory.
Kerrier.

           29 H. 8.   Thomas Skelton forfeited his Tenem* for Sellinge xij trees &
Trematon.   was admitted again vpon a newe fine.

           Ibm.   John Thomas tooke two Mills forfeited by William Serritoe, because the said William had leased them for xiiij yeres.

           Ibm.
Helston in   John Hayne forfeited his Tenem* for digginge of Tynn vpon
Kerrier.   the same without the King's license.

      Prince Edward grants a Comission so sundry persons to assesse his landes in Cornewall and Devon for Term of life or yeres, & to put the fines of such Tenem*ᵗᵉˢ as they should let for life, and which were formerlie wont to be let for vij yeres amongst other Rents payable yerelie to thend no man might alien his Tenem* wᵗʰout license; and that yf the Reiue were behind for the space of one Month after any the Termes assigned, and noe sufficient distresse, it might be lawfull for the sᵈ Prince & his heires to enter.

   Clause 7.   Lastlie; There are ffewe Tenem*ᵗᵉˢ wᵗʰin all the said Manners, wᶜʰ have not bean either leased for life or remayned in the Duke's hand for want of Takers, or Escheated, or forfeited vnto the lord, or newlie taken in out of the wasts, as may appeare by perusall of the Records, and though there were a Custome for the rest yet for theis it is gone.

Section IV.   5 E. 4.   There remayned above ij^m v^c acres of the Manners of Helston in Kerrier, beinge severall Groundes in the lordes handes because the same would not be taken at the Old Rents, and in sundry other Manners at the same Tyme a greate Quantitie.

Section V.   The Inconveniencies arysinge by reason of the said Custome & the Losse vnto his Matie are these:

Clause 1.   The losse of the Inheritance Claymed by the Ten^{tes} by Collour of the said Custome, the same beinge worth above the Rate of xxx^{ti} yeres purchase of the rent.

Clause 2.   The smalenes of the ffines and Casualties wch doe hardlie equall the some of halfe the Rents of Assize Communibus Annis, whereas in other lands in the same Countrie the Casuall profitts doe double & trebble the some of the Rents Communibus Annis, and theise Manners are very lowe rented.

Clause 3.   The Tenn^{tes} of the said Manners doe pretend That they, by virtue of there Custome, doe wthout the Lord's licence (payinge only a small some vnto him for an acknowledgment), may surrender any parte of theire Tenem^t vnto a Straunger, wherevpon followeth the dismembering of the Tenem^t and decay of the dwellinge house, and a generall povertie amongst theise Tenn$^{ts.}$

Clause 4.   The tenn^t so surrendringe (that he may make the Greater some in present,) dischardgeth the whole Rent out of that which remayneth in his handes, wherevppon the purchaser, in short tyme (yf he have land adioyninge) ioynes it to his owne land, and Claymes it as his Inheritance.

Clause 5.   One Tenn^t havinge gotten sundrie Tenem^{tes} in his hand setteth the same without licence, to sondry Tenn^{tes}, as his owne ffee simple, Callinge it his Manner, and taketh sondrie heriots of the Tenn^{ts} payinge but one himselfe to the Lord.

Section VI.   The Casuall Profitts and Benefits which his Matie may haue out of the said Manners as the Custome nowe standeth are theise:

Clause 1.   The ffines and Tallages accordinge as they are set downe in the Table next followinge, taken out of the Records, wherein all the Casuall profitts are also ioyned in one some payable in vj yeres by equall porcions, the vijth yere free.

Clause 2.   The old Recognitions or acknowledgm^{tes} paid by ye Tenn^{tes} as a guift, or gratuitie, for takinge there Tenem^{tes} w in the aforesaid Manner: vizt, from vij yeres to vij yeres. This is a very small some & certain & begunn as it

9 Hen. 5, Hel-   seemeth in the Tyme of H. 5.
ston in Trigge.

Clause 3.   The newe Recognition, or acknowledgm^t, is double ye rent & the fine vpon every Surrender, to be paid wthin three yeres next after the Assessions. This some is almost as much as the ffines, and was just begunn, as it seemes, in the Tyme of H. 8, but it was not then as much as it is nowe.

3 E

SECTION VI.   The Revennewe of the s^d Manners in the xliij^th yere or (sic) her late Maties Raigne, when as all theise profits and Casualties were answered together wth the Rents, did amount vnto vij^c xxiij^li xiij^s vj^d ob.

The Revennewe of the said Manners, Consistinge only of rents and perquisites and noe fines, or other Casuall proffits as they were answered vnto the late prince in the viij^th yere of his Maties Reigne, did amount vnto the some of v^c xxxj^li xi x^d qr.

I have added a Table wherein are set downe the present Rentes compared wth those that were answered in the vij yere of King E. 3., & all the Casuall proffits as they are nowe answered, compared wth the fines made then. And lastlie what the said ffines and casualties doe amount vnto in yerely proffitt Comunibus Annis.

Manor.	Reddus ano xliij° Eliz.			Reddus ano vij E. 3.			ffines & Recog. dict. An° xliij			ffines & Tallag. dc° an° vij° E. 3			valor. Coibz. annis casual.			ffines an° xliij° Eliz.		
	li.	s.	d.	li.	s.	d.	li.	s.	d.	li.	s.	d.	li	s.	d.	li.	s.	d.
Rillaton	vj	ix	v	iiij	x	xj	xxviij	xiiij	viij	vj	x	x	iiij	ij	j	xxiij		xvj
Climsland ..	xix	viij	v ob.	..		..	cciiij	xviij	x	..		..	xxix	v	vj ob.	cxliiij	iiij	ix
Helston in Trigge	xlv	iiij	ix ob.	xxxvij		xvij	cviij	viij	viij ob.	lxi	xviij	viij	xv	ix	vj ob.	lxxj	v	ij
Liskeard	xxx	xij	xi	..		..	clxij	vij	vj	..		..	..		..	clxij	vij	vj
Tibesta	xxvij	x	x	xxiij	ix	j	lx	xvij	iiij ob.	lxv	xij	ii	..		..	xxvij	x	vij ob.
Tywarnhayle ..	xiij	vij	iiij	xiij	iiij	ii	xj	xij	vij	xviij	ix		..		..	lxxix		ix
Talskedie ..	lxxiij	vi		lxviij			lxix	iiij		lxxiiij			..		..	lx		
Polmeane ..	cxi	x		lxv	viij		ix	xiij	vij	iiij	xiij	x	..		..	vj	viij	iiij
Calstocke ..	xliij	ij	ix ob.	xxj	v	xi	ccxij	x	vij ob.	lxvij		i	..		..	lxxx	xj	j
Trematon ..	xxx	v	vj	xxxj	xj	vij	cxxxvj	vij	2 ob.qr	lxxxiiij		xvj	..		..			18 ob.qr
Restormell ..	vj	viij	iiij	vj	xvj	ix	iiij	iiij	v	xxxij		viij	..		..		iiij	viij
Penkneth ..	iiij	iij	x		xlij	vj		ij	iiij	iiij	vj	viij	..		..		ij	
Penlyne	v	xv	viij	vj	iij	iiij		cxij		vj	x	iiij	..		..		vj	viij
Tewington ..	xxij	xij	v ob.	xxj	xix	x ob.	xxij	iij		xxx	vij	vj	..		..	xix	xv	
Helston in Kerr	xlvj	xiiij	ix	lxiij	viii	vij ob.	cxj	ix	vj ob.	lxxxiiij	xvj	viij	..		..	xxxiij	vj	x
Tintagle	xxxj	ix	ix	xxv	ij	iij	xxxj	iiij	vj	l		viij	..		..	xx	xvij	vj ob.
Moreske ..	xxiij	v	xj	xxx	ij		xx	x	viij	xxxj	j	vij	..		..	vj	viij	

The some of the Rents of the Customary Tenn^tes only as they are now paid } ccclxvj^li xviij^s

The some of the ffines of the same Tent^tes as they were answered in 43 E. is } c^v xx iiij^li vij^s viij^d x

The some of the Casuall proffits except perquisites of the ⎱ xj^c $xliiij^{li}$ vij^s x^d qr.
same Manners dewe accordinge to the s^d Custome is   ⎰

The said Casualle proffits beinge equallie Rated Communibus ⎱ $clxiij^{li}$ ix^s $viij^{d.}$ ob.
             Annis doe amount vnto ⎰

The said Record of **vij** Ed. 3 was defaced & worne out in the places where the Rents of Climsland & Liskeard were set downe.

APPENDIX II.

Walter Bodulgate's Charter for the Endowment of a Chantry in the Chapel of St. Thomas the Martyr at Camelford. The original is now in the possession of John Jope Rogers of Penrose, Esq., who has kindly collated with it this impression.

Omnibus Christi fidelibus præsens scriptum indentatum visuris vel audituris Walterus Bodulgate salutem. Sciatis me præfatum Walterum dedisse concessisse et hoc præsenti scripto meo confirmasse Johanni Jaybien et Stephano Trenewith omnia messuagia terras et tenementa mea redditus et servicia ac reverciones omnium tenencium meorum in Mochiltrewynt Tresterlek Torre et Algarsmylle in parochia de Seint Athwanne et Southertrewordra in parochia de Egleshaille cum omnibus suis pertinentiis habenda et tenenda omnia prædicta messuagia terras tenementa redditus et servicia ac reverciones cum omnibus suis pertinentiis præfatis Johanni et Stephano et eorum assignatis ad terminum vitæ mei præfati Walteri absque impeticione vasti seu vexatione aut perturbatione aliquali de capitalibus dominis feodorum illorum per redditus et servicia inde debita et de jure consueta ita quod post mortem mei præfati Walteri volo et concedo quod omnia prædicta messuagia terræ tenementa redditus et servicia ac reversiones cum omnibus suis pertinentiis integre remaneant Thomæ Bodulgate et hæredibus de corpore suo exeuntibus tenenda de capitalibus dominis feodorum illorum per redditus et servicia inde debita et de jure consueta sub modo forma et condicione subsequentibus videlicet quod idem Thomas et heredes de corpore suo exeuntes post mortem mei præfati Walteri infra annum ex tunc proximum sequentem de exitibus et proficuis ex messuagiis terris tenementis redditibus et serviciis ac reversionibus prædictis cum pertinentiis annuatim pervenientibus inveniant sustentent et manuteneant unum Capellanum idoneum cotidie missam in Capella Sancti Thomæ Martyris apud Camelford celebraturum pro anima mei dicti Walteri necnon animabus parentum antecessorum et benefactorum meorum et animabus omnium et singulorum quorum nomina patebunt in quadam parva tabula sive cedula super altum altare in dicta capella ponenda sive erigenda qui quidem capellanus missam suam ad altare prædictum cotidie secundum usum Sarum seu aliam missam secundum ejus discrecionem dicet et celebrabit hoc semper excepto et proviso quod quolibet die Mercurii per annum missam de Requiem ac Placebo et Dirige cum commendatione animarum et oratione Absolve quæsumus Domine pro animabus prædictis una cum psalmo De profundis cotidie pro eisdem animabus ad missam vel immediate post missam in capella prædicta dicet nisi causa rationabilis et specialis de præmissis se rationabiliter excusari poterit. Et prædictus Thomas et hæredes sui prædicti præfato capellano qui pro tempore fuerit annuatim ad omnia supradicta divina obsequia et servicia bene et fideliter celebranda dicenda et observanda septem marcas legalis monetæ Angliæ de exitibus et proficuis supradictis pervenientibus ad quatuor anni terminos principales videlicet ad festa Nativitatis Domini Paschæ Nativitatis Sancti Johannis Baptistæ et Sancti Michaëlis Archangeli equis porcionibus dabunt solvent et satisfacient. Et si probatum vel inventum fuerit aliquo tempore futuro coram Rectore Ecclesiæ parochiæ de Lanteglis qui pro tempore fuerit quod prædictus capellanus pro tempore ut præmittitur existens missas suas et obsequias ut predictum est pro animabus prædictis non celebraverit nec dixerit et predicta omnia non observaverit absque causa rationabili tunc sex denarii sterlingorum de salario ipsius capellani qui pro tempore fuerit per dictum Thomam aut heredes suos predictos abbregientur et fabricæ dictæ Capellæ dentur et solventur et hoc totiens quotiens hujusmodi Capellanus defectivus in premissis seu aliquo præmissorum inventus fuerit, proviso semper quod hujusmodi Capellanus qui ad altare predictum in forma prædicta celebrabit nominetur eligatur et ordinetur per prædictum Thomam et heredes suos prædictos totiens quotiens necesse fuerit. Et post mortem ipsius Thomæ et hæredum suorum prædictorum vel si contingat ipsum Thomam sine hærede de corpore suo exeunte obire vel si contingat dictum Thomam aut hæredes suos prædictos in inventione sustentatione manutencione et ordinacione dicti capellani in forma prædicta aut in observatione perimpletione et sustentatione omnium et singulorum onerum præmissorum seu eorum alicujus deficere abbreviare minuere seu ea minime perimplere prout superius dictum et declaratum est Tunc ego præfatus Walterus volo et concedo per præsentes quod status ipsius Thomæ et hæredum suorum prædictorum in prædictis messuagiis terris tenementis reddititibus et serviciis ac revercionibus cum pertinentiis omnino et totaliter cesset et pro nullo habeatur. Et quod tunc omnia prædicta messuagia terræ tenementa redditus et servicia ac reverciones cum omnibus suis pertinentiis integre sint et remaneant Thomæ Rescarrek et Isabellæ uxori ejus et hæredibus de corpore Isabellæ legitime exeuntibus. Et quod iidem Thomas Rescarrek et Isabella et hæredes de corpore ipsius Isabellæ legitime exeuntes in omnibus messuagiis terris tenementis reddititibus et serviciis ac revercionibus supradictis poterint intrare et seisire et ea pacifice retinere absque reclamatione seu perturbatione prædicti Thomæ Bodulgate aut hæredum suorum prædictorum Tenenda de capitalibus dominis feodorum illorum per redditus et servicia inde debita et de jure consueta sub modo forma et condicione supradictis scilicet quod iidem Thomas Reskarrek et Isabella et hæredes de corpore ipsius Isabellæ exeuntes unum capellanum idoneum missas et alia divina, et obsequia ut prædictum est faciendo et celebrando invenient sustentabunt et manutenebunt ac omnia et singula onera præmissa prout superius declaratum et expressatum est de et cum reddititibus exitibus et proficuis ex messuagiis terris tenementis reddititibus et serviciis ac revercionibus supradictis pervenientibus quolibet anno bene et fideliter in forma prædicta observabunt facient invenient solvent et perimplebunt. Et si contingat dictos Thomam Rescarrek et Isabellam sine hærebibus de corpore ipsius Isabellæ legitime exeuentibus obire vel si contingat præfatos Thomam Rescarrek et Isabellam aut hæredes de Corpore ipsius Isabellæ legitime exeuentes in inventione sustentatione manutencione et ordinacione prædicti Capellani in forma prædicta aut in observatione perimplecione et sustentacione omnium et singulorum onerum præmissorum seu eorum alicujus deficere abbreviare minuere seu ea minime perimplere prout superius dictum et declaratum est Tunc ego præfatus Walterus volo et concedo per præsentes quod status prædictorum Thomæ Reskarrek et Isabellæ et heredum de corpore ipsius Isabellæ exeuntium omnino et totaliter cesset et pro nullo habeatur. Et quod tunc omnia prædicta messuagia terræ tenementa redditus et servicia ac reverciones cum omnibus suis pertinentiis integre sint et remaneant Edwardo Coryton et Johannæ uxori ejus et heredibus de corpore ipsius Johannæ legitime exeuntibus. Et quod iidem Edwardus et Johanna et heredes de corpore ipsius Johannæ legitime exeuntes in omnibus messuagiis terris tenementis redditibus et serviciis ac revercionibus supradictis poterint intrare seisire et ea pacifice retinere absque reclamatione seu perturbatione prædicti Thomæ Rescarrek et Isabellæ aut hæredum suorum prædictorum Tenenda de capitalibus dominis feodorum illorum per reddittus et servicia inde debita et de jure consueta sub modo forma et condicione supradictis scilicet quod iidem Edwardus et Johanna et heredes de corpore ipsius Johannæ legitime exeuntes unum capellanum idoneum missas ac alia divina et obsequia ut prædictum est facienda et celebranda invenient sustentabunt et manutenebunt ac omnia et singula onera præmissa prout superius dictum et declaratum est de et cum redditibus exitibus et proficuis ex messuagiis terris tenementis redditibus et serviciis ac revercionibus supradictis pervenientibus quolibet anno bene et fideliter in forma prædicta observabunt facient invenient solvent et perimplebunt. Et si contingat præfatos Edwardum et Johannam sine heredibus de corpore ipsius Johannæ legitime exeuntibus obire vel si contingat ipsos Edwardum et Johannam aut hæredes de corpore ipsius Johannæ legitime exeuntes in inventione sustentatione manutenencione et ordinacione prædicti capellani in forma prædicta aut in observacione perimplecione et sustentatione omnium et singulorum onerum præmissorum seu eorum alicujus deficere abbreviare minuere seu ea minime perimplere prout superius declaratum et expressatum est Tunc ego præfatus Walterus volo et concedo per præsentes quod status prædictornm Edwardi et Johannæ et hæredum de corpore ipsius Johannæ legitime exeuntium omnino et totaliter cesset et pro nullo habeatur. Et quod tunc omnia prædicta messuagia terra tenementa redditus et servicia ac reverciones cum omnibus suis pertinentiis integre sint et remaneant Thomæ Dannant et heredibus de corpore suo legitime procreatis. Et quod idem Thomas Dannant et heredes sui prædicti in omnibus mesuagiis terris tenementis redditibus et serviciis ac revercionibus supradictis poterint intrare et seisire et ea pacifice retinere absque reclamacione seu perturbacione ipsorum Edwardi et Johannæ aut hæredum suorum prædictorum tenenda de capitalibus dominis feodorum illorum per reddittus et servicia inde debita et de jure consueta sub modo forma et condicione supradictis scilicet quod idem Thomas Dannant et hæredes sui prædicti unum capellanum idoneum missas ac alia divina et obsequia ut prædictum est faciendo et celebrando invenient sustentabunt et manutenebunt ac omnia et singula onera præmissa prout superius declaratum et expressatum est de et cum redditibus exitibus et proficuis ex messuagiis terris tenementis redditibus et serviciis ac revercionibus supradictis pervenientibus quolibet anno bene et fideliter in forma prædicta observabunt facient invenient solvent et perimplebunt Et si contingat præfatum Thomam Dannant sine hæredibus de corpore suo legitime procreatis obire vel si contingat ipsum Thomam Dannant aut hæredes sui prædicti in inventione sustentacione manutenencione et ordinacione dicti capellani in forma prædicta aut in observacione perimpletione et snstentacione omnium et singulorum onerum permissorum seu eorum alicujus deficere abbreviare minuere seu ea minime perimplere prout superius dictum et declaratum est Tunc ego præfatus Waterus volo et concedo per presentes quod status prædicti

3 F

Thomæ Dannant et hæredum suorum prædictorum omnino et totaliter cesset et pro nullo habeatur. Et quod tunc omnia prædicta messuagia terræ tenementa redditus et servicia ac reverciones cum omnibus suis pertinentiis integre sint et remaneant rectis hæredibus prædicti Walteri Bodulgate et eorum assignatis in perpetuum. Et quod iidem recti hæredes in omnibus messuagiis terris tenementis redditibus et serviciis ac revercionibus supradictis poterint intrare et seisire et ea pacifice retinere absque reclamacione seu perturbacione prædicti Thomæ Dannant aut hæredum suorum prædictorum Tenenda de capitalibus dominis feodorum illorum per redditus et servicia inde debita et de jure consueta ad inveniendum sustentandum dandum solvendum supportandum et perimplendum de et cum redditibus exitibus et proficuis ex messuagiis terris tenementis redditibus et serviciis ac revercionibus supradictis pervenientibus omnia et singula onera superius declarata expressata et contenta singulis annis modo et forma quibus superius expressantur et declarantur Et in casu quo iidem recti hæredes ipsius Walteri Bodulgate aut eorum assignati vel aliquis alius superius separatim ut premittitur nominatus per quem seu per quos omnia et singula onera prædicta sustentari et perimpleri deberent in inventione sustentacione manutencione observacione et implecione omnium et singulorum onerum præmissorum aut eorum alicujus defecerit et ea non perimpleverit Ita quod omnia et singula onera supradicta aut eorum aliquod sint vel sit infectum et non executum nec observatum prout superius declaratum existit ipsum quoque ob cujus defectum prædicta onera remanent non facta supportata nec perimpleta prout superius dictum et declaratum est ego antedictus Walterus coram Deo omnipotente et omnibus sanctis ejus appello ut ipse qui inde culpabilis existit in die summi judicii michi præfato Waltero respondeat et anima ejus e eat ad locum ubi erit fletus et stridor dentium gemitus et ululatus ejulatus luctus et cruceatus stridor et clamor timor et tremor dolor et labor ardor et fœtor obscuritas et anxietas acerbitas asperitas calamitas et egestas angustia et tristitia oblivio et confusio tortores et puniciones amaritudines et terrores fames et sitis frigus sulphur et ignis ardens in secula seculorum imperpetuum duratura. In quorum omnium et singulorum præmissorum fidem et testimonium adhibendum præsentibus indentatis sigillum meum apposui. Et quia sigillum meum pluribus est incognitum ideo sigillum prioris prioratus Sancti Germani præsentibus apponi procuravi. Et ego Johannes prior prioratus antedicti ad specialem rogatum prædicti Walteri præsentibus indentatis sigillum meum apposui. Datum apud Trecorum vicesimo die Januarii Anno regni Regis Henrici sexti post Conquestum Angliæ terciodecimo [1435].

APPENDIX III.

(Subsidy Roll, 1st Edward III. (1327.) $\frac{87}{7}$

In 1st Edward III, a statute was passed granting a Subsidy of a twentieth of all move-able goods for the defence of the realm against the Scotch rebels, and was assessed upon all the Commons who possessed goods of the value of ten shillings or upwards, but the armour, mounture, jewells, and robes of knights and gentlemen and of their wives, and all their vessels of gold, silver, and brass were excepted; and all the goods of lepers who were governed by a Sovereign a leper, were also excepted, but those of lepers who were governed by a healthy Master were taxed like others, according to the Statute 25th Edward I. (Rot. Pat. 25th Edward I, Part 2, m. 11, ced.) 1st Edward III, Part 3, m. 18, ced.

COLLECTORS FOR CORNWALL RICHARD HYWISH AND ROBERT BILKMORE.

Parochia de Lanteglos.

D. Stephano Trewynt	ij*s*	D. Johanne Caydorel	-	vj*d*
D. Willelmo Trewergonon	xiij*d*	D. Willelmo Brown	-	x*d*
D. Johanne filius ejusdem	xij*d*	D. Ricardo Londre	-	xviij*d*
D. Stephano Kyttou	xvj*d*	D. Andrea Tregarth	-	xij*d*
D. Johanne Richard	xv*d*	D. Johanne Trofreu	-	vj*d*
D. Stephano Corun	ij*d*	D. Johanne Trefarlyche	-	xiij*d*
D. Nicholao Fentewensant	x*d*	D. Willelmo Heraund	-	viij*d*
D. Willelmo Wolger	vj*d*	D. Willelmo filius ejusdem	-	viij*d*
D. Waltero Reynold	xij*d*	D. Rogero Habick	-	xv*d*
D. Warino de Bodulget	xij*d*	D. Dauid Richard	-	viij*d*
D. Johanne Roberd	x*d*	D. Johanne Brounyng	-	vij*d*
D. Willelmo Roger	vj*d*	D. Johanne Reynold	-	xij*d*
D. Willelmo Wille	xviij*d*	D. Henrico Duk	-	xij*d*
D. Willelmo Trewenna	x*d*	Tax. { Johannis Trehuthond	-	ix*d*
D. Johanne de Eadem	xij*d*	{ Thom Trefreu	-	ix*d*

Summa xxix* ix*d* prob.

Camelford.

D. Waltero Peat	-	-	vj*d*	D. Rogero Cobba	-	-	xij*d*
D. Nicholas Jan	-	-	xij*d*	D. Johanne Bauton	-	-	ij*s*
D. Rogero Bolle	-	-	vj*d*	D. Willelmo Waltre	-	-	vj*d*
D. Thoma Doger	-	-	vj*d*			
D. Thoma Charl	-	-	xvj*d*	Tax. { D. Johanne Mariot	-	ix*d*
D. Andrea Smyth	-	-	xvj*d*	{ D. Rogero Burgeys	-	xi*d*

Summa x*s* prob.

Parochia Sancti Adwyny.

D. Stephano Trewynt	-	-	ij*s*	D. Waltero Hurna	-	-	vj*d*
D. Christophero fullore	-	-	viij*d*	D. Stephano Treta	-	-	vj*d*
D. Willelmo Grysa	-	-	viij*d*	D. Rogero Mauynges	-	-	xij*d*
D. Stephano Sanka	-	-	vj*d*	D. Ricardo Hykye	-	-	viij*d*
D. Willelmo Blakeby	-	-	xij*d*	D. Johanne Pencayrou	-	viij*d*
D. Thoma Resterlok	-	-	xij*d*	D. Stephano Pe	-	-	x*d*
D. Thoma Wydewales	-	-	xviij*d*	D. Johanne ffox	-	-	vj*d*
D. Henrico Dogel	-	-	xij*d*	D. Stephano Kryk	-	-	viijd
D. Johanne Cok	-	-	vj*d*	D. Thoma Windyf	-	-	x*d*
D. Willelmo Wada	-	-	xij*d*	D. Thoma Pers	-	-	x*d*
D. Waltero Sibily	-	-	viij*d*	D. Waltero Crehydan	-	xij*d*
D. Waltero Mona	-	-	vj*d*	D. Willelmo Langa	-	-	xij*d*

Summa xx*s* prob.

Parochia de Lysnewyth.

D. Jordano Treyarap	-	-	ij*s* vj*d*	D. Geruasio Mercatore	-	viij*d*
D. Andrea de Eadem	-	-	ij*s*	D. Ricardo Glasta	-	-	ij*s*
D. Johanne de Trelay	-	-	xij*d*	D. Simone Giffard	-	-	xij*d*
D. Roberto Treworel	-	-	viij*d*	D. Waltero Treglaste	-	-	xij*d*
D. Simone Trebyan	-	-	xx*d*	D. Gervasio Peneton	-	-	viij*d*
D. Johanne de Lamelyn	-	-	xij*d*	D. Johanne Menedu	-	-	ij*s*
D. Johanne Tracy	-	-	xij*d*	D. Waltera Wyta	-	-	ij*s*
D. Henrico de Lusum	-	-	xviij*d*			
D. Thoma de la Watere	-	-	viij*d*	Tax. { Rogerus Goladon	-	ix*d*
D. Waltero Molend	-	-	viij*d*	{ Rogerus Wegellsly	-	ix*d*

Summa xxiij*s* vj*d* prob.

PARISH OF LESNEWITH.

This parish derives its name from the Manor of Lesnewith, from which also the Hundred in which it is situate[1] is designated. The parish is very compact and contains in the aggregate 2028a. 0r. 31p. It is bounded on the north and east by the Parish of St. Juliott, from which it is divided by the little river Valency, which empties itself into the creek at Boscastle. On the south-east and south Lesnewith adjoins Davidstow, and on the west it is bounded by ·Minster.

The following terrier is preserved in the Bishop's Registry at Exeter:

LESNEW[TH] PARISH. } A note of the bonds and lymits of the pish aforesaid.

The pish of Lesnew[th] aforesaide is bounded by three pishes, viz., of St. Julett, Dewstowe and Minster. The pish beginneth to bound at Burdenhold where the two Rivers come into one, and so upwards by the River untill it com to the head of Meryfields where Dewstowe pish beginneth, and from thence along by Hellsett hedge vnto Tettesbourough, and from Tettesbourough downe by the King's highwaie vnto Hender Corner to the foot of a cross, and from thence over Hender downe to the cross hedge betwen Gonvellock and Hender, a little aboue St. Austen's Well, and from thence downe along by the brooke vnto Grills foord, and from thence up by Grills lane vnto Cobstone higher corner, and from thence along by Cobstone hedge to the little brooke w[ch] cometh downe to Burdenhold as aforesaide.

Johannes Hobbe, Gard.

Thomas Patchcot, icon.

This doth agree wth the original examined by me

Zacharius Forwaye, Rector of Lesneweth, predict.

2 Septembris 1628.

The sign of Abel ⊏ Michell, Churchwarden.

The sign of James Ⅎ Colman, Sideman.

The only villages, if villages they may be called, are Treworla, Treworwell, Treworla, or Treworld, and Trewanion, at each of which places are a few scattered houses.

The geological features of this parish are of considerable interest. In general character they resemble those of Minster, though differences and distinctions are observable. The parish is about equally divided between the carboniferous series of Devon and the grauwack slates and grits of the neighbourhood of Trevalga and Tintagel; the whole being forced

---

[1] Carew says the Hundred derives its name from the Parish, and that the latter is famous for nothing else.

seaward, in a great curve, by the protrusion of the neighbouring granite at a more recent period. The line of junction, in this parish, between the carboniferous system and the grauwack, where the latter emerges from beneath the former, follows very nearly the course of the road which leads from the Stratton turnpike to Trewanion, whence it extends, in nearly a straight line, as already noticed (vol. i, p. 580), to the western Black pit at Forrabury, at which place the strata assumes, in patches, quite a carbonaceous appearance. The grauwack series, especially in the parish of Davidstow, and extending into this parish, is intersected by large beds of schistose trappean rock of a peculiar calcareous character, consisting of hornblend and calcareous spar, either distinctly conjoined in a granular or laminated form, or, so intimately blended as to form a homogeneous greenstone. A large bed of this peculiar rock extends from Davidstow to Grylls, at which place it is so impregnated with calcareous matter as to induce an attempt to burn it as limestone for agricultural purposes. After several trials, however, the attempt was abandoned, for it was found that unless great care was taken in selecting those parts alone in which calc spar mainly abounded the whole charge of the kiln vitrified, and ran into slag owing to the great fusibility of the hornblend.[1]

The land of about two-thirds of the parish is described as arable, but it is chiefly suitable for pasture. The parish is very hilly and the high lands are thin and coarse, though some of the meadows in the low grounds afford good grass. The chief landowners are Lord Churston, Colonel Grylls, E. A. Magor of Lamellen, and Michael Williams of Halwell, Esquires.

INDUSTRIAL PURSUITS.

There is no other branch of industry than the cultivation of the soil. There is no surplus of labour. All the laborers are fully employed and are well cared for. They receive regularly 12s. a week. There is not a public house in the parish nor is there a pauper. There are no almshouses, schools, or charitable endowments.

The Census Tables give the following as the population, &c., at the several periods:

		1801	1811	1821	1831	1841	1851	1861	1871
Population		104	105	123	127	137	131	114	129
Houses	Inhabited ..	18	20	20	22	20	25	23	9
	Uninhabited ..	nil	nil	nil	nil	5	2	1	nil
	Building ..	..	1	nil	nil	1	..		nil

[1] Dr. Boase, Davies Gilbert's History of Cornwall, vol. iii, p. 23; and De la Beche, Geological Report, pp. 56, 57.

			£	s.	d.
The annual value of real property as assessed in 1815	1400	0	0
Present rateable value	1454	0	0
County Assessment	1520	0	0
Land Tax, net sum £52 8s. 11d. Redeemed £18 14s. 5d.	71	3	4
House Duty	nil		
Property Tax Assessed upon Schedule A	1389	0	0
,, ,, ,, B	911	0	0
,, ,, ,, D	nil		
,, ,, ,, E	nil		

ANCIENTS ROADS AND TRACKS.

The parish of Lesnewith is touched on its south-eastern and southern sides by the great roads leading from Stratton to the south through Camelford and that which crossed it at Tichbarrow leading from Warbstow to Tyntagel; whilst, at its north-western corner, the boundary, for a short distance, abutted on the road, which, branching out of that last mentioned, led to Boscastle Creek. Two ancient roads, or tracks, also intersected the parish, crossing it at right angles near its centre. The first branched out of the coast road from Stratton to Tyntagel on Tresparret Down, and entering the parish near Anderton traversed it, on account of the hilly nature of the ground, in a zig-zag manner, to Grylls Ford, whence, for about half-a-mile, it formed the south-eastern boundary of a spur on that side, to the road to Boscastle from Tichbarrow abovementioned; crossing which it fell into the Tyntagel road on Waterpit Down. The other track, which we have mentioned above, also very hilly, led from near Tichbarrow through Penpole, Lesnewith, and Treworrel by Minster Church to Boscastle.[1]

PRE-HISTORIC REMAINS.

The only pre-historic remains, which have fallen under our notice, in this parish are the barrows formerly called Tettesborough now softened into Tichbarrow, situate on a hill rising to an elevation of 1010 feet above the level of the sea. This hill, of course, commands extensive views, and the barrows form conspicuous objects at great distances. There are four barrows, three on the summit of the hill in the parish of Lesnewith, and the other about a quarter of a mile on the south, in the parish of Davidstow, which is at a little lower elevation. This is larger than the others, and an attempt would appear to have been recently made to open it and to have been abandoned. It would, however, seem to have been disturbed by digging in the centre. All the barrows are on the

[1] Compare with the descriptions, ante vol. i, pp. 586, 587, and vol. ii.

3 G²

western side of the road leading to Stratton. On the eastern side there is a deep excavation some of the rubbish taken from which remains heaped on the sides. Was material taken from this place to construct the barrows?

The Lesnewith barrows are disposed in a straight line lying north-east and south-west, and are about 100 yards apart. Two of them are fine large barrows, the third, and south-westerly one, is much smaller. That on the north-east was opened a few years ago by Mr. Cook, late of the *Saturday Review*. In the centre was discovered a rude cist built of stones, in which were found human remains, but no weapon or ornament. A large heap of stones covered the cist.

There was a fire beacon on this hill hence it is called Tichbarrow Beacon.

ANCIENT CHRISTIAN MONUMENTS.

No. 37. We have already (ante vol. ii, p. 586) described the head of a cross which is now set up in the churchyard of this parish. We believe this to have been the head of the magnificent cross which once stood on Waterpit down (see Engraving, No. 27, vol. ii. p. 585).

No. 38. This rude monolith formerly stood near Auderton Mill, in the parish of Lesnewith, and was carried thence in 1852, for the purpose of preservation, by the Rev. G. W. Manning, and set up in the Churchyard of St. Juliott, where it still remains. It is 5 ft. 9 in. in height above the ground, 2 ft. in width, and 8 in. in thickness. The head is very indefinitely formed, and the symbol, which is of the Latin type, extends down upon the shaft. The head is 1 ft. 10 in. in length, and 1 ft. 8 in. in breadth.

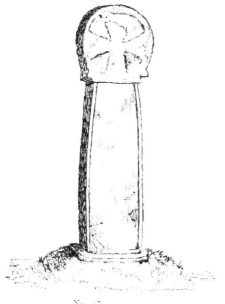

No. 37.

No. 38

St. Austen's Well.—This well, which is mentioned in the terrier (ante page 387) is situate in the valley between Lesnewith and Davidstow, a furlong north of the farm house at Hendra Chapel.[1] It is a fine spring of water, and forms the source of the brook which on that side forms the parish boundary.

MEETING HOUSES OF DISSENTERS.

Bible Christians.—By deed dated 2nd April 1838, Henry Burdon of Lesnewith, yeoman, conveyed to Thomas Wooldridge of the Michaelstow Circuit, Preacher of the Gospel, a portion of a field at Treworwall, with the Chapel then being built thereon, to hold for the term of 1000 years; and by another deed, dated three days later, the said Wooldridge conveyed the same to Jacob Hunt Prior and others in trust for the people called Bible Christians.[2] The plot of ground measured 28 ft. by 22 ft. The Meeting House was opened 25th October 1838. It is not now (1874) used, and there are no registered members.

MANOR OF LESNEWITH, *alias* LISNEWYTH *alias* LESNEWTH.

From this manor having given its name to the Hundred, it must be of very great antiquity, and was probably of greater importance in early Saxon times than it was in its later history. To it the Bailiwick of the Hundred was annexed. We also find it mentioned as a separate Tithing in 1283.[3] It was held by Brictric in the reign of King Edward the Confessor, and was given by the Conqueror to the Earl of Moreton, under whom Brictric continued to hold it at the time of the Domesday Survey, but it had considerably decreased in value. The record states: "The Earl has one manor which is called Lisniwen, which was held by Brictric on the day on which King Edward was alive and dead, and he still holds it of the Earl. There is one virgate and it renders gild for half an acre. This two ploughs can plough, and Brictric has thereof half a virgate and half a carucute in demesne, and the villans have the other land and three oxen in plough. There Brictric has three bordars, and one bondservant, and 3 unbroken mares, and 3 animals, and 20 sheep, and 15 acres of pasture, and 2 acres of meadow, and the value is 10 shillings and when he received [it] 25 shillings."[1]

In 1346, when an aid of 40s. for each knight's fee was granted for making the

---

[1] This farm derives its name from an ancient Chapel about a quarter of a mile on the north-west of the farm house. The Chapel is now in ruins, and has been for a long while. It is about 20 ft. long and 12 ft. wide. When we visited it in October 1871, Mr. Michael Williams was causing some of the stones to be removed for the restoration of the "Holy Well" at Davidstow. There was a winding stair at the south-western angle, two steps of which remained. The stone which covered the doorway was still upon the spot. It formed a semicircle in one stone from the Pentuan quarry, the outer lower edge being chamfered. It was rude in workmanship.

[2] Rot. Claus. 1838, Part 42, No. 1.   [3] Assize Roll, 11th Edward I, m. 6.

[4] Exon Domesday, vol. iv, p. 222, orig. fo. 242 b.

King's eldest son a knight, Henry de la Pomeroy held half a fee in Lesnewyth and Trebighan, which his father had held 1290, when an aid was levied for marrying the eldest daughter of King Edward I.[1]; and when the aid was levied in 6th Henry VI. (1427), this fee had become divided. The King held a quarter part by reason of the minority of Richard son and heir of Richard Denys, John Penpoll, John Dyar, John Maiowe, John Trevyrek, John Tregonwell, William Moys, and Richard Douncombe held separately between them another quarter part, and the remainder, being held in smaller portions than quarter parts, was not assessable.[2]

It would seem that from the thirteenth century the Manor, together with the Advowson of the Church thereto annexed, had been in the possession of the family of Denys, held of the family of Pomeroy as of their Manor of Tregony. Henry le Denys was rector in 1297, and was one of those clergy who, in that year, in obedience to the Pope, refused to pay the subsidy levied by the King. Benedict Reynward became surety for the payment of his fine.[3] In 8th Henry V, (1420) all the messuages in Lesnewth, and the office of Bailiff of the Hundred of Lesnewth, were in the hands of the King by reason of the death of Thomasia relict of John Denys of Orleigh (who in his life-time had enfeoffed her, conjointly with himself, for the term of her life and the heirs of the said John Denys), and the minority of Johanna and Margaret daughters and heirs of John St. Aubyn, of whom the Manor of Lesnewth was held, as of their Manor of Tregony, and who were then in the King's wardship, by military service, and by reason also of the minority of John Denys, son of Richard Denys, son of the aforesaid John Denys, deceased ; and on 16th November in that year, the King granted the custody of the said messuages and lands and the Bailiwick of the Hundred to Arnulphus Chagestry.[4]

In 1577, John Denys, Esq., and Dorothy his wife, suffered a fine in the manor and bailiwick of the Hundred[5] to John Gifford and others.[6] The property continued vested in the family of Denys until the death of Anthony Denys of Orleigh, in June 1641,[7] leaving, by Gertrude his wife, daughter of Sir Bernard Grenville, three daughters, of whom, Mary, the eldest, became the wife of Sir Thomas Hampson of Taplow, co. Bucks, Bart., and Gertrude, the youngest, married Nicholas Glynn of Glynn, Esq., and the third, Elizabeth, wedded Sir John Hern. The elder co-heir inherited, *inter alia*, the Manor and Advowson of Lesnewth, and, surviving her husband, who died on 22nd March 1670, she suffered in the following year a fine in this manor and advowson, and bailliwick of the Hundred of Lesnewith, probably for purposes of settlement, to Thomas Turner and Philip Vennying, Gentlemen.[8] She had several children, and dying in 1694, by her will, dated 4th March 1678,[9] devised her Cornish lands to her second

---

[1] Book of Aids, pp. 33, 36.   [2] Inquisitions for levying a Subsidy, 6th Henry VI.

[3] Prynn's Records, vol. iii, p. 719, see also ante vol. i, p. 368, note †   [4] Rot. Fin., 8th Henry V, m. 9.

[5] John Denys was bailiff of the Hundred of Lesnewith in 6th and 7th Edward IV. (1467) and accounted to the Exchequer for lxxij[s] viij[d] for that year. Ministers' Accounts for the Duchy of Cornwall, 6th and 7th

Edward IV. $\frac{95}{9}$ [6] Pedes Finium, 19th Elizabeth, Easter.

[7] Will dated 30th April, Cod. 15th May, 1641. Proved 4th July following. (P.C.C., 88 Evelyn).

[8] Pedes Finium, 23rd Charles II, Trinity.   [9] Proved 16th October 1694, (P.C.C., 171 Box).

son Henry Hampson. He dying s.p., and his elder brother also in 1719, the estates in Cornwall devolved upon William Glynn, grandson of Nicholas Glynn and Gertrude Denys,[1] which William Glynn and Rose his wife, for purpose of settlement, in 1722 suffered a fine,[2] *inter alia*, in this manor and advowson and in the Bailiwick of the Hundred to Edmund Prideaux, Esq., brother of the said Rose.[3] From William Glynn the manor, &c., descended to the late Edmund John Glynn of Glynn, Esq., upon the sale of whose estates, in 1828, it was purchased by the late Lord Churston, then Sir John Yarde Buller, Bart., and is now the property of his grandson, and successor, the present Lord Churston.

The following is a description of the manor, &c., as offered for sale at Bodmin, on 23rd January 1823, extracted from the Particulars of sale.

Manor and Bailiwick of Lesnewth.

Tenements.	Tenants.	Terms.	Rents.			Contents.		
			£	s.	d.	A.	R.	P.
	FREE TENANTS.							
Tregoll	Rev. Mr. Marshall ..	.. ..	0	1	0			
Ditto	Heirs of Lord Rolle ..	.. ..	0	0	8			
Ditto	Sir A. O Molesworth ..	.. ..	0	3	0			
Black Down Moor in Trewint in Poundstock.	Ditto ..	.. ..	0	2	0			
Tregoll	William Gay ..	.. ..	0	0	8			
Blackdown in Trewint in Poundstock.	Paul Orchard ..	.. ..	0	2	0			
Tregoll	William Webb..	.. ..	0	6	8			
Ditto	James Stacy ..	.. ..	0	1	0			
Ditto	Mr. John Burgoyne ..	.. ..	0	1	0			
Ditto	James Webb ..	.. ..	0	4	0			
Taway	Charles Honey..	.. ..	0	1	0			
A Watercourse	John Harris ..	.. ..	0	1	0			
	RACK TENANTS.							
Halamellin	⎫					68	0	10
Menadew	John Gill	14 years from Michs. 1813	100	0	0	26	0	28
Delaboll	⎭					13	0	36
Hamley's Tenement ..	⎫							
Coleman's Tenement ..								
Bettenson's Tenement ..	Peter Brown	14 years from Michs. 1813	210	0	0	256	0	0
Warrent's Two Tenements ..								
Part of Treskiddy and Menadew	⎭							

[1] See Pedigree of GLYNN, ante pp. 68, 71. [2] Pedes Finium, 8th George I, Hil.

[3] See Pedigree of PRIDEAUX, ante pp. 228, 229.

The Advowson and right of presentation to the Rectory of Lesnewith. The present Incumbent is about 45 years old.

RECTORY.

In the year 1237, Fulco Abbot of Valle suffered a fine, for himself and his Church of Valle, to Henry le Daneys in the Advowson of the Church of Lysnewyth, reserving to himself and his successors and the Church of Valle the ancient pension by custom payable out of the same,[1] and from that time the Rectory has been appurtenant to the Manor of Lesnewith as before stated. In the taxation of Pope Nicholas, cir. 1290, " Ecclesia de Lesnewid " is valued at £4 6s. 8d. In 15th Edward III. (1341) the Church of Lesnewyth was taxed for the ninth sheaf, the ninth fleece, and the ninth lamb at the same rate, which were so sold to John Menadieu, Robert Artur, Henry Kena, and Roger Chelle. Of fifteenths it is said there were none.[2] And when in 1379, the clergy granted a subsidy to the King of 16d. upon the mark in all benefices, the Church of Lesnywit paid 8s. 8d. upon the said value of £4 6s. 8d.[3] In the valuation of Cardinal Wolsey, the parish is rated at £8, as it is also in the return to the Crown made by Bishop Vesey on 3rd November 1536, in obedience to the King's writ, dated 20th July in that year.[4]

The estimated quantity of land subject to the payment of all manner of tithes in kind, exclusive of the glebe, is 1724 acres: viz., arable land 1190 acres, pasture 528 acres, and woodland 6 acres; all which tithes are payable to the Rector for the time being, and in 1841 were commuted at £200 per annum.

The glebe lands consist of 44a. 2r. 24p., the Church and Churchyard occupy 2r. 33p., and the roads and wastes 22a. 2r. 36p.

The following Terriers, which are preserved in the Bishop's Registry at Exeter, show the extent and boundaries of the Glebe, and the furniture and utensils of the Church at various dates.

LESNEWITH PARISH.   } A Terrier of the Gleebe Lande belonginge to the Parsonage of Lesnewith aforesaide.

There are six closes and one meadowe, being bounded wth the Church Towne on the north side, Penpoll on the east side, Treskerdie on the south side, and Choidon on the west side. And one aker and quarter Land, or therabouts, lying in Trebesen, w^thin the Parish aforesaide, in a close there called the Church land. Exhibited in anno domini 1613.

John Hill   Thomas O Patchet
Warden.   Sidesman.

<hr/>

[1] Pedes Finium, 22nd Henry III, Trinity.   [2] Inquis. Nonarum, p. 345.

[3] Subsidy Rolls, Clerical, 3rd Richard II $\frac{20}{3}$ [4] Bishop Veysey's Reg. vol. ii, fols. 86, 100.

ix die Aprilis   A Terrier of all the Glebe landes, Meadowes, Gardens, Howses, and all
1622.   other implements belonginge to the Parsonage & Rectorie of Lesnewith, w^{th}
                 the bondes & lymits thereof, &c.

           Imprimis the Glebe land is in quantity Thirty-two acres.
           Item, in closes six, one meadowe and one Towne place.
           Item, Three gardens. Item ffive howses.
           And it is bounded on the East with a Tenem^t called Penpoll, and on the
                 south with Treskedye, on the west wth Choldon, and on the north
                 wth Lesnew^{th} and the King's high way leadinge towardes Botreaux
                 Castle.
           Item, one parcel of land more, being in quantitye one acre and quarter
        of Land, or thereabout, lying in Trebiffine and bounded on every side w^{th}
        the Lands of Richard Southcott & Humphry Prowse Esquires.
           Zacharias Forway, Rector, ibidem.
           Will'm betenson.
                 The sign of Degory S Taylor.
                 The sign of Tho. ∽ Langman senior.
                 John Langman.
                 The sign of James Ɪ Colman.
                 per me John R * * * * Churchwarden.

There is a similar Terrier, dated 16th March 1679, with the exception that it is
stated that the close of land in Trebiffin is bounded on every side with the lands of
Sir Walter Moyle, Knight.

            Signed John Dinham, Rector of Lesnewth.
                 William Bettenson.

Thomas Taylor.   James Colman.
                 Humphry Betenson.
                 Christopher Langman.
                 Edward Langman, Warden.

A Terrier of the Parsonage of Lesnewth.

The parsonage house is built with stone and covered with tile, in the front has six rooms,
a Kitchen, a Hall (which have lime-ash floors) and a parlour (floored with deal) each of which
rooms has a chamber over it (plaistered and floored with deal) on the back part is a Kitchen,
a dairy, and a cellar with a Chamber over each. At the north-east corner is a Hogstie built
with stone and covered with tile. The Barn is built with stone and covered with thatch, consists of five bayes. Adjoining to it is a stable built with stone and covered with thatch, at
the end of each is a Hogstye built with stone and covered with tile.

(Then follows a description of the glebe as before given).

There is a high rent of six shillings & eight pence per annum payable at Mich's out of
a field belonging to Trebiffin called "Higher Church park" or "Church land."

Easter Offerings are two pence every single person, and three pence for every married
couple: the fees for marriages, churchings, and burialls, are one shilling each.

3 H

If colts, calves, piggs, lambs, fleeces, or the like, be seven, eight, or nine, the Rector takes one and pays the parishioner, pro rata. If under seven the parishioner pays the rector, pro rata.

There are three bells, a purple plush cushion for the pulpitt, a green cloth for the Communion Table, a Linnen Cloth, a pewter flagon and Bason, and silver Chalice weighing thirteen ounces, &c., &c.

Signed Aprill y⁵ 12ᵗʰ 1727,

> Will Cruwys, Rector
> James Dinham Churchwarden
> Edward Langman
> Christopher Langman
> William Symons
> Edward Jose

The following later Terrier gives further particulars:

A true Terrier of the Glebe, Parish Church, &c., of Lesnewth in the County of Cornwall and Diocese of Exeter taken this tenth day of April in the year of Our Lord one thousand seven hundred fourty six.

The Parsonage house is built with stone and covered with heling Stones, consists of seven under rooms, floored only with earth except the Parlour, which is floored with boards, & five chambers neither wainscotted nor ceiled, the outhouses are a barn, stable, & two pigs houses, built with stone & cover'd with thatch.

The glebe of thirty-one acres and quarter, or there about, of meadow, arable and pasture, bounded on the east by Penpoll, on the south by Garles-Skiddy, on the west by Chapple hill & Tom's ground, and on the north by the Church towne, is divided into eight fields; and one acre & quarter, viz., Lane Park about five acres of arable and pasture, the marsh field, about two acres of pasture, higher Crookedpark about one acre and half of meadow, Middle park about five acres of arable, Quarry park about four acres of arable, Church park about six acres & half of meadow and pasture, Toorpark about four acres & half of pasture, and one acre and quarter of meadow in Trebeffen, in a field there called Church land. The homestall is about one acre fenced with stone hedges.

The furniture & utensils of the Church are one surplice, one large bible, two large Common Prayer books, five bells, one silver cup marked 1630, one flagon, one bason, one plate, each of pewter, one blue carpet, one linnen cloth & napkin, a pulpitt cushion covered with green plush.

The Church and Church Yard are maintain'd by the parish, except the Chancel which is maintain'd by the Rector.

The Clerk's wages is twenty shillings a year, paid by the parish, chosen by the Rector. The sexton's wages is ten shillings a year, paid and chosen by the parish.

Antho: Hosken Vic^r

W. Betenson.

(another named erased.)

The Parsonage House has been recently built upon another site, and stables have been erected where the Parsonage formerly stood.

LESNEWITH INSTITUTIONS.

1297   -   Henry le Denys.[1]

               Richard de Cersyaus.

1308, March 19th   -   Sir Thomas de Stapeldon, Priest,[2] was instituted to Church of Lesnewyth, vacant by the resignation of Richard de Cersyaus, the last Rector, upon presentation of Richard le Deneys, the true patron.

unknown   -   John Deneys,[3] who exchanged for the Parish Church of Ellerky.

1330, August 14th   -   John Cooke, of Exeter, Priest,[4] was instituted to the Church of Lisnewith, vacant by the resignation of John Denys, the late Rector.

1333, January 29th   -   Roger de Esse, Clerk,[5] was instituted to the Church of Lisnewith, vacant through the resignation of John Cokes, of Exeter, the late Rector, upon the presentation of Alan de Esse

1343, November 13th -   Thomas Podding, Vicar of the Church of Ellerky, upon exchange with Roger de Esse.[6]

1361, March 8th   -   William de Tredethy, Priest,[7] was admitted to the Parish Church of Lisnewith, upon the resignation of Thomas Poddynges, last Rector, to which he had been presented by John de Penhirgard by reason of his custody of certain lands belonging to Richard son and heir of Henry Denys, who was a minor, and to whom this turn belonged.

unknown   -   Thomas Edward.[8]

1422, December 1st   -   John Mayowe[9] was admitted to the Parish Church of St. Michael

---

[1] Prynn's Records, vol. iii, p. 719.   [2] Bishop Stapledon's, Reg. fo. 39.

[3] 1310, September 19th, John le Deneys, Rector of the Church of Lesneuwith, Deacon, had dispensation to study from feast of St. Michael following for one year, and in the interim to receive Priest's orders and then to reside. (Bishop Stapledon's Reg. fo. 56).   [4] Bishop Grandison's Reg. fo. 18.

[5] Ibid. fo. 27   [6] Ibid. fo. 50.   [7] Ibid. fo. 139.

[8] Thomas was Rector of Lesnewith in 1380, (Sub. Roll 4th Richard II. $\frac{24}{5}$) and Thomas Edward is mentioned as Parson of Lisnewyth in Assize Roll, 8th Richard II, (1384) m. 40; and again in that of the 22nd of the same King's reign (1398) m. 48 d. In 1400, John Denys of Orleigh took proceedings against Thomas Edward, Clerk, to obtain from him an account for the time that he was Receiver of the moneys of the said John. He did not appear, and the Sheriff said that he was beneficed by the Bishop of Exeter, and had no lay fee in his bailliwick. (De Banco Roll, 1st Henry IV, Easter, m. 277).

[9] Bishop Lacy's Reg. vol. ii, fo. 32. John Mayowe was admitted to the Parish Church of St. Michael, of Lesnewyth, then vacant by the death of Sir Thomas Edward, on 14th December 1421, upon the presentation of Edward Pomeroy, Knight, and Margaret his wife, true patrons, (Lacy ii, fo. 32). On the 18th of the same month, William Whittyng was admitted, and the same day it was commanded the Archdeacon of Cornwall to induct him (Ibid. fo. 48), but on the 1st December in the following year, the Bishop instituted the aforesaid John Mayowe upon the presentation of the King, (Ibid. fo. 70). The institution of Thomas Edward has not been found.

3 H[2]

of Lesnewyth, vacant by the death of Sir Thomas Edward, late Rector, upon the presentation of King Henry VI. Died 6th February 1444.

1445, April 30th - Thomas Clement,[1] was admitted to the parish Church of Lesnewith, vacant by the death of John Mayow, last Rector, upon the presentation of John Denys, gent.

1461, March 6th - Michael Colay, Clerk,[2] was instituted to the Church of Lesnewth vacant by the death of Thomas Clement, the last Rector, upon the presentation of John Denys of Orley, the true patron.

1469, April 8th - John Bigwell, Chaplain,[3] was instituted to the Church of Lesnewth, vacant by the resignation of Michael Colay, upon the presentation of John Denys of Orley.

unknown - - William Cullow, died 4th April 1489, (Bishop Booth's Reg. fo. 138)

1489, May 5th - William Bylke, Chaplain,[4] was instituted to the parish Church of Lesnewth, vacant by the death of William Cullow, last Rector, upon the presentation of John Denys of Orley, *alias* Orleigh, gent, the true patron.

unknown - - Robert Pudñ.[5]

1541, August 15th - William Crossying, Priest,[6] was instituted to the Rectory of Lesnewth, vacant by the death of Robert Pudñ, Clerk, last Rector, upon the presentation of Nicholas Denys of Orley, Esq.

1565, April 17th - Sir John Sutton, Clerk,[7] was instituted to the Parish Church of Lesnewth, vacant by the death of the last Incumbent, upon the presentation of John Denys of Orleigh, Esq.

1584, April 2nd - Christopher Dingle, Clerk,[8] was admitted to the Church of Lesnewth, vacant by the death of John Sutton, last Incumbent, upon the presentation of (blank) Bitensonne, yeoman, of the said Church, for this turn, the true patron by the assignment of the advowson by Thomas Dene, Gent., who had it of the gift of Richard Dene by his last will, which said Richard had it of the grant of John Denys of Orleigh, Esq., the true patron.

---

[1] Bishop Lacy's Reg. fo. 216. He was one of the jurors on 23rd June 1457, on an inquisition concerning the vacancy and right of presentation to the Church of St. Maben, (Bishop Nevill's Reg. fo. 71).

[2] Bishop Nevill's Reg. fo. 17.   [3] Bishop Booth's Reg. fo. 15.

[4] Bishop Booth's Reg. fo. 106. 1489 April 13th, Certificate upon an Inquisition into the vacancy and right of patronage of the Church of Lesnewth, made by Thomas Ponteshed of Bliston, William Morton of Mynster, Rectors; William Merefyld of Bodmin, Richard Nycoll of Mynfre, Robert Reke of Kew, Henry Ley of Bruard, Nicholas Hawke of Dyndanyll, John Person of Tetha, Vicars; who say that the Church of Lesnewth is vacant by the death of William Colow, who died on the 4th April in this year, and that John Denys of Orley is the true patron by hereditary right; that there is no objection to William Bylk, who has been presented by the said John Denys, and that the said William is 28 years of age (Ibid. fo. 138).

[5] In the Ecclesiastical Survey returned to the Crown on 3rd November 1536, by Bishop Vesey, this Rector is called Robert Pounder (Vesey's Reg., vol. ii, fo. 86—100).   [6] Bishop Voysey's Reg., fo. 102.

[7] Bishop Alley's Reg., fo. 9. He was also Vicar of St. Gennys. Upon his death the two benefices were put under sequestration. (Bishop's Act Book A.)   [8] Bishop Babington's Reg., fo. 16.

1585, December 30th	Digory Betenson, Clerk,[1] was admitted to the Church of Lesnewth, vacant by the resignation of Christopher Dingle, last Incumbent, upon the presentation of William Betenson, the true patron by grant of William Denys of Orleigh.
1617, December 18th -	Zacharias Torway, Clerk,[2] was admitted to the Rectory of Lesnewth, vacant by the death of Degory Betenson, upon the presentation of Mary Denys, widow, relict of William Denys of Orleigh, in Devon, deceased, the true patron.
unknown	John Dinham, Clerk.[3]
1699, June 4th	Christopher Tregian, Clerk,[4] was admitted to the Rectory of Lesnewth, vacant by the death of John Dinham, Clerk, upon the presentation of Alexander Tregian the true patron.
1724, June 5th	William Cruwys, Clerk,[5] A.B., was admitted to the Rectory of Lesnewth, now vacant, upon the presentation of William Glynn of Glynn, Esq., the true patron.
1737, April 30th	Joseph Silly, Clerk,[6] was admitted to the Rectory of Lesnewth, void by the death of William Cruwys, Clerk, upon the presentation of Nicholas Glynn of Glynn, the true patron.
1738, July 21st	Anthony Hosken, Clerk,[7] M.A., was admitted to the Rectory of Lesnewth, void by the cession of Joseph Silly, Clerk, upon the presentation of Nicholas Glyn of Glyn.

[1] Ibid. fo. 24. Matriculated from Broadgate Hall, 17th January 1583-4, aged 20, "Pleb. fil," of co. Cornwall. Buried at Lesnewith 17th June 1617.   [2] Bishop Carey's Reg., fo. 109. He was sequestrated by the Puritans (Walker's Sufferings of the Clergy, Part ii, p. 375). Died in 1651.

[3] We have no record of the institution of John Dinham. He, doubtless, obtained the benefice upon the expulsion of Mr. Torway. He signed the Registers in 1653, and having conformed in 1662 retained it. He signed the Terrier in 1679 (ante p. 405). He was buried at Lesnewith 8th September 1697. Margaret, wife of John Dinham, Rector, was buried there 2nd March 1692.

[4] Bishop's Reg. N.S., vol. iv, 42, B.A., Pembroke College, Cambridge, 1696. Christopher Tregian, Rector of Lesnewith, married Cordelia, daughter of John Trewren of Trewardreva in Constantine, in which Parish she was baptized 20th February 1677, and married 22nd April 1708. The following entries occur in the Parish Registers of Lesnewth:

1708, John son of Christopher Tregian, Rector, born 18th, baptized 30th January.

1709, Alexander son of Christopher Tregian and Cordelia his wife, born 31st December, baptized 7th January.

1711, Cordelia daughter of Christopher Tregian and Cordelia, born 31st August, baptized 18th September.

1712, Christopher son of Mr. Christopher Tregian and Cordelia, born 27th January, bap. 8th February.

1714, Cordelia daughter of Mr. Christopher Tregian, born 17th October, baptized 26th October.

1715, Susanna daughter of Mr. Christopher Tregian, baptized 31st December.

1717, Grace daughter of Mr. Christopher Tregian, baptized 7th September.

1719, Alexander son of Mr. Christopher Tregian, baptized 11th November.

1713, Alexander son of Christopher Tregian, Rector, buried 29th April.

1715, Susanna daughter of Mr. Christopher Tregian, buried 14th February.

1719, Alexander son of Mr. Christopher Tregian, buried 18th November.

1720, Christopher Tregian, Rector of this Parish, buried 1st May.

[5] Bishop's Register, N.S., vol. vi, 18, Matriculated from Balliol College, Oxford, 4th June 1709, aged 18 son of John Cruwys, Gent. Buried at Lesnewith 2nd December 1736. Par. Reg.

[6] Bishop's Register, N.S., vol. vii, fo. 9.   [7] Ibid. fo. 25. Also Vicar of Bodmin. (See ante vol. i, pp. 142, 149, 159, 169.)

1767, June 16th	- Henry Oglander, Clerk,[1] B.A., was admitted to the Rectory of Lesnewth, vacant by the death of Anthony Hosken, Clerk, upon the presentation of John Glyn of Glyn, Esq.
1786, March 6th	- Henry Oglander, Clerk, B.D.,[2] was admitted to the Rectory of Lesnewth, void by his own cession, upon the presentation of Edmund John Glyn, of Glyn, Esq. (by his mother Susanna Glyn of Bath, his lawful attorney) the true patron.
1791, February 2nd	- Anthony William Glyn, Clerk, S.C.L.,[3] was admitted to the Rectory of Lesnewth, void by the resignation of Henry Oglander, upon the presentation of Edmund John Glyn of Glyn, Esq.
1802, May 11th	- Anthony William Glyn, Clerk, B.LL.,[4] was admitted to the Rectory of Lesnewth, void by his own cession, upon the presentation of Edmund John Glyn of Glyn, Esq.
1804, August 29	- Anthony William Glynn, Clerk,[5] was admitted to the Rectory of Lesnewth, void by his own cession, upon the presentation of Edmund John Glyn of Glyn, Esq.
1809, January 18th	- John Pomeroy, Clerk, B.A.,[6] was admitted to the Rectory of Lesnewth,, void by the cession of Anthony William Glyn, upon the presentation of Edmund John Glyn of Glyn, Esq.
1813, December 7th	- Charles Worsley, Clerk,[7] was admitted to the Rectory of Lesnewth void by the death of John Pomeroy, Clerk, upon the presentation of Edmund John Glyn of Glyn, Esq.
1854, November 18th	- Henry Farwell Roe, Clerk, M.A.,[8] was instituted to the Rectory of Lesnewth, void by the death of Charles Worsley, Clerk, last Incumbent, upon the presentation of Sir John Buller Yarde Buller, of Lupton House, co. Devon, Bart., the true patron.
1871, May 19th	- John Tracey, Clerk,[9] (late Vicar of Townstal, Dartmouth, with St. Saviour's) was admitted, void by the resignation of Henry Farwell Roe, upon the presentation of the Right Hon. Lord Churston.
1874, February 24th	- Charles John Perry-Keene, Clerk, B.A.,[10] was admitted, upon the death of John Tracy, last Rector, upon the presentation of John Baron Churston.

---

[1] Bishop's Register, vol. ix, fo. 24. Third son of Sir John Oglander of Nunwell, Isle of Wight, Bart Fellow of Winchester College. Died 16th March 1814.

[2] Bishop's Reg., vol. x, fo. 39.

[3] Ibid. fo. 73. Son of John Glynn, Sergeant at Law, *Vide* Pedigree of GLYNN, ante p. 70.

[4] Ibid. fo. 152.   [5] Ibid. fo. 179.

[6] Bishop's Register, vol. xi, fo. 13. Also Vicar of Bodmin. (See ante vol. i, pp. 149, 164.)

[7] Ibid. fo. 61.   [8] Bishop's Register, vol. xiii, 106.

[9] Ibid. vol. xiv, 61.   [10] Ibid. fo. 147.

THE PARISH CHURCH.

The Parish Church of Lesnewith, which is dedicated to S. Michael,[1] was originally cruciform and of the Norman period, having a small Chapel on the east of the south transept, a south porch, and western tower. The nave, chapel and tower were of third-pointed work. The Chapel and the south transept were separated from the Chancel by two Norman arches springing from responds and resting on a massive central column, having a square abacus. The Chancel, which was divided from the nave by an ancient rood-screen, much decayed, was lighted by an eastern window of early second-pointed date, consisting of three very pointed lights intersecting each other, and there was also a three-light window of third-pointed work on the south side; whilst a four-light modern window had been inserted in the south wall of the transept. The Chapel also had two three-light windows. In the south wall of the Chancel are the remains of what was once an elegant piscina of second-pointed work. The upper part had been cut off and converted, probably, into an aumbry, or the shelf used as a credence table, nevertheless the lower parts of the side shafts yet remain; the bason was of the fluted pattern and partially projected, but it has been cut down flush with the wall. On the north side was a square aumbry. The Chancel measured 18 ft. by 13 ft. 4 ins., the Chapel 9 ft. by 7 ft. 6 ins., and south transept 17 ft. by 13 ft. The north transept, which measured 17 ft. 6 ins. by 11 ft. 6 ins., was 18 inches above the floor of the nave. It was lighted by a small narrow window on the east, probably a lancet, and had an altar in the thickness of the wall beneath it, the slab of which, measuring 3 ft. in length and 1 ft. 9 ins. in breadth, with its five crosses thereon, remained in situ. In the north wall was a third-pointed window of three-lights. The nave measured 42 ft. by 14 ft. It was of third-pointed work, and was lighted on the north side by two three-light windows, having a door between them, and on the south side, close on the west of the porch, which itself was in the angle of the nave and transept, was another similar window. The porch was modern; 9 ft. by 7 ft. (see Plate XLI, fig. 1). The tower is of third-pointed work, of three flights, besides a crenelated parapet, on the angles of which are crocketted pinnacles. The stair turret is at the north-east angle, and is lighted by a narrow loop-hole and a quatrefoil opening in each flight. The basement has a three-light cinque-foil window over the door with tracery in the head, and in the second flight, on each face, is a narrow trefoil niche, or blank window, with circular hoodmoulding, and on the eastern face is a second with a square hoodmoulding. The bell chamber has a two-light window without any foliation, but with a quatrefoil, unpierced, in the tympanum, on each face.

The roofs were fine examples of the wagon pattern, but in a very decayed condition. In the part between the transepts the principals sprung from corbels at each angle, and, converging, terminated in a central boss. All the original benches had been removed and the church was chiefly filled with high square pews, whilst the portion of the nave west of the

---

[1] Bishop Lacy's Reg. vol. ii, fo. 32.

doors was filled with a hugh gallery, of the worst type, which shut off the tower arch. The whole of the walls and fittings were in such a dilapidated and decayed condition as to render unavoidable the almost entire rebuilding of the fabric, which was effected from designs by Mr. J. P. St. Aubyn in 1862.

The new Church in plan differs entirely from the old one. It consists of a chancel raised three steps above the nave, sanctuary two steps above the chancel, with a vestry on the south side, Nave, South porch and western Tower, (see Plate XLI, fig. 2). The Chancel and Sanctuary measure 22 ft. by 15 ft., vestry 17 ft. by 10 ft., nave 30 ft. by 17 ft. The only portions of the old Church which are preserved in the new are the tower and some portion of the walls of the chancel, the eastern window, the piscina in the south wall of the chancel, the square recess above, (which has been pierced through the thick wall with a very small opening about 8 ins. in diameter,) the chancel arch and the arches of the south transept and chapel with the column which supports them, and the south door within the porch, which is of late third-pointed work.

The square aumbry on the north side of the chancel has been converted into a window and therein has been inserted the small window and the altar slab removed from the north transept; and the slab is now used as a credence table. The vestry is separated from the chancel by a glazed screen. The fittings, throughout, are of red pine varnished. The font, which is octagonal, stands west of the south door.

The alterations made in the plan of the Church will be seen upon reference to Plate XLI, in which that of the old Church and the new are delineated.

It appears from the Inventory of Plate and Bells belonging to the Churches in the Hundred of Lesnewth, dated 6th May 3rd Edward VI. (1549), that at that time the parish of Lesnowyth possessed one Chalice of silver and three Bells.[1] The foregoing Terriers (ante p. 406) shew that there were no more in 1727, but that there were five bells in 1746. It would seem, however, from the following inscriptions, which are upon the existing bells, that they were cast into five in 1734:

							DIAMETER.
1st Bell	MDCCXXXIIII	..	..	..	..	..	2 ft. 2 in.
2nd ,,	MDCCXXXIIII	..	..	...	..	..	2 ft. 3½ in.
3rd ,,	JOHN VENNING & SAMUEL LANGFORD C. W. .:. J. P. :. 1805					..	2 ft. 6½ in.
4th ,,	JOHN DINHAM: WILLIAM TREMERE: CH: WARDENS				..	..	2 ft. 7⅝ in.
5th ,,	JOHN TAYLOR OF OXFORD FOUNDER 1830: SAMUEL LANGFORD. SAMUEL HAMBLY, C. W. S.						

The second bell is slightly, and the fifth much, cracked.

ALTAR PLATE.

There is a curious old chalice and cover. On the latter is the date 1638. The stem is formed of three serpents knotted in the middle with a head at each extremity. They are disposed in the form of the letter S—Hall, or maker's mark (m) three times repeated.

---

[1] Queen's Remembrancer's Office. Church Goods, Cornwall, $\frac{1}{50}$

XII

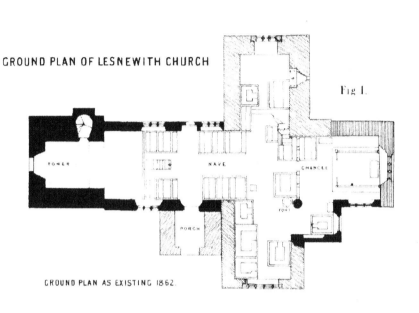

GROUND PLAN OF LESNEWITH CHURCH

Fig 1.

TOWER NAVE CHANCEL

PORCH FONT

GROUND PLAN AS EXISTING 1862.

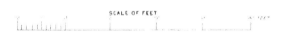

SCALE OF FEET

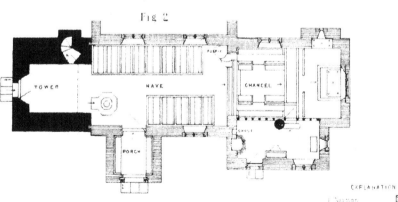

Fig 2

TOWER NAVE CHANCEL

PORCH

GROUND PLAN AS REBUILT.

EXPLANATION

PARISH REGISTERS.

The Old Registers of this parish consist of two volumes. Vol. i commences with a transcript made in 1642. There is a title to each division: viz., "The Register Booke of the pish of Lesnewth, as itt was in the Old Register: and the yeere when it was written, for Christings." The baptisms commence in 1573. The other titles give the dates of the transcripts: viz., burials 7th, and weddings 17th, June 1642. The entries of the former commence in 1564, and the latter in 1569. The earliest names which occur in the Registers are Langman, Keene, Pearse, Barber, Hamblie, Secombe, Swaine, Pyne, Meager, Garland, Colman, Fryer, Bilkie, Patchcott, and Bath, several of which names we find in the Subsidy Roll of 1524, and some yet remain in the parish and neighbourhood. A note in the Register states that the trees and shrubs in the churchyard were planted about the year 1850, by the Rev. G. W. Manning, now Rector of St. Petrock Minor, then stipendiary Curate of this parish.

MONUMENTAL INSCRIPTIONS.

IN THE CHURCH.

1. Upon a marble tablet set in slate:

Jesus said I am the true Vine.

In memory of Philippa the beloved wife of John Harris, late of Trewannion in this Parish, who died Nov. 19, 1855, aged 48.

I know that my Redeemer liveth

Dum vivimus vivamus

IN THE CHURCHYARD.

2. Here lyeth the Body of Humphry Prowse of Mamhead in Devon, Gent., who was buried the 23 Day of May 1638.

3. Here lyeth the body of Thomas Taylor of this parish who was Buried before the toure the 12 day of May 1683.

Thou sayst wee're dead, may't not bee rather saide
that as a sundred clock is peece-meal laide
Not to be lost, but by the maker's hand
Repolish'd, without error then to stand:

so, though our bodyes be resolu'd to dust,
Yet at the Resurrection of the Just
Rais'd and reioyned, more celestial
Shall be than Angels were, for they could fall.
Thus after timely sleep, wh. thou call'st death,
wee 'ue life again more permanent than breath.

Degory ye son of Thomas taylor was buried ye viii January 82.

ON AN ALTAR TOMB.

4. In Memory of Thomas Pearse of Holwell who was buried the 20th of August 1715, aged 73.

And of Mary his wife, she was Daugher of Degory Bettenson of Griles, Gent.; who was buried the 19th of Nov. 1693, aged 54.

And also of Richard Pearse their son, who was buried the 2nd of Feb. 1720, aged 48; and likewise of Joan the daughter of Hender Pearse of Holwell and Joan his wife, who was buried the 5th of Augt 1740, aged 13.

This stone is erected by their Daughter, Mary Chapelman of Clovelly, in 1742.

ON AN ALTAR TOMB.

5. In Memory of Thomas Pearse of Holwill in Davidstow, Gentleman, who was Buried August 4th 1789, aged 73 years.

Also, nigh this Place Lieth the Body of Mary Pearse, who was Buried June 4th 1753, in the 27th yeare of her age.

Also, nigh this Place Lieth the Body of Hender Pearse, Gentleman, who was Buried May 28th 1762, in the 84th year of his age.

Also nigh this Place Lieth the Body of Joan Pearse, the Wife of Hender Pearse, Gentleman, who was Buried April 25 1770, aged 81 years, and they were Father and Mother to the above Thomas and Mary Pearse.

6. In memory of William Betenson Esq. of Grylls in this Parish, who was buried here May the 13th 1771, aged 65.

And of William Gilbert Betenson, Gent., Son of the said William Betenson and Grace his wife, who was buried Dec. the 1st 1759, aged 27. Also of Anne Betenson Daughter of the said William and Grace Betenson, who was buried August the 5th 1767, aged 38.

Let who so list think Death a dreadful thing
And hold the Grave in Horrow [sic] and in hate;
We think them both worth welcoming.
Where end our Woes our Joys begin.

ARMS: A Fess, in chief a lion passant. CREST: A horse's head couped.

7. Sacred to the Memory of Samuel Langford of Grylls in this Parish, Yeoman, who departed this life Nov. 14th 1843, aged 61.

Also of Mary his wife. She died March 8th 1847, aged 61 years.

THE MANOR OF HELSET.

This Manor in the 13th century formed parcel of the possessions of the family of Giffard of Helland,[1] and in 1302 Simon Gifford of Hellisete, commenced proceedings against William Prempa and others that they should do service for the manor mill.[2] Simon Giffard of Helset presented to the Church of Helland in 1348.[3]   Ingreta, granddaughter of the said Simon, and co-heir of her father John Giffard, carried it in marriage to Thomas Colyn,[4] and it formed part of a settlement made by the said Thomas and Ingreta in 1411.[5]   It descended to Elizabeth Colyn their great grand-daughter who was thrice married.[6]   Her third husband was Edward Ap Rice, *alias* Apryse, *alias* Preys, who, in her right, presented to the Church of Helland in 1499.[7]   In the following year Edward Preys and Elizabeth his wife suffered a common recovery to John Wyllemer and Roger Cheverell of the Manor of Helset with appurtenances in the parish of Lesnewith, also all messuages, &c. in Helset, Treworwell, Trenguen, Denbeth, Trewanyon, Peneton, Wogolowe, Trebuhan and Anderton,[8] and by their charter, dated 21st February 18th Henry VII, (1502-3).   John Wyllemer and Roger Cheverell granted the same manor and lands to Peter Courteney[9] and his heirs and assigns for evermore,[10] and in the following April the said Edward Preys and Elizabeth his wife suffered a fine to the said John Wylmer of the same manor and lands.[11]

The manor thus became vested in Peter Courteney, who died, in 1508, without surviving issue, thereof seized, and by will, dated 16th August in that year, after directing that his body should be buried in the Chapel of St. Saviour at Dartmouth before the ymage of St. Saviour in the choir, if he dye there, devises all his lands in Cornwall to Johan his wife for the term of her life, and directs that in her lifetime she shall make an estate to the churchwardens of Uploman, in the county of Devon, of all his lands in Uploman, Kalenge and Dartmouth, and of the Manor of Helsete in the parish of Lesnewyth in the county of Cornwall, for the term of four-score years, to find a Priest to sing for him, his wife and children, and all his friends in the parish Church there; and he directs that after sixty years of the said term shall have expired, the churchwardens shall make another estate of the said lands to others of the said parish, at the discretion of the parishioners, for a further term of four-score years, and so on from four-score to four-score years, one

---

[1] Assize Rolls, Devon and Cornwall, 23rd Edward I, 2 N 9   [5] See also ante p. 9, note.

[2] Assize Rolls, Cornwall, 30th Edward I, 2 M 21 1, m. 22. See also ante p. 35, note 3.

[3] See ante p. 11.   [4] See ante p. 41.

[5] Ibid. p. 7.   [6] See pedigree, ante pp. 40, 41.

[7] See ante p. 12.   [8] De Banco Rolls, 16th Henry VII, Trinity. m. 252.

[9] Son of Sir William Courteney of Powderham by Margaret daughter of Lord Bonville, and brother of Edward Courteney of Landrake.

[10] Rot. Claus. 18th Henry VII, m. 22.   [11] Pedes Finium. 18th Henry VII, Easter.

term after another, immediately following, and he makes his said wife Jane sole executrix.[1]
Jane his wife survived him a few days only.   By her will, dated 30th August 1508, after
directing that her body shall be buried in the Chapel of St. Saviour of Dartmouth in the
choir where the body of her husband Piers Courteney lieth buried, and giving to the said
Chapel her husband's best chain of gold, she desires her executors to see and help her
husband's will to be fulfilled and performed to the Church of Uploman, as in his testament
is contained, and gives them full power and authority so to do.   She makes Sir William
Courteney, Knight,[2] overseer of her will, and gives him a young horse colt of gray, that
she had going in Cadley park, to the intent that he should help her husband's executors
and her's to fulfil her husband's will and her own.[3]

These intentions were accordingly fulfilled, and the chantry founded, but, of course,
the lands forming the endowment fell into the King's hands under the Act for suppressing
the Chantries, Colleges, &c.   In the certificate of the Commissioners, appointed 14th
February 37th Henry VIII, under the head of Uploman appears the following entry:
"The Chauntrye called Courteney's.   Founded by Peers Courteney, Esquyer.   To fynde
pryste to praye for hym wythein the parish Church of Uploman.   The yerelye value of
y° lands and possessions, vj[u] xvj[d]."[4]

This, however, could have been a moiety of the manor only.   The other moiety was
vested in the issue of Elizabeth Colyn by her first husband, and, like the Manor of
Helland, &c., devolved upon Johanna daughter and heir of Humphry Calwodely, who
carried them in marriage to Roger Arundell, whose son and heir, Humphry Arundell, for
the share which he took in the Cornish rising in 1549, was attainted and executed, and
his estates forfeited to the Crown.

The King being, by these means, in the possession of the two moieties of the
Manor of Helset, by Letters Patent, dated 5th March 1549-50, granted it, *inter alia*, to
Sir Gawen Carew, Knight;[5] and, in 1560, the said Sir Gawen Carew, George Carew,
Clerk,[6] and Ann daughter of Sir Nicholas Harvey, Knight, wife of the said George,
suffered a fine to George Southcott, Gent., and John Prowse of the Manor of Helset with
appurtenances, also of twenty messuages, eight cottages, 100s. rent, &c., in Helset, &c.,
whereby they quitclaimed and warranted the same to the said George and John and the
heirs of the said George for ever.[7]   George Southcott and John Prowse appear to have
made this purchase jointly, for on 2nd April 1572, a licence was granted to John Prowse
to alienate to John Walrond, Richard Ap Powell, and Thomas Harknell, and their heirs
all that part, purparty or portion of all those messuages, &c., in Lesnewith, called
Hilsett, which the aforesaid John, together with George Southcote, lately purchased to

---

[1] Proved 2nd October 1508, P.C.C. Bennett, 5.

[2] Sir William Courteney of Powderham her husband's brother ob. 1512, direct ancester of the Earl of Devon.

[3] Proved 2nd October 1508, by Adam Raley her brother and executor, Bennett, 5.

[4] Augmentation Office, 37th Henry VIII, Certificate No. 15, 43.

[5] Rot. Pat. 6th Edward VI, Part 6, m. 39.

[6] George Carew of Upton Hillion, Clerk, D.D., Dean of Windsor, next brother and heir of Sir Gawen,
he having no issue. (*Vide* Ped. CAREW in "Life", and Times of Sir Peter Carew Knight, 1857.)

[7] Pedes Finium, Cornwall, 2nd Elizabeth, Easter.

them and their heirs, to hold to the use of the said John Prowse for the term of his life, remainder to Robert Prowse, son of the said John and the heirs male of his body,[1] and in 1570 John Prowse suffered a fine, *inter alia*, in this manor to the said John Waldron and others.[2] In 1620 Humphry Prowse[3] held parcel of Helset, after the death of Robert Prowse his father, John Prowse his brother, and John his grandfather;[4] and in 1649 Robert Prouse suffered a recovery to Henry Bligh, Gent., of a moiety of this manor.[5] In 1613, Thomas Southcott, Esq., and Richard Southcott, Gent., suffered a fine, *inter alia*, in the manor of Calwodely and this manor, to Thomas Whitfield, Esq., and John Whitfield, Gent.,[6] which was probably for purposes of settlement, for, in 1632 Richard Southcott suffered a fine in the same manors to John Cowling and William Ley, Gent.,[7] probably for a like purpose. These Southcotts were of Calwodely[8] at the Visitation of the Heralds in 1620, and registered their descent from John Southcott of Bovye Tracy;[9] and we find that John Prouz of Chagford married Margaret daughter of John Southcott of Bovye Tracy, which may account for the Prowses having a moiety of the manor.

In 1621 Humphry Prowse, Gent. and Grace his wife suffered a fine of one messuage in Helset, and the moiety of one messuage in Trebiffin, to John Moyle, Esq.,[10] and in 1679 the entirety of the manor had passed to Sir Walter Moyle of Bake, Knight,[11] who, in conjunction with Walter his son and heir, sold the same to Sir John Carew of Antony, Bart., whose son, Sir William Carew, held courts of the manor in 1714, (*see* Rental and Court Roll post), and on 30th January 1732 granted a lease of a tenement in Trewanion, *alias* Trewanguyon, said to have been previously granted on lease by Richard Southcote to a tenant then deceased, together with the eighth part of Tettes-boroughdown, all which premises are described as being parcel of the manor of Helset and then in the tenure of Martha Langman widow, to the said Martha for the term of 99 years if Edward Langman and Thomas Langman, sons of the said Martha, so long should live.[12] Sir William Carew died in 1744, intestate, and the estates devolved upon his only surviving son Sir Coventry Carew, Bart., who died s.p. in 1748, having by his will devised to his cousin,[13] Jonathan Rashleigh of Menabilly, Esq., *inter alia*, the lordship and manor of

---

[1] Rot. Pat., 14th Elizabeth, Part 10.   [2] Pedes Finium, Divers Counties, 14 Elizabeth, Trinity.

[3] Humphry Prowse of Mamhead, co. Devon, Gent., was buried at Lesnewth, 23rd May 1638   (M. I., No. 2, p. 413) He doubtless died at Helset.

[4] This family of Prowse was of Tiverton, but claimed descent from the house of Chagford, and were allowed the same arms: sa. three lions ramp. ar. (Heralds' Visitation of Devon, 1620. Harl. Soc. Pub. 1872, p. 224.)   [5] Recoveries 1649. Hilary, m. 11.

[6] Pedes Finium, Divers Counties, 10th James, Trinity.

[7] Ped. Finium Cornwall, 7th Charles, Michaelmas.

[8] Which was also parcel of the forfeited possessions of Humphry Arundell, and formed part of the grant to Sir Gawen Carew.

[9] Heralds' Visitation, Devon, Harl. Society, 1872, p. 269.   [10] Pedes Finium 18th James, Hilary.

[11] See Terrier of that date ante page 405. Sir Walter was knighted at Whitehall 4th February 1663. Arms: gules a mule ar.

[12] Deed in the possession of Mr. Rickard of Trehane, in Trevalga.

[13] Jonathan Rashleigh was the eldest son of Jonathan Rashleigh of Menabilly, by Jane one of the daughters of the aforesaid Sir John Carew, and aunt and one of the co-heirs of the said Sir Coventry Carew.

Hellcett, otherwise Hellsett, together with the rents and services of all the free tenants of the said manor, which high rents amounted to about 18s. 8d. yearly, or thereabouts, and one red rose, and all those messuages, lands, &c., known by the names of Tregline* and Trevanger* in the parish of St. Minver purchased of William Peters, Rowe's Helland* and Kestell's* tenements in Blisland purchased of Francis Reynolds and Obadiah his son, Boskier* in the parish of Bodmyn,[1] together with the capital messuage and barton and demesne lands of Helsett, and all those messuages called Trebiffin, Anderton's mills, Trewenguen, and Treworle, together with all courts, courts-leet, view of frank pledge &c., &c., to hold to the said Jonathan Rashleigh his heirs and assigns for ever, chargeable with certain annuities.

Philip Rashleigh, son and successor of Jonathan Rashleigh, by Indentures of lease and release, dated respectively 24th and 25th December 1772, conveyed the fee of the Barton to Digory Langman of Lesnewth, Gent., who already held the lease thereof for the residue of a term of twenty-one years, at the yearly rent of £57 4s., to hold of the chief Lord of the fee subject to the rents and services theretofore due and accustomed.[2] Digory Langman died in May 1811, having by his will, dated 30th March 1802, devised this estate to his two youngest sons, Digory Langman and Jose Langman, subject to certain charges, who, under the description of Digory Langman, yeoman, and Jose Langman, yeoman, both of the parish of St. Juliott, by Indentures of lease and release, dated respectively 24th and 25th December 1818, conveyed the fee to William Pitt Bray, Clerk, who, dying on 22nd July 1844, by his will, dated 4th May 1844, devised this estate to William Sloggatt and Claudius Crigan Hawker of Boscastle, Gent., in trust for sale; and, Mr. Sloggatt having disclaimed, it was sold the following year by the said Claudius Crigan Hawker to John Pemberthy Magor of Redruth, afterwards of Lamellen, Gent., whose son is the present proprietor.

We select for publication the following from among the Rentals and Court Rolls of the Manor:[1]

| Manor of Helset | The Court Baron of the honor[d] S[r] William Carew, Baronet, held for said Manor at the house of John Bray, Reeve of the said Manor, the 27th day of October 1715 |

Homage

John Bray jur.   Abel Michell jur.
William Simons jur.   Edwar Langman jur.

The Presentments of the said Jury

We present all our ancient customes to be good and ought to be continued.

---

[1] The tenements marked thus * would not appear to have been parcel of the ancient manor of Helset, but to have been purchased and annexed thereto by the Carew family.

[2] The Manor of Helset was subject to a Fee Farm Rent of 4s. 6d. per annum, which was reserved upon the grant by the Crown to Sir Gawen Carew after the attainder of Humphry Arundell. This rent, *inter alia*, was granted by Letters Patent, 11th November 23rd Charles II. (1671) to Francis Lord Hawley and others for sale, who, by Indenture dated 23rd February 24th Charles II, (1671-2) conveyed the same, *inter alia*, to Edward Boscawen, Esq. (Rot. Claus. 24th Charles II, Part 22, m. 34). Upon the sale to Mr. Langman this rent had not been paid, or demanded, for many years.

We present all free and Convencionary Tenants that owe Suit & Service at this Court & have made default this day.

We present the death of Christopher Langman, his son Christopher to be taken Tenant jur.

We present John Bray junʳ to be taken Tenant for the moyety of Treworle jur :

We present Edward Joce to be taken Tenant for the moyety of Trebiffin.

We present Elizabeth Joce to be Reeue for the year ensuing.

We present all former presentments that are not withdrawn.

John Bray
William Symons
his
Abel × Michel
sign
Edward Langman

30ˢ due for Heriot on the death of Christopher Langman recᵈ 8ᵇʳ 18ᵗʰ 1716.

MANNOR OF } High & Conventionary Rents recᵈ November 8ᵗʰ 1714 payable att
HELLSETT. } Mich'. last past.

Willliam Simons Reeve.

Tenemᵗˢ & Tenants.	Rents.	Rates Allowed.	Recᵈ Cleare.
Trewinian : Martha Langman	£1 9 3		
2 Tenᵐᵗˢ one year		....	£1 9 7
pᵈ Short 4ᵈ	4		
Anderton } John Bray one year & Mills }	£2 8 2	£0 3 00	£2 5 2
Trewinian Eliz. Joce one year	£0 12 3	....	£0 12 3
Ibidᵐ John Paynter ...	£0 11 9	....	£0 11 9
Ibidᵐ } Christ' Langman 2 Tenemᵗˢ } one year	£1 2 6	....	£1 02 6
Treworle Hugh Hony ..	£0 4 10	....	£0 04 10
Trebiffin. Wᵐ Symons in part			
for three leases, rent	£2 8 4		
& in part of arrears ...	£3 10 2		
	£5 18 6		£5 18 06
			£12 04 03

Zacharias Coleman, in hand, Trewore £0 4 10

The High Rents & Suits amounting to £1 00 02 to be paid by William Simons, Reeve of yᵉ sᵈ Manor, at the next Court as according to Custome.

Not paid 1715.

Convencionary rents & dues amount to £9 2 3 : deduct for Treworle 4s. 10d. & pᵗ of Joce's Tenemᵗ in hand :

Recᵈ 8 14 5
Allowᵈ 03 0
Z. Coleman in hand 4 10
—————
£9 2 3

Accounted with Edwᵈ Langman this 8ᵗʰ day of Nov. 1714 : and find to be due from him for rent to Mich'mas last for the Barton of Helset : £20 05 05

¹ In the possession of W. H. Pole-Carew of Antony, Esq.

GRYLLS *alias* TREGRYLLS.

This estate gave its name to an ancient family of gentlemen, the probable representative of which served the office of Sheriff of Cornwall last year (1873). When the aid was levied in 31st Edward I., (1303) for marrying the King's eldest son, John de Grylles held one knight's fee, of the fees of Moreton, in Grylles, for which, in the first instance, he paid an aid of 25s., the fees of Moreton being small fees and not assessed at so high a rate as the other fees. Afterwards, however, he paid a further sum of 15s.[1] which made his contribution equal to the ordinary rate. In subsequent aids we do not find Grylls mentioned as a separate fee, nor do we know when it passed away from the family of Grylls. Indeed, we have been able to glean but very scanty information concerning its ancient history. It was perhaps in the possession of the family of Betenson as early as the reign of Queen Elizabeth, William Betenson having been assessed to the subsidy in Lesnewith in 1572 and 1600. It continued in this family for many descents; William Betenson died seized of it in 1710, as did his son of the same name, being the last of his race, in 1771.

From the family of Betenson the estate passed by purchase to the family of Glynn.[2] In the particulars of the sale of the lands of Edmund John Glynn Esq. in 1823, Grylls is described as a "Barton and Tithing," and is shewn as annexed to the Manor of Halwell. Grylls was eventually purchased by Sir John Yarde Buller, Bart., afterwards Lord Churston, by whose representative it is now possessed.

[1] Pipe Roll, 31st Edward I, Cornwall.

[2] Mr. Betenson lost his son, who was drowned on a pleasure cruise to Wales, and, surviving all his issue, adopted a person of his own name, said to have been a weaver at Tiverton, but no relation, who, upon the death of Mr. Betenson, succeeded to his estates, subject to the payment of an annuity to Mr. Betenson's widow, who survived him seven years. The weaver soon became involved, and sold his interest in the lands to Mr. Glynn for an annuity of £30 a year for life, and at the same time his son and heir sold his reversionary interest and became Steward to the family of Glanville of Catchfrench. This account is derived from local information.

FAMILY HISTORY.

GRYLLS.

The family of Grylls, which, probably, derived its name from the estate of Grylls in the parish of Lesnewith, is of great antiquity in Cornwall;[1] in various parts of which county they held lands at an early date. In 1303, John de Grilles held one knight's fee in Grilles and another knight's fee in Treudered (in Blisland).[2] From proceedings taken in the previous year he would seem to have let on lease for thirteen years, certain lands belonging to the last named manor, to Walter de St. Margaret, viz., certain messuages in Treudered, Penstradou, Greeneborough, and Lawalles, and Walter complained that in the following year the said John de Grilles had, by craft, ejected him, and he obtained a verdict.[3] In 1316 an assize of view of recognizance was granted to enquire if John de Grelles and John and William his sons, Henry Tyrell and Lawrence Penhyrgbard had unjustly disseized William, son of Walter, de St. Margaret of his free tenements in Trehudred, Kernek, and Penstradou. The interest held by the family of St. Margaret in the manor of Trehudreth not long after this date had passed to the family of Carburra, but litigation still continued, for in 1361 John, son of William, de Grillys took proceedings against Walter Carburra, senior, Richard Hendyman, Chaplain, Stephen Madek, Chaplain, and Walter Carburra, junior, and Meroda his sister, concerning five messuages and two carucates of land in Trehudreyt which he claimed as his right, and a day was given for the trial in the following Hilary term.[5] And, at the same Assize, John, son of John, de Grylls petitioned against William Cyteller and Alice his wife concerning one acre of land in Boduf, juxta Brounyr (Bodeve near Burnayre in Egloshayle) which he claimed as his right.[6] It is shewn, however, on the levy of the aid in 20th Edward III, that the fee in Treuderet which John de Grilles had formerly held was then held by Roger de Carburra.[7]

[1] Warine de Griles, Priest, was admitted to the Vicarage of St. Tethe in 1257, upon the presentation of the Prior and Convent of Bodmin.—Bishop Bronescombe's Reg.

[2] Subsidy Roll, 31st Edward $\frac{87}{4}$

[3] Assize Roll, Cornwall, 30th Edward I. $\left.\begin{array}{c} M \\ 1 \\ .21 \end{array}\right\}$ 1, m. 18.

[4] Ibid. 10th Edward II, $\left.\begin{array}{c} N \\ 2 \\ 16 \end{array}\right\}$ 5, m. 142.

[5] De Banco Rolls, 35th Edward III, Michaelmas, m. 133.

[6] Ibid., m. 160.

[7] Book of Aids.

3 K

Soon after this date the family of Grylls would seem to have left Cornwall and settled in Devonshire, for we do not find any further mention of the name (except that John Grilles was chaplain, or stipendiary curate, in the Deanery of Trigg Minor in the 3rd and 4th of Richard II, 1380-1381), in Cornish records until 1569, when William Grylls of Tavistock, who heads the pedigree recorded at the Heralds' Visitation of Cornwall in 1620, held one ferling of land, Cornish, in Downe of the Manor of Bodulgate in socage.[1] His son Charles Grylls was a Councillor at Law and acquired Court and other lands in Lanreath, and there seated himself. By Agnes his wife, daughter of George Tubbe of Trengoffe, besides three daughters, he had four sons, some of whom founded other branches of the family. His eldest son, John Grylls of Court, married Grace daughter and co-heir of William Bere of Pengelly in St. Neot, the representative of several ancient Cornish families.[2] He was a devoted loyalist and took an active part in the cause of the King in the great rebellion of the 17th century. In recognition of his patriotism and loyalty the King, when he visited Cornwall in August 1644, conferred upon him the honour of knighthood, and for the same cause, upon the overthrow of the kingdom, the dominant party seized all his estates. He died, however, on 30th December 1649 before any further steps could be taken. He was described by the Sequestration Committee as "one of the violent men against the honest party that stood for the Parliament in Cornwall," and was said to have "made little or no satisfaction to the State for his delinquency, or to such persons as were injured or undone by them."[3] His son and heir, Charles Grylls, was one of the gallant defenders of Pendennis castle, which, under the brave old Governor, John Arundel of Trerice, a gentleman nearly four-score years of age, was the last but one to surrender, which it did on 16th August 1646.[4] Charles Grylls being in the castle at the time claimed and was allowed on 2nd June 1657 to compound for his estates under the articles of capitulation, and paid the sum of £582 16s. 3d. being one third the value of his unsettled estates.[5] Charles Grylls was succeeded by his eldest son of his own name who married Elizabeth daughter and heir of Richard Gerveys of Benathlek, *alias* Benallack, in Constantine, by whom he had two sons and several daughters. Charles, his eldest son, married Mary daughter and sole heir of Edmund Spoure of Trebartha, but died without surviving issue. Richard, his second son, was Rector of Lanreath, and by his wife, Ann Mohun, had a son Richard Gerveys Grylls who settled at Helston where he married Cordelia only daughter and heir of Thomas Glynn of Helston,[6] one of devisees under the will of Elizabeth Glynn of Trewane before mentioned. From this marriage the fourth in descent is Shadwell Morley Grylls of Lewarne Esq., late a Lieut.-Colonel in the army, who was sheriff of Cornwall in 1873, and is the present representative of the family of Grylls.

---

[1] See ante p. 342.
[2] See Descents ante vol. i, p. 311.
[3] Royalist Comp. Papers, first series, vol. lii, 673.
[4] Ragland Castle held out until the following day.
[5] Ibid, second series, vol. xlix 585, 591.
[6] See Ped. of GLYNN, ante p. 73.

GEIRVEIS *alias* GERVEYS OF BENATHLEK *alias* BENALLACK IN CONSTANTINE.

The family of Gerveys is of great antiquity in Cornwall. The original name, as appears from the pedigree recorded in the Herald's College, was Antrenon (incorrectly written Antrewon) descended from Peter Lord of Antrenon who is stated to have married a daughter of Hugh Peverel. This Peter was probably the son of Roger de Antrenon, who, with Nicholaa his wife, in 1230 levied a fine of Godfrey, Prior of St. Germans, of the Advowson of the Church of St. Sythyn of Merthersithune,[1] in which the said Prior acknowledged the right of the said Nicholaa to the said advowson, and remised and quitclaimed the same to them and the heirs of Nicholaa for ever, for which acknowledgment, &c., Roger and Nicholaa granted to the Prior and Church of St. Germans 4s., to be received as alms for ever of the parson of the said Church of St. Sythyn, whoever should be made parson. The Lord William Briwere, then Bishop of Exeter, was present when the fine was made, as were also Walter Colsweyn and Bellesaund his wife, and Salamanda, sisters of the said Nicholaa who recognised the said Advowson as the right of the said Nicholaa and her reasonable portion.[2] From this it would appear that Nicholaa, Bellesaund and Salamanda were coheirs, but whose daughters they were we have no knowledge. Gerveis de Antrenon, second son of Joceus, son of the abovementioned Peter, had three sons: John Gerveis of Helston, founder of the family of Gerveys, Michael, and Joceus. The latter is not named in the officially recorded pedigree. By Charter dated at Helstonburgh on Thursday next after the feast of the Translation of St. Thomas the Martyr (7th July) 5th Edward III, (1331), Stephen de Trefusa granted to Joceus son of Gervas de Antrenon and Matilda his wife certain premises, particularly described, in Helstonburgh, some of which abutted on premises held by Gervas de Antrenon and John Gerveys, to hold to the said Joceus and Matilda and the heirs of their bodies, in default, remainder to John Gerveys, brother of the said Joceus, and the heirs of his body; thus confirming the change of name shewn in the pedigree. John Gerveys married Nicholaa daughter and heir of John Benaleck, or Benathleck, in Constantine. She was probably the grandaughter of Nicholas de Benathlek, who, in 1297, gave the King half a mark for a writ,[3] which Nicholas was probably the son of Henry de Benathlek, who in 1244 suffered a fine in Benathlek to Geoffry de Pridias and Isabella his wife.[4] In 1312 John Gerveys and Nicholaa his wife suffered a fine to John Bethwer of seven messuages, &c., in Benathlek and Boscasek, &c., except the third part of two messuages in Benathlek and Boscasek, which Alice, relict of John, Benathlek held in dower, whereby the said messuages, and the reversion of the lands held in dower, were settled upon the said John

---

[1] Dr. Oliver assigns the dedication of the Parish Church of Merther to St. Coanus (Mon. Exon. p. 441), and we do not trace that he anywhere mentions the grant of 4s. payable to the Priory of St. Germans upon the institution of every Incumbent.   [2] Pedes Finium, 14th Henry III, Trinity.

[3] Rot. Fin. 25th Edward I.   [4] Pedes Finium, 28th Henry III.

3 K[2]

Gerveys and Nicholaa and the heirs of their bodies, remainder to the right heirs of the said Nicholaa.[1] John Gerveys, according to the pedigree, was living in 1323. He left three sons, James, who carried on the succession, Michael and Thomas. The latter is stated to have died s.p., and we have no trace of issue from Michael. He is stated in the pedigree to have been Mayor of Helston. In 1384, he was one of the Collectors of Subsidies.[2] In 1390 he took proceedings against one John Langwyth of Helston, to compel him to render an account for the time that he was Receiver of the moneys of the said Michael.[3] He was dead in 1400, for in January 1400-1 we find Johanna, relict of Michael Gerveys, James Gerveys, and Martin Pellour, executors of the will of the said Michael, sueing one Michael Mellour of Helston for a debt of £40.[4]

James Gerveys married Isabel daughter and co-heir of Roger Trevighoe. In 1367 a fine was levied in which James Gerveys and Isabella his wife were querists and Thomas Gerveys deforcient, whereby five messuages &c. and one mill in Treneglos woos, Bosdrenelon, and other lands were settled on the said James and Isabella and the heirs of their bodies, and in default of such issue remainder to the right heirs of the said Isabella.[5] These lands were, of course, her inheritance. By charter dated on Monday next after the feast of St. Michael 10th Richard II, (1386) John Skywys, Lord of Skywys, granted to James Gerveys of Benadlek all his messuages &c. in Benadlek, which charter, upon inspeximus, John Skywys, son and heir of the said John, on the Friday following, confirmed. We find also that in a deed, dated on Saturday next before the feast of St. Luke the Evangelist in the following year, reference is made to a grant by John Skywys, Lord of Skywys, to the same James Gerveys, as Lord of Benadlek, of a rent of £10 per annum payable out of Skywys and other lands. By his charter dated at Benathlek on Tuesday next before the feast of the Purification of the Blessed Virgin Mary 5th Henry IV, (1405-6) James Gerveys granted to John Rosmaryn all his lands and tenements in Benathlek which he had of the inheritance of Nicholaa his mother, to hold to the said John during the whole time of the life of Isabella wife of the said James.[6] Isabella died in 7th Henry IV, (1405) before her husband. How long he survived her we cannot tell. They left two sons and two daughters. John the eldest son married Margaret daughter and heir of William Mewthing. In 1401 John Gerveys (during the life of his father) and Margaret his wife gave the king 10s. for a writ of convention.[7] ·In the same year a fine was levied in which John Gerves and Margaret his wife were querists and Thomas Jon of Helston deforcient, whereby five messuages in Argaun, Trewothen, &c., together with the reversion of two messuages in Trewothen held by Thomas Burwyk and Johanna his wife, were settled on the said John and Margaret and the heirs of their bodies, in default, remainder to Margaret and the heirs of her body, in default, remainder to the heirs of the said John.[8] Of this John

[1] Pedes Finium, 6th Edward III, Michaelmas.   [2] Rot. Fin. 7th Richard II.
[3] De Banco Rolls, 13th Richard II, Hilary, m, 167 d.   [4] Ibid., 2nd Henry IV, Trinity, m, 299.
[5] Ped. Fin. 41st Edward III, Mich.   [6] Charters penes Colonel Grylls.
[7] Rot. Fin. 2nd Henry IV.

[8] Ped. Fin. 2nd Henry IV, Trinity. These lands were probably of the inheritance of Margaret, and Johanna wife of Thomas Burwyk was probably the relict of William Mewthing.

we have no further note. It appears from the pedigree above cited that he was alive in 11th Henry VI, (1433). We know not when he died.

Peter Gerveys succeeded. By charter dated 35th Henry VI. (1460) James Rosmeryn quitclaimed to him all the right he, the said James, had in Benathelek.[1] In 1467, John Emotte sued Peter Gerveys of Benathlek, gent., and Simon Gerveys of the same place, yeoman, on a plea of trespass at Helstonburgh;[2] and in 1472 the same Peter and Simon, together with James Gerveys and Henry Gerveys, described also as of Benathlek, yeomen, were sued by John Carowe, Clerk, for a trespass at Helstonburgh and the removal of the goods and chatels of the said John;[3] and in the same term the same Peter was sued by John Bere of Bodmin in a plea of debt.[4] These actions were not closed in 1475.

Peter Gerveys was succeeded by his son William, who married Emlyn daughter of Michael Petit, whose widow Thomasine after his death, intermarried with Peter Bevil, who in his will, proved in 1515, bequeaths to William Gerveys " his best gowne lyned with Sasnet." Thomasine Bevil, the widow, in her will in 1517 names her daughter Emlyn, and says: " I bequeath to William Gerves children begotten of Emlyn £6 13s. 4d. between them."[5]

It would seem to be unnecessary to trace further in detail the descents of this family, and the reader is referred to the accompanying pedigree, which will shew that Richard Gerveys, the fourth in descent from the above mentioned William, in whom the estates became vested, had an only child and heir named Elizabeth, who married Charles Grylls of Court, to whom she carried the said lands.

ARMS OF GRYLLS: Or, three bendlets, enhanced, gu. CREST: a porcupine argent.

Confirmed to William Grills, by Robert Cooke, Clarencieux King of Arms, 19th Elizabeth, A.D. 1577. 2 C. 1. 140.

NOTE: For Pedigrees of Gerveys and Grylls, *see* post pp. 427-431.

---

[1] Charter penes Colonel Grylls.
[2] De Banco Rolls, 7th Edward IV, Michaelmas, m. 372.
[3] Ibid., 11th Edward IV, Hil. m, 6 d.
[4] Ibid., m, 255.
[5] Heralds' Visitation of Cornwall, Harl. Soc. Pub. 1874, p. 76, n.

PEDIGREE OF BETENSON OF LESNEWITH.

William Betenson of ⊤ Jane, dau. of . . . .
Lesnewth, assessed to │ bur.[1] 25th Jan.
Subs. there 1572-1600. │ 1597.

Degory Betenson admitted to Rectory of Lesnewth, upon the presentation of William Betenson 1585. Bur.[1] 17th June 1617.

Alice, bur.[1] 19th Jan. 1578.

William Betenson of ⊤ Jane dau. of . . . . . .
Lesnewth, assessed to │ bur.[1] 24th Oct. 1646.
Subs. there 1624, 1625. │ Will dated 19th Jan.
Bur.[1] 7th March 1631. │ 1643. Prov. 12th Sept.
│ 1647, Archd. Cornw.

Thomas Betenson of ⊤ . . . .
Oterham, Rector of │
Minster, Forrabury, │
and Trevalga, 1614. │

Degory, bap.[1] 11th Feb. 1609, bur.[1] 28th June 1611.

Degory Beten- ⊤ Isota, dau. of
son of Lesnewth │ . . . . . Mabyn of
son and heir, │ Launcels. Mar.
bap.[1] 6th May │ Lic. 12th July
1612. Assessed │ 1638, mar.[1] same
to Subs. in Les- │ day. Bur. 24th
newth 1641. │ Dec. 1693. Admo.
Named in │ granted 30th April
mother's will. │ 1694 to Richard
│ Betenson of Les-
│ nowth, M.D., her
│ son.

Elizabeth, bap.[1] 8th Oct. 1614, bur.[1] 31st July 1624,

Dorothy, bap.[1] 24th June 1617. Ex[x]. with brother Humphry to mother's will.

Humphry Bet- ⊤ Christine
enson born 5th │ dau. of
bap.[1] 13th Feb. │ . . . . . .
1619. Named in │ Pearse.
mother's will, of │ Mar.[1]
which he was │ 18th
joint exr. Assess. │ Oct.
to Subs. in Les- │ 1655.
newth 1641, │ Bur.[1]
bur.[1] 10th April │ 13th
1692. │ Feb.
│ 1700.

William Betenson, born 25th May, bap.[1] 1st June, 1623. Admitted to the Vicarage of Ilsington co. Devon, 28th March 1663?

Mary, bap.[1] 6th Dec. 1610.

Mary Betenson, bap.[1] 8th Dec. 1639. Mar. Thomas Pearse of Halwell, in Davidstow, mar. lic. 17th Oct. 1671. Mar.[1] 3rd Sept. 1673. Bur.[1] 19th Nov. 1693, aged 54.

Isatt, bap.[1] 1st March 1642.

Elizabeth, bap.[1] 20th Oct. 1641. Will dat. 22nd Nov. 1681. Prov. 19th April 1682, Archd. Cornw.

William ⊤ Elizabeth,
Betenson- │ dau. of . . . .
born 23rd, │ Bur. 28th
bap.[1] 30th │ Jan. 1713.
Dec. 1648, │ Will dated
bur.[1] 20th │ 25th Jan.
July 1680. │ 1713. Prov.
│ 13th Oct.
│ 1735.

Richard Betenson born 8th, bap.[1] 23rd Sept. 1652, of Les- newth, M.D.

Jane, born 21st and bap.[1] 30th Jun. 1654. Bur.[1] 5th May 1721, unmar.

Richard, born 18th, bap.[1] 25th Feb. 1657. Bur.[1] 10th Nov. 1678.

William, bap.[1] 27th Sept. 1659, bur.[1] 11th June 1691.

William Betenson of ⊤ Anne dau. of . . . . . . Blinch. of Buckland
Grylls. Bap.[1] 8th Jan. │ Brewer, Devon. Mar. lic. 8th Oct. 1705,
1678. Bur.[1] 18th Aug. │ named in will of Elizabeth Betenson, her
1710. │ mother-in-law 1713. Remar. Edward Amy
│ of Botreaux Castle 1735. Bur.[1] 23rd March
│ same year.

William Betenson of Grylls, ⊤ Grace, dau. & co-h. of Samuel
bap.[1] 10th April 1706. Bur.[1] │ Gilbert of Tackbear. Mar.
13th May 1771, aged 65, │ lic. 22nd Feb. 1727. Bur.[1]
M.I., s.p. │ 29th Nov. 1778.

George Betenson, bap.[1] 19th Aug. 1710. Died, s.p. Admo. to brother William, 13th Oct. 1735. Archd. Cornw.

Ann, bap. 1st July 1729. Bur.[1] 5th Aug. 1767, aged 38, M.I.

William-Gilbert, bap.[1] 16th March 1732, bur.[1] 2nd Dec. 1759, aged 27, M.I.

---

[1] At Lesnewith.

PEDIGREE OF GERVEIS OF BENATHLECK.

Peter, Lord of Antrewon.—.... dau. of Hugh Peveril.

Joceus de Antrewon.—Alice, dau. Roger le Archdekne of
Treworton Hall, co. Cornwall.

Peter, eldest son=.... dau. of .. Basset Gervasius de Antrewon in Cornwall,—
  2nd son.

Joceus de Antrenon, living 1331.—Matilda. Michael, 2. John Gerveis of—Nicholaa, dau. and sole heir of John Benalek. Nicholas de
Collector of Subs. 1349. Rot. Helston, 17th Benathlek, probably grandfather of Nicholaa, gave half
Fin. 23rd Edward III, m, 23.   Edw. II, 1323-4. a mark for a writ, 25th Edward I. Rot. Fin. m. 14.

Thomas, Michael, 2. Mayor of Helston. Living=Johanna, ex. James Gerveis, Anno.=Isabel, dau. and co-heir of Roger
ob. s.p. 13th Richard II. De Banco Roll, Hil. to husband's 8th Richard II, living | Trevighoe, ob. 7th Henry IV,
 m. 167 d. Dead 2nd Henry IV. will. 5th Henry IV. before her husband.

Henry Gerveis of John Gerveis, A°. 11th Henry VI. =Margaret dau. and Margaret, wife of Margery, wife of
Helston, 2nd John Gerveys and Margaret his wife had | heir of William Richard Flamock. John Trefusis.
sonne. a writ 1401. Rot. Fin. 2nd Henry IV. | Mewthing.

Peter Gerueis, living 1472. De Banco=Joane, dau. of James.
Roll, 12th Edward IV, Easter. | William Garland.

William Gerueis.=Emlyn daughter of Michael Petit. James.
A°. 20th Henry VIII,

John, eldest son and Margaret, wife Richard Gerueis. By deed dated 22nd June, 1st Elizabeth,=Jane dau. of Thomasine,
heir, mar. Mulier, of .... Hoare made settlement on his children, and by deed dated 12th | Thomas wife of
dau. of John Tre- of St. Ervan. June, 15th Elizabeth, made further settlement on Nicholas | Trefusis of Raufe
sithney, ob. s.p. his son, and Grace his youngest daughter. Bur. at Constan- | Trefusis. Couche of
  tine, 2nd Oct. 1574. Brass in Constantine Church. Glasney.

John Ann dau. of=Thomas Gerueis of Benathleck. Bur.=Isett, dau. of Nicholas, Melior wife of John Jane. A
 Nicholas Herle | at Constantine 26th Aug. 1616. | Richard Pollard 2nd sonne. Pendarves. Died 17th [
Emlya, of Trenouth, | Will prov. in Archd. Court of | of Langlis, co. March 1607. Brass in Grace.
wife of 2nd wife. | Cornwall, 17th March 1816-7. | Devon, 2 w. s.p. Constantine Church.
Trewick.

John Gerueis=Jane, dau. and sole Richard Gerueis, died 1608. =Wilmot, dau. of Thos. Richard. Jenophat, wife Jane,
of Benathleck, heir of William Admo. granted 11th Jan. 1608, | Trenance of Lanhy- of .... wife of
2nd son. Trevanion, bur. to Wilmot his relict. Archd. | drock. Settlement Westcott of ......
 14th Dec. 1658. Court of Cornw. Bur. at Con- | after marriage 20th St. Issey. Harris.
  stantine 26th Nov. 1608. | Aug. 1578.

John, 2, Francis Gerueis=Eliza- Richard, 3,=Sara, dau. of George Ursula, Thomas Gerveis, eldest son. Æt. 36. John,
bap. 1st eldest son æt. | beth. of Benath- | Yeo of Huish, co. wife to John anno. 1620. By deed dated 25th
Jan. 5, anno 1620 leck, son | Devon. Mar. settl. Trewinan. April 1612, and Recovery there George,
1633. Executor to and heir in | dated 21st March Constance. upon, and by Deed Poll dat. 26th bap. 22nd
 his grand- 1652. Bur. | 1652, and 14th April Jane. Jan. 19th James, released and quit- May 1592
 father's will. at Constan- | 1653. Bur. at Con- William, claimed Benathleck, &c. to John
  tine 19th | stantine 9th May ob. s.p. Gerveis his uncle and Francis son Richard,
  Jan. 1658. | 1656. of John. Will proved Archd.
    Cornw., 1st Nov. 1661. Louis,

Mary, bap. at Constantine,
28th March 1639.

PEDIGREE OF

William Grylls of Tavistock in the co. ⊨ *Elizabeth, rel. of*
of Devon. 2, C.I. 373.   *...... Knight.*

Charles Grylls of Lanreath co. Cornwall, Counsellor at ⊨ *Agnes, dau. of George Tubb*
Law, born at Tavistock, eldest son and heir of William | *of Trengoff, co. Cornwall.*
Grylls. Bur. there 2nd March 1611 M.I. Will dated | *Bur. 13th June 1607 at*
21st Feb. 1611-2. Prov. 14th May following. | *Lanreth, M.I.*

Francis Grylls, | *George Grylls of Lanreth afore-* | *Charles Grylls*
instituted to the | *said, bur. there 11th June 1616.* | *of Carven in*
Rectory of Lanreth | *Will dated 6th June 1616.* | *Lanreath. Liv.*
4th June 1614. | *Prov. 26th April 1617, by his* | *1649.*
Prov. his brother | *brothers Francis and Charles, in*
Geo. will 1617, | *the Archdeaconry Court of*
living 1649. | *Cornwall.*

John Grylls, | *Jonathan Grylls,* | *Anne, dau.* ⊨ *Charles Grylls of Lanreth aforesaid also son and*
bap. 23rd Dec. | *2nd son 1620,* | *of ......* | *heir 1620, bap. there 24th Nov. 1611. Aged 8*
1611 at | *bap. 24th Nov.* | *Bur. 8th* | *at Heralds' Visitation, anno 1620. Bur. 25th*
Lanreth. 2nd | *1617 at Lanreth* | *July 1692* | *Dec. 1687 at Lanreth. Will dated 29th Sept.*
son ob. s.p. | *and bur. there* | *at* | *1684. Prov. 11th June 1687 by his son Charles*
 | *26th Jan. 1619.* | *Lanreth.* | *Exor. in Archd. Court, Cornwall.*

A

Charles Grylls of Court in the parish of Lanreth aforesaid. | *Bap.* ⊨ *Elizabeth, dau. and heir of Richard Gerveys of Benallack in Con-*
there 13th Oct. 1642. Matriculated at Queen's College,-Oxford, | *stantine co. Cornwall, grand dau. of George Yeo, of Heaish co.*
2nd Apr. 1661, then aged 19 years. Bur. 18th Aug. 1712 at | *Devon. Mar. Settl. dated 1st Aug. 1671. Will in which she is*
Lanreth. Admo. granted 20th Oct. 1712 to his son Charles and | *des. of Constantine co. Corn, dated 1st Oct. 1722. Prov. 7th Jan.*
Elizabeth his widow and rel. in the Archd. Court, Cornwall. | *1733 by his son Richard Exor. in the Archd. Court of Cornwall.*

Charles Grylls of Trebartha, ⊨ *Mary, dau. and heir of* | *Rev. Richard Grylls, Rector* ⊨ *Ann, dau.* | *Sarah, mar.* | *Elizabeth, mar.*
co. Cornwall, eld. son, bap. | *Edmund Spoure of Trebar-* | *of Lanreth, youngest son, 9th* | *of ......* | *John Rich-* | *Joseph Bastard*
16th May 1672 at Lanreth. | *tha, and rel. of Renatus* | *Nov. 1719, bap. there 18th* | *Mohun, she* | *ards of* | *of Yampton,*
Bur. 24th Feb. 1727 at | *Bellot of Bochym, in the* | *Sept. 1692. Matric. at* | *remar.* | *Liskeard,* | *co. Devon,*
Northill. Will dated 23rd | *parish of Cury, co. Corn-* | *Balliol Coll. Oxford, 22nd* | *........* | *co. Corn-* | *Surgeon, she liv.*
April 1726. Prov. 5th | *wall. Bur. 6th May 1729,* | *March 1709-10, then aged 17* | *Allen.* | *wall, she* | *1732-54, a*
June 1728, by Mary Grylls | *at Northill nr. Laun-* | *years. Bur 19th Jan. 1735* | | *liv. 1732-35* | *widow 1754.*
his widow, rel. and executrix. | *ceston, co. Cornwall.* | *at Lanreth. Will dated* | |
 | | *13th July 1735.* | |

Gerveys Grylls died an infant, buried
18th March 1729, at Northill.

a

GRYLLS.

Sir John Grylls of Lanreath, Knt, eldest son and heir, aged 30 at his father's death. Entered his Pedigree with Arms at the Heralds' Visitation of Cornwall in 1620. Knighted 3rd Aug. 1644 at Liskeard, being then Sheriff for Cornwall. Bur. at Lanreth 30th Dec. 1649 M.I. Will dated 27th Dec. 1849, prov. 11th June 1652 by Dame Grace Grylls his widow and rel. and his dau. Joan Grylls, Exors. (133 Bowyer).	Grace eldest dau., (with Philippa youngest dau. wife of Renatus Bellot, of Bochym co. Cornwall), and co-heirs of William Beare of S. Niott co. Cornwall, son and heir of William Beare of the same place, by Joan Killiowe. Bap. there 20th Feb. 1581, mar. 4th Feb. 1610 at Lanreth, and was bur. there 19th Nov. 1653, M.I. Will, in which she was described of the parish of Lanreth co. Cornwall, was prov. 4th Dec. 1658, by her son William Grills.			Elizabeth, mar 12th Jan. 1600 at Lanreth, John Scawen of Trehane co. Cornwall. Died s.p. bur. there 11th July 1602.	Mary, mar. 7th May 1600 at Lanreth. William Cann of Plymouth co. Devon, she Bur. there 22nd July 1601.	Agnes, mar. 16th Jan. 1610 at Lanreth, Henry Reade.

Grace, bap. 31st March 1614 at Lanreath, mar. there 13th June 1637, Mark Cottle. Agnes, bap. July 1615 at Lanreth, wife of Walter Glyn in 1649.	Mary, bap. 12th Jan. 1622 at Lanreth.	Elizabeth, bap. 6th Oct. 1616 at Lanreth, and bur. there 7th Nov. 1610.	William Grylls, bap. 23rd Sept. 1621 at Lanreth, liv. 1658.	Mary, bap. 2nd Feb. 1618 at Lanreth, and bur. there 12th Sept. 1620.	Johan, bap. 28th May 1620 at Lanreth. Mar. Settl. dated 14th May 1653, with Lewis Pollard of Jacobstow. co. Devon.	Philippa, bap. 28th May 1625 at Lanreth, and died and bur. there 6th Oct. 1691.

William Grylls 2nd son, Matric. at Queen's Coll. Oxford, 19th Oct. 1671 then aged 17. Bur. 18th June 1683 at Lanreth.	Grace, bap. 9th May1641 at Lanreth, and bur. there 17th Dec. 1655.	Elizabeth & Philippa, bap. 7th Sept. 1645 at Lanreth. Elizabeth bur. 14th Sept. 1648.	Ann, bap. 19th May 1644 at Lanreth, mar. .... Porter, and bur. 4th May 1687 at Lanreth.	Joane, bap. 27th Dec. 1649 at Lanreth. Liv. unmar. 1682.	Elizabeth, bap. 1st Nov. 1646 at Lanreth.	Mary.

Katherine, bap. 21st Sept. 1694 at Lanreth, bur. there 2nd Oct. 1713.	Ann, bap. 10th March 1673 at Lanreth, and bur. there 10th May 1680.	Philippa, bap. 5th July 1685 at Lanreth and will in which des. of Constantine sp. dated 13th Dec. 1754, prov. 8th May 1755, in the Archd. Court of Cornwall.	Anne, bap. 16th July 1682 at Lanreth, ob. unmar., bur. 8th July 1732. Will dated 6th Feb. 1732, in which she is described of Lanreth. Prov. 7th Jan. 1732-3, by her brother Richard, Exor, in the Archd. Court of Cornwall.	Joan, bap. 27th April 1687, at Lanreth, bur. there 8th July 1730.	Warwick Grylls bap. 6th Jan. 1680, at Lanreth, and bur. there 10th Jan. 1680-1	Grace, bap. 9th Oct.1683, at Lanreth, and bur. there 22nd October following
						Gerveys, bap. 26th Aug. 1688, at Lanreth.

3 L

a

Richard Gerveys Grylls of Helston, co. Cornwall, only=Cordelia, only dau. of Thomas Glynn and heir to her brother Thomas
son and heir, bap. 1st Dec. 1735, at Lanreth. Died 3rd.   Glynn, both of Helston, co. Cornwall. Bap. there July 1734, and mar.
bur. there 6th April 1771. Will dated 12th March   there 17th Jan. 1758, and bur. there 19th Jan. 1802, æt 67. Will
1771. Proved 3rd May 1771 in the Archdeaconry   dated 10th Jan. 1801, 3rd codl. 1801. Prov. with 3rd codl. 12th April
Court of Cornwall.   1802, by her sons Richard Gerveys and Thomas Grylls. (276 Kenyon.)
                                                         See Ped. of GLYNN ante p. 72.

Rev. Richard Gerveys Grylls, Vicar and Patron of St.=Charity dau. of William   Thomas Grylls of   =Mary, dau. and co-heir
Neot, and Rector of Helston aforesaid, LL.B., bap.   Hill of Carwythenack   Helston, aforesaid, At- of Humphry Millett of
20th Nov. 1758, at Helston. Matriculated at Uni-   in Constantine. Born   torney at Law, bap.   Enys, in the parish of
versity College, Oxford, 22nd March 1777, then aged 20th Nov. 1761. Mar.   there 5th June 1760.   St. Hilary, and Mary
18 years. Died 20th, bur. 28th Dec. 1841 at Helston, 24th July 1783, St.   Died 10th and bur.   his wife. Mar. 8th
æt 83. Will dated 24th Jan. 1840, codl. 25th Jan.   Clement Danes, Strand.   there 15th Nov. 1813   May 1786, at Madeira.
1840, 2nd cod. 10th July 1841. Prov. C.P.C. 10th   Bur. 13th Aug. 1849,   æt. 53.   Living in 1840.
March 1842.   æt 88, at Helston.

Rev. Richard Gerveys Grylls, LL.B.=Sophia, youngest   Rev. William Grylls, M.A.,   Rev. Henry Grylls, Vicar=Ellen Mary, 2nd
Jan. 1809, Vicar of Luxulyan, co.   of the three   Vicar of Crowan, co. Corn-   of St. Neot, co. Cornwall.   dau. of Joseph
Cornwall, eldest son. Born 30th March dau. of Charles   wall, 2nd son. Bap. 12th   3rd and youngest son.   Boulderson of Bed-
and bap. 5th May 1785, at Helston. Rashleigh of   Sept. 1786, at Helston.   Born 1st Feb. and bap.   ford Row, in the
Sometime at Jesus College, Cambridge. Duporth. Mar.   Sometime of Trinity College, 26th March 1794, at Hel-   parish of St.
Died 4th s.p., and bur. 12th Nov. 1852 29th Aug. 1816 Cambridge. B.A. 1808,   ston. Matric. at Exeter   Andrew's, Holborn.
æt 67, at Luxulyan. Will dated 24th at St. Austle.   M.A. 1812. Died unmar.   College, Oxford, 19th Oct.   Mar. 30th Dec.
Oct. 1844. Prov. with 5 codls. 19th   Will dated 27th Sept. 1861. 1812, æt. 18. Vicar of   1820, at St. An-
April 1853. 1st codl. 19th July 1847,   Prov. 18th Jan. 1864, C.P.C. St. Neot, 21st Dec. 1820.   drew's, Holborn,
2nd codl. 13 Dec. 1847, 3rd cod. 14th   1st cod. 19th June 1863,   Bur. 19th June 1862, at   co. Middlesex. Died
July 1852, 4th cod. 26th April 1852,   2nd cod. 6th Oct. 1863.   St. Neot, æt. 68.   at Plymouth, 22nd
5th cod. 10th May 1852.   Feb. 1841.

William Henry   Charles Gerveys   =Anne,   Horatio Glynn   Shadwell Morley Grylls of Le-=Isabella Ellen, Born 9th
Gerveys Grylls   Grylls, a Commander   dau.   Grylls, born 27th   warne, in St. Neot, co. Cornwall.   Oct. 1843, at Ceylon,
Born 14th   H.M. Royal Navy.   of   Jan., and bap.   Born 11th and bap. 13th Feb.   dau. of Sir Arthur
Sept. 1824, bap.   Born 1st July and   James   26th June 1828,   1831 at St. Neot, Lieut.-Col. in   William Buller, Knt.
8th March followg. bap. 15th Aug. 1826, Robin-   at St. Neot.   the Royal Regt. of Artillery.   Judge of the Supreme
at St. Neot. Died   at St. Neot. Died at son.   Lieut. in 64th   Appointed 2nd Lieut. 19th Dec.   Court of Calcutta, and
s.p. 11th Sept. 1839 Cheltenham s.p., bur.   Reg. of Foot.   1848, 1st Lieut. 3rd Nov. 1849,   sometime M.P. for Lis-
at Lisbon. Mid-   14th Feb. 1860, at St.   Died s.p. and   2nd Capt. 13th Aug. 1855, 1st   keard, 2nd son of
shipman on board   Neot, æt 33. Entered   Bur. at St. Neot,   Capt. 20th June 1862, Mayor 6th   Charles Buller and
the "Ganges," Dec. Royal Navy as a Vol-   8th Jan. 1852, æt   June 1866, Lieut.-Col. 1st Jan.   Barbara Isabella
1838.   unteer, Sept. 1840.   24.   1868. Sheriff of Cornwall,   Kirkpatrick.
                                                                        1873.

Charles Bere Grylls, born
2nd Nov. 1866.

Mathew Grylls of Helston, Attorney, 3rd son, bap. 3rd Aug. 1765, at Helston. Died s.p., 8th Jan. 1795, at Champagne, in France and bur. there.	Rev. Thomas Trevenen, Rector of Cardinham, co. Cornwall, afterwards of Mawgan in Meneage, Born at Camborn, co. Cornwall, 27th Feb. 1758, 2nd son of Rev. John Trevenen, of Camborn, aforesaid.	=Cordelia, born 10th and bap. 11th July 1762, at Helston, mar. there by lic. 19th Feb. 1784. Died at Mawgan 24th and was bur. 28th April 1810, æt 47, at Helston.	Ann, bap. 31st March 1764, at Helston. Died 17th and was bur. there 23rd June following.	Sarah, bap. 24th July 1768, at Helston. Died unmar. at Clifton in Bristol, 20th Aug. 1823, æt. 55.	Anne, born 12th Sept. 1770, ob. 8th Feb. 1771, bur. at Helston.

Charity, bap. 29th, and bur. 30th March 1784, at Helston.	Ann Hill, born 8th Aug. and bap. 19th Sept. 1788, at Helston, and buried there 11th June 1789.	Rev. William=Frances, born 12th March, Veale of and bap. 27th April 1790, Trevayer at Helston. Married there in Gulval, 6th Oct. 1814. Died 20th and co. Cornwall. bur. 28th June 1841, at Living 1840. Helston.	Elizabeth, born 27th Feb. and bap. 19th April 1792, at Helston, and bur. there 27th Dec. following.

Henry Chamond Grylls, born 12th Aug. and bap. 26th Sept. 1833, at St. Neot, and bur. there 10th Jan. 1851.	Richard Gerveys Grylls, eldest son, born 24th Oct. 1821, at Helston. Died 3rd Jan. 1842, at Chatham.	Lucretia Frances Gerveys, eldest dau. Born 16th Dec. 1822, at St. Neot. Died 4th and bur. 12th May 1834, at St. Neot.	Ellen, born 2nd July and bapt. 30th Sept. 1829, at St. Neot. Mar. there 2nd July 1850, Rev. Francis Paul James Hendy, Vicar of St. Neot aforesaid, sometime Incumbent of Par with St. Blazey, co. Cornwall.	Emma, born 15th March, bap. 27th April 1836, at St. Neot. Mar. there 1st Nov. 1859, Samuel Broadperal Hill of Bach Hall, co. Chester, and of Liverpool.	Adelaide Frances, born 22nd and bap. 26th Feb. 1841, at St. Neot. Mar. Vivian D. Majendie, Capt. in Royal Artillery. Died at Woolwich 1866.

I hereby certify that the foregoing Pedigree of Gerveys, so far as printed in *italics*, agrees with the records in this Office; and that the Pedigree of Grylls is a true copy of that registered here, and further, that the Arms are correct as allowed to the family of Grylls at the Heralds' Visitation of Cornwall in 1620. (2. C.I. fo. 373.)

Herald's College,
  6th February 1875.

GEORGE HARRISON,
Windsor Herald and Registrar.

3 L²

WILLIAMS.

The family of Williams of Gwennap, a member of which, Mr. Michael Williams, holds a considerable estate in Lesnewith and the neighbourhood, has, during the present century, acquired great influence and landed property in Cornwall. During several generations, the Williamses of Scorrier have been actively instrumental, and eminently successful, in developing the mining resources of the county, and thus, whilst acquiring great wealth to themselves, have become large public benefactors.[1] A few particulars, therefore, as to their earlier history will be of general interest.

It is said that when the former house at Scorrier was removed a few years ago to make way for the present mansion, a great quantity of old papers were destroyed, as of no immediate use, hence much evidence respecting the early history of the family has been lost. According to tradition three brothers immigrated from Wales about the middle of the seventeenth century, and settled in the parish of Stythians, where we find James, Davy, and Richard Williams, these three brothers, were residing 1650. John Williams, the grandson of James, born 1685, may be said to have originated the prosperity of his family.

Mr. John Williams having settled at Burncoose in the adjoining parish of Gwennap, in 1715 he became actively engaged in various mining enterprises, carried on during a long life with untiring industry and judgment, whereby he realized no inconsiderable fortune. More especially he managed the mineral property of the Hearle family, afterwards inherited, by marriages with the co-heirs of John Hearle of Penryn, by the families of Tremayne, Rodd, and Wallis; the latter subsequently devolving upon Mr. Stephens by marriage with Ann daughter and heir of Mr. Commissioner Wallis.[2] In this management Mr. Williams was succeeded by his son and grandson. The County Adit, a work most important in its results to Cornish mining, commenced in 1748, was originated by Mr. Williams of Burncoose, though, subsequently, carried out by the founder of the Lemon family. Mr. Williams was twice married, by his first wife, Thomasine Paynter, he had seven sons, and having by his will, dated 25th January 1760, made ample provision for his eldest sons, he constituted his youngest son, Michael, his executor and heir, and even in a deed, now in the possession of Sir Frederick Williams, dated as early as 1753, notwithstanding that five of his brothers were alive, this Michael is described as: "Michael Williams, Gent., *son and heir* of John Williams, Gentleman."

Michael Williams, who appears to have been like his father a man of considerable energy and marked character, died at Bath in the prime of life in 1775. He married

---

[1] Hitchins, writing of Mr. John Williams of Scorrier, before 1826, says: "About 10,000 persons are employed under his management, and a sum amounting to half a million per annum passes through his hands." (History of Cornwall, vol. ii, 306.)   [2] See ante pp. 372, 374.

Susanna daughter of Henry Harris of Cusgarne, Gent.,[1] by his wife Elizabeth only child of Edward Kempthorne of Chymder in Gunwalloe, son of Renatus Kempthorne of the same place; which Henry Harris was son and heir of John Harris of Cusgarne by his wife Elizabeth, daughter of John Beauchamp of Trevince. By this marriage Mr. Williams had several children, with reference to whom see annexed pedigree.

Mr. Williams was succeeded at Burncoose by his eldest son, John Williams, who married Catherine daughter of Martin Harvey of Killifreth in Kenwyn, a family which afterwards became intimately associated with the Williams family in their various mercantile undertakings, and is now extinct.[2]

John Williams, after his marriage, resided at first entirely at Burncoose, but in the year 1778, with the view of being in the immediate vicinity of the several important mines which he was then superintending, he enclosed and planted Scorrier, and erected the house in which he subsequently resided, altogether, during a period of many years. Scorrier House held, during the life of its first owner, a position altogether unique among the

[1] This family of Harris was previously of Trevance in St. Issey. Hals mentions "Trevance as the dwelling of Richard Harris, gent. of Tolskiddy, that married Vivian, his father Moyle." (Davies-Gilbert's, Hist. of Cornwall, vol. ii, p. 255). Richard Harris, a member of this family, was Vicar of Gwennap, and dying in 1646 made many bequests of landed property to various nephews and other relatives of the name, and to Richard, son of John Harris of St. Issey, lands at "St. Dye," upon which he resided. Richard Harris thereupon settled at St. Day, and dying in 1672 left a son, John Harris of St. Dye, gent., who in 1704 purchased a small estate called Bargus Vein in Perran Arworthal, which is now in the possession of his direct descendant, Sir F. M. Williams, Bart. Mr. Henry Harris, whose daughter Susanna, as stated in the text, married Michael Williams of Burncoose, on his death, in 1768, left two surviving sons, Edward, who succeeded him at Cusgarne, and John. Edward inherited his maternal grand-father's lands in Gunwalloe, and having married Eleanor, daughter of Stephen Johns of Trewince in St. Gerrans, died s.p. at Cusgarne in 1798. John also died s.p. in 1805. Of the daughters, who thus became co-heirs of their brothers, Susanna, the eldest, married Michael Williams, as before stated, and Catherine married Isaac Head of St. Mary's, Scilly Islands.

[2] Mr. Martin Harvey of Killifreth was a member of an old yeoman family resident there for several generations, but originally from St. Burian, where they at one time owned considerable property. In Martyn's Map of Cornwall, Trevore, in St. Burian, is marked as the seat of "Mr. Harvey." The present representative is Jane Harvey Andrew, granddaughter and heir of the late James Harvey of St. Day, Esq., who married, 18th May 1870, James Charles Archibald Hewitt, Esq., grandson of James second Viscount Lifford, and has issue.

The following extracts from the will of Mr. Michael Williams are somewhat curious and will be read with interest.

"I hereby make and appoint Francis Beauchamp of Trefince in the county aforesaid (Cornwall), Esquire, John Beauchamp and Joseph Beauchamp, Esquires, his two sons, together with my mother-in-law (step mother) Anne Williams, and my wife Susanna Williams (during her widowhood) the survivors or survivor of them, to be executors of this my last will and testament, to whom I commit the care and government of my children, hoping, as they have hitherto shewn the greatest regard and affection for them, they will not refuse this favour after my death.

"It is my will, and I do hereby declare it so to be, that if after my death, my said son John Williams, should take to wife, or be joined in marriage to any person without the approbation or consent of his mother, and the Mr. Beauchamps, whom I have made Trustees in my said will over my children, or such of them as shall be living, which approbation and consent shall be had and obtained under their hands properly attested, and also signed by the minister before the marriage shall be solemnized, Then I do hereby, immediately from and after such marriage, revoke, make void and annull all and every bequest in my said will in my said son John's favour.

"And whereas there is no kind of friendship that I have not received in my own person from that worthy gentle-man, the Rev. Henry Hawkins Tremayne of Heligan in the said county, Clerk, now I take the liberty to desire he will extend his friendly care to my family and children, and act in the capacity of trustee over them in conjunction with the

houses of the county. C. S. Gilbert, writing about 1810, describes it as "a rather irregular building," and says: "it is known to contain the most valuable variety of Cornish minerals that was ever collected by any gentleman in Europe."[1] For this, and for the striking abilities, the extensive information, and the extraordinary practical knowledge of mining possessed by Mr. Williams, which had given him a reputation little less than European, Scorrier became a great attraction; consequently few strangers of distinction,

[1] History of Cornwall, vol. ii, p. 206.

other trustees mentioned in my said will, and I do make his approbation and consent also necessary respecting the marriage of my son John Williams as aforesaid."

Accordingly, in conformity with the above rigid limitations, the following certificate was obtained, and is now preserved in the family.

"Whereas by the last Will and Testament of the late Mr. Michael Williams of the parish of Gwennap, in the county of Cornwall, it was directed and appointed that his son John Williams should not take to wife or be joined in marriage to any person without the approbation and consent of Susanna Williams, his mother, John Beauchamp and Joseph Beauchamp, and Henry Hawkins Tremayne, the trustees therein and for that purpose named; We, therefore, the said Trustees, do hereby consent and approve of the said John Williams taking to wife Catherine the daughter of Martin Harvey of Kenwyn in the said county. As witness our hands this 20th day of January 1776.

"SUSANNA WILLIAMS.
"JOSEPH BEAUCHAMP.
"JOHN BEAUCHAMP.
"H. HAWKINS TREMAYNE."

The signatures were all duly attested and the marriage was recorded in the Parish Registers of Kenwyn in these words:

"John Williams of the parish of Gwennap, in the county of Cornwall, Gent., and Catherine Harvey of this parish, a minor, were married in this Church by license, with consent of parents, this 23rd of January in the year 1776 by me,

"F. WEBBER, Curate."

An account of the family of Williams would be incomplete without relating the remarkable dream experienced by Mr. Williams, notwithstanding that it has been several times narrated. The subjoined account of it is reprinted from Mr. Spencer Walpole's "Life of Spencer Perceval," from an attested statement drawn up and signed by Mr. Williams, in the presence of the Rev. Thomas Fisher and Mr. Charles Prideaux-Brune, and given by the latter of these gentlemen to Mr. Walpole.

"Some account of a dream which occurred to Mr. John Williams of Scorrier House, in the county of Cornwall, in the year 1812, taken from his own mouth, and narrated by him at various times to several of his friends:

"Being desired to write out the particulars of a dream which I had in the year 1812, before I do so, I think it may be proper for me to say that, at that time my attention was fully occupied with affairs of my own, the superintendence of some very extensive mines in Cornwall being entrusted to me. Thus I had no leisure to pay any attention to political matters, and hardly knew who, at that time, formed the administration of the country. It was, therefore, scarcely possible that my own interest in the subject should have had any share in suggesting the circumstances which presented themselves to my imagination. It was, in truth, a subject which never occurred to my waking thoughts. My dream was as follows:

"About the 2nd or 3rd of May 1812, I dreamed I was in the lobby of the House of Commons, a place well known to me. A small man, dressed in a blue coat and white waistcoat, entered; and immediately I saw a person, whom I had observed on my first entrance dressed in a snuff-coloured coat and yellow metal buttons, take a pistol from under his coat and present it at the little man above-mentioned. The pistol was discharged, and the ball entered the left breast of the person at whom it was directed. I saw the blood issue from the place where the ball had struck him; his countenance instantly altered, and he fell to the ground. Upon inquiry who the sufferer might be, I was informed that he was the Chancellor. I understood him to be Mr. Perceval who was Chancellor of the Exchequer. I further saw the murderer laid hold of by several of the gentlemen in the room. Upon awaking I told the particulars related above to my wife. She treated the matter lightly, saying it was only a dream. I soon fell asleep again, and again the dream presented itself with precisely the same circumstances. After awaking the second time, and stating the matter again to my wife, she only re-

English or Foreign, visited Cornwall without bringing an introduction to, and receiving a hospitable welcome from, this remarkable man. Amongst other, about the year 1800, the Comte de Lille and the Comte d'Artois, afterwards, respectively, Louis XVIII, and Charles X, of France, honoured Scorrier with a visit. The contemporary local historians of Cornwall bear honourable testimony to the character and standing of Mr. Williams, and it will suffice, without reprinting what they have respectively stated, to refer to their works.[1] Mr. Williams's wife died in 1826, a few years after which he retired to Calstock, which manor he had purchased in 1809, and dying there in 1841, left by his wife Catherine, a family of four sons and five daughters.

John, the eldest son of John Williams, inherited the paternal estate of Burncoose, which he greatly improved and beautified, and which has been still further augmented by his nephew and successor. He married Phillippa, daughter of Mr. William Naudin, descended from a French Protestant family, who settled in England on account of the religious persecutions in France, towards the end of the seventeenth century.[2] Having shortly before his marriage joined the Society of Friends, Mr. Williams lived a private retired life, respected and beloved by all who knew him for his gentle and benevolent disposition, and for his spotless integrity. He died at Burncoose in 1849, s.p.

Edward Williams, third son of Mr. John Williams, married Elizabeth daughter of

peated her request that I would compose myself and dismiss the subject from my mind. Upon my falling asleep the third time, the same dream, without any alteration, was repeated; and I awoke, as upon former occasions, in great agitation. So much alarmed and impressed was I by the circumstance above narrated that I felt much doubt whether it was not my duty to take a journey to London and communicate upon the subject with the party principally concerned. Upon this point I consulted some friends, whom I met on business at the Godolphin mine on the day following. After having stated to them the particulars of the dream itself, and what were my own feelings in relation to it, they dissuaded me from my purpose, saying I might expose myself to contempt or vexation, or be taken up as a fanatic. Upon this I said no more, but anxiously watched the newspaper every evening as the post arrived. On the evening of the 13th May, as far as I recollect, no account of Mr. Perceval's death was in the newspaper. But my second son, at that time returning from Truro, came in a hurried manner into the room where I was sitting, and exclaimed, "Father, your dream has come true, Mr. Perceval has been shot in the lobby of the House of Commons! There is an account come from London to Truro, written after the newspapers were printed." The fact was, Mr. Perceval was assassinated on the evening of the 11th.

Some business soon afterwards called me to London; and, in one of the print shops, I saw a drawing for sale, representing the place and the circumstances which attended Mr. Perceval's death. I purchased it, and upon a careful examination, I found it to coincide in all particulars with the scene which had passed through my imagination in my dreams. The colours of the dresses, the buttons of the assassin's coat, the white waistcoat of Mr. Perceval, the spot of blood upon it, and the countenance and attitude of the parties present, were exactly what I had dreamed. The singularity of the case when mentioned among my acquaintance naturally made it the subject of conversation in London; and in consequence my friend, the late Mr. Rennie, was requested by one of the Commissioners of the Navy, that they might be permitted to hear the circumstances from myself. Two of them accordingly met me at Mr. Rennie's house, and to them I detailed at the time the particulars, then fresh in my memory, which form the subject of the above. I forbear to make any further comment upon the above narration, further than to declare solemnly that it is a faithful account of facts as they actually occurred." (Spencer Walpole's Life of Spencer Perceval, vol. ii, p. 329, n.)

[1] C. S. Gilbert's History of Cornwall, ii, 806. Davies-Gilbert's History of Cornwall, ii, 134. Hitchin's and Drew's History of Cornwall, ii, 385.

[2] On 17th November 1681, Letters of denization, in the usual form, were granted to Elias Naudin, master of a ship, being an alien born. (List of Foreign Protestants and Aliens resident in England in 1688, p. 33, Camd. Soc. Pub. 1862).

John Pearson Foote of Harewood, near Tavistock, of the same family as Samuel Foote the celebrated actor. One of his grandsons, Edward Mansell Williams, is now resident at Flushing.

The third and fourth sons, Michael and William, married respectively, Elizabeth and Caroline, daughters of Richard Eales of Eastdon, co. Devon. Their mother was Elizabeth daughter of Peter Young of Netherex, by Salome only child and heir of Thomas Martyn of Kenton, co. Devon, a gentlemen of ancient and illustrious descent, derived from Martin de Turon who came to England with William of Normandy, and was made by him Baron of Kemeys, or Camaes, in co. Pembroke, having first made a conquest of that territory.[1] On the death of her first cousin, William Clifford Martyn of Netherex and Oxton, in 1770, she inherited the former estate with other lands; Oxton having been devised to the Tripp family, descended from testator's grandfather Nicholas Martyn. Many heirlooms of the Martyns are preserved in the Williams family. By these alliances the Williams's acquired a royal descent from King Edward I. and Eleanor of Castile, for which see pedigree annexed.

Mr. Michael Williams, the elder of the two brothers just mentioned, was, in many respects, one of the most remarkable men, amongst a remarkable family, of his day. To his great energy, determination, foresight and prudence, his faculty of seeing the opportunity and seizing it at the right moment, may the success of his family be, in a great measure, attributed; and these qualities may, in good truth, be said to have descended to all his sons. He inherited Scorrier from his father, and purchased, in 1854, Caerhayes Castle, the ancient seat of the Trevanion family, with its demesne lands &c., as well as many estates, at various times, but he resided through life at Trevince, which he held on lease from the representatives of the Beauchamp family. Dying in 1858 he left three sons, the eldest, John Michael of Burncoose and Caerhayes Castle in Cornwall, and Gnaton Hall in Devon, married Elizabeth daughter of Stephen Davey of Bochym, by his wife Charlotte daughter of William Horton, Clerk, third son of Joshua Horton of Howroyd, co. York, who was next brother of Sir William Horton, first Baronet of Chadderton, and has issue. Mr. Williams is a Deputy Lieutenant for Cornwall, and a Deputy Warden of the Stannaries, and served the office of Sheriff in 1865. Michael Henry, the second son, of Tredrea and Arrallas, who is in the Commission of Peace for Cornwall, married Catherine daughter of Richard Almack of Melford, co. Suffolk, Esq.; and George the youngest, of Scorrier and Lanarth, who is also in the Commission of Peace, married Charlotte another daughter of the abovementioned Stephen Davey, and has issue. He built the present very handsome house at Scorrier about 1862, and has greatly improved the gardens and grounds, since which date he has been master of the well-known "Four-Barrow" Fox hounds, as his uncle, the late Sir William Williams, had previously been from 1854.

William the youngest son of John Williams at the time of his marriage in 1826 enclosed Tregullow and built the house there. As the junior partner he necessarily occupied in business a position subordinate to that of his brothers, nevertheless his opinion was

---

[1] Dugdale Bar. i. 729. See also Prince's Worthies of Devon, p. 574.

constantly sought by them, since his advice was always felt to be sound and his judgment unerring. He was in the Commission of the Peace for Cornwall during the greater part of his life, and was Sheriff of the County in 1851. By Letters Patent, dated 4th August 1866, the Queen was pleased to confer upon him the dignity of a Baronet. Sir William Williams died on 24th March 1870 leaving a large family, and was succeeded in his title, and the greatest portion of his large estates, by his second and eldest surviving son and heir Sir Frederick Martin Williams of Tregullow, Bart., the now representative in Parliament of the Borough of Truro. To his fifth son, Michael, Sir William Williams devised Halwell and his lands in Davidstow and Lesnewith.

The memory of Sir William Williams will long be cherished in his native county, his character having, during a long and most useful career, been distinguished by a rectitude of conduct and a simple courtesy of manner which never failed to gain the respect and esteem of all classes with whom he came into contact. His generous hospitality and his genuine kindness not only rendered him popular among the richer of his neighbours, but his munificent, though judicious, charity to the needy and destitute around Tregullow, caused him justly to be revered as the father of his parish, and "the poor man's friend." Beyond the ample provision which this good man left to his children he bequeathed to them, in the recollection of his blameless life, the yet richer inheritance of an example which it should be their daily effort and their proudest distinction always to follow.

ARMS: Quarterly, 1st and 4th, Vair three crescents or, two and one; for Williams.

2nd and 3rd sa. a tilting spear, fesswise, between three crescents ar.; for Harris.

CREST: A demi Eagle, displayed, az., winged sa., each wing charged with four bezants.

MOTTO: "Nil desperandum."

PEDIGREE OF

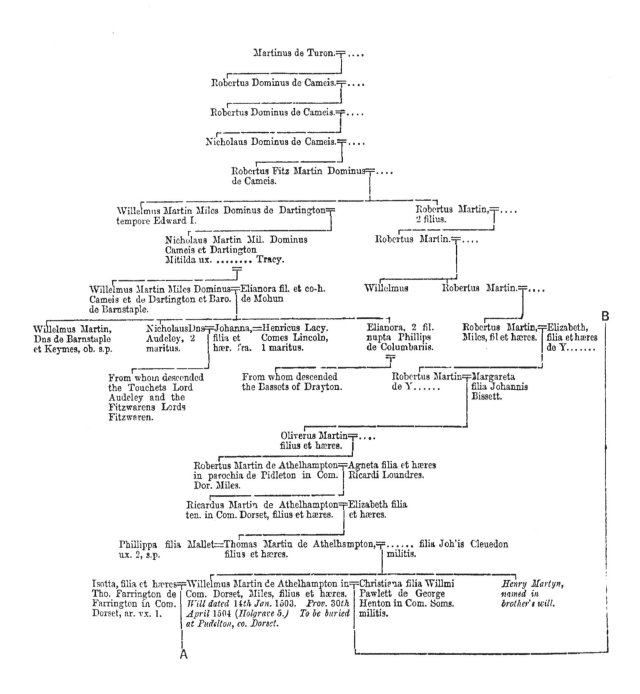

Martinus de Turon. =....

Robertus Dominus de Cameis. =....

Robertus Dominus de Cameis. =....

Nicholaus Dominus de Cameis. =....

Robertus Fitz Martin Dominus =.... de Cameis.

Willelmus Martin Miles Dominus de Dartington = tempore Edward I.

Robertus Martin, =.... 2 filius.

Nicholaus Martin Mil. Dominus Cameis et Dartington Mitilda ux. .... Tracy.

Robertus Martin. =....

Willelmus Martin Miles Dominus = Elianora fil. et co-h. Cameis et de Dartington et Baro. | de Mohun de Barnstaple.

Willelmus   Robertus Martin. =....

Willelmus Martin, Dns de Barnstaple et Keymes, ob. s.p.

NicholausDns = Johanna, = Henricus Lacy. Audeley, 2 | filia et Comes Lincoln, maritus. | hær. fra. 1 maritus.

Elianora, 2 fil. nupta Phillips de Columbariis.

Robertus Martin, = Elizabeth, Miles, fil et hæres. | filia et hæres de Y.......

B

From whom descended the Touchets Lord Audeley and the Fitzwarens Lords Fitzwaren.

From whom descended the Bassets of Drayton.

Robertus Martin = Margareta de Y...... | filia Johannis Bissett.

Oliverus Martin =.... filius et hæres.

Robertus Martin de Athelhampton = Agneta filia et hæres in parochia de Pidleton in Com. | Ricardi Loundres. Dor. Miles.

Ricardus Martin de Athelhampton = Elizabeth filia ten. in Com. Dorset, filius et hæres. | et hæres.

Phillippa filia Mallet = Thomas Martin de Athelhampton, =...... filia Joh'is Cleuedon ux. 2, s.p. filius et hæres. | militis.

Isotta, filia et hæres = Willelmus Martin de Athelhampton in = Christiana filia Willmi Tho. Farrington de | Com. Dorset, Miles, filius et hæres. | Pawlett de George Farrington in Com. | *Will dated 14th Jan.* 1503. *Prov.* 30th | Henton in Com. Soms. Dorset, ar. vx. 1. | *April* 1504 *(Holgrave 5.)* To be buried | militis. | *at Pudelton, co. Dorset.*

Henry Martyn, named in brother's will.

A

MARTYN.

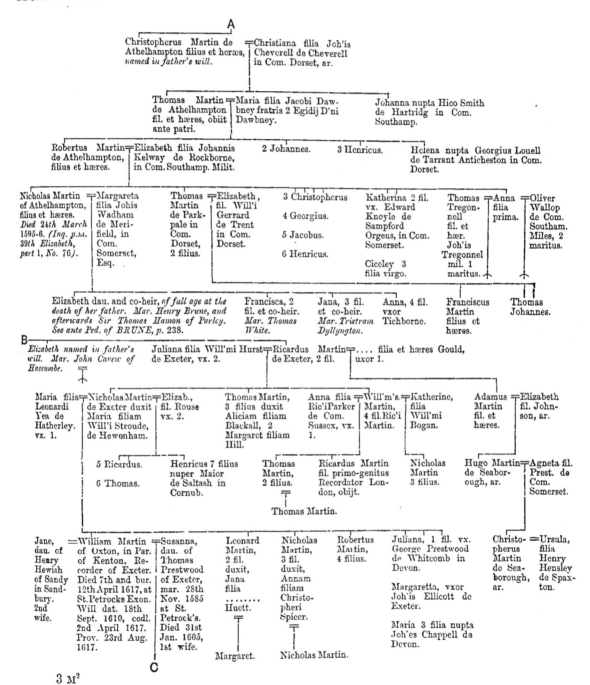

3 M²

PEDIGREE OF

Francis Godolphin **of** Treveneage, co. Corn-=Ann dau. of Richard Carew of Antony.
wall, son and heir of William Godolphin of | Mar.lic. dated 10th, and mar. at Antony 18th,
the same place by Jane dau. and co-heir of | Nov. 1616. Exon. See ante p. 366.
Walter Gaverigan of Gaverigan.

John St. Aubyn of Clow-=Katherine, æt 6 weeks, 9th
ance and St. Michael's | Oct. 1620, daughter and heir.
Mount.

Gertrude dau. of John St.Aubyn=Nicholas Martyn of Netherex	Elizabeth, eldest dau.	Gertrude, 2nd dau.	Susanna, 3rd dau.
of Clowance, co. Cornwall, by	and Oxton. In the Commission	unmar. and under	mar. John Martyn	mar. Richard South-
Katherine dau. and heir of	of the Peace for Devon. Eldest	24 in 1666. Mar.	of Exeter. Bur. at	cott of Dawlish, and
Francis Godolphin. Mar. lic.	son, aged 10 years in 1662. Bur.⁴	Peter Atwell of Ken-	St. Petrocks, Exeter,	bur. there 27th Aug.
dated 29th July 1675. Exon.	17th Nov. 1717.	ton. Died 17th Nov.	18th Oct. 1678, s.p.	1704.
		1673. Bur.⁴ M.I.		

Rev.Nicho-=Susanna,	Gertrude,	Elizabeth,	Richard=Catherine.	Margaret, =Thomas Martyn=Salome Hart, of St.
las Tripe,	mar. lic.	born 1677,	mar. Wm.	Young of	Bap.⁴ 24th	2nd wife.	of Kenton, aged	Paul's, Covent Gar-
Vicar of	dated 1st.	mar. 18th	Southcott	Mam-	May 1694.	Bur. 9th	25 years, and a	den. Mar. lic. dated
Chudleigh.	mar. 7th	May 1718.	of Dawlish.	head, co.	Mar. 30th	April 1758.	bachelor in 1718.	10th Feb. 1718. She
Bur. there	Dec. 1710,	at St Ed-	Named in	Devon.	June 1716,	at St.	Will dated 4th	a spinster then aged
26th April	at Dawlish.	mund's,	the will of		at St. Pet-	George's in	December 1729.	24 years. Mar. same
1713.		Exeter, to	her uncle		rocks,	the East,co.	Proved 6th Dec.	day at St. Bencts,
		Mathew	John Mar-		Exeter.	Middlesex.	1730.	Paul's Wharf. Died
		Hillson of	tyn in 1725.			Will dated		before 1729.
		Honiton,co				4th Oct.		
		Devon.				1757.		
		Bur. there						
		19th Feb.						
		1732-3.						

Catherine. Bap.	Richard Young,	Peter Young of the=Salome, **only child** and	William Clifford =Elizabeth dau. of ..
13th April 1724,	2nd son, bap. 2nd	city of Exeter, after-	heir, bap. 20th Sept.	Martyn of Oxton,	Paul's, Covent Gar-
at Dawlish.	Oct. 1721, at Daw-	wards of Netherex,	1721, at St. Mary	bap.⁴ 20th July 1706.	den. Mar. lic. 30th
	lish.	bap. 20th Jan. 1719, at	Steps, Exon. Bur.26th	Died s.p.. Bur.⁴ 18th	Aug., mar. 8th Sept.
		Dawlish. Bur. 18th	Feb. 1806 at Netherex.	April 1770. Will	1733, at St. Alphage,
		Feb. 1784 at Netherex.	Will dated 9th March	dated 11th Oct. and	London Wall, she
		Will dated 16th June	1792. Prov. 7th March	codl. 29th Oct. 1769.	then aged 24 years,
		1780. Codl. 5th Dec.	1806 in Archd. Court,	Prov. 9th May 1770.	and a spinster. Bur.
		1782. Prov. 23rd	Exon. Her son	Peter Young exr.	at Kenton 18th Oct.
		March 1784 in Archd.	Thomas Young sole		1753.
		Court of Exon.	executor.		

Richard Eales of Eastdown, co. Devon, for-=Elizabeth, 2nd dau. of Peter Young, born
merly of St. Paul's, Exeter. Bap. 19th | 30th Sept. 1763, bap. at Netherex. Mar. 2nd
Sept. 1759, at Ashburton. Died 21st Feb. | July 1785 at St. Paul's, Exon. Bur. 11th
1852, aged 92. Bur. at Starcross, co. Devon. | Jan. 1843, aged 80, at Starcross.

---

⁴ At Kenton.

MARTYN.

C

Sir Shilston Calmady of Wembury, co. Devon, Knight, son of Josias Calmady of Wembury. Knighted at Theobalds 11th Nov. 1618. Will dated 12th April 1641. Prov. 16th Feb. 1647-8. = **Honour** dau. of Edmund Fortescue of Fallopit, Devon. Relict of Humphry Prideaux of Soldon, Devon, and Prideaux Place, Cornwall. Descended from King EDWARD I, and ELEANOR of Castile. For descent see ante pp. 240, 241.

Sir Nicholas Martyn of Oxton, Knight, born 12th April 1593, aged 27 at the Herald's Visitation of Devon 1620. Knighted at Newmarket 15th Feb. 1624-5. Sheriff of Devon 1646, to his death 25th March 1653 aged 60. Bur.[4] = **Elizabeth** dau. of John Symes of Poundsford, co. Somerset.

William Martin, 2nd son, an° 1620.

Edward Martin, 3rd son, an° 1620.

Susan, wife of Peter Bevis of Exeter.

Elizabeth, youngest dau. a minor and unmar. in 1641. Executrix and proved her husband's will 1662. Died 26th April and bur.[4] 3rd May 1695. M.I. = **William Martyn** of Netherex co. Devon, born at Oxton, in the parish of Kenton, 22nd Oct., and bap.[4] 1st Nov. 1626. Will dated 28th Sept. 1661. Prov. 14th May 1662 at Exon. by Elizabeth his widow, during minority of their son Nicholas.

Susanna, mar. circa May 1654, Charles Staynings. Died May 1685, at Holnicote, co. Somerset.

Richard Turner of Totteridge, co. Herts. Died 20th and bur. there 25th May 1676, aged 66. = **Dorothy,** mar. 8th Aug. 1644. Died 24th Feb. 1689-90, aged 65.

Honor, 4th and youngest dau. Died unmar. Bur.[4] 13th July 1706. Will dated 31st July 1705. Prov. 19th Nov. 1708, at Exon.

William Martyn of the city of Exeter and of Holnicote, co. Somerset. 2nd son, a minor in 1661. = **Theodosia** dau. of .... Smyth of Thaddlesthorp, co. Lincoln. Will dated 27th Feb. 1735-6. Prov. 18th March 1740, by her son Charles.

John Martyn of King Street, in St. Paul's, Covent Garden, 3rd son. Bur. there 3rd Oct. 1735. Will dated 16th Sept. 1725. Prov. 10 Nov. fol. = **Philipe** dau. of Edward Hooper of Heron Court, co. Southampton. Executrix and proved her husband's will 1725. Bur. 28th Aug. 1732, with her husband. Will dated 12th June 1729. Prov. 21st Aug. 1732.

William Martyn of Oxton. Bur.[4] 25 Oct. 1710. Will dated 11th Oct. 1710. Admo. with will annexed granted at Exon 25th Nov. 1710, to William Martyn his father-in-law. = **Susanna,** mar. lic. Exon, 26th June 1705. Extrix. and renounced. Prob. to will of her husband, 1710. Bur.[4] 10th Feb. 1748.

Charles Martyn of St. Andrew's, Holborn, merchant. Died s.p 1st May 1765. Will dated 4th May 1764, codl. 27th July following. Prov. 7th May 1765. = **Rebecca** his wife ex[x]. and proved her husband's will in 1765.

John Martyn, bur. 6th Oct. 1700 at Kenton.

William Martyn of the city of Exon, born 1690, bur. 31st Oct. 1737, at St. Paul's, Exon. Will dated 27th Oct. 1737 Prov. 31st Oct. 1738, Exon. = **Dorothy** his wife, mar. 21st June, 1719, at St. Stephen's, Exon, and prov. her husband's will.

Charles Martyn of the Close in the city of Salisbury. Will dat. 16 June 1723. Prov. 18 June 1724, s.p. = **Rebecca,** sister of Richard Woodford. Extrix. and prov. her husband's will 1724.

Elizabeth and Philippa Both bur. at St. Paul's, Covent Garden.

John Martyn, bap.[4] 27th March 1708, and bur. there 23rd April following.

Rev. William Martyn, Rector of Dunkerton, co. Somerset, and Netherex. Will dated 24th Feb. 1768. Codl. 23rd March 1769. Prov. 3rd April 1770. = **Jane** his wife, executrix and proved her husband's will 1770.

Theodosia Martyn of Yealmpton, co. Devon, spinster. Will dat. 5th July 1765. Prov. 9th Nov. 1768, by her sister Elizabeth.

Rev. John Collins, Rector of Mamhead, co. Devon, 1738-1755. Bur. there 11th Dec. 1755. = **Dorothy,** eld. dau. Liv. his widow 1769.

Elizabeth, 2nd dau. Prov. her sister Theodosia's will in 1768. Unmar. 1769.

D

---

[4] At Kenton.

PEDIGREE OF

NIL DESPERANDUM.

1 AND 4 WILLIAMS
2 AND 3 HARRIS.

.... Williams.⊤ ....

James Williams of St. Stythians, co.⊤Mary his wife, Bur.⁷ 22nd
Cornw. Bur.⁷ 20th June 1673. | Aug. 1656.

Richard Williams of St. Sty-⊤Elizabeth Donking of Camborne.
thians, bap.⁷ 7th Feb. 1654. | Mar.⁵ March 1684.

Thomasine Payn-⊤John Williams of Burncoose and⊤Ann Skews, widow
ter, aged about 24 | Cusgarne, both in the parish of Gwen- | Mar. at St. Cle-
years a°. 1716. | nap. Bap.⁵ 17th Mar. 1685, aged | ments Cornwall,
Mar. before April | about 32 years, a°. 1716. Bur.⁵ 24th | 7th Nov. 1743,
1716. Bur. 28th | June 1761. Will dated 25th Jan. 1760 | Liv. May 1761.
Oct. 1742. 1st | Codl. 6th May 1761. Prov. in Archd. | Original will dat.
wife. | Court of Cornw. 16th Jan. 1762. | 2nd Oct. 1781.

John Williams of Geare Tre- | Richard Williams, | James Williams,
fusis in the parish of Gwennap, | 2nd son, bap.¹ 12th | 3rd son, bap.¹ 1719
afterwards of Gilly Tresamble | May 1717. Liv. | Liv. Jan. 1760.
in the parish of Perran Arwor- | Jan. 1760. |
thal. Bap.¹ 2nd of Feb. 1714. |
Liv. 1760. ⊤

John Williams of Burncoose and of⊤Catherine dau. of Martin Harvey of
Scorrier House, eldest son born 23rd | Killefreth, co. Cornwall. Born 12th
Sept. 1752. Purchased the Manor of | Jan. 1757. Mar.⁴ 23rd Jan. 1776.
Calstock, co. Cornw. in 1809. Died | Died Sept. 1826, bur.¹
April 1841. Bur. at Calstock.
D

John Williams⊤Philippa dau. of | Edward Wil-⊤Elizabeth dau. of
of Burncoose | John Naudin, mar. | liams of Honey- | John Pearson Foote
House, eldest | in the Quaker's | combe, 3rd son, | of Harwood in
son born there | Meeting House, | born 5th Aug. | Calstock, co. Corn-
3rd Aug. 1777, | Perran Wharf, co. | 1787 at Burn- | wall. Mar. at
and died there | Cornwall, 27th | coose House. | Tavistock 15th
11th Aug. 1849, | June 1810. Died | | July 1814. Died
s.p. Bur.¹ | 7th Dec. 1861, | | 25th Dec. 1851 at
| aged 87. s p. | | Weston-super-
| | | Mare, Somerset.

Edward Williams of | John Williams, 2nd⊤Caroline, only dau. of | Elizabeth, mar.³ 9th June | William John Wil-
Honeycombe, mar. | son, born at Plymouth | Michael Williams of Tre- | 1840, Thomas Somers of Men- | liams, eldest s. born
Emma White. | 10th Jan. 1821, bur.¹ | vince and Scorrier House, | dip Lodge, co. Somerset. He | 3rd Nov. 1827 at
⊤ | 20th Oct. 1849. | uncle to her husband. Mar.² | died 2nd Dec. 1862. Bur. at | Tregullow. Died
| | Sept. 1846. | Burrington in same county. | unmar. 25th Sept.
| | | | 1847. Bur.¹

Edward Mansel | William Robert | Frederick Law, | Edward Harvey | Leonard Al- | Claude Albert, | Caroline Sydney
Williams, only | eldest son born | born 10th May | born 2nd Feb. | fred, born 9th | born 5th Oct. | born 22nd Mar.
issue. Born | 21st Feb. 1860, | 1862, bap. at | 1865, bap.⁵ | April 1867. | bap.⁵ 10th Nov. | 1859, bap.⁵
June 1847, at | bap.¹ | Christian Mal- | | | 1870.
Tiverton, co. | | ford. | |
Devon. | |

¹ At Gwennap.   ² At St. George's, Hanover square   ³ At St. James', Westminster.
⁴ At Redruth.   ⁵ At Perran Arworthal.   ⁶ At Kenwyn.   ⁷ At St. Stythians.

WILLIAMS.

Davy Williams of St. Stythians.

Richard Williams of St. Stythians.

Richard Williams of St. Stythians, 2nd son.═Anne, dau. of Walter Martyn, mar.[1] 3rd
Bap.[7] 25th Dec. 1693.   January 1718.

Henry Williams,
4th son, bap.[1] 13th
Aug. 1722. Liv.
Aug. 1761.

Thomas Williams,
5th son, bap.[1] 21st
Mar. 1724, and
bur.[1] 12th Feb.
1748.

William Williams,
bap.[1] 14th Jan.
1727-8. Liv. Jan.
1760.

Michael Williams of Burncoose, youngest═Susanna, bap.[1] 23rd   E
son, born Aug. and bap.[1] 20th Oct. 1730. | Nov. 1732, mar. at
Died at Bath and Bur.[1] 28th Feb. 1775. | Cury, 30th Nov.
Will dated 6th Oct. 1773, and prov. with a | 1752. Bur.[1] Feb.
codl. 9th Aug. 1775. | 1814.

William Williams of Penryn, bap.[1] 6th May
1756, mar.[1] 11th April 1786, to Catherine
Paul.

Michael Williams, bap.[1] 14th April   F
1770. Mar. at St. Saviours Jersey, 18th
Feb. 1787, to Jane Turner of Tregony.

Michael Williams of Scorrier House, and═Elizabeth, eldest dau. of
of Carhayes Castle, Cornwall, and Gnaton | Richard Eales of East-
Hall, Devon. Deputy Lieut. for Cornw. | down Devon, mar. 5th
and Deputy Warden of the Stannaries. | March 1813 at St. Law-
2nd son born 5th June 1785. Sheriff of | rence, Exon. Died 20th
Glamorgan 1839, M.P. for West Cornw. | July 1852. Bur.[1]
1853, till his death 15th June 1858. Bur.[1]

Sir William Williams of Tre-═Caroline, 2nd dau. of Rich-   G
gullow, Cornwall, and Heanton | ard Eales of Eastdown. Born
Court, Devon. Deputy Lieut. for | 30th Jan. 1796. Mar. 26th
Cornwall, and Deputy Warden of | Sept. 1826 at Dawlish.
the Stannaries, 4th son born 3rd
Aug. 1791 at Scorrier House.
Sheriff of Cornwall 1851. Created
a BARONET 4th Aug. 1866. Died
24th March 1870. Bur.[1]

Sir Frederick Martin Williams of Tregullow═Mary Christian, youngest dau. of Rev.
Bart., J. P. and Deputy Lieut. for Cornw. | Robert Vanburgh Law, M.A., Rector
Deputy Warden of the Stannaries, M.P. | of Christian Malford, co Wilts, and
for Truro, 2nd but eldest surviving son and | Preb. of Wells, son of George Henry
heir, born at Tregullow, 25th Jan. and bap. | Law, D.D. Bishop of Bath and Wells,
24th Mar. 1830, succeeded to the Baronetcy | mar. 10th June 1858, at Christian
on the death of his father. | Malford.

Richard Michael Wil-═Georgiana Sophia,   H
liams, Lieut.-Col. of 3rd | 3rd dau. of Rev.
Hussars, born 18th Dec. | Thomas Phillpotts of
1830, bap. 26th Jan.1831. | Porthgwidden, mar.
Died 25th Dec. 1867. | 19th Jan. 1858, at
                      | Feock.

Mary Christian,
born 25th March
1861, bap.[5]

Beatrice Julia,
born 20th Sept.
1863, bap.[3]

Amy Gertrude, bap.
6th May 1869, at
Sutton Verney, co.
Wilts.

Ernest Martin,
born 17th Dec.
1871, bap.[5] 4th
March 1872.

Victor George,
born 28th Jan.
and bap.[5] 8th
April 1874.

Georgiana Caroline   I
Mary, born 27th
March at Borrahard
near Newbridge, co.
Kildare, bap. at
Feock 5th June 1859

[1] At Gwennap.

[2] At St. George's, Hanover square.

[3] At St. James', Westminster.

[4] At Redruth.

[5] At Perran Arworthal.

[6] At Kenwyn.

[7] At St. Stythians.

PEDIGREE OF

Richard Harris of St. Day, co. Cornwall, son of John Harris of
St. Issey, to whom Richard Harris Vicar of Gwennap, by his will
dated 16th Dec. 1645, and prov. 25th Feb. 1646, P.C.C. leaves his
tenement called Crowgiers in the parish of St. Day. Bur.[1] 2nd
Feb. 1672.

John Harris of St. Day and Gwennap, purchased the estate=Alice, dau. of Henry Pelloe of Mabe,
of Bargus vean in 1704. Bur.[1] 3rd July 1705. Adm° | mar. there 26th Nov. 1677. Registered
granted in Archd. Cornwall, 17th April 1706, to sons John | at Gwennap. Died 28th June 1734.[1]
and Henry Harris, his relict Alice renouncing.

John Harris of Cusgarne, bap.[1] 14th=Elizabeth, dau. of John Beauchamp of Trevince, co.   Henry Harris of St. Day, bap.[1]
Oct. 1678. An officer in the Cornw. | Cornwall, and sister of William Beauchamp, whose will   1st Nov. 1683. Adm°r to his
Militia. Bur.[1] 5th Aug. 1732. | is dated 28th July 1726. Prov. in P.C.C. 21st Feb. 1729- father's effects in 1706. Mar. Joan
                                     | 30. Bap.[1] 13th April 1675. Mar.[1] 27th April 1703   dau. of Stephen Harris of Redruth
                                     | Bur.[1] 6th July 1735.   Bur.[1] 11th April 1729.

Henry Harris of Cusgarne, bap.[1]=Elizabeth, only child of Edward Kempthorne of   John Harris, 2nd son, bap.[1] 19th
27th Dec. 1703. Bur.[1] 6th May | Chimder in Gunwalloe, whose will is dated 31st   April 1705. Bur.[1] 9th April 1716.
1768. Intestate adm° granted 25th | March 1753, and prov. in Archd. Cornwall, 6th June
May 1768, to his son Edward, at | 1760. Mar. at Gunwalloe 1st May 1728.
Exeter.

E ——

Elizabeth, bap.[1] | Catherine, bap.[1] 25th March | Edward Harris of Cusgarne in Gwennap.=Eleanor Johns of Trevince,
13th Nov. 1741. | 1729. Mar.[1] 15th April 1758, | Captain in the Cornwall Militia, eldest son, | Cornwall, mar. at St. Gerrans,
Bur. 24th Aug. | to Isaac Head of St. Mary's, in | bap.[1] 27th July 1730. Prov. his grand- | 6th Jan. 1769. Bur. from
1765 at St. Mul- | the Scilly Islands, Collector of | father's will in 1760. Died s.p. and was | Penryn at St. Mullion, 27th
lion. | Customs there. | bur. from Gwennap, at St. Mullion 5th | April 1809, aged 75.
                     | | July 1798. Will dated 27th June 1798.
                     | | Prov. 23rd Nov. 1798 in Archd. Cornwall.

F ——

Edward Harris Williams, bap.[1] | Richard Pellowe, a Captain=Elizabeth, bap.[1] 6th July
17th June 1773. An officer in the | in the Royal Navy.   1767.
87th Regt. of Foot. Died s.p.

G ——

Susan, born at Burncoose, 30th | Ann, born 4th Nov. 1779. Mar. 23rd Dec. | Catherine, born 10th July 1781, Mar.
Dec. 1776. Died unmar. Jan. | 1811, to Benjamin Tucker of Trematon | 21st May 1806, to Rev. Josiah Hill, of
1829. Bur.[1] | Castle, sometime Secretary to the Admiralty | Barnet. Died 16th Dec. 1828.
                                   | and Deputy Lieut. for Cornwall.

H ——

Arthur Edward, born | Charles Henry Williams, of Pilton=Harriet Mary dau. of Arthur | Michael Williams of Halwell,
20th Aug. and bap. | House, co. Devon, M.P. for Barn- | Davie Bassett of Umberleigh, co. | co. Cornwall. Born 10th Jan.
24th Sept. 1832. | staple 1868 to 1874. Born 16th | Devon. Mar. at Berrynarbor, co. | 1839. Bap. 2nd Oct. 1840 at
                       | Nov. 1834, and bap. 13th Oct. | Devon, 7th Jan. 1858. | St. Day. J.P. for Cornwall.
                       | 1835 at St. Day. | | Liv. 1874.

I ——

William Phillpotts, born at the | Lionel Arthur born 29th Dec. | Edith Bassett, born 13th June | Walter Bassett, born
Curragh, 5th Aug. and bap. there | 1861, at Newbridge, bap. at | and bap. at Atherington, co. | 20th Sept., and bap. at
23rd Sept. 1860. | Moorfield Newbridge, 30th Jan. | Devon, 14th July 1861. | Atherington 7th Nov.
                                 | 1862. | | 1863.

[1] At Gwennap.

HARRIS.

Susanna, bap.[1] 1st Dec. 1681. Bur.[1] 17th Dec. 1696.	Katherine, bap.[1] 17th Dec. 1685. Mar.[1] 17th May 1716, to Richard Banbury, junr. of Redruth.	Alice, bap.[1] 10th Dec. 1688. Bur.[1] 11th March 1747.	Elizabeth, bap.[1] 4th April 1691.	Loveday, born 1693. Bur.[1] 26th Nov. 1767.

Richard Harris, 3rd son, bap.[1] 26th June 1707. Bur.[1] 14th Dec. 1717.	William Harris, 4th son, Bap.[1] 2nd Aug. 1711. Bur.[1] 3rd June 1714.	Elizabeth, bap.[1] 23rd Feb. 1708. Bur.[1] 26th Oct. 1710.	Catherine, bap.[1] 7th May 1713. Bur.[1] 31st March 1716.

John Harris of H.M. Dockyard, Ply-mouth, 2nd son bap.[1] 6th Feb. 1734. Died s.p. and bur. 6th Feb. 1805 at Mylor. = Elizabeth Leverton of Gwennap, mar.[1] 18th Feb. 1762.	William Harris, bap.[1] 8th Oct. 1736. Bur.[1] 12th Nov. 1746.

Elizabeth, born 10th July 1788. Mar.[1] to Joseph Moore, D.D.	Mary, born 9th Nov. 1789. Mar. 27th Jan. 1813, to Rev. Henry Beaufort, Vicar of Eaton Socon co. Beds.

Caroline, born 4th Jan., bap.[1] 6th Oct. 1829. Liv. unmar. 1866.	Mary Elizabeth, born 15th Aug. and bap. 8th Sept. 1833. Died 15th of same month.	Catherine Ann, born 4th April and bap. 5th May 1836. Mar. at St. Day, 9th June 1859, to James Hornby Buller, a Lieut.-Colonel in the army. *Died 9th Dec. 1874, at Down Hall, Epsom.*	Susanna Elizabeth born 3rd March 1837, bap. 24th January following at St. Day.

I hereby certify that the foregoing Pedigree, as printed in *Roman* type, and the Arms agree with the Records in this Office.

Heralds' College,
9th February, 1875.

GEORGE HARRISON.
Windsor Herald.

---

[1] At Gwennap.

3 N

APPENDIX I.

SUBSIDY ROLLS OF THE PARISHES OF LANTEGLOS AND ADVENT AND LESNEWITH, 1543. $\frac{87}{152}$

CORNUBIA : Extractum Indenturæ prime solucionis subsidii domini regis infra hundredum de Lesnewith in comitatu predicto factæ vltima die Octobris anno regni regis Henrici VIII. tricesimo quinto quod quidem subsidium concessum fuit dicto domino regi in ultimo parliamento suo ac per Johannem Chamond militem Humfridum Trevelyan & Thomam Chamond Armigeros Commissionarios assignatos ad predictum subsidium taxandum assessatum. Et dicti Commissionarii nominaverunt & eligerunt Johannem Beauchemp armigerum generalem Collectorem Hundredi predicti ad colligendum & recipiendum subsidium predictum & dimidium subsidii ad vsum dicti domini regis in scaccario suo ante sextum diem mensis ffebruarij proximi sequentis soluendum.

Parochia de Lanteglos.

Christopherus Cocke[1]	pro bonis	xiijs iiijd	Willelmus Edward	- pro bonis	iiijd
Hugo Hockyn[2] -	- ,,	xiijs iiijd	Ricardus Cocke -	- ,,	iiijd
Johannes Hutford	- ,,	xiijs iiijd	Hugo Cocke -	- ,,	iiijd
Johannes Sloget	- ,,	viijs	Henricus Cocke -	- ,,	iiijd
Thomas Walles[3]	- ,,	viijs	Johannes Hathendy	- ,,	iiijd
Johannes Perse	- ,,	vjs viijd	Nibles Grene -	- ,,	iiijd
Henricus Harfy	- ,,	ijs viijd	Johannes Baker -	- ,,	ijd
Thomas Blake -	- ,,	iijs viijd	Johannes Jose -	- ,,	ijd
Henry Hycke -	- ,,	ijs	Willelmus Roby -	- ,,	ijd
Gensonus Dawe -	- ,,	ijs	Johannes Chapell -	- ,,	ijd
Johannes Waren	- ,,	ijs	Johannes Wordesale	- ,,	ijd
Johannes Colman	- ,,	xxd	Johannes Cocke -	- ,,	ijd
Johannes Blake	- ,,	xxd	Deonisius Harrys -	- ,,	ijd
Regnaldus Edward	- ,,	viijd	Robertus Stere -	- ,,	ijd
Willelmus Perse	- ,,	viijd	Thomas Collyn -	- ,,	ijd
Johannes Saunder	- ,,	viijd	Johannes Welle -	- ,,	ijd
Willlelmus Walles	- ,,	viijd	Johannes Barweyke	- ,,	ijd
Agneta Walles -	- .,	viijd	Thomas Peres -	- ,,	ijd

[1] See Pedigree, p. 369. Buried 1566.
[2] Hugh son of Robert Hockyn, buried 1563. See Pedigree, p. 367.
[3] Buried 1560, see Pedigree 374.

Thomas Jose -	- pro bonis	vj*d*	Johannes Jeffrey -	-	pro bonis	ij*d*
Johannes Shorte -	,,	vj*d*	Johannes Serpell -	-	,,	ij*d*
Johannes Sloget -	,,	vj*d*	Johannes Colman -	-	,,	ij*d*
Johannes Renold -	,,	vj*d*	Stephanus Hebell -	-	,,	ij*d*
Johannes Toker -	,,	vj*d*	Johannes Havys -	-	,,	ij*d*
Rogerus Layn -	,,	vj*d*	Helvet Tregrugon -	-	,,	ij*d*
Willelmus Dyer -	,,	vj*d*	Christopherus Battoyll -	-	,,	ij*d*
Willelmus Lanston -	,,	vj*d*	Johannes Hyll -	-	,,	ij*d*
Christopherus Roby -	,,	iiij*d*	Thomas Keyte -	-	,,	ij*d*
Johannes Roby -	,,	iiij*d*	Johannes Peprylle -	-	,,	ij*d*
Margareta Hycke -	,,	iiij*d*	Johannes Ronolde -	-	,,	ij*d*
Henricus Marke -	,,	iiij*d*	Thomas Donot -	-	,,	ij*d*
Stephanus Rouse -	,,	iiij*d*	Johannes Colman -	-	,,	ij*d*
Nicholaus Hender -	,,	iiij*d*	Johannes Cocke -	-	,,	ij*d*
Henricus Toker -	,,	iiij*d*	Alsen Colman -	-	,,	ij*d*
Hugo Colman -	- ,,	iiij*d*	Willelmus Leuyn Alien -	-	,,	xvj*d*
Willelmus Dawe -	,,	iiij*d*				

Summa iiij^{li} xvj^s iiij^d

Parochia de Sent Adven.

Willelmus Hockyn	- pro bonis		x*s*	Nicholaus Hodge	-	pro bonis	viij*d*
Ricardus Hodge -	,,		xx*d*	Thomas Burges -		,,	viij*d*
Rogerus Hamley -	,,	vj*s*	viij*d*	Thomas Rooke -		,,	ij*d*
Johannes Cowlyng, Senr.	,,		iij*s*	Ricardus Hamley -		,,	ij*d*
Johannes Batyn -	,,	vj*s*	viij*d*	Johannis Notyng -		,,	ij*d*
Johannes Jory -	,,		iij*s*	Willelmus Cowlyng -		,,	vj*d*
Henricus Edward -	,,		iiij*d*	Johannes Charta -		,,	iiij*d*
Johannes Bedlacke -	,,		iiij*d*	Thomas Garre -		,,	xx*d*
Hugo Peers -	,,		ij*d*	Johannes ffote		,,	iiij*d*
Johannes Knebone -	,,		vj*d*	Peter Ylle -			ij*d*
Johannes Blake -	,,		iiij*d*	Johannes Denysell -		,,	ij*d*
Thomas Penwaren -	,,		vj*d*	Johannes Cowlyng -		,,	iiij*d*
Willelmus Nyell -	,,		ij*d*				

Summa xxxviij^s viij^d

Parochia de Lesnewth.

Johannes Longeman	- pro bonis	iij*s*	Johannes Bylkey	- pro bonis		iiij*d*
Thomas Taylor	- ,,	ij*s*	Robertus Waryn			ij*d*
Willelmus ffreer	- ,,	xx*d*	Christopherus Pyker	-	,,	ij*d*

Johannes Dawe	-	pro bonis xx*d*	Johannes Rube	-	pro bonis vj*d*
Ricardus Garrowe	-	,, ij*s*	Johannes Dawe	-	,, ij*d*
Willelmus Harry	-	,, iij*s*	Jacobus Colyn	-	,, ij*d*
Willelmus Barber	-	,, ij*s*	Robertus Hobbe	-	,, ij*d*
Willelmus Longeman	-	,, viij*d*	Johannes Bylkey	-	,, viij*d*
Willelmus Belkey	-	,, iij*s*	Johannes ffreer	-	,, viij*d*
Thomas Rawe	-	,, iiij*d*	Johannes Longeman, Jun'	-	,, xx*d*
Johannes Rowe	-	,, viij*d*	Willelmus Rube	-	,, iiij*d*
Willelmus Hamley	-	,, vj*d*	Johannes Rube	-	,, ij*d*
Willelmus Hamley, Jun'	-	,, vj*d*	Johannes Garrowe	-	,, ij*d*
Johannes Packet	-	,, vj*d*	Johannes Dawe	-	,, iiij*d*
Johannes Packet, Jun'	-	,, vj*d*	Willelmus Waren	-	,, ij*d*
Ricardus Bylkey	-	,, iiij*d*	Johanna Colyn	-	,, ij*d*

Summa xxviij*s* iiij*d*.

This Subsidy was levied by Act 34 & 35 Henry VIII, cap 27, which Act granted one entire subsidy, the payment of which was to extend over three years. It was levied on all real estate of the annual value of 20s. and upwards; and upon all personalty of that value, or above. Every *subject* possessing personalty worth 20s. and under £5, including plate, stock, merchandise, corn severed from the ground, household goods and all other moveable goods, or sums of money due to him after deducting such sums as he owed and felt in conscience bound to pay, and the value of the apparel of himself, his wife and children, save jewells of gold, silver, stone, &c., was charged at the rate of four pence for every pound. If his possessions were of the value of £5 and under £10, eight pence for every pound. If worth £10 and under £20, sixteen pence for every pound. If of the value of £20 and upwards, two shillings for every pound. Every alien was charged at double the above rates, and every alien of the age of sixteen years and upwards not being contributory as abovesaid, paid a poll rate of four pence. Every person who held in fee-simple, fee-tail, or for term of life or years, or by copy of Court Roll, &c., any castles, manors, lands, tenements, rents, services, &c., &c., of the yearly value of 20s. and under £5 was charged at the rate of eight pence for every pound. Of the value of £5 and under £10, sixteen pence for every pound; of the value of £10 and under £20, two shillings for every pound; and of the value of £20 and above, three shillings for every pound. Estates of aliens were charged at double rates.

The first levy was charged at half the entire subsidy. Hence these rolls give a clear view of the value of the possessions of every person in each of the parishes at the date in question. Of course allowance must be made for the difference in the value of money. It will be observed that not a single person in either of the parishes is assessed upon lands. This circumstance, to a greater or lesser degree, pervades the whole of the Subsidy Rolls from the earliest to the latest date, and our endeavours to ascertain the principles upon which the tax was assessed upon landholders have been completely baffled.

VIEW OF THE CHURCH OF ST MARBON.

J Ferguson lith.

PARISH OF ST. MABEN _ALIAS_ ST. MABYN.

The Parish of St. Mabyn, which derives its name from the dedication of the Church, contains by admeasurement 4067a. 2r. 7p. It is irregular in form, and is bounded on the north by St. Tudy, on the east by Blisland, on the south-east by Helland, on the south-west by Egloshayle, and on the north-west by the last named parish and St. Kew.

The land, generally, is fertile and adapted either to pasture or corn. The chief land owners are: The Viscount Falmouth, the Trustees of the late Sir William Molesworth, John Tremayne of Heligan, Esq., the Heirs of the late John Peter-Hoblyn, Esq., Francis John Hext and Richard Hambly Andrew, Esqs., and Mrs. Hooper. There is no other industry practised than the culture of the soil. Laborer's wages are 12s. or 13s. a week, and sometimes they have a cottage and garden free of rent. Besides this there are about two acres of land, contiguous to the Church Town, let as garden allotments, in portions of ten perches each, at five pence the perch.

The geological character of the parish is precisely the same as that of the neighbouring parishes of Egloshayle and St. Kew, being altered Devonian traversed by beds of greenstone lying nearly north and south; whilst two elvan dykes, issuing from the granitic formation at Trehudreth, in Blisland, protrude into this parish in parallel lines, in a westerly direction, one of them reaching nearly to the centre of the parish.

The population, &c., at the several decennia in the present century, as shewn by the Returns, is as under:

			1801	1811	1821	1831	1841	1851	1861	1871
Population ..	..	..	475	560	715	793	870	772	714	765
	Inhabited	..	91[1]	103	128	149[2]	180	162	153	169[3]
Houses	Uninhabited ..		12	7	..	6	15	21	13	6
	Building	..	..	3	2	2	2	..	..	1

[1] The increase of the population during the 40 years ending in 1841 was 83 per cent. In the following 20 years there was a decrease of 18 per cent, which, in 1841, was attributed to Emigration. In the last decade there has been an increase of 51 persons or 7 per cent.

[2] Occupied by 108 families.   [3] Occupied by 157 families.

3 o

ASSESSMENTS, &c.

	£	s.	d.
The Annual Value of Real Property as Assessed in 1815 was ... 6,051	6,051	0	0
Rated Value from County Rate ... ... ,, ... 5,160	5,160	0	0
Gross Estimated Rental in 1863 6,089	6,089	7	3
Rateable Value ... ... ,, ... 4,322	4,322	7	8½
Gross Estimated Rental in 1874 5,948	5,948	0	0
Rateable Value ... ... ,, ... 5,247	5,247	0	0

Parochial Assessments for the year ending Michaelmas 1874

		£	s.	d.
Common Charges	...	427	15	11 [1]
Police Rate ...	...	53	15	0
County Rate ...	...	48	7	6
		529	18	5

		£	s.	d.
Land Tax Redeemed £107 11s. 1d. Payable £51 7s. 11d.		158	19	0
Assessed Taxes		not known		
Inhabited House Duty assessed upon the Annual Value of		160	0	0

Property and Income Tax assessed upon

		£	s.	d.
Schedule A	Gross amount ...	5,940	0	0
,, B	,,	5,228	0	0
,, C	,, ...	not known		
,, D	,, ...	not known		

At St. Maben "Church Town," which, in ancient times, was often called "Tremaben," a Fair is held on St. Valentine's Day. When that day falls on a Sunday the fair is held on the Monday following. We do not know whether on this day the dedication feast of the Church was formerly kept.

ANCIENT ROADS AND TRACKS.

Several important roads intersect this parish. We have already alluded to the ancient road, or track, which, passing by the earthworks at Dunmere and Pencarrow extended to Dinham's Bridge (ante, vol. i., p. 405.) At this bridge, or ancient ford, two other roads converge, one entering the parish at Helland bridge, before mentioned (vol. ii., p. 61,) passing by Tredinnick and St. Mabyn Church Town; and the other entering the parish from St. Tudy, near Trevisquite, passing through Littlewood and Trethevy. Another road enters the parish from Blisland, at Tresaret Bridge, and unites with the road above mentioned from Helland Bridge, a little east of St. Mabyn Church. A fourth road from the great junction at "Five ashes," close to the castle at Pencarrow, extends through the parish, intersecting the two last mentioned; the former near Tredethy and the latter at

---

[1] The amount levied in this parish for the maintenance of the poor in the year 1831 was £383 1s. 0d.

Longstone, and enters the parish of St. Tudy at Hendra. There are other intersecting roads and tracks which it is unnecessary particularly to specify in detail, and it shall suffice to allude to one before mentioned, as winding down the hill opposite Penhargard to an ancient ford (ante, p. 6,) crossing the river Alan; and to another, which, branching out of the road from Tresaret to St. Mabyn, above mentioned, near Tregaddock, passes through that place and West Polglaze to Kelligren, in St. Tudy, where it falls into the road referred to ante, p. 81.

PRE-HISTORIC REMAINS.

There are no castles or earthworks in this parish, and the only pre-historic remains, of which we have any knowledge, are two stones called "Longstone" and "Shortstone." The first was formerly situate at the intersection of the roads above mentioned, to which it gave its name. Previously to the erection of the cottages there it was within a field, but was then enclosed in one of the gardens. A few years ago it was removed by Mr. Abraham Hambly, then owner of the property, to his residence at Treblethick, when it was either broken up, or it now forms one of the stones covering a well. There were some ridiculous legends connected with this stone, and it was the object of much superstitious awe and veneration, to brave which, we have been given to understand, was one of the causes leading to its removal. It is said to have been inscribed. The second is at the junction of a road from Slade's Bridge, in Egloshayle, with the road alluded to above as extending from Pencarrow to Dinham's Bridge. From it the place is called "Shortstone." The stone was formerly erect, but is now prostrate.

37.

3 o²

ANCIENT CHRISTIAN MONUMENTS.

37. At a place called "Cross Hill," on the road mentioned above as leading from St. Tudy to Dinham's Bridge through Littlewood and Trethevy, is an ancient cross. It remains in situ. Formerly it stood on an open piece of waste, but the waste having been recently enclosed it is embraced within the enclosure, and stands inside a gate in the side of the hedge. It is 3ft. high, 1ft. 4in. wide, and 9in. thick; and the symbol is of the Greek type.

38. There is another cross on the left hand side of the road, leading from St. Mabyn Church town to Long-

stone, about 200 yards east from "Lane End." The symbol is of the Greek type, and without a rim It is 4ft. high, and the head 1ft. 10in. in diameter. The head has been broken off the shaft.

38.

39. At Tredethy is a portion of a cross which was dug up some years ago at Lancarfe, in Bodmin. It is 1ft. 10ins. in height and four sided, each side measuring 10ins. On each face is a trefoil-headed niche, or panel, containing a subject—on one side is the Crucifixion, with SS. Mary and John at the foot of the cross, and on the opposite side the Virgin, crowned, bearing the

39.

Holy Child, whilst on each of the other faces is a single figure, both mitred, one bears the pastoral staff, and has the hand raised in benediction. It is much worn and defaced.

The base of a cross, with the mortice in it, remains in the churchyard; it is of wrought granite, about 2ft. 10ins. square, and was dug up some years ago when a pathway was made through the Churchyard. The mortice is about 12ins. square and 6ins. deep. We failed to discover the Cross, which probably remains buried in the Churchyard.

MEETING HOUSES OF DISSENTERS.

On 5th February 1811, a house at Helland Bridge, in the parish of St. Mabyn, belonging to Thomas Harvy, was registered in the Court of the Archdeaconry of Cornwall, under the various Acts of Parliament in that behalf,[1] by James Evans and others, as "a place of meeting of Protestant Dissenters called Methodists." On 3rd October 1816, a dwelling house in the possession of William Cornelius, situate at Longstone, was registered by Richard Martyn of St. Mabyn, Yeoman, for the meeting of Protestant Dissenters, the denomination not being stated. And on 20th March 1820, William Metheral, of Poughhill, registered a house, in the occupation of Thomas Scantlebury, in the town of St. Mabyn, for Armenians.

United Methodist Free Church.—The first building specially devoted to this purpose in the parish of St. Mabyn was erected, at considerable expense, about the year 1820,

[1] 1st William III, Cap. 18. 19th George III, Cap. 155. 52nd George III, Cap. 14.

by Richard Hambly Andrew of Tredinnick, Gent., on some fields belonging to his estate near the Church Town, and to this building he attached a burial ground. On 21st April 1821 it was registered in the Court of the Archdeaconry by John Hodson of Bodmin, Minister, as a place of meeting for Methodists. By Indenture dated 9th March 1839, Mr. Andrew, "for the purpose of ensuring the regular service and preaching according to the usages of the Society called the Wesleyan Methodist Association," conveyed this building and burial ground attached to James Andrew, Yeoman, John May Andrew, Yeoman, Edmund Harry, Yeoman, Arthur Gaved, Gent., all of the parish of St. Mabyn and several other persons, as Trustees, to hold the said premises, and to permit such persons as should be regularly appointed preachers by the Wesleyan Methodist Association in their General Assembly, and the local preachers appointed by the preachers at the quarterly meetings of the circuit, to preach therein under certain limitations as to doctrines, &c.[1]

This Chapel is licensed for the celebration of Marriages. It will seat two hundred and fifty persons, and there are now (1875) attached to it fifty registered members.

Wesleyan.—We have mentioned above that in 1816 a dwelling house at Longstone was registered as a Meeting House. This was probably for the Wesleyans. By Indenture dated 6th October, William Perry of St. Tudy, Yeoman, with the consent of William Kirkness of Falmouth, Esq., granted a piece of waste land, 30 ft. in length and 20 ft. in breadth, by the side of the road leading from Longstone to Tresallett (Tresarret) Bridge, contiguous to two fields belonging to a tenement called Tregaddock, on which then a Chapel was partly built, to William Perry of St. Mabyn, Yeoman, Joseph Bennett of Helland, Yeoman, and several other persons as Trustees, to hold the said piece of ground and the building to be erected thereon for the term of ninety-nine years, at the rent of 2s. per annum, subject to the provisions of the Wesleyan Model Deed enrolled in Chancery.[2]

This building will accomodate fifty persons and there are now (1875) belonging to it twenty-three registered members.

A new building is in course of erection which is intended to supersede the one last mentioned.

MANOR OF TREVISQUITE.

This manor, to which is annexed the advowson of the Church of St. Mabena, is called Trauiscoit in Domesday, and was one of the manors of the Earl of Moreton, of whom it was held by Richard (de Tracy). "The Earl has one manor which is called Trauiscoit, which was held by Merlesuain on the day on which King Edward was alive and dead. There are there two hides of land, and it renders gild for one hide. This twelve ploughs can plough. There Richard has in demesne one virgate and three ploughs, and the villans have the rest of the land and three ploughs. There Richard has eight villans, and nine

---

[1] Rot. Claus. 1862, Part 163, No. 16. [2] Rot. Claus. 3rd William IV., Part 42, No. 3.

bordars, and eight bond servants, and five animals, and five hogs, and one hundred sheep and one mill which renders per annum 2s., and twenty acres of coppice, and fifty acres of pasture, and the value per annum is 25s., and when the Earl received it, 30s."[1]

The above mentioned Richard was Richard de Lacy, to whom was granted several other manors in the County, and his descendants continued to hold Trevisquite of the Earls of Cornwall for a considerable period.   In 1210 Robert the son of Walter held eleven Knights' fees in the County, of the fee of Richard de Lasci, his uncle.[2]   Upon the death of Edmund Earl of Cornwall, on 13th September 1300, it was found that he held two fees in Trevisquite and Hamatedie, which were held of him by John Tracy and Hugh Peverel.[3] John de Tracy, in Trinity term 1306, suffered a fine to Simon Fitz Roger and Isabella his wife of two mills, ten acres of wood, and sixteen marks rent in Treuescoyt, and of the Advowson of the Church of the same ville, at the rent of one red rose for all services, to hold jointly to the said Simon and Isabella during their lives, remainder to the heirs of their bodies, in default remainder to the heirs of the body of the said Isabella, remainder over to the said John and his heirs.[4]

According to Pole this John de Tracy was a son of Sir Henry Tracy of Wollecombe, and died, s. p., leaving his two sisters, the above mentioned Isabella, and Isold, his heirs. Isabella was thrice married.   1st, to Sir Herbert Mauris; 2nd, to Sir Simon Roges; and lastly, to Sir Edmond Botiler; Isold was twice married.   She had to her first husband Sir Richard Fitz Stephen, and to her second John Mauger; and according to the same authority, the two sisters made partition of the estates in 5th Edward III.[5] (1331.)

Sir Symon Roges, or Rogos, died immediately after the above mentioned settlement was made, and it was found upon the inquisition taken at Trevescoyt on 26th September 1306, that he died seized, conjointly with his wife Isabella, of a moiety of the Hamlet of Treuescoyt, which they held of the King in capite by the service of half a Knight's fee as of the Earldom of Cornwall, and that they were enfeoffed of the said moiety by John de Tracy, brother of the said Isabella, and that Johanna daughter of the said Isabella was their nearest heir, and was aged three years at Easter preceding.[6]   In 1325 a presentation was made to the Church of St. Maben, by the grant of Sir Edmond le Botiller,[7] the third husband of the aforesaid Isabella, and in 1334 the same Edmond suffered a fine in the said manor and advowson to William Casse.[8]

When the Aid was levied in 20th Edward III. (1346), on the King's eldest son being made a knight, it was found that the Duke of Cornwall, by reason of the minority of the heir of John le Jeu, held half a fee in Treuiscoid which John de Tracy had held before; the other moiety of John de Tracy's fee there being held by Matilda Lercedekne,[9]

---

[1] Exon. Domesday, p. 239, orig. fo. 260.   See also Excheq. Dom., vol. i, p. 122 b.

[2] Inq. made 12th and 13th John of the services of Knights and others, who hold in Capite. Lib. Rub. pp. 132, 149.

[3] Inq. p. m. 31st Edward I, Sub. Rolls $\frac{84}{4}$

[4] Pedes Finium, 34th Edward I, Trinity.

[5] Pole's Devon, p. 512.

[6] Inq. p.m., 34th Edward I, No. 31.

[7] See List of Institutions, post, p. 460.

[8] Pedes Finium, 7th Edward III, Hilary.

[9] Book of Aids, Queen's Remcmb. Office.

which Matilda presented to the Church of St. Maben in 1340, and in 1361.[1] On 11th August 11th Edward III. (1354)[2] John Jeu did homage to the Duke for a moiety of this manor, but he was dead on 16th July 1356, for on that day a *writ diem clausit extremum* was ordered to be issued,[3] and on 30th November following, dower of lands in Treuiscoyt was granted to Margaret widow of John Jeu. On 12th February 1356-7 it was ordered that a moiety of the manor of Treuisquyt should be delivered to Isabella Roges next heir of John Jeu.[4]

We have, at this early date, and in the intricacy of the abovementioned five marriages, been, as yet, unable to trace the descent either of Matilda Lercedekne or John le Jeu. On 4th October 1365 the wardship of Henry, son and heir of Nicholas Marreis of Treuiscoit, was granted by the Duke of Cornwall to John Whisshele, one of the gentlemen of his wardrobe, for five years.[5] The Nicholas here mentioned must, we conceive, have been the son of Isabella de Tracy by her first marriage with Sir Herbert Mauris.

In 1381 the entire manor and advowson had descended to Johanna Courtenay, who in that year presented to the Church of St. Maben, as she did again in the following year, being then described as relict of Thomas Courtenay, the true Patron; and two years later Philip Walweyn presented as Lord of the manor of Trevisquite, and of the Church of St. Maben, the true Patron in right of inheritance of his wife Johanna.[6] The said Johanna afterwards became the wife of Thomas Beaumont, who presented to the Church of St. Maben on 13th April 1415, and she died on the day next after the Nativity of our Lord 9th Henry V. (1421.) Upon the inquisition taken after her death it was found that certain John Daucombe and Peter Sylverlock were seized of the manor of Trevysquyt and the Advowson of the Church of St. Maben to the said manor pertaining, and by their Charter, dated on Monday next after the Nativity of Our Lord (1381), granted the same to the said Johanna, then the relict of Thomas de Courtenay, for the term of her life, remainder to John son and heir of the said Thomas Courtenay, and the heirs of his body, in default remainder to Edmund brother of the said John, in default remainder to Thomas brother of the said Edmund, and the heirs of his body, in default remainder to Clemencia sister of the said John, Edmund, and Thomas, and the heirs of her body, in default remainder to Robert Scrobehulle' and the heirs of his body, and in default of such issue, remainder to Peter Courtenay, Knight, and his heirs and assigns for ever.[7] In virtue of this grant the said Johanna was seized in demesne as of a free tenement, and the aforesaid John, Edmund, Thomas, and Clemencia died without heirs of their bodies, and Robert Scrobehull had issue Isabella, Johanna, Elizabeth, and Isabella; and that Johanna daughter of Robert Scrobehull took to her husband William Holbeme, then living, and had issue John Holbeme, and died; and afterwards the said Johanna Beaumont died seized, as aforesaid,

---

[1] See Institutions, post, p. 460.
[2] Council Book of the Black Prince, fo. 161.
[3] Ibid. fo. 159.
[4] Ibid. fo. 284.
[5] Ibid. fo. 551.
[6] See List of Institutions, post, p. 461.
[7] We have not succeeded in tracing the descent of Johanna Courtenay, though we conceive she must have been a Tracy, nor have we been able to identify her husband, nor trace the relationship which undoubtedly existed between Johanna Courtenay and Robert Scrobehulle.

of the said manor and Advowson, which she held of the King as of the Duchy of Cornwall by the service of one Knight's fee. The jury found that there were rents of assize of the value of £16 per annum issuing out of free tenements, that there was a corn mill of the clear annual value of 10s., that there were four acres, English, of moor of the value of 3s. 4d. per annum, and that there was one acre of wood, whereof the pasture was of the value of 4d. per annum; and that Matilda, wife of Ralph Durburgh, sister of the said Johanna, was her nearest heir, and was aged 60 years and more. They say, further, that the aforesaid Isabella, senior, Elizabeth, Isabella, junior, and John son of the aforesaid William Holbeme and Johanna his wife, were the nearest heirs of the said Robert Scrobehulle, and they say that Isabella, senior, was then the wife of Nicholas Specote, and aged 34 years and more, that the aforesaid John Holbeme was aged 14 years more, and that the said Elizabeth was aged 20 years and more, and that the said Isabella, junior, was aged 18 years and more.[1] This inquisition having been returned into Chancery in the usual manner, and the King having received the homage and fealty of Nicholas Specote for the proparty of his wife Isabella, and the homage of Elizabeth and Isabella, junior, for their respective proparties, it was, on 5th February 1432-3, commanded the escheator to take security for their reliefs, respectively, and make legal partition of the said manor and Advowson, and deliver seizin of their respective shares to the said Nicholas and Isabella his wife, Elizabeth, and Isabella, junior, and to retain in his hands the portion of the said John Holbeme.[2] Thus the manor became divided into fourths, and accordingly we find that a vacancy occurring in the Rectory, King Henry V presented in the minority of John Holbeme, son and heir of Johanna, eldest daughter of the aforesaid Robert Scrobehulle, and a vacancy again occurring in 1457, John Specote son and heir of Isabella, second daughter of the said Robert Scrobhull, presented. Elizabeth, married first John Trebell, who, with her, in 1429, did homage for her share of the lands.[3] By this marriage she had no issue, and afterwards she married Robert Kirkham, but we do not find that she had her turn in the presentation, for the benefice becoming void by the death of the last Rector, in 1477 John Holbeme again presented. Three shares appear to have remained for a considerable period in the families of Holbeme, Specott, and Kirkham. In 1515 a presentation was made by the grant of Nicholas Specote, grandson of the beforementioned John, and in 1565 George Kirkham, Esq., Humphry Specote, Esq., and John Holbeme Esq., and James Kirkham, Gent., suffered a fine in three parts of four of the advowson of the Rectory to Leonard Loveys, Gent.[4]

Isabella, the youngest daughter of Robert Scrobehulle, married Thomas Chedder, who with her, in 1429, did homage and had seizin of her proparty of the lands of her father.[5] In 1440 Thomas Chedder Esq., and Isabella his wife levied a fine of Alice who was the wife of John Golepynne, and Nicholas Golepynne of the manor of Trevysquyd and the advowson of the Church of St. Maben, whereby the said Alice and Nicholas quitclaimed the same to the said Thomas and Isabella, and warranted the same against the

---

[1] Inq. p.m. 1st, Henry VI, No. 50.
[2] Rot. Fin. 1st Henry V, m. 10.
[3] Lord Treas. Remb. of Excheq., 7th Henry VI, Easter, m. 5
[4] Ped. Fin. 7th & 8th Elizabeth, Michaelmas.
[5] Lord Treas. Remb. of Excheq. 7th Henry VI, Easter, m. 5.

Prior of Launceston and his successors for ever.[1] Thomas Chedder died on 3rd June 1443, and upon the Inquisition taken upon his death it was found that he had died seized of the Manor of Trevysquyd, and also of a fourth part of the advowson of the Church of St. Maben, which he held as of the right and inheritance of Isabella his wife, who still survived, and that Johanna, late wife of Robert Stafford Esq., and Isabella wife of John Newton, son of Richard Newton, Knight, Chief Justice of the Common Pleas, were the daughters and heirs of the said Thomas Chedder, and that on the said 3rd June the said Johanna was aged 18 years, and the said Isabella 14 years and more.[2]

Johanna, by her first husband, Robert Stafford, left no issue. She married secondly John Talbot, Viscount L'Isle, whose daughter, and eventual heir, Elizabeth, became the wife of Sir Edward Grey, Knight, who, in her right, in 1475, was created Baron L'Isle. Upon the partition of the estates between the two co-heirs of Thomas Chedder, Trevisquite was allotted to Lord L'isle and his wife, but because the allotment to Sir John Newton was of less yearly value than that to Lord L'Isle by the sum of £7 11s. 8½d. per annum, he and his wife granted to Sir John Newton and his wife, a yearly rent of that amount out of the Manor of Trevesquite, which rent descended to Richard son of the said Sir John Newton. Edward Grey, Viscount L'Isle, died in 1491, leaving an only son John who succeeded him, and three daughters, viz., Ann wife of John Willoughby; Elizabeth who married first Edmund Dudley and afterwards Arthur Plantagenet, natural son of King Edward IV; and Muriel, wife of Henry Stafford, Earl of Wiltshire. John Grey, Viscount L'Isle, by Muriel daughter of Thomas Howard, Duke of Norfolk, had a daughter Elizabeth, who married Henry Courteney Marquis of Exeter, who must have died v.p. and s.p., for on the death of John Lord L'Isle in 1504, it was found, upon inquisition, that he had died seized of the Manor of Trevysquyte with appurtenances, and of the advowson of the Church of St. Maben, and the fourth turn in the presentation to the said Church when it happened to be void; and that Elizabeth, wife of Edmund Dudley, Esq., and Ann, wife of John Willoughby, Esq., were his sisters and heirs, the said Elizabeth being aged twenty years, and the said Ann twenty-seven years.[3] In 1532, Sir John Dudley, Knight., son and heir of Sir Edmund Dudley, Knight, suffered a fine to Henry, Marquis of Exeter, inter alia, of the Manor of Trevisquyte, also sixty messuages, two mills and 100s. rent in Trevisquyte, and of the advowson of the Church of St. Maben. The Manor of Trevisquite being thus in the possession of the Marquis of Exeter by the attainder of that nobleman, in 1538, it fell into the King's hands, and the abovementioned yearly rent having, inter alia, descended to Sir Henry Capell and Dame Jane Griffen, as cousins and next heirs to the abovementioned Richard Newton; viz., Sir Henry Capell as son of Isabel daughter and one of the heirs of the said Richard, and the said Jane Griffen as daughter and other heir of the said Richard, they held the said rent, inter alia, in coparcenery, and in 1545 petitioned the King that the said rent might continue to be paid to them and their heirs, which was granted by a decree in the Exchequer dated 20th February 1545-6.[4]

---

[1] Pedes Finium, 19th Henry VI, Michs.

[2] Inq. p.m. 21st Henry VI, No. 55.

[3] Inq. p.m., 20th Henry VII, No. 47.

[4] Exch. Decrees, 37th Henry VIII.

3 P

The Manor of Trevisquite being, by the attainder of Henry, Marquis of Exeter, in the hands of the Crown King Edward VI, by letters patent dated in June 1553, granted a lease of the capital messuage and all the lands to Richard Arscott, Gent., for a term of 21 years, at the rent of £14 13s. 2d. per annum. And upon the restoration in blood and honours of Edward Courteney, son and heir of the Marquis, in 1553 he was created by Queen Mary, Earl of Devon, and had his estates restored, *inter alia*, the Manor of Trevisquite and advowson of the Church of St. Mabyn, to hold to him and the heirs males of his body;[1] but dying, unmarried in 1556, they again reverted to the crown.

By her Charter, dated 13th May 1564, Queen Elizabeth, after reciting the abovementioned lease to Richard Arscott, granted the reversion of the capital messuage, &c., of Trevisquite, together with the lordship and manor with all its members and appurtenances, and the beforementioned rent of £14 13s. 2d., to Leonard Loveys of Ogbeare, co. Devon, reserving, however, the advowson of the Church, and subject to the payment of the beforementioned rent of £7 12s. 8d., annually, to the heirs of Thomas Greffeth, and an annuity of 26s. 8d., for life, to John Spiller then bailiff there.[2]

Richard Loveys would thus seem to have acquired the entirety of the Manor and three fourths of the advowson of the Rectory,[3] and being so seized, by his charter dated 28th September 12th Elizabeth (1570), *inter alia*, granted the same to Roger Prideaux, Humphry Specote, and others to hold, as Trustees, to certain uses specified in an Indenture dated two days previously: viz., as regarded the Manor of Trevisquite and the three parts in four of the advowson of the Church of St. Mabyn, to the use of the said Leonard Loveys for life, with remainder to Richard Loveys, fourth son of the said Leonard and the heirs male of his body, unless, and until, any attempt were made by the said Richard or his heirs to bar the entail, and upon the determination of such estate remainder to William Loveys and Humphry Loveys, second and third sons of the said Leonard, under like limitation, in default of such issue remainder to the heirs males of the body of the said Leonard begotten of the body of Ibott his then wife.[4] Leonard Loveys died at Ogbeare, on 14th April 1576, when Thomas Loveys was found to be his son and nearest heir, and to be of the age of thirty years and more;[5] but, in virtue of the abovementioned settlement, the Manors of Trevisquite and Willsworthy devolved upon the beforementioned Richard Loveys, who died at Beardon, in Boyton, thereof seized on 20th May 1607, when Robert Loveys, Esq., was found to be his son and nearest heir, and to be of the full age of twenty-one years and more.[6]

---

[1] Rot. Pat. 1st Mary, Part 10.   [2] Rot. Pat. 6th Elizabeth, Part 6, m. 11.

[3] By Privy Seal, dated 8th August 1622, King James I granted the next presentation to the Church of St. Mabin to John Porter his heirs and assigns, in order that he might prefer to the said Church Thomas Porter, M.A.; and upon the death of Thomas Ducke, the then Rector, in 1629, Thomas Porter was admitted upon the presentation of Elizabeth Porter, relict and administratrix of the aforesaid John Porter, deceased. (Privy Signets, Bund. xii No. 23.)

[4] Ibott daughter of Humphry Specote, second wife, by whom he had a daughter, Elizabeth, who married Richard Coffin.—Visit. Devon, 1620. Harl. Soc., p. 64.

[5] Inq. p.m. 18th, 19th, and 20th Elizabeth, Wards and Liveries, No. 161.

[6] Inq. p.m. 1st to 6th James, Wards and Liveries, Bundle 2, No. 266.

Robert Loveys of Beardon registered his pedigree at the Heralds' Visitation of Cornwall in 1620, when Richard his son and heir, by Grace daughter of Andrew Luttrell of Hartland, upon whom eventually the estates devolved, was aged 9 years. In 1649 he conveyed two messuages and two water mills, &c., in Trevisquite and Netherwood to John Nicholl, Gent.;[1] and in 1659 a fine was levied, in which the said Richard Loveys was plaintiff and Arthur Lord Capell and Elizabeth Capell, widow, defendants, whereby, in consideration of the sum of £150, the said Arthur Lord Capell and Elizabeth Capell remised and quitclaimed to the said Richard all the annual rent of £7 11s. 8½ payable, as aforesaid, out of the Manor of Trevisquite to the heirs of Griffith.[2]

In 1670 Richard Loveys suffered a recovery in the Manor of Trevisquite, and in three parts of the advowson of the Rectory of St. Mabyn to Hugh Boscawen of Tregothnan,[3] who being thus in possession of the right of presenting three persons, King Charles II, by letters patent dated 10th June 1673, granted to him the right of presenting the fourth, and granted, also, to him the entire Advowson of the said Rectory.[4] From which date the manor and advowson has been vested in the family of Boscawen, and is now parcel of the possessions of the Viscount Falmouth.

THE RECTORY.

Having traced the descent of the advowson under our account of the Manor of Trevisquite, little more remains to be said respecting it. In Pope Nicholas's Valuation (1288-1291) the Benefice was rated under the following description: "Ecclesia de Sabene" (Mabene) at £8, tenths 16s.; and in 1340, under the designation of "Ecclesia de Sancte Mabene" the ninth fleece, sheaf, and lamb were assessed at the same rate, and so sold to William Bere, Lawrence Maynby, John Hobbe, and Roger Gonvena. Of fifteenths there were none.[5] In Wolsey's Taxation of 1535, it is rated at £36,[6] and in Bishop Veysey's Return of 3rd November of the following year, it stands at the same rate, Thomas Gressam being the Incumbent.[7]

According to the Tithe Survey the whole area of the parish is 4067a. 2r. 7p., and the estimated quantity subject to the payment of tithes is 3563 acres, which are cultivated as under, viz.:

[1] Pedes Finium, 1649, Easter.
[2] Pedes Finium, 1659, Easter.
[3] Pedes Finium 22nd Charles II, Easter.
[4] Rot. Pat. 25th Charles II, Part 6, m. 1. Notwithstanding this grant, John Hill, Rector of St. Maben, by his will dated 31st December 1709, devised to his grandson all his right in the perpetual Advowson of St. Mabyn, which, he says, he held by patent from the crown. We have not been able to trace this Patent.
[5] Inq. Nonarum, p. 345.
[6] Valor Ecclesiasticus, vol. ii, p. 402.
[7] Bishop Veysey's Register, vol.   fo. 86-100.

3 P²

						ACRES.
Arable	...	...	...	...	...	3021
Meadow	...	...	...	...	...	43
Pasture	...	...	...	...	...	132
Wood	...	...	...	...	...	344
Orchard	...	...	...	...	...	23
						3563

228 acres are cultivated as coppice.

The Rector of the parish, for the time being, is entitled to all the tithes, which, on 9th June 1842, were commuted at £798 10s. 0d. per annum, exclusive of the tithes of the glebe (consisting of 49a. 2r. 9p.) which were commuted at £18 10s. 0d., when not in the occupation of the Rector. The Church and Churchyard occupy 2r. 2p.

The Rev. Granville Leveson-Gower on his institution in 1818 pulled down the old parsonage house, which was situate near Greenwix, and erected a more commodious house on a new site.

INSTITUTIONS.

9th year, Bp. Brones-combe, die Resurrectionis Dominicæ. (Easter Day 1267)	Roger de Worlegan, Priest,[1] was instituted to the Church of St. Habene [Mabene in the margin] on the presentation of Thomas de Tracy, in right of his wife,[2] the true patron.
13th year. Vigil of St. Lawrence. (9th Aug. 1271)	Peter Haym, Clerk,[3] was admitted to the Church of St. Mabene upon the presentation of Sir Stephen Haym, granted in commendam.
unknown - -	John de Tracy.[4]
1325, 17 Kal. Nov.	William de Glynyon, Clerk,[5] instituted to the Church of St. Mabene, vacant by the death of John Tracy, last immediate rector, upon the presentation of Thomas de Stapildon and Richard Glynyon, by the grant of Edward le Botiller, the true patron.

[1] Bishop Bronescombe's Reg., fo. 34.   [2] Isolda, daughter and heir of Andrew de Cardinan.

[3] Bishop Bronescombe's Reg., fo. 48.

[4] John de Tracy, Parson of the Church of St. Mabena, was one of those who, in obedience to the Pope, refused to pay the subsidy. (Prynne's Records, vol. iii, 713.) 1317 September 15th, License of non-residence granted to John Tracy, Rector of St. Mabyn, till the 1st Monday in Lent then next following, and he gave, of his free will, to the fabric of the Church of Exeter 60s. Stapledon's Reg., fo. 121.

[5] Bishop Stapeldon's Reg. fo. 16.

1340, January 9th	-	John de Aldestowe, Clerk,[1] was instituted to the Church of St. Mabene, vacant by the resignation of William Glynyon, the last rector, upon the presentation of Matilda Lercedeckne, the true patroness.
1361, June 13th	-	Walter de Baunton, Priest,[2] was instituted to the rectory of St. Mabene, upon the presentation of the Lady Matilda Lercedeckne.
Unknown	-	Nicholas Ferrers.[3]
1381, July 12th	-	John Grey, Rector of St. George in the City of Exeter,[4] was admitted, upon exchange with Nicholas Ferrers, Rector of St. Mabene, upon the presentation of Johanna Courteney.
1382, July 18th	-	James Cobham, Rector of the Church of Samford Courteney,[5] was admitted to the Church of St. Mabene upon the presentation of Johanna relict of Thomas Courteney, the true patron.
1383, Sept. 14th	-	John Rescorrek, Priest,[6] was admitted to the Parish Church of St. Mabene, vacant by the death of James Cobham, last Rector, upon the presentation of Philip Walweyn, Senr., Lord of the Manor of Trevisquite, and of the same Church the true patron in right of the inheritance of his wife Johanna.
1415, April 13th	-	Thomas Hendeman, Priest, s.t.p.,[7] admitted to the Parish Church of St. Mabene, vacant by the resignation of Mr. John Rescowrek, upon the presentation of Thomas Beaumont, Esq.
1445, June 23rd	-	John Weymond, Rector of St. Mabene,[8] on a commission to enquire into the right of patronage of the Church of St. Tudy.
1457, June 24th	-	Thomas Colles, b.l., Chaplain,[9] admitted to the Parish Church of St. Mabene, vacant by the death of John Wymound, the last Rector, upon the presentation of John Speccotte, Esq., for this turn the true patron.[10]

[1] Bishop Grandison's Reg., fo. 44. Sir John de Aldestowe, Rector of St. Maben, in 1346 was one of the Commissioners for the installation of Thomas de Burdon in the Priory of Launceston, vacant by the resignation of Adam Knolle.

[2] Ibid. fo. 143. In accordance with a Commission directed by the Bishop to the Dean of Trigg Minor and Sir Ralph Mayndy, Rector of St. Tudy, they inquired into the presentation of Walter de Baunton, and found the presentation in that turn sufficient.

[3] There was an institution cir. 1370, which was probably that of Nicholas Ferrers, but vol. iii of Bishop Brentingham's Reg., on folio 15 of which it was recorded, is unfortunately lost.

[4] Bishop Brentingham's Reg., fo. 66.   [5] Bishop Brentingham's Reg., fo. 73.

[6] Bishop Brentingham's Reg. fo. 81.   [7] Bishop Stafford's Reg., fo. 164.

[8] Bishop Lacy's Reg., vol ii., fo. 217.   [9] Bishop Neville's Reg., fo. 5.

[10] 1457. June 24th. Certificate upon an inquisition to enquire into the vacancy and right of presentation to the Church of St. Maben. The jurors present that the Church is vacant by the death of John Wymond the last Rector, who died the 11th June in the year aforesaid, that John Speccote, Esq, is the true patron for this turn, it being remembered that King Henry V, deceased, last presented by reason of the minority of John Holbeme, son and heir of Johanna daughter of Robert Scobhyll, which said Johanna was the eldest daughter of the said Robert Scobhyll; and that the aforesaid John Speccote, Esq., to whom the right of presentation for this turn belongs is heir of Isabell Speccote his mother, second daughter of the said Robert Scobhyll; and that Thomas Colles, who has been presented, is in every way fit. Ibid. 71.

1477, March 28th - Robert Marke, Chaplain,[1] instituted to the Parish Church of St. Mabene, vacant by the death of Thomas Collys, late Rector, upon the presentation of John Holbeme, gent., the true patron.

Unknown   -   - John Waryn.

1500, August 31st - Barnard Oldon, Clerk,[2] instituted to the Church of St. Mabene, vacant by the death of John Waryn, last Rector, upon the presentation of Margaret mother of Henry VII, Countess of Richmond and Derby, for this turn the true patroness.

1515, June 13th - Oliver Pole, D.D.,[3] was instituted to the Church of St. Mabene, vacant by the death of Barnard Oldham, the last incumbent, upon the presentation of John Skewys, Humphry Wyngfield, and John Pakyngton, by the grant of Nicholas Specott.

1534, August 29th - Thomas Gresham, Clerk,[4] was admitted to the Rectory of St. Mabene, vacant by the death of Oliver Pole, last rector, upon the presentation of King Henry VIII.

1559, June 23rd - John Kennall, Doctor of Laws,[5] was admitted to the Rectory of St. Maben, vacant by lapse of time.

1583, March 10 - Thomas Ducke, Clerk, B.A.,[6] was admitted to the Rectory of St. Maben, vacant by the resignation of John Kenall, D.L., last incumbent, upon the presentation of the Queen.

1629, June 15th - Thomas Porter, Clerk, M.A.,[7] was admitted to the Rectory of St. Mabyn, vacant by the death of Thomas Ducke, last incumbent, upon the presentation of Elizabeth Porter, widow, relict and administratrix of John Porter deceased, for this turn the true patron by the grant of William Loveys,[8] of the same rectory the true patron.

1668, October 9th - John Hill, Clerk,[9] was admitted to the Rectory of St. Mabyn, vacant by the death of Thomas Porter, last incumbent, upon the presentation of Thomas Tocker, Gent., the true patron.

---

[1] Bishop Bothe's Reg., fo. 40.   [2] Bishop Redmain's Reg., fo. 16.
[3] Bishop Oldham's Reg., fo. 61.   [4] Bishop Voysey's Reg., fo. 74.
[5] Bishop Alley's Reg., fo. 45.

[6] Bishop Wotton's Reg., fo. 16. Matric. Exeter Coll. Oxford, 20th December 1577, aged 20. Pleb. fil. of Co. Devon. Bur. at St. Maben, 8th June 1629.

[7] Bishop Hall's Reg., fo. 9.

[8] This is an error. The grant was by King James I. (see ante p. 458 n.) Mr. Porter was sequestrated at the time of the rebellion (Walker's Sufferings, part 2, p. 327.), and a Mr. William Treis intruded into the Rectory. Calamy says: "Mr. Treis was reckoned a profound scholar, and his composures extraordinarily good; but he was unhappy in his delivery" (vol. i, p. 355). As Mr. Porter survived to the Restoration he was, of course, re-instated in his Benefice and was buried at St. Maben, 30th September 1668.

[9] Bishop's Reg., N.S., vol. i, fo. 108. In 1664 Richard Loveys and Francis his wife granted the Advowson of the Church of St. Mabyn to George Spry (Ped. Finium, 16th Charles II, Michs.) This was perhaps the next presentation only, and was probably assigned by Mr. Spry to Thomas Tucker.

1681, April 21st - John Hill,[1] was admitted to the Rectory of St. Mabyn, and his previous title corroborated, upon the presentation of King Charles II.

1710, June 9th - Simon Paget, Clerk,[2] M.A., was admitted to the Rectory of St. Mabyn, vacant by the death of John Hill, Clerk, last incumbent, upon the presentation of Hugh Boscawen, Esq., the true patron.

1716, April 25th - Walter Hewgoe, Clerk,[3] was admitted to the Rectory of St. Mabyn, vacant by the resignation of Simon Paget, upon the presentation of Hugh Boscawen, of Tregothnan, Esq.

1722, February 7th - John Hillman, Clerk, M.A.,[4] was admitted to the Rectory of St. Mabin, vacant by the death of Walter Hewgoe, upon the presentation of Viscount Falmouth.

1726, November 17th Charles Peters, Clerk, M.A.,[5] was admitted to the Rectory of St. Mabin, vacant by the death of John Hilman, upon the presentation of Viscount Falmouth.

1774, December 21st Nicholas Boscawen, D.D.,[6] was admitted to the Rectory of St. Mabyn, vacant by the death of Charles Peters, the last Rector, upon the presentation of the Right Honble. Hugh Viscount Falmouth, the true patron.

[1] Bishop's Reg., N.S., vol. iii, fo. 9. Son of Michael Hill of Croane in Egloshayle. He published two sermons, one preached at St. Mary le Bow, London, in 1679, on the Apostacy of the Church of Rome, &c., and the other before the Justices of Assize at Launceston in 1693. See Bibl. Cornub., vol. i, p. 240. Bur. at St. Maben 20th February 1709.

[2] Ibid. vol. v, fo. 31. Matric. Pembroke Coll., Oxford, 1685, aged 19, son of Simon Paget of Chipping Norton, co. Oxford (poor Scholar) B.A. 8th December 1691, M.A., 16th April 1695.

[3] Ibid. fo. 91. Of Queen's Coll., Cambridge, B.A., 1688, Rector of Michaelstow, 1695 to 1712. See post.

[4] Ibid 156. 1722, April 22nd. Upon an inquisition taken concerning the right of patronage, promoted by Viscount Falmouth against George Prince of Wales, it was found that the said Viscount Falmouth was the true patron, and that the Rectory had become vacant two months before.

[5] Bishop's Reg., .N.S, vol. vi, fo. 50. Charles Peters was educated at the Grammar School at Tregony, and matriculated at Exeter Coll., Oxford, 3rd April 1707, aged 16, described as "the son of Richard Peters, Pleb., of Tregonny," B.A. 27th October 1710, M.A. 5th June 1713. In 1714-18 he was presented by Elizabeth Baroness Mohun to the small Rectory of Boconnoc, on which he resided until 1723, when he removed to Bratton Clovelly, and afterwards, in 1726, he was instituted to St. Maben. Whilst resident at Boconnoc he built the south front of the Parsonage House, with the apartments behind it, which have been since altered and the house converted into a residence for the Steward. He held Bratton Clovelly, both with Boconnoc and St. Mabyn. In 1751 he published a Dissertation on the Book of Job, and about six years afterwards a new edition was published with corrections. Meanwhile a controversy arose with Dr. Warburton, then Dean of Bristol, afterwards Bishop of Gloucester, which was conducted by Mr. Peters with great learning, ability, and temper, whilst the Dean, for what he lacked in argument he endeavoured to make up by haughty superciliousness. Mr. Peters died 11th February 1774, and was buried at St. Mabyn two days afterwards. Mr. George Browne of Bodmin notes Mr. Peters's death in his diary, as that of "a very worthy, good, and great man." Mr. Peters also published a volume of Sermons and left in M.S. a further reply to Dr. Warburton. (Nichol's Literary Illustrations, vol. viii, p. 633. Gent.'s Mag., &c., vol. lxv, 2, p. 1085.)

[6] Ibid. vol. ix, fo. 118. Inducted 3rd March 1775 (G. B.) of Corpus Christi Coll., Cambridge, M.A., 1745, S. T. P. 1753, 5th son of Hugh 1st Viscount Falmouth, born 16th August 1720. He was also Dean of St. Burian. Married Jane Hatton daughter of .... Woodward of Stratford upon Avon, and left issue a son of his own name. Dr. Boscawen died at Quendon, Essex, 4th July 1793 (Gent.'s Mag.)

1793, November 21st   Charles Kempe, Clerk,[1] admitted to the Rectory of St. Mabyn, vacant by the death of the Hon. and Rev. Nicholas Boscawen, D.D., upon the presentation of the Right Hon. George Evelyn Viscount Falmouth, the true patron.

1818, May 22nd - Granville Leveson-Gower, Clerk,[2] admitted to the Rectory of St. Mabyn, vacant by the death of Charles Kempe, last incumbent, upon the presentation of the Right Hon. Lord Viscount Falmouth.

1842, March 12th - George Henry Somerset, Clerk, M.A.,[3] was licensed by the Bishop a Public Preacher in and throughout the Diocese of Exeter, who immediately afterwards admitted him to the Rectory of St. Mabyn, vacant by the death of Granville Leveson-Gower, the last incumbent.

THE PARISH CHURCH.

The Parish Church (see Plate XLII) is dedicated to St. Mabena, one of the daughters of Brychan. It consists of: a chancel of two bays, slightly projecting eastwards, nave of five bays, and north and south aisles to both; a western tower, and south porch. (see Plate XLIII, fig I.) The interior was barbarously altered by the late Rector Mr. Leveson-Gower soon after his institution in 1818. He reduced the floors of the chancel, nave and aisles to one common level, and all the ancient family monuments were destroyed. The aisles are divided from the chancel and nave by monolith granite columns supporting four-centred arches, somewhat more pointed than is usual.

The eastern window of the Chancel, which is a large and good example of the style, is of five lights, in two compartments of two lights each, 5 fo., with a quatrefoil in the head, the space above the middle light being filled with mullioned tracery. The window is filled with painted glass in memory of the late Francis John Hext of Tredethy, some-time Rector of Helland, and Margaret his wife.[4] On the north side of the altar is a piscina with drain complete. A pulpit, in Caen stone, carved, has been set up in the chancel. The work is fairly well executed, but the pulpit is small and undignified.

---

[1] Bishop's Reg., N.S., vol. x, fo. 90. Second son of Charles Kempe of Crugsillick (see ped. of KEMPE, ante vol. i, p. 77.) He was Curate of St. Tudy from 1765 to 1781.

[2] Ibid, vol. xi, fo. 102. Fourth son of Admiral John Leveson-Gower (son by the 3rd marriage of John 1st Earl Gower) by Frances eldest daughter of Admiral Edward Boscawen. Mr. Gower was born in 1788. Of Trinity Coll., Cambridge, B.A., 1808, M.A. 1812, died 28th September 1841, bur. at St. Mabyn, M. I. No. 14.

[3] Ibid. vol. xi, fo. 180. Eldest son of Lord Arthur John Henry Somerset (fifth son of Henry 5th Duke of Beaufort, K. G.) by Elizabeth eldest daughter of George Evelyn, 3rd Viscount Falmouth, born 1809. Of Jesus Coll., Cambridge, M.A., 1818. Mr. Somerset, in 1835, married Phillida Elizabeth daughter of Sir William Pratt Call of Whitford, co. Cornwall, Bart., and has issue.

[4] It is noted in the Parish Register under the year 1808. "I paid eleven guineas for new Chancel Window in St. Mabyn Church in July. Charles Kempe, Rector."

PLATE XLIII

GROUND PLAN OF ST MABEN CHURCH

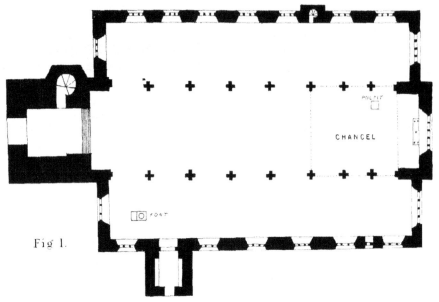

Fig 1.

GROUND PLAN OF MICHAELSTOW CHURCH

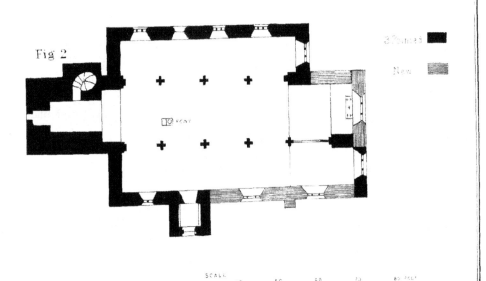

Fig 2

There is a Priest's door in the second bay of the south aisle and a north door in the next to the westernmost bay of the north aisle. The aisles are lighted by eastern windows, four-light, divided into two compartments, the heads being filled with mullioned tracery, three-light windows, of different type, at the western ends, and a three-light 5 fo. ogee window in each bay, except where interrupted by the doors. There was formerly an altar at the east end of each aisle. The piscina of that in the north aisle has been plastered over, but that in the south aisle yet remains open, though concealed by a high pew. The rood loft staircase in the north wall, for which there is an external turret, is walled up. All the roofs are of the cradle pattern and good of the kind.

The tower arch, which is circular and lofty, is walled up. On the north side is a large quatrefoil opening from the stair turret looking into the Church. The font, which is placed at the western end of the south aisle, is First Pointed. It is square, the sides being slightly panelled with pointed arches. It has a circular bowl and stands on a similar stem, raised on a step.

The tower, which is 75 ft. in height, is of three stages, battlemented and pinnacled; the pinnacles, which appear to be of modern work, are surmounted by crosses, as are also the gables of the Church. The tower has a demi-octagonal stair turret at the north east angle. The bell chamber stage is lighted by a three-light 5 fo. traceried window on each face, and there is a small, plain arched, window on the middle stage, whilst the lower stage has a four-light 5 fo. window in two compartments, with a quatrefoil in the head. The external door is of fine workmanship in Catacluse stone. The moulding is continuous, the deep cavetto being filled with strawberry leaves and quatrefoils. The hoodmoulding is terminated by figures of Angels bearing shields, that on the north charged with a Castle, and that on the south with the arms of Lucombe of Bodmin and Helligan: Ar. a saltier sa. between four estoiles gu. Over the door of the south porch is a bracket for a statue.

The angles of the tower are ornamented at each string-course with small figures. At the south-west angle, on the uppermost string-course, appears to be the figure of a man with long hair and bearded, having some animal at his feet. Upon the middle string-course is some grinning monster, and upon the lower one a talbot.[1] At the north-west angle, on the upper string-course, is a figure with full drapery holding a (lamb?) On the middle string-course is a ram's head, and on the lower one a bear muzzled.[2] At the north-east upper angle the figure is set off the string-course on the eastern side because of the turret stairs. It represents a figure holding an open book, said by tradition to represent a lady of the Heligan family. The figure on the middle string-course is a winged dragon, and that on the lower a (sheep?) At the south-east angle, on the upper string-course, is the figure of a man bearing a staff with an animal at his feet; that on the middle string-course is another winged dragon; whilst on the lower is the figure of an eagle rising but chained to the tower with an iron chain.

[1] The cognizance of Hamley of Treblethick? This family bore for their arms: ar. three talbots az.

[2] This is probably the cognizance of Barrett of Tregarden, seated there when the tower was built. They bore: ar. a chev. engrailed between three bears passant sa., muzzled or.; and a bear's head muzzled for a crest. See post.

3 Q

The tower in 6th of Edward VI possessed four bells,[1] there is now a ring of six. Until recast in 1787, there were five only. The casting was effected in a garden adjoining the village green, still called the "Bell garden." The second bell was cracked a few years ago in consequence of being struck by lightning, which also injured the tower, and was recast in London. The present bells bear the following inscriptions:

1st. I. P. : C. P 1787
2nd. C. & G. MEARS, FOUNDERS, LONDON 1854
3rd. I. P. : C. P 1787
4th. I. P. : C. P. 1787. PEACE AND GOOD NEIGHBOURHOOD.
5th. I. P. : C. P. 1787. JOHN BAWDEN SAMUEL PHILP.
6th. I. P. : C. P. 1787. JOHN SLYMAN & ANTHONY GUY.

This Church formerly contained many fine monuments, but it was entirely gutted by Mr. Leveson-Gower, the late Rector. The floor was reduced to a dead level throughout, and the church now arranged in a most extraordinary manner. All the old monuments were moved, partly to the old parsonage and partly to the new. Some portions of them were lying about the premises at the former place for many years, and fragments were seen there within the last ten years.[2] The following inscriptions we have recovered from fragments found in a hole in the Tower.

On an oval slab of black marble, which formed a portion of one of the monuments removed from the Church.

1. In memory of Mrs. Elizabeth Silly, the wife of Joseph Silly of Heligan, Gent., and daughter of Robert Shapcote of the City of Dublin, Esq., who died the third Day of August 1679.[3]

2. Some fragments of a very handsome monument in memory of William Hamley of Treblethick, consisting of two beautiful figures of weeping angels, which formed supporters to the monument, painted and gilt. Also a portion of the escutcheon of Arms with an Esquire's helmet surmounted by a Crest: a talbot sa. The Arms of Hamley: ar. three talbots sa. (should be az., probably discoloured) differenced with a mullet, impaling ar. in the dexter chief (the rest of the escutcheon being broken off and lost) a roundel sa.—Inscription:

Subtus jacet quicquid mortale fuit
Gulielmi Hamley
Viri non uno in laudis genere spectabilis
Prosapia enim longa oriundus gentilitiam nobilitatem
Cum humilitate conjunxit
Magnatibus non ignotus cujuscunq; ord'is hominibus

---

[1] Augmentation Office, Church Goods, 6th Edward VI, $\frac{1}{51}$.

[2] Information received from William Clemence, aged seventy years, an old inhabitant of parish, in 1865.

[3] C. S. Gilbert has printed this inscription. He says the monument stood in the north aisle, whereon were the arms of Silly impaled with: ar. a Chev. between three Castles, sa. (Hist. Cornwall, vol. ii, p. 615.) Instead of "impaled with," it is presumed we should read "impaling."

Familiariter usus est
Ille Ecclesiam amavit illum Respublica honoribus affecit
Et pium erga Deum, et principi fidelem
Fortem rapuit fortibus invisus morbus
Vxore, Liberis Patriâ desideratum
Ob. April 12° A.D. 1711. Ætatis 42°
P. Rebecca Conjux.

Repair'd at the joint expense of Mr. Osbertus Hamley of London in the parish of Duke Street St. James, and Mr. John Hamley of Lostwithiel. A.D. 1819.[1]

3.　　　　　　　　　　To the Memory of James Bligh
(late of Stone in this parish) who departed this life
the 24th day of March 1811, in the 73rd year of his age.[2]

C. S. Gilbert records that the south aisle contained monuments inscribed to Margaret wife of Giles Hamley, Gent., and daughter of Reginald Billing, who died in 1637; and Thomas Hamley of the Inner Temple, London, Esq., who died at Wokingham in Berkshire in 1656. He also says that in the same aisle was laid a brass plate with the following inscription:

4. Here lies the body of the lady Grace Carnsew, the daughter of Arthur Fowell of Fowelscombe, Esq., deceased, first married unto Richard Barrett of Tregarden, Esq., and, secondly, married unto Sir Richard Carnsew of Bokelly, Knt., who finished a most pious and exemplary life the 7th day of July 1656, and of her age 73.

After whose virtues, if the curious ask,
Angels assume the theme, and Saints the task.

Gilbert adds: (in the north aisle,) "is a large brass plate, on which, among other ornaments, are engraved the arms of Godolphin: it is inscribed to the memories of two infant sons of William Godolphin, Esq., interred here in the years 1631 and 1632. Near the altar are several monumental stones, in recordation of the Michel family."

5. In memory of John and Reginald Bligh both sons of Richard Bligh of Tinten in the Parish of St. Udy, Gent., and Jane his wife is this stone placed. Here John was buried underneath the 30th day of Nov. In the year of Our Lord 1739. In the 25th year of his age. Reginald was buried in the Parish Church of Allington near Bridport, in Dorsetshire, the 10th day of June in the year of Our Lord 1741, in the 24th year of his age.

6. A stone with the inscription, "27th Maye 1656." The following entry in the Parish Register probably has reference to it:—"Thomas Hamley of the Inner Temple, London, Gent., eldest son unto Giles Hamley of this Parish, Gent., died at Wokingham in the Co. of Berks, the 25 and was buried 27 Maye 1656."

---

[1] This monument is mentioned by C. S. Gilbert as at the east end of the south aisle, but he does not give the inscription.

[2] This inscription has been printed by C. S. Gilbert, and he adds that the monument bore the arms of Bligh. Hist. of Cornwall, vol ii, p. 615.

3 Q²

7. Here lies the Body of Joseph Lang of little Trevisquite in this Par: who was bury'd the 4 day of May Anno Domini 1769, in the 47 year of his age.

8. Here lies the body of Richard the Son of Richard & Agnes Philip of this Par: who was buried the 26 of June in yᵉ year 1743. Ætatis suæ 31.

9.   Memento Mori
Nigh this Stone lyeth yᵉ Body of Mary Peard of this Par: who was buried October the ninth in yᵉ year of Our Lord 1774, aged 72.

10. Without name or date:

> They joyed & grieved lov'd & liv'd both in one
> The one not beeinge the other is as none
> When death stroke her hee felt an equal smart
> He hers shee his both but one loving heart
> As to a center still his thoughts bend hither
> Shee dead hee lives yet both intombed togeather.

IN THE CHURCH YARD.

11. This Stone is erected in memory of John Martyn Bligh Esqʳ of the Parish of Bodmin, formerly of Stone in this Parish, who departed this life on the 6th day of May 1834, in the 54th year of his age.
Also in memory of Catherine, daughter of the said John Martyn Bligh and Mary Edyvean Bligh his wife, who died the 2nd day of July 1828. Aged 13 years.

12. Here lies the Body of Josias yᵉ son of John and Alice Toker of the Par. of St. Tudy who was buried yᵉ 4 day of March Anᵒ Dom. 1767, in the 24th year of his age.
Here also lies the Body of John Toker, the father of Josias, who was buried yᵉ 27 Day of Decem. Anᵒ Dom. 1775.

13. Here lies the Body of Mrs. Joan Andrew (wife of Mr. Christopher Andrew of this Par:) who departed this life yᵉ 25th Day of Oct. 1778. In the 42 year of her age.

14. Underneath this Stone lies the Body of the Revⁿᵈ G. Leveson Gower. M.A. 23 years Rector of this Parish. He died Sepᵗ the 28th 1841, aged 54 years.

15. Sacred to the memory of Louisa Bessy, who died Septʳ 26 1845, aged 24 years.
Mary Georgina, who died at Cannes April 25th 1867, aged 27 years.
Blanche Emma, who died at Pau Octʳ 26 1867, aged 19 years.
Arthur Wᵐ Henry, who died April 26th 1869, aged 26 years.
Children of the Revᵈ George Somerset & Phillida Elizabeth his wife. All died in faith. Thanks be to God which giveth us the Victory through Our Lord Jesus Christ.
Also in memory of George Edward, Lieut. R. N., son of the above, who died at Cape Town Jan. 19th 1870, aged 25 years.

16.   I. H. S.

In memory of Charles Henry Harris, infant son of John and Emily Peter of Colquite. Born April 25th. Died August 25th 1863. He shall gather the Lambs with his arm.

17. Joseph George Thompson, Lieut. R.N. Died July 16th 1827, aged 44 years. Joseph George Thompson, Surgeon, Died August 26th 1855, aged 29 years. Betsy Gaved, Died March 31st 1870, aged 75 years.

ALTAR PLATE.

In 1552, the Parishioners of St. Maben possessed "a chalice of sylver parcel gilte, and one other chalice of sylver;"[1] but these ornaments of the Church no longer remain. The altar plate now consists of: a cup with a cover, a paten, two flagons, and an alms' dish, all being of silver, and the cup and cover gilt.

The cup was not intended for a chalice but as an ordinary drinking vessel on festive occasions. It is of elegant form, 13 inches in height, the cover being surmounted by a boy, nude, holding a shield; the mouth of the cup is $3\frac{1}{2}$ inches in diameter. The bowl and cover are engraved in an Arabesque style, with birds and foliage, the birds consisting of two storks and another bird, and the stem and foot are ornamented in repoussé work. It bears the Hall mark of 1576, the maker's mark being a pair of compasses enclosing a mullet.

The paten is plain with simple rims, and is $6\frac{3}{4}$ inches in diameter. On the back of it is inscribed "Ex dono E. H. gent. hujus Ecclesiæ Guardiani 1702." The Hall mark is of the same year, and the maker's mark R.O. in roman letters, being the two first letters of his surname.

The two flagons are alike, $11\frac{1}{4}$ inches high, and engraved on the front "Church of St. Mabyn, A.D. 1757." They are not properly *flagons*, as they are made without lips, or spouts. As, however, as shewn by the stamps, the lion's head erased and the Britannia; with the year mark for 1756-7, they are of the standard silver, previous to the Act of 6th George III., which contains 11oz. 10dwts. of silver in the pound troy, instead of 11oz. 2dwts. as afterwards sanctioned, we may conclude they were made for sacred use. The maker's mark is "J. W." in cursive characters, being the initial letters of his christian and surname.

The alms' dish is plain with simple moulded edges. Around the dish is engraven "The gift of Nathaniel Lang to the use of St. Mabyn Church." The Hall mark is of the year 1765-6, the maker's mark being "W. F." in cursive characters, being his initials, as in the last case.

[1] Queen's Remb. Office. Church Goods, Cornwall $\frac{1}{50}$

PARISH REGISTERS.

The old Registers of this parish consist of two volumes. The first volume is intituled: "The Register Booke of names & surnames of all them that were christened wedded & buried w^{th}in the pish of Saint Maben Anno Dom^l 1562."

The entries from the commencement in 1562 to 1598 are in the same handwriting, shewing the entries thus far to have been transcribed from earlier records. They are all in English. The book seems to have been kept with tolerable regularity until 1645, between which date and 1664 few entries of baptisms were made. There are no records of marriages from 1641 to 1646. In the latter year, one; in 1647 and 1648, nil; in 1649, one; from 1650 to 1653 inclusive, nil; in 1654, four; afterwards with greater regularity. There are three entries of burials in 1645, one in 1646, and no other until 1653, when five occur; after which the entries are made with more order. This volume extends to 1758, and is in good condition, having been rebound, as recorded on the title page, in 1703, by:

> JOHN BEWES,   ⎫
> GEORGE HAMLEY, ⎬ Churchwardens,
>   ⎭

Whose names deserve to be held in remembrance.

The second volume commences in 1758, and extends to 1812. There are no entries of marriages after 1790.

The earliest names in these registers are Browne, Hamley, Tamlyn, Billing, Barrett, Poyle, Cardew, Tresloget, Hill, and Arundell.

CHAPELS.

There were two domestic Chapels in this parish, one at Colquite, and the other at Heligan. In 1373, Sir Richard Cergeaux received from the Bishop a license to have the Divine Offices celebrated in his presence by a fit Priest in all his Chapels within the diocese for one year,[1] and the following year this license was renewed,[2] and on the 16th November 1379, a similar license was granted to the said Sir Richard Sergeaux and his wife, specifically for their Chapel within their Manor of Kilquid in the parish of St. Mabene,[3] and on 1st May 1425, Bishop Lacy granted a like license to Robert Treatte[4] and his wife, for the Chapel of St. Mary of Kilquyt, in the parish of St. Mabene. On the 24th of October 1374, a similar license was granted to Reginald Heligan and his wife, for the Chapel of the blessed Virgin Mary, within his Manor of Helygane, in the parish of St. Maben.

---

[1] Bishop Brentingham's Reg., fo. 41.   [2] Ibid, fo. 62.
[3] Ibid, fo. 77.
[4] This was some occupant during the time of Sir John Marny.

CHARITIES.—ALMSHOUSES.

William Parker, described as of St. Mabyn, Esq., by his will, dated 4th July 1688, after devising to his sons, William Parker and Robert Parker, his lands in Tredinnick, and giving a few small legacies, bequeathed all the residue of his personal estate to Sir John Molesworth, Knight, and others, in trust for his two said sons, under certain limitations, and in the event of his said sons both dying without lawful issue, after giving several legacies, he bequeathed £100 more to be bestowed on an Almshouse for the poor of St. Mabyn; residue to his daughter Opie if she survived her husband, but not otherwise; and appointed the said trustees executors of his will.

The history of this legacy is very extraordinary, and will, we think, be read with interest.

All the trustees renounced the trust and refused to prove the will, and administration, with will annexed, was granted on 10th September 1688, to William Parker, eldest son of the testator. The said testator died possessed of considerable personal estate subject to the payment of the legacies, and, in particular, of a mortgage term of 2,000 years in the capital messuage of Trequites, in St. Mabyn, for securing the sum of £1,500 with interest, which being more than the value of the mortgaged premises the said William Parker, the son, applied for and obtained from the Court of Chancery a decree of foreclosure. Both William and Robert Parker having died without issue, the contingent bequests in their father's will took effect. John Anstis, Garter King of Arms, obtained possession of Trequites, and surrendered it to Elizabeth Opie as residuary legatee, which she released to her son, John Opie, by Indenture dated 27th June 1717, who thereby became liable for the payment of the various legacies. Such legacies, however, were not paid, and the Churchwardens and Overseers of the poor of St. Mabyn, and the other legatees under the will of William Parker, in 1743 filed a Bill in Chancery against the said John Opie and John Anstis. The case came on for hearing on 26th June 1750, when it was decreed that it should be referred to Mr. Edwards, one of the Masters of the Court, to compute interest on the £100 given to be bestowed on an Almshouse, from Lady-day 1718, at £5 per cent. per annum, and also to take account of what was due to the other legatees; that the mortgage foreclosed should be sold to the best purchaser, and that a scheme should be laid before the Master for the application of what should be coming to the Charity. The Master reported, on 17th February 1755, that he had computed the sum due to the Charity and the legacies, from Lady-day 1718 to 5th April 1755, *being old Lady-day*, and that the whole amounted to £2,092 14s. 11d.; that he had advertised the estate to be sold, and that the best offer he had received was £1,450, which had not been accepted; therefore the consideration of the scheme for the Charity had been deferred. On 11th June 1755 it was decreed that a Receiver should be appointed to the estate, that John Opie should deliver up possession, and that he should pay the sum of £1,095, the balance reported to be due from him, to the Accountant-general.   One Christopher Bawden of St. Mabyn, Yeoman, was appointed Receiver.

The matter now stood over for nearly forty years, when a bill was filed in Chancery to revive the original suit, all the parties to which had died: from which bill it appeared that John Opie never paid the sum of £1,095, in accordance with the decree of 11th June 1755, and had been committed to the Fleet Prison for default, and that he died in the Prison, having made his will and appointed Rachel Opie his wife executrix,[1] who proved the will: the said Rachel soon afterwards died, having made her will and appointed her daughter, by a former husband, Rachel (then the wife of William Hulke) executrix, who proved the same.   That Christopher Bawden let the estate and received the rents, but never rendered any account into Chancery, but that upon certain representations of Sir John Molesworth that he was entitled to rents, paid him a sum of £200, and that the said Christopher died about the year 1770, having a sum of about £100 balance in his hands, which had never been paid.   That upon his death Sir John Molesworth took upon himself to receive the rents until his death in 1775, and that he never rendered any account of the same.   That Christopher Bawden, during the period of his Receivership, had let the estate to one Mr. Tucker, and that in 1770, one Alexander Menhinnet had made an arrangement with Tucker for his corn and stock, and had entered into possession of the estate, and that not only had he not ever paid any rent but that he had cut great quantities of timber from off the estate; and the said plaintiff prayed that the suit might be revived, and the representatives of the parties called upon to answer to the matters in question, which was decreed accordingly.[2]

After various intermediate orders and decrees by a decree, dated 3rd March 1792, the case was referred to a Master (Ord.) to adjust the accounts, and on 7th May 1794, he made his report and certified that the sum due to the various Legatees on 5th April 1794, amounted altogether to £3,827 1s. 11d.; that he had advertised the estate to be sold, and that it had been purchased by Henry Hooper for the sum of £2,205, which purchase had been confirmed, and the amount paid to the Accountant General; that he had postponed the consideration of any scheme for the application of the legacy and interest due to the poor of St. Mabyn, as directed by the decree of 20th June 1750, until the exact sum to be paid in respect to such legacy could be ascertained, and that the sum available would not meet all the claims in full.   It was accordingly ordered, on 25th June 1794, that the claims should be abated in proportion, and that the Master do settle the proportions in which they are to be abated.[3]

We cannot trace that any scheme was ever settled in Chancery, but on 10th February 1795 the Master reported, *inter alia*, that on apportioning the estate he found that the proportion due to the Churchwardens and Overseers of St. Maben, being the amount of the legacy and interest at 4 per cent. per annum, was £370 10s. 7d.,[4] which amount, on 2nd March 1796, was accordingly paid to Messrs. John Slyman and Thomas Olver, Church-

---

[1] See Pedigree of OPIE, ante p. 53.   [2] Chancery Bills and Answers 1758—1800, No. 176.
[3] Chancery Decrees, Book A. 1793, p. 551.   [4] Chancery Reports, 1795, Hil. Letter G.

wardens, and Christopher Andrew and John Rowe, Overseers of the Poor.[1] An alms house was soon afterward built in the Church Town for the accommodation of several occupants, having on its front a slate slab, bearing the following inscription: "This building was erected in pursuance of the will of Wm. Parker, Esq. The ground upon which it is built is the gift of Sir Wm. Molesworth, Bart. of Pencarrow."[2] As early 1838 it had been diverted from its purpose as an alms house, and was used by the Parish as an ordinary workhouse; consequently when the new Poor Law Act, creating Unions, came into operation, it being no longer required for this purpose, it was, by deed dated 18th November 1843, sold to Messrs. Richard Hambly Andrew, James Andrew and Christopher Andrew, and the purchase money applied in aid of the rates. The whole now, partly by devise and partly by purchase, is vested in Mr. Richard Hamley Andrew of Tredinnick.

Mayne Charity.—William Mayne of Polglase in this parish by his will, proved in the year 1818,[3] bequeathed to John Kempe, Clerk, then Rector of St. Maben, the sum of £100, the interest to be applied annually in the education of William Mayne, Mary Tabb, and Joseph Belmore, poor children of the said parish, the management to be vested in the said John Kempe, his heirs and executors for ever. The Charity Commissioners have appointed as Official Trustees the Rector and Churchwardens for the time being, and the sum of £101 3s. 4d. is invested in Consols in their names, the interest whereof is applied to educational purposes.

Godolphin Charity.—Although through some mischance or mismanagement this Charity, which would have been a very valuable one, has been lost to the parish, its remarkable history can scarcely fail to be read without interest.

Sir William Godolphin, second son of Sir William Godolphin of Tregarden, previously to his going to Madrid as Ambassador at that Court, did by a writing under his hand declare his intention of leaving a sum of £3,000 for the education and maintenance of poor scholars, the relief of decayed and virtuous gentlemen, or other pious uses, under the direction of certain persons therein named, and did also express his intention of giving £20 to the poor of Camelford, £10 to the poor of Liskeard, and a like sum to the poor of St. Maben. Before his death at Madrid in 1696 being, as is alleged, surrounded by Friars, Priests, and Jesuits, as he lay bed-ridd, was influenced to execute, about 30th March in that year, a notarial instrument, whereby he appointed Don Matthias des Escolar, Abbot of the Basillians, Geronimo Guerero, Procurator General of the Jesuits, Don Balthazar de Cabredo, a secular Priest, and Don Antonio de Cendoya, a Lawyer, to be what are called his Testamentarios, which is explained in the instrument to be for the purpose that as soon as he should be dead those persons should make his last Will, expressing therein the gifts and legacies which he had communicated to them, giving to each of such persons a legacy for what are called superstitious uses and constituting his soul his universal heir. In the latter end of June or beginning of July following, Sir William Godolphin made a

---

[1] Chancery Reports, 1796, Hil., Letter I.   [2] Charity Commissioners' Report, 1838.
[3] In Archdeaconry Court of Cornwall.

3 R

nuncupative will, whereby he gave to his nephew Francis Godolphin all his lands in England, together with £7,000 in money, and besides £1,000 each to his four children; and to Elizabeth wife of Charles Godolphin, Esq., younger brother of the first Earl Godolphin, and sister of the said Francis, £4,000, and to the said Charles £1,000, with a few other legacies. He died soon afterwards, and administration with will annexed (no executor having been named) was granted by the Prerogative Court of Canterbury, on 26th November 1696, (223 Bond) to the above mentioned Francis Godolphin and Elizabeth Godolphin, the two principal legatees named in the said nuncupative will. An attempt having been made to set up the said Notarial Act, proceedings were instituted to set it aside and confirm the letters of administration; and a private Act of Parliament was obtained to the same end, in which it was provided, *inter alia*, that the sum of £3040, the aggregate amount of the aforesaid charitable gifts, should be paid in moieties to the administrator and administratrix, who should give their separate bonds in Chancery for the disposal of the said moneys in conformity with the intention of the Donor, and that such bonds should not be discharged except upon the certificate of the Archbishop of Canterbury, the Lord Chancellor, or the Lord Keeper, that the money had been vested, or disposed of, to such pious and charitable uses as might answer the intentions of the Donor.

After the Act had passed in the House of Commons, and whilst it was passing through the House of Lords, Francis Godolphin added a codicil in his will, dated 14th March 1697, in which he declared his desire that the sum of £1500, mentioned in the said Act to be disposed of by him, should, if the said Act passed, be laid out by his executors for a Free School, or for a Hospital in the Parish of St. Mabyn, near Tregarden, in the County of Cornwall, and that it might be in memory of his dear uncle, Sir William Godolphin.

On 2nd August 1699, the Master in Chancery, to whom the matter was referred (Sir John Hoskyns), reported that Charles Godolphin and Francis Godolphin should, before the 8th April 1701, enter respectively into recognizances in the court in the sum of £3040, for the due application of the sums given for charities, the former to pay £10 for the poor of Liskeard and £10 for the Poor of St. Mabyn, and £1500 to be applied for the education of the poor, &c., as provided in the above mentioned Act, to the satisfaction of the Archbishop of Canterbury; and the same, *mutatis mutandis*, for Francis Godolphin, except that he should pay £20 to the poor of Camelford instead of the two sums to Liskeard and St. Maben. On 14th February 1703-4, the said Master reported that the Archbishop of Canterbury had certified that the payments to the Parishes of Liskeard and St. Maben had been duly made and the sum of £1500 disposed of by Charles Godolphin and Elizabeth his wife to his satisfaction, and the recognizance given by them was accordingly vacated.[2]

Francis Godolphin, however, died before 8th April 1701, and we are unable to trace

---

[1] Chancery Reports, 1699, Letter G.

[2] Charles Godolphin was M.P. for Helston, and appropriated a considerble portion of the £1500 for charitable uses in that Borough. He also gave £100 to a subscription raised for the maintenance and education of Sir Robert Henley, Bart, who died in 1740, s.p., when the title became extinct. Moreover Charles Godolphin dying s.p., both he and Elizabeth his wife devoted a considerable portion of their wealth for charitable purposes. By a part of it the Godolphin Grammar School at Hammersmith was founded in 1856.

that any recognizance was entered into by him or his representatives touching these charitable bequests, although, as concerning his estate, there were proceedings in the court of Chancery extending over twenty years. It is stated, however, in Gilbert's Returns of 1786, in which the charity is entered as the gift of *Lord* Godolphin and consisting of £1,000 for the purchase of the land and £500 for building, that the money was offered to be paid to the Rev. Mr. Peters between thirty and forty years previously, who refused the principal because no interest was allowed.

SCHOOLS.

The only school in the parish is the National School. Under the authority of the Act 5th Victoria, for affording further facilities for the conveyance and endowment of sites for schools, George Henry, Earl of Falmouth, the Rev. the Hon. John Evelyn Boscawen, of Wotton, county Surrey, and Evelyn Boscawen his son, by deed poll dated 31st July 1846, and inrolled in Chancery,[1] granted to the Archdeacon of Cornwall and the Rector of St. Mabyn a piece of land adjoining the road leading to Egloshayle, as a site for a school for poor persons in the parish of St. Mabyn and such other poor persons as the committee of managers may think fit, and for a residence for a master or mistress, or both, of the said schools. It is provided that these schools shall be always in union with the "Incorporated Society for the Education of the Poor in the principles of the Church of England;" that the master and mistress shall hold their appointments at the discretion of the Earl of Falmouth, his heirs and assigns, being members of the Church of England, and the Rector of St. Mabyn; that the Rector of the parish shall have the care and direction of the religious instruction of the scholars; and that, in other respects, the management of the school shall be vested in a committee consisting of the Rector, his Curates, if appointed by him, the Earl of Falmouth and his heirs males, and the Churchwardens, if, respectively, members of the Church of England.

The school was constructed for the accommodation of 112 children, 56 of each sex. It is now conducted upon the mixed principle by a certificated master, and there are about 70 names in the books.

MANOR OF KILCOED, *alias* KILCOYT, *alias* KILQUYT, *alias* COLQUITE.

The manner of spelling the name of this Lordship has to some extent varied. In Domesday it is written Chilcoit. It was one of the manors granted to the Earl of Moreton under whom it was held by Richard [de Tracy,] and in the time King Edward was held by one Colo.

---

[1] Rot. Claus. 1846. Part 104, No. 4.

3 R²

"The Earl holds one manor which is called Chilcoit, which was held by Colo on the day when King Edward was alive and dead, and it renders gild for one hide and half. This ten ploughs can plough. This is held by Richard of the Earl. Thereof Richard has one virgate and two ploughs, and the villans have the rest of the land and one plough. There Richard has six villans, and eight bordars, and three bond servants, and four animals, and eight pigs, and sixty sheep, and twenty acres of brushwood, and forty acres of pasture; and the value per annum is 20s., and when the Earl received 40s."[1]

Thomas de Tracy, living in 1260, married Isolda daughter and heir of Andrew de Cardinan, son and heir of Robert, who held two Baronies in Cornwall, containing seventy-one Knights' fees; and the daughter and heir of whose second son, Robert, married Odo de Treverbyn.[2] Thomas de Tracy appears to have died s.p., and Isolda, in her widowhood, conveyed the lands to Oliver de Dinham, or Dinam, who died (1299) leaving Joceus de Dinham his son and heir aged 24 years.[3] He died two years later seized, besides of various manors and lands in Devon and Cornwall, of some twenty Knights' fees in the latter County, of which Richard de Ceresceaux (Sergeaux) held of him one and half fees in Kilcoyt.[4] These fees in chief continued to be held by the Dinham family and their heirs for several centuries, if not until military tenures were abolished. Richard Sergeaux died in, or before, 1307, seized of this manor and the manor of Lanrethou (Lanreath) which he held of the heir of Joceus de Dynham, then a minor in the wardship of the King, as of the Barony of Cardinham, by the service of five and half Knights, and by making suit at the Court at Cardinham three weeks by three weeks. An extent of the possessions of Richard Cerizeaux was taken at Lanrethou on 6th February 1st Edward II (1307-8), which gives us a very interesting account of the then condition, and the value, of the manor. The jury say upon their oaths that in the manor of Kilcoit is one messuage with a garden, and the value per annum is 2s., that there are four score acres of arable land, value per annum 20s., price per acre 3d.; that there are six acres of meadow, value per annum 3s., price per acre 6d.; that there are ten acres of pasture, value per annum 20d., price per acre 2d.; and fifty acres of high wood with the pasture, value per annum 10s.; and that there are two water mills for corn, value per annum 60s.; and that there are there six free tenants who render per annum 15s. at the usual quarterly terms by equal payments; and that there are there nineteen conventionaries who render per annum £5 4s. 8d., at the said four quarterly terms, and each of the conventionaries owe ploughing for one day in winter, the value of which work is 3s. 2d., and for each person 2d., that they owe mowing for one day in autumn for food for the lord, and that the value for all is 19d., and for the work of each 1d.; and they owe carriage for the corn of the lord for one day in autumn, and the value of all is 3s. 2d., and of each man's work 2d.; and that there are there seven natives who render per annum 76s. 2d. at the said four terms, and that each of the said native's work per annum is the same as the conventionaries', and that the value of their work is 2s. 11d., and the price of the work for each 5d.; and they say that the pleas and perquisites of the Courts is of the value per annum of

---

[1] Exon. Domesday, vol iv., p. 230, orig. fo. 260.   [2] *Vide* Pedigree, ante p. 219.

[3] Inq. p.m. 27th Edward I, No. 42.   [4] Inq. p.m. 29th Edward I, No. 59.

4s.; and that the sum of the value of the said manor per annum is £25 0s. 4d.; and the jury say that Richard, son of John, son of the said Richard de Cerizeaux, is nearest heir of the said Richard, and is of the age of seven years. Richard de Sergeaux, besides the manors of Lanrethou and Kilquite, held the hamlet of Trenvennek and no other lands in Cornwall, and the total value of all his possessions was £46 11s. 6½d. per annum.[1]

Sir Richard Sergeaux, who was found to be the heir of the above mentioned Richard, died in 1362, leaving a son of the same name who died on 30th September 1393, seized, *inter alia*, of the manor of Kelquit, which he held of Sir John Dynham, Knight, by military service, reversion of it after the death of Philippa his wife to Richard Sergeaux, son and heir of the said Richard; and the value per annum of all receipts beyond reprises was £46 6s. 8d.[2] so that in the period of 86 years the value of the manor had increased nearly two fold.

Sir Richard Sergeaux, Knight, son of the last named, granted the manor of Kelquyt to Henry Nanfan and John Pollard for the term of the life of Philippa wife of the said Richard, who granted their whole estate therein to the said Philippa, after whose death, in consequence of the pre-decease of her son Richard Sergeaux, who died in the same year as his father, it devolved, in common with the other Sergeaux estates, upon Elizabeth, Philippa, Alice and Johanna, daughters of the said Sir Richard Sergeaux and the said Johanna his wife, and coheirs of their brother Richard Sergeaux.

Upon the partition of the Sergeaux lands the manor of Colquite, with the moiety of Pencarrow, *inter alia*, were allotted to Elizabeth the elder coheir, then the wife of Sir William Marny of Layer Marny, co. Essex, Knight, and in consequence of the death of his granddaughter Margaret, in infancy, eventually devolved upon Sir John Marny, Knt., second son of the said William, whose son Sir Henry Marny in 1522 was created Baron Marny, and died 24th May 1523,[3] seized, *inter alia*, of the Manor of Kylqwyte, which he held of the heirs of Lord Dynham, and leaving his son Sir John Marny, Knight, then Lord Marny, his nearest heir and aged 30 years and more.[4] He devised his manor of Kylqwyte to trustees for the payment of his debts and legacies, and for building a chapel on the north side of the chancel of the Church of Layer Marny, and also for the erection of an Alms house for five poor persons, with five chambers and one common kitchen, and one chamber for two Chantry Priests. John Lord Marny died 27th April 1525, s.p.m., when the title, which had only existed two years, became extinct. By his last will he charged his manor of Colquyte with an annuity of £9 6s. 8d. to his then wife Margaret, daughter of Sir William Waldegrave, Knight, sometime Lord Mayor of London, to make up an annuity to her of £20 a year, according to a bond which he had given her father. It was found that he held this manor of the heirs of Lord Dynham, as of the manor of Cardinham, but by what service the jurors declared themselves ignorant. By his first wife Christine, daughter and sole heir of Sir Roger Newburgh, he acquired great accession to his estates. By her he left two daughters, Katherine and Elizabeth, who were found to be his nearest heirs, and to be aged respectively ten and eight years.[5]

[1] Escheats. 1st Edward II, No. 56.   [2] Inq. p.m., 17th Richard II., No. 53.   [3] See ante, Vol. i., p. 443

[4] Inq. p.m., 15th Henry VIII., No. 10.   [5] Inq. p.m., 17th Henry VIII., No. 93.

Katherine, the eldest daughter of Henry Lord Marny, married, first, George Ratcliffe, Esq., who had special livery of seizin, *jure uxoris*, 21st Henry VIII, and dying soon afterwards s.p. she wedded Sir Thomas Poynyngs, Knight, who, in 1545, was created Baron Poynings; and the second daughter, Elizabeth, became the wife of Thomas Howard, second son of Thomas third Duke of Norfolk, in 1559 created Vicount Bindon, county Dorset. An Act of Parliament was obtained in 1536[1] for the partition of the estates, as well those of Newburgh, as of Marny, in which partition both Bindon and Layer Marny were allotted to Sir Thomas Poynyngs and Katherine his wife, and it was provided by the Act that the parties should not make any change in the apportionment. This not giving satisfaction, a further Act was obtained in 1540[2] to amend the apportionment. In this partition Colquite, *inter alia*, fell to the share of Thomas Howard and his wife Elizabeth. In 1547[3] by a further Act it was enacted that Thomas Howard, one of the sons of Thomas Viscount Bindon, should, immediately after the death of the said Viscount, have and enjoy, for his life, the lordship of Colquite with its appurtenances, &c., and have power to make joincture for term of life only to any wife he should marry. Thomas Viscount Bindon and Henry his son being greatly in debt, in 1575 obtained another Act of Parliament for empowering Lord Burleigh, then Lord High Treasurer, and others, during a period of five years from the 18th February 1575-6, to sell, *inter alia*, the manor of Cowlequite, and apply two thirds of the sum realized to the use of the said Viscount, and the other third to the use of his son Henry, saving the contingent rights of Thomas Howard, under the Act of 1st Edward VI.[4] Thereupon a special commission was issued to make a survey of the manor, which survey we here give:—

Maner de } A breefe abstract of the Man[r] of Colquyte made by Sir Arthure Bassett Knight
  Colquyte }   Will[m] Mohun and Richard Grenville Esquyres and Antonye Gyffarde Gentleman in the moneth of September laste past Anno Regin. Dne nr'o El. Regine nunc xviij by vertue of a special Commission to them directed for vewe and survey of the same.

Will[m] Bawden holdeth percell of the barton for three lyves by the rent } clxxxvi acres
of vij[li] xiiij[s] iij[d] w[ch] conteynes by estemacion

Nicholas White holdeth percell of the barton one toft and ij Tenements } cvi acres
for term of his owne lyfe by the rent of v[li] xiiij[s] viij[d] w[ch] conteynes by estemacion

Walter Whytford holdeth percell of the barton and two other ten[ts] for } lxxxxij acres
three lyves by the rent of iiij[li] xij[s] ij[d] w[ch] conteynes by est.

Barnard Hamlye holdeth percell of the barton and one other tent for three } xliiij acres
lyves by the rent of xxxvij[s] ix[d] conteyninge by est.

[1] Act 27, Henry VIII.   [2] Act 32, Henry VIII.
[3] Act 1, Edward VI.   [4] 18th Elizabeth, No. 34.

Henrye Cundye holdeth percell of the barton and one tenement for two lyves by the rent of xliiij^s conteyninge by estem. } xlv acres

Willyam Hamlye holdeth percell of the barton and ij other tent^s for three lyves by the rent of xxviij^s iiij^d conteyninge by est. } xlviij acres di.acre woode copised

Nicholas Dawby holdeth percell of the barton and one other ten^t for three lyves by the rent of xxvj^s viij^d conteyninge by estem. } xxv acres

Gyles Bettye holdeth percell of the barton for three lyves by the rent of xiij^s iiij^d conteyninge } xvj acres

Humfrye Thomas holdeth one tent for his owne lyfe by the rent of xiij^s iiij^d conteyninge by est. } xxx acres

William Panston holdeth one ten^t for three lyves by the rent of xiij^s iiij^d conteyninge by estemacion } xxij acres di. acre woode copised

Nicholas Maye holdeth one ten^t for his owne lyfe by the rent of xiij^s iiij^d conteyninge by estem. } xxij acres di. acre woode copised

John Pawlye holdeth one ten^t for three lyves by the rent of xiiij^s conteyninge by estem. } xxij acres di. acre woode copised

Thomas Otes holdeth one ten^t for ij lyves by the rent of xvj^s conteyninge by estemacion } xx acres

John Maye holdeth one ten^t for ij lyves by the rent of xvj^s conteyninge by estemacion } xx acres

Thomas Sabye holdeth one ten^t for three lyves by the rent of xij^s conteyning by estemacion } xx acres

John Croppe holdeth one tenem^t for two lyves conteyninge by estemacion lij acres by the rent of xlv^s } lij acres

Willm Hamblyn holdeth one ten^t for two lyves by the rent of xx^s w^{cn} conteynes by estem. } xxvj acres

Henrye Moyse holdeth one ten^t for three lyves by the rent of xxiiij^s conteyninge by estem. } xxxvj acres, wode copysed v acres

John Trebble holdeth one ten^t for three lyves by the rent of xiij^s iiijd wch conteynes by estem. } xix acres

Nicholas Marshall holdeth one ten^t for three lyves by the rent of liij^s iiij^d conteyninge by estem. } lxxvij acres

Margery nowe the wyfe of Thomas Martyn holdeth one ten^t for two lyves by the rent of xvj^s conteyninge by estem. } xx acres

John Bennett holdeth one ten^t for three lyves by the rent of xiij· iiij^d } xxx acres
conteyninge by estem.

Emblyn Cocke widowe holdeth one ten^t for two lyves by the rent of ix· } lx acres
conteyninge by estemacion

Willm Rawlyns holdeth one ten^t for three lyves by the rent of xiij· iiij^d } xxx acres
conteyninge by estem.

John Denham holdeth one corne myll and two closes of land for three } xx acres
lyves by the rent of xxxiij· iiij^d conteyninge by estem.

Thomas Hambly holdeth one ten^t for three lyves by the rent of xvj· con- } xx acres
conteyninge by estem.

Richard Langdon Gen. holdeth one toft and a corne myll for three lyves } x acres
by the rent of xxxv· containing by estemacion

John Pawlye holdeth one ten^t for three lives by the rent of xiij· iiij^d } xxvij acres di.acre
conteyninge by estemacion   } woode copysed

Elizabeth ffletcher holdeth one ten^t for two lyves by the rent of viij· iiij^d } v acres
conteyninge by estem.

Roberte Tucker holdeth one cottage by the rent of ij· iiij^d   x yerdes

Walter Wade holdeth one ten^t and at this servey was absent so as no
wrytinge of the same was sene, the rent is xj· vj^d and it conteynes by } xxij acres
estemacion

There is reserved vppon every lease an heriote or fourty shillinges for } heriotes
the same

There is younge woode vppon the barton by estemacion ccxx acres of
(blank) yeres growth for the wch it is thoughte there wilbe for everye acre } ccxx acres
geven xiij· iiij^d the herbage of wch woode is leassed vnto Willm Bawden for
the rent of one penny yerely

ffor a fountayne or well thereys payde to the L. of Colquyte yerely   iijd

By the rentall wherewth the reves do yerely make theire collection and
accomptes yt apeareth that the yerely Rent Convencionarye amountes vnto } xlvij^l xiiij· v^d
the some of

By the same rentall yt also appeareth the highe rentes of the free tenam^{ts} } iij^l xvij· vij^d ob.
amountes to the some of

Summa totalis   .. lj^{li} xij· ij^d ob. q;

Oute of the wch some there is alowed yerely to the Reves for rentes repayed and rentes denyed as followeth in this accompte

Rentes repayde	To the mano^r of Trewosell	- - ij^s vj^d	
	To the heirs of Cardynham	- - ij^s ij^d	
	To the mano^r of Parke	- - ij^s vj^d	
	To the mano^r of Lanowe	- - xx^d ob.	x^s viij^d ob.
	To the mano^r of Lanno St.	- - xiij^d	
	To the mano^r of Trevisquite	- - vj^d	
	To the heires of Lukye	- - iij^d	
	By John Treffrye Esq.	- - v^d ob. q ;	
	By Richard Roscradock, Esq.	- - ix^s	xj^s ix^d ob. q ;
	By George Speake Knight	- - xvj^d	
	By the heires of Wynslade	- - xij^d	

These perticulers beinge deducted and alowed there then remayneth of cleare yerely rent for the mano^r and lordshipp before sayd the some of } l^h x^s viij^d

ARTHUR BASSETT

WYLLYAM MOHUN   R. GREYNVILE.[1]

Every effort was made to sell the manor of Colquite, but owing to the estate held in it by Thomas Howard no sufficient sum could be obtained.[2] Sir Richard Grenville on 5th January 1579-80 reported that they could get no more than £1500, and consequently the Act lapsed. Thomas Viscount Bindon died 28th January 1581-2,[3] when, in virtue of the Act of the 1st Edward VI., Colquite devolved upon Thomas Howard, who, in 1587, with Grace his wife suffered a fine therein to his brother Henry, the Viscount Howard of Bindon, ceding the same for a term of 89 years, from 29th March in that year, to the said Viscount, for which the said Viscount paid them the sum of £1600.[4] Henry Viscount Bindon died 1590, leaving by Francis his wife an only daughter and sole heir, Douglas Howard, who married Arthur Gorges, one of the Gentlemen Pensioners to the Queen, and had issue a certain Ambrosia Gorges, who, upon the inquisition taken on 6th October 1591, was found to be the sole heir of her grandfather (her mother having died 13th August 1590), and to be then aged two years nine months and eleven days.[5] We have some difficulty now in tracing the descent of the manor. In January 1593-4 a fine was passed in which Thomas Harris, Serjeant at Law,[6] was querist, and Arthur Gorges, Esq. defendant, by which the

---

[1] State Papers, Dom. Corr. Elizabeth, vol. cix, No. 10.

[2] The tenants of the manor offered forty years' purchase, provided the estate of Thomas Howard were redeemed and the manor sold absolutely. Richard Carye, Esq. (Richard Carew of Antony, the historian of Cornwall), if he might have immediate possession of the estate, subject only to the payment of the rent to Thomas Howard and his wife for their lives, offered 1,500. Thomas Roscarrock offered fifty-five years' purchase, amounting to the sum of £2,779 6s. 8d. for the absolute sale, and Mr. Edgcombe bid £20 more (State Papers, Devon, Cornwall, Elizabeth, vol. cix., No. 11.) Thomas Howard himself desired to have the preference in the sale and offered £20 more than any other one would give. (Ibid. cxxii, No. 8.)   [3] Inq. p.m., 33rd Elizabeth, No. 33.

[4] Ped. Finium, 29th Elizabeth, Easter.   [5] Inq. p.m., 33rd Elizabeth, Part 2, No. 22.

[6] This Sir Thomas Harrys was called to the dignity of a Serjeant at Law in 1589 (Foss's Judges, v., 414). He was the son of Edward Harrys by his first wife, which Edward was the son of Walter Harrys of

3s

said Arthur Gorges remised and quit-claimed for himself and his heirs all the right he and they had in the manor of Colquite with appurtenances, fifty messuages, &c., and £5 annual rent.[1] And in 1594, the said Thomas Harrys, described as of Blackwaie, co. Herts, Serjeant at Law, Lord of the manor of Colquite, granted to one John Berry a lease for ninety-nine years of a messuage in Tredethy;[2] and in Michaelmas term 1597, we find that the said Thomas Harris and Edward Harris his son suffered a fine, *inter alia*, in the same manor to Arthur Fowell, Esq.[3] This was clearly for purposes of settlement, for by a deed dated 2nd March 5th James (1607) Edward Harrys, Esq., described as Lord of the manor of Colquite, conveyed to William Lugger of St. Mabyn, Yeoman, a tenement in Tredethy, for a term of ninety-nine years, determinable upon the deaths of the said William Lugger, Gilbert Marshall, and Phillippa Lugger daughter of the said William, at the annual rent of 13s. 4d., a capon, and suit at the Court of the manor of Colquite twice a year.[2] And, further, by deed dated 28th June 8th James (1610) the said Edward Harrys, described as " of Colquite, Esq.," granted a lease to Thomas Pomeroye of Landrake, of another tenement in Tredethy under similar conditions.[2]

Meanwhile, on 10th May 1600, there was a decision in the Court of Wards to make the young daughter of Sir Arthur Gorges a ward of the Queen, and a proposal was made for her marriage to Sir Philip Herbert, younger brother of William, third Earl of Pembroke (and afterwards Earl of Pembroke and Montgomery) who offered the Queen £5000 in money and jewels. Sir Arthur Gorges endeavoured to have himself the disposal of his daughter, and intended to give her to the son of Thomas Lord Howard of Walden, but she died in November of the same year, by which her father sustained considerable loss, though he had some compensation in an annuity of £400 a year to be paid him by the young lady's uncle, Thomas Viscount Bindon, upon whom the estates devolved.[4] This Viscount died in 1610, when the title became extinct, but during his life time he demised his estates to his kinsman Thomas Howard Earl of Suffolk, and entailed them on Henry Viscount Howard, Giles Howard, Henry Howard Earl of Northampton, William Lord

Monmouthshire. Sir Thomas, by a daughter of Sir Henry Pomeroy, had a daughter named Ann who married Sir Thomas Southwell, and a son Edward, named in the text, who was appointed by Lord Falkland (Lord Deputy of Ireland), Chief Justice of Munster (Pat. dated 27th October 1623, Rot. Pat. 21st James, Part I., m. 32, Ireland). This appointment by the Lord Deputy gave great offence to the King, who wrote to the Lord Deputy on 11th December 1623, rebuking him for having presumed to make the appointment, as the office should have been disposed of by the King himself; nevertheless, the King added, to preserve the Lord Deputy from disgrace, he would allow Sir Edward to hold the appointment upon the condition that he should surrender the former patent; and a new one passed the Great Seal 28th January 1623-4.

Arthur Harrys, half-brother of Sir Thomas, was of Churston in Devon, and registered his Pedigree at the Heralds' Visitation of that County in 1620. (Harl. Soc. Pub., vi., 138). ARMS: Sa. an antelope salient ar. maned and armed or.

[1] Pedes Finium, 36th Elizabeth, Hilary.　　　　　　　　　[2] Deeds at Tredethy.
[3] Pedes Finium, 39th and 40th Elizabeth, Michaelmas.
[4] 1600, November 8th. "Sir Arthur Gorge's daughter is dead, which works him shrewd effects, but he hath some releef by a composition made between him and the Viscount, who must pay him £400 a yeare during his lyf, which will keep the staff from the dore" (Sir Robert Cecil's Letters to Sir George Carew. Camden Soc. 1864.)

Howard and their heirs.[1] Whether or not Colquite was included in this settlement we have no knowledge, but in January 1618-9 Edward Harrys, Esq., suffered a fine in the manor of Colquite fifty messuages, 100s. rent, &c., to Sir Henry Spiller, Knt., and Michael Humphry, for which fine they gave the said Edward £1600,[2] and in January 1619-20 a recovery was levied, in which George Long, Gent., and Henry Carter, Gent., were petitioners, and Sir Richard Weston and Sir Henry Spiller, Knights, defendants, concerning the same manor, who called to warrant Thomas Earl of Suffolk, who called Theophilus Lord Walden his son and heir.[3] By Indenture 3rd December 1629, Sir Henry Spiller, described as of Lalcham, county Middlesex, Knight, John Page, Esq., one of the Masters in Chancery, George Longe and Philip Maynewaring of London, Esquires, and Thomas Stich of London, Gent., granted to William Lugger of St. Mabyn, Yeoman, a tenement in Tredethy, parcel of the manor of Colquite, for a term of 99 years, if William Lugger, Nathaniel Lugger, and Alexander Lugger, sons of the said William, so long should live.[4]

This would seem to indicate that at this date the manor was held under trust, but Sir Henry Spiller died seized thereof, *inter alia*, in 1653, and by his will dated 18th April 1649,[5] devised the same, specifically, under the name of the manor of Colquite, *alias* Kilquite, and all his lands in the county of Worcester, to certain trustees to hold to the use of Ann his wife for her life, with remainder to his cousin and godson Henry Spiller and his heirs for ever. In the same year Henry Spiller, Esq., and Elizabeth his wife suffered a fine, *inter alia*, in this manor to Henry Martyn, Esq.[6] Very soon after the death of Sir Henry Spiller the manor would seem to be, to some extent at least, in process of dismemberment. By Indenture dated 4th June 1656, Henry Spiller of Elsfield, county Worcester, and Elizabeth his wife, Dame Ann Spiller, widow, relict of Sir Henry Spiller, of co. Middlesex, Knight, deceased, Richard Porter and William Le Hunt of Gray's Inn, Esquires, and William Spry of Blisland, Gent., granted to William Lugger of St. Mabyn, Gent., a tenement called Pool Parks in Tredethy, being parcel of the barton of Colquite, to hold to him and his heirs and assigns;[4] and about the same time a fine was suffered by the same parties of the manor of Colquite to Edward Hoblyn, Gent., and Grace Barrett, Spinster.[7] And by Indenture dated 20th August in the same year, Edward Hoblyn, described as of St. Columbe, Gent., in consideration of a nominal payment to Henry Spiller of Elsfield, county Worcester, Esq., granted and confirmed the said premises to the said William Lugger.[8]

---

[1] This settlement is referred to in his will dated 14th June 1607, proved 10th March 1610-1. (22 Wood.) P.C.C.

[2] Ped. Fin., 16th James, Hil.

[3] Recoveries 17th James I. Hil. m. 86. Theophilus Howard when, in 1603, his father was created Earl of Suffolk, had summons to Parliament as Lord Howard of Walden.

[4] Deeds penes F. J. Hext, of Tredethy, Esq.

[5] Proved 7th May 1653 (Brent 298) P.C.C. He devised his capital messuage of Finventon, in Brodoke, and his messuage of Bodergy, in Boconnoc, to the same trustees, to the use (after the payment of debts and legacies) of his wife Ann for life, with remainder, as regard Finventon, to Ferdinando Spiller, son of his cousin William Spiller, and the heirs males of his body; and as regards Bodergy, remainder to George Spiller, son of his cousin William, and the heirs male of his body, in default of such issue, remainder, in both cases, to Henry Spiller, another son of the said William, and his heirs for ever. He gave to his granddaughters Catherine Dutton, Dorothy Reynell, Frances Reynell, and Ann Proctor £500 each.

[6] Pedes Finium 1653, Michs. (Divers Counties.)   [7] Pedes Finium, 1656, Trinity.

3 s[2]

The manor of Colquite thus became vested in Edward Hoblyn of St. Columb and afterwards of Bodmin, who married Bridget daughter of John Carew of Penwarne, second son of Richard Carew of Antony, Esquire. His grandson, Edward Hoblyn of Penhargard and Colquite, left one only daughter and sole heir, who married her cousin Samuel Peter of Percothen. Upon her death she settled her estates upon her second son Deeble Peter, who fixed his residence at Colquite, and died there in 1832. By his will dated 19th July 1832, he devised the manor of Colquite and all his other lands to his nephew Deeble Peter, youngest son of Hoblyn Peter of Percothen, for life, remainder to his first and other sons in tail male, with divers remainders over, in grateful remembrance of his mother, from whom he says all his property in this world sprung, he directed that the said Deeble Peter his nephew, and every other person or persons who might become entitled to any estate in the said manors and lands under the limitations of the said will, shall take upon himself and themselves, respectively, the surname of Hoblyn, and use the same in addition to the name of Peter, and bear the arms of Hoblyn quartered as he then bore the same, with a clause of forfeiture in default of compliance. Accordingly, immediately after his uncle's death, Deeble Peter, Junior, applied for and obtained a royal license, dated 13th September 1836, to assume the name of Hoblyn in addition to that of Peter and bear the arms Hoblyn in the first quarter. Deeble Peter-Hoblyn served the office of Sheriff of Cornwall in 1839, and died unmarried and s.p. on 18th September 1864, when the estates, under the will of the aforesaid Deeble Peter, devolved upon John Harris Peter, third son of Samuel Peter, grandson of the beforementioned Samuel Peter and Sarah Hoblyn his wife, who, being in actual possession, by royal license dated 18th July 1865, was granted authority to him and his heirs to use the name and arms of Hoblyn in addition to those of Peter, in conformity with the testamentary injunctions of his great uncle Deeble Peter. Mr. Peter Hoblyn died in 1871, and the estates have devolved upon his son and heir Cyril Onslow Peter-Hoblyn now (1875) a minor.

Some remains of the old mansion house still exist a little west of the present residence, which was erected by the late Deeble Peter. These remains consist of two rooms having access from without. One of the doorways has a flat four-centred arch; the other is within a porch opening at the sides, the masonry of which is very substantial, the doorway itself has an acutely pointed arch. There is evidence that there were chambers above these two rooms and in each a wide chimney place.

MANOR OF HELIGAN.

We are unable to trace this manor in Domesday. Perhaps it was taxed under Trevis-quite, but inasmuch as it formed two separate Knights' fees, and appears as a separate tithing of the Hundred of Trigg in 1283,[1] it would seem more probable that it appears

---

[1] Assize Roll Cornwall, 11th Edward I, m. $\frac{1}{20}$ 4. m. 8.

in the survey under some name not now recognisable. It was clearly part of the grant to the Earl of Moreton, and passed to the Dinham family, for when in 1292 the aid was granted on the making of the eldest son of King Edward I, a Knight, Robert de Heligan paid the aid at 25s. each for two fees of Moreton there, and he afterwards accounted for a further sum of 30s. to make up his assessment to the usual rate of 40s. for each fee.[1] When the aid was granted, 1332, for making the eldest son of King Edward III a Knight,[2] Adam de Heligan paid upon two fees, which Robert his father held before. It appears from an Inquisition taken at Camelford on Saturday next after the feast of Pentecost 6th Henry VI (1428), that John Trelawny, Isabella Helygan, Thomas Paget, Nicholas Raulyn, James Tresslogat, John Beauchamp and Robert Hardwick held separately, between them, a moiety of one small fee in Helygan, which Adam de Helygan formerly held, and paid the subsidy; and that the other moiety was held by Andrew Helygan. Moreover that Isabella Helygan, John Bere, Benedict Giffard, and others held respectively between them the moiety of another small fee in Helygan, which Adam Heligan formerly held. We seem here to lose a moiety of the second fee.

Having thus disposed, as far as we can, of the *Fees* we will return to the Manor. It was held by the family of Heligan, who from it derived their name, from a much earlier date than we have been able to trace the fees. Nicholas de Heligan, who held it in the early part of the reign of King Henry III, had issue by his wife Maud daughter of Alan Bloyou, a son, Robert de Heligan, mentioned above, and a daughter Millicent who became the wife of Jordan de Farndone, or Faringdon, and in 1254 Nicholas de Heligan suffered a fine to Jordan de Farndone and Milesent his wife of one carucute of land in Heligan, and one carucute of land in Portkeliok, whereby he granted to the said Milesent the said lands. And Nicholas and Milesent re-granted the land in Heligan to the said Nicholas, to hold of them during his life by the rent of one pair of white gloves at Easter, with remainder, after his death, to the said Jordan and Milesent and the heirs of the body of Milesent, to hold together with the land in Portkelliok of the chief Lords of the fees, and in default of heirs of the body of the said Milesent all the said lands to revert to the heirs of the said Nicholas.[3]

Robert de Heligan, son of Nicholas, died 1314, seized of the hamlet of Heligan, which he held of the heir of Joceus de Dynham, which heir being then a minor and a ward of the King, Adam de Heligan, son and heir of Robert, on 18th April 1315, did homage to the King and had livery of seizin;[4] and four years later he paid ten marks for his relief.[5] In 1331, Adam de Heligan held one fee in Heligan of John de Dynham, the heir of Joceus to whom allusion is above made.[6] This Adam was twice married. By his first wife, Sybel, he had two children Richard and Emma. His second wife was Isabell

---

[1] Rot. Pip. 29th Edward I. See also Subs. Roll, 31st Edward I, $\frac{87}{4}$

[2] Excheq. Queen's Remb. Office, vol iii.

[3] Ped. Finium. 38th Henry III, Easter.

[4] Rot. Fin., 8th Edward II. *Vide* also

[5] Rot. Origin., m. 14, 22, and Rot. Pip. 13th Edward II.

[6] Inq. p.m., John de Dynham, 6th Edward III, No. 59.

daughter of Sir John Carmynow, by whom he had issue John, Nicholas, and Isolda. Joan the daughter and sole heir of Nicholas de Helygan, son of John, married John Trelawny, second son of Sir John Trelawny, and it is stated in an old "Book of Evidences" at Trelawne,[1] that Richard, eldest son of Adam de Helygan is supposed to have been born before marriage, "as," it is said, "by certain instruments it doth appear." This Johan, it is further remarked, "added a blessing to our family by bringing with her the manor of Treserrett, and the third part of the manor of Tregrilla." There would seem to be some ground of doubt, or suspicion, as to the legitimacy of Richard, but there does not appear to have been any conclusive evidence, and, as we shall presently see, he was acknowledged by Nicholas, son and heir of John, as the son and heir of Adam de Heligan. Adam de Heligan, by his charter, dated 5th Edward III, granted to Richard his son and Johan daughter of James Peverell, his wife, all his messuages, mills, &c., in Porthkulyock and Tregoyth (Trequites) the higher, to hold to them and the heirs of their bodies.[2] He also granted to him the manor of Heligan with the same limitations. To John, his son, Adam de Heligan granted the manor of Tresarrett. Richard de Helygan would appear to have had two sons, Reginald and John. Reginald, by his charter dated at Helygan on Sunday in the vigil of the Nativity of the Blessed Virgin Mary 39th Edward III (1365), granted to Sir Hugh Peverel, John Giffard of Helland, and John de Penharghard, all his manor of Helygan with all his messuages, lands and tenements in Helygan, Nythera Tregoyt, Overa Tregoyt, Frogeham, Treslogget, Bocouan, Spytal, Restorbet and Pybenlycka, with the dovecote, mills, &c., together with the fealty and rents, and all the service of Isabella, who was the wife of Adam Helygan, for all the messuages, &c. which she held in Overa Tregoyt for the term of her life, together with the reversion of the same messuages, &c., to hold to the said Hugh and others and their heirs and assigns for ever.[3] This was doubtless a conveyance in trust for uses of which we had no knowledge. The same Reginald, by a charter dated at Bodmin on Monday next after the feast of St. Dionisius 7th Richard II (1383), granted certain premises in Tremaben (St. Maben Church Town) to John Seys and Walter Robyn, and appointed Robert Tremaben and Mark Helygan to deliver seizin. And by their charter, dated at Tremaben on Thursday in the feast of St. Thomas following, the said John Seys and Walter Robyn re-granted the same premises to the said Reginald Helygan and Johanna his wife and their heirs. He would seem to have died s.p. and to have been succeeded by his brother John, who then became the heir of his father.[3]

By Indenture dated at Bodmyn on Friday next after the Invention of Holy Cross (2?) Henry IV (1401) between John Heligan, son and heir of Richard Heligan, son and heir of Adam Heligan of the one part, and Nicholas, son and heir of John Heligan, son of the aforesaid Adam Heligan, of the other part, whereby the said John son of Richard confirmed to the said Nicholas son of John all the messuages and lands which belonged

---

[1] In a list of deeds is "An Indenture authentically proving, by the depositions of divers deponents, the illegitimacy of Rychard de Helligan, borne before marriage by Sybil wife of Adam de Helligan, and that John de Holligan was son and heir of the said Adam, begotten in true matrimony. Dated anno Dom. 1401."

[2] Charter at Trelawne.   [3] Charters at St. Benet's Priory, Lanivet.

to Adam Heligan in Spetell, Treceret, Bocouan, Tresloget, and other lands particularly described pertaining to the manor of Tresarrett to hold to the said Nicholas and the heirs of his body for ever, in default of such issue remainder to the heirs of the body of the aforesaid John Heligan, son of Adam Heligan, for ever; and also the aforesaid Nicholas, son and heir of John, son of Adam, granted, confirmed and quit-claimed to the aforesaid John, son and heir of the aforesaid Richard, son and heir of the aforesaid Adam, and the heirs of his body, and also to the heirs of the body of the said Richard, son and heir of the said Adam, according to the form of a certain charter which Nicholas Heligan thereof made to the aforesaid Adam Heligan and Richard his son and heir, and the heirs of the body of the said Richard, all his right and claim which he had, or might have, in the manor of Heligan with its appurtenances, except the aforesaid messuages lands and tenements which the aforesaid John son of Richard granted by this charter to the aforesaid Nicholas son of John, and except the lands in Porthkulyck, with appurtenances, which were under other conditions. And also the aforesaid John, son of Richard, granted and quit-claimed for himself and his heirs to the aforesaid Nicholas, son of John, and the heirs of the body of the said John, son of Adam, all his claim which he had, or might have, in all the messuages lands &c. which the said Nicholas then had in his possession of the manor of Tregrilla and in the glebe of the church of Mahynyet.[1]

This arrangement clearly leaves the manor of Heligan in the possession of John son and heir of Richard in 1401, from whom it descended to his son Sir Andrew de Helligan, who left an only daughter and sole heir, Jane, who married Thomas Lucombe of Bodmin, to whom she carried the manors of Helligan, Trehudreth, Cabilia, and Lancarf, and other lands, of which Thomas Lucombe died seized (temp. Edward IV) leaving two daughters and coheirs, of whom Mary married William Vaughan, and died s.p., and Johanna became the wife of Richard Flamank of Boscarne, by whom she had three sons, Thomas, John, and Bartholomew.[2] Thomas married Elizabeth daughter of John Trelawny of Menwynek by Blanche daughter and coheir of John Powna of Brightorre. The Heligan estates were so settled upon Thomas Flamank and his issue as not to be affected by his attainder, but were carried by Johanna his daughter and heir in marriage to Peter Fauntleroy, whose daughter and heir carried them in marriage to Robert Hill. In 38th Henry VIII (1546) Robert Hill, described as of Heligan, and Margaret his wife were complainants in a case in Chancery against Gilbert Flamank, concerning, *inter alia*, the manor of Heligan, when the said Margaret was found to be the heir, not only of Peter Fauntleroy and Johanna his wife, but also of Richard Flamank and Johanna his wife, father and mother of Thomas Flamank, grandfather of the said Margaret, and it was decreed that the said Robert Hill and Margaret his wife should quietly enjoy the said manors and lands,[3] and that all evidences, deeds, and rolls, &c., should be delivered up to them. In 1566 Robert Hill and

[1] Charter at St. Benet's Priory, Lanivet.

[2] In 1509, a fine was levied, in which Thomas Tregian was querist, and William Vaughan and Mary his wife, one of the daughters and heirs of Thomas Lucombe, and Peter Fauntleroy and Johanna his wife, daughter and heir of Thomas Flamank, son and heir of Johanna the other daughter and heir of the aforesaid Thomas Lucombe, concerning six messuages, &c., in Lancarf, Norton, &c. (Pedes Finium, 1st Henry VIII, Divers Counties, Michaelmas.)

[3] Chancery Decrees, 38th Henry VIII, 1 Div. No. 3, 105. See ante, vol i, p. 44.

Margaret his wife suffered a fine to Humphrey Nichols in the manors of Heligan, Cabilia, and Trehudreth, whereby the said manors were settled upon the said Robert and Margaret for life, with remainder to Humphry Hill, third son of Robert and Margaret, and the heirs of his body, in default remainder to John Hill, second son, for life, remainder to Maurice Hill and his heirs males, in default remainder to the right heirs of the said Robert and Margaret.[1] Humphry Hill and John Hill both died before their father. The latter died in 1575, when, under this settlement, the manor devolved upon his wife Margaret for life, and a complaint was laid in Chancery by Maurice Hill, son and heir of Giles Hill, son and heir of the said Robert and Margaret, that the said Margaret had secretly granted estates for life in the said lands unto John Lavelis and Mary his wife, and Thomas Harrys and Ann his wife.[2]

Humphry Hill, son and heir of Maurice Hill, in 1626 suffered a fine in one messuage, one dovecote, &c., in Heligan to John Peryman, Gent.[3] In 1630 Humphry Hill, suffered a fine in two messuages in Heligan and Trequites to John Lord Mohun, Baron of Okehampton.[4] And in 1636 the same Lord Mohun and Cordelia his wife, Humphry Hill, jun^r., Gent., and Maurice Hill, suffered a fine in the same premises to John Tredinham, Esq.,[5] and in the following year a recovery was levied in which Richard Tristrean, Gent., and William Legeawe were petitioners, and John Tredinham, defendant, of six messuages in Heligan and Trequites, when Humphry Hill was called to warrant.

In 1641, John Tredinham, Gent., and Elizabeth his wife, Humphry Hill, Senior, Esq., and Humphry Hill, Junior, Gent., suffered a fine to Richard Silly, Junior, Gent., in the manor of Helligan, and of eight messuages, two mills, one dovecote, &c., &c., in Helligan, Trequite, Helligan Mills, Frogham, Tresloggett, and Stone,[6] and soon after this date the family of Silly removed hither from Trevelver in St. Minver. The lands continued in this family until 1801, when, by Indentures of lease and release, dated respectively 24th and 25th September in that year, all the said lands, described as that capital messuage, barton, farm, and demesne lands called Helligan, with the coppice woods thereto belonging, and all those mills called Helligan mills, &c., and all that messuage called Talquites, &c., were, in consideration of the sum of £5,550, conveyed by Julia Silly, the last surviving heir of the family, to Edmund John Glynn of Glynn, Esq., who, by Indenture dated 28th April 1818, in consideration of the sum of £10,250, conveyed all the said lands to John Hooper of Penhargard, Gent., to hold to him and his heirs and. assigns for ever.[7] Mr. Hooper died in 1859, and by his will, dated 2nd February, and proved 17th May in that year, devised all his estates to his wife, who is now the possessor, *inter alia*, of the barton of Helligan and the lands above described.

[1] Ped. Fin., 8th and 9th Elizabeth, Michaelmas.
[2] Chancery Proc. Elizabeth, H. h. 17, No. 55.
[3] Ped. Finium., 2nd Charles I, Michaelmas.
[4] Ibid. 6th Charles I, Easter.
[5] Ibid. 12th Charles I, Hilary.
[6] Pedes Finium, 17th Charles, Easter.
[7] Deeds in possession of Mrs. Hooper.

MANOR OF TRESARRET.

The late Rev. John Carne, in his attempt to identify the Domesday Manors of Cornwall, suggested that, possibly, the manor of Tresarrett might be the same as appears in the Survey under the name of Tretwerit. We do not think there is sufficient ground for this conclusion, which, indeed, Mr. Carne, with his usual care, put it very doubtfully. There is, however, an Indenture (exact date not known[1]) made by Alan, Commander of the Brethren of House of Jerusalem in England, by which, with their common consent, he granted to Reynolde son of Nicholas and his heirs five acres of land Cornish in Treserrett, yielding yearly 16d. for all services,[2] which rent, as appears by the annexed rental, was paid to Queen Elizabeth, in respect to the manor of Temple, as late as 1598.

Adam de Heligan, as we have already seen, granted Tresarret and other lands to his son John, who would seem at one time to have resided at Treblethick in St. Mabyn, and by his charter dated at that place on Wednesday next after the feast of St. Martin 3rd Richard II (1379), granted to Nicholas his son, and Elizabeth daughter of Thomas Mayndy, *inter alia*, all his lands in Treceret, Boscoven, Spytal, &c., &c., with common of pasture for all animals in the ville of Helygan, and reasonable estover for "husbote" and "haybote" in the woods of Helygan, &c., to hold to the said Nicholas and Elizabeth and the heirs of their bodies, and in default of such issue remainder to the right heirs of the said John Helygan for ever. Nicholas Helygan, by his charter dated at Trebleythek on Monday next after the feast of St. Thomas the Martyr 19th Richard II (1395) granted to Mr. John Rescourek, parson of St. Maben, Robert Michel, parson of Helland, Thomas Rescarek, and Thomas Mayndy, senior, all his messuages, *inter alia*, in Tregrilla, Tresseret, Tresputel, Boscoûen, &c., &c., with the services of all his free tenants in the county of Cornwall, together with all his men and his chattels moveable and immoveable, to hold for the life of the said Nicholas, rendering to him an annuity of £20 sterling, with reversion after his death to Robert his son and the heirs of his body, in default remainder to Roger, brother of the said Robert and his heirs for ever.[2] Both Robert and Roger[3] would appear to have died s.p., before their father, and the lands devolved upon Joan daughter and heir of the said Nicholas, who carried, *inter alia*, the manor of Tresarret in marriage to John Trelawny second son, and eventually heir of Sir John Trelawny, Knight, in which family it continued until 1654, when Sir John Trelawny, Knight and Bart., suffered a fine therein to John Roe of Trewornan, Esq.,[4] who having taken part with the King in the great rebellion compounded for his estate, but in 1650 he made a further return of particulars, stating that since his last composition and discharge he had absolutely purchased

---

[1] Alan was appointed Prior in 1192, and made Bishop of Bangor in 1195, in which year he died. His case is a solitary exception of the Priors of England being in Holy Orders. His designation as "Commander" is also remarkable at this early period. Those Knights who held Proceptories were generally termed "Proceptores" or "Magistri."

[2] Charters at Trelawne.

[3] Perhaps it was this Roger who was trustee for the manor of Hamatethy before 1422 (See ante, vol. i, p. 356.)

[4] Pedes Finium, 1654. Trinity.

3 T

to himself and his heirs the manor of Tresallet *alias* Tresaret in the parish of St. Mabyn, the yearly value thereof, being rents of assize, are, and were, of the yearly value of £9 1s. 4d.[1] In 1668 however, Sir Jonathan Trelawny, Bart., levied a fine of Thomas Darrell, Esq., and Elizabeth his wife, in this manor and lands,[2] to which Thomas Darrell the Roe estates had descended; and in 1727 Sir John Trelawny, Bart., Edward Trelawny, Esq., and Hele Trelawny, Clerk, suffered a fine therein to John Treise of Lavethan, Esq.[3] From John Treise the manor descended, with the other Treise estates, to Sir John Morshead, Bart., upon the sale of whose lands this manor, *inter alia*, was purchased by the late Mr. Wallis of Bodmin, by whom it was sold in 1840 to James Hayward of Loudwater House, co. Herts, Esq., the present owner.

TRESERRET—A rental of the manor aforesaid, made the 7th day of February, in the one and fortieth year of the reign of our most gracious Sovereign Queen Elizabeth, 1598.

Free Tenants.

Treslogett	Mawris Hill Esqre. holdeth there one acre of land Cornish in Knight's service, doth suit at two law courts by the year and yieldeth by the year	2s. 6d. and for work days yearly 8d.
Porthkulyock	The same Mawris holdeth certain lands in special tail in Porthkulyock and Porthkulyocke Mill in Knights' service and yieldeth at two terms of the year equally	£0 6s. 10d.
Penvose	The heirs of Roger Trewynycke holdeth one acre of land Cornish in tail general in Penvose in Elerky parish and yieldeth yearly at the feast of Easter	3 capons

Sum of the free rents yearly   ...   ...   £0 10s. & 3 capons

Customary Tenants.

Overspyttle	William Rowe holdeth there one tenement doth common suit to the Courts and yieldeth yearly at the four terms of the year by equal portions	£0 10s. 0d. 8 acres & half.
	Agnes Cavell holdeth there one other tenement doth suit as as before, and yieldeth as before yearly	£0 10s. 0d. 5 acres & half
Netherspytle	Nicholas Philp holdeth there one tenement containing 11 acres and a half doth suit as before and yieldeth yearly	£1 0s. 0d.
Coldrenycke	Robert Powle holdeth there one tenement containing 19 acres and half doth suit as before and yieldeth by the year	£0 13s. 4d. 2 capons
	David Kestle holdeth there one tenement containing 24 acres and three quarters of land doth suit as before and yieldeth by the year	£0 13s. 4d. 2 capons

[1] Royalist Comp. Papers. 2nd Series, vol. xxxiv, fo. 819.   [2] Pedes Finium, 20th Charles II. Trinity.
[3] Pedes Finium, 1st George II. Mich.

Bocoven	Humfry Sloggett holdeth there one tenement containing 50 acres of land doth suit as before and yieldeth yearly	£3 13s. 8d.
Treslogett	Lawrence Holman holdeth there one tenement and a half containing 32 acres of land doth suit as before and yieldeth by the year	£1 5s. 6d. 3 capons
Trethanycke	Walter Curling holdeth there one tenement containing 17 acres of land Doth suit as before and yieldeth yearly	£0 18s. 0d. 1 capon
Treserrett	John Tom holdeth there the capital house and the Barton con⁸ 47 acres Doth suit as before and yieldeth yearly	£2 6s. 0d.
Helligan Down 42 Acres	John Sharrocke holdeth there three parts in eight being divided of the said Down Doth suit as before and yieldeth yearly	£0 14s. 0d.
	Humphry Sloggett holdeth there two parts in eight being divided of the said Down Doth suit and yieldeth yearly	£0 9s. 4d.
	John Teague holdeth two parts in eight divided of the said Down Doth suit as before and yieldeth yearly	£0 9s. 4d.
	Johan Tom holdeth there one-eighth part of the said Down Doth suit as before and yieldeth by the year	£0 4s. 0d.
Treserrett Woods 27 acr.	One wood there called the South Wood containing 16 acres, one other wood called the North Wood containing six acres & quarter the Down Copse containing four acres & half all in the Lords' hand	£0 10s. 0d.

Sum of the Customary Rents by the year	£13 17s. 2d. 8 Capons
Sum as well of Free as Customary Rents yearly	£14 7s. 2d. & 11 Capons

Whereof

Reprises	To our Sovereign Lady the Queen's Majesty as to her Manor of Temple for high Rent out of Treserrett Bocoven Treslogett Porthkulyocke and Spyttle yearly	£0 1s. 4d.
	To our said Sovereign Lady as to her Hignesses Manor of Pendevy for high Rent out of Trethanycke by the year, with 6d for Suit at Courts	£0 7s. 6d.
	To John Trevillyan Esq. as to his Manor of Lancarfe for high Rent out of Coldrynnick by the year	£0 1s. 0d.
	Summa	£0 9s. 10d.
	And yet remaineth clearly by the year, over and above all Reprises	£13 6s. 8d. & 11 capons

3 T²

TREGARNE, *alias* TREGAREN, *alias* TREGARDEN.

This place, at a remote period, was a seat of the family of Bere. William le Bere would seem to have been of Tregaren in 1302, when he was defendant in a suit brought at the assizes at Launceston, concerning an acre of land in Nancedeny juxta Tregaran (See ante, vol. i, p. 556), whilst William Bere of Tregaren and Richard his brother, probably sons of the above William, in 1347 were defendants in a suit at the instance of John, Vicar of St. Neot.[1] In 1365 William Bere of Tregaren was witness to a deed of Reginald de Heligan. In 1385 John Bere of Tregaren was plaintiff in a case versus Stephen Bodulgate and Johanna his wife.[2] In the following year Johanna Bere of Tregaren sued John Bodulgate and Johanna his wife in a plea of waste.[3] In 1390 John Bere of Tregaren sued John Wilcok for trespass on his turbary at St. Neot.[4] Four years afterwards John Bere of Tregaren sued the Prior of Bodmin for detention of his animals.[5] In 1398 we find John Bere sueing Stephen Bodulgate for the recovery of a pix, containing charters and other muniments.[6] In 1431 John Oppy and Claricia his wife suffered a fine in seven messuages in St. Maugan, &c., to Walter Kene, Chaplain, in which they quit-claimed the said lands to the said Walter to hold to the use of the said Claricia for her life, remainder of a portion to James Meyndy and the heirs of his body; as regards another portion, remainder to the aforesaid John for life, remainder to the aforesaid James and the heirs of his body, in default remainder of a moiety to John Bere, junior, son of John Bere, senior, of Tregaren, and the heirs of his body, in default remainder to the heirs of the body of Alice relict of John Bere, senior, in default remainder to Thomas Penles and Johanna his wife and the heirs of their bodies, in default remainder to the right heirs of the said Claricia; as regards the other moiety, remainder after the death of John Oppy to Thomas Penles and Johanna his wife and the heirs of their bodies, in default remainder to John Bere, junior, and the heirs of his body, in default remainder to the heirs of the body of the aforesaid Alice, in default remainder to the right heirs of the aforesaid Claricia as before.[7] John Bere, described as of Tregarne, was one of the witnesses to a Charter dated at Alternon 20th Henry VI[8] (1422). It seems more than probable that Thomasine Bere, who became the wife of Nicholas Barrett, was the daughter and coheir of this John Bere. We find their son, John Barrett, described as of Tregarne, Franklyn, in 1474.[9] His great grandson, of the same name, by Joan daughter of Hugh Boscawen and relict of John Gaverigan of Gaverigan, had three sons and a daughter. Richard, his

[1] Assize Rolls, Cornw. 21st Edward III, $\frac{N}{2}$ $\left.\begin{array}{}\\23\end{array}\right\}$ 3 m. 2 d.

[2] De Banco. Roll, 9th Richard II, Michs. m. 384. A John Bere was Escheator in 10th Richard II.

[3] Ibid. Trinity, m. 309.   [4] Ibid. 13th Richard II, Hil. m. 166 d.

[5] Ibid. 17th Richard II, Hil. m. 377 d.   [6] Ibid. 22nd Richard II, Hil. m. 172 d.

[7] Ped. Finium, 10th Henry VI, Michs.   [8] Original penes, the Right Rev. Bishop Kestell-Cornish.

[9] De Banco Rolls, 14th Edward IV, Hilary m. 451.

eldest son, succeeded him at Tregaren; Nicholas would seem to have died s.p.; and John was the founder of the family of Barrett of St. Tudy, who, being the representative of the family, in the male line, at the time of the Heralds' Visitation of the County in 1620, registered the pedigree. Of that branch we propose to treat hereafter under St. TUDY.

Richard Barrett married Grace daughter of Arthur Fowell of Fowelscombe, co. Devon, who afterwards re-married Richard, subsequently, Sir Richard Carnsewe (*vide* Pedigree of CARNSEWE, ante p. 173), and dying in 1611, left two daughters and co-heirs, of whom Mary, the elder, married Richard, afterwards Sir Richard, Prideaux of Theuborough in the parish of Sutcombe (*vide* Pedigree of PRIDEAUX, ante pp. 204, 224), to whom she carried a moiety of the barton of Tregaren or Tregarden, the other moiety being carried to Sir William Godolphin in marriage by Grace the second daughter and co-heir of the said Richard Barrett, who, however, died a few years after her marriage, s.p.

Richard Prideaux made Tregarden his chief residence for several years after his marriage. He had several children baptized at St. Maben between 1635 and 1644, and he would seem to have been resident at Tregarden in 1645, when he received a protection from Fairfax for his person and property both at Tregarden and Theuborough.[1] Having received the honour of knighthood he died in 1667, leaving two surviving sons. Richard, the elder, died three years later, s.p., and the estates devolved upon his brother Jonathan, who had a son Richard, who died a minor and unmarried in 1702, and eight daughters. In the following year, Jonathan Prideaux and Ann his wife, Digory Slade, Clerk, and Anna Maria his wife, Frances Prideaux, Spinster, Thomas Pollard, Gent., and Sarah his wife, and Mary Prideaux, four of the surviving daughters[2] and co-heirs, presumptive of the said Jonathan, suffered a fine in Tregarden, Tregellen, and other lands in St. Mabyn, Egloshayle, and St. Kew, to Edward Hoblyn, Gent.[3] of Croane, in Egloshayle, from whom it descended, in like manner as Croane, to John Tremayne of Helligan, Esq., the present possessor of this moiety.

As to the other moiety: Sir William Godolphin, by his will dated 15th October 1663,[4] after reciting that he was seized of certain lands of the ancient inheritance of Richard Barrett, *inter alia*, of a moiety of the manor of St. Niott Barrett, and a moiety of the Barton of Tregarden, now, it is added, divided from the other moiety, and of one field called New Park, and of one house called the Oxenhouse, and of the pear garden behind the same, and of the dwelling houses and gardens in Tregarden as now divided, devises

---

[1] Theis are to require on sight heerof to forbeare to prejudice Sir Richard Prideaux of Tregard, in the Countie of Cornwall, or his living at Thuborough in the Countie of Devon, either by plundering his house, or taking away his horses, sheepe, or other cattell, or goods, whatsoever, or by offering any violence to his person, or the persons of any of his familie, as you will answer the contrarie, provided hee bee obedient to all orders and ordinances of Parliament. Given under my hand and seale att Truro, this 16th day of March 1645.

FAIRFAX.

To all Officers and Soldiers under my command. (Royalist Comp. Papers, vol. xxxix, p. 391.)

[2] There was another and younger daughter named Ann, who being at the time a minor, was no party to the fine. She was living in 1710, and is named in her father's will, but was dead, unmarried, in 1716. Frances married Charles Davie of Bideford, and Mary became the wife of Vaughan Kestell, Clerk, second son of James Kestell of Kestell in Egloshayle by Elizabeth daughter of John Vaughan of Ottery St. Mary, co. Devon.

[3] Pedes Finium, 2nd Anne, Trinity.   [4] Proved Archd. Cornw., 23rd December 1663.

the said lands and tenements of Tregarden to his third son, John Godolphin and the heirs of his body, in default remainder to his daughter Ruth Greatrex and the heirs of her body, and, in default of such issue to his own right heirs.

John Godolphin, who attained the degree of knighthood, having died in 1679, s.p.m., and his only daughter, Elizabeth having died a few years afterwards unmarried, his estates devolved upon his nephew Francis Godolphin of Coulston, co. Wilts (see Pedigree of GODOLPHIN post). And William Godolphin of Coulston, by Indentures of lease and release, dated, respectively, 4th and 5th August 1738, conveyed all his divided moiety of Tregarden to John Mitchell of St. Mabyn, Gent., to hold to the said John Mitchell and his heirs for ever of the chief Lords of the Fee at the services due and accustomed. John Mitchell died intestate, and the land devolved upon John Mitchell his eldest son and heir at law, who, at his death, by his will dated 9th June 1793, devised his lands to his nephew Henry Mitchell of Padstow, Tanner, who, in conjunction with certain mortgagees, by Indentures of lease and release, dated, respectively, 10th and 11th August 1794, in consideration of the sum of £2,810 10s. paid as therein prescribed, granted, &c., the said moiety to Christopher Andrew of St. Mabyn, Esq., to hold to him and his heirs for ever; and it is now possessed by his grandson Mr. James Andrew of Tregarden.

The old mansion house, which is of the date of the 16th century, still remains. It consisted of a central part, containing the hall, and two wings, and is approached through a quadrangular enclosure having a handsome gate. Like the estate it was divided, and is now converted into a farm house. In the hall is a large achievement of arms: Barrett quartering Bere and eight other coats; which is flanked by two other shields, one charged with Barrett and Bere quarterly, and the other with Barrett impaling a bull, a stag, or a goat;[1] on a chief a roundel; the same coat occupying the last quarter of the large achievement. All these coats, except the last, are quartered on a handsome escutcheon, carved in wood, which was formerly over the fire place in the parlour, but when we inspected the house, a few years ago, we found it lying broken in an outhouse, where it still remains. In lieu of the omitted coat, abovementioned, upon this shield appear two other coats: viz., a single roundel; and the arms of Fowell of Fowelscombe: ar. a chev. sa., upon a chief gu. three mullets of the first—shewing this escutcheon to have been set up subsequent to the marriage of Richard Barrett and Grace Fowell about 1609. It is clear that the quarterings on these shields do not commemorate heiresses, but simply *alliances*. Several of them, probably, relate to the family of Bere. In consequence of the escutcheon having been re-painted without heraldic skill it is difficult to identify several of the coats from the want of an accurate knowledge of the tinctures. (See Engraving annexed.)

---

[1] The shields being much defaced, it is difficult to say, with certainty, which of these animals is represented, and from the position of the line dividing the shield, it is uncertain whether it was meant to divide the sinister side of the shield, fesswise, into two coats, representing two marriages, or whether the roundel is borne on a chief. As the roundel forms a distinct coat in the achievement from the parlour, it is possible the former was intended. It should be also observed that in the fifth quarter of the achievement in the hall, the pears have their stems upwards instead of downwards as in the other shield.

ACHIEVEMENT OF ARMS FROM THE PARLOUR AT TREGARDEN.

1. Barrett, ar. a chev. betw. 3 bears passant sa.
2. Bere, ar. a bear ramp. muzzled or.
3. ? a chev. gu. betw. 3 eagles' gambs sa. is quartered by Coryton.
4. ?
5. Calmady ? az a chev. betw. 3 pears slipped or.
6. ?
7. ?
8. Flamank, ar. a cross betw. four mullets gu.
9. Winslade, three falcons volant.
10. ?
11. Fowell, ar. a chev. sa. upon a chief gu. three mullets ar.

TREBLETHICK.

Treblethick, in the latter part of the 14th century, was one of the seats of the younger branch of the family of Heligan,[1] after which it became, and long continued, a seat of the family of Hamley. Osbert Hamley was resident here as early as the reign of Edward IV, and the family continued to reside here until towards the end of the last century, though, in 1721, John Hamley, Gent, and Elizabeth his wife, daughter and coheir of Henry Bond of Tresunger (see ante, vol. i, p. 570) suffered a fine to John Treise, Esq., of one messuage, &c., in Treblethick.[2] John Treise, however, thereupon granted to John Hamley a lease of the said estates during the term of his life. He also, by deed dated 24th March 1732, agreed with the said John Hamley that, for certain considerations, he should receive to his own use the rent due on the lease of that part of the capital messuage and demesne lands of Treblethick called Longstone, where one Nicholas Menheniot then lived, consisting of a dwelling house and smith's shop, and should at any time have power to change and alter the lives thereon. And the said John Hamley, by deed dated 12th January 1776, from the natural love which he bore towards his son Richard Hamley of Bodmin, Gent., granted to him a lease of the said premises for the term of 99 years determinable upon the deaths of the said Richard Hamley, then aged 39 years, William Hamley, another son of the said John Hamley, aged 29 years, and William Wood son of William Wood then late of Callington. By deed dated 30th April 1777, Sir Christopher Treise of Lavethan, Knight, in consideration of the sum of £1,050, granted a lease thereof, excepting the tenement above referred to held by John Hamley, Gent., to Joseph Edyvean of Bodmin, Merchant, for a term of 99 years from the date of the death of the said John Hamley, determinable upon the deaths of Joane Edyvean, aged 12 years, and Lydia Edyvean, aged 10 years, daughters of the said Joseph Edyvean. This estate, like other of the Treise lands, devolved upon Sir John Morshead, Bart., upon the sale of whose possessions the reversion, after the expiration of the leases referred to, was purchased by Abraham Hambly of Treore, in Endellion, Gent., to whom, by deed dated 1st August 1811, Thomas Commins of Bodmin, Gent., and Lydia his wife, one of the daughters and executrix of the will of Joseph Edyvean, deceased, in consideration of the sum of £3,800, conveyed the estate they had in the said capital messuage, &c., of Treblethick, for the remainder of the aforesaid term. Moreover, by Indenture, dated 23rd September 1811, Richard Hamley of St. Columb, Gent., reciting the Indenture above recited of the 29th January 1776, conveyed to the said Abraham Hambly the tenement held by him for the residue of the term which he had therein. Abraham Hambly, being thus in possession of the whole estate, in fee, by his will, dated 9th October 1827, and proved 16th January following, devised the same to his younger son of the same name, who, upon entering into possession, pulled down the old house of the Hamleys, which had fallen into decay, and built thereon an excellent

---

[1] See post, p. 513.　　　　　　　[2] Pedes Finium, 8th George I, Michs.

farm house, and there he resided for some years; but by deed, dated 29th September 1859, conveyed the estate to Richard Hambly Andrew of Tredinnick, Esq., the present possessor.

TREDETHY.

The present estate of Tredethy consists of several tenements acquired at various times by William Lugger of St. Mabyn, Gent., who died in 1639. His grandson, of the same name, by Deborah his wife, daughter of .... Squire, left three surviving daughters and co-heirs, Margaret wife of William son of Thomas May of Bodmin, Mercer, Deborah wife of William Randall of Great Torrington, and Elizabeth wife of Robert Venn of South-molton, Maltster. The two latter died s.p. By indentures of lease and release, dated respectively, 6th and 7th July 1727, Deborah Randall, described as of St. Mabyn, widow, conveyed to William May, described as of Bodmin, Mercer, all those messuages called Tredethy, and certain fields some time parcel of the barton of Colquite.[1] William May had a son of his own name, and three daughters, of whom Margaret, the youngest, married to her second husband Elias Lang of Plymouth, who left two children: Elias, who succeeded his father in Tredethy, and Margaret who became the wife of Francis John Hext of Bodmin. Elias Lang the younger died at Tredethy, s.p., in 1792, and by his will devised Tredethy to his nephew Francis John Hext, who resided at Tredethy until his death in 1842 s.p., when Tredethy devolved upon his next brother Capt. William Hext, R.N., then of Lancarfe, afterwards Rear-Admiral, who, dying in 1866, was succeeded by his eldest son, Francis John Hext, late of the 83rd Regiment, who has recently enlarged the house, and gives great attention to the improvement of the property. (See Ped. of HEXT, post.)

TREDINNICK.

This place formerly consisted of several tenements, but the chief house has, at various times, formed the residence of families of gentility. Nicholas Vivian of Tredinnick was buried in 1628, as was Humphry Vivian, Gent., in 1634. Later in the century it was for some time the residence of the Parker family. William Parker of Tredinnick, Esq., was buried in 1688. By his will, before cited, (ante, p. 471) he devised Tredinnick to his two sons, William Parker and Robert Parker. Robert died on 20th March 1716, in the life time of his brother, s.p., and intestate, when the land devolved upon William, who soon afterwards, also, died intestate and s.p. It afterwards formed part of the possessions of Philip Rashleigh of Menabilly, Esq., from whom it was purchased, by deed dated 29th September 1775, by Christopher Andrew of St. Tudy, who, about the same time, acquired Tregarden and other extensive bartons and farms in this parish. He combined all the tenements in Tredinnick into one large farm, and fixed his residence there. He died in 1810, at a very advanced age, but before his death he settled Tredinnick and other lands

[1] Deed penes F. J. Hext, Esq.

3 U

upon his eldest son, Richard Hambly Andrew; and Tregarden upon his second son, John May Andrew. Richard Hambly Andrew improved the property by planting and extension of the gardens. On his death, in 1851, he devised his real estate to his great nephew, Richard Hambly Andrew, Barrister-at-Law, eldest son of Christopher Thomas Andrew, eldest son of John May Andrew abovementioned, who has extended the improvements of his predecessor, and is the present owner of Tredinnick and other lands in this parish, including the greater part of the Church Town.

TREQUITES.

This farm is a portion of the manor of Heligan. Lysons mentions this place as sometime a seat of the Parkers.[1] It appears from certain proceedings in Chancery in 1718, that Joseph Silly, then late of Heligan, Esq., deceased, purchased of William Parker, then late of St. Mabyn, Esq., deceased, certain lands for a sum of £1,700, whereof he paid £200 only, and for securing the further payment of £1500 by indenture dated 23rd November 20th Charles II. (1668) did grant the barton of Trequites to the said William Parker, for the term of 2000 years, by way of mortgage, which mortgage, by deed poll, the said William Parker assigned to Sir John Molesworth. William Parker, by his will dated 15th July 1688, devised all his estate, goods and chattels unto Sir John Molesworth and others in trust for certain uses therein defined, and appointed such trustees executors of his will, and his daughter Elizabeth Opie residuary legatee. William Parker soon afterwards died, and the said executors having renounced, administration with will annexed was granted, on 10th September 1688, to William Parker son of deceased, to whom Sir John Molesworth did re-convey the said mortgage. The said Joseph Silly being dead, and a sum of upwards of £2,000 for principal and interest being due, which was more than the value of the said mortgaged premises, William Parker applied for and obtained in the Court of Chancery a decree of foreclosure. William Parker and Robert his brother having died s.p., the fee of this estate devolved upon Elizabeth Opie, as residuary legatee under her father's will, who, by deed dated 27th June 1717, conveyed it to her son John Opie of Egloshayle.[2]

The manner in which this estate passed from the Parkers to Mr. Henry Hooper we have already detailed in our account of the Parker charity (ante pp. 471, 472). From Mr. Henry Hooper it devolved upon his son and heir, Mr. John Hooper, and it is now the property and residence of his widow.

TREGADDOCK.

There were two messuages in Tregaddock, one of which was formerly held by the family of Toker, and the other by that of Tamlyn.

In 1622 Nicholas Martyn and Grace his wife suffered a fine in one messuage, &c.,

---

[1] For an account of the PARKER Family, ante vol. i, p. 67
[2] For Pedigree of OPIE of Egloshayle, see ante p. 53

in Tregaddock, in St. Mabyn, to Stephen Toker of Helland, Gent.,[1] from whom it passed to his son and heir Christopher Toker, who, with Honour his wife, in 1640, suffered a fine therein, *inter alia*, to Stephen Toker his son and heir.[2] From him it passed to his grand nephew John Toker, who, as John Toker, junior, Gent., was buried at St. Maben in 1688. He left an only daughter, aged three years, and by his will gave to her certain articles in his house at Tregaddock, to be delivered up after the deaths of John Toker his father and Elizabeth Toker his mother, to whom he entrusted the education and government of his daughter. John Toker the father died in 1698, and as "Mr. John Toker of Tregaddock" was buried at St. Maben, the property now passed to Stephen Toker, second son of the last named John Toker, who, in 1706, suffered a fine in Tregadock *alias* Tregathick, in St. Mabyn, to William Hamley, Gent.[3]

Another messuage at Tregaddock was the residence of the Tamlyn family. It was parcel of the manor of Trevisquite, and how long it had been occupied by the Tamlyns we know not, but the fee simple was sold by Richard Loveys, Lord of the manor, in 1659, to Richard Tamlyn (see ped. TAMLYN post.)

Tregaddock is now divided into several tenements, which we are unable to identify with those above mentioned.

TOSTONE *alias* STONE.

This messuage was formerly parcel of the manor of Heligan, and appears in old terriers and descriptions of the manor under the above names. In the beginning of the present century it belonged to Mr. Thomas Harry, by whom it was sold to Mr. John Martyn Bligh, an attorney at Bodmin, who built thereon a genteel cottage, which he made his residence for some time. It was purchased a few years ago of the representatives of Mr. Bligh by Mr. Pollard, who is now the owner.

PENWYNE.

Hals says of this place that it was "the dwelling of ... Porter, Gent., that married Spry, and giveth for his arms in a field Sa. three bells ar. and a canton erm. This place is now sold to Cole." In 1716 Arthur Porter and Elizabeth his wife suffered a fine to John Cole, Gent., of two messuages, &c., in Penwyne.[4] In 1812 Mr. Ralph Cole was tenant for life, with remainder to his son Francis Cole, Clerk, by whom it was sold to Nankivell, and is now by bequest, vested in trustees to the use of Thomas James Nankivell Harris, son of Mr. William Harris of St. Maben, and a minor.

[1] Pedes Finium, 20th James, Michs.
[3] Ibid. 5th Anne, Michs.
[2] Ibid. 16th Charles, Easter.
[4] Ibid. 2nd George I, Trinity.

3 U²

FAMILY

TABLE SHEWING THE DESCENT OF THE MANOR OF TREVISQUITE,

Warine de L'isle, son of Robert, son of Alice, dau. of Henry =Alice, sister and heir of
younger son of Henry Fitz Gerald, ob. 1st Edward III.   Henry Baron le Teyes.

Gerald de L'isle, summoned to Parl. 31st Edw. III.,=....
ob. 34th Edward III.

Warine de L'isle, Lord of Kingston L'isle, co. Berks, summoned to=Margaret, dau. of Sir William Pipard, died 3rd Aug. 1375.
Parl. 43rd Edward III. to 5th Rich. II. ob. 1383.   Inq. p.m. 49th Edward III. Part 1, No. 73.

Gerard, son and heir, aged 15 years on   Thomas de Berkeley, =Margaret, dau. and heir.
his mother's death. Died v.p. s.p.   12th Lord Berkeley.

Richard Beauchamp, 14th Earl of Warwick; creat. Earl of Albemarle,=Elizabeth, dau. and heir
K.G. ob. 1439; Inq. p.m. 17th Henry VI., No. 54.   of her mother.

John Talbot, 1st Earl of Shrewsbury,Wexford=Margaret, dau. and   THOMAS CHEDDAR, died 3rd June=ISABELLA, Junr. youngest
Waterford and Valence, slain at Chatillon   heir of her mother,   1443, Inq. p.m. 21st Henry VI.,   dau. and coh. aged 18 in
1453.   2nd wife.   No. 55.   1413.

JOHN TALBOT, cr. Baron=JOAN, dau. and coh.   SIR JOHN=ISABELLA, dau. and coh. aged   JOHN SPEOOTE,=Johanna.
L'isle 1443, and Vis-   aged 18 years in 1443,   NEWTON.   14 years 1443; died 14th May   Presented to St.
count L'isle 1452, slain   relict of Robert   1498, Inq. p.m. 14th Henry   Maben 1457.
at Chatillon 1453.   Stafford.   VII. No. 133.

THOMAS,   SIR EDWARD=ELIZABETH,   Sir =Marga-   Sir William Capel,=Margaret,   RICHARD NEWTON=Elizab. died
2nd Visct.   GREY, created   sister and   George ret, sister   Lord Mayor of   dau. of Sir   aged 30 years   17th June
L'isle, ob.   Baron L'isle &   heir.   Vere. and heir.   London, ob. 6th   John Arun-   1498; Died 26th   1524, Inq.
1469, s.p.   Viscount L'isle   Sept. 1515, Inq.   del of Lan-   Sept. 1500, Inq.   p.m. 16th
   1483, ob. 1491.   p.m. 7th Henry   herne.   p.m. 16th Henry   Hy. VIII,
     VIII, No. 43.   VII, No. 32.   No. 147.

JOHN =Muriel,   ANN, aged   ELIZABETH,aged   Muriel, mar. 1st   SIR GILES CAPEL, aged=ISABEL,   JANE, aged
GREY,   dau. of   27 in 1504,   20 in 1504, mar.   Edward Stafford   30 years 1515, of   dau. and   5 years
2nd Vis-   Thomas   mar. JOHN   SIR EDM. DUD-   Earl of Wilts,   Rumsford, co. Essex,   coh. aged   1500, mar.
count   Duke of   WILLOUGH-   LEY, KT., 2ndly   and 2nd his cousin   Sheriff of Essex 1529;   13 years   SIRTHOMAS
L'isle,   Norfolk.   BY   Arthur Planta-   Henry Stafford   Died 29th May 1556.   in 1500.   GRIFFITH.
ob.1504.   genet.   Earl of Wiltshire,   Inq. p.m. 3rd & 4th P.
     ob. s.p.   & M. Part 1, No. 110.

Elizabeth, =HENRY =Gertrude   Sir John   Henry Capel,=Ann, dau.   SIR EDWARD CAPEL,=Ann, dau. of
ob. s.p.   COURTENEY   dau. of   Dudley.   aged 19 years,   of Sir   Knt., Sheriff of Herts   Sir William
   Marquis of   William   in1524.ob.s.p.   George   and Essex 1566; died   Pelham of
   Exeter;   Blunt Lord   Manners   19th March 1576-7,   Laughton,
   attainted   Mountjoy.   Lord Roos.   Inq. p.m. 19th Eliz.   co. Sussex.
   1538.   Part 2, No. 72.

EDWARD COURTENEY, restored   Mary, dau. of Sir Anthony Browne,=HENRY CAPEL, died=Catherine, dau. of
in blood and cr. Earl of   relict of John Lord Grey, 2nd wife.   22nd June 1588. Inq.   Thomas Manners .
Devon 1553, ob. 4th October   Died 4th Feb. 1616-7, Inq. p.m. of   p.m. 30th Eliz. Part   Earl of Rutland.
1556 s.p.   Sir Henry Capel, 20th James.   1, No. 96.

SIR ARTHUR CAPEL, KNT.1603,aged 30 years in 1588 Knt.1603 ; Sheriff of Herts=Margaret, dau. of Lord John
1592. Will dated 4th Mar. 1631, prov. 3rd May 1632 (Awdley 60) Died 9th   Grey of Pirgo. Died 12th
April 1632 ; Inq. p.m. Wards and Liveries 8th Charles, Bundle 52, No. 220.   Aug. 2nd James (1604.)

Dorothy, dau. of John Aldersey and relict of=SIR HENRY CAPEL, ob. v.p. 29th April=Theodosia, sister of Edward Lord Montague of
Sir Thos. Hoskins ; mar. settl. dated 20th   1622, Inq. p.m. Wards and Liveries, 19th   Boughton ; mar. settl. 2nd May, 42nd Eliz.
Jan. 14th James (1616-7).   and 20th James, Bundle 35, No. 208.   (1600.) Died 16th Jan. 13th James(1615-6.)

ARTHUR CAPEL, born 19th Feb. 1604-5, aged 18 years on the=ELIZABETH, dau. and sole heir of Sir Charles Morrison
death of his grandfather. Created Baron Capel of Hadham   of Cashiobury, co. Herts, Knt. and Bart., mar. settl.
6th Aug. 1641. Beh. 9th Mar. 1648-9.   dated 5th Nov. 1627.

ARTHUR LORD CAPEL, created Viscount Malden and Earl of Essex 20th
April 1661. *Sold interest in Manor of Trevisquite 1659.*

ISTORY.

ND THE ADVOWSON OF THE RECTORY OF ST. MABEN.

N.B.—The names of those who held the Manor, or the Advowson, are printed in small capitals.

Sir Thomas Scrobhull══Edith, dau. of Sir Roger Prideaux of Orchardon, vide Ped. of PRIDEAUX ante p. 221.

Robert Scrobhull of Scrobhull,══Elinor. co. Devon.

NICHOLAS SPECOTE,══ISABELLA, Senr. of Specote, co. Devon. dau. and coh. aged 34 1413.

WILLIAM HOLBEME══JOHANNA, of Holbeme, co. eld. dau. Devon. and coh.

Robert Kyrkham, died 3rd══ELIZABETH, dau. and Jan. 1443, Inq. p.m. 22nd coh. mar. 1st Wm. Henry VI. No. 12. Trebell.

OHN HOLBEME of Holbeme,══Elizabeth, dau. ged 14 1413, born 30th Nov. and coh. of John 407, Died 20th April 1472, Inq. Gambon of More-.m. 12th Edward IV, No. 23. ston, Devon.

ROBERT KYRKHAM, son and heir, aged 11 years on his father's death. Died 21st Dec. 1451, Inq. p.m. 33rd Henry VI. No. 33.

NICHOLAS KYRKHAM, of Blacka-══Jane, da. & don, heir of his bro., born 4th Mar. h. of Rob. 1433-4. Died 15th Mar. 1515-6, Weye of Inq. p.m. 8th Hen. VIII, No. 121. Marsh, Devon.

NICHOLAS NEWTON, ob. s.p.

JOHN SPECOTE.

══Anne, dau. and coh. of John Boys of Buriton.

JOHN HOLBEME of Hol-══Elizabeth, beme, æt. 30 years in 1472; dau. of Sir Died 31st Jany. 1493-4, Inq. John Pese-p.m. 10th Henry VII, No. mersh, co. 13. Presented to St. Maben, Stafford. 1477.

SIR JOHN KYRKHAM,══Lucy, dau. aged 44 years on his of Sir John father's death; died Tremayle, 11th July 1529. Inq. 3rd wife. p.m. 21st Henry VIII, No. 78.

NICHOLAS SPECOTE══Anne, dau. died 20th Aug. of William 1517; Inq. p.m. Stretchley 10th Henry VIII, of No. 26. Granted Stretchley. next Presentation of St. Maben 1515.

JOHN HOLBEME of══Margaret Holbeme; aged dau. of Sir 24 years in 1494. William Died 26th July Fowell of 1526. Inq. p.m. Fowelscombe 18th Henry VIII, No. 122.

Cecilia dau. of Sir Wm. Carew of Mohun's Ottery 2nd w.

══THOMAS KYRKHAM,══Mary, dau. and aged 25 years in coh. of Nicholas 1529. Died 31st Jan. Ferrers by Jane 1551-2. Inq. p.m. dau. of Sir John 6th Edward VI, Malherbe. No. 18.

EDMUND SPECOTE,══Jane, aged 18 in 1517; dau. died 24th April of 1557. Inq.p.m. 4th ...... and 5th P. and M. No. 11.

JOHN HOLBEME, of Hol-══Mary, dau. beme, son and heir, aged of Gilbert 30 years 1526; died 18th St. Cleer of Nov. 1566. Inq. p.m. 9th Budley, co. Eliz. No. 201. Sold interest Devon, ob. in Trevisquite 1565 s.p.

Elizabeth, mar. John Marwood, and 2ndly Robert Pollard of Honyton, aged 74 years in 1566, heir of her brother.

John, ob. s.p.

GEORGE KYRKHAM══Margaret, aged 27 years in dau. of Sir 1552. Sold interest Thomas in Trevisquite 1565. Denys.

HUMPHRY SPECOTE, aged 25 years 1557.══Elizabeth, dau. of Sold interest in Trevisquite 1565. John Walter.

Elizabeth, daughter and sole heir.

CERIZEAUX, *alias* SERGEAUX.

We find this family mentioned in the Records in the beginning of the reign of King Edward II. In 1283 William de Ceryseux was defendant in a suit of novel disseizin against Lawrence Denysel and Dionis his wife, concerning a tenement in Trewalwat; and at the same assize Claricia, relict of John Merghon of Kestell, sued Richard de Ceriseaus for the third part of half an acre of land, Cornish, as dower, in Tremynek, which Richard compounded for the dower and had seizin of the land.[1] This was, probably, the same Richard who held of Oliver Dinham on his death in 1299 one and a-half Knights' fees in Kylcoyt.[2] He was a juror at the assize at Launceston in 1302, and dying in 1307 seized five and a-half Knights' fees in the manors of Kilcoit and Launceston was succeeded by his grandson.[3] In 1314 an assize of view of recognizance was held to enquire if Margery de Treverbyn, William de Ralegh and Elizabeth his wife, Walter de Treverbyn, Walter Kyldrynek, William de Cerizeus and Thomas de Lammentyn had unjustly disseized Henry Lym of Loo and Edith his wife of their free tenement in Porthbygan juxta Loo; and Henry and Edith recovered against the said Margery, Walter Kyldrynek, William Cerizeus, and Thomas de Lammentyn with damages.[4] This William was probably a younger son of the above-mentioned Sir Richard, as, perhaps, was also Richard de Ceresyaux, who resigned the rectory of Lesnewith in 1308.[5]

From certain proceedings at the assizes at Launceston in 1309 concerning a tenement called Trewhystan it appears that after the death of Sir Richard Cerizeux the manor of Kylcoyd, together with the wardship of Richard de Ceresyaux, son and heir of John de Ceresyaux, was granted by the king to John le Bret of Bosham and Johanna his wife.[6] This John de Ceresyaux had also a daughter Margaret, who married Stephen Podyford. In 1320 Richard, son of Richard de Podyford of Podyford, Stephen, son of the same Richard son of Richard and Margaret, daughter of John Cerciaus, gave 40s. for a license of covenant concerning the manors of Truthek and Podyford, &c.,[7] of which, however, 20s. remained unpaid in 1329.[8]

[1] Assize Rolls Cornw., 12th Edward I., 1 ${}^{M}_{O}$ } 6. m. 3.   [2] Inq. p.m. (of Oliver de Dinham), 29th Edward I., No. 59.

[3] See Pedigree post.   [4] Assize Rolls Cornw., 8th Edward II., m. 4d. 2 ${}^{N}_{16}$ } 1.

[5] See ante p. 407.   [6] Assize Rolls, Cornwall, 3rd Edward II. 2 ${}^{N}_{15}$ } 1. m. 17.

[7] Rot. Pip., 13th Edward II.

[8] Ibid. 3rd Edward III. In 1388 Richard, son of Richard Podyford of Trenythick, petitioned against Michael Trewenneleke and Cecilia his wife and Michael their son, of one messuage and one carucate of land in Pentirnen, which Richard, son of Richard de Podyford of Trenythick, gave Nicholas Heligan, Clerk, for the life of the same Richard, remainder to Stephen son of the said Richard son of Richard and Margaret his wife daughter of John de Sergeaus, and the heirs of their bodies, and which, he said, after the death of the said Richard, Stephen and Margaret, and Richard son and heir of the said Stephen, and James son and heir of the

In 1315 Richard de Cireseaux held eight Knights' fees in Cornwall,[1] as he did also in 1332.[2] In 1323, pursuant to a writ dated 9th May, he was returned by the Sheriff of Cornwall as summoned under the general proclamation to attend the great council at Westminster, he having lands of the value of £40 a year and upwards,[3] and in 1326, he paid a subsidy of 3s. 4d. in St. Maben, as a twentieth of all his moveable goods.[4] He married Margaret daughter and heir of John le Seneschal, Knt., and relict of James Peverel. In 1340, an assize of view of recognizance was held to enquire if Richard Ceriseaux, senior, Knt., Richard Ceriseaux, junior, Knt., John the son of Richard Ceriseaux, senior, and others had disseized Richard de Stapeldon of his free tenement in Truerdeuy Cropping juxta Trethynan, and in 1546,[5] Richard de Ceriseaux, Knt., and Margaret his wife, together with Ralph the son of Ralph Arundel, gave half a mark for a writ;[6] and on 11th September in the following year, Richard Sergeaux of Colquyt, jointly with Richard Trewynt of Bodmyn, were appointed assessors of 262½ sacs and six stone of wool, growing in Cornwall, of the 2000 sacs granted to the King by the Council on 3rd March preceding, the said wool to be delivered to John Bylon of Trethewol and others, Receivers of the King's wool in Cornwall.[7] He died in 1362, and was succeeded by his son Richard, described above as Richard Ceriseaux, junior, Knt., who, in that year, was called upon to pay the relief on his father's death for three-and-a-half Knights' fees in Tremodret, and twelve fees in Restronget, which had belonged to William de Bodrugan,[8] the payment of which was stayed in the following year. In addition to Richard he would appear to have had other children. William Cergeaux held the Prebend in St. Endellion Church, afterwards called Marny's, and died in 1391, when John Cergeaux was presented by Sir Richard Cergeaux, Knt.,[9] but we have no sufficient data to place either of them into the pedigree, even hypothetically.

Sir Richard Sergeaux, the younger, married to his first wife Elizabeth, daughter and

same Richard son of Stephen, which said James died s.p., to the aforesaid Richard son of Richard de Podyford, brother and heir of the aforesaid James, ought to descend.

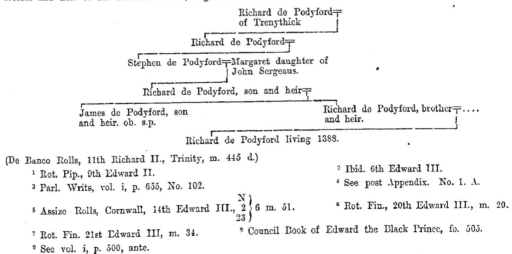

(De Banco Rolls, 11th Richard II., Trinity, m. 445 d.)

[1] Rot. Pip., 9th Edward II.

[2] Ibid. 6th Edward III.

[3] Parl. Writs, vol. i, p. 655, No. 102.

[4] See post Appendix. No. 1. A.

[5] Assize Rolls, Cornwall, 14th Edward III., 2 N 23 6 m. 51.

[6] Rot. Fin., 20th Edward III., m. 20.

[7] Rot. Fin. 21st Edward III., m. 34.

[8] Council Book of Edward the Black Prince, fo. 505.

[9] See vol. i, p. 500, ante.

sole heir of Sir William Bodrugan,[1] and had by her a daughter named after her mother, who died in childhood, but because he had issue he held the Bodrugan estates for the term of his life, according to the law of England, and upon his death, in 1393, they reverted to the heirs of Bodrugan.[2] His second wife was Philippa daughter of Richard Earl of Arundel by Philippa his wife, daughter of Hugh Lord Spencer.

The remainder of the pedigree is so complete, and we have already treated so fully of the last Sir Richard Sergeaux and his issue, that it will suffice here to say that on the division of the Sergeaux estates between the four coheirs of the said Sir Richard Sergeaux, Elizabeth, the elder, carried the manor of Colquite into the family of Marny of Lyre Marny in co. Essex.

MARNY.

The family of Marny, though not in early times of the highest standing in the county of Essex, was of great antiquity and of considerable position in that county. By his charter, dated 12th October 1264, King Henry III granted a license to William Marny to impark his wood at Lyre within the metes of the Forest of Essex.[3] Morant says that about this date William de Marny held a Knight's fee under Henry of Essex.[4] His grandson William de Marny, in 1329, had license to alienate thirty acres of land and the advowson of the Church of Leyremarny to three Chaplains to celebrate Divine Service there, daily, for the soul of the said William and the souls of his ancestors and of his heirs, which land and advowson were parcel of his manor of Leyremarny, which he held of the Bishop of London as of the Castle of Stortford, by the service of two suits at the court of the said Bishop in the said castle, and the payment of 8s. per annum to the Ward of the said castle. The land was stated to be worth per annum, according to the true value, 7s. 6d., or price per acre 3d., and the Church, per annum, in all issues, according to the true value, £10 13s. 4d.[5] To Robert de Marny, son of the last named, King Edward III, upon inspeximus of the above recited charter of 48th Henry III, by letters patent, dated 18th September 1335, confirmed, under the description of Robert de Marny, kinsman and heir of the aforesaid William de Marny, the same to him and his heirs for ever.[6]

---

[1] In the account of the Bodrigan family, ante vol. i, p. 550, through some inadvertence it is inaccurately stated that this Elizabeth was the daughter of *Henry* Bodrigan, and (p. 551) that Sir *William* died s.p.; and, unfortunately it is so shewn in the Pedigree, p. 554, notwithstanding that her parentage is correctly given in a note on an earlier page (530, note §).

[2] Vide Inq. p.m., 17th Richard II, and De Banco Rolls, 12th Richard II, Michaelmas 119.

[3] Rot. Pat. 48th Henry III, m. 2. An attempt has been made, to identify this family of Marny with that of Mareny (the Norman family of Marigny) but the evidences adduced are not, in our opinion, sufficient to establish it. Transactions of the Essex Archeol. Society, vol. iii, p. 2.   [4] Morant's Essex, vol. i, p. 406.

[5] Inq. ad quod damnum, 3rd Edward III, No. 122 (2nd numbers.)

[6] Rot. Pat. 9th Edward III, Part 2, m. 4.

Sir William Marny, Knt. by marriage with Elizabeth eldest sister and coheir of Richard Sergeaux, son of Sir Richard Sergeaux, Knt., acquired the third part of the manor of Tremodret, the manors of Trevelen and Kilquyt, one acre of land Cornish in Pencarrow, juxta Kilquyt, and one acre of land English in Trefryck, together with the advowson of one prebend called "Bodrugan prouendre" in the Church of St. Endellion, of all which he died seized according to the law of England, of the inheritance of Thomas his son and heir, in 1414. In his will, dated 19th August, and proved 19th December in the same year,[1] he directs that his body shall be buried in the Church of Lyre Marny, and names his sons Thomas and John, and his daughters Ellen and Ann; to the latter of whom he gives 300 marks as a marriage portion. The former was previously married to Sir Thomas Tyrell. To Sir William Mandeville the téstator gives an annuity of 40s. out of the manor of Leyre Marny for the term of his life. Sir Thomas Marny died seized of the same lands at the early age of 24 years, leaving his wife Margaret great with child. She was afterwards delivered of a daughter named Margaret, who dying in infancy the estates and the representation of the family devolved upon her uncle, Sir John Marny. To him succeeded his son Henry Marny, who, upon the death of his mother, in 1478, was found to be aged 21 years. Upon the landing of Henry Earl of Richmond in 1485, Henry Marny joined his standard at Nottingham; and he fought bravely against the Earl of Lincoln, in the cause of Lambert Simmel, at the battle of Stoke, on 6th June 1489, and also against Lord Audley and the Cornish men at Blackheath, on 22nd June 1497. He was one of the twenty-three Knights made at the creation of Henry Duke of York, on the Eve of All Saints 10th Henry VII (1494).[2] He was appointed Sheriff of Essex, 1487, Chancellor of the Duchy of Lancaster, Officer of the Countess of Richmond's Household, and Privy Councillor, in the reign of Henry VII. After the accession of King Henry VIII, he was again appointed a Privy Councillor, elected a Knight of the Garter on the 23rd, and installed on the 27th April 1510,[3] Lord Privy Seal, Captain of the Body Guard and Vice-Chamberlain in 1509.[4] In June 1513, when Henry VIII personally undertook another invasion of France, among those who went over to Calais with the King appears Sir Henry Marny's son with a retinue of 800 persons.[5] And on 23rd July 1514, a protection was granted to Sir Henry Marny, Knight of the Body, retained in the King's service beyond the seas.[6] In September of the same year he was appointed Steward of the Duchy of Cornwall,[7] as he was before for the Duchy of Lancaster. Finally on 12th April 1523 he was created Baron Marny of Leyre Marny, co. Essex. He died 24th May following, according to Newcourt, at his house in St. Swithen's, London, and was buried at Leyre Marny. Notwithstanding the antiquity of the Marny family, King Henry VIII, in answer to the complaint of the "Rebylles in Yorkshire" that he had not then as many noble Councillors as at the beginning of his reign, wrote, "Who were then Counsaillors I well remember, and yet of the Temporaltie I note none but two worthie calling noble

---

[1] Proved P.C.C. (29 and 31 Marche.)
[2] Cotton MSS. Claudius, C. III, fo. 27.
[3] Beltz's Memorials, p. clxxi.
[4] Rot. Pat., 1st Henry VIII, Parl. 2 m. 33.
[5] Cotton MSS., Faustina, E. vii, 6.
[6] Signed Bills, Record Office.
[7] Privy Seals.

3 v

...........others, as the Lords Marney and Darcye, but scant well borne Gentlemen, and yet of no great landes till they were promoted by us and so made Knights and Lordes."[1]

On the death of Henry Lord Marny he was succeeded by his son John, then aged 30 years. He did not, however, long enjoy the dignity of the peerage, for he died on 27th April 1525, s.p.m. when the title, after an existence of only two years and fifteen days, became extinct. Like his father, he was a favorite of the King. He was an Esquire for the Body in May 1509, when he was appointed Warden of Rochester Castle. We have mentioned above how he accompanied the King on his expedition into France in 1513. Soon after the *Battle of the Spurs*, at Tournay on 25th September, he received the honour of Knighthood.[2] By Christine daughter and heir of Sir Roger Newburgh he left two daughters, coheirs, Catherine, the elder married first George Ratcliffe, Esquire, and secondly Thomas Lord Poynyngs, and died s.p. Elizabeth, the younger became the wife of Thomas Howard second son of Thomas Fourth Duke of Norfolk, who, in 1558, was created Viscount Bindon. Her descendants became extinct upon the death of Ambrosia the young daughter of Sir Arthur Gorges, in 1600. See Pedigree annexed.

---

[1] State Papers, Henry VIII, vol i, 507.   [2] Harl MS., 6069, f. 112.

PEDIGREE OF SERGEAUX, MARNY, & HOWARD,

SHEWING THE DESCENT OF THE MANOR OF COLQUITE.

N.B.—The Names of those who held the Manor are Printed in Capitals.

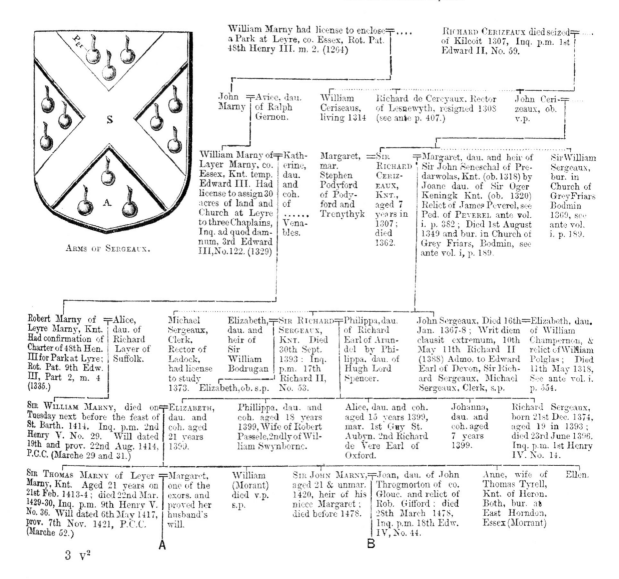

ARMS OF SERGEAUX.

William Marny had license to enclose a Park at Leyre, co. Essex, Rot. Pat. 48th Henry III. m. 2. (1264) ==....

RICHARD CERIZEAUX died seized of Kilcoit 1307, Inq. p.m. 1st Edward II, No. 59. ==....

John Marny ==Avice, dau. of Ralph Gernon.

William Ceriseaus, living 1314

Richard de Cereyaux, Rector of Lesnewyth, resigned 1308 (see ante p. 407.)

John Cerizeaux, ob. v.p.

William Marny of Layer Marny, co. Essex, Knt. temp. Edward III. Had license to assign 30 acres of land and Church at Leyre to three Chaplains, Inq. ad quod damnum, 3rd Edward III, No. 122. (1329) ==Katherine, dau. and coh. of ...... Venables.

Margaret, mar. Stephen Podyford of Podyford and Trenythyk

SIR RICHARD CERIZEAUX, KNT., aged 7 years in 1307; died 1362. ==Margaret, dau. and heir of Sir John Seneschal of Predarwolas, Knt. (ob. 1318) by Joane dau. of Sir Oger Keningk Knt. (ob. 1320) Relict of James Peverel, see Ped. of PEVEREL ante vol. i. p. 382; Died 1st August 1349 and bur. in Church of Grey Friars, Bodmin, see ante vol. i, p. 189.

Sir William Sergeaux, bur. in Church of Grey Friars Bodmin 1369, see ante vol. i. p. 189.

Robert Marny of Leyre Marny, Knt. Had confirmation of Charter of 48th Hen. III for Park at Lyre; Rot. Pat. 9th Edw. III, Part 2, m. 4 (1335.) ==Alice, dau. of Richard Layer of Suffolk.

Michael Sergeaux, Clerk, Rector of Ladock, had license to study 1373.

Elizabeth, dau. and heir of Sir William Bodrugan. Elizabeth, ob. s.p. ==SIR RICHARD SERGEAUX, KNT. Died 30th Sept. 1393 : Inq. p.m. 17th Richard II, No. 53. ==Philippa, dau. of Richard Earl of Arundel by Philippa, dau. of Hugh Lord Spencer.

John Sergeaux, Died 16th Jan. 1367-8 ; Writ diem clausit extremum, 10th May 11th Richard II (1388) Admo. to Edward Earl of Devon, Sir Richard Sergeaux, Michael Sergeaux, Clerk, s.p. ==Elizabeth, dau. of William Champernon, & relict of William Polglas ; Died 11th May 1318, See ante vol. i. p. 554.

SIR WILLIAM MARNY, died on Tuesday next before the feast of St. Barth. 1414. Inq. p.m. 2nd Henry V. No. 29. Will dated 19th and prov. 22nd Aug. 1414, P.C.C. (Marche 29 and 31.) ==ELIZABETH, dau. and coh. aged 21 years 1399.

Phillippa, dau. and coh. aged 18 years 1399, Wife of Robert Passele, 2ndly of William Swynborne.

Alice, dau. and coh. aged 15 years 1399, mar. 1st Guy St. Aubyn. 2nd Richard de Vere Earl of Oxford.

Johanna, dau. and coh. aged 7 years 1399.

Richard Sergeaux, born 21st Dec. 1374, aged 19 in 1393 ; died 23rd June 1396. Inq. p.m. 1st Henry IV. No. 14.

SIR THOMAS MARNY of Leyer Marny, Knt. Aged 21 years on 21st Feb. 1413-4 ; died 22nd Mar. 1429-30, Inq. p.m. 9th Henry V. No. 36. Will dated 6th May 1417, prov. 7th Nov. 1421, P.C.C. (Marche 52.) ==Margaret, one of the exors. and proved her husband's will.

William (Morant) died v.p. s.p.

SIR JOHN MARNY, aged 21 & unmar. 1420, heir of his niece Margaret ; died before 1478. ==Joan, dau. of John Throgmorton of co. Glouc. and relict of Rob. Gifford : died 28th March 1478, Inq. p.m. 18th Edw. IV, No. 44.

Anne, wife of Thomas Tyrell, Knt. of Heron. Both, bur. at East Horndon, Essex (Morrant)

Ellen.

A

B

3 v²

A   B

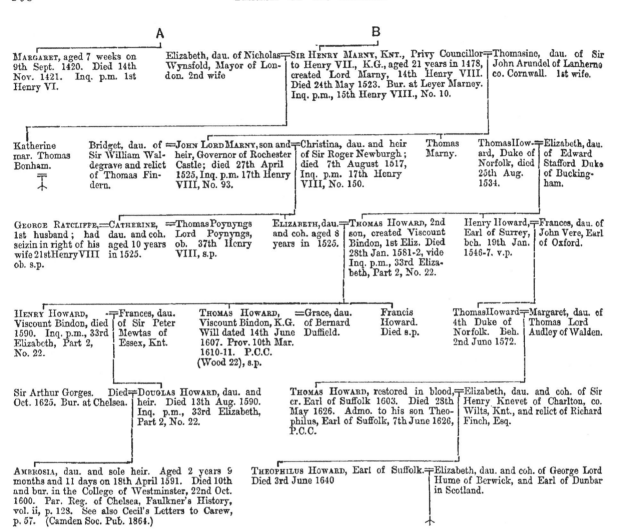

MARGARET, aged 7 weeks on 9th Sept. 1420. Died 14th Nov. 1421. Inq. p.m. 1st Henry VI.

Elizabeth, dau. of Nicholas Wynsfold, Mayor of London. 2nd wife

SIR HENRY MARNY, KNT., Privy Councillor to Henry VII., K.G., aged 21 years in 1478, created Lord Marny, 14th Henry VIII. Died 24th May 1523. Bur. at Leyer Marney. Inq. p.m., 15th Henry VIII., No. 10.

Thomasine, dau. of Sir John Arundel of Lanherne, co. Cornwall. 1st wife.

Katherine mar. Thomas Bonham.

Bridget, dau. of Sir William Waldegrave and relict of Thomas Findern.

JOHN LORD MARNY, son and heir, Governor of Rochester Castle; died 27th April 1525, Inq. p.m. 17th Henry VIII, No. 93.

Christina, dau. and heir of Sir Roger Newburgh; died 7th August 1517, Inq. p.m. 17th Henry VIII, No. 150.

Thomas Marny.

Thomas Howard, Duke of Norfolk, died 25th Aug. 1534.

Elizabeth, dau. of Edward Stafford Duke of Buckingham.

GEORGE RATCLIFFE, 1st husband; had seizin in right of his wife 21st Henry VIII. ob. s.p.

CATHERINE, dau. and coh. aged 10 years in 1525.

Thomas Poynyngs Lord Poynyngs, ob. 37th Henry VIII, s.p.

ELIZABETH, dau. and coh. aged 8 years in 1525.

Thomas Howard, 2nd son, created Viscount Bindon, 1st Eliz. Died 28th Jan. 1581-2, vide Inq. p.m., 33rd Elizabeth, Part 2, No. 22.

Henry Howard, Earl of Surrey, bch. 19th Jan. 1546-7. v.p.

Frances, dau. of John Vere, Earl of Oxford.

HENRY HOWARD, Viscount Bindon, died 1590. Inq. p.m., 33rd Elizabeth, Part 2, No. 22.

Frances, dau. of Sir Peter Mewtas of Essex, Knt.

THOMAS HOWARD, Viscount Bindon, K.G. Will dated 14th June 1607. Prov. 10th Mar. 1610-11. P.C.C. (Wood 22), s.p.

Grace, dau. of Bernard Duffield.

Francis Howard. Died s.p.

Thomas Howard, 4th Duke of Norfolk. Beh. 2nd June 1572.

Margaret, dau. of Thomas Lord Audley of Walden.

Sir Arthur Gorges. Died Oct. 1625. Bur. at Chelsea.

DOUGLAS HOWARD, dau. and heir. Died 13th Aug. 1590. Inq. p.m., 33rd Elizabeth, Part 2, No. 22.

THOMAS HOWARD, restored in blood, cr. Earl of Suffolk 1603. Died 28th May 1626. Admo. to his son Theophilus, Earl of Suffolk, 7th June 1626, P.C.C.

Elizabeth, dau. and coh. of Sir Henry Knevet of Charlton, co. Wilts, Knt., and relict of Richard Finch, Esq.

AMBROSIA, dau. and sole heir. Aged 2 years 9 months and 11 days on 18th April 1591. Died 10th and bur. in the College of Westminster, 22nd Oct. 1600. Par. Reg. of Chelsea, Faulkner's History, vol. ii, p. 128. See also Cecil's Letters to Carew, p. 57. (Camden Soc. Pub. 1864.)

THEOPHILUS HOWARD, Earl of Suffolk. Died 3rd June 1640

Elizabeth, dau. and coh. of George Lord Hume of Berwick, and Earl of Dunbar in Scotland.

PEDIGREE OF PETER-HOBLYN OF COLQUITE.

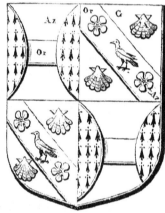

Arms as granted to Deeble Peter-Hoblyn of
Colquite, 1836.

John Peter of Torbrian ⹀ Joan, dau. of ....

John Peter of Torbrian, co. Devon ⹀ Alys, dau. of John Collinge of
Woodland, co. Devon.

| Sir William Petre, from whom descend the Lords Petre. | John Peter, Alderman of Exeter. Will dated 8th Dec. 1579. Prov. 4th Nov. 1581. (36 Darcy.) ⹀ Wyllmot. | Robert Peter, Auditor of the Exchequer. Died 16th Sept. 1593 s.p. Bur. at Ingatestone M.I. Will dated 16th Aug. 1583 Prov. 9th Oct. 1593. (69 Nevil.) ⹀ Margaret, dau. of Sir John Tirrell, Knt. Liv. 1581-83. Remar. Edward English, M.I., at St. Margaret's, Westminster. (Pingo Collec.) |

Otho Peter of Bowhay, co. Devon. Named in will of his uncle, John Peter. Customer of Exeter in 1570, and proved his father's will in 1581.

Thomas Peter, on whom ⹀ ...., dau. of his father settled Trewaran, Treator, and other estates in Cornwall. | Thomas Godolphin.

Robert Peter, Repres. in Parl. for Fowey, ⹀ Thomasine, dau. of John Kestell of 13th Elizabeth; for Dartmouth, 28th Elizabeth. | Kestell, co. Cornwall.

Henry Peter, M.P. for Fowey, ⹀ Debora, dau. of John Treffry of Place, temp. James. | Fowey, mar. there 9th Jan. 1609. (See Ped. of TREFFRY, ante p. 252.)

Thomas Peter of St. Merryn, co ⹀ Elizabeth, dau. of Henry Michell of St. Cornwall, eldest son, admo. at | Merryn, mar. ante 21st Charles I. nuncupative Exeter 10th Jan.1675, to Elizabeth | will dated 30th Nov. 1677. Prov. at Exon. his wife. | 22nd Feb. 1677-8.

Elizabeth, dau. of John Goove of Goovehayes, ⹀ Gregory Peter of Harlyn in St. Merryn. Bur.[1] ⹀ Jane his wife. Living 1712. Bur.[1] co. Devon, widow of William Woodland of | 19th Feb. 1712. Will dated 19th April 1710. | 9th Mar. 1737. Trevose, co. Cornwall. Mar. Art. dated 14th | Prov. 17th June 1712, at Exeter. July 1658. Living 1685.

John Peter of Harlyn, son and heir. Exr. to his father's will. ⹀ Ann, dau. of Sir John Coriton of Newton Ferrers, Cornwall, Bart. Bur.[1] 28th April 1733. Will dated 23rd Oct. 1728. Cod. 12th | Bapt. at St. Mellians, co. Cornwall, 11th August 1663. Mar. there April 1733. Prov. at Exeter 7th May 1733. | 14th April 1685, mar. articles dated 11th same month. Bur.[1] 18th Oct. | 1737.

A

---

[1] At St. Merryn.

[2] At St. Mabyn.

PEDIGREE OF PETER-HOBLYN

A

Henry Peter, bap.[1] 30th April 1688. Living 1712 & 1728.	William Peter, bap.[1] 25th July 1690.	Samuel Peter, bap.[1] 6th July 1696.	Genopher, bap.[1] 4th May 1694.	Elizabeth, mar.[1] 15th June 1706, to Richard Morshead	Susanna, bap.[1] 29th April 1699.

Mary, born 8th Feb. 1724, bap.[1] 10th same month.	Elizabeth, bap.[1] 16th Feb. 1727.	Jenny, bap.[1] 10th Dec. 1728.	Ann, bap.[1] 19th Jan. 1730.	Susanna, bap.[1] 6th July 1731.	Martha, bap.[1] 27th Dec. 1732

Hoblyn Peter of Percothen, born 5th April 1748, bap.[1] same day. *Died 10th Jan. and bur.[1] 14th Jan. 1804. Will dated 10th April 1801.* ═ Elizabeth, dau. and heir of John Pomeroy. Mar.[1] 9th July 1778. Died at Padstow and bur.[2] 6th Nov. 1821.		Deeble Peter of Colquite in S. Mabyn, born May 1750. Died 19th July 1836. Bur.[1] Will dated 19th July 1832. Cod. 17th Aug 1833. Prov. C.P.C. in Sep. 1836.

Samuel Peter, born 17th April 1779, and bap.[1] 24th same month. Died 1832. Bur. at Padstow. ═ Sarah Carbis, mar. at Falmouth, in 1804, *Died at Luxulian and bur. there.*	Hoblyn Peter of Percothen, born circa 1781. Liv. there 1836. unmar. *Bur.[1] 28th November 1846, aged 65.*	Pomeroy Peter, a Midshipman, R.N. Died at Plymouth cœl.	Edward Peter in the service of the East India Company. Died in India. cœl.

Elizabeth *Sarah,* eldest child, *born 30th April 1805, bap.[1] 4th Oct. 1806. Died in Childhood.*	Hoblyn Samuel Peter, eldest son, born 19th *July, bap. 4th Oct. 1806. Died at Plymouth 1870, and bur. there.*	Edward Pomeroy Peter, born 1st Oct. 1807, *bap. 17th April 1809. Living at Plymouth 1875, unmar.*	John Harris Peter, born 7th May 1809. *By Royal Licence dated 1865, assumed the additional name and arms of Hoblyn. Died at Colquite 3rd and bur.[2] 8th Sep., 1871. Will Prov. 15th Dec.* 1871. ═ Emily, dau. of Rev. John Kingdon, Clerk, Rector of Michaelstow. Mar. there 24th July 1862.	Henry Peter, born 14th July 1810. Bap.[1] *14th May* 1811. *Deceased s.p.*	Deeble Peter, born 4th May, bap.[1] 21st *Nov. 1817. Deceased s.p.*

Charles Henry Harris, born 25th April, and bap.[2] 24th June 1863. Died 24th and bur.[2] 28th Aug. 1863.	*Ellen Maude, born 4th April, bap.[2] 17th May 1864.*	*Caroline Emily, born 29th April, bap.[2] 30th May 1865.*	*Catherine Sarah, born 24th Oct. bap.[2] 5th Dec. 1866.*

---

[1] At St. Merryn.   [2] At St. Mabyn.

OF COLQUITE.—Continued.

Martha, bap.[1] 26th Nov. 1793.	Ann, bap.[1] 3rd August 1706. Mar. Edward Hoblyn of Tresadern. Died 1791, æt 85.	Jonathan Peter of Porthcothen, bap.[1] 10th June 1692. Living 1747. ═ Mary, dau. of Thomas Hoblyn of Penhargard, co. Cornwall. She was one of the admin. of her father who died in 1719, in admo. granted C.P.C. 26th Jan 1727, then wife of Jonathan Peter. Living 1747.

Jonathan Peter, bap.[1] 5th Nov. 1736.	Samuel Peter of Porthcothen, born 30th Dec. 1725, bap[1] 26th Jan. 1726, bur.[1] 3rd Oct. 1770. ═ Sarah, sole dau. and heir of Edward Hoblyn of Penhargard, admx. to her father 1754. *Mar. Lic. 30th March 1747. Died 13th Sep. 1803.*

Rev. Edward Peter, Clerk, Rector of Wigborough, co. Essex, born Sep. 1759, at Plymouth, ob. 1832. Bur. at St. Sidwell's, Exeter. Will dated 14th May 1831. Prov. 30th July 1832. (464, Tenterden).	Mary, bap.[1] 1st July 1754.	Sarah, bap.[1] Mar. Rev. Coplestone Radcliffe *of Plymouth.*

Jonathan *Humphry* Peter of Steps, near Bodmin, *born 18th; July 1792. Bap.[1] 9th June 1798.* ═ Mary, dau. of . . . . . Serpil.	Thomas Peter of Percothen born 11th Dec. 1793, bap.[1] 9th June 1798. Liv. there 1836 cœl. *Died* 24 and bur.[1] *30th June 1873.*	Elizabeth, mar. at Padstow to Robert Avery of Padstow. Both living 1836. *See ante vol. i, p. 655.*	Deeble Peter of Colquite, born 22nd Feb. 1798. By Royal License dated 13th Sep. 1836, assumed the name and arms of Hoblyn. Died unmar. *Aged 67, and bur.[1] 19th Sep. 1864.*	Mary, bap.[1] 21st Nov. 1817. Mar. John Stone of St. Mabyn.	Susan, mar. Thomas Dewston, Lieut. R.N.	Sarah and Sarah, died young.

Pomeroy *William* Peter, bap.[1] 4th June 1823.	Samuel Peter, born 13th Oct. 1825 bap.[1] 14th Jan. 1826 *Deceased s.p.*	Caroline Mary, born 4th, bap.[1] 10th Dec. 1811. *Mar... Seccombe.*	Anna Maria and Jane Louisa, Twins, born 19th Dec. 1812, *bap.* 4th Jan. 1815. *Both mar. and emig. to America.*	Mary, born in April 1815. *Mar. C. E. Hosken, Clerk, who died* 1870. *She living* 1875.	Ellen, youngest dau., born 19th Dec. 1820. Mar. 1848. *Sir Henry Onslow, Bart. He buried at St. Tudy, 26th Nov. 1870. She living* 1875.

Cyril Onslow, born 5th April, bap.[2] 12th May, 1868.	*Henry Godolphin, born 17th June, bap.[2] 3rd August 1869.*	*Ernest Pomeroy, born 21st and bap.[2] 24th June, 1870.*

I hereby certify that the portion of the above Pedigree which is printed in *Roman* type, and the Arms agree with the Record in this Office.

GEORGE HARRISON,

Heralds' College.

Windsor Herald.

7th June 1875.

[1] At St. Merryn.

[2] At St. Mabyn.

FAMILY OF HELIGAN.

Ancient documents in the possession of Sir John Trelawny, at Trelawne, state that about the year 1000 there was one Reynolde, the son of Nicholas de Heligan, who was Lord of the Manor of Treserret,[1] and, further, that about the time of King Henry II there was one Nicholas de Helligan, the son of William, who by his wife .... heir of Lamettyn, had issue Richard, called Lamettyn because he there dwelt, and also had issue John and Reynold. Richard de Lamettyn had issue Geoffry. Nicholas de Helligan gave all his land in Helligan and Porthkulyock to John his son, and he dying s.p., v.p. he gave the same, afterwards, to his younger son Reynold, which grant Richard de Lamettyn confirmed by his charter, as did, subsequently, Geoffry de Lamettyn.[2]

Reynold de Helligan had issue Nicholas de Heligan, who, by Matilda his wife, daughter of Alan Bloyou, had issue Robert and Millicenta, which Robert, in 1283, gave half a mark for a pone,[3] and he paid the aid upon two fees in Helligan in 1301. He married Emma daughter and coheir of William de Tregrilla, whose other daughter and coheir, Isabella, became the wife of Walter Doyngell. In 1313 an assize of view of recognizance was held to enquire if Robert de Heligan and Emma his wife, Adam de Helygan, Johanna de St. Winnow, and John her son, had unjustly disseized Adam Doyngel of his free tenement in Tregrilla juxta Mahynyet (Menheniot) and Adam recovered.[4] In 1278 Henry de Helligan, Clerk, had a dispensation from the Bishop of Exeter on account of defect of birth. Robert de Helligan died before 1314, for in that year Adam Helligan, as son and heir of Robert, made fealty for the hamlet of Helligan, which he held of the heirs of Joceus de Dinham then in the King's wardship.[5] In 1327 he paid 2s. as his share of the subsidy, being a twentieth of his moveable goods.[6] We have already in our account of the manor of Helligan treated of the marriage and issue of Adam de Helligan. We may, however, here mention that in 1346 Adam de Heligan and Isabella his wife, who had taken out a writ of novel disseizin against John Lowys, junior, concerning a tenement in Bodmin, did not appear to prosecute, and were in mercy, together with their sureties, viz., Richard

[1] This is more than doubtful. We consider that the Reynold son of Nicholas must be the same person so described in the Charter of Prior Alan, dated cir. 1193. See ante, p. 489, and note.

[2] These deeds are cited in a "Book of Evidences" at Trelawne, but the deeds themselves we have not seen. We are indebted for the information to the kindness of Sir John and Lady Trelawny. In 1201 Henry de Heligan gave one mark for want of a surety. (Coram Rege Roll, 3rd John) see ante p. 485

[3] Rot. Fin., 11th Edward I, m. 23. In the Assize Rolls of the same year $1\frac{M}{20}$ 4. m. 8., we find Jordan de Heligan mentioned.

[4] Assize Rolls, 7th Edward $2\frac{N}{15}$ 6. m. 2.   [5] Rot. Fin., 8th Edward II.

[6] Sub. Roll, 1st Edward III, $\frac{87}{7}$ see ante Appendix I., A, and C.

Heligan and John Heligan,[1] who, probably, were the sons of the said Adam. Isolda, his daughter by Isabell Carminow, married John son of Roger Blake of Bodmin, and Adam Heligan and Nicholas his son, by their charter dated at Helygan on Monday next after the feast of St. Lawrence the Martyr 21st Edward III (1347) granted to the said John Blake and Isolda daughter of the said Adam, one messuage, one corn mill, and one fuller's mill, &c., in Nytherkildreynek juxta Schulawode, and also the whole common of pasture of the manor of Lancarf, to hold to the said John Blake and Isolda and the heirs of their bodies for ever; in default of such issue to revert to the said Adam and Nicholas and the heirs of the said Nicholas.[2] Adam de Heligan also granted to Roger Blake and John his son, and Isolda the daughter of the same Adam, and the heirs of the bodies of the said John and Isolda, one acre of land Cornish in Tregrilla, to hold to the said John and Isolda and the heirs of their bodies, in default remainder to John Helygan son of the said Adam. Roger Blake, John, and Isolda died s.p., and in 1397 Nicholas Helygan petitioned against William Carminow for the recovery of the said land at Tregrilla, under the aforesaid charter. William Carminow appeared and defended his right against the said Nicholas and, whilst admitting the charter, pleaded that after that gift the said Roger and John his son and Isolda, by a certain Indenture of those and other lands, dated at Heligan on Saturday next after the feast of the Assumption of the B. V. Mary 21st Edward III (1347), for themselves and the heirs of the said John and Isolda, agreed that if a certain Adam Heligan, John his son, and Richard and Nicholas, brothers of the said John, should pay to the said Roger Blake, John his son, and Isolda, £60 at certain times prescribed, that then the said charter of feoffament should be void; which said sum of £60, he said, was paid by Adam Heligan, so that the aforesaid John son of Adam Heligan into the said lands entered as in his former estate, to hold to him and his heirs for ever, which said John's estate in those lands the said William then had. As Nicholas took no exception to this statement, William Carminow obtained judgment.[3]

John Helygan son of Adam appears to have been resident at Treblethick, where he made his charter dated on Wednesday next after the feast of St. Martin 3rd Richard II (1379), whereby he granted to Nicholas his son and Elizabeth the daughter of Thomas Mayndy, and the heirs of their bodies, messuages in Bocoven, Spytul, Tresloget, and Tresarret, which messuages form a considerable portion of the manor of Tresarret.[4] His son Nicholas also dated a charter there in 1395. They would appear also to have been sometimes resident at their mansion at Trencruke, in the parish of Menheniot; John Heligan and Isabella his wife had license for a Chapel there in 1387, which was renewed in 1396, and again in 1410, whilst on 10th March 1420, a similar license was granted to Isabella, relict of John Heligan.[5] Nicholas de Heligan had issue two sons and a daughter,

---

[1] Assize Rolls, 20th Edward III, $\frac{N}{2}$ } 6. m. 8 d.
$\frac{}{21}$

[2] Charter at Trelawne. Among the witnesses to this charter are the names of John Dillon of Trethewel and John Billon of Tregartha. See ante, vol. i, pp. 385, 386.

[3] De Banco Rolls, 21st Richard II. Michs. m. 377.

[4] Muniment Room, Trelawne; see also ante, vol. i, p. 557, and Rental of Tresarret, ante pp. 490, 491.

[5] Bishop's Registers.

3 X

and the sons dying s.p., the daughter, Joan, carried the manor of Tresarret, in marriage, to John Trelawny, second son of Sir John Trelawny, Knt.

Richard, the elder son of Adam de Helygan, remained, as we have already seen, at Helygan. He would appear to have had two sons, John, who, in 1401, is described as his son and heir, and an elder son Reginald. For further account see ante, p. 487, under the Manor of Helygan.[1]

HILL OF HELIGAN.

The pedigree of the family of Hill of Heligan, recorded at the Herald's Visitation of Cornwall in 1620, which is attested by "Humphrye Hyll," commences with Robert Hill, or Hyll, who married Margaret daughter and heir of Peter Fauntleroy. A pedigree in the British Museum[2] carries the pedigree several generations higher, stating that this Robert Hill, was the son of Giles Hill, the son of Robert Hill, the son of Ralph Hill, the son of John Hill of Spaxton, by a second marriage with Maud daughter of Sir Giles Daubenay. Whether any portion of these descents may be accurate or not we cannot say, but it is certain that John Hill of Spaxton had no son, as we have already shown (ante page 28). He died in 1455, leaving as his heir, by Margaret daughter of Sir William Rodney, an infant daughter, aged eight weeks.[3] This young lady, in due time, became the wife of Sir William Saye of Broxbourne, co. Herts, and died before her husband s p., and the estates devolved upon the [issue of her aunts as her nearest heirs. (Vide Ped. ante pp. 42, 43.)

It is not improbable that the Hills settled in St. Maben before the marriage of Robert Hill with the heiress of Fauntleroy, for we find a certain John Hill, senior, assessed to the subsidy there upon goods, at the comparatively high rate of £10 in 1524,[4] and from the Return, Appendix I. C., it appears that John Hyll, senior, John Hyll, junior, and Henry Hyll, had goods in common of that amount, and possessed arms for one man[6]. The marriage alluded to took place before 1543, for in that year we find Robert Hill assessed upon lands of the value of £20 per annum.[5] He was again assessed in St. Maben in 1559,[6] and in 1571, but at a reduced rate of £12. He died in 1575, and his grandson Maurice Hill probably succeeded him, as we have no mention of his son Giles. Maurice

---

[1] In 1415 Johanna, who was the wife of Peter Helygan, took out a writ in plea of lands against William Paynter and Johanna his wife. (Assize Rolls, 3rd to 10th Henry V, 2 $\frac{N}{48}$ } 1. m. 46.) In 1471 Philip Heligan was manucaptor for John Wyn, one of the Burgesses returned to Parliament for the Borough of Bodmin. (See ante vol. i, p. 242.)

[2] Harl MS. 1079, fo. 115.   [3] Inq. p.m., 34th Henry VI, No. 17.

[4] Sub. Roll. 16th Henry VII, $\frac{87}{131}$ See Appendix No. 1, C.   [5] Ibid. 35th Henry VIII, $\frac{87}{154}$

[6] Ibid. 1st Elizabeth, $\frac{87}{218}$ and 36th Elizabeth, $\frac{88}{253}$ [6] Appendix I. D.

was assessed upon lands in St. Maben at the further reduced rate of £10 in 1593,[1] and 1600[2]. He married Margaret daughter of John Carnsewe of Bokelly, who survived him, and was assessed to the subsidy in St. Maben upon lands of the value of £3 per annum in 1625, at which time her son Humphry Hill was assessed at the same rate.[3] It was this Humphry who attested the official pedigree in the College of Arms. Helligan was sold soon afterwards, and the Hills seem to have left the parish, for the name does not appear in the subsidy roll of 15th Charles I (1639).

Arms of Hill.—Gu. a saltier vairée between four mullets, ar.; quartering Flamank, Lucombe and Helligan.

SILLY OF TREVELVER AND HELIGAN.

This family claimed to have been descended from the family of Silly of Rackenford, co. Devon, though we know of no evidence on the subject. John Silly, alleged to have been the son of Richard Silly of Rackenford, in 1612 married Elizabeth daughter and heir of John Marke of St. Wenn, by which he acquired possessions in that parish. In 1630 he purchased of John Kempe the barton of Trevelver in St. Minver,[4] in which, in 1636, he, with Elizabeth his wife, suffered a fine to Alexander Carew and William Courtenay, doubtless for purposes of settlement.[5] These gentlemen were afterwards trustees to his will. We find him first assessed to the subsidy in that parish in 1641, when, as John Silly, Esq., he was rated upon lands of the value of £7 per annum, and his son, as Richard Silly, Gent., was, at the same time, assessed upon lands of the value of £1 per annum.[6] By his will, dated in 1640, and proved 15th April 1646 (in which he mentions his wife, his sons Richard and John, his sister Richard, and his daughter Elizabeth) he stipulates that if his son Richard releases to his brother John his right to lands in St. Wenn, John is not to have Penlease, in St. Breoke, nor any of the lands in St. Minver. Richard appears to have done so, and to have settled at Trevelver, and John settled in St. Wenn, where he was residing in 1646 and in 1659. Richard was twice married, by his first wife, Gertrude the daughter of Richard Carew of Antony, he left one surviving son, named Marke after his grandmother's family, and one daughter, Mary, the wife of Thomas Ceely. By his second marriage, with Ann daughter of Humphry Nicoll of Penvose, he had a son, Joseph, and a daughter. Marke succeeded him at Trevelver, and upon Joseph he settled the manor of Heligan which he had purchased in 1641. Marke died s.p., and by his will, dated 15th July, and proved 18th September 1667, after making certain specific bequests to the children of his sister Mary Ceely, he devises all his real and personal estate to his uncle John Silly, who thereupon removed to Trevelver.

[1] Ibid. 36th Elizabeth, $\frac{88}{253}$ 7, and [2] 42nd Elizabeth, $\frac{88}{265}$ [3] Ibid. 1st Charles $\frac{89}{312}$

[4] Pedes Finium, 6th Charles, Easter.   [5] Pedes Finium, 13th Charles, Trinity.

[6] Sub. Roll, 17th Charles, $\frac{89}{334}$

3 x[2]

John Silly married Jane daughter of William Cotton, Precentor of Exeter Cathedral, and coheir of her brother Sir John Cotton (see Ped. of COTTON, ante vol i, p. 653). He was Burgess in Parliament for Bodmin in 1660, and dying 1672, with other children, left a son William Silly, who succeeded him at Trevelver.[1] This William, as William Sylly, Esq., under the charter of 27th March 1685, was appointed one of the free burgesses of Bodmin, to whom, to the exclusion of the capital or other burgesses, together with the mayor, was granted the privilege of electing the two burgesses to represent the Borough in Parliament.[2] He married first, Jane daughter of ...... Kekewich, by whom he left a son named Hender; and secondly, Honour daughter and coheir of John Carter of St. Columb, by whom he had two sons, John and William, and two daughters, of whom Honour became the wife of Antony Tanner of St. Enoder. By deeds of settlement, dated respectively 19th and 20th September 20th Charles II (1668), upon the marriage of William Silly and Jane Kekewich, all the manors and lands of the said John Silly, father of the said William, in Cornwall, (except as therein excepted) were limited after the deaths of the said John Silly and Jane his wife, to the issue male of the marriage of the said William and Jane his then intended wife. William Silly became greatly involved, and Trevelver and his other estates were mortgaged, in sums which had accumulated to £2,500, to Josias Calmady and Richard Doidge, as trustees for John Buller, and by Indentures of lease and release, dated respectively 25th and 26th March 1699, between William Silly and Hender Silly his son and heir apparent, it was arranged that the whole of the estates should be conveyed in fee to the said Hender, who undertook: 1st, to pay off the mortgage, 2ndly, to pay the other debts of his father; 3rdly, to pay his father a further sum of £1,500;[3] 4thly, during his father's life to pay Jane and Honour his sisters of the half blood £15 per annum each, besides washing, lodging, &c.; or, if they did not choose to live with him, £25 each; 5thly, to pay his father £80 per annum, besides keeping his horses, &c.; 6thly, to pay the heir in tail male of his father's second marriage with Honour Carter £2,000; 7thly, to pay his half sisters Honour and Jane £500 each at the age of 21 or on marriage; in virtue of which arrangement William the father conveyed to Hender his son all the said lands for the term of forty-one years, if the said William should so long live, remainder to such uses as the said Hender should by deed or will appoint, and for want of such appointment to the said Hender in tail male, in default remainder in tail male to William the father, remainder to the right heirs of the said William; Hender to pay to his half brother John £2,000 within one year after his father's death; and by Indenture of lease and release, dated, respectively, the 17th and 18th April 1699, the third part of

---

[1] He would appear to have had some interest in the Office of Registrar of the Archdeaconry of Cornwall (See ante, vol i, p. 343.)   [2] See ante, vol i, p. 216.

[3] In order to effect this arrangement, by Indenture dated 17th June 1699. reciting the Indenture of settlement of 25th and 26th March named in the text, William Silly and Hender Silly mortgaged to John Hussey of Marnhull, co. Dorset, Esq., the manors of Heligan and Hender, and other lands, for the sum of £1,500 to be paid to William Silly. The money was not repaid at the time prescribed, and by a decree in Chancery, dated 3rd November 1712. the mortgage was foreclosed. (Deed in possession of William Coode of St. Austell, Esq., brought to our knowledge since the foregoing account of Heligan was printed.) It is not understood what interest William Silly had in Heligan, and the foreclosure appears not to have disturbed the possession of that estate.

the Carter estates was conveyed to the said Hender Silly for the same term under like limitations.

Hender Silly died in 1705, and by his will, dated 10th November in that year, he bequeathed £100 to his uncle Edward Amy in trust for his sister Honour Tanner, and £500 to his sister Jane. All his lands and tenements he devised to his brother William, together with the residue of his personalty, and constituted him sole executor, provided he were alive at the time of testator's death. In the event of William's death, he devised all his real estate and the residue of his personalty to his sister Jane, and appointed her sole executrix. Jane, as Jane Silly, proved her brother's will on 13th April 1706,[1] and soon afterwards married Nathaniel Shepherd of Little St. Botolph, Bishopsgate, London. She died in 1707, for on 30th December in that year administration of her effects was granted to her husband, as was also, on the same day, administration of the will of Hender Silly, with will annexed, in which the said Jane had been named executrix.[2] It would thus appear that John, eldest son of William Silly and Honour Carter, was already dead, s.p., when his brother Hender made his will, that William died between the date of that will and the date of probate, and that Jane died very soon afterwards intestate, and probably s.p.; and as Honour Tanner also died s.p., this branch of the Silly family would seem to have become extinct.

Richard Silly of Trevelver settled the capital messuage and barton of Heligan from the time of his death upon Ann Silly his relict, in dower, who resided there in 1677, and by Indenture dated 21st January 1677-8, released the same to her son Joseph to whom the reversion belonged, as also certain chatel estates in St. Breoke, St. Merryn, and St. Breward, reserving to her own use certain apartments in Heligan. Joseph Silly, by his second wife Dorothy daughter of John Elford, had two sons, Joseph who succeeded him at Heligan and was Sheriff of Cornwall in 1714, and John who married Mary daughter of Hubert Glyn of Brodes in Helland, and resided at Kernick in that parish, which was the property of her father.[3]

Joseph Silly by his wife Elizabeth, daughter of John Clobery of Bradstone, besides several daughters, had a son Clobery Silly, whose only son John Samuel Silly, Lieut. R.N., dying s.p. devised all his property to his sister Julia Silly, when this branch in the male line became extinct, and Julia in 1801 joined in the sale of Heligan to Edmund John Glynn, Esq.

ARMS :—There are no arms recorded to this family, but they used : az. a chev. between three mullets or., being the coat of Ceeley.

[3] See ante, p. 32.

---

[1] Proved P.C.C., (99, Eedes.)

[2] Act Books P.C.C.

PEDIGREES OF HELLIGAN, HILL
SHEWING THE DESCENT OF THE

Nicholas de Helligan.

Reynold de Helligan.

William de Helligan.

Nicholas de Helligan, temp. Henry II. ═ .... dau. and heir of .... Lamettyn.

Richard de Lamettyn ═ ....   John de Helligan. ob. v.p. s.p.

Geoffry de Lamettyn.

Millicent, mar. Jordan de Farndone, 1254, ob. s.p.   Robert de Helligan, ob. 1314. ═ Emma, dau. and coheir, remar. Rob. Trelawny.

Sybil ═ Adam de Helligan had seizin of his lands as son and heir of Robert 1315. Assessed at Sub. in St Maben 1327. Living 1347. ═ Isabella, dau. of John Carminow, living 1365, held Over Trequites in dower.

Richard de Helligan. ═ Johanna, dau. of James Peverel.   Emma, mar. H. Mayndy.   John de Helligan, living 1379. ═ Isabella, dau. and coh. of Thomas de Cartuther, relict of .... Bodrugan. As relict of John Helligan, had a writ 16th Henry V. Living 1428.   Nicholas de Helligan, living 1347.   Isolda, mar. John, son of Roger Blake of Bodmin. Cart. 21stEdward III 1347.

Reginald de Helligan. living 1365. ob. s.p. ═ Johanna.   John de Helligan, living 1401. ═ Elizabeth.

Thomas Lucomb ═ Alice, dau. of William de Carbuna. See ped. of CARBURRA, ante, vol.i, p.276.   Andrew de Helligan held one Fee in Helligan, 1428. ═

Thomas Lucombe, who granted Manor of Cabilia to Thomas Flamank, son of Richard Flamank and others. Cart. dated Easter Monday 3rd Henry VI (1425). ═ Jane de Helligan, dau. and heir.

LUCOMBE.

Richard Flamank living 5th Henry VIII. See ped. of FLAMANK, ante, vol. i, p. 283. ═ Joane, dau. and coheir.   Mary, dau. and coheir, mar. William Vaughan. Ped. Fin., 1st Henry VIII. ob. s.p.

FLAMANK.

Thomas Flamank, executed 1497. ═ Elizabeth, dau. of John Trelawny and Blanche his wife, dau. of John Powna of Brightorre.

FAUNTLEROY.

Peter Fauntleroy, dead before 1543. ═ Jane, dau. and heir.

HILL.

Robert Hill, son and heir of Giles Hill, mar. ante 1546. ═ Margaret, dau. and heir of Fauntleroy and to her mother, who was dau. & heyre of Flamock. Bur.[1] 13th Dec. 1582. Assessed to Subs. in St. Maben, 1543-59-71. Bur.[1] 4th Oct. 1578.

Giles Hill, son and heir. ═ .... dau. of Littleher of Essex.   John Hill, 2nd son. ob. s.p.   Humphry, 3rd son, bur.[1] 1st Nov. 1576. s.p.   Joyce, wife to John Yeo.   Catherine, wife to Alexander Arundel of Ley.   Phillip, wife to William Biell.

Robert Hill, 2nd son. Bur.[1] 8th June 1611.   Morris Hill of Helligan, in co. Cornwall, assessed to Subs. in St. Maben, 1593, 1600. ═ Margaret, dau. of John Carnsew of Bokelly of 2 House (See ped. of CARNSEWE, ante p. 173.) Assessed to Subsidy in St. Mabyn 1625. Living 1635.

Katherine, mar. Peter Toker brother of Christ. Toker. (See ped. of TOKER, ante p. 57.)   Honour mar. Christ. Toker of Helland. (See ped. of TOKER, ante, p. 57.)   Morris Hill, 2nd son.   Humphry Hill of Helligan, eldest son. Assessed to Subs. in St. Maben 1625. Sold Helligan 1641. ═ Grace, dau. of Peter Corylon of Newton in Cornwall.   Richard Hill, 2nd son, bap.[1] 2nd Jan. 1595.

Humphry Hill, æt. 6, Ano 1620. Joined in sale of Helligan 1641.   John Hill, bap.[1] 12th July 1621.

[1] At St. Maben.

OF HELLIGAN AND TRELAWNY.
MANORS OF HELLIGAN AND TRESARRET.

I certify that the pedigree of Hill, so far as it is printed in *italics*, agrees with the record in this Office.　　　　　　　　　　GEORGE HARRISON,

Herald's College.　　　　　　　　　　　　　　　　　Windsor Herald.

　　10th June 1875.

Reynold de Helligan had grant⊤.... of Tresarret, cir. 1193.

Sir Otto de Tregrilla,⊤ Knt.

Nicholas de Helligan.⊤Maud, dau. of Alan Bloyou.

William Tre-⊤Johanna. grilla.

Isabella, dau. and⊤Walter Doyngell coheir.

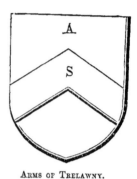

ARMS OF TRELAWNY.

Nicholas de Helligan,⊤Elizabeth, dau. of Thomas Meyndy. living 1403.　　　Mar. Settl. 3rd Richard II (1379)

Robert, ob. s.p.　　Roger. ob. s.p.　　Joan⊤John Trelawny, son of Sir John Trelawny, Knt.

John Trelawny 2nd⊤Florence, dau. of Sir Hugh Edward IV.　　Courteney of Boconnoc.

Walter Trelawny, son and heir,⊤Isabell, dau. of .... 20th Henry VII.　　Towser of Taunton.

John Trelawny 22nd⊤Margery, dau. and heir Henry VIII.　　of Thomas Lamellyn.

John Trelawny.⊤Ann, eldest dau. and coheir of William Reskymer.

Sir Jonathan Trelawney, Sheriff of Cornwall,⊤Elizabeth, dau. of 37th Elizabeth, & Knt. for Shire, 39th Elizabeth. Sir H. Kelligrew.

| Agnes, wife to Richard Langdon. | Ann, wife to Nicholas Fortescue. | Mary, mar.[1] John La-velis, 30th June 1579. | Isabell, Ann, Thomasine, Dorothy. | Sir John Trelawny, created a Baronet 1628. *Sold Tresarret* 1654. | ⊤Elizabeth, dau. of Reginald Mohun of Boconnoc. |

Sir Jonathan Trelawny,⊤Mary, dau. of Sir Edward re-purchased Tresarret 1668. Seymour, Bart.

| Anthony, bap.[1] 27th Aug. 1583, bur.[1] 28th Aug. 1583. | Giles, bur.[1] 8th Feb. 1601. | Sir Jonathan Trelawny, Bishop of Exeter,⊤Rebecca, dau. and coh. of Thomas Hele of Winchester, &c. Born April 1650, died 19th July 1721, bur. at Pelynt. | Bascomb, co. Devon. |

John Trelawny sold Tresarret 1727　　Charles.　　Edward.　　Hele.　　Letitia.

---

[1] At St. Maben.

PEDIGREE OF SILLY OF

ARMS USED BY THE FAMILY OF SILLY.

Richard Silly of Rackenford, ⊤ co. Devon.

Phillippa, dau. of ═ John Silly. Will dat. ⊤ Elizabeth, dau. of John   .... dau. mar.
Humphry Nicoll of | 1640. Prov. 15th April | Marke of St. Wenn.   .... Richards.
Penvose, mar.[3] 4th | 1646. Archd. Cornw. | Mar. 1612.
Jan. 1639. Bur.[3] 1669.
Will dated 12th May
1661. Prov. 30th May
1669. Archd. Cornwall.

Ann, dau. of Humphry Nicoll ⊤ Richard Silly of Trevelver in ⊤ Gertrude, dau. of Rich-
of Penvose. Bap.[3] 1610. Mar.[3] | St. Minver. Bur.[1] 8th July | ard Carew of Antony.
25th Jan. 1649. Released Heligan | 1659. Will dated 1st July, | Mar Lic. 1st Dec. 1636.
to son Joseph 29th Jan. 1677. | Cod. 5th July 1659. Prov. 9th | Vide ante p. 366.
Bur.[2] 8th June 1685. | May 1661. P.C.C. (May, 85.)

Anne, bap.[1] 3rd	Elizabeth, dau. of ═ Joseph Silly of ⊤ Dorothy, dau. of	John Silly,	Elizabeth.	Marke, bap.[1] 25th
April 1651. Liv.	RobertShapcote of	Heligan, bap.[1] 7th	John Elford. Mar.	bap[1] 14th	Died unmar.	April 1639, of Tre-
1672. Named in	Dublin, died 3rd,	Sep. 1652. Bur.[2]	Settl. 8th Feb.	Feb.	Will dated	velver. Bur.[1] 5th
sister Eliza-	bur.[2] 5th Aug.	8th June 1688.	1680. Lic. 29th	1637-8.	15thApril and	Aug. 1667. Will
beth's will.	1679. s.p. M.I.	Admo. 11th June	Jan. 1680. Bur.[2]		prov. 2nd	dated 15th July,
Bur.[2] 23rd July	No. 1, p. 466.	1688 to Dorothy his	24th Mar. 1716.		Aug. 1672,	proved 18th Sept.
1677.		rel. Archd. Cornw.	Will dated 1st		Exon.	1667. Archd. Cornw.
			Nov. 1714. Prov.			
			14th Aug. 1721.			

Joseph Silly of ═ Elizabeth, dau.	Dorothy,	Sarah, bap.[2] 3rd	Anne bap.[2]	John Silly of Ker- ⊤ Mary, dau. of
Heligan bap.[2] 15th	of John Clobery	bap.[2] 20th.	Nov. 1687. Admo.	18th Oct.	nick in Helland,	Hubert Glynn of
June 1685. Sheriff	of Bradstone.	Nov. 1681.	to brother John	1683. Mar.	bap.[2] 2nd Aug.	Brodes in Helland,
of Cornwall 1714.	Mar. Settl. 28th	Admo. 17th	Silly of Helland,	7th Oct. 1711	1686. Admo.	seePed. of GLYNN,
Bur.[2] 24th Oct. 1731.	June 1710. Mar.	April 1784,	21st March 1725.	William	granted to Dennis	ante, p. 74.
	Lic. 8th Sep.	to Ann	Archd. Cornw.	Phillips of	Stephens of Apple-	
	1710.	Phillips.	Further admo.	Bodmin.	dore, grandson	
			17th April 1784,		and next of kin,	
			to Ann Phillips.		26th March 1784.	

Clobery Silly ⊤ Anne dau.	Dorothy,	Joseph,	Sarah,	Elizabeth,	Richard,	John,	Hender.	Mathew,
of Heligan,	of	bap.[2]	bap.[2]	named in	bap.[2] 8th	bap.[2] 8th	bap.[2]	bap.[4] 1st	bap.[4]
son and heir,	Preston of	26th	June	Deed	Dec. 1714.	Dec.	27th Sep.	Oct. 1717.	20th July
bap.[2] 30th	St. George	March	1713.	1724.		1716.	1718.		1726.
April 1711,	the Martyr,	1712.							
Diedintestate	Middlesex.								
cir. 1771.									

Anne, bap.[2] 27th Oct.	Isabella Mary, bap.[2] 5th	William Calverly, bap.[2]	John Samuel Silly, son ⊤ ...... dau. and
1739, mar. William	May 1741, mar. at Bod-	14th Jan. 1742, bur. 14th	and heir, bap.[2] 5th April	coheir of Samuel
Martyn of Launceston,	min 1764, Henry Slog-	Nov. 1747.	1744, Lieut. R.N. Will	Harris of Smale-
mercer.	gett, Purser, R.N.		dated 29th March 1797.	combe, co. Devon.
			s.p.	

TREVELVER AND HELIGAN.

Elizabeth, mar. William Parker of St. Maben, son of James Parker of Trengoff.

John Silly, of St. Wenn in 1646 and 1659,=Jane, dau. of William Cotton, Precentor of afterwards of Trevelver. M.P. for Bodmin | Exeter. Bur.[5] 16th May 1689. Will prov. 27th 1660. Died 11th and Bur.[1] 13th April 1672. | May 1689. Archd. Cornwall. (See Ped. ante M.I. Will dated 6th Mar. 1671. Prov. 22nd | vol. i, p. 653. April 1672. Archd. Cornw.

Phillipa, named in brother Marke's Will, and in sister Elizabeth's.

Bridget, bap.[1] 14th May 1640, bur.[1] 13th Sep. 1650.

Mary, mar.[1] Thomas Ceely 5th Oct. 1658

Jane, dau. of .... Kekewich, mar. Settl. 19th and 20th Sep., 20th Charles II. Bur.[1] 10th Aug. 1672.

=William Silly of Trevelver, exr. to his father's Will. Free Burgess of Bodmin 1685.

=Honour, dau. and coheir of John Carter of St. Columb, bap. there 24th Oct. 1650. Mar. Settl. 23 March 1675-6, and mar. there 27th March 1675-6. Bur.[1] 4 Oct. 1681

John Silly, living 1671.

Marke of Middle Temple, died at Kensington, co. Middlesex. Admo. to sisters Jane and Catherine 16 Feb 1687-8 by sentence. (Ent 167.) P.C.C.

Elizabeth, mar. William Ball of St. Minver, Mar. Lic. 9th Feb. 1670.

Jane, mar. Peter Williams of Padstow. Mar. lic. 6th Dec. 1676.

Catherine, mar.[5] 13th April 1704. Edward Amy. Bur.[5] 5th Feb. 1727. See ante, vol. i, p. 653.

Hender, son and heir, bur. 24th Nov. 1705. Will dated 10th Nov. 1705. Prov. 13th April 1706. P.C.C. (Eedes 99.) s.p.

William, bap.[1] 27th June 1672, bur.[1] 2nd Aug. 1672.

Jane,[1] bap. 27th March 1677, mar. Nathaniel Shepherd of Little St. Botolph, Bishopsgate, London. Died 1707. Admo. to her husband 30th Dec. 1707. P.C.C.

John Silly, bap.[1] 6th July 1678, not named in brother Hender's will, then dead ? s.p.

Honour, bap.[1] 26th Oct. 1679, mar.[1] Anthony Tanner of St. Enoder, living 1705 died s.p.

William Silly, bap.[1] 16th Sept. 1681. Died cir. 1706. s.p.

Joseph Silly, Clerk, Inst. to the Rectory of Lesnewith 1737. Resigned for the Rectory of Lanivet 1738, bur. there 16th April 1739. Admo. to his brother John Silly of Lostwithiel, his mother, Mary Silly, having renounced, 19th April 1739. Exon.

Dennis Silly, Mariner. Admo. granted 23rd June 1746, in Arch. Court of Corw. to Mary Silly his mother.

Anne.

Dorothy, mar. .... Stephens.

Alice, mar. Nicholas Phillips of Bodmin.

John Silly of Lostwithiel, admr^d. to effects of brother Joseph 1739.

Frances Wade, bap. at Blisland, 13th Jan. 1747. Bur[2] 23rd Aug. 1759.

Elizabeth Colwill, bap. at Bodmin, 10th July 1750, mar. Clement Jackson of Looe.

Julia, bap. at Lanivet, 26th April 1753 Mar. William Lyddon.

[1] At St. Minver.   [2] At St. Maben.   [3] At St. Tudy.   [4] At Helland.   [5] At Minster.

Y

PEDIGREE OF GODOLPHIN.

ARMS OF GODOLPHIN.

Sir William Godolphin, Knt., Capt. of the Islands of Scilly 1549. = Margaret, dau. of John Glyn of Morval. See Ped. of GLYN ante p. 72.

Thomas Godolphin, 2nd son, Captain of the Scilly Islands, 6th Edward VI. = ... dau. and heir of Edward Bonython, I.W.

Sir Francis Godolphin, granted lease of Scilly Isles for 38 years, 14th Dec. 1570. = Margaret, dau. of John Killigrew of Arwenick

William Godolphin = Jane, dau. and co-heir of Walter Gaverigan, mar. 11th Dec., 1587.

Sir William Godolphin, eldest son, knighted by the Earl of Essex in Ireland 1599, ob. 1613. = Thomasine, dau. and heir of Thomas Sidney of Wrighton, co. Norfolk.

John Godolphin, 2nd son = Judith, dau. of Thomas Meredith of Ashley Castle, co. Chester.

Sir Francis Godolphin, eldest son, created K.B. at Coronation of King Charles II. Bap. at St. Margaret's, Westminster, 27th Dec. 1605. Will prov. Nov. 1667 (13 Carr). = Dorothy, dau. of Sir Henry Berkeley of Yarlington.

Ruth, dau. of Sir John Lambe of Coulston, co. Wilts, 1st wife. = Sir William Godolphin, eldest son, æt. 15, 1620. Knighted at Oxford 6th May 1644. Will dated 15th Oct. and Prov. 23rd Dec. 1663. (Archd. Cornwall). = Grace, dau. and co-heir of Richard Barratt of Tregarden, mar. at Sutcombe, co. of Devon. 25th March 1658. Died 11th. Bur. 13th Oct. 1663.

Elizabeth. Margaret. Thomas.

John Godolphin, 2nd son, of St. Thomas near Launceston, afterwards of London. Doctor of Laws. Living 1671-2 Mar. Settl. 7th May 1640 Mar. 10th May 1640. = Honour, dau. of John Molesworth of Pencarrow by his 2nd wife Phillippa dau. of Henry Rolle of Heanton, Devon, which Honour was relict Edmond Denys. Bur. 15th May 1642

Elizabeth, dau. of Sir John Gayer, Lord Mayor of London. Died 27th Jan. 1667

Francis Godolphin, eld. son, of Coulston co. Wilts. Will dated 3rd Feb. 1667. Cod. 20th April 1669. Prov. 31st Jan. 1672 (4 Eure.)

Sir William Godolphin. Bap. 2nd Feb. 1634. 2nd son. Amb. to Spaine. Kntd. 1668. Died at Madrid 1696. s.p. Will nunc. dat. June or July. Admo. with will annexed to nephew and niece, Francis Godolphin and Elizabeth, wife of Charles Godolphin. 26th November 1696. (223 Bond.)

Ruth, bap. 14th Oct. 1633. Mar. .... Greaterex.

Barnard, bap. 24th Feb. 1638.

Sir John Godolphin, bap. 24th April 1636. Devisee of Tregarden under will of his father. Will dated 1st, and proved 12th Aug. 1679. (106 King).

William, bur. 29th Sep. 1631. William, bap. Died in infancy. Bur. 1632. M.I.

Ann, bap. 12th Jan. 1611.

Margaret bur. 31st Oct. 1641.

Charles Godolphin, 5th son, M.P. for Helston, Commr. of Customs. Died 10th, and buried in Westminster Abbey 28th July 1720, æt. 69. Will dated 21st June 1719. Last cod. 31st May 1720. Prov. 22nd Oct. 1720. P.C.C. = Elizabeth, mar. lic. Vic. Gen. 27th June, 1687. Died 29th July and bur. in Westminster Abbey 16th Aug. 1726, æt. 63. Will dated 1724. Cod. 22nd July 1725. Prov. 18 Aug. 1726. P.C.C.

William Godolphin, eldest son, Governor of Scilly Isles, ob. s.p.

Charles, named in his father's will, but died before it was proved.

Francis Godolphin, of Coulston, 2nd son. Governor of Scilly, Will dated 14th Mar. 1697. Died same year. Admo. with will annexed to relict. = Elizabeth, sister of John Dixey of Market Bosworth, co. Leic.

Elizabeth Godolphin, only child. Maid of Honour to Queen Katherine. Proved her father's will. Will dated 15th Mar. 1683. Prov. 28th Nov. 1684. Admo. 15th May 1686. Unmar.

William Godolphin, born 25th March, bap. at St. Martin's-in-the-Fields, Middlesex, 8th April 1694. Bur. in Cloisters, Westminster Abbey, 16th May 1694.

Anne, born 9th, and bap. 12th Aug. 1688 at St. Martin's-in-the-Fields, Middlesex. Died 8th, and bur. in Westminster Abbey, 12th Dec. 1690.

William Godolphin, of Coulston, eldest son, Died 4th Sept. 1781, aged 88 years, and bur. at East Coulston. s.p.

Francis Godolphin, 2nd son, Deputy-Governor of Scilly, born after 1696. Died s.p.

James Burslem of Stanton, co. Derby. = Elizabeth mar. in 1719

John Mapletoft, Clerk = Barbara

Issue extinct.

Richard Chaloner Cobbe. = Mary.

TRESLOGET.

An ancient local family derived its name from Tresloget in this parish, though the name was sometimes written Sloget, and as "Sloggett" is still extant, probably Stephen Slegha, who was assessed to the subsidy in St. Maben in 1327 (Appendix I. A.) was of this family. James Tressloget held a portion of the fee of Heligan in 1428. (see ante, p. 485.) In the return of 1521-3 (Appendix I. D.) Richard Tresloget is included as possessing goods of the value of ten marks and arms for one man, and William Tresloget as having goods of the value of £4, whilst John Sloget, senior, and John Sloget, junior, are also returned at the latter rate. The names of the two last mentioned persons appear in the Subsidy Roll of 1524 as Tresloget, shewing that the spelling was, at least at that date, to some extent, indiscriminate; and in this document, in addition to the above names, we observe those of Robert Tresloget and Nicholas Tresloget. The name is found as Tresloget in the early part of the parish Registers, but soon afterwards the affix "Tre" appears to have been dropped.

HILL OF WENDRON, AND CROANE IN EGLOSHAYLE.

This family derives its descent from a certain John Hill, who married Jane daughter and heir of John Bedow, by Jane daughter and heir of Richard Seneschall of Trevenethek (now called Trenethick) in Gwendron, whilst John Bedow was great grandson of Vincent de Bedow. John Hill of Gwendron, the seventh in descent from the abovementioned John and Jane, registered his pedigree at the Heralds' Visitation of Cornwall in 1620. He had, at that time, four sons and four daughters, Francis his eldest son, then aged 23, was married, but was then without issue. He afterwards had a son named Michael, to whom his grandfather, by his will, dated 4th June 1652,[1] devised his messuage in Trevenethick and Boswen in Gwendron, and all his lands in Peran Arworthal, Kea, Gerrans, and several other parishes, subject to an annuity of £30 a year payable to his father Francis Hill. Davies Gilbert says Trevenethick continued in his descendants until the beginning of the last century, when the last of the family, Mr. John Hill, devised it by will "to a family long seated in Constantine of the same name, but from their bearing different arms supposed not to be related."[2]

[1] Proved 11th June 1653 (Brent 190.)

[2] Hist. of Cornw., vol. ii, p. 139.

3 Y²

To Michael, his fourth and youngest son, the abovementioned John Hill devised Besorow in Maugan in Meneage, and property in Gwendron, and made him executor and residuary legatee, and appointed Thomas Flamank his brother-in-law, Edward Penrose his brother-in-law, William Flamank his son-in-law, overseers. Michael Hill, the year after his father's death, purchased Croane in Egloshayle. He died in 1672. In his will, dated 14th March 1671,[1] he directed that his body should be buried in the Church or Chancel of St. Mabyn, mentioned some of the lands devised to him in his father's will, made a bequest to the poor of Gwendron, and named his brother-in-law, William Flamank, thus establishing his identity. Amongst other bequests, he gave to his son John Hill his gold signet ring. His son John Hill, on 9th October 1668, was instituted to the rectory of St. Mabyn, and dying in 1710, left a large family. By his will, dated 31st December 1709, he devised to his grandson all his right in the perpetual advowson of St. Mabyn, which he held by patent from the crown, and bequeathed to him his (testator's) grandmother's ring, given him by his father's will to be continued for ever in the family.

Michael Hill son of Michael Hill of Croane settled in Brodoke, and in his will, dated 6th November 1723, mentioned his sister Barrett's children, his nephew John Hill, and his daughters Dorothy and Elizabeth, his brother Alexander's two daughters; and his wife Ann whom he made residuary legatee and executrix.

John Hill son and heir of the Rector of St. Mabyn, resided at Croane. He married Agnes daughter of John Colwell of Horberton, co. Devon, and by deed dated 7th June 1690, some years after marriage, in performance of certain marriage articles, he conveyed to trustees the capital messuage, &c., of Croane, to the intent that Dorothy Hill his mother, if she survived her husband, should receive thereout an annuity of £20 for life, residue to the use of the said John Hill and Agnes his wife for life, remainder to their first and other sons in tail male. Three years afterwards, however, John Hill the elder, Clerk, and Dorothy his wife, and John Hill the younger of Croane, Gent., and Agnes his wife, by deed dated 30th April 5th William and Mary (1693) conveyed the said capital messuage of Croane to Edward Hoblyn of the Middle Temple, Gent.[2]

ARMS:—We know not of any arms assigned to this family of Hill. Lysons says they bore the coat of Seneschall; or, a fess betw. two chevrons sa. We have never, however, seen these arms used in the execution of any will or deed by any member of the family. The seal used by Michael Hill, on his will, is a merchant's mark, and this is probably the seal referred to in this will, and in that of John Hill, Rector of St. Maben, whilst the latter seals his will with a chev. betw. three birds, (but the arms are imperfect and indistinct,) and a castle for a crest; which are, apparently, the arms of Kestell of Kestell in Egloshayle.

---

[1] Proved 1st July 1672, Exon. P. R.

[2] Deeds in the possession of John Coode of St. Austell, Esq. See also Pedes Finium, 5th W. and M., Easter.

PEDIGREE OF HILL OF TREVENETHICK IN WENDRON AND OF CROANE IN EGLOSHAYLE.

Vincent de Bedow.

Robert de Bedow.

James de Bedow.=Jane, dau. of Reginald de Rosiwike.

John Bedow.=Jane, dau., of Richard Seneschall of Trevenethek in Wendron.

John Hill.=Jane, dau. and heir.

John Hill son and heir.

N.B.—The portion printed in *italics* is taken from the Herald's Visitation in 1620.

John 4th son.	*Thomas, 5th son.*	*Robert Hill, eldest son, ob. s.p.*	*William Hill,=Alice, dau. of .... 2nd son. Carance.*	*Paul Hill, 3rd son.*

Thomas Hill,=Jane, dau. of son and heir. Otes Trefusis.

Michael Hill,=Jane, dau. and coheir of 2nd son. Gerance Bodrigie.	*Thomas Hill, son and heir, ob. s.p.*

Michael Hill,=Margerie, dau. of son and heir. Robert Vivian.

John Hill son and heir, ob. s.p.	*Paul Hill, 2nd son.* =*Dorothy, dau. of James Erisey of Erisey, by Christian, youngest dau. of Roger Grenville of Stowe.*

John Hill of Wendron, son and heir. Will dated=Alice, dau. of Thomas 14th May 1652. Prov. 11th June 1653 (Brent190.) | Penrose.

Francis Hill, son=Grace, dau. of and heir, æt. 23. Thomas Rendall. 1620.	*Thomas,2nd son, æt. 15.*	*John, 3rd son, æt. 12.*	*Michael Hill, 4th son, æt. 6.=Sarah, dau. of Bought Croane, 1654. Bur.[1] Exec. to 23rd April 1672. Will dated husband's 14th March 1671. Prov. 1st will. July 1672.*	*Agnes. Jane. Dorothy. Margaret.*

Michael, named in grand-father's will.	William, named in grand-father's will.	Alice, named in father's will. Mar. .. Bawden.	Ann, under 21 years of age in 1671. Named in father's will. Mar. at St. Tudy, 23rd May 1677, to John Barrett of that parish.	John Hill, Rector=Dor-othy, dau. of ... of St. Maben. Inst. 9th Oct. 1668. Bur.[1] 20th Feb. 1709-10. Will dated 31st Dec. 1709. Prov. 12th Feb. 1710-11. Exon.	Charles. Richard, named in father's will.	Michael =Ann, Hill of exec. to Brodoke. husb. Will dat. will. 6th Nov. 1723. Prob. 2nd July 1724. Exon. s.p.	Alexander, named in father's will, then under age. De-visee of lands in St. Mabyn.	Nicholas =Mary, Hill of Eg-dau. of loshayle. .... Bur.[1] 30th Bur.[1] May 1718. Dec. 1698.

Elizabeth, bap.[1] May 1669. Mar.[1] 14th Aug. 1701, to Christopher Penning-ton of Bod-min.	Dorothy, bap.[1] 26th March 1672	Sarah, bap.[1] 30th June 1674.	Ann, bap.[1] 6th Oct. 1676.	Bridget, bap.[1] 20th Nov. 1684.	John Hill, =Agnes, dau. of Croane, of John bap.[2] 22nd Colwell Sept. 1663, of Horber-Bur.[1] 6th ton, co. May 1731. Devon. Settl. after mar. 7th June 1690. Bur.[1] 18th March 1722.	Richard, bap.[2] 24th March 1667.	Catherine. =Michael dau. of Wil-Hill, liam Lynam of bap.[2] St. Kew, and 12th relict of Mat-Nov. thew Hutton. 1665. Mar.[3] 3rd Bur.[1] 6th March 1673. May 1723 Bur.[2] 30th March 1719.	=Ann, dau. of .. Williams of Eglos-hayle, mar.[2] 5th Jan. 1719.	Mary, bap. .. Bur.[1] 26th July 1720.

Agnes, bap.[1] 27th Feb. 1684.	Henrietta, bap.[1] 5th June 1686, named in grandfather's will.	James, bap.[1] 1st Nov. 1692, named in grandfather's will as Devisee of Rectory of St. Mabyn.	Dorothy, bur.[1] 15th Sept. 1697.	Elizabeth, named in will of great-uncle Michael Hill.	Ann, named in grand-father's will.

---

[1] At St. Mabyn. [2] At Egloshayle. [3] At St. Kew.

HEXT OF TREDETHY AND LANCARFE.

The family of Hext of Tredethy and Lancarfe is descended from Francis John Hext of Bodmin, who was the second son of Francis Hext of Trenarren, which family claims descent from Hext of Kingston in Devon.

Francis John Hext married Katherine daughter of William Mounsteven of Lancarfe, and settled in Bodmin, of which borough he was several times Mayor. His son of the same name, who was also of Bodmin, Town Clerk of that borough in 1769, and several times Mayor (see ante, vol i, pp. 238, 239), married Margaret sister and sole heir of Elias Lang of Plymouth and Tredethy, and daughter of Elias Lang and Margaret his wife daughter of William May of Bodmin by Margaret daughter and coheir of William Lugger of Tredethy. Francis John Hext and Margaret his wife had four sons and four daughters. Their eldest son Francis [John] Hext was sometime a captain in the Royal Miners' Militia, but he afterwards took Holy Orders and became Rector of Helland. He inherited Tredethy by the bequest of his uncle Elias Lang, the younger, and died unmarried in 1842.

Samuel Hext, the third son, was commissioned to an Ensigncy in the 50th Foot with which he served in the Egyptian campaign. Afterwards he was gazetted to a company in the 53rd Regiment, with which regiment he served in all the battles of the Peninsula, from Talavera to Toulouse. He was present also in Ceylon during the Candian war in 1803, and was at the capture of the Cape of Good Hope in 1806. He received a gold medal for Badajoz, where he stormed the citadel, and gold clasp for Orthes and Toulouse, and was made a Companion of the Most Honorable Order of the Bath. Eventually he became Major of the 83rd Foot. This distinguished Officer, having escaped all the dangers of the field, died from an accident in 1822, aged 40 years.

George, the fourth son, twin brother of Samuel, entered the Royal Navy, and was a Lieutenant of the Barrosa frigate. He fell by a rifle shot while leading a boat attack in the Potomac, in America, in 1813.

William Hext, the second son, in 1791, also entered the Royal Navy, and was present in Lord Howe's glorious victory of 1st June 1794. He was continuously in active service from the date of his joining until the peace, and received the war medal with two clasps. On 12th April 1862, he was promoted to the rank of Rear-Admiral on the Retired List. He married Barbara, daughter and heir of James Read of Tremeere in St. Tudy, M.D., and left three surviving children. George, his second son, after a distinguished University career, entered Holy Orders, and is now (1875) Rector of Steeple Langford, co. Wilts, Francis John, son and heir of Admiral Hext, succeeded his father at Tredethy and Lancarfe. and is in the Commission of the Peace and a Deputy-Lieutenant for Cornwall.

ARMS:—The arms used by this family are the same as were allowed to Hext of Kingston in Devon and Constantine in Cornwall at the Herald's Visitation of 1620, viz.:—
    Or, a tower between three battle axes sa. (Hext) quartering: ar. a fess, per fess indented, or and gu., in chief three trefoils slipped sa. (Tilly) and; vairée ar. and sa. a chief of the second guttée de sang (Colswell.)

PEDIGREE OF HEXT AND LUGGER OF ST. MABYN.

ARMS ALLOWED TO HEXT OF KINGSTON 1620.

.... Lugger.

Elizabeth,† 2nd wife named in her husband's will.	William Lugger of Tredethy. Bought Tredethy 1607. Bur.¹ 29th Jan. 1639-40. Will dated 10th Aug. 1639. Prov. 12th May 1640. P.C.C.	Honour, bur. 3rd Oct. 1630.	Nathaniel Lugger of Bodmin, Mayor of Bodmin 1661, 1670. Bur.² 1693. Had a grant of arms 24th Nov. 1645. See ante, vol. i, p. 340. = Ann, bur.² 1676.

| Wilmot, bur.¹ 13th June 1625. John,† bap.¹ 12th Aug. 1626. | Grace, bap.¹ 11th Oct. 1612. Mar. Ralph Plumleigh. Elizabeth, bap.¹ 17th Sept. 1627. | Jane, bap.¹ 13th June 1613, bur.¹ 29th July 1614. | Margery,† bap.¹ 23rd March 1613. Honour.† | William Lugger† of Tredethy, bap.¹ 4th May 1617. Will dat. 17th Feb. 1674. Prov. 2nd Feb. 1676 Exon. =Elizabeth, dau. of Alexander Lang. | Nathaniel,† bap.¹ 13th May 1617. Philippa, life on Tredethy, 1607. | Alexander† bap.¹ 16th April 1620. life on Tredethy, 1639. | Elizabeth, bur.² 1644. William, bap.² 19th Nov. 1639, bur.² 22nd June 1642. | Honour, bur.² 1663. |

| Honour, bap.¹ 16 Jan. 1611. | Elizabeth, bap.¹ 6th Jan. 1646 | Ann,¹ bap.¹ 14th March 1647, mar.¹ George, Baron of Tintagel, 16th Nov. 1670. | William Lugger¹ of Tredethy,† born 13th and bap.¹ 25th July 1651. Will dated 23rd March 1719. Proved 12th May 1721. Exon. =Deborah dau. of .. Squire. Bur.¹ 21st Aug. 1714. | John,† bap.¹ 20th Jan. 1660. Grace.† | Jane, bap.¹ 24th Dec. 1669. Mar. Eliezer Hancock Margery † |

| William Lugger, bap.¹ 6th May 1683. | John Lugger, bap.¹ 1st Mar. 1684. | William May of Bodmin Merchant, son of Thomas May of Bodmin, Gent. Will dated 6th May 1740. Cod. 20th April 1757, and 28th May 1758. =Margaret, bap.¹ 13th Dec. 1680. Mar. Settl. 20th April 1698. mar.¹ 31st May 1698. Bur. 26th March 1754. | Deborah, bap.¹ 3rd April 1687, mar. at Helland, 1st Oct. 1713, to William Rundall of Great Torrington. Living a widow 1727. Will dated 4th July 1767. Exccr. to father's will. | Nathaniel, bap.¹ 16th April 1689. | Elizabeth, mar. Robert Venn of Southmolton.. Mar. Settl. 7th March 1737, ob. s.p. Bur. at Southmolton, 11th July 1758. | Hugh bur.¹ 18th Dec. 1691. |

A

Those marked thus † named in father's will.

¹ At St. Maben. ² At Bodmin. ³ At St. Tudy.

PEDIGREE OF HEXT AND

Francis John Hext of Bodmin,=Catherine, dau. of William
second son of Francis Hext of | Mounsteven of Lancarfe. Mar.[3]
Trenarren. Born 8th Jan. 1703. | 26th June 1728. Bur.[1] 1773.
Mayor of Bodmin 1762, 1768. | Will proved 27th Jan. 1773.
Bur.[2] 1770. Will proved March
1770.

```
                              A
  John      Grace      Elizabeth
        died young.
```

Samuel, bap.[3] 4th April   Elizabeth, bap.[2] 1739,   Anne, bap.[2]
1747, bur.[1] 9th March   mar. 1st, William Cole   1737, mar. .....
1804, aged 57, un-   of Plymouth, 2nd, Ste-   Bellringer of
married.   phen Hewett. ob. s.p.   Bodmin.

Ann,   Francis [John] Hext, Clerk, of Tredethy, Rec-   William Hext of Lancarfe and after-=Barbara, dau. and heir of James
bap.[1]   tor of Helland. Born 10th April 1779, bap.[2] 3rd wards of Tredethy. Born 5th July 1780 Read, M.D., of Tremere in St.
15th   April 1781, died at Bath 27th Jan. 1842. Aged   and bap.[2] 3rd April 1781. Entered R.N. Tudy. Died 22nd Feb. 1852.
April   63. Bur. at Helland. unmar. Many years in the   1791. Lieut. 8th Aug. 1799. Comm.
1771.   Com. of the Peace and a Dy-Lieut. for Cornwall. 28th April 1809. Cap. 23rd Nov. 1841.
                                                           Rear-Adm. 12th April 1862. Died 31st
                                                           Oct. 1866. Many years in the Com. of
                                                           the Peace for Cornwall.

Francis John born   Francis John Hext of Tredethy,=Mary Francis Elizabeth, only   Loveday Mar-   Barbara Read, born
13th Sep. 1815.   son and heir, born 28th Aug. | dau. of Sir Joseph Sawle   garet. Born 15th   at Lancarfe 17th
Died in infancy.   1817. Bap.[2] Sometime of the | Graves Sawle of Penrice, Bart., Feb. 1814, died   Dec. 1821, died 19th
                     83rd Regt. J. P. and D. L. for | mar. 9th Dec. 1852.   3rd Oct. 1822.   July 1842.
                     Cornwall.

Francis John Hext, son and heir, born   George Hext, born 22nd   William Hext, 12th Sep.   George Kendall Hext.
19th March and bap.[3] 29th June 1854.   Jan. and bap.[3] 8th August 1862, died 9th Feb. 1865.   Born 21st Sep. 1864.
Lieut. Royal Cornwall and Devon   1855. Lieut. R.N. March
Miners, 11th Sep. 1871.   22nd 1875.

At St. Mabyn.　　　　　　[2] At Bodmin.　　　　　　[3] At St. Tudy.

LUGGER OF ST. MABYN—Continued.

Benjamin Stone=Margaret, of Great bap.[2] 8th Torrington, Clerk, Jan. 1705. mar.[1] 22nd June Bur.[2] 15th 1736. Bur.[2] 20th Dec. 1773. April 1737, s.p. 1st Husband Admo. to Margaret his relict, 28th Sept. 1737. P.C.C.	=Elias Lang of Plymouth. Mar. Settl. dated 9th March and mar.[2] 23rd June 1742. Bur. at Plymouth 11th June 1762. Will dated 1759.	William May of Bodmin, bap.[2] 11th Oct. 1703, bur.[1] 24th Feb. 1785. Exec and Residuary Legatee, appointed by last Codicil to his father's will. Died unmar. and intestate.	Deborah, bap.[2] 2nd Jan. 1702, bur.[1] 21st May 1750, unmar.	Jane, bap. 27th Aug. 1699, Mar. Settl. 13th Sept. 1736, mar.[2] same day Samuel Carkeet of Totnes, Clerk. Bur.[2] 9th Aug. 1780. Admo. granted to her brother William, 10th Oct. 1780. P.C.C. ob. s.p.
Francis John Hext of Bodmin and Lancarfe, bap.[2] 1731. Mayor of Bodmin, 1773, 1779, 1785, 1789, 1791. Died 25th Jan., bur.[1] 31st Jan. 1803. Will dated 14th March 1803. Prov. P.C.C.	=Margaret Lang, born at Plymouth and bap. at Meeting House there, 3rd July 1744. Mar.[2] 24th Jan. 1769. Bur.[1] 8th March 1794.	Elias Lang of Plymouth and Lancarfe. Born at Plymouth and bap. at the Meeting House there 22nd Dec. 1747. Bur.[1] 25th Oct. 1791, ob. s.p. Will proved P.C.C.	Ann Lang, named in her father's will.	
Samuel Hext, C.B. Born 11th May 1782, bap.[1] 5th Oct. 1786. Major 83rd Regt. Died 24th July 1822. Aged 40.	George Hext, born 20th Aug. 1785. Bap.[1] 5th Oct. 1786. Lieut. Royal Navy. Killed in action 1813.	Anne, bap.[1] 14th Mar. 1770, mar.[2] 1795. Charles Kendall, Clerk.	Jenny, bap.[1] 30th Sept. 1774. Died 1824.	Elizabeth, bap.[1] 11th March 1776. Died 1779.	Margaret, bap.[1] 9th Sep. 1778. Died 1810.

George Hext, B.D., born 15th Jan. 1819, 1st= Class Lit. Hum. 1840, late Fellow and Tutor of C. C. Coll., and Pub. Exam. Univ. Oxford 1852. Vicar of St. Veep, 1857-73. Rector of Steeple Langford, co. Wilts.	=Elizabeth Furnis, dau. of John Penberthy Major, of Lamellen in St. Tudy.	Samuel Hext. Died in infancy.	Susanna Read, born 28th Jan. 1824. Mar.[1] David Horndon of Pencreber, co. Cornw.
Edward Francis Amyas, born 20th Aug. 1867, 2nd son.	Barbara Elizabeth. Born 20th March 1860.	Mary Constance, born 20th March 1861.	Margaret, born 15th Feb. 1866.	Lyonel John, born 16th July 1871.

[1] At St. Mabyn. [2] At Bodmin. [3] At St. Tudy.

3 z

PROSPICE.

ARMS OF ANDREW OF TREDINNICK.

PEDIGREE OF

William Andrew of St. Tudy,⹌
bur.[1] 17th Oct. 1584.

John Andrew of Penhale in⹌Alice his wife, bur.[1]
St. Tudy, bur.[1] 16th April | 17th May 1601.
1594.

John Audrew of St.⹌Margery, dau. of .... Jeffry
Tudy, bap.[1] Aug. 1580. | of St. Tudy. Mar[1] 16th Oct.
Bur.[1] 8th March 1650. | 1615, bur.[1] 4th Feb. 1655.

Avis Andrew, bap.[1]   Mary Andrew. Bap.[1]
11th Aug. 1622.   22nd May 1625, bur.[1] 4th
                                    Mar. 1657.

Jonathan Andrew of St.⹌*Magdalen, dau. of ......*
Tudy, bap.[1] 4th Nov. 1655. | *bur.[1] 13th Nov. 1710.*

Margaret, bap.[1]   *Jonathan Andrew*⹌*Joan, dau. of ..*
14th May 1687.   *of St. Tudy, bap.[1]* | *Hawken of St.*
                        14th May 1690. | *Breward, mar.*
                                         | *there 16th Sep.*
                                         | *1719.*

Mary, bap.[1] 18th   *Susannah, bap.[1]*
April 1718.   *19th Sep. 1724.*

Richard Hambly Andrew of⹌*Ann, dau. of Abraham Browne*
Tredinnick. Bap.[1] 24th Nov. | *of Endellion. Died 21st Dec.*
1772. Died 10th Aug. 1851. | *1836. Aged 49 years.*
Will dated 12th April 1848, and
proved with 5 Codicils 15th Sep.
1851, s.p.

Elizabeth, born 8th | Amelia, born 12th and bap. | Mary Ann, born 26th and | Christopher Thomas⹌Mary, dau. of
May, and bap. at | 24th Feb. 1817, mar. 1st | bap.[3] 27th May 1812. | Andrew of Menkee. | Thomas Lawry of
Lanivet 1st Aug. | Robert Woodman Grose 12th | Mar. 1st William Warne | Born 9th Aug. and | Brodes in Helland.
1803. Died unmar. | Nov. 1839 ; he died 1851 | of St. Issey. He bur. | bap.[1] 22nd Oct. 1805. | Born 15th March
6th Oct. 1838. | and bur. at Bodmin. 2ndly, | there 5th Jan. 1832. Mar. | Died 6th and bur.[1] | and bap. at Helland.
| Aaron Weston, 25th July | 2ndly John Rowe, formerly | 11th Nov. 1870. | 30th March 1808.
| 1854. Died at Manchester | of Bodmin now (1875) of | Will dated 5th Nov. | Mar. there 4th Nov.
| 11th Feb. 1874. | Frognal House, Hamp- | 1876, prov. 7th Mar. | 1827. Died Sept.
| | stead. | 1871, Bodmin. | 1871. Bur.[3]

Richard Hambly Andrew of Tre⹌Henrietta, dau. of Francis Wool- | Ellen Mary, born 6th | George John, born
dinnick. Born 14th Jan. and bap. | cock Pye, Clerk, Rector of Blisland. | Dec. 1829, mar.[1] 28th | 3rd Aug., and bap.
17th Feb. 1829. Bar.-at-Law of the | Born 20th Sep. 1839, bap. at Blis- | July 1869, Thomas | at St. Columb. 6th
Inner Temple and Capt. in the Royal | land, and mar. there 29th April | Spears Rundell. | Sep. 1831, unmar.
Cornwall Rangers. | 1858.

Richard Hambly Andrew, son and heir, born 17th Sep.
1868, priv. bap. the same month, and publicly received
into the Church at St. Mark's, Regent's Park, London,
16th June 1869.

At St. Tudy.   [2] At St. Minver.   [3] At St. Mabyn.   [4] At Endellion.

ANDREW.

Christopher Andrew of St.⹀Margaret, dau. of .... Pawley
Tudy, bur.[1] 17th Aug. 1699. | of St. Tudy. Mar.[1] 20th Oct.
1654, bur.[1] 4th June 1687.

Margery, bap.[1] 30th
Jan. 1658.

Margaret, bap.[1]
1659.

Edward, bap.[1] 18th Feb.
1700.

Christopher Andrew of⹀Elizabeth, dau. of ....
St. Tudy, bap.[1] 24th | Stephens, bur.[1] 29th
May 1684, bur.[1] 10th | Mar. 1775.
Nov. 1770.

Christopher Andrew of St. Tudy. Bap[1] 19th Sep. 1727.⹀Joan, dau. of John May of St. Minver. Bap.[2] 5th March
Purchased Tregarden and Tredinnick in St. Mabyn 1794. | 1738, mar.[2] 21st May 1769. Died 25th Oct. 1778 in
Bur.[1] 13th Aug. 1810. Aged 86. | the 42nd year of her age. Bur.[3] M.I.

John May Andrew of Tregarden,⹀Mary, dau. of James
bap.[1] 5th Jan. 1775. Died 21st | Thomas of Lanivet. Bap.
and bur. 23rd April 1842. Will | there 25th July 1777, mar.
dated 30th Dec. 1841, and prov. | there 24th March 1801.
27th Aug. 1842. Archd. Corn- | Died 16th May 1844.
wall.

John May Andrew of Menkee.⹀Mary, dau. of John George of
Born 13th and bap.[3] 25th Oct. | Endellion. Bap.[4] 1807, mar.[4]
1809. Died 22nd and bur.[3] | 1st Dec. 1834. Remar. ....
26th Nov. 1840, s.p. and intes- | Brown.
tate.

James Andrew of Tregarden.⹀Mary Ann, dau. of George
Born 13th Sep. and bap.[1] | Hambly of St. Mabyn.
15th Dec. 1807. | Mar. at Tavistock Nov.
1833.

John May of 8,⹀Mary Adeliza, dau.
Queen's Crescent, | of Michael Bradford
Haverstock Hill, bap[4] | of Tickencote, co. Rut-
5th Feb. 1833. | land, mar. there 1st
Jan. 1857. Died 1st
June 1867. s.p.

Christopher
Thomas, born
5th Nov., and
bap.[1] 20th
Nov. 1834.

Thomas Lawry, bap.
3rd Oct. 1839, died
6th May 1863.
Bur.[3] unmar.

Samuel Lawry,
born 6th Sep.
1840, and bap.[1]
6th Jan. 1841,
unmar.

Charles James,
born 1st Sep.
1844, died 12th
Sep. 1859.

I hereby certify that the portion of this Pedigree which is printed in *Italics*, and the Arms, are
recorded in this Office.   GEORGE HARRISON,
Heralds' College.   Windsor Herald.

[1] At St. Tudy.   [2] At St. Minver.   [3] At St. Mabyn.   [4] At Endellion.

3 Z[2]

BALDWYN, *alias* BAWDWIN, *alias* BAWDEN OF COLQUITE.

The family of Bawdwyn held a large portion of the barton of Colquite and all the wood, on a lease for lives, and William Bawden held this lease in 1576 (see ante, pp. 78 and 80.) His daughter and heir married Giles Hamley of Treblethick, who was allowed by Sir John Borough, Garter King of Arms, to quarter, in respect of this alliance; gu. two bendlets within a bordure ar. for Bawdwyn. Nicholas Bawdwyn was dwelling in St. Mabyn in 1586, and probably at Colquite. He is mentioned in the confession of John Hamblye (see post) as having been a Scholar of Exeter College, Oxford, and his sister Emlyn is also named in the same document. Both were Roman Catholics.

PLUMLEIGH OF ST. MABYN.

At the time of the Herald's Visitation of Cornwall in 1620, a family of Plumleigh was settled in St. Maben, shewn in the pedigree, then recorded, to be descended from Thomas son of John Plumleigh of Dartmouth, by his second wife Ann, daughter of John Fortescue of Fallopit. In the pedigree of Plumleigh of Dartmouth, however, recorded by the same Heralds in the Visitation of Devon, this Thomas is shewn as the second son of the said John Plumleigh by his first marriage with the daughter of ...... Eastchurch of Chudleigh. We must leave this discrepancy to be reconciled by the Heralds. At the date of the Visitation John Plumleigh was Mayor of Dartmouth, and William Plumleigh, elder brother of the whole blood of Thomas (according to the Devon Pedigree) was one of the Capital Burgesses. The above mentioned Thomas Plumleigh, by Elizabeth daughter of Robert Shapleigh of Dartmouth, had a son John Plumleigh, who married Joane daughter of John Sture of Huishe in Devon (called in the Devon Visitation " John Steourt of Bradley ") and settled in St. Maben in the beginning of the 17th century. He had a daughter buried there in 1610, and his father and mother were both interred at St. Maben, the former in 1615 and the latter in 1628. John Plumleigh, Gent., was assessed to the subsidies in St. Maben, *upon goods*, in 1625, 1629, and 1642. We have traced his descendants to the third generation, but at the end of the century they would seem to have become almost extinct in the male line, though the name lingered in the parish until 1736. We have not discovered at what place in the parish the family was seated.

ARMS:—Ermine, a bend lozengy gu.—Crest, a dexter arm, embowed, ppr. habited of the second, and cuffed ar., grasping a dart of the second, barbed of the fourth.

PEDIGREE OF PLUMLEIGH.

ARMS AS ALLOWED AT THE VISITATION AT 1620.

John Plumleigh of ... *Dartmouth in co. Devon.* = ... *dau. of John Fortescue of Fallopit.*

Thomas Plumleigh Bap.[1] *24th July 1615.* = *Elizabeth, dau. of Robert Shapleigh of Dartmouth. Bur.[1] 28th April 1628.*

John Plumleigh of St. Mabin in Cornwall, living Ano. 1620. Assessed to Subs. in St. Maben in 1625, 1629, and 1642. Bur.[1] 7th Feb. 1658. = *Joane, dau. of John Stare of Haish in Devon. Bur.[1] 7th Nov. 1667.*

William, bap.[1] 14 July and bur.[1] 28th Sep. 1611.	Margaret, bur.[1] 20th March 1610.	*Gilbert Plumleigh, æt. 16. Ano. 1620.*	*Elizabeth æt. 13. Eldest dau.* Mar.[1] 1641. Giles Betty.	*Ralph* Plumleigh, *æt. 10. Second son,* bap.[1] 13th May 1611, bur.[1] 16th Aug. 1658. Admo. to Grace his relict 27th Oct. 1658. P.C.C. = Grace, dau. of William Lugger, mar.[2] .. 1636, bur.[1] 24th Jan. 1697-8.	*Grace, æt. 8.* Bap.[1] 20th Sep. 1612 mar.[1] 21st June 1654, John Seamer.	*Joane, æt 5.* Bap.[1] 9th July 1615, mar.[1] 20th Jan. 1633, William Hender of Tintagel.	John Plumleigh of St. Maben. Bap.[1] 15th March 1620 bur.[1] 4th Sep. 1689 Admo. granted 2nd Jan 1690 to Humphry Borlase a Creditor. = Ann dau. of .. bur.[1] 21st Jan. 1694	Frances, bap.[1] 21st Feb. 1625. Mary, bp.[1] 12 July 1627.

John Plumleigh, bap.[1] 20th April 1638, bur.[1] same day.	Elizabeth bap.[2] 1st June 1641, bur.[1] 5th Sep. 1660.	Joane, bap.[1] 4th July 1639, mar.[1] 20th Jan. 1664, William Parnell.	Honour, bap.[3] 6th June 1644, mar.[1] 16th Nov. 1675, John Helman of Lanlivery.	Grace, bap.[1] 6th Mar. 1651. Mary, bap.[1] 21st Dec. 1652 Mary, bap.[1] .. 1654.	John, bap.[1] .. 1652. John, bap.[1] 18th Nov. 1659.	Mary, bap.[1] April 1651. Thomas, bap.[1] 14th Oct. 1654, bur.[1] 12th March 1659.	Joseph, bap.[1] 6th June 1656.	Joane, bap.[1] 1st April 1658, mar.[1] 12th Oct. 1682, Henry Stevens.	Charles, bap.[1] 5th June 1662, bur.[1] 16th April 1685. William, bap.[1] 18th Nov. 1659, bur.[1] 19th Jan. 1659-60.

I hereby certify that the portion of this pedigree printed in *italics*, and the Arms, agree with the Records in this Office.

Heralds' College,

GEORGE HARRISON,
Windsor Herald.

[1] At St. Maben.   [2] At St. Teath   [3] At St. Breward.

TAMLYN.

The family of Tamlyn was of long continuance in the parish of St. Maben. Henry Temelyn was a tenant of the manor of Trevisquite in 1422.[1] John Tamlyn was assessed to the subsidy in St. Mabyn 1541,[2] and we find the name at the very commencement of the parish Registers. Roger Tamlyn had a son baptized in 1565, which same Roger was probably also the father of Thomas, the grandfather of Richard, to whom Richard Loveys, Lord of the manor of Trevisquite, and Frances his wife sold Tregaddock in 1659,[3] possibly the same tenement which had been held by his ancestor in 1422. This Richard, in the entry of his burial in the parish Register in 1664, is described as " Richard Tamlyn of Tregaddock, Gent." He would seem to have died s.p., and Tregaddock devolved upon his elder brother John Tamlyn, who died in 1671, and is described in the same manner as his brother. By his will, dated 16th August 1670, John Tamlyn demised to Susanna Tamlyn and Elizabeth Tamlyn, his two unmarried daughters, the reversion of a tenement in Tregaddock (then held on lease by Thomas Philpe and Richard Philpe his son for life) as security for the payment to his said two daughters of £100 each, with remainder to testator's grandson John Tamlyn (then an infant) and the heirs male of his body, in default of such issue remainder to the heirs of the body of testator's son John Tamlyn, in default remainder to the right heirs of the said John Tamlyn. It was probably for the purpose of carrying out this settlement that, in 1659, as John Tamlyn, senior, Gent., and John Tamlyn, junior,[4] Gent., they were deforcients in a fine levied in Tregaddock by William Arthur, Gent., and William Beale, Gent. John Tamlyn had also a daughter Anne, whom he does not name in his will. She married in 1661 Chamond Penhallow, whom, as his son-in-law, John Tamlyn appointed one of the overseers of his will,[5] and gave his grandson John Penhallow a small legacy. She was the mother of Samuel Penhallow, the most remarkable man, perhaps, which St. Maben has ever produced.

John Tamlyn the grandson, who was constituted tenant for life of Tregaddock under the above mentioned will, would appear to have died in childhood, as his father had another son of the same name baptized in 1693. The property consequently devolved upon the father under the above mentioned limitations.

ARMS:—John Tamlyn sealed his will in 1677, with an armorial seal: three bars in fess.

---

[1] Inq. p.m. of Johanna Beaumont, 1st Henry VI, No. 50.

[2] Sub. Roll, 33rd Henry VIII, $\frac{87}{148}$ [3] Pedes Finium, 1659, Hilary.

[4] John Tamlyn, junior, married a daughter of William Arthur of St. Ervan, and William Beale of St. Teath married the sister of the said John.

[5] Probate, 3rd November 1671. Exon.

SAMUEL PENHALLOW.

Samuel Penhallow was born, probably at Tregaddock his grandfather Tamlyn's house, on 2nd July 1665. His father Richard Penhallow, of whom he was the second son, was the representative of an ancient family, deriving their name from Penhallow in Filleigh, which they had for centuries possessed. His mother, the second wife of Richard Penhallow, was Mary the daughter of Walter Porter of Launcelles, by Gertrude daughter of Richard Chamond son of Sir John Chamond, who was sometime Steward for the Priory of Bodmin.

Chamond Penhallow was of puritan proclivities, and was intimate with Charles Morton, who sometime held the rectory of Blisland during the interregnum; and when that gentleman established a school at Newington Green, co. Middlesex, young Penhallow, in 1683, was placed under his care. He continued at Newington for about three years, when the school was broken up because the Ecclesiastical authorities did not consider it proper that dissenters should be allowed to take part in the education of the young. Penhallow made diligent application to his studies, and by his progress and conduct gained the affection of his master, consequently upon the latter determining to emigrate to America he was invited, with others, to accompany him, to which, with the consent of his parents, he acceded and arrived in New England in July 1686.

Before Penhallow left England, the New England Society for the Propagation of the Gospel[1] offered him £20 a year for three years if he would acquire a knowledge of the Indian language, and promised him £60 a year afterwards for life if he devoted himself to the Ministry and preached to the Indians at times.

Soon after their arrival in America, Mr. Morton had an invitation to take charge of the Church of Charlestown, which he accepted, and young Penhallow accompanied him thither. The political troubles, however, which took place in Massachusetts about that time, discouraged him from entering the Ministry, and he removed to Portsmouth. Soon after his settlement there he married Mary daughter of John Cuff, a native of Wales, at that time President of the State. She inherited from her father a valuable patrimony, a part of which consisted of a large tract of land upon which the town of Portsmouth was built. Mr. Penhallow engaged in trade and accumulated a large fortune. He lived in a style superior to most of his fellow-townsmen, exercising hospitality on a liberal scale. He

---

[1] This Company was first formed under a pretended Act of Parliament in 1649, but, through the influence of Sir William Morice, Secretary of State, was incorporated, by letters patent dated 7th February 1661-2, (Rot. Pat. 14th Charles II., part 2, No. 17.) under the title of "The Company for the Propagation of the Gospel in New England and parts adjacent" The Company acquired a considerable extent of lands, including the manor of Eriswell in Suffolk, and its funds have considerably accumulated. By a Decree in Chancery in 1836, Canada, as being the part of the British Dominions nearest adjacent to New England, was placed within the limits of the operations of the Company. It is, perhaps, unnecessary to say that this Company is quite distinct from the Society for the Propagation of the Gospel in Foreign Parts,. which was not incorporated until 1701. The New England Company is little known.

acquired great influence, and taking an active part in the management of the town, was soon made a Magistrate, in which office he displayed great prudence, promptness, and decision of character. He was appointed by the House of Representatives Recorder of Deeds. In 1714 he was made Justice of the Superior Court of Judicature, and in 1717 Chief Justice of the same court, which office he held until his death. It is said that "a strong mind improved by education added to his long acquaintance with public business, enabled him to discharge the duties of the office with as much credit to himself as could be expected from any one not bred to the profession of the law." Mr. Penhallow likewise held the office of Treasurer of the Province for several years. His last account was rendered to 9th November 1726, and he died at Portsmouth on 2nd December in the same year, aged 61 years and 5 months. By his first wife, who died in 1713, he had 13 children.

His son, John, was Clerk of the Superior Court at Portsmouth in 1729, and Registrar of the Court of Probate there from 1731 to 1735, in which year he died. He married a daughter of Hunking Wentworth, and had two sons, John, who, in 1770, was the largest taxpayer in Portsmouth, and Samuel, who is called the "good deacon." John had two, probably three, sons: Hunking, Benjamin, and perhaps Thomas W. (Wentworth?) It is related that "Benjamin Penhallow one day saw a lady who stopped at Mrs. Parker's, on her way to Portland. He sought an introduction, and in due time was married to Susan, the daughter of Colonel William Pearce of Gloucester. They were visited by a young lady, Miss Harriet Pearce, daughter of David Pearce of Gloucester, and Hunking Penhallow took her for his helpmeet. When Miss Mary Beache of Gloucester was afterwards on a visit to Mrs. Hunking Penhallow, she was first seen by Thomas W. Penhallow, who became her husband. This matrimonial alliance with Gloucester made him acquainted with his second wife, who was half-sister of Hunking Penhallow's wife."[1]

These particulars of a Cornish worthy and native of this parish, and the extension of the pedigree annexed, collected from sources not readily accessible, will be of interest to Cornish genealogists, as shewing the continuation with credit in the New World of an ancient Cornish family, which, as far as we know, has become extinct in the Old.

Chief Justice Penhallow, in 1725, published in Boston, a History of the Wars of New England with the Eastern Indians. The first edition of this work having become exceedingly scarce, in 1859 it was reprinted in Cincinnati.[2]

ARMS OF PENHALLOW :—Vert, a Rabbit squat, ar.

---

[1] Brewster's Rambles about Portsmouth, p. 340.   [2] Bibl. Cornub, vol. ii,

PEDIGREE OF PENHALLOW AND TAMLYN.

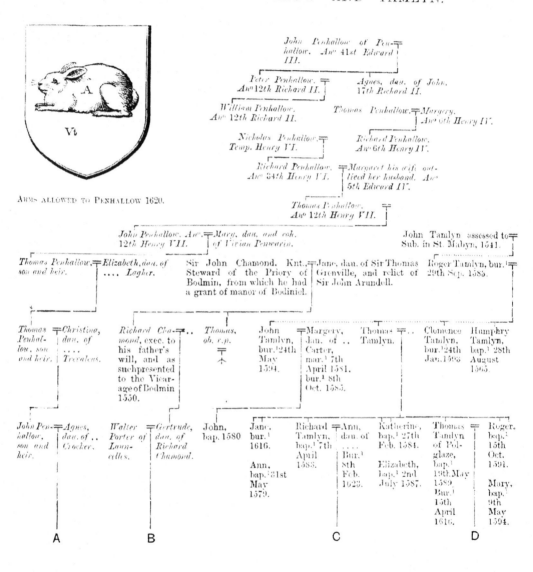

ARMS ALLOWED TO PENHALLOW 1620.

A   B   C   D

PEDIGREE OF PENHALLOW

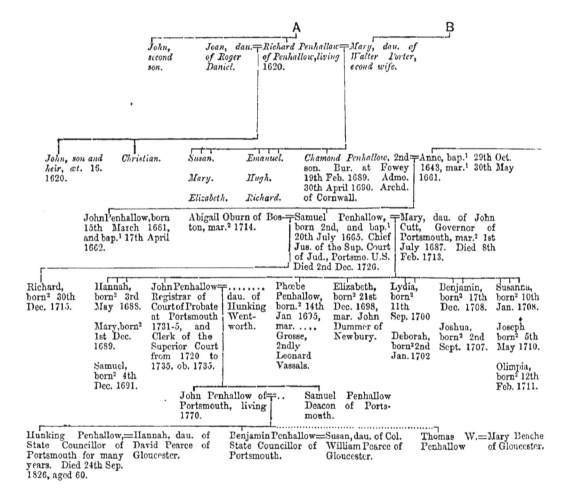

AND TAMLYN.—Continued.

C   D

| John Tamlyn of=Mary. | Christiana, bap.[1] 14th April 1611. | RichardTam-=Elizabeth lyn,bap.[1] 11th Feb. 1612. Bought Tregaddock 1659 Died 13th,and bur.15th Feb. 1664. | Grace,bap.[1] 13th May 1615. Joan, bap.[1] 28th Dec. 1617. | Anne, bap.[1] 15th Oct. 1620. | Thomasine, bap.[1] 17th Sep. 1615. | Jane, bur.[1] 1st April 1816. |

John Tamlyn of=Mary. Tregaddock, bap.[1] 10th May 1609, died 24th, bur.[1] 25th Sep. 1671. Will dat. 16th Aug. 1670. Prov. 3rd Nov. 1671. Exon.

RichardTam-=Elizabeth lyn,bap.[1] 11th dau. of .... Feb. 1612. Bur.[1] 11th Bought Tre- March 1658. gaddock 1659

| Mary, mar.[1] 4th Feb. 1668, Justinian Webber of Bodmin. | Elizabeth, mar.[1] William Beale of St. Teath, Mar. Lic. dated 25th June 1668. | John Tamlyn of=Issott,dau.of...Arthur of St. Ervan, Mar. Lic. dated 26th Aug. 1669. | Susanna,bap.[1] 11th Feb. 1650, bur.[1] 15th Feb. 1672. | Katherine, bap.[1] 29th June 1652. |

John Tamlyn of=Issott,dau.of..Arthur Tregaddock, bap.[1] 11th April 1648. Died 22nd, and bur.[1] 24th Feb. 1706-7.

| JohnTamlyn, bap.[1] 13th Jan. 1669-70. | Mary, bap.[1] 1674, mar.[1] 27th May 1695, John Williams. | Elizabeth, bap.[1] 29th Oct. 1678, bur.[1] 24th Jan. | Loveday, bap.[1] 7th Jan. 1679-80. | William Tam-=Grace, lyn, bap.[1] 7th dau. of Feb. 1683, bur.[1] .. bur.[1] 23rd Feb. 1732. 22ndOct. 1738. | Richard bap.[1] 13th Nov. 1689. | John, bap.[1] 18thJuly 1693. |

Honour, bap.[1] 4th Aug. 1707. Mar.[1] 26th Dec.1723. Richard Bastard of Lanteglos.

William,bap.[1] 29th Aug. 1708, bur.[1] 9th Feb. 1708-9.

I certify that the portion of the above Pedigree which is printed in *Italics*, and the arms, agree with the Records in this Office.   GEORGE HARRISON,
Herald's College,   Windsor Herald.
        24th June 1875.

---

[1] At St. Maben.

4 A[2]

HAMELEY *alias* HAMLEY.

The family of Hamley, usually in ancient times written Hamely, and sometimes Hamelyn, is of great antiquity in Cornwall. The name would appear to have been derived from Hamelin de Trewasac, otherwise called Hamelin de Boetun, who, about the year 1245, confirmed to Osbert de Alba Launda 7s. rent which Flora his mother paid from Trenant, 5s. rent which the said Osbert paid from Tresodorn, and 6s. 6d. rent which Peter de Cleher paid from Caerlin and Tresudun;[1] and by another charter Hamelin de Trewasec confirmed to Sir Osbert de Laund, Carlin in the hundred of Kerrier, to be held, freely and hereditarily, with Trenant, Tresodorn and Treudnou, at the rent of 2d. per. annum.[2] By another charter we find that 11s. 8½d. rents from the tenants of Osbert de Landa in Carlin, Treudnou and Tresodorn, were mortgaged by him for sixteen years to Richard son of John Reskemer.[3] A further charter shews that Tresodorn was acquired by Ewerin de la Land of William FitzEylet,[4] which Ewerin was husband of the above mentioned Flora the mother of Osbert,[5] who was the daughter and heir of the aforesaid Peter de Cleher[6]. Osbert de Laund would appear to have had a son, or grandson, named Ewerin, for in 1307-8, John Hamely,[7] whom we take to have been the son, or grandson, of Hamlin de Trewasac, granted to Sir Michael le Petit the homage and services of Ewerin de Launde in Carlyn, Treydnou, Trenansmur and land in Tresodern, and gave him notice to render the same to the said Michael;[8] and there is an acknowledgment, dated in 1309, of Sir Michael le Petit to Ewerin de la Landa that he had received the homage and fealty of of the said Ewerin in the places named, which he formerly held of John Hamely, and then held of the said Michael, of his court of Predannet.[9]

This would seem clearly to establish the descent of John Hamely from Hamelin de Trewasec, otherwise de Boetun. There is nothing to prove, so far as we are aware, that any relationship existed between John Hamely and Osbert de la Laund, but such relation-

---

[1] Charter No. 16.   [2] Charter No. 18.

[3] Charter No. 5.   [4] Charter No. 15.

[5] Both were alive in 1221, for in that year Richard Pincerna and Simolda his wife gave the King half a mark for a pone against Everarius de la Laund and Flora. (Rot. Fin., 5th Henry III. Part 2, m. 3.)

[6] Charter No. 13.

[7] John Hamely is cited in a charter dated in 1274, relating to Trenancemur (No. 1911,) and in another, dated in 1308, relating to Blanchland.   [8] Charter No. 7.

[9] Charter No. 22. These particulars are gleaned from an Index to the transcribed charters in the Muniment Room at Tregothnan, kindly given to the author by his late friend the Rev. Lambert Larking, the eminent and learned Kentish antiquary. but the author has not been fortunate enough to obtain from Lord Falmouth the privilege of inspecting his valuable collection of Cornish charters, or, he doubts not, this history would have been much improved thereby.

ship is not improbable, and it is not unlikely that the christian name "Osbert,"[1] which for centuries has been a leading name in the Hamely family, was derived from him.

A pedigree of the family, illuminated with the arms of the several matches, was certified by Sir John Borough, Garter King of Arms, in 1638,[2] and a memorandum thereon states that it is "proved, from Evidences then in possession of Mr. Giles Hamley of Treblethick, from Osbert Hamley," who was living in 9th Edward IV (1469) and married Joane Hockin, and to this extent only does the certificate confirm the pedigree; but it is further stated that "the upper part of the Pedigree is taken out of divers Ayncient Bookes of Arms gather'd out of Old Records and deeds of Antiquity." To the lower part, which is certified by Garter, we cannot take exception. Very little evidence upon the subject, so far as we know, is now extant, but, so far as it goes, it supports the descents. We have printed the pedigree as it stands, but are constrained to pronounce the upper part exceedingly inaccurate. It will be sufficient to say, with reference to this, that Matilda Pipard, shewn in the pedigree as the wife of Osbert son of the first John Hamely, was, as is proved by the inquisition taken on the death of her sister, aged 30 years in 1375, whilst the inquisition taken on the death of her grandson, Sir John Hamely, Knt., shews that his son and heir Ralph Hamely, was born in 1323; moreover the alleged sons of the latter, Sir John Hamely and Osbert Hamley, were living in 3rd Edward IV (1463) and 9th Edward IV (1469) respectively. The last is said to have married Joane Hockin, sister and heir of William Hockin, Rector of Helland. As, however, William Hocken was not instituted to Helland until 1521, and lived until 1555, his sister could scarcely have been born early enough to have been the wife of a gentleman who flourished in 1469. As it would be hopeless to attempt to correct this pedigree, we have printed it as it stands, and have added an alternative table shewing the descents so far as we have been able to support them by evidence.

John Hamely, whose name we have mentioned above (page 540), in connection with Sir Michael Petit, as the descendant of Hamelyn de Trewasac, had a son named Osbert. In 1302 Thomas Peticru of Brongolon petitioned against Osbert the son of John Hamely concerning a moiety of one acre of land in Lanyghan juxta Langargala as his right, and in which, he said, the said Osbert had no entrance except by the disseizin which a certain Cenota Peticru unjustly made against William Peticru father of the said Thomas. Osbert pleaded that he held the tenement jointly with Margaret his wife, who was not named in

---

[1] At these early dates the use of certain *Christian* names in families was sometimes more permanent than surnames. The latter, especially in Cornwall where territorial names were very general, frequently changed with change of residence. The spelling also of the same names greatly varied. It has been said that the name of Cholmondely is written twenty-five different ways in the deeds of that family. The variations in spelling the same names are equally numerous and remarkable in the will of Henry VII, published by Mr. Astle in 1775. Besides a multitude of other words the single one of "alms" is written in five different ways: "almons," "almose," "elemoss," "elemosse," "elemesse."

[1] This pedigree is now in the possession of Major General F. Hamley, and is doubtless the same which is mentioned by the Rev. Thomas Tregenna Hamley, who, in 1812, in a letter to Lysons, says: "there was also a pedigree of my paternal family, but no researches at present can discover it I believe." Lysons Corr., Addl. MSS. 9417, fo. 304.

the writ, and therefore Thomas Peticru was nonsuited.[1] In 1309 Osbert Hamely was defendant with others in a suit of novel disseizin at the instance of William le Poer of Trengothel of a tenement in Trewheran;[2] and he is again twice mentioned in the following year.[3] He is also named in 1322,[4] and in 1327 he was attorney for Henry de la Pomeroy, in a plea of novel disseizin against William the son of Walter de St. Margaret.[5] This Osbert died in 1331, and was succeeded by his son John Hamely, begot of Margaret daughter of Ralph Glynn.[6] In 1333 we find John the son of Osbert Hamely, senior, a defendant with John Chamond and others in a suit of novel disseizin by William de Carburra. He is stated to have married "Margaret daughter and heir of Walter Idles." His wife was really Margery, the elder daughter and coheir of Walter de Alet, who was aged 9 years in 1308, when the inquisition was taken upon her father's death.[7] This marriage brought to the Hamely family the manor of Alet and lands in Kilmonsac.

In 1331 John Hamely and Margery his wife suffered a fine to John de Aldestowe, of one messuage and one acre of land in Kylmonseg, and a moiety of the manor of Alet, whereby the said messuage and land were settled upon John Hamely and Margery his wife for life, remainder to John the son of the said John Hamely for his life, and after his death remainder to Ralph the brother of the said John the son of John, and the heirs of his body, in default remainder to the right heirs of the aforesaid Margery; and as concerning the moiety of the manor of Alet, to the said John Hamely and Margery, and the heirs of their bodies, in default remainder to the right heirs of the said Margery;[*] and by another fine, passed in the same term, John Hamely settled one messuage in the Island of St. Agnes in Scilly upon himself and the heirs of his body, in default of such issue upon Andrew his brother and the heirs of his body, and in default upon his own right heirs. John Hamely died on 27th May 1346, as shewn by the Inquisition taken thereupon, seized of the third part of the manor of Tregynnou, whereof Holwyn (Halwyn), Trewyas, and Penhale were parcel, which he held of William Bodrugan by military

---

[1] Assize Rolls, Cornw., 30th Edward I, $\begin{smallmatrix}M\\1\\21\end{smallmatrix}\Big\}$ 1. m. 18d.   [2] Ibid. 3rd Edward II, $\begin{smallmatrix}N\\2\\15\end{smallmatrix}\Big\}$ 1. m. 16d.

[3] Ibid. 4th Edward II, $\begin{smallmatrix}N\\2\\15\end{smallmatrix}\Big\}$ 2. m. 10.   [4] Ibid. 16th Edward II, $\begin{smallmatrix}N\\2\\17\end{smallmatrix}\Big\}$ 6. m. 11.

[5] Ibid. 2nd Edward III, $\begin{smallmatrix}N\\2\\18\end{smallmatrix}\Big\}$ 3. m. 23.   [6] See ante, p. 58.

[7] It appears from this Inquisition that Walter Alet, on the day on which he died, viz: Friday next before the Feast of All Saints 1st Edward II (1307), was seized, inter alia, conjointly with his wife Isota, of the third part of one acre of land in Kilmonseg, and that Margery his daughter, "antenata," and Alianora his daughter, "postnata," were his nearest heirs, and that the said Margery was aged 9 years, and the said Alianora was aged 6 years. (Inq. p. m. 2nd Edward II, No. 31.) It appears from a further Inquisition, taken after the death of Isolda (sic) who was the wife of the aforesaid Walter de Alet, that John de Alet father of the said Walter granted, by his charter, to Serlone de Nansladron, the manor of Alet for the term of the life of the said John, that after the death of John Walter, as son and heir, entered upon the manor, but that Serlone ejected him, and that upon the death of Serlone, it fell into the King's hands by reason of the minority of the heirs of Walter de Alet, and then still remained in the King's hands. (Inq. p. m. 10th Edward II, No. 26.)

[8] Pedes Finium 5th Edward III, Michs.

service; and also of a moiety of the manor of Alet, as of the right of inheritance of Margery his wife, which he held of the Duke of Cornwall, as of the Castle of Launceston, by military service; and Ralph Hamely, son of the said John Hamely, was found to be his nearest heir, and to be of the age of 23 years and more.[1] In 1346, when the aid of 40s. for each Knight's fee was granted for making the King's eldest son a Knight, Ralph de Hamely paid 20s. for half of a small fee in Trekinneu which John Hamely, his grandfather[2], held when the aid was levied by King Edward I, on the marriage of his eldest daughter;[3] and at the same time Margery Hamely and Eleanora her sister paid 13s. 4d. for the third part of one Knight's fee in Alet, which Serlon Lansladron had held when the previous aid was granted.[4] Margery survived her husband, and on Wednesday next before the feast of the Nativity of the B. V. Mary 1347, had assigned to her as dower, *inter alia*, a moiety of the manor of Tregynneu and all the chambers within the gate of Helwyn, together with the chapel there.[5]

Ralph Hamely, son and heir of John Hamely, was born in 1323, and it is clear that there is an hiatus in the pedigree between him and Osbert who married Joan Hocken. Two or three descents have evidently been omitted. This Ralph would appear to have had several brothers. In 1365, an assize of view of recognizance was held to enquire if Osbert Hamely, William Hamely, and others had unjustly disseized John Durant of his free tenements in Kylmonsek, &c., and two years later a similar assize was taken to enquire if John[6] the son of John Hamely had unjustly disseized John the son of Richard Attemore and Alice the daughter of John Hamely of their free tenement in Southmore, and John the son of · Richard and Alice recovered seizin.[7]

We have no mention of Ralph Hamely subsequent to the year of his father's death. He probably died s.p., and was succeeded by his brother Osbert, which Osbert, we conceive, was identical with Osbert Hamely who married Matilda the daughter and heir of Sir William Pipard.[8] This gentleman is described in the pedigree as " of Cornwall." We

---

[1] Inq. p. m. 21st Edward III, No. 20, (2 Nos.)   [2] He must have been his great grandfather.

[3] John Hamely, in 1303, paid an additional charge of 7s. 6d. upon half of a small fee in Trekynneu on 12s. 6d. which he had paid before, and Ralph Arundell paid a like amount for the other half of the fee. (Rot. Pip., 31st Edward I.)

[4] Queen's Rememb. Office, Book of Aids, p. 34.

[5] Assign. Dower. Escheats, 21st Edward III, No. 68, (1st Nos.)

[6] On 19th June 1365, an annuity of £20 was granted to John Hamlyn, the valet of the Prince of Wales, (Council Book of the Black Prince, fo. 545.)

[7] Assize Rolls, Cornw. 40th Edward III et. seq. $\frac{N}{2 \quad 27}$ } 7

[8] This Sir William Pipard, though described as of the county of Cornwall, would rather appear to have been of Wilts. He was the son of Stephen Pipard and had two daughters and heirs: Margaret, the eldest married, first Robert le Fitz Elys; Sir William Pipard, by his charter, settled upon them and their issue, the manor of Nethercote in Wilts, in default remainder to Stephen Pipard father of the said William for life, and after his death to revert to the grantor. By Robert le Fitz Elys she had no issue, after whose death she took to her second husband Warine de L'Isle. She died 3rd August 1375, leaving a son Gerard aged 15 years, and a daughter Margaret. (See ante, p. 500.) Matilda, the other daughter and coheir of Sir William Pipard, became the wife of Osbert Hamely, and was aged 30 years on her sister's death. (Inq. p. m. 49th Edward III, part 1, No. 73.)

have no knowledge that he held lands in that county, but he was seized of Larkbeare, North Bovey, and other lands in Devon, and of the manor of Nethercote in Wilts. The latter was carried away by the other coheir, but Matilda inherited the two former. In 1370, an inquisition was taken at Exeter to enquire what lands were held by Osbert Hamely, who had been convicted of divers felonies. The jury found that he held divers lands in Larkbeare, North Bovey, &c., of the inheritance of Matilda his wife, and that he held, as of his own right, four ferlings of land at Uppeton near Tavistock, and also in Salcome an annual rent of 4s. of the grant of John Cheueryston, for the term of the life of Matilda wife of the said Osbert.[1] It would appear, however, that he did not forfeit his estates, for in 1384, we find him taking proceedings against John Davy of Whympel, to compel him to render an account for the time he was the said Osbert's bailiff at Larkbeare.[2]

Osbert Hamely is again mentioned in 1380, in connection with Reginald Heligan.[3] By his charter, dated on Saturday nearest the feast of the Purification of B. V. Mary 7th Richard II (1383-4), Osbert Hamely, described as of the county of Cornwall, granted to Richard Welyngton, Parson of the Church of St. Tudy, and others, certain lands in Trenulgois, &c., and the rents and services of various tenants, which was probably for purposes of settlement.[4] In the same year he sued Aldestowe de Plymouth in a plea of trespass[5] and in the following January, he appointed Stephen de Fall and others as his attornies in another plea of trespass.[6] We do not find him again mentioned, but at the end of this year Arthur Hamely, described as kinsman and heir of John Hamely, Knt., was sued by Richard Trenewyth of Denezel for £100, being the value of 8,000 lbs. of white tin, coined.[7] It is recited in the inquisition taken after his death, that being seized of the manor of Helwyn, and a moiety of the manor of Alet, by his charter, dated at Helwyn on Thursday in the Vigil of SS. Simon and Jude 6th Henry V (1418), he granted to Henry Nanskelly, Vicar of the church of St. Ide, the said manor and moiety, and also all messuage lands, &c., *inter alia*, in Helwyn, Trewyns, Kilmonsek, and St Agnes Isle, to hold to the use of the said Arthur and Isabella his wife during their lives, remainder to Margaret, the daughter of the said Arthur and Isabella; and the jury found that the said Arthur died on 5th March 1427, that Isabella still survived, and that Margaret Hamely was the daughter and nearest heir of the said Arthur, and was aged 18 years.[8]

We conceive that after the death of Arthur Hamely, Isabella, his relict, married a certain John Sprygy, and that Margaret became the wife of John Champernon of Insworth; for in the inquisition taken at Lytelbrygge, county Cornwall, 17th October 1468, after the death of Richard Champernon, it is recited that John Talcarn and John Trenewyth

---

[1] Escheats, 44th Edward III (2nd Nos.), No. 39.

[2] De Banco Rolls, 7th Richard II, Easter, m. 303.

[3] Assize Rolls, Divers Counties, 4th Richard II, 2 $\left.\begin{array}{c} N \\ 27 \end{array}\right\}$ 7. m. 17d.   [4] Inrolled De Banco Roll, 7th Richard II, Trinity.

[5] Coram Rege Rolls, 7th Richard II, Easter m. 38.   [6] Ibid, 8th Richard II, Hil. m. 51.

[7] De Banco Roll, 8th Richard II, Michs. m. 299, continued 9th Richard II, Easter m. 293.

[8] Inq. p. m. 6th Henry VI, No. 48.

of Padistowe, being seized of the manor of Helwyn, otherwise called Tregenowe, and a moiety of the manor of Alet, had granted the same to John Sprygy and Isabella his wife for their lives, remainder to John Champernon and Margaret his wife and the heirs of the body of the said Margaret, and in default of such issue remainder to the right heirs of John Arundel late of Lanherne, Knt., deceased;[1] that in virtue of this grant John Sprygy and Isabella were seized in demesne as of a free tenement, and that John Sprygy died so seized, and Isabella survived and was solely seized; that John Champernon and Margaret his wife had issue Richard Champernon, and that Isabella, by her charter, dated at Helwyn, on Thursday next after the feast of All Saints 38th Henry VI (1459), granted the said manor and moiety to the said Richard Champernon, he paying the said Isabella an annual rent of £8 during her life, and that she was still living; that in virtue of this grant the said Richard Champernon was seized of the said lands, and by his charter, dated 15th May 2nd Edward IV (1461), granted the same to Michael Hals for the term of his life, and that the said Michael was seized as of a free tenement. The jury further found that the said Richard Champernon died 26th May then last past (1468), and that Margery, Margaret, Elizabeth, Johanna, and Mary, were his daughters and heirs, and were aged, respectively, Margery 7 years, Margaret 5 years, Elizabeth 3 years, Johanna 2 years, and Mary 3 months.[2]

It is evident from the foregoing, that Arthur Hamely was in the line of succession, and that, by his death in 1427, s.p.m., the estates went out of the family, hence Sir John Hamley, Knt., Osbert Hamley and Ralph Hamley, shewn on the pedigree as the sons of Ralph son and heir of Sir John Hamley, who died in 1346, could not have been so related. We have no evidence concerning either. We may, however, notice the following persons, who, though not traced to the elder branch, are indicated by their peculiar Christian names as belonging to the same family.

In 1351 we find Andrew Hamely and John Hamely, Knt., concerned in a suit relating to one acre of land Cornish in Trewayther (Trewethern) juxta Bodannan.[3] As this Sir John was living subsequent to the death of Sir John Hamely abovementioned, it is certain he was a different person, and he was, perhaps, identical with the Sir John Hamely who married Johanna daughter and heir of Sir Nicholas Plecy, Knt.,[4] by whom he acquired the manor of Hethelan in the county of Surrey. They had issue a son named John, or Thomas, who died in infancy, and the said Johanna died on Thursday next after the Assumption of the B. V. Mary (1373) s.p., and the manor reverted to Peter Plecy the uncle of Johanna,[5] who, in 14th Richard II (1390), suffered a fine to John Hamely, acknowledging his right to the said manor during his life.[6] After the death of Johanna Plecy, Sir John

[1] Ped. Finium, 21st Henry VI, Michaelmas.

[2] Inq. p. m. 8th Edward IV, No. 35.

[3] Assize Rolls, 25th Edward III, $\frac{N}{2}$ } 6. m. 56.
23

[4] She was sister and heir of Nicholas, brother and heir of John de Plecy, son and heir of Nicholas de Plecy. John Hamely did fealty for her lands, and had livery of seizin 30th September 1362. (Rot. Fin. 36th Edward III, m. 15.)

[5] Inq. p. m. 48th Edward III, No. 35 (1st Nos.)

[6] Inq. p. m. 22nd Richard II, No. 25. (Surrey.)

4 B

Hamely took to wife a certain Elizabeth, and, together with his wife, suffered a fine, in 1393, *inter alia*, in the manor of Upwimborne, co. Dorset, together with the advowson of the church of Upwimborne, to John Alet and Thomas Ramesay, by means of which the said manor and advowson were settled upon the said John and Elizabeth and the heirs of their bodies, in default remainder to John Lovell, Knt., and his heirs for ever. The said Sir John Hamely died 15th January 1398-9, and Egidia the daughter of the said John and Elizabeth was found to be their nearest heir.[1]

Geoffry Hamely and Martin Hamond and Matilda his wife, in 1353, gave half a mark for certain writs.[2] In 1400, William son of Jordan Hamely recovered lands in Westcoryth against John Foghell.[3] Benedict Hamely was one of the jurors on the Inquisition, post mortem, of Thomas Cheddar, held at Bodmin on 21st June 1443;[4] and in January 1470-1, as executor of the will of John Hamely, he took proceedings to recover from Roger Stone of Trevigy in St. Minver, and Johanna his wife, daughter and heir of John Wytheyng, a debt of £20.[5]

Accepting the pedigree as certified by Sir John Borough as being substantially correct from Osbert Hamely who married Joan Hocken, we find that Benedict Hamley, son of the said Osbert and Joane, was assessed to the subsidy in St. Maben as early as 1524, and Thomas son of Benedict in 1571.

We have occupied so much space in the critical examination of the early part of Sir John Borough's pedigree, that we must hasten over the latter part, but we cannot refrain from mentioning John Hamblye, *alias* Tregwethan, a Seminary Priest, described as of St. Mabyn, Clerk, whose singular confession, dated 18th August 28th Elizabeth (1586), is preserved in the State Paper Office.

We all know that very severe measures were enacted against the Roman Catholics in the reign of Queen Elizabeth, and especially against Priests educated in seminaries abroad. John Hamblye, who calls himself, *alias* Tregwethan,[6] of the parish of St. Mabyn, was on the 18th August 1586, taken before the Bishop of Salisbury and Giles Estcourt, Esq., two of the Justices of the Peace for Wilts. He stated that he had, from his infancy, been brought up at divers schools in Cornwall learning the Latin tongue, and that about four years previously one Nicholas Bawdwyn, dwelling in the same parish, who had been a scholar in Exeter College, Oxford, had given him several books relating to the Romish religion which unsettled him in his faith, so that he ceased to attend the Church of England, and being afraid of the penal laws in that behalf, he proceeded to London, where he met one Davie Tomson, a Priest, and a Cornish man born at Blisland, whose name, in truth, was David Kempe, and one Foskewe (Fortescue) another priest, by whom he was duly admitted into the Romish Communion. He mentions various occasions when he was present at mass in London, on some of which he met Mr. Bawdwyn. He relates,

---

[1] Inq. p. m. 22nd Richard II, No. 25 (Dorset.)   [2] Rot. Fin. 27th Edward III.

[3] Assize Rolls, Div. Cos. 1st Henry IV, $\frac{N}{2}$ $\left.\right\}$ 2. m. 48d.   [4] Inq. p. m. 21st Henry VI, No. 55.
36

[5] De Banco Rolls, 49th Henry VI, Hil. m. 171d.

[6] This name was probably assumed for purposes of concealment.

FAMILY HISTORY.—HAMLEY. 547

in great detail, a journey he made to Rheims, in France, and names all the English persons he saw, and the books which he read, relates how he was admitted to the diaconate, and how he was ordered to return to England, which he did in disguise, "to convert those that are in error, and to save souls;" that he afterwards celebrated mass on several occasions in London and in the country, that he received from Mr. Bawdwyn £10 being part of a legacy given him by his own father, that he went to Charde to meet one Mr. Fulford, and a gentlewoman which the said Mr. Fulford intended to have married, and whilst accompanying them to one Mr. Maunday's house, where the marriage was to have been solemnized, he was apprehended and committed to the common gaol at Ilchester, was tried at the assizes at Taunton, and there condemned for being a seminary priest, and had his judgment; that he made his submission and promise of reconcilement to Her Majesty's laws, and was reprieved; and for that "he lay there vppon the bare bordes and had but the allowance of a peny a day & colde not have the allowance of 2d. a day more, & a bedde as yt was allowed and appoynted unto him," he escaped and was again apprehended at Knowle. The Bishop in sending this deposition to the Privy Council concludes his letter by saying: "yet the man is not so obstinate at this tyme but he can be contented (so he may obtaine mercye of her Matie and pdon for his lyfe) to forsake the Pope, come to the Church, and willingly follow her Maties proceedings as he beareth vs in hande."[1]

We are unable to identify this gentlemen. He was probably a younger son of Thomas Hamley of Treblethick, whose eldest son Giles married, in 1573, Elizabeth daughter of William Baldwin, *alias* Bawdwyn of Colquite; hence there existed a family connection.

William Hamley of Treblethick, who died in 1711, as well as daughters, had several sons. John Hamley, his eldest son, succeeded him at Treblethick, and, by his improvidence, was obliged to sell his estate. He died in 1777, leaving two sons, whom he describes in his will as Richard Hamley of Bodmin, shopkeeper, and William Hamley of Lostwithiel, saddler. The former afterwards removed to St. Columb, where he was living about 1816, aged 81, being then the representative of the family. We do not know if he left issue. Probably Mr. Osbertus Hamley and Mr. John Hamley, who, in 1819, repaired the monument of their ancestor in St. Maben Church, were his sons, or the sons of his brother William.[2]

Giles Hamley, second son of William Hamley of Treblethick, settled at St. Columb as an attorney, and was twice married. His grandson Thomas Tregenna Hamley, Clerk, was curate of St. Ervan and St. Eval nineteen years, and died at St. Ervan in 1818, aged 59, and s.p. He was the last representative of this branch of whom we have any trace. Of Joseph and William, younger sons of William Hamley of Treblethick, we are unable to speak with certainty. We, however, believe they were identical with Joseph and William Hamley, who settled at Bodmin, as surgeons, of whom Joseph was the progenitor of the present family of Hamley of Bodmin, a family greatly distinguished for their naval and military services, whose pedigree we annex.

[1] State Papers, Dom. Corr., Eliz., vol. 192, No. 46.
[2] See ante, p. 467.

4 B²

PEDIGREE OF HAMELEY

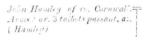

John Hamley of co. Cornwall.⊤
Arms: ar. 3 talbots passant, az.
(Hamley)

*The upper part of this Pedigree or descent was taken out
of divers ancient bookes of armes, gathered out of
olde records and dooinge antiquities and good proves.*

Sir John Hamley, Knt. Died⊤Margaret [Margery] dau. and
20th Edward III. 1346. | heir [coh.] of Walter Idles [Alet
Died 27th May 1346. Inq. | assignment of dower, Sep. 1347.
p.m., 21st Edward III. | Escheats 21st Edw. III. Part
Part 1, No. 20. | 1, No. 68.

Ralfe Hamley, son and heire of⊤Margaret, daughter of
Sir John Hamley. Aged 23 at | William Trelazzus.
his father's death. Born 1323. |
Held half a Knight's fee in
Trekinnen in 1346.

Sir John Hamley of Hamley,
Knt., married ye daughter
and heire of Sir Humfrey
Talbot, Knt., 3rd Edward
IV. Arms: Hamley im-
paling: per chev. or and ar. a
chev. betw. 3 talbots sa.

*Richard Champernon of Insworth marryd ye daus. and heire of Sir John Hamley of
Hamley, Knt., and of his wife Fauge, and heire Sir Humfrey Talbot, which Richd.
Champernon was son and heir to Joe. son and heir to Richard, sonne and heir to Joan,
that came to Richd. sonne and heire to Henry, sonne and heir to Thomas, sonne and
heire to Richard Champernon and of Joan his wife, daugr. and heir of Fulk Vautort
and of Joan his wife, daur. to Edward Lisle of Cornwal, lord of Insworth, sonne
and heir to Richard Knox of the Knoxes sonne to John Knox of England.*

*The arms of Hamley are quartered by divers, ancient and worthy families both in
Devon and Cornwall, viz. by Nicholas Champernon, Monke, and Trevillion and others, and are
very conspicuously painted in glass in the windows of the Church of St. Mabyn in Cornwall
in severall places, and likewise in glass windows at Sent Peters in Exeter, and in many
other places in Devon.*

*This descent of Webber and the match with
Hamley is in the book of Cornwall, remayning
in the Office of arms.*

William Webber of ye parish of St. Kew⊤. . . dau. of
in Cornwall. Arms: Gu. upon a chev. | [William]
eng. or, betw. 3 plates, 3 annulets az. | Mathew of St.
(Webber) impaling: sa. within a bordure | Kew.
a stork ar. membred gu. (Mathew). Died
1596. (See ante, vol. ii, p. 168.)

John Webber of Am-⊤Joane, dau. of . . . .
ball in St. Kew. | Trewbodie of St.
| Clere.

Giles Hamley of Treblethick. Arms:⊤Elizabeth, dau. and heire of William
Hamley differenced with a mullet | Baldwin, alias Bawdwin, of Col-
impaling: gu. two bendlets within a | quit in St. Mabyn.
bordure or.

John Webber of Amball, his⊤Susan, dau. of Pol-
first wife Henry, dau. of | whale of Trevorgan,
John Culprodden of Padstow. | second wife.

Margaret, dau. of John⊤Alexander Hamley of Treblethick.
Webber of Amball, in ye | Arms: Hamley impaling Webber.
parish of St. Kew. Mar.[1] | Bur.[1] 29th Oct. 1624. Will
18th June 1596. Executrix | dated 20th Oct. 1624. Prov. 23rd
to husband's will. | Feb. 1624-5. Archd. Cornw.

A

[1] At St. Mabyn.

alias HAMLEY.

Sir *William Pipard of Corn-*=*Joan, dau. of John*
wall, Knt. Arms: Per Saltier, | *de Adsully.*
az and or.

Osbertus Hamley of co. Corn-=*Maud, dau. and heir of Sir*
wall. Arms: Hamley im- | *William Pipard. Aged 30*
paling Pipard. | *years in 1375.*

Osbertus Hamley, of co. Cornwall=*Margaret, dau. of Ralph*
[ob.] 5th Edward III, 1331. Arms: | *Glynn. She died 23rd*
Hamley, impaling: ar. 3 Salmon spears, | *Edward III, 1349.*
sa.

*Hamley hath byn sondry wayes
written as thus: sometymes hemley
and hemele, Hamlyn, Haluyn,
Helwyn, Hamely and Hamele, as
by olde writings and deeds may
appear.*

Alice, wife of John
AtteMore. Living
1367.

*This Ioane Hocking, widdow of Osbert
Hamley is proued by a letter of admin-
estracion granted to the said Ioane, after
the death of hir brother William Hockin,
Clarke, Rector of Helland in ye co. Cornwall. She being heire to hir brother and
mother to Benedict.*

Osbertus Hamley, third son, 9th=*Joan Hockin, widow*   *Ralfe Hamley, second*
Edward IV. Arms: Hamley | *of Hamley, heir to*   *son. Arms: Hamley*
differenced with a mullet; im- | *her brother, William*   *differenced with a*
paling: ar. a lozenge buckle, sa. | *Hockin, temp. Edward*   *cresent.*
| *IV.*

Benedict Hamley of Treblethick in=*.... the daughter of*
Cornwall. Assessed to Subsidy | *Raymward, wife to*
in St. Maben in 1524, 1541, and | *Benedict Hamley.*
1545.

*The nether part of this Pedigree is taken and
collected out of the deeds and euidences of Mr.
Gyles Hamley at Treblethick in Cornwall, who
dooth enioye the lands and possessions of his
ayncesters this day. Proved from Ioane Hockin
downewards.*

Thomas Hamley of Treble-=*Margery, dau. of*   *John Billing of Tre-*=*[Margery] daughter*
thick in Cornwall. Arms: | *William Proute*   *uorder, Arms: or,* | *and heir of [Thomas]*
Hamley differenced with a | *of North Peder-*   *upon a bend sa. 3* | *Blewett of Cornwall.*
mullet, impaling: sa. a | *win in Co.*   *stags' heads couped* | *(See Ped. of BILLING,*
stag ramp. ar. attired or, | *Devon.*   *or. impaling: or,* | *ante vol. i, p. 389.)*
debruised by a fess emb. | *a chev. betw. 3*
Assessed to Subsidy in St. | *eagles, displayed*
Maben in 1571. | *vert. (Blewett).*

*This descent of Billing and
the match with Hamley is in
the booke of Cornwall, remayning in the Office of
Arms. (See ante vol. i.
p. 289.)*

William Billing of Hanger in ye parish of St.=*Elizabeth, dau. of*
Tuddie in Cornwall. Arms: Billing impaling: gu. | *.... Babb of Tin-*
a fess ar. within a bordure engrailed (Babb). | *grase in Devon.*

John Hamley, 2nd son. Gentleman of the   *Reynald Billing of St.*=*Ann, dau. and heir of*
moving wardrobe to King James and King | *Mabyn. Arms: Billing:* | *[Thomas] Hockin [of*
Charles. Died 1627. Will dated 12th | *impaling: ar. a lozenge* | *St. Breward.]*
Feb. 1627-8. Prov. 6th Feb. 1628-9. | *buckle ar. (Hocken).*
(12 Ridley)

B

---

[1] At St. Mabyn.

PEDIGREE OF HAMELEY,

A

Thomas, bur.[1] 9th Feb. 1596-7. William, bap.[1] 10th April 1611. Named in father's will.	Richard, bap.[1] 24th July 1613. Named in father's will Alexander, bap. 24th Aug. 1619. Named in father's will.	*Oliver Hamley, 3rd sonn, maried Bridget, dau. of John Rouse of co. Bucks. Arms differenced with a mullet charged with a mullet. Named in father's will.*	*Humfrey Hamley, 2nd sonn, married Margaret, dau. of ..Blake of St. Kew. Arms: Hamley differenced with a mullet charged with a crescent. Bap.[1] 23rd July 1601. Named in father's will.*

ACHIEVEMENT OF THE ARMS OF HAMLEY.
Hamley quartering Hocken and Bawdwin as above.

William, bap.[1] 16thNov. 1643.	Grace, bap.[1] May 1622. Mar. .. Orchard. Named in grandfather's and father's wills.	Ann, bap.[1] 1st Jan. 1623. Bur.[1] 24th Nov. 1625. Named in grandfather's will.	Elizabeth, bap.[1] 30th April 1626. Mar. William Arnold. Named in father's will.	Philadelphia, bap.[1] 16th March 1627. Mar. .... Warne. Named in father's will.	*Thomas Hamley, son and heir. Arms differenced with a mullet, and a label in chief.* Bap.[1] 14th May 1629, of the Inner Temple, London. Died at Wokingham, co. Berks, 25th and bur. 27th May 1656, v.p., and s.p.

Giles Hamley, born 9th and bap. 17th Feb. 1657-8.	Margaret, bap.[1] 14th Dec. 1659.	Katherine, bap[1]. 23rd Jan. 1662.	John Hamley bap.[1] 10th Feb. 1663.

Barbara, dau. of Philip Hawkins of Pennance.	=Giles Hamley, 2nd son, of St. Columb. Died 20th Sept. 1738. Aged 40, M.I. Bur.[3] admo. to Grace his relict, 4th March 1738-9. Archd. Cornw.	=Grace, dau. of RichardHoblyn of Tresaddern. Died 20th Nov. 1786. Aged 86, M.I. Bur.[3]	Rebecca, bap.[1] 25th March 1700. Mar.[2] 18th Aug. 1721,Lewis Blight of Bodmin. See Pedigree of BLIGHT, ante, vol. i, p. 289.	John Hamley of Treblethick. Bur.[1] 3rd June 1777. Will dated 30th Jan. 1776. Prov. 5th July 1777. Archd. Cornw.	=Elizabeth dau. and coh. of Henry Bond of Tresunger, by Lucy sister and coh. of Richard Mathew of that place. See Ped. of MATHEW, ante, vol. i, p. 570.

John, bap.[3] 10th Jan. and bur.[3] 4thMar. 1723.	Ann, bap.[3] 15th July 1726.	Johanna, bap.[3] 5th Feb. 1727, bur.[3] 26th May 1760. M.I.	Anne, bap.[3] 14thDec. 1731.	Elizabeth, bap.[3] 6th May 1736. Mar.[3] 8th. Aug. 1761, Rev. Dr Robert Bateman, Rector of S. Columb.	Grace, bur.[3] 11th Dec. 1741.

Thomas Tregenna Hamley, Clerk, bap.[3] 4th Aug. 1756.=Mary, of Henry Braddon Curate of St. Ervan and St. Eval, 19 years. Died at of Camelford. Died 12th St. Ervan, 23rd Dec. 1818. Aged 59, and bur. there, Dec.1813. Aged 57. Bur. M.I.   at St. Ervan.

---

[1] At St. Mabyn.   [2] At Bodmin.   [3] At St. Columb.

alias HAMLEY.—Continued.

B

Frances, 2nd wife. Named in husband's will. Bur.[1] 18th Feb. 1684.	*Giles Hamley of Treblethick, in the parish of St. Mabyn* Bap.[1] Dec. 1597. Assessed to Subsidy in St. Mabyn 1625, 1628, and 1641. Died 7th and bur.[1] 10th July 1658. Will dated 3rd Feb. 1657-8. Prov. 31st Jan. 1658-9. (63 Pell.)	*Margaret, dau. of Ray Billing of St. Mabyn.* Bur.[1] 22nd Nov. 1637.	Margery, bap.[1] 1st June 1612, named in father's will. Ann, bap.[1] Aug. 1614. Bur.[1] 10th April 1639. Named in father's will.	Jane, mar. .. Philp. Named in father's will.	Elizabeth named in father's will.	John named in father's will.

ACHIEVEMENT OF THE ARMS OF BILLING,
Billing quartering Blewett and Hocken, as above.

John Hamley of Treblethick, son and heir. Bap.[1] 6th April 1632. Died 6th and bur.[1] 7th Mar. 1674. Executor to father's will.	Katherine, dau. of .... Brook. Mar.[1] 19th May 1657. Bur.[1] 21st Nov. 1711. Named in Giles Hamley's will.	Giles Hamley, bap.[1] 31st Aug. 1634. Named in father's will.	Loveday, bap.[1] 25th Sept. 1636. Mar.[1] 14th Dec. 1659, Henry Isaacke. Named in father's will.	Ann, bap.[1] 10th Nov. 1637.

CERTIFICATE OF SIR JOHN BOROUGH.
According to affidavit made and severall evidences exhibited unto me for proofe of the premisses, I do allow of this Pedigree. JOHN BOROUGH, Garter Principall King of Arms 8 March 1638. for Englishmen
N B.—This Certificate applies to the portion printed in *Italics.*

William Hamley of Treblethick. Bap.[1] 10th March 1668. Died 11th and bur.[1] 14th Apr.[1] 1711. Aged 42. M.I. ante, p. 466, No. 2.	Rebecca, dau. of .... remar. Joseph Drake.	John Hamley bap.[1] 3rd May 1670.	Alexander, bap.[1] 8th April 1672.	Thomas, bap.[1] 10th March 1667.

Thomas Hamley bap.[1] 20th Feb. 1701-2. Bur.[1] 21st April 1719.	Joseph Hamley, bap.[1] 22nd April 1703. Probably settled at Bodmin. See Table II.	Alexander, bap.[1] 9th Feb. 1705-6.	Katherine, bap.[1] 1st Feb. 1707-8. Unmar. in 1729. Named in brother John's will.	Margaret, bap.[1] 5th Jan. 1708-9. Mar.[1] 24th July 1725, John Harry of St. Kew.	William. Probably settled at Bodmin. See Table II.

Grace, dau. and coh. of John Tregenna, Clerk, Rector of Maugan. Bur.[3] 22nd April 1761.	Thomas Hamley of St. Columb, Clerk. Bur.[3] 11th June 1766.	Mary, dau. of	Richard Hamley, of Bodmin, afterwards of St. Columb. Eldest son, born 1741. Named in father's will. Lived to a great age, and died at St. Columb.	William, bap.[1] 10th Dec. 1736. Died young.	Mary, bap.[1] 15th Jan. 1738. Living unmar. 1773.	William Hamley of Lostwithiel born 1775, named in father's will. Living 1808

Thomas Hamley, bap.[1] 4th Aug. 1759.	Edward, bap.[3] 25th Oct. 1764.	Giles, bap.[1] 15th Mar. 1766.

---

[1] At St. Mabyn. [2] At Bodmin. [3] At St Columb.

ALTERNATIVE PEDIGREE OF HAMELY.

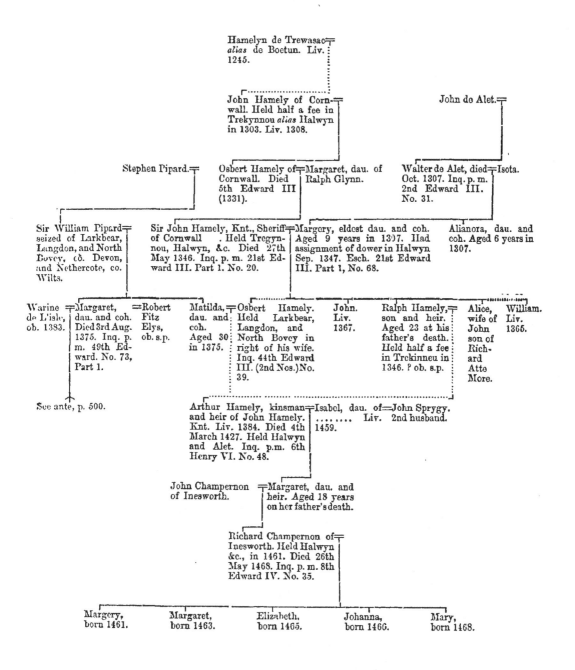

Hamelyn de Trewasac alias de Boetun. Liv. 1245.

John Hamely of Cornwall. Held half a fee in Trekynnou alias Halwyn in 1303. Liv. 1308.

John de Alet.

Stephen Pipard.

Osbert Hamely of Cornwall. Died 5th Edward III (1331). ═ Margaret, dau. of Ralph Glynn.

Walter de Alet, died Oct. 1307. Inq. p. m. 2nd Edward III. No. 31. ═ Isota.

Sir William Pipard seized of Larkbear, Langdon, and North Bovey, cð. Devon, and Nethercote, co. Wilts.

Sir John Hamely, Knt., Sheriff of Cornwall . Held Tregynnou, Halwyn, &c. Died 27th May 1346. Inq. p. m. 21st Edward III. Part 1. No. 20. ═ Margery, eldest dau. and coh. Aged 9 years in 1307. Had assignment of dower in Halwyn Sep. 1347. Esch. 21st Edward III. Part 1, No. 68.

Alianora, dau. and coh. Aged 6 years in 1307.

Warine de L'isle, ob. 1383. ═ Margaret, dau. and coh. Died 3rd Aug. 1375. Inq. p. m. 49th Edward. No. 73, Part 1. ═ Robert Fitz Elys, ob. s.p.

Matilda, dau. and coh. Aged 30 in 1375. ═ Osbert Hamely. Held Larkbear, Langdon, and North Bovey in right of his wife. Inq. 44th Edward III. (2nd Nos.) No. 39.

John. Liv. 1367.

Ralph Hamely, son and heir. Aged 23 at his father's death. Held half a fee in Trekinneu in 1346. ? ob. s.p. ═ Alice, wife of John son of Richard Atte More.

William. Liv. 1365.

See ante, p. 500.

Arthur Hamely, kinsman and heir of John Hamely. Knt. Liv. 1384. Died 4th March 1427. Held Halwyn and Alet. Inq. p.m. 6th Henry VI. No. 48. ═ Isabel, dau. of John Sprygy. .... Liv. 2nd husband. 1459.

John Champernon of Inesworth. ═ Margaret, dau. and heir. Aged 18 years on her father's death.

Richard Champernon of Inesworth. Held Halwyn &c., in 1461. Died 26th May 1468. Inq. p. m. 8th Edward IV. No. 35.

Margery, born 1461.

Margaret, born 1463.

Elizabeth, born 1465.

Johanna, born 1466.

Mary, born 1468.

PEDIGREE OF HAMLEY OF BODMIN.

Joseph Hamley of Bodmin, Surgeon, supposed son of William Hamley of Treblethick, see ante p. 551. Died 18th July 1771, aged 68. Bur.¹ .. Will dated 20th March 1770. Prov. 5th July 1777. Archd. Cornwall ═ Susan, dau. of William Wymond. Bap.¹ 1703. Mar.¹ 3rd April 1727. Died 20th December 1769, aged 66. Bur.¹

William Hamley of Bodmin, Surgeon, supposed son of William Hamley of Treblethick, see ante p. 551. ═ Cecilia.

William Hamley, of Bodmin, Surg., Bap.¹ 1st June 1741. Died 19th July 1810, aged 70. Bur.¹ M.I., No. 43. Will dated 14th July 1810. Names all his children. Admo. to Sarah his relict. Exrs. named having renounced. Archd. Cornw. ═ Sarah, dau. of John Pomeroy of Bodmin, bap.¹ 29th Nov., 1757. Admrd. to husband's will. Died 28th July 1812, aged 65, M.I.

Joseph, bap.² 1729. Bur.¹ 1732.

Susanna, bap¹ 1732.

Betty, bap.¹ 1735.

Frances, bap.¹ 1739.

Joseph, bap.¹ 24th Jan. 1743. Bur.¹ 1747. Rebecca, bap.¹ 1739. Mar. Powne.

Mary, bap.¹ 1720. William, bap.¹ 1721.

Elizabeth, bap.¹ 1725. Bur.¹ 1727. Nicholas, bap.¹ 1729.

Nicholas, bap.¹ 1726. John, bap.¹ 1735. Bur.¹ 1735.

Sally Pomeroy, bap.¹ 16th June 1779. Died 21st Dec. 1870, aged 91. Unmar.

Elizabeth, bap.¹ 5th Nov. 1784, mar. .. Turtle.

Susanna, bap.¹ 3rd July 1781. Died 19 Jun. 1871. Unmar.

Elizabeth, dau. of John Basset Collins, Clerk, born 1781. Died 1st Feb. 1810. Bur.¹ M.I., No. 43. 1st wife. (See vol. i, p. 335.) ═ Joseph Hamley of Bodmin, Surgeon and Coroner for Cornw., bap.¹ 10th April 1782. Died Jan. 7th 1854. Selina Glubb. 3rd wife. Died 1863. Bur.¹ ═ Elizabeth, Garnet, dau of Edmund Gilbert, Clerk, 2nd wife, mar.¹ 1813. Bur.¹ 1823, aged 41. (See vol i, p. 303.)

William Hamley, born 9th Aug. 1784, bap.¹ 28th Sep. 1786. Cap. R.N. 28th Oct. 1834 Retired Rear-Adm. 1856. Retired Vice-Adm. 1863. Died in London 8th Nov. 1866. Bur. at Brompton Cemetery. ═ Barbara, dau. of Charles Ogilvy of Lerwick, Shetland. Born 3rd June 1788. Mar. 1814. Died 12th June 1842. Bur.¹ M.I. No. 42.

Caroline, bap. 16th July 1787. Mar. John Bennett. He bur.¹ 1797. She bur.¹ 1814.

John Pomeroy, bap.¹ 16th Mar. 1790. Drowned at sea a minor. Catherine Pennington, bap. 6th Jan. 1794.

Mary Charity, bap. 2nd Jan. 1792. Died unmar. 23 June 1868. Wymond, bap.² 2nd Jan. 1797. Com. R.N. 9 Nov. 1846. Cap. 1st Aug. 1860. Died 3rd Mar. 1865. Unmar.

William George Hamley, born 28th June 1815. 2nd Lieut. Royal Engineers 5th Aug. 1833. 1st Lieut. 25th May 1836. 2nd Capt. 22nd May 1845. Major 1st May 1845. Lieut.-Col. 10th June 1856. Col. 10th June 1861. Major.-General 27th Jan. 1872. A Companion of the Most Hon. Order of the Bath. ═ Olivia Arbuthnot, dau. of Thomas Gallwey, Cap. R.N. Mar. 1847.

Charles Ogilvy, born 1817 Lieut.-Col. R.M.L.I. 12th May 1862. Retired 10th June 1862. Died 1863. ═ Georgina, dau. of Hanbury Williams. Died 1853.

Barbara Jane, born 1852.

Wymond Thomas Ogilvy, bor. 1818. Coll. of Customs British Columbia.

Edward Bruce Hamley, born 1824. Lieut. R. A. Lieut.-Cap. May 1850. Major 12th Dec. 1854. Bt.-Lieut.-Col. 2nd Nov. 1855. Col. 2nd Nov 1863. A Companion of the Most Hon. Order of the Bath 13th Mar. 1867. Knt. 5th Class of the Leg. of Honour, & 5th Class Medjidie. Professor of Military History Staff Coll., Sandhurst 1858-64.

Barbara Charlotte Caroline, born 16th Dec. 1828. Died 2nd Dec. 1837. Bur.¹ Aged 9 years. M.I.

Wymond Thomas Ogilvye.

William Wymond, 1849. B.A. Cantab.

Walter Raleigh Gilbert, born 1851. ═ Ellen, dau. of George Andrew of Ernicroft Compstall, co. Derby. Mar. 1873.

Alice Emma Pomeroy, born 1853.

Edward Charles. Born 1855.

Walter Raleigh Thornhill, born 1874.

Edward Collins, bap.¹ 30th Dec. 1807.

Caroline Frances, bap. 30th Dec. 1807.

William, bur.¹ 1831. Aged 25.

Francis Gilbert Hamley, born 1815. Major 50th Regt. 7th Dec. 1858. Lieut.-Col 31st Aug. 1860. Major-Gen. 9th Aug. 1873. ═ Matilda Whyte, eldest dau. of Hon. James Wilson, Chief Justice of Mauritius. Born in Edinburgh 27th April 1822. Mar.¹ at Mauritius 10th Mar. 1846.

Elizabeth, died young Bur.¹ 1817.

Edmund Gilbert of Bodmin, born 1817 One of the Coroners for the County of Cornwall, and an Attorney. ═ Ann, dau. of James Carter Barton of Hopwas House near Tamworth. Mar. 7th March 1843.

Joseph Osbertus Hamley, born 1819. Apptd. Controller of Army Stores 1st Jan. 1871. A Companion of the Most Hon. Order of the Bath. ═ Martha, dau. of Thomas Morgan of Bristol, born there 13th Sep. 1826. Mar. 27th April 1848, at Wellington N. Zealand.

Francis Joseph Cuninghame, born at Mauritius 17th Feb. 1847. Died at Aldershot 15th April 1871, and bur. in the Cemetery there.

Joseph Hamley, Clerk, born 23rd Sep. 1853. Bap.¹ Stipend. Curate at St. Paul's, Truro.

Flora Ann, born 22nd Nov. 1845. Bap.¹

Louisa Mary, born 27th Nov. 1847. Mar.¹ 2nd July 1868 Preston J. Wallis of Bodmin, Attor.-at-Law.

Francis Gilbert, born 1st Feb. 1851. Bap. at Wellington, New Zealand.

Elizabeth Garnett Blanche, born 1st Jan. 1856. Bap. at Wellington, New Zealand.

¹ At Bodmin.

4 C

PORTER OF PENWYNE.

This family was introduced into the parish of St. Mabyn through the induction of Thomas Porter into the Rectory in 1629, the right of presentation, for that turn, having been purchased of the crown, in 1622,[1] by John Porter, for the express purpose of presenting thereto the said Thomas Porter. John Porter dying before the benefice fell vacant, the presentation was made by his relict (see ante 458 n., 462). We have no evidence to shew what relationship existed between these parties, but conclude that Thomas was the son of John and Elizabeth. According to Hals, a contemporary, their arms were: *sa. three bells ar. a canton erm.* As, however, these arms are borne by several families of the name, they afford very slender assistance in tracing the descent of this family. Thomas Porter may have been the same who, as the son of a Gloucestershire gentleman, matriculated at Magdalen Hall, Oxford, on 7th November 1600, aged 15.

PEDIGREE OF PORTER.

John Porter purchased the next ⊤ Elizabeth, adm[rd]. to her hus-
presentation to St. Mabyn in band. Presented Thomas
1622. Died ante June 1629. Porter to St. Mabyn in 1629.

Thomas Porter, M.A., instituted to the ⊤ Sarah, bur.[2]
Rectory of St. Mabyn 15th June 1629. 12th May
Will dated June 1668. Prov. 20th Jan. 1668-9. 1668.

Thomas, bap.[2] 15th May 1639 Bur.[2] 23rd Jan. 1666.	Grace, bap.[2] 8th and bur.[2] 20th Dec. 1633.	Christopher =Elizabeth, Porter of dau. of Arthur Penwyne, sold Spry of Place. Trethevy, Bur.[2] 17th 1706. Bur.[2] May 1701. 6th March See Ped. of 1710. SPRY, ante vol. i, p. 72.	Judith, bap.[2] 4th July 1641. Alice, bur.[2] 3rd Oct. 1643. Ann, bur.[2] 27th May 1638.	John, bur.[2] 5th July 1639. Mark, bur.[2] 21st Oct. 1644. Mary, bap.[2] 7th Oct. 1632. Bur.[2] 14th Jan. 1632-3.	Sarah, mar. .... Eord
Ann, bap. 27th May, 1638, mar.[2] Walter Langollen, 15th June 1658.	Mary, bap.[2] 15th Feb. 1634. Mar.[2] 30th Dec. 1658 Thomas Fortune.				

| Charles, bap.[2] 17th June 1690. Mar.[2] Mary Chaffinder of Launceston, 24th June 1714. | Mary, bap.[2] 5th June 1671 Bur.[2] 1st Jan. 1671. Endymion, bap.[2] 1st Oct. 1692. | Lucy, bap.[2] 13th Oct. 1673 Thomas, bap.[2] 28th Dec. 1672 Bur.[2] 1st Nov. 1673. | Arthur =Elizabeth. Porter of Penwyne bap.[2] 30th April 1682. Sold Penwyne in 1716. | Thomas, bap.[2] 20th Aug. 1683. Elizabeth, bap.[1] 30th Sept. 1684. | Christopher, bap.[2] 20th Jan. 1686. John, bap.[2] 19th June 1688. | William, bur.[2] 14th May 1706. |

[1] Privy Seal, 8th August 1622, and Rot. Pat. 20th James, Part 7, No. 11.   [2] At St. Mabyn.

PARISH OF HELLESBURY *ALIAS* MICHAELSTOW.

The ancient name of this parish would appear to have been Hellesbury. In the early part of the fourteenth century it was called Stow St. Michael, but it was not until nearly the end of that century that it attained its name in the present form. It is entirely embraced within the manor of Helston in Trigg. The parish is bounded on the north by Lanteglos, on the east and partly on the south by St. Breward, on the remainder of the south and the southwest by St. Tudy, and on the west by St. Teath.

The following careful survey, preserved in the Bishop's Registry at Exeter, shews the boundaries in detail:—

MICHAELSTOW IN CORNUBLÆ. } A view taken the xxiij daye of Maii 1613 of all the boundes limits & precinctes of the parish aforesaide by the seven whose names are heerevnder written.

The said parish of Michaelstowe Joyning wth St. Vdy & St. Teath is bounded & limited from the flood yeat against Trennick Mill vp to a flood yeat neare to Knights Mill bridge, the water being the bound all the waye betwene the parish of St. Teath & Michaelstow aforesaid. The ground of the sayd Treurenick, Karkeene, & bowmers, lying on the west and northwest syde of the sayd water, & the parish of Michaelstowe on the other syde of the sayd water; and from the sayd flood yeat neare Knightes mill bridge, turninge straight easte vp to a certaine yeat commonly called the Mill yeat, bordering on the parishes of St. Teath, Tintagel & Michaelstow, & betwene the said flood yeat & Mill yeat, The mill meadowe hedge being the bounde, leavinge the said Knights Mill bridge and the high waye on the north & northeast side, & the parishe of Michaelstowe on the other side. And from the said Mill yeat, leavinge the parishe of St. Teathe, only Joyning with Lanteglos, the hedge that runnes straight east from thence so farre vp as the high waye next to helsbury parke hedge, the foresaide hedge beinge the bound all the waye, leavinge the ground of ffentenwansen & Helston on the north & north east side & the parish of Michaelstowe on the other side. And from Helsbury parke hedge right downe over the said Helsbury parke vnto an oke tree[1] wth a springinge well thereto commonly known by the name of ffentonadle well in the said parke of Helsbury beinge the bound between the said parish of Michaelstow & Lanteglos or Advent; and from thence vnto the great River of Helsbury the lake that runnes from the foresaid well

---

[1] The oak tree is now gone, and the well also, the ground having been drained, but the boundary remains the same.

4 C²

vnto the said River beinge the bound, leavinge the parish of Lanteglos or Advent on the north east & the parish of Michaelstow on the south west side of the said well and lake. And from thence leavinge Lanteglos or Advent & Joyning with Breward the great River running right south from the foresaid lake vnto Gam Bridge the said River beinge the bound all the waye, leavinge the said parishe of Breward on the east side of the said River & Michaelstowe on the west side. And from Gam Bridge to the cross next to and from thence vp to Gam lane head the said lane being the bound the ground of longpill in the parish of Breward lying on the south side of the said lane & the parishe of Michaelstow on the other side. And from Gam lane head, leavinge Breward & Joyning the parish of St. Vdy, vnto certain boundes in the heath parke within the parish of St. Vdy, the highwaye beinge the bound, the said parishe of St. Vdy lyinge on the south side of the said highwaye & southwest side of the said boundes in the heath parke aforesaid & the parish of Michaelstowe on the other side. And from thence the hedge that runnes westward full to the flood yeat over against Trerenick mill aforesaid, and the said heath parke, Polsheath, litelyes hayes, and libbyespark in the said parish of St. Vdy on the south side of the said hedge, & Banoke's Downe, *alias* Polrode, Tregavena neither, & Treveleck of the said parish of Michaelstow on the other side; the said hedge being the bounde all the waye betwixe the sayde parishes of Michaelstowe and St. Vdy.

	Richard Burton, Clerck.	
	Wittm. Mulles	John Mulles
Witnesse	Trestrane Beane	John Olver
	Xpr Mulles	Thomas Philp
		John Symons

The entire area of the parish, according to admeasurements, is 1617a. 2r. 0p.

The geological character of the parish is of the altered Devonian series, precisely like the western part of Advent and Lanteglos, merging on its western side into true Devonian. Three very wide greenstone dykes intersect the parish north and south. The soil generally is good and suited either to corn or pasture.

The following particulars of the population, &c., are extracted from the census returns for the several decennia in the present century.

	1801	1811	1821	1831	1841	1851	1861	1871
Population	151	181	216	215[1]	225	218	219	240
Houses { Inhabited ..	28[2]	30	26	41	47	43	46	47
Uninhabited ..	4	10	2	1	3	5	5	4
Building ..	..	..	..	Nil	1	1	Nil	Nil

[1] Davies Gilbert notes that in the 30 years ending 1831, the increase in the population was 36 per cent. (Hist. of Cornw., vol. iii, p. 223.) His computation appears to be inaccurate. The increase was 64, which, upon 151 in 1801, was 42 per cent. The increase in the 40 years from 1831 to 1871 was 25 only, or a little more than 11 per cent. [2] Occupied by 40 families.

PLATE XLIV.

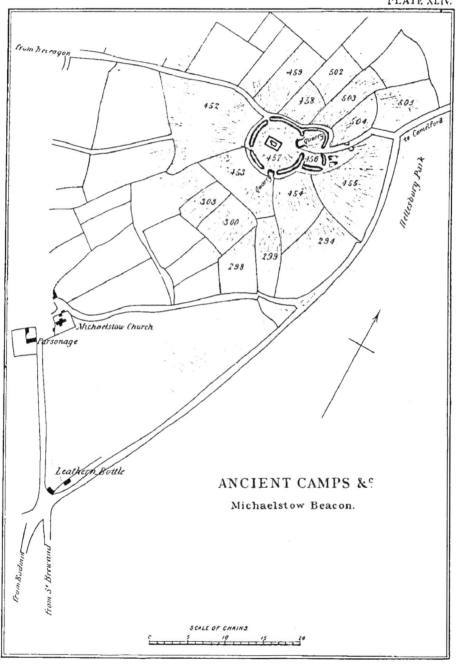

from Helligon

459   502
458   503
452   505
        504
Quarry
457   456
453
Quarry   to Camelford
454   455
303   Hellesbury Park
300
294
298   299

Michaelstow Church
Parsonage

Leathern Bottle

ANCIENT CAMPS &c.

Michaelstow Beacon.

from Bodmin
from St Breward

SCALE OF CHAINS
0   5   10   15   20

The annual value of real property assessed in 1815 was ... £1564
Gross Estimated Rental in 1874 1999
Rateable value in 1874 1839
Amount of Poors' Rate levied in 1874 ... ... 245[1]
Land Tax—Redeemed £21 9s. 3½d., unredeemed £50 10s. 8½d., Total 72
Assessed Taxes ... ... not known
Inhabited House Duty assessed upon the annual value of ... 40
Property and Income Tax assessed upon ... ... { Schedule A 2207
{ „ B 2112

Agriculture is the only branch of industry practised in the parish. Agricultural laborers receive wages at 12s. a week, without any other advantages. They have not cottages and gardens free of rent, nor are there any field allotments.

The chief landowners are: the Duke of Cornwall, in respect to the manor of Helston, John Gatley, Esq., Mr. John Seccombe, and Mr. Harry Hocken.

PRE-HISTORIC REMAINS.

In this parish is situate the important castle, or earthwork, known as Hellesbury, or Michaelstow, Beacon. It is situate three miles south of Camelford, and is distinct from Tregaer, in St. Kew, 3 miles; from Castle Gof 2 miles; from Tyntagel 6½ miles; from Titchbarrow Beacon 6½ miles; from Warbstow 10 miles; from Castle Canyke 8½ miles; and from Pencarrow 6½ miles. In consequence of its elevation, which is 684 ft. above the sea, it commands a view of all those fortresses. It is circular in form, and consists of a single lofty rampart and a deep ditch. The diameter of the inner, and principal, work, is about 460 ft. On the east side is an outwork, or barbican, which is about 400 ft. from north to south, and about 200 ft. in depth. Through this was the entrance. And external to the outwork are traces of other works too much effaced to admit of their plan being understood. Its commanding position must have rendered it a place of great importance in the system of defence of the country.[2] (See Plate XLIV.)

William of Worcester speaks of a castle here as being in ruins when he wrote (1478) "Castellum Hyllysbery dirutum per 4 milaria ultra Tyntagele."[3] Lysons says: "it is said to be what is called St. Syth's;"[4] and C. S. Gilbert suggests that it was one of the residences of the ancient Earls of Cornwall.[5] There certainly never was a walled castle on this spot, nor was it ever a residence of the Earls of Cornwall. There is no knowledge now of the designation "St. Syth's." On the top of the hill are ruins of a small quadrangular enclosure, measuring 85 ft. by 65 ft., within which are the remains of a small building, 40 ft. in length and about 20 ft. in breadth at the eastern end, and 15 ft. on the western. If this were a chapel, as has been supposed by some, dedicated to St. Syth, it would account for the name assigned to the hill, and although we do not

[1] The amount of Poors' Rate levied in 1831 was £141 11s. 0d. (Davies Gilbert's Hist. of Cornw., vol. iii, p. 223).
[2] Mac Lauchlan. 32nd Report of the Royal Institution of Cornwall, p. 35.
[3] Itinerary.   [4] Mag. Brit. pp. 182, 234.   [5] Hist. of Cornw., vol. ii, pp. 594.

know of any ancient authority for the designation, we conceive there must have been some traditional use, though now died out. The only Saint in the Roman Calendar, whose name is at all suitable, is S. Ositha, Queen and Martyr, who was commemorated on 7th October, but, she being a Saxon princess, it is not likely a British chapel would be dedicated to her.[1] In the Retour[2] of James Earl of Linlithgow, November 1696, we have mention of the patronage of St. Syth, who must, we think, have been the Saint in question. He was, probably, an Irishman. A few years ago excavations were made within the building by Mr., now Rev., E. T. Gibbons, but nothing distinctive of a chapel was discovered. There is, on the site, a circular-headed arch, cut in a solid piece of granite, of an octagonal form externally, having a span of 2 ft. 6 ins. and a height of 10 ins., the edges being chamfered; and also part of the head of another arch, of a wider span, with mouldings of the Third-pointed period. This earthwork is on a farm called Tredarrap, long the property of the Hocken family, and lately sold by Mr. William Hocken of Tregenna House, to Mr. John Gatley.

ANCIENT ROADS AND TRACKS.

We have before mentioned the road from the north, which, passing through Camelford, led to Michaelstow Beacon. After skirting the Beacon on the east, it passed through the parish and entered St. Tudy, about half-a-mile north of Hanger. A road branched off from

this road on the east side of the Beacon, and entered the earthwork on that side. Another road branched out of the road before described as leading from Camelford through St. Teath, &c., to Wade (ante, vol. ii, p. 283) near Tregreenwell, and passed through the parish of Michaelstow, due north and south. From this road, another road branched off, near Trevegon, which led to the castle on the west side. (See Plate XLIV.)

ANCIENT CHRISTIAN MONUMENTS.

The only cross known to us in this parish is a very fine shaft which now forms the lower step of a flight leading from the village green into the Churchyard. It measures 10 ft. in the length of the shaft. It is 20 ins. in breadth at the bottom, and 13 ins. at the top below the fillet, and in thickness it is 12 ins. at the bottom and 7 ins. at the top. This cross, which was a monolith of the holed type, has lost the greater part of its head. It was probably the village cross, and it is greatly to be desired that it should be removed from its present degraded position and set up either on the village green or in the Churchyard.

[1] She was the daughter of Frewald, a Mercian Prince, and neice to Editha, to whom belonged the town and manor of Ailsbury, where Ositha was brought up with her pious aunt. Ositha was married, while young, to a King of the East Angles, but the same day obtained his consent to live always a Virgin. She suffered about the year 870. (Butler ii, 601.) The Church of Merther is said to be dedicated to St. Sythyn=St. Swithin. (See ante, p. 423, and note.)

[2] Retours Linlithgow 283. Bishop of Brechin's Calendar of Scottish Saints, p. 449.

MEETING HOUSES OF DISSENTERS.

On 1st April 1820, upon the application of William Metherall, a house in the occupation of Edward Hocking in the village of Trevegon *alias* Treveighan, was registered in the Archdeaconry Court as a place of meeting for Armenian Bible Christians (Brianites). A Chapel was afterwards erected here in 1828, and on the 18th September 1830, it was registered in the Archdeaconry Court, being then in the possession of Edward Hocken of the parish of St. Tudy, by William Hooper Daniel for Brianites. It is not in trust, but is the private property of the representatives of the late Mr. Edward Hocken.

This building will receive a congregation of 100, and there are 20 registered members attached to it.

United Methodist Free Church.—The Wesleyan Methodists long had a place of meeting in a cottage at "Leathern Bottle." A Chapel was erected here, however, in 1842, which, on 6th December 1845, was registered in the Court of the Archdeaconry, by John Hawkey of Michaelstow for the use·of the Wesleyan Methodist Association. It is not under trust, but is proprietary, or on the share-holding principle.

This building will seat 75 persons, and the number of registered members is 14.

THE RECTORY.

The Advowson of this Church, like that of Lanteglos, has always been annexed to the Manor of Helston in Trigg. In Pope Nicholas's Taxation (1288-1291) the benefice was rated at £3, and in 1341, the ninth sheaf, fleece, and lamb were valued at the same amount, and so sold to Ralph Tregrynewen, Robert Tregrynewen, and John Stevyn. Of fifteenths there were none.[1] In the caption of seizin of Edward the Black Prince 11th Edward III. (1337), the Church of St. Michael, in the manor of Helliston in Trigg, is valued at 25 marks per annum. In the Bishop of Lincoln's taxation, the Church of St. Michael is rated at 60s.[2] On the levy of the Subsidy of the Clergy (1387) the Rector was assessed upon the same rate.[3] In Wolsey's taxation 1535, it is rated at £10 13s. 8d.,[4] and in Bishop Veysey's return of 3rd November 1536, it is valued at £10 13s. 9d., John Wade being Incumbent.[5]

[1] Inquisitiones Nonarum, p. 346.   [2] Bishop Bronescombe's Register.

[3] Sub. Roll, Clerical, 4th Richard II. $\dfrac{24}{5}$

[4] Valor Ecclesiasticus, vol. ii, p. 402.   [5] Oliver's Eccl. Antiquities, vol. ii, p. 191.

The total area of all the lands in the parish subject to the payment of tithes is 1348a. 3r. 23p., viz.:

	A.	R.	P.
Arable	793	0	9
Meadow and Pasture	250	0	0
Orchards and Gardens	30	0	0
Woods and Plantations...	30	0	0
Roads, Rivers, Hedges, and Wastes ...	245	3	14
	1348	3	23

All the lands in the parish, except Hellesbury Park, which contains by estimation 216a. 1r. 26p., the tithes of which are covered by a modus, or customary payment, of 13s. 4d. per annum, are subject to all manner of tithes, and the Rector for the time being is entitled to all the said tithes, which were commuted, on 30th June 1843, at the annual rent charge of £235 per annum.

The tithes of all the glebe lands, containing by estimation 48a. 1r. 4p., have been merged in the freehold.

INSTITUTIONS.

1280 Christmas Day	Mr. William le Brun, Sub-deacon,[1] admitted to the Church of St. Michael of Hellesbury, upon the presentation of Edmund Earl of Cornwall.
1281 9th Kal. March	William de Cryditon, Sub-deacon,[2] was admitted by Bishop Quivel to the Church of St. Michael of Hellesbury, upon the presentation of Edmund Earl of Cornwall.
1320 September 21st	Walter de Plompton, Priest,[3] was admitted to the Church of St. Michael juxta Hellisbury, vacant by the death of William the last Rector, upon the presentation of Isabella Queen of England.
Unknown -	- John de Nelond.
1341 -	- Peter Sevenoks, Vicar of the Church of Stoke sub Hamedon, Diocese of Bath and Wells,[4] was admitted to the rectory of Stow St. Michael, in exchange with John de Nelond.
1344 June 30th	- John de Arnhale, Rector of the Church of Hampstede Marshall in the Diocese of Sarum,[5] was admitted to the rectory of Stow St. Michael, in exchange with Peter Sevenoks, with consent of the patrons.

[1] Bishop Bronescombe's Reg., fo. 94.

[2] Bishop Quivil's Reg., fo. 116. On 30th August 1315, at the prayer of William, Priest, Rector of Stow St. Michael juxta Hellesbury, Nicholas de Chaillou, Priest, was appointed to assist him, both in person and in goods, on account of his age and infirmity of his body. Bishop Stapeldon's Reg.

[3] Bishop Stapeldon's Reg., fo. 152.   [4] Bishop Grandisson's Reg., fo. 45.   [5] Ibid, fo. 51.

1345 May 29th   -   Roger de Silby of Gatton, Diocese of Wynton,[1] was admitted to the Rectory of Stow St. Michael, in exchange with John de Amhall, with consent of patrons.

1354 April 29th   -   William de Middleton, Vicar of Karsaul, Diocese of Winton,[2] was admitted to the Rectory of Stow St. Michael, in exchange with Roger de Silby, with consent of patrons.

1371 July 13th   -   Roger Baconn, Chaplain,[3] was instituted to parish Church of Michaelstow, upon the presentation of the Prince of Wales.

1371 August 9th   -   John Baconn, Rector of the Church of Fornham, Diocese of Norwich,[4] was admitted to the Church of Michaelstow, in exchange with Roger Baconn, Rector of the said Church.

1371-2 January 3rd   Roger de Shouldham, perpetual Chaplain, or custos cancarie, or perpetual benefice in the Chapel in the Guild Hall, London, founded by John Wythorne and others,[5] was admitted to the Rectory of Michaelstow, in exchange with John Baconn, Rector of the said Church.

1382 May 26th   -   Bartholomew Porter, Rector of Thrandeston, Diocese of Norwich, was admitted to the Rectory of Michaelstow, in exchange with Roger de Shouldham, Rector of the said Church.

1382 October 23rd - John de Balsham, Rector of the parish of Brokedysham, Diocese of Norwich,[7] admitted to the Rectory of Stow St. Michael, in exchange with Bartholomew Porter.

unknown   -   Simon Barton.

1404 August 25th - Robert Bulle,[8] was admitted to the parish Church of Michaelstow, vacant by the death of Simon Barton, upon the presentation of Henry Duke of Cornwall.

1407 December 25th   John Nowers, Clerk,[9] was admitted to the parish Church of Michaelstow, vacant by the death of Robert Bole, upon the presentation of Henry Duke of Cornwall.

1430 December 18th   John Carbure of Dudcote, Diocese of Sarum,[10] was admitted to the Church of Michaelstow, in exchange with John Nowyers.

1437 August 13th - John Kelly, Dean of the Collegiate Church of Carentoc, co. Cornwall,[11] was admitted to the Rectory of the parish Church of Michaelstow, in exchange with John Carbura.

[1] Bishop Stapeldon's Register, fo. 53.   [2] Ibid., fo. 103.
[3] Bishop Brentingham's Register, fo. 15.   [4] Bishop Brentingham's Register, fo. 15.
[5] Ibid., fo. 18.   [6] Ibid., fo. 71.
[7] Ibid. fo. 76.   [8] Bishop Stafford's Register fo. 78.
[9] Bishop Stafford's Register, fo. 99.   [10] Bishop Lacy's Register, vol. ii, fo. 93.
[11] Ibid., fo. 153.

1445 May 3rd　　-　Hamiline Kirkeby, Chaplain,[1] was admitted to the Rectory of Myghelstowe, vacant by the resignation of John Kelly, last Rector, upon the presentation of the Duke of Cornwall.

1489 April 27th　-　Thomas Janyn, Chaplain,[2] was admitted to the parish Church of St. Michael of Michaelstow, vacant by the death of Hamelyn Kirkeby, last Rector, upon the presentation of Arthur Prince of Wales and Duke of Cornwall, the true Patron.

1507 October 2nd -　Christopher Borlase,[3] was admitted to the Rectory of Michaelstow, vacant by the death of the last Incumbent, upon the presentation of Henry King of England.

1513 Feb. 20th　-　John Wade, Chaplain,[4] was admitted to the Church of Michaelstow, vacant by the death of the last Incumbent, upon the presentation of Henry King of England.

1562-3 March 23rd-　Reginald Aldridge,[5] was admitted to the Rectory of Mighelstow, vacant by the death of the last Rector, upon the presentation of Queen Elizabeth. .

1565 January 21st -　Thomas Washington, Clerk,[6] was instituted to the parish Church of Michaelstow, vacant by the deprivation of Reginald Aldridge, last Rector, upon the presentation of Elizabeth Queen of England.

1568 March 4th　-　Sir Thomas Boden, Clerk,[7] was admitted to the parish Church of Michaelstow, vacant by the resignation of the last Incumbent, upon the presentation of the Queen.

1589 June 16th　-　Richard Burton, M.A.,[8] was admitted to the Parish Church of Michaelstow, vacant by the death of Thomas Bawden, last incumbent, upon the presentation of the Queen.

1630 May 8th　　-　Thomas Harrison, Clerk,[9] was admitted to the Rectory of Michaelstow, vacant by the death of Richard Burton, Clerk, last incumbent, upon the presentation of the King.

1639 March 16th　-　John Davies, Clerk, M.A.,[10] was admitted to the Rectory of Michaelstow, vacant by the cession of the last incumbent, upon the presentation of the King.

[1] Bishop Lacy's Register, vol. ii, fo. 217.

[2] Bishop Fox's Register, fo. 111. Thomas Janyn, Rector of Michaelstow, included in a commission concerning the patronage of the Church of Tindagell, 19th May 1498.

[3] Bishop Oldham's Register, fo. 13. Presentation dated 9th September 1507 (Rot. Pat., 23rd Henry VII, Part I. m. 12.)

[4] Ibid., 54. Sir John Wade, Parson of Michaelstow, was buried 16th November, 1562, P.R.

[5] Bishop Turberville's Register, fo. 80.

[6] Bishop Alley's Register, fo. 13. He was again instituted on 5th June following.

[7] Ibid., fo. 22.　　　　　　　　　　　　　　　[8] Bishop Woolton's Register, fo. 41.

[9] Bishop Hall's Register, fo. 21.

[10] Bishop Hall's Register, vol. ii, fo. 22. Jone, the wieff of John Deaves, Preacher of the Word of God in this parish, was buried May 12th 1647. John Deeues, Minister of Michaelstow, was buried 16th February 1663. P.R.

1664 April 6th   - Christopher Hill, Clerk,[1] was admitted to the Rectory of Mighelstow, *alias* Michaelstow, vacant by the death of the last incumbent, upon the presentation of the King.

1678 July 15th   - Moses Horway, M.A.,[2] was admitted to the Rectory of Mighelstow, vacant by the death of Christopher Hill, upon the presentation of the King.

1695 August 2nd   - Walter Hewgoe, Clerk,[3] was admitted, upon the resignation of Moses Holway, upon the presentation of the King.

1712 July 9th   - Christopher Chilcott, Clerk, M.A.,[4] was admitted to the Rectory of Michaelstow, vacant by the cession of Walter Hewgoe, upon the presentation of the Queen.

1726 July 8th   - John Clode, Clerk,[5] was admitted to the Rectory of Michaelstow, vacant by the death of Christopher Chilcott, last incumbent, upon the presentation of the King.

1755 January 10th - John Fisher, Clerk, B.A.,[6] was admitted to the Rectory of Michaelstow, vacant by the death of John Clode, Clerk, last incumbent, upon the presentation of the King.

1775 October 13th - John Fisher, the younger, B.A.,[7] was admitted to the Rectory of Michaelstow, vacant by the resignation of John Fisher, upon the presentation of the King.

1801 June 1st   - Isaac Tyeth, Clerk, B.A.,[8] was admitted to the Rectory of Michaelstow, vacant by the death of John Fisher, Clerk, last incumbent, upon the presentation of the Prince of Wales.

1818 December 22nd   Edmund Spetigue, Clerk, B.A.,[9] was admitted to the Rectory of Michaelstow, vacant by the death of Isaac Tyeth, Clerk, last incumbent, upon the presentation of the Prince of Wales.

1849 November 5th   John Kingdon, Clerk, B.A.,[10] was admitted to the Rectory of Michaelstow, vacant by the death of Edmund Spetigue, Clerk, last incumbent, upon the presentation of the Prince of Wales.

---

[1] Bishop's Register, N.S., vol. i, p. 73.

[2] Bishop's Register, N.S., vol. ii, fo. 87. Of Cath. Hall, Camb., M.A., per Literas Regias 1677.

[3] Ibid. vol. iv, fo. 9. Rector of St. Mabyn from 1716.

[4] Ibid. N.S., vol. v, fo. 52. Matric. Mag. Hall, Oxford, 13th July 1683, aged 18, son of Robert Chilcott, of Byminster, co. Dorset. B.A., 11th April 1687, M.A., 2nd April 1690, Vicar also of Tintagel. (See post.)

[5] Ibid. vol. vi, fo. 43. Matric. at Balliol. Coll., Oxford, 27th May 1704, aged 19, son of Edward Clode "Pleb" of Chardstock, co. Dorset, (took no degree.) Buried 8th August 1754. Mrs. Elizabeth Clode was buried 18th January 1769. P.R.

[6] Ibid. vol. viii, fo. 37. He was probably the same John Fisher, Clerk, who was Master of the Grammar School at Bodmin. (See ante, vol. i, p. 282.)

[7] Ibid. vol. ix, fo. 108. Matric. at Exeter Coll., Oxford 17th December 1759, aged 18, son of Rev. John Fisher. B.A., 3rd June 1763.

[8] Ibid. vol. x, fo. 149.   [9] Ibid. vol. xi, fo. 105.   [10] Ibid. vol. xii, fo. 63.

4 D²

1871 April 14th - Charles Joseph Gillett, Clerk,[1] was admitted to the Rectory of Michaelstow, vacant by the death of John Kingdon, Clerk, last incumbent, upon the presentation of the Prince of Wales.

THE PARISH CHURCH.

The Parish Church (see Plate XLV.) which is situate on the south of the Beacon, near the centre of the parish, is dedicated to St. Michael. A great portion of it has been rebuilt; the north wall of the chancel some fifty years ago, and the south wall of the aisle very recently. Before the late alterations it consisted of Chancel, partially disengaged, 15 ft. by 13 ft., nave 44 ft. by 14 ft., south chapel 15 ft. by' 10 ft. 6 in., south aisle 39 ft. by 10 ft. 6 in., north aisle 42 ft. by 10 ft., south porch and western tower. The Chancel and Chapel were separated by a parclose, and divided from the rest of the Church by carved screens, the bottoms of which remained until the recent alterations. (See Ground Plan XLIII., fig. 2.)

The east window of the Chancel is a modern one of three lights. No piscina or other adjunct of the altar remains, but, built into the north wall on the inside, there is a pierced quatrefoil, and outside a small arch, which probably covered a piscina.

The Chapel was lighted by a three-light window in the east wall, and another on the south. The former contained remains of painted glass. The subject was probably the last scenes in the life of Our Lord, as the fragments contained several heads with the legend " Hic ductus est ante Pilatum." In the tracery of this window were two angels bearing shields, with the monograms of Our Lord and the Blessed Virgin. The window has been re-glased, and the ancient glass is gone. All distinction between the Chapel and aisle has been removed, and in rebuilding the wall two new square-headed windows have been introduced. The aisle was of four bays, and the Chapel one, divided from the nave and chancel by granite pillars of the usual type, the capitals of Caen stone beautifully foliated.

The north aisle is also of four bays. The pillars are, however, of workmanship inferior to that of those on the south. It has a north door under a plain equilateral arch. This aisle has a three-light window at the east end. The lights are circular-headed 5-fo. with openings of the same type above. In the north wall are three three-light 5-fo. ogee windows, two on the east and one on the west of the door.

The nave contains several of the ancient oak benches with well carved ends, though some of them are somewhat decayed. The designs are emblems of the passion, sacred monograms, crowned M's, &c. Upon one of them are two escutcheons; one charged with the letter " L " over a rose, and the other with a letter " T " over a taw cross.

The roofs throughout the Church are of the wagon type, and good of their kind. Those of the Chancel and nave are plastered, except the principals. The roof of the north aisle is open, with well carved principals and bosses, nearly complete, but those of the south aisle are not so well carved, and nearly all the bosses are lost.

The outer door of the south porch has an equilateral arch with continuous mouldings.

[1] Bishop Register, N.S., vol. xiv, fo. 60.

Plate XLV

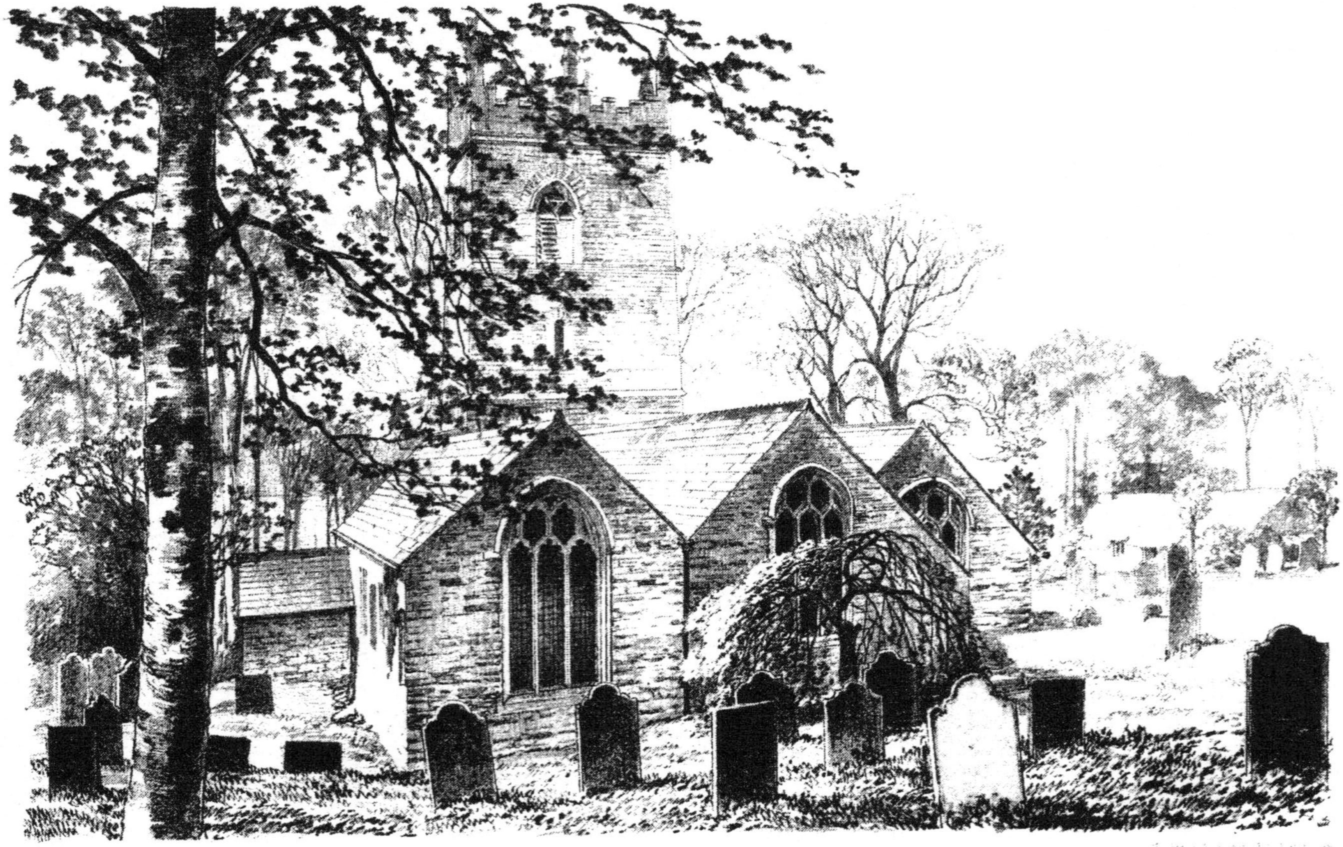

The inner door has a depressed four-centred arch under a square hood-moulding. The mouldings are continuous, the cavetto being filled with quatrefoil and cinquefoil ornaments. In the spandrils are elongated trefoils. The whole is well cut in Catacleuse stone.

The tower is of three flights, fifty-four feet in height, with a stair turret, at the north east angle, lighted with circular-headed openings. It is battlemented and possesses six pinnacles, three on the east side, and the same number on the north, one being at each external angle of the stair turret. The tower door has an equilateral arch with a dripstone over, and above it a new window, three-light 5-fo., with tracery in the head. The bell chamber has on each face a large two-light window.

The font is octagonal, of third-pointed date, and stands on a circular shaft on a square cushioned-patterned base, of the Norman period.

In the Churchyard is a Holy Well.

In the year 1550, this Church possessed three bells and two chalices of silver. Of these bells one, the *First*, still remains, which is a bell of considerable interest, and not common. There is one at S. Dennis in this county, one at Marldon, and another at Townstal in Devon, by the same founder, and they occur in other counties. The Michaelstow bell bears the legend: "Sancta Margareta ora pro nobis," and the three stamps underneath. The shields,

Fig. 1.   Fig. 2.   Fig. 3.

figs. 1 and 3, appear to be trade marks, but the founder has not yet been identified. Ellacombe calls these bells: "Jesu mercy, Lady help bells,"[1] from the legend which encircles the elegant foliated cross on the principal stamp, fig. 2.[2] The Michaelstow bell is 2 ft. 6½ in. in diameter at the mouth.

The two other Michaelstow bells have been recast at different periods, and bear respectively the following inscriptions:

2. ROGER . SANDY . ROGER MAY ÷ WARDS ▱ ÷ A ◬ GOODING ÷ 1739.

3. RICHARD . MAYOW : GENT. ÷ WILLIAM . PARSONS : Ch : WARDENS ÷ C. P. ÷ 1750.

The latter was recast by Christopher Pennington, as his initials indicate. The note of this last mentioned Bell is B flat.

[1] Ellacombe's "Church Bells of Devon," 1872, p. 28.

[2] We are indebted to the kindness of Mr. Ellacombe for the use of the blocks for these stamps. That numbered 2 is a trifle larger than the similar stamp on the Michaelstow bell, but, in other respects it is precisely the same.

COMMUNION PLATE.

The present Communion Plate consists of a chalice with a cover and a paten. The chalice is of the seventeenth century, and is very quaint in its form, and ornamented with arabesque foliage. The cover, which was intended to be used as a paten, bears the following inscription :

✠ MEY HIL STO ✠

There is also a paten which is quite new, having been bought at Exeter about four years ago.

INSCRIPTIONS ON MONUMENTS AND GRAVESTONES.

1. In the north aisle is a loose slate slab, removed from the Chancel in the recent alterations, having incised thereon the figures of two females, and circumscribed as under:

Here lyeth Jane yᵉ daughtʳ of John Killiow Esqʳ, and late wife to Thomas Merrifield of Collomb Majᵒʳ, Gent, who died yᵉ 26ᵗʰ of March 1662.

2. On the floor of the north aisle circumscribed:

Here lyeth Phillip the sone of Richard Mounsteven, who was buried yᵉ 26ᵗʰ Novʳ 1660.

3. Another slab circumscribed:

Here lyeth the Bodye of Honor the wife of Richard Mounsteven, who was buried the 19 day of June 1654.

In the centre.——

Here also lieth the Body of Ioseph Mayow, Gent, who Was buried august The 5ᵗʰ 1689, in yᵉ 52ᵈ year of his Age.

4. Just within the north door is a large and handsome slab, much worn, in memory of Margery Symons, widow, who died 28th January, in the year of our Lord 1629.

IN THE CHURCH YARD.

5. On a stone now loose is the following inscription :

Here ly the Bodies of John Brod,[1] gentleman, who died the 5 day of May 1577: and John Brod......................... John who died the 8 day of Aprill añ 1582, having issue by Jone his wyf, daughter unto Henry Trefry Esquire, 6 sonnes & 4 daughters.

---

[1] These Brodes were of Trenowith in this parish, which they inherited from a family of that name as early as 1469. John Brode held Trenowith in 1539, and John Brode the younger, named in the inscription, was succeeded by his son and heir, Walter Brode. (See post under TRENOWITH.)

6. Upon a granite slab in large letters, in relief, some of them conjoined:

ELIZABETH THE WIFE OF ROGER MAY WAS BVRIED THE 12 DAY OF APRIL IN THE YEAR OF OVR LORD 1656. ROGER MAY WAS BVRIED THE 15 DAY APRIL IN THE YEAR OF OVR LORD GOD 1661.

Here lyeth the body of Christopher Alee,[1] of this Parish, who was buried the fourth day of July in the year of our Lord God 1706, aged neer 75.

> Take notice all from dust wee came
> To dust we must return again.
> Under this stone the dust doth ly
> Of him whose vertues cannot dye;
> His alms, his prayers, his pietye
> Hath sent his soul above the skye.

7. On an altar tomb the arms of Lower: a chev. eng. between 3 roses, and the following inscription:

Here lyeth the body of John Lower, Gent, of Tregreenwell, in this P^{sh}, who departed this life the 20th day of January in the 48th year of His Age, anno Domini 1724.

> Low here my dearest friend is Gone,
> His days are past his Race is Rune.
> May you be holders well Think on
> Your dayes Expire and will be done.
> Now Lett his body undisturb'd remain
> Till the last Trump calls him to rise again.
> Memento mori.

8. On another altar tomb:

Here lies ye Body of John ye son of John and Ann Lower, of Tregreenwell, in this Parish, Gent, who was buried ye 23 day of June 1747, Ætatis suæ 26.

> Of manners gentle, of affections mild,
> In wit a man simplicity a child.
> With Native Humour tempering Virtue's rage
> Form'd to Delight at once and Lash the age,
> Aboue Temptation in a Low Estate
> And Uncorrupted even a mong the Great.
> A safe Companion and an easy Friend,
> Unblamed thro' Life Lamented in the End.
> These are thy Honours not that here they Boast
> Is mixt with Heroes or with Kings thy Dust
> But that the worthy and the good shall say,
> Striking their pensive Bosoms, Here I lye.

9. On a massive calvary Cross of granite are the letters I. H. C. within a circular panel; and upon the upper step this inscription:

John Kingdon, Twenty one years Rector of this Parish, fell asleep October 21st 1870, aged 62. In such an hour as ye think not the Son of Man cometh ✠

---

[1] Christopher Alee, in 1683, held lands in Tregreenwell. A son of the same name succeeded him, and held the same land in 1718 (see post).

10. William the son of William Hocken of Tregreenwell, and Priscilla his wife, was buried May the 3rd 1770, in the 4th Year of his age.

11. Sacred to the memory of Henry Hocken of this Parish who departed this life October the 12th 1789, aged 74 years. Also in memory of William Hocken of this Parish who departed this life November 14 1795, aged 56 years. Also in memory of Mary Bonear, the daughter of Henry & Elizabeth Hocken, of Tregreenwell in this Parish, who departed this life Oct. 2 1814, aged about nine months.

12. Underneath are deposited The mortal Remains of Wm. Hocken, Son of Wm. and Priscilla Hocken of this Parish, who exchanged Earth for Heaven June the 7th 1804, aged 24 years. Also in memory of Mary Ann his daughter whose mortal remains was [sic] deposited May the 17th 1804, aged six months.

13. On an altar tomb :

Sacred to the memory of Priscilla Hocken the wife of Wm. Hocken of Tregreenwell, in this Parish, who departed this life the 28 Decr 1816, aged 63.

Also to the memory of Henry Hocken of Tregreenwell, their son, who departed this life August 2d 1817, aged 45.

14. On an altar tomb :

Sacred to the memory of Mary the Daughter of William Hocken and Priscilla his wife, Late of Tregreenwell in this Parish. She departed this life at Sowdons, in the Parish of St. Tudy, on the 24th day of Novr 1837, aged 54 years.

PARISH REGISTERS.

The old Registers consist of three volumes, the first being very imperfect. The entries of burials commence in 1544, and are continued, in regular order, to 1736. The entries of marriages extend from 1548, and are perfect to 1735; but those of baptisms begin only in 1682, are complete to 1693, then imperfect to 1718, and end in 1734. The second volume contains entries of baptisms and burials from 1740 to 1812, and of marriages from 1737 to the same date. The third volume contains the record of marriages under the Act 26th George II., cap. 33, from 1754 to 1812.

It appears from a memorandum left by Mr. Thorne, who was Curate in 1813, that the injury to the first volume was done during the incumbency of Mr. Fisher, the book having been left with the Parish Clerk, from whom Mr. Spettigue recovered it, 2nd May 1841.

The earliest names occurring in the Registers are Kelly, or Killiowe, Pomeroy, Hocken, Brode, and Tooker.

SCHOOLS.

On 13th April 1852, Earl Fortescue, under the Acts 5th Victoria and 8th Victoria for affording facilities for the conveyance and endowments of sites for Schools, granted to the Minister and Churchwardens of the parish of Michaelstow, and their successors for ever, a cottage, and garden enclosure in front, in the village of Michaelstow, for a school for the education of children and adults, or children only, of the labouring, manufacturing, and other poorer class in the parish of Michaelstow, and as a residence for the teachers: and it is provided that "such school shall always be in union with, and conducted upon the principles, and in furtherance of the ends and designs of the Incorporated National Society for promoting the education of the poor in the principles of the Established Church."

The school is still conducted as a Church School, and in union with the National Society, but the Education Department, considering that the building is not sufficiently large to accommodate all the children in the parish who ought to attend school, has proposed that a School Board shall be formed for the united parishes of Michaelstow and St. Teath, and that children in the former parish, above nine years of age, be sent to St. Teath, where they would be accommodated in a new school house about to be erected in that parish, and to this proposal the ratepayers have agreed.

CHARITIES.

There are no public charities or bequests belonging to the Church.

TRENOWITH.

This estate at an early date was held by a family of the same name. In 1337 Ralph de Trenowith held one acre of land Cornish there at a rent of 15½d. per annum, and a fine of 6d.[1] The free tenements of the manor are not shewn in the Assession Rolls until 1469, when the same lands were held, at the same rent, by John Trenowith and Stephen Brode, as kinsmen and heirs of Ralph de Trenowith.[2] In 1539, the premises had passed to John Brode, who had acquired them of John Trenowith and Henry Brode, Chaplain, son and heir of Robert Brode, kinsman and heir of John Brode, and they remained in the tenure of John until his death in 1582,[3] when they passed to Walter Brode, his son and heir.[4] Seven years later they had been acquired by John Hendy, Gent.,[5] upon whose daughters and coheirs the land had devolved in 1617. At the Assession in that year, William Stoninge, in right of Abigail his wife, Ralph Cozens and Patience

---

[1] Caption of Seizin, Edward the Black Prince.
[2] Assession Roll, 9th Edward IV.
[3] See Mon. Inscrip., No. 5, p. 566, ante.
[4] Assession Roll, 30th Elizabeth.
[5] Ibid., 37th Elizabeth.

4 E

his wife, and Frances North, daughter of Elizabeth Hendy, held the same acre of land by the accustomed services, and the aforesaid rent of 15½d.[1] Abigail Hendy, after the death of her first husband, William Stoninge, married Emanuel Davies, who, in her right, in 1624, held the third part of the land, the other properties being held by John Billing, Gent., whose father Richard Billing,[2] deceased, had purchased of Ralph Cozens and Patience his wife their third part share. The other third part had passed to Richard Marke and Frances his wife,[3] and had, by them, been sold, one moiety to the aforesaid John Billing, and the other to Emanuel Davies.[4]

From the last mentioned date the Assession Rolls cease until 1683, when the premises in question were held by Lady Smith after the death of Sir James Smith her husband.[5] In 1725, the lands had passed to John Phillipps, Gent.,[6] and are now the property, by recent purchase, of John Gatley, Esq.

TREGRENEWEN *alias* TREGREENWELL.

Tregrenewen, in ancient times, was held in free tenure of the manor of Helston in Trigg, and gave its name to its possessors (see pp. 559, 573). In 1335 Roger Probyt held half an acre of land Cornish in Tregreenewen, at the annual rent of 2s. 6d., aid one half-penny, suit at Court and fealty.[7] In 1491 Stephen Brode, as kinsman and heir of Roger Probit, held it,[8] and his descendant, John Brode, died seized in 1582, and was succeeded by his son and heir, Walter Brode, who held it in 1588,[9] and from whom, in 1595, it had passed to George Carnsew.[10] Not long afterwards it had become broken into parcels. In 1617, a portion was held by Francis Carnsew, as son and heir of George Carnsew, another portion by Robert Mullis, by purchase of John Mullis, and a third part by John Carneck.[11] In 1624, it was held by Michael Inch, Gent., by purchase from Francis Carnsew, Gent., George Mullis after the death of George Mullis his father,[12] and Thomas Carneck.[13] In 1637, Francis Carnsew, Gent., and Mary his wife suffered a fine in two messuages in Trelill and Tregreenwell to William Inch, Senior, Gent., and William Inch, Junior, Gent.[14] In 1650, Elizabeth Mullis held one acre at the rent of 1s., William Jack, Gent., held an acre at the rent of 2s. 6d., and John Kernick, Gent., held another acre at the rent of 2s.[15] In 1668, William Lower held in Tregrenewen in his own right.[16] In 1683, it was

---

[1] Assession Roll, 15th James. John Hendy, Gent., was buried 1st November, 1616. P.R.

[2] See Pedigree of BILLING, ante vol. i, 389.

[3] Frances, wife of Richard Marke, Gent., was buried 2nd Oct. 1636.　　[4] Assession Roll, 22nd James.

[5] Ibid., 35th Charles II.　　　　　　　　　　[6] Ibid., 11th George I.

[7] Caption of Seizin, Edward the Black Prince.　　[8] Assession Roll, 7th Henry VII. (Record Office).

[9] Ibid., 30th Elizabeth.　　　　　　　　　　[10] Ibid., 37th Elizabeth.

[11] Ibid., 15th James. Nicholas Carnyk was Prepositus of the Manor in 1345, and again in 1352.

[12] 1643. George Mullis son of George Mullis deceased, and Ann his wife (who afterwards was married to William Lower, Gent.) A vertuous yong man, and one that feared God, departed this life, October 27th, and was buried October 28th. P.R.

[13] Assession Roll, 22nd James.　　　　　　[14] Pedes Finium, 12th Charles, Hil.

[15] Parliamentary Survey.　　　　　　　　　[16] Copy of Assession Roll. Original lost.

held by William Beile, by purchase from William Inch, Gent.; Christopher Allee and William Salmon, Clerk, by purchase from Charles Carnecke, after the death of John Carnecke his father; Ralph Pike after the death of Digory Glyn; Humphry Carnecke after the death of John Carneck his father;[1] and at the following assession in 1688, it continued to be held by the same parties.[2] William Beale of Trewinnell, in St. Teath, died seized in 1713, and by his will, dated 1st May 1712, devised it to his eldest son William Beale and the heirs male of his body, in default remainder to his sons, John and Joseph, successively, in tail male, in default remainder to his daughter Dorothy and her heirs for ever.[3] We have no further Assession Roll until 1717, when John Lower, Junr., Gent., held a certain portion, and Richard Betenson, Junr., and Ann his wife, John Glanville, Junr., and Phillippa his wife, daughters and heirs of Christopher Allee, held other portions,[4] and it was held in the same manner in 1724.[5] In 1731, the portion held by John Lower, by his death, had passed to Richard Lower his son; Richard Dow held a portion by purchase from Richard Betenson in right of Ann his wife, and John Glanville in right of Phillippa his wife held as before.[6] In 1784, William Hocken held a third part, Giles Bawden, after the death of his wife Mary Symons, held a third part, Henry Hocken held a sixth part, and the other sixth part was held by James Baron, Gent., in right of Elizabeth his wife after the death of John Spiller.[7] Some portion continued to be held by the Hocken family until within a few years,[8] which is now the property of Mr. Button.

MICHAELSTOW.

Hals states that "in this parish formerly lived the genteel family of Michaelstow, that married one of the heirs of Gifford of Fewborough (Thenborough) in Devon."[9] It is not improbable that the family alluded to derived their name from this parish, but, if they ever lived here, it was at a very early date, and we have never seen any record of the fact. In 1337, William de Treythian held one acre of land Cornish in Mighelstow of the manor of Helston in Trigg, at the annual rent of 4s.,[10] rendering the usual services, which land, in 1469, had descended to Philip Copleston as his kinsman and heir.[11] In 1574 it had passed in marriage with Isotte daughter and heir of Richard Coplestone to John Wood.[12] In 1624 it had passed to Christopher Wood by purchase from his father,[12] and in 1683, Hugh Boscawen held it, from whom, in 1718,[14] it had passed to Hugh Fortescue of Filleigh, by marriage with Bridget only daughter and heir of the said

---

[1] Assession Roll, 35th Charles II.
[2] Ibid., 3rd and 4th James II.
[3] Proved 22nd March 1713-14. Archd. Cornwall
[4] Assession Roll, 4th George I.
[5] Ibid., 11th George I.
[6] Ibid., 5th George II.
[7] Ibid., 25th George III.
[8] See grave-stone inscriptions, ante p. 568.
[9] The Michaelstows were, we believe, settled in Devon. Their arms: sa three wings ar., are quartered by Treffry (See ante, p. 252) and by Prideaux.
[10] Caption of Seizin, Edward the Black Prince.
[11] Assession Roll 9th Edward IV.
[12] Ibid. 16th Elizabeth. In the Roll of 37th Elizabeth she is called "Isabella."
[31] Ibid. 22nd James.
[14] Ibid. 4th Geo. I.

4 E²

Hugh and Margaret his wife, fifth daughter and eventually coheir of Theophilus Clinton, Earl of Lincoln, by whose death the Barony of Clinton fell into abeyance, which, in 1721, was terminated in favour of Hugh Fortescue, son of the abovementioned Hugh and Bridget, who, in 1725, held Michaelstow after the death of his father.[1] His son Hugh Fortescue was, in 1746, created Baron Fortescue and Earl of Lincoln, the Barony of Fortescue to revert, in the event of his dying s.p., to his half brother Mathew Fortescue, which limitation took effect, and by his descendant Earl Fortescue the Michaelstow lands are now held.

TREGENNA.

A very substantially built and convenient mansion has recently been erected here by Mr. William Hocken, upon lands which have been in the possession of his family for several generations. The principal front is constructed of fine granite ashlar, and the other portions of local stone of considerable beauty of colouring. The whole is completed in the most costly manner, whilst the stables and other auxiliaries are very perfect of their kind, the gardens being well stocked and prolific.

FAMILY HISTORY.

Several names of gentle families occur in the early register, but none of them except the Lowers, of whom we hope to treat under St. Tudy, were seated for more than one or two descents in the parish. A Mr. Vincent Calmadie would seem to have been resident here in the early part of the 17th century. He was, doubtless, of the Wembury House in Devon. His wife, as Mary wife of Vincent Calmadie, Esq., was buried 30th June 1636, and we have Philip, wife of Vincent Calmadie, buried 20th June 1640, and Vincent Calmadie, Esq., was buried 14th May 1651. We should name, also, the Mayows, who were seated at Tregone. Joseph Mayow, attorney, was buried in 1689, and Mrs. Jane Mayow in 1692; Richard Mayow, Gent., in 1751, &c. Tregone passed to the Hockens, a very ancient family of this and the neighbouring parishes, whose name we have frequently mentioned. Besides Tregone they held Tredarrap, Bearoke, Tregreenwell, Tregenna, and other lands in this parish, some of which are still in their possession. The family of Trenowith and Brode we have already adverted to (ante, pp. 569, 570), as we have also to that of Mullis, which name is found in the Return of 1525, see p. 575.

[1] Assession Roll, 11th George I.

APPENDIX.

A.

Subsidy Roll 1st Edward III, $\frac{87}{7}$ consisting of a Twentieth of all Moveable Goods.

See ante, p. 395.

Parochia Sancti Maubani.

De Ricardo Gones	-	·· - ix*d*	De Waltero Dogy -	- - viij*d*
De Ricardo Cereseaux	-	iij*s* iiij*d*	De Juliano Dogy -	- - ix*d*
De Willelmo Homet	-	- vj*d*	De Johanne Whityng	- - vij*d*
De Henrico Kyng -	-	- vj*d*	De Briano Kene -	- - vj*d*
De Willelmo Pores -	-	- vj*d*	De Radulpho Mostard	- - xij*d*
De Laurencio Meyndy	-	- xij*d*	De Johanne Gones -	- - vij*d*
De Henrico Berty -	-	- vj*d*	De Johanne Hikedon	- - vj*d*
De Emma Walsha -	-	- xij*d*	De Martino de Stone	- - vj*d*
De Waltero Yonge -	-	- vj*d*	De Adam Heligan -	- - ij*s*
De Stephano Yonge -	-	- vj*d*	De Willelmo Scott -	- - viij*d*
De Willelmo Watta -	-	- vj*d*	De Rogero Dola -	- - x*d*
De Nicholas Watta -	-	- vj*d*	De Hugone -	- - vij*d*
De Eustachio Watta	-	- viij*d*	De Ricardo Wyot -	- - vij*d*
De Thoma Kynt -	-	- vj*d*	De Waltero Jay -	- - vj*d*

Taxatores { Stephanas Treysek - vij*d*
{ Willelmus Sent Maban - vij*d*

De Waltero Pillond - - - xv*d*

De Rogero Tant . - - xij*d*

De Stephano Slegha - - - viij*d*

Summa xxv*s* vji*d* probatur.

B.

Parochia de Michestouce.

De Johanne de ffentonadul	-	- xij*d*	De Nicholas Jumore	- - vj*d*
....		vj*d*	De Rogero Thomas	- - xij*d*
....		vj*d*	De Johanna Kyka -	- - vj*d*
....		vj*d*	De Nicholao Bissop -	- - vj*d*
....		vj*d*	De Stephano Tregenwer	- - xij*d*
....		xij*d*	De Martino de eadem	- - xij*d*
De Radulpho Lune -	-	- xij*d*	De Willelmo Kyttou	- - vj*d*

De Stephano Trenewyth	-	- xij*d*	De Willelmo Dreyn -	-	- vj*d*
De Radulpho de eadem	-	- xij*d*	De Martino Jumore -	-	- vj*d*
De Roberto Jon ' -	-	- xij*d*	Taxatores { Johannes Bagga -		- vj*d*
De Radulpho Hanky	-	- xij*d*	{ Radulphus Clork -		- vj*d*
De Stephano Treuelek	-	- xij*d*			

Summa xvij*s* probatur.

C.

HUNDREDUM } Secunda Solutio Subsidii hundredi predicti Domino Regi nuper concessi de terris
DE TRIGGE. } tenementis bonis et Catallis coiatus ejusdem hundredi juxta formam et effectum
cujusdam actus in vltimo parliamento facti sive editi quod quidem subsidium per Rogerum
Arundell Johannem Roscarek Johannem Flamank et Nicholaum Opy Commissionarios assignatos
infra Hundredum predictum taxat' et assessat' fuerunt.   Et per Petrum Bevyll generalem
collectorem inde predictos Commissionarios assignatos et deputatos colligendum et ad receptum
scaccarii dicti domini Regis ante Octabas Purificationis beate Marie proximo futuræ computandum
et soluendum juxta vim formam et effectum actus predicte prout inferius sequentur.

Parochia de Scynt Mabon. 16th *Henry VIII,* $\frac{87}{131}$

Thoms Mayowe	in bonis	xl*s*	subsid' xij*d*	Nicholaus Tresloget	in bonis v *mks.* subsid xx*d*
Nicholaus Otys	in Stipend'	xx*s*	,, iiij*d*	Stephanus Dawe	,, lx*s* ,, xviij*d*
Johannes Hendy	,,	xx*s*	,, iiij*d*	Willelmus Bettewe	,, lx*s* ,, xviij*d*
Johannes Pethe	in bonis	xl*s*	,, xij*d*	.... Berwyk vidua ,,	lx*s* ,, xviij*d*
Willelmus Hay	,,	xl*s*	,, xij*d*	.... Taillor ,,	iiij*li* ,, ij*s*
Robertus Treslogett	,,	vj*li*	,, ij*s*	Willelmus Barrett in terris p ann. xl*i* ,,	x*s*
Paschasius Bennett	,,	lx*s*	,, xviij*d*	Nicholas Whyt	in bonis xx*li* ,, xx*s*
Robertus Phelipp	,,	vj*li*	,, ij*s*	Johannes Wrothe	,, vj*li* ,, ij*s*
Johannes Tresloget, Sen'	,,	iiij*li*	,, ij*s*	Johannes Trewenck	in Stipend' xx*s* ,, iiij*s*
Johannes Tresloget, Jun'	,,	iiij*li*	,, ij*s*	Johannes Croppe	in bonis c*s* ,, ij*s* vj*d*
Thomas Hendy	,,	x*li*	,, v*s*	.... ,,	xl*s* ,, xij*d*
Willelmus Luky	,,	xl*s*	,, xij*d*	Johannes Cradoke	,, x*mks* ,, xl*d*
Stephanus Isak	,,	lx*s*	',, xviij*d*	Johannes Hoper	,, vj*li* ,, ij*s*
Johannes Hill, Sen'	,,	x*li*	,, v*s*	Thomas Vymen	,, c*s* ,, ij*d*
Willelmus Dyver	in Stipend'	xx*s*	,, iiij*s*	.... in Stipend' xx*s* ,, iiij*d*
Johannes Antony	,,	xx*s*	,, iiij*d*	.... in bonis c*s* ,, ij*s* vj*d* .
Robertus Dawe	in bonis	iiij*li*	,, ij*s*	Thomas Carthew	,, xl*s* ., xij*d*
Ricardus Bulke	in Stipend'	xx*s*	,, iiij*d*	Willelmus Murty	,, lx*s* ,, xviij*d*
Johannes Oly[ver]	in bonis	x*mks*	,, xl*d*	Johannes Tom	,, xvj*li* ,, viij*s*
Robertus Dawe	in Stipend'	xx*s*	,, iiij*d*	Ricardus Tom	,, c*s* ,, ij*s* vj*d*
Ricardus Slee	in bonis	xl*s*	,, xij*d*	Willelmus Weber	,, lx*s* ,, xviij*d*
Johannes Oliver	in Stipend'	xx*s*	,, iiij*d*	Thomas Martyn	,, lx*s* ,, xviij*d*

.... in bonis		lx*s*	,,	xviij*d*	Johannes Cowlyn	in bonis	c*s*	,, ij*s* vj.*l*
Thomas Trevethek	,,	xl*l*	,,	v*s*	Johannes Bennett, Sen*r*	,,	xm*k*s	,, xl*d*
Benedictus Hendy	,,	xx*li*	,,	xx*s*	Ricardus Tresloget	,,	c*s*	,, ij*s* vj*d*
Walterus Hendy	in Stipend'	xx*s*	,,	iiij*d*	Johannes Phelipp	,,	lx*s*	,, xviij*d*
Johannes Bettewe	in bonis	vij*li*	,,	iij*s* vj*d*	Willelmus Browne	,,	lx*s*	,, xviij*d*
Henricus Bettewe	,,	lx*s*	,,	xviij*d*	Ricardus Edwardes	,,	iiij*li*	,, ij*s*
Willelmus Jak	,,	xl*s*	,,	xij*d*	Willelmus Treslogett	,,	lx*s*	,, xviij*d*
Johannes Luky	,,	lx*s*	,,	xviij*d*	Benedictus Hamley	,,	xv*li*	,, vij*s* vj*d*
Stephanus Brabon	,,	lx*s*	,,	xviij*d*	Stephanus Ruby	,,	xl*s*	,, xij*d*
Thomas Brabon	,,	xvj*li*	,,	viij*s*	Johannes Mayowe	,,	xl*s*	,, xij*d*
Benedictus Harry	,,	iiij*li*	,,	ij*s* ·	Robertus Otys	in Stipend'	xx*s*	,, iiij*d*

Summa ix*li* v*s* x*d*

D.

87

Hundred of Lesnewith.—Parochia of Mychelstow, — dated 26th November 16th Henry VIII.

130

Johannes Brode	in bonis	vij*li*	subsid	iij*s* vj*d*	Johannes Elnat,	in bonis	vij*li*	subsid	iij vj*d*
Johannes Hamley ⎱ *alias* Harvey ⎰	,,	vij*li*	,,	iij*s* vj*d*	Johannes Dawkyn	in terris	iij*li*	,,	iij*s*
					Johannes Brode jun*r*	in bonis	vj*li*	,,	iij*s*
Henricus Wade	,,	xl*s*	,,	xij*d*	Stephanus Molys	,,	v*li*	,,	ij*s* vj*d*
Johannes Haukyn	,,	xl*s*	,,	xij*d*	Harry Robyn	,,	xl*s*	,,	xij*d*
Wyllelmus Atgave	,,	xl*s*	,,	xij*d*	Stephanus Sonder	,,	xl*s*	,,	xij*d*
Thomas Slogat	,,	vij*li*	,,	iij*s* vj*d*	Rolandus Hervy	,,	xl*s*	,,	xij*d*
Johannes Rychard	,,	vj*li*	,,	iij*s*					

Summa xxxiiij*s* vj*d*

E.

RETURN OF THE POSSESSIONS OF THE INHABITANTS OF ST. MABEN, 1521—1523.
Augmentation Office, Miscellaneous Books, vol. lxxvii, p. 47.

PAROCHIA DE ⎱
SEYNT MABEN ⎰ *Valencia Spiritualium possessionum ibidem per annum.*

Oliverus Person, Rector ibidem valet per annum in proficuis eiusdem ecclesie - xxx*li*

Valencia terrarum et tenementorum ibidem per annum.

Henricus Marney miles valet ibidem per annum -	-	xx*li*	Willelmus Tredennek	- x*s*
			Johannes Martyn -	- viij*s*
Arturus Plantagenet Miles	-	viij*li*	Henricus Burgh	- iij*s*
Vmfridus Collys -	-	lx*s*	Johannes Stone	- x*s*
Egidius Hyll -	-	xx*s*	Johannes Cripse -	- xij*s*
Nicholaus Willughby	-	v*li*	Willelmus Barret -	- lx*s*
Johannes Beachamp -	-	xl*s*		

Summa.

Valencia bonorum et Catallorum dictæ parochiæ et de eorum armis.

Johannes Hendy Capellanus curatus ibidem in bonis nil in Stipendio vj*li*

Willelmus Barret valet in bonis	-	x*li*
arma pro vno homine		
Nicholaus White „	-	xx*li*
arma pro vno homine		
Stephanus Hockyn „	-	xl*s*
Johannes Herry „	-	x*li*
arma pro vno homine		
Johannes Croppe „	-	v *marcas*
Hamelinus Mathew „	-	v *marcas*
Johannes Pawle „	-	x *marcas*
Johannes Hoper „	-	vj*li*
Thomas Symon „	-	v*li*
Johannes Browne „	-	iiij*li*
Willelmus Martyn „	-	xl*s*
Johannes Tomlyn „	-	iiij*li*
Johannes Tom „	-	xvj*li*
arma pro vno homine		
Ricardus Tom „	-	c*s*
Willelmus Webber „	-	xl*s*
Thomas Martyn „	-	xl*s*
Johannes Benyt, senr. „	·· x *marcas*	
arma pro vno homine		
Johannes Benyt, junr. „	-	xl*s*
Ricardus Tresloget „	- x *marcas*	
arma pro vno homine		
Ricardus Pawly „	-	xl*s*
Johannes Phelipp „	-	iiij*li*
Robertus Browne „	-	vj*li*
arma pro vno homine		
Willelmus Browne „	-	xl*s*
Ricardus Edward „	-	lx*s*
Willelmus Tresloget „	-	iiij*li*
Henricus Phelipp „	-	xl*s*
Benedictus Hamley „	-	xv*li*
arma pro vno homine		
Stephanus Ruby „	-	xl*s*
Johannes Mayowe „	-	xl*s*

Johannes Hendy valet in bonis	-	lx*s*
Johannes Pethe „	-	xl*s*
Willelmus Haye .,	-	xl*s*
Robertus Sloget „	-	iiij*li*
arma pro vno homine		
Robertus Phelipp „	-	vj*li*
Johannes Sloget, sen. „	-	iiij*li*
Johannes Sloget, jun. „	-	iiij*li*
Thomas Hendy „	-	x*li*
arma pro vno homine		
Willelmus Luky „	-	xl*s*
Stephanus Isak „	-	lx*s*
Johannes Hyll, senr.⎫		
Johannes Hyll, junr. ⎬ in bonis communie		x*li*
Henricus Hyll ⎭		
arma pro vno homine		
Robertus Dew „	-	iiij*li*
Johannes Gibbe „	x *marcas*	
Willelmus Pawly „	liij*s* iiij*d*	
Thomas Trevethyk „	-	x*li*
arma pro vno homine		
Benedictus Hendy „	-	xx*li*
arma pro vno homine		
Johannes Bettow „	-	vij*li*
Willelmus Isak „	-	c*s*
Johannes Luky „	-	lx*s*
Stephanus Brabyn „	-	x*s*
Robertus Hamly „	xx *marcas*	
arma pro vno homine		
Thomas Brabyn „	-	xvj*li*
arma pro vno homine		
Benedictus Herry „	-	lx*s*
Nicholas Tresloget „	v *marcas*	
Stephanus Dawe „	-	lx*s*
Willelmus Harry „	-	iiij*li*
Henricus Bettow „	liij*s* iiij*d*	
Thomas Mayowe „	-	xl*s*

Summa.

Numerus armorum

Numerus hominum abilium

Numerus alieneginorum.

END OF VOLUME II.

INDEX TO SUBJECTS.

NOTE.—That in this and the following Indices, no attempt is made to distinguish the different modes of spelling the same name, and that one reference only is given, notwithstanding the name may occur more than once on the same page.

INDEX TO NAMES OF PLACES.

INDEX TO NAMES OF PERSONS.

Lightning Source UK Ltd.
Milton Keynes UK
UKOW05f0918090916

282528UK00003B/46/P